‏‏‎IS

D1581656

VOLUME 2

The rise of classes and nation-states, 1760–1914

Distinguishing four sources of power in human societies – ideological, economic, military, and political – *The Sources of Social Power* traces their interrelations throughout history. This second volume of Michael Mann's analytical history of social power deals with power relations between the Industrial Revolution and World War I, focusing on France, Great Britain, Hapsburg Austria, Prussia/Germany, and the United States. Based on considerable empirical research, it provides original theories of the rise of nations and nationalism, of class conflict, of the modern state, and of modern militarism. While not afraid to generalize, it also stresses social and historical complexity. Michael Mann sees human society as "a patterned mess" and attempts to provide a sociological theory appropriate to this. This theory culminates in the final chapter, an original explanation of the causes of World War I. First published in 1993, this new edition of Volume 2 includes a new preface by the author examining the impact and legacy of the work.

Michael Mann is Distinguished Professor of Sociology at the University of California, Los Angeles. He is the author of *Power in the 21st Century: Conversations with John Hall* (2011), *Incoherent Empire* (2003), and *Fascists* (Cambridge 2004). His book *The Dark Side of Democracy* (Cambridge 2005) was awarded the Barrington Moore Award of the American Sociological Association for the best book in comparative and historical sociology in 2006.

The sources of social power

VOLUME 2

The rise of classes and nation-states, 1760–1914

MICHAEL MANN

University of California, Los Angeles

CAMBRIDGE
UNIVERSITY PRESS

CAMBRIDGE UNIVERSITY PRESS
Cambridge, New York, Melbourne, Madrid, Cape Town,
Singapore, São Paulo, Delhi, Mexico City

Cambridge University Press
32 Avenue of the Americas, New York, NY 10013-2473, USA

www.cambridge.org
Information on this title: www.cambridge.org/9781107670648

First edition published 1993
Reprinted 1995, 1996, 1998, 2000, 2003
New edition published 2012

Printed in the United States of America

A catalog record for this publication is available from the British Library.

Library of Congress Cataloging in Publication data
Mann, Michael, 1942–
    The sources of social power / Michael Mann.
        v. cm.
    Contents: v. 1. A history of power from the beginning to AD 1760 – v. 2. The rise of
    classes and nation-states, 1760–1914 – v. 3. Global empires and revolution, 1890–1945 –
    v. 4. Globalizations, 1945–2011.
    Includes bibliographical references and index.
    ISBN 978-1-107-03117-3 (hardback : v. 1) – ISBN 978-1-107-63597-5 (pbk. : v. 1) –
    ISBN 978-1-107-03118-0 (hardback : v. 2) – ISBN 978-1-107-67064-8 (pbk. : v. 2) –
    ISBN 978-1-107-02865-4 (hardback : v. 3) – ISBN 978-1-107-65547-8 (pbk. : v. 3) –
    ISBN 978-1-107-02867-8 (hardback : v. 4) – ISBN 978-1-107-61041-5 (pbk. : v. 4)
    1. Social history.   2. Power (Social sciences)   I. Title.
    HN8.M28   2012
    306.09–dc23   2012028452

ISBN 978-1-107-03118-0 Hardback
ISBN 978-1-107-67064-8 Paperback

Contents

Preface to the new edition   *page* vii

Preface   xix

1   Introduction   1
2   Economic and ideological power relations   23
3   A theory of the modern state   44
4   The Industrial Revolution and old regime liberalism in
     Britain, 1760–1880   92
5   The American Revolution and the institutionalization
     of confederal capitalist liberalism   137
6   The French Revolution and the bourgeois nation   167
7   Conclusion to Chapters 4–6: The emergence of classes
     and nations   214
8   Geopolitics and international capitalism   254
9   Struggle over Germany: I. Prussia and authoritarian
     national capitalism   297
10   Struggle over Germany: II. Austria and confederal
     representation   330
11   The rise of the modern state: I. Quantitative data   358
12   The rise of the modern state: II. The autonomy of
     military power   402
13   The rise of the modern state: III. Bureaucratization   444
14   The rise of the modern state: IV. The expansion of
     civilian scope   479
15   The resistible rise of the British working class,
     1815–1880   510
16   The middle-class nation   546
17   Class struggle in the Second Industrial Revolution,
     1880–1914: I. Great Britain   597
18   Class struggle in the Second Industrial Revolution,
     1880–1914: II. Comparative analysis of working-class
     movements   628
19   Class struggle in the Second Industrial Revolution,
     1880–1914: III. The peasantry   692
20   Theoretical conclusions: Classes, states, nations, and
     the sources of social power   723

21   Empirical culmination – over the top: Geopolitics,
      class struggle, and World War I   740

Appendix Additional tables on state finances and state
      employment   803

Index   816

Preface to the new edition

This book is bold and ambitious. It charts and explains the development of power relations in the advanced countries of the world over 150 years and interprets this with the aid of a general theory of power in human societies. Readers of my first volume will be familiar by now with my argument that the development of human societies can be explained in terms of the interrelations of four sources of social power – ideological, economic, military, and political (the IEMP model). These sources generate networks of interaction whose boundaries do not coincide. Instead, they overlap, intersect, entwine, and sometimes fuse, in ways that defy simple or unitary explanations of society given by social scientists. More importantly, they also defy the ability of social actors to fully understand their social situation, and it is that uncertainty which makes human action somewhat unpredictable and which perpetually develops social change.

And yet this book is not as big in scope as my other three volumes. Unlike them, it is not global. One enthusiastic reviewer did begin his review of this one with the word "Colossal!" and ended saying "this volume stands alone for its heroic scope, and the depth of its analysis attests to the author's vision and determination" (Snyder, 1995: 167). Yet others were disappointed with what they saw as a narrowing of my scope compared to Volume 1. Here I am resolutely focused from beginning to end on Europe and America. I narrowed my focus firstly because in the "long nineteenth century" Europe and its white settler colonies constituted the "leading edge" of power in the world. This was the first period in world history in which one regional civilization came to dominate all four sources of social power across the world – ideological, economic, military, and political. This dominance was not to last long but it was still firmly in place in July 1914 at the end of the period covered by this volume. Yet this volume is even more tightly focused, for it largely ignores the global empires of these Powers. I have been criticized on both counts as being "Eurocentric," but I feel that this is misplaced for this is avowedly a book about only a part, albeit the most important part, of the world at that time. It was never my intention to ignore the global empires or the globe as a whole, and they are the subject matter of Volumes 3 and 4.

However, in my decision to focus on the leading advanced countries, methodological issues also played a part. I am often asked about my method. I confess to being methodologically unconscious. I just do what

vii

I do without thinking much about my method. Joseph Bryant (2006) and Tim Jacoby (2004) give a much better explanation of my methodology and my ontology than I could ever provide. However, there are certain practical patterns to what I do. First, I cut down on the range of countries and regions by focusing on the leading edge of power, the most advanced civilizations at any one point in time. I have most obviously done that in Volume 2 where I only discuss the five leading countries in European civilization: Britain, France, Prussia/Germany, Austria-Hungary, and the United States (with Russia playing a more intermittent role).

Second, I then read everything I can on this edge within the limits of my linguistic abilities, but I stop reading when the result becomes simply to add detail or minor qualifications to my argument. I reached this point much sooner for earlier historical periods than later ones because in early history I could read almost everything published. But preparing Volume 2 was a learning experience for me. Even after deciding to focus on a few countries, my aspiration to read even half of what was available on them meant I was spending an inordinate amount of time and writing too much to be able to accomplish my original intent of including imperial history too, and of reaching the present day in my narrative. So I left the empires to Volume 3 (adding the American and Japanese empires), and I only reach up to today in Volume 4.

So with Volume 2 half-finished but already too long, I realized that if I was ever to reach the present day, I had not only to write more volumes but also to be much more selective in my reading. Luckily, technology then came to my aid. The development of online capabilities has added useful shortcuts to my reading task. In Volumes 3 and 4 I have been able to enter a period or problem by searching for relevant online university syllabi. The syllabi give me a sense of what every student is expected to read on the topic and the better ones also give me a preliminary sense of current debates. I then use recent book reviews and review articles in journals available to me online through UCLA's fine library resources to read further on current thinking. I soon learned to greatly prefer the type of book review that states clearly the book's arguments and data to the more self-indulgent review in which the author concentrates on giving his/her own opinions on the topic. Then I read the selected works. This method is probably the reason why I cite more books than journal articles, which I had not realized until Rogers Brubaker pointed it out to me. However, "read" is not always the most appropriate description for my treatment of books, because very often I "pillage" them, glancing though the table of contents and the index for sections that bear on the themes I am pursuing, neglecting the rest. This is a scholarly sin, of course, but it is absolutely necessary in any very general work, given the immensity of today's scholarly production.

The third aspect of my method in all my volumes has been to continuously zig-zag between theory and data, developing a general idea, then testing and refining it on the historical evidence, then back to theory, then once again to data and so on, and so forth. In one respect here this volume differs from Volume 1. There I had noted that explanations of why Europe pioneered the way to modernity cannot employ the comparative method, because there are no other "pristine" cases of such a breakthrough (Japan's remarkable breakthrough came through conscious adaptation of European institutions). All one could do was to compare Europe to the one case that might have broken through to industrial capitalism but did not do so – Imperial China. In Volume 2, however, I can deploy the comparative method, because Europe became divided into nation-states, which had enough boundedness and enough similarities and differences in their development to permit a comparative analysis of them. Some readers took my rejection of the comparative method in Volume 1 as being principled. But no, it was pragmatic, and in this volume reality allows me to do comparative research.

Once again, however, this volume expresses a distinctively sociological view of history, one that is more concerned with theoretical questions than is the case among historians, yet is more concerned with history than is the case among sociologists. This is true even in this volume, which does not have great geographical or historical breadth.

Let me state what I consider to be its strengths. I continue here my argument established in Volume 1 that "societies" are not unitary or systemic. Human societies are constituted by power networks – ideological, economic, military, and political power – which do not have the same boundaries. These networks are overlapping, intersecting, and entwining, forming much looser units than most sociologists have accepted. In the period covered in this volume, as I say on page 9, states harden into nation-states with a certain degree of boundedness. But they nonetheless entwine with a broader transnational "Western civilization" which was in a sense competing as a basic membership unit. Thus sociology's master concept, "society" kept metamorphosing between the nation-state and the civilization. But the similarity and the distinctiveness of each national unit, and the fact that they were erecting what I call "cages" around part of the lives of their subjects/citizens, enabled me to do comparative analysis of them.

These comparisons centre on what I identify as the two main actors of modern times: classes and nation-states. I argue that the two cannot be seen, as is conventional, as utterly separate from each other. Nor are they opposites, the one undercutting the other. Instead, economic and political power relations have developed entwined with each other, influencing rather than undercutting each other's development.

Recent trends in the disciplines of sociology and history have served to obscure this. When I began writing this volume, class analysis dominated. What was called "social history" focused overwhelmingly on class relations, and especially on the working class. There was then a reaction against this overemphasis in the form of a general "cultural turn" in which culture took over from the economy as the main object of study. Insofar as classes were discussed at all, this was in terms of discourses, symbolic communication, and the like rather than concrete labour relations or the material means of production. This was one result of the decline of the traditional left in Western society, which was occurring from the 1980s onward. But a new left was also emerging, centred not on class but on "identity" rights, especially those of gender and ethnicity. Writers on gender relations then took much attention away from class analysis, though some were concerned to specify the relations between class and gender. But those focusing on ethnicity virtually ignored class relations, and that has been especially true of those working on nations and nationalism. Thus class and nation have been kept apart, in separate boxes, class predominating at first, then nation, thus obscuring the fact that class and nation have developed together, entwined. It is now conventional, for example, to say that World War I represented the triumph of nation over class. Yet we shall see in both this volume and Volume 3 that their interrelations were far more complex than this.

I believe that this book remains the best treatment available of the development of the modern state. Chapter 3 presents my own theory of the modern state. My notion that states "crystallize" in different forms as a result of both their different functions and the pressure of different constituencies on them is better able to cope with the real-world messiness of political life. Second, my treatment of the five states is rooted in a detailed statistical analysis of their finances and employment records, and on this quantitative basis I can launch into some grand historical generalizations. In the course of this period, the main functions of the state changed radically. At the beginning of the period, its main function was in the financing and the fighting of war. Charles Tilly famously remarked that "war made the state and the state made war" (1975: 42). But I find this was only so in Europe up to the mid-nineteenth century. Nor did I think it likely that either his model or mine would fully apply to other continents. In fact, Centeno (2002) found that it only applied to the history of Latin America in a negative sense. There states rarely made war and they remained puny, and Herbst (2000) says more or less the same thing about postcolonial Africa. So the question there turns to "why did they not make war?" By the end of the century, Western state civilian functions, like building infrastructures, education, public health, and the first stirrings of the welfare state, had emerged to rival warmaking. It was now a dual civil-military state, a character it retained during most of the twentieth century, although near the end of that century many states were predominantly pursuing civilian roles. They have lost their historic backbone. We can also see from my data that states developed greater infrastructural power over their territories, even though, surprisingly, their overall financial size was no greater as a proportion of the overall economy than it had been at the beginning of the period – because the growth of the economy was actually slightly greater than the growth of the state. It was not yet a Leviathan, nor was it as bureaucratic as is often assumed. On Sundays, U.S. President Harrison (in office from 1889 to 1893) would open the White House front door himself, because it was the butler's day off.

The third strength of my analysis of political power is the emphasis I place on the rise of the nation-state. This offers further justification of my oft-criticized, unconventional distinction between political and military power. The role of political power relations in this period is more in terms of collective power (power through people) than of distributive power (power over people). The rising costs of war followed by the growth of state infrastructures meant that people and their interaction networks were gradually mobilized into nations. The metaphor I use is that they were "caged" and "naturalized" within the nation-state. This was consequential because social relations – especially class relations – came to vary mainly according to the configuration of political power in each country. Although the economic power relations of capitalism varied across the advanced world, they were less important than national variations in political power in determining the various outcomes of labour conflict.

In the realm of classes, the period of this volume saw the phenomenal growth of a capitalism, which generated the first and the second industrial revolutions and massive economic growth. This led to the development of modern social classes like the capitalist, middle, working, and peasant classes. I focus for much of the time on the relations between workers and capitalists, although I discuss the middle class in Chapter 16 and the peasantry in Chapter 19. I show that the peasantry was capable of much more collective organization than Marx had argued, and that the middle class was very diverse, and not nearly as nationalistic as is often believed. In my book *Fascists* (2004), I show that they were not more susceptible to fascism than were other classes. All these classes were extremely important from the time of the French Revolution to World War I, because industrial capitalism became the fundamental economic power structure of society. Those sociologists who have criticized me for writing at length on class relations (on the grounds that class is passé) do not seem to grasp the realities in the long nineteenth century.

Yet class relations between workers and their capitalist employers have been ambiguous, in two different senses. First, workers do feel exploited, yet they must cooperate on a daily basis with their employer in order to obtain their daily bread. Thus conflict versus cooperation is a perennial choice for both workers and their employers. Secondly, when workers do organize, three possible forms of solidarity emerge: class solidarity among the working class as a whole, sectional solidarity among workers in a particular trade, and segmental solidarity among workers in a particular enterprise. Here I argue that whether conflict or cooperation predominates and which combination of these three forms conflict takes are explained more by political than economic power relations. Most specifically, the more workers are excluded from sharing in political power, the more likely they are to form class-based organizations, to find plausible the claims of socialists or anarcho-syndicalists, and to be attracted by the prospect of revolution rather than reform. Thus, the ordering in terms of the emergence of class, socialist and revolutionary sentiments runs from Russia, through Austria-Hungary and Germany, to France and Britain, and finally to the United States.

I now turn to considering criticisms and misinterpretations of the volume. Some have interpreted my analysis in variations in class consciousness as my saying that political power relations are more important than economic ones and so they conclude that this book is "state-centric" (e.g., Tarrow, 1994; Mulhall, 1995). I reject this. In my conclusion on page 737, I identify two phases of what I call dual determination. In the first phase, lasting until 1815, economic and military power relations predominated in the structuring of societies. But in the course of the nineteenth century, power shifted and by the end of the century economic and political power relations (capitalism and nation-states) predominated. On the face of it this would seem to give economic power relations some priority, which is not surprising given that these two phases correspond to the onset of the first and second capitalist industrial revolutions. It also implies that the advanced world became *more* state-centric and that is one of my main arguments in this volume. But these dualities are heroic simplifications of a very complex reality, and I should admit that I have always been a little uneasy with them. And comparable heroic simplifications of other times and periods would look rather different.

As far as class relations are concerned, I should point out that it is principally the variations between countries that are more explicable in terms of political power relations. That there was everywhere in this period pronounced labour discontent is explicable in terms of the nature of the economic power relations intrinsic to capitalism, while I also acknowledge that to explain the emergence of sectional and segmental organization, we need to also pay attention to craft and corporate structure. The structure of capitalism is obviously also a *necessary* part of any explanation, and when we combine this with political power relations, we have a *sufficient* explanation of class outcomes. But I do not intend to elevate political over economic power in this period.

George Lawson (2006: 491) airs the possibility that my work as a whole contains an implicit hierarchy with military power at the top, followed by political power, then economic power, and finally ideological power. I think this would be a misinterpretation. Given that military power is neglected in most social science, I may mention it too much for most tastes. But my own view is that both military power and ideological power are rather more erratic in their effects than are the other two. They sometimes emerge powerfully in world-historical moments, militarism launching great transformative wars and ideological power turning occasionally transcendent and leading revolutionary changes in the way that people view the world. But otherwise military power stays on the sidelines in the form of a military caste minding its own business. Similarly, for the most part, ideological power largely reproduces dominant power relations (as Marxists argue). In this volume military power was important at the beginning and the very end of the period (except in the colonies, where it was continuously important), and it became more important again in the twentieth century, while ideological power never really matched the heights of the period of the much earlier emergence of the world religions or the heights of twentieth-century secular ideologies. I make more general comments on the interrelations and relative importance of the power sources at the end of Volume 4, but I reject the idea of any simple hierarchy among them.

Within Europe after 1815, this was largely a period of peace, so military power relations actually figure less in this volume than they did in Volume 1 or than they will in Volume 3. Their main entrances are at the beginning and the end. In the latter case we see evidence of the relative autonomy of militaries from civilian state control, and this was important in helping cause World War I. I discuss this in Chapter 21. In Volume 3, I briefly revisit these causes. And I should note that there I added to the explanation of the causes of this war greater emphasis on the thousand-year European tradition of militarism and imperialism. Europeans had long been from Mars. This chapter has received much praise and it is in many ways the clearest vindication of my overall model of human society. As I conclude, on page 796, the war "resulted from the unintended consequences of the interaction of overlapping, intersecting power networks." No one could control the whole or could predict the reactions of other nations, classes, statesmen, and militaries. That was why in August 1914 a disastrous war began, one that was to ensure the demise of European power, whose rise I had charted in Volume 1. Military power relations were also to play a role in the denouement of class relations in the first half of the twentieth century. Only in countries that were effectively defeated in the two world wars were there serious attempts at revolution. This I show in Volume 3. These are examples of my most fundamental point: that we cannot explain major social developments in any period without considering the entwinings of more than a single source of social power. Ideological, economic, military, and political determinisms must all be rejected. However, in this period, having excluded colonies from my purview, military power and political power are closely entwined. In the advanced countries armies are no longer feudal, and paramilitaries and civil wars are rare. The wars discussed here are between states. It is really only the tendencies toward military castes, distinct from the civilian authorities, that maintain the autonomy of military from political power in this place, in this period.

Turning to ideological power, some criticize me for being too materialist, too instrumental, and too rationalist. In principle my model is none of these things, although my practice has sometimes faltered. I prefer the term "ideology" to "culture" or "discourse," not because I view ideologies as false or a cover for interests, as materialists sometimes say. By ideology I mean only a broad-ranging meaning system that "surpasses experience." "Culture" and "discourse" are too all-encompassing terms, covering the communication of all beliefs, values, and norms, even sometimes all "ideas" about anything. When used so generally, they presuppose a contrast between only two realms, the "ideal" and the "material," leading to the traditional debate between idealism and materialism. The material might be conceived of as "nature" as opposed to "culture," or as the "economic base" versus the "superstructure," or as joint economic/ military interests (as in international relations "realism") as opposed to "constructivism" – or even as "structure" as opposed to "agency."

These dualist debates are perennial. After a period dominated by materialist theories of everything, we now have cultural theories of everything. As noted earlier, "nation" and "ethnicity" have largely replaced "class" as objects of research; they are said to be "cultural," whereas classes are said to be "material"; they are usually discussed without any reference to classes; and "cultural" and "ethno-symbolist" have largely replaced "materialist" theories of nations and ethnicities. Thirty years ago, fascism was explained in relation to capitalism and classes; now it is seen as a "political religion." My books *Fascists* and *The Dark Side of Democracy: Explaining Ethnic Cleansing* suggest that this is not progress, but a shift among equally one-sided theories.

Nonetheless, I may have given the impression of being a materialist in four different ways.

(1) I use the word "material" when, to avoid confusion, I should have written "concrete" or "real." That is just an error of language, not of substance.

(2) I endorse John Hall's and Perry Anderson's description of my theory as "organizational materialism," and this often involves emphasizing the "logistics" and "infrastructures" of ideological power, sometimes at the expense of the content of their doctrines. My originality here lies clearly with the organization of power, and I continue to emphasize that. I also find myself at least as drawn to Durkheim's emphasis on religious rituals as to Weber's emphasis on doctrine. Nonetheless, I should not neglect either.

(3) I declare here on page 35 (as I also had in Volume 1, pages 471–2) that ideological power declined through the eighteenth and nineteenth centuries. I still think this is broadly true within the most advanced countries, yet I did not discuss in this volume the major ideology of the period – racism. Lawson (2006: 492) goes further. He suggested to me that I neglect a whole series of nineteenth-century ideologies. He lists racism, Darwinism, colonialism, imperialism, nationalism, Marxism, and liberalism as the main ones. In one sense I do neglect the first four of them. But they form an interrelated group that was largely significant because of Europe and America's overseas empires. For example, racism was only important in this period in colonies and not mother countries, except for the United States. I do exclude empires from this volume, but I deal extensively with them and with this cluster of ideologies in Volume 3. As for nationalism, Marxism, and liberalism, I think I do discuss them in this volume.

(4) I declare that the extensive power of religion has continued to decline since the nineteenth century in the face of rising secular ideologies like socialism and nationalism. Having subsequently researched twentieth- and twenty-first-century fascism, ethno-nationalism, and religious fundamentalism, I now disown half of this statement. My emphasis on rising secular ideologies is correct, but I accept Gorski's (2006) criticism that religion has not generally declined in the world. I was generalizing only on the basis of traditional Christian faiths in Europe, which indeed still are declining, although much of the rest of the world differs. More specific criticisms with some force are that I have sometimes been too rationalistic about religions in earlier periods, and that I neglected the religious content of eighteenth-century politics (Bryant, 2006; Trentmann, 2006). Edgar Kiser (2006) is also right to see me as trying to lessen the rationalism and moving toward greater recognition of value- and emotion-driven behaviour in my later work on fascism (2004) and ethnic cleansing (2005).

My model of power ultimately abandons the distinction between ideas and materiality in favour of one between "ideas and practices combined" (or "action and structure combined") in each of four power networks. Nonetheless, ideological power is clearly more idea-heavy than the others. It comprises networks of persons bearing ideologies that cannot be proved true or false, couched at a sufficient level of generality to be able to give "meaning" to a range of human actions in the world – as religions, socialism, and nationalism all do, for example. They also contain norms, rules of interpersonal conduct that are "sacred," strengthening conceptions of collective interest and cooperation, reinforced, as Durkheim said, by rituals binding people together in repeated affirmations of their commonality. So those offering plausible ideologies can mobilize social movements and wield a general power in human societies analogous to powers yielded by control over economic, military, and political power resources. This is when ideology is what I call "transcendent," for it cuts right through institutionalized practices of economic, military, and political power.

The period discussed in this volume is not one of major ideologies. I hope that in this volume, ideological power autonomy comes through in my conception of an "ideological power elite" steering the direction of the French Revolution in Chapter 6. Elsewhere in this volume I stress that European states sometimes crystallize in terms of religious disputations, but if I do not deal extensively elsewhere in this volume with religion, it is because I believe that, with the exception of racism (which I discuss extensively in Volume 3), Europe did not see much ideological power in this period and place. Religion was declining and the great twentieth-century ideologies of nationalism, socialism, and fascism were just beginning to stir. Though people were beginning caged within the nation, nationalism was still a rather shallow emotion among the working and middle classes, becoming virulent (I argue in Chapter 16) largely among those deriving their employment from the state. I do not claim to discuss *all* ideas, values, norms, and rituals, only those mobilized in macro-power struggles. Schroeder (2006) gives my defence of this neglect: ideas cannot *do* anything unless they are organized. This is why the label "organizational materialism" still seems partly apposite, whatever the economic images it might set up in the reader's mind, for ideas are not free-floating. Nor are economic acquisition, violence, or political regulation – they all need organizing. But maybe I should drop the word "materialism" and just say that I have an organizational model of power and society.

I must acknowledge one final omission: the absence of gender relations from this book. I admit on page 34 that I have omitted in this volume the more intimate aspects of human life. To a certain extent I repair this neglect in Volumes 3 and 4, although I doubt if this extent will satisfy my critics. In the end, my defence against this charge of neglect is only that I cannot do everything! But I think you will agree that I do a lot of things in this book.

Bibliography

Bryant, Joseph 2006 "Grand, yet grounded: ontology, theory, and method in Michael Mann's historical sociology" in John Hall & Ralph Schroeder (eds.), *An Anatomy of Power. The Social Theory of Michael Mann*. Cambridge: Cambridge University Press.

Centeno, Miguel 2002 *Blood and Debt: War and State-Making in Latin America*. University Park: Pennsylvania State University Press.

Gorski, Philip 2006 "Mann's theory of ideological power: sources, applications and elaborations" in Hall & Schroeder, op. cit.

Herbst, Jeffrey 2000 *States and Power in Africa: Comparative Lessons in Authority and Control*. Princeton, NJ: Princeton University Press.

Jacoby, Tim 2004 "Method, narrative and historiography in Michael Mann's sociology of state development," *The Sociological Review*, **52**: 404–21.

Kiser, Edgar 2006 "Mann's microfoundations: addressing neo-Weberian dilemmas" in Hall & Schroeder, op. cit.

Lawson, George 2006 "The social sources of life, the universe and everything: a conversation with Michael Mann," *Millennium – Journal of International Studies,* **34**: 487–508.

Mann, Michael 2004 *Fascists*. New York: Cambridge University Press.

2005 *The Dark Side of Democracy: Explaining Ethnic Cleansing*. New York: Cambridge University Press.

Mulhall, Terry 1995 "Review of *The Sources of Social Power*, Vol II," *The British Journal of Sociology*, **46**, 362–3.

Schroeder, Ralph 2006 "Introduction: the IEMP model and its critics" in Hall & Schroeder, op. cit.

Snyder, Wayne 1995 "Review of *The Sources of Social Power*, Vol II," *The Journal of Economic History*, **55**, 167–9.

Tarrow, Sidney 1994 "Review of *The Sources of Social Power*, Vol II," *American Political Science Review*, **88**, 1031–2.

Tilly, Charles 1975 "Reflections on the history of European state-making" in Tilly, ed., *The Formation of National States in Western Europe*. Princeton, NJ: Princeton University Press.

Trentman, Frank 2006 "The 'British' sources of social power: reflections on history, sociology, and intellectual biography" in Hall & Schroeder, op. cit.

Preface

This is the second volume of what is intended as a four-volume study of the sources of social power. It delivers, however, only 63 percent of the coverage promised in Volume 1, ending in 1914, not in 1990, as I announced there. Volume 3 will cover the twentieth century (perhaps the whole century, by the time I finish). The theoretical conclusion to *The Sources of Social Power* will be Volume 4. I hope all who have expressed interest in my conclusions will still be around then.

I have worked on the research for this volume for more than a decade, beginning in the mid-1970s, when I believed *Sources* would be one normal-sized book. Over the years, I have benefited from the labors, advice, and criticism of many. Roland Axtmann and Mark Stephens helped me collect the comparative statistics in Chapter 11, and Mark also aided me with Chapter 5. Jill Stein helped to collect data on the French revolutionaries for Chapter 6. Ann Kane contributed substantially to Chapter 19, as well as elsewhere, especially Chapter 16. Marjolein 't Hart, John Hobson, and John B. Legler showed me unpublished data for Chapter 11. Joyce Appleby and Gary Nash set me almost straight about the American Revolution; Ed Berenson and Ted Margadant, about the French Revolution; James Cronin and Patrick Joyce, about British labor history; and Kenneth Barkin and Geoff Eley, about German history. Christopher Dandeker commented generously on Chapter 12; Ronen Palan, on Chapters 3, 8, and 20; and Anthony Smith, on Chapter 7. John Stephens was extraordinarily helpful for Chapters 18 and 19. Randall Collins and Bill Domhoff have been helpful in their responses to both volumes. I also thank an anonymous reviewer of the first draft of this book. His or her critique forced me to clarify some of my central ideas.

I thank the London School of Economics and Political Science and the University of California at Los Angeles for providing me with supportive working environments over the last decade. Both also provided seminar series whose excellent discussions helped me clarify many ideas. The LSE Patterns of History seminar flourished principally because of the excitement provided by Ernest Gellner and John A. Hall; the seminars of the UCLA Center for Social Theory and Comparative History have depended especially on Bob Brenner and Perry Anderson. My secretaries, Yvonne Brown in London and Ke-Sook Kim, Linda Kiang, and Alisa Rabin in Los Angeles, have treated me and my work perhaps better than we deserve.

I owe the greatest intellectual debt to John A. Hall, who has continued for many years to provide me with perceptive criticisms entwined with warm friendship. To Nicky Hart and to our children, Louise, Gareth, and Laura, I owe love and perspective.

1   Introduction

This volume continues my history of power through the "long nineteenth century," from the Industrial Revolution to the outbreak of World War I. Focus is on five Western countries at the leading edge of power: France, Great Britain,[1] Habsburg Austria, Prussia-Germany, and the United States. My overall theory remains unchanged. Four sources of social power – ideological, economic, military, and political – fundamentally determine the structure of societies. My central questions also remain the same: What are the relations among these four power sources? Is one or more of them ultimately primary in structuring society?

The greatest social theorists gave contrary answers. Marx and Engels replied clearly and positively. In the last instance, they asserted, economic relations structure human societies. Max Weber replied more negatively, saying "no significant generalizations" can be made about the relations between what he called "the structures of social action." I reject Marxian materialism, but can I improve on Weberian pessimism?

There is both good news and bad news. I want you to read on, so I start with the good news. This volume will make three significant generalizations concerning primacy. I state them outright now; the rest of the book will add many details, qualifications, and caveats.

1. During the eighteenth century, two sources of social power, the economic and the military, preponderated in determining Western social structure. By 1800, the "military revolution" and the rise of capitalism had transformed the West, the former providing predominantly "authoritative" power and the latter predominantly "diffused" power. Because they were so closely entwined, neither can be accorded a singular ultimate primacy.

2. Yet, into the nineteenth century, as military power was subsumed into the "modern state" and as capitalism continued to revolutionize the economy, economic and political power sources began to dominate. Capitalism and its classes, and states and nations, became the decisive

---

[1] I discuss only mainland Britain, excluding Ireland, which Britain ruled throughout this period. After hesitation I decided to treat the only major European colony as I treat other colonies (except for the future United States) in this volume: excluding them except as they impacted on the imperial country.

1

power actors of modern times – the former still providing more dif-
fuseness and ambiguity; the latter, most of the authoritative resolution
of this ambiguity. Again, because they too were entwined, neither can
be accorded a singular ultimate primacy.

3. Ideological power relations were of declining and lesser power
significance during the period. Medieval Europe had been decisively
structured by Christendom (as Volume I argues); in 1760, churches
were still (just) revolutionizing the means of discursive communication. No comparable ideological power movement appeared later in
this period, although churches kept many powers and literacy had
considerable impact. The most important modern ideologies have concerned classes and nations. In terms of a distinction explained later,
ideological power (except in rare revolutionary moments; see Chapters
6 and 7) was more "immanent" than "transcendent" in this period,
aiding the emergence of collective actors created by capitalism, militarism, and states.

Now for the bad news, or, rather, complicating news from which we
can actually construct a richer theory more appropriate to deal with
the mess that constitutes real human societies:

1. The four power sources are not like billiard balls, which follow
their own trajectory, changing direction as they hit each other. They
"entwine," that is, their interactions change one another's inner shapes
as well as their outward trajectories. The events discussed here – the
French Revolution, British near hegemony, the emergence of nationalism or of socialism, middle-class or peasant politics, the causes and
outcomes of wars, and so forth – involved the entwined development
of more than one power source. I criticize "pure" and monocausal
theories. Generalizations cannot culminate in a simple statement of
"ultimate primacy." The three statements I made earlier turn out to be
rough and "impure" generalizations, not laws of history.

2. My rough and impure generalizations also fail to distinguish between Parsons's (1960: 199–225) distributive and collective power; yet
their histories differ. *Distributive power* is the power of actor A over
actor B. For B to acquire more distributive power, A must lose some.
But *collective power* is the joint power of actors A and B cooperating
to exploit nature or another actor, C. In this period Western collective
powers grew simply and dramatically: Commercial capitalism, then
industrial capitalism, enhanced human conquest of nature; the military
revolution enhanced Western powers; the modern state fostered the
emergence of a new collective power actor, the nation. Though other
sources of social power helped cause these developments, these three
"revolutions" in collective power were primarily (and respectively)
caused by economic, military, and political power relations (the

"revolution" in ideological power – the expansion of discursive literacy – was less "pure"). Distributive power changes were more complex and "impure." The growing collective powers of states actually lessened the powers of political elites over their subjects, as "party democracies" began to displace monarchies. Nor did military or ideological elites generally enhance their distributive power over others. Yet two major and impure distributive power actors, classes and nations, did emerge – first in response to military and economic power relations, then as institutionalized by political and economic power relations. Their complex history requires more than a few sentences to summarize.

3. Classes and nation-states also emerged entwined, adding more complexity. Conventionally, they have been kept in separate compartments and viewed as opposites: Capitalism and classes are considered "economic," national-states "political"; classes are "radical" and usually "transnational," nations "conservative," reducing the strength of classes. Yet they actually arose together, and this created a further unresolved problem of ultimate primacy: the extent to which social life was to be organized around, on the one hand, diffuse, market, transnational, and ultimately capitalist principles or, on the other, around authoritative, territorial, national, and statist ones. Was social organization to be transnational, national, or nationalist? Should states be authoritatively weak or strong, confederal or centralized? Were markets to be left unregulated, selectively protected, or imperially dominated? Was geopolitics to be peaceful or warlike? By 1914, no simple choice had been made – nor has one yet been made. These considerations remain the key ambivalences of modern civilization.

4. Classes and nation-states did not go unchallenged throughout the history of Western civilization. "Sectional" and "segmental" actors (rivals to classes) and transnational and "local-regional" actors (rivals to nations) endured. I treat such organizations as notable political parties, aristocratic lineages, military command hierarchies, and internal labor markets as segmental power organizations. I treat such social movements as minority (and some majority) churches, artisanal guilds, and secessionist movements as essentially local-regional alternatives to national organizations. All affected the makeup of classes and nation-states, reducing their power and their purity.

5. The cumulative effect of all these interactions – among the sources of social power, between collective and distributive power actors, between market and territory, and among classes, nations, sectional, segmental, transnational, and local-regional organizations – produced an overall complexity often exceeding the understanding of contemporaries. Their actions thus involved many mistakes, apparent accidents, and unintended consequences. These would then act back to

change the constitution of markets, classes, nations, religions, and so forth. I attempt to theorize mistakes, accidents, and unintended consequences, but they obviously provide yet more complexity.

Thus the discussion in this volume will broadly push forward my three rough, impure generalizations while recognizing these five additional complications. They cope with the patterned mess that is human society, as must all sociological theory.

I discuss sociological theories in this and the next two chapters. Then follow five groups of narrative chapters. Chapters 4–7 cover the period of the American, French, and Industrial revolutions, which I situate amid transformations of all four sources of power. Two had begun far earlier – capitalism and the military revolution – but during the eighteenth century they helped foster ideological and political transformations, each with its own partly autonomous logic – the rise of discursive literacy and the rise of the modern state. I take all four "revolutions" seriously. From the Boston Tea Party to the Great Reform Act, from the spinning jenny to George Stephenson's "Rocket," from the Tennis Court Oath to the Karlsbad Decrees, from the field of Valmy to that of Waterloo – events were impure, presupposing varying combinations of the four power revolutions, carrying classes, nations, and their rivals forward in complex forms that often escaped their own control. Chapter 7 presents my overall account of power developments during this early part of the period, putting final causal emphasis on military states and commercial capitalism.

Chapters 9 and 10 focus on Prussian-Austrian rivalry in Central Europe and on the complex developing relations between class and national actors. They explain the eventual triumph there of relatively centralized nation-states over more decentralized confederal regimes. The conclusion to Chapter 10 summarizes the arguments of these two chapters and discusses whether Central European resolutions were general across Western civilization.

Chapters 11–14 analyze the rise of the modern state. I present statistics on the finances and personnel of the five states, and I disaggregate state growth into four distinct processes: size, scope, representation, and bureaucracy. The massive growth in size was military-led, occurring up to 1815, politicizing much of social life. It fostered extensive and political classes, as well as nations, at the expense of local-regional and transnational actors. Contrary to general belief, most states did not grow again until World War I. But after 1850, states – mainly responding to the industrial phase of capitalism – vastly extended their civilian scope and, quite unintentionally, this integrated the nation-state, fostered national classes, and weakened transnational and local-regional power actors.

Most functionalist, Marxian, and neo-Weberian theories of the modern state emphasize its increasing size, scope, efficiency, and homogeneity. Yet, as states grew and then diversified, their two emerging control mechanisms – representation and bureaucracy – struggled to keep pace. Representative conflicts centered on which classes and which religious and linguistic communities should be represented and where they should be represented; that is, how centralized and national should the state be? Although the "who" has been much theorized, the "where" has not. True, there are many empirical studies of states' rights in the United States and of nationalities in Habsburg Austria. But struggle between the centralized nation and local-regional power actors was actually universal, and the representative and national issues were always entwined. Because neither issue was resolved during this period, as states grew they became less coherent. This became glaringly evident in the disjunction between domestic and foreign policy: Classes became obsessed with domestic politics while political and military elites enjoyed privacy in foreign policy. Marxism, elite theory, and pluralist theory see states as too coherent. I apply my own "polymorphous" theory, presented in Chapter 3, to show that modern states "crystallized," often messily, in four main forms – as capitalist, as militarist, and with differing solutions to the representative and national issues. The conclusion of Chapter 14 summarizes my theory of the rise of the modern state.

The fourth group, Chapters 15–20, deals with class movements among middle and lower classes and with the emergence of popular nations after 1870. Commercial and industrial capitalism developed class, sectional, and segmental organizations simultaneously and ambiguously. I attribute outcomes mainly to authoritative political power relations. Chapter 15 discusses the "first working class," in early nineteenth-century Britain. Chapter 16 treats three middle-class fractions – petite bourgeoisie, professionals, and careerists – and their relations with nationalism and the nation-state. Chapters 17 and 18 describe the three-way competition for the soul of the worker among class, sectionalism, and segmentalism, which was authoritatively resolved by the varying crystallizations of modern states. Chapter 19 analyzes a similar resolution of the competition for peasants' souls among "production classes," "credit classes," and "segmental sectors." Chapter 20 presents a generalization of all this material and summarizes the relations among the sources of social power throughout the "long nineteenth century."

Thus Chapter 7, the conclusions to Chapters 10, 11, and 14, and Chapter 20 generalize the conclusions of this volume. But there was another conclusion, a truly empirical one, to the period. Western society went over the top into the Great War, the most devastating conflict in history. The previous century had also culminated in a devastating sequence of wars, the French Revolutionary and Napoleonic wars, and these culminations are discussed in Chapters 8 and 21. Chapter 21, explaining the causes of World War I, is a final empirical exemplification of my general theory. It rejects explanations predominantly centered on either geopolitics or class relations. Neither can explain why the actions taken were objectively irrational and were recognized as such by the protagonists amid calmer times. The entwining of classes, nations, and their rivals produced a downward spiral of unintended domestic and geopolitical consequences too complex to be fully understood by participants or controlled by polymorphous states. It is important to learn lessons from this decline and to institutionalize power so as not to repeat it.

The rest of this chapter and the next two explain further my IEMP model of power. I repeat my advice to the reader given at the beginning of Volume I: If you find sociological theory hard going, skip to the first narrative chapter, Chapter 4. Later, it is hoped, you will return to the theory.

The IEMP model of power organization

In pursuit of our goals, we enter into power organizations with three characteristics of form and four of substance that determine the overall structure of societies:

1. As noted earlier, organization involves collective and distributive power. Most actual power relations – say, between classes or between a state and its subjects – involve both, in varying combinations.

2. Power may be extensive or intensive. *Extensive power* can organize large numbers of people over far-flung territories. *Intensive power* mobilizes a high level of commitment from participants.

3. Power may be authoritative or diffused. *Authoritative power* comprises willed commands by an actor (usually a collectivity) and conscious obedience by subordinates. It is found most typically in military and political power organizations. *Diffused power* is not directly commanded; it spreads in a relatively spontaneous, unconscious, and decentered way. People are constrained to act in definite ways, but not by command of any particular person or organization. Diffused power is found most typically in ideological and economic power organizations. A good example is market exchange in capitalism. This involves considerable constraint that is yet impersonal and often seemingly "natural."

The most effective exercises of power combine collective and distributive, extensive and intensive, authoritative and diffused power. That is why a single power source – say, the economy or the military – is rarely capable of determining alone the overall structure of societies. It must join with other power resources, as in the two overall dual determinations I identify throughout this period. In fact there are four substantive sources of social power: economic, ideological, military, and political.

1. *Ideological power* derives from the human need to find ultimate meaning in life, to share norms and values, and to participate in aesthetic and ritual practices. Control of an ideology that combines ultimate meanings, values, norms, aesthetics, and rituals brings general social power. Religions provide most examples in Volume I and figure here along with secular ideologies like liberalism, socialism, and nationalism – all increasingly grappling with the meaning of class and nation.

Each power source generates distinct organizational forms. Ideological power is predominantly diffused, commanding through persuasion, a claim to "truth" and "free" participation in ritual. Its diffusion has two principal forms. It may be sociospatially "transcendent." That is, an ideology may diffuse right through the boundaries of economic, military, and political power organizations. Human beings belonging to different states, classes, and so forth face similar problems to which an ideology offers plausible solutions. Then ideological power spreads transcendentally to form a new, distinctive and powerful network of social interaction. Second, ideological power may solidify an existing power organization, developing its "immanent morale." Transcendence is a radically autonomous form of power; immanence reproduces and strengthens existing power relations.

2. *Economic power* derives from the need to extract, transform, distribute, and consume the resources of nature. It is peculiarly powerful because it combines intensive, everyday labor cooperation with extensive circuits of the distribution, exchange, and consumption of goods. This provides a stable blend of intensive and extensive power and normally also of authoritative and diffused power (the first of each pair centers on production, the second on exchange). Volume I calls such economic power organizations "circuits of praxis," but the term is too abstruse. I now abandon it in favor of more conventional labels for the forms of economic cooperation and conflict discussed in these volumes: classes and sectional and segmental economic organizations.

All complex societies have unequally distributed control over economic resources. Thus classes have been ubiquitous. Marx distinguished most basically between those who own or control the means of production, distribution, and exchange and those who control only their own labor – and we can obviously go into more detail distinguishing further classes with more particular rights over economic resources. Such classes can also be broken down into smaller, sectional actors, like a skilled trade or a profession. Classes relate to each other vertically – class A is above class B, exploiting it. Yet other groups conflict horizontally with one another. Following anthropological usage, I term such groups "segments."[2] The members of a segmental group are drawn from various classes – as in a tribe, lineage, patron-client network, locality, industrial enterprise, or the like. Segments compete horizontally with each other. Classes, sections, and segments all cross-cut and weaken one another in human societies.

Volume I showed that segments and sections had hitherto usually predominated over classes. Classes were generally only "latent": Owners, laborers, and others struggled, but usually semicovertly, intensively, confined to an everyday, local level. Most extensive struggle was between segments. But if class relations begin to predominate, we reach a second stage: "extensive" classes, sometimes "symmetric," sometimes "asymmetric." Asymmetric extensive classes generally arrived first: Only owners were extensively organized, whereas laborers were locked into sectional and segmental organizations. Then, in symmetric extensive class structures, both main classes become organized over a similar sociospatial area. Finally we reach the "political class," organized to control the state. Here again we may distinguish symmetric and asymmetric (i.e., where only owners are politically organized) class structures. In his more grandiose moments Marx claimed that political, symmetric, extensive classes, and class struggle provided the motor of history. Yet, as discussed in Volume I (with the exceptions of classical Greece and early Republican Rome), classes were only becoming political and extensive just before the Industrial Revolution. In most agrarian societies a dominant class, organized extensively, "caged" subordinate latent classes inside its own segmental power organizations. This volume describes an uncompleted drift toward Marx's full, symmetric class struggle and the linked transformation of sections and segments.

3. *Military power* is the social organization of physical force. It derives from the necessary of organized defense and the utility of aggression. Military power has both intensive and extensive aspects, for it concerns intense organization to preserve life and inflict death and can also organize many people over large sociospatial areas. Those

---

[2] Rather confusingly, American class theorists have begun to use the term "segment" to refer to a portion of a class, what Europeans term a "class fraction." I stick to anthropological and European usage here.

who monopolize it, as military elites and castes, can wield a degree of general social power. Military organization is essentially authoritative and "concentrated-coercive." The military provides disciplined, routinized coercion, especially in modern armies. (Chapter 12 stresses the role of military discipline in modern society.) In its impact on the broader society, military power is sociospatially dual. It provides a concentrated core in which coercion ensures positive cooperation – for example, in slave labor in earlier historic societies or in ritualized "shows of force," as discussed in this volume. But it also provides a far larger military striking range of a more negative, terroristic form. Volume I stresses this especially in its Chapter 5, "The First Empires of Domination." In the modern West military power differs. It has been formally monopolized and restricted by states, yet military elites have kept considerable autonomy inside states, impacting considerably on society, as we shall see.

4. *Political power* derives from the usefulness of territorial and centralized regulation. Political power means *state* power. It is essentially authoritative, commanded and willed from a center. State organization is twofold: Domestically, it is "territorially centralized"; externally, it involves geopolitics. Both have impact on social development, especially in modern times. Chapter 3 is devoted to theorizing about the modern state.

The struggle to control ideological, economic, military, and political power organizations provides the central drama of social development. Societies are structured primarily by entwined ideological, economic, military, and political power. These four are only ideal types; they do not exist in pure form. Actual power organizations mix them, as all four are necessary to social existence and to each other. Any economic organization, for example, requires some of its members to share ideological values and norms. It also needs military defense and state regulation. Thus ideological, military, and political organizations help structure economic ones, and vice versa. Societies do not contain autonomous levels or subsystems, each developing separately according to its own logic ("from the feudal to the capitalist mode of production," "from the dynastic to the nation-state," etc.). In major transitions the fundamental interrelations, and very identities, of organizations such as "economies" or "states" became metamorphosed. Even the very definition of "society" may change. Throughout this period the nation-state and a broader transnational Western civilization competed as basic membership units. Sociology's master concept, "society," kept metamorphosing between the two.

The power sources thus generate overlapping, intersecting networks of power relations with different sociospatial boundaries and dynamics;

and their interrelations produce unanticipated, emergent consequences for power actors. My IEMP model is not one of a social system, divided into four "subsystems," "levels," "dimensions," or any other of the geometric terms favored by social theorists. Rather, it forms an analytical point of entry for dealing with mess. The four power sources offer distinct, potentially powerful organizational means to humans pursuing their goals. But which means are chosen, and in which combinations, will depend on continuous interaction between what power configurations are historically given and what emerges within and among them. The sources of social power and the organizations embodying them are impure and "promiscuous." They weave in and out of one another in a complex interplay between institutionalized and emergent, interstitial forces.

A revolutionary long century?

We have an obvious discontinuity from Volume I: Whereas it covered 10,000 years of human social experience and 5,000 years of civilized history worldwide, Volume II covers a mere 154 years and only the core area of a single civilization, Western Europe and its principal white colonial offshoot. Many broad-ranging issues discussed in Volume I are outside the scope of this volume. I cannot chart further (except in limited ways) one of its principal themes, the dialectic between empires of domination and multi-power-actor civilizations, since my civilization was merely an example of the latter. This volume replaces the macro with the micro.

There are good reasons for narrowing the scope. Western civilization now transformed the globe, and its wealth of documentation allows a finer grained narrative, linking macrostructures, group decision making, and individual human agency. I can also assay more comparative analysis. Some reviewers of the first volume assumed I opposed comparative analysis on principle. I do not. The more the cases and the closer they are in world-historical time, the more we can compare them. Provided we remember that my five cases were merely "countries" or "Powers," and not total "societies," they can be fruitfully compared. Most historians and sociologists also regard this period as essentially discontinuous from earlier history. They believe overall social development was ultimately determined by a singular, usually an economic, revolution. This is a simpler explanation than my IEMP model: not four sources but one fundamental source of power; not impure, interstitial entwining and metamorphosing, but a single dialectical system. Is their model of a single revolution useful?

Within about seventy years, first in Great Britain between about 1780 and 1850, then in Western Europe and America over the next seventy years, occurred what is generally acknowledged as the most momentous revolution in human history, the Industrial Revolution. It transformed the power of humans over nature and over their own bodies, the location and density of human settlement, and the landscape and natural resources of the earth. In the twentieth century all of these transformations spread over the globe. Today, we live in a global society. It is not a unitary society, nor is it an ideological community or a state, but it is a single power network. Shock waves reverberate around it, casting down empires, transporting massive quantities of people, materials, and messages, and, finally, threatening the ecosystem and atmosphere of the planet.

Most sociological and historical theory considers such changes "revolutionary" in the sense of their being qualitative, not merely quantitative. It dichotomizes human history around 1800. Classical sociological theory arose as little more than a series of dichotomies among societies existing before and after then, each considered to have a unitary, systemic character. The main dichotomies were from feudal to industrial society (Saint-Simon); from the metaphysical to the scientific stage (Comte); from militant to industrial society (Spencer); from feudalism to capitalism (Smith, the political economists, and Marx); from status to contract (Maine); from community to association (Tonnies); and from mechanical to organic forms of the division of labor (Durkheim). Even Weber, who did not dichotomize, saw history as a singular rationalization process, although he traced its development back farther.

There has been no letup. In the 1950s, Parsons identified a fourfold dichotomy revolutionizing interpersonal relations. These shifted from being particularistic to universalistic, from ascriptive to achievement-oriented, from affective (i.e., emotion-laden) to affectively neutral and instrumental, from being specific to a particular relationship to being diffuse across most relations. Preindustrial relationships were dominated by the former qualities; industrial societies, by the latter. Then the ghosts of Comte and Marx reappeared in Foucault's (1974, 1979) distinction between the classical and the bourgeois age, each dominated by its own "episteme" or "discursive formation" of knowledge and power. Giddens (1985) draws on all these writers in his avowedly "discontinuist" distinction between premodern societies and the modern nation-state.

Recently, some trichotomies have appeared, that is, arguments for a third type of society in the late twentieth century. These all suggest two transitions – from feudal to industrial to postindustrial; from feudal to capitalist to monopoly capitalist, disorganized capitalist, or postcapitalist; and from premodern to modern to postmodern. Postmodernism is now rampaging through academe, although it only scuttles through sociology. Its vitality depends on whether there was indeed a preceding "modern" era. These third stages are outside the scope of this volume (they will figure in Volume III). But the revisions do not question the revolutionary, systemic nature of the first transition; they merely add a second one.

I begin to unravel these dichotomies and trichotomies by critiquing their two main assumptions and their one internal disagreement. First, they assume that this period qualitatively transformed society as a whole. Second, they locate the transformation in an economic revolution. Most are explicit; a few, covert. For example, Foucault never explained his transition, but he repeatedly described it as a "bourgeois" revolution in an apparently Marxian sense (but because he had no real theory of distributive power, he never made clear who is doing what to whom). I contest both assumptions.

But the unraveling can start with the disagreement between the dichotomies. Whereas some see the essence of the new economy as industrial (Saint-Simon, Comte, Spencer, Durkheim, Bell, Parsons), others label it capitalist (Smith, the political economists, Marx, neo-Marxists, Foucault, Giddens, most postmodernists). Capitalism and industrialism were different processes occurring at different times, especially in the most advanced countries. Britain had a predominantly capitalist economy long before the Industrial Revolution.

In the 1770s, Adam Smith applied his theory of market capitalism to an essentially agrarian economy, apparently with little inkling that an industrial revolution was in the offing. If the capitalist school is correct, we must date the English revolutionary transformation from the eighteenth or even the seventeenth century. If the industrial school is correct, we may retain an early nineteenth-century dating. If both are partly correct, however, then there was more than one revolutionary process, and we must unravel their entwinings. Actually, economic transformations may have been even more complex. Current economic historians downplay the impact of the (first) Industrial Revolution, whereas others emphasize a "Second Industrial Revolution" that affected the leading economies from about 1880 to 1920. Relations between capitalism and industrialization also differed between regions and countries, and I shall show that economic transformation was not singular or systemic.

Was it a qualitative change? Yes on collective power, but no on distributive power. There was now indeed an unparalleled, truly exponential transformation in the logistics of collective power (as

Giddens 1985 emphasizes). Consider three measures of collective powers: the capacity to mobilize large numbers of people, the capacity to extract energy from nature, and the capacity of this civilization to exploit others collectively.

Population growth measures the increasing capacity to mobilize people in social cooperation. In England and Wales the entire process of human development had achieved 5 million population by 1640. After 1750, growth curved upward, reaching 10 million by 1810 and 15 million by 1840. What had first taken millennia now took thirty years. Across the globe the first billion of world population was not reached until 1830; the second took a century; the third, thirty years; and the fourth, fifteen years (McKeown 1976: 1–3; Wrigley and Schofield 1981: 207–15). During the previous millennia life expectancy mostly stayed in the 30s, then it improved through nineteenth-century Europe to fifty years and in the twentieth century to more than seventy years, a massive change in human experience (Hart, forthcoming). Similar acceleration occurred in virtually all forms of collective mobilization. Between 1760 and 1914, statistics on the communication of messages and goods, gross national product, per capita income, and weapon-kill ratios reveal a takeoff beyond all known historical rhythms. The growth of collective power mobilization, of what Durkheim called "social density," became truly exponential.

The ability of humans to extract energy from nature also greatly increased. In the agrarian societies discussed in Volume I, energy output depended overwhelmingly on human and animal muscle. Muscles required calories provided by agricultural produce, which required almost everyone's labor. There was an energy trap, with little left to spare for nonagricultural activity beyond supporting small ruling classes, armies, and churches. Landes (1969: 97–8) points out the difference coal mines and steam engines made: By 1870, British coal consumption exceeded 100 million tons. This generated about 800 million calories of energy, enough to supply the energy requirements of a preindustrial society of 200 million adults. The actual British population in 1870 was 31 million, but this energy was generated by only 400,000 miners. Humans' current ability to extract energy even threatens to exhaust the earth's reserves and destroy its ecosystem.

In historical terms, this rate of energy extraction is simply staggering. Agrarian societies might occasionally match the energy concentration of a coal mine or a large steam engine – for example, a Roman legion building a road or Egyptians constructing a pyramid – but these sites would be teeming with thousands of men and beasts. The approach roads, ending at great storehouses, would be choked with supply wagons. For miles around agriculture would be organized to deliver its surpluses there. Such agrarian logistics presupposed an authoritarian federation of local-regional and segmental power organizations, coercively concentrating their powers onto this one extraordinary task. Yet, by 1870, steam engines were found everywhere in Britain, each involving perhaps fifty workers and their families, a few beasts, a shop, and a couple of supply vehicles. Energy output no longer required concentrated, extensive, and coercive mobilization. It diffused throughout civil society, transforming collective power organization.

This single civilization could now dominate the world. Bairoch (1982) has assembled historical statistics of production (discussed in Chapter 8). In 1750, Europe and North America contributed perhaps 25 percent of world industrial production and, by 1913, 90 percent (probably a little less, as such statistics understate the production of nonmonetary economies). Industry could be converted into massive military superiority. Quite small European troop contingents and fleets could cow continents and divide the globe. Only Japan, inland China, and inaccessible, unattractive countries remained outside the empires of the Europeans and their white settlers. East Asia then rebounded and joined the select band of pillagers of the earth.

Western collective power had been revolutionized, as dichotomous theories suggested. Societies were qualitatively better organized to mobilize human capacities and to exploit nature, as well as to exploit less developed societies. Their extraordinary social density enabled rulers and people actually to participate in the same "society." Contemporaries called this revolution in collective power "modernization," even "progress." They perceived movement toward a wealthier, healthier, and otherwise better society that would increase human happiness and social morality. Few doubted that Europeans, in their homelands and colonies, were inaugurating a qualitative leap forward in general social organization. We may be skeptical, even alarmist, about such "progress," but in the long nineteenth century few doubted it.

The time span of change was short, major transformations often occurring within single lifetimes. This was different from most structural changes described in Volume I. For example, the emergence of capitalistic social relations in Western Europe had taken centuries. People might experience some aspects of this (say, the commutation of their labor services into cash rent or forcible enclosure of their land), but it is doubtful if anyone comprehended the macrochanges under way. By contrast, nineteenth-century macroprocesses were identified by thoughtful participants – hence the emergence of the dichotomous theories themselves, which were really just relatively scientific versions of contemporary modernization ideologies.

Increasing self-consciousness and reflectiveness bring feedback effects. If social actors become aware of ongoing structural transformations, they may seek to resist them. But if, as here, transformations enhance collective powers, they are more likely to seek to harness modernization to their own interests. Their ability to do so depends on their distributive power.

At first sight, distributive power also seems to have transformed near the beginning of this period. Classes and nations appeared as relatively novel actors in power struggles, generating the sociopolitical events we call "revolutions." Volume I demonstrated that both class and national organization had been rare in agrarian societies. Now, as Marx, Weber, and others noticed, class and national struggles became central to social development. Distributive power, like collective, moved from particularism toward universalism.

Yet the results were curiously unrevolutionary. Consider the first industrial nation, Great Britain. Many distributive power relations found in Britain in 1760 were still there in 1914 – indeed, they are still there. Where they have changed, the transition was usually under way long before 1760. Henry VIII had introduced state Protestantism, the Civil War confirmed it, and the eighteenth and early nineteenth centuries half secularized it. Constitutional monarchy was institutionalized in 1688; the erosion of the monarchy's powers, along with confirmation of its symbolic dignity, proceeded throughout the eighteenth, nineteenth, and twentieth centuries. Agriculture and commerce early became capitalist; industry was molded by eighteenth-century commercial institutions, and modern classes have been absorbed into such capitalism. The House of Lords, the two ancient universities, the public schools, the City, the Guards, the London clubs, the administrative class of the civil service – all survive in power as a mixture of the old and of the nineteenth century. True, genuine power shifts also resulted – the rise of the middle class and of labor and the growth of party democracy, popular nationalism, and the welfare state – but the overall trend was less the qualitative transformation that dichotomous theories envisaged than more gradual changes indicating the massive adaptability of ruling regimes.

Perhaps Britain is extreme, in many ways the most conservative European country; but we find many similar patterns elsewhere. The religious map of Europe was settled in 1648, with no significant changes appearing since. The Christian religion has been half secularized ever since. True, there were two great overthrows of monarchies near the beginning of our period; but the American and French revolutions occurred before industrialization in those countries, and (as we shall see) the French Revolution needed a whole century to achieve rather more modest changes than it first promised, and the American revolutionaries' Constitution rapidly became a conservative force on later distributive power relations. Elsewhere capitalism and industrialism shocked but rarely overthrew old regimes – two sociopolitical revolutions in France and Russia, compared to a host of failed ones and of more limited reforms elsewhere. Old regime and new capital usually merged into a modern ruling class in the nineteenth century; then they made citizenship concessions that also partly domesticated middle and working classes and peasantries. There has been even greater continuity in the major non-Western capitalist country, Japan.

Perhaps I have been selective, downplaying genuine distributive power shifts. But the opposite case, for a transformation in distributive power – especially in the Marxian dialectical sense of opposites clashing head-on in social and political "revolution" – seems implausible.

This also seems true for power distributed geopolitically. States became nation-states but continued to rise and fall while a few remained to contest the leadership over many centuries. France and Britain remained contenders from the medieval period right through this period, whereas the success of Prussia, the emergence of the United States, and the decline of Austria were more novel. The post–sixteenth century trend toward fewer, larger Powers was actually slowed by the Industrial Revolution (Tilly 1990: 45–7). The Industrial Revolution privileged the nation-state over the multinational empire and it privileged those states with large economies. We shall see, though, that these trends also depended on noneconomic power relations.

There is one main exception to the surprising continuity of distributive power. Power relations between men and women began a rapid, even revolutionary, transformation during this period. I have briefly described elsewhere (1988) the end of "patriarchy," its replacement by "neopatriarchy," and then the emergence of more egalitarian gender relations. The simplest indicator is longevity. From the earliest prehistoric times until to the end of the nineteenth century, men outlived women, by about five years over a life span of thirty to forty-five years. Then the discrepancy was reversed: Women now outlive men by five years over a life span of seventy years, and the differential is still widening (Hart 1990). I have abandoned my original intent to focus on gender relations in this volume. Gender relations have their own history, currently being rewritten by feminist scholarship. Now is not the time to attempt grand synthesis – although I shall comment on the connections among gender, class, and nation during this period. Except for gender, however, distributive power was transformed less during this period than theoretical tradition suggested. Classes and nation-states did not revolutionize social stratification.

Some sociologists and historians have remarked this. Moore (1973) argues that political development was affected more by older land-holding patterns than by industrial capitalism. Rokkan (1970) distinguishes two revolutions, the national and the industrial, each generating two political cleavages. The national revolution involved center-periphery and state-church conflict, the Industrial Revolution brought land-industry and owner-worker conflicts. Rokkan unravels the revolutionary dichotomy into a complex combination of four struggles, earlier ones setting down parameters for later ones. Lipset (1985) believes variations in twentieth-century labor movements were caused by the presence or absence of earlier feudalism. Corrigan and Sayer note the durability of the British ruling class – its "supposed reasonableness, moderation, pragmatism, hostility to ideology, 'muddling through,' quirkiness, eccentricity" (1985: 192 ff.). Mayer (1981) argues that European old regimes were not swept away by industrialism: Only by perpetrating World War I and by overreacting to socialism by embracing fascism did they ensure their demise.

These writers make two points. First, tradition matters. Neither capitalism nor industrialism swept all away but were molded into older forms. Second, these writers go beyond the economy, adding various political, military, geopolitical, and ideological power relations to modes of production and social classes. Their arguments are often correct. Later chapters draw from them, especially from Rokkan, who perceived the significance of national as well as class struggles.

Nonetheless, distributive power relations were altered. First, classes and nations could not simply be ignored or repressed by old regimes. To survive, they had to compromise (Wuthnow 1989: III; Rueschemeyer, Stephens, and Stephens 1992). But national struggles also entwined with classes, thus changing all power actors, not "dialectically," systemically but in complex ways often having unintended consequences. Second, the traditional rival power organizations of classes and nations – segmental or sectional and transnational or local-regional – were not eliminated but transformed. Loose networks controlled particularistically by old regime notables became more penetrative notable and clientalist political parties, keeping class parties at bay. Armed forces tightened from loose confederations of regiments "owned" by great nobles or mercenary entrepreneurs to modern, professional forces imposing highly centralized line and staff controls and discipline. The Catholic church buttressed its transnationalism with greater local-regional mobilizing powers to organize decentralizing power against the nation-state. All such organizations transformed the relations between regimes and masses.

In sum: Economic transformation was not singular but multiple;

collective power was revolutionized; most forms of distributive power were altered but not revolutionized; traditional dominant power actors survived better than expected; and power actors were aware of structural transformations but these were extremely complex. All of this carries implications for a theory of social change.

Social change: strategies, impure entwinings, unintended consequences

At the beginning of the period occurred three revolutions, all surprises to their participants. Britain's Industrial Revolution, initiated by Adam Smith's "hidden hand," was intended by no one and would have astonished Smith himself. Second, British settlers in America stumbled unintentionally into the first colonial revolution. Third, the French old regime was surprised by a political revolution intended by few of its participants. Power actors now debated whether further revolutions were repeatable or avoidable. Colonial revolutions are outside the scope of this discussion, but I do consider industrial and political revolutions.

Industrialization had been hard to initiate but was easy to imitate and adapt, provided some commercialization existed already. The successful adaptors ranged across Europe from northern Italy and Catalonia to Scandinavia and from the Urals to the Atlantic, and across America and Japan. Regimes strove to maximize profits and minimize disruption. Industrialization was adapted according to local traditions. Political revolution was the opposite, seemingly easy to initiate, difficult to imitate – once old regimes were alerted to its dangers. The revolutionary program could be modified: Regime and emerging power actors could choose or drift between modernization paths placing differing emphases on monarchical rule, the rule of law, economic liberalism, democracy, and nationalism. Half-conscious incorporative-repressive strategies ensured varied nonrevolutionary patterns of development.

Thus traditions were neither overthrown nor merely reproduced. They were modified or amplified according to clashes between "regime strategies-drifts" and the strategies-drifts of emerging classes and nations. By "regime" I mean an alliance of dominant ideological, economic, and military power actors, coordinated by the rulers of the state. These rulers, as we see in Chapter 3, comprised both "parties" (in Max Weber's sense) and "state elites" (in the sense used by elitist state theory). They sought a modernizing alliance to mobilize the emerging powers of classes and nations, or the state would fall to internal revolt or foreign powers. Regimes generally have greater logistical capacities than do those down below. However, their resilience depended on their cohesion. Party factionalism in an era of rising classes and nations encouraged revolution. I term their attempts to cope with the challenge of emergent social classes and nations "regime strategies." Not all regimes possessed them, and even the most far-sighted found themselves buffeted by complex politics into different tracks of which they were not wholly conscious. Thus most power actors drifted as well as schemed – hence strategies-drifts.

At first, almost all regimes ran along a continuum between despotic and constitutional monarchy. T. H. Marshall (1963: 67–127) argued from the British experience for a three-phase evolution toward fuller citizenship. The first involved legal or "civil" citizenship: "rights necessary for individual freedom – liberty of the person, freedom of speech, thought and faith, the right to own property and to conclude valid contracts, and the right to justice." British civil citizenship was obtained through a "long eighteenth century," from 1688 until Catholic Emancipation in 1828. The second phase obtained "political" citizenship, comprising voting and participating in sovereign parliaments, over the century from the Great Reform Act of 1832 to the Franchise Acts of 1918 and 1928. The third, twentieth-century phase secured "social" citizenship, or the welfare state: "the right to a modicum of economic welfare and security to . . . share to the full in the social heritage and to live the life of a civilized being according to the standards prevailing in the society."

Marshall's theory has excited considerable interest in the English-speaking world (the best recent discussions are Australian: Turner 1986, 1990, and Barbalet 1988). Two of his types of citizenship turn out to be heterogeneous. Civil citizenship may be divided into individual and collective subtypes (Giddens 1982: 172; Barbalet 1988: 22–7). As we shall see, although most eighteenth-century regimes conceded individual legal rights, none yielded collective organizing rights to workers until the end of the nineteenth century or even until well into the twentieth. (See Chapters 15, 17, and 18.) I also subdivide social citizenship (Marshall's "sharing in the social heritage") into ideological and economic subtypes – rights to an education, allowing cultural participation and occupational attainment, and rights to direct economic subsistence. Through the long nineteenth century, ideological-social citizenship was attained by all middle classes (see Chapter 16), but economic-social citizenship remained minimal (as Marshall noted; see Chapter 14). Citizenship developed varied forms and rhythms, some of which undercut others. Citizenship perhaps has not been as singular a process as Marshall argues.

Moreover, as I have already (1988) argued, Marshall's evolutionism, neglect of geopolitics, and Anglo centrism can all be faulted. Let us begin by asking a simple question: Why should classes – or indeed any other power actor – *want* citizenship? Why should they consider the state relevant to their lives? Most people had not hitherto. They had lived amid predominantly local or regional power networks, as influenced by transnational churches as by the state. We shall see that through wars eighteenth-century states enormously increased their fiscal and manpower exactions, caging their subjects onto the national terrain and thus politicizing them. Thus classes flexed their growing muscles on politics instead of concentrating as traditionally on fighting other classes in civil society. This "militarist" phase was then followed by other encouragements of the caged nation: office-holding disputes, tariffs, railways, and schools. As states transformed first into national states, then into nation-states, classes became caged, unintentionally "naturalized" and politicized. The nation was vital to citizenship (as Giddens 1985: 212–21 recognizes). We must theorize national as well as class struggle.

There were actually two citizenship issues: representation and the national question of who is to be represented and where. *Where* turned on how centralized and national or how decentralized and confederal the state should be. Despotism might be fought by decentralizing the state onto local assemblies, while linguistic, religious, or regional minorities normally resisted the centralized nation-state.[3] Enlighten-ment modernizers believed the two issues went together: the future belonged to representative and centralized states. Later evolutionary theorists like Marshall believed the nation-state and national citizen-ship were inevitable. Indeed, most Western countries today *are* cen-tralized, representative, and citizen nation-states.

But such "modernization" has not been one-dimensional or evolu-tionary. The Industrial Revolution did not homogenize; rather, it modernized disparate regime strategies. The boost to collective powers provided by the revolution could be used by any regime – party democratic or despotic, centralized or confederal – to amplify its initial characteristics. Outcomes depended on both domestic politics and geo-politics. So did the undoubted overall movement toward the centralized nation-state. Regimes competed, flourished, and perished according to domestic class and national power struggles, diplomatic alliances, wars, international economic rivalry, and ideological claims resonating across

---

[3] Turner (1990) rightly criticized my neglect of religion and ethnicity in my 1988 essay. I now seek to remedy this by taking seriously the national question. Turner also criticized my emphasis on ruling class at the expense of lower-class strategies. This volume considers both, but continues to stress the former.

the West. As Powers rose, so did the attractiveness of their regime strategies; as Powers declined, so their strategies disintegrated. One Power's successful strategy might then change subsequent industrialization. German semiauthoritarian monarchy and greater American centralization were both partly the result of war. They then fostered the Second Industrial Revolution, the large capitalist corporation and state regulation of economic development.

Finally "impure entwinings" also muddied contemporaries' perceptions. Thus I edge away from "strategies" – from cohesive elites with transparent interests, clear vision, rational decisions, and infinite survival. Ideological, economic, military, and political transformations and class and national struggles were multiple, entwined, and developing interstitially. No power actor could comprehend and take charge of all this. In acting they made mistakes and generated unintended consequences, changing their very identities below the level of consciousness. The whole was a nonsystemic, nondialectical process between historically given institutions and emergent interstitial forces. My IEMP model can confront and then begin to make sense of this mess; dichotomous theories cannot.

Bibliography

Bairoch, P. 1982. International industrialization levels from 1750 to 1980. *Journal of European Economic History* 11.
Barbalet, J. 1988. *Citizenship*. Milton Keynes: Open University Press.
Corrigan, P., and D. Sayer. 1985. *The Great Arch*. Oxford: Blackwell.
Foucault, M. 1974. *The Order of Things*. New York: Pantheon.
    1979. *Discipline and Punish*. London: Allen Lane.
Giddens, A. 1982. *Profiles and Critiques in Social Theory*. London: Macmillan.
    1985. *The Nation-State and Violence*. Cambridge: Polity Press.
Hart, N. 1990. Female vitality and the history of human health. Paper presented to the Third Congress of the European Society for Medical Sociology, Marburg.
    Forthcoming. *Life Chances and Longevity*. London: Macmillan.
Landes, D. 1969. *The Unbound Prometheus: Technological Change and Industrial Development in Western Europe from 1750 to the Present*. Cambridge: Cambridge University Press.
Lipset, S. M. 1985. Radicalism or reformism: the sources of working-class politics. In his *Consensus and Conflict: Essays in Political Sociology*. New Brunswick, N.J.: Transaction Books.
McKeown, T. 1976. *The Modern Rise of Population*. New York: Academic Press.
Mann, M. 1986. *The Sources of Social Power*. Vol. I, *A History of Power from the Beginning to A.D. 1760*. Cambridge: Cambridge University Press.
    1988. Ruling class strategies and citizenship. In my *States, War and Capitalism*. Oxford: Blackwell.

Marshall, T. H. 1963. *Sociology at the Crossroads and Other Essays*. London: Heinemann.

Mayer, A. J. 1981. *The Persistence of the Old Regime*. London: Croom Helm.

Moore, B., Jr. 1973. *Social Origins of Dictatorship and Democracy*. Harmondsworth: Penguin Books.

Parsons, T. 1960. The distribution of power in American society. In his *Structure and Process in Modern Societies*. New York: Free Press.

Rokkan, S. 1970. *Cities, Elections, Parties: Approaches to the Comparative Study of the Processes of Development*. Oslo: Universitets forlaget.

Rueschemeyer, D., E. Stephens, and J. Stephens. 1992. *Capitalist Development and Democracy*. Chicago: University of Chicago Press.

Tilly, C. 1990. *Coercion, Capital and European States, AD 990–1990*. Oxford: Blackwell.

Turner, B. S. 1986. *Citizenship and Capitalism*. London: Allen & Unwin.

1990. Outline of a theory of citizenship. *Sociology* 24.

Wrigley, E. A., and R. S. Schofield. 1981. *The Population History of England, 1541–1871*. London: Arnold.

Wuthnow, R. 1989. *Communities of Discourse*. Cambridge, Mass.: Harvard University Press.

2 Economic and ideological power relations

It became conventional in the eighteenth century – and it has remained so ever since – to distinguish between two fundamental spheres of social activity – "civil society" (or just "society") and "the state." The titles of this chapter and the next would seem to conform to that convention. Though Smith, other political economists, and Marx meant by "civil society" only economic institutions, others – notably, Ferguson, Paine, Hegel, and Tocqueville – believed it comprised the two spheres discussed in this chapter. For them, civil society meant (1) decentered economic markets resting on private property and (2) "forms of civil association . . . scientific and literary circles, schools, publishers, inns, . . . religious organizations, municipal associations and independent households" (Keane 1988: 61). These two spheres carried vital decentered and diffused freedoms that they wished secured against the authoritative powers of states.

Yet, such a clear division between society and state carries dangers. It is, paradoxically, highly political, locating freedom and morality in society, not the state (obviously Hegel differed in this respect). This was so among the eighteenth-century writers resisting what they saw as despotism, and it has recently been so again as Soviet, East European, and Chinese dissidents sought to mobilize decentralized civil society forces against state repression. Yet states are not as distinct from the rest of social life as these ideologies suggest. Volume I showed that civil societies had first risen entwined with modern states. This volume shows that through the long nineteenth century, civil society became more substantially, though far from entirely, the province of the nation-state. This had implications for both economic and ideological power relations, and this is the central theme of this chapter. Thus the actual text of this chapter and Chapter 3 often refutes the separation implied by their titles.

Economic power: capitalism and classes

By 1760, Western economic power relations were becoming dominated by capitalism. Following Marx, I define capitalism in the following terms:

1. *Commodity production.* Every factor of production, including labor, is treated as a means, not an end in itself, is given exchange value,

and is exchangeable against every other factor. Thus capitalism is a diffuse form of economic power, except that it requires authoritative guarantee of:

2. *Private exclusive ownership of the means of production.* The means of production, including labor power, belong exclusively to a private class of capitalists.
3. *Labor is "free" but separated from the means of production.* Laborers are free to sell their labor and withdraw it as they see fit, without authoritative prohibitions; they receive a freely negotiated wage but have no direct claims of ownership over the surplus.

Marx correctly argued that capitalism revolutionized society's "productive forces" – collective economic power. That was the most obvious claim to "ultimate primacy" that this particular mode of economic production possessed in modern times. But Marx also argued that capitalism's "relations of production" – distributive economic power – was also revolutionizing society. Now the surplus could be extracted by "purely economic means" through production and markets themselves, without the need for assistance from independent ideological, military, and political power organizations. His contrast between capitalism and previous modes of production has been endorsed by many (Poulantzas 1975: 19; Anderson 1979: 403; Giddens 1985: 181; Brenner 1987: 227, 231, 299). I will disagree. Marx also argued that commodity production diffuses the *same* relations over the whole terrain of capitalism. Thus economic class struggle could become "pure," extensive and political, transnational, and eventually symmetrical and dialectical, as it had been but rarely before (though Marx did not quite admit this last point). He saw class conflict as the motor of modern development, generating its own ideologies, politics, and military struggles. Their forms would be determined "in the last instance" by the class dialectic of the capitalist mode of production. This would end, Marx hoped, and sometimes predicted, in the overthrow of capitalism by a revolutionary proletariat, instituting socialism and communism.

Obviously, Marx went wrong somewhere. He overestimated the revolutionary tendencies of the proletariat – and before it, of the bourgeoisie. Even where revolutions came close to success, they did so for reasons other than just class conflict. He exaggerated the economic contradictions of capitalism and he neglected ideological, military, political, and geopolitical power relations. All this is well known. But a conventional demolition job on Marx clouds our understanding of where *exactly* he went wrong and of how we might improve on him. Even if history is not the "history of class struggle," classes do exist, competing with other power actors over human souls. In these days of Marxian retreat and postmodern nihilism, some historians seem to abandon class altogether (e.g., Joyce 1991). Yet this is to throw out the baby with the bathwater. It is better to make more precise our conceptions of classes and of their power rivals.

Marx was most explicit about class when describing the French peasantry:

In so far as millions of families live under economic conditions of existence that separate their mode of life, their interests, and their culture from those of the other classes, and put them in hostile opposition to the latter, they form a class. In so far as there is merely a local interconnection among these small-holding peasants and the identity of their interests begets no community, no national bond, and no political organization amongst them, they do not form a class. They are consequently incapable of enforcing their class interests in their own name. [1968, 170-1]

Chapter 19 shows that Marx was wrong about the "smallholding peasants" – they were actually prolific in their organization. But this passage is of more general interest. Historians and sociologists have often quoted it in connection with two other distinctions Marx made. The smallholding peasantry, they say, constituted a class "in itself" but not "for itself," with a common relationship to the means of production but incapable of collective class action. Marx was indeed saying this. But the commentators proceed to a second distinction: The peasantry were "objectively" but not "subjectively" a class. We must analyze, they say, two dimensions of class, objective economic conditions and subjective class consciousness, both necessary for class formation. Hunt, a historian of the French Revolution, says: "For Marx, class formation depended on both economic condition and culture, social category and consciousness" (1984: 177). The sociologists Westergaard and Resler announce that their major analysis of twentieth-century class structure starts from the question of "how objective cleavages of power, wealth, security and opportunity give rise to groups whose members are conscious of a common identity. [Is] 'class in itself' translated into an active consciousness of 'class for itself'?" (1975: 2-3).

It is appropriate that Marx should be misinterpreted, for his own polemic against idealism helped establish the dualism of objective economic reality versus subjective consciousness that underlies these commentaries. But Marx is not arguing this in the passage quoted. He explicitly included the "culture" of the peasantry in the supposedly objective aspect of class. Conversely, the "merely local interconnec-tion" of the peasants, which prevented them acting (supposedly subjectively) as a class, is actually economic. Marx said nothing about economic versus ideological aspects of class. Instead, he distinguished two predominantly economic preconditions of class: "similarity," which peasants possessed, and "collective interdependence," which he says they did not. Peasants' economic similarity gave them a sense of their class interests plus a broader cultural identity. But their ability to organize, equally economic in origin, was partial and locally confined. For Marx, classes were economic power organizations, and as such were defined by two criteria, the economic and the organizational.

Marx's broad economic criterion was "effective possession" of economic resources. In capitalism, the model generates two main antagonistic classes, capitalist owners and nonowning proletarians. He also identified an intermediary class of petits bourgeois owning its own means of production but not controlling the labor of others; and he left guidelines for coping with the emergence of the middle class(es) (see Chapter 16). Such classes might be considered "objective," but we might choose to define classes by other "objective" criteria. So-called industrial society theorists distinguish classes according to their specialized role in the division of labor, which method yields numerous occupational classes. Weberians identify classes according to market capacities, producing many classes based on ownership of property, scarce job skills, professional powers, and educational levels. How do we choose among these equally "objective" schemes?

In the extended passage quoted earlier, Marx gave us a second criterion: Classes possess organizational ability. The economic without the organizational criterion gives only what I term a "latent class" – corresponding roughly to the term "objective class" or "class in itself." Such a latent class is of little sociological interest. Theorists may develop what analytic categories they like, as ideal types, but only some of these help explain the real world. If classes are significant power actors in the real world they must be *organized*, extensively or politically. Throughout this volume I dissect the organizational capacities of class and other movements. What are their logistics? How and over what geographic and social terrain can they communicate messages, exchange personnel, and organize petitions, strikes, riots, revolutions?

Marx thought modern classes were involved in a head-on *dialectical* struggle with one another. The emergence of the capitalist mode of production gave bourgeoisie and workers organizational capacities rooted in production but totalized throughout society and throughout their life experience. He was partly correct. Such class organizations did emerge, capable of changing history. True, his view of the working class was absurdly utopian – how unlikely that an exploited class would confound all of previous history and rise up to destroy all stratification. Nonetheless, Marx had discovered an essential truth: Capitalism had created potentially extensive, political and (occasionally) symmetrical and dialectical classes. Rare in earlier societies, such classes have been ubiquitous ever since.

Thus class consciousness is also a perennial feature of modern societies, though it is never pure or complete. Most dominant classes show ambivalent consciousness. They share a cohesive community and a keen defense of their own interests. What social group could be more class conscious than, say, the eighteenth-century English gentry or the nineteenth-century Prussian Junker landlords? Yet they usually deny that society is divided into opposing classes, claiming that segmental and local-regional organizations (perhaps underpinned by normative consensus) are more significant. Indeed, subordinate classes are usually embedded in such organizations, but Marx believed they could attain class consciousness. His model of rising class consciousness implicitly contained the four components I identified in an earlier book on the working class (1973: 13):

1. *Identity*. The definition of self as working class, as playing a distinctive role in common with other workers in the economy.[1] This self-conception need not be associated with class conflict.
2. *Opposition*. The perception that capitalists and their managers constitute the workers' enduring opponent. Identity plus opposition will generate conflict, but this may not be extensive. It may be limited to workplace, trade, or local community, not generalized to whole classes, legitimating sectional, not class, conflict.
3. *Totality*. The acceptance of the first two elements as the defining characteristics of (1) the workers' total social situation and (2) the whole society. The addition of (1) adds intensity to consciousness of sectional conflict, and (2) converts sectional consciousness to extensive class conflict.
4. *Alternative*. Conceiving of an alternative form of power relations to existing capitalism. This will reinforce extensive and political class conflict and legitimate revolutionary struggle.

I shall analyze the extent to which rising classes exhibit these components of class consciousness. Most people probably sense more of the first than of the second and of the first and second more than of

---

[1] In 1973, I wrote "in the productive process," a phrase I now replace with a more diffuse term, *economy*, in line with one of the general arguments of this volume.

the third and fourth. But it is rare that they single-mindedly drive anyone. We are also members of families, of cross-class communities and workplaces, of churches, of other voluntary associations, of nations, and so forth. Most of these identities confuse, some oppose, a clear-cut sense of class. Societies are confusing battlegrounds on which multiple power networks fight over our souls. In modern societies, class is just one of the more important forms of self-identity. But people in similar economic circumstances will also be influenced by other identities. Only a few will experience their lives as dominated by a class – or by a religious, national, or any other single – identity. When describing classes "acting" in later chapters, I am not conjuring up images of masses of people resolutely acting as if in heroic Soviet proletarian paintings. I am usually describing a few militants who really are so motivated, able to move large numbers by persuading them that their class sentiments are a more significant part of themselves than they had previously believed. Even then, most such persons may dearly wish they could continue being loyal producers, Catholics, citizens, and so forth.

I identify six main class actors: the *old regime* and the *petite bourgeoisie*, emerging through conflicts between old and new modes of production and political regimes in the first part of the period; the *capitalist class* and the *working class*, the two great extensive groups emerging in the second half of the period; the *middle class*, emerging throughout the nineteenth century; and the *peasantry*, of considerable significance throughout the period. I define these classes near the beginning of three chapters: the peasantry in Chapter 19, the working class in Chapter 15, and the other classes in Chapter 4.

These classes may seem familiar enough, especially within the Marxian tradition. But, unlike Marxists, I do not see classes as pure, defined only in terms of relations to the means of production. Whole, pure classes never organize major social change. Social movements we recognize as classlike can be distinguished at two levels. Where whole class movements emerge, they are impure, their force contributed by noneconomic as well as economic power networks. Considered as purely economic organizations, they are heterogeneous, incapable of much collective action (although fractions among them may possess their own particular organization). Four economic fault lines persistently weaken the solidarity of whole classes:

1. Economic sector fragments classes. Fractions of both capital and labor persistently organize differently, sometimes in conflict with one another. Agriculture usually generates its own subculture. Farm laborers rarely conceive of themselves as "proletarians," alongside industrial workers; peasant proprietors and smallholders generate

their own distinct movements. (See Chapter 19.) Interindustry differences and the rise of the public and service sectors add their own heterogeneity,

2. The direct relations of economic production may generate much smaller collectivities than a whole class – defined by a single enterprise, industry, or occupation. This may strengthen segmental, not class, organization. Solidarity may be highly developed within these boundaries but have few organizational connections with those supposedly in the same class. At the most they will constitute a militant sectional union movement; at the least they may form a segmental alliance with their employer, against other workers and employers.

3. Strata and fractions divide classes. The late eighteenth-century petite bourgeoisie actually comprised a varied collection of professionals, merchants, factors, shopkeepers, artisan masters, artisan men, and many others. Later, the "middle class" contained an elongated occupational hierarchy and three distinct fractions (professionals, careerists, and petite bourgeoisie). The working class contained groups with different labor-market powers, especially separating skilled from unskilled workers, and workers entrenched in internal labor markets from newcomer workers – often reinforced by ethnicity and gender. Such differences lead to distinct organizations – to the profession, the career, the craft union – separating them from other members of "their class." Internal labor markets, managerial careers, and other forms of hierarchical dependence have generated segmental organizations, reducing the prospects for class organization.

4. The nation-state crosscuts classes, forming national segments. There has never been one great transnational bourgeoisie or proletariat, although transnational class tendencies do exist (perhaps nowhere stronger than among the contemporary capitalist class). Normally the largest class actors have been nationally limited, thus the "British working class," the "French bourgeoisie," and the like. The national fragmentation of class has actually been rather complex, as we shall see later.

For these four reasons, relations of production do not merely generate whole classes. They too are a confused battleground on which our identities are fought over. Purely economic actors have been normally smaller, more specific, and more fragmented by internal sectionalism and crosscutting segmentalism than Marx's great classes. Nonetheless, his classes have played important historical roles. Why? Not because the "law of value" or some other economic law polarized all these economic particularities into great class camps. Instead, *noneconomic* organizations have welded solidarities among these economically heterogeneous fractions, strata, and segments. Class conflict arose in societies with ideological, military, and political power relations and was also molded by them. This point is usually made to explain why classes *lack* solidarity – for example, because they are split by religion. Yet noneconomic networks may also *generate* class solidarity. Marx's neglect of ideological, military, and political power is not merely of phenomena external to capitalism and class. Their organizations helped metamorphose disparate economic actors, often with opposing conceptions of identities and interests, into relatively cohesive classes. All my classes were created by the entwined development of the sources of social power. The "purity" of modern classes, though in historical terms rather developed, has been only partial.

We shall see that states, especially the developing nation-states, played a very substantial structuring role in the development of civil society and its classes. Not even revolutionary politics flow simply from the conflict between classes already "out there" in civil society. The class actors aroused during the French Revolution barely existed before the Revolution. They were created by its power processes – partly because militant ideologists worked hard to mobilize class sentiments, but mostly because they were unintentionally fostered by political power relations. States are also impure, being economic as well as political. They own property, they spend, and they tax. In the eighteenth century, rights to office, monopolies, and tax privileges provided economic rewards and generated factional, segmental politics. "In" parties were pitted against "outs," "court" against "country" parties. "In" parties were from landowning families, commercial oligarchies, or professions allied to the crown, whereas "out" parties began to consist of discontented factions of the same groups leading the petite bourgeoisie. Thus factional politics became entwined with class and sectional struggles generated by the transition from commercial-landed to manufacturing capitalism. "Ins," landed gentry, and commercial oligarchs solidifed into an old regime class, and "outs" and diverse fractions and strata solidified into a broadly petit bourgeois movement. This was not merely a class struggle; it also derived, in some cases predominantly, from the state's political economy. "Class" only became extensive and political as economic and political power struggles became entwined. Where factional political struggles were weaker, as in Germany (or Japan), there was no revolution, class politics were feebler, and feudalism changed into capitalism with little class struggle.

Parallel, if lesser, points can be made concerning ideological and military power relations. Marx believed that classes create their own ideology, articulating their own practical activity and interests. They might be aided by intellectuals like himself, but these are only articulating an ideology already immanent in an already constituted class. This view poses two problems: First, as in other "instrumental" theories of action (e.g., neoclassical economics, exchange theory, rational choice theory), it is not clear that interests alone can drive forward the kind of action Marx was envisaging. Is it ever in the interests of the individual worker to expose himself or herself to employer and state power by starting a union, still less by erecting barricades or attacking cossacks? Classes do exist, but they have shared norms and passions, inspiring them to recklessness, sacrifice, and cruelty. These help them overcome their diverse economic membership to generate passionate collective behavior. Ideology may be immanent and transcendent among classes. Second, if ideology matters, so do ideologists. Eighteenth-century ideologists, secular and religious, found messages and communication media that transcended the diverse grievances of petite bourgeois segments, class fractions, taxpayers, those deprived of lucrative office, and so forth. Journalists, coffeehouse keepers, teachers, and others mobilized class consciousness. A century later, middle-class dependence on state education helped transform its own class and national consciousness (see Chapter 16).

Similarly, Engels believed that some types of military power aided class consciousness: Mass conscription in the Prussian army could train revolutionaries. I believe the reverse: In this period militaries tended to provide effective segmental discipline over subordinate classes, aiding the survival of regimes and dominant classes. Nonetheless, other military power organizations – guerrilla warfare and defeated armies – have assisted class formation, as we will see.

Thus classes were imperfectly, haltingly formed as multiple economic identities were welded together by the political, ideological, and military power networks with which economic struggles were always entwined.

This also renders problematic the culminating quality of class struggle for Marx: its symmetrical, *dialectical* nature. If class A is organized in relation to different power networks to class B, they may not meet head-on over the same terrain. Marx took the arena of conflict for granted, and so have most others. Capitalism is invariably defined transnationally, penetrating state frontiers sociospatially wherever there are commodities to exchange and profits to be won. But capitalism actually emerged within and between the territories of states. It became sociospatially structured by their domestic and geopolitical relations. Its classes could have three sociospatial forms, as could segments and, indeed, all power actors:

1. *Transnational*. Organization and struggle proceed right across state boundaries, without significant reference to them. Classes occupy

the global reach of capitalism. States and nations are irrelevant to class struggle, their power weakened by its global reach. With the use of a distinction explained later, interests are defined more by market than by territory. An example of a predominantly transnational class was the medieval nobility, linked by kin relations stretching across Europe, conducting its own class diplomacy and many wars. More pacifically this was how most classic theorists – from Smith to Marx to Durkheim – saw the future of capitalism. Modern classes would be transnational.

2. *Nationalist.*[2] All or some of the inhabitants of one state become a quasi-class whose economic interests conflict with those of inhabitants of other states. "Nations," or the more restricted "class-nations," compete with and exploit one another, each with its own distinctive praxis in the international division of labor. Nationalist classes encourage what I term "territorial" definitions of interest (to be discussed shortly) and aggressive geo-economic and geopolitical rivalry. An emphasis on the nationalist organizations supposedly dominant in their own times suffused the work of turn-of-the-century writers like Gumplowicz (1899) and Oppenheimer (1922), formalized by Rüstow (1981) into the notion of "superstratification," domination by one nation over another. The same historical tendencies informed Lenin's theory of imperialism and then more recent Marxian theory like Wallerstein's and Chase-Dunn's theories of the "world system" and contemporary theories of Third World dependency.

3. *National.* Class organization and struggle are territorially confined within each state, without significant reference to class relations in other states. Here class praxis is not "anchored" in international space. Classes might get caught up in domestic struggles over the identity of the nation, but their sense of nationhood is inward-looking – divorced from, and incompetent in, international affairs. They have no serious geopolitical or geo-economic interests in relation to either markets or territory and no considered predisposition toward war or peace. No major school of theory conceptualizes this model of class organization, but I emphasize its importance throughout this period.

These are ideal types. Real classes (and other power actors) normally embody elements of all three organizations. A class may contain

---

[2] In previous work, I used the label "inter-national" for this type of organization. For readers to understand such a label required them to pay close attention to its hyphen. The word "international," without a hyphen, is conventionally used to denote something close to my transnational organization (as in "liberal internationalism"). As "nationalist" conventionally conveys the rough sense of what I mean in this second type, it is to be preferred.

distinct fractions, one relatively transnational, another nationalist. Or class actors may feel the tug of two or three organizational forms simultaneously, reducing class coherence. Or one class may be far more nationally confined than another, as labor is when compared with capital today. Thus classes are less likely to meet dialectically head-on than Marx expected.

The structuring role of nation-states means that their geopolitics are also entwined with classes. It has been common to analyze the impact of class struggle on geopolitics (e.g., in the theory of social imperialism, discussed in Chapter 21). It is less common, but as necessary, to reverse the causality (as Skocpol 1979 and Maier 1981 have done). Capitalism and industrial capitalism were "made in Britain." British near hegemony, and the resistance it provoked in France, Germany, and elsewhere, reshaped the nature of class struggle. So has the more recent American hegemony. We cannot tell either story, of class struggle and geopolitics, without the other. Here I make the immodest claim that this was never attempted on such a broad scale before this volume.

Not only classes but the very conceptions of economic "interest" and "profit" are affected by geopolitics. We can distinguish two ideal-typical conceptions of economic profit and interest, here termed "market" and "territorial" (cf. Krasner 1985: 5; Rosecrance 1986; Gilpin 1987: 8–24). A market conception sees interest as privately held and furthered by possession of resources on markets, without regard to state territories, war, or aggressive diplomacy. It is transnationally and peacefully oriented. Capitalists will pursue profit wherever there are markets, regardless of state boundaries. Geopolitics do not here define "interest." Yet a territorial conception of economic interest sees profit secured by authoritative control of territory by the state, often by aggressive diplomacy and, in extremis, by war. The tension between market and territory, capitalism and geopolitics, is a theme of this volume.

Again, these ideal types do not exist in the real world. Capitalism and states cohabit the world, influencing each other. Six main strategies may be distinguished:

1. *Laissez-faire*. The state merely endorses (or is unable to change) existing market terms, and does not try to change them authoritatively.

2. *National protectionism*. The state interferes authoritatively but pragmatically and peacefully with existing market terms to protect its own economy (when dealing with nineteenth-century Germany, I subdivide protectionism into "selective" and "general coordinated" protection).

3. *Mercantilist domination*. The state attempts to dominate international markets, authoritatively controlling such resources as it can, moving toward diplomatic sanctions (perhaps in concert with allied states), even shows of force, but short of war and territorial expansion. The old mercantilist formula was that "power and plenty" were conjoined.

Most international political economy regimes combine these three strategies in varying degrees. Although they embody conflict, they do not usually spark off war (as in the conflict of "The Third World Against Global Liberalism" analyzed by Krasner 1985), but three other political economies imply further aggression:

4. *Economic imperialism*. The state conquers territory for direct motives of economic profit.

5. *Social imperialism*. Conquest is aimed primarily at controlling existing more than new territories and populations. It seeks to distract attention from conflict between classes or other groups within existing state territories. Lenin and Marxists have emphasized class distraction; Weber saw social imperialism as employable by whoever controls the state against whoever are the enemies. Regime motives primarily concern domestic politics, *Innenpolitik*; geopolitics, *Aussenpolitik*, are their by-product.

6. *Geopolitical imperialism*. The state attempts to conquer territory as an end in itself.

These six strategies reveal that "power and plenty," geopolitics and capitalism, territory and market, have been usually entwined. Even the two extremes are not entirely "pure." The British were largely attached to laissez-faire in the nineteenth century because the more warlike strategies (3 and 4) had helped form the British Empire and the Royal Navy, which now ensured that the international terms of trade were mostly *its* terms. At the other extreme Hitler adopted geopolitical imperialism, obsessed by world power and paying little attention to economics. Yet, even he thought this would bring profit to Germany. International political economy – for example, laissez-faire or protectionism – does not result from a "pure" calculation of economic interest. Real-life definitions of interest are affected by territory, by senses of national identity, and by geopolitics, just as geopolitics is affected by economic interest. Both are also affected by ideologies. No strategy was self-evidently economically superior to its principal rivals. Choosing or drifting into it normally resulted from the entwining of *Innen-* and *Aussenpolitik* and of ideological, economic, military, political, and geopolitical power networks. Thus later chapters will interweave the stories of emerging extensive, political, yet still "impure" classes and nation-states.

Ideological power relations

As I indicated in Chapter 1, I believe that ideological power declined somewhat in significance during this period. This does not render it insignificant, however. Chapters 4–7 treat ideological power as an essential and autonomous part of the rise of bourgeois classes and nations, especially influential in shaping their passions. Chapters 16 and 20 then continue this argument through the nineteenth century, describing the importance of state educational institutions for the rise of the middle class and discussing nationalism as an ideology. Chapter 15 distinguishes the main forms of socialist ideology found among working-class and peasant movements of the long nineteenth century; and Chapters 17–19 trace their development. I do not fully explore the potential autonomy of these later ideologies in this volume. That task is reserved for my third volume, which will treat socialist and nationalist ideologies together over the terrain of the twentieth century. The discussion that now follows concentrates on earlier periods.

I make two general points about ideological power in 1760. First, just like the other principal aspect of civil society, the capitalist economy and its classes, ideological power networks were split between transnational and national terrains. On the one hand, Europe – increasingly the "West" – was a normative community, its ideologies diffusing interstitially, "transcendentally" across states. On the other hand, states erected barriers to the free flow of messages – more effective if linguistic communities coincided with state boundaries. Then, throughout the period, the national tended to strengthen at the expense of the transnational, though the latter always survived. Second, the media of discursive communication were undergoing revolutionary expansion during the eighteenth century, enabling ideological power to play a somewhat autonomous role.

Europe had been an ideological community for a millennium. Values, norms, rituals, and aesthetics diffused across the continent. It had been a single Christian *ecumene*, then split into Catholic and Protestant halves. We see churches losing power within states but remaining entrenched within the family and at the local-regional level, especially in the countryside. The historic power and then partial decline of Christendom left an important legacy: Communication media were interstitial, not controlled by any single power organization. Because much literacy was church-sponsored, the media were not fully controlled by state or capitalism, hard though both were to try. Europeans had also diffused their ideologies through their settler colonies, modifying "Christian" to "white" and "Europe" to the "West." Ideological messages diffused throughout the West, relatively unconfined by national boundaries. In comparative terms such autonomy of ideological power was unusual; neither Japan nor China possessed it to a comparable degree in early modern times. To be a Westerner was to participate in a partly transcendent ideological power organization, interstitial to the reach of other power organizations. This also means that the international arena was far from normless, as realists tend to argue.

Theorists emphasizing the rapid diffusion of ideologies throughout this period often claim it indicates "the autonomy of ideas" in society (e.g., Bendix 1978). That is not quite my own position. But I do not counterpose to such "idealism" a "materialism" that reduces ideas to their social base. My position is one of "organizational materialism": Ideologies are attempts to grapple with real social problems, but they are diffused through specific media of communication and *their* characteristics may transform ideological messages, so conferring ideological power autonomy. Thus the particularities of ideological power organization should be our object of study.

This means we must focus around 1760 on an ongoing revolution in "discursive literacy" – the ability to read and write texts that are not mere formulas or lists but presuppose literate mastery of conversation and argument. This volume charts various discursive ideologies across the long nineteenth century. Some were religious: Puritanism influenced early American history; moral Protestantism affected Britain; the Protestant-Catholic divide had an enduring role in Germany. Others were secular, usually disputing with religions: the Enlightenment, utilitarianism, liberalism, and the two greatest modern ideologies, of nation and class. All these ideologies were shared across extensive territories linked by the communication of discursive literacy.

Benedict Anderson (1983) famously observed that the nation is an "imagined community" in time and space. People who have never met, who have no direct connection – even the living, the dead, and the yet-to-be-born – supposedly become linked together in a "nation." As a secretary at UCLA explained to me about the American Thanksgiving holiday: "It's when we remember our ancestors who came over on the *Mayflower*." Her imagination was impressive since she is black. I add what Anderson, a Marxist, does not: If the nation was an imagined community, its class rival might seem even more metaphorical, a veritable "*imaginary* community." Nations were reinforced by enduring historical traditions, state boundaries (past or present), or linguistic or religious communities. How were classes, with little prior history (apart from ruling classes), which always live among and cooperate with other classes, to be conceived and created as communities? We shall observe the two imagined communities arising together as discursive literacy diffused across societies beyond the particularistic old regime networks to which it had been hitherto confined.

Most ideological infrastructures were now provided, as Anderson says, by "print culture," though not simply by his "print capitalism." Texts were duplicated and circulated into the thousands. The usual measure of literacy is minimal: the ability to sign one's name in the marriage register. Throughout the late seventeenth and eighteenth centuries this more than doubled in most countries, resulting in about 90 percent male and 67 percent female signing literacy in Sweden and New England, 60 percent and 45 percent in Britain, and 50 percent male literacy in France and Germany (Lockridge 1974; Schofield 1981; Furet and Ozouf 1982; West 1985). The male rise preceded the female, but by 1800, females were catching up. Signing does not measure discursive literacy – many signers could do little other writing and no reading – but it situates it amid a rapidly growing basic literacy. Discursive literacy was carried by nine principal media:

1. *Churches*. From the sixteenth century on, Protestant and then Catholic churches encouraged Bible reading and the reading and writing of simple catechisms. This was the basic cause of the surge of signing literacy. Church schools were responsible for most early growth in discursive literacy and dominated elementary education in most countries until the end of the nineteenth century. In 1800, devotional works still comprised most literary best-sellers.

2. *The military*. The "military revolution" of 1540–1660 centralized and bureaucratized armies and navies. Drills and logistical support became standardized; technology developed artillery and navies; the division between staff and line institutionalized written orders and map reading. Drill and naval signaling manuals became common among officers and noncommissioned officers, quartermasters and artillery and naval officers needed full literacy and numeracy, and higher officers increasingly "studied" in the modern sense. Increasing military manpower, reaching 5 percent of the total population at the end of the eighteenth century (Chapter 11), made this a significant medium of discursive literacy.

3. *State administration*. Before the mass expansion of the lower bureaucracy in the late nineteenth century (see Chapter 11), there was only a modest increase, concentrated in fiscal departments supplying armed forces. But the literacy of higher administrators became secularized as universities replaced churches and upper-class family life in educating administrators.

4. *Commerce*. Its massive seventeenth- and eighteenth-century expansion spread discursive literacy through contracts, accounts, and marketing methods. Literacy was greater in commercial areas and

occupations than among agriculture or manufacturing industry. Commerce also involved women, though less so as the workplace became separated from the household with industrialization.

5. *The profession of law.* Law occupied the ideological interface between church, state, and commerce. It doubled in size in most eighteenth-century countries, and its education broadened in scope.

6. *Universities.* Controlled by either church or state and supplying young adults for them and the law profession, universities rapidly expanded in the eighteenth century to become the principal trainer of higher level discursive literacy.

7. *The literary media.* The writing, printing, circulation, and reading of literary products rapidly expanded from the late seventeenth century on, transformed by capitalist production and market methods. It diffused down through middle-class households. Although its producers were mostly men, its consumers may have become mostly women (Watt 1963).

8. *Periodical media.* Newspapers, periodicals, and secular pamphlets virtually began at the end of the seventeenth century and expanded exponentially through the eighteenth.

9. *Discursive discussion centers.* Academies, clubs, libraries, salons, taverns, and coffeehouses all rapidly expanded as public discussion centers of printed discursive materials. Even barbers and wig makers stocked newspapers and pamphlets and served as discussion centers. All but salons were male-dominated.

Such diverse and only sporadically quantifiable rates of increase cannot be summed up into an overall index of discursive expansion. Nonetheless, throughout the eighteenth century, discursive literacy probably expanded much faster than basic literacy. A mass communications network was emerging. Who participated in it, and who controlled it?

Primary demand came first from churches, then from states, especially their militaries, and commercial capitalism. This marked out two broad alternative tracks. I take Britain as the prototype of a diffused "commercial capitalist" (similar to Anderson's "print capitalist") track, Austria and Prussia as the prototype of an authoritative "military-statist" route, with old regime France combining both. Both received a large moral-religious input from churches. In Britain commercial expansion generated a mass literate petite bourgeoisie, lawyers, universities, schools, and entrepreneurial mass-market techniques for the literary media. In Austria and Prussia army and administrative expansion linked lawyers, universities, schools, and the literary media more closely to the state. France, commercial and statist, experienced both expansions. Both routes linked the new to the old. "New" power networks – of petite bourgeoisie and of professional officers and civil servants – were also linked with merchant and noble classes and with clerics. The result was different ideological fermentations, none entirely harmonious, in all three cases.

By 1760, states and capitalist classes were probably ideologists' main clients. Yet demand did not lead simply to effective control. Britain did not lack a state or churches, nor did Austria lack capitalism and churches. In each country churches, state, and classes had distinct, sometimes conflicting, demands and were themselves factionalized over modernization strategies. The result was interstitial space within which ideologists could operate.

But factionalism also split the ideologists. This was especially evident in the religion-science, capitalist-statist, and market-territory dilemmas implicit in the Enlightenment (Cassirer 1951; Gay 1964, 1967; Payne 1976). The philosophes privileged human reason. Reason was conceived, firstly, as a scientific "formal rationality" – they called it the *esprit systematique*, the systematic application of methodical calculation, a relentless questioning of all social arrangements to see whether they brought human happiness. But reason was also conceived of as "substantive," moral, and strongly influenced by religion. Reason could tell us what happiness and the good society actually were. Not everyone possessed full reason, but the stupidity of the populace, the naïveté of the savage, and the often defective reason of women were improvable by culture and education. Thus argued Kant's famous pamphlet "What Is Enlightenment?" Although most of the prominent philosophes were antireligious, their moralism was clearly derived from European religiosity and was paralleled by considerable moral ferment within the churches themselves. Ideology, like morality and passion, as well as science, was flourishing.

When applied to society, reason also contained a contradiction. On the one hand, formal rationality was decentered, fostered especially by the "invisible hand" of commercial capitalism. In the Anglo-American heartland of capitalism this encouraged a predominantly liberal regime strategy: laissez-faire political economy, individual civil citizenship, developing political citizenship for property owners, moral (often Protestant) individualism, and the duty to spread enlightenment and morality through private charity and voluntary work. These ideas also resonated in other countries because the philosophes were transnational, advocating programs regardless of state boundaries and communicating easily via their linguistic skills and incessant traveling. Yet, in absolutist Europe, the potential for substantive reason was identified more with modernizing states. While almost all philosophes respected the "freedom" and material progress of capitalism and of private associations, most also saw that enlightened social responsibility invited legislative action. Kant embodied this ambivalence, believing both in enlightened absolutism and in the transnational diffusion of the Enlightenment to bring "perpetual peace" to the world. Philosophes using a "civil society versus the state" model could not sustain its fundamental dualism.

Ambivalence passed onto a new plane when capitalism's "hand" later became "visible." Though its ideologists presented laissez-faire as a natural law, it presupposed a class society in which some owned the means of production and others owned only their labor. Thus the "hand" embodied, while concealing, class power. It also embodied the geopolitical power of "national" capitalists, able to set the terms of trade over lesser capitalist nations. Free trade was then seen as British-dominated trade. Nineteenth-century ideologists of both rising classes and states contested the rule of the "hand" by advocating greater authoritative, territorial state power.

The entwining of classes and nation-states produced emergent dilemmas for power actors to which clear solutions did not exist. Indeed, as we saw with regard to classes, the very identity of classes and nations was still fluid, influenced by ideologists. Interstitial space existed for ideologists to propose their solutions and influence social identities. The Western ideological community explored developing, transcendent contradictions. Economic theory was riven between the market theory of Adam Smith and two more authoritative ideologies, the "national territorial" alternative of Friedrich List and the class alternative of Karl Marx. Their three-way disagreements soon resonated globally amid the struggles of Powers and classes.

Here is Ito Hirobumi, the principal author of Japan's Meiji constitution of 1889:

We were just then in an age of transition. The opinions prevailing in the country were extremely heterogeneous, and often diametrically opposed to each other. We had survivors of former generations who were still full of theocratic ideas, and who believed that any attempt to restrict an imperial prerogative amounted to something like high treason. On the other hand there was a large and powerful body of the younger generation educated at the time when the Manchester theory [i.e., laissez-faire] was in vogue, and who in consequence were ultra-radical in their ideas of freedom. Members of the bureaucracy were prone to lend willing ears to the German doctrinaires of the reactionary period, while, on the other hand, the educated politicians among the people having not yet tasted the bitter significance of administrative responsibility, were liable to be more influenced by the dazzling words and lucid theories of Montesquieu, Rousseau and similar French writers. . . . It was in these circumstances that the first draft of the Constitution was made and submitted to His Majesty. [quoted in Bendix 1978: 485]

Was there ideological *autonomy* in this? Alternatively, were the philosophes – Hirobumi's Manchester theorists and German doctrinaires – mere aides, "organic intellectuals" in Gramsci's sense, to the Meiji and their Western equivalents? Did they merely offer intellectual schemes that dominant regimes were free to accept, reject, or amend? The ideological media were, after all, fulfilling specialized technical functions. They were expanding the ability to read catechisms, drill manuals, and commercial contracts. Perhaps ideologists were offering mere *immanent* morale to already formed classes and political regimes.

Yet ideologists also had two creative powers. First, classes and state factions were not already constituted but interstitially emergent. Ideologists helped create their "imagined communities," especially in the American and French revolutions (see Chapters 5 and 6), but also more generally. Second, discursive media also had emergent properties, partially freeing them from control. Most were not segregated, merely communicating technical knowledge for specialized clients. They were also jointly diffusing debates about general meanings, norms, rituals, and aesthetics. Modernizing ideologies – cameralism, the Enlightenment, the evangelical movement, social contract theory, political and "economical" reform, "improvement," political economy – diffused throughout the media. Their claims were universal, applying to both morality and science, influencing ideologies of nation and class. The three-way debates among the schools of Smith, List, and Marx did not merely concern the economic interests of classes and states. Much social experience was interstitial to class and state; Europe quested for modernization and the "holy grail" of progress. These writers were not mere economic pragmatists. They saw ideological conflict as moral and philosophical, concerning cosmological truth and morality as well as economics. All three were anchored in the Enlightenment: The world was improvable if reason was placed at the head of a social movement. As potentially *transcendent* ideologists, they might have more formidable resonance.

Thus the principal personnel of discursive media developed a sense of their own community. An ideological power elite – the intelligentsia, the intellectuals – appeared as a collective actor, just as the clerical, priestly caste had done in earlier ages. True, intellectuals were not united or "pure"; many remained loyal to their clients, and their clients battled to control them with rewards and punishments, licensing, and censorship. Nonetheless, the battle was recognized by the protagonists as real and novel: a struggle over enlarged powers of ideological mobilization. Entwined classes, nations, states, churches, and others were struggling for power. Solutions were proffered by a transcendent, revolutionized Western ideological community. I assess its precise degree of autonomy and power in my narrative chapters. They were generally greater early in the period than later, when regimes had developed coping strategies, centered on confining most ideological power networks within state institutions.

Conclusion

Capitalism and discursive literacy media were the dual faces of a civil society diffusing throughout eighteenth-century European civilization. They were not reducible to each other, although they were entwined, especially in the more capitalistic westerly countries. Nor were they more than partly caged by dominant classes, churches, military elites, and states, although they were variably encouraged and structured by them. Thus, they were partly transnational and interstitial to other power organizations – only partly, however, and later chapters will chart a decline in both qualities. Civil societies were always entwined with states – and they became more so during the long nineteenth century.

Bibliography

Anderson, B. 1983. *Imagined Communities*. London: Verso.

Anderson, P. 1979. *Lineages of the Absolutist State*. London: Verso.

Bendix, R. 1978. *Kings or People: Power and the Mandate to Rule*. Berkeley: University of California Press.

Brenner, R. 1987. The agrarian roots of European capitalism. In T. Aston and C. Philpin, *The Brenner Debate*. Cambridge: Cambridge University Press.

Cassirer, E. 1951. *The Philosophy of the Enlightenment*. Princeton, N.J.: Princeton University Press.

Ferguson, A. 1966. *An Essay on the History of Civil Society, 1767*. Edinburgh: Edinburgh University Press.

Furet, F., and M. Ozouf. 1982. *Reading and Writing: Literacy in France from Calvin to Jules Ferry*. Cambridge: Cambridge University Press.

Gay, P. 1964. *The Party of Humanity*. London: Weidenfeld & Nicolson.

   1967. *The Enlightenment: An Interpretation*, Vol. I: *The Rise of Modern Paganism*. London: Weidenfeld & Nicolson.

Giddens, A. 1985. *The Nation-State and Violence*. Oxford: Polity Press.

Gilpin, R. 1987. *The Political Economy of International Relations*. Princeton, N.J.: Princeton University Press.

Gumplowicz, L. 1899. *The Outlines of Sociology*. Philadelphia: American Academy of Political Social Science.

Hunt, L. 1984. *Politics, Culture, and Class in the French Revolution*. Berkeley: University of California Press.

Joyce, P. 1991. *Visions of the People: Industrial England and the Question of Class, 1848–1914*. Cambridge: Cambridge University Press.

Kant, I. 1963. What is Enlightenment? In *Kant on History*, ed. L. W. Beck. Indianapolis, Ind.: Bobbs-Merrill.

Keane, J. 1988. Despotism and democracy. In his *Civil Society and the State: New European Perspectives*. London: Verso.

Krasner, S. 1985. *Structural Conflict: The Third World Against Global Liberalism*. Berkeley: University of California Press.

Lockridge, K. 1974. *Literacy in Colonial New England*. New York: Norton.

Maier, S. 1981. The two postwar eras and the conditions for stability in twentieth century Western Europe. *American Historical Review* 86.

Mann, M. 1973. *Consciousness and Action Among the Western Working Class*. London: Macmillan.

Marx, K. 1968. The 18th Brumaire of Louis Bonaparte. In *Marx and Engels, Selected Works*. London: Lawrence & Wishart.

Oppenheimer, F. 1922. *The State*. New York: B. W. Huebsch.

Parkin, F. 1979. *Marxism and Class Theory: A Bourgeois Critique*. London: Tavistock.

Payne, H. C. 1976. *The Philosophes and the People*. New Haven, Conn.: Yale University Press.

Poulantzas, N. 1975. *Classes in Contemporary Capitalism*. London: NLB.

Rosecrance, R. 1986. *The Rise of the Trading State: Commerce and Conquest in the Modern World*. New York: Basic Books.

Rüstow, A. 1981. *Freedom and Domination: A Historical Critique of Civilization*, English ed. Princeton, N.J.: Princeton University Press.

Schofield, R. S. 1981. Dimensions of illiteracy in England, 1750–1850. In *Literacy and Social Development in the West*, ed. H. J. Graff. Cambridge: Cambridge University Press.

Skocpol, T. 1979. *States and Social Revolutions*. Cambridge: Cambridge University Press.

Watt, I. 1963. *The Rise of the Novel*. Harmondsworth: Penguin Books.

West, E. G. 1985. Literacy and the Industrial Revolution. In *The Economics of the Industrial Revolution*, ed. J. Mokyr. London: Allen & Unwin.

Westergaard, J., and H. Resler. 1975. *Class in a Capitalist Society: A Study of Contemporary Britain*. London: Heinemann.

3 A theory of the modern state

Chapter 1 distinguishes clearly between military and political power. Yet modern states seem to merge the two, since they formally monopolize the means of military violence. This did not end the autonomy of military power organization, as Chapters 12 and 21 make clear, but it redirected it through organizations that were formally the state's. Hence this chapter treats military power within a broader discussion of political power.

I review five current theories of the state, plus the political concepts of Max Weber. I then proceed in three stages to my own theory. I begin with an "institutional" definition of the state and seek to specify the many institutional particularities of modern states. Then I seek to simplify this complexity by moving to a "functional" analysis, offering a polymorphous view of state functions. I assert that modern states "crystallized" (over the area covered in this volume) in several principal forms. Responding to the other three sources of social power, they crystallized as capitalist, as moral-ideological, and as militarist. Responding to their own political struggles, they crystallized at variable points on two continua, one "representative," running in this period from autocratic monarchy to party democracy; the other "national," from centralized nation-state to a loosely confederal regime. Most diffusely, they also crystallized as patriarchal, regulating gender and family relations. Finally, I discuss whether we can detect relations of hierarchy among these, so that one or more crystallizations may ultimately determine the overall character of the state.

Five theories of the state

It has become common to distinguish three theories of the state: class, pluralist, and elitist (sometimes called statism or managerialism) (Alford and Friedland, 1985). Because elitism is similar to realist international relations theory, I discuss the two together. But I divide elite theories into two, each with a distinct view of state autonomy. I call these two "true elitism" and "institutional statism." I also add a fifth theory, implied by many empirical studies, which I label cock-up or foul-up theory. I borrow from all five, especially from institutional statism.

Most class theories have been Marxist. Marx tended to reduce states to economic power relations. States are functional for modes of

economic production and for classes. Modern states have been determined by two phases of politicized class struggle, between feudal
lords and capitalist bourgeoisie and then between bourgeoisie and
proletariat. Applied to modern Western states, class theory has one
tremendous virtue: It recognizes that they are in some fundamental
sense capitalist. All five of my principal states during the long nineteenth century were already or rapidly becoming capitalist. But the
vice of class theory is to regard this as their *only* fundamental property.
True, Marx sometimes wrote as if other powers might be lodged in
the state. I discuss the rather limited autonomies he allowed to the
"Bonapartist state" in Chapter 9. Marxists see modern states as having
only relative autonomy: Ultimately states service capital accumulation
and class regulation. Marxists add "historical contingencies" and
"conjunctures," but these are rarely theorized – they are added on
empirically (as in Wolfe's 1977 history of modern states). Although
class-plus-contingency indicates more empirical sensitivity than class
alone, it does not transform the theory.

Most Marxists deny allegation of economic reductionism, but when
they define the state they give the game away. Poulantzas (1978:
18–22), Jessop (1982), and Offe and Ronge (1982: 1–2) claim that
states can be defined only in relation to specific modes of production –
the "capitalist state" and the "feudal state" are possible concepts, they
all say, but not the "state" in general. Those who do define the "state"
do so only in terms of class relations: "The 'state' is a concept for the
concentrated and organized means of legitimate class domination,"
says Zeitlin (1980: 15). In recent years some Marxists have become
more hesitant. Jessop (1990) now emphasizes "contingency" in politics,
arguing that the Marxian notion of state "relative autonomy" still
offers too rigid an economic determinism. The capitalist class essentially
pursues the "value form" but may have alternative accumulation projects (as I also emphasize in this volume). Dominant classes have
"hegemonic projects" for which they may organize cross-class alliances,
even sometimes for noneconomic purposes such as enhancing military
power or morality. But he still only theorizes, and then qualifies,
classes. Despite relative autonomy, conjunctures, or contingencies,
Marxists have offered theoretically reductionist views of the state. This
volume attempts to do better.

Most Marxists have become pessimistic about the chances for a
proletarian revolution and advance "instrumental" or "structural"
views of the capitalist state. Either modern state personnel are the
direct instrument of the capitalist class (Miliband 1969), or they
function structurally to reproduce capitalist relations of production
(Poulantzas 1973). It is extraordinary that sociologists ever regarded

the "Miliband-Poulantzas debate" as being a significant controversy in state theory, as their debate was over such a narrow area when viewed from the perspectives of all other theories. Either way the state helps accumulate capital and regulate class struggle, sometimes even repressing capitalists whose sectional interests frustrate the interests of capital in general (there are many disputations on such points; for reviews, see Jessop 1977, 1982). These functions "required" a vast expansion of what Althusser (1971: 123–73) termed "repressive and ideological state apparatuses" – police, welfare agencies, education, mass media, and the like. The state is not an actor, but a place where classes and class "fractions" or "segments" (Zeitlin 1980, 1984) organize. Actually, states are *both* place and actor.

Class theorists who retain more optimism emphasize that capitalism still contains contradictions and class struggle, which is politicized and displaced onto the state as the "fiscal crisis of the state" (O'Connor 1973), "legitimation crisis" (Habermas 1976), or "crisis management" (Offe 1972, 1974; Offe and Ronge 1982). Offe distinctively accepts that the state has also become an actor, leading to a contradiction between its own institutional interests in compromising class struggle through developing welfare programs and the dynamic of capitalist accumulation, which continually seeks to subvert this and reduce state expenditure. Class theory has also generated an empiricist radical school, associated especially with C. Wright Mills (1956) and Domhoff (1978, 1990), who see states as less unified, composed of diverse institutions and branches colonized by power elites and class fractions. Apart from these radicals, most class theorists treat the state as passive and unitary: It is largely the central politicized place of capitalist society. State-society relations form a single system: The state, at the center of a "social formation" defined by its modes of economic production, reproduces their cohesion and their systemic contradictions. The modern Western state, thus, has, in the last instance, been defined by a single crystallization, as capitalist.

Unlike class theory, which seeks to explain all states, pluralist theory claims to explain only modern democratic ones. Pluralism is liberal democracy's (especially American democracy's) view of itself. Modernization shifted political power "from kings to people" (as Bendix's 1978 title suggests). Dahl noted that this consisted of two processes: (1) the emergence of institutionalized "contestation" between parties and pressure groups representing a plurality of interest groups in society and (2) the widening scope of "participation" by the people in this contestation. Combined, contestation and participation generate genuine democracy (which Dahl calls "polyarchy"). Since, as Dahl observes, contestation appeared early in the West, while participation remained very limited, its history is more critical in my present period. I term Dahl's contestation "party democracy." For pluralists, a broadening party democracy is the ultimately defining crystallization of most modern Western states.

Through party democracy, states ultimately represent the interests of individual citizens. Classes may be seen as the most important interest groups behind parties (as for Lipset 1959) or as merely one among many types of countervailing interest groups whose composition varies among states (others being economic sectors, religious, linguistic, and ethnic communities, regions, gender, age cohorts, etc.). Few pluralists claim that all interest groups have equal powers or that party democracy confers perfect political equality on all. But most assert that Western liberal democracy generates enough competition and participation to produce government by competing and responsive elites, not government by a single elite or dominant class. Power inequalities are not cumulative but dispersed, says Dahl (1956: 333; 1961: 85–6; 1977).

Pluralism correctly recognizes the importance of party democracy in Western history (though perhaps it exaggerates how ultimately "democratic" modern states are). It also recognizes that there is more to society than classes. But it makes two mistakes. First, though it suggests a more complex state, like class theory it is ultimately reductionist and functionalist. It credits the state with no autonomous power – the state is still a place, not an actor; party and pressure group politics radiate inward to control the state. Second, it sees classes, sectors, religions, regions, and so forth, as analogous and systemic in their competition with one another. Again, like class theory, the state is unitary and systemic. Relations between government and plural interest groups form a democratic functional *system*. Plural interest groups have powers in proportion to the muscle of their constituency. These sum up to a single totality, "society." Democratic government reflects "society" and its "needs" as a whole.

For Easton (1965: 56), "the political system" is the "most inclusive system of behavior in a society for the authoritative allocation of values." Coherence is attributed to the "political system," the "polity," the "political community," or the "government." Pluralists eschew the word "state," probably because it conveys a more Germanic sense of "power." Nothing whatever flows from choosing one of these words rather than any other; I use the shortest one, state. Whatever word pluralists use they agree with the substance of Poulantzas's functionalist statement: The state is the "factor of cohesion" in society. Only the pluralist view of society differs from his. As we shall see, neither state nor society is usually that cohesive.

By contrast, writers in the third school, "elitists" or "statists," focus on autonomous powers possessed by the state. Yet they contain two quite different views of autonomy that need distinguishing. There would be no point in my distinguishing political power as the fourth source of social power unless one or both of these possessed considerable truth. Although both contain some truth, one contains much.

Elite theory first flourished at the beginning of the twentieth century. Oppenheimer (1975) emphasized the increasing powers through history of the "political class." Mosca (1939) located political power in centralized organization. A centralized, organized, and cohesive minority will always defeat and control the disorganized masses, he correctly argued. Yet Mosca and Pareto emphasized that the power of political elites originated elsewhere, in civil society, and is eventually vulnerable to new counterelites arising therefrom. Control over other resources (economic, ideological, or military) enabled rising elites to overthrow the fading political elite and organize their own power in state institutions. Thus classical elitists saw political power as a dynamic relation *between* the state and civil society – and this is indeed correct.

Yet, about 1980, sociological attention concentrated on centralized state powers. Theda Skocpol (1979: 27, 29–30; cf. 1985) defined the state as "a set of administrative, policing, and military organizations headed and more or less well co-ordinated by an executive authority . . . an autonomous structure – a structure with a logic and interests of its own." She wished to correct "society-centered" pluralist and Marxist theories with a "state-centered" approach. Although neither Skocpol nor her critics seem to have realized it, these remarks actually contain two quite different versions of state autonomy, which I term "true elitism" and "institutional statism."

True elitists emphasize the distributive power of state elites *over* society. Thus states are seen as actors. Krasner (1984: 224) states this flatly: "The state can be treated as an actor in its own right." Levi (1988: 2–9) also insists that "rulers rule." She sees states as rational actors, maximizing their own private interests, becoming "predators" despoiling civil society – a very American viewpoint. Kiser and Hechter (1991) have advanced a "rational choice" model of states that assumes states are single, unitary, rational actors. Poggi (1990: 97–9, 120–7), while recognizing that states are also "serviceable" (i.e., serving plural interests) and "partisan" (benefiting classes), argues that states are ultimately "invasive," preoccupied with "their own" interests. True elitists invert class and pluralist theory: Distributive power now primarily radiates outward from, not inward to, the state.

True elite theorists have one tremendous virtue. They emphasize one aspect of states on which almost all class and pluralist writers have been inexcusably silent: that states inhabit a world of states and that states "act" geopolitically (Shaw 1984, 1988 is an honorable exception to Marxian silence, as are the radicals Mills and Domhoff). The few class theorists who discuss international relations tend to reduce them to modes of production and classes extended into the globe – the most recent such analysis being world systems theory. By contrast, theorists influenced by true elitism have emphasized geopolitics, war, and war finances (Giddens 1985; Levi 1988; Tilly 1990).

Elitists are reinforced by "realist" international relations theorists. Though little interested in the internal structure of states, realists see states as unitary power actors enjoying "sovereignty" over their territories. "Statesmen" are empowered to represent internationally an overall "national" interest. But among sovereign states there is no higher rationality or normative solidarity, only the exercise of distributive power, normlessness, and anarchy (Poggi 1990: 23–5). Thus foreign policy is made by states and statesmen systematically, "realistically" pursuing "their own" geopolitical interests against those of other states. The primary interest is security – vigilant defense coupled with intermittent aggression. Morgenthau (1978: 42) declared: "All history shows that nations active in international politics are continuously preparing for, actively involved in, or recovering from organized violence in the form of war." Realism thus emphasizes cohesion of states within, zero-sum games, normlessness, and war without. Most international relations theorists, realists or not, stress the difficulties of establishing international norms. Where norms exist, they tend to attribute them to "hegemony" or coercion (e.g., Lipson 1985) or to "realistic" calculations of national interest such as develops in balance of power systems. Ideological solidarity among Powers can be only transient and interest-determined.

Realism has been criticized by a countertrend in international relations theory, emphasizing interdependence among states. Realists are blamed for neglecting transnational and transgovernmental power networks around the globe. These crosscut state sovereignty, reducing their cohesion and providing an alternative source of norms and hence of world order (Keohane and Nye 1977: 23–37). Because interdependence theorists focus on modern global capitalism, they rarely apply their arguments to previous centuries. They seem to agree with realists that balance of power or hegemonic powers usually ruled then. Rosecrance (1986) is an exception. He regards trading and imperial states as present in varying degrees throughout history, both embodying distinct normative systems. I develop similar arguments in Chapters 8 and 21. In multi-power-actor civilizations, like Europe or the modern West, geopolitical relations exist within a broader civilization embodying transnational and transgovernmental power networks and norms.

Realist and interdependence theorists also share a curious blind spot: They concentrate on how benign pacific international norms appear. Interdependence theorists see contemporary norms of co-operation as reflecting shared plural, material interests; realists see norms as generalized calculations of state interest. Yet many transnational or transgovernmental norms and ideologies might not be benign or reflect material interests expressed peacefully on markets. They might embody repressive class and other power-actor interests, they might encourage war in the name of higher ideals, they might even idealize war itself. Normative solidarities might lead to disorder. Disorder might not result from the absence of an international regime but from the presence of one. Realists prefer to avoid this problem. For example, in Morgenthau's realist historical narrative, periods of calm, rationalistic balance of power or hegemonic power are abruptly shattered by more violent interregna, as during 1772–1815 or 1914–45. But Morgenthau makes no attempt to explain these interregna. Since he has earlier described ideologies as mere legitimations or "disguises" of interests, he has no theoretical concepts with which to interpret periods in which diplomacy and war were themselves deeply infused with violent revolutionary and reactionary ideologies (1978: 92–103, 226–8). Indeed, I show that calculations of interest were always influenced by all of the entwined sources of social power, and always involved norms – sometimes peaceful, sometimes violent – emanating from complex attachments to the "imagined communities" of class and nation.

Realism and true elitism also tend to share with pluralism and Marxism an emphasis on a cohesive, systemic state – this time in the form of a singular elite actor. Krasner has argued that the autonomy of the state elite is greater in foreign than in domestic policy; it is relatively "insulated" from domestic class and interest group pressures. The state is a "set of roles and institutions having peculiar drives, compulsions and aims of their own that are separate and distinct from the interests of any particular group" (1978: 10–11). I use Krasner's "insulation" metaphor later in this volume, while qualifying his conclusion. Statesmen also embody social identities emanating from beyond the state itself; and statesmen are not cohesive.

On the first point, as Jessop (1990) has argued, central state resources are rarely adequate for ambitious statist projects. State elites need alliances with powerful groups "out there" in society. These are not usually alliances between two quite distinct groups. Laumann and

Knoke (1987) show that in contemporary America networks constituted by multiple organizations typically penetrate the formal division between state and society. State actors normally are also "civilians," with social identities. Domhoff (1990: 107–52) shows that most modern American "statesmen" are recruited from big business and corporate law firms. They form a "party" "representing" an international capitalist class fraction more than America.

All class theorists stress the dominant class identity and interests of statesmen. As a sociologist believing that social identities cannot be reduced to class, I broaden their line of argument in this volume. Though I support Krasner by demonstrating that nineteenth-century statesmen were indeed somewhat insulated from both popular and dominant classes, they could not be wholly insulated because they themselves possessed social identities. They were all white males, overwhelmingly drawn from the old regime and from dominant religious and linguistic communities. All these social identities mattered in their conduct of foreign policy, shaping the norms uniting them with, or dividing them from, other domestic and foreign power actors, sometimes reducing, sometimes increasing, international violence.

On the second point, few states turn out to be unitary actors. Keohane and Nye (1977: 34) pointedly ask of arguments asserting that "states act in their own interest": "which self and which interest?" State elites are plural, not singular. Some moderately statist writers acknowledge this. Tilly (1990: 33–4) accepts that reification of the state is ultimately illegitimate, as also, he acknowledges, is his neglect of social classes. These are just pragmatic and heuristic simplifications, he says. Skocpol recognizes that elite powers and cohesion vary. Constitutions matter. Democratic constitutions prohibit elite autonomies allowed to authoritarian ones. Her analysis (1979) of early modern revolutions centered state autonomy, reasonably enough, on the powers of absolute monarchs. In the period discussed here, monarchical powers usually approximate most closely true elitist notions of state autonomy, although autonomy is never absolute. But Skocpol's more recent collaborative work (Weir and Skocpol 1985), on twentieth-century welfare programs, locates elite autonomy among specialized bureaucrats, a more surreptitious, lesser form of autonomy. In Trimberger's analysis (1978) of "revolutions from above" in developing countries, the state elite differs yet again: It is a revolutionary alliance of bureaucrats and military officers. Thus state elites are diverse and they may be incoherent – especially in the period under discussion, when monarchies, the military, bureaucrats, and political parties cohabit states.

But Skocpol has also moved, seemingly somewhat unconsciously, toward a more fundamental revision of state autonomy. Let me again quote her statement that the state "is a structure with a logic and interests of its own." "Interests" are obviously properties of actors – an expression of true elitist theory – yet "logic" need imply no actor or elite. State autonomy might reside less in elite autonomy at all than in the autonomous logic of definite political institutions, arisen in the course of previous power struggles, then institutionalized and constraining present struggles. Skocpol and her collaborators (Weir et al. 1988: 1–121) emphasize how American federalism and the party patronage system, institutionalized in the nineteenth century, then held back the development of U.S. state powers, especially in the area of welfare policies. Though they still intermittently assert that state elites (bureaucrats, technocrats, and party leaders) possess some autonomy as actors, Skocpol and her associates focus more on the autonomous effects exerted by state institutions on all political actors. Federalism, parties, the presence or absence of cabinet government, and many other features of what we call the "constitutions" of states structure power relations in quite distinctive ways. Laumann and Knoke (1987) offer a more empiricist institutional approach. They look for formal patterning of the interactions between state departments and pressure groups, concluding that the contemporary American state consists of complex "organizational" networks.

This is "state power" though rarely "elite power," as it relates more to collective than to distributive power. It affects more the forms in which politicized actors collaborate than who has power over whom. This theory would predict less that state elites dominate civil society actors and more that all actors are constrained by existing political institutions. Because states are essentially ways in which dynamic social relations become authoritatively institutionalized, they readily lend themselves to a kind of "political lag" theory. States institutionalize present social conflicts, but institutionalized historic conflicts then exert considerable power over new conflicts – from state as passive place (as in Marxian or pluralist theory) to state not quite as actor (as in true elitism) but as active place. Chapter 20 endorses such a view of the Western state.

I call this approach to state power "institutional statism," and I embrace it as part of my overall "organizational materialism." Because this period saw the emergence of a truly massive set of political institutions – the nation-state – the theory will prove to have considerable explanatory power in our discussion. True elitism may be usefully applied to the most authoritarian and dictatorial states – for example, to the Nazi or Stalinist state (though even there its assumption of elite coherence must be relaxed). Even in some of the states of my present period true elitism has useful things to say about absolutist and authoritarian monarchs. But overall I shall rely far more on institutional statism to identify the predominant forms of state autonomy.

Naturally enough, many writers do not fit neatly into any of these schools of theory. Some draw from more than one. Rueschemeyer and Evans (1985) argue that capitalism imposes limits on states, yet elites possess some autonomy. Laumann and Knoke (1987) draw on all four of the theories I have so far identified. Dahl has qualified his earlier pluralism by acknowledging that the concentrated power of corporate capitalism now jeopardizes democracy. And anyone with empirical sensitivity – like Dahl, Domhoff, Offe, or Skocpol – sees that all three schools have something valid to say about states: that states are both actors and places, that these places have many mansions and varying degrees of autonomy and cohesion, yet also respond to pressures from capitalists, other major power actors, and more general expressed social needs.

But much of the empirical work on state administrations does not stress any of the actors privileged by these theories – a state elite, the interests of capital, or the interests of society as a whole. Rather states are portrayed as chaotic, irrational, with multiple departmental autonomies, pressured erratically and intermittently by capitalists but also by other interest groups. Under the microscope, states "Balkanize," dissolving into competing departments and factions (Alford and Friedland 1985: 202–22; Rueschemeyer and Evans 1985). For example, Padgett's (1981) dissection of the budgets of the U.S. Department of Housing and Urban Development does not find that singular cohesive actor, *the* state, but multiple, sprawling, fragmented administrations. Adding foreign policy often worsens the confusion. In Albertini's (1952–7) painstaking reconstruction of the diplomacy leading to World War I, states are riven by multiple disputes, some geopolitical, others domestic, entwining in unanticipated ways far from the cohesion portrayed by realist-elite theory and as implied by class and pluralist theory. Thus, said Abrams (1988: 79), the very idea of *the* state mystifies: "The state is the unified symbol of an actual disunity. . . . Political institutions . . . conspicuously fail to display a unity of practice – just as they constantly discover their inability to function as a more general factor of cohesion."

Therefore, we might advance a fifth theory, which I describe with a traditional English expression: The state is not conspiracy but "cock-up." As this metaphor conveys quite the wrong meaning in American English, I translate it as: The state is not functional but "foul-up."

Most sociologists would regard cock-up or foul-up theory with disdain. They believe social life is patterned and ordered. Obviously, some states are more orderly than others, but is there not a certain consistency to state blunders as well as state strategies? Surely, modern Western states are in some fundamental sense "capitalist" and "party democratic" (as Marxists and pluralists assert). They have contained monarchal and bureaucratic elites (as elitists observe). They are major or minor Powers, secular or religious, centralized or federal, patriarchical or gender-neutral. Such states are patterned. Granted the excesses of systemic theories, can we pattern states while not reifying them? Do we have to abandon substantive theory and construct our theory merely from the formal properties of maps of the dense organizational networks of modern political influence, as Laumann and Knoke (1987) do? Despite the considerable virtues of their organizational theory, and the parallels between their enterprise and my own, does it not sometimes miss the wood for the trees? The American state surely is at some "higher," macro level capitalist; it is also essentially federal and it possesses the most powerful militarism in the world. I would not have guessed this from their maps of complex organizational power networks. Indeed, by dismissing the notion that this might essentially be a capitalist state because organizational networks are rarely configured for the defense of capitalism (and so may sometimes react belatedly to a threat to their property rights), Laumann and Knoke (1987: 383-6) are in danger of repeating the old pluralist error of mistaking the terrain of open political debate and organization for the entire terrain of politics.

My more substantive version of organizational materialism comes in two stages. First, I identify the particular characteristics of political institutions. Marxism and pluralism, being reductionist, tend to neglect political particularities. True elitism-realism regards them as singular, exaggerating the power and cohesion of state actors; cock-up–foul-up theory overproliferates particularities. In beginning to identify general patterns of political particularities, we cannot do better than start with Max Weber. Weber has been sometimes identified as a true elitist, yet this characterization is wrong. Weber did not produce a coherent state theory, but he left us concepts with which to fashion one. An institutional approach tends to proliferate organizational complexity, as do Laumann and Knoke (using much more sophisticated data than I can aspire to for historical states). So in the second stage I look to simplify institutional proliferation, using my polymorphous theory of "higher-level state crystallizations."

Weber's political concepts: an institutional analysis

Above all, Weber was a theorist of the historical development of social institutions. He began his discussion of the state by distinguishing three stages in its institutional development, characterized by the terms "political power," the "state," and the "modern state." In his first stage, political power existed though a state did not:

A "ruling organization" will be called "political" insofar as its existence and order is continuously safeguarded within a given *territorial* area by the threat and application of physical force on the part of the administrative staff. [This and the next two quotations are from Weber 1978: I, 54–6; his emphases.]

Thus political power is essentially territorial, and it is physically imposed by a specialized (implicitly centralized) staff. The "state" then emerged in the second stage:

A compulsory political organization with continuous operations will be called a "state" insofar as its administrative staff successfully upholds the claim to the *monopoly* of the *legitimate* use of physical force in the enforcement of its order.

This institutional definition of the state has been widely endorsed (MacIver 1926: 22; Eisenstadt 1969: 5; Tilly 1975: 27; Rueschemeyer and Evans 1985: 47; Poggi 1990, Chapters 1 and 2). Along with Giddens (1985: 18), I differ on one point: Many historic states did not "monopolize" the means of physical force, and even in the modern state the means of physical force have been substantially autonomous from (the rest of) the state.

Thus I loosen the ties between military and political power to generate my own definition, much influenced by Weber:

1. The state is a differentiated set of institutions and personnel
2. embodying centrality, in the sense that political relations radiate to and from a center, to cover a
3. territorially demarcated area over which it exercises
4. some degree of authoritative, binding rule making, backed up by some organized physical force.

This is an institutional, not a functional, definition of the state. It does not mention what the state does. True, the state uses force, but only as means to back up its rules, which are given no particular content. Of the theories considered here, only Marxist class theory and some realists specify state functions: to reproduce the social relations required by dominant modes of production (Marxists), or to pursue territorial security needs (realism). Yet states have undertaken multiple functions. Though states have indeed class and security functions, they also adjudicate disputes, redistribute resources among regions, age groups, and other interest groups, sacralize some institutions and secularize others, and do many other things. As different states pursue different functions with differing degrees of commitment, it is not easy to define the state in terms of functions. Later I move to a functional analysis to identify different functional crystallizations of states.

From my definition of the state we can derive four particularities, shared by all states, of political institutions:

1. The state is territorially centralized. It does not wield an analogous resource to ideological, economic, and military power. Indeed, it must draw on these very resources, which are located outside itself. But the state nonetheless possesses another distinct power resource: It alone is inherently centralized over a delimited territory over which it has binding powers.

2. The state contains two dualities: It is place and persons and center and territory. Political power is simultaneously "statist," vested in elite persons and institutions at the center, *and* it is composed of "party" relations between persons and institutions in the center and across state territories. Thus it will crystallize in forms essentially generated by the outside society *and* in forms that are intrinsic to its own political processes.

3. State institutions are differentiated, undertaking different functions for different interest groups located within its territories. Whatever centrality, whatever private rationality, the state possesses, it is also impure, different parts of its body politic open to penetration by diverse power networks. Thus *the state need have no final unity or even consistency*. It might do so if societies possessed such final unity or consistency, but my model of societies as overlapping, intersecting power networks suggests that they do not.

4. The very definition of the state as a delimited territory suggests a further set of "political" relations between this state and other states – that is, *geopolitics*. Throughout his work, and especially when dealing with his own Imperial German state, Weber emphasizes that geopolitics help shape domestic politics. Collins (1986: 145) suggests that, for Weber, "politics works from the outside in," though Weber also sometimes emphasizes the reverse causation. Politics and geopolitics are entwined; the one should not be studied without the other.

I shall expand on these points after explaining Weber's third stage, the "modern state." It additionally

possesses an administrative and legal order subject to change by legislation, to which the organized activities of the administrative staff, which are also controlled by regulations, are oriented. This system of orders claims binding authority, not only over the members of the state, the citizens . . . but also to a very large extent over all action taking place in the area of its jurisdiction. It is thus a compulsory organization with a territorial basis.

Thus the modern state added routine, formalized, rationalized institutions of wider scope over citizens and territories. It *penetrates* its territories with both law and administration (embodying what Weber calls "rational-legal domination"), as earlier states did not. Tilly (1990: 103–16) aptly describes this as "direct" rule and contrasts it to the indirect rule embodied in earlier states. But this is not merely a matter of the state increasing rule over society. Conversely, "citizens" and "parties" also penetrate the modern state. The state has become a *nation-state*, also representing citizens' internal sense of community as well as emphasizing the distinctness of their external interests in relation to the citizens of other states. Whereas the "legitimacy" problem in most historic states is, for Weber, primarily a problem of the cohesion between a ruler and his staff, he argues that in the modern state it principally concerns relations among rulers, parties, and the nation.

Weber sometimes selects one institution of the modern state for extraordinary emphasis: "monocratic bureaucracy," that is, bureaucracy centralized under one head. He famously wrote:

The monocratic variety of bureaucracy is, from a purely technical point of view, capable of attaining the highest degree of efficiency and is in this sense formally the most rational means of exercising authority over human beings. It is superior to any other form in precision, in stability, in the stringency of its discipline, and in its reliability. It thus makes possible a particularly high degree of calculability of results for the heads of the organization. . . . The development of modern forms of organization in all fields is nothing less than identical with the development of and continual spread of bureaucratic administration. . . . Its development is, to take the most striking case, at the root of the modern Western state. . . . [T]he needs of mass administration make it today completely indispensable. The choice is only that between bureaucracy and dilettantism in the field of administration. [1978: I, 223]

Weber saw bureaucratization dominating the entire West. Although he viewed the German state as a bureaucratic pioneer, he took pains to demonstrate that two states that might seem decidedly unbureaucratic – tsarist Russia and the confederal party–ridden United States – were also falling under its sway. Everywhere competing political authorities were subordinated to bureaucracy. A democratic regime, by centralizing responsibility, only furthered monocratic bureaucracy. He anguished over this "irresistible advance," asking rhetorically, "How can one possibly save any remnants of 'individualist' freedom in any sense?" and again, "What can we oppose to this machinery, in order to keep a portion of humanity free from this parcelling out of the soul, from this total domination of the bureaucratic ideal of life?" (1978: II, 1403; Beetham 1985: 81).

At one point Weber seems to have sensed that his argument was weak. He mused whether modernization increased the *power* of bureaucracy – without explaining what this sudden italicization means.

But then he concluded plainly that it did: "The power position of a fully-fledged bureaucracy is always great, under normal conditions overtowering. The political 'master' almost always finds himself vis-à-vis the trained official, in the position of a dilettante facing the expert" (1978: II, 969–1003, quoted from p. 991; for an excellent commentary, see Beetham 1985: 67–72).

Weber went badly wrong in suddenly endorsing a true elitist theory of bureaucracy. Bureaucrats have rarely dominated modern states, and state administrations have rarely been monocratic (see Chapter 13). There are both conceptual and empirical objections.

Curiously, empirical objections are found in Weber's dissections of his own Imperial German state. There he identified not just a powerful bureaucracy but three distinct political institutions: bureaucracy, a dual political executive (kaiser and chancellor), and parties (especially the Junker party). Weber did not confine the term "party" to formal political parties fighting elections. He meant any group collectively organized for the acquisition of power, including factions at court or in ministries or high commands. As Chapter 9 shows, at different times he stated that each of these three actors dominated the *Kaiserreich*. Note, however, that parties differ from the other two actors. The bureaucracy and the executive are compatible with true elitism, but party power derived from a two-way relation between center and territory: The Junkers were a class "out there" in civil society, yet were also entrenched in the military and other key state institutions. In his work Weber gave greatest weight to parties; they, not bureaucracies or executives, comprised the third actor in his tripartite model of social stratification, along with classes and status groups.

Although Weber did not have a final theory of the modern state, his ideas differed from the state theories identified earlier. He was not a reductionist: Unlike proponents of Marxism and pluralism, he saw that states had powers of their own. And unlike those of true elitism and realism, he did not lodge those powers merely in a central elite; nor were they necessarily cohesive. Like many other modern writers, Laumann and Knoke (1987: 380) identify Weber as a realist elitist and criticize his supposed neglect of the blurring of boundaries between the public and the private. But this was precisely his point when analyzing parties. Political power was simultaneously a centralized resource, a two-way relationship between center and territories, and a relationship among states. Weber did not mold these institutional elements into a coherent state theory. Yet, by remedying his key conceptual confusion, we are able to do so.

Weber's remarks confuse two conceptions of state strength, expressed in his cited quote as "penetration" and "power." Weber is right in saying that bureaucracy increased penetration but wrong in saying that it simply increased power. He was confusing collective infrastructural and distributive despotic power. The former is emphasized by institutional state theories; the latter, by true elitism.

Despotic power refers to the distributive power of state elites over civil society. It derives from the range of actions that state elites can undertake without routine negotiation with civil society groups. It derives from the fact that only the state is inherently territorially centralized, fulfilling useful social functions that require this form of organization and that ideological, economic, and military power actors, organized on different bases, cannot themselves fulfill. Actors located primarily within states have a certain space and privacy in which to operate – the degree varying according to the ability of civil society actors to organize themselves centrally through representative assemblies, formal political parties, court factions, and so forth. They can alternatively withhold powers from central politics (discussed later) or undercut state powers by strengthening transnational relations abroad. A state with despotic power becomes either an autonomous actor, as emphasized by true elitism, or multiple but perhaps confused autonomous actors, according to its internal homogeneity.

Infrastructural power is the institutional capacity of a central state, despotic or not, to penetrate its territories and logistically implement decisions. This is collective power, "power through" society, coordinating social life through state infrastructures. It identifies a state as a set of central and radial institutions penetrating its territories. Because the infrastructural powers of modern states have increased, Weber implied this also increased their despotic power over society. But this is not necessarily so. Infrastructural power is a two-way street: It also enables civil society parties to control the state, as Marxists and pluralists emphasize. Increasing infrastructural power does not necessarily increase or reduce distributive, despotic power.

Effective infrastructural powers, however, do increase collective state power. Because more of social life is now coordinated through state institutions, these will structure more of it, increasing what might be called the "territorial centralization" or the "naturalization" of social life. Infrastructurally more powerful states cage more social relations within their "national" boundaries and along the radial lines of control between center and territories. They increase national and geopolitical collective powers at the expense of local-regional and transnational ones while leaving open the distributional question of who controls them. Thus the explanatory power of institutional statism increases in the modern state as its collective, infrastructural powers massively expand.

Table 3.1. *Two dimensions of state power*

Despotic power	Infrastructural power	
	Low	High
Low	Feudal	Bureaucratic-democratic
High	Imperial/absolutist	Authoritarian

Despotic and infrastructural powers combine into four ideal types, as shown in Table 3.1.

The feudal state combined feeble despotic and infrastructural powers. It had little capacity to intervene in social life. It had considerable autonomy in its own private sphere but little power over or through society. The medieval king possessed the state; it was his household, his wardrobe, his estates, generating his own revenues. He could do as he pleased within it, but he could not do much to society outside. His rule there was indirect, depending on the infrastructures of autonomous lords, the church, and other corporate bodies. His army depended on their levies and these might decline his orders. The imperial state of Rome or China and European absolutism approximate to the second ideal type, with pronounced despotic but little infrastructural power. They could roar "off with his head," and if the person was within range, off came his head – but few were within range. Their armies were formidable but tended to fragment as generals became rival imperial pretenders. The modern Western liberal-bureaucratic state approximates to the third type, with massive infrastructures largely controlled by either capitalists or the democratic process (I shall not yet judge which). The modern authoritarian state – the Soviet Union when at its height – had both despotic powers and substantial infrastructures (though their cohesion was less than we often assumed).

From the sixteenth century on, a monarchical surge toward greater despotism provoked a representative backlash and massive political conflict. But infrastructural power grew fairly consensually as states partook in the exponential growth of the general collective powers discussed in Chapter 1. As Table 3.1 indicates, the unusual strength of modern states is infrastructural. Agrarian states could not even know the worth of their subjects, let alone tax them accurately. They could not tax income at all, assessed only crude indicators of wealth (size of landholding or house, value of goods brought to market, etc.), and relied on autonomous local notables to extract it. Yet today the

American and British states can both tax my own income and wealth "at source" – they know my approximate worth – and extract their cut without my even laying hands on it. Whoever controls these states has infinitely more control over me than agrarian states had over my ancestors. As Huntington (1968: 1) observed, the British, U.S., and Soviet (before 1991) states were more similar to one another than either were to historic states or to many states in developing countries – "the government governs," actually implementing cabinet, presidential, or Politburo decisions, capable of far more power mobilization at home and abroad than were their historic predecessors.

But not only state infrastructures expanded. A revolution in collective power logistics increased the infrastructural penetration of all power organizations. Civil society's capacity to control the state also increased. Modern societies contain both authoritarian states, effectively dominating everyday life in their territories (as no historic states did), and democratic-party states, routinely controlled by civil society (as only small city-states had been previously). This spelled the end for states in the upper left portion of Table 3.1 – autonomous and fairly cohesive, yet feeble, enjoying privacy from civil society but little effective power over it. Modern states and civil societies interpenetrate too tightly for autonomy without power.

This muddies our analysis. Given such interpenetration, where does the state end and civil society begin? The state is no longer a small, private central place and elite with its own rationality. "It" contains multiple institutions and tentacles sprawling from the center through its territories, even sometimes through transnational space. Conversely, civil society also becomes far more politicized than in the past, sending out diverse raiding parties – pressure groups and political parties – into the various places of the state, as well as outflanking it transnationally. Modern political power as place and actor, infrastructure and despot, elite and parties is dual, concerning both a center, with its multiple power particularities, and center-territory relations, with their power particularities. "Its" cohesion is always problematic. Only in one respect is "the state" singular: As infrastructural interpenetration increased, "it" tended to "naturalize" social life. The "power" of the modern state principally concerns not "state elites" exercising power over society but a tightening state-society relation, caging social relations over the national rather than the local-regional or transnational terrain, thus politicizing and geopoliticizing far more of social life than had earlier states.

Starting from Weber, in this section I identified the institutional particularities shared by all states. I then added the particularities of modern nation-states. Beyond these broad similarities states will differ

Table 3.2. *Power networks in nineteenth-century states*

Political institutions	Despotic state	Particularistic state–civil society alliance	Dominant classes	Multiple interest groups
Supreme executive	Absolute monarch, dynasty	Embedded in court and old regime	Embedded in feudal-capitalistic society	Constitutionally embedded in estates, parliaments, corporate privileges
Judiciary-police	Insulated royal courts	Embedded in corporate legal profession and universities	Embedded in property law	Civil citizenship (individual and collective)
Civil administration	Insulated corps of royal or bureaucratic officials	Embedded in old regime, new professionals, and universities	Functional for capitalism	Meritocratic bureaucracy answerable to parliaments
Parties, assemblies	One-party regimes (none in this period)	Limited legislatures, divide and rule, party oligarchies, court intrigue	1. Property franchise 2. Capitalist limits to parliamentary sovereignty	Political citizenship
Diplomacy	Insulated "statesmen"	Embedded in old regime	Embedded in propertied classes	Answerable to parliaments
Military	Insulated caste	Embedded in old regime and other particularistic groups	Embedded in propertied classes, answerable to civilian executives	Answerable to parliaments
Despotic power	High	Medium	Low	Low
Theory of state	True elitist-realist	Institutional statism	Class	Pluralist

considerably, according to time and place. In the next section I go into more detail, to list the main political institutions of Western societies during the long nineteenth century, beginning with those involved in domestic policy.

Nineteenth-century political institutions

Domestic policy

Table 3.2 gives the major institutions of central government (I deal later with central-local government relations). The first column lists the institutions, and the remaining columns analyze who controls them – with the aid of a distinction between "insulated" and "embedded" power. For a state to be despotic (as in true elitism), its networks must be insulated from civil society (as Krasner argued occurred in foreign policy). Column 2 lists forms of insulation that might free the state elite from civil society pressures and interests. But if state institutions are "embedded" in civil society, they will be controlled, as class and pluralist theories argue (columns 4 and 5).

But full despotism and complete insulation are unlikely. Because the state is both center and relations between center and territory, autonomy would require its territorial reach as well as its center to be insulated. Most fundamental of all, the state's resource base – its fiscal and manpower networks penetrating throughout civil society – must be insulated from civil society control. Yet such insulation has been rare historically. Raising revenue and troops normally required the help of local-regional notables. Insulation became even rarer in this period as political representation developed – aimed precisely at controlling such fiscal and manpower exactions. Full state autonomy or insulation, as specified in the second column of Table 3.2 and by the true elitist-realist theories, is unlikely. It presupposes insulation of all column 1 institutions. It is more likely that some are relatively insulated, others embedded in dominant classes, and still others in plural power networks (cf. Domhoff 1990: 26–8). Thus the state would be less coherent than any of the first three theoretical schools suggests. Insulation and autonomy might be possessed by parts, rather than by all, of the state.

More plausible is a "medium" level of despotic power, specified in the third column. State institutions may be embedded in more particularistic civil society power actors, as in Weber's account of the Junker party. According to him, the German monarchy had much autonomy from capitalists and from the citizenry in general because it had formed a particularistic alliance with the Junkers, a class formerly dominant in society, now greatly declined in economic power though still controlling the military and most civilian ministries. Through particularistic, embedded alliance regimes may attain moderate insulation and autonomy from the broader social forces specified by class and pluralist theories. Regimes may divide and rule to secure particularistic segmental allies, political insiders, and to encourage "outs" to moderate their opposition in the hope of getting back in. Of course, the balance of power contained in this alliance may work in the opposite direction: The particularistic civil society group may effectively "colonize" part of the state, using it against other state elites or more general power actors – as, for example, in the historic control exercised by American southern politicians, embedded in the merchant-planter oligarchies in southern states, over the congressional committee structure (Domhoff 1990: 53, 104–5). Column 3 lists the main particularistic embedded or semiinsulated segmental alliances found in the long nineteenth century.

The first row in Table 3.2 deals with the supreme executive, the chief model for true elitist-realist theory. Here is where we might expect true elite autonomy to center. All state constitutions then (as now) conferred certain powers on their chief executive, especially (as Chapter 12 reveals) in foreign policy. Most Western executives were emerging from an absolutist phase of monarchy. Louis XIV's "*L'état, c'est moi*" contained three truths. Absolute rulers possessed more despotic power than constitutional monarchs or republican executives. Constitutions matter, as contemporaries believed, entrenching different degrees of state autonomy. Second, in absolute and later in authoritarian monarchies, more depended on the abilities and energies of the monarch or the chief ministers to whom monarchs delegated powers. As historians aver, the talents of a Maria Theresa or a Bismarck (considerable) or a Louis XVI or a Bethmann-Hollweg (negligible) made a difference – more so than did the abilities of a constitutional monarch or even of a parliamentary prime minister. Third, hereditary monarchs and their families were unique in not being a relationship between center and territory, for they actually were centralized actors, constituting a core, insulated state elite, with their own power particularities.

But to exercise power over society, monarchs had to control further state institutions. At the center they relied on the court. Courtiers were usually aristocrats, high clerics, and military commanders, embedded in the dominant class, as class theory asserts. Monarchs sought to counter this embedding by segmentally dividing and ruling, using kin and client networks to split the dominant class into loyal "in" and displaced "out" parties. As society and state became more universalistic, this strategy shifted to embedding monarch and court in the old regime, a court-centered party alliance between monarch and the old landed, rentier class plus the hierarchy of established churches and the officer corps.

The old regime dominates most of column 3's semiinsulations. This "party-cum-elite" survived well into the twentieth century (as Mayer 1981 has forcefully argued). It remained more important in authoritarian monarchies. Yet even constitutional monarchies retained old regime tinges, and republics exhibited "old" elements – "Republican notables," "the 100 (or 200 or 400) families," "the Establishment," and the like. In all countries some political power was or is wielded by an "upper class" centered on "old money," usually landed or banking, coupled with traditional status – the term "Establishment" conveys its role in Britain, and in relation to foreign policy making in America. Old regimes retained considerable powers over diplomacy, as Chapter 12 explicates.

Class theorists argue that old regimes became incorporated as a fraction into the increasingly dominant capitalist class. Though pluralists have rarely applied their theory to nondemocratic regimes, plural power networks may also have pervaded even absolute monarchies. Absolutists were pressured by multiple interest groups and so granted political rights and privileges beyond landed aristocracy and capitalists, to churches and to lesser estates – municipalities, professional bodies, merchant corporations and guilds, even to peasant farmers. Like courtiers, their privileges were particularistic, and their politics tended to factional, segmental intrigue. Subsequent chapters in this volume evaluate these class and pluralist views of the old regime.

The second row of Table 3.2 concerns judicial-police institutions – law courts and law-enforcement agencies. In this period police forces emerged distinct from armies but were not major power players. (See Chapter 12.) Law courts mattered more. Law had a dual role: expressing the monarch's will, yet also embodying customary and divine law. The monarch might prevail in his or her highest court, but lower justice was dispensed by or in cooperation with local-regional notables, often church notables. Europe was a law-governed community; even absolute rulers did not like to be seen infringing law and custom (Beales 1987: 7). Its hybrid character made law a central site of ideological struggle and gave lawyers a corporate identity reducible to neither state nor civil society. Monarchs granted lawyers corporate privileges, seeking to reduce their social embeddedness. The French monarchy went the farthest, granting patents of nobility carrying material privileges (*noblesse de la robe*) and rights to corporate assemblies (parlements). The collapse of their particularistic alliance in the 1780s was a necessary precondition of the French Revolution. (See Chapter 6.) The success of this despotic semiinsulation strategy varied. In some states, lawyers and courts allied with despotism (as in Austria and Prussia); in some, with its enemies (as during the American and French revolutions). If judicial institutions acquired a little autonomy, it might on occasion be their own, not the state's.

Rising eighteenth-century classes and interest groups aimed much of their energy at the law, to secure the first of T. H. Marshall's triumvirate of citizen rights: civil citizenship. They demanded judicial rights for individuals, not for collectivities. Old regimes proved co-operative because they were becoming capitalist themselves, readier for that equation of personal and property rights labeled by C. B. MacPherson as "possessive individualism." Monarchs were also seeking to develop more universal contractual relations with their subjects. Modern states began to embody Weber's "rational-legal domination" (Poggi 1990: 28–30). There was little head-on class collision over individual civil rights in this period (unlike earlier centuries). Old regimes became factionalized as rising classes pressured. Civil-law codes were sometimes promulgated by absolute monarchs themselves. But the language of law codes was universal even if designed to protect male property holders (and sometimes the dominant ethnic or religious community). Law had emergent power, useful for extending the rights of lower classes, religious communities, and women. For a time legal organizations – half inside, half outside the state – exerted radical pressures. After about 1850, however, they became conservative, wedded to whatever combination of old regimes and capitalist classes had been institutionalized. Individual civil citizenship proved a barrier to the development of further collective civil and political citizen rights.

The third row in Table 3.2 concerns civil administration. Apart from judicial and military activities, previous states had not administered much; then nineteenth-century states greatly increased their infra-structural scope. But all states need fiscal and manpower resources (as Levi 1988 emphasizes). Despotism requires that revenue and expenditure allocation be insulated from civil society. Royal domains and regalian rights (e.g., state ownership of mining rights and the right to sell economic monopolies) had conferred some revenue insulation, as did ancient, institutionalized forms of taxation. War making was a state prerogative, and successful war might increase revenue through booty and using the army to coerce at home (though unsuccessful war might diminish powers). Few eighteenth-century monarchs had to submit budgets to parliaments. Yet for the increased scale of modern warfare, traditional insulated revenues proved insufficient. New forms of taxation and borrowing embedded administrations among taxpayers and creditors, though particularistic alliances with tax farmers and merchants could stave off dominant class control. Thus fiscal balance sheets were complex and varied. I examine them in Chapter 11.

State officials were formally responsible to the monarch, yet they actually needed to administer through local-regional notables. In 1760, administrations were embedded in local property relations through office-holding practices we today call corrupt. Administrations then became substantially "bureaucratized," as Chapter 13 shows. Bureaucratization involved conflicts among monarchs, dominant classes, and plural pressure groups. The monarch sought to insulate officials as a dependent corps, although even this involved partial embeddedness, in the legal profession and higher educational organizations, and through them in classes and other power networks. Dominant classes tried to ensure that bureaucracy was run by people like themselves and was answerable to parliaments they controlled. More popular political movements sought to embed bureaucracy in universal criteria of performance, answerable to democratic assemblies. There emerged moderate state autonomy through semiinsulated, particularistic alliances between the executive and highly educated sons of the old regime, then broadened by admitting highly educated sons of the professional middle class. Control over secondary and tertiary education became crucial to these semiinsulation strategies.

So developed a distinct "technocratic-bureaucratic" institution within the state, in principle accountable at the top but actually with some bureaucratic insulation. Even where states represented the interests of society or its ruling class, states are nonetheless centralized and civil societies and classes are not. Their ability to supervise is limited. Two technocratic monopolies identified by Weber (1978: II, 1417–18) – of technical know-how and administrative channels of communication – permit the surreptitious and limited form of insulation emphasized by Skocpol and her collaborators. Classes and other major power actors are not routinely organized to supervise all state functions. They may stir themselves to legislate a desired policy. Having achieved that, they disband or turn to another issue, leaving civil servants in peace. These may act with quiet autonomy. If power actors do not once again stir themselves, then departmental autonomies may emerge. These are probably greater in authoritarian than in parliamentary regimes. Without centralized cabinet government with ultimate responsible to parliament, authoritarian monarchs proved to have less control over "their" technocratic-bureaucratic organizations than did constitutional supreme executives. Constitutional regimes proved more cohesive, if less autonomous, than authoritarian ones.

Thus elite autonomies may be *plural*, reducing state cohesion. Though the growth of bureaucracy may seem centralized, it actually sprawled. Thousands, then millions, of civil servants implemented policy. Technocracy and bureaucracy is inherently specialized and multiple, increasing state complexity, as stressed by cock-up–foul-up theory. Nothing has more misled analysis of actual states than Weber's notion of monocratic bureaucracy. State administration almost never forms a single, bureaucratic whole.

The fourth row in Table 3.2 concerns legislative assemblies and parties. I extend the term here, as Weber did, to indicate not just political parties but any pressure groups. Absolutism did not formally acknowledge parties, and (unlike in the twentieth century) there were no attempts to rule despotically through single-party regimes. But executive attempts to build up particularistic embedded alliances proliferated segmental factions composed of court and parliamentary cliques, embodying intriguing, behind-stairs clientelism. More formal and often less segmental were the formal political parties emerging in the nineteenth century, enabling diffuse civil society actors to control state executives (and each other) through Marshall's "political citizenship." This established sovereign legislative assemblies, elected secretly by widening franchises, usually enshrined in constitutions. These ensure that modern Western states are democratic, pluralists assert.

Yet political citizenship did not advance as smoothly as Marshall implied. Authoritarian executives could divide and rule between factions and parties, allying particularistically and segmentally with party oligarchies of notables. Constitutions also had emergent properties that could prevent further citizen development. Property and gender restrictions on franchises remained to the end of the period, as did restrictions on the sovereignty of assemblies. If "entrenched" to protect the rights of the contracting parties, constitutions proved resistant to social change. The U.S. Constitution preserved a federal capitalist-liberal state across two centuries into very different social conditions, resisting movements demanding collective and social citizen rights. The (unwritten) British constitution entrenched parliamentary sovereignty, which preserved a relatively centralized, two-party state.

Marxists also argue that parties and assemblies are limited in a more fundamental sense by their dependence on capitalism. Most political power actors in this period believed property rights and commodity production were "natural." They rarely considered encroaching on them. But even had they tried, their powers might have been limited, as capitalist accumulation provided their own resources (as Offe and Ronge 1982 emphasize). This is a key Marxian argument against both true elitist and pluralist positions. Neither state elites nor anticapitalist parties can abrogate the "limits" set by the need for capitalist accumulation, they argue (short of mounting a revolution). I have already suggested that states had only limited chances of generating their own independent fiscal resources. This supports the Marxian argument. The modern state did crystallize as capitalist, though not only as capitalist.

Foreign policy

The fifth and sixth rows in Table 3.2 concern diplomatic and military institutions. As I have previously polemicized (in essays reprinted in Mann 1988; cf. Giddens 1985), most state theory has neglected diplomacy and military power. Yet states inhabit a world of states, oscillating between war and peace. Agrarian states raised at least three-quarters of their revenues to make war; and their military personnel dwarfed their civilian officials. States looked like war-making machines. Yet the machines were started up and wound down by diplomacy, often oriented to conciliation and peace. This was the essential duality of foreign policy.

European diplomats inhabited a "multi-power-actor civilization," not an anarchic black hole (as envisaged by some realists) but a normative community of shared norms and perceptions, some very general, others shared by specific transnational classes or religions; some peaceful, others violent. Many power networks operating across international space did not go through states. Chapter 2 notes that this was especially true of ideological and economic power networks. States could not fully cage the exchange of messages, goods, and personnel, nor interfere much with private property rights or with trade networks. Statesmen had social identities, especially of class and religious community, whose norms helped define conceptions of interests and morality.

Thus diplomacy and geopolitics were rule-governed. Some rules defined what reasonable national interests were and were shared by statesmen across the civilization. Others added normative understandings among kin-related aristocrats, among Catholics, among "Europeans," "Westerners," even occasionally among "human beings." Even war was rule-governed, "limited" in relation to some, righteously savage in relation to others. The stability of the civilization over many centuries aided what some realists assume to be universal human abilities to calculate rationally "national interest." In particular, European diplomacy had a millennium of experience of two particular geopolitical situations: balances of power among two to six near-equal Great Powers and attempts at hegemony by one of them, countered by the others. These common understandings are sometimes labeled the "Westphalian system," after the 1648 Treaty of Westphalia ending the wars of religion (Rosecrance 1986: 72–85). But they embodied older European norms.

Diplomacy was *alliance* diplomacy. Almost all wars were between groups of allied Powers, unless one protagonist succeeded in diplomatically isolating its opponent. Diplomacy sought to make friends and isolate enemies; in war a Power sought to use its friends, ideally to force the enemy to fight on more than one front. These are very realist tactics, of course. But some alliances also rested on shared norms, hitherto on religious solidarity, in this period on the solidarity of reactionary monarchs or of the "Anglo-Saxon" community, and on the increasing reluctance of liberal regimes to go to war with one another (see Chapters 8 and 21).

But, the seventeenth and eighteenth centuries saw an increase in the lure of war. Europe was expanding east into Asia, southeast into Ottoman lands, south into Africa, and by naval staging posts and colonies of settlers throughout the globe. By 1760, war costs (financial and mortal) were escalating, but so were the benefits. Colonial wars were not usually zero-sum for the European Powers. They could all gain: If Britain and France conflicted in North America, or Russia and Austria in the Balkans, the winner took the choicest prizes, the loser took lesser ones. Colonialism was unusually profitable, and Europeans also congratulated themselves that they were furthering Christian or Western or "white" civilization and "progress" over savages, natives, or decadent civilizations.

Aggression within Europe also rewarded the bigger states. There were about two hundred independent states in Europe in 1500, only about twenty by 1900 (Tilly 1990: 45–6). The winners also appropriated history. When Germans, in 1900, reflected on their national identity, few conceived of themselves as ex-citizens of the thirty-eight German states defeated since 1815 by the kingdom of Prussia. They were German winners, not Saxon or Hessian losers. In a history written by winners, warrior aggression looked better than it really was. War has been ubiquitous among states. It looked entirely normal to most Europeans during the long nineteenth century.

The ubiquity of war and aggressive diplomacy infused the very notions of material interest and capitalist profit with territorial conceptions of identity, community, and morality – though these coexisted with the more market-oriented conceptions of interest and profit fostered by the multi-power-actor civilization. Thus flourished all six international political economies distinguished in Chapter 2: laissez-faire, protectionism, mercantilism, and economic, social, and geopolitical imperialism. All were "normal" strategies-drifts.

Five major organized actors participated in diplomatic decisions:

1. *Classes.* I return to the three types of class organization distinguished in Chapter 2. Most early theorists expected that modern

capitalist or industrial society would be dominated by transnational classes and other interest groups, defined without reference to national boundaries. Aggressive transnational classes do sometimes exist – for example, the European warrior nobility of the Middle Ages, or the French revolutionary bourgeoisie seeking to export revolution. But over most of this period transnational classes were mainly cosmopolitan, internationalist in their expertise and interests, conciliatory, even pacific, in their diplomacy. Liberals expected this of the capitalist class, socialists of the working class. Classical Marxists and interdependence theorists emphasize such pacific transnationalism.

Then, about 1900, when the world seemed more violent, theorists began to emphasize the opposite: "nationalist" classes defined in opposition to inhabitants of other states. These were also believed to have expertise and interest in diplomacy, but this was aggressive, expansionist, and even militarist. The central theory deriving from this perspective is economic imperialism.

Transnational and nationalist diplomacy is supervised by organized actors in civil society possessing diplomatic expertise and interests. For example, the end of a major war often produces an upsurge of interest by dominant classes among the victorious Powers. Chapter 8 narrates the attempt to restore the old regime by the victorious Powers of 1815. Domhoff (1990: 107–52) and Maier (1981) have argued that a new world order was implemented by American capitalist class fractions at the end of World War II. But diplomacy will be much less expert if national classes dominate. If classes and other interest groups are largely caged by their state boundaries, they may have little interest in diplomacy. National classes are obsessed with domestic politics. They may leave diplomacy to others, increasing the "insulation" of statesmen, or they may express foreign policies that merely displace their domestic problems and so are rather shallow, unrooted in geopolitical reality, and volatile.

This volume narrates the entwined development of all three forms of class organization. But amid this, national classes emerged especially powerfully, allowing four other organized actors with stronger foreign policies more powers. One was rooted predominantly in civil society, two in the state, and one embodied an active relationship between the two.

2. *Particularistic pressure groups.* Amid the national indifference of classes and other major power actors, more particularistic parties might form around foreign policy. Economic sectors, industries, even individual corporations may have specific interests, usually in particular regions or countries. The broadest are class fractions – as in Domhoff's identification of an international fraction among modern

capitalists, located in large corporations and banks with global interests. Eighteenth- and early nineteenth-century "gentlemanly capitalism" was a comparably broad class fraction influencing British foreign policy (see Chapter 8); while three alternative German foreign policies from the 1890s (*Weltpolitik, Mitteleuropa*, and liberalism) partly derived from class fractions (see Chapter 21). Similarly, Weber argued that economic imperialism – what he called "booty capitalism" – was supported by capitalists with material interests in state power: "military-industrial complexes" we call them today. Noneconomic pressure groups also abound; notably ethnic, religious, or linguistic groups linked to other countries.

Pressure groups may be more decisive than in domestic policy, usually more closely supervised by classes and other broad power actors. They may also be activated rather more erratically. In recent U.S. foreign policy, for example, mining corporations have influenced policy toward Chile; blacks, toward South Africa; Jews, toward the Middle East; and so forth. But the attention span of pressure groups is narrow: Jews and blacks are uninterested in U.S. policy toward Chile, and most mining corporations have little interest in Middle East policy. Foreign policy dominated by pressure groups may be a series of short, sharp jabbing crystallizations with little overall pattern. As Durkheim remarked: "There is nothing less constant than interest."

3. *Statesmen*. Realism focuses on state actors concerned professionally with diplomacy, speaking for, even (as their title suggests) personifying, the state. Statesmen cluster round the chief executive. Monarchs had long possessed the prerogative to make foreign policy, including war. The growth of nationally caged classes allowed the prerogative to survive even into the democratic era, even though insulation was reduced by other power actors. Social pressures often came through statesmen's own identities. Almost all were drawn from the old regime class. They expressed its values, norms and rationality, and some of its transnational solidarities. Again, as with domestic policy, the particularistic alliance, rather than the wholly controlled or wholly insulated state, emerges – and again it is between chief executive and old regime. They conducted routine diplomacy, made and broke alliances or threatened war, and even occasionally went to war, without overmuch consultation with other power actors. Because they were cosmopolitan and multilingual specialists, statesmen were "experts" wielding technocratic-bureaucratic powers, possessing the broadest attention span over the whole range of foreign policy. Different foreign policies resulted when their insulation was at its peak than when it was disrupted.

But even old regime statesmen were changed by the rise of the nation-state. As Weber observed, statesmen came to represent the *nation*, as well as the state. Their own political power came to depend on their success in Great Power relations as perceived by the other power actors distinguished here (cf. Rosecrance 1986: 86–8). Weber emphasized that statesmen had become more active as imperialists, identifying their own political power with the brute power of their nation-state, aware that military victory would be their greatest triumph but also that defeat might overthrow them (Collins 1986). This, Weber argued, was equally so for monarchs, for their appointed chief ministers, and for elected leaders. This is a rather pessimistic view of the nation: Some nations generated a more liberal and pacific view of their world mission, and their statesmen could strike poses, attain prestige, and win elections as exemplars of pacific national virtues. Weber was a German nationalist; his politics should not color our entire view of national political prestige.

4. *The military*. Here I move on to the sixth row in Table 3.2, to the state monopolization of organized military power – gone were feudal levies and private armies. The military became centralized under a high command under the formal control of the chief executive. Modern techniques of insulation through salaries, pensions, and state employment upon retirement were developed for military personnel. Most eighteenth- and early nineteenth-century officer corps were heavily recruited from old regimes. (See the data in Chapter 12.) They favored a strong military posture in foreign policy, but lacked interest in routine diplomacy and were often rather sober about the reality of war, cautious about starting it and desirous of "limiting" it with rules.

Nineteenth-century high commands were close to statesmen, as both were recruited overwhelmingly from old regimes. They also developed closer links to industrial capitalists as they became major customers for the products of the Second Industrial Revolution. "Military-industrial complexes" were only named by U.S. President Dwight Eisenhower; they had existed long before him. Nonetheless, militaries also generated quasi-caste insulation within the state. They possessed a technocratic self-confidence, and their skills became removed from everyday social practices and controls. They developed segmental discipline over their mass soldieries; their lower cadres became recruited from marginal social backgrounds. As the kill ratios of weapons grew, so did their potential impact on society. Nineteenth-century strategic thinking began quietly to prefer attack over defense. In deteriorating diplomatic situations, high commands advised mobilizing and striking first, as happened in late July 1914. So, although militaries were close to the executive and to old regimes and capitalism, their professionalism encouraged caste autonomy within the state, normally inconspicuous, occasionally devastating. Military power autonomy survived the state monopoly of organized violence.

5. *Nationalist parties.*[1] In the absence of classes with strong material diplomatic interests, a more politically rooted nationalism emerged, first in the Revolutionary and Napoleonic wars, then in the later nineteenth century. As classes and other actors attained civil and political citizenship, the state became "their" nation-state, an "imagined community" to which they developed loyalties. Its power, honor, humiliations, and even material interests came to be sensed as their own, and such feelings were mobilizable by the statesmen, pressure groups, and militaries. Nationalist parties and pressure groups pressed these feelings on statesmen. Yet aggressive nationalism in this period was never as broadly popular as is often believed. It had particular core carriers, who I identify as "statist nationalists," directly implicated in state institutions – the increasing numbers in state employment and socialized in state educational institutions. Rather milder nationalism emerged among classes enjoying citizenship and also among centralizing interest groups – the middle class and dominant religious, linguistic, ethnic, and regional communities. In the twentieth century, as the working class, women, and minorities also attained citizenship, this mild nationalism broadened.

The growth of national identities and of core carriers of statist nationalism sometimes gave diplomacy a popular, passionate, national tinge. But this lacked the precise rationality of interests pursued by classes or particularistic pressure groups and the precise, normatively rooted understandings of insulated old regime statesmen. Class, pluralist, and realist theories all suggest that foreign policy was dictated by material collective interests. But political nationalism might dictate conceptions of material collective interests, rather than vice versa. If another Power seemed to impugn "national honor," aggression or firm defense could be backed by popular, shallow, volatile, yet nonetheless, passionate nationalism. The extreme, perhaps, is where the nation is invested with a very broad crusading stance toward the world – defending Christianity or the Aryan race, carrying liberty and fraternity to the world, or fighting communism. In this period only the French Revolution generated such extreme sentiments.

These five organized actors jointly determined foreign policy over the long nineteenth century, as they mostly do today. Their interrelations were complex. And because the extent of their interest and

---

[1] Again, the word "parties" is used here in Weber's sense of any politically organized group. Nationalists usually pressured through lobbying groups (navy leagues, empire leagues, etc.) than by sponsoring formal political parties.

attention span varied, there was relatively little systemic consensus or head-on collision among them. Unless substantial class fractions or moral national crusades intervened, routine foreign policy might be left to the statesmen, with others more sporadically, erratically jabbing them into and out of alliances, crises, and wars. This does not seem conducive to a very systemic foreign policy, as suggested alike by elitism-realism, Marxism, and pluralism.

I have identified diverse organized actors in domestic and foreign policy. Domestic policy institutions often differed from those in foreign policy, nor were the same institutions always found in different states – and this could create difficulties in the ability of regimes to understand each other. Realist calculations of state interests require accurate perceptions of each other, especially in changeable diplomatic crises. This was often lacking, as we see especially in Chapter 21 in the slide toward the Great War. Clearly neither state nor civil society were autonomous or cohesive entities. Despotic powers derived less from a centralized elite than from particularistic semiinsulated alliances among organized actors in states, national civil societies, and transnational civilization. State personnel can exercise autonomous power by virtue of the centrality they alone possess. Monarchs, bureaucrats, high commands, and others emerged as distributive power actors, if rarely as a singular, cohesive state elite. But institutions of central power have little distributive power unless enhanced by constituencies in civil societies channeling them fiscal and manpower resources. The singular state elite, that critical personage of true elitism, will barely figure in this volume. Far from being singular and centralized, modern states are polymorphous power networks stretching between center and territories.

Functional analysis: a polymorphous crystallization model

In chemistry a polymorph is a substance that crystallizes in two or more different forms, usually belonging to different systems. The term conveys the way states crystallize as the center – but in each case as a different center – of a number of power networks. States have multiple institutions, charged with multiple tasks, mobilizing constituencies both through their territories and geopolitically. As Rosenau (1966) observes, and Laumann and Knoke (1987) formally prove, different "issue areas" or "policy domains" mobilize different constituencies. States are thus thoroughly polymorphous. Perhaps, as Abrams has suggested, in describing any particular state, we should cease talking about "the state." But by shifting away from an institutional toward a functional approach, maybe we can simplify multiple institutions in terms of the underlying functions undertaken by particular states. These may pervade multiple institutions and constituencies, activating states in simpler overall crystallizations.

In this period states crystallized enduringly and importantly as "capitalist," "dynastic," "party democratic," "militarist," "confederal," "Lutheran," and so forth. When later identifying the most fundamental one or more crystallizations in a state, I use the term "higher-level crystallizations." Marxism, pluralism, and realism assert that modern states have ultimately crystallized as, respectively, capitalist, party-democratic, and security-pursuing states. That is, they see patterned, hierarchical relations existing among multiple institutions. Cock-up–foul-up theory explicitly denies this, while pluralism adds that party democracy is the way there is systematic compromise between many other crystallizations. Marxism, realism, and pluralism ultimately imply a singular cohesive state making "final" decisions between crystallizations. There are two methods of adjudicating whether some crystallizations or compromises between them are ultimately decisive – two tests of "hierarchy" and "ultimacy." One method is direct, the other indirect.

The direct test might confirm that the state ultimately crystallized as x rather than y, say, as capitalist rather than proletarian. Since x and y are diametrically opposed, they collide head-on. In general we know that x (capitalism) triumphed over y, not invariably but in some "last instance" sense, systematically preventing proletarian revolution and setting limits to what proletarian parties can do. Can such a direct test be applied more generally?

Steinmetz has tried to submit rival class and ("true") elitist theories of Imperial Germany's welfare state policies to such a test. He says that to support elite theory we would have to identify

policies that directly challenge dominant class interests. . . . [S]tate-centered theory ultimately rests upon showing cases of "*non-correspondence*," meaning instances when state officials and policy-makers directly contravene the interests of the class that is economically dominant. [1990: 244]

Steinmetz argues that elite theory fails this test in Imperial Germany because there was not "noncorrespondence." Welfare policies were actually agreeable to many capitalists and were permeated by principles of capitalist rationality. There was actually "correspondence" between capitalism and welfare. In Chapter 14, I mostly agree with Steinmetz's empirical conclusions. Yet I disagree with his methodology of resolving the "ultimate" nature of the state. The problem is whether we can apply his test of noncorrespondence, head-on challenge, and ensuing victory–defeat–dialectical synthesis to the entire state. This implies a social system placing holistic limits on its state. The Marxian class model does envisage this as it sees class struggle as a dialectical totality, systematically structuring the whole society and state. *Provided* theoretical disputes remain within these dialectical terms, we can adjudicate them.

Head-on class conflict can be stated in dialectical terms. States cannot be feudal and capitalist or capitalist and socialist or monarchical and party democratic. They must be one or the other or some systemic compromise between them. In this period they became and remained predominantly capitalist, rather than feudal or socialist. We can also specify the conditions under which systemic conflict might breach the "limits" normally exercised by capitalism on such states. Rueschemeyer and Evans (1985: 64) list these as (in ascending order of the threat to capital) where the capitalist class is divided; where threat from below induces the capitalist class to hand over power to the political regime (and the regime acts autonomously to compromise class conflict); and where subordinate classes acquire the power in civil society to capture the state themselves. Capital-labor struggle has been systemic in modern countries. They can function efficiently only if they produce, and efficient production presupposes solving class struggle. States require the struggle between capital and labor to be resolved, one way or another. Capital and labor have persistently struggled for over a century over the whole terrain of the state. We can analyze their repeated head-on (x versus y) collisions and "noncorrespondences," see who wins, and come to a systematic conclusion of one kind or another.

How far can this Marxian model of conflict be applied across the board to all politics? The problem is that, considered in itself, every crystallization of function is systemic and limiting, in the sense that it must be stably institutionalized. Just as states must be capitalist, socialist, or some relatively stable compromise between these, so they must be secular, Catholic, Protestant, Islamic, and so forth, or some institutionalized compromise. They must stably divide political authority between national center and localities-regions; they must institutionalize relations between men and women; they must achieve efficiency of justice, administration, military defense, and diplomatic security. Each of these crystallizations is intrinsically systemic and contains head-on challenges and noncorrespondences that contemporary Western countries have managed to institutionalize broadly.

But relations *between* functional crystallizations are not systemic. Class and religious crystallizations, for example, differ and sometimes they conflict. But their conflict is rarely systemic, their collisions rarely constitute a head-on dialectic. States do not usually make "ultimate" choices among them. Italy today, for example, remains party democratic, capitalist, *and* Catholic, just as it remains patriarchal along with various other crystallizations. Steinmetz may find capitalistic rationality embodied in welfare policies. This is highly likely because these were economic policies substantially aimed at reducing class conflict (though he does not consider whether they were also patriarchal, as they were).

Nor is it surprising that over that war-horse of modern state theory, disputes over American New Deal welfare or agricultural policies, most writers have emphasized class crystallizations. These policies are primarily economic, mostly framed with classes or economic sectors in mind. Nonetheless, U.S. welfare policies have been also (if rarely explicitly) patriarchal and often they have been racist. How do these three crystallizations over welfare policy relate to one another? Some of the best American sociology and political science have wrestled with these entwinings of class, gender, and race and have not emerged with a consensual ultimate conclusion. Steinmetz may also not find correspondences or noncorrespondences in Imperial Germany among policy areas – among, say, class interests, the Kulturkampf, and Bismarckian diplomacy. These were different, not in head-on collision, yet entwined. We might say the same of American class, federal, and diplomatic policy areas.

Even without head-on confrontation, though, states might still allocate priorities, ranking crystallizations in ultimate importance. Four state mechanisms allocate priorities:

1. *Legal codes and constitutions* specify rights and duties. The civil and criminal law are precise about what they proscribe and what broad civil and political rights they allow. But they do not indicate exactly how power will be allocated. Constitutions are supposed to locate where sovereignty lies, but they do not indicate how its priorities are to be set. And, as Anderson and Anderson (1967: 26–82) demonstrate, eighteenth- and nineteenth-century constitutions were actually vague because they embodied an unfinished struggle against executive powers.

2. *Budgets* allocate fiscal priorities. All state activities cost money, so budgets may reveal where ultimate power and limits lie. A choice between a regressive or progressive tax or between spending on "guns or butter" may evoke head-on conflict and reveal the systemic distribution of power. This is the working assumption of my analyses of state finances. But finances also have their own particularities. The cost of functions cannot be equated simply with their importance. Diplomacy needs little money but may be devastating in its consequences. In any case, through most of this period states did not have unified budgets, or if they did, some items were constitutionally entrenched, not available for reallocation.

3. *Party-democratic majorities* might indicate the hierarchical dis-

tribution of power, as pluralists assert. The policies of majority parties may indicate ultimate priorities. But party intrigue normally avoids head-on confrontation and ultimate decision making. Governing parties slide by issues of principle by making ad hoc compromises and logrolling. Regimes rarely choose between guns and butter; they seek both, in combinations varying according to complex changing political crystallizations. Moreover, majorities were only an imperfect indicator over this period. No major state enfranchised women; several did not enfranchise whole categories of men. Did the excluded have no political power at all? In several countries access to the monarch was also as important as a parliamentary majority. The state had many mansions. Parliaments did not routinely control diplomacy or military practices; classes and other interest groups lobbied court, army, and administrations as well as parliament. Parliaments were not actually, sometimes not even constitutionally, sovereign.

4. *Monocratic bureaucracy* might rationally allocate priorities within state administration. Though Weber exaggerated the autonomy of bureaucrats, they are arranged rationally by hierarchy and function, with priorities set authoritatively by the chief executive. Throughout this period, substantial state bureaucratization occurred. But as Chapter 13 shows, it remained incomplete, especially near the top of state administrations. Authoritarian monarchies divided and ruled to prevent cohesive bureaucracy; parliamentary regimes were careful to staff the highest administrative levels with political loyalists. Administrations were not fully insulated; they embodied the principal crystallizations of the rest of the state.

Of course, some states were more coherent than others. Such states can be distinguished according to how clearly they locate ultimate decision making – their *sovereignty*. We shall see that eighteenth-century Britain and Prussia located sovereignty more clearly in determinant sets of relations (concerning monarchs and parliament or higher officials) than did France or Austria, and that by 1914, party democracies did this more clearly than authoritarian monarchies. In these comparisons the latter sets of cases embodied more cock-up–foul-up than did the former. Overall, however, although the modern state was attempting to increase its allocative coherence in all four mechanisms just discussed, this was actually in response to assuming more diverse functional crystallizations (as Chapter 14 argues). Thus it was (and still is) incomplete. I argue that overall state coherence was probably decreasing throughout the period, so priorities could not usually be allocated systematically.

No single universal measure of political power exists comparable to money for economic power or concentrated physical force for military power. There is no final measure of ultimate state power. For diverse crystallizations to result in a singular systemic state would require not only extraordinary organizing abilities by state officials but also extraordinary political interest by civil society actors. Why should the capitalist class, or the working class, or the Catholic church care about routine diplomacy? Why should nationalist parties or the military care about factory safety legislation? States do not routinely allocate fundamental priorities among such functions as class regulation, government centralization, or diplomacy. Powerful political actors pursue most of the multiple functions of states pragmatically, according to particular traditions and present pressures, reacting pragmatically and hastily to crises concerning them all.

Thus political crystallizations rarely confront each other dialectically, head-on. We cannot routinely apply the direct test of "who wins." States rarely embody x *rather than* y. The states I focus on were capitalist, but they were also patriarchical; they were Great Powers, and all but Austria became nation-states (and they might be Catholic, federal, relatively militaristic, and so forth). The logic of capitalism requires no particular gender, Great Power, or national logic – and vice versa. These xs and ys did not clash head-on. They slid through and around each other, the solutions to crises over each having consequences, some unintended, for the other. Even crystallizations that in principle were in head-on opposition often were not in practice perceived as such, since they came entwined with other crystallizations. I find Rueschemeyer and Evans's three conditions (noted earlier) by which labor might triumph over capital to be too restrictive. I find that wherever two of Marx's opposed classes collided head-on, the dominant class – possessing all the major sources of social power (especially the state and the military) – triumphed. Where subordinate classes had more chance is where their threat came entwined with other threats, from other classes but more importantly from religious or military factions, political decentralizers, or foreign Powers. In such circumstances political regimes and dominant classes could lose their power of concentration on the potential class enemy and be overwhelmed by their interstitial emergence. This happened in the French Revolution (see Chapter 6) and did not happen in Chartism (see Chapter 15).

Of course, different crystallizations might dominate different state institutions. That might be ordered by a perfectly bureaucratic state with a rationalized division of labor. But this did not exist in the nineteenth century and does not exist now. As often, the left hand of the state has not known what the right hand is doing. American insulated diplomats (jabbed intermittently by pressure groups) took care of relations with Iraq, until suddenly, in August 1990, the consequences of their (plus foreigners') actions compelled the president's entire attention. In recent years, NATO nuclear submarine commanders have carried sealed orders to be opened if their communications with headquarters were broken. It is believed these orders read: "Launch your missiles at the enemy targets designated here." In this case, the small finger on the right (military) hand of states can act autonomously to terminate the state, capitalism, and perhaps the world. The state is unaware of what its members are doing.

The direct test failing, can we apply the second, indirect test? State crystallizations may not often collide dialectically head-on, but are the effects of one or more crystallizations so devastating for the rest that they limit and pattern the whole, perhaps through their powerful unanticipated consequences? Was there at least one "higher-level crystallization"?

Higher-level state crystallizations

This volume gives suitably nuanced answers to the questions just asked. Different states crystallized differently. Yet I guardedly reply yes: Over this period I identify six higher-level crystallizations of Western states. The first five were as capitalist, ideological-moral, militarist, and at variable positions on a representative continuum (from autocratic monarchy to party democracy) and on a "national" continuum from centralized nation-state to confederal regime. I identify varied ideological-moral crystallizations, some religious (e.g., Catholic, Lutheran), others more mixed religious-secular. But they somewhat declined in significance over this period, as religions and ideologies became more (though never entirely) reducible to representative and national issues. The ideological-moral crystallization emerged most strongly when entwined with the sixth higher-level crystallization, which, unfortunately, I touch on only lightly in this volume: the state as patriarchal, which we shall find significant in linking the mobilization of intensive to extensive power relations. At the extensive level I generally emphasize four higher-level crystallizations: capitalist, militarist, representative, and national.

Each of these four crystallizations produced its own head-on dialectical conflict, which in combination constituted the essential politics of the period. True, some states were also Catholic, others Protestant, others secular, naval or land Powers, monolingual or multilingual, with varying old regime or bureaucratic colorings – all generating distinctive crystallizations. But through this diversity I discern four broad tracks: toward the maturation of capitalist economic relations, toward greater representation, toward intensifying national centralization, and toward professionalizing and bureaucratizing state militarism. Modern Western states might vary their religions, their languages, and so forth, but a common capitalist and (with more room for variance) a more representative national and militarist character seems to have been forced on them by the general development of the sources of social power. If they did not modernize all four, they did not survive.

That states became capitalist is too obvious to belabor. Throughout this period, Western states consistently privileged private property rights and capital accumulation. European states had not traditionally possessed many powers over the property of their subjects. By the time capitalist property and market forms were thoroughly institutionalized (by 1760 in Britain, by 1860 almost everywhere in the West) almost all political actors had internalized their logic. Countries became more similar on this crystallization, as they all commercialized and industrialized. I shall introduce adjectival qualifications of capitalism – liberal capitalism, industrial capitalism, and so forth. National (and regional) economies also differed. Britain was the only truly industrial society of the period; Germany and Austria were distinctively late developers. Such variations among capitalist crystallizations will matter, although we shall see that they usually mattered less than the many economistic theories of modern social science have argued. Marx and Engels wrote in the *Communist Manifesto*: "The executive of the modern state is but a committee for managing the common affairs of the whole bourgeoisie" (1968: 37). Except for the "but" this is correct. Western states were and are capitalist, a crystallization relatively unthreatened by head-on oppositional challenges. In this period, we shall find little head-on conflict from feudal movements. In fact, feudalism tended to transform itself into capitalism with far less conflict than Marx seems to have believed. We find more socialist opposition to capitalism, though before 1914 this was not life-threatening for capitalism. The capitalist crystallization draws our attention toward class conflict, but also toward capitalist hegemony in this period.

Western states were and are not *only* capitalist, though. Pluralists seek to add many crystallizations. To classes they add segmental power actors, some economic, some non-economic: urban versus rural, interregional conflicts, Catholic versus Protestant versus secular, linguistic and ethnic conflicts, politicized gender conflicts – all forming parties, sometimes reinforcing, sometimes cross-cutting classes. There were also more particularistic pressure groups. An industry, corporation, occupation, sect, even an intellectual salon may dominate a party holding the political balance, or enjoy good communication channels to decision making – especially in foreign policy. Each state, even each regional and local government, may be unique. But are these pluralist additions adding mere detail, or do they change the parameters of political power? Religious communities, regional parties, even salons may make a difference, but were these essentially capitalist states?

Precise answers will differ according to time and place. In this period in the West, power networks also crystallized around other higher-level issues. Two concerned citizenship: *Who* should enjoy it, and *where* should it be located, I term these the "representative" issue and the "national" issue.

Representation turned on Dahl's two democratic preconditions, contestation and participation. Contestation began as a struggle against monarchical despotism, generating "in" and "out," "court" and "country" parties. Contestation emerged fully when alternative parties could form a sovereign government upon winning a free and fair election – first guaranteed in the U.S. Constitution and effectively established in Britain over the following decades. Participation concerned which classes and which ethnic, religious, and linguistic communities should be enfranchised and entitled to public office and (later) to state educational credentials. At the very end of the period, it also came to concern the issue of woman suffrage.

Some regimes yielded more on contestation, others on participation. Over the long nineteenth century contestation was a far more significant concession. A regime in which an opposition party could become the sovereign government involved a degree of openness denied to a universal male suffrage regime whose parties could not claim sovereignty. This was recognized by authoritarian monarchs themselves, far more willing to concede universal male suffrage than parliamentary sovereignty since it still allowed them significant despotic powers (this has been even more true of twentieth-century dictatorial regimes). Thus, though Britain had a more restricted franchise than Prussia-Germany in the second half of the period, I shall term Britain as a party democracy but not Prussia-Germany. Parliament was sovereign, the Reichstag was not. We shall see a fundamental difference between their politics: British politics concerned parties, German politics concerned parties *and* monarchy.

Representation can thus be arranged in this period along a continuum running from despotic monarchy to full party democracy, along which my countries unevenly moved.[2] First Britain, then the United States

---

[2] Over this period it is a single dimension because all these countries emerged from one toward the other. Things get more complex in the twentieth century, when most despotic regimes have been not monarchies but party dictatorships or military regimes, each with distinctive "nondemocratic" properties differing from those of monarchies.

led the way, while France zigzagged behind. By 1880, all three "liberal" countries (except for the American South) had improved the freeness and fairness of their elections and had attained sovereign legislatures (although they differed as to who should enjoy suffrage). Because they clustered on the representative continuum, I often contrast them to the two enduring monarchies, Austria and Prussia-Germany, which had not conceded parliamentary sovereignty and where the monarchs formed their own ministries. However, we can distinguish degrees of despotism within the period: The Russian "autocracy" possessed more power and more autonomy than Austrian "dynasticism," which possessed more autonomy (not more "power over") than German "semiauthoritarian" monarchy. Yet in all countries conflicts between advocates and opponents of more party democracy dominated much of the politics of the period.

But much domestic controversy also turned on *where* to participate. How centralized, uniform, and "national" should the state be? Centralization versus confederalism produced civil war in the United States and wars across Germany, Italy, and Habsburg lands. It persistently structured mundane politics. Confederalism remained important in the United States throughout. German party politics seemed complex: Some parties were class-based, others were explicitly religious (most notably the Catholic Center); others were implicitly religious (Protestant parties like the Conservatives, the National Liberals, and the ostensibly secular Socialists); others were ethnic (Danes, Poles, Alsatians); and still others, regional (the Bavarian Peasant People's party, Hanoverian Guelphs). Yet much of this swirled around the "national" issue. Catholics, South Germans, and ethnic parties were decentralizers, opposed to North German Protestant centralizers.

The nineteenth-century House of Commons spent more time discussing religion than political economy or class. Though religion did matter, it also expressed the issue of how uniform, centralized, and national Britain should be. Should the Anglican church be "established" also in Wales, Scotland, and Ireland? Should education and social welfare be uniform, state-guided, and religious or secular? Across all states most active Catholics opposed state centralization. The church retained transnational while strengthening local-regional organization.

All states were riven by struggles over centralized versus local-regional powers. This was because there had been two historic ways to fight despotism: by centralizing democratic representation or by reducing all central state powers and boosting plural local-regional party democracy. The massive nineteenth-century growth of state infrastructural powers made this especially troublesome. Where to locate them? Religious, ethnic, linguistic, and regional minorities, for example,

Table 3.3. *The national question: central versus local infrastructural power*

	Central government		
	Infrastructural power	Low	High
Local government	Low	(Premodern state)	Federal nation-state
	High	Confederal state	Centralized nation-state

consistently favored "antinational" decentralization. Yet these vital issues concerning the relations between central and local government have been ignored by almost all theories of the state (though not by Rokkan 1970: 72–144). Class and pluralist theorists use the same model for analyzing local as central government; elite theorists and Weber barely mention local government. Yet politics in the modern state fundamentally concerned the distribution of power between levels of government. Table 3.3 lists the principal options.

All eighteenth- and nineteenth-century states expanded their infra-structures and so the upper left box is empty. Most expansion might be of local-regional government, developing a confederal state, as in the nineteenth-century United States when most political functions were undertaken by state and local governments rather than in Washington. Or expansion might be predominantly of the centralized nation-state, as in France since the Revolution. Or it might occur fairly evenly at both levels, to produce a federal nation-state, as in Imperial Germany or in the United States in the later twentieth century. During the eighteenth and nineteenth centuries the enemy of representative movements in Austria-Hungary (and at first in the United States) was believed to be centralization; yet in France democracy *was* centralization. In these debates class and nation became entwined, each having unintended consequences for the other, influencing the way in which each crystallized. Classes and nations were not "pure," but formed by their mutual entwinings.

In foreign policy the national issue focused on how nationalist, how territorial, how much dominated by aggressive *Geopolitik* diplomacy should be. It raised the six forms of international political economy identified in Chapter 2 and connected to the fourth higher-level state crystallization, *militarism*. At the beginning of the period, states spent at least three-quarters of their revenues on their military; by the end, this had declined, but only to about 40 percent. Thus militarism still pervaded states, fiscal politics, and the dual representative-national crystallizations over citizenship.

Militarism also related to domestic representative and national crystallizations, as repression was an obvious way to deal with them. Different countries had different mixes of foreign and domestic repression and so it is not possible to rank them on a single militarist continuum (as I did with representation). The United States was least involved and least threatened by military geopolitics, yet was committing domestic genocide throughout the period against native Americans, while slavery required considerable local repression and there was a pervasive violence across American life. Thus American geopolitical militarism was low, while its domestic militarism was probably the highest – certainly the most violent – of my five countries. Other paradoxes are that the greatest Power of the age, Great Britain, was the most pacific domestically, and that for Austria domestic and geopolitical militarism merged as the regime became threatened by cross-border nationalism. Militarist crystallizations were dual and then complex.

Militarism mobilized not only the military. In the first half of the period military old regimes (allied particularistically to monarchy) helped give a relatively territorial definition to capitalists' conceptions of interest and to the foreign policy of emerging nation-states. At the beginning of the twentieth century these were reinforced by nationalist parties advocating geopolitical militarism and some capitalist classes advocating domestic militarism. All militarists were challenged by more pacific liberals and socialists, rarely straightforwardly pacifist, more often seeking limits to repression, military budgets, conscription, and wars. It was difficult to ban militaries in the West, because they had brought so much profit to the Powers, but they could perhaps be relegated to last-resort instruments of policy. That was the hope of most liberals and diplomats alike, though 1914 proved them wrong.

It would be nice to develop a general theory of the "ultimate" relations among these four higher-level state crystallizations. There are, however, four obstacles. First is the problem of the number of cases. I have identified four major crystallizations. Even if each were only a dichotomy, they would yield sixteen possible combinations. Capitalism, it is true, varied relatively little, but militarism contained two separable dimensions (geopolitical and domestic), while representation and the national issue crystallized in multiple forms. The possible combinations of variables are numerous. Thus, once again, macrosociology pushes beyond the limits of the comparative method. There are just not enough states to test the impact of each crystallization while holding the others constant.

Second, these states were not fully autonomous, analogous cases. All four sources of power – a transnational economy, a Western civilization, a military community, and diplomacy – spread rapidly among them. A single shattering event, like the French Revolution, or the rise of a single state, like the Prussian-German state, might have massive consequences for all states. Theorizing the particular has obvious limits.

Third, all four crystallizations entwined to produce emergent, unanticipated consequences that then affected each others' development – "interaction effects" producing yet more "variables." Nation-states developed and changed as they internalized partial and contested capitalist, representative, and militarist rationalities. Capitalist classes changed as they internalized partial and contested representative, national, and aggressive territorial conceptions of interest. Militaries changed as they defended property, enfranchised classes, and the nation. The capitalist state, party democracy, the nation-state, and the military caste do not appear in this volume in "pure" form. Nineteenth-century states were constituted nondialectically by entwined contests over all four.

Fourth, the impurity of classes, representation, nation-states, and military-civilian relations increased as they participated in both domestic and foreign policy. Foreign policy remained more insulated and particularistic – more dominated by old regime statesmen, military castes, volatile nationalist parties, and pressure groups; domestic policy was dominated more by capitalism, representation, and national centralization. Domestic and foreign policy struggles rarely met head-on but in overlapping, entwining crystallizations in which all affected one another's development in unintended ways. My culminating example of this will be the causes of World War I, in which outcomes escaped the control of any single actor – of "elites" like absolute monarchs or bureaucracies, of classes, of parliaments, of high commands, of plural interest groups. The modern state has emerged in forms intended by no one and has in turn transformed all their identities and interests.

These four obstacles push me toward an intensive rather than an extensive methodology, based on relatively detailed knowledge of five countries rather than on the more superficial knowledge involved in covering many countries and variables. Even on only five cases (sometimes supplemented by hasty coverage of a few others) I can refute single-factor theories and make broad suggestions about general patterns. But this is also a history of a particular time and place, and one with a singular culmination: World War I.

Conclusion

I have borrowed from all the principal state theories to generate my own partly institutional, partly functional polymorphous theory. I accept class theory's insistence that modern states are capitalist and that politics are often dominated by class struggles. One higher-level crystallization of the modern state is indeed capitalist. But I reject any notion that the capitalist, or other class, crystallization, is in some sense "ultimately determining." I accept pluralism's identification of multiple power actors, multiple state functions, and a (partial) development toward democracy. This led toward a second higher-level crystallization as representative, in which monarchy fought a rearguard action against party democracy (entwined with the class struggles of the first crystallization). Pluralism is also comfortable with the third crystallization over the national issue. Yet I reject pluralism's conception of democracy as ultimately decisive; more forms of power than voting and shared norms help decide outcomes. With true elitists I accept that central state personnel may constitute autonomous power actors. However, I identified two rather different state actors in this period. Monarchies hung on in some countries, resisting party democracy and generating distinct representative crystallizations. Also, geopolitics and domestic repression, though usually in particularistic alliances with civil society actors, generated the fourth higher-level crystallization, as militarist. Yet the first power is, on its own, usually puny, whereas the latter is more erratic. It is the combinations of all these higher-level crystallizations (plus inputs from moral-ideological and patriarchal crystallizations) that provide such "ultimate" patterning of modern states as we can find.

Like cock-up–foul-up theorists, however, I believe that states are messier and less systemic and unitary than each single theory suggests. I thus borrowed from another type of statist theory and from Max Weber to develop what I labeled "institutional statism." To understand states and appreciate their causal impact on societies, we must specify their institutional particularities. Because the modern state has massively enlarged its institutional infrastructures, it has come to play a much greater structuring role in society, enhancing the power of all crystallizations. My history of Western society will focus increasingly on the entwined, nonsystemic development of capitalist, representative, national, and militarist state crystallizations.

Bibliography

Abrams, P. 1988. Notes on the difficulty of studying the state. *Journal of Historical Sociology* 1.

Albertini, L. 1952, 1956, 1957. *The Origins of the War of 1914*, 3 vols. Oxford: Oxford University Press.

Alford, R., and R. Friedland. 1985. *Powers of Theory: Capitalism, the State, and Democracy*. Cambridge: Cambridge University Press.

Althusser, L. 1971. *Lenin and Philosophy and Other Essays*. London: New Left Books.

Anderson, E. N., and P. R. Anderson. 1967. *Political Institutions and Social Change in Continental Europe in the Nineteenth Century*. Berkeley: University of California Press.

Beales, D. 1987. *Joseph II*. Vol. I: *In the Shadow of Maria Theresa, 1740–1780*. Cambridge: Cambridge University Press.

Beetham, D. 1985. *Max Weber and the Theory of Modern Politics*. Cambridge: Polity Press.

Bendix, R. 1978. *Kings or People: Power and the Mandate to Rule*. Berkeley: University of California Press.

Block, F. 1977. *The Origins of International Economic Disorder*. Berkeley: University of California Press.

Collins, R. 1986. Imperialism and legitimacy: Weber's theory of politics. In his *Weberian Sociological Theory*. Cambridge: Cambridge University Press.

Dahl, R. A. 1956. *A Preface to Democratic Theory*. Chicago: University of Chicago Press.

1961. *Who Governs? Democracy and Power in an American City*. New Haven, Conn.: Yale University Press.

1977. *Polyarchy*. New Haven, Conn.: Yale University Press.

Domhoff, W. 1978. *The Powers That Be: Processes of Ruling Class Domination in America*. New York: Random House.

1990. *The Power Elite and the State*. New York: Aldine de Gruyter.

Easton, D. 1965. *A Framework for Political Analysis*. Englewood Cliffs, N.J.: Prentice Hall.

Eisenstadt, S. N. 1969. *The Political Systems of Empires: The Rise and Fall of the Historical Bureaucratic Societies*. New York: Free Press.

Giddens, A. 1972. *Politics and Sociology in the Thought of Max Weber*. London: Macmillan.

1985. *The Nation-State and Violence*. Cambridge: Polity Press.

Habermas, J. 1976. *Legitimation Crisis*. London: Heinemann.

Huntington, S. 1968. *Political Order in Changing Societies*. New Haven, Conn.: Yale University Press.

Jessop, B. 1977. Recent theories of the capitalist state. *Cambridge Journal of Economics* 1.

1982. *The Capitalist State*. Oxford: Martin Robertson.

1990. *State Theory: Putting the Capitalist State in Its Place*. University Park: Pennsylvania State University Press.

Keohane, R., and J. Nye. 1977. *Power and Interdependence*. Boston: Little, Brown.

Kiser, E., and M. Hechter. 1991. The role of general theory in comparative-historical sociology. *American Journal of Sociology* 97.

Krasner, S. D. 1978. *Defending the National Interest: Raw Materials Investments and U.S. Foreign Policy*. Princeton, N.J.: Princeton University Press.

1984. Approaches to the state: alternative conceptions and historical

dynamics. *Comparative Politics* 16.
1985. *Structural Conflict: The Third World Against Global Liberalism.*
     Berkeley: University of California Press.
Laumann, E. O., and D. Knoke. 1987. *The Organizational State.* Madison:
     University of Wisconsin Press.
Levi, M. 1988. *Of Rule and Revenue.* Berkeley: University of California Press.
Lipset, S. M. 1959. *Political Man.* London: Mercury Books.
Lipson, C. 1985. *Standing Guard: Protecting Foreign Capital in the Nineteenth
     and Twentieth Centuries.* Berkeley: University of California Press.
MacIver, R. M. 1926. *The Modern State.* Oxford: Oxford University Press.
Maier, C. 1981. The two postwar eras and the conditions for stability in
     twentieth-century Western Europe. *American Historical Review* 86.
Mann, M. 1988. *States, War and Capitalism.* Oxford: Blackwell.
Marshall, T. H. 1963. *Sociology at the Crossroads and Other Essays.* London:
     Heinemann.
Marx, K., and F. Engels. 1968. *Selected Works.* Moscow: Progress Publishers.
Mayer, A. J. 1981. *The Persistence of the Old Regime.* London: Croom Helm.
Miliband, R. 1969. *The State in Capitalist Society.* New York: Basic Books.
Mills, C. W. 1956. *The Power Elite.* Oxford: Oxford University Press.
Mommsen, W. 1984. *The Age of Bureaucracy: Perspectives on the Political
     Sociology of Max Weber.* Oxford: Blackwell.
Morgenthau, H. 1978. *Politics Among Nations: The Struggle for War and
     Peace*, 5th ed. New York: Knopf.
Mosca, G. 1939. *The Ruling Class.* New York: McGraw-Hill.
O'Connor, J. 1973. *The Fiscal Crisis of the State.* New York: St. Martin's
     Press.
Offe, C. 1972. Political authority and class structure: an analysis of late
     capitalist societies. *International Journal of Sociology* 2.
     1974. Structural problems of the capitalist state. In *German Political Studies*,
     vol. 1, ed. K. Von Beyme. London: Sage.
Offe, C., and V. Ronge. 1982. Theses on the theory of the state. In *Classes,
     Power and Conflict*, ed. A. Giddens and D. Held. Berkeley:
     University of California Press.
Oppenheimer, F. 1975. *The State.* New York: Free Life Editions.
Padgett, J. F. 1981. Hierarchy and ecological control in federal budgetary
     decision making. *American Journal of Sociology* 87.
Poggi, G. 1990. *The State. Its Nature, Development and Prospectus.* Stanford,
     Calif.: Stanford University Press.
Poulantzas, N. 1973. *Political Power and Social Classes.* London: New Left
     Books.
     1978. *Political Power and Social Classes.* London: Verso.
Rokkan, S. 1970. *Citizens, Elections, Parties: Approaches to the Comparative
     Study of the Processes of Development.* Oslo: Universitetsforlaget.
Rosecrance, R. 1986. *The Rise of the Trading State: Commerce and Conquest
     in the Modern World.* New York: Basic Books.
Rosenau, J. 1966. Pre-theories and theories of foreign policy. In *Approaches to
     Comparative and International Politics*, ed. R. B. Farrell. Evanston,
     Ill.: Northwestern University Press.
Rueschemeyer, D., and P. Evans. 1985. The state in economic transformation:
     towards an analysis of the conditions underlying effective
     transformation. In *Bringing the State Back In*, ed. P. Evans, D.

Rueschemeyer, and T. Skocpol. Cambridge: Cambridge University Press.

Shaw, M. 1984. War, imperialism and the state-system: a critique of orthodox Marxism for the 1980s. In *War, State and Society*, ed. M. Shaw. Basingstoke: Macmillan.

1988. *Dialectics of War: An Essay on the Social Theory of War and Peace*. London: Pluto Press.

Skocpol, T. 1979. *States and Social Revolutions: A Comparative Analysis of France, Russia, and China*. Cambridge: Cambridge University Press.

1985. Bringing the state back in: strategies of analysis in current research. In *Bringing the State Back In*, ed. P. Evans, D. Rueschemeyer, and T. Skocpol. Cambridge: Cambridge University Press.

Steinmetz, G. 1990. The myth and the reality of an autonomous state: industrialists, Junkers and social policy in Imperial Germany. *Comparative Social Research* 12.

Tilly, C. 1975. *As Sociology Meets History*. New York: Academic Press.

1990. *Coercion, Capital and European States, AD 990–1990*. Oxford: Blackwell.

Trimberger, E. K. 1978. *Revolution from Above: Military Bureaucrats and Development in Japan, Turkey, Egypt and Peru*. New Brunswick, N.J.: Transaction Books.

Weber, M. 1978. *Economy and Society*, 2 vols. Berkeley: University of California Press.

Weir, M., and T. Skocpol. 1985. State structures and the possibilities for "Keynesian" responses to the Great Depression in Sweden, Britain and the United States. In *Bringing the State Back In*, ed. P. Evans, D. Rueschemeyer, and T. Skocpol. Cambridge: Cambridge University Press.

Weir, M., et al. 1988. *The Politics of Social Policy in the United States*. Princeton, N.J.: Princeton University Press.

Wolfe, A. 1977. *The Limits of Legitimacy: Political Contradictions of Contemporary Capitalism*. New York: Free Press.

Zeitlin, M. 1980. On classes, class conflict, and the state: an introductory note. In *Classes, Class Conflict and the State: Empirical Studies in Class Analysis*, ed. M. Zeitlin. Cambridge, Mass.: Winthrop.

1984. *The Civil Wars in Chile*. Princeton, N.J.: Princeton University Press.

4 The Industrial Revolution and old regime liberalism in Britain, 1760–1880

The British paradox is laid out in Chapter 1: Britain pioneered the Industrial Revolution – the greatest surge in collective power in world history – yet its distributive power relations saw no revolution. On the mainland, excluding Ireland, there was gradual representative reform and national consolidation. Why?

Revisionist economic historians have offered the simplest solution to the paradox: They take "Revolution" out of the Industrial Revolution. Industrialization, they say, was also gradual, with only moderate structural change. Some Marxists also downplay industrialization, emphasizing the earlier transition from feudalism to capitalism, now ending with a shift from agrarian-commercial to commercial-industrial capitalism, disturbed by early proletarian stirrings (E. P. Thompson 1963). Whigs see a more diffuse evolutionary modernization, seeing industrial capitalism as interacting with the early achievement of civil rights and constitutional government to develop steadily greater citizenship and democracy (Plumb 1950: 140; Marshall 1963). Moore (1973: chapter 1) combines Whig and Marxian views: Britain evolved through reform to democracy because of the absence of a landholding nobility using labor-repressive agriculture and the presence of a large bourgeoisie. Marxists and Whigs believe industrial capitalism forced democracy on the state. Tories disagree: The old regime still commanded ideology and the state and extracted deference well into the nineteenth century. Its eventual decline came more through its own mistakes and divisions than through pressures exerted by industrial society (Moore 1976; Clark 1985).

I borrow freely from all these views and add my own emphasis on military and geopolitical power relations. Industrialization was indeed structured by an older market capitalism. The British state had early institutionalized civil rights and a rudimentary party democracy. Yet there was conflict between the old regime and the petite bourgeoisie (more than the "bourgeoisie"), but these classes were "impure," partly molded by noneconomic sources of social power. Class identities were first intensified, then compromised by war pressures, leading both to favor the development of a modern nation-state. By the 1840s, the cores of the two classes were merging into a single capitalist ruling class embodying an "old regime liberalism" that survives today. My explanation entwines ideological, economic, military, and political power organizations. I pay special attention to the particular institutions of the state. Neither old regime liberalism nor the triumph of reform can be reduced to industrialism or capitalism. The entwined development of all four sources of social power led old regime and petite bourgeoisie toward compromise, to state modernization, and toward the nation.

The Industrial Revolution

Because we know most about the simplest datum, I start there – with the size of the population. This reveals much. Wrigley and Schofield (1981: table A3.3) and Wrigley (1985) show that population growth between 1520 and 1700 was dominated by London; from 1700 to 1770, by historic regional centers or ports like Norwich, York, Bristol, or Newcastle; and only after 1770, by the new manufacturing and commercial towns like Manchester, Liverpool, and Birmingham. Through all three phases, from 1520 to 1801, as the proportion in agriculture declined from 76 percent to 36 percent, so those living in rural areas (in places of less than 5,000 population) who were not employed in agriculture grew from 18 percent to 36 percent of the national population. By 1801, the countryside was as concerned with services, commerce, and "protoindustries" as with agriculture, and the towns still contained only 28 percent of the population. Capitalism was as much rural as urban, as much agrarian and commercial as industrial. The world-historical shift of population from the agrarian shires to the manufacturing Manchesters had a commercial capitalist prehistory of three centuries, including two centuries of London domination, only then culminating in a manufacturing-centered urban population explosion. This is a more complex, less revolutionary shift than implied by those dichotomous theories discussed in Chapter 1. Perhaps Britain's distributive power institutions would be able to handle the Industrial Revolution after all.

Indeed, revisionist economic historians have been taking some of the "Revolution" out of the Industrial Revolution. Annual economic growth after 1760, they say, did not reach 3 percent before 1830, about the same as population growth. Exports were sluggish, largely from a single industry, cotton. There was no "takeoff" and little factory and steam-power mechanization, output growth, or structural change. By 1841, mechanization had "revolutionized" well under 20 percent of the labor force, mostly in textiles (Harley 1982; Crafts 1983, 1985: 7–8; Lee 1986). Nonetheless, if we use a slightly longer time frame, the changes surely were dramatic. By 1850, most labor and investment had switched to towns, commerce, and manufacturing. There had never been such a prolonged period of agrarian growth as over the previous three centuries; never such commercial expansion as over two centuries; and never the emergence of an urban, manufacturing-centered economy. In world-historical terms, if this combination doesn't count as a social revolution, nothing can. Provided we treat "it" not as a single, one-dimensional event but as multiple continuing processes, we must call these events a revolution.

The causes of the revolution remain controversial. Most historians point to improvements in agriculture and to the demand of middling farming households (Eversley 1967; John 1967; McKendrick 1974, 1982: 9–33; Pawson 1979; for a more European view, see Hagen 1988). Others claim agricultural growth slowed after 1710 and ceased altogether from 1760. They stress supply-side pushes from industrial productivity and international commerce (Mokyr 1977, 1985; McCloskey 1985; O'Brien 1985). The controversy itself reveals the most general cause of the revolution: the emergence of a market capitalist economy in which supply and demand in all three sectors were closely integrated. The classical laws of political economy – supply and demand, market competition, profit as incentive, marginal utility, and the like – *could* now describe the late eighteenth-century British economy. Most of the population – for the first time in extensive societies – were acting in a market-integrated civil society as buyers and sellers of commodities. Few economists appreciate how peculiar such market mechanisms are. Yet they had almost never dominated human societies hitherto.

Volume I identified the long-term enabling circumstances of such an economy: the emergence of decentralized parcels of private property, the expropriation of laborers from the land, the integration of local village-manor networks inside the normative regulation of Christendom, the Continent's "dispersed portfolio of economic resources" (Jones 1982), and the drift of advantage to wetter soils and open-seas navigation. All these developed a capitalist economy, especially in northwestern Europe and especially in Britain.

Medium-term causes came first from agriculture, which doubled its yields over the 150 years to 1710, releasing people into towns and commerce and thus allowing the rural diversification revealed by the population growth. The integrated demands of agricultural, commercial, and protoindustrial sectors generated mass consumption markets and discursive literacy and new communications infrastructures – turnpikes, canals, and postal services (Albert 1972; O'Brien 1985). Finally Britain began to dominate international shipping and commerce; this also had geopolitical and military causes and consequences (e.g., the Military became the largest consumer of iron and textiles). By 1770, Adam Smith's "invisible hand" ruled civil society. Classical political economy arose to describe it.

Immediate causes came from three industries: coal, iron, and cotton. They centered on

the substitution of machines – rapid, regular, precise and tireless – for human skill and effort: the substitution of inanimate for animate sources of power, in particular, the introduction of engines for converting heat into work, thereby opening to man a new and almost unlimited supply of energy; the use of new and far more abundant raw materials, in particular, the substitution of mineral for vegetable or animal substances. [Landes 1969: 41]

These inventions were marginal but multiple improvements on much earlier technological breakthroughs (Lillee 1973: 190–1; cf. my Volume I: 403–8). The steam engine itself is a good example of continuous, incremental innovations linking different industries, with the military adding the penultimate shove. As demand for coal increased, deeper seams were dug, but they flooded. The first steam engine (Newcomen's atmospheric engine) pumped water out of them. The increased coal supply, however, led to a bottleneck in moving coal to furnaces. Newcomen-Watt pumping engines were modified into traction engines to haul coal. Cheaper coal prices made it possible to produce coke from coal, rather than charcoal from wood, to achieve sustained higher burning temperatures. But this required better furnace design and iron casting. The steam engine was adapted to improved casting methods developed within military ordnance factories. Throughout, market pressures had been important: the interconnected demands of coal and iron consumers (especially the armed forces) and of their spinoff industries (principally railways). On the supply side, innovation remains mysterious. Inventions do not simply flow from demand. But we do not fully understand how Newcomen, Watt, Boulton, Arkwright, Wedgwood, and the others hit on their discoveries (Musson 1972: 45, 56, 68; McCloskey 1985).

We do know that big capital and complex science played only limited roles until much later. The revolution was mostly financed by small entrepreneurs and their families and friends – less well capitalized than subsequent ones in other countries (Crafts 1983; Mokyr 1985: 33–8). Nor did organized science play much of an early role (Musson and Robinson 1969; Musson 1972). Most experiments were confined to a small workshop, even a single workbench. Watt's famous kettle actually existed: a miniature boiler in an experiment. Science was important in chemicals, intermittently in engineering, and rarely in textiles. Few inventors were mere "practical tinkerers" (Landes's description). Most had trained in a technical trade but had read widely in

Enlightenment natural philosophy. Access to the free market for ideas pioneered by the seventeenth-century scientific revolution and the eighteenth-century Enlightenment (transmitted by expanding infra-structures of discursive literacy) mattered more than organized science.

Without big science, complex technology, and concentrated capital, industrial enterprises remained small and shaped by existing commercial institutions. The entrepreneur ("taker between") often originated as a general merchant. Enterprises were family-based, often with women in charge, retaining personal links with suppliers (Wilson 1955; Pollard 1965; Payne 1974; Chandler 1977; Davidoff 1986). Steam power enabled greater production runs and a larger work force in a few factories (I give numbers in Chapter 15), often ad hoc partnerships between families. The roles of the general merchant were usually broken down into small, specialized enterprises. An entrepreneur might cooperate with a skilled artisan-inventor, supervising a few artisans who employed their own laborers. The enterprise rarely totaled fifty persons. Sales and distribution were left to separate job-bing agencies at home and abroad.

Bestriding this world were small masters, jobbers, traders, engineers, and independent artisans, mixing their own labor with small amounts of family capital – the classic petite bourgeoisie. It was *their* Industrial Revolution – perhaps the greatest class achievement in world history – and yet they were not organized as a class. They did not need their own extensive organization. A civil society was already institutional-ized in agriculture and commerce, its "invisible hand" promoting development intended by no one. In Britain, unlike France, the old regime was already thoroughly capitalist, treating resources as com-modities, defending absolute property, and pursuing overseas profit. The petite bourgeoisie made money by using the organization of other classes.

Eighteenth-century classes

Thus there was no self-styled bourgeoisie or capitalist class in Britain. The closest singular term was the "nation," meaning those who had a stake (i.e., property) in the emerging national state. However, most of the new petite bourgeoisie, excluded from the vote and state offices, were not full members of the nation. Beyond that, contemporary class terms were diverse and plural. I identify five broadly "capitalist" class actors in this volume.

1. The *old regime*, the British ruling class in 1760, comprised monarch and court, established church, aristocracy, country gentry, and commercial merchant oligarchies. They owned substantial property

and used it capitalistically. They controlled the state through "place-men." Many higher professionals and functionaries (including higher military officers) were in, or were dependents of, this class, whereas much "new" capital was outside it. Its church penetrated almost every area of society, though with declining intensity. Hostile contemporaries called it "old corruption." Later the term "old regime" resonated throughout Europe. The label is not meant to indicate great homo-geneity; its politics were factionalized.

2. The *petite bourgeoisie* embraced small capitalists from trading and manufacturing, including independent artisans. Their numbers, wealth, literacy, and confidence were rising, but they were excluded from the state, and on occasion they opposed the old regime. They included what Gramsci called "organic intellectuals," lesser lawyers, teachers, and journalists articulating a bourgeois liberal ideology. In France and, to a lesser extent in America, these intellectuals might lead revolu-tions. The "middling class(es)" was the commonest label used at the time in Britain, but "petite bourgeoisie" is more precise, suggesting small, urban-centered capitalists. It is not ideal, though, for it re-sonates less in Britain and America than in continental Europe. But I reserve "middle class" (used by Neale 1983 for these people) for a later development (class 5 in this list).

3. *Peasant farmers* owned or controlled (as secure tenant farmers) small property in land, using mostly family labor, perhaps augmented with a little hired labor. In continental Europe the term "peasant" suffices, but in Britain and America the word is slightly derogatory and "farmer" substitutes adequately. Most British small farmers were not proprietors. They rented from a landlord, but with some security of tenure.

These three were the main eighteenth-century capitalist actors, though each country had its peculiarities. Peasant farmers retained their class identity (see Chapter 19). But between 1830 and 1870, other property owners in most countries realigned themselves to form two new classes:

4. A *capitalist class* merged old regime and upper petite bourgeoisie across land, commerce, and industry. By about 1870, the capitalist class ruled Britain, and the powers of the "invisible hand," court, church, landed aristocracy, financial institutions, industrial corpora-tions, and the national state were largely centered in its hands. Such merging took different forms in different countries. I call the British variant "old regime liberalism."

5. A *middle class* formed in mid-Victorian Britain and elsewhere (though normally pluraled to "middle classes" by contemporaries). This class and its three fractions – petite bourgeoisie, professionals,

Table 4.1. *Percentage of British families and family income by social class of male household head, 1688, 1759, and 1801–3*

| Contemporaries' classes | | My classes | 1688 | | 1759 | | 1801–3 | |
Whig politicians	Sociologists		% Families	% Income	% Families	% Income	% Families	% Income
The people	High titles and gentlemen Professionals, greater merchants[a]	Old regime	5	28	5	27	5	28
	Freeholders, farmers	Farmers	16	22	16	25	15	26
	Lesser merchants, manufacturers, greater artisans[b]	Petite bourgeoisie	15	26	19	27	16	23
(Marginal)	Lesser artisans[c]	(Marginal)	12	8	17	9	21	13
The populace	Laborers, cottagers, paupers, vagrants	Laborers	45	12	37	8	36	8
—	Military and maritime	—	7	4	6[d]	3	11	5

Notes: [a] Merchant groups earning an average at least £400 per annum in 1688 and 1759 and £800 per annum in 1801–3.
[b] All groups earning £40–£399 per annum in 1688 and 1759 and £80–£799 per annum in 1801–3. King grouped together "all manufacturing trades," with average income of £38 per annum. I have split their numbers equally into "greater artisans" (with assumed income of £50 per annum) and "lesser artisans" (assumed income of £25 per annum).
[c] Also includes miners and building tradesmen.
[d] An obvious underestimate given the military buildup of that year.
Sources: Contemporary estimates of Gregory King (1688), Joseph Massie (1759), and Patrick Colquhoun (1801–3); revised by Lindert and Williamson (1982) and Crafts (1985).

and careerists – are discussed in Chapter 16. Artisans, originally part of the petite bourgeoisie, became proletarianized.

These classes are ideal types. They did not stride resolutely over eighteenth-century society. Yet they are not mere artifices. They had contemporary resonance, and the first three appeared in the "political arithmetic" of three early British sociologists. Gregory King (in 1688), Joseph Massie (1759), and Patrick Colquhoun (1801–3) calculated the numbers and incomes of what they called the principal social classes of Britain. (See Table 4.1.)

My "old regime" was identified by all three sociologists. All distinguished "high titles and skills/professions," divided into similar subcategories: levels of nobility and gentility, the clergy, government officials, lawyers and other professionals. I have amended their classification slightly, making the old regime a little more "classlike," a little less closely tied to status gradations, by adding the few thousand "greater merchants" kept separate by them. All three estimates, thus enlarged, put the old regime at 5 percent of families and 27 percent to 28 percent of national income. The titled and gentry were only slightly over 1 percent of families but accounted for 15 percent of national income. Service professionals remained the next wealthiest group throughout the period, though "greater merchants" were not far behind.

At the bottom of society, the decline of the laborers is probably an artifact of the different classifications. The figures also mask the major shift of the period among the poor: the relative decline of agricultural laborers. When dealing with the "populace," these sociologists were relatively uninterested in differentiating by economic sector. Only Colquhoun attempted to put some industrial laborers and miners into a separate sectoral category. In Britain and France, liberal or Whig writers often distinguished the propertied, educated "people" from the "populace" below. Here is the philosophe Holbach being particularly clear:

By the word people I do not mean the stupid populace which, being deprived of enlightenment and good sense, may at any moment become the instrument and accomplice of turbulent demagogues who wish to disturb society. Every man who can live respectably from the income of his property and every head of a family who owns land ought to be regarded as citizens. [*Système Sociale* 1773: vol. II]

The genuinely propertyless were regarded as of little importance. It did not matter whether most were rural and agricultural, as in 1688, or whether they were as likely to be drawn from urban, commercial, or manufacturing sectors, as later. But they were only a little more than 40 percent of the population, not its vast majority, matched in numbers by the "middling" categories.

In the "middle," the sociologists had no difficulty identifying farmers as a distinct class – about 15 percent of population with 25 percent of wealth. They tried with less success to distinguish commercial from industrial middling classes. King undercounted and Massie over-counted shopkeepers. Most of Massie's tradesmen were classified by King as "manufacturing tradesmen" and by Colquhoun as "artisans, handicrafts, mechanics and labourers." If we compromise between their classifications, those in commerce comprised 9 percent to 12 percent of the population, representing perhaps 20 percent of national wealth. In industry and building the sociologists blurred masters and independent artisans and sometimes artisans and laborers. King alone put most industrial and building trades among common laborers. Massie separated manufacturers by their family income; Colquhoun, by whether they possessed capital. As four-fifths of them lacked capital, he put them into an enormous "working class" category: "artisans, handicrafts, mechanics and laborers employed in manufactures, buildings, and works of every kind."

Thus contemporary sociologists were unsure about how to handle new occupational strata, about how distinct manufacturers and builders were from those in commerce, and they blurred artisans and laborers. They were unsure about where the "people" ended and the "populace" began.

Their dilemmas were real. There is no single best solution to the actually competing economic identities of much of the population. I have produced a partial solution in Table 4.1 by combining the commercial and industrial categories into an overall "petite bourgeoisie," 15 percent to 19 percent of population and 23 percent to 27 percent of wealth. Its size and wealth probably increased through time (this is obscured in the table by the high military conscription of 1801–3) as manufacturing and building artisans expanded. Together with the farmers and old regime, they were called the "people" in contemporary Whig parlance, distinct from the "populace" below. But within this petite bourgeoisie lay a potential fault line. Those in industry and building, increasing in numbers, were not as propertied as those in commerce, their incomes being around the national average rather than twice it. Three-quarters of manufacturers and builders, half the overall petite bourgeoisie, were probably artisans, more propertied and more secure than the "lesser artisans" I label "marginal" in the table, but sharing many life experiences with them.

These "middling" groups could potentially break in either of two main ways: into a broader petit bourgeois–artisan movement against old regime and farmers, or with the fault line appearing lower, ranging the commercial petite bourgeoisie against artisans plus laborers, with the working class, or "populace," below. "Classes" were ambivalent, variable through time and across countries, as is shown in later chapters. It is a question – as Moore (1973) and Rueschemeyer, Stephens, and Stephens (1992) suggest – not just of classes being strong or weak but of their very identity and existence as classes. In this chapter and in Chapter 15, we perceive in Britain a petite bourgeoisie, then a working class, as collective actors, but we often find the same occupations in both of them. Let us see how these latent classes (with some significance in contemporary theory) came, hesitatingly, partially, into extensive and political existence.

Classes in the economy, 1760–1820

Commercial capitalism dominated eighteenth-century Britain (Perkin 1968; Abercrombie, Hill, and Turner 1980: 104–19; Hill 1980). Old regime, farmers, and petite bourgeoisie all sold commodities on the market, and most bought free wage labor. Bonded labor was declining (Kussmaul 1981: 4). Centuries of enclosures had ended rights to common land; most feudal privileges and restrictions on alienability were abolished by 1700. Absolute individual property was still re-strained by laws protecting the family through "strict settlement," binding the heir to provide for brothers and sisters (Bonfield 1983). But Britain, unlike old regime France, lacked privileged "orders" enshrining noncapitalist property.

Between 1760 and 1820, capitalist laissez-faire also triumphed – not bourgeois but old regime. The old regime did the legislating and aimed it less at agrarian than at industrial traditionalism. States had long regulated wages, apprenticeships, and prices, established monopolies, and granted licenses for large enterprises; but by 1820, wage, ap-prentice, and union restraints were removed, and most international trade was freed from monopolies. This was legislated by an unreformed Parliament, whose members were merchants or bankers, or land-owners or professionals with merchant or banking interests. There were virtually no industrialists. When, in 1804, Peel (the Elder) intro-duced legislation to abolish guild regulation, to protect the "health and morals of apprentices," he may have been the only member of either house employing apprentices. "Laissez-faire" is perhaps not the right label for a state whose navy ruthlessly enforced the near monopoly of the carrying trade enacted by the Navigation Acts. The most bourgeois state, the new American state, was committed not to international free trade but protective tariffs. Wolfe more appropriately uses the term "accumulative state" to describe these Anglo-American states (1977: 13–41). It is simpler to say that they were capitalist.

There was no fundamental economic opposition between old regime and petite bourgeoisie. Common legislative needs pushed them toward regarding the state and its bounded territory as delimiting *their* civil society. They were becoming, largely unconsciously, naturalized. Most "North British" and Welsh were now clearly "British," although most Irish were not. The English were becoming the "most national people in Europe" a contemporary claimed, unthinkingly equating English with British (as we have done ever since). This class-national identity preceded the more overt nationalism of the French Revolution (Colley 1986: 97, 100; Newman 1987). The propertied nation-state was beginning to emerge, behind the backs of the men who comprised it.

Yet Britain had its economic squabbles. The agrarian interest and most industries favored protective tariffs, whereas cotton sought free trade. Many industries switched sides, and the conflict came to a head in the 1840s over the Corn Laws. There was also a controversy with high moral-ideological tone over the Poor Law. Laissez-faire urged minimal interference with markets and work incentives for the able-bodied poor, whereas much of the old regime, especially the church, favored local paternalism. The Poor Law remained contentious right through to the 1830s. Yet neither dispute produced class struggle between petite bourgeoisie and old regime.

Was there significant economic class conflict between them? I shall argue that their economic conflict was not direct but, rather, mediated by the political economy of the state. McKendrick, Brewer, and Plumb (1982) disagree, however. They see a direct conflict arising between an old regime "client economy" and a petit bourgeois "free market," reinforced by a consumer economy and mass literacy. They document an eighteenth-century surge in consumption – of goods as diverse as clothes, pottery, books, garden seeds, shaving utensils, and iron coffins. "Safety for the dead . . . the right to inter in iron" was a typically insistent marketing slogan of undertakers exploiting fear of grave robbers. This economy supposedly conflicted with old regime clientelism, in which tradesmen and professionals depended personally on notables and could not enforce credit against them. Thus, says Brewer (1982: 197–8), "The middling sort or bourgeoisie," "men of moveable property, members of professions, tradesmen and shop-keepers," agitated to replace the old regime with "a broadly based market and a more equitably grounded politics" – implicitly a class struggle.

Mass consumerism also subverted qualitative divides between old regime status orders, introducing finer, diffuser, quantitative measures of wealth. As a contemporary put it:

In England the several ranks of men slide into each other almost imperceptibly, and a spirit of equality runs through every part of their constitution. Hence arises a strong emulation in all the several stations and conditions to vie with each other; and the perpetual restless ambition in each of the inferior ranks to raise themselves to the level of those immediately above them. In such a state as this fashion must have uncontrolled sway. And a fashionable luxury must spread through it like a contagion. [Quoted by McKendrick 1982: 83, 11]

Plumb suggests that "fashion" contained an ideology of "improvement":

"Improvement" was the most over-used word of eighteenth-century England – landscapes, gardens, agriculture, science, manufacture, music, art, literature, instruction both secular and religious, were constantly described as improved . . . after "improvement," the phrase in which salesmen put their faith was "new method," after that "latest fashion" . . . quite humble activities played their part in the acceptance of modernity and of science: growing auriculas or cucumbers, crossing greyhounds with bulldogs, giving a child a microscope or a pack of geographical playing cards, taking a look at the first kangaroo seen in England or to watch a balloon rise in the skies did much to create one of the greatest revolutions in human life. [1982: 332–3]

Historians of ideas often ask: Why no Enlightenment in England, unlike France or Scotland? They conclude that as England was actually modern, it did not need a modernizing ideology. But perhaps England did declaim the Enlightenment – as advertising slogans. The "English Enlightenment" was less philosophy and formal ideology than shaving, dressing, and mourning its dead, implicitly encouraging principles of merit, utility, and reason rather than the particularisms of status and corporate privilege.

McKendrick and his collaborators argue there was petit bourgeois economic subversion, not frontal class attack. But could the old regime take this on board without jettisoning its interests? Essential to the consumer economy were infrastructures of discursive communication. How did these articulate class interests?

A revolution in ideological power

Throughout the West, discursive literacy was greatly expanding through the nine infrastructures listed in Chapter 2. As elsewhere, churches provided the first and most enduring boost, then British expansion added the commercial capitalist track of "print capitalism." Did this divide petite bourgeoisie from old regime, encouraging distinct class identities, as McKendrick and his collaborators suggest, or did it integrate them?

The lowest level of literacy, signing one's name in the marriage register, had risen in the eighteenth century to around 60 percent for men and 45 percent for women (Schofield 1981; West 1985). It was substantially higher in commercial towns than in the countryside or industrial towns, especially among artisans and merchants (Houston 1982a, 1982b). More significant was the spread of discursive literacy. Religious homilies provided most best-sellers, then narrative moralizing novels, especially among women, and men read nonfiction books, newspapers, periodicals, and pamphlets. A Birmingham bookseller boasted in 1787 that his stock consisted of 30,000 volumes, and that 100,000 books and pamphlets were read in Birmingham every month – two items per inhabitant (Money 1977: 121). The reading of discursive texts and the writing of letters filtered down to farming and petit bourgeois families and then to servants. Market-attuned writers and publishers strove for messages of broad social appeal, embodying universal values (Cranfield 1962, 1978; Watt 1963; Wiles 1968; Brewer 1976: 139–53, 1982; Money 1977; 52–79).

Newspapers and periodicals grew more than tenfold over the century. Aimed first at old regime and merchants (shipping movements were newspaper staples), they spread downward. By the 1760s, newspapers were in fifty-five provincial towns, and London had four dailies, five or six triweeklies (also circulating in the provinces), and many more weeklies and fortnightlies. Annual sales of dailies exceeded 10 million (Cranfield 1962: 175–6). Readership appeals were broadly addressed "to the worthy Body of Merchants and Citizens," "Gentlemen, Tradesmen and Others," and "all Persons of all Orders and either Sex." The provincial press was wary of politics and did not have leader columns until the 1790s, and government bribes ensured that conservative views circulated widely. But most circulation was among middling provincial readers who affirmed "the Radical principle that every individual had a right to a knowledge of affairs of state" (Cranfield 1962: 184, 273). Short pamphlets sold 500 to 5,000 copies by the 1770s, and handbills and cartoons reached much larger numbers. A copy of a newspaper or pamphlet might be read and discussed by twenty to fifty persons.

There were about 600 libraries and subscription book clubs by 1800, with perhaps 50,000 members spread among gentlemen, professionals, merchants, manufacturers, and securer artisans. Dissenters were overrepresented and women were seriously underrepresented, with most of their reading private (Kaufman 1967: 30–2). More numerous were inns and taverns, coffeehouses, clubs, barbershops, and wig-making establishments, all stocking newspapers, periodicals, and pamphlets and serving as debating centers. In 1739, London had 551 coffeehouses and 654 inns and taverns (Money 1977: 98–120; Brewer 1982: 203–30). Most claimed to bridge ranks, bringing together gentlemen, professionals, tradesmen, and educated artisans and developing rituals of fraternity (there were few women). Visitors from continental Europe commented on their openness to middling groups compared to clubs back home.

Something new had emerged: As in the later Roman Empire (see Volume I, Chapter 10) an interstitial communications network centered on traders, manufacturers, and artisans, this time with more evenly diffused infrastructures of discursive communication. It amounted to a revolution in ideological power relations: a potent means of passing messages around a diffuse network, inherently difficult for any authoritative regime to control. Regimes attempted censorship and licensing and restricted assembly and discussion. But states had few infrastructures outside tax gathering. Churches could exercise more effective formal or informal censorship, but all censorship remained partial. These infrastructures were up for grabs by contending power actors.

McKendrick, Brewer, and Plumb (1982, especially Brewer) believe they encouraged radical petit bourgeois politics – much as I showed Roman networks activating the subversive religion of Christianity. Emerging groups in Rome had been denied access not only to office in the empire but also to official culture and community associations. Thus they developed ideologies that ran counter to official imperial ones. But there was no such segregation in eighteenth-century England. The petite bourgeoisie was not consistently deprived of voting and political office (as we shall see later). It participated in the same economy and culture, read the same printed documents, joined similar clubs, and discussed the same ideas.

These infrastructures expanded from old regime networks, just as mass consumerism expanded from its consumption. True, they often discussed more leveling doctrines than suited the regime. But they implied three sets of class relations: national cooperation between modernizing old regime and bourgeois and petit bourgeois factions; local-regional cross-class organization, counterregime in some newer manufacturing areas (like Manchester), more cooperative elsewhere; and petit bourgeois class organization in alliance with radical artisans.

This combination produced ambiguous "impure" ideologies. At one extreme a combative sense of class identity and opposition to the old regime formed among a smallish radical petite bourgeoisie, especially among independent artisans. They identified themselves proudly in newspapers and pamphlets as the "industrious classes." The label, like "nation" and "people," included only those of independent means and education, excluding laborers (dependent on others for their subsistence). It comprised independent capitalists who also worked, whether as masters or as artisans, as opposed to the supposedly idle and parasitic rentiers, office placemen, and East India nabobs who used capital passively. "Old corruption" exploited the diligence of others and encouraged dependence on patronage. Commerce was free if left open to the market and to work, corrupt if commanded by particularistic patronage. A Birmingham radical paper described two candidates in an election with metaphors drawn from a booming consumer industry, horse racing. The race was between "Mr. Kelly's horse Independency, got by Freedom upon Commerce, and Mr. Rous' black horse Nabob, descended from a bloody shoulder'd Arabian, full brother to tyranny and corruption, back'd by Lord Jaghire and other Asiatic sportsmen" (Money 1977: 105).

This was petit bourgeois ideology, even at times suggesting a "transcendent" image of an alternative society. Newman (1987) shows that this class ideology entwined with Protestantism and nationalism, now encouraged by geopolitical rivalry with France. As old regime culture had cosmopolitan and French overtones, petit bourgeois resentments acquired national coloration. English sincerity, bluntness, and hard work and Protestant simplicity contrasted with French aristocratic Catholic luxury, decadence, superciliousness, and idleness. The virtue of England lay in its "people," principally its petite bourgeoisie.

Yet such elements of class ideology could not form a totality, for they coexisted with conceptions more congenial to the old regime. Both included overlapping versions of the "Protestant constitution." After a fierce by-election Birmingham manufacturers and tradesmen captured the Warwick County seat from the county gentry. Yet their MP promptly pledged to support

the Laws and Liberties of this Country upon the solid principles of our most excellent Constitution, by preventing . . . every inroad to innovation and abuse which designing or visionary men propose, and . . . by promoting the commercial interests of this extended Empire in which this County claims so considerable a share. [Money 1977: 211]

Here Birmingham and petit bourgeois interests were seen as realizable within the framework of the old "commercial" regime and the constitution. Alternative transcendent ideologies could not easily flourish. Later chapters show this became less so in America or France.

Principled, moral-ideological but ambiguous messages were also carried by churches and sects. Dissenters were 10 percent of the population and more than 20 percent of regular church attenders (Currie et al. 1977: 25). They first recruited among the poor and uneducated, then became more petit bourgeois, with small businessmen and self-employed artisans overrepresented (Gilbert 1976: 59–67). But sects varied and some were predominantly workers. A more elevated "Rational Dissent" movement printed best-selling pamphlets, sponsored subscription libraries, literary and philosophical societies, dispensaries, and schools (Seed 1985). A few sects chose radical politics, mostly the working-class ones. More generally many Whig politicians depended on radical dissent to get elected. Yet Wesley (a Tory) and most chapel leaders steered their congregations away from national politics (Ward 1973: 70–104). Dissent was varied, more involved in local community activism than national politics, by no means a "religion of consolation" for the oppressed (as suggested by E. P. Thompson).

The established church was also becoming more varied. Although much of its hierarchy was identified as "old corruption," Evangelicals were active in humanitarian causes, occasionally in political reform. Overall, the more active religious communities centered on family and local community concerns. This generated political diversity and more cross-class and local-regional than class ideologies. Along with most discursive infrastructures, churches fostered more class cooperation and local-regionalism than conflict. What kind of state were such diverse politics addressed toward?

Political sovereignty and representation

All European states had established basic territorial sovereignty by about 1700. State writs, tax collectors, and recruiting officers had fanned out over their territories. Their foreign embassies enjoyed special "extraterritorial" status negotiated with other sovereign states; there were agreements over frontier waterways and seacoasts; their generals were monopolizing military power and their statesmen diplomacy. Sovereignty cohered around the person of the monarch, his family, and his clients – approximating a "state elite," as emphasized by the elitist school of state theory discussed in Chapter 3. Sovereignty was wielded domestically and geopolitically by a sovereign.

But the effective scope of sovereignty remained narrow. States had virtually no rights of interference in what were termed "private"-property relations and laid no claim to ultimate knowledge and meaning – hence the contemporary distinction between state and civil society. State infrastructural powers were mostly for erratic execution of justice, maintenance of minimal order, tax levying, and recruitment of soldiers and sailors. There were few infrastructures to implement any further policy goals, though these were often proclaimed. To implement actual policy, the sovereign had to cooperate with a much larger political penumbra, composed of semiautonomous notable courtiers or parliamentarians. These also enjoyed property rights over offices of state and they dominated provincial administration.

Hence we are not dealing with a single, unitary state in this period. Its unity and cohesion were reduced in two ways. First, the *total* state – court, parliamentary assemblies, and the various administrative tiers – was effectively dual. There were really two states, a potentially autonomous monarchical *elite* in the center and a set of radial networks stretching between that center and civil society that I term, following Weber, *parties*. Eighteenth-century parties principally organized relations with and among dominant classes and secondarily with and among churches. Second, these parties rendered the state polymorphous, crystallizing in plural forms as party networks, lying both outside and inside state institutions, mobilized to influence them. The greater the variety and scope of state functions, potentially the more parties and the more polymorphous the state. Eighteenth-century state functions and parties were relatively few, yet there were "ins" and "outs," "court" and "country" parties organizing rivalries between and within elites and parties. Because transnational churches had long penetrated more intensively into localities than states did, state intervention in religion had hitherto generated the most agitated politicization, boosting representative pressures through the seventeenth century. Now European and colonial society was rather apolitical.

Notables were politicized. In despotic monarchies the court and royal administration were *the* political institution in which elites and parties interacted. In more representative regimes courtiers were subordinated to parties of parliamentary notables. Through the eighteenth century, the British state developed an embryo form of party democracy. Its despotic power was restrained by legal, political, and administrative rights enjoyed most notably by the dominant classes and by the established church. Legislatively (less so administratively) this was a fairly centralized state in which sovereignty resided symbolically with the "king in Parliament," where parties openly competed, although the king's ministers could still usually "buy" a parliamentary majority. Only at the end of the century could a genuinely oppositional party win an election and form a government.

Effective sovereignty, backing constitutional doctrine with real state infrastructural power to penetrate territories and mobilize resources, thus rested on coordination between state elite and party networks. The British state managed this, but not uniquely, as Table 4.2 shows.

British and (recently) Prussian state elites had centralized their rela-

Table 4.2. *Eighteenth-century relations between states and dominant classes and clerics*

Despotic power	Infrastructural relations with dominant classes and clerics	
	Centralized	Decentralized
High	Prussia	Austria, France
Low	Britain	American colonies

tions with parties of dominant classes and clerics, bringing them right into the state. Though the power base of dominant classes remained local, some collective organization was central – in Prussia, inside the royal administration (and increasingly in the universities), and in Britain, inside Parliament and through office "ownership." By contrast, the powers of Austrian notables and churches were expressed more autonomously through provincial diets and administrations, mostly distinct from royal administration; and in France they were largely organized outside monarchical institutions, enjoying privileged exemption from political obligations. These central states were more controlled by a dynastic "elite" than jointly by state elite and class clerical "parties."

Thus the infrastructural power of eighteenth-century states correlated less with despotism by the dynastic elite than with the ability to coordinate centrally party relations involving dominant classes. Chapter 11 shows that the eighteenth-century British and Prussian states could extract a higher proportion of national income for state expenses. Prussia was absolutist, Britain was not. The decisive difference from Austria and France lay not in their degree of despotic power but rather in the embedding of their states in the collective organization of dominant classes. Their state elites were actually less autonomous. The Austrian and French state elites were more autonomous; they were "suspended" above, relatively insulated from their civil societies. Despite the rival polemics of true elitist and class theories, states are *simultaneously* centralized actors and places where civil society relations are coordinated. As in most times and places, eighteenth-century state autonomy indicated more weakness than strength.

It also meant Austrian and French state institutions might be less adept at coping with new pressures coming from their civil societies. The British and Prussian states had stabilized institutions that directly "represented" dominant classes and churches. Thus if civil society began to generate new, broader pressures, these could potentially feed through parties directly into central state institutions. In Prussia those pressures fed through administrative institutions. In Britain they mostly fed through Parliament and its embryo party democracy. Who did Parliament represent?

Did the state's representative crystallization divide old regime from petite bourgeoisie and contribute to conflict between classes? Most petit bourgeois men were excluded from voting and office holding (as were all women), and the conflicts leading to the Great Reform Act of 1832 are often portrayed as class struggle. Yet British political institutions were particularistic. About 500,000 propertied males (15 percent of adult males) could vote and hold office. Franchise inequities were grounded in custom and geography as well as class discrimination. Borough electorates varied from the 12,000 ratepayers of Westminster to the zero electorate of Old Sarum, whose patron could allocate the seat as he pleased. By 1830, fifty-six borough seats owned by patrons or corporations had fifty or fewer voters; yet forty-three had more than 1,000 voters, and seven had more than 5,000. Uneven population growth left newer towns like Birmingham, Manchester, and Leeds unrepresented, though their forty-shilling freeholders could vote in surrounding county constituencies. The worst-off region was Scotland, with only 4,500 voters; yet the Welsh franchise was broader than the English (Brock 1973: 20, 312).

Thus the franchise was a mess. The more propertied petits bourgeois were variably enfranchised; the remainder, in newer manufacturing towns, were excluded, as were artisans almost everywhere; older ports, county towns, and small towns were more varied. Overall only a minority had the vote but many more were "virtually represented" by participating in long-established segmental patron-client networks. Many might operate comfortably through existing "parties," as we saw in Birmingham-Warwickshire. Thus some messages flowing through petit bourgeois communications networks would be aired in Parliament. They could not easily embody the grand politicized principles of excluded classes.

Thus even radicals felt the lure of two rival politics. First was a tradition of struggle for (individual) civil citizenship centering on Parliament, the law courts, and Protestant dissent – the first two inside the regime, the third on its respectable periphery. They could ally with "out" parliamentary factions, with lawyers, and with popular chauvinism. Englishmen were not "slaves" or "papists," nor did they wear the "wooden shoes" of less free countries. They had a "birthright" of liberty, even the regime acknowledged. The jurist Blackstone defined liberty of the subject in terms of civil citizenship: freedom of the person and private property, enforceable against the monarch, the great, or anyone else, primarily in the law courts and by petitioning crown and Parliament for redress of grievances (Gash 1986: 11). Second, if this proved insufficient, petit bourgeois radicals could demand "reform" – political citizenship for the "people." Few wanted full "democracy." They argued for a property qualification, to give all independent men a "stake in the nation," and in a sovereign but limited party democracy.

Both rhetorics spread unevenly through localities and regions, competing for the souls of emerging classes. Whereas the Birmingham petite bourgeoisie was split between the two, Manchester and Sheffield were attracted more by reform. There was not much British "genius for compromise" in this. True, Britain was constitutional, giving universal minimal (predominantly civil) rights, but the dividing, and eventual compromising, of potentially subversive class ideologies was primarily the unintended consequence of the mess that was the British franchise. As yet we have seen little economic bite given to class resentments. Most petit bourgeois interests were apparently being serviced already, by however "unrepresentative" a state, although this appearance misleads, as I have not yet touched on the political economy of the state.

Could the old regime have lasted much longer? In other countries, segmental patronage politics has been long-lived. Mouzelis (1986) observes that Latin American and Balkan commercialization and urbanization developed quasi-parliamentary institutions that survived for a considerable period before industrialization. Traditional oligarchies were faced by rising commercial classes not powerful enough to capture state power yet capable of disruption. The oligarchies developed two strategies of segmental incorporation: clientelism and populism. In clientelism, particularism was widened so that local oligarchies could "speak for" clients with a more popular base, whereas populist leaders who could control mass followings were admitted into power sharing. Mouzelis argues that such politics still dominates in parliamentary regimes in semideveloped countries. But he believes the evenness of British commercialization and industrialization created a civil society too powerful for the existing regime and classes too powerful for patronage.

Clientelism did decline in Britain (although it never disappeared), and populism never assumed importance. Was the decline of segmental and the rise of extensive and political class organization the inevitable outcome of deep-seated evolutionary or revolutionary processes? I will give a very qualified answer. I start by noting that evolutionary (or revolutionary) theories explaining politics in terms of economic and class development neglect the particularity of states.

European states had long been rather feeble. Even in the eighteenth century their scope remained narrow; they did not do much. The British king in Parliament headed the established church, conducted foreign policy, defended the realm (especially in Ireland), made law, enforced minimal public order and charity, and collected taxes. The church was in practice largely autonomous and at its higher levels rather somnolent. Foreign policy rarely concerned many on the mainland. The realm was not threatened after 1745; there was mainland consensus over Ireland; most defense was entrusted to a navy stationed abroad; most public order and charity were delegated to local authorities, secular and sacred.

Thus much legislation was particularistic, as the acts passed in 1763–4 reveal. "Private acts" permitted, for example, the executors of John Newport to lease his estate during his lunacy and dissolved the marriage of John Weller. But most "public acts" were not much broader. Tax legislation involved the levy of 2d. Scots or 1/6d. sterling on every pint of ale sold at Dunbar, as well as general customs and excise duties. Public order concerned the rebuilding of the road from Shillingford to Reading as well as renewing the Mutiny Act. Of the 176 statutes of this session, 145 were aimed at local and personal matters (Gash 1986: 14). Few were implemented by centralized bureaucracies, far more by local notables holding (often owning) public office, mobilizing segmental patron-client relations. The relationship of the state to class interests was problematic. It possessed too few infrastructural powers to be much concerned with general economic development or the regulation of class struggle.

Why would the excluded masses want participation in this particularistic state? They rarely had in the past (except where mobilized by religious ideologies). Emerging capitalist classes at first showed little interest. But when they did, the principal medium through which state and class struggle became linked was the issue then labeled "economic reform." This takes us to the particularistic heart of eighteenth-century state institutions, away from the notion that pure economic or class conflict became inevitably politicized.

The political economy of the state

Old regime states were not merely political but also economical: They distributed economic patronage; they taxed and borrowed. Both revenue and expenditure offered financial benefit to those who controlled the state and costs to those who did not. Access to the spoils of office and to the terms of government bonds and privileged exemption from taxation were the most important reasons for political activity.

Exclusion from these benefits in a period of rising state expenditures was the most important reason for wanting reform and for activating networks of discursive literacy to demand it.

There was less sale of offices, tax farming, and conferment of economic privilege in Britain than in France. Yet, on the expenditure side, similar practices existed, if on a smaller scale. Perhaps half the 16,000 civil offices of state were distributed by patronage. The best church livings went to relations and clients of political patrons. Promotion in the army and navy was swifter for an officer with a powerful patron. Government granted privileges and monopolies in colonial commerce. Membership of either house helped; support for the king's ministers helped more, for the Hanoverian kings were the fountainhead of office and honor and they personally scrutinized them.

On the revenue side the British state was not very corrupt, but it was regressive. About a quarter of revenue was borrowed (more in wartime) organized into a national credit system by the Bank of England from 1697. Taxation made up the rest, falling predominantly upon trade, through customs and excise taxes, backed up by land taxes. (See Table 11.6.) It allowed few exemptions, though revenue officers themselves benefited. But there were political choices between land taxes, at the direct expense of landowners (and indirectly of tenants and laborers), customs, and excise taxes, borne most visibly by commercial interests, though affecting the masses because generally regressive and levied on subsistence goods, and credit, benefiting the wealthy who could save, at the expense of the rest, who could not. Regressiveness worsened during wartime but seemed most regressive immediately after wars, when taxes remained high in order to repay bondholders. These choices divided classes and sectors who might assert self-interest in principled, constitutional terms.

At first, fiscal issues fed into an embryo party democracy, not through dissident classes but through segmental parties of "ins" and "outs." Their faction fighting had earlier generated principled ideologies of "court" and "country" or of religions, but these declined through the eighteenth century. Dissenters and Catholics remained "outs." Though voting restrictions were being removed, Catholics remained excluded from the legislature and both religions from public office and the universities (and therefore from law and medicine). With this exception, conflict of the king, his permanent majority in the Lords, and his ministerial faction in the Commons against the Commons opposition concerned patronage more than principle. As ideology weakened, local-regional patronage had sewn up more constituencies. Contested elections became fewer and turnout declined between 1715 and 1760; then they increased, for reasons I will explore (Holmes

1976; Speck 1977: 146–7, 163; Clark 1985: 15–26). Before the 1760s, politics concerned segmental parties arguing over spoils, though with potentially more principled, "excluded" classes and religions lurking outside.

The largest Commons party comprised 200–250 "outs," independent country gentlemen, outside national spoils though holding local office as justices of the peace, and land tax commissioners. They favored low taxes and denounced ministerial corruption and "despotism." Yet they included an old Tory faction and favored church and king against "radicals." Then came the 100 or so members of the court and treasury party – civil servants, courtiers, merchants, lawyers, and military officers seeking preferment, sinecures, or honors. Most offered loyalty to ministries and king. Finally came 100–150 political activists – land-owning faction leaders and their clients who provided ministers and orators, the famous men of the period. Few were like Edmund Burke, declaiming consistent principles. Most articulated principle as they generalized the problems of office or of exclusion from office and of revenue interests. They represented perhaps 200 ruling families. The independents represented 5,000–7,000 gentry families and, together with the treasury party, the 3,000–4,000 families of richer merchants, tradesmen, and professionals. In total the parties directly represented the material interests of perhaps 1 percent of British families (Smith 1972: 68–102).

These parties then competed, sometimes perfunctorily, for the support of the 15 percent of men who could vote. The remaining 85 percent were their segmental clients or powerless. This was not a democracy, but it had stably institutionalized political contestation. As Dahl (1971) observes, this was of supreme importance because it is the usual first step toward the achievement of democracy in the world. Britain had the rudiments of party democracy. But we must also note the important fact that the excluded 85 percent were not simply defined by class. Thus institutionalized contestation was not totally closed to rising classes. But, as yet, parties and rising classes showed little interest in each other.

Government depended on party contests over what I term in Chapter 3 "particularistic embedding." The king's ministers had to preserve court and treasury spoils, bribe "in" factions yet satisfy "outs" with low taxes, national success, and adherence to the Protestant constitution, and avoid too much overt discontent among the "excludeds." Most governments succeeded rather well and became admired throughout Europe as stable, balanced, and modern. Yet these qualities arose as factions institutionalized and embedded corruption. It *was* "old corruption."

It came to be denounced as such only because two pressures conjoined – the fiscal pressures of militarism and the emergence of ideologies linking these to political exclusion. Between 1760 and 1832, they
fused in economic and political reform, intensifying political struggle
between parties that became less segmental, half like classes led by
ideologists espousing principles. The fiscal-military pressures came in
three waves: the aftermath of the Seven Years' War, the American
Revolution, and the French Revolution and the Napoleonic Wars.
Through these wars many old regime members themselves came to
lobby for a more modern state. Under geopolitical pressures, their
modernizing principles became joined to those of the predominantly
excluded petite bourgeoisie, the "nation without doors."

War and reform, 1760–1815

Abroad, the British state had crystallized as essentially militarist. Wars
made Britain "Great." The Seven Years' War ended in 1763 with
glorious success and a massive empire. The loss of the American
colonies during 1776–83 was recompensed by final triumph in the
French Revolution and Napoleonic Wars lasting from 1792 to 1815.
These massive wars had the normal historical effects on state finances
documented in Volume I, for Britain magnified out of all its historical
experience by becoming a great imperial Power. As the wars started,
expenditures more than doubled, at first entirely the result of military
expenses. Then debt repayments took over and lasted well into peacetime. Wartime surges then settled back, but always at a higher level
than before the war. Over the period the state trebled in financial size,
more than double national economic growth. As Table 11.3 reveals,
in peacetime the British central state extracted about 11 percent of
national income, in wartime at least 22 percent, and in the Napoleonic
Wars well over 30 percent. Moreover, most exactions were regressive
and divisive, through indirect taxes and borrowing.

How could this militarist state now fail to be relevant to social life?
The sudden surges created political problems more acute than anything
that the slow Industrial Revolution could throw at the state. Yet the
state did raise money to win the wars, and defeat in North America did
not cause much trouble at home. The wars never caused actual regime
breakdown, as in the American colonies, France, and some Austrian
provinces. In comparative terms the fiscal-military crisis, as in Prussia,
was only moderate. That was principally because parties were already
institutionalized in the sovereign decision-making bodies of this state
and, under pressure, could bend and extend, without breaking the

state apart. Militarism could be handled by a rudimentary but sovereign party democracy.

Moderate pressures developed moderate reform politics in two phases. The regime itself was most concerned at costs at their highest point, during wars, and sought then to improve administrative and fiscal efficiency. During successful wars taxpayers grumbled but paid up extra taxes. It was in the second phase, with the war ended but taxpayers subsidizing bondholders, that radical reformers arose. The level of taxes as a proportion of gross national product did not significantly rise through this period (overall revenue did), but because the taxes were especially regressive in the aftermath of war, the proportion then taken from middling and poorer classes' incomes rose. Popular discontent resulted.

Reformers from both old regime "ins" and "outs" and from more radical "excludeds," passing messages and principles across cross-class ideological power networks, produced a movement for economic reform around the fringes of the regime. "Ins" sought administrative improvements to cut costs; "outs" railed at corruption and particularism; "excludeds," encouraged by the factionalism above them, began to demand popular fiscal control. As we see in Chapter 15, "excludeds" became enraged as taxes got more regressive. The state and class had mattered little to most people in the mid-eighteenth century; by 1815, the state mattered considerably and was organizing class exploitation on a national scale. Military-fiscal extraction drove forward a political and national class struggle.

The wars varied in popularity and ideology. The Seven Years' War was a traditional war among Great Powers with dynastic rulers. It was faintly religious, mostly ranging Protestant against Catholic. Yet, unlike later wars, it involved no divisive political ideologies. The instrumental rationality of the participants made it a "limited war" (Mann 1988b). In Britain the propertied "people" generally supported the war; the "populace" still lacked more than local organization. Politics concerned only strategy and whether peace was being too hurriedly sought and the burdens were reluctantly accepted until after war ended. But in the mid-1760s, the war over, "outs" and "excludeds" wanted cheaper government. When it did not arrive, they denounced corruption. Some also wanted franchise reform. Ministries responded by escalating patronage and coercion. The cry of despotism was added.

The county of Middlesex had a broad franchise and John Wilkes as its MP. In 1763, he was arrested for publishing seditious libels. Claiming parliamentary privilege, with support from "out" factions, he successfully challenged his arrest, proceeding to legal victories against government press harassment and forcing publication of House of Commons debates. Though centering on civil citizen rights, Wilkes also activated a national organization with widespread urban support for franchise reform, shorter parliaments, the exclusion of placeholders from the Commons, and curbs on ministerial authority. In the early 1770s, it supported the rebellious Americans. The London leadership was

exemplified by the newspaper proprietor, the printer of cartoons, the producer of artefacts, the brewer, the tavern proprietor, and the city merchant, all of whose conceptions of politics differed substantially from that of the political elite. Thanks to Wilkes, these men, . . . of little political significance before 1750, came into their own during the 1760s. [Brewer 1976: 268; cf. Christie 1962]

Alarmed government agents reported that "sober discreet master traders and artificers" supported Wilkes (Christie 1982: 75). Neither Wilkes's nor, later, Wyville's organization contained many ordinary artisans or laborers. Wilkes's core was petit bourgeois, small and middling merchants and tradesmen in London and other commercial cities and lesser freeholders in urban and rural districts. Yet agitation sometimes spread downward. Most arrested from London mobs were artisans and laborers, often also protesting labor disputes (Rudé 1962: 172–90, 220–3). Both "people" and "populace" could be mobilized but not yet together.

Wilkes's organization centered on discursive literacy – on the distribution of printed handbills, pamphlets, and petitions. In 1769, 55,000 inhabitants of fifteen counties and twelve boroughs signed a petition to free him from prison. Wilkes mobilized the towns; an "out" faction, the Rockingham Whigs, mobilized counties. The regime was forced to imitate, expanding its own publishing and petitioning enterprises. Whig factions and ministries competed for popular support, Whigs flirting with excluded radicals by proposing economical reform. By the 1790s, both sides were using mass mobilization tactics in Manchester (Bohstedt 1983: 100–25). The first mass public of history, diffused across an extensive society, was activated in Britain (and in America; see Chapter 5).

Wilkes himself faded away in 1779, moving from "out" to "in" by obtaining the profitable sinecure of chamberlain to the City of London. His organization had been ambiguous, using both reform channels identified earlier – popular press, petition, and mob, along with the law and Parliament. Parliament might increase civil citizenship but feared the mob and franchise extension. English lawyers were no radicals, unlike some in France and America. They defended custom and precedent. They could secure rights within the ancient constitution, no more; and such has been the generally conservative role of British law ever since. Wilkes's movement was thus contradictory and petit bourgeois radicals frightened off "out" sympathizers. Amid the peaceful mid-1770s state expenditures declined, and with it, discontent.

The American war at first strengthened the government. But by 1779, British armies were foundering, France had declared war, and the Irish Volunteer movement threatened rebellion. The war involved high regressive taxation, disrupted trade, and seemed incompetently run (although the logistics of a 3,000-mile supply line would have overstrained any contemporary state). Taxes fueled demands for economic reform. Discursive networks were again activated. A Birmingham tavern and coffeehouse keeper announced a debate at his tavern in verses evoking the conflict between taxpayers and bondholders. The words he emphasized were those of an antiwar Commons motion:

> ... as a friend
> To my country, the war I would wish at an end,
> For taxes we find e're the work is half finished,
> Have *increased*, and *increasing*, and should be *diminished*.
> But those who each year taste the sweets of the loan
> Undoubtedly with the same work may go on.
>
> [Money 1977: 104]

But this war, unlike the Seven Years' War, also raised principles. The American rebels mixed traditional defense against despotism with claims for universal contractual rights. These resonated in the market experience of property owners, in moral Protestantism, and in established civil citizen rights. The colonists demanded "no taxation without representation." The regime countered by arguing that taxpayers were "virtually represented": MPs represented men of independence and therefore indirectly represented the whole nation (Brewer 1976: 206–16). The Rockingham and Chatham Whigs had been out of office long enough to have espoused principles. They proposed to reduce crown influence by mixed economical and franchise reforms, barring government contractors from sitting in the Commons and disenfranchising revenue officers.

The second radical movement, the Association movement led by the Reverend Christopher Wyville, took off in 1779–80 (Christie 1962). Committees of correspondence in nearly forty counties and boroughs organized petitions for economical reform, mobilizing country "outs" and "excluded" property owners. Wyville seems to have depended more on religious radicals than Wilkes and he reckoned he received disproportionate support from Dissenters. He linked up with radicals to press for annual elections and one hundred new county constituencies. But this worried his Rockingham Whig allies and some of his own county associations. Even his astute leadership could not paper over these cracks. The "outs" withdrew, leaving radical urban "excludeds" in charge. They were finished off by the Gordon riots of June 1780 – pillaging and burning supposedly in defense of the Protestant constitution against Catholics. The propertied drew together in fright, compromised over minor economic reform, but backed off franchise reform.

The French Revolution revived reform and radical discursive literacy, typified by the mass organization the Society for Constitutional Information. Tom Paine's *Rights of Man*, published in 1791, sold a phenomenal 200,000 copies by 1793. But the execution of Louis, the Terror, and the successes of the revolutionary armies alienated "outs" and propertied "excludeds." Reform was forced back to artisan corresponding societies. Wartime patriotism ground them into insignificance. With the example of France before them, regime party disputes would not at this point go principled. The very success of the French Revolution made a British bourgeois or petit bourgeois revolution (unlikely anyway) impossible. Popular pamphlets congratulated Britain on achieving prosperity and liberty without violence or leveling. As the *Anti-Gallican Songster* of 1793 declaimed:

> Long may Old England possess good cheer and jollity.
> Liberty and property, and no equality.
> [Dinwiddy 1988: 62]

The rise of Bonaparte lessened fear of revolution but worsened geopolitical danger. The war, paid for by the masses, became almost national, as it did in France. Some nationalism emerged, ill at ease with corrupt and particularistic state administration. Ministries sought economies. Pitt's piecemeal reforms whittled away "old corruption" from the ministries prosecuting the war. Patronage remained in the legal profession, church, India Company, and all those sinecures from the Cinque Ports to the Band of State Pensioners, once the citadel of the state, now its nooks and crannies. Corruption was difficult to defend when citadel modernization was underway. The leading Conservative, Lord Eldon, moaned, "Touch one atom and the whole is lost." The regime came to accept bureaucracy, accountability, and national uniformity (Rubinstein 1983). The nation-state was cultivated by economic reform pressured by national war. (See Chapter 13 for administrative details.)

Yet the link between economic reform and franchise reform had been severed by the French bogey. The Foxite Whig party, out of power for two decades, developed principled opposition but would not join with "excluded" radicals organized in corresponding societies and Jacobin Clubs. Attempts at reform in Parliament brought only a handful of votes; class riots by urban poor and handloom weavers were isolated and repressed.

Reform, not revolution, 1815–1832

War's end again put reform on the agenda, ushering in the second phase of the military-fiscal cycle. Direct military costs declined, but peacetime debt repayments provoked. In 1816, the Commons abolished income tax, a tax on the propertied, only increasing the regressiveness of the taxes paying off fundholders. Improvements in wartime budgeting had exposed the costs of placeholding. Lord Liverpool's postwar government wished to cut costs, but its members benefited from "old corruption." Radical pamphlets claimed two hundred Tory peers and bishops received upward of £2 million annually from sinecures, official salaries and offices, and church livings – more than from their agricultural rent rolls – even without counting the pickings of the India Company (Rubinstein 1983: 76–7). This was now widely defined as corrupt, especially in the press. In 1820, Peel wrote:

Public opinion never had such influence on public measures, and yet never was so dissatisfied with the share which it possessed. It is growing too large for the channels that it had been accustomed to run through ... the engineers that made them never dreamt of various streams that are now struggling for a vent. [Brock 1973: 16]

The *Manchester Guardian*, founded in 1821, and the *Westminster Review* (1824), respectable reform journals circulating among educated people, confirmed Peel's observation. Between 1819 and 1823, Whig leaders committed themselves to franchise reform, though petit bourgeois radicals still gave priority to economic reform. Cobbett's *Political Register*, "read in every ale-house," hammered away: Parliamentary reform was a means to an end – the elimination of corrupt fundholders and "tax-eaters." As the *Extraordinary Black Book* put it in 1832: "Cheap government – cheap bread – cheap justice – and industry unfettered and productive will reward our efforts in the triumph of the Reform Bill" (Gash 1986: 45–6). Lord John Russell wrote in 1823:

The few enthusiastic Jacobins of 1793 were converted, in 1817 and the following years, into hundreds and thousands of malcontents. The pressure of sixty million taxes have indisposed more sound and loyal men to the constitution of their country, than the harangues of Citizen Brissot ... could have done in a hundred years. [Dinwiddy 1988: 70]

But postwar discontent still met repression, supported by many reforming "outs." To see how broader unity among reformers was built I turn first to changes in popular movements.

As in most agrarian societies, normally the masses were incapable of their own extensive or political organization. For an illiterate disenfranchised populace, the best way to demonstrate grievance forcibly was via the local mass procession leading to riot. Bohstedt (1983) counted riots in England and Wales between 1790 and 1810. The most common type, 39 percent, was over food, most protesting high prices. Twenty-two percent had military targets – press gangs and quasi-conscription methods. "Political and ideological" riots (Whig, Tory, radical, and "king and country" mobs) comprised 10 percent, just ahead of labor riots. The pattern in London differed. "Miscellaneous" riots comprised 25 percent, directed at unpopular prominent persons, helping prisoners escape from the authorities, or "occurring at theaters." Many of these should be added to the political and ideological category, bringing them from 14 percent to perhaps 25 percent of London riots. Then came "brawls" (mostly Irish-English conflicts) at 16 percent. There were far fewer food riots in London and slightly more labor riots.

Food and military riots had the lowest social base, mobilizing the ordinary populace. Women (who did the marketing) were also active in food riots and participated in all but labor disputes (of employed artisans and laborers). Political and ideological riots and "miscellaneous" riots in London mixed petit bourgeois leaders and a rank and file drawn from the populace. Riots intensively mobilized family, street, and neighborhood. As we shall see in other countries and in Chartism in Britain, this intensity could give an insurrectionary bite to popular protest, more than in later periods.

But riots were rarely extensive. They were undercut by class differences. The "populace" rioted most over food and conscription, yet these worried the "people" less. Farmers benefited from higher prices and the petite bourgeoisie could afford them. Neither were likely to be press-ganged. Labor disputes divided people from populace because the former employed the latter. Such class divisions helped the authorities activate segmental organizations and repress rioters. Only some riots were even aimed at the state. Demonstrating workers often petitioned the local regime to intervene against their employers. Most food riots were apolitical. The bread riots of 1766 had been caused by changes in customs regulations, which led grain middlemen to switch to exporting. This raised bread prices in towns and among rural populations specializing in other produce. But the ensuing riots were aimed not at the state but at visible market figures like millers and merchants, sometimes asking the local regime for help against them (Williams 1984; cf. Stevenson 1979: 91–112; Bohstedt 1983: 211–2, 296). The authorities, not themselves attacked, were sometimes sympathetic.

These class and target differences among popular movements were the decisive, *organizational* cause of the lack of political revolution in Britain. Yet they have been neglected by historians committing their characteristic vice: leaving implicit in their writings the theoretical and political assumptions of the twentieth century. They assume class struggle must have involved politics in the eighteenth and early nineteenth centuries, just as it does in the twentieth. On the one hand, Marxian historians like E. P. Thompson (1963) and Foster (1974) exaggerate political radicalism among the populace, or they explain its failure by exaggerating consoling ideologies like Methodism. On the other hand, conservatives like Clark (1985) and Christie (1984) assume the absence of revolution must be due to the opposite: political contentment, deference, and material well-being. Let us consider Christie's book, which explicitly addresses the question of why there was no revolution in Britain.

Christie mobilizes various conservative arguments drawn from twentieth-century experience. A revolution was averted, he argues, because Britain was a society of plural, not qualitative, stratification (the twentieth-century "decline of class"); of deference for squire, church, and king (the "deferential Tory voter"); of rising prosperity ("post–World War II affluence"); of a generous Poor Law (the "welfare state"); and of legitimate workmen's combinations ("institutionalization of industrial conflict"). These are pertinent to the twentieth century because all relate everyday life experience to the state. National stratification structures, universal suffrage, national political parties, a government-regulated economy, welfare state, and institutionalized union-management relations all embed national politics in popular practical experience.

Some of Christie's arguments apply also to the eighteenth century, but rarely to the British *state*. The Poor Law was important in popular economic life, although it appeared local rather than national. Plural distinctions in wealth, reproduced by the market, and the absence of legal privilege meant that material issues did not necessarily involve reform of the state – as they did in France, where legal privilege permeated the economy. Other Christie arguments barely apply to the eighteenth century. He exaggerates prosperity, which scarcely touched most of the populace. If the die was so cast for conservatism, why was there such a Chartist insurrection from below in the 1830s and 1840s? (See Chapter 15.) And if material prosperity prevented revolution, why did one occur in the most prosperous country in the world

(America), and in the second most prosperous country in Europe (France)? Periods of slump, bad harvests, and severe price rises did lead to popular discontent in all three countries. Only in the French countryside in 1788–9 was this causally related to revolution – for a political reason peculiar to France. To improve their lot, the French peasantry attacked their lords' legal privileges and this involved a frontal assault on the *state.*

But the economic condition of the British populace had no great relevance to *political* power, one way or the other. Usually they appeared content and deferential, but this was not why the regime survived. At other times they switched to insolence and riot; but as we have seen, their collective riots and class grievances were only rarely directed against the state, only rarely involved all their class, and only rarely allied them with discontented, politically excluded elements of the propertied "people." Their level of contentment had little to do with it. The "people" controlled segmentally most of the extensive and political organizations of protest, centering on networks of discursive literacy. Most "populace" discontent was channeled through them; it was not yet extensively or politically organized. This was sufficient cause of the absence of revolutionary movements in Britain before Chartism.

Nevertheless, organizational changes were under way. Food riots were declining, labor and political disputes increasing. Manufacturing districts were taking the lead from London and the commercial towns. New factory towns terrified old regime observers, especially religious ones. Their descriptions invoked the worst analogies they could draw upon. Factories were like the fires of hell, tended by the working damned – men, women, and children, except that in their previous images of hell, little children had never been among the damned. The towns smoked and stank like battlefields, dotted with degraded, drunken survivors. Rapid population growth had brought disorder, irreligion, and the "dangerous classes." They were "dangerous" precisely because they were initially outside of the regime's segmental organizations. Even the army had only small numbers quartered in the industrial areas, and they had to counter more organized protests and demonstrations.

Mass processions turning to riot gave way to mass meetings addressed by agitators presenting resolutions and petitions, coordinated regionally, even nationally. Journalists joined their platforms and publicized grievances and regime atrocities. The word "Peterloo" was a journalist's invention to convey how British troops had perverted their victory at Waterloo by their ferocity four years later in dispersing a demonstration is St. Peter's Square, Manchester. Mass demonstrations and press campaigns expanded discursive infrastructures across and down the nation. The American and French revolutions had expanded the dual organization of printed word and oral assembly. (See the next two chapters.) British radical leaders like Place, Hunt, Cobbett, and O'Connor circulated reform proposals as radical as any French revolutionary of the period 1789–90. But "confronting an undefeated and potentially repressive government the only option to fruitless rebellion was organisation," says Stevenson (1979: 317) – plus appearing moderate. They restrained alternative principles and demanded limited economic and political reform backed by the "language of menace." Old regime modernizers and substantial petits bourgeois argued they could not preserve local-regional order until property was fully represented. Respectable rational reform and popular agitation remained separate but developed symbiosis through the 1820s, both with more national and class, less segmental, and local-regional organization.

Then came a breakthrough in ideological power. In the American and French wars the enemy had been secular. Religion was no longer a geopolitical threat. Dissenters and Catholics had shown wartime loyalty, and laws against them had not been enforced for decades. Governing Ireland was widely acknowledged to be made more difficult by discrimination against Catholics, and the moral decay of the hierarchy of the established church was widely publicized. Bills for repeal of Test and Corporation Acts against Dissenters and for Catholic emancipation got nearer success. O'Connell's landslide victory in the County Clare election of 1828 made a mockery of the law: A Catholic could be popularly elected but not take his seat. Catholics might sweep the Irish seats at the next election. The Tory duke of Wellington moved to forestall such a constitutional crisis. His emancipation bill passed in 1829. The old regime abandoned its Protestant soul as well as potent segmental controls over the souls of its subjects (Clark 1985).

Whig modernizers were emboldened. Once in government, they presented a reform bill in the 1830–1 session. Grey and his cabinet were determined and the popular movement had strengthened as artisan discursive networks, friendly societies, and unions had expanded (see Chapter 15). The Whigs used the mass demonstrations to pressure both houses. For the first time, there was actual collusion between an old regime faction and an "excluded" popular movement. But this divided artisan radicals, many rightly fearing that the bill would delay their own representation if middling property owners were enfranchised. Yet they could hardly oppose the bill. Although Conservatives realized that only alternative reform proposals would head off the bill, they could not agree on their form. They defeated the first bill in 1831, but the government called a new election. The election was fought amid demonstrations and riots, and the results decimated the declared Conservatives. This persuaded many country members to switch sides and support the second bill. With assistance from the streets, the Parliament of "old corruption" reformed itself. It seemed, as Carlyle put it, an "abdication on the part of the governors" (Perkin 1969: 183–95).

The regime was not converted to full democracy. Rather it was impressed by two arguments, one progressive and usually implicit, the other reactionary and explicit. It implicitly accepted the reform view of modernization and progress, equating particularism with corruption. Uneven population growth had made the existing franchise unrepresentative of any general principle of political citizenship. It was either irrational or corrupt. Having abandoned absolutism, then particularism in major government departments, then a hieratic church, the regime had no principles left. It also recognized the contributions of the petite bourgeoisie to Britain's rising prosperity. Britain could now dominate the world through free trade backed by economic government. The petite bourgeoisie had a property stake in the nation. It should no longer be excluded – provided it broke with the "populace." So, second, explicitly, the rulers looked to detach the petite bourgeoisie from the mob.

Property – whatever its source, lineage, or patronage – was to rule the nation. Research revealed a £10 property franchise in the boroughs would preserve voter "independence," admitting most of the petite bourgeoisie but only one in fifty to one hundred employed artisans (mostly in London, where better education would also encourage "independence"). The new property qualifications were higher than a few existing ones, which actually disenfranchised several thousand electors; but in all, 300,000 men were added to the electorate of 500,000. The elimination of 140 rotten boroughs was the death knell for royal and ministerial patronage over the Commons. In political (though not symbolic) terms, Britain was no longer a monarchy; segmental dividing and ruling, flourishing in central Europe, was finished there. The defeated House of Lords also declined before party democracy. But the distribution of seats between counties and boroughs remained unchanged, while county "virtual representation" and segmental organization remained. Personnel and parties did not greatly change. Landowning notables formed a Commons majority until the 1860s (Thomas 1939: 4–5). Yet the state had changed from particularism and segmentalism, centered on the king in Parliament, to universalism, centered on a capitalist class-nation.

The triumph of old regime liberalism, 1832–1880

The petite bourgeoisie seemed triumphant: Free trade in everything; the abolition of patronage; reform of the civil service, of municipal government, of the church, of Oxford, Cambridge, and the public schools; the abolition of the landed property qualification for MPs, of church rates, of enclosure of urban common land, and of the "taxes on knowledge" – all had seemed revolutionary in 1760 yet were being achieved a century later. The state would not intervene particularistically but "hold the ring" for diffused market forces.

Yet liberalism was legislated by a state dominated by old regime notables. Their patronage networks still controlled most counties and some towns, they had the leisure and wealth for politics, and they dominated London. Thompson (1963: 298) asserts that the petit bourgeois electorate ruled not through the "composition of the House but in the course of legislation." But this is not quite right, for the regime itself had converted to the new principles. The regime was secularizing across midcentury, not without retaining a certain moral sense, but the church declined as Britain became probably the most secular country in the world. Its regime also now acquiesced in the originally bourgeois view that "one species of wealth, namely passive property in land had no right to exact a toll from another, namely active capital in industry and commerce" (Perkin 1969: 315–6). But the old regime lost little from its conversion and gained by harnessing the petit bourgeois Industrial Revolution to its distinctive commercial form of capitalism (Ingham 1984; see also "The Decline of Great Britain" in Mann 1988a).

During Victoria's long reign (1837–1901), the British economy boomed. Until the 1860s, the rich did best and inequalities widened, as they did in most industrializing countries (Kuznets 1955, 1963; Lindert and Williamson 1983). Landowners prospered best of all. Rubinstein (1977a, 1977b) estimates that, in 1815, 88 percent of all persons worth £100,000 or more drew most of their fortune from land. Among millionaires dying in 1809–58, 95 percent had remained great landowners. Even to the 1880s, most millionaires and half millionaires were landowners. In 1832, land and farms contributed 63 percent of total national capital (Deane and Cole 1967: 271). This had to be tapped for industrial expansion. Eighteenth-century changes in mortgage laws and interest rates, the advent of West End and country banks, insurance companies, the provincial mortgage market, and professional estate management enabled the old regime to handle agricultural revenue with a more diversified capitalism (Mingay 1963: 32–37). Mines converted a few landowners into colliery owners, while urbanization raised land values and enabled landowners to buy into urban transport industries.

Then canals and railways brought windfalls to adjacent landowners and increased agricultural profits and rents by slashing distribution costs to urban markets (F. M. L. Thompson 1963: 256–68). Landowners' investments went more into commerce than industry, through private banks and solicitors, through the City, into government stocks, commerce, and foreign trade. Until 1905, the City's "invisible earnings" from banking, insurance, and shipping exceeded its income from foreign investments, and both far exceeded income from domestic manufacturing industry. Thus the City, secure under British naval hegemony, converted to free trade, hitherto alien to the older part of the regime. The City and the treasury began to cement the alliance that has dominated British political economy ever since. Investment went through country and city banks, discount houses, bill brokers, and solicitors to banks that lent to industry, usually over the short term, or more commonly to manufacturers' merchant suppliers and commercial distributors. Because land was easily mortgaged, landowners' debts channeled reverse flows: petit bourgeois savings went through solicitors and insurance companies into landowners' consumption and investment (Crouzet 1972, 1982: 335–41; Cannadine 1977: 636–7).

Commercialization affected all property owners, embedded in diffuse, decentralized circuits of capital. The particularistic, ascriptive categories of genealogy and rank became less decisive in social differentiation. Capital also diffused through the family. The patriarchal head had been responsible for the landed estate, but capitalist shareholding separates management and ownership. Any person can hold shares, regardless of ascriptive position. All those ticklish problems regarding property flow through life cycle and generations could be handled more easily by the shareholding person. Younger sons, cadet lines, the elderly, and ailing patriarchs could be given shares without long-term implications for control of the estate. Even more momentous was the impact on women in propertied families. Marriage portions, unmarried daughters, maiden aunts, and widows could be provided for. This required legal changes, legislated in midcentury, so that individual women could become property owners. The regime was composed more of individual entrepreneurs, less of corporate lineages. It could rule less through segmental organization, more through class and market.

Railways introduced economic concentration because all the track and rolling stock had to be in place before revenue could flow. By 1847, gross expenditure on railway capital formation (even excluding land purchase) was 7 percent of national income. After the British boom subsided, railways were exported abroad. New provincial stock exchanges and joint-stock companies (first with unlimited liabilities) moved into railways, as did the London Stock Exchange, hitherto mostly dealing in government stocks. The most numerous group of shareholders mixed gentry, professionals, businessmen, and merchants from London and commercial rather than industrial areas. Then came great local landowners, useful for influencing Parliament, as each company had to be set up by private act of Parliament. A "new corruption" appeared: By 1865, 157 MPs and 49 peers were directors of railway companies. The third investing group was the propertied petite bourgeoisie, those with sufficient savings to buy at least one share (typically valued at £100), again from commercial more than manufacturing areas (Pollins 1952; Barker and Savage 1974: 77–9; Reed 1975; Crouzet 1982: 335–41). Rentier capital diffused through civil society, moving wealth from land and commerce to the major industrial venture of the age. The separate interests of the old regime were fused by commercial capitalism.

"Old corruption" had not faded away but had slipped sideways into the City, where it remains today. The placeholders, the younger sons of landowners, loosened their particularistic connections with the state and moved into City commerce. Throughout the nineteenth century the wealthy outside of agriculture earned fortunes in commerce, finance, and transport, as merchants, bankers, shipowners, merchant bankers, and stock and insurance brokers, rather than as manufacturers. Manufacturing never led commerce as a source of wealth (Rubinstein 1977b: 102–3). Old regime fortunes amassed in colonies and overseas trade had bought landed estates, titles, and government stocks, then made mortgage loans. Now their City successors could do the same. They built "more Fonthills than factories," says Crouzet (1972: 176). They married more into land than industry (F. M. L. Thompson 1963: 20–1). Aristocrats and landowners were far more likely to join the boards of City than manufacturing enterprises. As the radical MP for manufacturing Rochdale John Bright used to remark, the City was a "system of outdoor relief for the aristocracy."

This fusion of land, finance, and commerce eased the effects of the decline of agricultural revenues and the capital value of land that began in the late 1870s. Those who diversified relied less on land for wealth and position; others sold urban land to invest in shares and government bonds. Though the lesser gentry and squirearchy suffered real decline, the great families slipped sideways. So did the Tory party. By 1895, finance had replaced land as the main business interest of its MPs (Thomas 1939: 15). Capitalists in land, commerce, and finance fused as a single extensive political class, with national economic, familial, and educational (the "public" schools) organizations, committed to a bureaucratic state and to free trade under British near hegemony. Old regime liberals were the new ruling class.

Manufacturers were in this class, but in its margins. Few were in Parliament. Most MPs were in finance, commerce, and railways rather than manufacturing – more so at first in the Tory than the Liberal party (Thomas 1939: 13–20). The Liberals represented broader property; the Tories, land, commerce, and finance. But the parties were also divided by region and religion. Neither parties nor economic sectors differed much on economic policy. Between the repeal of the Corn Laws in 1846 and the Tariff Reform movement from the 1890s, Parliament barely concerned itself with economics. The dominant issues, remaining important until 1914, were religion, education, and Ireland (the British version of the "national" state crystallization emphasized in Chapter 3) and working-class representation (part of the capitalist state crystallization). Even after tariff reform surfaced, industry did not seriously challenge the City's gods of free trade and the gold standard.

The government of the "first industrial nation" has never been as thoroughly industrial as those of its main rivals. Britain has lagged in devising policies of authoritative industrial organization: corporatism, state education, and state funding for hi-tech industry (Longstreth 1983; Ingham 1984; Lee 1986; Mann 1988a). British capitalist organization has been unusually diffuse, pledged to preserve markets. The strength of the market had been the main reason why the Industrial Revolution had occurred first on that island. Britain took the customary step of institutionalizing the structures that had made it "Great" in the first place. In a changed world they assisted decline.

Thus neither petite bourgeoisie nor manufacturing industry constituted an organized class or class fraction in Victorian Britain. Since Victoria's maturity they have been "virtually represented" by an essentially commercial old regime liberalism, relying less than earlier regimes on segmental organization. Property owners had consolidated into a single, national, capitalist class organized into mass political parties controlled by liberal old regime notables.

Conclusion

Britain passed through the Industrial Revolution without a bourgeois revolution; political reform permitted the old regime to survive in new liberal colors. The first industrial country institutionalized national capitalist liberalism with an old tinge without undue turbulence in this period. Mild reform and old continuity have also characterized its more recent history. It may appear as an evolutionary process; yet the seventeenth century had seen civil war, the execution and exile of kings, and religious schisms. Jacobite uprisings in 1715 and 1745 were reminders of that past. From the 1830s, Chartism also proved a revolutionary movement, defeated by the very unity of old regime and petite bourgeoisie here described. (See Chapter 15.) Thus the period from the 1750s to the 1830s, establishing that unity, was decisive in modern British history. Indeed it became a turning point in world history, as liberalism became a viable global strategy of modernization.

My explanation has involved all four sources of social power. I have not yet sought to rank their relative causal weights; that attempt is begun in Chapter 7. First, economic power: Through the late seventeenth century and the eighteenth, British agriculture institutionalized commercial market capitalism. This was the main medium-term cause of the Industrial Revolution. It also ensured that economic organization would be unusually diffuse rather than authoritative: The "invisible hand" constrained all power actors. True, it also produced an emergent class, the petit bourgeois class, but the market ensured that old regime and petite bourgeoisie remained half latent, not engaging in head-on, dialectical economic class struggle. The old regime did not exclude the petite bourgeoisie from the main route to economic advantage, the market; and the petite bourgeoisie prospered. In the early nineteenth century their parallel preoccupation with market advantage developed into mutuality. Land and industry alike became subordinated to finance and commerce, and the merged British capitalist class developed its distinctive obsession with free trade and the gold standard – the political economy of British old regime liberalism.

Religion and then state expansion and especially market capitalism generated the second principal power networks discussed here: the mass ideological networks of discursive communication. On occasion, these could transmit moralizing ideologies of class among the petite bourgeoisie. In other countries, they helped destroy the moral cohesion of old regimes and provided revolutionary leadership and principles of social reorganization. But British networks were driven by consumer markets in which old regime and petite bourgeoisie alike participated. To a much greater degree than in France, bourgeois consciousness and modernization of old regime values could coalesce to generate a common "half-principled" movement of compromise reform spreading through mixed class-segmental organization. Ideological power relations were perhaps the least autonomous of the four, as they were largely generated by capitalist and state organizations.

Third, the particularities of states, as suggested by institutional statist theory (discussed in Chapter 3), also helped produce "reform, not revolution." The British state had already institutionalized centralized, competitive "party" relations between the state elite and (primarily) dominant classes. I have not sought to explain this early, rudimentary "party democracy," for it occurred in an earlier historical period (which my first volume did not much discuss). Perhaps a class reductionist theory of the rise of these institutions might have some force, although I believe such causes had become entwined with both military-fiscal pressures and ideological-religious disputes. But the political *result* of this earlier process attained its own "lagged" power autonomy. Because this period so enhanced the relevance of the state for social life, the particularities of its existing institutions came to play a considerable determining role in Western society. This was a general feature of this period; later chapters demonstrate the same process occurring in other countries.

In Britain, the franchise and "virtual representation" were messy, not entirely closed to rising classes. After 1832, the mess was tidied up with a property franchise and closure resulted (until the mid-Victorian boom conferred property franchise on more workers). Before 1832 (and from the 1860s), "parties" located at the heart of the state might be bent and extended if pressured from below – proving less brittle than French or Austrian or British colonial states. Moreover, reform agitation centered less on the class franchise than on another particularity of state institutions – common to all late eighteenth-century states – the escalating significance of its political economy. "Economic reform" movements demanded the elimination of state corruption, with the intention of reducing taxes, and unintentionally furthering the centralization and "naturalization" of government. This was the core petit bourgeois class grievance against the old regime and the key issue over which modernizing regime parties abandoned "old corruption" for alliance with the petite bourgeoisie.

But this was driven by the logic of the fourth source of social power. The militarist crystallization, created by the geopolitical rise of Great Britain, created fiscal and political pressures. The state was primarily modernized and reformed the better to win wars. Without the French wars a more segmental, less "national" old regime might have survived, largely unreformed, into industrial society. A prosperous petite bourgeoisie, enjoying individual civil and perhaps partial political citizenship, could have continued, as small farmers had done before them, as clients of a segmental, constitutional-monarchical but non-democratic regime. Prussian-German development showed the viability of a similar trajectory.

Extensive political class conflict between old regime and petite bourgeoisie had been intensified, then compromised. But it was not "pure": It had been also molded by ideological, military, and political power networks. British modernization was not one-dimensional evolution; industrial capitalism did not determine state structures. Rather, the British state was polymorphous; it had crystallized as enduringly capitalist and militarist. Their joint impact had furthered the development of its representative crystallization toward party democracy and of its "national" crystallization toward the more centralized nation-state.

In this period state and social modernization depended fundamentally on the conjunction of market capitalism and geopolitical struggle. Each reinforced the other: the rise of Great Britain to geopolitical near hegemony was partly due to its pioneering market capitalism and the Industrial Revolution, whereas capitalism and industrialism were greatly assisted by the Royal Navy, shrewd alliances abroad, and sophisticated state finances. Yet, in the Iron Duke's words, Britain's geopolitical success was a "damn close-run thing." As Chapter 8 shows, it depended critically on Britain's naval and diplomatic skills in acquiring allies to force France into two-front wars. Whenever France fought on two fronts, it lost. On the one occasion Britain fought on two fronts, in the American Revolution, it lost. The viability of old regime liberalism was not an evolutionary necessity, nor the result merely of the agricultural and industrial revolutions and the balance of class forces. It resulted in the last instance from a more contingent conjunction of two fundamental power struggles – between classes and between states – in which each helped reduce the other's segmental and local-regional rivals.

Bibliography

Abercrombie, N., S. Hill, and B. S. Turner. 1980. *The Dominant Ideology Thesis*. London: Allen & Unwin.

Albert, W. 1972. *The Turnpike Road System of England, 1763–1844*. Cambridge: Cambridge University Press.

Barker, T., and C. Savage. 1974. *An Economic History of Transport in Britain*. London: Hutchinson.

Bohstedt, J. 1983. *Riots and Community Politics in England and Wales, 1790–1810*. Cambridge, Mass.: Harvard University Press.

Bonfield, L. 1983. *Marriage Settlements, 1601–1740: The Adoption of the Strict Settlement*. Cambridge: Cambridge University Press.

Brewer, J. 1976. *Party Ideology and Party Politics at the Accession of George III*. Cambridge: Cambridge University Press.

1982. Commercialization and politics. In *The Birth of a Consumer Society: The Commercialization of Eighteenth Century England*, ed. N. McKendrick, J. Brewer, and J. H. Plumb. London: Europa Press.

Brock, M. 1973. *The Great Reform Act*. London: Hutchinson.

Cannadine, D. 1977. Aristocratic indebtedness in the nineteenth century: the case re-opened. *Economic History Review* 2nd ser., 30.

Chandler, A. D., Jr. 1977. *The Visible Hand: The Managerial Revolution in American Business*. Cambridge, Mass.: Harvard University Press.

Christie, I. R. 1962. *Wilkes, Wyville and Reform: The Parliamentary Reform Movement in British Politics, 1760–1785*. London: Macmillan.

1982. *Wars and Revolutions: Britain 1760–1815*. London: Arnold.

1984. *Stress and Stability in Late Eighteenth Century Britain*. Oxford: Clarendon Press.

Clark, J. C. D. 1985. *English Society, 1688–1832*. Cambridge: Cambridge University Press.

Colley, L. 1986. Whose nation? Class and national consciousness in Britain, 1750–1785. *Past and Present*, no. 113.

Crafts, N. 1983. British economic growth, 1700–1831: a review of the evidence. *Economic History Review* 36.

1985. *British Economic Growth During the Industrial Revolution*. Oxford: Clarendon Press.

Cranfield, G. A. 1962. *The Development of the Provincial Newspaper, 1700–1760*. Oxford: Clarendon Press.

1978. *The Press and Society: From Caxton to Northcliffe*. London: Longman Group.

Crouzet, F. 1972. Capital formation in Great Britain during the Industrial Revolution. In his *Capital Formation in the Industrial Revolution*. London: Methuen.

1982. *The Victorian Economy*. London: Methuen.

Currie, R., et al. 1977. *Churches and Churchgoers: Patterns of Church Growth in the British Isles Since 1700*. Oxford: Clarendon Press.

Dahl, R. 1971. *Polyarchy*. New Haven, Conn.: Yale University Press.

Davidoff, L. 1986. The role of gender in the "first industrial nation," agriculture in England 1780–1850. In *Gender and Stratification*, ed. R. Crompton and M. Mann. Oxford: Polity Press.

Deane, P., and W. Cole. 1967. *British Economic Growth, 1688–1959*. Cambridge: Cambridge University Press.

Dinwiddy, J. 1988. England. In *Nationalism in the Age of the French Revolution*, ed. O. Dann and J. Dinwiddy. London: Hambledon Press.

Eversley, D. 1967. The home market and economic growth in England, 1750–1880. In *Land, Labour and Population in the Industrial Revolution*, ed. E. Jones and G. Mingay. London: Arnold.

Foster, J. 1974. *Class Struggle and the Industrial Revolution*. London: Weidenfeld & Nicolson.

Gash, N. 1986. *Pillars of Government and Other Essays on State and Society, c1770–c1880*. London: Arnold.

Gilbert, A. D. 1976. *Religion and Society in Industrial England: Church, Chapel and Social Change, 1740–1914*. London: Longman Group.

Hagen, W. 1988. Capitalism and the countryside in early modern Europe: interpretations, models, debates. *Agricultural History* 62.

Harley, C. 1982. British industrialization before 1841: evidence of slower growth during the Industrial Revolution. *Journal of Economic History* 42.

Holmes, G. 1976. The Electorate and the National Will in the First Age of

Party. Inaugural lecture, University of Lancaster.

Houston, R. A. 1982a. The development of literacy: northern England, 1640–1750. *Economic History Review*, 2nd ser., 35.

1982b. The literacy myth: illiteracy in Scotland, 1630–1760. *Past and Present*, no. 96.

Ingham, G. 1984. *Capitalism Divided?: The City and Industry in British Social Development*. London: Macmillan.

John, A. H. 1967. Agricultural productivity and economic growth in England, 1700–1760. In *Agriculture and Economic Growth in England 1650–1815*, ed. E. L. Jones. London: Methuen.

Jones, E. 1981. *The European Miracle*. Cambridge: Cambridge University Press.

Kaufman, P. 1967. The community library: a chapter in English social history. *Transactions of the American Philosophical Society* 57.

Kussmaul, A. 1981. *Servants in Husbandry in Early Modern England*. Cambridge: Cambridge University Press.

Kuznets, S. 1955. Economic growth and income inequality. *American Economic Review* 49.

1963. Quantitative aspects of the economic growth of nations: VIII – distribution of income by size. *Economic Development and Cultural Change* 11.

Landes, D. 1969. *The Unbound Prometheus: Technological Change and Industrial Development in Western Europe from 1750 to the Present*. Cambridge: Cambridge University Press.

Lee, C. H. 1986. *The British Economy Since 1700: A Macroeconomic Perspective*. Cambridge: Cambridge University Press.

Lillee, S. 1973. Technological progress and the Industrial Revolution, 1700–1914. In *The Fontana Economic History of Europe*. Vol. 3: *The Industrial Revolution*, ed. C. M. Cipolla. London: Fontana.

Lindert, P. H., and J. G. Williamson. 1982. Revising England's social tables, 1688–1812. *Explorations in Economic History* 19.

1983. Reinterpreting Britain's social tables, 1688–1913. *Explorations in Economic History* 20.

Longstreth, F. 1983. State Economic Planning in a Capitalist Society: The Political Sociology of Economic Policy in Britain, 1940–1979. Ph.D. diss., London School of Economics.

McCloskey, D. 1985. The Industrial Revolution, 1780–1860: a survey. In *The Economics of the Industrial Revolution*, ed. J. Mokyr. London: Allen & Unwin.

McKendrick, N. 1974. Home demand and economic growth: A new view of the role of women and children in the Industrial Revolution. In his *Historical Perspectives. Studies in English Thought and Society*. London: Europa Press.

1982. Commercialization and the economy. In *The Birth of a Consumer Society*, ed. McKendrick, Brewer, and Plumb.

McKendrick, N., J. Brewer, and J. H. Plumb, eds. *The Birth of a Consumer Society: The Commercialization of Eighteenth Century England*. London: Europa Press.

Mann, M. 1988a. The decline of Great Britain and

1988b. The roots and contradictions of modern capitalism. Both in my *States, War and Capitalism*. Oxford: Blackwell.

Marshall, T. H. 1963. Citizenship and social class. In his *Sociology at the Crossroads*. London: Heinemann.

Mathias, P., and P. K. O'Brien. 1976. Taxation in Britain and France, 1715–1810. *Journal of European Economic History* 5.

Mingay, G. E. 1963. *English Landed Society of the Eighteenth Century*. London: Routledge & Kegan Paul.

Mokyr, J. 1977. Demand versus supply in the Industrial Revolution. *Journal of Economic History* 37.

1985. The Industrial Revolution and the new economic history. In *The Economics of the Industrial Revolution*, ed. J. Mokyr. London: Allen & Unwin.

Money, J. 1977. *Experience and Identity: Birmingham and the West Midlands, 1760–1800*. Manchester: Manchester University Press.

Moore, B., Jr. 1973. *Social Origins of Dictatorship and Democracy*. Harmondsworth: Penguin Books.

Moore, D. C. 1976. *The Politics of Deference*. Hassocks, Sussex: Harvester.

Mouzelis, N. 1986. *Politics in the Semi-Periphery*. Basingstoke: Macmillan.

Musson, A. E. 1972. Editor's introduction. In his *Science, Technology and Economic Growth in the Eighteenth Century*. London: Methuen.

Musson, A. E., and E. Robinson. 1969. *Science and Technology in the Industrial Revolution*. Manchester: Manchester University Press.

Neale, R. S. 1983. *History and Class: Essential Readings in Theory and Interpretation*. Oxford: Blackwell.

Newman, G. 1987. *The Rise of English Nationalism. A Cultural History, 1740–1830*. New York: St. Martin's Press.

O'Brien, P. K. 1985. Agriculture and the home market for English industry, 1660–1820. *English Historical Review* 100.

Pawson, E. 1979. *The Early Industrial Revolution*. New York: Harper & Row.

Payne, P. L. 1974. *British Entrepreneurship in the Nineteenth Century*. London: Macmillan.

Perkin, H. 1969. *The Origins of Modern English Society*. London: Routledge & Kegan Paul.

Phillips, J. A. 1982. *Electoral Behavior in Unreformed England: Plumpers, Splitters and Straights*. Princeton, N.J.: Princeton University Press.

Platt, D. C. M. 1972. *Latin America and British Trade, 1806–1914*. London: Black.

Plumb, J. H. 1950. *England in the Eighteenth Century: 1714–1815*. Harmondsworth: Penguin Books.

1982. Commercialization and society. In *The Birth of a Consumer Society*, ed. McKendrick, Brewer, and Plumb.

Pollard, S. 1965. *The Genesis of Modern Management*. London: Arnold.

Pollins, H. 1952. The finances of the Liverpool and Manchester railway. *Economic History Review*, 2nd ser., 5.

Reed, M. C. 1975. *Investment in Railways in Britain, 1820–44*. London: Oxford University Press.

Rubinstein, W. D. 1977a. The Victorian middle classes: wealth, occupation and geography. *Economic History Review*, 2nd ser., 30.

1977b. Wealth, elites and the class structure of modern Britain. *Past and Present*, no. 76.

1983. The end of "old corruption" in Britain, 1780–1860. *Past and Present*, no. 101.

Rudé, G. 1962. *Wilkes and Liberty*. Oxford: Clarendon Press.

Rueschemeyer, D.; E. Stephens, and J. Stephens. 1992. *Capitalist Development and Democracy*. Chicago: University of Chicago Press.

Schofield, M. 1981. Dimensions of literacy in England, 1750–1850. In *Literacy and Social Development in the West: A Reader*, ed. H. J. Graff. Cambridge: Cambridge University Press.

Seed, J. 1985. Gentlemen dissenters: the social and political meanings of rational dissent in the 1770s and 1780s. *The Historical Journal* 28.

Smith, R. A. 1972. *Eighteenth-Century English Politics: Patrons and Place-Hunters*. New York: Holt, Rinehart & Winston.

Speck, W. A. 1977. *Stability and Strife: England, 1714–1760*. London: Arnold.

Stevenson, J. 1979. *Popular Disturbances in England, 1700–1810*. London: Longman Group.

Thomas, J. A. 1939. *The House of Commons, 1832–1901: A Study of Its Economic and Functional Character*. Cardiff: University of Wales Press Board.

Thompson, E. P. 1963. *The Making of the English Working Class*. Harmondsworth: Penguin Books.

Thompson, F. M. L. 1963. *English Landed Society in the Nineteenth Century*. London: Routledge & Kegan Paul.

Ward, W. R. 1973. *Religion and Society in England, 1790–1850*. New York: Schocken Books.

Watt, I. 1963. *The Rise of the Novel*. Harmondsworth: Penguin Books.

West, E. G. 1985. Literacy and the Industrial Revolution. In *The Economics of the Industrial Revolution*, ed. I. Mokyr. London: Allen & Unwin.

Wiles, R. M. 1968. Middle class literacy in eighteenth century England: fresh evidence. In *Studies in the Eighteenth Century*, ed. R. F. Brissenden. Canberra: Australian National University Press.

Williams, D. E. 1984. Morals, markets and the English crowd in 1766. *Past and Present*, no. 104.

Wilson, C. 1955. The entrepreneur in the Industrial Revolution in Britain. *Explorations in Entrepreneurial History* 3.

Wolfe, A. 1977. *The Limits of Legitimacy*. New York: Free Press.

Wrigley, E. A. 1985. Urban growth and agricultural change: England and the Continent in the early modern period. *Journal of Interdisciplinary History* 15.

Wrigley, E. A., and R. S. Schofield. 1981. *The Population History of England, 1541–1871*. London: Arnold.

5 The American Revolution and the institutionalization of confederal capitalist liberalism

On the British mainland, war and reform were separated – the one abroad, the other at home. Yet in other countries, including British Ireland, armed struggles fused the two. In France and America occurred the two great revolutions of the period. The outcome in America was that the United States became, probably, the most capitalist of countries, with one of the least national, most confederal of states. I characterize the new American state as crystallizing as capitalist-liberal, confederal, and party democratic, adding an uneven militarism, more pronounced domestically than geopolitically. I seek to explain how it acquired these characteristics.

The American colonies

In 1760, 2 million people were counted as living under the British crown in the colonies of North America. Native Americans ("Indians") were not counted. (They numbered upward of 100,000 in the colonies, more farther west.) Slaves of African descent comprised 20 percent of those counted. Of whites, about 75 percent were of British or Irish descent. So, except for native Americans and slaves, most inhabitants were accustomed to British rule. America was British. Its ideological and economic institutions were similar to those of the mother country – this was the second home of that diffuse "civil society," comprising capitalism and the commercial capitalist route to mass discursive literacy, introduced in Chapter 2. Its military and political institutions were also modeled on Britain's. We might expect an American variant of the moderately centralized old regime liberalism described in Chapter 4. Yet fiscal-military pressures erupted into a "revolution" that first amplified American distinctivenesses and then finally retracked them into a capitalist and confederal liberalism. But even before the crisis, five American power particularities had already arisen, mostly underscoring the ways in which Britain differed from most European countries:

1. The colonies were three thousand miles from the mother country, with considerable logistic autonomy and therefore de facto civil and political freedoms. Under eighteenth-century communications conditions, America could not be run from London. Local conditions were

137

so different that to make major decisions in London required constant consultation. Yet sailing ships took at least four months to complete the round trip, virtually an entire campaigning or agricultural season. London was, anyway, interested more in commercial profit than in imperial organization, adopting the policy it described as "salutary neglect," allowing autonomy to people who, after all, were colonial cousins, not foreigners or "natives." Despotic rule would not have been legitimate for a British crown, whereas the election of colonial MPs to sit at Westminster was considered impracticable (though the French revolutionaries later adopted that centralized solution). The American colonies were substantially free.

Autonomy meant plural, decentralized autonomies, for there was never a capital colony – indeed, no clear separation between these colonies, Canada, and the British Caribbean. The seaboard was also twelve hundred miles long. As Table 4.1 indicates, America had a decentralized, constitutional state. Each colony ran its own affairs, with its own elected assemblies and police and tax authorities. The routine of these ministates – their fiscal sinews, their judicial process, and their passing of bills – was American. Only 5 percent of assembly laws were disallowed by the British Parliament (Palmer 1959: 190). Most colonial assemblies were formally subordinated to a governor representing the crown, though a few were still under proprietary or charter government. The governor had great formal powers: He could veto bills, dissolve the assembly, and appoint an upper house or legislative council as the executive authority. But he could not implement his will except by agreement with the notables of the colony. The British Parliament had refused to add the salaries of governors, their staffs, and judges to the civil list. The local legislatures voted their salaries. Thus the governor became a "rather strong negotiator in a foreign country" (Pole 1966: 503), ruled in practice by local parliaments. The nominally sovereign state at Westminster was not much institutionalized in local life. Amid such autonomy, local-regional variations could bloom.

2. The colonial economy was unique – fundamentally agrarian, even primitive, yet highly capitalistic. More than 90 percent of white Americans were farmers, extracting from an environment that was less domesticated than any in Europe. Manufacturing remained insignificant. Yet natural abundance and labor skills made white Americans more prosperous than Europeans. American army recruits were on average more than two inches taller than their British counterparts, indicating substantial dietary superiority (Sokoloff and Villaflor 1982). Farming generated larger surpluses for the market. Its two dominant forms, small farming and southern plantations of cotton and tobacco

producing for world markets, generated three classes with no exact European counterpart: planters, plantation slaves, and highly autonomous peasant farmers. Britain was the most capitalist country in Europe; once peasant farmers began producing for world markets, America was even more so.

3. The colonies had institutionalized racism. Europeans all over the globe theorized their evident power superiority over the peoples of other continents into ideological racism. But the American experience involved mass European settlement amid two very different races: fierce competition for land with often warlike "red Indians" and exploitation of the labor of black African slaves. Their triangular relationship was longer-lived than in Central or South America. The climate was more benign for Europeans; Indians remained more resilient a military threat, and slave labor remained useful to grow cotton and tobacco. The dual horror of Indian genocide and African enslavement remained central to North American society right through the period covered by this volume. The effect on the Europeans was profound, fostering a pervasive violence in power relations – blatant in coping with Indians, barely concealed in the institutions of slavery, and routinized in the bearing of arms by whites. It enhanced domestic militarism and a racial definition of solidarity and normative community. Despite their diversity of background, whites comprised a more homogeneous community amid "alien races" than existed in any eighteenth-century European country.

4. The white community was strengthened by common religiosity and relative economic equality. Almost all were Protestant. Most denominations settled together, solidifying communities around institutions of worship and encouraging mass literacy. The first of the three great ideological infrastructures of the eighteenth century, religious-sponsored literacy, here expanded to its greatest extent. By the late eighteenth century, white Americans were as literate as the English, despite living in a far more agrarian society. About two-thirds of all men, not much fewer women, and virtually all men in Puritan New England were literate (Lockridge 1974: 72–101). Expanding ideological power networks (discussed in Chapter 2) could diffuse discursive ideologies through the white community, as in the mid-eighteenth-century Great Awakening, a religious revival movement. Sermons and pamphlets expanded the free market in salvation. Although the Anglican church was established there too, it was dominant in only a few areas, its hierarchy undermined by a religious ferment cutting across church divisions. Nondenominational Protestantism could potentially divide colonists' souls from the rulers'.

Relative economic equality also integrated whites. True, the settlers included most of the British classes distinguished in Table 4.2. The old regime was represented by aristocrats and gentry, especially in Virginia and the Carolinas (many had retained wealth and position over several generations), by coastal merchant oligarchies dominating overseas trade, and by the clerics, lawyers, and army officers who sought official patronage and staffed administrations. But among the ordinary propertied "people" were far more small independent farmers than in Europe, comprising about 40 percent of whites and a third of the whole counted population and fewer petit bourgeois traders, shopkeepers, artisans, and town laborers. Thus among the poorer "populace" America differed, having Indians and slaves but few white casual laborers or paupers. Although inequality worsened through the eighteenth century (Henretta 1973: 102–12, Nash 1975–6), the abundance and beneficence of land plus labor shortages ensured subsistence for almost all whites. No large excluded white populace existed, and so neither did as clear a conception of an opposed class, the propertied "people" to set against it, as in Britain. Whites were inside civil society and could participate in its routine activities, more so than even in Britain. Blacks and Indians could not.

5. Migration had freed more whites from dependence on segmental power organizations. The local regime was not "old," rooted in custom and deference – although it was striving hard to cultivate these, especially in long-settled areas of the South and in the patriarchal townships of Puritan New England. It lacked the church-state and county gentry networks of "old corruption." The Anglican church, backed by the British, was established only in the South. Individual civil citizenship was wholly achieved by the early eighteenth century in America (Bailyn 1962: 348), as it was in Britain, whereas political citizenship was more developed because more could vote. Office patronage was also limited. Yet there was, instead, market-oriented corruption. Colonial administrations were the major source of land grants and trading and slaving privileges. The regime embodied "new capitalist corruption" as against the old Engligh variety.

Farmers had been especially liberated by migration. Up to 20 percent of migrants had been poor tenant farmers squeezed off their land in England, Scotland, and Ulster by landlords. Now most were genuinely free, and a little richer, on their small farms in the backwoods and frontiers. A larger group – Bailyn (1986) estimates them as about half of British migrants – had been impoverished artisans and tradesmen from urban areas. In return for their passage they hired themselves out as indentured servants. They were sold off the decks like slaves and then endured personal subjection to their employer, usually for four years. On serving their time, most abandoned their trade and bought small farms in the interior. By the 1770s, indenturing was declining before free wage labor (as it was in English farming).

All these variations were movements away from segmental power organization, a mobility far more significant than the mere occupational shifts that the term "mobility" signifies in modern sociology (although Main 1965 argues that there was also considerable occupational mobility). As in other colonies in their formative years, various opportunities arose for personal advancement. Hard work, talent, luck, and minimal resources could more easily transform artisan into master, small dealer into shopkeeper, and anyone into an independent farmer than in more institutionalized Europe. Among the upper classes, the same combination enabled talented young men of respectable but not wealthy families to use extended family connections to achieve wealth and position, as several of the Founding Fathers had (Mann and Stephens 1991). America, though rural, lacked the relatively closed aristocracy of Europe. For whites in America the countryside represented mobility and independence rather than stability and deference. European eighteenth-century small farmers – that is, peasants – were often independent economically but rarely politically from their betters. America reversed the politics of town and country. "Petite bourgeoisie" is too urban a term to delineate the vanguard of American capitalism – small, independent farmers, free from segmental power organization.

These five variations ensured that, although the white American colonists were recognizably British, they constituted a civil society more cohesive, less segmentally organized, more regionalized, and more fluid than that in the mother country, let alone in most of continental Europe. Small capitalists were more numerous and locally independent, especially in the middle states and in interior farming. Their independence had been hard-won, in life histories of struggle against poverty and subjection. Yet larger property concentrations, political patronage, and legal subjection also played a role in defining what counted as a commodity in towns and ports and in southern agriculture. Thus American capitalism contained four distinct elements:

1. A predominantly agrarian petty commodity capitalism, whose spirit has been made famous by Weber's use of Benjamin Franklin's writings in his *The Protestant Ethic and the Spirit of Capitalism*
2. Larger concentrations of private property, employing free labor, its owners usually combining at least two among farming, merchant, financial, and manufacturing interests

3. A repressive slave capitalism in the South producing staples for the world market
4. State and "quasi old regime" patronage of capitalistic activity, initially containing much indentured labor

That these varied by locality and region, over thirteen colonies and over such a large land area, ensured that America was more economically varied, less politically centralized, and less "national" in certain respects than Britain. Through revolution the colonists began to cut down on this variety. Roughly put, the American Revolution saw the victory of the first and third forms of capitalism over the fourth. The second form of capitalism split down the middle, but its revolutionary faction succeeded in hanging onto power in the new state. Thus the state remained confederal and decentralized. Later, the Civil War destroyed the third, slave, form of capitalism.The United States eventually emerged with a capitalism combining decentralization and large property concentrations paradoxically infused with the spirit of petit bourgeois capitalism: It became distinctively capitalist-liberal and remained confederal.

Before the Revolution politics tended to pit those engaged in the first form of capitalism (petty production) against the other three. Colonial assemblies were elected on British property qualifications. Because there were many more small propertied farmers, 40 percent to 80 percent of white adult males (varying between colonies and averaging perhaps around 50 percent) were enfranchised. This was far broader than anywhere else in the world. (The British enfranchised around 15 percent of adult males.) In town meetings (an American invention) all property owners could normally participate and small farmers and the urban petite bourgeoisie formed the majority. Yet notable families whose members normally combined the roles of merchants, landowners, officials, and lawyers (and who were usually slave owners in the South) had sewn up the governors' legislative councils and administrations; and they were the majority elected to serve in the assemblies and on the committees of town meetings. Government was effectively ruled, just like an English county, by a small network of intermarrying extended families.

Large seaports saw the most conflict. Parties of conservatives and reformers appealed to class-defined followings amid sporadic violence. Yet the same confused dynamics were in evidence as in English radicalism: The mob could protest but not organize for alternatives; and the main reform leadership, drawn from notable "outs," would only rarely cooperate with petit bourgeois and artisan activists whose class consciousness was in any case ambiguous and varied among towns (as it did in England). Of the three major seaports, Philadelphia was moving Leftward in the early 1770s, Boston was moving Rightward, and New York's direction was unclear (Nash 1986: 200–47).

In most other areas, the mass electorate accepted its political powerlessness, failed to turn out to vote, and accepted the patronage and deference networks of the colonial notable regime (Dinkin 1977). In the words of a contemporary, it was "a speaking Aristocracy in the face of a silent Democracy" (Fischer 1965: 4). Most colonists were getting on with the business of conquering nature, cooperating with their white neighbors, and exploiting or exterminating the others. As I have emphasized, politics and the state were not vital matters for most people in any early eighteenth-century Western country. For Americans living in the most prosperous, least taxed, most logistically isolated, and most dispersed outpost of Western civilization, both the British state and the government of the individual colony seemed insignificant. So, by default, government was not illegitimate.

Amid mass political indifference segmental old regimes were emerging. The colonies could have continued thus for many years, deferring to the light, corrupt rule of Great Britain. True, there were early American peculiarities, as listed earlier, but there was no steady evolution from them to the flowering of nineteenth-century American capitalist liberalism, as Hartz (1955) has argued. Local-regional colonial regimes had begun to institutionalize themselves atop a prosperous, settled agrarian society. Regimes need time and stability to become old, but this was happening among southern gentry and New England Puritan patriarchs. A rather decentralized old regime liberalism, modeled on Britain's, could have flourished, with varied local-regional colorations.

We can extend the counterfactual argument to geopolitical power. Without the Revolution, at some point in the mid-nineteenth century the growth of the colonies would have outstripped the grasp of the queen in Parliament. By then British governments would have been probably ready for looser forms of political association, like those then granted to their remaining white dominions. Modern political and geopolitical power might have turned out very differently: dominated continuously by a vast English-speaking confederal commonwealth, its center shifting across the Atlantic – perhaps avoiding the destabilizing period of Great Power conflict occurring between British decline and American hegemony that terrorized and changed the world.

Rebellion

Even more than in Great Britain, though, the military-fiscal extraction cycle, driven by geopolitics, intervened to steer power relations down different tracks. It pressured the British government into policies that pointed up the American peculiarities. In turn, this forced many Americans into regarding the colonial state first as significant and then as illegitimate. They then overthrew it and institutionalized a different regime.

During the Seven Years' War of 1756–63 (called in America the French and Indian Wars), the colonists paid emergency taxes in return for an increase in the power of their local assemblies – increasing their decentralized political autonomy. The British victory ended French and Spanish subsidies to hostile Indians and settled colonial boundaries. The military threat to the colonies was virtually over. From the British point of view in America, victory was a disaster. The colonists now barely needed British protection or rule; in fact, many saw the British government as interfering unnecessarily with the displacement of the Indians and with westward expansion. Yet the war enabled the British government to acquire a global empire and free trade area, plus a resident army in America. It sought to organize this empire as a coherent whole. It wished colonials to contribute their fair share to its upkeep, and it believed it possessed a new means of enforcing its wishes, a standing army.

The British government never asked Americans to pay anywhere near as high taxes as its subjects did in Britain. In comparative terms, the direct fiscal pain was less than in my other cases, even than in Prussia (where much revenue came from royal domains). But, as we will see also in the case of France, fiscal pain results from the combination of rising exactions and the degree to which states can institutionalize their extraction. The colonies lacked the latter. There was no institutionalized national debt, so colonials were asked to pay increased taxes. Yet most were now oblivious to geopolitics and empire, had a local conception of interest, and had long practiced local fiscal control and evaded customs duties. American logistic autonomy was attacked by a regime driven, as it saw the situation, by geopolitical necessity. Fiscal-military pressure yet again escalated political struggle and centralization of discontent.

Through the late 1760s and the 1770s, this direct conflict of fiscal interest became more principled and extensive. It mobilized an alternative ideological power network, just as in Britain (discussed in Chapter 4) and in France (Chapter 6). American writers and speechmakers generalized interests into principles. They could draw on the five American peculiarities discussed earlier. Interests and principles could be debated amid the democratic spirit and de facto logistic sovereignty of their assemblies. The half-buried tradition of seventeenth-century Puritan radicalism combined with the more respectable tradition of Locke and the Scottish Enlightenment to resonate amid practical economic independence and the contractual spirit of petty capitalism and moral Protestantism. Under fiscal pressure, American traditions amplified British traditions to proclaim the principle of "no taxation without representation," a principle that also won much support in Britain. The homogeneity of a religious, literate, and fairly egalitarian white community then diffused principled moral protest throughout two levels of American ideological and political power networks.

The more popular level of protest centered on small farmers, lesser petits bourgeois, and artisans. They were mobilized primarily through oral assemblies – mobs, demonstrations, tar and featherings, and other intimidations of royal officials and their local clients – bridging the gap between "people" and "populace," as in the French revolutionary crowd or the British demonstrations of the Peterloo period. In America, as to an extent in Britain, clubs and taverns, plus the American institution of town meetings, were the crucial petit bourgeois-small farmer contact points with the second level, networks of notable families. These centered at first on the colonial assemblies, but as these began to stalemate, the notables expanded their network across the colonies through extended family connections, infrastructures of discursive literacy, and the profession of law.

Discursive ideologies boomed. Between 1763 and 1775, the number of newspapers doubled (Davidson 1941: 225). In 1776, about four hundred pamphlets were published, most ten to fifty pages long, predominantly of the discursive, explanatory type that investigated premises, explored the logic of arguments, and considered conclusions. Their style presupposed a literate, propertied, sophisticated audience (Bailyn 1967: 1–21). Tom Paine's *Common Sense*, published in that year, sold a massive 120,000 copies (a number equaling about 3 percent of the entire colonial population, the same proportion as his *Rights of Man* was later to sell in Britain). Pamphleteers and journalists were rarely professionals. Pamphlets were written by notables who still had leisure time even after filling their varied roles as lawyer, minister-teacher, merchant, and planter; the newspapers were filled by their letters and extracts from their speeches, sermons and official reports. They were not really radicals but, rather, a progressive "party" among the colonial ruling regime. As among their modernizing, "enlightened" counterparts in the French old regime, they were being pushed into "national" opposition, toward alternative principled ideologies, by government pressure.

Lawyers became critical. Through the eighteenth century, they had become a useful adjunct to the colonial regime, just as the British legal profession serviced Britain's old regime. Training in law became a stepping-stone to royal patronage, political preferment, and status. At first most lawyers were loyal Tories. Yet British taxes caused lawyers ideological difficulties. The taxes were compatible with British parliamentary sovereignty but were contrary to local political and legal practice. Custom was being violated, and custom was essential to English conceptions of legal rights. As in the mother country, radicals used the English legal framework to defend existing liberties against "despotism." But when the legitimate political authority, the king in Parliament, would not concede those liberties, some lawyers were forced beyond custom to devise new principles of liberty. They actually had ready-made theories available from Locke and the Scottish Enlightenment, but the lawyers made these resonate by grounding them in essentially commercial notions of contracts made between free individuals.

Lawyers became the main practical theorists, the "organic intellectuals" (to use Gramsci's term), of a more bourgeois conception of liberty. Most prominent lawyers were substantial and active property owners, not specialized professionals. The interests of older lawyers were entangled with the colonial regime and most became Loyalists. But younger men, trained in the 1770s and not yet as entangled, became leaders of dissent and eventually rebel patriots (McKirdy 1972; Murrin 1983). As in France, there is no evidence that these men were suffering from "blocked mobility"; most appear to have been highly successful. They were, rather, genuine practical ideologists. As the British General Gage complained to his superiors after the Stamp Act: "The lawyers are the source from whence the clamours have flowed in every province." They were to be well represented among revolutionary leaders.

Stable British rule depended on an alliance between the crown and local-regional notables. But these now disintegrated into Loyalist and Patriot parties. Patriots mobilized discursive literacy networks and the law and liaised with, and sometimes controlled, the more popular oral assembly networks. Because there were fewer impoverished "dangerous classes" among whites, notable Patriots were less disciplined by the fear of revolution from the "populace" below than were their counterparts in most of Europe.

The first major organized resistance was to the Stamp Act, in early 1766. The Sons of Liberty established links across the colonies through newspapers, pamphlets, and correspondence networks among men of property – gentlemen, freeholders, master artisans, and independent tradesmen. Yet against the British army they needed the support of those below, the mob. Their combined protest worked. The act was repealed in 1776, and the Sons were disbanded. They were revived when the government switched to the Townshend Acts, taxing consumption, the following year. As the taxes fell on all consumers, it was easy to enlist mass support. Tactics now switched to a boycott of British goods and to discipline those who broke the boycott. Tribunals gave this a judicial air, elected by those eligible to vote for assemblymen and staffed by notables usually also practicing law (Davidson 1941: 63–82; Maier 1973: 77–112, 280–7). A rebellion was under way, but it was conducted by members of the colonial regime and organized across the colonies, with mass support and novel methods of ideological mobilization.

The British government, however, would not yield to their principles. Birch (1976) and Pocock (1980) argue that British politicians had principles of their own. Representation and sovereignty were indivisible in the formula the "king in Parliament." If colonial assemblies were allowed to ratify and veto taxes, this would divide parliamentary sovereignty, on which the centralized British conceptions of liberty depended. I am skeptical, however, of the view that the Revolution was caused by a clash of principles. That is too static a view of powerful ideologies, normally created out of power struggles themselves. As we saw in Chapter 4, the British old regime was largely unprincipled. It had been its opponents – exactly as in America – who had gradually articulated their resentments at exclusion from power into principle. The British government had two more cynical views of events. First, it believed American principles were a smoke screen for unwillingness to pay their fair share for imperial defense and it was reluctant to increase the burden of taxation in Britain. Second, it sought pragmatically the least painful form of fiscal extraction, but in the last resort it now had a resident army to enforce it. It went through its repertoire of taxes, from land, customs, and excise taxes to stamp duties.

Either the British government miscalculated, failing to perceive American peculiarities, or it ultimately had no alternative. Unlike in Britain, in the colonies such fiscal schemes were not already institutionalized into infrastructures of tax collection supervised by the segmental organizations of local notables. Thus armed coercion was not merely a threat held in reserve (as in Britain); it had to be used to actually collect the taxes. Each expedient, each marshaling of the troops, hurt and offended, contradicting the sense of local autonomy and freedom and provoking more resistance, more British coercion, and then more principled opposition. Americans now realized two things: (1) that a small regular army was ill-equipped to collect taxes in such a large country amid widespread resistance and (2) that the taxes were demanded not just by ill-intentioned ministers but by the king in Parliament. Resistance was forced toward principled rebellion against the sovereignty of Parliament.

In the summer of 1775, the British resorted to full-scale military repression. Yet they did not possess enormous military superiority. Americans were quite well equipped, mostly bearing sidearms, many with militia experience, a few with the militia authority to appropriate hastily cannon, ammunition, carts, horses, and maps (uniforms and drill manuals could come later). Eighteenth-century armies had no other resources. Enough resisted with enough military resources to foil the first British thrusts and give time to create a more organized rebellion.

The resort to arms divided the colonists. At least 20 percent of whites became Loyalists. It was not a division based simply on class or region or sector. Various writers have suggested that Patriots and Loyalists were divided by economic sector, with Patriots materially involved in westward expansion – being frustrated by British policy (e.g., Egnal 1988). Yet their evidence is thin and conflicts with what Stephens and I (1991) found to be the essentially diverse economic interests of the Patriot leaders. Perhaps the clearest, though still rough, divide separated two capitalist modes of production from the third. The "ins," who ran and profited from state political economy – colonial administration and commerce – were more likely to be Loyalists (Brown 1965). Most independent farmers, urban petit bourgeois, and slave owners, who were little involved in administration and commerce, were Patriots. (Slavery was so institutionalized in the South that it no longer needed crown military support.) The clearest distinction was probably segmental – an "in" party versus an "out" party. As elsewhere, "outs" proclaimed universal principles, "ins" particularistic tradition. But such distinctions were sometimes fuzzy: A cohesive group of local notables could organize its community round to its position, silencing majority opponents.

As Brown notes, judgments were influenced by who they thought would win, and this varied according to the visible balance of local terror. The Patriots centered on a curious alliance of Virginia gentlemen and New England democrats, whereas the Loyalists carried New York and many middle colony communities. On both sides almost all prominent leaders were drawn from the very wealthiest, most prominent notable families. The rebellion was not yet a revolution. So far, the military and fiscal pressures had amplified, not retracked, American peculiarities into war.

War and "revolution"

Armed conflict escalated into civil war. At each stage both sides believed the other would back down. Both then risked full-scale war, believing they could win it – and that warfare was closely contested. Historical tradition stresses British mistakes and the superior will and staying power of the rebels. Recent revisionism has emphasized broader geopolitics. The British government feared that rebellion might spread to Ireland, from which French intrigue could threaten Britain itself. Thus more troops were stationed to cope with the Irish threat than were made available to British generals in America. The balance tipped when France and Spain entered the war. The French fleet, carrying a French army, broke through to secure the decisive surrender of General Cornwallis at Yorktown in 1781. Without the French the war would have dragged on, perhaps to eventual compromise. The war had important consequences for America. Its process and outcome were determined predominantly by military and geopolitical power relations – in the last instance by the fortunes of war. This was the essential discontinuity of early American history.

The war also moved the rebels closer to revolution. Whether the War of Independence was "revolutionary" has always, rightly, been controversial. A revolution can be defined sociologically as a violent transformation of dominant power relations; bur real-world revolutions are a matter of degree. American events were decidedly ambiguous. Reluctance to term them revolutionary derives from four sources:

1. The War of Independence contained three distinct struggles: overthrowing the British old regime, establishing a new political constitution, and establishing new social relations among classes. Had the three fused into a single, violent cataclysm, as they did in the events we know as the French and Russian revolutions, we would unhesitatingly call this a "revolution." But they never quite did.

2. Although the struggle with the British was settled violently, the other two struggles were compromised and then further institutionalized through the conflict of subsequent generations. This "revolution" started violently, then stuttered semiturbulently over several decades, at the end of which political and ideological power had been substantially transformed but class relations far less so.

3. Although such changes were substantial, it might be argued that they were occurring anyway, the result of deep evolutionary processes, given perhaps a jab of assistance by violent conflict.

4. The leaders of the Revolution, the Founding Fathers, remained white men of substantial property from beginning to end. The research of Stephens and myself (1991) shows that the Founding Fathers were

even more upper class and more organized as an upper class than the earlier researches of Beard (1913), Solberg (1958: 387ff.) and McDonald (1958) had indicated.

One hundred and twenty-nine Founding Fathers signed the Declaration of Independence in 1776 or the Articles of Confederation in 1783 or were delegates to the Constitutional Convention in 1787. Almost all were drawn from the wealthiest, most prominent colonial families. None was poor or did manual work (apart from doctors and a handful of active, middling farmers). Only about twenty even had an occupation or occupational career in the modern sense. The rest combined the diverse economic activities of the gentleman – on average, three of the roles of planter, lawyer, merchant, financier, manufacturer, high official, and other professional position. They also belonged to wealthy extended families almost always prominent in the local community, and they received patronage, made marriages, and received inheritances through such connections. Only two Founding Fathers appeared to have been genuinely self-made; the remaining upwardly mobile men of talent were relatively "poor relations" benefiting from extended family connections. Their education was almost always to the highest level, available to well under 1 percent of colonists, and their cultural networks were elevated, extended, and dense. Although it is impossible to draw up a comparable leadership group of Loyalists, they could not possibly have come from more propertied families, although Loyalist leaders, too, seem mostly wealthy (Brown 1965). Was this not mere factionalism among an emerging old regime? After all, Burch (1981: vol. I) has shown that the same upper class continued to dominate American cabinets well after the Revolution.

But four countervailing, potentially "revolutionary," forces also impacted:

1. During the war, the participants used extreme socially, and politically, directed violence. The war was not just between Britain and America, it was also a civil war among communities, neighbors, and friends, and it was fought to the death. Even excluding the battles, in comparative terms the violence was as great as in events generally accepted as revolutionary – for example, the French and Russian revolutions. Loyalists were as likely to have their property expropriated and were almost five times as likely to flee into exile as were Royalists in the French Revolution (Palmer 1959: I, 188, 202). Land redistribution, generally from wealthy Loyalists to farmers and petite bourgeoisie, also constituted at least as substantial and as violent an expropriation of economic power as did similar events in France (though not Russia).

2. Such actions were legitimated by reference to revolutionary politi-

cal ideology. Patriots referred to the moral authority of the "people" against "despotism," "slavery" (though not of blacks), "privilege," "corruption," and "conspiracy" – all much as in France. Loyalist and British principles were merely to defend duly constituted authority, and they were little interested in grand ideological battles. Such ideological asymmetry also resembles revolutions elsewhere.

3. Events amounted to a sudden transformation in political legitimation. Throwing out the British and the Loyalists involved having to found the state anew, to "constitute" it in a written document. Power was vested in "We, the people" and in its popularly elected assemblies, whose vote was proclaimed sovereign, capable of creating a state. In 1780, the Massachusetts rebels, driven by British intransigence beyond ad hoc political reorganization, introduced their "constitution" with the statement "We the people ordain and establish." It was a departure from the conservatism of the Western rebel tradition. Europeans had long defended rebellion in terms of customary rights legitimated by long traditions. Indeed, the Americans had begun thus.

As Bailyn puts it (though justifying a conservative, nonrevolutionary account of events), they claimed to seek not "the overthrow or even the alteration of the existing social order but the preservation of political liberty threatened by the apparent corruption of the constitution and the establishment in principle of the existing conditions of liberty" (1967: 19). Indeed, had the crown stopped taxing them in novel ways, all could have been restored. But as the crown did not desist, political order could not be restored. Despite their best intentions rebels became political revolutionaries. They were forced in creating their state to introduce the "people" as an active political force, not the mere passive embodiment of customary liberties. From now on rebels in other countries also became revolutionaries when they consciously imitated this American invention and set up "constituent assemblies," as did the French and the Russian revolutionaries.

4. Letting the "people" onstage proved more than mere symbolic legitimation. It led toward political democracy and more democratic political economy. The wealthy notables who proclaimed rebellion in the name of the "people" were not democrats. By "people," they meant what the English meant – white male property owners, "men of education and fortune." But they were in combat against the greatest power in the world, even if most of its troops were three thousand miles away. They needed more people than this. In fact they needed the "people" plus the "populace." In America these were a violent lot, used to bearing arms, useful to rebellion. On the rebel side there was now something of a class struggle between upper-class leaders and rank-and-file militants (Countryman 1981, 1985; Nash 1986; Rosswurm

1987), explicit and recognized but contained (just) by the discipline required by military cooperation against a more dangerous enemy.

The organization of military power relations now entwined with all these anti- and prorevolutionary forces as the war developed ambiguously "revolutionary" outcomes. This became the first mass mobilization war of modern times, though of a distinctively decentralized, often guerrilla kind. During the main crises the rebels proclaimed universal militia service in the areas they controlled, and they gradually made this stick. The militia's main role was not to win battles (although some detachments provided a valuable screen for the regular Continental Army) but to mobilize coercively the indifferent majority to minimal military action. Once they had been persuaded or trapped into local marauding against British detachments or Loyalist neighbors, there could be no turning back: They were rebels at war against the crown (Shy 1973).

Mass-mobilization warfare has had variable effects on domestic power structure. It need not have radicalizing consequences if the hierarchical command structure of the regime can prosecute the war successfully. We see in Chapter 12 that the Austrians and Prussians kept control of their mass armies in 1812–13 and were able both to defeat the French and resist reform. But the American war produced more varied military organizations. It was far more decentralized, fought amid thirteen autonomous colonies, involving numerous loosely defined fronts and skirmishes, with important guerrilla elements on both sides. Even the rebel Continental Army was somewhat decentralized, riven by regional factions and forced by inadequate supplies toward local self-sufficiency. It was also led by Washington, a commanding general whose genius lay in military politicking rather than in any integrated campaign strategy. Thus when the "people" fought, they did so in fairly autonomous local groups, as free men (and sometimes women), hounding and even killing local notables to whom they had previously deferred.

Thus, as Palmer (1959) emphasized, the war quickly destabilized local colonial patronage networks and enormously amplified the popular, democratic strand of local colonial power relations. "When the pot boils, the scum will arise," as one disgruntled Massachusetts rebel notable complained (Handlin and Handlin 1969: 11). The young men enlisting in the army and conscripted in the militia were those least likely to be property owners and enfranchised voters. Their demands for political citizenship were clear – and for a time hard to resist.

The campaign also depended logistically and strategically on ports and other towns on communications routes, and on farmers in the interior for supplies and outflanking movements. In most areas this elevated numerical organizational strength at the expense of notables.

Two groups marginal to the colonial regime became key to rebel success. First, urban artisans, mechanics, and small shopkeepers – the lower petite bourgeoisie – were able to pressure town meetings and organize violence against Loyalists as each locality declared for king or for rebellion. Second, small farmers in newly settled western areas, as yet with no or restricted voting franchise, had autonomous community and trade organizations. They could prevent Loyalists from operating in their areas, and they enlisted in and supplied rebel forces. They were sympathetic to the cause, especially the abolition of government-conferred economic privileges and monopolies – what I call "new capitalist corruption." What was revolutionary about the wartime situation was that petit bourgeois and farmer demands could be implemented by their local political and military organizations. Popular town meetings and rural community organizations became local organs of the emergent rebel state and militia. In town and countryside restricted networks of the printed word – of newspapers, pamphlets, and correspondence committees – became overtaken by popular oral assemblies. (See Henretta 1973: 162–5; essays in Young 1976; and Steffen 1984.)

Thus, when Patriot notables appealed to the people to fight, gradually – without full consciousness of its significance – they began to justify rebellion in terms of popular principles of government. Their rhetoric became by degrees more populist in tone, more democratic in substance. Ideological principles became generalized and transcendent in an appeal for help. Some formal political ratification followed. Property requirements were lowered slightly in a majority of states, increasing the proportion of enfranchised white adult males from the range of 50 percent to 80 percent to 60 percent to 90 percent, abolishing local religious disbarments, and even enfranchising a few blacks and women (Williamson 1960; Dinkin 1982: 27–43). Local segmental notable control through patronage and deference networks was undermined by a more than doubling of electoral turnout through the 1780s, by the spread of the practice of mandating representatives (begun in the town meetings of the 1760s and 1770s), and by mass electioneering on issues.

Dahl's "contestation," my "party democracy," was institutionalized. True, the leadership descended only slightly down the class structure, being still dominated by the "better sort," but their organized relationship to the electors had changed, as Cook explains for New England: "When the Revolution destroyed the foundations of the hierarchical notions of social arrangements, deferential politics began to disappear. Political leaders ceased being regarded as social superiors and became explicitly servants of the people" (1976: 192).

Small proprietors increased their numbers in the legislatures. In 1765, more than 50 percent of Massachusetts assemblymen owned wealth in excess of $2,000; by 1784, the proportion was only 22 percent. Fewer than 20 percent of the delegates to colonial assemblies during 1750–75 had been artisans and small farmers. By 1784, they were 40 percent of all legislators, but a majority from the North (Main 1966: 406–7; Henretta 1973: 168). Political power was still local, but it was shifting toward the petite bourgeoisie and small farmers. In a rural country whose institutions were basically British, this was partly an evolutionary process. But it was speeded beyond a British-style compromise between old regime and emerging petite bourgeoisie as a consequence of an avoidable war with a conjunctural, contested military outcome.

This was reinforced by economic reforms. Struggling against despotism, the rebels favored economic freedom. They reduced state mercantilism, abolished quitrents and primogeniture, increased the proportion of elected officials, and attempted to free land grants from patronage. The effects were greatest in the middle states, where more notables had been Loyalist. Their lands and offices were expropriated and local power shifted to the small farmers and petite bourgeoisie. Outside the South, there was no longer a qualitative difference in power between big and small capital. Weber's "spirit of (petty commodity) capitalism" predominated in the North and West; and it shared the South with slave capitalism. This shift was reinforced by a European trend unrelated to the war. European population growth now outstripped the capacities of its agriculture. American grain producers, mostly small farmers, could export profitably. By the 1790s, the northern had overtaken the southern states in per capita wealth and exports (Appleby 1984). The growth was again greatest in the middle states, especially in Pennsylvania. Their economies became dominated by small agrarian capital. The new electoral system could translate this into political power.

Leftward shifts, however, were reversed by the centralization of military power relations during the latter stages of the war, as campaigning became more integrated and as its strategic center moved into the more conservative South. Upper-class Founding Fathers, in command of the military and political headquarters, now found greater local support for their social conservatism among the segmental organizations of southern planters. The increasing military discipline of the Continental Army also bolstered their power. Radical proprietors might dominate local assemblies elsewhere, but not the centralized heights of the later Patriot war effort.

Constitutional settlement

The war ended in 1783. The British and Loyalists were expelled, and the popular militias were dispersed. Although radicals remained influential in individual states, they lost influence on the leadership. Some state assemblies now edged toward radical political economy, cancellation of debts (mostly owed by poor farmers) and progressive taxation and land grants. The interim constitution represented by the 1783 Articles of Confederation contained only a feeble central state. Threatened by local class radicalism, the notables organized to strengthen the state.

The making of the Constitution at the Philadelphia Convention in 1787 was their main response. There was broad consensus that the state should be a representative one (for white males), that ideologically it should not entrench any one religion, and that it should enjoy little military power over its white citizens (and enough to coerce its nonwhites). Of course, its patriarchal nature remained unquestioned. Debate centered on the remaining two of what Chapter 3 identifies as the "higher-level crystallizations" of modern states – as capitalist and as nation-states.

The first turned not on capitalism versus some other mode of production but on alternative capitalist political economies: whose model of economic development the state should assist, that of small or substantial proprietors (with slave owners complicating the issue). This did involve the question of who should be represented in this state, and also what the state's economic powers should be. This was closely linked to the other problematic crystallization, how centralized and "national" this state should be. Because all parties had just fought a war against despotism, they would avoid a state as centralized as French revolutionaries later introduced, or even as centralized as the British state. Most notables favored a more centralized state than radicals wanted, as the notables controlled the continental level. But slave owners and some notables from small states differed. Because both crystallizations were entwined, there was no head-on class confrontation.

The Constitutional Convention was the only major decision-making process of the period taken behind closed doors, without direct popular pressure or consultation (for a graphic account, see Collier and Collier 1986). After two weeks of intensive debate, fifty-five participating delegates produced a new constitution for ratification by the states. The delegates were all substantial property owners, the wealthiest, most notable of the three Founding Father groups. They all wanted powers to restrain the "anarchist" tendencies revealed by local legislatures. Dangerous scenarios had just been presented, as exemplified by Shays' Rebellion, largely a class insurrection against taxes and debts in Massachusetts. But their debates did not center on class issues, on which delegates shared common unspoken assumptions. Nor did they dwell much on religion. Though from a diversity of churches, they were nonsectarian, members of multichurch state delegations. They quickly agreed the state should be secular.

Instead, delegates debated the "national" centralization issue that divided them. A relatively centralized state was feared by delegates from small states, wary of the "tyranny" of the electorate from big ones, and especially by southern delegates, who believed a strong central state might legislate against slavery. To emerge with an agreed-on constitution, and so head off radicals, they had to compromise on states' rights. They did so pragmatically, leaving loopholes (especially over the constitutions of future states) and thus ensuring that the states' rights issue – and its connection to slavery in the South and in new western states – would remain troublesome. But they did emerge almost united behind a Constitution that could avoid class confrontation – part by design, part unintentionally.

Fully intended was the separation of powers, producing a divided central state designed to appeal to radical decentralizers as well as to conservatives by preventing equally despotism and sudden expressions of popular will. Public powers were divided among no fewer than five representative institutions – the presidency, the two houses of Congress, the thirteen states, and the local governments. The division was not by consistent principles that might allow hierarchies to develop among them. Economic powers at present with state legislatures were divided among various institutions. The Senate and House of Representatives had differing suffrages ad staggered elections; the House originated budgets; the Senate had more powers over presidential appointees and foreign treaties, yet a more restricted franchise; the president was elected indirectly by an electoral college, which it was assumed would better represent property; the president could not initiate legislation but could veto congressional legislation (unless both houses passed it by two-thirds majorities). No franchises were significantly extended (except for removing religious disabilities). Electoral constituencies were deliberately enlarged so that they would be cross-class, supposedly invulnerable to mob control.

The final separation of powers created the Supreme Court. This proved a stroke of genius, but it was less conscious strategy than a consensus about the nature of rights that proved to have enormous unintended consequences. It stemmed from the predominance of notable lawyers-cum-property owners in the Revolution and in the drafting of the Constitution itself – at least 33 of the 55 delegates had practiced law, but only 4 of them had been *only* lawyers (Mann and Stephens 1991). Rebellion had been against the sovereign despotism of king in Parliament; it had been followed by a period in which local legislatures had acted against property law. Thus the delegates thought it prudent to "entrench" their Constitution as the rule of law, supervised by a Supreme Court – if necessary (though the implications of this appear not to have been recognized by the opposition) against executive and legislatures alike.

The Constitution would change as social power changed, but modifications had to be broadly consistent with the principles laid down by these propertied Founding Fathers. The Constitution demanded such substantial majorities for constitutional change that this needed considerable consensus across class (and across state) lines. The president appointed the justices of the Supreme Court, but for life, so they usually outlasted their benefactor. They could veto legislation or government action or decide that actions undertaken by government or a private body were in accord with the spirit of the Constitution. Lesser courts exercised similar regulatory judgments over lesser bodies.

Thus the law profession, up to the Supreme Court, became active regulators of private, corporate, and government agencies – a surrogate for a more centralized state administration (as Skowronek 1982: 24–30 observes). It took some decades for legal institutions to attain their full preeminence. But by the mid-nineteenth century, law was above politics and therefore in certain senses ultimately above party democracy. It might seem (T. H. Marshall believed so) that America had early institutionalized both civil and political citizenship. But its civil citizenship remained highly individualistic and capitalistic and it was entrenched even against sovereign political citizenship. "Popular majorities . . . would be for ever constrained" concludes Appleby (1987: 804).

In his observations of American democracy, Tocqueville emphasized lawyers' power, famously declaring the "bench and the bar" were the "American aristocracy." But this was not quite accurate, for American law was then, as it is now, inseparable from capitalist property. These propertied lawyer notables had a distinctive conception of rights. They had been reared on that equation of personal human freedom and individual property rights labeled by MacPherson (1962) as "possessive individualism." Although MacPherson located this ideology too early, distorting the views of Hobbes and Locke to place it in the seventeenth century, it did dominate the thinking of the Founding Fathers. Private property became truly sacred, inviolate from state and anarchism alike. Entrenching the rule of law in this context protected the liberty of the person and of his or her property. The main radical opposition rested among petite bourgeoisie and small farmers. They were also individual property owners, so they did not oppose this principle. On this vital issue there was no head-on, dialectical class conflict of the Marxian variety. The solution, which gradually proved to favor big property (as financial and industrial property became more concentrated, and as small farmers became once again indebted), slid largely unnoticed through the postrevolutionary conflicts.

Once exploited social groups – lower classes, women, blacks, perhaps even eventually the few surviving native Americans – were admitted to the status of individual civil and political citizenship, no regime would be more active in advancing their individual property rights and freedoms than the American. But collective rights would always be subordinate to individual rights, as labor unions (see Chapter 18), radical farmers (Chapter 19), and twentieth-century advocates of a more social citizenship discovered to their cost. They would experience not collective rights but fierce military-judicial repression. Contrary to Marshall's evolutionary theory of the spread of citizenship, America never developed much social citizenship, while the collective powers of its labor and farm movements remained hamstrung by entrenched individual civil citizenship longer than in any of my other countries. State legislatures could not constitutionally cancel debts, nor could they (until well into the twentieth century) pass laws legalizing picketing or other "conspiracies" against the property freedoms of employers. Big capitalist property became entrenched against the main nineteenth-century grievances of labor and small farmer alike, as Chapters 18 and 19 reveal. As interpreted by lawyers, the entrenched Constitution became the best possible guarantee of the power of capitalist property in America (as Hartz 1955: 103 also observes). Lawyers became in this period, and have remained ever since, the "organic intellectuals" of capitalism. Within forty years, this switched them from the revolutionary to the conservative camp – and this was achieved largely without opposition from petit bourgeois radicals.

Though the Constitution was written in a Philadelphia vacuum, popular pressures could not be ignored. Delegates narrowly secured ratification of the new Constitution by the individual states, sometimes against considerable opposition. They were also forced to make concessions to protect individual rights against the new government secured in the first constitutional amendments, known collectively as the Bill of Rights. But because no part of the Constitution appeared to proscribe directly the political economy goals of the radicals, they did not oppose it as energetically as they might have done.

Through the 1780s, two broadly equal "parties" emerged, comprising about three-quarters of representatives in the legislatures. Main (1973: chapter 2) terms them "commercial-cosmopolitans" and "agrarian-localists." The cosmopolitans were predominantly urban merchants and professional men, with support from planters and landowners near cities – in effect, an old regime similar to local colonial regimes before 1776. The localists were new politicians, predominantly representing small capitalist farmers in inland counties. Artisans, small manufacturers, and lesser tradesmen (the lower petite bourgeoisie) were torn between the two factions, their class drawing them to localists, their urban interests to cosmopolitans. Through the 1790s, the two turned into loose political parties, many cosmopolitans becoming Federalists, many localists (joining with southern planters) becoming first Anti-Federalists, then Jeffersonian Republicans and Democrats. American politics crystallized, thirdly, earlier than anywhere else, as a fairly full party democracy.

The problematic crystallizations – What was the form of capitalism and how "national" should government be? – still divided the parties. Federalists favored a strong central government and restricted franchise, to secure economic development and property rights; their opponents favored the reverse. Their conflict proved paradoxical. The Federalists got most of their desired ends, yet with neither chosen means.

Fear of resurrecting centralized despotism was widely shared by all classes and regions. Therefore, the state remained largely decentralized. Most government infrastructures and functions (education, health, family, law, most public works, police, care of the poor) were devolved by the Constitution to individual state administrations (see Lowi's 1984 summary of the power of all three government levels). Indeed, the Constitution devolves "residual" powers – powers not elsewhere specified – in these matters to the individual states. By European, even British, standards, the American national state was born puny. Chapter 11 shows that it remained less powerful than its European counterparts throughout the period under discussion.

Nevertheless, Federalists triumphed over two narrower fronts, which proved decisive for attaining their goals. First, law embodying secure individual property rights was entrenched, as described earlier. It did not seem like centralization and the potential class opposition did not resist. Second, the Federalists (especially Hamilton) originated "late development" theories. Believing that Britain provided the model of the future economy, they wished government to encourage financial concentration and manufacturing industry. They concentrated their centralizing offensive quite narrowly, on securing federal government infrastructures for large-scale economic activity, especially on obtaining a national banking, currency, and credit structure, but also seeking protective tariffs for manufactures (Ferguson 1964; McGuire and Ohsfeldt 1984). Less controversially, they also favored an enlarged postal service, customs, and land offices, plus a small navy to protect shipping and a small standing army to kill Indians and undertake civil engineering works. This narrower "modernizing" centralism won many converts. Tom Paine, supposedly their political enemy, came to see his rural democratic allies as parochial, indifferent to the economic needs of the emerging nation (Foner 1976). Individual states in the first half of the nineteenth century also became active subsidizers of roads and canals and charterers of corporations, though less so in the South than elsewhere (Pisani 1987; their expenditure figures are provided in Holt 1977). Federalists got property rights and infrastructural development, but through a predominantly *confederal* state – through the courts and a division of labor between federal and state governments – not in the anticipated form of a centralized nation-state.

With regard to the franchise, the Federalists overestimated their segmental powers over elections. Their patronage networks struggled to control the emerging mass electorate. Ideological power networks expanded, partly because of Federalist policies: Post offices increased twelvefold over the 1790s, newspapers two-and-a-half-fold. Republican and Democratic correspondence societies and campaign meetings spread. Farmers, petits bourgeois, and mechanics had alternative organizations. Notables were also split by region. Southern planters favored the Federalists on class grounds, but the overriding threat that centralization posed to slavery brought them into the Democrats' camp. An electoral alliance of the propertied classes and their clients (such as dominated nineteenth-century Britain) never materialized. This lessened head-on, political class struggle. It also placed the Federalists in electoral trouble. Geopolitics worsened this. The Federalists took Britain as their model of a modern capitalist society, capable of legitimate taxation and strong state action, constitutional yet without democracy. But Britain had just been the main enemy; Britain was still the enemy of France, the revolutionary heir of America; and Britain was now the main trade rival. Federalist foreign policy could be smeared as un-American.

Jeffersonian Democrats achieved a sweeping victory in the election of 1800. "Never again would any group of Americans seriously seeking power in a national election champion hierarchical values or deferential political practice," concludes Appleby (1984: 3). Intense party

competition resulted in consistent voting turnouts of more than half
the adult white males by 1810, a far higher proportion than in the
colonial period (Fischer 1965: 182–92). Jacksonian Democrats, leading
small farmers and the urban petite bourgeoisie and artisans, strove to
further suffrage reform in the 1830s. Jeffersonians and Jacksonians
could sometimes express a populist anticapitalist ideology contrasting
the "industrious" and "agrarians" with parasitic "capitalists" (Hartz
1955: 120–5). American parties could sometimes sound quite like
British radicals and French sans-culottes. But their franchise goal
could be achieved with less violence, broadly within the institutions of
colonial America as amplified by the war and institutionalized by the
Constitution. As the Constitution entrenched property law and rigorously divided powers, Federalists and notables had less to fear from
franchise reform. By 1840, all adult white males possessed the vote
and the first modern two-party democracy existed. The "spoils" segmental system distributed offices between them. (See Chapter 13.)
Class struggle, crosscut by party democracy and segmental clientelism,
did not threaten the rule of property.

By 1840, this was adding up to a fairly coherent regime strategy. The
American regime could not be "old," save in the South. Rule by birth,
religion, customary patronage, and deference was destroyed by a colonial war, followed by a petty capitalist electoral onslaught. The petite
bourgeoisie, led uniquely by small farmers, achieved mass democracy
in advance of anywhere else in the world. This had further potentially
radical implications. Yet radicalism was not anticapitalist. The state,
being a real separation of powers, became conservative. Its divided
infrastructures were quietly turned toward the projects of large-scale
capitalism. And the rule of law entrenched conceptions of capitalistic
private property. The combination amounted to the hegemony of
capitalist liberalism everywhere outside the South. The Constitution as
rule of law – and not as elsewhere the state or sovereign parliament –
became by the late nineteenth century the symbolic, venerated heart of
the nation.

Neither Constitution nor state proved of much help on the national
issue of states' rights. Slavery became increasingly at odds with northern capitalism, yet this weak federal state had no resources to solve
the conflict or even to authoritatively allocate constitutions (containing slavery or not?) to new western states. The Union became
engulfed in a civil war that only temporarily increased state centralization. American geopolitics did not involve challenges to other
Great Powers and required little national mobilization and little high-
tech militarism until the twentieth century. Thus the nation-state
lagged. As state and local government infrastructures strengthened

throughout the late nineteenth century, American government moved from the confederal to a more federal form, in the senses I specify in Table 3.3. Its federal institutions met the Second Industrial Revolution – and the challenges of discontented farmers, workers, and others – with a coherent capitalist-liberal and party-democratic regime strategy buttressed by pronounced domestic militarism. These challenges and responses are discussed in Chapters 18 and 19.

American conclusion

I have addressed three main problems in the founding of the American Republic: how to characterize its emerging regime, how to explain its rise, and whether it was truly revolutionary.

In terming the new American regime confederal, party democratic, and capitalist-liberal, I have done little more than accept conventional wisdom. As subsequent chapters show, the capitalist-liberal strategy has successfully absorbed all that industrial society (and massive ethnic immigration) threw at it. Since the United States eventually became the hegemonic Western Power, its capitalist liberalism has influenced much of the globe. Its parties, the capitalist liberalism enshrined in its law courts, and its confederalism also survived most of the Second Industrial Revolution, although confederalism was finally modified by the New Deal and the acquisition of superpower status (which also ended the unevenness of its militarism).

In explaining its rise I took sides in a debate among historians, with Bailyn (1967) and Appleby (1984) against the evolutionism of Boorstin (1959), Degler (1959), Hartz (1955), and Lipset (1964), who traced capitalist liberalism back through the Founding Fathers to early colonial settlement and to the supposed absence of "feudalism" in the New World. Instead I argued that the War of Independence and subsequent political struggles intervened to destroy viable local-regional regimes that were becoming recognizably "old." Without this intervention, these regimes might have developed quite similarly to their counterpart in Britain, whether or not under British control. True, the colonies also contained alternative power organizations that, when amplified, led into more purely capitalist tracks, but this amplification occurred through three additional, contingent processes:

1. The geopolitical and fiscal-military pressures operating on the British Empire factionalized its American clients and, reinforced by French military power in war, rendered the British (narrowly) unable to defend their colonies.

2. The military pressures of semiguerrilla warfare increased moderate reform toward democracy. The old regime could not simply be trans-

ferred to local American control once rebellious notables were forced to seek the help of the "people" (in the early twentieth-century sense of the masses) in an armed struggle against the British and Loyalists. Outside of the South, the locality was more captured by class than by segmental organization. Yet to win the war, the popular and notable power actors had to compromise.

3. At the end of the war the roughly equal yet confused balance of political power between entwined class and national forces ensured that the victors did not fall out among themselves. Instead, their power relations and conflicts became institutionalized into a capitalist-liberal regime strategy through postwar compromises combining capitalism with democracy. The notables had the initial constitution-making field to themselves. Through a mixture of intent, miscalculation, and unintended consequences, they devised a constitution whose separation of powers carried conservative consequences. They compromised on the states' rights issue, institutionalizing North-South (and other regional) political crystallizations that crosscut and weakened class struggle. Federalists and notables also reduced their proproperty, procentralization offensive to two areas, entrenching property law in the Constitution and providing central state infrastructures for the development of big capitalism (then unexpectedly reinforced by the individual states). But they miscalculated their capacity to segmentally control elections, and the (white male) masses secured a two-party democracy. The confused result was to consolidate a capitalist-liberal, party-democratic, and confederal regime hegemonic outside of the South. Because power struggles entwined disparate elements, class conflict had never been "pure" or transparent. Notables and masses never faced one another head-on, dialectically as class enemies. They first allied in war, then slid past one another, concentrating their energies on different, though entwined, political crystallizations and networks of political power.

More generally, I have traced a transition in the relations of primacy among the four sources of social power. Ideological power relations had a declining role in structuring overall power relations. Early outcomes – the downward spiral to rebellion, the changing balance of wartime power between notable and popular rebels, and the military result of the war itself – were predominantly determined by the entwining of economic and military power relations. In a very confused way – and always remembering that economic relations had strong segmental, regional and national components as well as class ones – they jointly shaped the institutions of the new Republic. Yet thereafter (as institutional statism might suggest), its political institutions had their own power autonomy, significantly constraining American development. In a country unthreatened by other Great Powers, geo-political militarism, though not domestic militarism, proved to have less general power significance through the nineteenth century. Now American development was predominantly capitalist development, yet constrained by institutionalized confederal, party-democratic, and domestic military state organization. This was the American version of the general transition noted over this period in Chapter 1 in a very rough "ultimate" dual determination – from economic–military to economic–political power relations.

Finally, was this a revolution? The completeness of American trans-formation to capitalist liberalism – its "revolutionary" aspect in the everyday sense of that word – was due to the absence of revolution in the sociological sense of a violent transformation of power relations. Opposed class forces had not squarely faced and fought, as they were to in France. Moreover, capitalist liberalism soon became conservative. After forty or so years it was more thoroughly institutionalized, more resistant to change, than any other regime. It discovered how to avoid class struggle – not altogether, of course, but how best to avoid a single, extensive, head-on political conflict. The commercialization of agriculture proved as disruptive, small farmers as discontented, the Industrial Revolution as brutal, the proletariat as discontented, as elsewhere. But their aspirations were more tracked by political and military institutions into nonclass organizations than in any other coun-try. The early institutionalization of a colonial revolution decisively structured later American power structure.

Bibliography

Appleby, J. A. 1984. *Capitalism and a New Social Order: The Republican Vision of the 1790s.* New York: New York University Press.
    1987. The American heritage: the heirs and the disinherited. *Journal of American History* 74.
Bailyn, B. 1962. Political experience and enlightenment ideas in eighteenth-century America. *American Historical Review* 67.
    1967. *The Ideological Origins of the American Revolution.* Cambridge, Mass.: Harvard University Press.
    1986. *Voyagers to the West: A Passage in the Peopling of America on the Eve of the Revolution.* New York: Knopf.
Beard, C. 1913. *An Economic Interpretation of the Constitution.* New York: Macmillan.
Birch, R. C. 1976. *1776: The American Challenge.* London: Longman Group.
Boorstin, D. 1959. *The Americans: The Colonial Experience.* New York: Random House.
Brown, W. 1965. *The King's Friends.* Providence, R.I.: Brown University Press.

Burch, P. H., Jr. 1981. *Elites in American History*. Vol. I: *The Federalist Years to the Civil War*. New York: Holmes & Meier.

Collier, C., and J. L. Collier. 1986. *Decisions in Philadelphia*. New York: Ballantine Books.

Cook, E. M., Jr. 1976. *The Fathers of the Towns: Leadership and Community Structure in Eighteenth-Century New England*. Baltimore: Johns Hopkins University Press.

Countryman, E. 1981. *A People in Revolution: The American Revolution and Political Society in New York*. Baltimore: Johns Hopkins University Press.

1985. *The American Revolution*. New York: Hill & Wang.

Davidson, P. 1941. *Propaganda and the American Revolution, 1763–1783*. Chapel Hill: University of North Carolina Press.

Degler, C. N. 1959. *Out of Our Past: The Forces That Shaped Modern America*. New York: Harper.

Dinkin, R. J. 1977. *Voting in Provincial America: A Study of Elections in the Thirteen Colonies, 1689–1776*. Westport, Conn.: Greenwood Press.

1982. *Voting in Revolutionary America: A Study of Elections in the Original Thirteen States, 1776–1789*. Westport, Conn.: Greenwood Press.

Egnal, M. 1988. *A Mighty Empire: The Origins of the American Revolution*. Ithaca, N.Y.: Cornell University Press.

Ferguson, E. J. 1964. *The Power of the Purse: A History of American Public Finance, 1776–1790*. Chapel Hill: University of North Carolina Press.

Fischer, D. H. 1965. *The Revolution of American Conservatism. The Federalist Party in the Era of Jeffersonian Democracy*. New York: Harper & Row.

Foner, E. 1976. *Tom Paine and Revolutionary America*. New York: Oxford University Press.

Handlin, O., and M. F. Handlin. 1969. *Commonwealth: A Study of the Role of Government in the American Economy: Massachusetts, 1774–1861*, 2nd ed. Cambridge, Mass.: Harvard University Press.

Hartz, L. 1955. *The Liberal Tradition in America*. New York: Harcourt, Brace & World.

Henretta, J. A. 1973. *The Evolution of American Society, 1700–1815*. Lexington, Mass.: D. C. Heath.

Holt, C. F. 1977. *The Role of State Government in the Nineteenth-Century American Economy, 1840–1902*. New York: Arno Press.

Lipset, S. M. 1964. *The First New Nation*. London: Heinemann.

Lockridge, K. A. 1974. *Literacy in Colonial New England*. New York: Norton.

Lowi, T. J. 1984. Why is there no socialism in the United States? A federal analysis. In *The Costs of Federalism*, ed. R. T. Golombiewski and A. Wildavsky. New Brunswick, N.J.: Transaction Books.

McDonald, F. 1958. *We, the People*. Chicago: University of Chicago Press.

McGuire, R., and R. Ohsfeldt. 1984. Economic interests and the American Constitution: a quantitative rehabilitation of Charles A. Beard. *Journal of Economic History* 44.

McKirdy, C. R. 1972. A bar divided: the lawyers of Massachusetts and the American Revolution. *American Journal of Legal Library* 16.

MacPherson, C. B. 1962. *The Political Theory of Possessive Individualism*. Oxford: Clarendon Press.

Maier, P. 1973. *From Resistance to Revolution: Colonial Radicalism and the*

Development of American Opposition to Britain. London: Routledge & Kegan Paul.

Main, J. T. 1965. *The Social Structures of Revolutionary America.* Princeton, N.J.: Princeton University Press.

1966. Government by the people: the American Revolution and the democratization of the legislatures. *William and Mary Quarterly* 23.

1973. *Political Parties Before the Constitution.* Chapel Hill: University of North Carolina Press.

Mann, M., and M. Stephens. 1991. American revolutionaries: social class and the Founding Fathers. Unpublished paper, Department of Sociology, University of California, Los Angeles.

Murrin, J. M. 1983. The legal transformation: the bench and bar of eighteenth-century Massachusetts. In *Colonial America: Essays in Politics and Social Development,* ed. S. N. Katz and J. M. Murrin. New York: Knopf.

Nash, G. 1973. The transformation of American politics, 1700–1765. *Journal of American History* 60.

1975–6. Urban wealth and poverty in pre-revolutionary America. *Journal of Interdisciplinary History* 6.

1986. *The Urban Crucible: The Northern Seaports and the Origins of the American Revolution.* Cambridge, Mass.: Harvard University Press.

Palmer, R. 1959. *The Age of the Democratic Revolutions,* 2 vols. Princeton, N.J.: Princeton University Press.

Pisani, D. 1987. Promotion and regulation: constitutionalism and the American economy. *Journal of American History* 74.

Pocock, J. G. A. 1980. 1776: The revolution against Parliament. In his *Three British Revolutions: 1641, 1688, 1776.* Princeton, N.J.: Princeton University Press.

Pole, J. R. 1966. *Political Representation in England and the Origins of the American Republic.* London: Macmillan.

Rosswurm, S. 1987. *Arms, Country and Class: The Philadelphia Militia and the "Lower Sort" During the American Revolution.* New Brunswick, N.J.: Rutgers University Press.

Shy, J. 1973. The American Revolution: the military conflict considered as a revolutionary war. In *Essays on the American Revolution,* ed. S. G. Kurtz and J. H. Hutson. Chapel Hill: University of North Carolina Press.

Skowronek, S. 1982. *Building a New American State: The Expansion of National Administrative Capacities, 1877–1920.* Cambridge: Cambridge University Press.

Sokoloff, K., and G. Villaflor. 1982. The early achievement of modern stature in America. *Social Science History* 6.

Solberg, W. 1958. *The Federal Convention and the Formation of the Union of the American States.* New York: Liberal Arts Press.

Steffen, C. G. 1984. *The Mechanics of Baltimore: Workers and Politics in the Age of Revolution, 1763–1812.* Urbana: University of Illinois Press.

Williamson, C. 1960. *American Suffrage: From Property to Democracy, 1760–1860.* Princeton, N.J.: Princeton University Press.

Young, A. F. (ed.). 1976. *The American Revolution: Explorations in the History of American Radicalism.* DeKalb: Northern Illinois University Press.

6   The French Revolution and
the bourgeois nation

The central issue in analyzing the French Revolution traditionally has
been whether it was a class revolution. Historians from Jaurès to
Lefebvre said yes, analyzing the Revolution as a class struggle between
a feudal old regime and a capitalist bourgeoisie. But three revisions
have disputed this. Since Cobban (1964), empirical studies showed
that the Revolution began as old regime factional fighting and continued under nonbourgeois leadership. The second revision, centered
on Behrens (1967) and Skocpol (1979), sees the Revolution triggered
by a fiscal crisis caused by Great Power rivalry. Only through this
fiscal crisis did class struggle emerge. The third revision, offered by
Ozouf (1976), Furet (1978), Agulhon (1981), Hunt (1984), and Sewell
(1985), sees the Revolution as essentially ideological, driven by ideas,
emotions, and cultural forms, classes being mobilized more symbolically than materially. This has become the new conventional wisdom:
codes have replaced classes among historians of France. The intelligentsia has turned inward.

   I accept some of all these arguments. As usual, my explanation
entwines ideological, economic, military, and political power networks. The Revolution did not begin as a class struggle, except for the
peasantry, but it became a class struggle, just as it became a national
struggle. Classes were not "pure" but also were defined by ideological,
military, and political forces. The Revolution became bourgeois and
national, less from the logic of development from feudal to capitalist
modes of production than from state militarism (generating fiscal difficulties), from its failure to institutionalize relations between warring
elites and parties, and from the expansion of discursive ideological
infrastructures carrying principled alternatives. I also provide evidence
to support a general argument about class conflict made in this volume:
Where class conflict is relatively "pure" – where classes emerge more
directly out of modes of production to confront one another head-
on – they more accurately perceive one another. The organizational
advantages of the dominant class, in control of the state, permit it to
repress or incorporate, thus evading revolution. Where class conflict is
entwined confusingly with other conflicts, dominant classes lose concentration on their class interests. Then popular discontent may push
them off balance, induce mistakes, and fuel a revolutionary situation
as in France. I return to mistakes shortly.

I accept much of the fiscal-military revisionism of Behrens and Skocpol; indeed, this volume generalizes it to all countries of the period. Yet I also build on Goldstone's (1991: 172–4) criticisms of Skocpol. Because she then had a true elitist theory of the state, Skocpol viewed the fiscal crisis as an "objective" one confronting a singular state elite. She neglects intraelite and party struggles. French finances were in a mess, but they collapsed – bringing down the entire old regime – only because of deteriorating factional relations between and among the two main elements of the French state, the monarchical state elite and a party of privilege deeply entrenched in French society. Because the French state had not institutionalized sovereign representative mechanisms for settling factional disputes, fiscal disputes that other states could resolve brought it crashing down. Skocpol's true elitism explains less of the Revolution than her institutional statism.

With class revisionism I have three disagreements. I disagree with Cobban's vision of revolutionary leadership as a declining old regime fraction and with Goldstone's view of the revolutionaries suffering "blocked mobility." I also disagree with Skocpol's and Goldstone's curious "one-class" model: they rightly stress the peasantry but largely ignore the bourgeoisie and petite bourgeoisie. In the towns and in Paris, where the Revolution acquired its basic direction, theirs is a top-down theory of revolution, not a bottom-up theory (like class theories). Yet the failure to institutionalize elite-party struggles let in the excluded classes, the peasants and petite bourgeoisie. The Revolution in both towns and countryside moved from top-down to bottom-up. Third, the rise of bourgeois and petit bourgeois parties was continuous, not a "skidding off course" beginning after 1791, unconnected to the events of 1789, as Furet and Richet (1970; cf. Furet 1981) argue, wishing to support the goals of the Revolution before but not after 1791.

I accept some of the empirical arguments of the now-dominant ideological school. Because ideological power did play a substantial role in the Revolution (more than in events in Britain and America), I wish now to briefly consider the arguments of the cultural school. The problem is that it has been idealist. Now idealists could make useful, testable causal arguments, emphasizing the role of ideological institutions, of symbolic and ritual practices, and of the content of ideologies. Yet they have rarely done this, for their causal arguments usually have been subsumed under a more totalizing idealism, eschewing causal analysis and, instead, redescribing entire social processes in cultural terms. This is the legacy of Hegel and of German idealism, carried into contemporary social science by discourse analysis and by writers like Foucault and Geertz.

Thus Lynn Hunt analyzes the Revolution as "text": "in terms of its internal patterns and its connections to other aspects of political culture." The importance of her work is to demonstrate that the revolutionaries showed great interest in symbolic culture and morality. We must take these seriously. But she rejects "looking underneath or outside the words" for causes. Thus her conclusion that the origins of revolution "must be sought in political culture" is not a causal argument but a tautology. She has established no causal relations between culture and anything else (1984: 24–5, 234). To establish the importance of culture, we must look outside revolutionary words and texts, to see where they came from. Did they merely articulate economic, military, and political power relations? Or did they express the needs of specifically ideological institutions? Such causal issues are evaded by Hunt.

Furet also tends to redescribe the Revolution as cultural-symbolic process, but he adds causal arguments. For example, he suggests that when royal power collapsed at the onset of the Revolution, it was replaced by *la parole*, the spoken word. Whoever could claim to speak successfully in the name of the nation spoke for the general will and could assume power. Thereafter the Revolution became, literally, a battle of words, he says (1978: 83).

This usefully focuses our attention not on a totality made up of texts and symbolic discourses but on specific media and messages of communication, interacting with other sources of social power. If people are to be moved by cultural messages, they need to be reached. We cannot assume they share the same culture. We know from countless sociological, historical, and anthropological studies (and despite normative functionalist theory) that extensive societies almost never do. Communications infrastructures should be the object of our analysis of ideological power (or culture, if that is the preferred term). Thus (building on the work of Eisenstein 1986) my analysis begins with the eighteenth-century expansion of infrastructures, the creation of "public opinion," and its escape from absolutist control.

Both Furet and Hunt correctly emphasize that the Revolution escalated politics of principle rather than pragmatic compromise. As crisis deepened, and as practical politics could not cope, power actors turned to principled solutions. "Principle" carries its double meaning of a general and a moral rule, for the revolutionaries became obsessed with "virtue" and "purity" as well as with schemes of rational reconstruction, with the "politics of authentic emotions" (Hunt's phrase) as well as of ideologies. When principles are evoked, we may indeed suspect that ideological institutions and elites are exercising some power. Unlike practical economic, military, and political actors, they pursue general, transitive, principled knowledge.

To test this suspicion, we must answer two questions: First, is the content of principles merely the experience of practical power actors, as generalized by ideologists? Or are they created by ideologists out of their own distinct experience? Second, do ideologists possess collective or distributive power techniques over practical actors such that they influence which principles are to be evoked and implemented? By exploring ideological infrastructures, and by answering these two questions, I will assess the causal significance of ideological power. I begin this task in this chapter and complete it in Chapter 7.

Finally, I return to mistakes. The French Revolution was a unique world-historical event. It was the first, and virtually the only, successful bourgeois revolution. Its power actors were "unconscious," unlike subsequent power actors in any country. They did not know at the beginning that they were in a revolution. Therefore, they made what hindsight may portray as ghastly miscalculations – the king and privileged orders especially. Their miscalculations contributed to the exhaustion of practical politics and the recourse to ideological principles of revolution. Had the king and the privileged orders known what lurked in the wings, they would have acted differently, as their counterparts in other countries did later (with the example of the French Revolution before them). There were deep-rooted power processes – of class, of geopolitics, and of ideology – and I attempt to explain them. But they could have been stopped or redirected by power actors making different decisions. I enunciate this not as a universal principle of sociology but as applying to a specific type of structural situation in which power actors are unconscious of the emergence of novel interstitial power networks and so are prone to miscalculate power possibilities. As revolutions occur when regimes lose their powers of concentration on their interests, mistakes are *essential* to revolutions.

Economic and political power under the old regime

The Revolution did not happen in a backward or in a late or uneven developing country (as Skocpol asserts). By 1789, France had been the greatest Power and one of the most prosperous countries in the world for a century. Yet France seemed to have one "backwardness": It was lagging behind its Great Power rival, Britain. In the 1780s, the chemist Lavoisier estimated the productivity of English land at 2.7 times that of French. Indeed, some historians rate the whole British economy as more advanced (Crouzet 1966, 1970; Kindleberger 1984). Others disagree, seeing the two as near equals (O'Brien and Keyder 1978).

Goldstone's economic calculations seem the most persuasive (1991: 176–92; but see Vovelle and Roche 1965; Crouzet 1970; Léon 1970; Chaussinand-Nogaret 1985: 90–106; Dewald 1987). Goldstone estimates that the French economy grew in real terms by 36 percent between 1700 and 1789 but was unevenly distributed by sector – trade doubled; industry rose by 80 percent; agriculture, by only 25 percent. Each sectoral growth rate was similar to that in Britain, so no sector was particularly backward (though earlier data would have found more agricultural growth in Britain). But only a third of the British population was in agriculture, the low-growth sector, compared to four-fifths of the French. The French economy lagged because of the size of its agriculture. Hence a modest population growth of 30 percent, less than Britain's, bore down hard on this agrarian population, causing agricultural output per capita to fall by 4.3 percent between 1700 and 1789. The economic problem was not low or lagging gross national product but burdensome sectoral inequalities. Yet this "problem" was more severe in almost every other European country – and did not result in revolution. We cannot attribute the French Revolution to the general state of the economy. What mattered more, and what directly underlay all the causes of the Revolution, was state finances.

French geopolitical militarism brought fiscal difficulties. Throughout the eighteenth century Britain and France struggled for global supremacy. Britain was victorious in three of the four wars, losing only when confronted also by rebellious American colonists. Even in that war, France made no gains to pay for its high cost. Britain acquired a global empire; France acquired debts. Though both luck and geopolitics contributed to the outcome (discussed in Chapter 8), the British state possessed greater infrastructural power centered on its fiscal efficiency. The French state could only extract in taxes a far smaller fraction of national wealth (Mathias and O'Brien 1976; Morineau 1980). France levied as much but obtained less, spending far more on paying its tax gatherers and creditors.

As Anglo-French rivalry intensified, British state finances improved and those of the French visibly worsened (Behrens 1967: 138–62; Riley 1987). Most commentators deduced that the British were helped by their parliamentary regime. British property owners consented to indirect customs and excise duties and loans organized by the Bank of England. Geopolitical success then made military-fiscal extraction even less painful. But, as Table 4.1 suggests, other forms of sovereign "representation" might have been just as effective. In Prussia there was no parliament, but the dominant classes were effectively "represented" within central royal administration. Monarchism and party democracy offered alternative forms of "representative" crystallization. Both could stably institutionalize elite-party relations, as Prussia and Britain showed. But this was not true of France.

Because finances were the sinews of the French state, their crisis involved all of its institutions. France had developed as a bigger, looser kingdom. As the monarchy had expanded outward from the Ile de France, it struck particularistic deals with local-regional power networks, creating a rather decentralized absolutism of "corporations" and "orders." The consent of regions, the three estates (clergy, nobility, and commoners), and urban and professional communities (especially the assemblies of lawyers known as parlements) was bought with "privileges," rights over peasants and exemptions from civic duties, especially taxation. Unlike in Britain and Prussia, consent was based on exclusion from, not participation in, the central state. Despite absolutism and the intendants (royal officials supervising the provinces), I reject Tocqueville's famous argument that the French state was already highly centralized before the Revolution (1955). It was institutionally dual: a centralized monarchical state elite and privileged, decentralized notable parties. Both became less coherent through the eighteenth century.

Most taxes were direct land taxes, generating less and less revenue as landowners secured exemptions and powers to assess themselves. As Goldstone (1991: 196–218) observes, France's fiscal problem was not a lack of wealth but a tax system bearing down hardest on those who were becoming the least able to pay: the peasants. Salvation could have come, as partially in England, from indirect taxes on trade, but merchant and urban corporations also possessed privileges. The crown's response reinforced the particularistic, corporate embeddedness of the state. It sold its own offices for cash, granted annuities to those who would lend it funds, and granted rights of tax collection to anyone who would advance their receipts to the crown. The closest counterpart of the Bank of England was an autonomous corporation of wealthy men, the Company of General Farmers (i.e., tax farmers), who negotiated with foreign bankers to raise loans for the state.

The sale of offices and tax farming had paid for the wars of Louis XIV and his successors (Chaussinand-Nogaret 1970; Bien 1987), but they had consequences for class structure. I estimate there to have been more than 200,000 venal public offices. (See Chapter 11.) Office owning and tax farming involved virtually all wealthy families, cementing them into a massive "party of privilege" blocking state modernization (Matthews 1958: 249; Durand 1971: 282–362; Doyle 1980: 120). The bureaux de finances were transformed from judicial and administrative offices into lending institutions from the propertied to the crown (Bossenga 1986). This absolutism differed from Prussian or even Austrian absolutism. Its treasury had only 264 employees; Austrian equivalents in ministries and the state bank numbered in the thousands (Dickson 1987: I, 306–10). The French state elite was a monarch, a court, a few clerics, and a small administration at the center of sprawling party networks of privileged notables (the best account is of its Languedoc branch, in Beik 1985). Nobility and bourgeoisie merged into a "proprietory class," mostly noncapitalist, deriving most of its income from feudal dues, rents, offices, and annuities. Venality even fostered the "modern" cash economy, as offices were marketable commodities (Taylor 1967; Beik 1985: 13).

Because they shared privileges, merchants and manufacturers voiced little opposition to the nobility or commitment to alternative "capitalist" values. They wanted ennoblement, and the dowry system favored mésalliance between wealthy bourgeois and poor nobility (Barber 1955; Lucas 1973: 91). There was little sign of feudal old regime versus the bourgeoisie before the Revolution, no obvious bourgeois class identity or opposition, no "sharp clashes" between privileged and upwardly mobile families (as Goldstone 1991: 237 suggests) except for the army (whose more complex factionalisms are discussed later). Darnton claims a contemporary account of Montpellier reveals class tension. Its bourgeois author says wealth should be more significant than honor and mildly criticizes noble privileges. Yet he shows greater fear of the common people, "naturally bad, licentious, and inclined toward rioting and pillage" (1984: 128–30). The bourgeoisie was worming its way into segmental regime organizations, exhibiting "manipulative deference," seeking material advantage through acquiring privileges. "The quest for nobility was part of a bourgeois investment perspective," concludes Favier of a Gap merchant family (1987: 51; cf. Bonnin 1987). The quest for privilege stifled universal identities like class and nation.

For their part, nobles urbanized, distancing them from peasants. Some became rentier industrialists. More than half the forges and mines were owned (rarely managed) by aristocrats. This was now as much an aristocracy of wealth as of birth. Chaussinand-Nogaret (1985: 23–34) calculates that a quarter of noble families in 1789 had been ennobled since 1700, and probably two-thirds since 1600; adding that "a noble was now nothing but a commoner who had made it." Darnton (1984: 136–40) suggests they were becoming a little bourgeois, as fashion and cuisine became plainer. But the term "bourgeois" referred as much to people "living nobly" off rents, annuities, and offices as to merchants, tradesmen, and manufacturers. Taylor (1967) calculates that, even in commercial Bordeaux, the third estate contained eleven hundred nonnoble proprietors and professional men against seven hundred merchants and traders, many of them ennobled. Urban propertied classes were merging, not conflicting.

Rural life was more discordant. Old regime France had three kinds of exploitation. The oldest derived from the feudal mode of production: Landowners exploited peasants through rents and dues amid a hierarchy of birth and privilege. The second, politically determined, derived from the fiscal needs of late absolutism and was organized by privilege and corporations. Much of what we consider feudal was produced and sustained by the state (Bien 1987: 111). The word "feudalism" now came into use (spreading to other countries) as a term of abuse for this fusion of feudal and absolutist exploitation. The third was capitalist petty commodity production, often dominating production and markets but politically and socially subordinate to the first two (Dewald 1987). There was little large-scale capitalist production, so few farmers controlled the labor power of others (Cominel 1987). Land and produce, rarely labor, were commodities. Peasants and lords, and even many merchants, manufacturers, artisans, and workers, were bound into customary regulation of labor.

Rural capitalism now began to conflict with the other two kinds of exploitation. Pressured by expanding population and rising prices, peasants chafed at feudal-absolutist exploitation. They paid ancient feudal dues, now mainly in cash or crops rather than labor, and complied with the hated seigneurial monopolies, the *banalités* – obligations to use the seigneur's mill, oven, or press. The burden was not crushing unless poor harvests pushed them close to subsistence, as they did in 1787 and 1788. But France was not Eastern Europe. Serfdom, manorial estates, and corvée labor had almost disappeared. Almost all peasants were personally free and farmed and sold produce autonomously from their lord. These free petty commodity producers were then subjected to seigneurial privileges that were rooted in neither production nor local community relations. Except for the church – the greatest landholder in the country and entrenched in every village – there was little direct segmental power exercised over them, restraining class action. Privilege seemed to come from outside, from Paris and the court. As Barrington Moore (1973: 73) observed, discontent came from "their half-way position: they possessed the land without really owning it."

Rural class conflict was thus boiling up from its customary latent level. Maintaining the old regime's class crystallization of proprietorial privilege depended increasingly on external reinforcement, on three further crystallizations as politically absolutist, as militarist, and as ideologically Catholic. As long as the old regime held its own body politic, its right arm and its soul together, peasants, with only local class organization, could do little. Yet it would be a dangerous time for monarchical elite, proprietary class, officers, and clerics to squabble.

Ideological and military power in the old regime

Ideological power contributed to revolution in four stages. First, the regime lost authoritative control over most of its own networks of discursive literacy through the second half of the eighteenth century. Second, in the 1780s, the legal profession and the Enlightenment joined to espouse alternative ideological and political principles to those of the state elite. Third, suddenly from 1789, more popular ideological networks pushed this union Leftward, developing the dual organization of printed word and oral assembly that we saw emerge in the American Revolution. Fourth, the fusion of all these networks amid a crisis that practical politicians could not resolve produced a recourse to transcendent ideologies by which state and society could be reorganized. The role of ideologists escalated through all four stages.

As in other advanced eighteenth-century countries, basic signing literacy surged, reaching 70 percent to 80 percent among urban males by 1750. Discursive literacy grew even faster. The church sponsored most growth, employing schoolmasters and increasing church attendance among the masses. European churches began a local-regional revival, even while losing influence over states. But it was not one-way indoctrination. Priests and schoolmasters "gradually tended to secularize the morality they were teaching children and families" (Furet and Ozouf 1982: 80). Popular literacy was not directly subversive, because its messages were mainly religious and practical. But it was under less secure authoritative control.

Chapter 2 identifies two predominant later routes in the expansion of discursive literacy. Because France had a commercial economy and a large state and army, it combined both the commercial capitalist and the military statist route. The growth of trade and state – of the officer corps, civil officeholders, and semiofficial legal institutions – rapidly expanded secondary schooling, book and periodical publishing, sub-scription libraries, and academies (literary clubs). Media and messages under absolutism differed from constitutional regimes. Commerce and law were more integrated into the proprietary old regime; schooling was monopolized by the Catholic church, also entwined with the regime. This might seem effective authoritative control, but it also brought ideological problems into the regime itself.

The Enlightenment was long blamed by conservatives for fathering the Revolution. In *Les Misérables* Victor Hugo parodies them:

> I fell on the ground,
> It was Voltaire's fault,
> My nose in the water,
> It was Rousseau's fault.

But if the philosophes pushed, the regime pulled. The Enlightenment was half inside the regime. Almost all philosophes were born noble or bought themselves titles (Rousseau was exceptional). Many of their ideas – condemnation of feudalism, superstition, metaphysics, and Scholasticism, and the praise of reason – were current among educated people. Seven of the last eighteen finance ministers claimed to be partisans of the Enlightenment (Behrens 1967: 136). Though philosophes were persecuted and censored, they were capable of reversing this. They had Malesherbes in charge of censorship during 1750–63 and they captured the French Academy during 1760–72 (Gay 1967: I, 22–3, 76). Malesherbes claimed (as did other men of letters): "What the orators of Rome and Athens were, in the midst of a people *assembled*, men of letters are in the midst of a *dispersed* people" (Eisenstein 1986: 200; cf. Starobinski 1987). Philosophes strutted through aristocratic salons, including that of the duke of Orléans, the king's cousin. Madame de la Tour du Pin, lady-in-waiting to Queen Marie Antoinette, records princesses and duchesses styling themselves philosophes, which she explains meant "freethinkers" (1985: 81). Versailles lost cultural preeminence to Parisian salons (Lough 1960: chapter 8). Tension rose between the principles of the salons and the particularism, "luxury," and supposed "moral laxity" of the court. While the court and the king's council ruled regime politics, the salons and academies ruled its theory and morality. The Enlightenment was becoming the conscience of the regime, if not its heart. Modernization could be thought and valued; it was less easily done.

The *Encyclopédie* was the Enlightenment's manifesto. Its articles covered every branch of knowledge, arguing that everywhere human reason, "the organized habit of criticism," could defeat superstition, particularism, and privilege. Reason cultivated by education could establish a society governed by rational, universal principles, administered by merit. As Darnton's research (1979: esp. 273–99) reveals, such subversive ideas penetrated through the old regime. By 1789, fifteen thousand copies had been sold, with much better sales in older administrative towns with parlements than in ports or industrial towns, and among nobles and clergy than among tradesmen or manufacturers. Copies then spread downward – through bookclubs, accounting for half the sales – to lower lawyers, clerics, officials, and local notables servicing the regime rather than in trade or manufacturing.

Roche's study of provincial literary academies reveals a similar pattern. Twenty percent of academicians were from the first (clerical) estate, 37 percent from the second (noble) estate, and 43 percent were commoners of the third estate. Less than 4 percent of the commoners were in commerce or manufacturing, 29 percent lawyers and officials (35 percent of the nobles were officials), 23 percent lower clergy, 26 percent doctors and surgeons, and 18 percent simply men of independent means. Though women were active in salons, the clubs, academies, and Masonic Lodges were masculine. Thus the intelligentsia were "a service bourgeoisie everywhere assimilated into the consecrated social hierarchy" (Roche 1978: I, chapter 4, quote from 245). Expanding Masonic Lodges, predominantly discussion centers, had a similar composition except for fewer clergy because of mild anticlericalism (Le Bihan 1973: 473–80). The number of journals steadily increased (Censer and Popkin 1987: 18), but until the late 1780s, they portrayed an urban noble world, unlike their larger, more petit bourgeois English and American counterparts (Botein et al. 1981). Secondary education differed. According to Palmer (1985: 23): "The sons of noblemen and of tradesmen met in the same classroom." Thereafter they entered different cultural networks. But they would converse again in the Revolution.

These media espoused both modernization routes mentioned in Chapter 2: one state-led, the other embedded in civil society. Some philosophes praised monarchs embodying "benevolent absolutism." D'Alembert said that Voltaire's adulatory *Peter the Great* made him want to vomit, although d'Alembert himself received a French royal pension. The legislator should promulgate civil rights, patronize education and social welfare, and sweep away particularistic corporations and privileges. "Absolute government" was good, if it respected the law. Thus Voltaire supported monarchy against privilege and criticized the parlements (assemblies of lawyers) as archaic, selfish checks on efficient administration (Gay 1967: II, 67, 474). Yet the philosophes found it easier to apply this program to states of which they knew little (like Russia or Austria) than to their own venal court and administration. The French state required major overhaul in order to become benevolent absolutism.

The second Enlightenment program saw reason as decentralized in civil society. Education could enlighten men (and even women) by cultivating their inherent reason. Personal autonomy should be encouraged, merit rewarded, and economic, political, religious, and sexual freedoms cautiously increased. Most philosophes were paternalistic, wishing to lead the people gradually toward enlightenment. None believed in democracy. Most advocated Anglo-American constitutionalism. As all adults possessed a common humanity, all should have equal civil or "passive" citizenship. Literate, property-holding household heads possessing "independence" should have political or "active" citizenship now. To base rights on "rational" principles contradicted the actual society of orders and privilege: All should be equal before the law; all were eventually capable, through self-improvement, of political participation. The success of the American Revolution thus encouraged this civil society path to reform.

The monarchical elite was not blind to the ideological ferment within the regime. It censored. It incarcerated more than eight hundred authors, printers, and book and print sellers in the Bastille between 1600 and 1756 (Eisenstein 1986: 201). Most tacitly agreed to keep alternative ideologies from the masses. As Becker (1932: 31) remarked: "They courageously discussed atheism, but not before the servants." Absolutism had always considered secret decision making an essential prerogative. But the appearance of the term "public opinion" now presaged the possibility of government restrained by what Baker (1987: 246) optimistically terms "the politics of national consensus" (cf. Ozouf 1987). But there was no consensus. The regime no longer knew what to believe.

This was especially true in the church. The hierarchy opposed the Enlightenment's attack on its own wealth, corruption, and manipulation of superstition. Most philosophes endorsed Hume's description of religion as "the sick man's dream," which healthy, enlightened men could throw aside. Much of the church also chafed at court secularization, halfhearted censorship, and toleration of Protestants. It tacitly withdrew sacralization of royal authority (Julia 1987). Yet reason had also penetrated the church. Jansenist-Jesuit struggles had relativized doctrine, attacking the literal truth of the Bible and incorporating science into justifications of belief (Cassirer 1951: 140–84). Among the proprietary class church attendance fell after midcentury (Vovella 1984: 70–1). As most high prelates were aristocrats, nonattendance had unfortunate effects. Several archbishops (including two prominent ministers of state in the 1780s) no longer believed in God. Lower-down curés and schoolteachers resented the irreligion and privileges of aristocratic superiors without genuine religious qualifications (McManners 1969: 5–18). Discontent within the church was dangerous, for local segmental control over peasants depended critically on it. Secular modernization and Enlightenment ferment were dividing monarchy and church, weakening the immanent morale of regime and state. Their ideological power was wavering.

And so was their military power. Army modernization, essential for all states, produced conflicts. Although European regimes bickered over fiscal modernization, they quickly overhauled their armies. After the disasters of the Seven Years' War, French army tactics and techniques were reformed, noncommissioned officers and many junior officers became professional, and recruits now came disproportionately from the literate, skilled urban petite bourgeoisie. (See Chapter 12.) But offices remained venal, regiments were controlled by noble patrons and remained effectively independent, and there were many incompetent higher officers. Ministers of war aided by some generals tried to eliminate corruption and encourage professionalism.

The reform was divisive (Corvisier 1964; Bien 1974, 1979; Scott 1978: 4–45). Three regime factions possessed military privileges. Great nobles presented at court dominated the highest ranks; wealthy, recently ennobled men could buy rank; and old, often poor, noble families with a tradition of military service sought promotion using connections and experience. There was never much chance in any old regime that appointments and promotions might be on some direct measure of experience and merit. But the military experience of the third faction, the old nobility, offered an approximation to competence. Thus reform combined (bizarrely, to modern eyes) the abolition of venality with the Segur Decree of 1781, requiring four generations of nobility of anyone entering directly the officer corps (promotion from the ranks remained for a few *officiers de fortune*). This increased professionalism, but intensified the gap between officers and other ranks, simplified it into a quasi-class conflict between "birth" and "merit," and created enemies among both rich and commoners. Because officers and noncommissioned officers were literate, these conflicts were widely aired in pamphlets, books, and academies. The regime's right arm proved feeble in 1789.

Fiscal crisis and the growth of principled resistance

Army and church did not cause the struggles of 1788 and 1789. All they did was contribute to the regime's feeble response. The cause lay squarely in the crown's inability to solve its fiscal problems. Around the 1730s, finances had reached a tipping point. Now the costs of collecting taxes, of repaying loans made by tax farmers and financiers, and of extracting taxes amid privileged exemptions became a serious drain. The Seven Years' War (1757–63), a massive defeat, brought on crisis. Lacking universal taxation, the government borrowed, particularistically, at high cost and interest rates. Debt service rose from a prewar 30 percent of total revenue to more than 60 percent after the war (Riley 1986: 231). At this level, debt was self-sustaining, for the government could only pay for normal expenditures by further borrowing. This was the main problem, although the costs of the American Revolution worsened it. Between 1776 and 1787, only 24 percent of direct and indirect taxes raised reached the treasury; the rest was used to pay off accumulated debt, principally tax collectors' commissions.

Ministers now realized that the peasants had been pushed danger-ously near subsistence. From the late 1760s to the Revolution, ministers suggested reform schemes. Turgot, controller general during 1774–76, and Necker, controller general during 1777–81, reduced venal and tax offices, attempted to free transport and the grain trade from tax farmer control, and limited the autonomy of the GCF (the principal tax-farming company) (Bosher 1970: 90, 145–62). Privileges were the main problem, as Finance Minister Calonne explained to the Assembly of Notables in 1787:

In this vast kingdom it is impossible to take a step without finding different laws, contrary customs, privileges, exemptions . . . and this general disharmony complicates administration, interrupts it, clogs its wheels and multiplies expense and disorder everywhere. [Vovelle 1984: 76]

For half a century the state elite erratically attacked the party and class of privilege, its traditional pillar. The political unity of feudalism and absolutism and of the proprietorial and absolutist state crystal-lizations weakened, affecting also their ideological and military sup-ports. Reform ministers faced opposition from privileged proprietors in control of the parlements and the court. The king – and it must be counted as a necessary cause of the Revolution – dithered, caught between elite and party interests, an absolutist yet the protector of proprietorial rights. At each crisis he would first support reform and defy parlements, then bow to court intrigue, dismiss the reforming minister, and abort the reform plan.

Like his fellow executed monarchs, Louis has received a bad press. This was deserved after 1789, but before then he had had to cope with a severe institutional problem of state, unique among my five states. All states contain warring elites and parties. The question is whether they have means of resolving them. An extraordinary chief executive – in this period a Frederick William, a Bonaparte, or a Bismarck – might succeed. Louis was clearly not in their class, but not many chief executives are. Most states find more institutional solutions. They locate "sovereignty" in particular state institutions, so that decisions taken somewhere in the state may be authoritative. British parliamentary sovereignty is an obvious example. The United States developed complex, specialized sovereignties whose interrelations are specified by the Constitution and Supreme Court. We shall see that foreign policy was the Achilles' heel of sovereignty in such constitutional states.

But there was also an absolutist version of sovereignty. Eighteenth-century Prussian kings located it in the relations between the king and his ministers in a form often (though wrongly) called "bureaucratic." (See Chapter 13.) They were able to do this because ministers were really "party representatives" of the whole noble class. Though the Prussian king divided and ruled between ministers, and though court intrigue weaved through their relations, nonetheless most decisions made within these institutions would stick. The institutions would not falter until the late nineteenth century, when state functions would have greatly expanded. Even Austrian institutions possessed coherence by virtue of a fairly clear division between two levels of sovereignty, the royal and the provincial. Maria Theresa and Joseph II knew what institutions were theirs. But Louis faced institutional incoherence, with a proprietorial class whose factionalism pervaded almost every office of state. His ministers did not control their own departments (see Chapter 13), his legal officers belonged to autonomous corporate assemblies, and his church and army were divided. Louis's ditherings were understandable because they coincided with failure to institutionalize the conflict of elites and parties.

A consequence was that, from the 1750s on, Louis's ministers were abdicating their proclaimed reform program, the deficit worsened, and their incompetence was increasingly denounced. The monarchy repeatedly declared its intention of abolishing privileges but could not. The Prussian route, "conservative modernization from above," was blocked from within (Moore 1973: 109), by institutional incoherence. Thus the old regime could not implement the first "statist" Enlightenment program, and more of its members turned toward the second, civil society program, and toward representation.

Thus elite-party conflict became principled and centralized. Turgot was a leading philosophe, Necker's home an Enlightenment salon. Their regime opponents also grew principled. Private property, office holding, tax farming, and privilege had become entwined. A royal assault on one involved all. The bureaux des finances responded with outrage to reform: The crown was arbitrarily interfering with fundamental property rights and with local guarantees against despotism. Their language turned from defending particularistic privilege to appealing to fundamental laws and customs, and thence to enunciating the "imprescriptible" rights of property holders against despotism (Bossenga 1986). The parlements shifted their defenses, from ancient privileges to "liberties" to a single universal "liberty," acquiring brief popularity in the 1780s. Law was no longer a small corporation. Through the eighteenth century the profession more than doubled as it became the dominant route to office holding and as legal education broadened. Younger lawyers participated in Enlightenment discursive networks.

The lawyers who later became revolutionary leaders had already begun their old regime careers, buying the first offices off whose fruits they would live. But Robespierre, Bailly, Brissot, and Barère were also writing prize essays on the nature of truth, justice, and liberty for their local academies. Thompson (1936: 40) argued that the profession of law divided into two, the *gens de lettres* and the practical winners of cases, Robespierre being one of the former. But legal practice and social, philosophical, and aesthetic principles were fused. After a brilliant education, Robespierre took on cases defending the poor. This was common among lawyer-revolutionaries, indicating a social conscience developing alongside political theories.

Where did this come from? It was not class interest, for the young lawyers were from privileged families, enjoying the early stages of seemingly successful careers. There is no evidence they became embittered and radical because they were unsuccessful (as Goldstone 1991 suggests). Rather, their politics emerged through interaction between their practices and principles. Their practices widened as France became commercial and prosperous, involving peasants and urban classes in litigation (Kagan 1975: 54, 68). Their principles were influenced by paternalist morality, originating in the church, now carried by Enlightenment discursive infrastructures.

Thus, while practicing, Robespierre also attended an Arras salon discussing philosophy, aesthetics, and political reform. He began to think of himself as a writer after assisting an enlightened Arras lawyer defend against local superstition a man who had put up a lightning rod on his house. His brief was published in a periodical (he sent a copy to Benjamin Franklin), and he joined a literary club and the Academy of Arras, where he won prizes and was eventually elected director (Matrat 1971: 11–35). A youthful essay on criminal shame reveals Enlightenment influence and the origins of his Republican faith. He argued:

The mainspring of energy in a republic, as has been proved by [Montesquieu] is *vertu*, that is to say, political virtue, which is simply the love of one's laws and of one's country. . . . A man of high principle will be ready to sacrifice to the State his wealth, his life, his very self – everything, indeed, except his honour.

Robespierre was ready for the "Republic of Virtue," but he was less clear about how to create men of virtue, relying lamely on Enlightenment idealism: "Reason and eloquence – these are the weapons with which to attack . . . prejudice" (Thompson 1936: 23–4).

A less high-minded motive was that of Vadier, the future police chief of the Revolution's Committee of General Security (Lyons 1977; Tournier n.d.). Vadier's politics developed partly from the factional fighting of local landowning lawyer notables. The Vadiers were the "outs" and the Darmaings the "ins" of small-town Pamiers, in the Pyrenean foothills. Thus, says Lyons, Vadier became a revolutionary in order to guillotine the Darmaings (which he did). Yet this is too cynical. After a provincial religious and legal education, Vadier's intellectual horizons expanded during a spell in the army. He returned to Pamiers, read Voltaire, Hume, and the *Encyclopédie*, and attained local prominence after he took on a case involving a local hospital in which he championed the poor. As a local judge he was considered liberal. Though a man of few words and fewer speeches, Vadier demonstrated a political conscience, narrowly securing his election to the Estates General. He signed the Tennis Court Oath and willingly surrendered his family's privileges. He moved Left while the Darmaings became Rightists. Through the Revolution local "in" and "out" factional politics became far more principled than in England and more than in America.

Enlightened lawyers like Robespierre and mildly malcontented lawyers like Vadier were not yet thinking as revolutionaries. But the monarchy's inept offensive was crystallizing old regime tensions from Paris to Pamiers, pushing lawyers gradually toward asserting principles. Similarly, philosophes were moving away from the monarchy. Diderot had first supported the attack on parlement privileges, then believed it a threat to liberty (Gay 1967: II, 474). Reformers turned from the statist to the civil society route to modernization. The monarchy became isolated as Enlightenment and law joined forces to lead an increasingly principled old regime movement claiming to speak for the "people," demanding representation. On the fringes were radical journalists and lawyers like Marat and Brissot, ready to replace old regime with principled blueprints. In 1780, Brissot replied to a friend who urged that change be built on present practice: "You have a poor idea of my judgement if you think I would prefer to accept present-day practice, which I know too well. However monstrous the new theories may be, they will never equal practice in absurdity and atrocity" (Palmer 1959: I, 261). Few yet listened to Brissot. They would later.

In 1787, a desperate finance minister, Calonne, summoned an ad hoc Assembly of Notables. There had been peace for four years and Necker, his predecessor, had published optimistic fiscal accounts (to keep up the regime's credit rating). Therefore, the assembly was shocked by the size of the deficit. Members demanded to see the books, refused to believe them, and through court intrigue, forced Calonne's dismissal. His successor, the unbelieving Archbishop Lomenie de Brienne, was pressured by shortage of funds. He sought to steal the cause of representation. He appealed beyond the highly privileged Notables by summoning the only representative assembly France had known, the antique Estates General. The crown was pursuing absolutist divide-and-rule tactics into the uncharted waters of representative government. Each local community was also invited, as in ancient tradition, to send written grievances to Paris. Both tactics had unintended consequences. Had the regime realized these in advance, it would have done differently. The French monarchy could have survived, as the Prussian monarchy did, by reforming its administration along more universalistic principles.

The grievances were published in *cahiers de doléance*, "grievance books," drawn up by local representatives of each estate (Taylor 1972; Chartier 1981; Chaussinand-Nogaret 1985: 139–65; and, on peasants, Gauthier 1977: 131–44). Some were written at a "primary" meeting, others were carried forward for discussion at district, *bailliage*, meetings, and these also elected representatives to the Estates General. This unexpectedly started a "national" political process with its own dynamic. It hastened the expression of ideological principle and the fusion of three communications infrastructures that eventually provided an ideological, revolutionary elite: regime enlightenment, political-rights lawyers, and literacy diffused among the petite bourgeoisie, lower clergy, and upper peasantry. Third estate assemblies brought in bourgeoisie and upper peasantry, but drafting was mainly by lawyers and royal officials. There seemed little to worry the regime – grievances would be in the hands of its own officials. It suspended censorship to allow circulation of the *cahiers*. Periodicals and newspapers proliferated. The ideological infrastructures were streaming beyond authoritative control.

Most of the *cahiers* survive. Their content did not seem very bad news for the regime. Most professed loyalty to the king and complained about local injustices without referring to general principles. Peasants railed at the privileges of lords and church and against taxes. Noble and third estate *cahiers* complained of royal arbitrariness. But about half the *bailliage* documents, more in Paris and major towns, referred to a more principled reform program: generally asking for regular meetings of the Estates General and sometimes for a written constitution, freedom of the press, and equality of tax burdens. There is no hint of democracy or revolution, and their language was more that of old regime lawyers than of philosophes.

Nevertheless, many of the *cahiers* drafted after *bailliage* meetings reveal the universalizing of political discourse and the underground growth of capitalism and nation. Peasants complained that privilege and feudalism were remnants of a barbaric past, an offense against natural equality and economic development. Most *cahiers* accepted France as a single country and people or "nation" whose natural rights, including consent to taxation, should be respected. The word "nation" had undergone a similar transformation that comparable fiscal politics had wrought in England, the Netherlands, and Hungary. Originally meaning a people of the same origin – united by blood but not necessarily by territorial or political ties – it was now proclaimed by disaffected privileged taxpayers claiming "national liberties" based on ancient constitutions (Dann 1988: 4–7).

The main reform instrument was supposedly the Estates General, ancient but hardly traditional. Not having met since 1614, nobody knew how to control it. Its antique rules proved to have two "institutional statist" unintended consequences. First, everyone knew it had three estates, but who was to be eligible for each, and how should they vote? Many feared the king would establish arbitrary rules, so the Parlement of Paris declared for the rules of 1614. This was accepted before its consequences were realized. But the 1614 rules confined membership of the noble second estate to the old "nobility of the sword." France was vastly more developed in 1789 than in 1614. Many proprietors of substance were not noble, and many ennobled in the eighteenth century were ineligible for the second estate. An unexpected political divide emerged among old regime proprietors, as it was revealed that only a minority were eligible (Lucas 1973: 120–1; Goldstone 1991: 243–7 – though he suggests their faction fighting had begun earlier). Aristocracy and clergy were granted corporate political powers. At a stroke feudalism versus the bourgeoisie was given some political reality, centralized in Versailles.

Some critics demanded more third estate representatives; others, that the estates be merged into one assembly. This was too radical, but Necker (back in favor) persuaded the king to enlarge the third estate so as to represent proprietors better and to act as a counterweight to the first two, should he need to divide and rule. Thus its numbers exceeded those of the other two estates combined, though the three met separately. It seemed a reasonable compromise, but it increased the volume of the third estate voice protesting at suddenly entrenched privileges.

Second, no one foresaw the effects of open elections. In the first estate curés outvoted prelates and supplied most representatives, including many malcontents. Second estate elections were unexpectedly

Table 6.1. *Percentage of pre-1789 occupations of French revolutionaries*

	Crown officials	Independent lawyers	Other professionals	Business, trade, agriculture	Private means or unknown	Total %	N
1. National Assembly, 1789	49	23	7	20	—	100	648
2. Constituent Assembly activists, 1789	44	33	16	6	—	100	62
3. Constituent Assembly unwavering revolutionaries 1789–91	23	26	18	20	12	100	287
4. National Convention, 1792–4	27	27	24	15	7	100	749
5. National Convention activists, 1792–4							
5(a). Prominent in Kuscinski	23	27	43	6	3	100	162
5(b). Members of CPS, core members of CGS, or executed 1792–94	25	26	38	7	4	100	80

Note: "National Assembly" and "Constituent Assembly" essentially refer to the same body, meeting from June 1789, restyling itself the Legislative Assembly in October 1790, and replaced by the National Convention in September 1792. The convention was finally dissolved in October 1795.

Sources:

1, 2: Lemay (1977), who probably includes those of private means in "agriculture."

3: Named in a document of 1792, *Le Véritable Portrait de nos Législateurs*, as "patriots who have not varied" over the period 1789–91. Data supplied in Dawson (1972: 238–9), who attributes it speculatively to the deputy Alquier. However, the memoirs of the patriot deputy Prieur de la Marne attribute it to Dubois-Crancé.

4: Patrick (1972: 260), using Kuscinski's (1916) biographies.

5a: Those *conventionnels* whose biographies are given two or more column space by Kuscinski (plus Robespierre, omitted by Kuscinski).

5b: All 23 members of the Committee of Public Safety (CPS), the 36 longest-serving members of the Committee of General Security (CGS) (see Patrick 1972: 374–5), and those *conventionnels* guillotined or murdered between 1792 and 1794 (the leading Dantonists and Girondists, plus Philippe Egalité, formerly the duke of Orléans).

dominated by conservatives, leaving the vocal, urban, Enlightened nobles only about a third in the estate. These two estates were factionalized, and the gap between second estate nobles and their coproprietors in the third estate had widened. Underlying their factionalism was the king's attempt to carry absolutist divide-and-rule segmental tactics into uncharted representative terrain. The parlements and aristocracy had resisted particularism. This produced open conflict with the universalism now forced on the "excluded" third estate, which was now potentially "bourgeois." It was looking a bit more like class struggle even though it had been produced by old regime parties.

The emergence of the ideological elite

The third estate, however, did not yet seem much of a class or a threat. The emerging bourgeoisie was too much entwined with the old regime to generate independent consciousness or organization and so the elections did not produce a bourgeois opposition. This is evident in the backgrounds of the Revolution's elected representatives. Table 6.1 analyzes the pre-1789 occupations of the revolutionary assemblies. Its first row categorizes the backgrounds of third estate deputies (after they had turned themselves into the National Assembly in late June 1789).

Half the deputies were crown officials, normally legal officers of the local *bailliages*. A quarter were lawyers in independent practice. At least 72 percent had received legal training. There were 14 percent engaged in private business or trade and only 6 percent (all large farmers) in agriculture, which represented three-quarters of the French population. The 7 percent who were "other professionals" were a disparate collection of doctors, military officers, academics, and philosophes. Cobban (1964: 59–61) used figures like these to stand class theories on their head: The Revolution was made not by the bourgeoisie but by a class of officials and lawyers embittered at declining social and economic status. Goldstone (1991: 247–9) has, alternatively, credited the Revolution to youthful elites whose "rush for credentials" had resulted in "blocked mobility." But the evidence supports neither suggestion. Third estate deputies were freely elected, usually without great conflict, by the entire propertied classes. Among the deputies were members of the most celebrated legal families of France. Lawyers who joined the Revolution did not differ significantly in terms of age, family ties, and wealth from those who did not (Seligman 1913: I. 118–86; Berlanstein 1976: 177–82; Fitzsimmons 1987: 34–8).

Who would voters, without prior electoral experience, choose to represent them? Reasonably enough, they went for locally prominent men with relevant skills. First, they chose lawyers holding public office, the persons with greatest experience of public duties and, under absolutism, the closest thing to politicians. They had just become prominent doing what they could do best: draft documents of complaint (the *cahiers*). A second valued skill, as an ideologist, was also emerging, exemplified by Robespierre – not yet a radical orator but a reformer prominent in academies and literate salons, practiced in their rhetorical techniques. The electorate had already been considering issues of principle as *cahier* meetings were succeeded by debates over how the estates should meet. Almost all deputies arrived in Paris favoring reforms, affected by alternative political principles. Who better to deliberate principle than prize essay contestants from respectable families – like Robespierre?

There had been what Doyle (1980: 155) terms "a landslide victory for the noncommercial, professional and proprietary bourgeoisie." Cobban was right: A Marxian-type bourgeoisie did not lead the Revolution. Right up to 1794, from Right to Left (terms invented from the seating plan of the National Assembly), from constitutional monarchists and Thermidorians on the Right, through the Center of Brissotins and Girondists, to Leftist Jacobins and *enragés*, the leaders were not a cross section of the bourgeoisie, the petite bourgeoisie, or any class fraction. The fourth row of Table 6.1 shows that directly productive and commercial classes remained only 15 percent of elected deputies in the 1792 National Convention – predominantly businessmen plus a few farmers. Only a handful of artisans and petite bourgeois entered the Constituent Assembly despite their providing the shock troops of the Revolution. These classes provided even fewer leaders, as rows 2 and 4 of Table 6.1 reveal. Sixty-two National Assembly deputies are classified as activists by Lemay (she does not explain how she measured activism). Farmers, traders, and merchants comprised only 6 percent of these. I estimate they made up 20 percent of the revolutionary deputy Dubois-Crancé's list of "patriots who have not varied" in their support of the Revolution between 1789 and 1791. Perhaps here was the core of a revolutionary bourgeois-peasant movement. Yet, in the National Convention, they then declined to only 3 percent to 4 percent of activists on both measures used in rows 5(a) and 5(b).

So who were most of the revolutionary leaders? The lawyers and officials who had stumbled into revolution remained important, though Table 6.1 shows their combined weight dropped from 72 percent to 54 percent in the National Convention. Pre-revolutionary officials declined most, from 49 percent to 27 percent (almost all legal officers). The table may exaggerate the shift by analyzing only pre-1789 occupations, as some new leaders made their way into the National Convention after service in Revolutionary offices. If we include post-1789 occupations, the proportion of officials rises from 27 percent to at least 43 percent while independent lawyers drop to under 5 percent (estimates kindly supplied by Ted Margadant from ongoing research).

Lawyers were now joined by other learned professions, contributing 24 percent of the National Convention and including few post-1789 officials. Among them were 55 clerics, 46 doctors, 41 academics and literary figures, and 36 military officers. Independent advocates and other learned professions contributed even more activists. In the National Assembly, they provided half the activists (as classified by Lemay) though only 30 percent of members, increasing in the National Convention to two-thirds on both measures. The other learned professions now provided about 40 percent of activists on their own. Among them writers and clerics were predominating over more technical professions like law and the military. These trends are especially marked among *conventionnels* from Paris and surrounding *départements*. Leadership had shifted, as legal officials declined and ideologists increased. "The men of the conference room" gave way to the "men of the podium" (Dawson 1972: 125), as rhetorical persuasion replaced factional fighting among officials.

How many of them participated in discursive Enlightenment networks of the printed word? The figures that follow are bound to be underestimates of works and activities many of which have not survived. Masonic membership lists reveal a substantial, though hardly overwhelming, presence of Freemasons among the leaders. In the Estates General, they comprised 28 percent of the second, noble, estate, as compared to 17 percent to 19 percent among the third estate and only 6 percent in the clergy (Freemasonry was anticlerical). These are Lamarque's figures (1981). He has not collected systematic data for the National Convention but provisionally puts Masons at 15 percent of membership. I find Masons comprise at least 20 percent of both my two groups of activist *conventionnels*.

I also investigated *conventionnels'* publications, starting from Kuscinski's monumental *Dictionnaire des Conventionnels* (1916), which lists most of the known published works of the members of the National Convention. I supplemented him with numerous autobiographies and biographies of the revolutionaries. I ignored memoirs and published works that were merely political commentaries on the issues of the day – although Darnton (1987) argues that even the political publications of two *conventionnels*, Rivard and Fabre d'Eglantine, exemplified literary genres and the cult of absolute virtues more than they did practical politics. I have not restricted publications

Table 6.2. *Percentage of* conventionnels *known to have published cultural, social, or scientific works*

Publishing	Percentage	Total
1. National Convention, 1792–4	23	892
2. National Convention activists (Kuscinski)	56	162
3. National Convention activists (CPS, CGS, executed)[a]	58	80

[a] See note 5b in Table 6.1.
Source: Kuscinski (1916) and numerous memoirs and biographies.

to pre-1789. How many *conventionnels* published at any time scientific, cultural, or social works indicating intellectual interests similar in breadth to the concerns of the Enlightenment? The results are in Table 6.2, row 1. Again, they must be a severe underestimate.

At least one-quarter of the National Convention deputies published works indicating broad intellectual interests. Some indicate professional learning. Arbogast's *Essay on the New Principles of Differential Equations . . .* and Barailon's *Observations on a Type of Epilepsy . . .* are the works of a mathematician and a doctor. But we may nonetheless ask why such publications seem to amount to a qualification for office. Their volume was far in excess of comparable works by members of modern assemblies like the U.S. Congress or the British House of Commons. Other works were more general. Some wrote about almost everything under the sun, like Bonet de Treyches in his *General and Perpetual Peace Between Nations Founded on Natural Law* or Bonnemain in his *Republican Institutions, or the Analytical Development of the Natural Civil and Political Faculties of Man.* Others generalized out from politics, like Bresson's *Reflections on the Bases of a Constitution*, or wrote about earlier philosophers – as Deleyre on Bacon and Montesquieu. Some wrote about the arts, like Eschasseriaux in his *Opinion on Theatres and the Encouragement of Dramatic Art*, or Bouquier in his *Epistle to M. Vernet, Painter to the King*. Some wrote fictional works: Himbert's tragedy *The Death of Henry of Guise*, or Deville's *Fables*. These *conventionnels* were Enlightenment underlaborers.

These were all "backbenchers," whose politics were dwarfed by deputies like Brissot or Robespierre and whose oeuvres were dwarfed by deputies like the philosopher Condorcet or the painter David. But was prominence related to breadth of intellectual interests? Did activists publish more? They did. Rows 2 and 3 in Table 6.2 indicate that more than half the activists, more than twice the proportion among the rank and file, published nonpolitical works. But, it is easier to discover the achievements of leaders than those of back-benchers. I have not found any published works by Merlin de Thionville other than a memoir. Yet he was a professor of Latin, mixed with philosophes, and became a Freemason. Did he really write nothing cultural himself? Did not Pinet or Petit or Reubell, whose library had 1,500 books (and whose biographer, Homan 1971 is silent on this matter)? Perhaps all of them contributed essays to journals or published poems at their own expense. But I found nothing in the libraries of London and Los Angeles (extensive research in France might reveal otherwise), and so I have counted these men as non-publishers. We know most about the greatest leaders, the "twelve who ruled," the core members of the Committee of Public Safety ruling France from 1793 to 1794. Table 6.3 contains their curricula vitae.

No fewer than 11 of the 12 – Lindet is the exception – wrote for publication on nonpolitical matters. Even the committee's administrative workhorses – Couthon, the Prieurs, and Carnot, the "organizer of victory" – were academicians with broad-ranging cultural interests. Even the youngest, Saint-Just, only twenty-two in 1789, had rushed into enlightened print. The twelve amount to a fine "Department of Western Civilization"! Just like the members of a modern department, no one two centuries later would read any of their works had their authors not become world-historical terrorists. By 1789, only Saint-André had ever engaged in trade (unsuccessfully), and none had tried production. They were comfortably off, living from rents, pensions, and offices – middling members of the old regime. Their other common identity was that "all twelve were intellectuals . . . steeped in the philosophy of the eighteenth century" (Palmer 1941: 18).

Either the trend revealed is genuine – the more prominent the leader, the more his qualifications for office included being an Enlightenment intellectual – or the trend is an artifact and fuller research would reveal virtually all *conventionnels* as Enlightenment activists. Even the few merchants and manufacturers included "cultural capitalists," drawn from printing, or from consumer industries whose premises were revolutionary discussion centers and whence crowds would emerge – most prominently the brewer Santerre and the butcher Legendre. Virtually all *conventionnels* had income from property, including venal offices. They did not work full time in the modern sense, but had leisure to write pamphlets and essays and orate in assemblies.

Either way, revolutionary leaders constituted an ideological elite, the shock troops of two major eighteenth-century ideological power networks, the profession of law and the circulation of the discursive

Table 6.3. *Cultural activities of the "twelve who ruled" (pre-1789 unless otherwise stated)*

Robespierre	Independent lawyer. President, Academy of Arras; wrote at least three essays for academy prizes (awarded one second prize) plus an unpublished poem on beauty.
Saint-Just	Law student. Published *Organt*, a lengthy, satirical, sexy epic poem.
Barère	Lawyer, then judge. Leading member of Academy of Floral Games, Toulouse; wrote numerous essays on legal and penal reform and on Rousseau (one comparing *La Nouvelle Héloise* to Richardson's *Clarissa*); won an academy prize. Freemason.
Carnot	Army officer. Active in Academy of Arras. Published songs, poems, *Essay on Machines*, *Eulogy to Vauban*, and a scheme for army reorganization.
Billaud-Varenne	Professor. Active in academies; published numerous plays (e.g., *Women, As She No Longer Exists*) and a polemic against the church, *Last Blow Against the Prejudiced and Superstition*. Published *Regenerative Principles of the Social System* (1795).
Hérault de Séchelles	Nobleman and judge. Active in literary salons and academies; published *Reflections on Declamation*, *A Theory of Ambition*, travel books, and a book on the geologist Buffon.
Collot d'Herbois	Actor-director-impresario. Published many plays (e.g., *Lucy, or Imprudent Parents*, *The Peasant Magistrate*, *The Good Angevin*).
Jeanbon Saint-André	Sea captain, then Protestant pastor. Published sermons and *Considerations on the Civil Organization of the Protestant Churches*. Member of Academy of Montauban. Freemason.
Couthon	Independent lawyer. Active in Academy of Clermont-Ferrand, entered prize competitions, gave lauded "Discourse on Patience." Published a political comedy in two acts, *The Aristocratic Convert*. Freemason.
Prieur of the Côte-d'Or	Army officer. Member of Academy of Dijon and Paris Society of Natural History. Published articles in *Annals of Chemistry* and *Journal de l'Ecole Polytechnique*. Later wrote on military strategy and *Of the Decomposition of Light Into its Most Simple Elements*.
Prieur of the Marne	Independent lawyer. Academy member. Freemason. Later in exile wrote *Study of the Flemish Language*, a history of Freemasonry, a *Dictionary of Law*, and numerous poems.
Lindet	Prosecutor. No known cultural activities before 1789, beyond local publication of a speech advocating reform. Later published *Memoirs* and *Essay on Public Credit and Subsistence*.

printed word. As the Revolution developed, Enlightenment principles began to predominate over the "semiprinciples" of the law (a distinction explained in Chapter 7). The elite had distinct "ideal interests" (to use Weber's term). Lawyers turned against the king, generalizing legal precepts into political principles; men of letters believed reason could reconstruct state and society. They purveyed Enlightenment ideas in the prose style of the old regime. Speeches in revolutionary assemblies were written down ahead of time, followed Quintilian's rules of argument and classical rhetorical techniques, paradigms, and examples (Hunt 1984: 33). The enlightened leaders were obsessed with *vertu*, political virtue. They risked lives on political rather than economic issues. Against king and particularistic privilege they counterposed the "rights of man and the citizen," "justice," "liberty, equality, fraternity," and citizenship for the "people" and "nation." Networks of discursive literacy throughout Europe were extending the potential span of the "nation" from the privileged to all with property and education. In a fight against privilege, third estate leaders extended it further downward. People and nation were one, as Rousseau had uniquely argued. The old regime motto *"Un roi, une foi, une loi"* (One king, one faith, one law) was replaced by *"La Nation, la loi, le roi"* – with only the Nation capitalized (Godechot 1973, 1988).

The leaders mixed values and norms with fact – Hunt's "politics of authentic emotions." The Jacobins expressed the "flaming sense of the immediacy of the ideal," as Brinton (1930) put it. Robespierre and Saint-Just declaimed virtue and purity as their political and economic philosophy. Virtue and the Terror eventually merged. Saint-Just apparently believed moderates carping at the Terror were financially and sexually corrupt: "One would think that each one, frightened by his conscience and the inflexibility of the laws, said to himself: We are not virtuous enough to be so terrible; philosophic legislators, take pity on my weakness; I dare not say to you, I am corrupt; I prefer to say to you, you are cruel!" (Curtis 1973: 189).

Saint-Just believed his moralizing perorations. A trimmer like Barère probably did not, but he made regular reports from the Committee of Public Safety to the National Convention in this vein: "The Committee is busy with a vast plan of regeneration, the result of which would banish from the Republic both immorality and prejudice, superstition and atheism. . . . We must found the Republic on principles and morality. If you lend it your support, it will dedicate itself to the great design" (Gershoy 1962: 226).

Some revolutionaries believed, others found it useful to believe, in the "Republic of Virtue." Elevation of moral principles is not found in all revolutions. The Bolsheviks claimed scientific laws, but their moral principles (notably comradeship) came directly from their "scientific" theory of class struggle. French revolutionaries differed: They came out of the Enlightenment as a fusion of religion, science, philosophy, and the arts. That is the significance of the essays and poetry of Robespierre, Saint-Just, Collot d'Herbois, and the rest. There was an ideological causal chain from the church to Enlightenment academies to "Republic of Virtue." Practical politicians of royal court, law courts, and streets had to come to terms with its power to morally inspire and coerce.

Did the ideological elite also represent the bourgeoisie? Narrative histories persistently describe the leaders during 1789–92 as the "bourgeoisie" or as representing bourgeois class fractions (Furet and Richet 1970; Boiloiseau 1983; Vovelle 1984). Indeed, provincial revolutionary cadres were becoming bourgeois. In 1789, royal municipal administration was replaced by ad hoc permanent committees dominated by merchants and lawyers. Then came a second wave, replacing lawyers with lesser merchants and shopkeepers, artisan masters, and lesser professionals like schoolteachers and barber-surgeons. By 1791, most city councils were dominated by whoever ran the local economy, plus literate professionals; and rural towns, by small farmers, artisans, shopkeepers, and increasingly schoolteachers (Hunt 1984: 149–79). Provincial politics reflected class structure more directly than did national politics. Even national leaders often mouthed bourgeois slogans. They favored merit and work over privilege, universalism over particularism, laissez-faire over mercantilism and monopoly. Above all, they believed in absolute private property, to be defended against privileged and propertyless alike.

For a long time, though, the elite were unaware of the class forces emerging around and through their power. That is perhaps the main reason that such propertied men nevertheless led a genuine revolution. They began to identify quasi-class actors: court and aristocracy, bourgeois notables, and the "people" (a combination of petite bourgeoisie and crowd). But they did not form the obvious class alliance. Rightists like Ferrières, Malouet, and Mirabeau did seek mild reform to cement a "party of order" between court and notables against the people. Even Leftists like Barnave and Robespierre at this stage wanted more radical reform to ally the whole bourgeoisie against both court and mob. Right and Left differed in their assessments of the threats from court and streets. What was uniquely revolutionary about France was that from 1789 up until 1794 most political leaders feared the streets less than the court. Even the choice of venue for the Constituent Assembly revealed this: The clamor of the Parisian gallery was preferred to the intrigue of the Versailles court. Unlike in Britain, the old regime–bourgeois party of order did not prevail.

Ideological principles and class strengthened as a result of a downward spiral of practical politics. The ineffective hostility of king and aristocracy escalated moral principles and class ideology. An emerging bourgeoisie was goaded by old regime intransigence and led by the ideological elite toward defending capitalism against feudalism. Without these two political and ideological power processes the French bourgeoisie could have continued as a latent class, enmeshed in segmental old regime organization. Lucas (1973: 126) has observed that "the Revolution made the bourgeoisie even if it was not made by the bourgeoisie." More precisely: A political opponent and an ideological leadership made revolution and bourgeoisie.

As soon as the Estates General assembled in Paris at the beginning of May 1789, the king's ministers disappointed reformers. The crisis was fiscal, they argued, and the estates should discuss only that in their separate assemblies. The crown produced no reform plan from now to its fall. The king appeared deaf to the pleas of the constitutional monarchists "to place yourself at the head of the general will," that is, to head a national party of order. His failure doomed them, and himself.

The first clash was over whether the estates should meet separately or together. A group of lawyers and men of letters, styling themselves the Commons after the British model, argued that, since the nation was indivisible, the estates should be merged. Votes revealed nobles opposed three to one to merger and beginning to rally around the king. The clergy proved the weak link. Many of the lower clergy were closer to their parishioners than to the hierarchy. As one pamphlet argued:

It is a mistake to attribute a united *esprit de corps* to the clergy. . . . Why talk of three orders of citizens? Two suffice. . . . [E]veryone is enlisted under one of two banners – nobility and commons. [These] are the only rallying cries dividing Frenchmen. Like the country itself, the clergy is divided. . . . The *curé* is a man of the people. [McManners 1969: 18]

From June 13 on, clerics drifted over to the third estate, which renamed itself the National Assembly on June 17. On June 19, the clergy voted narrowly to join the National Assembly. The king asked whether a disaffected army would repress a body called the "Assembled Nation," led by self-styled "patriots." His generals counseled caution. As Enlightened nobles also drifted over, Louis appeared to give in, advising all nobles and clerics to join the National Assembly. The old regime had caved in before the revolutionaries had really attacked it, and before the bourgeoisie became conscious.

But king and court were not sincere. In early July, twenty thousand troops were assembled around Paris (Scott 1978: 46–80). Yet the soldiers and noncommissioned officers saw more of civilians than of their noble officers. Half the officers were on leave, as was the custom in 1789 and, incredibly, 1790. Most soldiers were literate and were reading Parisian pamphlets. The officers advised it would be wiser to move French regiments *away* from Paris! Foreign regiments seemed loyal. But after July 14 (the storming of the Bastille), the crowd and the new Paris municipal authority were armed and stiffened by army deserters. To use foreign regiments against citizen militias in the Paris streets seemed politically risky (though if the king was unprepared to compromise, this was the only alternative). The regime's military power melted away and political and ideological power could remain primary.

On August 4, 1789, the National Assembly voted almost unanimously "to destroy entirely the feudal regime." Noble after noble rose, amid great enthusiasm, to propose the abolition of yet more feudal dues and privileges. The scene has entranced historians. Sewell (1985) argues that it was a sudden emotional statement of principle, which, once offered, constrained practical politics by the need to be consistent with the metaphysical "natural, inalienable and sacred rights of man" as promulgated in the Declaration of Rights. Cynics note that nobles proposed the abolition of their neighbors' privileges. Emotions may have been genuine and surprising, but the stage had also been set by third estate "patriots" scheming with Enlightened nobles, pressured by urban mob and peasant revolt (discussed later). Reform was needed to head off anarchy. They agreed that nobles should do the talking so that class hostility would not mar the unity of the nation.

Their expectations were far exceeded. The ideological elite discovered its basic power technique: moral persuasion to evoke a grand declaration of principle, which then proved coercive and self-fulfilling. Popular pressure ensured that later "betrayal" would risk dignity, position, even life. The leaders did not anticipate just how successful a strategy it would be. The renunciation was practical politics – a solution to fiscal crisis and peasant insurrection. But its content came straight out of the Enlightenment: the end of feudalism, and the denunciation of privilege and localism as barriers to the *nation une et indivisible*. The "nation" and "feudalism" had been imaginatively created, the first as moral and unifying, the second as immoral and divisive. The boundaries of pragmatic alliances were now redrawn. Instead of all three estates being natural allies (with the king) against the propertyless, they had divided into the privileged versus the nation – with an ambiguous lower boundary. The principled nation had emerged interstitially.

As Fitzsimmons (1987: 41) notes, principle had its own momentum: It abolished corporate bodies like the Order of Barristers even though there was no apparent hostility to the order. It was a statement of principle in its dual sense, evoking a new social and moral order. The emotions did not come merely from assembly speakers but from dynamic interaction between their words, the slogans of emergent discursive networks (centered on clubs, pamphlets, and newspapers), and the slogans shouted by crowds outside. After the National Assembly moved from Versailles to Paris in October, interaction intensified. The galleries – partly paid claques, partly representing popular forces outside – intervened in debates. Partly by accident, revolutionary leaders discovered that principled slogans could forge emotional links between disparate power actors. But those who proclaimed them were forced past points of no return – and the privileged into political oblivion. Ideological power techniques provided a transcendent moment. Principle was an emergent property of revolutionary politics, an unintended consequence of action.

Louis stood out, declaring "I will never allow *my* clergy and *my* nobility to be stripped of their assets." Louis was right in his analysis of what was going on, wrong in his belief that he could stop it. The clergy were swiftly stripped. By October the sale of church property was binding many families of wealth, including rich peasants, to the Revolution. But the patriots unwisely displayed their Enlightenment secularism, in November 1790 compelling clerics to take an oath of loyalty to the nation, above church or pope. Half (two-thirds of the assembly's clerical members) refused to swear. The church split in two – the Revolution's "constitutional church" versus the "nonjuring" counterrevolutionary church. Most local clergy turned toward counterrevolution, the more effective now that they had no privileges alienating them from peasants. Nobles were not so swiftly dispossessed, but their powers faded. They were supposed to receive compensation for loss of privilege, but peasant control of the countryside made this a dead letter. Conservative nobles retired to their estates or emigrated to organize counterrevolution. Liberal nobles became less prominent in the Constituent Assembly and had no separate role in the Assembly elected in October 1791.

Revolution becomes class struggle

The key to the revolutionary process after 1790 was interaction among five power actors. Four began to approximate to classes – the old regime, with its core at court; the substantial bourgeoisie; the petite bourgeoisie, with its sans-culotte core, and the peasantry – though all resulted from distinctly political power processes. Their conflict led to the breakup into Right and Left factions of the fifth power actor, the ideological elite who initially led the Revolution. I begin with the old regime.

By mid-1790, there were dual state institutions. Monarch, aristocracy, and clerical hierarchy had lost control of the new institutions of elections, assemblies, and clubs. They retreated into the traditional one, court intrigue. The king and his family feigned compliance with the Revolution and covertly financed and negotiated with moderates from Mirabeau and LaFayette to the Brissotins and Danton. None of this was sincere, for the king actually saw foreign armed intervention as his deliverance and schemed with aristocratic emissaries to raise provincial and foreign armies. One court faction, the Austrian committee around the queen, was believed especially intransigent. Many plots were revealed, many more suspected. Furet (1978) argues that the plot became the central myth of the Revolution, but this is misleading – and hardly ideologically innocent. The plot was not invented. The revolutionaries had to cope with real attempts by the court to split them, to raise revolt in the provinces, and to get armed intervention by the princes of Europe.

These plots also contrasted with the genuine openness and "morality" of the Revolution's own infrastructures: freedom of speech in the assembly (imitated in assemblies and clubs throughout France) and freedom of the press. These really did involve the "people," extending beyond the men of property to embrace the populace. The intrigues of the king and aristocracy were demonstrating what was true: They were opposed to the "people"; they were immoral, covertly scheming and bribing. During the king's trial Saint-Just's denunciation resounded throughout France: "No one can rule innocently: the folly is too evident. Every King is a rebel and a usurper" (Curtis 1973: 39). The contrast between aristocratic plot and revolutionary open communication made the "people" sacred and plotters demons. By 1791, Robespierre saw all men of wealth as plotters: Virtue resided in the people, in the sense of the populace.

As this contrast became clearer, it undermined pragmatic politicians seeking to bridge the two sets of state institutions. The memoirs of Ferrières (1822) and Malouet (1874) are long lamentations: Their constitutional monarchist party is continually frustrated by court intrigue and Louis's insincerity. The king's abortive attempt to escape abroad, followed by foreign invasion, showed Centrists what they could expect from the old regime. Most moved Leftward, to believe or parrot general principles they had earlier regarded as impractical. Those still negotiating with the king could expect the worst if exposed. They were traitors to the "nation." Eventually the king and his family caused their own heads to tumble. Their intransigence had broken apart the propertied party of order, polarized political and ideological infra-structures, converted their enemies into principled representatives of the sacred, and turned their own party into demonic agents. The old regime was finished by late 1791.

Three organized classes now remained. First in size and early impact was the peasantry (see Lefebvre 1924, 1954, 1963: chapter 4, 1973; Moore 1973: 70–101; Skocpol 1979: 118–28; Goldstone 1991: 252–68). Bad harvests in 1787 and 1788 and a severe winter in 1788, assisted by rising demographic pressure and prices, had exacerbated rural suf-fering and unemployment. But why would this lead to a *revolutionary* peasant movement? As Chapter 4 shows, bread riots in England were not aimed at the state, but at classes supposedly dictating the market. French absolutism accepted responsibility for the bread supply, making bread a *political* issue. So was "privilege"; feudal dues and taxes bore down hard when harvest yields were low. Yet segmental controls were now weak, with most nobles absent and divisions in the army and the church – all crucial in the villages. Peasants were freer to explore class identities and oppositions. Peasant *cahiers* reveal pro-found discontent, mostly aimed at the state. Peasants supported the third estate stand against king and nobles. The summer of 1789 also saw scattered rural insurrections, known as *la grande peur*. Across France spread rumors of bands of brigands led by aristocrats looting peasant property. Peasants took up arms, but finding no brigands, they burned chateaux and destroyed manorial records of their feudal obligations.

Urban forces were immobilizing the regime; peasants faced weakened segmental control. A peasant revolt could be rewarded, unusually, with success. Peasants seized control of the countryside and the old regime was deprived of its rural power base. The urban Revolution could continue. As Moore (1973: 77) observes, "The peasantry was the arbiter of the Revolution, though not the main propelling force." Its militant core was now class-conscious.

Peasants wanted freedom from privilege and absolute property rights. So did the ideological elite. It abolished feudal dues in principle – peasants enforced the practice – and sold church and émigré noble lands in fairly small lots at moderate prices. Until 1791, the Revolution was popular among peasants capable of organization (we don't know what others thought). Without this "capitalist connection" between urban and rural movements, the Revolution could not have continued its forward motion. The urban revolution had activated politically and ideologically a conflict between feudalism and commercial and petty commodity capitalism in the countryside that otherwise would have remained latent, as it did in most of Central Europe.

Thereafter, rural disillusion and splits appeared. Feudalism's collapse brought few gains to most peasants. Land sales only benefited those who could afford to buy. They created a new exploiting class composed of richer peasants and bourgeoisie buying into land. The urban revolutionaries now had to settle conflict over enclosure of common land, of which they had little understanding. They also desperately needed bread for army and towns. The bourgeoisie favored free-market supply; sans-culottes favored price and quantity controls backed by coercion. Both rich and poor farmers favored a market that would keep prices up. As the Revolution moved Leftward in 1792 and 1793, it moved toward controls and alienated peasants. Under the Terror, it attempted to distribute confiscated goods and lands to the poor but lacked infrastructures to implement this. The Leftist peasant option, favoring community collectivism against nobles and richer peasants, was abortive. The countryside moved Rightward, and clerics with denser local-regional organization led counterrevolutions. The sans-culottes were isolated in the towns. Most organized peasants welcomed the Thermidorian Rightist coup of August 1794, yet urban-rural tensions remained throughout the 1790s. Peasant power had been a necessary cause of early revolution; now it was a necessary cause of its collapse. From beginning to end, the rural revolution had favored agrarian petty capitalism. Peasant proprietors seized and held control of the land. But, as Chapter 19 shows, they adhered to diverse local-regional politics.

From 1790 on, the Revolution centered on the three remaining power actors in the towns. It was led by the ideological elite with substantial bourgeois and petit bourgeois backing. The new legitimating principle was the "people" or the "nation." But, as in Britain and America, the identity of the people was ambiguous, ranging from men of substantial property to the whole male populace. Substantial property owners led the Revolution but needed the crowd for support against a hostile court. They interacted through five main political organizations: clubs, press, assemblies, national guard, and urban crowd. All but the crowd were first controlled by the ideological elite, but they then spread downward among petite bourgeoisie and artisans, creating an autonomous sans-culotte class movement that divided the ideological elite and intensified class struggle between substantial and petite bourgeoisie.

The urban crowd was essential to the Revolution because only it could coerce the king. To the mob, bread mattered most. In all countries during the eighteenth century (as we saw in England in Chapter 4), food riots predominated in popular disturbances. The Parisian artisan spent half his wage on bread; if its price rose, starvation threatened. Bread riots sparked many of the revolutionary *journées*, especially providing female militants. Consumption, rather than production, provided popular community-centered mobilization. The intensity of popular movements in this era derived from family and community reinforcement of class (Chapter 15 takes this argument farther). Rioters first shouted the ideologists' slogan of "freedom" from privilege and corruption. The "interests" of the old regime – noble and church privilege, the wealthy merchant, the bourgeois monopolist – were preventing fair food distribution. The mob marched to Versailles to capture the royal family chanting "Cherchons le boulanger, la boulangère et le petit mitron" ("Let's get the baker, the baker's wife, and the baker's boy"). After the good harvest of 1790, the market worked and the ideological elite and petite bourgeoisie fought as allies. But the bad harvest of 1791, counterrevolutionaries, and the instability of the currency produced food shortages. Rioters demanded government intervention, anathema to most of the ideological elite. Who would prevail?

The clubs were the organized core of the Revolution. In 1790, the Confédération des Amis de la Verité had 3,000 to 6,000 members. Of its leading 121 members, at least 100 are known to have been highly educated publicists, politicians, and writers, enamored of the Enlightenment, especially of Rousseau, extolling discursive literacy: "The great tribune of humanity has been found: it is the press," "without journals and gazettes the American Revolution would never have occurred" (Brissot); "a sparsely populated people in a large territory can now be as free as the residents of a small city. . . . It is through the printing process alone that discussion among a great people can truly be one" (Condorcet, solving Rousseau's problem of how to achieve democracy in anything larger than a city-state) (Kates 1985: 83–5, 177, 180; Eisenstein 1986: 191). Brissotins and Girondists centered on publishing houses. The Jacobins then dwarfed all of them – from 24 clubs in February 1790 to over more than 200 by December 1790, 426 by March 1791, and more than 6,000 by early 1794, reaching down to the villages. The larger clubs had reading rooms and printing presses, and their meetings were timed with the arrival of major periodicals. Resolutions were communicated through a correspondence network to regional centers and to Paris. The clubs were oral assemblies discussing the printed word.

Most early Jacobins were propertied, then membership broadened.

There were few nobles and virtually no peasants, laborers, or servants. Of the members of thirteen clubs during 1789–91, 16 percent were officials or salaried employees, 16 percent substantial bourgeois (wholesale merchants, investors, manufacturers, and rentiers), 14 percent artisan masters and tradesmen, 13 percent liberal professionals (mostly lawyers), 7 percent priests, and 5 percent officers and noncommissioned officers. A further 24 percent were lower artisans, among whom small master blurs into man (Kennedy 1982: 73–87 and appendix F). Thus Jacobins came from all across the bourgeoisie and petite bourgeoisie, especially after clubs opened their membership to "passive" citizens in late 1791. Most leaders remained substantial bourgeois but, pressed by their galleries, moved to favor democracy.

National guard units and local government section committees were more petit bourgeois. Most activists in the Paris sections (Soboul 1964: 38–54) and in crowds and sections in Provence (Vovelle 1976) were master craftsmen, skilled workers and small shopkeepers producing and selling to their neighborhoods. Their leaders were small manufacturers and lower-level professionals and administrators (Andrews 1985). They mobilized local crowds whose arrest records mostly reveal them as workshop masters, craftsmen, shopkeepers, and small traders, people of moderate substance who mixed property and labor. Wage earners were underrepresented, and riots were centered in petit bourgeois neighborhoods, not in the industrial suburbs (Rudé 1959). Their ideology contrasted their own hard work and sturdy independence with the idle parasitism of the rich. Militants labeled themselves sansculottes – literally, without knee breeches (wearing trousers instead) – indicating the pride of productive workers. These neighborhood politics and ideologies involved women as well as men. But though formidable in Paris and ferocious in their attacks on the substantial bourgeoisie, these *enragés* lacked coherent national organization. Although the "people," they could not organize the nation.

Revolutionaries were divided between dual institutions. The ideological elite, largely from the substantial bourgeoisie, controlled national discursive infrastructures in clubs and the National Assembly/ Convention. But they shared administration and army with an unreliable king. To pressure the king they needed popular violence, but this was wielded by turbulent petit bourgeois institutions, linking an inflammatory press to the sections, the semidisciplined national guard units, and the mob. The split between these two organized bases of class power could be bridged only by the Jacobin Left, whose Parisian and national organization supported some aspirations of both classes. From late 1792, Jacobin successes and ultimate failure became those of the Revolution itself.

Revolution becomes national struggle

Yet even now class struggle was not "pure." The franchise issue was successfully compromised; conflict was restrained by the lack of petit bourgeois national organization, allowing the elite to preserve market "freedom"; and unity was required against counterrevolutionaries. Yet a second phase of military and geopolitical power relations intervened to intensify and centralize class and nation.

Within the ideological elite, power shifted from constitutional monarchists to Jacobins in late 1791. They responded to aristocratic plots by turning the slogans of "people" and "nation" Leftward. The nation was a community of free, independent citizens, from which nobility, clergy, and probably also the king should be excluded. Emigré property was expropriated. At the fringes of France, this made the conflict national and geopolitical, for the "nation" was confiscating the French estates of German nobles. Alsatians *wanted* to be French, but this revolutionary principle of voluntary citizenship abrogated property and ancient treaty rights. The Austrian and Prussian monarchs were persuaded (against their better judgment) that their cause was also that of Louis, émigrés, and German nobles. It was dynastic particularism against the universal nation.

The émigré leader, the duke of Brunswick, threw caution aside. His manifesto called for a general uprising against the Revolution, promising no mercy for Paris if it resisted. This strengthened the unity of Parisian revolutionaries, sounded the death knell for the king if the émigré army failed, and weakened bourgeois conservatives. Petit bourgeois organizations mobilized to defend the nation. National guard and Paris section militants stormed the Tuileries on August 10, 1792. The king was taken; France, declared a republic; and universal adult male suffrage was announced. A petit bourgeois commune remained alongside a convention led by an ideological elite defending property. The moderate Brissotins now sought war, believing this would strengthen national unity under their leadership, divert popular agitation toward the foreign threat, and enhance the prestige of the army. They and the court willed each other toward war.

On September 20, 1792, the invading Prussian and émigré army (the Austrians delayed) reached Valmy, a village in the northern Department of the Marne. There they found drawn up a motley French army, representative of the Revolution. One section of the old royal army was mostly intact, the bourgeois-officered artillery. It was supported by battalions cobbled together from old regiments of the line and revolutionary volunteer units. The line officers remaining loyal to the Revolution were largely bourgeois, drawn especially from professions and towns. With noble privileges swept away, they could expect promotion based on merit and combat experience. Many were newly promoted from noncommissioned-officer status, rare before the Revolution. Most volunteers were shopkeepers, artisans, and liberal professionals from Paris and the other towns. The "nation in arms" was bourgeois and petit bourgeois and highly literate (Scott 1978).

Luckily for the nation, it was an artillery battle, played to France's strength. For twelve hours the cannons pounded one another around the Valmy windmill. The French stood their ground, shouting *Vive la Nation*. At the end of the day, the Prussians, reluctant combatants, retreated out of France in good order. Revolution and nation were saved; Louis's fate, sealed. He and his family were executed in January 1793. There could be no turning back for regicides. Whatever happened now, the old regime had passed away. "The cannonade at Valmy" was a minor military engagement, but it was one of modern history's turning points. Goethe was an eyewitness. The end of the day found him sitting amid dejected Prussian soldiers around a campfire. He thought to cheer them up by saying: "From this place and from this day begins a new era in the history of the world, and you will be able to say, I was there" (Bertaud 1970; Best 1982: 81).

Valmy's significance outlasted the Revolution. A nation's citizens, mobilized by their state, triumphed on the battlefield. They repeated the triumph a year later when the Austrians took their turn. They were repulsed by the *levée en masse*, a mass mobilization of 300,000 to 400,000 soldiers, predominantly artisans and peasants with bourgeois officers. In 1799, the nation in arms drove out invaders for a third time. For fifteen years, this army was composed only of Frenchmen (plus "legions of patriots" from "sister nations"), the only national army in Europe. Even between crises, when the army was smaller and professional, it remained penetrated by pamphlets and clubs, committed to *la grande nation*. I return to it in Chapter 8.

With war and *levée en masse* the revolutionaries had again drawn on their ideological experience to emerge with a coercive and self-fulfilling transcendent principle. Brissot did not win the support of the assembly, the clubs, the sections, and the national guard by pragmatic arguments. Robespierre, opposing the war, showed how flimsy these were, how dangerous it was to rely on generals whose loyalty was suspect, and how defeat would end the Revolution. In words of universal application, Robespierre argued:

It is in the nature of things that the diffusion of reason should proceed slowly. The most pernicious government is powerfully supported by the prejudices, the habits, and the education of its people. . . . The wildest idea that can form in any politician's mind is a belief that the people of one country, to induce the people of another to adopt their laws and constitution, need only to subject them to armed invasion. Nobody takes kindly to armed missionaries. [Gauthier 1988: 31]

But the assembly chose bellicosity as a statement of high emotional principle to unite disparate power factions and protect property. According to the minutes, the assembly erupted when a Girondist deputy cried out that the nation was ready to die for its constitution:

All members of the Assembly, inspired by the same sentiment rose and cried: *Yes, we swear it!* This surge of enthusiasm communicated itself to all those present, firing their hearts. The ministers of justice and of foreign affairs, the ushers, the citizens male and female who were present in the Assembly joined with the deputies, rose, waved their hats, stretched their arms to the President's table and swore the same oath. The cry was: *We shall live free or we shall die. The Constitution or death*, and the chamber resounded with applause. [Emsley 1988: 42; emphases in original]

The enthusiasm actually joined principle to calculation. Many moderates saw war as activating an Enlightenment principle. As Pocock (1975) has shown, an idealized classical notion of propertied citizen-soldier republics had long circulated among European intellectuals. A propertied citizen militia could hold the center against monarchy and mob. Yet petit bourgeois sections and national guard also saw mobilization as enhancing *their* role in the Revolution. Jacobin ideological leadership, papering over cracks between bourgeoisie and petite bourgeoisie, created a novel and powerful offensive weapon, a nation in arms against old regimes everywhere. The creative principle undermined its initiators, just as had earlier the abolition of feudal privilege. Against Brissotin expectations the war moved leadership Leftward and brought petit bourgeois national guard and section committees into the state. The "nation" had changed in class composition, now including the (male) urban populace. A new collective actor had emerged interstitially, taking by surprise most of the power actors whose actions had created it.

Now a struggle developed between Right and Left, Girondist and Montagnard, factions among the Jacobins. To some extent this was a class conflict, though entwined with, and focused on, the period's other major political issue: how centralized or local-regional the state should be. The Parisian crowd and sections were essential to Leftist conceptions of the Revolution. Hence the Right sought to fight mob rule by decentralizing the state. This was the exact opposite of the conservative strategy in the United States after its revolution, where the answer to mob rule in individual states had been to centralize political power. This is why federalism, in both countries conservative, at first meant centralization in the United States and decentralization in France. The Girondists sought a federal, decentralized state better able to protect property.

The Girondists were disadvantaged by the growing centralization of politics since 1789 and by having to fight in their enemy's heartland, Paris. Yet, before 1789, the French state had been dual, its absolute monarchy centralized, most administration and law courts local-regional. Though the assembly legislated away much of this, it could not abolish localism at a stroke. The struggle was evenly matched, but the war tipped the scales. It strengthened Parisian Montagnard institutions and also the logic of the centralist case. The federal United States and Switzerland had admirable domestic liberties, pamphleteers noted, but they were geopolitically weak. To resist invasion required the "nation indivisible" (Godechot 1956, 1988: 17–18). Their Brissotin allies worsened the Girondist predicament by wavering in their prosecution of the war, some negotiating with the enemy. Charges of conspiracy led to the Terror, directed against the Girondists, substantial bourgeoisie, and aristocracy. The Girondists had lost.

France was further centralized as the war added government economic intervention. Armies had to be provisioned, as did their main recruiting bases, the towns. The remaining ideological elite still wished to protect property and free markets, but had to provide bread to avoid popular wrath. The Committee of Public Safety, led by Robespierre, organized economic intervention and the Terror while still fudging class divisions. Robespierre declared: "The state must be saved by whatever means and nothing is unconstitutional except what can lead to its ruin" (Boiloiseau 1983: 9). The "Republic of Virtue" extolled "purity" and purged "corruption," but policy was less principled. Robespierre steered between bourgeois property freedoms and petit bourgeois radicalism. Radical Jacobin deputies and armed detachments of sans-culottes roamed the provinces to ensure there were supplies, organize activists, and dispose of opponents. They succeeded well enough, but by varied tactics, here by Terror, there by conciliation, according to local exigencies and their predilections. The committee struck out at whatever seemed the current threat, now purging bourgeois conciliators, now sections, enragés, and terrorists, here enforcing grain quotas and price maximums (harming farmers and merchants), there enforcing wage maximums (harming workers and artisans). Though they kept the armies well supplied, the towns suffered.

Activist support drifted away and the sans-culottes did little to stop Thermidor, the rather confused 1794 coup that overthrew Robespierre and fatally weakened the ideological elite. In came a bourgeois regime that ended the Revolution. The Revolution's class ambiguities finally collapsed before a class-conscious bourgeoisie, shorn of connection to privilege, wielding the powers of the centralized nation-state as once its enemies had.

The war continued. Furet argues: "It is the war that survives the Terror and constitutes the last refuge of revolutionary legitimacy" (1978: 128). But war had also changed that revolutionary legitimacy, now resting on a stronger, more centralized nation-state. Under Bonaparte its military discipline gave it an authoritarian tinge. After Thermidor its centralized administration also enforced bourgeois liberalism more directly than in Britain. After 1815, it proved only a difference of degree, but it was the source of an enduring division among capitalist states: on the one hand the Anglo-Saxon model of the state as the center and territorial location of a capitalist civil society and nation; on the other hand a Continental model of a more centrally organized, explicitly nationalist, and slightly more despotic state, centrally setting and enforcing more capitalist norms (Birnbaum 1982). Still, the restored monarchy and revived church were to fight many battles against this centralized Republican nation-state before it finally triumphed.

French conclusions

In its origins, the French Revolution was neither bourgeois nor national, nor was it dominated by classes. It began because state militarism produced a fiscal crisis in which failure to institutionalize the normal factionalism among state elite and privileged parties immobilized the entire old regime. This was reinforced by unresolved factionalism in army and church. By 1789, the usual segmental defenses against political opposition, urban riots and peasant jacqueries, were down. Head-on class confrontation was interstitially emerging. The peasants made their class revolution early and held onto their gains. In the towns power was seized by an ideological elite, partly bourgeois, partly old regime modernizers, but not from the mainstream of either class, and with distinct Enlightenment preoccupations with moral principle.

Over the next five years, this ideological state elite was buffeted on the Right by the ineffective intransigence of king and court, backed halfheartedly by foreign armies, and on the Left by a petit bourgeois class increasingly strong on identity and opposition but weak on political totality and alternatives. Under the strain the ideological elite made creative power discoveries, developing transcendent, principled ideologies and power techniques to enforce them. (I discuss these further in Chapter 7.) The elite's interaction with classes intensified the reality of a second interstitial power actor, the bourgeois and petit bourgeois nation. This overthrew the monarchy and forced the church back to a local-regional segmental organization. In the process, though, the unity of the ideological elite disintegrated. Its leadership was finally forced toward a more bourgeois class identity.

Thus conflict *became* defined by both class and nation emerging interstitially entwined with ideological, military, and political power relations. The final struggle between substantial bourgeois and petit bourgeois class fractions displaced the ideological elite and allowed the victory of a national bourgeoisie and the end of the Revolution. France was, and remained, a bourgeois nation – its state crystallizing as capitalist and as nation-state – whether its constitution was subsequently Republican, imperial, or monarchical.

As part of the same process, the French state and even the French identity changed. The link between old regime and postrevolutionary bourgeoisie was provided by the ideological elite. It solidified and then became bourgeois under the geopolitical pressure of old regimes. These mediations ensured that absolutist elements were transmuted into the bourgeois age in the form of a despotically strong nation-state. After the war defeated the Girondist federal alternative, political citizenship was conceived of as centralized – the opposite of the American solution. Thus the French state was able to mobilize national sentiments to a degree hitherto unknown in the world (as we shall see in Chapter 7). France was not now an aggregation of particularistic, authoritative corporations, welded together by monarchy and church. It was a capitalist civil society like Britain, but with a civil society depending more on a nation-state. Europe now had more than one model of modernization.

Bibliography

Agulhon, M. 1981. *Marianne in Combat: Imagery and Republican Symbols from 1789 to 1880*. Cambridge: Cambridge University Press.

Andrews, R. M. 1985. Social structures, political elites and ideology in revolutionary Paris, 1792–94. *Journal of Social History* 19.

Baker, K. M. 1987. Politics and public opinion under the old regime: some reflections. In *Press and Politics in Pre-Revolutionary France*, ed. J. R. Censer and J. D. Popkin. Berkeley: University of California Press.

Barber, E. G. 1955. *The Bourgeoisie in Eighteenth-Century France*. Princeton, N.J.: Princeton University Press.

Becker, C. L. 1932. *The Heavenly City of the Eighteenth-Century Philosophers*. New Haven, Conn.: Yale University Press.

Behrens, C. B. A. 1967. *The Ancien Regime*. London: Thames & Hudson.
    1985. *Society, Government and the Enlightenment: The Experiences of Eighteenth-Century France and Prussia*. London: Thames & Hudson.

Beik, W. 1985. *Absolutism and Society in Seventeenth-Century France*. Cambridge: Cambridge University Press.

Berlanstein, L. 1976. *The Barristers of Toulouse, 1740–1783*. Baltimore: Johns Hopkins University Press.

Bertaud, J. P. 1970. *Valmy*. Paris: Julliard.

1979. *La Révolution Armée*. Paris: Laffont.

Best, G. 1982. *War and Society in Revolutionary Europe: 1770–1870*. Leicester: Leicester University Press.

Bien, D. D. 1974. La réaction aristocratique avant 1789: l'exemple de l'armée. *Annales E.S.C.* 29.

1979. The army in the French Enlightenment: reform, reaction and revolution. *Past and Present*, no. 88.

1987. Offices, corps and a system of state credit: the uses of privilege under the *Ancien Régime*. In *The French Revolution and the Creation of Modern Political Culture*. Vol. I: *The Political Culture of the Old Regime*, ed. K. M. Baker. Oxford: Pergamon Press.

Birnbaum, P. 1982. *La Logique de l'Etat*. Paris: Fayard.

Boiloiseau, M. 1983. *The Jacobin Republic, 1792–94*. Cambridge: Cambridge University Press.

Bois, P. 1960. *Paysans de L'ouest. Des structures economiques et sociales aux options politiques depuis l'époque révolutionnaire dans la Sarthe*. Paris: Vilaire.

Bonnin, B. 1987. Un bourgeois en quête de titres et de domaines seigneuriaux: Claude Perier dans les dernières années de l'Ancien Régime. In *Bourgeoisies de Province et Révolution*, ed. M. Vovelle. Grenoble: Presses Universitaires de Grenoble.

Bosher, J. F. 1970. *French Finances, 1770–1795*. Cambridge: Cambridge University Press.

Bossenga, G. 1986. From corps to citizenship: the Bureaux des Finances before the French Revolution. *Journal of Modern History* 58.

Botein, S., et al. 1981. The periodical press in eighteenth-century English and French society: a cross-cultural approach. *Comparative Studies in Society and History* 23.

Brinton, C. 1930. *The Jacobins: An Essay in the New History*. New York: Russell & Russell.

Cassirer, E. 1951. *The Philosophy of the Enlightenment*. Princeton, N.J.: Princeton University Press.

Censer, J. R., and J. D. Popkin. 1987. Historians and the press. In *Press and Politics in Pre-Revolutionary France*, ed. J. R. Censer and J. D. Popkin. Berkeley: University of California Press.

Chartier, R. 1981. Cultures, lumières, doléances: les cahiers de 1789. *Revue d'Histoire Moderne et Contemporaine* 24.

Chaussinand-Nogaret, G. 1970. Capital et structure sociale sous l'ancien régime. *Annales E.S.C.* 25.

1985. *The French Nobility in the Eighteenth Century*. Cambridge: Cambridge University Press.

Cobban, A. 1964. *The Social Interpretation of the French Revolution*. Cambridge: Cambridge University Press.

Cominel, G. 1987. *Rethinking the French Revolution: Marxism and the Revisionist Challenge*. London: Verso

Corvisier, A. 1964. *L'Armée francaise de la fin du XVIIe siècle au ministère de Choiseul: Le Soldat*, 2 vols. Paris: Presses Universitaires de France.

Crouzet, F. 1966. Angleterre et France en XVIIIe siècle: essai d'analyse

comparée de deux croissances économiques. *Annales E.S.C.* 21.
  1970. An annual index of French industrial production in the 19th century.
    In *Essays in French Economic History*, ed. R. Cameron. Homewood,
    Ill.: Irwin.
Curtis, E. N. 1973. *Saint-Just, Colleague of Robespierre*. New York: Octagon
    Books.
Dann, O. 1988. Introduction. In *Nationalism in the Age of the French
    Revolution*, ed. O. Dann and J. Dinwiddy. London: Hambledon
    Press.
Darnton, R. 1979. *The Business of Enlightenment: A Publishing History of
    the Encyclopédie, 1775–1800*. Cambridge, Mass.: Harvard University
    Press.
  1984. A bourgeois puts his world in order: the city as a text. In his *The Great
    Cat Massacre and Other Episodes in French Cultural History*. New
    York: Basic Books.
  1987. The facts of literary life in eighteenth-century France. In *The French
    Revolution and the Creation of Modern Political Culture*. Vol. I: *The
    Political Culture of the Old Regime*, K. M. Baker, ed. Oxford:
    Pergamon Press.
Dawson, P. 1972. *Provincial Magistrates and Revolutionary Politics in France,
    1789–1795*. Cambridge, Mass.: Harvard University Press.
Dewald, J. 1987. *Pont-St.-Pierre, 1398–1789*. Berkeley and Los Angeles:
    University of California Press.
Dickson, P. G. M. 1987. *Finance and Government Under Maria Theresa,
    1740–1780*, 2 vols. Oxford: Clarendon Press.
Doyle, W. 1980. *The Origins of the French Revolution*. Oxford: Clarendon
    Press.
Durand, Y. 1971. *Les fermiers-généraux au XVIIIème siècle*. Paris: Presses
    Universitaires de France.
Eisenstein, E. 1986. On revolution and the printed word. In *Revolution
    in History*, ed. R. Porter and M. Teich. Cambridge: Cambridge
    University Press.
Emsley, C. 1988. Nationalist rhetoric and nationalist sentiment in revolution-
    ary France. In *Nationalism in the Age of the French Revolution*, ed.
    O. Dann and J. Dinwiddy. London: Hambledon Press.
Favier, R. 1987. Un grand bourgeois à Gap à la fin de l'Ancien Régime:
    Pierre-Daniel Pinet. In *Bourgeoisies de Province et Révolution*, ed.
    M. Vovelle. Grenoble: Presses Universitaires de Grenoble.
Ferrières, Marquis de. 1822. *Mémoires*, 2nd ed. Paris: Baudouin Frères.
Fitzsimmons, M. P. 1987. *The Parisian Order of Barristers and the French
    Revolution*. Cambridge, Mass.: Harvard University Press.
Furet, F. 1978. *Penser la Révolution Française*. Paris: Gallimard. Translated
    as:
  1981. *Interpreting the French Revolution*. Cambridge: Cambridge University
    Press.
Furet, F., and J. Ozouf. 1982. *Reading and Writing: Literacy in France from
    Calvin to Jules Ferry*. Cambridge: Cambridge University Press.
Furet, F., and D. Richet. 1970. *French Revolution*. London: Weidenfeld &
    Nicolson.
Gauthier, F. 1977. *La voie paysanne dans la révolution francaise: l'exemple
    picard*. Paris: Maspero.

1988. Universal rights and the national interest in the French Revolution. In *Nationalism in the Age of the French Revolution*, ed. O. Dann and J. Dinwiddy. London: Hanbledon Press.

Gay, P. 1967. *The Enlightenment: an Interpretation*, 2 vols. London: Weidenfeld & Nicolson.

Gershoy, L. 1962. *Bertrand Barère: Reluctant Terrorist*. Princeton, N.J.: Princeton University Press.

Godechot, J. 1956. *La grande nation*. Paris: Aubier.

1973. Nation, patrie, nationalisme et patriotisme en France au XVIIIe siècle. *Actes du colloque Patriotisme et nationalisme en Europe a l'époque de la Révolution française et de Napoléon.*

1988. The new concept of the Nation and its diffusion in Europe. In *Nationalism in the Age of the French Revolution*, ed. O. Dann and J. Dinwiddy. London: Hambledon Press.

Goldstone, J. 1991. *Revolution and Rebellion in the Early Modern World*. Berkeley: University of California Press.

Homan, G. 1971. *Jean-François Reubell*. The Hague: Nijhoff.

Hunt, L. 1984. *Politics, Culture and Class in the French Revolution*. Berkeley: University of California Press.

Julia, D. 1987. The two powers: chronicle of a disestablishment. In *The French Revolution and the Creation of Modern Political Culture*. Vol. I: *The Political Culture of the Old Regime*, ed. K. M. Baker. Oxford: Pergamon Press.

Kagan, R. L. 1975. Law students and legal careers in eighteenth-century France. *Past and Present*, no. 68.

Kates, G. 1985. *The Cercle Social, the Girondins and the French Revolution*. Princeton, N.J.: Princeton University Press.

Kennedy, M. L. 1982. *The Jacobin Clubs in the French Revolution: The First Years*. Princeton, N.J.: Princeton University Press.

Kindleberger, C. 1984. Financial institutions and economic development: a comparison of Great Britain and France in the eighteenth and nineteenth centuries. *Explorations in Economic History* 21.

Kuscinski, A. 1916. *Dictionnaire des conventionnels*. Paris: Société de l'histoire de la Révolution francaise.

Lamarque, P. 1981. *Les francs-maçons aux états-généraux de 1789 et à l'assemblée nationale*. Paris: EDIMAF.

La Tour du Pin, Madame de. 1985. *Memoirs*. London: Century.

Le Bihan, A. 1973. *Francs-maçons et ateliers parisiens de la Grande Loge de France au XVIIIe siècle*. Paris: Bibliothèque Nationale.

Lefebvre, G. 1924. *Les Paysans du Nord pendant la Révolution Française*. Lille: Librairie Papeterie.

1954. *Questions Agraires au Temps de la Terreur*. La Roche-sur-Yon: Henri Potier.

1963. *Etudes sur la Révolution Francaise*. Paris: Presses Universitaires de France.

1973. *The Great Fear of 1789: Rural Panic in Revolutionary France*. New York: Pantheon.

Lemay, E. 1977. La composition de l'Assemblée Nationale Constituante: les hommes de la continuité? *Revue d'histoire moderne et contemporaine* 24.

Léon, P. 1970. L'élan industriel et commercial. In *Histoire économique et sociale de la France*, ed. F. Brandel and E. Labrousse. Paris: Presses Universitaires de France.

Lough, J. 1960. *An Introduction to Eighteenth-Century France*. London: Longman Group.

Lucas, C. 1973. Nobles, bourgeois and the origins of the French Revolution. *Past and Present*, no. 60.

Lyons, M. 1977. M.-G.-A. Vadier (1736–1828): the formation of the Jacobin mentality. *French Historical Studies* 10.

McManners, J. 1969. *The French Revolution and the Church*. London: SPCK.

Malouet, P. V. 1874. *Mémoires*. Paris: Plon.

Mathias, P., and P. O'Brien. 1976. Taxation in England and France, 1715–1810. *Journal of European Economic History* 5.

Matrat, J. 1971. *Robespierre, or the Tyranny of the Majority*. Paris: Hachette.

Matthews, G. 1958. *The Royal General Farms in Eighteenth-Century France*. New York: Columbia University Press.

Moore, B., Jr. 1973. *Social Origins of Dictatorship and Democracy*. Harmondsworth, Middlesex: Penguin Books.

Morineau, M. 1980. Budgets de l'état et gestation des finances royales en France au dix-huitième siècle. *Revue historique* 264.

O'Brien, P., and C. Keyder. 1978. *Economic Growth in Britain and France, 1780–1914*. London: Allen & Unwin.

Ozouf, M. 1976. *La Fête révolutionnaire, 1789–1799*. Paris: Gallimard.

1987. Public opinion. In *The French Revolution and the Creation of Modern Political Culture*. Vol. I: *The Political Culture of the Old Regime*, ed. K. M. Baker. Oxford: Pergamon Press.

Palmer, R. R. 1941. *Twelve Who Ruled: The Committee of Public Safety During the Terror*. Princeton, N.J.: Princeton University Press.

1959. *The Age of the Democratic Revolutions*, vol. I. Princeton, N.J.: Princeton University Press.

1985. *The Improvement of Humanity: Education and the French Revolution*. Princeton, N.J.: Princeton University Press.

Patrick, A. 1972. *The Men of the First French Revolution: Political Alignments in the National Convention of 1792*. Baltimore: Johns Hopkins University Press.

Pocock, J. G. A. 1975. *The Machiavellian Moment: Florentine Political Thought and the Atlantic Republic Tradition*. Princeton, N.J.: Princeton University Press.

Riley, J. C. 1986. *The Seven Years War and the Old Regime in France*. Princeton, N.J.: Princeton University Press.

Roche, D. 1978. *La Siècle des lumières en province: Académies et académiciens provinciaux, 1680–1789*, 2 vols. Paris: Mouton.

Rudé, G. 1959. *The Crowd in the French Revolution*. Oxford: Clarendon Press.

Scott, S. F. 1978. *The Response of the Royal Army to the French Revolution*. Oxford: Clarendon Press.

Seligman, E. 1913. *La justice en France pendant la Révolution*, 2 vols. Paris: Plon.

Sewell, W. H. Jr. 1985. Ideologies and social revolutions: reflections on the French Revolution. *Journal of Modern History* 57.

Skocpol, T. 1979. *States and Social Revolutions*. Cambridge: Cambridge University Press.

Soboul, A. 1964. *The Parisian Sans-Culottes and the French Revolution, 1793-4*. Oxford: Clarendon Press.

Starobinsky, J. 1987. Eloquence ancient and modern: aspects of an Old Regime commonplace. In *The French Revolution and the Creation of Modern Political Culture*. Vol. I: *The Political Culture of the Old Regime*, ed. K. M. Baker. Oxford: Pergamon Press.

Taylor, G. V. 1967. Non-capitalist wealth and the origins of the French Revolution. *American Historical Review* 72.

  1972. Revolutionary and nonrevolutionary content in the *cahiers* of 1789: an interim report. *French Historical Studies* 7.

Thompson, J. M. 1936. *Robespierre*, 2 vols. New York: Appleton-Century.

Tocqueville, A. de. 1955. *The Old Regime and the French Revolution*. New York: Doubleday.

Tournier, A. n.d. *Vadier Sous le Terreur*. Paris: Flammarion.

Vovelle, M. 1976. *Les Métamorphoses de la fête en Provence, 1750-1830*. Paris: Flammarion.

  1984. *The Fall of the French Monarchy, 1787-1792*. Cambridge: Cambridge University Press.

Vovelle, M., and D. Roche. 1965. Bourgeoisie, rentiers and property owners: elements for defining social categories at the end of the eighteenth century. In *New Perspectives on the French Revolution: Readings in Historical Sociology*, ed. J. Kaplow. New York: Wiley.

7 Conclusion to Chapters 4–6: The emergence of classes and nations

Many have hailed the half century beginning in 1770 as a revolutionary epoch in both Europe and the Americas. Some identify this with class and democracy – the "era of democratic revolutions" is Palmer's (1959) label – others with the revolutionary rise of nations across the two continents (Anderson 1983). Some countries did move toward nationalism and democracy; but most revolutions did not succeed, the French Revolution remained incomplete and the American was only ambiguously revolutionary. Moveover, these events inspired other regimes to avoid revolution by compromising with rising classes and nations. Their compromises proved of world-historical significance, for they were institutionalized in enduring forms. This chapter sums up what proved to be the main creative phase of modern Western history. The four greatest modern state crystallizations – capitalism, militarism, representation, and the national issue – were institutionalized together. And far from being opposites, classes and nations rose together, structured by all four sources of social power; and though rival segmental and local-regional organizations were diminished, they survived, transformed.

To explain all this, I start from the three power revolutions of the period. First, the economic revolution turned more on capitalism than on industrialism. Only in Britain (and lesser regions of Europe) did industrialization occur now, yet British distributive power changes were no greater than elsewhere. Chapter 4 shows how British industrialism was molded by a commercial capitalism that was already institutionalized. In this period industrialization greatly enhanced collective and geopolitical power only in Britain. Its impact on distributive power was minor everywhere else: Manufacturing capitalists and workers barely figured in my narrative. A more broadly diffused agrarian, protoindustrial and commercial capitalism generated denser networks of organization as well as new bourgeois and petit bourgeois classes whose confrontation with the old regime was the period's main domestic power struggle.

Second, intensifying geopolitical militarism spurred massive state growth and modernization. In earlier centuries, state expenditures had consumed under 3 percent of gross national product in peacetime, perhaps about 5 percent in wartime. By the 1760s this had risen to 10 percent in peacetime and 20 percent in wartime (30 percent in Prussia), and during the Napoleonic Wars it rose to 30 percent to 40 percent (see Table 11.3). Almost all the increase went to armed forces, in peace and war alike. Military manpower doubled across midcentury and doubled again during the Napoleonic Wars, reaching 5 percent of total populations. (See Table 11.6.) These exactions, far higher than those of any Western state today, are identical with those of the most militarized societies of 1990: Iraq in expenditures, Israel in manpower. If we consider the transformations such military commitments wrought in Iraq[1] and Israel, we can appreciate their impact on eighteenth-century Europe: States became far more significant to their subjects; regimes desperately economized and modernized; and political protest broadened into extensive and political class struggle, displacing segmental organization, and into national struggle, displacing local-regional organization. Representation and the national question came fully onto the Western agenda, the product of increasing state militarism.

Third, the entwined growth of capitalism and states fueled a revolution in ideological power, already begun by churches. Their joint demands expanded and transformed networks of discursive literacy – the ability to read and write nonformulaic texts – which then developed autonomous powers. After the church-led phase, discursive literacy grew in two ways. One, predominant in Britain and its American colonies, was mostly stimulated by commercial capitalism; the other, predominant in Austria and Prussia, was mostly stimulated by the growth of militaries and state administrations. France mixed both. These capitalist and statist routes to discursive literacy were preconditions of the development of class and nation as extensive communities.

Concerning classes and nations, I adhere more to "modernism" than "perennialism" or "primordialism" (for these distinctions, from the literature on nationalism, see Smith 1971, 1979: 1–14). A nation is an extensive cross-class community affirming its distinct ethnic identity and history and claiming its own state. Nations tend to conceive of themselves as possessing distinct claims to virtue, and many have gone one step farther into persistent aggressive conflict with other, "inferior" nations. Nations, aggressive or not, arose only from the eighteenth century in Europe and America, and much later elsewhere, as most writers have agreed (e.g., Kohn 1944; Anderson 1983; Gellner 1983; Hroch 1985; Chatterjee 1986; Hobsbawm 1990). Before then, dominant classes, but only rarely subordinate classes, could organize extensively and politically. As dominant class culture had been largely insulated from the culture of peasant masses, few political units were defined by

---

[1] This was written before the Gulf War of 1990–1, after which Iraq was militarily transformed in other ways.

the sharing of culture, as occurs in nations (see Volume I of this work: 527–30; see also Gellner 1983, chapter 1; Hall 1985; Crone 1989: chapter 5). Beneath an extensive and political dominant class had descended particularistic segmental networks whose building blocks were localities and regions, not classes.

These broad assertions need qualifying. As we saw in Volume I, class struggle could develop in unusual societies like classical Greece or early Republican Rome; elsewhere it could appear if structured heavily by religious communities. As Smith notes, "ethnic consciousness," the sense that a population shares a common identity and history (usually mythical), was not uncommon in prior history, especially given the presence of a shared language, religion, or political unity. Then (as in England, with all three) a diffused sense of "nationality" might emerge. Yet this was only one among several "specialized" identities, considerably weakened by local, regional, corporate, and class identities.

Before the French Revolution the term "nation" generally meant a kin group sharing a common blood connection. A term like "political nation," found in eighteenth-century Britain, referred to those with franchise and office-holding rights (conferred by blood connections and property). Nations were as yet predominantly (in Smith's term) "lateral," confined to dominant classes. Smith also identifies "vertical" (i.e., cross-class) ethnic communities, which he claims were common in agrarian societies, thus advancing a compromise "perennialist" theory (as does Armstrong 1982). I generally disputed such perennialism in Volume I – and indeed Smith agrees that "nationalism, both as ideology and movement, is a wholly modern phenomenon" (1986: 18, 76–79).

Yet I concede some "premodern" history of the nation. I identify two "protonational" phases in the development of nations already underway before my period begins. I label these the religious and the commercial-statist phases. Then I argue that the "long nineteenth century" turned protonations into fully fledged nations in two further phases, the militarist and the industrial capitalist phases. In this chapter I fully discuss the militarist phase, dividing it into two subphases, pre-1792 and post-1792. The fourth, industrial capitalist, phase is reserved for future chapters; its history is summarized in Chapter 20.

In the first, religious, phase, beginning in the sixteenth century, Protestantism and the Catholic Counter-Reformation created two kinds of potential protonation. First, the Christian churches spread networks of discursive literacy laterally across the reach of each major native vernacular language and (more variably) downward to middling class persons. Whereas Chaucer and his contemporaries wrote in three languages (English, Anglo-Norman French, and Latin), Shakespeare and his wrote only in English, a language that became fully standardized in its written form by the late seventeenth century. In most countries the written vernacular of regime and church spread gradually out from the home counties at the expense of other dialects and languages, principally because it was the language of God. Provincial and border languages like Welsh and Provencal were left to the lower classes on the periphery. Where the triumphing vernacular roughly corresponded with state territories as a whole, this somewhat increased a sense of shared community among its literate subjects. Second, where different churches organized different states or regions, their conflicts could attain a more popular protonational force, as they did in the Wars of Religion. Yet both "naturalizing" tendencies were highly variable, as most churches (and the entire Catholic church) were essentially transnational, whereas state, linguistic, and church boundaries only sometimes coincided.

If we look at Western history teleologically, from present to past, then this religious phase of nation building appears as a massive imposition of ideological power upon the world. Yet, in itself, it produced only rudimentary protonations. Even in England, where state, language, and church probably coincided more than anywhere else, the sense of being "English" in the seventeenth or early eighteenth century was still somewhat limited by class and deeply infused by Protestantism and by its schisms. The state was not yet sufficiently relevant to the whole of social life to be fused with, and reinforce, such a protonational identity. Yet the most important legacy of this phase was probably in the realm of mobilizing what I call "intensive power." The churches had long been deeply implanted in the rituals of the family life cycle and the community seasonal cycle, especially in the villages. By inculcating literacy, churches were beginning to link the intimate, moral sphere of social life with broader, more secular social practices. I will chart the growing significance of this mobilization, as the broadest "family" unit eventually became the nation.

In the second, commercial-statist, phase, begun around 1700, this limited sense of shared community was further secularized as commercial capitalism and military state modernization took over much of the expansion of literacy, each predominating in different countries. Contracts, government records, army drill manuals, coffeehouse business discussions, academies of notable officials – all these institutions secularized and spread slightly downward the shared literate culture of dominant classes (as earlier chapters demonstrate in detail). Because all states now ruled by law, an elementary shared "civil citizenship" had also diffused farther across state territories, and shared religions variably diffused more universal solidarities. Yet under capitalism, the discursive literacy of dominant classes and churches remained somewhat transnational, and "naturalization" remained limited. Anderson's "print capitalism" could as easily generate a transnational West as a community of nations. The nation still did not mobilize society.

The transformation of such protonations into cross-class, state-linked, and finally aggressive communities began in the third phase covered by this chapter. By 1840, all the leading Powers contained quasi nations, but of three different types. Mainland British and French nations reinforced existing states; they are examples of the nation as state-reinforcing. In Prussia-Germany, nation was bigger than any existing state and was moving from an apolitical to a state-creating (or pan-state) role. In Austrian lands, nations were smaller than state boundaries and became state-subverting. Why did nations develop, but in these varying forms? My answer centers on the insertion of the increasing militarism of this third phase into different economic, ideological, and political power relations.

The central drama for classes was the French Revolution. Chapter 6 shows that this was not initially a class struggle, but it became the principal example of class struggle in Marx's sense – extensive, symmetrical, and political. Yet it was the only such event of its era, its main emulator being the slave revolt of Haiti. In America, capitalist liberalism rose up, but revolution there was less class-based and less socially revolutionary. The French was the only bourgeois revolution to succeed largely on its own merits. Others were assisted by French armies and faded when they left. (We saw a similar sequence occurring from 1945 to 1989 in Eastern Europe.) Having analyzed more moderate reform outcomes in Britain and America, and anticipating my later discussion of more conservative Germany and Austria, I assess in comparative perspective Marx's vision of class struggle between feudalism and capitalism and between old regime and rising bourgeoisie. How was a bourgeois revolution seemingly possible in France, but not elsewhere? I argue that such varied class and national outcomes were closely entwined. I explain their joint emergence in four stages, beginning by focusing more on classes and then on nations.

1. From feudalism to capitalism

As Marx saw, capitalism was revolutionary, accelerating the forces of production, first in agriculture and commerce, then in industry, and diffusing its freer market relations and its production relations of absolute private property more universally across civil society. Capitalism also helped spread discursive literacy (print capitalism) and its common ideological messages more extensively. Collective powers became revolutionized, fairly uniformly. Nor could any regime survive without accommodating to capitalism's distributive powers, wielded by its emerging classes; their struggles provided much of the period's drama, including most of the politics of representation. These arguments are too familiar to belabor.

But Marx was wrong to suggest that the transition from feudalism to capitalism revolutionized distributive power in the sense of bringing extensive and political class conflict between "feudal lords" and "capitalist bourgeoisie." In Germany (as, later, in Japan) and to some extent in Britain, such lords actually *became* capitalists in agriculture and commerce, then in industry, changing their power base without social upheaval. Class tensions remained latent, sometimes disruptive, but local and apolitical. Even where lords spurned capitalism, conflict remained surprisingly quiescent. In eighteenth-century France, as later in Austria-Hungary and Russia, bourgeois capitalists were subordinated to old nobles, yet reacted with manipulative deference within segmental organizations rather than with class hostility. True, they came to terms with the old regime partly because both feared "people" and "populace" below. But this was not the overriding concern it was to become in 1848. The lack of such fear, and of a broad "party of order," made the French Revolution possible. Lacking their own extensive organizations, bourgeois capitalists used those of the old regime to achieve their goals. They ingratiated their economic practices and their sons and daughters into the old regime, buying patronage, offices, titles, and noble marriage partners. They were not sacrificing wealth for status, but getting inside the regime to secure the fruits of state offices and secure privileges against market uncertainties.

The point can be broadened. The capitalist mode of production requires only private property ownership and market competition. It has little extensive organization beyond law courts and the market and tends not to revolutionize but to accommodate to other distributive power organizations. If, say, ethnic differences are institutionalized as apartheid, or if patriarchy is already institutionalized, then capitalists build them into their market calculations. Alternatively, in other circumstances they calculate around assumptions of ethnic and gender equality. Their manipulations may reinforce old regimes, apartheid, and patriarchy, but capitalists are not responsible for these. If those distributive power organizations begin to crumble, then alert capitalists shift their manipulative strategies so as to make profits without them. Capitalism was not such a powerful transformer of distributive power relations as Marx believed – nor is any mode of economic production.

Nowhere in this period did the substantial bourgeoisie conceive of itself as belonging with the petite bourgeoisie in a class struggle of bourgeoisie against a feudal old regime. The bourgeoisie in Marx's classic sense, uniting "grande" and "petite" fractions, was not a significant power actor – in the very period when it should have been. Although a few substantial bourgeois railed against feudalism, they did so in alliance with a modernizing old regime faction rather than with the petite bourgeoisie (unless noneconomic power relations intervened, as detailed later). This was not a failure of class consciousness but of class organization. Capitalists were inserted in old regime political economy, buying court or parliamentary influence to win commercial monopolies and privileges, acquiring tax farms and government offices, and using marriages to enter patron-client networks. True, these "corrupt" practices gradually declined, but more from pressure by old regime modernizers-become-capitalists than by an independent bourgeoisie. The new manufacturing capitalism was based on a plethora of small enterprises linked by a diffuse market. The manufacturing bourgeoisie lacked authoritative organization. The bourgeoisie was only a "latent class." Those who might have belonged to it did not need class or their own state to achieve their goals.

Petit bourgeois capitalists exhibited more class identity and organization. As McKendrick, Brewer, and Plumb suggested for England, Soboul for France, and Nash for the American colonies, small shopkeepers, traders, and artisan masters smoldered at how the corruption and parasitism of the old regime economy subordinated their labor and the markets on which they sold their products to privilege. In crises this sense of production-cum-market class identity and opposition could erupt into political denunciations of "old corruption" and "aristocratic plots." Yet perceptions of direct economic exploitation occurred more through market than production relations. Petit bourgeois eruptions, especially if supported by the populace below, were most often precipitated by bread riots. These were market-centered, mobilized through intense petit bourgeois penetration of their local communities, aided by discursive networks of communication through broadsheets, pamphlets, and other print materials. This involved families, women alongside men, organizing locally, by street and neighborhood, more than by employment. The integration of intimate family with extensive politics (also evident in conscription riots) gave such movements considerable moral force.

But these class eruptions had limited goals: to demonstrate grievance to the old regime and to seek pragmatic concessions, not new structures of representation, still less revolution. They were locally organized, although rioting in the capital might be directed at the central state, and if the state distributed or priced bread it was more politicized. Bread riots might worry, even destabilize, old regimes; they did not institute bourgeois ones. If politicized, most came under the control of cross-class power organizations centered on the transmission of discursive literacy (discussed later). Yet, as this assisted extensive and political protest, it also tamed its moral ferocity, lowered its intensity, and narrowed its base, especially by excluding women. (I pursue this argument further in Chapters 15 and 17.)

So combining the economic organizations of production and market can explain latent class conflict plus intensive local protests that might lead toward regime concessions. But it cannot explain extensive, still less political, classes or structural democratic reform or revolution. Petits bourgeois operated within diffuse markets whose broad parameters were set diffusely by their betters, with only limited state assistance. The resentment they sometimes displayed was a necessary condition for all further class conflict, but it did not directly, "purely," produce the period's extensive and political class conflict. Because states were not central in economic life, the capitalist revolution did not unaided propel forward popular "nations." Petit bourgeois malcontents did struggle against old regime and for citizenship; their struggles did generate "national" consciousness. Yet they were stirred into action as militarism and ideologies intervened.

2. Pre-1792 militarism

Why *should* a class organize extensively and politically? Marx thought this was obvious: Class organization emerged directly from the relations of production. He was wrong. As we have seen, the bourgeoisie was more likely to choose segmental than class organization. Later chapters reveal more proletarian class organization but always in competition with sectional-segmental or local-regional organizations. Yet it should surprise no one that political organization by classes also has specifically political causes, involving the institutional particularities of states.

These institutional particularities now centered on state militarism. I first discuss the pre-1792 subphase, before the French Revolution and Napoleonic Wars. Tilly (1975, 1990) and I (in Volume I) have shown that for centuries political struggles had been structured by fiscal crises induced by war making. Similarly, we have seen that in this period petits bourgeois organized extensively and politically only when states, pressured by the manpower and fiscal needs of Great Power rivalry, failed to obtain resources by institutionalized means and sought to levy novel taxes, loans, and conscriptions. As state extraction increased and became more regressive, social tensions were forced to the "national" political level. Discontent focused on state costs (taxes and military service) and benefits (profitable office holding, economic monopolies, bondholding, and tax and conscription exemptions). These, not the production and market relations of capitalism, constituted the most contentious political economy of the period. Let me make one point perfectly clear: I am not asserting that these discontents were greater than discontent leveled against direct economic exploitation; in fact, they were almost certainly lesser in the lives of most people. But I am asserting that such discontent more consistently evoked *politics*.

Militarism also encouraged monarchical state elites to rationalize administration and attack the costly particularistic privileges hitherto sustaining them. Political struggles thus began with semiprincipled elite and party conflict *within* old regimes. Further fiscal and conscription pain and the opportunity presented by regime faction fighting then forced broader tax-paying classes out of their historic political indifference to question state legitimacy. If state institutions could not resolve elite-party factional fighting, petit bourgeois ideologists and organizations appeared, extending two demands of the regime modernizers. They claimed civil citizenship to freely protest political economy, and when protest was ineffective, they demanded political citizenship.

Only this route might potentially lead toward revolution because only it could mobilize the populace – urban and rural laborers and small peasants – behind the demands of the propertied people. Neither the French nor the American Revolution could have succeeded without the support of the populace. The French peasant revolt of 1789 pressured regime modernizers Leftward into structural reform; urban sans-culottes kept up the pressure. The American urban populace and small farmers provided troops and supplies to win the war and pressured rebel notables Leftward throughout the 1780s. Their main target was political economy – taxation, bondholding and economic privileges, debt laws, and monopolies and prices conferred by the state. The class alliance of petite bourgeoisie, peasant farmers, and sometimes the urban poor was politicized by the institutional particularities of states.

Fiscal crises had two components. First, the rate of increase in exactions had to be substantial to cause discontent. But given rates did not produce identical political reaction. Britain was the most highly taxed country, Prussia the most highly conscripted, followed by France and Austria, with the American colonies the least taxed or conscripted. This ranking by level of exaction does not correlate with degree of political outrage. Tax rates are particularly poor predictors of revolution or riot in the period, for most tax rates were rather stable. The majority of increased expenditures were financed by loans.

Thus, second, the degree to which a state had institutionalized elite-party conflicts also explains the severity of crisis. In terms of the distinctions expressed in Table 4.1, those regimes – Britain and Prussia

– that had centralized infrastructural coordination between state elites and parties of the dominant classes could steer higher revenues through these institutions, reducing old regime factional disputes. In Britain Parliament continued to vote taxes and the bank continued to raise loans – the one to pay off the other. Negotiations over both were institutionalized, with ultimate sovereignty located in Parliament, where state elite, "in" parties, and "out" parties interacted. In Prussia sovereignty lay in the relations between king and nobles, institutionalized within state administration at all levels. They had agreed to extract taxes from the rest jointly. The king could also extract considerable resources from the institutionalized management of his own domains.

Yet, in France and the American colonies, supposedly sovereign state institutions were less embedded among local notables. Attempts to levy moderate (France) or even mild (America) increases hit notable parties "from outside," to end their privileges or levy new taxes on them. Austria lay in the middle. Though its central state was but feebly embedded among local notables, it had institutionalized particularistic contracts with provincial notables whereby taxes and conscription could be increased in wartime, though only up to a point.

Loans, when taken to a vast scale, created distinctive equity problems. Because wealthy bondholders were paid off by the mass of taxpayers, loans were regressive. This situation endured beyond the war itself, and it became less easy to legitimate. Britain and France borrowed more than the others and so invited more peacetime discontent in this respect.

Thus exaction crises differed among states. Prussian exactions were managed through existing fiscal institutions. Prussia also had the most statist church among the countries, with little moral grounding of discontent in religion. Protest resulted, but it was largely expressed "within" the state in the form of an administrative reform movement and in the final fusion of the two Protestant churches into a single state church. This secured new rules for access to administrative office (and also to local representative assemblies), fused state elite and propertied class parties, and insulated their politics and morality from broader class discontent. Because the Prussian state borrowed little, taxpayers were not subsiding bondholders. In Britain substantial exactions were levied by state elite and "in" parties, but regressive borrowing and indirect taxes caused discontent among "out" and "excluded" parties. These could mobilize large emerging classes now capable of collective organization, especially the petite bourgeoisie, ideologically grounded in the notion of the "Protestant constitution," morally reinforced by everyday religious rituals. But its class organization never quite became autonomous, remaining torn between alliances with "out" and even "in" parties composed of old regime modernizers and the excluded populace below, its religious organization also generating ambiguous moral messages. Democratic reform resulted, often turbulent but not revolutionary.

Austrian exactions eventually exceeded the capacities of institutionalized provincial arrangements. Crisis appeared as plural provincial struggles rather than as singular and centralized. Discontent was expressed less by classes than by regional-nations (as we shall see soon). But in the American colonies and France old regimes began to disintegrate under protest at uninstitutionalized, "illegitimate" fiscal exactions and reforms, morally grounded in lower-level church discontent (France) and Protestant sects (the American colonies). The excluded petite bourgeoisie and peasant farmers then appeared, initially encouraged by old regime modernizers, then autonomously.

Without fiscal-military crisis the state and "national" politics were not sufficiently salient to popular experience to provoke class struggle over representation. Without such politicization, capitalists could ingratiate themselves segmentally into old regime economies, enfeebling autonomous class organization. Most persons would probably prefer to continue ignoring the state. Now, willy-nilly, they were "caged," politicized, and "naturalized" by state fiscal exactions.

As in most comparative macrosociology there are few cases on which to base such sweeping generalizations. However, I am emboldened by comparable variations in the early twentieth century. By then these fiscal-military pressures were no longer the principal mechanism by which classes were politicized. But an analogous mechanism had developed as the logic of military geopolitics had shifted state extraction toward mass mobilization of manpower. In the aftermath of World War I the degree of revolutionary turbulence, instigated this time by the proletariat, varied directly with the severity of regime breakdown in mass mobilization warfare. Between these two major revolutionary phases in Western history the Paris Commune and the Russian Revolution of 1905 resulted from comparable pressures. With the exception of the 1830 revolution in France and the Low Countries and of some failed revolutions of 1848,[2] all Western revolutions have had a similar triggering mechanism: military geopolitics putting class pressures – first fiscal, then manpower – on state institutions. Given the vagaries of

---

[2] The French revolution of 1848 was not so caused, nor were most of the German disturbances; but the most severe disturbances, in the Austrian lands, were primarily a fiscal-constitutional crisis (see Chapter 10) and Chartism in Britain was partly so caused (see Chapter 15).

history and the uniqueness of cases, it is as consistent a relationship as we find in macrosociology.

Many of these same processes also propelled the first *nations* beyond the protonational level into cross-class self-consciousness. Those capable of resisting state exactions were property owners; but their numbers were now exceeding the capacities of traditional particularistic segmental politics, which in any case did not respond promptly to their demands. They turned toward universal rallying cries like "people" or "nation." If fiscal crisis was averted, as in Prussia, these barely appeared. Where fiscal compromise occurred, as in Britain, their radical import could be weakened. But in America, and even more in France, fiscal crises politicized "people" and "nation." In both Britain and France the nation was thus state-reinforcing. "Nation" broadened its meaning from blood to citizenship. Yet it retained family metaphors – the nation became "motherland" or "fatherland" to all, joined in a single national family, along with other national families. Instead of kings, nobilities, and clerics symbolizing the family of kin, in the French Revolution they were formally excluded from the family of citizens. The abbé Volfius declared, "The true *patrie* is that political community where all citizens, protected by the same laws, united by the same interests, enjoy the natural rights of man and participate in the common cause" (Kohn 1967: 43).

Fiscal crises drove forward what might be called "rising class-nations." Self-conscious nations were thus essentially born of the struggle toward representative government. Whatever atrocities were later committed in the name of the nation, we should not forget that its emergence lay with those democratic ideals of this period that we most value today.

Yet the nation's dark side arose precisely because democratic ideals were born of war. Without the pressures of conscription, war taxes, and regressive war loans, the "people" would have remained apolitical, content to largely ignore the state. Now a limited "people" was in partial control of the state – yet the state's main function was war making. Thus the nation became a little more aggressive. Foreign policy could not remain quite so limited, dynastic, and private. The eighteenth-century struggle between Britain and France became supported by extra-regime pressure groups and patriotic demonstrations, though state exactions also brought popular opposition to war. Networks of discursive literacy generated stereotypes of one's national virtues and the enemy's national vices (as both Newman and Colley, referred to in Chapter 4, indicate). Nations had the qualities of intimate individuals and were loved and hated. Aggressive nationalism had not gone far by 1792, even in these countries, but it had emerged.

Yet the pre-1792 part of the militarist phase also began to generate a major, enduring complication. The drive for political citizenship created both a representative and a "national" issue, bifurcating nations into state-reinforcing and state-subverting. Mainland Britain and France were examples of the former; the Austrian case exemplifies the latter. The Austrian fiscal crisis was distinctive, not in its scale, but in its organizational consequences. Most military spending derived from taxes known as the "military contributions" of what were called the historic provinces; most of the rest was borrowed (Dickson 1987). But the contributions' formulas (usually fixing the numbers of troops that could be raised) proved insufficient, and the monarchy's credit was poor (it declared bankruptcy in 1811). Higher exactions had to be negotiated through the unwieldy confederal structure of provincial diets and ad-ministrations. Thus Austrian dissidents organized by region.

Slogans of "no taxation without representation" came from notables entrenched in provincial assemblies and administrations. In fact, in the 1780s, Joseph II actually had provoked the first two "patriot" move-ments in Europe – one in the most economically advanced province, the Austrian Netherlands, the other in one of the most backward, Hungary. What they shared was powerful provincial political organ-ization, in the Netherlands among all propertied classes, in Hungary confined to the nobility. As yet only the so-called nations with his-tories (i.e., of political autonomies) organized dissent. From such diverse regional actors the first state-subverting nations would emerge.

This early militarist phase of the emergence of self-conscious nations built on the two protonational phases. For example, Austrian provin-cial movements did not emerge from nowhere – they resonated amid ancient Magyar, Bohemian, Moravian, and similar nobilities and churches (with burghers added in the Austrian Netherlands and richer peasants and other middling strata intermittently elsewhere). But what was distinctive about this period (and here I depart from Anthony Smith's "perennial" theory of nationalism) was the exponential growth of the vertical nation existing across class lines. Cross-class nations were propelled forward more by the states' military than by their capitalist crystallizations. Because fiscal-military pressures hit states more directly and more uniformly than did commercial or industrial capitalism, nations appeared amid all of them with regional political institutions, not only in the more economically advanced. Nations appeared in different guises because state institutions differed: state-reinforcing, as in Britain; state-subverting, as in Austria. But emerging nations shared with classes a further emergent commonality: They mobilized unusually fervent ideologies. Since this impacted considerably, if variably, on post-1792 militarism, I pause to discuss ideological power.

3. Ideological power

Even when inflamed by the fiscal and conscription consequences of militarism, the petite bourgeoisie and the "people" still needed further organizational resources. To struggle successfully as a class or nation requires a meaning system embodying ultimate values, norms, and ritual and aesthetic practices. It requires ideology in the dual sense of immanent collective morale and a transcendent message to confer morality on one's own collective identity, to deny it to the opponent, to totalize the struggle, and to conceive of an alternative society worth the struggle. Indeed, the moral force of classes and especially of nations has been perfectly evident. "Interest-driven" theories of society – like Marxism or neoclassical economics or rational choice theory – cannot explain why members of collective organizations such as classes and nations are swept by intense collective emotions, break strong taboos about torture, killing, even genocide, and sacrifice their own lives on the barricades or in the trenches. The only serious attempt to explain the emotional force of nationalism has come from the "primordialist" and "perennialist" schools – nationalism is so strong because it is so old, so deeply rooted (Armstrong 1982; Smith 1986). But I do not believe this is correct.

I claim to do a little better. I say "a little better" because a full explanation requires more rigorous analysis of the intimate sphere of social life than I undertake here. We see in this volume that extensive classes and nations have possessed more moral fervor, more passion, when they can also mobilize the more *intensive* networks of their members. I shall trace a decline in proletarian class fervor when its roots shifted away from family and local community toward employment relations. In this early period, as we have seen (and will see again in Chapter 15), lower and middling class protest was most passionate and riotous when exploitation was of families, when it concerned men and women together, and when its organization was fundamentally that of street, village, and neighborhood. Protest was more passionate because the injustice of bread prices, of regressive sales and land taxes, and of conscription immediately concerned not merely self but also intimate loved ones. The family was the principal moral and emotional agent because it was the site of most socialization, including the experiencing and social channeling of love and hate. Nationalism also everywhere generated a fictional family: The nation is supposed, erroneously, to be a community of descent; it is also our symbolic mother or father. I believe the moral fervor of nationalism derived from its ability to link family, local community, and extensive national terrain.

Intensive family and community organization may generate strong emotions, perhaps rick burning or rioting, but not extensive solidarity across entire class and nation. This intensity must be mobilized by more extensive power organizations. This is where the first two proto-national phases of the nation proved so significant. Churches had long dominated the linkages between family, neighborhood, and the arena of extensive power. They had long monopolized formal social morality; their rituals centered on the stages of the individual and family life cycle (baptism, marriage, death); "class" and regional discontent had been expressed through heretical and schismatic mobilization from the Albigensians to the English Civil War. More recently churches had become the principal teachers of socially useful knowledge by sponsoring mass literacy. This instruction was also moral because its main instrument, the book, remained dominated by the Bible, homilies and sermons.

Church hierarchies were too closely associated with old regimes to encourage directly either class or national identities, but regimes from Henry VIII to Napoleon expropriated church property and substituted royal for canon law. Now they were also encroaching on church education. The most extensive protonational power relations were being secularized. Churchmen who were influential in states were increasingly seen as secular and immoral, often by their own clerical subordinates or parishioners, as were late eighteenth-century French and English bishops. Eighteenth-century religious innovators and dissident sects were generally less interested in doctrinal transformation of the church, more concerned with local social improvement, than had been their earlier counterparts (Jansenism would be an exception to this). The Great Awakening, Methodism, alienated French village curés – all were linking their moral concerns to popular social practices while religiously performing the rituals that implanted them in the family and community cycles. Religion had begun the retreat into local-regional power relations that I chart in later chapters, but it was leaving a large legacy of moral communication among family, locality, and more extensive power relations.

In the second protonational phase commercial capitalism and military states displaced churches as the principal communicator of messages between the intensive and the most extensive levels of power. Yet neither's own authoritative organizations proved suitable for the task. Commercial capitalism provided only tiny productive organizations linked by a diffuse, amoral market. The military state's growing authoritative organization was experienced as exploitative and immoral. Thus both capitalism and state mobilized less directly, principally through the expanding networks of discursive literacy they had generated. Writing, reading, and oral assembly networks became the principal links between the intensive and the extensive, between the secular instrumental and the sacred moral; and because churches and religiosity remained influential, an ideological contest between religious and secular moralities proceeded within these networks. A disputatious intelligentsia arose, providing ideological power resources for class and national development. As we saw, their ideologies were not just advanced as scientific principles; they were extraordinarily moralizing.

Preceding chapters show that much of the ideology and leadership of rising class and national movements came from outside the petite bourgeoisie, especially where they became radical. I assessed radicals' social backgrounds. They are typified by this list of occupations of a Vonckist cell (radical patriots in the Austrian Netherlands) rounded up by the Brussels police in the 1780s: 8 lawyers, 4 doctors or apothecaries, an architect, 3 merchants, 3 rentiers, 3 wig makers, 3 coffee shop proprietors, 2 printers, and 3 priests (Palmer 1959: I, 353). Only the merchants and rentiers seem at the heart of major social classes, and they were split equally between bourgeoisie and old regime. Can this really be a rising bourgeoisie? The other patriots were all at least semiprofessional ideologists. Their work presupposed discursive literacy and learning; their premises were vital to networks of communication. The wig makers (active radicals in several countries) puzzled me until I realized that their shops (like coffee shops and taverns) stocked journals and pamphlets, to be read and discussed during the long process of wig fitting. Chapters 5 and 6 show that revolutionary leaders in France and America were extraordinarily well educated. Many French revolutionaries had written nonpolitical essays and literary works. Many political organizations were "literary" – the pamphlets, mass petitions, and letter-writing networks, the societies of correspondence, the oratorical devices of the revolutionaries. These radicals seem less bourgeois than literati, an intelligentsia in the sense of a distinct stratum of moralizing intellectuals.

An ideological vanguard led bourgeoisies and some nations – a rather Leninist scenario. To paraphrase Lenin on the working class (discussed in Chapter 18): Left to itself the bourgeoisie was only capable of economism – in the eighteenth century of segmental manipulative deference. Revolutionary consciousness, said Lenin, presupposed leadership by vanguard intellectuals from outside the class. He did not explain where they came from. The Marxist Lucien Goldman (1964) tried to do this. Although the contradiction between modes of production underlay social crises, Goldman believed, it was best articulated not by the rising class but by intellectuals experiencing "maximum possible consciousness" by virtue of their exposed position and their professional ideological role. But, he says, the rising class then appropriated their ideas and dispensed with them. This argument needs broadening because the contradictions were not merely economic. An ideological vanguard might articulate best the experience and needs of other power actors (economic, military, and political), but its ideology was then appropriated by them. Alternatively, we might credit the vanguard with autonomous power: Its ideas and solutions were articulated and imposed from within its own discursive networks rather than from the contradictions of classes or states.

I explored both rival arguments most fully in discussing the French Revolution. Both had some force, varying among countries. Ideologists' slogans and principles were adopted as plausible solutions to the real problems of economic, military, and political power actors. Yet the recourse to ideology also involved two emergent powers conferred by expanding networks of discursive literacy.

1. Ideologists' principles were *transitive*, transgressing the essentially particularistic and segmental nature of old regimes. Knowledge was universal: The same principles could be applied across all human experience to philosophical, moral, aesthetic, scientific, sociological, or political problems. Discursive networks diffused not only rational but also moral reconstruction. Old regimes were aware of the danger and censored, licensed, and patronized, seeking to insulate each infrastructure and prevent transitivity. The old regime would be safely modernized if lawyers confined themselves to the courts, if peasant and petit bourgeois literacy meant better accounts and contracts, if church schooling increased the reading of homilies, if newspapers posted shipping arrivals and official communiqués. Particularistic patronage, corruption, and coercion could discipline each segmental infrastructure. But insulation did not succeed; eighteenth-century infrastructures contained three transitivities:

a. Specialized became generalist moralizing knowledge. Homilies and sermons concerned broad social morality, not just dogma. Homilies, sermons, novels, social essays, pamphlets on everything – all enjoyed mass sales. Questions of meaning and social morality were entwined in theology, in philosophy, in poetry whose meter was adapted to the native vernacular, in large circulation satiric stories like *Candide*, and in satiric paintings, reproduced with novel printing techniques, like Hogarth's. Legal training became entwined with the humane education of a gentleman, and legal concepts became universal rights. Newspapers discussed and advertised everything.

b. Discursive literacy diffused through and down from the old regime. Regime modernizers articulated reform ideologies in disputes with conservative factions at court, in law courts, parliaments, state administration, academies and salons, officer corps, and churches. If their factional dispute could not be institutionalized, they appealed downward for support. Religious sects, coffee shops, taverns, some academies, and newspaper and pamphlet sales of five thousand mobilized middling farmers, artisan masters, traders, schoolteachers, priests, officials, officers, and women.

c. Networks of discursive literacy used comparative reference points, relativizing social practices. Religious, especially Protestant and Puritan, networks exhorted members to live the simple unadorned lives of the early Christian communities. The secular Enlightenment practiced cultural anthropology, comparing Europe, its colonies, and its contacts with other cultures. How the English, the French, the Americans, the Persians (Montesquieu's *Persian Letters*), even the Huron Indians (Voltaire's *Ingénue*) supposedly behaved was considered relevant to how we should behave. In fact, these supposedly factual portrayals were actually moral and political tracts. The Huron were not so ingenuous, so naturally virtuous. Voltaire's point is that *we* should renounce luxury, deceit, and corruption. Thus networks of literacy disscussed what Bendix (1978) has termed alternative "reference societies." The American and French revolutions then supplied two particularly attractive or unattractive reference societies (depending on one's perspective) for political modernization.

Yet transitivity varied between ideological infrastructures and according to the intensity of fiscal-military crisis. The transitivity of religious infrastructures usually stopped short of explicit class or national politics, though they had political implications. The literacy drive of the Gallican church, the Great Awakening in the American colonies, and the growth of English Methodism all implicitly democratized religion, vesting ultimate knowledge in the individual and ultimate morality in an improved family and local community and desacralizing old regime hierarchies. In any case, state encroachments in secondary education and family law and appropriation of church property also desacralized hierarchy. The Catholic church moved toward being a transnational confederation of local-regional power networks, intensely implanted in family and communal life, dominating rituals of the family life cycle and the seasonal cycle of the rural community, and controlling most elementary education. Minority Protestant churches mostly did likewise, though established Protestant churches retained greater statism. Popular ideologies thus remained more susceptible to religious influence than Enlightenment intellectuals realized. But that influence might not merely reinforce old regimes.

Austrian and Prussian statist infrastructures generated ideologies like cameralism and "enlightened absolutism," attacking the particularism of churches, aristocracies, and privileged corporations, but limited by absolutism. The intelligentsia sometimes proposed radical reforms, but rarely publicized them to potential class movements. They did not become popular or "national." Thus statist transitivity was limited.

Statist and commercial capitalist routes intersected in the legal profession. Emerging from royal control, legal practice increasingly concerned civil contracts and rhetoric generalized this. Rights and liberties resided less in particularistic customs of corporations and communities, more in universal rights of property and person. Though incorporated into Austrian and especially Prussian statism, lawyers were important in moderate reform: in the early phases of English reform and of the French Revolution and in the American Revolution. In their practice American, British, and French lawyers felt the clash between old and new modes of production and political regimes (though they rarely articulated it so). They articulated a kind of "half-ideology" – semioppositional, semiprincipled. But as regimes learned to cope with capitalism, they incorporated this into the practices of state institutions like the U.S. Supreme Court, Napoleon's Civil Code, or the Prussian *Rechtstaat*. By the 1840s, law had lost its destabilizing, half-ideological role and supported the new regimes.

Commercial capitalism was the major generator of most other infrastructures of discursive literacy – networks of discussion (academies, reading circles, taverns, and coffee houses), newspapers, pamphlets and journals, and the literary media. In Britain, especially when reinforced by religious moralizing, they disseminated cross-class reformism and "improvement," a pragmatic program of personal achievement and social and political reform. Where commercial capitalism became entwined with military absolutism, across western continental Europe, the Enlightenment program proper emerged – metaphors of struggle justifying principled social changes toward a better form of society. Its mottos were the transitivity of knowledge, the *Sapere aude* (Dare to be wise) of Kant, the *Ecrasez l'infâme* (Crush the infamy, i.e., superstition) of Voltaire. It combined comparative politics, sociology, and ethics, encouraging the downward spread of cultivated, moralizing reason. It did not carry explicit class messages, and its radicalism was limited by absolutism; but where fiscal crisis deepened out of institutionalized control by practical elite and party politicians, as in France, the Enlightenment spawned alternative, principled ideologies espoused by a professional intelligentsia.

Discursive literacy was generated first by churches and then by states and capitalism, but it developed an emergent power transitivity. Without this the separate tensions of modernizing church, economy, military, and state could remain segmental, insulated from each other. Bourgeois men grumbling at economic privilege could believe there was no alternative to manipulative deference, liberal aristocrats could retreat to improve their estates, questing clerics could adopt Jansenist retreat and meditation. Remember Vadier, the discontented small-town notable lawyer-soldier who read Enlightenment texts and drifted toward politics, eventually to become the Revolution's police chief. Transitivity became a potent ideological weapon. Ideologists could find allies to outflank old regimes, expose their particularistic corruptions to moral principles, mobilize democratic sentiments, and relativize sacred traditions.

Emergent classes and nations were actually rather disparate. The petit bourgeois movement comprised small merchants, shopkeepers and small traders and middlemen, lesser professionals, small manufacturers, artisan masters, and artisan men. Their relations of production were diverse and sectionalized. Most were independent entrepreneurs employing little labor, but many lesser professionals (teachers, journalists, lawyer officials, pamphleteers) were employed, and many artisans were employed by other artisans. Only limited class identity, alongside sectional and segmental identities, might derive from such relations to the means of production. Much more class identity was generated by fiscal crisis. But the transitivity of ideological infrastructures encouraged moral, principled notions of systemic conflict between old and new societies, between the particularism, dependence, sophistication, idleness, and corruption of feudalism and the sturdy independence, honesty, and hard work of the industrious classes and the nation. Contemporaries usually pluraled the bourgeoisie into industrious or middling classes; but the entwining of rising classes with fiscal political crisis and ideological infrastructures could on occasion make them one community, one class, and one nation.

Classes, even when generated by capitalism, are not "pure." The class actors of this period were not merely economic but were created by the added entwining of ideological, military, and political power relations in a sort of "trialectic" among class, fiscal-military crisis, and ideological principles. Ideologists helped integrate the disparate experience of "middling" families into a coherent petite bourgeoisie. The battle between new and old forms of society was joined primarily through ideological, not economic, organizations, and the first emergent autonomy of ideological power went beyond Goldman's reductionist notion of "maximum possible consciousness." The intelligentsia did not merely aid an existing class and nation to develop immanent morale. It also helped imagine and so create that class and nation.

2. Only in rare revolutionary crises, when practical politics failed, did a second emergent ideological power appear – an ideological van-

guard with powers over other power actors. Ideologists had confidence in superior, principled knowledge and morality. Morality, science, and history were on their side; they despised pragmatists and trimmers. Practical politicians knew that not principles but compromises, corruptions, and coercion governed the world. But as the fiscal-military crisis worsened and the regime refused to budge, their practical institutionalizing skills became played out, escalating resort to principles and those who wielded them. Privilege *could* be abolished, the nation summoned to arms, superstition abolished – by declaring so. True, the rhetoric of Barnave, Brissot, Danton, and Robespierre was often calculated. But with practical politics in abeyance, they possessed a distinctive ideological power – the ability to move people into self-fulfilling actions by invoking principles and emotions flowing between written and verbal infrastructures generated by the crisis.

The mob, the pamphlet, and classical rules of composition and rhetoric came together in the French revolutionary assemblies as speeches, motions, and galleries interacted amid intense emotions. Here the enunciation of principle attained an emotional, ritualistic, and ethical content that would have been ridiculed in nonrevolutionary situations. It went too far even in France. For Robespierre and Saint-Just the pursuit of "virtue" and "purity" became obsessive, contributing to their downfall. Often rejecting practical compromise, they were suspected of plotting dictatorship, yet remained curiously passive as the Thermidorian coup developed against them.

Thus the second level of ideological power in France and sometimes in America rested on the ability to move people with self-fulfilling principles. Ideologists manipulated and morally coerced followers into bold declaratory, initiatory steps, past points of no return, from which retreat was difficult. Once privilege was declared abolished, no politician in the Revolution could be seen to support it. Practical politicians could backtrack over details but not over the principle of abolition. France was permanently changed. Once aristocratic or propertied neighbors were declared traitors to the nation or the cause, they could be dragged to the tumbrels, their property confiscated, shattering segmental deference networks. Louis was executed as a traitor to the nation, so declared the National Assembly, thus polarizing Europe into two armed camps. The nation was declared armed, and was armed, with global consequences. Constitutions were written, embodying the grandest principles, the fundamental rights of all persons. The American Constitution still constrains practical politics. Nineteenth-century French class struggles turned on rival constitutions.

In these "moments," ideological power elites arrived at principled messages that they derived partly from their prior experience in networks of discursive literacy. The Americans turned to predominantly legal and Protestant principles, the French to moral Enlightenment ones. Of course, there was also a substantial economic-political content to "self-evident" rights, to a nation equal without privilege, to a nation in arms. They had resulted as taxpaying classes generalized their discontents. But generalization occurred as the writings and speeches of the ideological vanguard interacted with the slogans of the popular assemblies, the pamphlets, and crowds. In this dynamic interaction of written and verbal communications, ideologists stumbled upon and exploited simple formulas and popular emotions, devising a power technique for implementing ideological principles. They had discovered "transcendent" principles of power organization.

Naturally, revolutionaries depended on economic, military, and political organizations to institutionalize their rule. But their ideology also changed these. French and, to a lesser extent, American transcendence fused economic and political power into a more active citizenship mobilizing class and nation, especially in armies, as in modern revolutions in general. This nation-state mobilized greater collective power than old regimes could muster. They had to reform in self-defense. Ideological power could only sway revolutionary moments, but they proved world-historical moments.

Yet Central Europe had developed more conservative ideologies, diffused more through statist channels. Lutheranism, traditionally state-reinforcing across North Germany, confirmed this; most churches cooperated more uneasily with states and became increasingly divided at lower levels. Administrations, church schools, armies, and capital cities grew faster than commercial capitalism. Discursive literacy flourished among the clients of old regimes, less among the petite bourgeoisie. The German literacy rate was only around 25 percent, though increasing steadily. Academies, clubs, and newspapers were dominated by officials, officers, teachers, and clerics (Blanning 1974). Radical ideologies had limited appeal to the employees and clients of absolutist regimes, though many referred to a conflict between education and privilege and referred to themselves interchangeably as the *Mittelstand* or *Bildungsstand* – "middle estate" or "educated estate" (Segeburg 1988: 139–42). Fiscal discontent was low in most German states (though not in Austria) because they drew more of their revenue from regalian rights and crown lands (see Chapter 11). Thus German political reformers, sparked as everywhere by fiscal and conscription issues, were less enraged than elsewhere.

Still, networks of discursive literacy were beyond state control in another sense in Central Europe. Unlike in Britain and France, state boundaries and linguistic communities did not roughly coincide among the propertied classes. The Austrian state was bigger than any language community; German states were much smaller. Austria ruled over nine major languages plus many minor ones. Germany had more than 300 states plus 1,500 minor principalities in 1789; 39 survived in 1815. Both contained at least two major religious communities, Protestant and Catholic (in Austria there were also Eastern Orthodox churches). So in Austria (at first) and Germany, unlike in Britain or France, discursive literacy was in a sense apolitical, not oriented positively or negatively toward the state, producing what is usually described as a less worldly, more narrowly "cultural" national ferment among a smaller intelligentsia.

In the German and Central European Romantic movements, intellectuals explored emotions and the soul more than reason and politics. Schiller defined German "greatness" as deriving less from politics than from "delving into the spiritual world." The absence of a central state left intellectuals free to invent a "world spirit": *Bildung* (combining formal education and moral cultivation) not geopolitics would triumph. For Hölderlin the "priestess Germania" would guide "peoples and princes." Germany would wield ideological not military or political power – a cosmopolitan ideal. Schiller and Goethe jointly wrote, "Forget, O Germans, your hopes of becoming a *nation*. Educate yourselves instead . . . to be human beings" (from Segeburg 1988: 152).

German intellectuals studied history, literature, philosophy, and the medium of communication itself, language. They grammaticized and codified German and were imitated across Central Europe as others codified Polish and Magyar, then Czech, Slovak, and other Slav languages. The materials for their task lay, of course, in existing linguistic communities. Czechs of various regions and classes did speak dialects of a mutually intelligible language, which gave them some sense of shared community; but overall, as Cohen (1981) shows, few Czech speakers imagined this was a total, "national" identity. Czech was the language of specialized identities emerging from the private household and the local community, German the language of specialized identities arising from the public sectors of capitalism and state. Those using the latter often classified themselves as "Germans," despite having Czech surnames. Intensive and extensive identities were not one. Philologists and protonationalist intellectuals did not seem to threaten states. Indeed, states, churches, and even some old regime nobles favored language standardization to ease their rule. But it subtly subverted state powers because it encouraged community identities that cut across or subverted state boundaries.

The "national" identities of these ideologists were ostensibly apolitical, yet they carried varied political implications. They imbibed

Enlightenment advocacy of reason, education, and literacy to modernize, usually with liberal political implications. But other ideological currents had conservative implications (Droz 1966). German Romantics saw progress carried less by the individual than by the community, the *Volk*. Herder discovered a *Volksgeist* expressed in folk songs and vernacular dialects and projected it back into history. He believed he was reviving, not creating, the German nation. In a different political context this might encourage radical-bourgeois demands for limited democracy, but amid German statism, clericalism, and lower fiscal discontent, it often romanticized a past order: The absolute ruler articulated a spiritual union among ruler, ancient community, and religion. Austrian and Catholic Romantics idealized a Holy Roman Empire of community comprising emperor, church, and estates.

All this might have mattered little. Central European protonationalism concerned small groups of intelligentsia, mostly loyal to their rulers, busying themselves with abstruse forms of knowledge. Hroch (1985: 23) calls this "Phase A nationalism (the period of scholarly interest)," later developing into "Phase B (the period of patriotic agitation)" and then "Phase C (the rise of a mass national movement)." He rigorously pursues economic and class explanations, admitting they yield few simple conclusions. Unfortunately, he ignores most political and all geopolitical causes. The latter is especially odd because the scholars made their first dramatic impact as French revolutionary militarism intensified class and national identities across Europe.

4. Post-1792 militarism

Britain, then briefly America, had begun what Bendix termed "reference societies" for modernizers, but after 1789, French influence dwarfed theirs. The Revolution attracted modernizers, but when it turned violent and attacked old regimes abroad, France became a terrible example except for radicals. From then on, old regimes and substantial bourgeoisies realized that their factional fighting might lead into the abyss. This caused them to compromise, mobilizing more "national" state administrations and armies. France was defeated, but by half-nations.

France became a nation-state quickly, then slowly. A purely bourgeois counterrevolution might have adopted the American strategy and decentralized France as a precaution against future "mobs." But Napoleon represented himself, not the bourgeoisie. He was a general and dictator, relying on a formidable national army and a central state, expanding both. The Directory's legal reforms were developed into the Code Napoléon, a comprehensive legal code; the revolutionaries' attempts to centralize administration were partly implemented

(Chapter 14); education became centralized; and church and state hierarchies were reconciled. Napoleon institutionalized the nation-state while emasculating political citizenship. After his fall the nation-state was weakened up to 1848 by monarchism and more enduringly by a clericalism forced back to the local-regional level. From the 1870s, the Republican nation-state began its final triumph.

British and Russian social structures were the least directly affected by French armies. Neither experienced routine occupation, and neither was militarily humiliated. Their traditional military formations proved adequate – the British navy, plus paying Europeans to do much of the land fighting; and the Russian autocracy, helped by "General Winter," leading nobility and peasants in defense of the homeland. The Terror and Bonaparte made France a negative reference society, slowing domestic reform. Autocracy allowed Alexander to switch from reform to reaction without causing serious unrest or encouraging a Russian nation.

During the wars, the British petite bourgeoisie split and radicals were repressed. But fiscal pressures eventually forced economic and political reform. Petite bourgeoisie and old regime compromised, and political citizenship was granted to property owners. The new "ruling class-nation" saw itself as uniquely capable of compromise and gradual evolution, morally qualified to rule the global empire of uncivilized and "colored" peoples now under its sway. With laissez-faire institutionalized, the British nation appeared pacific; already enjoying global power, it had less need of aggression. Its nationalism was complacent, achieved – only turning nasty in far-off colonial places. The British conversion from national to full nation-state proceeded relatively smoothly. (See Chapter 16.)

The French impact was much greater on the Continent. France propagandized freedom of opinion, of the press, and of association, equality before the law, an end to privilege, expropriation of church property, freedom of worship, economic freedom from guilds and other corporate bodies, and political citizenship for propertied males. Bonaparte abrogated political but not civil citizenship. In 1808 he wrote to his brother Jerome, just created king of Westphalia:

In Germany, as in France, Italy and Spain, people long for equality and liberalism. The benefits of the Code Napoleon, legal procedure in open court, the jury, these are the points by which your monarchy must be distinguished. . . . Your people must enjoy a liberty, an equality unknown in the rest of Germany. [Markham 1954: 115]

Much of Europe was ruled by distant dynasties. Discontent smoldered among powerful local-regional aristocracies and burgher oligarchies and where the local church was not that of the dynasty. Here intensive local-regional power relations did not reinforce the extensive state. Across much of Italy, the Austrian Netherlands, Poland, and Ireland, nobilities or substantial bourgeoisies – relying at village level on clerics – rallied local forces to greet the French as "national" liberators. Their "nations" were often traditional, segmental, and particularistic: Notables united by common territorial residence and blood relationships should govern themselves. Yet bourgeois and petit bourgeois groups in economically advanced areas – the Netherlands, parts of Switzerland, and some Italian towns – embraced more secular and democratic Jacobinism. The nation should embody civil and political citizenship for all males or all male property owners. By the 1790s, few even of these areas were industrialized, but they were commercial and urban. Their radicals believed that rule should pass from dynasties, aristocracies, and particularistic clients to the universal propertied "people."

Among conservative clerical and radical "patriots" alike, just as among class movements, leaders were drawn disproportionately from the ideological professions – priests, lawyers, professors, printers, and journalists – often with students and seminarians as shock troops. In backward Ireland this presented the curious spectacle of Wolfe Tone, a Protestant lawyer and zealot for the secular Enlightenment, leading a peasant-clerical revolt against the British. Almost everywhere in patriot movements the "rising bourgeoisie," that is, the manufacturing bourgeoisie, was poorly represented. So were Germans. None of the several hundred German states (including some feeble ones) were toppled by patriots, only by French armies. The predominantly statist, Lutheran route to discursive ideologies in Germany had created few patriots (Blanning 1974: 305–34).

Elsewhere patriots mobilized locally intensive transnational federations of discursive literacy networks. As the French army neared, networks of Masonic lodges, clubs of illuminati, Jacobins, and secret societies exploded. Though small and unrepresentative (only in the Austrian Netherlands did they organize a large popular party, the Vonckists), their risings distracted the local states. Later they formed auxiliary militias and client administrations. Around French borders patriots staffed "sister republics" protected by French arms.

A second, intensive linguistic spark was sometimes added. Appealing downward for local support, patriots expressed their demands in the local written language, often not the language of the ruling dynasty. Nor was it the spoken language of most of the populace, whose many dialects were often mutually intelligible. That the patriot appeal was rather restricted led them into greater linguistic activity. The French revolutionaries had sought to extend the French language downward.

The abbé Grégoire's linguistic survey of 1790 had revealed that three-quarters of the population knew some French, but only just over 10 percent could speak it properly. As the Committee of Public Safety declared in 1794:

The monarchy had good reason to resemble the Tower of Babel; but in a democracy, to leave the citizens ignorant of the national language and incapable of controlling the government means to betray the fatherland. It means to fail to recognize the blessings of the printing press, for every printer is a teacher of the language and the legislation. . . . In a free people language must be one and the same for all. [Kohn 1967: 92]

In Italy, the Low Countries, and Poland this enhanced the political relevance of the linguistic community, of clerics still providing the most education, and of obscure philologists.

The term "nationalism" seems to have been used first in Germany in 1774 and in France in 1798. It was not yet used aggressively. The leaders of France, described as *la grande nation* from 1797, did not consider themselves opposed to other nations; nations were allied against reactionary dynasties in a struggle to establish universal freedom and peace (Godechot 1956; Mommsen 1990). But as the wars intensified mass mobilization, two developments occurred. First, fiscal and manpower needs forced limited economic and political reforms. These inched states away from segmental particularism, seen increasingly as immoral "corruption," toward more universal principles of administration, military service, and morality. Second, the scale of war mobilization – 5 percent of total populations conscripted, perhaps half agricultural and manufacturing surpluses fed into the war machines – meant whole "peoples" were organized to fight each other. In Britain and France, the most advanced combatants, this fed popular aggressive nationalism after about 1802 – after British Jacobinism and French counterrevolution had faded and when it became clear that the two states would fight unto death. Negative national stereotypes of the enemy became more widely shared. Local legend has it that the citizens of West Hartlepool, finding a ship's monkey in a uniform washed up on their beach, hung it for a Frenchman.

The growth of nationalism on the Continent was more complex.[3] At first, most populations were split, especially in more advanced areas. Many French reforms were popular, particularly civil law codes.

---

[3] Hobsbawm (1962 101–16) provides a fine short overview of these nationalisms, Palmer (1959) a fine longer one. Godechot (1956) is good up to 1799; thereafter for detailed cases see Dunan (1956), Connelly (1965), Devleeshovwer et al. (1968), and Dovie and Pallez-Guillard (1972). For a contrasting study of the Rhineland, loyal to France, see Diefendorf (1980).

Napoleon's Confederation of the Rhine allowed medium-sized states (like Baden, Württemberg, and Bavaria) to modernize and mop up tiny states, counterweighting Austrian power. Industries benefited from the French demand for uniforms, guns, and fodder. But the French fueled local nationalisms as "liberation" turned into imperialism. Bilateral trade treaties favored France. Wealth, inventions, and skilled workers were often simply carted off to France. By 1799, revolts against the French were widespread. Some attacked under the conservative banners of old regimes and religions, some radically proclaimed national self-determination. As in England, contrasting stereotypes of "national character," based on individual character, appeared. Germans characterized themselves as open, upright, and God-fearing, the French as sly, frivolous, and unreliable. The nation and *la grande nation* were no longer one.

Bonaparte worsened the contradiction. His own career inspired radical patriots across Europe, proof that bourgeois birth plus merit could rule. Yet he opposed nationalism and helped patriot movements only when they suited his personal interests (Godechot 1988: 23–6). He favored a dynastic empire, not a confederation of sovereign national states. He appointed his family and marshals as kings and married them into the royal families of Europe, and he divorced Josephine to marry Francis of Austria's eldest daughter in 1810. As the Viennese ditty expressed it:

> Louise's skirts and Napoleon's pants
> Now unite Austria and France.
> [Langsam 1930: 142]

As imperial rule descended into cycles of revolt and repression, even his client-kings advised concessions to patriots. But Bonaparte only tightened his despotism. This would have mattered less had it brought peace and prosperity, but wars brought taxes, conscription, and British blockade. By 1808, nearly all patriots were turning against the French; after 1812, even active collaborators were deserting a losing cause.

But to whom could they turn? Conservative patriots – nobles and clerics mobilizing peasants – could mobilize segmental, intensive, local-regional guerrilla warfare in backward Spain and mountainous Switzerland and the Tyrol. Elsewhere big armies were required to kick out the French. As in the Revolution, and as later in the century, war between large armies favored the "one and indivisible" state. A Milanese patriot perceived the military weakness of Italian federalism:

The ease with which Italy can be invaded, the . . . national jealousies which actually arise between confederated republics, the slowness with which federations operate, lead me to reject the federalist plan. [Italy] needs to be given a form of government which can offer the strongest possible resistance to invasion; and the only such government is a *republic one and indivisible*. [Godechot 1988: 23]

He recommended an Italian constitution modeled on the 1793 constitution of France – the state that had most successfully resisted foreign invasion.

What was utopian in Italy could be reality in Central Europe under the powerful states, Prussia and Austria. German patriots had realistically to choose French rule or to support these absolute monarchies. The auspices were not good for either the smaller German states or for radical patriots, compromised by their support for Bonaparte, weakened by his downfall. Liberalism seemed allied with the particularism and military failure of smaller states. Liberalism and radical nationalism had only just got going in Germany; by 1815, they were badly faltering.

The decisive French victories at Ulm and Austerlitz and at Jena and Auerstadt had, respectively, devastated Austria and Prussia in 1805–6. Yet the two monarchies were not finished. They were shocked by defeat to contemplate reform, learning to harness a modicum of nationalism to absolutism. In Central Europe, the French had rarely abrogated noble privileges (they had needed noble support). But the Civil Code and sale of common and church lands had created a more capitalist environment for nobles and bourgeoisies alike. In France, the Revolution had encouraged capitalism plus legal and political liberalism. With careful regime management, German modernization might secure more capitalism and more bureaucracy but no more liberty. Administrative, not parliamentary, representation might suffice.

Prussian reformers, mostly university-educated officials, made headway after Jena, then had to compromise (Gray 1986; for more details, see Chapter 13). Their plan to enfranchise all property owners in a national assembly was defeated but partly implemented at the municipal level. Central administration was rationalized, subjected to the law and opened to the educated bourgeoisie. Public education was expanded and German discursive literacy extended downward under Lutheran and Prussian leadership. Serfs (and Jews) were emancipated and corvée labor abolished. In return, peasants handed over one-third of their land to their nobles. Nobles now had free landless laborers, not serfs. Agrarian capitalism advanced. In the army general conscription, meritocratic promotion rules, and staff colleges were introduced. All subjects were permitted for the first time to wear the Prussian colors as a national cockade. The Landwehr militia was created, in pale imitation of the French citizen army. (See Chapter 12.) In 1813, the king declared war against France, appealing "to my people" – "My" and "people" being somewhat contradictory. The enthusiasm of the Landwehr during the campaigns of 1813–15 raised liberal hopes. Hegel, a supporter of Bonaparte in 1806, now saw the Prussian bureaucracy as a "universal class" realizing the potentialities of the human spirit. Though this seems bizarre to us, many German liberal nationalists looked hopefully toward Prussia.

Some reaction occurred after 1815. As in Austria, monarch and court were fearful of arming the rabble. The commander of the guard corps and the minister of police warned; "To arm a nation means to organize and facilitate rebellion and sedition" (Ritter 1969: I, 103). Yet many professional officers favored change, so the Landwehr stayed, but as a reserve force not a permanent militia. There developed a Lutheran Prussian-German national identity, linking religious and national sentiments to loyalty to a strong state.

The Habsburgs had different options. When somebody was recommended to Emperor Francis as a patriot for Austria, Francis replied, "He may be a patriot for Austria, but the question is whether he is a patriot for me" (Kohn 1967: 162). The Habsburgs could not rule a national state. They were dynasts ruling a multilingual, multiprovincial empire, in some provinces aided by the Catholic church. Though the Austrian core was Germanic, most of the population spoke other languages. But the dynasty had possessed the titular headship of the Holy Roman (German) Empire for almost four hundred years and Austrians could conjure up an alternative German nationalism. Here is a French report on the activities of a confidant of Archduke John and later a leader of revolts against the French:

Baron Hormayr . . . has undertaken the editorship of a periodical called *Archives of Geography, History, Politics and Military Science*. Under this rather innocent-sounding title he continues to ape Thomas Paine in the preaching of revolutionary doctrines. These doctrines, he claims, should bring about the regeneration of Germany and the reunion of that vast country under one new constitution. Rarely does M. de Hormayr himself speak. Instead, he very cleverly quotes from many justly esteemed German writers who thought of anything but revolution. Even Luther is laid under contribution. . . . The favorite themes of these extracts are the *unity* and *indivisibility* of Germany, and the conservation of its *mores*, its usages and its language. As historian and imperial archivist, M. de Hormayr has access to many details regarding the ancient unity of Germany of which we are entirely ignorant. [Langsam 1930: 49]

Thus could an archivist worry an army of occupation – but he also worried his own emperor.

Francis wanted to be rid of the French but not on popular terms. He compromised, reforming the army, creating a Landwehr in Austria and Bohemia, promising general reform (which he never implemented), and in 1809, launching an uprising against the French, appealing to the

"German nation" as "allies" and "brothers" of the Habsburgs and Austria. Archduke Charles inflicted the first major battlefield defeat on Napoleon at Aspern, a defeat that broke the myth of invincibility. Napoleon recovered, grinding down the Austrian generals to sue for peace. Yet Austria remained the leader of German resistance, with the largest armies, able to appoint Archduke Charles as the supreme allied commander in the final pursuit of Napoleon. As Habsburg military power revived, the "German card" was resisted. Francis refused the German imperial crown. Officials were instructed to refer only to Austrian patriotism – and even to speak respectfully of Napoleon "since, after all, he is the son-in-law of our monarch" (Langsam 1930: 160). Segmental dynasticism had revived.

But Austria's regional-national problems had been worsened by the wars. The Habsburgs suffered most from Jacobin patriots, in the Netherlands, Poland, and Italy. The departure of Napoleon eased the pain briefly, but dissidents were emboldened throughout the Napoleonic period and their grievances remained. Through the next (and last) century of their rule the Habsburgs were assailed by nationalists asserting that a people, defined by ethnic-linguistic culture but ruled by foreigners, should have its own state. Eventually these state-subverting nations triumphed.

The movements in the Austrian lands were not directly caused by the development of capitalism or industrialism (as Marxists and Gellner 1983: chapter 2 argue) because they appeared among diverse economies and classes. Nationalism arose right across Europe amid different levels of capitalist and industrial development (Mann 1991) – and this is the only perverted sense I can make out of the revisionist Marxist notion that nationalism resulted from "uneven development" (as advocated by Nairn 1977). Nationalists said virtually nothing about classes or capitalism or industrialism (until mass peasant nationalisms appeared far later). Why, then, should we believe them reducible to these forces?

Hroch (1985) gives the most careful analysis of economies and classes, relying mainly on samples of the adherents of nationalist societies in eight state-subverting small nations across Europe (including two Austrian minorities, Czechs and Slovaks). His Phase B nationalism, when significant patriot movements began popular agitation but before they had mass followings, roughly corresponds to the first half of the nineteenth century across most Austrian lands. Hroch sustains some generalizations. Most cases still involved the intelligentsia (its clerical wing now usually fading), and most disproportionately involved literate urban occupations at probably the highest levels to which the oppressed minority could reach. The directly productive bourgeoisie was underrepresented as were almost all manufacturing sectors. But nationalists were usually more active in areas where markets were most developed.

Yet Hroch's countries do not include the most advanced and state-subverting regions in the Austrian lands, the Austrian Netherlands and northern Italy. They were commercialized and urbanized at the time of their first patriotic ferment (so were the Czechs by the time ferment reached them). But Poland, Hungary, Slovakia, and the Balkans hosted nationalist movements while they were still far more agrarian and backward. There was probably a threshold level of market-aided literacy and communication beyond which patriots could credibly organize – as Hroch seems, finally, to conclude. But beyond that level of mobilization there was economic and class diversity. Indeed, Hroch's nationalist societies were not always the most significant actors. In the Revolution of 1848, most leaders of provincial "national" movements were nobles seeking representation only for themselves (Sked 1989: 41–88). The Magyar nobles remained in control, though most nobilities did not. As Hroch observes, mass state-subverting nationalism (his Phase C, mostly occurring in the later nineteenth century) acquired a peasant base. What common class motivation could possibly lead them all to proclaim themselves nationalists (cf. Sugar 1969)?

My explanation centers on the political impact of the militarism and ideologies discussed earlier. Most grievances concerned the political economy of the state: its growing fiscal and manpower exactions and its office-holding spoils – costs and benefits. But fiscal discontent was here expressed territorially, by region. This had unfortunate consequences for the state's "national" crystallization. Fiscal or manpower discontent in Britain might produce class riots that local gentry and yeomanry could handle. But territorially based discontent led to revolts by provincial notables, wielding militias, sometimes regular troops, with initial sympathy from lower-level clerics, and mobilizing intense local sentiments that families and homes were under attack from strangers. Political representation was structured as much by local community and region as by class – *where* to locate citizenship was as important as *who* would obtain it.

Austria was not unique, for the United States was also riven by regional-national struggles. During the mid-nineteenth century in the United States, states' rights mobilized intense local passions, dominated politics, and ended in civil war. Across the Austrian lands, civil disturbances peppered the nineteenth century – in 1821, 1830, 1848–9, 1859, 1866, and 1908 – usually abetted by foreign Powers. Local-regional resistance to a centralizing state recurred in all five countries, though only in these two did it generate civil war.

Yet Austrian regional nationalism also uniquely (among the five countries) involved linguistic issues, especially through office spoils. Two issues arose: What should be the language of the public sphere, especially government, and what languages should be taught in public schools? As Gellner (1983) argues, literacy was cultural capital, realizable in employment in army, civil administration, law courts, and capitalist economy. As capitalism and states expanded, they were staffed by more non-German speakers. More nobles, bourgeois, and petit bourgeois had a vested interest in the local language's being the state's. The Habsburgs were not unsympathetic, encouraging bilingualism in the army. Yet to extract taxes they turned intermittently to repression, pushing them to depend on the mainly Austro-German officer corps and central administration. Other linguistic communities were blocked from administration and law courts, so the revolutionaries of 1848 protested (Sked 1989: 41–88).

Yet linguistic nationalism was not just an instrumental demand (as in Gellner's model). As clerics and philologists labored to produce standardized local vernaculars, these became the cement of public local-regional interaction networks, reproduced in elementary schools, churches, and market exchanges. Language gradually became a unifying ideology of a locally rooted cross-class community, pointing to the contrast between "us," speaking intelligibly, and "alien" unintelligible conquerors. Movements legitimated themselves in terms of the "nation" even where (as in Hungary) they permitted only the nobility political citizenship, even where (as in Slovakia) the "nation" was invented by a handful of intellectuals. The fusion of regional and linguistic identities meant the Habsburgs came to be assailed less by classes than by passionate, state-subverting "nations."

In this post-1792 part of the militarist phase revolutionaries and Bonaparte had loomed large. Though the nation's rise seems inexorable when viewed teleologically from the twentieth century, in this period it advanced contingently, as decisions made by leaders of the principal aggressor Power had enormous geopolitical repercussions. Had Louis XVI compromised, had the Brissotins foreseen that war would destroy them, had the French troops at Valmy run away (as they were expected to do), had the Directory not produced a consummate general who proved an insensitive conqueror and who made one terrible decision to invade Russia . . . these and other "might have beens" might have stemmed the national tide.

Events in 1815 seemed to reverse the tide anyway. With the defeat of France concerted political decisions strove to cut down nationalism. The Concert of Powers and the Holy Alliance of dynasts acted decisively against radical patriots (see Chapter 8). Though Britain was becoming a nation-state, it did not advocate national principles of government for Europe. The Prussian regime might be tempted to play the German card in its rivalry with Austria, but for the moment, fear of the people kept its state true to segmental dynasticism. Habsburg power was self-consciously dynastic; Russia knew only dynasticism. The United States was an ocean away, no longer infecting Europe with democratic germs. The world seemed embarked on cautious modernization, ruled by two transnationalisms, old regime dynastic networks and the global, liberal British economy.

But there were three reasons why nationalism would not be dispelled. First, the many contingencies of this short subphase had transformed power organizations. Britain, France, and the United States were now national states and could not return to being particularistic old regimes. Though the United States remained regionally confederal, Britain and France were increasingly centralized. Though the Austrian and Prussian situations were more open-ended, nations within them had also been strengthened. Second, capitalism and state modernization were unstoppable, identified with material and moral "progress," making states better at fighting wars. Their conjunction meant that classes and nations would continue to develop extensive and political organization. It was not inevitable that democratic nation-states would dominate, for more statist Prussia and more confederal Austria long survived. But the old particularistic, segmental order had substantially declined. Third, industrial capitalism was later to increase the density of social interaction and to transform state functions. The unintended consequences of this fusion produced full-fledged nation-states in the fourth phase of development, chronicled in later chapters.

Conclusion

This period saw the emergence of classes and nations. As Marx perceived, eighteenth-century capitalism did (roughly) displace what was now called feudalism, and there was extensive and political class struggle between old regime and bourgeois elements. Yet this almost always involved the petite bourgeoisie, not the bourgeoisie as a whole. The bourgeoisie, Marx's historical paradigm case of the rising class, was largely absent from the macrohistorical record. We shall see that Marx also exaggerated the powers of his other rising class, the proletariat. Even in the capitalist mode of production, classes proved far less extensive and political than he and many others have asserted.

Little old regime–petit bourgeois conflict emerged directly from an economic dialectic. Militarist state crystallizations intervened, generating fiscal crisis and severe conflict between state elites, "in" and "out" parties, the "people," and the "populace." Direct relations of economic production were more particularistic, diverse, and amenable to segmental and sectional compromises. Most conflict between petite bourgeoisie and old regime derived from the political economy of the state. Expanding networks of discursive literacy then helped some regime modernizers and emerging petites bourgeoisies to transcend their conflict and modernize the state. Where elite-party conflict was not institutionalized, fiscal crisis deepened, permeating class structure and generating class hostilities. Revolutionaries wielding ideological powers then might seize command and transform social structure. The French Revolutionaries then marched on all old regimes. The French Revolution and Napoleonic Wars intensified militarism and thickened the heady, impure brew.

No revolution was fully completed, most class conflict remained muted and partial, and nations only half emerged. Party democracy tottered unsteadily and unevenly forward as emerging classes and nations compromised with old regimes. Regimes became more capitalistic, as classes were partially incorporated into their segmental and local-regional organization. States and militaries modernized, professionalized, admitted highly educated sons of professionals, and became less particularistic and corrupt. Intermarriage between old regime, substantial bourgeoisie and professionals increased. British capitalism retained an old regime commercial tinge, German capitalism acquired statist tinges. Nineteenth-century nouveaux riches in all countries were incorporated into both national regimes and local-regional and segmental power networks.

The incorporation of the petite bourgeoisie (and later of the middle class; see Chapter 16) seemed more problematic. Their numbers were far greater and their demands for citizenship more radical. The regime did not want to marry its sons to *their* daughters. Yet even their loyalties could be bound by full individual civil and partial political citizenship. Legal codes enshrined "possessive individualism" combining personal and property freedoms, although regimes varied in their concessions of more collective civil rights like freedom of association or of the press (none allowed workers untrammeled organizing rights). Limited, varying degrees of party democracy were conceded to the petite bourgeoisie.

Now began the era of "notable" political parties, predominantly segmentally controlled by substantial property owners, using bribery, patronage, status deference, and mild coercion (usually the ballot was not secret) to persuade middling classes to vote for their betters. The United States was pushed to adult male suffrage outside the South, but region, religion, and ethnicity crosscut class and kept its parties segmental and notable. In Britain two notable parties extended the franchise to "dish" each other. Austria and Prussia lagged, but eventually conceded some local and then central representation. Two noted antidemocrats, Bismarck and Napoleon III, were the first to introduce universal adult male suffrage (though to assemblies of limited sovereignty). Notable parties segmentally incorporated most of the petite bourgeoisie (although in Austrian provinces they were often antiregime). The massive increase in social density and the emergence of classes and nations meant greater collective and distributive power mobilization. The "people" and the "populace" had more direct relations with old regimes. But these remained more cooperative and more varied than either Marx or any of the other dichotomous theorists referred to in Chapter 1 realized.

I have presented a predominantly modernist theory of the emergence of the nation into world history. Nations are not the opposite of classes, for they rose up together, both (to varying degrees) the product of modernizing churches, commercial capitalism, militarism, and the rise of the modern state. Thus my theory has combined all four sources of social power. Ideological power had dominated the first protonational phase, as churches diffused broader social identities through sponsorship of mass discursive literacy. In the second protonational phase, varying combinations of commercial capitalism and modernizing states continued to diffuse more universal protonational (and class) identities, enveloping particularistic economic roles, localities, and regions. In the decisive third, militarist phase, the increasing costs of eighteenth- and early nineteenth-century geopolitics propelled broader identities toward the national state, just as they politicized class and regional grievances. Intensifying geopolitical rivalries gave national identities the first aggressive sentiments toward each other. Thus protonations became actual self-conscious, cross-class, somewhat aggressive nations. Yet emerging nations (and classes) also mobilized a distinctive moral passion, as ideological power relations linked intense familial and local community networks to perceptions of extensive exploitation by capitalism and military state. Extensive and political class and national discontent were principally organized by discursive literacy networks staffed by secular and religious intelligentsia.

Emerging classes and nations now influenced, and were themselves influenced by, state institutions. Galvanized by militarism, their moral passions intensified by ideologies, classes and nations demanded more representative government and aimed toward democracy. Thus nations essentially originated as movements for democracy. However, nations were at this point confronted by a choice: to democratize a central state or to reduce the powers of a central state and seek to democratize local-regional seats of government. Their choices were principally determined as political and ideological power relations entwined.

Politically, the choices depended on whether state institutions were already fairly centralized. British ones were; Austrian and American colonial ones were not. In the latter, advocates of representation could fall back on local-regional institutions that they felt were more controllable than would be any central state. Ideologically, the legacy of the first two protonational phases was now strongly felt because political territories related variably to religious and linguistic communities, both able to mobilize local intensity for extensive purposes. The language issue also generated the politics of public education and qualifications for public office. If these political and ideological power relations centralized the entire (or the core) state territories, state-reinforcing nationalism resulted, as in mainland Britain and (after revolutionary vicissitudes) France. Where they decentralized state-subverting nationalism resulted, as in Austria. The United States and Germany represented intermediate cases. The United States had political decentralization without much ideological reinforcement, and so its sense of "nation" remained ambiguously poised between the two. Germany was a different intermediate case because political decentralization lay within a broader ideological community. Its nationhood also remained ambiguous, although it soon moved down the third, state-creating, track.

Most theories have explained nationalism in terms of either economic or political power relations or both. Yet nations emerged as all four sources of social power entwined. Relations among these sources changed over the period. Before and at the beginning of this period geopolitics had generated a military revolution causing repeated state fiscal crises that politicized and "naturalized" class relations. The last and deepest crisis came at the end of the eighteenth century. Earlier states had been relatively puny at home; though often fairly autonomous even from dominant classes, they had exercised few powers over them. The nature of state elites or of state institutions had mattered little for society. Now they mattered a great deal. The rise of citizenship is conventionally narrated as the rise of modern classes to political power. But classes are not "naturally" political. Through most of history subordinate classes had been largely indifferent to or had sought to evade states. They were now caged into national organization, into politics, by two principal zookeepers: tax gatherers and recruiting officers.

Throughout the same period, and beyond, class relations were also revolutionized by commercial, then industrial capitalism. Capitalism and militarist states began to shape ideologies around classes and nations. As yet they were much influenced by moral-religious mobilization of intensive power, but at the beginning of the period it is perhaps possible to isolate two sources of social power, the economic and the military, as in a sense "ultimately primary."

Yet the entwined military and economic revolutions had generated the modern state, which proved to have emergent power properties. On the representative issue states crystallized at various positions between more mobilized authoritarian monarchy and an embryo party democracy (plus colonial settler variants). On the national issue they crystallized between centralized nation-states and confederalism. The last phase of fiscal-military crisis vastly increased the scale of states and politicized and naturalized classes. This did not increase the distributive power of state elites, but it did increase the collective structuring powers of state institutions, enhancing the relevance of what I called institutional statist theory. Thus ultimate primacy arguably may have shifted toward a combination of economic and political power. Later chapters show that whereas capitalism continued to revolutionize economic life, political institutions exerted conservative effects. The institutions by which early class representation and national conflicts were resolved – the American Constitution, the contested French constitution, British old regime liberalism, Prussian authoritarian monarchy, and Habsburg dynastic confederalism – endured. They interacted with the Second Industrial Revolution to determine the outcomes of the next phase of class struggle, between capitalists and workers.

Finally, I have shown that modern societies have not strained toward democratic and national citizenship as part of some general human evolution toward the realization of freedom. Rather, modern societies reinvented democracy, as the ancient Greeks had reinvented it, because their states could not be escaped, as medieval states could be escaped. What we call "democracy" is not simply freedom, because it had resulted from social confinement. Giddens describes the modern state as a "power container." I prefer the more charged "cage." In the early modern period people became trapped within national cages and so sought to change the conditions within those cages.

This had also happened in two earlier phases of state growth, described in Volume I. The first permanent states, in the world's "pristine civilizations," resulted from caging by alluvial and irrigated river valley cultivation. Those first states seem to have had representative institutions, later subverted by warfare, trade concentration, and the emergence of private property. A second phase, Greek democracy, was also the product of caging, partly economic, partly by hoplite warfare. In Volume I, I argue that Greeks were not necessarily politically freer than their great adversaries, the Persians. The despotism of the Persian

Great King mattered less than would despotism in Greek city-states, because Persian subjects had weaker relations with their state than did Greeks. In all three cases – the pristine civilizations, Greece, and the late eighteenth century – the cage tightened. As it did so, the same popular reaction occurred: The inmates cared more about conditions within their cages than about the cages themselves.

Bibliography

Anderson, B. 1983. *Imagined Communities*. London: Verso.
Armstrong, J. 1982. *Nations Before Nationalism*. Chapel Hill: University of North Carolina Press.
Bendix, R. 1978. *Kings or People: Power and the Mandate to Rule*. Berkeley: University of California Press.
Blanning, T. C. W. 1974. *Reform and Revolution in Mainz, 1743–1803*. London: Cambridge University Press.
Chatterjee, P. 1986. *Nationalist Thought and the Colonial World*. Totowa, N.J.: Zed Books for the United Nations University.
Cohen, G. 1981. *The Politics of Ethnic Survival: Germans in Prague, 1861–1914*. Princeton, N.J.: Princeton University Press.
Connelly, O. 1965. *Napoleon's Satellite Kingdoms*. New York: Free Press.
Crone, P. 1989. *Pre-Industrial Societies*. Oxford: Blackwell.
Devleeshovwer, R., et al. 1968. *Les pays sous domination française (1799–1814)*. Paris: CDU.
Dickson, P. G. M. 1987. *Finance and Government Under Maria Theresa, 1740–1780*, 2 vols. Oxford: Clarendon Press.
Diefendorf, J. M. 1980. *Businessmen and Politics in the Rhineland, 1789–1834*. Princeton, N.J.: Princeton University Press.
Dovie, J., and A. Pallez-Guillard. 1972. *L'épisode napoléonien. Aspects extérieurs*. Paris: Presses Universitaires de France.
Droz, J. 1966. *Le Romantisme allemand et l'Etat: Résistance et collaboration dans l'Allemagne napoléonienne*. Paris: Payot.
Dunan, M. 1956. *L'Allemagne de la Revolution et de l'Empire*, 2 vols. Paris: Centre de Documentation Universitaire.
Gellner, E. 1983. *Nations and Nationalism*. Oxford: Blackwell.
Godechot, J. 1956. *La Grande Nation. Expansion révolutionnaire de la France dans le monde de 1789 à 1799*, 2 vols. Paris: Aubier.
  1988. The new concept of the nation and its diffusion in Europe. In *Nationalism in the Age of the French Revolution*, ed. O. Dann and J. Dinwiddy. London: Hambledon Press.
Goldman, L. 1964. *The Hidden God*. New York: Humanities Press.
Gray, M. 1986. Prussia in transition: society and politics under the Stein reform ministry of 1808. *Transactions of the American Philosophical Society*. 76.
Hall, J. A. 1985. *Powers and Liberties*. Harmonsworth: Blackwell.
Hobsbawm, E. J. 1962. *The Age of Revolution, 1789–1848*. New York: Weidenfeld & Nicolson.
  1990. *Nations and Nationalism Since 1780*. Cambridge: Cambridge University Press.

Hroch, M. 1985. *Social Preconditions of National Revival in Europe*. Cambridge: Cambridge University Press.

Kohn, H. 1944. *The Idea of Nationalism*. New York: Collier.

1967. *Prelude to Nation-States: The French and German Experience, 1789–1815*. Princeton N.J.: Van Nostrand.

Langsam, W. C. 1930. *The Napoleonic Wars and German Nationalism in Austria*. New York: Columbia University Press.

Mann, M. 1991. The emergence of modern European nationalism. In *Power, Wealth and Belief: Essays for Ernest Gellner*, ed. J. Hall and I. C. Jarvie. Cambridge: Cambridge University Press.

Markham, F. 1954. *Napoleon and the Awakening of Europe*. London: English Universities Press.

Mommsen, W. J. 1990. The varieties of the nation state in modern history: liberal, imperialist, fascist and contemporary notions of nation and nationality. In *The Rise and Decline of the Nation State*, ed. M. Mann. Oxford: Blackwell.

Nairn, T. 1977. *The Break-up of Britain*. London: Verso.

Palmer, R. 1959. *The Age of the Democratic Revolution*, 2 vols. Princeton, N.J.: Princeton University Press.

Ritter, G. 1969. *The Sword and the Scepter: The Problem of Militarism in Germany*. Vol. I: *The Prussian Tradition, 1740–1890*. Coral Gables, Fla.: University of Miami Press.

Segeburg, H. 1988. Germany. In *Nationalism in the Age of the French Revolution*, ed. O. Dann and J. Dinwiddy. London: Hambledon Press.

Sked, A. 1989. *The Decline and Fall of the Habsburg Empire, 1815–1918*. London: Arnold.

Smith, A. D. 1971. *Theories of Nationalism*. London: Duckworth.

1979. *Nationalism in the Twentieth Century*. Oxford: Martin Robertson.

1986. *The Ethnic Origins of Nations*. Oxford: Blackwell.

Sugar, P. F. 1969. External and domestic roots of Eastern European nationalism. In *Nationalism in Eastern Europe*, ed. P. F. Sugar and I. J. Lederer. Seattle: University of Washington Press.

Tilly, C. 1975. Introduction. In his *The Formation of National States in Western Europe*. Princeton, N.J.: Princeton University Press.

1990. *Coercion, Capital and European States, AD 990–1990*. Oxford: Blackwell.

8 Geopolitics and international capitalism

Theoretical perspectives

This chapter is an attempt to explain the overall relations between geopolitics and capitalism through the "long nineteenth century." Yet it also weaves a third term into the equation: European (becoming Western) civilization. Europe had long been a multi-power-actor civilization embodying an inherent contradiction: geopolitically highly competitive unto war, yet regulated by common norms. Eighteenth-century war became more destructive and costly, yet also more profitable for the Great Powers and also partly regulated by transnational institutions and by multistate diplomacy. Society had two levels, of the state and of Europe. The enormous surge in collective power generated by capitalism and industrialism burst into this half-regulated, two-level world, carrying contradictory transnational, national, and nationalist implications.

1. Revolutions in ideological and economic power relations boosted a partly transnational civil society (as Chapter 2 notes). Networks of discursive, moralizing literacy penetrated state boundaries; private-property rights were institutionalized throughout Europe, largely autonomous of states. Thus capitalist expansion might blow away state rivalries. Europe might industrialize transnationally to become the core of a global economy and society, as most nineteenth-century writers expected.

We can separate "strong" and "weak" versions. The strong version would predict the virtual demise of states. Transnational classes would be pacific. Universal peace might ensue, hoped liberals from Kant to John Stuart Mill. State infrastructures might remain to aid capitalist development, but the old military states would be swept away. Laissez-faire conceptions of interest would displace mercantilist and imperialist ones – now and then perhaps invoking a little selective protectionism. Under "weak" transnationalism states might continue their private foreign policies, even make war, but without major implications for economy or society. Power structure would be dual: a transnational capitalist economy and limited rivalries between states.

2. But capitalist industrialization, when entwined with state modernization, also strengthened national organization. Nineteenth-century state infrastructural expansion unintentionally "naturalized" economic

254

actors (I explain this in Chapter 14). Capitalism also threw up extensive classes, politicized by state finances, demanding citizenship. Old regimes countered by incorporating them into the more mobilized segmental organizations of authoritarian monarchy. Both class demands and regime responses led Europe toward nation-states in the three ways distinguished in Chapter 7. In countries like Britain and France an existing state controlled by a homogeneous cultural and linguistic "ruling class nation" was broadened into a state-reinforcing nation. Second, in countries like Germany and Italy an ideological community united by culture and language but divided into many states became politically united, forming a state-creating nation. Third, large confederal states like the Austrian and Ottoman empires were broken apart by regional nationalisms, state-subverting nations, later forming their own nation-states. Nation-states dominated virtually the entire West by 1918. Classes had become more nationally confined, forcing states away from their traditional autonomy and society away from transnationalism.

3. Capitalism and industrialism also entailed nationalist organization. Capitalism developed entwined with aggressive geopolitics. Its mobilizing powers might enhance territorial conceptions of interest and struggles between nations. Mercantilism might now really become, as Colbert put it, "*un combat perpetuel.*" Europe was steadily consolidating through war into fewer, larger states, and profitable colonialism enhanced militarism. As world systems theorists (Wallerstein 1974; Chase-Dunn 1989: 201–55) have demonstrated, the "capitalist world system" became dual – free markets, free labor in its Western core, unequal exchange, coerced labor in its periphery. This might impact back upon the West, enhancing its aggressive nationalist organization.

Thus capitalism and industrialism were three-dimensional. Market competition was inherently transnational, offering diffuse profit opportunities to property owners wherever commodities could be produced and exchanged, regardless of political boundaries. Second, politicized social classes organized at the level of the authoritative, territorial state. The more they agitated there, the more territorialized and "naturalized" they became. Third, as capitalism became caged by state boundaries, it picked up colonial and European territorial rivalries. Capitalism and industrialism were always and simultaneously transnational, national, and nationalist, generating complex, variable power relations.

Yet "strong" versions of theories 1 and 3 have mostly ruled social theory, as rivals and with occasional compromises emerging between them. Theorists from Vico through the Enlightenment to Saint-Simon, Comte, Spencer, and Marx expected the triumph of strong transnationalism. At the beginning of the twentieth century this liberal-Marxian view seemed dramatically wrong, so nationalists proclaimed and liberals and Marxians bemoaned the coming triumph of nationalism (often also of racialism), that is, "superstratification" by one nation-state over another. Fascism and Nazism took this to extremes. With the triumph of the liberal-Marxian allies in World War II, explicit nationalism became unfashionable, but its influence lingers on. Much history is written as the history of rival national states. Realism also theorizes diplomatic history as the power of the sovereign state set amid international anarchy. Giddens (1985) has also offered a compatible theory of the state: Nation-states, the "great power containers," the "discipliners," and the "surveillers" of social life have ever strengthened their domestic and geopolitical grip on society. But liberal-Marxian transnationalism has also made a comeback in the post-1945 world, in the form of interdependence and world systems theories. And a liberal-Marxian-realist compromise has emerged: Global interdependence depends on the presence of a single, benign hegemonic Power.

Because of Marxian-liberal dominance, most recent theories of geopolitics have been ostensibly economistic, reducing "power" to economic power. Marshaling military and economic statistics, Kennedy concludes:

All of the major shifts in the world's military-power balances have followed alterations in the productive balances; and . . . the rising and falling of the various empires and states . . . has been confirmed by the outcomes of the major Great Power wars, where victory has always gone to the side with the greatest material resources. [1988: 439]

Wars merely "confirm" changes in productive powers, which determine geopolitics. Actually, however, Kennedy's theory is ultimately dual. Because he treats Great Power rivalry and war as constants in social development, economic power merely provides the means to prosecute ends defined by them. Kennedy does not try to theorize relations between the two, nor does he discuss how order and peace rather than disorder and war sometimes characterize international relations.

This last issue has been addressed by realism and Marxism, explaining nineteenth- and twentieth-century alternations of war and peace in terms of hegemony or hegemonic stability. Hegemonic states, or hegemons, are powerful ones that can set norms and exercise government functions in the overall international arena. Kindleberger (1973) originated the theory by explaining the crisis of the 1930s as the failure of the United States to step into Britain's discarded hegemonic shoes. The United States could now have set international norms but refused, accepting its hegemonic role only after 1945. "The British couldn't, the United States wouldn't." International capitalism needed a hegemon to avoid competitive devaluations, tariff wars, and even real wars.

Realists have developed this argument in what has become an enormous literature (twenty articles in the journal *International Organization* alone). Most writers identify two hegemons setting global free trade norms and avoiding economic instability and major wars: Great Britain through most of the nineteenth century and the United States since 1945. The case of Britain indicates that the hegemon must be not the biggest but, rather, the most advanced economy, able to set new economic norms and institutions. Britain established sterling as the world's reserve currency, the City of London as its financial center and shipping as its primary carrier. Conversely, when multi-Power rivalry prevailed, capitalist development was unstable and wars resulted – in the eighteenth century, in Anglo-German rivalry leading up to World War I, and between the two world wars (Calleo and Rowland 1973; Gilpin 1975: 80–5, 1989; Krasner 1976; Keohane 1980). Yet many writers have come to be skeptical (e.g., Keohane 1980; Rosecrance 1986: 55–9, 99–101; Nye 1990: 49–68; Walter 1991) – and I borrow from their skepticism.

Marxian world system theorists take hegemony a step farther, seeking to end its theoretical dualism. They explain Great Power rivalry in terms of the "single logic of the capitalist world-economy" (Wallerstein 1974, 1984, 1989; Chase-Dunn 1989: 131–42, 154, 166–98; Arrighi 1990 retains more dualism). They add another hegemon, the late seventeenth-century Dutch republic, whose currency, financial institutions, and shipping ruled contemporary capitalism. For the Dutch, British, and American hegemons, naval power is the main link between economic and military hegemony (Modelski 1978, 1987; Modelski and Thompson 1988). The most advanced capitalist national economy confers power, especially naval power, on its state, which then provides geopolitical order in the international economy. Wallerstein concludes, in terms identical with Kennedy's:

It is not the state that leaps ahead politically and militarily that wins the race, but the one that plods along improving inch by inch its long-term competivity. . . . Wars may be left to others, until the climactic world war when the hegemonic power must at last invest its resources to clinch victory. [1984: 45–6; cf. Goldstein 1988 and Modelski 1987]

These are great-man, Hobbesian, theories of history transferred to states. They are nationally self-serving – almost all the theorists are

American, pleased to celebrate the world-historical significance and benign rule of the United States. The British join in, pleased that their history is regarded as so great and benign. But the theory is ultimately pessimistic. Realists assume that Powers will continue slugging it out until the end of time unless one becomes so hegemonic as to institute world government. They are dualists: Anarchic Great Power rivalry is a near-eternal determining feature of human power relations; the outcomes of rivalry and bursts of order are determined by economic power relations. World systems theorists, as befits Marxians, see an eventual utopian, economistic outcome when the capitalist economy finally and equally penetrates the entire globe, permitting world revolution and world government.

Such economistic and dual theories are wrong, at least about the past discussed here. Geopolitics and international political economy were more varied, complex and intermittently hopeful, dynamically determined by all sources of social power. Capitalism, states, military power, and ideologies contained contradictory, entwined principles of social organization. Let us see how they jointly determined geopolitical power.

The determinants of power

I identify five major determinants of geopolitical "power": my four sources plus a distinctive combination of two of them, in military and diplomatic leadership. (This section draws freely upon Knorr 1956 and Morgenthau 1978: 117–70.)

1. *Economic power.* Considerable power is indeed conferred by varying combinations of the size and modernity of a state's economy. Genuinely poor or backward Powers almost never become Great Powers – and only if all other power sources are so favorable as to compensate. But in geopolitics, geo-economics – how an economy is inserted into regional and global geography – also affects economic size and modernity, perhaps increasing their relevance to geopolitics. Britain "waited" centuries until the navigational revolution and the "discovery" of the New World meant wealth and power might be conferred by its offshore geo-economy. Economic power translates into power only if geopolitically relevant, as we will see with all the sources.

2. *Ideological power.* Actors engaged in power ventures may be boosted by ideological resources relevant to geopolitics: a strong sense of collective identity – immanent morale – and morally transcendent beliefs legitimating aggression. If a wealthy capitalist class does not have a national identity, its resources are less mobilizable for a Great

Power project; if a large, well-equipped army does not have good morale, it will be brittle.

3. *Military power.* Amid aggressive geopolitics rich countries without effective armed forces will be defeated and absorbed into more militarily effective states. Some militaries are especially effective for the immediate power Project, as was eighteenth-century Britain or Prussia-Germany then and later. Some are ineffective, like late nineteenth-century Russia. Military power has its own logic: Its organization "coercively concentrates" resources. Economic power, however great, must be mobilized as manpower, armaments, and supplies, coercively disciplined, and then concentrated as effective coercion against the enemy. This requires not just gross national product but also a military able to concentrate it on training and on the battlefield. In 1760, Prussian economic resources were less than Austrian, but as they were better applied to precise military projects, Prussia became the greater Power, acquiring territories over which substantial economic development later occurred. When the two Powers fought their final battle in 1866, the Prussian economy only just led the Austrian one. But Prussian military (and political) mobilization of that economy was decisively superior. Military power resources must also be relevant to the geopolitical task in hand – one needs gunboats, not massed artillery batteries (or nuclear weapons), for gunboat diplomacy.

4. *Political power.* Modern states convert economic and ideological resources, gross national product and morale, into military power – a task at which they may be more or less effective. Organski and Kugler (1980: 64–103) show that in wars fought since 1945, economic resources did not predict outcomes. What they call superior political organization (although it is actually a mix of ideological, military, and political power) was decisive, as in the victories of Israel over Arab states and of North Vietnam over South Vietnam and the United States. Regime and state administration must effectively supply resources relevant to the geopolitical task at hand. That generally advantaged the more cohesive political regimes, those whose crystallizations and whose faction fighting were more institutionalized.

This was especially relevant to state diplomacy. Economistic theorists seem to forget that all major modern wars have been fought between alliances. Kennedy – rather oddly, as he is a diplomatic historian – takes for granted the fact that France under Napoleon took on all other major Powers; that Austria, without allies, took on both Prussia and Italy in 1866; that Austria and Germany took on Britain, France, and Russia (and, later, Italy and the United States as well) in World War I. By adding up their combined economic resources he accurately predicts who will win. But the alliances won. They require, but do not get, an explanation. Only after such an explanation, which they do not offer, could hegemonic theorists describe France or Germany as a "failed hegemonic challenger" rather than as an actual hegemon. Had the losers negotiated themselves more powerful allies, they could have been winners, plausible candidates for hegemony.

As we shall see, they failed in diplomacy for two reasons, one political and one ideological. First, their states were incoherent, different political crystallizations pulling them in contrary diplomatic directions, without sovereign institutions to settle the faction fighting. Second, distinctive nationalist ideologies made them inward-looking, neglectful of the usefulness of "foreigners" in alliances. Diplomacy also helps determine peace. Nineteenth-century peace may have resulted more from diplomacy among the Great Powers than from any British hegemony; it may have faltered when that diplomacy shifted rather than when Britain declined.

5. *Leadership*. Complex causality introduces the short term and the contingent. Diplomatic and military decisions in crises become critical. Then the international arena resembles the normless "anarchy" favored by realism. Diplomats then take decisions according to their conceptions of the interests of their state, independently of one another. They cannot easily predict outcomes, for each decision has unintended consequences for the others. (Chapter 21 discusses this further, in the case of the slide toward World War I.) Campaigning uncertainty is even greater. In *War and Peace*, Tolstoy left memorable accounts of the battles of Austerlitz and Borodino, culled from personal experience as an artillery officer in Russia's Turkish wars. Once the cannons fire, the battlefield is covered with dense smoke. Commanders cannot even see what is happening, let alone make appropriate tactical decisions. Sometimes they get it right, more often (according to armchair military historians, who can see the whole field) they get it wrong.

Amid contingent small-group and individual decision making, some outcomes appear as chance and accidents – not strictly random but emanating from the concatenation of many weakly related causal chains (the decisions of several commanders on both sides, the morale of their troops, the quality of their guns, the changing weather, varied terrain, and the like). This requires unusual diplomatic and military abilities. In the absence of objective, comprehensive knowledge, some make decisions that appear disastrous and incompetent. The defeats of a sorry succession of Austrian generals (from Tolstoy's "*le malheureux* Mack" at Austerlitz onward and the Archduke Charles excepted) are often attributed to their blunders. Other statesmen and generals develop a kind of vision of diplomacy or war, a kind of sensing of what will work, what will inspire troops, which they do not fully articulate, but which does actually work. Tolstoy credited General Kutuzov with a remarkable combination of lethargy, old age, and shrewdness that brought down the great Bonaparte.

We conventionally ascribe such "genius" to idiosyncratic personality characteristics (Rosenau 1966), although it flowers in socially prescribed leadership roles. Vision and genius may occur in any power organization, inventors and successful entrepreneurs may possess it. But in economic power networks, competition, imitation, and adaptation are more patterned, repetitive, and slower paced. Vision can be checked and restrained by market forces. What generals and diplomats decide in a few hours (even minutes) may change the world – as did the flawed military genius of Bonaparte and the diplomatic genius of Bismarck.

Thus the rise and fall of Great Powers was codetermined by five entwined power processes. Because economic power has been crucial to theories of hegemony, and because it can be measured statistically, I start there. Then I move to a narrative combining all five.

Economic power and hegemony, 1760–1914

I assess the economic strength of the Powers with the aid of Paul Bairoch's heroic compilations of economic statistics. Given the imperfections of the data, figures can only be crude indicators and some are controversial. (French figures are a battleground for scholars, and Third World figures are largely guesswork.) Because gross national product figures are unreliable when comparing countries at far different levels of development, I focus on sectoral statistics. Economic power helps determine power. In this period that means large manufacturing industries and an efficient agriculture. Which Powers had these?

The most striking finding in Tables 8.1–8.4 is the global expansion of Western economic power. Table 8.2 shows that total Western industrial production was lower than China's until after 1800. Then Europe and North America overtook and rapidly outdistanced the rest of the world. By 1860, they contributed two-thirds of global industrial production, by 1913, more than nine-tenths. These figures may exaggerate the change because they probably underestimate the production of subsistence economies (which consume most of the surplus before it is marketed or before we can measure it). But the overtaking is indisputable. The figures may also indicate geopolitical power better than they do economic power, because states and armed forces depend on marketable, measurable surpluses. Bairoch argues that Western capitalism deindustrialized the Third World, as Table 8.4 indicates.

Table 8.1. *National share of powers in total European gross national product, 1830, 1913*

	1830		1913	
	% GNP	Rank	% GNP	Rank
Russia	18.1	1	20.4	1
France	14.8	2	10.7	4
United Kingdom	14.2	3	17.2	3
Germany	12.5	4	19.4	2
Austria-Hungary	12.4	5	10.1	5
Italy	9.6	6	6.1	6
Spain	6.2	7	2.9	7

Source: Bairoch 1976a: 282.

Table 8.2. *Gross volume of national industrial production, 1750–1913, (U.K. in 1900 = 100)*

	1750	1800	1830	1860	1880	1900	1913
All developed countries	34	47	73	143	223	481	863
Austria-Hungary	4	5	6	10	14	26	41
France	5	6	10	18	25	37	57
Germany	4	5	7	11	27	71	138
Russia	6	8	10	16	25	48	77
United Kingdom	2	6	18	45	73	100	127
United States		1	5	16	47	128	298
Japan	5	5	5	6	8	13	25
Third World	93	99	112	83	67	60	70
China	42	49	55	44	40	34	33
World	127	147	184	226	320	541	933

Source: Bairoch 1982: table 8.

China and India were flooded with cheap Western goods and were reduced to exporting raw materials. This unprecedented shift in geo-economic power made the nineteenth-century West decisive for the globe, the leading edge of power, a hegemonic civilization.

Within Europe, Russia predominated in overall resources throughout the period, owing to population size and a not totally backward economy. Table 8.1 indicates that the Russian gross national product was easily the highest in 1830 and still barely led in 1913. Table 8.2 shows that the gross volume of Russian industry slipped behind that of

Table 8.3. *Per capita level of development of national agriculture, 1840–1910 (100 = net annual production of 10 million calories per male agricultural worker)*

	1840	1860	1880	1900	1910
Austria-Hungary	75	85	100	110	—
France	115	145	140	155	170
Germany	75	105	145	220	250
Russia	70	75	70	90	110
United Kingdom	175	200	235	225	235
United States	215	225	290	310	420
Japan	—	—	16	20	26

Source: Bairoch 1965: table 1. Austrian figures from Bairoch 1973: table 2.

Table 8.4. *Per capita industrialization, 1750–1913 (U.K. in 1900 = 100)*

	1750	1800	1830	1860	1880	1900	1913
All developed countries	8	8	11	16	24	35	55
Austria-Hungary	7	7	8	11	15	23	32
France	9	9	12	20	28	39	59
Germany	8	8	9	15	25	52	85
Russia	6	6	7	8	10	15	20
United Kingdom	10	16	25	64	87	100	115
United States	4	9	14	21	38	69	126
Japan	7	7	7	7	9	12	20
Third World	7	6	6	4	3	2	2
China	8	6	6	4	4	3	3
World	7	6	7	7	9	14	21

Source: Bairoch 1982: table 9.

Britain, then behind that of the United States and Germany, yet it remained that of a great power. By contrast, Tables 8.3 and 8.4 show Russian per capita levels in agriculture and industry falling far below those of other powers. In a century where modernization greatly expanded organizational capacity, this proved costly. Russian military mobilization remained large, but its efficiency lagged.

Around 1760, Russia was followed in total economic resources by two near equals, Britain and France. But nineteenth-century France slipped out of the leading group, outdistanced by Britain, Germany, and the United States. Britain became the first Power to attain clear economic leadership, with a significant industrial advantage from 1830 to 1880 and (along with the United States) the most efficient agriculture until 1900. (See Table 8.3.) The United States was an ocean away, not much involved in European geopolitics after 1815. But the tables reveal the phenomenal growth in its economic power. By 1913, its industrial economy was twice the size of any other – a giant Power, though still slumbering. The third success story was Germany, rising from parity with its Central European rival, Austria, to lead Europe in gross industrial and agricultural output by 1913 (though still behind Britain in per capita industry). Austria remained the fourth ranked European economic Power throughout the period, its industry even gaining on France's. But as Table 8.3 shows, Austrian agriculture remained backward. This plus political weakness (discussed in Chapter 10) severely weakened Austria.

The undisputed hegemon revealed in these tables is not a single state or Power in the usual sense but Western civilization as a whole, able to "pacify" the globe under its own terms. From the point of view of Indians or Africans it might matter little whether their trader–employer–colonial administrator was British, French, or indeed Danish. Domination was Western, Christian, and white, presenting essentially similar power institutions. From a global perspective the struggles among France, Britain, and Germany might seem epiphenomenal. Whoever won, Europeans (or their colonial cousins) ruled the world, in rather similar ways. Much of the hegemony of this multi-power-actor civilization did not derive from the individual state.

Yet the tables also reveal a potential second-level hegemon within the West. Though Great Britain never attained in the West the overwhelming economic predominance that the West attained globally, it was the clear nineteenth-century economic leader. Did this amount to hegemony? It depends on how we define "hegemony." I first adopt a somewhat arbitrary measure. From 1817 to the 1890s, British governments required the Royal Navy to meet Castlereagh's "two-power standard," possessing more capital ships than the next two navies combined (it usually had more than the next three or four). That was indisputably naval hegemony – and nobody did dispute it until after 1900. Did Britain's economy meet that standard? Was its economy bigger or more advanced than the next two Powers combined?

Britain's overall gross national product did not meet the two-power standard. It was never even the largest of the Western economies (that distinction passed from Russia to the United States). But Britain's economic modernity did meet the standard. Table 8.2 shows that the volume of British industrial production between 1860 and 1880 was greater than that of the next two Powers combined. But by 1900, Britain's industry did not even rank first; and by 1913, this industrial two-power standard had passed to the United States, which kept it for fifty years. Britain's per capita industrial two-power standard, a better measure of economic modernity, lasted longer, from the 1830s to the 1880s. Britain still retained first rank in 1900, falling just behind the United States by 1913. (See Table 8.4.) In the most modern industries British dominance around 1860 was even more striking, producing half the world's iron, coal, and lignite and manufacturing half the world's supply of raw cotton. Thus Britain's statistical qualifications for hegemony would be something of a compromise between economic size and modernity.

This indicates a borderline, short-lived British overall economic hegemony, which I call near hegemony. Yet it must have far exceeded the economic dominance possessed by the seventeenth-century Dutch republic, suggested by world systems theory as the preceding hegemon. Though the Dutch had the most modern commercial capitalist economy of the period, their overall economic power and their military power on land did not outstrip Spain's. The Dutch economy could not have met my two-power standard, although its navy did. Even earlier, the Portuguese had dwarfed all other navies while remaining a minor economic and land Power. Whatever the later American achievement, no Western Power since the Roman Empire had yet achieved overall economic and military hegemony. As we shall see again in this chapter, Europeans had long experience of preventing overall hegemony.

Yet specialized British hegemonies were present. First, hegemony was regionally specialized, in diplomatic agreement with other Powers, as in the recent tacit agreements between the United States and the Soviet Union to leave each other to dominate their own spheres of the globe. In this period Britain entered diplomatic arrangements whereby Britain ceded Continental in return for naval global dominance. Second, hegemony was sectorally specialized, as hegemonic theorists themselves recognize. In manufacturing, Britain acquired a massive but short-lived historic lead; others imitated and caught up. But other British specialisms were longer-lived, some surviving beyond 1914. Most concerned the circulation of commodities, what Ingham (1984) calls "commercial capitalism": financial instruments, shipping and distribution, and sterling as a reserve currency. These were distinctively transnational instruments of capitalism. Hence the paradox: transnational capitalism was also distinctively British.

So, in economic terms, this was only "specialized near hegemony" by Britain. It presupposed a specialized but absolute military hegemony – the two-power naval standard. This guaranteed British shipping and international commercial transactions, while sterling's reserve role derived much from the conquest of India, giving a favorable balance of trade and substantial gold reserves. It also had political preconditions: City power was entrenched in the treasury and Bank of England (Ingham 1984). It was also accepted abroad. Others have noted that hegemony seems to need little coercion – the norms of the hegemon appear in everyone's interest, benign, even "natural" (Keohane 1984; Gilpin 1987: 72–3; Arrighi 1990). But, I have argued, this was a little less than "hegemony"; Britain was only the leading Power, fixing transnational rules in *negotiation* with other Powers. Britain was not as powerful as hegemonic theorists assert. The West was hegemonic in the world, but it was still a multi-power-actor civilization. Its diplomacy, its transnational norms, helped structure capitalism. How did it work in the preceding period of intense rivalry?

Anglo-French rivalry

The eighteenth century
Around 1760, three Powers – Britain, France, and Russia – stood above the rest. In the east, vast land and population made Russia defensively invulnerable and able to expand south and east as Ottoman Turks and central Asian states declined. Russia stood somewhat geo-economically and geopolitically apart, half in Asia, leaving the west to Anglo-French rivalry. After these three came Austria and Prussia, whose struggle for Central Europe I discuss in Chapters 9 and 10. The struggles and alliances of these five formed the Western geopolitical core. Next came the peripheral United States, with only an intermittent geopolitical role outside its own continent, and then Powers, with only walk-on parts in this volume – Spain, the Netherlands, Sweden, and a host of smaller states.

For almost the entire eighteenth century, Britain and France contested Western European and colonial leadership, generally leading coalitions of other Powers engaged in European land warfare. According to Holsti's (1991: 89) count of wars between 1715 and 1814, territorial aggrandizement was a significant motive in 67 percent of wars, followed by commercial or navigational issues at 36 percent. Then came dynastic-succession issues at 22 percent, followed by more minor issues. With territory leading commerce, but both important, conceptions of profit were significantly infused by territorial options. Rivalries mixed elements drawn from five of the six international political economies identified in Chapter 3. Territorial dominance within Europe was intermittently attempted by France and other Powers, across the rest of the globe by Britain and France, driven by economic and geopolitical imperialism (regimes did not yet attempt to mobilize popular social imperialism). "The kingdom's commerce has been made to flourish through war," Burke bluntly observed. From relatively cheap military and commercial staging posts, European navies coerced the terms of trade with non-Europeans. There were two especially profitable colonies, in India and North America. French and British trading companies encroached on India as its Moghul Empire decayed. As states monopolized military power, the French and British states took over. Indian wealth and trade proved immensely profitable. The flow of European settlers to North America, some exploiting slave labor, also led to profitable trade there. The economic lure of modern imperialism rested substantially on these two profitable bases.

But the Powers were not always at war. In peacetime, they embraced the more moderate form of mercantilism arising in the eighteenth century: The state, while no longer actually encouraging piracy against its rivals, should actively use "power" to secure "plenty" by enouraging exports and discouraging imports with tariffs, quotas, and trade and shipping embargoes – all backed by diplomatic posturing and occasional boarding of foreign ships. Mercantilism did not make self-evident sense, as, without this policy, the actual economy would have consisted of multiple local-regional and transnational markets in which state boundaries would have had little significance. Yet states were still puny. They could but little restrain private-property rights and they had few infrastructural powers of enforcement. Smuggling probably always exceeded registered trade; and transnational ideologies evaded censorship. States developed two more market-oriented political economies – moderate national protectionism and laissez-faire. Toward the end of the century, a number of bilateral treaties reduced some tariffs, though more often from geopolitical than economic motivations.

Thus eighteenth-century international political economy oscillated considerably, but colonial expansion was easy: Islamic and Spanish decline provided power vacuums; the bigger still mopped up the smaller states. Three Powers (Britain, France, and Spain) generated most colonial wars; the rest specialized in European land war. Although war was still "limited" and "gentlemanly" in its methods, as Holsti comments, land war was not limited in its goals, as Powers now sought to dismember each other totally. The lure of aggression strengthened and wars intensified. Only alliance deterrence, the cost of war, and perhaps also a diffuse civilizational sentiment that peace was intrinsically preferable to war held Powers back from more continuous war (Holsti 1991: 87–95, 105–8).

Who would win? France was at first the greatest, more populous and richer in overall resources. The French state mobilized these resources into an effective military, becoming the leading Power of the late seventeenth and early eighteenth centuries, containable only by grand alliances assembled by Holland and Britain. Then Britain began to threaten. Its agriculture became more efficient, and its seaborne commerce facilitated naval predominance. (Skilled seamen could be trained in peacetime in the merchant marine.) Its manufactures crept ahead after midcentury, though agriculture and services still outweighed industry everywhere. British economic advance was necessary but insufficient to sustain a challenge to France.

Second, the British state became more cohesive than the French (as Chapter 4 argues). The territory of France faced two ways, into Europe and across the Atlantic. Both these "two Frances" crystallized factions within the French state and their pressure made France into both a European land Power and a naval colonial Power. With Britain's rise, France became stretched between its two ambitions. It lacked sovereign political institutions to settle conflicting policies authoritatively. Britain was less stretched and had a sovereign "king in Parliament." Aside from retaining Hanover (its dynasty's home), it had abandoned European territorial aspirations in favor of naval-commercial expansion across the Atlantic, plus acquiring naval stations around the European fringes where other Powers were declining. This strategy was labeled at the time as "bluewater policy" (Brewer 1989). The army was small, the regime concentrating more on its navy to defend the channel so that no enemy could land on British soil. The prestige, resources, and efficiency of the Royal Navy grew. The "ruling class-nation" disputed but resolved its disputes in parliamentary majorities. There formed a geopolitical purpose and a military instrument.

Third, this was also helped by the structure of British capitalism. With more commerce, Britain developed financial institutions that harnessed agrarian and commercial wealth to naval power by way of the Bank of England, City, and treasury (as we saw in Chapter 4). In what Cain and Hopkins (1986, 1987) call the "landed interest" phase of "gentlemanly capitalism," old regime, military, and capitalist state crystallizations fused. They agreed that taxes and loans should finance naval expansion. Rocketing war costs meant that states with greater access to liquid wealth (commerce) could extract more military resources than a state whose wealth was tied up in land. This gave an advantage to Britain over France, just as it had to Holland over Spain. Although no war financed itself, successful naval war over the globe brought more commercial returns than did fighting over European land. Eighteenth-century wars stretched all Powers, but they stretched Britain less per sum expended than any other Power.

Through the mid-eighteenth century astute leadership combined these three advantages to bring decisive victories. British governments used their liquid merchant capital to subsidize Continental allies (first acquired to defend Hanover), tying down French resources in Europe while the Royal Navy struck at the French Empire and blockaded French ports, thus reducing France's liquid merchant wealth to pay its own allies. Pitt correctly remarked, "Canada will be won in Silesia," where his Prussian allies were fighting. Indian wealth seized after the Battle of Plassey enabled Britain to buy back its national debt from the Dutch (Davis 1979: 55; Wallerstein 1989: 85, 139–40, 181). Moreover, Prussia, faced with defeat, unexpectedly fought its way to victory. Britain and Prussia rose as allies through war, while France and its allies fell. The British responded with the traditional vote of thanks, naming London pubs "The King of Prussia" and "The Princess of Prussia."

During the eighteenth century, Britain won all three wars in which old regime France was trapped into a two-front army and navy war; it lost the only war in which France turned the tables by financing American and Irish rebels. Britain stretched its army between America and Ireland and its navy over the globe. A French fleet slipped unopposed to land its army to which General Cornwallis surrendered at Yorktown. But the Seven Years' War, 1756–63, had secured British dominance over North America, the West Indies, and India, damaged the economies of French ports, and devastated French state finances. The loss of the American colonies proved not to be disastrous, because trade continued to flow between America and Britain. Britain controlled the two most profitable eighteenth-century pickings: India and trade with North America.

This abbreviated summary of British ascendancy includes all five determinants of power. The British economy grew and modernized, geo-economically linked to naval-commercial expansion. This increased the ideological cohesion of state elites and dominant class, and it increased state efficiency in converting wealth and ideology into naval power. Its diplomats grew skilled at redirecting liquid commercial assets to a militarily effective ally on the second front. As Kennedy emphasizes, geopolitical power is relative to other powers. British power had the edge relative to the specifics of its rivalry with France.

By the 1780s, the Franch still led in continental Europe, but Britain and its navy dominated the sea-lanes and expanding empires. We should not overstate the power of either. British cotton, iron, and mining industries were beginning their revolution. But much of their power was expressed transnationally rather than through state power; and the French government was still confident enough (perhaps wrongly) to sign the Anglo-French Commercial Treaty of 1786, which reduced mercantilism and tariffs between the two countries. Neither economy or power was hegemonic. Both Powers depended on allies to secure further gains, but the allies would not assist either to be hegemonic. The French had learned the diplomatic lesson and focused on the British threat, maintaining a low profile on the Continent. (They were also short of money.)

Neither Power could inflict damage on the other's territory, as the British army could not defeat the French army and the French army could not cross the channel. As Kennedy describes a similar standoff around 1800: "Like the whale and the elephant, each was by far the largest creature in its own domain" (1988: 124). The Royal Navy whale might look imposing, but it had a lot of ocean to cover. The logistic difficulties were immense. Warships were tiny, under three thousand tons, and fleets comprised fewer than thirty ships. They communicated by flag signals within telescope range. Navies could rarely even find each other in the vast oceans, let alone fight decisive engagements. The French avoided them; the British sought but rarely achieved them. Britain had risen to being France's equal.

The old regime diplomats of Europe had good normative under-standings: Preserve the balance of power against a possible hegemon. Geopolitics might rest there for some time, the rising costs of war and the lesser global spoils now available deterring further militarism.

This raises counterfactual speculations. What if the French Revo-lution had not intervened? If there had been no further wars, would the Industrial Revolution, transnational instruments of capitalism, and global empires have been quite so British? Would there have been any question of British hegemony? We cannot be sure. Wallerstein (1989), in a volte-face from the economism of his earlier writings, argues that British hegemony resulted from two geopolitical triumphs, which, he says, cannot be explained economistically. The first triumph I have just described; the second, involving Napoleon, I come to in a moment. I incline to a less optimistic view of French manufacturing than Waller-stein and I separate manufacturing from commercial-naval leads. The Industrial Revolution was aided in Britain and harmed in France by geopolitics, but the British manufacturing lead would have occurred anyway because it resulted from their different domestic economies and the more sympathetic attitude of the British state. But without colonial-commercial war gains, the British could not have so domi-nated nineteenth-century shipping, international trade, and inter-national credit, and British norms would have been less significant in the international economy. There might have been more disorder (as realists argue) or (more probably) more regulation by transnationalism and by negotiation between Powers sharing social identities and norms.

Bonaparte's failed hegemony

The French Revolution unexpectedly intervened. As we saw in Chapter 6, its diversion into war and conquest had sources quite other than traditional diplomacy or realist power strategies. It introduced for the first time since the Wars of Religion major value- rather than profit-oriented wars. It also introduced into the modern era the final regime of political economy: social imperialism. Its class, secular, and national threats to old regimes led to a ferocious class confrontation and to a French revolutionary army seeking to overthrow old regimes and their diplomacies. War was now less limited, less professional, and less separated from the markets and the classes of rising capitalism. At first, confrontation ranged revolutionary France and its "patriot" allies against an alliance between old regime Austria and Prussia and smaller princely and ecclesiastical states. But when the Revolution faltered, its officer-savior was revealed as a would-be hegemon. The other European regimes responded as customary, but with realism reinforced by class interests.

Napoleon Bonaparte exemplifies my fifth determinant of power – leadership genius. He ruled uniquely, without monarchical legitimacy but absolute, an extraordinary general only defeated by heavy odds, a politician able to institutionalize revolution while personally dominating all rivals. Napoleon's qualities probably had greater significance for world history than anyone else's in the period covered by this volume. We must examine his motives, his successes, his mistakes.

Bonaparte seems to have actually intended global hegemony as early as 1799; the British part schemed, part drifted into theirs. He pursued geopolitical imperialism. Though aware that "power" would bring "plenty" for France, he thought little about this and did not choose precise targets of economic profit. He was clear: "My power depends on my glory and my glory on the victories I have won. My power will fail if I do not feed it on new glories and new victories. Conquest has made me what I am and only conquest can enable me to hold my position." He would then institutionalize hegemony with French civil law, a French common market (the Continental System), and state institutions modeled on French ones. Integration at the top was dynastic – his generals and family were appointed rulers of his client states – though lower down he mobilized disconcerting class and national identities.

Bonaparte's economic power was only that available to the Bourbons before the Revolution. France was wealthy, a necessary condition for his success, but French resources were only equal to Britain's, far less than those of Britain, Prussia, and Austria combined and allied, even without his other intermittent enemy, Russia. Bonaparte's Continental hegemony was based mainly on his extraordinary ability to mobilize resources as concentrated coercion, as *military* power. He expanded the excellence and ideological élan of the revolutionary armies in three ways, each impacting on the problem of order:

1. He exploited the revolutionary national ideals of citizen-officers in France and in client "sister republics," giving them careers, autonomy, and initiative. After about 1807, his ordinary soldiers were conscripts and mercenaries not dissimilar to soldiers in other armies – though still with a distinct morale based on apparent veneration of "their" emperor. But the officer corps, professionals committed to modern values and guaranteed meritocratic careers, remained more politically committed than officers in most other armies, especially in Central Europe where many were doubting whether their unreformed regimes were sufficiently "modern" to survive. Bonaparte harnessed ideological to military power, enhancing the "immanent morale" of citizen soldiers, especially among lower officers and noncommissioned officers. This further alienated his old regime enemies. Not merely an external realist enemy, he also appeared to incite class and national subversion in their realms. This war brought ideologies and the specter of a new social order.

2. He mobilized militarily the economic power conferred by Europe's agricultural revolution, linking it to officer morale. In Volume I, Figure 12.2 (page 401) reveals that population in northwestern and Eastern Europe rose by almost 50 percent during the eighteenth century, mostly owing to a similar increase in the yield ratios of crops shown in Table 12.1 of that volume (page 400). As population density and food surpluses increased, they eased the major logistic constraint on historic warfare – the difficulties of moving food supplies over more than fifty miles. Large armies could still move freely only in a campaigning season from late spring to mid-autumn. But during that period supplies for men and horses could be found locally throughout Europe. Bonaparte's divisional tactics exploited this. Eighteenth-century armies had been moving toward a looser divisional structure, but he took it much farther. He relied on a war of *movement* to preserve the tactical initiative. He dispersed self-contained armies with only general orders and then divided into corps and divisions with similar autonomy across a wide front and many communications routes. Officers were to use their initiative to live off the countryside, ignoring fortresses (to sit still exhausted local food supplies). He reckoned a corps of 25,000–30,000 men could be left on its own indefinitely if it avoided battle and for most of a day if attacked by a superior force. All this vastly increased the size of mobilized armies and economies. This war brought more economic disorder, though it could potentially

reorder the economy more than eighteenth-century wars had brought.

3. He then linked officer morale, agrarian surpluses, and divisional tactics and mobility into a distinctive campaign strategy. Several army corps would be sent separately across a wide front to envelop the enemy and force an engagement by threatening his capital and court (capitals were now too big to be defended as fortresses). When the enemy was preparing to give battle, Napoleon rapidly concentrated his army against one part of the enemy's line to outnumber him there, break the line, and induce a general flight. After victory, the French were supplied by the defeated enemy. In Western and Central Europe it worked, especially against allied, loosely coordinated armies. The French attacked before the allies could join forces. Wherever an opponent retreated, the French found supplies for advancing upon him. When the ruler lost his capital or ran out of territories, he sued for terms. (On logistics, see van Creveld 1977: 34–35, 40–74; on tactics, see Chandler 1967: 133–201; and Strachan 1973: 25–37.) This happened to lesser Powers and to the two great Central European Powers, Austria and Prussia. Even the immense Russian army was worsted, forcing the tsar to sue for terms. Bonaparte had defeated greater economic power and larger military forces by superior concentration and mobility of military power. His mobilization of all sources of social power meant that states could be more easily invaded, defeated, and then imperially integrated and restructured than in eighteenth-century wars.

On land, Napoleon imposed his imperial order. But his pretensions foundered at sea. After 1789, the French navy stagnated because it could not defend the Revolution. Though Napoleon rebuilt the navy, he had no naval experience or vision. His Middle Eastern and Baltic pretensions were sunk by Nelson's ships at the battles of the Nile and Copenhagen. He then decided (as Hitler did later) that the easiest way to acquire the British Empire was to invade Britain. Across the channel the British would be no match for the *Grande Armée* (Glover 1973). But the Royal Navy commanded the channel and had to be attacked or lured away from home waters. The allied French, Dutch, and Spanish fleets outnumbered the British but did not match British seamanship and battle experience – the pusillanimity of his admirals indicated they also believed this. Bullied by Napoleon, the main French and Spanish battle fleets finally sallied out near Cape Trafalgar.

Like all battles, Trafalgar had chance elements and might have gone differently, but its outcome seemed likely to the combatants, as it does to us. It was not long in doubt once superior British maneuverability had exploited Nelson's bold tactic of sailing straight through the French and Spanish line of battle. After six hours more than half the French and Spanish ships were destroyed or taken, with heavy loss of life. (See Keegan 1988 for a graphic account.) By 6 P.M. on October 21, 1805, Nelson was dead, but there would be no French hegemony, no European empire of domination. Sea air still made one free – within the lesser cage of a multi-power-actor civilization.

British naval power had triumphed. The British economic blockade could now be enforced by command of the seas and the Continental System undermined by smuggling. Russia abandoned it in 1810, indicating how the tsar sensed the wind blowing. French international trade was destroyed (a process begun in 1793 when the British took Santo Domingo, the major French port in the Americas). The British blockaded Amsterdam, the main financial rival to the City of London. British exports doubled before 1815. Some French industry prospered amid protectionism, but techniques fell behind British and access to global markets and credits diminished. Most French possessions in the Caribbean, the Indian Ocean, and the Pacific were mopped up. Britain's naval-commercial hegemony was ensured and its manufacturing lead furthered, by force. Britain's victories were sealing the connection between manufacturing lead and commercial dominance, ensuring overall near hegemony.

With the Mediterranean, Baltic, and Atlantic blocked, Napoleon either could try again at sea or attempt hegemony within continental Europe. (Again like Hitler) he chose the latter. After 1807, only Spain and Russia held out, the two largest and most backward countries. Spain was a special problem because British naval power could supply and land troops to support revolts there. Bonaparte had conquered Spain and enthroned his brother Joseph. But Joseph struggled to cope with a popular revolt aided by British troops under Wellington, supplied by sea. While guerrillas and Wellington's evasive tactics were tying down 270,000 French troops, Bonaparte invaded Russia.

This was the decisive mistake, the first of three strikingly similar mistakes made by would-be Central European empires of domination over the next 130 years. Bonaparte's decision to fight simultaneously in the East and the West resembled that of the German high command in 1914 and Hitler's in 1941. Relying on confidence engendered by a string of rapid successes, their common strategy was to inflict swift, decisive victory on an enemy they underrated and then turn on the more persistent foe. But the swift victory did not materialize. In a war of attrition the big battalions would be likely to triumph (as Kennedy argues). In 1914, the German high command underestimated its Western enemies (misjudging the strength of the French army and of British diplomatic commitment). In 1812 and 1941, the failure was to misunderstand a Russian regime significantly different from all others encountered. Russia was backward. The Russian autocracy and noble officer corps were undivided by modernization politics and in full control of their peasants.

In June 1812, Napoleon crossed the Russian frontier with 450,000 men (half French, half allies), leaving another 150,000 to cover his flanks and rear – the biggest army then known to Western history, perhaps to world history. (I am skeptical that Chinese armies of "millions" could mobilize this number in one campaign.) They carried enough provisions (though not enough animal fodder) for twenty-four days – wagons and barges carrying twenty days, the men four days, supplemented by living off the country. The Russian generals divided over tactics, but the (perhaps unintended) effect was to copy Wellington's Spanish tactics and avoid battle. Extended lines of communication, logistic difficulties, and Russian harassment whittled down Napoleon's actual field army. He had 130,000 available on the eightieth day, as he arrived before Moscow. Under pressure from the court, Kutuzov reluctantly drew up his forces on the field of Borodino. As usual, Russian officers and soldiers did not flee but stood and died, inflicting heavy losses on the French. Kutuzov, appalled by horrendous casualties, finally withdrew. The French army occupied yet another capital.

But the Russian regime, unexpectedly to Bonaparte, did not surrender; Kutuzov dispersed his forces and moved eastward at the beginning of winter. Russia's economic, geo-economic, and political advantages – its size, its winter, and its economic and political backwardness – now became more relevant. As in 1941, the Russian regime was autocratic, less embedded in civil society than any European regime. It could abandon territory, burn its subjects' houses and cities, and destroy its peasants' crops more easily than Bonaparte's other enemies could theirs. The tsar and his court, unlike their cousins in Berlin and Vienna, did not seriously contemplate negotiation.

For the first time, Napoleon could not follow his enemy. Nor could he stay the winter in a Moscow the Russian Army had fired. In October he ordered his field army, now 100,000 strong, to withdraw. As it gathered momentum, the retreat drew in the rest of the *Grande Armée*. It had few supplies and little prospect of living off the country. The Russian "General Winter" has two tactics. At the beginning and end, rain and thaw produce mud that immobilizes guns, transports, and supplies and starves an army of equipment and food. In the middle, snow and ice freeze it to death. Both devastated the French. "General Winter" was aided by dispersed Russian troop detachments avoiding battle and laying waste the countryside (and the peasantry) around the line of march. As Napoleon and his staff abandoned their men, as the men abandoned their cumbersome artillery and transports, as the fit abandoned the weak, as the cavalry ate their horses, the *Grande Armée* disintegrated into a formless straggling rabble.

Marshal Ney wrote to his wife with anguish of the rear guard he commanded, "It is a mob without purpose, famished, feverish.... General Famine and General Winter have conquered *la Grande Armée*" (Markham 1963: 184–5). It was literally decimated: Fewer than 40,000 limped back into Germany, the most complete loss of a major army since A.D. 9, when the legions of Varus disappeared into German forests.

Once the Russian campaign was lost, so was the hegemonic opportunity. The monarchs, fearing their own patriots as well as Napoleon, wanted old regime "balance" back, even with Bonaparte. They offered terms, but Napoleon would not accept the loss of his empire. He raised new armies, but his enemies were now copying him. As we saw in Chapter 7, they were forced toward patriotic mobilization. Napoleon's unique advantages were disappearing. Austria and Prussia had their confidence stiffened by the victories of Russian and British armies (and British subsidies) converging on France from east and south. All four plus Sweden ganged up on Napoleon. Between 1812 and 1815, an alliance of Powers restored the European multi-power-actor civilization. The allies joined on battlefields from Leipzig (the "Battle of the Nations") to Waterloo (where Wellington's troops withstood the French until the Prussians arrived). The old regime allies then institutionalized the balance in the diplomatic halls of Versailles.

Let me again speculate counterfactually. With hindsight we see that Bonaparte's leadership abilities had failed him. He had chosen the wrong diplomacy. He should have taken things more slowly, concentrating first either on the Spanish-Portuguese or the Russian front while conciliating the other enemy. Then he could turn on the other. His main army could have forced Wellington's withdrawal; a rebuilt navy could protect his coastline. Perhaps he could not have conquered Britain or Russia anyway, but his ability to win land battles and occupy European Russia would have made Britain wary and the tsar his client. This might have inaugurated a period of French Continental hegemony against British overseas hegemony – a two-Superpower confrontation comparable to that of recent years. Britain and France might have accepted a cold-war modus vivendi. If not, the blockades would continue; France would have to build a massive fleet or Britain increase its Continental commitments. Client states would be sought; expeditionary forces, despatched; and blockades, escalated against the Continental System. Transnationalism would have been weakened by domestic and geopolitical intervention by the two states. Industrial development would have been retracked from its predominantly transnational destiny.

Probably French Continental hegemony would not have lasted. The major humbled states – Austria, Prussia, and Russia – would have risen up, with British support, just as the first two actually did with British and Russian support. We cannot be sure about hypothetical outcomes. Only one thing is clear: The diplomatic and military strategy of those who attempt hegemony in an essentially multistate system must be near faultless. Bonaparte's was not. In the Middle Ages, the papacy had excommunicated overmighty rulers, this being the diplomatic signal for other Powers to pounce. Now British and Russian secular diplomacy signaled the same pounce in 1812 when Bonaparte made his fatal mistake. Geopolitical power involves diplomacy as well as the mobilization of economic resources as military power. As Pareto noted, the qualities of the fox and the lion are rarely combined in the same person – or Great Power. Napoleon rose through leonine militarism; he despised diplomatic foxes. Hegemony was the strategy of the French lion, but he was overthrown by Anglo-Russian foxes. Diplomatic cunning was fundamental to Western power relations.

Napoleon's defeat did not derive from economic power. As they were for the Germans in the twentieth century, the economic odds were only stacked against him *after* he had created so many allied enemies. In a war of attrition the economy of any single Power, no matter how militarily effective its armed forces, would be overstretched by a contest with several Powers. But unfortunately Bonaparte, like the kaiser and Hitler, had himself converted blitzkrieg into a war of attrition. He had pursued a hegemonic quest similar to that of three Germans: the medieval Emperor Henry IV, Kaiser Wilhelm, and Hitler. Perhaps, as Wellington famously remarked of his own victories, each was "a damned close-run thing," but the geographic similarity of failure is striking.

A Power centrally located in Europe, its principal rivals on both flanks, mobilized considerable economic resources into unusually effective military power; but this provoked a diplomatic alliance among rivals able to wage war on two fronts. Two-front allies cannot easily coordinate tactics; given early nineteenth-century logistics, they could not even transport troops and supplies to each other's front in time to counter danger (as could be done by the time of World War I). But they can throw in resources frontally to wear down their enemy and prevent him (with the advantage of interior lines of communication) from transferring troops. If they are greatly superior in overall economic and military resources, this war of attrition will normally bring victory. All the extraordinary abilities of a Bonaparte or a Hitler, all the fighting powers of French and German armies, labored against this crucial diplomatic, converted into military, disadvantage. All but Henry compounded this inferiority by striking east and west simultaneously. Henry alone was a fox, capitulating, merely falling on his knees before the pope. The others fought like lions, and lost everything.

This near miss at hegemony was determined by ideological, economic, military, political, and diplomatic power relations, compounded by leadership in crises – in this case, by a flawed genius. His crucial mistake gave the prize of near hegemony to his enemy. As the Prussian General Gneisenau commented sardonically:

Great Britain has no greater obligation than to this ruffian. For through the events which he has brought about, England's greatness, prosperity and wealth have risen high. She is mistress of the sea and neither in this dominion nor in world trade has she now a single rival to fear. [Kennedy 1988: 139]

The concert and balance of power, 1815–1880

The period 1815–1914 was not quite a "century of peace." Holsti (1991: 142) shows that war was only 13 percent less likely across the international system between 1815 and 1914 than in the preceding one hundred years. Yet peace predominated in Europe's core (though not its periphery). The Great Powers had learned caution in relation to each other. Though the core saw wars between 1848 and 1871, they were short, sharp, and decisive. International tension then rose, culminating in the conflagration of 1914. The variations make the nineteenth an interesting century in which to explore the causes of international peace and order. Many writers attribute peace and order in the core after 1815 to the development of transnational industrial capitalism under British hegemony and attribute the increase of tension after 1880 to Britain's loss of hegemony. But this is too economistic and too concerned with British power. The nineteenth-century world order actually depended on three entwined power networks: a diplomatically negotiated Concert of Powers (underpinned by the normative solidarity of restored old regimes), the specialized near hegemony of the British Empire, and a diffused capitalist transnationalism. Post-1880 tensions were caused by the entwined decline of all three.

To most liberals, the period of relative peace heralded a new world order – hence the transnational pacifism of nineteenth-century social theory discussed in Chapter 2. Hindsight about 1914 and 1939 makes such carefree optimism seem misplaced. But how reasonable was it in its own time? In the mid-Victorian period, did transnational pacifism nearly conquer the West?

As we shall see in Chapter 12, the statesmen of this period were drawn overwhelmingly from the old regime class. Their common social identity reinforced balance of power realism. They constructed an elaborate alliance system to prevent any repetition of the alarming conjunction of devastating war and revolutionary class and national mobilization. France had transformed statesmen's attitudes toward war, international political economy, and class relations. The three had been subversively connected, as they had not been in the eighteenth century. War had brought social disaster. They determined to stabilize European and even (to some extent) colonial territories and to police class relations repressively, but then to let markets rule the economy (with a dose of pragmatic protectionism). Russia confined its expansion outside of Europe, in what was largely its own sphere of influence. Prussia and Austria pursued more covert expansion against small rather than Great Powers. The normative solidarity of the European Powers strengthened, rooted in shared class and geopolitical interests. Their balance of power was thus both geopolitical – among Powers – and class-bound – among old regimes, bourgeoisies, and petite bourgeoisies.

Their labors were strikingly successful.[1] In the core the Concert and balance of Powers among Britain, Russia, Austria, and Prussia inaugurated thirty years of peace and domestic stability. Constitutionalism crept in, but the crowned heads remained attached to their bodies and to most of their powers, and churches remained attached to souls. Unusually conscious, concerted regime strategies gave Europe class stability, despite capitalist and industrial disruption, and international peace, despite the rise and decline of Powers. France was ringed by states whose sovereignty was guaranteed by the Great Powers – enlarged kingdoms of the Netherlands and Sardinia-Piedmont, a restored Bourbon Spain, and a Rhineland given to Prussia. Revolution from below and outside was replaced by repression mixed with mild reform from above. By midcentury abortive revolutions had been repressed and a house-trained France admitted to the concert.

It is not obvious how to rank the concert Powers, but none approached geopolitical hegemony. There could be no doubting where power resided in the events of 1815: 200,000 Russian troops marched with their tsar through Paris (there were another 600,000 mobilized

---

[1] This judgment is not shared by many international relations specialists who have greater ambitions for the international order, expecting more ideals from diplomacy than it can surely deliver. Morgenthau (1978: 448–57) was especially disappointed by the concert, but he focused on Britain and Russia, which were not much constrained by it, rather than on southern or Central European liberals, who were. Holsti (1991: 114–37) devotes more space to the dashing of Tsar Alexander's youthful Kantian ideals than to his own data: The Powers did not go to war with one another, and they jointly regulated those regions whose instabilities threatened war.

elsewhere) while Wellington's army remained nearby and British war-ships ringed the French coasts. But the Russian army marched back home, Tsar Alexander became enveloped by his dreams, and Russian military power declined through midcentury. The two dominant figures at Versailles were the representatives of the two Powers that most favored the status quo – the Austrian minister, Prince Metternich, and the British foreign secretary, Castlereagh. Metternich's dominance on the Continent continued for two decades. Austria was sapped by internal disturbances, and the settlement of Central Europe turned out to favor Prussia more than Austria. Yet, as late as 1850, Prussia backed down and demobilized its army rather than risk war with Austria in the incident known as the "humiliation of Olmutz." The Continental Powers were rough equals. The United States, though steadily growing in power, contributed only occasionally to the concert, as befitted its distant interests.

The vacant leadership position was not filled by Britain, which withdrew from most Continental affairs. Foreign Secretary Canning (Castlereagh's successor) left the concert because he believed it would be dominated by Russia. Britain was never hegemonic over Europe in the sense that Bonaparte had aimed at and the United States later achieved. It is wrong to assert, as does Arrighi (1990), that the concert "from the start, was primarily an instrument of British overrule in Continental Europe." Britain was still counting the costs of its in-terventions on the Continent and was content with its cheaper naval presence in the Mediterranean and naval dominance elsewhere. True, the Continental Powers were in worse economic straits, indebted to British bondholders. Canning considered using British financial power to blackmail the Powers. But he backed away from this, fearing, significantly, that it would destabilize the balance of power.

British power felt few constraints elsewhere. No colonial or naval rivals remained. The French, Spanish, Portuguese, and Dutch empires had been much reduced. The British Empire now grew massively (Shaw 1970: 2). At its outer limits, in the eastern Mediterranean, the Far East, and the Indian North-West Frontier, the main rival seemed Russia – a sign of how global Britain's reach had become. Britain had attained a specialized naval-commercial, intercontinental, and colonial hegemony. It had cause to thank "that ruffian" Bonaparte. Yet Britain *jointly* ruled the geopolitical order by a negotiated division of powers with a concert of equal European dynasties.

The concert endured, not merely as a general undertaking to preserve the status quo, but as a series of detailed treaties and joint operations. The 1815 Congress of Vienna was followed by one in Aix-la-Chapelle in 1817. In the Holy Alliance, Orthodox Russia, Catholic Austria, and

Protestant Prussia announced their right to intervene against liberal, secular, or nationalist movements at home or abroad "in accordance with Holy Writ." The dynasts implemented not the alliance's lofty ideals (these were proclaimed only to appease the tsar) but its reactionary motives. Metternich's Karlsbad Decrees of 1819, banning liberal movements, were forced on all German states. Congresses authorized Austrian forces to crush revolt in Naples in 1821 and Piedmont in 1823 and joint Franco-Spanish Bourbon forces to crush revolt in Spain in 1823. In 1823, Britain demonstrated the European limits of the concert by announcing that its navy would intercept any French-Spanish expedition to repress revolt in Spain's New World colonies. The Atlantic was British.

The Powers coped with three main regional, becoming "national," instabilities. They often disagreed, but they were aware that such disagreements might lead them into war, which they wished to avoid. Low Country governments lacked legitimacy, small states survived right across Germany and Italy amid greater, predatory ones, and in the Balkans Ottoman decline continued. Throughout the 1820s and 1830s, the Powers jointly deterred French ambitions in the Low Countries. Prussia and Austria lay low in Central Europe. Britain, France, and Russia supported Greek independence against Turkey, secured in 1829 with Prussian mediation. But splits now appeared. The concert weakened into a substantially realist balance of power. Austrian and Russian interests diverged in the Balkans and liberal Britain and France (after the overthrow of Bourbon rule in 1830) often disagreed with the three reactionary monarchs. But they still managed to regulate the formation of a Belgian state, guaranteeing its "eternal neutrality" in 1830 (as they had in 1815 with Switzerland), and they finally settled Low Country boundaries in 1839. The three monarchs were often at odds but continued joint actions. In 1846, they jointly suppressed Polish revolts and agreed that Austria annex the free city of Kraków. Austria called Russian troops into Hungary to help crush the 1848 Revolution – the last attempt at revolution in nineteenth-century Europe (apart from the Paris Commune). Even in 1878 the other Powers by mere diplomatic declaration forced Russia to disgorge Ottoman territories it had just conquered. Some were declared independent states, and others were given to Austria in order to preserve the Balkan balance of power.

All these agreements had two objectives: to prevent any single Power becoming hegemonic in any region of Europe and to preserve order. "Order" meant regulating both international and domestic strife – for the reactionary monarchs it meant repressing reform, for the liberal Powers it meant avoiding revolution by allowing bourgeois and "national" self-determination. Diplomacy was consciously geared to the very opposite of hegemonic stability theory: Preserve peace and order, including reactionary class and market order, by *avoiding* hegemony. In fact, the diplomats had to work overtime throughout the nineteenth century. They had to cope with a new issue with potentially devastating impact: the rise of the nation at odds with the existence of many existing states. Holsti (1991: 143–5) calculates that more than half the wars between 1815 and 1914 – compared to only 8 percent of wars in the preceding hundred years – involved problems of new state creation. Such issues had far outstripped the territorial aggrandizement and commercial motives dominating eighteenth-century wars. In the Low Countries, the Balkans, and Italy, the fitting together of state and nation caused near-continuous armed conflict. That it did not yet lead to serious wars among the Great Powers can be counted their principal, negotiated achievement. Indeed, the concerted diplomacy only faltered as one Power, Russia, eventually saw opportunities in exploiting Eastern nationalisms, while a second, Prussia, turned its ambitions into "national" ones in Central Europe – and these two ambitions destabilized a third, multinational Austria. Order and a regional and "national" hegemony were inversely related in geopolitics throughout the nineteenth century.

States also shifted their international political economies toward more market, pacific options. As had recently been demonstrated, war among the Great Powers was just too dangerous for old regimes. Third World natives could be terrorized and colonized, but the Powers trod warily and accepted conciliation by a third Power if they crossed each other's colonial paths. Territorial conceptions of interest did not end but were stabilized in joint negotiations. There was a burst of commercial treaty making between 1814 and 1827: Britain negotiated commercial treaties with Argentina, Denmark, France (two), the Netherlands, Norway (two), Spain (two), Sweden (two), the United States (three), and Venezuela. This burst set the terms of Britain's international trade, as (with the exception of Venezuela and China) there were no further commercial treaties until after 1850 (Foreign Office 1931). No negotiations were purely commercial; on both sides geopolitical alliance interests were entwined with commercial ones.

Transnational capitalism, 1815–1880

The concert and the balance also received more diffuse transnational help from industrial capitalism. The Napoleonic Wars had decreased international trade and until about 1830 European production levels rose faster than international trade. In this phase, the first phase of

Table 8.5. *Foreign commodity trade as a percentage of gross domestic product, 1825–1910, in Britain, France, Germany, and the United States*

	Great Britain	France	Germany	United States
1825	23 (27)	10	n.a.	n.a.
1850	27 (33)	13	n.a.	12 (13)
1880	41 (49)	30	35	13 (14)
1910	43 (51)	33	36	11 (12)

Notes: 1. Kuznets does not give figures for the same years for all countries. My figures
are either for the year indicated or adjacent years or an inclusive period,
adjusted where necessary for the underlying trend. Therefore they are
approximations (as are all national account statistics).
2. British figures in parentheses add services; U.S. figures in parentheses add
most services.
3. French accounts calculated on net national product. Therefore, I have
adjusted slightly downward the percentage given in the source (by 5 percent).
Source: Kuznets 1967: appendix tables 1.1, 1.2, 1.3, 1.10, current price volumes.

the Industrial Revolution, the naturalization of economies actually
increased. Then, in Britain and France, as Table 8.5 reveals, international trade as a percentage of national product rose, especially after
midcentury. It leveled off in the 1880s.

British international trade had risen from a quarter to a half of gross
national product. Imports rose faster and longer than exports, peaking
in the 1880s, the balance coming from reexports and returns from
investment abroad. Though we lack good data from other countries,
overall international trade probably grew much faster than world production up to about 1880, when it stabilized. Kuznets estimates that
foreign trade rose from only 3 percent of world production in 1880 to
33 percent by 1913, most of the increase contributed by the European
states. The United States was exceptional, with no proportionate increase in foreign trade, still penetrating its own continent. As trade
expanded, it became less bilateral, needing fewer treaties and generating more transnational interdependencies. Trade between two
Powers deviated more from balance, so currencies and credit became
more important as means of settlement. Currencies became fully con-
vertible with the general adoption of the gold standard, begun by
Britain in 1821, continued by Germany in 1873, and ended by Russia
in 1897. With sterling as a reserve currency, monetary stability lasted
until World War I. All countries with significant foreign trade integrated
their banking and credit practices after 1850.

The expansion of trade coincided with British economic near hegemony and is usually attributed to it – certainly a cause, but along with

others. From 1815, Western industrialization was inherently transnational. Such massive expansion of interregional commodity exchange could not be controlled by the feeble infrastructures of contemporary states. Not states but private-property owners initiated economic growth, most of which emerged interstitially to state rule through fairly free markets. Of course, colonies were different, acquired and maintained by military force. But British exports and need for imports then diffused as opportunities less to states than to private-property owners, inventors, and skilled workers operating throughout European and American markets.

Industrialization spread mainly in response to three characteristics of transnational markets. First, the existing level of a region's agriculture and industry mattered. To trade profitably with Britain required advanced social organization. To compete with British products needed capitalist institutions only slightly behind Britain's. Second, industrialization depended on access to coal, later also to iron, on which steam power depended. Third, ease of communications with Britain, and then with other industrializing areas, reduced transaction costs. Thus industrialization diffused first to relatively advanced areas that possessed coal and were close to the original capitalist core.

Diffusion was regional rather than national; it passed through frontiers. It spread through the Low Countries – parts of the Dutch and Austrian Netherlands (the latter becoming Belgium in 1830) and northern France – not the territory of a single state; and then to the Rhineland, the Saar, and parts of Switzerland, also cross-frontier regions not the core territories of major states. Industrialization in Silesia, Saxony, and Czechoslovakia crossed the frontiers of Prussia, Austria, and minor states; northern Italy was contested territory; Catalonia was a frontier area, not fully integrated into the kingdom of Spain. Early industrialization mostly occurred outside the core areas of state infrastructural penetration. As Pollard (1981) emphasizes, in this period economic mechanisms were less national and international than regional and interregional. Capitalism diffused both interstitially and transnationally.

More market terms were set in Britain than anywhere else because industrial commodities and commercial capital disproportionately originated in, or passed through, Britain. In that sense most norms were "British." But this is only a convenient form of expression for norms that had no single place of origin and depended on the institutionalization of absolute private property and, in almost all the West, on formally free labor. What became transnational instruments of commercial capitalism had developed their fullest form in Britain but were not exclusively British. McKeown (1983) has shown that Britain had no major impact on the tariff and import quota policies of other countries – a crucial demolition of the notion that Britain enforced hegemonic stability. As Palmerston acknowledged, "The English government has neither the power nor the might to prevent independent states from entering into such arrangements with respect to their mutual commerce as may appear to them best calculated to promote their respective interests" (O'Brien and Pigman 1991: 95).

Yet Britain did not use "might." "Its" economy was widely regarded as beneficial for the world (as Arrighi 1990 observes). It was open and liberal. British foreign policy did not aggress against other Western Powers' territories. Britain's empire and Mediterranean influence were in place; they merely required defense. Scattered strategic ports and staging posts (later coaling stations for iron ships) like Aden, Singapore, and Hong Kong, not large new territories, were now sought by British governments (though white settlers sometimes dragged them further into continents). Gallagher and Robinson (1953) claimed that though Britain preferred "informal Empire," it moved to formal political control when necessary. But it almost never was necessary against other Western Powers. British naval power ensured free and equal trade, not discrimination in favor of British goods or intervention in Third World countries that could control their own territories and guarantee free trade (Platt 1968a, 1968b; Semmel 1970; Cain and Hopkins 1980: 479–81).

To other Powers, "British" terms of trade appeared merely technical. The Royal Navy pacified trade routes and stamped on recalcitrant non-Western states. Britain provided a model of the industrial capitalist future to be imitated – sometimes to be avoided. International transactions could be conveniently denominated in sterling backed by the promise of gold convertibility and credited through the world's major clearinghouse, the City of London. British techniques, skilled workers, managers, and capital were attracted and imitated by other states.

Why would most foreign countries wish it otherwise? Established foreign industries – for example, textiles in most advanced countries or the French iron industry – could compete with Britain's (often helped by mild protection from their state), local expertise and lower transport costs in their regions aiding them. Prosperity and demand for specialized consumer goods created boom conditions for the artisan and handicrafts industries of Western cities. Most countries could use British capital to develop their own infrastructures and manufacturing. Scandinavia, the Baltic Coast, Portugal, and America had long supplied primary goods for British manufacturers and consumers. Industrialization diffused across Belgium, the Netherlands, Switzerland, and lesser-state territories along the Rhine and the Saar. An economic belt stretched around northwestern Europe, in which the products of early comers such as Belgium and Switzerland could compete with British goods and primary producers in Denmark and Sweden could prosper. They accepted the transnational economy without considering over-much whether this was "British."

Why would foreign *states* wish it otherwise? The small states accepted leadership by Great Powers that claimed to guarantee their territorial integrity. All states' interest in trade was primarily fiscal. They milked it for revenue, benefiting from surging national and international trade (Hobson 1991). They were happy to exchange complicated monopoly licenses for general customs and excise taxes levied on the gross flow of trade. As trade increased, states' interest in keeping tariffs high declined. In periods of depression and therefore of declining trade and customs revenues, governments increased tariffs (McKeown 1983). As we shall see in Chapter 11, fiscal pressure on states at mid-nineteenth century was the lowest in centuries.

Thus geopolitical, economic, and fiscal motivations coincided across midcentury to move Western political economy away from protectionism toward laissez-faire. Between 1842 and 1846, Britain abolished the Corn Laws and proclaimed free trade in everything. States reduced tariffs in a series of bilateral trade treaties in the 1850s and 1860s in which geopolitical alliance motivations were secondary to commercial-fiscal ones. Negotiations also covered trademarks and recognition of one another's joint stock companies and laws regarding international rivers, straits, and people engaged in international trade – a second burst of commercial treaty making that lasted from the 1850s to the 1880s (Foreign Office 1931). Economic transnationalism was also negotiated among the Powers.

So optimism concerning the pacific and transnational implications of the economy was well grounded. Britain favored transnationalism, as did the major dynastic monarchies as well as most minor Powers, and it was the predominant tendency of capitalism itself. Strong trans-nationalism – the decline of the state amid a transnational society – was unlikely. But why not weak transnationalism, relatively private states engaging in diplomacy and even intermittent but limited wars, but without much salience for civil society? Wars were few, and mili-tary expenditures remained static or declined in absolute terms amid massive economic growth. (See Chapter 11.) Indeed, the first of these wars seemed to embody "weak transnationalism" perfectly, for govern-ments distinguished clearly between military and civil spheres. While British and French troops were fighting Russians in the Crimea, the British allowed the Russian government to raise a loan on the London stock market, and the French invited the Russian government to participate in an international exhibition of industry and the arts. "The ordinary way of business" should not be interfered with, declared the British Foreign Secretary (Imlah 1958: 10; Pearton 1984: 28). Limited warfare was back, popular nationalist mobilization seemed in decline. Laissez-faire political economy, called by Germans "*Manchestertum*," seemed to modernizers everywhere to embody natural economic laws, and to most regimes it did not look subversive.

But Manchester's laws rested, as all economic laws do, on social power: on the expropriating power of the capitalist class diffused transnationally and on geopolitical norms. Transnationalism was not "natural," a result of the interplay of private property, the commodity, the market, and the division of labor. Industrial capitalism presupposed coercive and normative regulation provided over international terrain by two main diplomatic mechanisms. The Concert of Powers and the balance of power regulated international relations of all types; and global trade routes, money, and credit were regulated by the specialized near hegemony of Great Britain. When both faltered, so did transnational capitalism.

Geopolitical and capitalist faltering, 1880–1914

Political economy had never been fully laissez-faire: Mercantilism had moderated into selective national protectionism; tariffs and import quotas were never absent; foreign economists advocated defending home produce against British goods; industrialists sought selective protection. But in the 1840s, the transnational economy changed gear. Railways boosted demand for more heavy capital goods than local industry could supply. British industry exported and took handicrafts and food in return. The potential threat to foreign manufacturers became actual when the mid-Victorian boom ended around 1873. Agriculture was hit by steamships and railways carrying North American and Russian grains. Competition was greatest in agriculture (Bairoch 1976b), yet agrarians were more than 60 percent of European consumers, so demand for manufactured goods declined. Greater efficiency enabled the British to lower prices, and Continental manufacturers joined agrarians to demand protection. State elites had their own interest in protection: Higher tariffs would keep up revenues threatened by economic depression.

Diplomacy also shifted as the balance of power faltered. This had little to do with British overseas and commercial hegemony, and much more to do with the balance on the Continent. The decline of Ottoman power, Austrian internal difficulties, and Prussian growth destabilized diplomacy and created fears of two regional hegemons, Russia in the east and southeast and Prussia in Central Europe. Neither expansion was aimed against Britain and neither was seriously connected to the question of capitalist leadership. Prussia was mopping up smaller states and menacing Austria and France. Russia was taking advantage of the decline of a precapitalist Power. The latter did affect British geopolitical interests. In 1852–54, Britain and France fought as allies in the Crimea to prevent Russia reaching the Mediterranean. Naval power enabled their success. But in continental Europe, Britain – at the height of its supposed economic and naval "hegemony" but with only a small army – could only passively watch as first France, then Prussia used Italian revolts to defeat Austria in 1859 and 1866; as Prussia and Austria confiscated Danish territory in 1865 (Palmerston did try meddling here, to no great avail); and as Prussia defeated France in 1870 (the British secured only a Prussian promise to respect Belgian neutrality).

Throughout this burst of calculated geopolitical imperialism, Bismarck set limited goals, so as not to shatter the decaying balance. But Prussian-German power was coming to dominate the Continent. Russia was also careful to expand through the Carpathians and across Asia, making British seapower irrelevant. Railways ended the logistic weakness of land powers. In the Crimea, Britain and France had more easily supplied their armies across a thousand miles of sea than Russia could in its own provinces. But those days were ending, as geopoliticians like Mackinder recognized. Britannia still ruled the waves, but no one ruled the Eurasian landmass, as hegemon or in collective concert or balance. Neither balance nor concert spelled trouble, since the rising Powers had done well with aggression. Germany was institutionalizing in its state two of the three main conditions of its success: Forgetting Bismarckian diplomatic care, it retained militarism and a segmental divide-and-rule strategy. The tendency of Great Powers to institutionalize what made them great in the first place was bad news for peace and for realism alike. (See Chapters 9 and 21.)

The decay of the concert spurred the Powers to enter into defensive alliances and increase military expenditures. Railways, artillery, and iron ships led to the industrialization of war. Costs rose after 1880 and so did civil expenditures (see Chapter 11). States needed more revenue – and tariffs would do nicely. Fiscal and economic motives jointly shifted political economy toward more territorialism, though only at first to protectionism. (I investigate this in the case of Germany in Chapter 9.) Tariffs were raised by almost all countries between 1877 and 1892. By 1900, levels were substantial, though not prohibitive. Only Britain, Belgium, the Netherlands, and Switzerland stuck to laissez-faire. As Table 8.5. shows, international trade now leveled off as a proportion of world production. The first fifty-year transnational surge of industrial capitalism was over.

This is the conventional account given by many economic historians and political scientists to explain how Europe got onto the slippery slope to 1914. However, it doesn't actually explain this. The move away from laissez-faire stopped well short of mercantilism – and a long way short of economic imperialism. Moreover, foreign trade was still growing, faster during the protectionist phase after 1879 than during the earlier free trade period (Bairoch 1976b). Continental European growth was now buoyant, and international institutions established around midcentury were still expanding. Tariffs were selective, pragmatic, cautious. They did not cage each national economy, nor did they seriously generate economic nationalism. The economy divided less into national economies than into spheres of interest of the Great Powers. These embodied differing degrees of territoriality.

The largest, most market-oriented economy was the Anglo-American. The British and American economies had always been closely integrated, despite high American tariffs. The countries shared a language and much of a culture. Across midcentury they agreed to divide geopolitical labors. Britain deferred to the United States in the Americas, the two negotiated amicably in the Pacific, and the United States deferred elsewhere. Table 8.6 shows that Britain and the United States remained each other's largest trading partner into the twentieth century. Their foreign investments interpenetrated in the two countries, in Latin America, and in Canada. Britain also tied itself more to its empire, less to Europe.

Between 1860 and 1913, the proportion of British exports going to the empire rose from 27 percent to 39 percent (Woodruff 1966: 314–17). Jenks (1963: 413) estimated that in 1854 55 percent of British overseas investment was in Europe, 25 percent in the United States, and 20 percent in Latin America and the empire. By 1913, investment in Europe had fallen dramatically, to 6 percent, the U.S. level had held steady, and investment in the empire had risen to 47 percent. (Different authors give slightly different figures: See (Woodruff 1966: 154; Simon 1968; Thomas 1968: 13; Born 1983: 115–19; Davis and Huttenback 1986.) Most direct investment by British companies in foreign subsidiaries also went into the empire (Barratt-Brown 1989). Because British and American investment institutions were independent of government, laissez-faire transnationalism ruled within the Anglo-American realm, moderated by its two internal fault lines, U.S. selective protectionism and the British Empire (Feis 1964: 83–117).

With Britain leading, global tentacles spread out from the Anglo-American sphere, especially to the Third World and smaller, free-

Table 8.6. *Percentage of a state's total trade carried out with other major states, 1910*

State	Trading with these states								
	Austria-Hungary	Belgium	France	Germany	Russia	U.K.	U.S.	All other	Total %
Austria-Hungary	—	−3	−3	42	5	14	6	33	100
Belgium	−3	—	18	19	6	14	5	38	100
France	−3	11	—	12	−3	16	8	53	100
Germany	10	4	6	—	12	11	11	46	100
Russia	3	−3	6	33	—	15	−3	43	100
United Kingdom	−3	−3	6	8	5	—	12	69	100
United States	−3	−3	7	12	−3	23	—	58	100

Source: Mitchell 1975, 1983: tables F1, F2.

trading European countries. In 1914, Britain alone contributed 44 percent of world foreign investment (around its nineteenth-century norm), France 20 percent, Germany 13 percent, Belgium-Netherlands-Switzerland combined 12 percent, and the United States 8 percent (Woodruff 1966: 155; Bairoch 1976b: 101–4). British and American trade were the most globally oriented, as the "all other" country column of Table 8.6 reveals. Their transnationalism diffused across the globe.

The second-largest sphere was the French. It was initially fairly market-oriented. French industry was less nationally organized than British or German. As Trebilcock puts it, "The international industrial revolution passed through France, leaving strong domestic pockets of manufacturing, but mobilizing men and money for a wider, trans-continental task" (1981: 198). French outward trade orientation in Table 8.6 ranks third, after that of Britain and the United States, but it was greater in investment. In 1911, 77 percent of stocks sold in France were for foreign enterprise, compared to only 11 percent in Germany (Calleo 1978: 64). French foreign investments were diplomatically supervised. As French military power declined, the French Foreign Ministry began to see capital as its secret weapon against Prussian divisions and British squadrons. It had to approve any foreign loan being floated on the Paris stock exchange. Arrangements for French investment figured largely in the Franco-Russian Dual Alliance of 1894. By 1902, French overseas investment reflected its diplomatic alliances. Substantial investment went to allies and clients – 28 percent to Russia, 9 percent to Turkey, 6 percent to Italy, and 6 percent to Egypt. Following the 1904 entente with Britain, trade with the Anglo-American sphere increased, 30 percent going to South America (Trebilcock 1981: 178–84; see also Feis 1964: 33–59, 118–59; Born 1983: 119–23). Geopolitics was bringing the French and Anglo-American spheres closer together.

The third sphere was German. It was the most territorially demarcated. German foreign investment was low and was supervised by the Reichsbank headed by the chancellor. Investment was steered by German diplomacy. By 1913, most went into adjacent client and buffer states – Austria-Hungary and the Balkans – although it was also expanding into Russia and Latin America (Feis 1964: 60–80, 160–88; Born 1983: 123–34). Germany was the only Great Power whose foreign trade and investment were both declining as proportions of gross national product as the twentieth century began. Table 8.6 shows that German trade spread out more than did its foreign investment, being equally divided between the Anglo-Saxon countries and Eastern Europe. But Eastern Europe (in Table 8.6, Austria-Hungary and Russia) depended on Germany. Germany's export trade involved subsidized dumping of manufactured products from about 1904. One of the three biggest economies was organizing against what it saw as the "sham" transnationalism of foreign Powers. Germany's political economy became more territorial than its two main Western rivals, as I explore further in Chapter 9.

But these Great Power contrasts are of degree only. Trade and investment patterns were only feebly segregated; and private capitalists everywhere traded and invested freely with one another and common third countries. Table 8.6 shows that British, American, French, and German trade diffused over the globe. This presupposed financial institutions. So as British near hegemony ended, its rivals sought to preserve "British" fiscal transnationalism. Sterling had never actually been as secure or as firmly based on gold as the American dollar was after 1945. It depended more on international "confidence." The gold standard required help from other governments, especially those with more controls over financial institutions than laissez-faire Britain possessed (Walter 1991). In the financial crises of 1890 and 1907, the Bank of England possessed insufficient reserves to secure international confidence. So the Bank of France and the Russian government loaned it gold and purchased sterling bills on the market. In 1907, the Bank of France specifically intervened to defend the British gold standard. Eichengreen (1990) comments: "The stability of the gold standard . . . depended on effective international collaboration by a core of industrial countries." What might seem transnational or hegemonic presupposed multilateral diplomacy. Such arrangements might have dominated the nineteenth century had not "that ruffian" Bonaparte so elevated "British transnationalism."

Financial capital was the most transnationally organized. The Rothschilds, Warburgs, Barings, and Lazards were almost stateless, deliberately placing family members in each major country. Financiers were a transnational peace lobby (Polanyi 1957: 5–19). They argued that war would massively harm every national economy. Indeed, threats of war invariably produced stock market panic, and stock markets and business cycles in each country were closely linked, more so than after World War I (Morgenstern 1959: 40–53, 545–51). Transnationalism was alive and dealing.

Yet the period ended with the catastrophic failure of transnationalism. Without entering here into the causes of World War I (discussed in Chapter 21), suffice it to say that transnational finance contributed two weaknesses. First, most overseas investment was "passive" – put into a portfolio of stocks, government bonds, or a single foreign company (usually a railway company). Only rarely would investors control companies abroad. Direct foreign investment by a company was uncommon, though growing just before the war (Barratt-Brown 1989). In this international rentier economy few capitalists controlled resources in other Western states – as do multinational corporations today. French and German governments controlled some investment abroad more directly. But this was overwhelmed quantitatively by the passive transnationalism of the British. Britain became more the passive rentier of international capitalism than the restructuring power it had earlier been. Second, capital depended on general geopolitical protection. Most flowed to the territory of friendly states, protected by the local or mother state. British capital moved toward its empire and to the United States and client Third World states; French and German capital moved to allied and client states within their spheres.

Thus the capitalist economy was becoming slightly less transnational as the economic significance of state boundaries grew. The Western economy had reached an ambiguous stage of complex coexistence between national and transnational networks. By 1910, Europe had not reached a level of territorial, nationalist economic rivalry sufficient to explain World War I. War probably did not result essentially from international capitalism (Chapter 21 confirms this suspicion). Yet we must differentiate by geopolitics. A world economy dominated by Britain and the United States would be more transnational than one dominated by France, which in turn would be more transnational than one dominated by Germany. As Germany was rising to challenge, the reasons for its rise and for its relatively territorial political economy and nationalist politics become crucial. I turn to this next. There is much more still to discuss before I can explain the collapse of the economic and geopolitical order whose rise this chapter has charted.

Conclusion

Although my narrative ends on a note of uncertainty, its theme is clear: The history of geopolitics marched to more complex rhythms than those suggested by economistic, dualistic, and hegemonic theories. The growing intensity of eighteenth-century wars resulted more from their unusual profitability, in both colonies and Europe, than from the absence of a hegemon. Yet they did not indicate international normlessness. War was regulated and coexisted with other sources of order. Napoleon's bid for hegemony was accompanied by the unexpected emergence of mobilizing class-national ideologies in revolution and value-oriented war. This threatened old regime order but failed because the Powers united to preserve that order, because they had well-established alliance norms to hand, and because of Bonaparte's diplomatic errors. I identified the ensuing period as seeing only "specialized near hegemony" by Great Britain. This provided order and peace only because of reinforcement by norms flowing from the concerted diplomacy of old regimes and from capitalist trans-nationalism. Peace and order faltered at the end of the century when all three of these preconditions also faltered, each for specific reasons needing further analysis.

The world was not dual. Neither capitalism nor the sovereign state emerges as powerful as diverse theoretical schools have suggested. Both were entwined with, and partly shaped by, all four sources of social power. In particular, I have rejected the self-serving imperial ideologies of nineteenth-century Britain and twentieth-century America. Peace and order have not depended on their benign hegemony; nor was "order" more complexly produced necessarily benign. Just as history has disconfirmed Hobbes's belief that domestic peace and order required a single powerful sovereign, so it disconfirms the notion that international peace and benign order need an imperial hegemon. Rather, it needs shared norms and careful multistate diplomacy.

Bibliography

Arrighi, G. 1990. Three hegemonies of historical capitalism. Paper presented at the ESRC Conference on States and International Markets, Cambridge, September 5–7.

294   The rise of classes and nation-states

Bairoch, P. 1965. Niveaux de développement économique de 1810–1910. *Annales ESC* 20.
  1973. Agriculture and the Industrial Revolution, 1700–1914. *The Fontana Economic History of Europe*. Vol. 3: *The Industrial Revolution*, ed. C. Cipolla. Glasgow: Fontana.
  1976a. Europe's gross national product, 1800–1975. *Journal of European Economic History* 5.
  1976b. *Commerce extérieur et développement économique de l'Europe au XIXe siècle*. The Hague: Mouton.
  1982. International industrialization levels from 1750 to 1980. *Journal of European Economic History* 11.
Barratt-Brown, M. 1989. Imperialism in theory and practice. Paper presented at the Center for Social Theory and Comparative History, University of California, Los Angeles, March 13.
Born, K. E. 1983. *International Banking in the Nineteenth and Twentieth Centuries*. New York: St. Martin's Press.
Brewer, J. 1989. *The Sinews of Power: War, Money and the English State, 1688–1783*. New York: Knopf.
Cain, P., and A. Hopkins. 1980. The political economy of British expansion overseas, 1750–1914. *Economic History Review* 33.
  1986. Gentlemanly capitalism and British expansion overseas. I: The old colonial system, 1688–1850. *Economic History Review*, 39.
  1987. Gentlemanly capitalism and British expansion overseas. II: New imperialism, 1850–1945. *Economic History Review* 40.
Calleo, D. 1978. *The German Problem Reconsidered: Germany and the World Order, 1870 to the Present*. Cambridge: Cambridge University Press.
Calleo, D. and B. Rowland. 1973. *America and the World Political Economy*. Bloomington: Indiana University Press.
Chandler, D. 1967. *The Campaigns of Napoleon*. London: Weidenfeld & Nicolson.
Chase-Dunn, C. 1989. *Global Formation: Structures of the World Economy*. Oxford: Blackwell.
Creveld, M. van. 1977. *Supplying War: Logistics from Wallenstein to Patton*. Cambridge: Cambridge University Press.
Davis, L., and R. Huttenback. 1986. *Mammon and the Pursuit of Empire*. Cambridge: Cambridge University Press.
Davis, R. 1979. *The Industrial Revolution and British Overseas Trade*. Leicester: Leicester University Press.
Eichengreen, B. 1990. Phases in the development of the international monetary system. Paper presented at the ESRC Conference on States and International Markets, Cambridge, September 5–7.
Feis, H. 1964. *Europe: The World's Banker, 1870–1914*. New Haven, Conn.: Yale University Press.
Foreign Office, U.K. 1931. *Handbook of Commercial Treaties etc. with Foreign Powers*, 4th ed. London: H.M.S.O.
Gallagher, J., and R. Robinson. 1953. The imperialism of free trade. *Economic History Review*, 2nd ser., 6.
Giddens, A. 1985. *The Nation-State and Violence*. Cambridge: Polity Press.
Gilpin, R. 1975. *U.S. Power and the Multinational Corporation*. New York: Basic Books.

1987. *The Political Economy of International Relations*. Princeton, N.J.: Princeton University Press.

1989. *The Economic Dimension of International Security*. Princeton, N.J.: Princeton University Press.

Glover, R. A. 1973. *Britain at Bay: Defence Against Bonaparte, 1803–1814*. London: Allen & Unwin.

Goldstein, J. 1988. *Long Cycles, Prosperity and War in the Modern Age*. New Haven, Conn.: Yale University Press.

Hobson, J. 1991. The Tax-Seeking State. Ph.D. diss., London School of Economics and Political Science.

Holsti K. 1991. *Peace and War: Armed Conflicts and International Order, 1648–1989*. Cambridge: Cambridge University Press.

Hopkins, T., and I. Wallerstein. 1979. *Processes of the World System*. Beverly Hills, Calif.: Sage.

Imlah, A. H. 1958. *Economic Elements in the "Pax Britannica."* Cambridge, Mass.: Harvard University Press.

Ingham, G. 1984. *Capitalism Divided?* London: Macmillan.

Jenks, L. H. 1963. *The Migration of British Capital to 1875*. London: Nelson.

Keegan, J. 1988. *The Price of Admiralty*. London: Hutchinson.

Kennedy, P. 1988. *The Rise and Fall of the Great Powers*. London: Unwin Hyman.

Keohane, R. 1980. The theory of hegemonic stability and changes in international economic regimes, 1967–1977. In *Change in the International System*, ed. O. R. Holsti et al. Boulder, Colo.: Westview Press.

1984. *After Hegemony*. Princeton, N.J.: Princeton University Press.

Kindleberger, C. P. 1973. *The World in Depression, 1929–1939*. Berkeley: University of California Press.

Knorr, K. 1956. *The War Potential of Nations*. Princeton, N.J.: Princeton University Press.

Krasner, S. 1976. State power and the structure of international trade. *World Politics* 28.

Kutznets, S. 1967. Quantitative aspects of the economic growth of nations. X: Level and structure of foreign trade: Long-term trends. *Economic Development and Cultural Change* 15.

McKeown, T. 1983. Hegemonic stability theory and nineteenth-century tariff levels in Europe. *International Organization* 37.

Markham, F. 1963. *Napoleon*. London: Weidenfeld & Nicolson.

Mitchell, B. R. 1975. *European Historical Statistics, 1750–1970*. New York: Columbia University Press.

1983. *International Historical Statistics: The Americas and Australasia*. Detroit: Gale Research.

Modelski, G. 1978. The long cycle of global politics and the nation-state. *Comparative Studies in Society and History* 20.

(ed.) 1987. *Exploring Long Cycles*. Boulder, Colo.: Rienner.

Modelski, G., and W. R. Thompson. 1988. *Seapower in Global Politics, 1494–1933*. Seattle: University of Washington Press.

Morgenstern, O. 1959. *International Financial Transactions and Business Cycles*. Princeton, N.J.: Princeton University Press.

Morgenthau, H. 1978. *Politics Among Nations: The Struggle for Power and Peace*, 5th ed. New York: Knopf.

O'Brien, P. K., and G. Pigman. 1991. Free trade, British hegemony and the international economic order in the nineteenth century. Paper presented at the ESRC Conference on States and International Markets, Cambridge, September 5–7.

Organski, A. F. K., and J. Kugler. 1980. *The War Ledger*. Chicago: University of Chicago Press.

Pearton, M. 1984. *Diplomacy, War and Technology Since 1830*. Lawrence: University of Kansas Press.

Platt, D. C. M. 1968a. *Finance, Trade and Politics in British Foreign Policy, 1815–1914*. Oxford: Clarendon Press.

1968b. Economic factors in British policy during the new imperialism. *Past and Present*, no. 39.

Polanyi, K. 1957. *The Great Transformation*. Boston: Beacon Press.

Pollard, S. 1981. *Peaceful Conquest: The Industrialization of Europe, 1760–1970*. Oxford: Oxford University Press.

Rosecrance, R. 1986. *The Rise of the Trading State: Commerce and Conquest in the Modern World*. New York: Basic Books.

Rosenau, J. 1966. Pre-theories and theories of foreign policy. In *Approaches to Comparative and International Politics*, ed. R. B. Farrell. Evanston, Ill.: Northwestern University Press.

Semmel, B. 1970. *The Rise of Free Trade Imperialism*. Cambridge: Cambridge University Press.

Shaw, A. G. L. (ed.). 1970. *Great Britain and the Colonies, 1815–1865*. London: Methuen.

Simon, M. 1968. The pattern of new British portfolio foreign investment, 1865–1914. In *The Export of Capital from Britain*, ed. A. R. Hall. London: Methuen.

Strachan, H. 1973. *European Armies and the Conduct of War*. London: Allen & Unwin.

Thomas, B. 1968. The historical record of international capital movement to 1913. In *The Export of Capital from Britain*, ed. A. R. Hall. London: Methuen & Co.

Trebilcock, C. 1981. *The Industrialization of the Continental Powers, 1780–1914*. London: Longman Group.

Wallerstein, I. 1974. *The Modern World System*. New York: Academic Press.

1984. *The Politics of the World Economy*. Cambridge: Cambridge University Press.

1989. *The Modern World System. III*. San Diego, Calif.: Academic Press.

Walter, A. 1991. *World Power and World Money: The Role of Hegemony and International Monetary Order*. Hassocks, Sussex: Harvester.

Woodruff, W. 1966. *Impact of Western Man: A Study of Europe in the World Economy, 1750–1970*. London: Macmillan.

Woytinski, W. S., and E. S. Woytinski. 1955. *World Commerce and Governments: Trends and Outlooks*. New York: Twentieth Century Fund.

9   Struggle over Germany:
I. Prussia and authoritarian
national capitalism

Three rivals, three theoretical issues

Just before 1900, the Second Industrial Revolution brought economic concentration, corporations, and cartels just when state infrastructures were "naturalizing" civil societies (see Chapter 14). Even Britain, the home of transnationalism, became more centralized and territorialized. But Germany, becoming the greatest European Power, went farther. By 1914, the German Reich was the leading exponent of "authoritarian national capitalism" – welding together semiauthoritarian monarchy, organized capitalism, and nation-state. The leading edge of power had shifted into Central Europe. Why? What was the nature of this power configuration, and what were its consequences?[1]

If we start around 1800, we have much explaining to do. The state that acquired the German Reich was the kingdom of Prussia, a second-rank Power, controlling only two-thirds of North Germany, mostly rather backward. Its territory, population, and economic resources were smaller than its pretensions to power. It was far from achieving German hegemony. Two rivals also blocked the way, Austria and confederal Germany. In 1815, Germany was a loose confederation comprising Austria (its president), Prussia, and thirty-seven smaller states. Most were puny; yet they were protected by neighboring Great Powers and by the belief of many Germans that confederation protected freedom of religion (Lutheran Prussia[2] and Catholic Austria had state churches); minor princes, cities, and merchant communities; and general civil liberties. With so many state boundaries, for example, censorship was ineffective; discursive literacy flowed right across Germany. In 1800, Austria was a Great Power, ruling more than double Prussia's territories and population. Yet Austria's economy was more backward and its provinces enjoyed considerable autonomy, so

---

[1] General sources used for nineteenth-century Germany were Hamerow (1958), Taylor (1961a), Henderson (1975), Berchardt (1976), Geiss (1976), Milward and Saul (1977: chapter 1), Böhme (1978), Kitchen (1978), and Snyder (1978: esp. chapter 3).

[2] Actually, Prussian and German Protestantism had comprised two main churches, Lutheran and Calvinist. In 1817, they merged in Prussia (and later in other German states) into a single Evangelical church. I shall refer to this church as Lutheran, as this indicates its main character and is a more familiar term.

Austrian resources were not as mobilizable by its state. The two rival Powers were evenly matched.

In the nineteenth century, Prussia overcame both Austria and the German confederation, at first by stealth, then more aggressively. Tables 8.1–8.4 indicate the economic overtaking. Before 1850 or 1860, there was little difference between the agricultural or industrial resources of Austria and Prussia. Yet by the 1890s Prussian Germany had doubled Austrian agricultural efficiency and gross and per capita industrial size and then raced farther ahead. In the wars of 1866–7 and 1870–1, Prussia gobbled up the smaller states, defeated Austria and France, and founded the German Reich. By 1914, Prussian Germany dominated continental Europe and Austria was not much more than its client state. This was also a victory for a more authoritarian, centralized nation-state with a closer relationship to industrial capitalism. Prussian Germany had welded a regime strategy of "authoritarian incorporation" onto industrial capitalism and nation-state. In Austria provincial nationalisms had now strengthened its confederal tendencies. Centralized "national" Prussia triumphed over confederal Germany and multinational Austria.

Was the triumph of authoritarian national capitalism secure and quasi-inevitable, or was it contingent and precarious? How viable in the long run were the three models of power development, the one that succeeded and the two that failed? This is the first set of issues addressed here.

A second set of issues arises from the increasingly "national" organization of the German economy. It actually drifted twice across that continuum of political economies, from market to territorial conceptions of interest, identified in Chapter 3. Most German states began as protectionist, then became laissez-faire. But then protectionism grew and became less selective; around 1990, it approximated mercantilism. Finally, it embodied elements of all three imperialisms – economic, social, and geopolitical – as political economy entwined with advocacy of territorial conquest. The drift also altered the balance of class organization, from predominantly transnational (proceeding through state boundaries) through predominantly national (confined within them) toward nationalist (where one state's citizens are organized against another's). Unsteady, contested, and only partial, these transitions nonetheless led toward what was in this period the final demonstration of national-territorial interest: the German rush to war in 1914. This chapter begins an explanation of the drift from market to territorial strategies and from transnational to nationalist classes. (Chapter 21 completes this explanation.)

There is tension between the terms "strategy" and "drift." *Strategy* indicates rational choice of means appropriate to a goal – to increase economic profit. *Drift* suggests those rational conceptions were being subtly, subconsciously changed by noneconomic power processes. This differs from most neoclassical and Marxian economic history, which tends toward a rational choice economism – "economic interest" explains development. It sees an economically rational "late development" strategy bringing authoritative capitalist organization, state planning, and protectionism (discussed further in Chapter 14). Gerschenkron (1962) originated the contemporary version of the theory, though its German antecedents stretch back to Friedrich List. Senghaas (1985) has revived List's theory, arguing that British laissez-faire, which he terms "associative," is less economically rational for most countries than "dissociative" protectionism. This is why Germany adapted the latter, he argues.

I make two different claims:

1. I show that the very concept of economic identity – of who the "we" is who might share an economic interest – is problematic and is structured by the entwined sources of social power. The emergent German "we," the "national' economic interest, was determined by power relations that were not merely economic but also ideological, military, political, and geopolitical.

2. Late development theorists do not explain the further drift of German policy making, from protectionism to mercantilism to imperialism and war. They believe this is not an economic problem but an outside interference with economic rationality. By contrast I explain the general nineteenth-century drift toward more territorial conceptions of interest. Economic questions, political economy, and class struggle were entwined with the national question, thus bringing in ideological, military, political, and geopolitical power relations. Power actors rarely confronted the one without the other. Drift resulted from the way these two struggles became conjoined in ways unexpected to any single power actor.

A purely economic theory cannot explain the drift from market to territory. At midcentury the very identification of the "economy" shifted from the transnational toward the national. The British political economists had seen the market and the division of labor as abstract and transnational. True, Adam Smith's famous tract, *The Wealth of Nations*, inscribed "nations" in its title. But his "nations" were mere geographic examples, playing no role in his theory. He used "Scotland" and "England" (national regions) interchangeably with "Great Britain" (a national state) to illustrate his points (as most British people do). He theorized individuals maximizing their utilities and classes forming around factors of production and transnational structures like markets and the division of labor. "Nations" were absent from the theories of classical economists.

This was not true of German theory. Cameralists (see Chapter 13) favored state economic intervention, quoted Alexander Hamilton, and pointed to the success of American tariffs. Friedrich List jibed that Smith had propounded not "political economy" but a "cosmopolitical economy" of disembodied individuals representing humanity as a whole – ignoring the reality of national societies. Laissez-faire was actually a smoke screen behind which the British could dominate the world. Germany should counter with selective tariffs adjusted to the needs of different sectors and regions. As development proceeded, selective protectionism could be relaxed (1885; cf. Snyder 1978: 1–34).

Listian views resonated more in the Lutheran statist ideology of North Germany than in the Catholic transnational south. But as Germans debated the needs of "national economies," they were implicitly conceding his fundamental point. Once the question was formulated in terms not of the "economy" but of the "*German* (or French or Russian) economy," the solution might be national rather than transnational. Yet "Germany" did not yet exist politically or culturally (at least for the masses). Goethe and Schiller remarked: "Germany? But where is it? I don't know how to find such a country" (Sheehan 1981). Who created Germany? The answer fuses all four sources of social power.

The third set of issues concerns the nature of the modern state. By 1900, Germany was "modern," its economy overtaking Britain's and its capital organization, technology, and human capital advancing faster. Yet it remained a rather militarist, semiauthoritarian monarchy. Was this a peculiar German *Sonderweg* (a special path)? What kind of state was it? I review Marxian theories that it was "Bonapartist," enjoying a limited power autonomy, and Max Weber's emphasis on its plural power autonomies. I show that its autonomy was not unitary, centering on a state elite. Although much focused on the center, its central institutions were unusually polymorphous (as defined in Chapter 3). Eventually Germany's lack of sovereign decision-making institutions brought it down, as Chapter 21 shows. The cataclysm of 1914 was the triumph of the unintended consequences of action, institutionalized in the polymorphous *Kaiserreich*.

"German" development

In 1815, "Germany" had a political half-life, in the feeble confederation and in the historical myth of the German/Holy Roman Empire. It had a more vibrant life amid networks of discursive literacy, barely touching the masses yet absorbing the professional and administrative bourgeoisie. As Chapter 7 shows, this tiny "German nation" existed ideologically before political unification and before an integrated economy. But the struggle against Bonaparte had driven it into the unwelcoming arms of the Habsburg and Hohenzollern dynasties. Out of that embrace came the German nation-state, by a circuitous route.

Both Austria and Prussia were dynastic monarchies, uninterested in popular nationalism, even though that was confined to propertied classes. Having mopped up Central Europe, Austria and Prussia now faced each other directly. Neither could easily expand at the other's expense. Geopolitics, in the narrow sense of the geographic structuring of interstate relations, steered them toward different projects. To the south and east, Prussia had Great Power neighbors, Austria and Russia. Expansion was easier among small western and southwestern German-speaking states. A dynastic accident, reinforced by geopolitics, made "German" expansionism more enticing. The Hohenzollerns had acquired by marriage scattered but prosperous Rhineland territories. The settlement of 1815, devised to counter French hegemony, enlarged these into a single bloc. Prussian territories spanned northern Germany but lacked contiguity. Joining them was the Prussian goal. It was implicitly a *Kleindeutsch* ("small German") strategy, ignoring the millions of Germans living under Austrian rule.

Austria would be the obvious leader for any *Grossdeutsch* ("great German") national integration because Austria had provided the Holy Roman/German emperors and was now president of the confederation. But the confederation was pluralistic and legalistic, hardly an instrument for Austrian hegemony (Austensen 1980). Austrian expansion would be better rewarded to the southeast, because Ottoman power in the Balkans was decaying and because in 1815 Austria had given up Flanders in return for Italian territories. Austrian expansion was not among Germans. Austria became even more multinational. Austria was even less interested than Prussia in playing the German card. Europe was still ruled by dynasticism and by economic transnationalism – but the latter carried unintended consequences for the former.

The German economy grew rapidly throughout the nineteenth and early twentieth centuries, as Tables 8.1–8.4 reveal. It also may have spurted around the 1850s, as it switched from transferring British innovations to Central Europe to developing its own industries. Cotton yarn exports as a proportion of home supplies grew from 25 percent in 1835 (dependent on British imports), to 44 percent in 1853 (breaking free), to 88 percent in 1874 (autonomy achieved) (Tipton 1974; Tilly 1978; Trebilcock 1981: 22–111; Perkins 1984). Such sustained growth was unparalleled in Europe. To some extent it was unsurprising. Western Germany had long prospered, and coal and iron deposits in the Ruhr and Saar made industrial development likely. But development became relatively "statist" and "national." Three main economic infrastructures were sponsored by the Prussian state and facilitated the integration of a *Kleindeutsch* nation: the Zollverein and railways (List's "Siamese twins" of German development) and education.

1. *The Zollverein.* By 1815, power actors in Germany agreed that industrialization was desirable but disagreed over international political economy. British-led free trade had been associated with economic advances, but it conflicted with the protectionist wisdom of mercantilism and with states' fiscal interests – most taxes came from customs dues. Yet thirty-nine sets of customs posts and tariffs was thought excessive, and North Germans, competitive in international markets, wanted lower external tariffs than did Austria and some southern states. Because Prussian territories were scattered across North Germany, Prussia had to negotiate economic arrangements with its neighbors; Austria and its neighbors with distinct blocs of territories did not have to do so. The northern states also controlled the outlets of Germany's main river and road routes to the most advanced European markets. Prussia could present customs reform as a technical matter and assemble a northern low tariff coalition to lead the German economy.

Prussia arranged with its neighbors to abolish internal customs posts while guaranteeing them their former revenues. In 1834, local agreements were expanded into the Zollverein, a customs union of eighteen states covering most of northern and western Germany. The states accepted low Prussian external tariffs and allowed Prussia to negotiate them with foreign Powers. A common administration collected the duties and distributed them according to the states' populations. Administrative savings were considerable, external trade was booming, and the states made a hefty fiscal profit. The Zollverein was a success, credited to Prussian leadership (Henderson 1959, 1975). It formed an embryo national economy and an actual national economic administration. It was the unintended consequence of entwined economic interests, the fiscal-political strategies of the confederated states, and Prussian geopolitics.

Unable to enter a German customs union without also involving its eastern, non-German lands, some of which favored greater protection, Austria had not joined. In 1850, Austria extended its own customs union to the Hungarian half of its empire. But southern German states communicated more easily with the northwest than with Austria and were gradually brought into the Prussian low-tariff union. Further, Austria was isolated by Prussia's ability to negotiate foreign tariffs.

When the Prussian tariff with France was ratified by the Zollverein in 1865, Austria, still president of the confederation, was not consulted. The Austrian economy was no longer German, and the Prussian was.

Did this matter much? The Zollverein had actually lowered tariffs, in step with the contemporary predominance of laissez-faire over mercantilism. Tariffs were selective and pragmatic, and markets were less impeded by frontiers. As elsewhere the main industrial regions straddled frontiers. In Rhineland-Westphalia, Saxony and Bohemia, and lower Austria, industries imported yarn, pig iron, and machinery from Britain; they finished the textiles and worked up the iron to sell regionally and farther east, usually in return for foodstuffs. The crucial raw material was coal, and by the coincidence noted in Chapter 7, most coalfields lay across or near frontiers.

To this interregional rather than international economy the Zollverein was only quietly subversive, with little immediate impact on economic growth (Trebilcock 1981: 37–41). Austria had suffered a reverse, and the confederacy had accepted Prussian economic leadership, but neither was decisive. The Zollverein was a useful fiscal technique, not anybody's model for a German state. Indeed, in 1867, when the German states went to war, their customs officials continued to collect the revenues – there was a wartime shortfall of only 10 percent. Such events conjure up weak transnationalism: Geopolitical struggles and wars might proceed, but with little social significance. For the geo-economic shift to Prussia to begin to have great significance, other forces must have aided the decline of transnational capitalism.

2. *Railways*. As elsewhere, railways boosted coal, iron and steel, and metal manufacture, and they commercialized agriculture by reducing marketing costs. German railways lowered freight costs by 5 percent to 10 percent of gross national product, a considerable saving. In western Germany, especially in the Prussian Rhineland, industry grew faster from the 1840s, aided by local coal and iron and proximity to the British–Belgian–northern French core. Railways widened markets, strengthened regional integration, and linked backward into agriculture and forward into iron and steel. Prussian grains moved westward, and semimanufactured goods from the west were finished in Germany and moved east with cheaper transport costs than western states faced and with a technological lead over the east. Railways encouraged a more integrated economy. They were the "hero of Germany's industrial revolution," says Fremdling (1983).

Railways were state-sponsored and usually state-financed and state-owned. Over most of Germany, unlike Britain, they existed *before* industrialization, and so state planning of lines was often more important than market forces. Three state crystallizations were involved – capitalist, monarchical, and militarist. Railway revenues brought profit to the monarchy: By 1910, they provided 44 percent of Prussian state revenue, increasing elite autonomy from parliamentary control. Like other states, Prussia soon saw railways in terms of military logistics, delivering troops and supplies to border and reserve locations for attack or defense on a massive scale. Little conflict was perceived among monarchical, military, and capitalist motives. The state saw that efficient distribution of the products of mines, iron and steel mills, metals factories, and textile mills also provided army equipment, geopolitical power, and autonomous fiscal resources. As the population urbanized, the logistics of transporting commodities, passengers, and troops and military supplies became nearly identical. The old regime core lay on the Junker estates. Railways enabled them to feed the growing towns. A more territorially centered economy and a more coordinated agrarian-industrial-military ruling class were emerging.

Railways also weakened transnationalism, consolidating economies within state boundaries. Railways resembled spiderwebs, each spun over a state's territories, with only a few threads connecting the national webs. This was deliberate. A Prussian line ran inside almost the whole length of the Saxon border, with many connections back into Prussia and only one into Saxony. Military and national economic considerations combined. This area of Saxony was more developed than adjacent Prussia, but the rail set up restricted its access to the Prussian market and enabled Prussians to turn elsewhere in the Prussian railway network for cheaper goods. And in war the Prussian army could flood over the Saxon border, as it did in 1866. Railways partly naturalized the economy, making it more statist.

3. *Education.* The same argument can be applied to canals, roads, the telegraph, and especially the educational infrastructures inherited from enlightened absolutism. Chapter 13 shows the Prussian monarchy centralizing its compromise with nobility and professionals in the universities and among the *Bildungsbeamten* (educated administrators). Much of bourgeois cultural nationalism moved inside the state. This was then diffused outward and downward as Prussia became the first large state to impose compulsory primary education and to develop a large cadre of trained teachers (29,000 by 1848). Its reading and writing literacy rate was 85 percent at midcentury, compared to 61 percent in France (reading only) and 52 percent in England (reading and writing); foreign visitors wrote admiringly of Prussian education (Barkin 1983). Education took a conservative turn after 1853 but still encouraged technical training well suited to the Second Industrial Revolution. Bismarck proclaimed, "The nation that has the schools, has the future." By "nation" he really meant "state."

After 1872, the *Kaiserreich* spent as much on education as on the military. It did not see the two as a "guns versus butter" alternative. Literacy among German army recruits was the highest in Europe, a proudly publicized fact. (See Chapter 14.) But this was not universal education in the modern sense. In 1882, average class size in Prussian schools was 66, it was reduced to 51 by 1911 (Hohorst et al. 1975: 157), and by then other countries were reaching this level. But Prussian education was statist, reinforced by the other carrier of literacy in the North, the pietistic Lutheran (Evangelical) church. Though unintentionally, the regime had harnessed "nationalist" loyalties.

These infrastructures did not merely aid economic growth. With few intending it, the infrastructures harnessed growth to the Prussian state, boosting the naturalization and statism of this originally multistate, regionalized economy and of its property owners. Prussian Junkers, Rhineland industrialists, merchants, traders, professionals, and officials throughout (*Kleindeutsch*) Germany, all increasingly speaking and writing a standardized language, attending the same schools and universities, were brought into a civil society whose main infrastructures were Prussia's.

There is both a weak and a strong version of this statist argument. The weak version, expounded by many economists, is that state policy was "permissive rather than propulsive" (Trebilcock 1981: 78; cf. Böhme 1978): State infrastructures merely "removed the fetters" (Schumpeter's phrase 1939: 280) from the diffusion of the "invisible hand" of market capitalism. Indeed, substantive state intervention in the economy was *declining* as protection and mercantilism retreated (Pounds 1959). Others take a stronger view, which I share. Kindleberger (1978: chapter 7; cf. Epstein 1967: 109) notes that intervention made economic integration national and thereby increased growth. But because this was largely unintentional and interstitial, it still had to overcome institutionalized political and geopolitical power relations.

The creation of the *Kaiserreich*: the *Sonderweg*

Between 1865 and 1871, Prussia conquered the confederation, expelled Austria from (*Kleindeutsch*) Germany, and established the Second Reich. The nature of this new state has occasioned two great controversies, raising major issues of sociological theory – arising from the *Sonderweg* and from the "autonomy" of this state. I deal with them in turn.

Many liberal historians and sociologists have viewed the *Kaiserreich* as a developmental aberration, seeing Anglo-Saxon and French liberalism as the normal track of capitalist development. They identify a German *Sonderweg*, a country with its "own special path" of development, semiauthoritarian rather than party democratic. They attribute this to rapid industrialization in a country dominated by reactionary state elites and propertied classes. The emerging bourgeoisie proved politically weak, unable to establish party democracy. Max Weber gave classic expression to this view (Beetham 1985: chapter 6); it has been repeated many times (Dahrendorf 1968; Böhme 1978; Kitchen 1978; Wehler 1985 gives a revisionist version). The argument presupposes that bourgeoisies are normally prodemocratic – the traditional view of comparative sociology (Moore 1973; Lipset 1980).

Marxian writers have attacked this liberal view of the *Sonderweg*. Blackbourne and Eley (1984) draw upon work denying any necessary relationship between capitalism and democracy (Poulantzas, 1973; Jessop, 1978). They say that the German bourgeoisie never seriously wanted liberalism, being content with a semiauthoritarian regime promoting capitalist development and minimal civil citizenship while restricting political citizenship and denying labor collective civil rights. Rueschemeyer, Stephens, and Stephens (1992) have extended this argument. Citing many historical and contemporary case studies, they show that the bourgeoisie has rarely pressed for democracy. If pushed from below by the working class, and more variably by peasants, it may favor more democracy. Without such pressure it rarely does. If emerging amid a powerful landholding nobility and military state, bourgeoisies freely embrace authoritarian rule, as in the *Kaiserreich*. There was no German *Sonderweg*; bourgeois authoritarianism has been as "normal" as liberalism.

But despite their differences, liberals and their critics offer alternative versions of the same underlying scenario. Both see the semiauthoritarian *Kaiserreich* emerging as a compromise between two power actors: an old regime and a rising bourgeoisie. Liberals see the old regime dominant, the bourgeoisie forced to compromise. The critics see old regime and bourgeoisie agreeing to divide the spoils: the old regime to control politics; the bourgeoisie, economics. Liberals see militarism as old regime, unstable, and doomed, for modern capitalism is in the end liberal. The critics see militarism as joint: the old regime as warlike, but the bourgeoisie favoring repression of the working class. Sharing the pessimism of much recent Marxism, Blackbourne and Eley see this as a viable track of capitalist development: "The orderly reproduction of capitalist productive relations could be guaranteed within a form of state which fell considerably short of pure representative democracy." It was a "bourgeois revolution from above," Moore's "conservative modernization from above" occurring here and in Meiji Japan and

Risorgimento Italy (Blackbourne and Eley 1984: 84, 90; Eley 1988). I draw on these views while correcting two shared flaws:

1. They are overconcerned with class relations, neglecting the national issue. They do not bring the identity of society into question. They differ over the relations between regime and bourgeoisie in a given state-society, Germany (Evans 1987: 114 also makes this criticism). But where was "Germany"? Wherever it was affected the identity of both capitalism and regime. *Two* sets of political incorporation were actually underway: bourgeois incorporation into an authoritarian state and incorporation into a single federal Germany of thirty-nine states, of two regional religions, and of Prussian, Austrian, and confederal geopolitics. Many of these writers, especially Blackbourne and Eley, are empirically well aware of this. But their theories ignore it. The old regime–bourgeois compromise was also over the national crystallization of the state, as in other countries. In this period, the German *Sonderweg* lay only in details. As Marxians point out, many states remained somewhat authoritarian. As Rokkan observed, and as I am extending in this volume, *all* states were riven by national conflict, differing according to peculiarities of region, religion, and the like. These we must specify.

2. Because they concentrate on class actors confronting one another head-on, these views overemphasize deliberate, rational collective strategies and interests. They assume regime and bourgeoisie knew what they wanted, struggled, and won or lost. But this was not what happened. When issues of class and nation were so entwined, collective identities became extremely complex, the outcomes of each struggle having unintended consequences for the other. Incorporation within authoritarian national capitalism (the outcome) was neither intended nor consistently fought against by *any* powerful actor. It was the product of several power networks whose crosscutting, intersecting relations were too complex to be controlled by anyone.

The 1848 Revolution is a good example of class and national entwinings. In many ways, the revolutions that broke out across Central Europe in 1848 were late-developing versions of the French revolutionary decade – and they were begun by another attempt at revolution in Paris. Yet if history repeats itself, in a multistate civilization it does so consciously. The three main class actors of 1848 – old regime, grande bourgeoisie, and petite bourgeoisie/crowd (including artisans and some laborers) – resembled those of the French revolutionary decade (although there was now greater artisan and proletarian participation, discussed in Chapters 15 and 18). A great expansion of networks of discursive literacy also preceded 1848, especially in Germany.

But there was a major difference: The actors of 1848 possessed precocious class consciousness based on earlier Western experience. Radicals immediately demanded civil and political citizenship, and regimes believed they must avoid the fate of their French cousins. When civil disorder erupted, old regimes and bourgeoisies made fewer "mistakes' about their own identities and interests. Most realized the greater threat was from below rather than from one another. The "party of order" consolidated in 1848 as it had not in 1776 or 1789. Most of the substantial bourgeoisie and some professionals, government careerists, and petite bourgeoisie deserted the revolutions, leaving radicals and their few thousand petit bourgeois, artisan, and student followers alone on the barricades (Stearns 1974; Price 1989). During the *Kaiserreich* most "liberals" did not endorse universal male suffrage, for fear of the masses (Sheehan 1978), as Blackbourne and Eley argued.

This process of class discovery came packaged with a second one, of national discovery – that the German propertied nation was best served by conservative Prussia. Northern Lutheran "national liberals" saw liberties and progress as coming through a reformed Prussia. Predominantly southern German "confederal liberals," often Catholics, saw freedom as interstitial to states and sought reform of the confederation. This split, over unification rather than class, stalemated the heady debates of the would-be revolutionaries in the Frankfurt Parliament during 1848 and prevented a coherent reform program from emerging. Many bourgeois leaders saw anarchy in this stalemate and called in the Prussian army. It repressed the revolution and exposed the German princes as depending on Prussia for their thrones. Advocates of confederation now split between defenders of the particularistic status quo and democrats favoring a sovereign Parliament in Frankfurt (Hope 1973).

Prussia was not a hopeless case for reform. Its *Bildungsbeamten*, teachers and civil servants, had played a prominent part in 1848, and they pressed for reform from within. The regime conceded a compromise constitution. A weak parliamentary system was established on the understanding that more radical movements would be repressed. The king could freely appoint ministers, officials, judges, and members of an upper house and he commanded the army. The lower house, the Landtag, could debate, participate informally in legislation, and approve or reject the budget (it was not so clear that the budget could not then be implemented). It was elected by universal male suffrage (for men over the age of twenty-five) but with weighted voting. Three "classes" had each the same number of votes: the 4 percent of major property owners, the 16 percent of minor property owners, and the remaining 80 percent of men. Some reformers settled for this; others pressed for more. From 1859, liberals, a majority in the Prussian Landtag, were rejecting the military budgets. The constitution was unclear. Bismarck (Prussian prime minister from 1862) argued that the "interest of the state" must prevail. Revenue was raised arbitrarily. Yet the stalemate needed a solution.

Bismarck turned to geopolitics. The Hohenzollerns had hitherto sought the consent of German states for gradually excluding Austria, France, and Denmark from German affairs. But in the 1860s, Bismarck shifted toward aggression. Popular outrage at supposed maltreatment of Germans in the Danish border provinces gave Prussia a pretext to invade, along with Austrian forces, in 1864. Victory obtained control over Schleswig for Prussia, Holstein for Austria (a dubious prize, as it was far away from other Austrian territories). Emboldened, in 1866, Bismarck took his greatest risk. He persuaded the king to invade Austria and its German allies, effecting a secret treaty with Italy to force Austria into a two-front war. Prussian mobilization was aided by better railways. The disparity was widened by Austria having to disperse its armies over two fronts. Even so, most of Europe, including France, the Berlin stock exchange, and Friedrich Engels, prepared for an Austrian victory. The Austrians defeated the Italians but were devastated by the Prussians at Königgrätz-Sadowa (Craig 1964; Rothenberg 1976: 67–73; McNeill 1983: 249–50).

This was not necessarily the end. Once well into Austria, Prussian armies were without their railway advantage and presented the usual chaotic spectacle of carts, beasts, men, and guns bogged down in muddy country lanes, intermittently short of food and ammunition, never in the positions requested by the grand campaign strategy. Had Austria continued the war, European general staffs might have absorbed the lessons of a recent American invention: industrial society's war of attrition, fought ruthlessly by the North in the American Civil War. Bismarck knew that Austria was in financial crisis, facing national disturbances in the southeast, but he also feared French intervention. He readily offered peace terms, asking for no Austrian territory but achieving his limited goal – to demonstrate Austrian impotence to its German allies. Most agreed to be swallowed into the Prussian-dominated North German Confederation.

Relations with an alarmed but isolated France now worsened. In 1870, seeing that neither demoralized Austria nor "bluewater" Britain would intervene, Bismarck moved frontally against France. The battle-hardened Prussian army triumphed more easily than was good for a Europe still ignorant of the horrors of industrial war. Prussia mopped up the last German states and unwisely took Alsace-Lorraine from

France. Bismarck's strategy had demolished – first by consent, then by manipulative diplomacy, then by "blood and iron" – confederal and Austrian alternatives for Germany. The Second Reich was in being – its regime, laws, communications networks, and coercion predominantly Prussian. The authoritative power of the Prussian monarchy and army, credited with achieving unification, led the nation.

These dramatic events had entwined four of the five causes of the rise and fall of Powers identified in Chapter 8. Ideological power differences seem small, though the morale of the Prussian troops was enhanced by victories. The economic modernization of Prussia gave the first principal edge, made relevant to the battlefield through railways and quick-reloading needle guns. Second, the balance of military power itself had tilted toward Prussia, as Moltke and his staff had developed tactics and training more relevant to the industrialization of war than had their opponents. Third, the Prussian state was more tightly integrated and more hospitable to industrial militarism than its adversaries. But its decisive political advantage came from diplomacy. Bismarck had carefully chosen when to fight and when to make peace, with allies in the first two wars, having neutralized other potential enemies in all three, leaving his generals with single focused objectives. By contrast, Austrian and French diplomacy left their generals with confused goals. Fourth, the decision-making abilities and authority of individuals – Moltke but especially Bismarck – made a difference amid complex, changing crises. Without Bismarck's political domination, the gamble would not have been made at this time, and the three German options might have remained viable (Pflanze 1976). There is a role for the individual – in institutionalized positions of high power – in world history. Again, as with the earlier British victories over France, it was an *ensemble* of advantages against particular foes in particular situations whose totality was skillfully mobilized into actuality. And again, superior alliance diplomacy was crucial to this mobilization.

The Prussian victories had immense consequences for Germany and for the world. Unification had been achieved and confederalism ended by force. Militarism now had great legitimacy, and transnationalism had been weakened. Bourgeois nationalists and modernizers were harnessed into the Prussian state. They saw Prussian superiority rested on its acceptance of industry, science, education, and capitalism. The authoritarian state was no longer the private property of a monarchy and old regime, unconnected to the bourgeoisie (as in liberal theory). Nor was it merely the product of their joint interest in repressing labor (as in Marxism). It was the unintended consequence of solutions to entwined class and national struggles.

Henceforth, said Bismarck, Prussia "will always be in a position to give Germany laws, not to receive them from others. . . . If revolution there is to be, let us rather undertake it than undergo it" (Gall 1986: I, 62, 278). His words led to the expression "a revolution from above" entering political vocabulary. Liberals split into minority recalcitrant Progressives and majority compliant National Liberals, declaring unconditional cooperation with Bismarck in national and foreign affairs, while observing the "duties of a vigilant and loyal opposition" in domestic ones. Its key decision was to support the regime's military appropriations budgets – so as not to "divide the nation." Its domestic priorities were more centralist than liberal: establishing the constitutional leadership of the imperial chancellor, unifying the civil code, and establishing the *Reichsbank*. With some restrictions in freedom of speech and collective association, a Prussian-led *Rechtstaat*, a state ruled by laws more than by parliament, embodying more civil than political citizenship, was established.

The Prussian political structure was extended to the North German Confederation in 1867 and to the German Reich in 1871. It was a federal constitution, with much routine administration, including police, justice, and education, in the hands of the individual states. Revenue raising was shared with the princes and representatives of the states, and municipal government was fairly autonomous. The class suffrage was abandoned in the Reichstag but retained in the important Prussian parliament. The distribution of constituencies was also biased in favor of rural areas. Reinforced by migration from rural to urban areas, this substantially underweighted workers' votes. There was broad suffrage but no parliamentary sovereignty. The Reichstag could not appoint ministers and had no right to debate foreign policy. The army was responsible not to a minister in the Reichstag but to the kaiser. The Hohenzollerns retained freedom of action, and the bourgeoisie was given a *Rechtstaat* (i.e., Marshall's civil citizenship) but only strictly limited party democracy. This state crystallized on the representative issue as semiauthoritarian.

The new regime's opponents might disparage it as a "customs parliament, a postal parliament, and a telegraph parliament" (Eley 1983: 282) – these were the civil state functions undertaken at the Reich level – but it won elections over the split confederal and radical oppositions. Its "liberalism" differed from British or French, tolerating a greater role in a modern state for authoritarian, even militaristic, practices and for more territorial conceptions of interest. The regime was strengthened. The bourgeoisie mobilized behind it, disparaging federalism as reactionary. The opposite was occurring in Austria, where modernizing ideologies were snatched from centralizing liberals by regional "nationalists."

Confederals did not disappear. They were now *within*, defending themselves against the central state. Alsatians, Danes, and Poles were reluctant subjects, organizing recalcitrant regional parties in the Reichstag. Some liberals defended regional, mostly southern autonomies against Reich centralization; Catholics resisted centralization by a Prussian Lutheran state. Struggles over class and nation were now entwined within a single state. The Prussian state had conquered but was now more polymorphous.

Moreover, the old regime–bourgeois alliance was still hindered by disagreements over international political economy. As heavy industry began to compete with Britain, it favored selective protectionism. A case was made (and has often been made since) for protecting infant industries while they were finding their feet and if they had potential markets to penetrate. After 1850, List was rediscovered. But was protection as necessary as lobbying or List made out? The German transition to industrial autonomy had occurred in midcentury free trade conditions. The debate was also influenced by the unintended consequences of modernizing nationalism. "Interests" became articulated as *German*. As industrialists were incorporated in the Prussian-German state they identified themselves and their economy as national rather than transnational. Most were Lutheran; most depended on state help against labor; most were socialized in the state's increasingly conservative education system; most appreciated the Zollverein and consulted regularly with the state over credit facilities and communications infrastructures; and many personnel moved back and forth between industry and civil service (Kocka 1981). Industrialists and state administrators generated "national" solutions to foreign competition.

Schmoller observed that protection was

state-making and national economy making at the same time. . . . The essence of the system lies not in some doctrine of money or of a balance of trade, or navigational laws, but in something far greater – namely in the total transformation of society and its organisation, as well as of the state and its institutions in the replacing of a local and territorial economic policy by that of the national state. [Ashley 1970: 55]

But at first the Junkers did not agree. They exported farm produce; tariff protection for industrial goods might invite foreign retaliation. Then the New World intervened. Table 8.4 shows that U.S. agriculture was far more productive than German. The steamship cheapened transatlantic freight in the 1870s. With cheap railway freight to and from ports, American grain and other primary goods entered Europe cheaper than local produce. Americans also developed a softer grain than Prussian rye. Junkers and peasant producers converted to selective protectionism on economic grounds in the late 1870s.

This, however, mattered less than their tax burden. Rather unusually, their desire to pay less tax coincided with the state's need for more revenue. What seems a straightforward sectoral "economic" interest came entwined with more complex state crystallizations – national, class, and military. The faltering of the balance of power, plus a technological arms race, raised military costs while revenue was falling – free trade diminished customs revenue, French indemnity payments ended in 1875, and depression increased tax defaulting. The federal government had a fiscal crisis. Its main direct taxes were the "matricular contributions" from the individual states. But these hit Junkers and peasant proprietors hardest, the very groups supporting Bismarck. They also decentralized state power, giving the states more say. Indirect customs taxes had neither disadvantage: They needed only minimal consent from the federal council of states and only initial consent from the Reichstag, and they hit consumers more than producers. Bismarck himself converted to protectionism on these political grounds.

National Liberals and Progressives, predominantly free traders and parliamentarians, were the main stumbling block to his plans. But Bismarck now had a stroke of luck. In 1878, there were two Leftist assassination attempts on the kaiser. The first led to the Anti-Socialist Laws. When Bismarck heard of the second attempt, he said, "Now I have got them." "The Social Democrats?" he was asked. "No, the National Liberals!" (Sheehan 1978: 183). He dissolved the Reichstag and organized a scaremongering election against Socialists and Liberals. It worked. With the fiscal support of the new majority, agrarian conservatives and Catholic Center, he raised tariffs to fund the military budget. The Reich government increased its fiscal autonomy from the confederal states (and to a lesser extent from the Reichstag), and got the unexpected bonus of a more consensual political economy as agrarian conceptions of interest switched to tariffs (my discussion of tariffs is indebted to the research of Hobson 1991: chapter 2). The alliance of "rye and iron" was formed, although it also included many western peasant farmers. German tariffs were raised in 1885, 1887, 1902 and 1906.

But these tariffs were no higher than those of other countries or than German tariffs of earlier periods (Barkin 1987). Their significance lies, rather, in their further unintended consequences. With unity achieved on selective protectionism, national bourgeoisie, old regime, and some peasants moved closer together. Far more industrialists, bankers, and merchants entered the nobility, bought rural mansions, and entered their sons in the army. The substantial bourgeoisie began to worm its way into the old regime, developing the same segmental manipulative deference as it had in eighteenth-century France. (See Chapter 6.) In what was called the "politics of rallying together," Junkers and industrialists exchanged produce, sons, and daughters, cooperated in political economy, conciliated peasants, and repressed workers. They still had disagreements, especially over taxes, but the opposition was even more split.

During the 1880s, authoritarian national capitalism was institutionalized. Industry, organized vertically into large corporations and horizontally into cartels, and coordinating closely with banks, penetrated an autocratic monarchy staffed by an agrarian nobility. Its success carried the middle classes behind it, deprived of some of the political participation enjoyed by their British, American, and French counterparts but sharing equal economic success, educational opportunities to forge careers as *Beamten* in public administration, management and the professions, and a growing sense of national community based on a strong, successful nation-state. Recent successes had been achieved by a two-pronged militarism popular among these groups: military adventure abroad and repression of the working class at home. Authoritarian incorporation was merging old regime, new capitalism, and middle class into a modern industrial society.

Yet German economic success also produced major class changes, destabilizing such cosy relations. Agriculture's contribution to gross national product halved, from 47 percent in 1850 to 25 percent in 1909. In the east the Junkers were turning inward, into their local economic problems at the same time as industrialists and financiers crowded into the state, restive at Junker-dominated political economy, taxes, and geopolitics. Agricultural commercialization diversified western class relations, producing both a rural proletariat and more independent peasant farmers. (See Chapter 19.) The middle class – petite bourgeoisie, professionals, and careerists in private industry and state bureaucracy – was increasing in power. First controlled by notable-led segmental parties, by 1900 it was responding to mass parties pressing for antiproletarian nationalism. (See Chapter 16.) Industrial workers were also increasing in power. Firmly excluded from political power, they united in class organization and Marxian socialism. (See Chapter 18.) This limited the regime's divide-and-rule options.

Class electoral strengths beginning in 1900 were about one-third agrarian, one-third middle class (including independent artisans), and one-third industrial proletariat, but class and voting correlated imperfectly. Segmental controls were still exercised by notables, now including industrialists, while all classes and most parties split over national versus local-regional power issues, especially expressed through churches. Class, religious, and regional identities competed. The two class extremes, regime and Social Democratic party, were both national statist centralizers, as both were predominantly northern and Lutheran. The Social Democrats opted firmly for statist socialism. They combined statist social democracy and Marxism, with few decentralizing economistic or syndicalist influences. Thus it resonated more in Lutheran than in Catholic communities.

Neither the regime nor the Social Democrats got much enthusiastic regionalist or Catholic support. The conflict between Lutheran Prussia and Catholic Austria, followed by the *Kulturkampf*, had strengthened a Catholic Center party. The Catholic church had been deprived of its vast estates and its secular powers within German states at the beginning of the century. Since then it had been consolidating its hold at the local community level, withstanding nineteenth-century secularization better than the more statist Lutherans. During the *Kulturkampf* priests and Catholic voluntary associations had drawn tighter together in defense of local rights, especially in rural areas, but even among Catholic industrial workers (Evans 1987: 142–50). Throughout Europe, the Catholic church was fighting against Marxism, an atheistic but also a statist doctrine. The Center opposed national centralization and statist socialism alike; it was clerically conservative yet had its own social program. Class and nation entwined in most persons' identities and all parties' programs.

To pass legislation in this semiauthoritarian regime needed a Reichstag majority. The regime segmentally manipulated and selectively repressed but still had to steer major domestic policies through the Reichstag parties. Because the Social Democratic party dominated Lutheran workers and because the parties of the ethnic minorities were firmly entrenched, the regime had to compromise with at least two among the middle class, the peasants, and Catholics. Its preferences were narrowed by its capitalism, monarchism, and militarism. Therefore, it did not try to undercut the Social Democrats by encouraging a Centrist alliance among moderate workers and regime, middle class, peasant, and Catholic liberals. Against the regime's opposition, no one else could move toward such an alliance. As Blackbourne (1980) notes, beginning in 1890, an alliance among the Social Democrats, the Catholic Center, and the bourgeois Progressives could have held a permanent Reichstag majority. But the Center preferred to compromise with the regime than defy it with the politics of class-cum-regionalist hostility. As we shall see in Chapter 19, the regime had considerable rural leverage. Lutheran peasants stayed loyal or were pressured from the Right; Catholic peasants were willing to make pragmatic accommodations. The regime allowed some local-regional autonomy in return for control at the center.

The Lutheran working class remained excluded, its militant core committed to an ostensibly revolutionary statist socialism. But the Social Democratic party worsened its own isolation. After 1900, Progressives made overtures to the Social Democrats but were rebuffed. Chapter 19 evidences the agrarian blindness of the Social Democrats, who remained committed to Marxist productivist orthodoxy: seeking the triumph of the urban industrial working class. The equally numerous agrarian proletarians and peasants were left to make alternative political arrangements. They went to conservative parties, regional peasant parties, and – the largest number – to the Catholic Center. Class politics were polarized between Lutheran workers and the rest. The bulk of the middle class was deterred from the liberalism found in Britain and France; Catholics stayed conservative on class issues, a "loyal opposition" on the national issue. Thus pressure lessened on the regime to dilute what I shall shortly identify as its capitalist, semi-authoritarian, monarchist, and militarist crystallizations. It diluted only its Lutheranism. Although its segmental divide-and-rule options were narrowing, its "additive" crystallizations remained intact.

The regime had two domestic priorities: to get the annual budget and the seven-yearly (later five-yearly) military appropriations through the Reichstag and Federal Council; and to modernize, industrialize, and undertake mild social reforms while orderly repressing labor and minority ethnicities. The main uncertainties lay with the Center, Right, and moderate regionalists. Conservatives supported the regime but opposed modernization. Junkers opposed privileges for industrial development and tax reform. Industry was impatient for all these. The Catholic Center and the South German states interpreted state modernization as centralization and opposed it. The regime's nightmare was that in a crisis an "out" party and temporarily alienated "ins" might unite with the "enemies of the Reich," the *Reichsfeinde*, to vote down the budget or military appropriations.

But nightmare never became reality. The regime coped, achieving its main goals while keeping freedom of action. Ministries fell, parliamentary majorities disappeared, and the kaiser's (short) temper was frayed by the humiliation of appeasing politicians. But the appropriations passed and no further advances to democracy occurred. Authoritarian incorporation appeared consolidated in what was now the greatest industrial nation in Europe. The working class might seem to threaten revolution; yet the more the Social Democratic party grew among urban, Protestant workers, the more bourgeoisie, peasants, Catholics, and decentralizers rushed toward the regime. The 1912 election left the Social Democrats the largest party, but drove Right and Center to the regime, enabling ministers to achieve long-desired tax reform. The regime seemed domestically secure. Its *Sonderweg* did not long stay "special": Many other authoritarian regimes, from Austria to Japan, sought to adapt its successful institutions.

The *Kaiserreich* and state autonomy

How much autonomous power did this state possess? The two main answers have been given by Marxists and by Max Weber. Marx allowed state elites the "limited" autonomy described in *The 18th Brumaire of Louis Bonaparte* (Marx and Engels 1968: 96–179). There he identified three autonomous political actors: the "official republican opposition," state officials, and Louis Bonaparte, stressing Bonaparte's ability to play off classes and class fractions against one another in a situation where no single mode of production or class was dominant. Marxists extend this analysis to other cases, always including Bismarck and the *Kaiserreich* (Poulantzas 1973: 258–62; Draper 1977: 311–590; Blackbourne and Eley 1984; cf. Wehler 1985: 55–62); but they view Bonapartist or Bismarckian manipulation of class conflict as structurally limited by the rising capitalist class. Bonaparte survived because he offered men of property the best guarantee of social order against popular insurrection. Bismarck generated a "creative independence of the state executive, inside the limits imposed by the political dynamic of capitalist social development" (Blackbourne and Eley 1984: 150). The form of such states may be liberal or authoritarian, but capitalism dictates the ultimate limits of their autonomy.

Weber credited the *Kaiserreich* (under which he lived) with rather more autonomy, but he also identified more bearers of autonomy. The first was the bureaucracy. Chapter 3 quotes his emphatic statement about bureaucrats "overtowering" political rulers in modern states. He argued:

In a modern state the actual ruler is necessarily and unavoidably the bureaucracy, since power is exercised neither through parliamentary speeches nor monarchical enunciations but through the routines of administration. . . . Since the resignation of Prince Bismarck Germany has been governed by "bureaucrats." [1978, II: 1393, 1400, 1404]

But we should not credit states of Weber's own lifetime with the powers implied by such sweeping statements. Chapter 13 shows that the number of bureaucrats was still far too small to permit effective infrastructural penetration by the state of its territories. Bismarck twice attempted to destroy alternative power organizations. Yet the Kulturkampf against the Catholic church and the Anti-Socialist Laws against the SPD failed, only strengthening their opponent. The bureaucracy was too small and politically unreliable to implement the legislation (Ross 1984).

Indeed, Weber himself undercut this stress on bureaucratic power. He noted that though efficient at implementing goals, bureaucrats did not set them. In Germany he identified two main policymakers: the chief executive – or, rather, the two executives allowed by the constitution, kaiser and chancellor – and "parties." For chancellor, read Bismarck. Weber believed Bismarck had dominated German politics, leaving "a nation *without any political will of its own.*" But then the folly of the kaiser and his circle, unrestrained by ministers or a sovereign parliament, then impacted disastrously on foreign policy (1978: II, 1385, 1392, 1431–8; for a review, see Mommsen 1984: 141–55). But bureaucrats *and* the two political executives were also subservient to the "party" of conservatives and Junkers. The monarch ruled as the patrimonial head of a kinship network of Junker lords, shared their assumptions and way of life, and staffed his court and higher bureaucracy with them or their clients:

Because a bureaucracy is all-powerful does not mean there is no *party* rule. Anything except conservative governments in Prussia [is] impossible, and German token Parliamentarism rests . . . on the axiom: every government and its representatives must of necessity be "conservative," apart from a few patronage concessions to the Prussian bourgeoisie and centre party. This and nothing else is meant by the "above party" character of bureaucratic rule. . . . The party interests of the conservative officialdom in power, and of the interest groups associated with them, control the direction of affairs alone. . . . Whenever the material or the social power interests of the stratum which stood behind the ruling party were at stake, the throne always remained powerless. [Beetham 1985: 165, 179]

Thus Weber also set limits to the elite autonomy of bureaucracy and chief executives: They could not defy, not capitalism, but rather the conservative party.

This party was not a state elite autonomous from social classes (as in the work of true elitist theorists). The Junkers *were* a class, hitherto dominant, now declining. But they retained power in Germany because their past economic dominance had been institutionalized in the state. Conversely, the capitalist bourgeoisie, now dominating the German economy, was politically feeble. The previously dominant class can cling to power against presently dominant classes by controlling state institutions. Such "parties" are relations *between* civil society and the state (as I argue in Chapter 3). Chapter 4 also notes that the British old regime clung to political power through an old regime liberalism that remained more laissez-faire than Britain's industrial needs have required (see also Mann 1988: 210–37). They had "party" power. In contrast, Weir and Skocpol (1985), also claiming lineage from Weber, argue that Britain's twentieth-century failure to adopt Keynesian corporatism resulted from the power of an autonomous state bureaucracy. Who is correct is an empirical matter – and is the only matter that really counts – but who is more Weberian is clear: me. State autonomy in Germany was plural, composed of two distinct elite elements, bureaucracy and dual chief executive, and a dominant institutionalized party.

In fact Weber's three political actors are an underestimate. If we pursue institutional statist theory, we can list no fewer than eleven significant political institutions in the *Kaiserreich*. The first two were Weber's chief executives:

1. The sovereign *kaiser* whose powers could be delegated to (and arrogated by)
2. the Reich *chancellor* and subordinate *ministers* – appointed by, responsible to, and dismissed by kaisers only exercising these powers erratically. They were usually drawn from the Junkers and western aristocracy and were predominantly Lutheran.

Then I add Reich administrative institutions, also embodying center-territory "party" relations in Weber's sense:

3. The *court* – not with a single administrative structure yet close to the kaiser, especially through the *Kabinetten*, his circles of personal advisers, and through faction and intrigue. The court represented most directly Lutheran Junkers and aristocrats, with a leavening of ennobled or influential industrialists, bankers, *Bildungsbeamten*, and (later) Catholics.
4. The *military*, essentially Prussian (though Bavaria, Saxony, and Württemberg retained their own contingents), responsible formally to the kaiser, the commander in chief, linked to the court, embedded in similar classes. Army and navy each had its separate command structure, with no formal relations between the two. Each was also crosscut at the top by aristocratic rank and by *Immediatstellung* – the right of senior officers to a private audience with the kaiser (see Chapter 13).
5. The *Bureaucracy*, the most coherent institution, partly responsible to ministers yet with its own collective legal rights and castelike solidarity. It represented a class compromise, through the universities, between old regime and professional bourgeoisie. Late nineteenth-century ministries then compromised religious differences, admitting some Catholics. At the top the bureaucracy was crosscut by *Immediatstellung* and at all levels by federalism. Most civil functions were administered by the individual states, while military, foreign policy, and material communication infrastructures were administered by the Reich. Prussian dominance, however, institution 10, counteracted this diversity.

Then I add parliamentary institutions – Reichstag and formal political parties – representing members and voters in civil society. The Reichstag was not sovereign. Its powers were limited and fuzzy, though its formal right to veto budgets conferred more power than the parties took up. Deference to the regime made most parties centralized and oligarchical. Most parties remained more segmental notable than mass electoral. Hence, the tripartite model used for eighteenth-century Britain (see Chapter 4) is again appropriate:

6. *"In" parties* of notables normally consulted by kaiser, chancellor, and ministers – the Conservative parties, representing Lutheran agrarian landlords and their dependents, and the National Liberals, representing mainly the Lutheran urban bourgeoisie. Both were statist.
7. *"Out" parties* normally not consulted but whose support might give a secure Reichstag majority without the regime making too many unpalatable concessions – the more antistatist Progressives, middle-class nationalists, the Catholic Center, and peasant parties. These gradually moved out of the control of notables and became mass electoral.
8. *"Excluded" parties*, called by the regime *Reichsfeinde*, enemies of the Reich, whose support the regime would not seek under any circumstances – the Social Democratic party plus ethnic minority and separatist parties.

Then I add federal institutions. Although federalism was partly formal and left little policy initiation to individual states, three distinct power institutions had to be reckoned with:

9. The *federal Council* (Bundesrat) – the upper house of representatives of the twenty-five confederal states. This cosigned legislation (with the kaiser) and declarations of war and martial law. The kaiser chaired it, however, and the Prussian representatives possessed a collective veto. Its main power lay in the complex revenue-sharing arrangements for direct taxes.
10. The *Prussian state* – this "provincial" government was actually larger than the Reich government and governed the regime's heartland, giving it more influence than the constitution indicated, defining the character of the Reich administration. Moreover, such civilian control as existed over the army was exercised through the Prussian War Ministry.
11. *Local government* – cities had considerable autonomy to decide their constitutions, levy supplementary taxes, and extend public ownership (Kocka 1986). Varying greatly across Germany this changed which parties might be locally "in," "out," or "excluded." Across Bavaria, for example, the Catholic church and its client parties were "in." Even the Social Democratic party was "in" in a handful of cities.

This state was polymorphous, its crystallizations emerging amid plural institutions. Modernization along semirepresentative lines, with multiple institutions responsible only to the kaiser, made this state much less unitary and cohesive than its eighteenth-century Prussian ancestor. Then sovereignty had resided in the relations between king and his higher officials; now it was more divided. The constitution divided powers, but unlike the American Constitution, did not clearly locate them. To implement policy required institutions whose constitutional powers had been left deliberately vague so as to preserve monarchical freedom of action, as in most nineteenth-century monarchical constitutions. This privileged the informal corridors of power and the centrality of monarch and chancellor. An upward-oriented segmental factionalism dominated the capital. Its intrigues, cabals, and attempts to get the ear of the kaiser were key political processes, subverting supposedly rational bureaucracies in ministries and military.

Segmental power relations at the center also encouraged corporate pressure groups. Power actors relied less on economic markets and mass elections than actors in most countries. Corporate organizations proliferated in the capital, to bend the ear of courtiers and to lurk in ministry corridors and Reichstag antechambers. Diefendorf (1980) shows that "corporations" early characterized relations between businessmen and German states in the Rhineland. Through the nineteenth century they grew at every level – from employers' organizations and cartels, through pressure groups like the Navy League or the Society of the Eastern Marches, right down to community organizations like the enormous number of choral societies. Germany was more authoritatively organized from top to bottom than liberal countries. The United States saw much lobbying by capitalist corporations, but its government was much smaller. In the 1920s, a German Marxist, Hilferding, coined the term "organized capitalism," which he believed began in this period. But for Germany he should have pluralized it. Wehler more aptly terms the regime "polycratic but uncoordinated authoritarianism" (1985: 62). It was actually less centralized than liberal states with sovereign decision-making bodies, like Britain or France. Policy resulted from complex segmental intrigues in which outcomes rarely matched intentions.

Yet polymorphous factionalism was not the same as chaos. The state's formal decision makers – monarch, chancellor, ministers – devised moderately coherent segmental power tactics to retain direction of affairs. Major policy initiatives like tariff or tax reform, a major naval program, a *Kulturkampf*, or welfare legislation required exercising arbitrary power. The Reichstag was dissolved; ministers were dismissed; opponents, harassed. Selective repression and inducements and divide and rule between parties became tactics Bismarck could use with great skill as less gifted or more ideological ministers struggled. Bismarck fluidly entwined class with national, domestic with foreign, policy – appropriate in a Reich whose opponents were fluctuating mixtures of "outs" and "excludeds," bourgeois liberals, peasants, workers, Catholics, southern regionalists, and ethnic minorities. Not all could be repressed, better to segmentally divide and rule. Policy seemed unstable because dictated by changing realities in which no one was in total command of all currents. Bismarck did not represent himself as master strategist but as someone able to *sense* general relationships and trends. In a metaphor he often used, he described himself as a man walking in a wood who, without knowing his exact way, senses his general direction.

But even without a Bismarck, politics did cohere around the pursuit of broad goals. Eleven can be reduced to four. Political institutions were committed to four diffuse, overlapping, and broadly compatible functional goals, what in Chapter 3 I call "higher-level crystallizations," each relating to one of the sources of social power. Their broad compatibility welded regime factions together, though eventually they destroyed them.

1. *Capitalism* was the state's economic crystallization. Anyone who counted was a substantial owner of land or industry or commerce, using all factors of production as commodities. Preserving private property was an unquestioned policy end; so was modernizing industry and agriculture to enhance private profit and state revenue.

2. *Militarism* seemingly had created the German nation-state. The court and the kaiser's entourage were stuffed with uniforms, medals, and swords. The bureaucracy was ranked and uniformed. Capitalists became reserve officers and their sons joined uniformed fraternities and acquired duelling scars at universities. This was not a state composed of foaming-at-the mouth, saber-rattling reactionaries. Military men were diverse; many officers were highly cultivated, and some were liberal – for example, Caprivi, a Prussian general and briefly chancellor. Yet military solutions to both domestic and foreign problems were reached for earlier in the German state than in most states to the west and south. When Weber, Hintze, and later observers wrote of German capitalists' becoming "feudalized" they really use the wrong word. "Militarized" would be better. "Feudalized" implies feudal *rather than* capitalist, as these are alternative modes of production. Germany was capitalist, not feudal. "Militarized" can imply military *as well as* capitalist, as the two are not alternatives. Thus as bourgeoisie became incorporated into the regime, many became socialized into more militaristic conceptions of interest in both domestic and foreign policy. They drifted toward authoritarian, territorial, repressive strategies. "Order" became sacred – more diffuse than mere property preservation – a value proudly proclaimed by the regime and oft criticized by foreign travelers.

3. *Semiauthoritarian monarchy.* On "representation" it was essentially dual. On the one hand, it was deeply monarchical, centered on

the kaiser. Political actors had to operate through upward-oriented networks centered on him and decked with monarchical trappings. A decisive monarch could have become a formidable power actor. The irascible Kaiser Wilhelm II proved only an erratic though occasionally dangerous one (as Weber noted). The kaiser's preferences had to be considered or manipulated, though German monarchy was more institutionalized, less dynastic than Austrian or Russian. Yet the constitution was also parliamentary. The Reichstag, though not sovereign, had to be consulted, even deferred to. This was why monarchists dreamed of coups. From such duality stemmed the fuzziness concerning the location of sovereignty in this state.

Although these three higher-level crystallizations themselves embodied ideologies, the regime also drew successively upon two autonomous ideologies:

4a. *Lutheranism*. German Lutheranism tended to sacralize the state.[3] This weakened somewhat after the failure of the Kulturkampf, as the regime sought to conciliate Catholics and as a rival statist ideology, Marxian socialism, came to dominate among Lutheran workers. As a legitimating state ideology, Lutheranism was increasingly displaced after about 1880 by:

4b. *Statist nationalism*. As citizenship widened and parties became mass electoral, a statist nationalism took root amid some classes and regions, urging that the state aggressively mobilize the power of the nation against *Reichsfeinde* within and Great Power rivals without. Though it supported capitalism, monarchy, and militarism, after 1900, this statist nationalism exerted disconcerting, independent "popular" pressure on them. (See Chapters 16 and 21.)

Thus the German state was somewhat autonomous – less as a coherent elite than as a polymorphous series of state elites and parties embodying compatible but distinct higher-level crystallizations. Let me add that the fifth crystallization, on the national issue, remained somewhat incoherent and volatile. The monarchy, aided by Lutheranism and statist nationalism, sought more national centralization than the constitution allowed.

Can I now further reduce these crystallizations along lines specified in Chapter 3? Does one finally impose itself on the others in some "ultimate," last instance sense? In the *Kaiserreich* did the chips ever come down, forcing the regime to choose among them? Marxists give positive answers, suggesting that ultimate "limits" were imposed by the class interests of capital. Indeed, this was a capitalist state. All

---

[3] Thus that later party of statist nationalism, the Nazis, also received far more support from Lutherans than Catholics.

European states were. They had proved it during 1848. The German state continued proving it through 1914 and beyond, continually intervening on the side of owners in industrial disputes, intermittently suppressing democratic and workers' movements. If it came to the crunch, all pre-1917 regimes were committed to such limits.

But states were not *only* capitalist states and this crystallization was not always at the forefront of minds and emotions. The *Kaiserreich* did not consistently fear workers or peasants. It was not so obvious to contemporaries as it is to Marxists that socialism was as viable an alternative mode of production to capitalism. Property was "natural," it did not need eternal vigilance. "Order" was primary in 1848, but thereafter little serious "disorder" came from below. Troops were not deployed as often against labor as in the United States during this period, and – because their deployment in Germany was ritualized and orderly – there was much less violence and killing. (See Chapter 18.) Bismarck's Anti-Socialist Laws and welfare state legislation were less a fearful onslaught on socialism than part of his normal segmental divide-and-rule strategy of selective repression and inducement emanating from the semirepresentative crystallization. The laws were intended to split the bourgeois parties, as the welfare program were intended to divide the Social Democratic leadership from the rank and file, and skilled from unskilled workers (Taylor 1961b; Gall 1986: II, 93–103, 128–9).

The weakest part of Blackbourne and Eley's Marxian case is the notion that the bourgeoisie allied with the old regime for fear of mass socialism. As Chapter 18 shows, it was mostly the other way around. A mass Marxian socialism arose *as a result of* this alliance, for labor unions and political associations could find fewer liberal allies than in Britain or France. Repression was not really necessary; conciliation would have worked as well. Rather, this militarist, semiauthoritarian, capitalist, and Lutheran statist-nationalist regime considered it the natural thing to do. It then became self-fulfilling – and in response the core Lutheran working class embraced revolutionary Marxism, eliciting further repression that was now perhaps necessary.

Such politics had unintended consequences for capitalism and, eventually, for its supposed "limits." It was a capitalist state, but it was not only that. These crystallizations were not identical; nor were they dialectical head-on opposites. They were just different. No "ultimate" choice had to be made among them, and fuzzy sovereignty ensured none was. The regime never faced them squarely, choosing among them. Only Lutheranism was downplayed, and that was replaced by statist nationalism. The regime drifted toward an additive strategy – capitalist *and* semiauthoritarian *and* militarist *and* statist nationalist.

Because it did not choose priorities, its institutions became more poly-morphous. But they embodied a more authoritarian, centralized, terri-torial, and aggressive capitalism. The *Kaiserreich* breached supposed capitalist "limits."

My proof of this will take several chapters. This chapter has begun it. Chapter 14 develops it in relation to economic development and social welfare; Chapter 16, in relation to supposedly bourgeois nationalism; and Chapter 18 in relation to the working class. The discussion in these chapters demonstrates the domestic strengths of the additive drift: It harnessed all four crystallizations into a successful, stable authoritarian national capitalism. Then Chapter 21 demonstrates the weakness of the additive strategy in foreign policy, as the regime failed to choose among alternative policies and its additive crystalli-zations increased the number of its foreign enemies. It drifted into a war that destroyed it. Later still (outside the scope of this volume), that war produced fascism in Germany and Bolshevism elsewhere – regimes that further infringed or abrogated altogether the "limits" of the capitalist mode of production.

A Prussian conclusion

I have narrated Germany's rise as the application of authoritarian incorporation to an industrial society, a compromise between "vertical" class relations and more "horizontal" segmental power relations. Industrial and commercial capital and much of the middle class came into or around the edges of the regime, religious and regional decen-tralizers were neutralized with segmental divide-and-rule inducements, and working class and ethnic minorities were excluded, isolated, and repressed. As the old regime modernized and schemed and muddled its way through complex class and national struggles, a new form of modern society, authoritarian national capitalism, was uninten-tionally created. It remained capitalist *and* militarist *and* it became semiauthoritarian – avoiding any "ultimate" choice among these higher-level political crystallizations. Only its ideological crystallization had changed, from Lutheran to statist nationalist. Segmental authoritarian powers were essential to it. Its militarism was deployed domestically – against labor and ethnic minorities, more selectively against others – and geopolitically against rival Great Powers and foreign capitalists. Its nationalism hastened the regime's drift from liberal conservatism toward a xenophobic sense of community, incorporating concepts of economic interest along the way. Its capitalism had become somewhat more repressive, territorial, and nationalist than most foreign capitalisms. It was probably in Germany to stay, unless overthrown by its own militarism.

Its rise was not uncontested or inevitable; its triumph, not total. I am not simply identifying Germany as authoritarian or militarist, or Britain as liberal or transnational. Their differences were of degree. Moreover, Germany's deflection from liberal conservatism and from transnationalism was slow and contingent on several entwined sources of power. Prussian advantages were at first almost accidental. They were then amplified by military, political, and diplomatic skills, especially by Bismarck. Midcentury economic development had a powerful autonomous logic but was also structured by these same forces. The combination of statism, nationalism, and modernization was intended by none of the principal participants in the great political compromises among Prussian old regime, capitalist classes, and local-regional decentralizers. Yet it changed their very identities. The combination proved itself by results as Germany became a great and prosperous nation-state. It was amplified by later entwined class and national conflicts and Great Power rivalries (discussed in Chapter 21). An alternative route toward advanced industrialism, besides those offered by liberalism or reformism, was institutionalized domestically – though in somewhat incoherent institutions. Its Achilles' heel had not yet been revealed.

But we have another methodological possibility to explain nineteenth-century German development. For there was another great German state, in many ways the antithesis of its rival. To narrate German history without Austria would be like narrating *Hamlet* without its irresolute, apparently doomed, yet eventually reckless prince.

Bibliography

Ashley, P. 1970. *Modern Tariff History: Germany – United States – France.* New York: Howard Fertig; reprint of 3d, 1920, ed.
Austensen, S. 1980. Austria and the struggle for supremacy in Germany: 1848–1864. *Journal of Modern History* 52.
Barkin, K. D. 1983. Social control and the *Volksschule* in *Vormärz* Prussia. *Central European History* 16.
  1987. The second founding of the Reich, a perspective. *German Studies Review* 10.
Beetham, D. 1985. *Max Weber and the Theory of Modern Politics.* Cambridge: Polity Press.
Berchardt, K. 1976. Germany, 1700–1914. In *The Fontana Economic History of Europe.* Vol. 4: *The Emergence of Industrial Societies*, Pt. I, ed. C. M. Cipolla. Brighton: Harvester.
Berghahn, V. 1973. *Germany and the Approach of War in 1914.* London: St. Martin's Press.
Blackbourne, D. 1980. *Class, Religion and Local Politics in Wilhelmine Germany.* Wiesbaden: Steiner.

Blackbourne, D., and G. Eley. 1984. *The Peculiarities of German History*. Oxford: Oxford University Press.

Böhme, H. 1978. *Introduction to the Social and Economic History of Germany*. Oxford: Blackwell.

Born, K. E. 1976. Structural changes in German social and economic development at the end of the nineteenth century. In *Imperial Germany*, ed. J. J. Sheehan. New York: Franklin Watts.

Calleo, D. 1978. *The German Problem Reconsidered*. Cambridge: Cambridge University Press.

Craig, G. 1964. *The Battle of Königgrätz*. Philadelphia: Lippincott.

Dahrendorf, R. 1968. *Society and Democracy in Germany*. London: Weidenfeld & Nicolson.

Diefendorf, J. 1980. *Businessmen and Politics in the Rhineland, 1789–1834*. Princeton, N.J.: Princeton University Press.

Draper, H. 1977. *Karl Marx's Theory of Revolution: State and Bureaucracy*. New York: Monthly Review Press.

Eley, G. 1980. *Reshaping the German Right*. New Haven, Conn.: Yale University Press.

1983. State formation, nationalism and political culture in nineteenth-century Germany. In *Culture, Ideology and Politics*, ed. R. Samuel and G. Stedman Jones. London: Routledge & Kegan Paul.

1988. In search of the bourgeois revolution: the particularities of German history. Paper presented at the Center for the Study of Social Theory and Comparative History, University of California, Los Angeles.

Epstein, K. 1967. The socio-economic history of the second German Empire. *Review of Politics* 29.

Evans, R. (ed.). 1978. *Society and Politics in Wilhelmine Germany*. London: Croom Helm.

1987. *Rethinking German History*. London: Unwin Hyman.

Fremdling, R. 1983. Germany. In *Railways and the Economic Development of Europe, 1830–1914*, ed. P. O'Brien. London: Macmillan.

Gall, L. 1986. *Bismarck: The White Revolutionary*, 2 vols. London: Allen & Unwin.

Geiss, J. 1976. *German Foreign Policy, 1871–1914*. London: Routledge & Kegan Paul.

Gerschenkron, A. 1962. *Economic Backwardness in Historical Perspective*. Cambridge, Mass.: Harvard University Press.

Hamerow, T. S. 1958. *Restoration, Revolution, Reaction: Economics and Politics in Germany, 1815–71*. London: Oxford University Press.

Henderson, W. 1959. *The Zollverein*. Chicago: Quadrangle Books.

1975. *The Rise of German Industrial Power, 1834–1914*. London: Temple & Smith.

Hobson, J. 1991. The Tax-Seeking State: Protectionism, Taxation and State Structures in Germany, Russia, Britain and America, 1870–1914. Ph.D. diss., London School of Economics and Political Science.

Hohorst, G. von, et al. 1975. *Sozialgeschichtliches Arbeitsbuch: Materialien zur Statistik des Kaiserreichs, 1870–1914*. Munich: Beck.

Hope, N. M. 1973. *The Alternative to German Unification: The Anti-Prussian Party, Frankfurt, Nassau and the Two Hessen, 1859–1867*. Wiesbaden: Steiner.

Howard, M. 1965. *The Theory and Practice of War*. London: Cassell.

Jessop, B. 1978. *The Capitalist State*. Oxford: Martin Robertson.
Kindleberger, C. 1978. *Economic Response: Comparative Studies in Trade, Finance and Growth*. Cambridge, Mass.: Harvard University Press.
Kitchen, M. 1978. *The Political Economy of Germany, 1815–1914*. London: Croom Helm.
Kocka, J. 1981. Capitalism and bureaucracy in German industrialization before 1914. *Economic History Review*, 2nd ser., 34.
   1986. La bourgeoisie dans l'histoire moderne et contemporaire de l'Allemagne. *Mouvement Social* 136.
Krasner, S. 1984. Approaches to the state: alternative conceptions and historical dynamics. *Comparative Politics* 16.
Lipset, S. M. 1980. *Political Man: The Social Bases of Politics*. Baltimore: Johns Hopkins University Press.
List, F. 1885. *The National System of Political Economy*. London: Longman Group.
McNeill, W. H. 1983. *The Pursuit of Power*. Oxford: Blackwell.
Mann, M. 1988. The decline of Great Britain. In my *States, War and Capitalism*. Oxford: Blackwell.
Marx, K., and F. Engels. 1968. *Selected Writings*. London: Lawrence & Wishart.
Milward, A., and S. B. Saul. 1977. *The Development of the Economies of Continental Europe, 1850–1914*. London: Allen & Unwin.
Mommsen, W. J. 1976. Domestic factors in German foreign policy before 1914. In *Imperial Germany*, ed. J. J. Sheehan. New York: Franklin Watts.
   1984. *Max Weber and German Politics*. Chicago: University of Chicago Press.
Moore, B., Jr. 1973. *Social Origins of Dictatorship and Democracy*. Harmondsworth: Penguin Books.
Perkins, J. 1984. The agricultural revolution in Germany, 1850–1914. *Journal of European Economic History* 10.
Pflanze, O. 1976. Bismarck's *Realpolitik*. In *Imperial Germany*, ed. J. J. Sheehan. New York: Franklin Watts.
Poulantzas, N. 1973. *Political Power and Social Classes*. London: New Left Books.
Pounds, N. 1959. Economic growth in Germany. In *The State and Economic Growth*, ed. H. G. Aitken. New York: Social Science Research Council.
Price, R. 1989. *The Revolutions of 1848*. Atlantic Highlands, N.J.: Humanities Press International.
Ross, R. J. 1984. Enforcing the Kulturkampf in the Bismarckian state and the limits of coercion in imperial Germany. *Journal of Modern History* 56.
Rothenberg, G. 1976. *The Army of Francis Joseph*. West Lafayette, Ind.: Purdue University Press.
Rueschemeyer, D., E. Stephens, and J. Stephens. 1992. *Capitalist Development and Democracy*. Chicago: University of Chicago Press.
Schumpeter, J. 1939. *Business Cycles*, Vol. I. New York: McGraw-Hill.
Senghaas, D. 1985. *The European Experience: A Historical Critique of Development Theory*. Leamington Spa: Berg.

Sheehan, J. L. 1978. *German Liberalism in the Nineteenth Century*. Chicago: University of Chicago Press.

1981. What is German history?: Reflections on the role of the nation in German history and historiography. *Journal of Modern History* 53.

Snyder, L. 1978. *Roots of German Nationalism*. Bloomington: Indiana University Press.

Stearns, P. 1974. *The Revolutions of 1848*. London: Weidenfeld & Nicolson.

Taylor, A. J. P. 1961a. *The Course of German History*. London: Methuen.

1961b. *Bismarck: The Man and the Statesman*. London: Arrow Books.

Tilly, R. 1978. Capital formation in Germany in the nineteenth century. In *Cambridge Economic History of Europe*. Vol. 7: *The Industrial Economies: Capital, Labour and Enterprise*, Pt. I, ed. P. Mathiason and M. Postan. Cambridge: Cambridge University Press.

Tipton, F. B. 1974. National consensus in German economic history. *Central European History* 7.

Trebilcock, C. 1981. *The Industrialization of the Great Powers, 1780–1914*. London: Longman Group.

Weber, M. 1978. *Economy and Society*, 2 vols. Berkeley: University of California Press.

Wehler, H.-U. 1976. Bismarck's imperialism, 1862–1890. In *Imperial Germany*, ed. J. J. Sheehan. New York: Franklin Watts.

1985. *The German Empire, 1871–1918*. Leamington Spa: Berg.

10 Struggle over Germany: II. Austria and confederal representation

What do we call it?

The political unit we are now discussing[1] had a long and powerful history but no secure name. The most accurate designation over the longest period would be dynastic, not territorial: It was ruled from the thirteenth to the twentieth century by the Habsburg family. Throughout, the Habsburgs ruled hereditary territories in present-day Austria, their capital being Vienna. Hence "Austria" is an acceptable shorthand designation for this state. But it became a Great Power by virtue of massive feudal and dynastic expansion. From 1438 on, Habsburgs were elected continuously as Holy Roman (i.e., German) emperors, giving them a German leadership role. Marriage alliances coupled with fortunate deaths led to two extraordinary enlargements. In the west, Burgundy, Flanders, and Spain fell into Habsburg hands; in the east, the crowns of Bohemia, Hungary, and Croatia did the same. Most of the west could not be held, but the eastern gains of 1526–7 were retained until the end.

In 1760, the Habsburgs held these possessions (save for Silesia, lost to Prussia) plus Belgian Flanders and part of northern Italy. They also gained from Polish dismemberment and Ottoman decline. Most of the empire was now non-German, and in 1806, Francis I proclaimed himself emperor of Austria, abandoning his German imperial title (of which Bonaparte had just deprived him). But Hungary and Bohemia were kingdoms with their own institutions, including assemblies, called diets. In 1867, Austria was forced to grant Hungary further autonomy and again to restyle itself. Its shortened title was now the dual monarchy of Austria-Hungary (the actual title would take up several lines). The Hungarian *Reichshalf* included Croatia, Slavonia, and Romania; the Austrian *Reichshalf* included everything else, running in a great arc from Bukovinia in the Ukraine, through Galicia (southern Poland), Bohemia (Czechoslovakia), and Austria to the Adriatic Coast (although most of Italy had been lost, as had Belgium). The only formula accept-

---

[1] General sources for this chapter were Kann (1964, 1974), Sugar and Lederer (1969), Macartney (1971), Bridge (1972), Gordon and Gordon (1974), Katzenstein (1976), and especially Sked (1989).

330

able in this half was constitutional rather than territorial: "The Kingdoms and Lands Represented in the Reichsrat" (Hungary had its own diet). In 1917, Charles I finally did proclaim this half as Austria. The next year he abdicated, and his state vanished.

Nomenclature reveals the character of this state, just as the great duke of Burgundy's earlier difficulties of nomenclature had revealed the character of his state. (See Volume I: 438–9.) This was not a national state like Britain or France or like what Germany became. It did not have a single constitution. Habsburgs were separately crowned and swore different coronation oaths in their main provinces. Joseph II refused to do this in Hungary, but his failure (see Chapter 13) forced compliance on his successors. Thus, by 1760, this state had crystallized in four main forms.

1. On the "national" issue, it crystallized at one extreme as *confederal* (as defined in Table 3.3). Habsburgs swore to defend each province and to respect its traditional customs, laws, privileges, and religion. In the terms of Table 3.1, their infrastructural powers to implement their pronouncements were also weak and particularistic, depending on deals made with parties of dominant classes and churches in each province.

2. On the "representative" issue, it crystallized as *dynastic monarchical*. Habsburg monarchs were absolute rulers, entitled to rule as they liked but within the laws laid down in the preceding paragraph. Their despotic power was near absolute, as a ruling house, a *Hausmacht*. Monarch, court, ministries, and high command comprised a fairly autonomous and insulated state elite, exercising despotic powers. But this dynasty sat above, less embedded in civil society than, for example, the Prussian Hohenzollerns; so its mobilizing infrastructural powers were less. Provinces accepted Habsburg dynastic rule because the alternatives were rule by a less benign Great Power (Russia, the Ottoman Turks, Prussia) or by smaller states representing a single "national" group of notables (Czechs, Magyars, Serbs). This is the enduring Eastern European problem, wedged between Great Powers and containing antipathetical "nations" of very different powers. There was benefit in the Habsburg protection racket; in modern times, it has so far proved the most benevolent solution to regional insecurities.

3. Nonetheless, this also implied crystallization as *militarist*, for geopolitical defense and for protecting small from large "nations." The army became the key Habsburg infrastructure, described by nineteenth-century observers as their "dynastic bodyguard" and "school of loyalty."

4. In economic terms, this state ruled over relatively backward lands in the transition from *feudal* to *capitalist* crystallizations, as agrarian lords and city merchants began to treat economic resources as commodities. Because Habsburg dynasticism was far more separate from

feudal privileges than French absolutism, there was not much political conflict between feudalism and capitalism.

On ideology, the Habsburgs crystallized weakly and uncertainly, reinforced in some provinces by a Catholicism they were also attacking with secularization policies, with wary relations with other churches, unable to mobilize nationalism, their generally "reactionary" preferences largely determined by dynasticism.

Throughout the nineteenth century, the Habsburgs maintained their militarism and moved with no difficulty toward capitalism. Their problems lay amid the national and representative issues. Under pressure they moved grudgingly toward a more representative confederalism, recognizing provincial "national" rights and liberties under a centralized monarchy. But the regime collapsed in 1918, before this was complete, into a series of small nation-states, now reemerged from the Soviet Empire.

This raises general issues. Were confederal states doomed when confronted by the power of the nation? Or did the Habsburgs perish because their dynastic monarchical version of confederalism was incompatible with representative pressures from classes and nations? Or did they perish contingently, even accidentally? Did the Habsburgs offer a viable confederal form of regime for advanced industrial societies?

On these issues objectivity has been difficult to come by. There is nostalgia for the grace and glitter of old Vienna, plus the understandable belief by East Europeans that they would have been better off under the Habsburgs than under Fascists or Communists. On the other hand lie teleological biases: Because the Habsburgs were reactionaries who failed, they seem to have been doomed – from some historic turning point of failure between 1790, when Joseph II revoked most of his enlightened reforms, and 1914, when Franz Joseph plunged into the Great War, which destroyed his dynasty. (See Sked 1981.) Because this was the Vienna of Freud, of the Secessionist painters, of Musil and Kafka (the latter actually from a provincial capital, Prague), as well as of the waltz and the white uniform, popular historical writers have delighted in metaphors of outward grace and inner turmoil, irrationality and decadence.

My argument lies between these positions. The Habsburgs were not doomed by the logic of development of modern industrial society. Indeed, they crystallized successfully as capitalist. Their Great Power militarism declined relatively to their rivals, but this was fiscally, not economically, caused and need not have ended in the catastrophe of 1918. The disintegrating power of regional nationalism has also been exaggerated; it was more the creation than the creator of Habsburg difficulties. In rather an old-fashioned argument I maintain the Habsburgs failed because of their militaristic dynasticism. They did not move to a citizenship appropriate to a modern society. This might have been liberal or semiauthoritarian, confederal or federal, achieved by agreement or force. In this period Prussia and the United States solved comparable class and national problems by such mixtures. But the Habsburgs developed only particularistic, inconsistent solutions to class and nation. This eventually destroyed them, first in war, then in the unexpected dénouement of war. Because these military dynasts chose war, this was not doom but hubris, self-induced.

Habsburg capitalism

Nineteenth-century economic failure brought a heavy political and military price. As Europe was a single ideological community, failure relative to other Powers was visible and punishable on the battlefield, for which modern industrial and agrarian resources became essential. Was economic failure a source of Habsburg decline and fall? The great economic historian Alexander Gerschenkron thought so. The title of his book, *An Economic Spurt That Failed* (1977), conveys his view that Austria, a halfhearted exponent of late development, failed to "take off." This used to be a common view among economic historians, but recent research proves it wrong.

First, it adheres to the theory of Rostow, Gerschenkron, and Kondratieff that industrializing economies suddenly "take off" (Rostow) or "spurt" (Gerschenkron) into the upswing phase of a "long wave cycle" (Kondratieff). Whatever the merits of this theory as applied to the economies of Britain, Germany, and the United States – and the doubters are increasing (see Tipton 1974 on Germany) – it cannot apply to France (as has long been recognized) and it does not apply to Austria. Austria experienced a steady rate of growth throughout the century, broken by recessions in the early 1860s and 1873–9 (Rudolph 1972, 1975, 1976; Good 1974, 1977, 1978, 1984; Gross 1976; Ashworth 1977; Huertas 1977; Bairoch 1982; Komlos 1983, especially his acerbic appendix C). Second, the charge of failure is leveled against Austria compared to its rival, Prussian Germany. Indeed Austrian growth lagged behind German from about 1850. But then so did almost all countries. German growth rates were virtually unique. In other comparisons Austria did quite well. As Table 8.1 indicates, it maintained its fifth rank in Europe in gross national product. Good (1984: 240) argues that from 1870 to 1914 its annual growth rate of 1.3 percent was matched only by Germany, Sweden, and Denmark. The Habsburg economy was a capitalist success.

But two more particular charges of economic failure might be made.

The first is fiscal. Fiscally induced recession in the early 1860s had geopolitical consequences, contributing to defeat by Prussia in 1866-7. Recession centered on stagnation in real per capita value added in industrial production, caused mainly by military commitments. Prussia remained at peace from 1815 to 1864, but Austria was embroiled in Italy, with minor revolts elsewhere – straining manpower and taxation – and government bonds drained investment from economic development. Fiscal crisis was worsened by restoring the currency to pre-1848 silver parity, so as to rival Prussian economic hegemony over Germany. Austrian debt issues crowded out private investment as German private investment followed a smooth upward path (Huertas 1977: 36-48).

But the charge of fiscal failure is incomplete. Austrian military spending was no higher than Prussian – or that of other Powers (see Chapter 11) – and did not necessarily endanger the economy. Rather, the fiscal system was inefficient at turning revenue into soldiers. The ancient military contribution, negotiated with provincial diets, was too cumbersome to deal with the escalating war costs of the period up to 1815 (see Chapter 11). The Habsburgs were forced to borrow more than any other Power; and they declared bankruptcy in 1811. After 1815, military pressure eased less for Austria than for other Powers. Bankruptcy was rumored in the 1840s and 1850s and was narrowly averted in 1859.

Austrian finances were like those of old regime France; not in the sheer level of extraction, but endless negotiations with particularistic power groups resulted in visibly "unfair" tax burdens, fiscal-political crises, and excessive borrowing. Intent on preserving privilege, diets and assemblies were slow to assent to new taxes, and the monarchy did not have local infrastructures to levy them without consent. The diets agreed to raise particular numbers of soldiers, but these numbers became inadequate whenever geopolitical and national pressures mounted. Thus the state borrowed again, draining investment resources (as Huertas argued). Fiscal strain was, at bottom, not an economic but a representative problem. I pursue this farther later on.

The other charge of economic failure relates to the substantial inequality among the provinces. By 1914, Czechoslovakia alone contributed 56 percent of Austro-Hungarian industrial output, its industrial horsepower exceeding France's. Savings deposits in inner Austria were ten times those in Galicia, income per head was three times as great, and literacy was twice as high (Good 1984: 150, 156). Kennedy (1988: 216), pursuing his economistic theory of Great Power rivalry (see Chapter 8), argues that regional inequalities were the "most fundamental flaw" in Austrian power. They might have three possible negative consequences: The Austrian and Czech cores might exploit and hold back the development of the periphery; the backwardness of the periphery might hold back the cores; or the disparities might reduce overall economic integration. Only the third has much substance.

Nationalists made the first two charges (according to where they lived) but were probably wrong. From 1850 on, Austrian development followed the German pattern, lagging by twenty to thirty years (Pollard 1981: 222–9). Czech lands and inner Austria were first intermediaries, importing semimanufactures and machinery from advanced Europe and sending finished manufactures to the southeast. Then they became industrially autonomous, supplying railways, machines, and high technology to the southeast. German-style bank cartels and state credit schemes channeled investment in the southeast, especially in railways. Industrialization benefited from late development strategies (nationalized railways, tariffs, and credit banks) – the "reactionary" Habsburgs appreciated how essential industrial capitalism was to their own health. Take Hungary as an example: At first, it exchanged agricultural produce for Austrian manufactured goods, becoming agriculturally efficient and thus penetrating international markets. Then, from 1900 on, light industries sprang up, using electricity, not needing proximity to raw energy sources, and using the agricultural profits and Habsburg financial expertise and communication infrastructures for exports (Komlos 1983). Good's (1981, 1984: 245–50) regional time-series data for 1867–1913 show that mutual benefit between regions was more general. Regional disparities declined (as they did in all countries in this period). By 1900, they were about the same as the American and less severe than the Italian or Swedish. Was the United States a capitalist failure during this period?

But such capitalist success brought an unexpected problem: It did not necessarily integrate the economy of the Habsburg lands. Rather, the economy became more *transnational*, integrating directly into the trans-European economy. Czech and Hungarian industries were becoming as linked abroad as to other Habsburg regions. And economic expansion exacerbated the monarchy's linguistic conflicts because more non-German speakers came into the public realm of civil society (more on this later). Austria was developing two capitalist economies, one transnational, the other "Habsburg" (the word "national" is not appropriate here) – the former leading away from loyalty to the dynasty and toward the atomized laissez-faire theory of the Austrian school of economists (Menger, von Mieses, Hayek), attacking the substantivism and nationalism of List's German successors (Roscher, Knies, Schmoller) (Bostaph 1978). While their sociologists mirrored regime similarities – the Prussian Gumplowicz and the Austrian Ratzenhofer stressed the military foundations of power – the economists mirrored differences in their economies. The Habsburgs assisted capitalist economic success in their lands but, unlike the Hohenzollerns, less in their economic integration. Yet this was perhaps of little political relevance. Regionalism would need considerable assistance from elsewhere if it were to threaten Habsburg centralism.

Nationalism and representation, 1815–1867

Habsburg political crises eventually became "national." Actors like the Hungarians, the Slovaks, the Slovenes (only sometimes qualified by class, economic sector, religion, etc.) stride across the pages of most historical works, combating one another and the Habsburg state and eventually destroying that state. These "nationalities" almost invariably became linguistic communities; some were also religious communities. But they were also rooted in regional political institutions. Nationalities barely existed at the beginning of my period, even as "imagined communities." Yet by the end they were real communities with considerable collective powers. Why? Because the development of all four sources of social power conferred social significance on both linguistic communities (sometimes on religious communities) and regional political institutions, welding them together into "nations."

The monarchy spoke many languages during the whole of the period under discussion. Of a population of 24 million in 1780, 24 percent spoke German; 14 percent, Magyar; 11 percent, Czech; 8 percent, Flemish or Walloon French; 7 percent, Italian; 7 percent, Ukrainian Ruthene; 7 percent, Romanian; 7 percent, Serb or Croat; 5 percent, Slovak; 4 percent, Polish; and there were sundry small language groups totaling 6 percent. As Flemish, French, and then most Italians were lost, more Slavs were acquired. Of 51 million in 1910, 23 percent spoke German; 20 percent, Magyar; 13 percent, Czech; 10 percent, Polish; 9 percent, Serb or Croat; 8 percent, Ruthene; 6 percent, Romanian; 4 percent, Slovak; and there were smaller groups totaling 7 percent. No other state contended with such linguistic diversity. In fact these figures even understate it. These "languages" were not at first unitary. Most of the population was illiterate and spoke varied dialects, some mutually unintelligible. Some written languages were only now being standardized and made grammatical. Nonetheless, as Chapter 7 shows, by 1815, the dominant classes of several provinces shared their own written and spoken language; and a few intelligentsia were claiming that their "ethnic-linguistic" community should have collective political rights.

Yet these dissidents were still insignificant. Before 1848, "nationalists" were few. Most were tiny groups of intelligentsia and professionals bemoaning the "national indifference" of the population around them. Where significant "national" dissidence occurred in this period it was either reinforced by the class cohesion of the old regime of a province – as among the Magyar nobility – or it indicated recent Habsburg rule, feebly institutionalized into civil society (as in Italy). In Bohemia, for example, there was little sense of overall Czech or German ethnic identities. German was the language of public space and economic opportunity – of administration, law, education, and commerce – Czech of the life of most families. Habsburg census categories did not confer total ethnic identity in this period. Many people with Czech surnames classified themselves as German speakers because German was the language of opportunity (Cohen 1981: chapter 1). After 1867, many in the Hungarian *Reichshalf* classified themselves as Magyar speakers for similar pragmatic reasons, accounting for the large jump in Magyar speakers revealed in the census figures cited earlier.

We cannot take these "national" actors for granted; we must explain their emergence. Various modernization processes contributed to their emergence across Europe – the expansion of capitalism, state modernization, the struggle for representation, the expansion of communications infrastructures, and mass mobilization warfare. In Austria, the decisive contribution was from a struggle for citizenship that had a *territorial* as well as a class base.

Most late eighteenth- and early nineteenth-century politics involved taxation and office holding – the costs and benefits of government. In Austria these politics became territorial and confederal. The provinces possessed or had possessed diets or assemblies of some historical pedigree. The Hungarian diet vigorously preserved its rights; the others mostly possessed only half a life, reasserting themselves in fiscal crises. These "parliamentary" institutions – though of limited, usually hereditary, franchises confined to the nobility – made Austria peculiarly comparable with the Anglo-American world rather than with other absolute monarchies like Prussia or eighteenth-century France. The Habsburgs encountered slogans of "no taxation without representation" among reactionary nobles dominating backward provinces and among noble–substantial bourgeois alliances in advanced ones. As elsewhere, representation meant only limited suffrages for parliaments and office holding. (See Chapter 13.) Until 1848, "liberals" demanded only a diet veto over taxation and a share in office spoils. But in a confederal state this was peculiarly threatening because regional discontent, unlike class discontent, might be expressed by provincial notables wielding paramilitary forces – even sometimes regular army regiments. The Habsburgs were confronted with virtual civil wars. They had to extract more taxes and manpower from nonrebellious provinces to suppress them. But these provinces were suspicious (they might be soon in a similar position) and slow to acquiesce, forcing the regime to borrow, make do with a barely adequate army, or cede particularistic rights to provinces.

The regime considered alternative strategies long and hard. Any ultimate failure was not through lack of consciousness or want of trying – unlike the ultimate failure of the German regime. One solution was to reduce geopolitical militarism, economizing until a constitutional settlement could be reached. This was the counsel of finance ministers, especially of Kolowrat, finance minister and virtual prime minister in domestic matters for most of 1815–48. This was sensible, but it tacitly acknowledged that the Habsburgs should not yet behave as one of the Great Powers. It might also have domestic consequences. Some rebellious ethnic-linguistic communities extended across Habsburg borders and received assistance from neighboring Powers. Late eighteenth-century French and Flemish rebels in Flanders were aided by the French revolutionaries while Hungarians entered into understandings with Prussia. Mid-nineteenth-century Italian rebels were supported by Piedmont and France; early twentieth-century South Slavs, by Russia. The national and military crystallizations were both geopolitical and domestic. A low geopolitical profile might encourage internal dissidents as well as rival Powers – so argued Metternich, who dominated foreign policy after 1815. While monarchs saw the need for economy and military restraint, they wished to maintain a strong diplomatic posture. Their failure to find a way around this contradiction, embedded in different departments of state, proved damaging.

Three possible constitutional strategies combined the representative and the national issue.

1. *Dynastic centralization*. Reinforce dynastic absolutism with infra-structural powers conferred by modernization. The state elite would impose centralization through the army and civil administration. But both were mostly officered by Austro-Germans. This would establish German as the official language of state. "Embedding" rule among Austro-Germans undermined confederalism and the neutrality of the dynasty, fueling fiscal and office-holding discontent among linguistic communities being created by economic growth. Civil society and the state became opposed.

2. *Confederal party democracy*. Become substantially democratic through a comprehensive agreement with provincial diets. Franchises and fiscal and office-holding rights would be spelled out universally, conceding considerable provincial autonomy.

3. *Federal semiauthoritarianism*. Compromise between solutions 1

and 2, accepting a semidemocratic constitution like the German one, though with greater real federalism – American federalism with a more authoritarian center.

The regime was not united, but until 1848 Metternich and monarchs led it toward the first solution, extending dynastic centralization without much pretense of an agreed-upon constitution. Metternich bluntly expressed his distrust of federalism: "Only by centralizing the various branches of authority is it possible to establish its unity and hence its force. Power distributed is no longer power" (Sked 1981: 188). The settlement of 1815 gave the dynasty time, easing geopolitical pressure and internal discontent. With some economizing, the strategy worked outside of Hungary, where concessions were made to the diet. But the strategy infringed on accepted understandings as to the essentially confederal crystallization of the state. The year 1848 brought massive resistance.

The Revolution of 1848 was a Europe-wide movement for civil and political citizenship led by whichever social classes lay just below the existing political citizenship line. But it also fused with the economic discontents of workers and peasants suffering from bad harvests, rising prices, and a downswing in manufacturing activity and employment. In France and in British Chartism, such fusions reinforced its character as class struggle. But in more confederal regimes this came packaged with "national" issues, as we saw in Germany. As revolution spread to more confederal Austria, it acquired more territorial, provincial, and "national" organization – which led to easily the most serious fighting of 1848. More than 100,000 persons were killed in the Austrian revolutions.[2]

The Italian provinces (aided by outside Italian states) and Hungary demanded their own parliaments and formed rebel armies out of imperial regiments and regional militias. But Vienna and Prague also saw the usual class conflicts of 1848, with petit bourgeois, artisan, and worker radicals demanding party democracy and social reforms, while the main bourgeoisie wavered before plumping for the "party of order." Because Prague radicalism entwined class with language discontent, it split between Germans and Czechs. Viennese radicalism, thoroughly German, split (as did its counterparts in Germany) between two alternative Germanic democracies. One was *Grossdeutsch* and looked to the Frankfurt parliament to develop citizenship among all Germans. The other remained Austrian and Habsburg, seeking a constitutional monarchy in Vienna. Because Germans were the "ruling" nationality,

---

[2] My main sources for the revolutions in the Austrian lands were Rath (1957), Pech (1969), Deak (1979), and Sked (1979, 1989: 41–88).

neither favored provincial autonomies. They made little appeal to revolutionaries in other provinces.

Thus the revolution split on class and on provincial "nationalism." Most provincial movements were led by notables, discontented with the centralization that excluded them from office holding and law courts. But to widen support without making economic concessions to the populace, notables used nationalist slogans, especially wielding the language issue – vital for all non-German literates seeking to obtain public office or to practice law. They demanded that public schools teach local languages as well as whatever "imperial languages" were agreed on. The cultural nationalism of a small intelligentsia thus became a universalizing ideology, stressing community among classes within provinces.

A multiclass, multinational compromise might have emerged from insurgent debates, creating federal parliaments with limited suffrage. But civil wars do not wait upon debates. The regime was confronted by four enemies – Italians, Hungarians, and Viennese and Prague radicals – struggling to develop compatible programs and military collaboration. But most of the military remained loyal to the dynasty. The officer corps carried most grumbling regiments with them; even half the Italian regiments stationed in Italy followed orders. Ably led by Radetsky, imperial troops defeated the rebel Italians (whose urban notables had foolishly alienated peasants). The Hungarian rebel forces remained more troublesome, controlling most of Hungary and threatening Vienna, which was just over the border. But they were led by noble reactionaries, with little appeal to Viennese or Prague radicals.

Meanwhile, events in Vienna unfolded as in Paris, Berlin, or Frankfurt. Bourgeois notables, petite bourgeoisie, and workers fought the regime and each other in the streets and in hastily formed militias and central committees. Rattled but seeking to divide them, the regime conceded a parliament (excluding Hungarians and Italians). There propertied peasants (bought off by the abolition of feudal dues) and loyal Slavs would outvote German radicals. Real sovereignty was now split between this Reichstag and the committees and militias. The monarchy then discovered that half the Vienna garrison were bandsmen. After chaotic street actions, the troops retreated out of the city. The regime temporized until the Hungarian army advancing on Vienna was turned back by imperial and Croatian forces (Croatian grievances were against the Magyars, their regional oppressors). Unnecessarily, the regime then called in a Russian army to help finish off Hungary. Vienna was stormed; the radicals, violently repressed. The revolution was over, destroyed by the class and national insurgents' failure to coalesce and by the loyalty of the army.

As in Prussia, the victorious dynasty promised reform. This was symbolized by the abdication of the Emperor Ferdinand in favor of his eighteen-year-old nephew Franz Joseph. Debate over rival constitutions continued. The liberal "Kremsier constitution" proposed a confederal semidemocracy. It left the monarch responsible for foreign affairs and war but limited him in domestic policy. Ministers were to be responsible to parliament. The monarch could delay but not veto its legislation. It guaranteed equality of languages in schools, administration, and public life but firmly within a single empire: "All peoples of the Empire are equal in rights. Each people has an inviolable right to preserve and cultivate its nationality in general and its language in particular." The Kremsier constitution would apply to all provinces except Hungary and Italy, which would develop their own constitutions.

The more conservative counterproposal, the "Stadion constitution," conceded parliaments but with a monarchical veto. It arranged government in a federal hierarchy: Below a bicameral parliament and ministries were provincial, then local, assemblies and administrations. It included Hungary and envisioned the Italian provinces entering later. It offered a more genuinely federal version of German semiauthoritarian incorporation. Several ministers favored it. With the balance of forces shifted to the conservatives but with vague expectations of reform, the Stadion constitution was implementable.

Yet the young Franz Joseph opposed concessions. He favored dynastic centralization. A vigorous dynast could always acquire a ministerial faction, and the triumph of his armies gave him crushing power. Generals were appointed as provincial governors and Austro-Germans led central and provincial administrations. These were made responsible only to a "crown council" of ministers and advisers appointed by the emperor – an advisory not an executive body, with uncertain membership and constitutional status.

But defeat in war in 1859 and 1866 led to fiscal crises and further reform pressures from provincial notables and German liberals. The monarchy conceded a *Rechtstaat* (like Germany) enshrining individual civil rights, but collective civil citizenship remained restricted. All associations had to register with the police and seek permission for meetings and demonstrations. As in Germany (until 1908), policemen normally attended protest meetings, able to declare them closed as soon as they decided "subversion" was occurring. In 1860, Franz Joseph decreed a parliament and municipal assemblies and councils and revived provincial diets, all with limited suffrage and sovereignty. The next year another decree reduced diet powers. Constitutions were all very well, but if they did not work to Franz Joseph's satisfaction, he would change them. The empire lacked an unequivocal political constitution.

Franz Joseph remained an active segmental divide-and-rule dynast throughout his long reign (1848–1916). He granted more than a hundred audiences a week, terminating them the moment he desired. He requested and diligently read hundreds of memos in his regular ten-hour working day. He used (and allowed courtiers and ministers to use) particularistic privileges, the *Protektion*, to interfere with bureaucratic routines. He enjoined secrecy on his administration (forbidding the writing of memoirs). He repeatedly intervened in the supposedly autonomous Viennese city administration. He peremptorily dismissed argumentative ministers (Johnston 1972: 30–44, 63; Deak 1990: 60). Franz Joseph did not institutionalize factionalized intrigue as thoroughly as the Hohenzollerns did; rather, he exemplified it in his person. His dislike of constitution and institution made him a genuine dynast. I cannot enumerate Habsburg state institutions as formally as I did the Hohenzollern. This was a highly polymorphous state, but its crystallizations were less institutionalized than in Germany. The state remained largely dynastic, militarist, and capitalist, while its multinational crystallization remained in flux – but all swirled and conflicted around the person of Franz Joseph, as well as in ministries, parliament, and diets.

To hindsight, this degree of dynastic discretion appears as a mistake – and fifty years later an elderly Franz Joseph tried to reverse it. The mistake and the blame are his. But dynastic centralization also depended on its two infrastructures: army and administration. They had powers and limitations that I explore in more general terms in Chapters 11 and 12. They kept this diverse empire surprisingly well ordered and administered, but they could not take two key initiatives: They could not reform state finances to achieve the higher taxes and military modernization required by Great Power rivalry and the industrialization of war. Nor could they much increase citizen loyalties except by making particularistic concessions, which they did to Magyars, to Poles in Galicia, and to Jews (whose lack of political nationality ensured their loyalty). These groups divided the labor of repressing other "nations."

If dynastic centralization were to work, Franz Joseph had to buy time with a low geopolitical profile. Military economizing would reduce the grievances of provincial nobilities and diets while he institutionalized authoritarianism. Yet he did not economize (Katzenstein 1976: 87–8). During the Crimean War, Austria mobilized in a posture of armed neutrality, just in case Balkan pickings appeared. There were none, yet Russia was alienated. The regime sold off much of the state railways to pay for the mobilization. This reduced revenues over the following period. "Selling off the family silver" is not much of an economic strategy, as Harold Macmillan caustically remarked of a more recent (Thatcherite) example of this policy. As tensions rose with

Piedmont, Austria became bellicose. War started in 1859. It went well against Piedmont, but when France predictably joined in, the comprehensive French victory at Solferino sealed the loss of most Italian provinces. The war virtually bankrupted the state. Minor reforms were extracted in return for consent to increased taxes. Franz Joseph now *had* to economize. But this was Bismarck's moment, and Austria did not conciliate him. Prussia and Piedmont invaded in 1866. Defeat produced fiscal collapse and major concessions to the Hungarian nobility. Dynastic centralization was over, defeated by provincial representation aided by Great Power rivals and by excessive military ambition.

In the "compromise" of 1867, the Hungarian nobility agreed to supply 30 percent of the joint budget (principally for the joint army controlled by Franz Joseph) in return for control over the diet and civil administration in its *Reichshalf*, the right to be consulted in foreign policy, and the right to form its own reserve army, the Honved. Hungarians were now free to oppress their own minorities. The compromise involved three institutions, the administrations of the two *Reichshälfe* and the monarch. If the administrations could not agree on matters of joint responsibility, Franz Joseph decided them. His overarching control over foreign policy and the army was unaffected. I therefore distinguish domestic from foreign policy.

Domestic politics in the dual monarchy, 1867–1914

Franz Joseph's domestic position was fundamentally altered: Now placed dynastically above two *Reichshälfe*, he lacked the required centralizing infrastructures to play a significant role within Hungary, and he had to renegotiate the Hungarian contribution to the joint budget every ten years. But he could still segmentally divide and rule, playing one province and one nationality against another and offering selective rewards and punishments. As one participant put it:

In this vast conglomerate called the Austro-Hungarian Monarchy . . . countries, provinces, nations, denominations, social classes, groups of interests all being factors in political and social life, put up to auction their loyalty for the grace of the court. [Mocsary, in Jaszi 1961: 135]

But dividing and ruling now had to include classes and nations. As in other nineteenth-century semiauthoritarian regimes, more concessions were made to local-regional than to central parliaments – they had more sovereignty (over local matters) and wider franchises. But in Austria this had unexpected consequences. Participation in local administration widened beyond Germans and client notables. Especially in Czech lands, commerce and industry was also extending economic power. Provincial languages were emerging from family and informal communal spheres into all public spheres, as were the middling classes. National identity could emerge as totalizing and the language issue could mobilize it. Those classified as Czech speakers increased, and German speakers decreased. German notables in Czech lands, especially liberal parties, lost power (Cohen 1981).

This changed the monarchy's own segmental power tactics. If it continued to rely on the Austro-Germans, it alienated minorities, now wielding local-regional economic and political powers – especially the Czechs, furious at not getting representation comparable to that of the Hungarians. Thus Franz Joseph's solidarity with Austro-German notables weakened, as theirs did with him. After 1867, Slavs became embittered at Magyar domination in their *Reichshalf*. By 1880, Hungarians and Austro-Germans were repressing others' political aspirations far more than Franz Joseph wished.

In 1879–80, he abandoned Austro-German "liberal" parties (there was not much of their liberalism left by now) and asked Count Taaffe to form a "conservative-nationalist" ministry, whereby the dynasty would receive support from Czechs and Poles. In 1882, the ministry greatly extended local suffrage, aware that (according to province) nobles or nationalists, not bourgeois notable–liberals, could now exercise segmental controls over peasant and petit bourgeois masses. They also soon staffed and controlled provincial and local administrations. As elsewhere (see Chapter 16), the core carriers of nationalisms were now public employees. All provincial dissidents now legitimated themselves in terms of the nation, even where, as in Hungary, they were only nobles, and even where, as in Slovakia, the "nation" and its language was being created by a tiny intelligentsia. Nations had been created as *real* communities by the unfolding of confederal representative struggles reinforced by language (and sometimes religious) communities. Nationalism was now peculiarly contradictory, often in alliance with the monarchy, yet also fragmenting it.

With dynastic centralization in ruins, Franz Joseph began to favor federal semiauthoritarianism. The Austrian suffrage was extended in 1897, though with a class-weighted franchise modeled on the Prussian scheme described in Chapter 9. In 1905, Franz Joseph finally announced: "I have decided to introduce the institution of general suffrage in both halves of the Monarchy," and he did so in 1907 in the Austrian *Reichshalf*. The Hungarian nobility, however, dragged its heels, aware that this might destroy its hegemony in its *Reichshalf*. Franz Joseph was moving to a more confederal version of the German Reich constitution. But this left him very different options. Because the main conservative opposition now came from the entrenched Hungarian nobility and German bourgeoisie, his allies on some issues were actually oppressed nations and classes. Moreover, as a genuine reactionary, increasingly out of sympathy with dominant national classes, he was not averse to paternalist social legislation moderating the capitalist crystallization of his regime – though budgetary constraints prevented full implementation and the dynasty still withheld parliamentary sovereignty and collective civil rights for labor.

Nonetheless, the entwinings of dynasty, classes, and nations had squeezed out liberalism. Originally centered in German resistance to absolutism, the liberal parties were now defending a status quo privileging their national identity. Thus class parties representing petite bourgeoisie, workers, and peasants emerged as opposed to liberalism as to the monarchy. They fused exploited class and exploited nation in diverse "social" parties – from the anti-Semitic Christian Socialism (Boyer 1981), to peasant and Slavic populism (described in Chapter 19), to Pan-Germanism, Zionism, and Marxist socialism (Schorske 1981: 116–80). The oddest outcome was the stance of the Marxist Austrian Socialist party. Marxism's proletariat is transnational. From 1899 on, the Socialists, under the ideological tutelage of Renner and Bauer, viewed the German and Magyar nationalisms as bourgeois. Other exploited nations were only temporarily analogous to the proletariat. Hence the Socialists opposed nationalism and supported confederal democracy. The Socialists were implicitly aiding Habsburg survival as a potentially constitutional monarchy.

Constitutions worked in some provinces; but the Hungarian diet refused to extend the franchise, and its extension in Austria and Bohemia resulted in chaos in the Reichstag and the Bohemian diet as Germans and Czechs failed to agree on the language issue and on public-office spoils. The stumbling block was now less a reactionary dynasty than dual entrenched exploitation by Hungarian and German dominant classes. Because each comprised only 20 percent to 25 percent of population in its *Reichshalf*, neither favored universal male suffrage, though they controlled each central administration. The compromise had only been a particularistic deal, to avoid further concessions. Its very success in that role blocked full democracy. Unless the entrenched nationalities would make concessions, especially to Czechs, Romanians, Croats, and Serbs, democracy was blocked *inside* the state. This was no longer a dynastic, militarist, capitalist, and multiprovincial state. It was no longer such a state besieged by nations. It was a dynastic, militarist, capitalist, and internally factionalized nationalist state. It remained thoroughly polymorphous but could not now resolve its factionalism.

The dynasty continued to divide and rule nations and classes segmentally but could not stably institutionalize this practice. I doubt that Franz Joseph's heart was fully in the semiauthoritarian strategy – he had been a dynast for fifty years and had proudly declared, "I am a German Prince" (though it has been calculated that he was only 3 percent German), without showing genuine sympathy for oppressed nations. Eventually he resumed the dynastic powers with which he felt at home, dissolving Reichstag and diet in 1913 and 1914. A solution did not seem in sight. Both heirs (Franz Ferdinand was assassinated in 1914; Charles succeeded in 1917) wished the Hungarians to compromise; their views on German-Czech conflict were less clear. But would they possess infrastructural powers to compel them? The Habsburgs had probably lost their chances of all three strategies. Hungarians had blocked dynastic centralization; several nationalities now blocked more democratic strategies.

But a more modest level of political viability remained open to the Habsburgs. Taaffe, prime minister from 1879 to 1893, defined political success as "keeping all the nationalities of the Monarchy in a condition of even and well-modulated discontent" (Macartney 1971: 615). The state could fudge its way through – Victor Adler defined it as "absolutism tempered by muddle" – providing two functions, domestic and geopolitical, which most nationalities and classes found useful.

Domestically, the monarchy held the balance among potentially more repressive "national" administrations. Hungarians, Germans, Czechs, Croats, and Poles could more effectively penetrate their local-regional civil societies and administrations. If their powers were unleashed, regional minorities would be more oppressed – as all could see in Hungary after 1867 (and as Central European minorities might see again at the end of the twentieth century). Some classes also appreciated this: Czech workers sought protection against German capitalists, as did Ruthenian peasants against Polish landlords. That languages and classes were spread out in so complex a geography – here a majority, there a minority – made principled solutions difficult to reach. But it prolonged "muddled" segmental rule. Its central state fostered economic development, and its civil administration grew rapidly at the beginning of the twentieth century. (See Tables 11.1–5 and Appendix Table A.1.) Except for the language issue, its growth was broadly consensual (as in other states of the period; see Chapter 14). It provided useful civil functions to subjects in a condition of "even and well-modulated discontent."

But the principal function of the Habsburg state was geopolitical militarism. Each nationality could provide only a small state. If Habsburgs did not rule them, someone else probably would. The historic Habsburg mission had been to coordinate regional Christian defense against the

Turks. Now the threat was from Germany and Russia (Taylor 1967: 132). Even South Slavs, recently acquired and of dubious commitment, were wary of reactionary Russia. The majority Croat-Serb Coalition party regarded the South Slav issue as an internal matter for the dual monarchy. Only after 1914 did it split and separatists emerge. After 1873, Poles, given local autonomy, proclaimed loyalty to Austrian mild rule – until they could recover their own Polish state. As this would involve defeating both Russia and Germany, it looked a long way off. Czechs, Slovaks, and Ruthenes also feared Russia or Germany. Most favored the Habsburg monarchy as a federation of Central European nations – requiring only a central state with supreme military and diplomatic authority and some budgetary powers. This, plus progressive economic policies, is what they had.

If they could not agree on a constitution for making that state properly representative and responsible, then it could not mobilize full citizen commitment. But perhaps that needn't matter. Nothing is more puzzling if we view Austria-Hungary from a modern nation-state perspective than the equanimity with which German, Czech, and other deputies reduced parliaments to shambles, then withdrew from them for years at a time. But their basic interests were ensured by Habsburg absolutism, which they could influence from within through local-regional administration and capitalism. For all the parliamentary strife, and for all the bickering between Austrian and Hungarian administrations, regime-threatening dissidence *declined* between 1867 and 1914 (Sked 1989: 231). The Socialists increasingly dominated the working class in the two industrial areas but were ghettoized (as in Germany). Labor violence declined from the 1880s. Unlike in 1848 or 1867, no major provincial movement claimed autonomy; no rebellion occurred in any historic land (there was more trouble in the new Balkan provinces). A ten-year "constitutional crisis" with Hungary ended in 1908 when the Hungarian budget contribution was raised from 30 percent to 36.4 percent, an eminently pragmatic settlement. Provincial nations and classes had settled in for Habsburg rule – but geopolitics dictated otherwise.

Final hubris: military geopolitics, 1867–1918

The 1867 compromise left Franz Joseph in sole charge of the army and in predominant control of foreign policy. The same militarist contradiction continued to dog him. Constitutional fiscal formulas still provided insufficient soldiers and military supplies for a Great Power strategy. (See Table 11.6; cf. Deak 1990: 64.) Hungary distrusted the joint army and dragged its fiscal heels, leaving the Austro-Hungarian military some way behind its rivals in quality of equipment, artillery, and logistic support, shielding the high command from adopting modern tactics. Yet the compromise did not lead Franz Joseph to economize. The end of geopolitical pretensions in Germany in 1867 shifted priorities to the southeast. Ottoman decline enabled Austria and Russia to move into the Balkans. The regime persuaded itself that the solution to the internal South Slav question was to acquire more South Slavs. Some argue that this shows the regime's reactionary, dynastic nature. Is not the very purpose of dynasts to acquire territory? asks Sked (1989: 265). But I doubt that any early twentieth-century government would refuse such territorial pickings – as the scramble for Africa and the U.S. Pacific expansion reveal. The extension of territory was implied by the very notion of geopolitics, as Chapter 21 argues.

But this did not bring economies or low-profile diplomacy. It might have been tolerable if it had brought cooperation with Russia to share the Balkans between their client states. Yet Austria entered into the opposite alliance structure. After 1867, Austria became allied with Germany, their disputes settled, sharing cultural and economic ties and similar political regimes. It seemed as natural an association as, say, the Anglo-American one. But it came to make no geopolitical sense, for the two Powers soon had opposite interests regarding Russia. Germany came to fear the Russian alliance with France and its rapid economic and military modernization. As German nationalism developed, this fear became almost racist: Teuton and Slav would fight to the death over Central Europe. Thus German regimes favored joint Austro-German–Magyar repression of Slavs. This was not in the interests of the Habsburgs and it antagonized Russia further. Austria was now too weak to withstand a Russian attack. Yet Austrian diplomacy became anti-Slav. Some attribute this to the increased influence of Hungarians in foreign policy. But Franz Joseph must take part of the blame, regarding Russia as his "natural enemy" and being personally anti-Slav. Austrian diplomacy not merely failed to economize; it had created a powerful enemy.

Events moved rapidly. In 1912–13, Turkish rule in the Balkans collapsed. Russia supported the emergent Slav states, especially Serbia, with designs on Austrian territory. Serbian patriots assassinated Archduke Franz Ferdinand, heir to the throne – ironically an advocate of less militarist diplomacy and of greater rights for South Slavs. The monarchy felt compelled to retaliate or lose its ability to overawe dissident nationalists. Russia's response was to be feared, but that was supposedly where the German alliance would protect Austria. As we shall see in Chapter 21, Austria's decision to strike coincided with

Germany's decision that it was better to strike now than later, when Russian military modernization would be complete. The two Central Powers egged each other on disastrously into World War I and to their ends. Franz Joseph and his ministers went deliberately into a major war. They were probably wrong: More skillful diplomacy could have shown strength while evading war. Perhaps Russia would have found another opportunity for demonstrating Austrian weakness to the Slavs. But in diplomacy tomorrow is another day.

I explore the slide toward World War I in Chapter 21, showing that decision making in all autocratic and semiauthoritarian regimes was factionalized. But at least Germany entered with a formidable fighting machine that came near victory. Austria declared war with the smallest, worst equipped, worst led army of the Great Powers. Most of it was entrained between two fronts as generals tried to catch up with diplomats' instructions as to whom they were actually fighting (Serbs or Russians?). Continued failure to reach a constitutional settlement meant a particularistic polymorphous state, well suited to muddling through, ill suited to crisis diplomacy and war – that is, to swift considered decision making and to the rational deployment of infrastructures to implement those decisions. Eighteenth-century Austrian war needs had created one of the first modern state administrations (see Chapter 13). By 1914, its enduring constitutional crisis had run it down; it could neither avert nor efficiently prosecute war.

Yet war brought not immediate collapse but patriotic enthusiasm. Sigmund Freud appropriately expressed his own surge of emotion: "All my libido is attached to the Monarchy" (Gerschenkron 1977: 64). Austrian soldiers repeatedly followed their officers in frontal attacks on Russian positions with inadequate artillery support (the artillery had been starved of modernization funds). They lost half their numbers in the first year, and most of their trained officer and noncommissioned officer cadres – an astonishing, unparalleled rate of loss. Thereafter Austrian soldiers, stiffened by Prussian officers and noncommissioned officers, fought surprisingly well to the summer of 1918, enduring heavy casualties on three fronts (Russian, Serbian, and Italian), but rent by fewer desertions and mutinies than the Russians. As the war dragged on, some loyalties weakened. Czech and Romanian deserters were formed into small armies to fight against the Habsburgs; most Slovaks and Croats remained loyal – more frightened of potential Czech and Magyar rulers. At the end, Austrian armies stood everywhere on foreign soil as they surrendered. They had not fought with great enthusiasm after the first year. Unlike the Entente armies, they were offered no vision of a better society, but they fought grimly on, with the professionalism of Habsburg military tradition, resembling an old regime more than a citizen army (Zeman 1961; Luvaas 1977; Plaschka 1977; Rothenberg 1977; Deak 1990: 190–204).

Had the Central Powers won, Austria would have survived; but Austria had chosen the wrong side in this war of alliances. From the highest moral principles Austria's enemies dismembered it. The Western allies, without autocratic multinational Russia from 1917, began to equate victory with democracy and national self-determination. In January 1918, President Wilson's Fourteen Points promised "the peoples of Austria-Hungary . . . the freest opportunity for autonomous development," though this was still envisaged as within an Austro-Hungarian confederal constitution. By summer, the Entente was recognizing national committees in exile, and they mostly favored independence, believing the Entente could protect them from Russia as well as Germany. The Social Democrats favored breakup if that meant peace (Zeman 1961; Valiani 1973; Mametey 1977). With the surrender, the emperor Charles was forced to abdicate. Each major national group received its own state. The nation-state everywhere triumphed.

By 1900, the potential weakness of the regime was that the essentially geopolitical loyalty of most nationalities was contingent and calculative. Until 1914, nationality struggles were fought on the assumption that Austria would survive. Therefore, national classes jockeyed for position within. In 1914, Austria was revealed as a client state of Germany, seemingly unable to maintain its military protection racket. Remaining uncertainties were removed when the war had a totally unexpected dénouement – the collapse of both Russia and Germany plus a new European order promised by the victors. Immediately the nationalities decided to take their chances without the Habsburgs. The regime had not reached a representative or semirepresentative constitution with classes and nations. Thus it could not mobilize citizen loyalty. In peacetime politics this was not essential, though disruptive. In mass mobilization warfare it proved a disadvantage, though not a decisive one (since Austria fought quite well). In defeat amid a new European order it brought instantaneous end.

Counterfactual regime strategies

Austria did not survive unexpected circumstances. To assess its more general viability, we must enter the treacherous terrain of counterfactual history. Could Austria have survived, and what would it have looked like if it had? Or was such a loose, confederal state an anachronism in a world in which advanced capitalism and modernization required a more organic nation-state? There are two levels at which Austria might have continued: to achieve one of the three ideal constitutions I specified or to muddle through as before.

The constitutional achievement was always difficult and became more so. The monarchy's own preference was for dynastic centralization, but it could not break through to a "nationally neutral" form of this. Its bias toward Austro-German centralization created provincial-national opposition and it failed to buy time with low-profile diplomacy and military economies. It overestimated its military power – not uncommon among declining Great Powers. Repeated opportunities between 1848 and 1866 to compromise rival constitutions were closed down by the regime's own diplomacy. It was forced into merely particularistic compromises, especially with the Hungarian nobility. This kept principled confederalism out of reach and trapped it in the embrace of the two ruling nationalities. At such points of opportunity had the dynasty gone for a version of the Stadion constitution, for federal semiauthoritarian rule, it would surely have saved itself.

In a sense any constitutional compromise would have done. A constitution is an authoritative basis for allocating sovereignty. It need not be absolutely authoritative. The German Reich worked domestically because of discretionary leeway conferred on its regime by its constitution. But the Habsburgs needed far more political institutionalization than they secured. From the 1870s on, the broadening of linguistic nationalism with the coming of industrialization, of the local-regional suffrage, and of state administrative expansion required more sovereignty than the regime could provide. Multinational representation might have been contained within Habsburg rule. But particularistic regime tactics had produced no satisfactory constitution when clashes *between* nationalities began to worsen the situation. This did push Franz Joseph into finally realizing – in head, though perhaps not at heart – that a constitution was the solution. But polymorphous particularism had now entrenched opposition within the state. The Habsburgs were contemplating this problem when their diplomatic folly, born of militarism, overwhelmed them.

So Austria was not killed off by the "internal" logic of the development of advanced capitalism or modernization. Superficially it seems that the Habsburgs did not die of natural causes, but were assassinated – the heir in 1914, the entire regime in 1918. Indeed, if left alone, they could have muddled along in mere survival, providing political and military functions even to nationalist dissidents. They may even have muddled their way through the era of bourgeois nationalism and proletarian and peasant class struggle onto a rather higher level of achievement: to emerge through the early twentieth century with a confederal semirepresentative state. Austria might not have been capable of mobilizing quite the level of commitment and sacrifice from its citizens as more centralized nation-states. But that demonstration is required not in peace but war. The fate of the Habsburgs reminds us that many forms of regime have cohabited with modernization, and that the demise of most of them has resulted most directly from geopolitics and war.

But the real weakness of the Austrian regime, the one that actually destroyed it, was self-induced. As Franz Joseph was the ruler for the whole of the period of opportunity, as he was an active dynast, personally responsible for much of the particularistic constitutional muddle and for the fatal militarism of Austrian diplomacy, Franz Joseph must bear much of the blame for his successor's demise. His identification of Great Power bellicosity with policies to control cross-border nationalities entailed costly wars for which the regime was ill equipped, and which deflected it erratically between contrary political strategies. It was not confederalism, per se, that was found wanting but Habsburg dynastic, militaristic confederalism, tarrying long after they were compatible with a requisite degree of multinational representation. Dynasticism was nearly obsolete. It could only continue to rule with extreme difficulty in the old particularistic way when confronted with classes and nations.

Modernization pressures required a more universal constitutional settlement with classes and nations. The constitution might be party democratic, as in Britain, France, and the United States, or it might be semiauthoritarian, as in the German Reich. It might be centralized like Britain or France or federal like the United States. But dynasticism could not embody the universal rights and duties appropriate to the four sources of social power in a modern society – to the bureaucratic state, the capitalist industrial economy, mass mobilized armed forces, and the imagined ideological community of shared citizenship. The pressures were not insupportable in peacetime. But war is the great tester of states, activated by the diplomacy of alliances. Habsburgs submitted themselves all too eagerly for the military and diplomatic tests and were found wanting. This state's polymorphous crystallizations, unlike the German state's, were ultimately in head-on collision. Dynasticism and militarism collided with confederal representation. The monarchy recognized this contradiction, but failed to surmount it. The Habsburgs did not develop a consistent regime strategy – and their drift was to disaster. Their epitaph had been pronounced twenty years earlier by the poet Grillparzer:

> That is the curse of our noble House,
> To strive on halfway paths to halfway deeds,
> Tarrying by halfway means.

German and global conclusions

This chapter and Chapter 9 have discussed the viability of three alternative modernizing tracks across German Central Europe. All were capitalist, but all involved other political crystallizations that then acted back to structure capitalism. One ensuing regime strategy, semiauthoritarian incorporation, apparently triumphed while the other two, democratic and dynastic confederalism, foundered. Thus German capitalism became more authoritative, territorial, and national than diffuse, market, and transnational – a trend that the triumph of either of the other regime forms would probably have reversed.

This was not a singular event. Indeed, in what seems a truly extraordinary convergence, during the same quarter century following 1848, other countries poised between comparable alternatives moved toward the authoritative, territorial, national alternative. The United States, also beset by regional disputes, lurched into a civil war with a mildly national centralizing (though still partly federal) outcome. Italy became united and its new regime strove toward the nation-state. In the Meiji Restoration from 1867 Japan emerged out of decentralized feudalism with a version of semiauthoritarian incorporation adapted from German practice. In Mexico and Argentina confederalism was also defeated. Conversely, democratic Britain and France began to centralize somewhat – though mostly slightly later, from the 1880s. So what happened in Germany begins to look like part of a logic of modernization, a global evolution of a unitary nation-state. It has been so described by Giddens (1985).

Because of the many contingencies involved, I prefer to view this as a global drift, in principle reversible, yet empirically occurring in this period (more recently it has been reversed). This drift operated through the conjunction of two distinct though entwined power processes:

1. Capitalist commercialization and industrialization, when entwined with state modernization, drifted toward nation-states, by "naturalizing" society with their infrastructures and by generating emergent classes struggling over taxation and office holding. Demands for party democracy (parliaments and office-holding rights) usually fused with the regime's own need for state modernization to create a sense of limited national citizenship. Confederal regimes, whether quasi-democratic or dynastic, had difficulty sitting astride this fusion of classes and nation, which seemed so "modern" to their internal dissidents. However, Austrian survival shows that, just as a formidable centralized and semiauthoritarian state like Prussia could wean the bourgeoisie away from much of its liberalism, so could an only moderately successful confederal regime apparently survive class-national emergence. With

only weaker resources the Habsburgs appeared able to confine disruptive nationalism to rhetoric and manageable political spaces.

2. At this point a second force intervened. States were involved in geopolitical militarism requiring greater mobilization of all power resources. The nation-state, coordinating capitalist industrialization and national citizenship, was at something of a logistic advantage over a confederal state like Austria or Tokugawa Japan, sitting loosely astride regional power networks extracting only those material or ideological commitments honored by traditional particularistic practices. The power of Commodore Perry's black ships off Kanagawa, of Prussian railways and needle guns at Königgrätz, seemed to reformers to be the very embodiments of national modernization and mobilization. Also, all the victors were boosted by the ideology of the nation-state as "modern." To be a Great Power – and in Central Europe or Japan merely to survive – it was useful to have a central government wielding greater infrastructural coordination of its territories than confederal regimes could muster. Self-styled "modernizers" everywhere regarded this as essential. Neither German nor Japanese confederations nor transnational dynasties could easily provide this. Their survival in war or anticipated war was in jeopardy, and so they fell. This is how Tilly has analyzed the entire process of the triumph of the European nation-state – warfare required and produced states that were centralized, differentiated, and autonomous, and it destroyed states of alternative forms (1990: 183, 190–1). The greatest irony revealed in these cases lay in the Confederate States of America. They had gone to war to defend weak confederalism (and slavery). Yet, as they fought against a superior foe, they developed a much more centralized, coercive, and mobilizing state than the one they resisted (Bensel 1990). The South was also buttressed by a common ideology amounting to a regional-nationalism – an incipient nation-state (only for whites).

We see the role of geopolitical militarism in the development of modern society. But we also see the influence of all *four* sources of social power – in ways that were rarely transparent to the participants. Typically the outcomes were not expected or aspired to by any of the principal power actors involved. The fusion of class and nation in citizenship, the emergence of democratic and semiauthoritarian incorporative regime strategies, the successive adaptive strategies of confederal regimes, were moments of clarity and resolve in a muddied stream of modernization. Particularly murky was the impact of diplomacy and war. Here "strategy" depended not only on devising institutions to cope with the entwined demands of classes and localities-regions. It also required, first, predicting and influencing the diplomacy of other Powers with which mutual understandings were often minimal;

and second, predicting the outcome of wars of alliances fought under changing military conditions. We have glimpsed Franz Joseph's difficulties in making the right decision (seemingly obvious from our late twentieth-century armchair) when confronted by all this. I address the issue further in Chapter 21.

Bibliography

Ashworth, W. 1977. Typologies and evidence: has nineteenth century Europe a guide to economic growth? *Economic History Review* 30.

Austensen, R. 1980. Austria and the struggle for supremacy in Germany: 1848–1864. *Journal of Modern History* 52.

Bairoch, P. 1982. International industrialization levels from 1750 to 1980. *Journal of European Economic History* 11.

Bensel, R. 1990. *Yankee Leviathan: The Origins of Central State Authority in America, 1859–1877*. Cambridge: Cambridge University Press.

Bostaph, S. 1978. The methodological debate between Carl Menger and the German historicists. *Atlantic Economic Journal* 6.

Boyer, J. 1981. *Political Radicalism in Late Imperial Vienna*. Chicago: University of Chicago Press.

Bridge, F. R. 1972. *From Sadowa to Sarajevo: The Foreign Policy of Austria-Hungary, 1866–1914*. London: Routledge & Kegan Paul.

Cohen, G. 1981. *The Politics of Ethnic Survival: Germans in Prague, 1861–1914*. Princeton, N.J.: Princeton University Press.

Deak, I. 1979. *The Lawful Revolution: Louis Kossuth and the Hungarians, 1848–49*. New York: Columbia University Press.

1990. *Beyond Nationalism: A Social and Political History of the Habsburg Officer Corps, 1848–1918*. Oxford: Oxford University Press.

Gerschenkron, A. 1977. *An Economic Spurt That Failed*. New Haven, Conn.: Yale University Press.

Giddens, A. 1985. *The Nation-State and Violence*. Cambridge: Polity Press.

Good, D. F. 1974. Stagnation and "take-off" in Austria, 1873–1913. *Economic History Review* 27.

1977. Financial integration in late nineteenth-century Austria. *Journal of European Economic History Review* 37.

1978. The Great Depression and Austrian growth after 1783. *Economic History Review* 31.

1981. Economic integration and regional development in Austria-Hungary, 1867–1913. In *Disparities in Economic Development Since the Industrial Revolution*, ed. P. Bairoch and M. Lévy-Leboyer. London: Macmillan.

1984. *The Economic Rise of the Habsburg Empire, 1750–1914*. Berkeley: University of California Press.

Gordon, H. J., and N. M. Gordon. 1974. *The Austrian Empire: Abortive Federation?* Lexington, Mass.: D. C. Heath.

Gross, N. T. 1976. The Industrial Revolution in the Habsburg monarchy, 1750–1914. In *The Fontana Economic History of Europe*. Vol. 4: *The Emergence of Industrial Societies*, Pt. I, ed. C. Cipolla. Brighton: Harvester.

Huertas, T. 1977. *Economic Growth and Economic Policy in a Multi-National Setting: The Habsburg Monarchy, 1841–1865.* New York: Arno Press. (Reprinted in *Journal of Economic History* 38, 1978.)

Jaszi, O. 1961. *The Dissolution of the Habsburg Monarchy.* Chicago: University of Chicago Press.

Johnston, W. 1972. *The Austrian Mind: An Intellectual and Social History, 1848–1938.* Berkeley: University of California Press.

Kann, R. A. 1964. *The Multinational Empire,* 2 vols. New York: Octagon Books.

1974. *A History of the Habsburg Empire, 1576–1918.* Berkeley: University of California Press.

Katzenstein, P. 1976. *Disjointed Partners: Austria and Germany Since 1815.* Berkeley: University of California Press.

Kennedy, P. 1988. *The Rise and Fall of the Great Powers.* London: Unwin Hyman.

Komlos, J. 1983. *The Habsburg Monarchy as Customs Union: Economic Development in Austria-Hungary in the Nineteenth Century.* Princeton, N.J.: Princeton University Press.

Luvaas, J. 1977. A unique army: the common experience. In *The Habsburg Empire in World War I,* ed. R. A. Kann et al. New York: Columbia University Press.

Macartney, C. 1971. *The Habsburg Empire, 1790–1918.* London: Weidenfeld & Nicolson.

Mametey, V. S. 1977. The union of Czech political parties in the *Reichsrat, 1916–1918.* In *The Habsburg Empire in World War I,* ed. R. A. Kann et al. New York: Columbia University Press.

O'Brien, P. K. 1986. Do we have a typology for the study of European industrialization in the nineteenth century? *Journal of European Economic History* 15.

Pech, Z. 1969. *The Czech Revolution of 1848.* Chapel Hill: University of North Carolina Press.

Plaschka, R. 1977. Contradicting ideologies: the pressure of ideological conflicts in the Austro-Hungarian army of World War I. In *The Habsburg Empire in World War I,* ed. R. A. Kann et al. New York: Columbia University Press.

Pollard, S. 1981. *Peaceful Conquest: The Industrialization of Europe, 1760–1970.* Oxford: Oxford University Press.

Rath, R. J. 1957. *The Viennese Revolution of 1848.* Austin: University of Texas Press.

Rothenberg, G. 1977. The Habsburg army in the First World War: 1914–1918. In *The Habsburg Empire in World War I,* ed. R. A. Kann et al. New York: Columbia University Press.

Rudolph, R. L. 1972. Austria, 1800–1914. In *Banking in the Early Stages of Industrialization,* ed. R. E. Cameron. London: Oxford University Press.

1975. The pattern of Austrian industrial growth from the eighteenth to the early twentieth century. *Austrian History Yearbook,* 11.

1976. *Banking and Industrialization in Austria-Hungary.* Cambridge: Cambridge University Press.

Schorske, C. 1981. *Fin-de-Siècle Vienna. Politics and Culture.* New York: Vintage.

Sked, A. 1979. *The Survival of the Habsburg Empire: Radetsky, the Imperial Army and the Class War, 1848*. London: Longman Group.

———. 1981. Historians, the nationality question, and the downfall of the Habsburg Empire. *Translations of the Royal Historical Society* 31.

———. 1989. *The Decline and Fall of the Habsburg Empire, 1815–1918*. London: Arnold.

Sugar, P. F., and I. J. Lederer, (eds.). 1969. *Nationalism in Eastern Europe*. Seattle: University of Washington Press.

Taylor, A. J. P. 1967. The failure of the Habsburg monarchy. In his *Europe: Grandeur and Decline*. Harmondsworth: Penguin Books.

Tilly, C. 1990. *Coercion, Capital and European States, AD 990–1990*. Oxford: Blackwell Publisher.

Valiani, L. 1973. *The End of Austria-Hungary*. London: Secker & Warburg.

Wangermann, E. 1969. *From Joseph II to the Jacobin Trials*. London: Oxford University Press.

Zeman, A. 1961. *The Break-up of the Habsburg Empire*. London: Oxford University Press.

11 The rise of the modern state: I. Quantitative data

The rise of the modern state is a commonplace of sociological and historical writing, yet it remains poorly analyzed. What is meant by state modernization encompasses four processes of growth: in state *size*, in the *scope* of its functions, in administrative *bureaucratization*, and in political *representation*. The struggle for representation is usually separated from the three administrative processes, which are assumed to constitute a single, overall modernizing process occurring more or less continuously over a long period of time (e.g., Beer 1973: 54–70; Eckstein 1982). In 1863, Adolf Wagner formulated his "law" of the ever growing expansion of the modern state, and this still influences statisticians contemplating ever larger sums in state budgets (e.g., Andic and Veverka 1963–4). Modern state development is described as "onward-and-upward" evolution.

Political scientists and economists have concentrated on the readily available financial statistics of the twentieth century. They explain growth in functional and pluralist terms. Higgs (1987) distinguishes four variants of their theories: *modernization theory* (states grew to coordinate greater social complexity and differentiation), *public goods theory* centered on national defense (public goods are provided by the state because they are in no one's private interest to pay for, yet are in the general interest, and their enjoyment by one consumer does not diminish their availability for others), *welfare state theory* (in complex societies the market undermines private charity and the state steps in), and *political redistribution theory* (the franchise enables the many to take from the few). Higgs shows that growth in the United States during the twentieth century has been more uneven than any of these four theories suggests. Rather, growth has been propelled by the ratchet effect of three great crises: two world wars and the Great Depression. These crises swung political ideologies toward state intervention (Peacock and Wiseman 1961 make the same point for Britain) and this, combined with entrenched bureaucratic interests (a borrowing from true elitist state theory), acted to prevent a return to lower levels of government.

The role of war in expanding states is very old, but whether it can be subsumed under a more general notion of "crisis" is questionable (Rasler and Thompson 1985 also make this point). Presumably social and economic crises apart from war had occurred before 1850. But they did not fuel state growth. Only war did this before 1850. The political interventionist response to the Great Depression seems peculiar, not part of a general phenomenon. Almost for the first time in history subordinate social classes demanded what Marshall called "social citizenship." Apart from war, nineteenth-century state growth was not a response to crisis. Higgs, to his credit, acknowledges this and concludes, "The development of Big Government was not a matter of logic, however complicated and multidimensional, but of History. . . . [R]eal political and socioeconomic dynamics are 'messier,' more open to exogenous influences or shocks and less determinant in their outcomes than the theorists suppose" (1987: 259). He is right. His four theories of state growth share the defects of all pluralist state theories. States do not systematically reflect their societies; they do not simply perform an underlying modernization, public goods, welfare, redistribution, or even crisis function. Nor do they systematically reflect a dialectical class struggle or the interests of state elites. They do all of these – and more – amid institutional and functional complexity that requires careful analysis.

Weber also had a systemic theory of state growth: It was part of a single "rationalization process" sweeping for centuries throughout the West. He feared the "overtowering" power of a bureaucratic state of ever increasing size and scope, and he referred briefly to three distinct causes of this state growth: the linked needs of a standing army, uniform law and taxation, the needs of capitalist enterprises for uniform technical and predictable services, and the pressure exerted by citizenship for uniformity of treatment. This was perceptive, but Weber subordinated this analysis to an essentially onward-and-upward story (though he wasn't sure he liked its outcome).

True elitist state theory (see Chapter 3) also tells an essentially onward-and-upward tale of growth. For Poggi (1990), this has been powered by the state's own "invasive" tendencies, though interacting with class and pluralist mechanisms and with some contingencies added. Skocpol (1979) provides a more discontinuous true elitist theory. She argues that revolutionaries from 1789 on increased state size, scope, and bureaucratization together (another version of Higgs's crisis theory). (I cast doubt on her explanation in Chapter 13.) Giddens merges Weber with Foucault (1975) to describe the rise of an all-powerful, all-surveilling, all-disciplining nation-state, which he believes is the greatest "power-container" of the modern world. It "absorbs" and actually "is" society (1985: 21–2, 172). But he is not too specific about precisely when and where this Leviathan emerged. Nor does he or Foucault make clear who this Leviathan is: Who controls it? Who is doing what to whom? Is there, in fact, a state elite in charge?

Marxists give an onward-and-upward account in terms of the development of capitalism. They point not to an "overtowering state" but to an ever expanding capitalism. Marx himself did not seriously analyze states, but he spiced descriptions of French and German states with Victorian diatribes against "bloated bureaucracies." He described the French state as "this appalling parasitic body, which enmeshes the body of French society like a net and chokes all its pores" (1968: 169). The tables in this chapter show that the French state was no larger than other European states of the period. Later Marxists invariably write of the "capitalist state." Miliband (1969) opens his book thus: "The vast inflation of the state's power and activity in the advanced capitalist societies . . . has become one of the merest commonplaces of political analyses." His title, *The Capitalist State*, reveals his explanation for this inflation. Wolfe's history of the capitalist state attributes growth and bureaucratization to the needs of concentrated, centralized capital for predictable, rationalized public goods and for an apparently neutral agency to regulate class struggle and to soften it with welfare reforms (1977: 59–79, 263). His history, like almost all Marxist accounts, barely mentions the state's military activities.

Such onward-and-upward stories reflect confidence that the state grew massively over this period. A few scattered numbers are generally marshaled in support (e.g., Poggi 1990: 109–11). Some refer to continuous growth in the number of state officials (e.g., Anderson and Anderson 1967), often citing Flora's (1983) compilation of historical statistics of public employment. The invaluable fiscal compilations of Bruce Mitchell (1975, 1983; Mitchell and Deane 1980) are also cited. They show enormous growth in the cash disbursements of most Western states throughout the period. The fiscal historian Gabriel Ardant has claimed further that state expenditures grew as a proportion of gross national product, even though that was considerably expanding, throughout the nineteenth century (1975: 221). After briefly presenting both types of statistics and acknowledging some of the unevenness of nineteenth-century growth, Grew (1984) moves to his main questions: Why was there so much state expansion in the nineteenth century, and why was it so strikingly similar in such different countries? Grew seems confident that states just grew and grew.

But did they? In this chapter, I present systematic quantitative data on state finances and employment to separate carefully size, scope, and bureaucratization to see which increased, when, and where. The rise of the modern state was a differentiated, complex, and uneven process. Rather surprisingly, the state did not become larger in relation to its civil society over the "long nineteenth century." Yet this overall lack of a trend confuses three processes – a declining but increasingly insulated military, an increase in bureaucracy, and a large increase in civilian scope. Each of these three is then analyzed in its own chapter.

For the five countries, I have gathered systematic data on size, scope, and bureaucratization for both central and regional-local government – all levels of government below the central or federal level. In the Austrian lands, "central government" before 1867 refers only to government in Vienna; after 1867, it refers to the two seats of the dual monarchy, in Vienna and Budapest. I expand the methodology of Volume I for grounding discussion of states in the statistics they generate. Revenue and expenditure accounts are analyzed as in Volume I. Revenue clues us in to the state's relation with power actors in civil society, revealing the extent to which it was insulated from or embedded in civil society power networks. (These concepts are explained in Chapter 3.) Expenditure reveals state functions. It gives a fiscal index of overall state size and of the relative importance of its functions. I adjust these fiscal totals for inflation and population growth; and I relate them to gross national product (GNP) or national income, measuring the size of the country's economy.

In modern times we can add statistics on state empolyment. The number of officials also seems to measure the size of the state, and is also controllable for population growth. However, personnel figures will prove extremely unreliable – and will actually tell us more about bureaucratic competence than size. I discuss personnel data further in Chapter 13 to illuminate the employment status of officials, their functions, organizational networks, and social backgrounds – revealing their homogeneity as either elite or bureaucracy and as either insulated from or embedded in civil society. We can now call the figures "statistics" without anachronism, for the word and its cognates emerged just before 1800 in English and all European languages as meaning data pertaining to the state – revealing the state modernization now under way.

This volume will tell a paradoxical tale of the development of the modern state. On the one hand the nineteenth century saw the emergence of a state justifiably termed modern – no larger in relation to its civil society, but undertaking many more civil functions, quasi-representative, becoming more centralized, bureaucratic and merito-cratic, its infrastructures able to penetrate efficiently all its territories. On the other hand, this modernization was not unitary but poly-morphous, in each phase responding to diverse political crystallizations. This resulted in an infrastructurally powerful state that was in certain respects less coherent than its predecessors.

The size of the state: expenditure trends

I first use expenditure trends as an indicator of overall state growth. Were states growing in the sense of spending ever larger sums of money?

Table 11.1 contains the available expenditure figures in current prices expressed in the national currencies of the mid-nineteenth century (several countries changed their currencies during the period). Figures for the central states of Austria, Britain, France, and Prussia-Germany are available virtually from the beginning, and figures for the U.S. federal government are available from 1790, immediately after its establishment. Austrian figures need to be watched carefully because they refer sometimes to the entire Habsburg lands and sometimes only to the western half (the Austrian *Reichshalf*, comprising just over 60 percent of the total population). Local-regional governments are less evenly documented. Figures for British local authorities, French departments and communes, and German *Länder* and *Gemeinde* and estimates for American state and local governments are available from various points across the mid-nineteenth century. Some Austrian local figures become available toward the end of the century, but I confess to not fully understanding their structure and have omitted them.

Like all the figures presented in this chapter, expenditure figures are to be treated with some reserve. Later figures tend to be more reliable than earlier ones, and central government figures are more reliable than local-regional ones. Generally, I have followed the guidance of specialist historians as to the meaning and accuracy of the surviving accounts. I do not claim that these figures are entirely accurate; none could be. I do claim, however, that they are the most comprehensive data yet assembled for this period.

All central states grew massively in money terms. In 1760, the British central state spent 18 million pounds; in 1911, it spent almost 160 million pounds. This eightfold increase also occurred in France. The other states grew even more: Austria and Prussia-Germany grew about fortyfold (making allowances for the fact that, from 1870 on, Austrian figures in Table 11.1 relate only to the Austrian *Reichshalf*); and the United States rocketed more than two-hundredfold (from a tiny beginning).

Adding local-regional governments increases the growth, but problematically. In the earlier part of the period there was local-regional government, but neither we nor central governments of the time could know its scale or cost because it was effectively autonomous (a significant finding discussed later). That part of local-regional government known, and in some sense accountable, to the central state started

Table 11.1. *Total expenditure of central states and all levels of government, 1760–1910, current prices*

Year	Austria Central (millions of florins)	Prussia- Germany Central (millions of marks)	All	France Central (millions of francs)	All	Great Britain Central (millions of pounds)	All	United States Central (millions of dollars)	All
1760	58	61		506		18.0			
1770		51		333		10.5			
1780	65	64		411+		22.6			
1790	113	90		633+		16.8	23.0	4.3	
1800	167	106		726		51.0	67.0	11.0	
1810	216			934		81.5	94.0	8.7	
1820	160	201		907		57.5	70.0	19.3	27.7
1830	138	219		1,095		53.7	65.0	17.0	33.1
1840	165	204	234	1,363		53.4	64.0	28.9	67.6
1850	269	252	334	1,473		55.5	66.0	44.8	89.2
1860	367	323	496	2,084		69.6	87.0	71.7	171.7
1870	332	1,380	2,360	2,482	3,348	67.1	92.0	328.5	611.7
1880	432	519	1,851	3,141	4,180	81.5	112.0	301.0	621.1
1890	560	1,044	2,690	3,154	4,289	90.6	123.0	378.9	854.1
1900	803	1,494	4,005	3,557	4,932	143.7	265.0	607.1	1,702.1
1910	1,451	2,673	6,529	3,878	5,614	156.9	258.0	977.0	3,234.0

Notes: All government = federal + state + local governments. For the United States in all tables, 1900 is actually 1902 and 1910 is 1913.

Sources:

Austria: Net normal and extraordinary expenditures of the central government.

1760   Janetschek 1959: 188.

1780–1860   Czoernig 1861: 123–7 (in this and subsequent tables, 1780 is actually 1781 and 1860 is actually 1858). Figures refer to the entire Austrian Empire.

1870–1910   Wysocki 1975: 109; the Austrian *Reichshalf* (disbursing about 70% of the fiscal revenues of the Austro-Hungarian dual monarchy). Hungarian figures are not available.

In 1858, 100 old florins were revalued at 105 new florins. I have not adjusted the figures either in this or subsequent tables.

Prussia-Germany: The following adjacent years were used in this and subsequent tables: 1821, 1829, 1852, 1862, 1872, 1881, 1892.

1760–1860   Prussian central government figures and 1870–1910 all German government figures: Riedel 1866: tables XV–XX; Leineweber 1988: 311–21; and Weitzel 1967: table 1a. Note that Andic and Veverka 1963–4 give somewhat higher figures for local government than do Leineweber and Weitzel.

1870–1910   German central government figures: Andic and Veverka 1963–4.

France

1760–70   Riley 1986: 56–7, 138–48, for the years 1761 and 1765.

1780–90   Morineau 1980: 315 – ordinary expenditures only for years 1775 and 1788, thus being a slight understatement of total expenses (because there was no war in either year).

1800–10   Marion 1927: IV, 112–3, 325; years are 1799–1800 (*L'an* VII of the Revolution) and 1811.

1820   Block 1875: I, 495–512.

1830–60   *Annuaire statistique de la France* 1913, "Résumé rétrospectif," 134.

1870–1910   Delorme and André 1983: 722; 1870, 1900, and 1910 are actually 1872, 1902, and 1909.

Great Britain

1760–1910   Central government: Mitchell and Deane 1980: public finance tables; up to 1800 net expenditure, thereafter gross expenditure.

(*Sources continue on next page.*)

Table 11.1. (cont.)

1790–1910	All government: Veverka 1963: 114, for the United Kingdom, including Ireland. As Veverka gives no references I have been unable to check his source material. His population figures are not accurate. 1800 figure is actually 1801 in all tables.

United States

1790–1910	Central (federal) government, 1790–1910, and all government, 1900 and 1910: U.S. Bureau of the Census 1975: tables Y350–6. As this standard source contains only postal profits, I have deducted these and added total postal expenditures from U.S. Department of the Treasury 1947: 419–22.
1820–90	State government, 1820–90: calculated from data in Holt 1977. Holt's incomplete data for states were converted to per capita figures and then aggregated up to the total U.S. population.
1820–90	Local government, 1820–90: calculated from Legler et al. 1988: table 4, and Legler et al. 1990: table 3. Note that (a) these are total revenue, not expenditure, figures, and (b) I have estimated the figures for 1820–40, assuming that per capita revenues for all local governments were 8% of the per capita figure for cities in 1820, 9% in 1830, and 10% in 1840 (the proportion was known to be 12% in 1850, 16% in 1860, 21% in 1870, and then continuing to slowly ascend). These figures thus can only be rough approximations.

small and then in the later part of the period usually grew faster than central government. It is unlikely that local-regional government costs declined in the earlier part of the period, so the cost of all government (central plus local-regional) must have escalated even more than Table 11.1 suggests.

Figures like these provide the main evidence for the onward-and-upward stories. They are not, however, very meaningful. We must control for inflation, which eroded the values of all currencies over this period, and we must control for population increase, rapid everywhere, though greatest in Prussia-Germany and the United States because of territorial expansion or massive immigration. If populations were growing faster than expenditures, then the real ability of states to penetrate their subjects' lives may have actually declined. I control for both inflation and population growth in Table 11.2, expressing expenditures as a percentage of their 1911 per capita level at constant prices.

These two controls eliminate much state growth, though to differing degrees according to country and level of government. In real per capita terms local-regional government grew more and later than central government except in France, where there was no significant difference between their growth rates. Growth was substantial and steady in France and Austria. Britain and Prussia experienced virtually no central government growth over the period and a pronounced decline after midcentury; but their local-regional governments grew substantially and steadily. There were two American trends, a mild secular trend upward, exaggerated by the rocketing effect of the Civil War on the

Table 11.2. *Trends in per capita state expenditure at constant prices, 1780–1910, central state and all government (1910 = 100)*

Year	France Central	France All	Great Britain Central	Great Britain All	United States Central	United States All	Prussia-Germany Central	Prussia-Germany All	Austria Central
1780			70						
1790			45	32	12		63		
1800			74	51	14		86		21
1810			96	61	9				19
1820	27		77	50	18	8	94		19
1830	31		76	48	14	8	80		14
1840	35		68	42	16	13	68	32	19
1850	43		87	53	22	14	82	46	25
1860	50		86	57	23	18	69	44	25
1870	67	63	69	50	57	35	118	83	35
1880	85	81	71	67	56	37	32	48	41
1890	92	89	75	63	68	51	63	66	54
1900	99	96	103	118	91	80	78	86	72
1910	100	100	100	100	100	100	100	100	100

Sources: Expenditure sources and notes as in Table 11.1. The following are sources for constant prices:
France: Lévy-Leboyer 1975: 64. Prices set to 1908–12.
Prussia/Germany: 1790–1860, Prussia; 1870–1910, Germany. 1790 is actually 1786; 1800 is calculated with 1804 prices. 1820 is actually 1821.
1790–1800 Weitzel 1967: table 1a.
1820–1910 Fischer et al. 1982: 155–7. Prices set to 1913.
Great Britain: 1780–1840, Lindert and Williamson 1983: 41 – their "southern urban, best guess" price index – spliced with 1850–1910, Deane 1968. These two indexes differ slightly during their overlap period of 1830–50.
United States: U.S. Bureau of the Census 1975: tables E52–89. Warren, Pearson wholesale price index for 1790–1890 spliced with Bureau of Labor Statistics Index for 1890–1910.
Austria: Mühlpeck et al. 1979: 676–9. Prices set to 1914.

figures. I explain these various trends later. For the moment I note that state growth was indeed real though it was variable. Over the century states did become bigger, though not spectacularly so, as measured by their expenditures, and local-regional state growth became greater than central state growth.

But I add a third control. The period saw massive economic growth, containing both the first and the second industrial revolutions, which actually centered in the five countries under discussion. Thus their economies might have been growing faster than their states, in which case the economic significance of the state might have actually declined.

Table 11.3. *Government expenditure as percentage of national income or national product, 1760–1910*

Year	Prussia-Germany NI Central	Prussia-Germany All	Great Britain NI Central a	Great Britain NI Central b	Great Britain NI All a	Great Britain NI All b	Great Britain GNP Central	Great Britain GNP All	Austria GNP Central	United States GNP Central	United States GNP All	France GNP Central	France GNP All	France CO Central
1760	35			22								12		16
1770	23			11								7		9
1780	22			22								8		
1790	24		19	12	29	16				2.3		12		13
1800	23		27	27	31	36			17	2.4		9		12
1810			20	37	24	43			27	1.5		10		14
1820	19		16	23	19	28	12	15		2.9	4.2	7		14
1830	17		12	19	14	23	11	13	9	1.8	3.5	7		12
1840	12	14	10		13		10	12	9	1.7	4.0	8		12
1850	9	12	11		13		9	10	11	1.7	3.4	9		13
1860	8	12					6	9	11	1.9	4.5	9		13
1870	15	18	7		10		6	9	11	4.5	8.3	10	13	14
1880	4	13	8		11		7	9	12	2.9	5.9	13	16	18
1890	5	13	7		10		8		13	2.9	6.5	14	18	19
1900	5	14	9					14	15	2.8	7.9	12	16	19
1910	6	16			16		7	12	17	2.5	8.2	11	15	15

Notes: In the late eighteenth and the nineteenth centuries, gross national product exceeded national income by about 15% and commodity output by 25%.

NI = national income; GNP = gross national product; CO = commodity output.

Sources: Expenditure sources and notes as in Table 11.1

Gross national product, national income, and commodity output

Prussia-Germany

1760–1800 Weitzel, 1967: table 1a, using the extrapolations he suggests for missing years.

1820–1910 Leineweber 1988: 311–21 – national income at factor costs.

United States: All years: Mitchell 1983: 886–9 (GNP).

Austria:

1780–90 National income: Dickson 1987: I, 136–7 – estimating national income in 1780 at 357 million florins (the midpoint of his estimate range) and in 1790 at 410 million florins. I have not used Dickson's own percentage estimates. They concern ordinary peacetime revenues, which were lower than actual expenditures.

1830–1910 GDP for Austrian *Reichshalf:* Kausel 1979: 692. I have calculated 70% of Czoernig's expenditure for 1830–60. After the 1867 division of the empire, Austria contributed 70% of the joint budget and Hungary 30% (in 1908, the Hungarian contribution was increased to 36.4%, but I have not adjusted my 1910 figure).

Great Britain: National income estimates: (a) Deane and Cole 1962: 166; (b) Crafts 1983 – extrapolating for 1770, 1790, 1810, 1820, 1830–1910. GNP: Deane 1968: 104–5.

France: GNP 1760–90: Goldstone 1991: 202. GNP 1800–10 (actually calculated from figures for 1781–90 and 1803–12): Markovitch 1965: 192. Expenditure for 1788 from Morineau 1980: 315; for 1820–1910 from Lévy-Leboyer 1975: 64. Commodity output = market value of agricultural and industrial products (i.e., excluding services). 1740–67: Riley 1986: 146 (1770 figure actually 1765). 1790–1910: Marczewski 1965: LXX.

Table 11.3 investigates this possibility by expressing state expenditures as a percentage of the national economy – of national income, gross national product (GNP), or total commodity production.

Here I sound a warning: Estimates of the size of national economies are even less accurate than expenditure figures. Economists do not agree about the best measures and they work with sometimes rudimentary sources differing between countries. Their figures aggregate the production, sales, or income figures of particular industries, areas, or occupations up to whole economic sectors. In this period it is particularly difficult to estimate the output of the service sector. Some economic historians confront these difficulties by estimating on the production side (GNP), others on the income side (national income), and still others omit services altogether (commodity output). Thus, unless the differences are large, country comparisons are hazardous. I am also wary of comparing different sets of estimates over time, as they are often based on use of different methods. Hence these figures cannot be used for subtle purposes. Luckily the overall trend is clear-cut.

The trend is striking and surprising. Contrary – I am fairly confident – to most readers' expectations, state activities *decreased* as a proportion of national economic activity between the mid-eighteenth and the early twentieth century. The data are not complete or unanimous, but most point in the same direction.

The British figures are the fullest. They jump around in the eighteenth century between high and average levels, rise to a peak at the beginning of the nineteenth century, and then decline fairly steadily. I am, however, somewhat skeptical about the most extreme set of British figures in Table 11.3, column b, derived from Crafts's (1983) estimate of national income during the Industrial Revolution. His downward adjustment of Deane and Cole's (1962) estimates would result in all government expenditures for 1811 (for which we have accurate figures) amounting to 43 percent of national income. Although 1811 was a year of major warfare, I doubt that any government before the twentieth century had the infrastructural power necessary to expropriate this proportion of national income. Even in World War I the British government's wholesale mobilization of the economy, plus proportionately larger armed forces, expropriated only 52 percent. At some point economic historians' addiction to numbers must give way before sociological plausibility. Nonetheless, whatever the exact proportion of British government activity, it declined substantially throughout the long nineteenth century.

The trend is even more marked for Prussia-Germany. Its early central government alone spent a substantially higher percentage of

GNP than all levels of government did in later Imperial Germany. The highest Austrian figure is also early, in 1790 (though the 1800 and 1810 figures, if available, would undoubtedly be higher). There is no overall French trend, although I argue later that available figures understate state activity during the the Revolutionary and Napoleonic wars. There was virtually no growth of the U.S. federal state, apart from the impact of the Civil War on 1870 figures. But what is striking about the United States is the one comparative difference big enough to be reliable: the small scale of American government at each level compared to European states. As conventional wisdom suggests, the United States really did have far less government than Europe – as we might expect from the capitalist-liberal regime identified in Chapter 5.

It is probable that late eighteenth-century states had the highest fiscal extraction rates the world had seen before the wars of the twentieth century. Obviously, we cannot make good estimates of GNP in earlier periods, but most guesses put European state expenditures before the seventeenth century well below 5 percent of national product or income (Bean 1973: 212; Goldsmith 1987: 189). The first calculation we can hazard is for 1688, when Gregory King estimated GNP in England and Wales. His figures have been revised by Lindert and Williamson (1982: 393). I gross up their estimate to Britain as a whole and then divide by average state expenditures during 1688–92 (the first years for which good expenditure data are available; see Mitchell and Deane 1980: 390). This yields an estimate that the British state extracted 5.5 percent of GNP. Rasler and Thompson (1985) may have done a similar calculation, though, unfortunately, they give no details of their methods. They estimate expenditures at 5 percent of GNP in 1700.

King also estimated Dutch GNP and revenue for 1695, but his GNP is considered too low and his revenue too high. He put government revenues at 25 percent of GNP (Goldsmith 1987: 226 accepts this at face value), but this is far too high. Grossing up per capita revenue figures for the province of Holland (Riley 1980: 275), and being agnostic about both schools of thought concerning Dutch GNP, yields a revenue estimate of 8 percent to 15 percent of GNP. I am more impressed by those of the high-GNP school (Maddison 1983; de Vries 1984) than by those staying closer to King (e.g., Riley 1984). I finally plump for about 10 percent – in a country considered to be very highly taxed. Seventeenth-century states may, therefore, have spent 5 percent to 10 percent of GNP, and this probably remained true in the early eighteenth century. Rasler and Thompson estimate British expenditure at 9 percent of GNP in 1720, though again with no explanation of methods. We can put French expenditure in 1726 at about 6.5 percent of GNP (expenditure in Morineau 1980: 315; GNP following Goldstone

1991: 202). Thereafter it rose: Riley (1986: 146) estimates peacetime years during 1744–65 at 8 percent to 10 percent and wartime years at 13 percent to 17 percent.

Thus the upward eighteenth-century trend revealed in the tables had begun earlier. The conclusion seems as clear as imperfect data sources allow. As measured by finances, states rapidly expanded throughout the eighteenth century, before 1815 playing their greatest role in societies until World War I; then in the nineteenth century they declined. *The first great sea change in the life of the state – in its size – occurred in the eighteenth century.* As Volume III will show, the next phase of growth in state size occurred in the mid-twentieth century, having begun during World War I. Thus Weber's fear of the "overtowering" state did not reflect reality through his own lifetime. Either he was responding to World War I or he was being remarkably prescient (he died in 1920). Similarly, those onward-and-upward stories of a state growing bigger and bigger, more and more looming over their societies during the period of industrial capitalism are wrong. Although the absolute financial size of states was growing at current prices and most were also growing modestly in per capita real terms, state fiscal size relative to civil society was now either static or declining.

This is such an important and counterintuitive finding that it might seem necessary to spend some time further evaluating data sources and methods to check the reliability and validity of the data, but I shall not do that. The downward trend is almost certainly real because it is easily interpretable and because it fits well with other trends. What we shall see are two contrary nineteenth-century trends that usually did not quite cancel each other out: A large increase in state civilian functions was more than counterbalanced in most countries by a larger decrease in its militarism.

Why did the state's traditional, military crystallization decline, after having rocketed upward in the eighteenth century? Three reasons explain the overall downward trend and the exceptions in Table 11.3. First, state expenditure varied, as it had done for millennia, according to whether the country was at peace or war, always rocketing with the onset of war. This is only partly revealed by Table 11.3, which somewhat obscures the role of war in Austrian and U.S. government finances. In Austria, the highest expenditure figure was in 1790, occasioned by the need to fight revolts in Flanders and Hungary. But the next two decades, fighting against Napoleon, would reveal even higher figures were GNP estimates available. The United States was at peace during all the years listed in the table. If we added expenditures for the Civil War period, then we should find the usual rocketing effect. In 1860, according to Table 11.1, U.S. federal expenditures were $72 million.

By 1864–5, those of the two warring factions had leaped thirtyfold, to
$1.8 billion – the Union's to $1.3 billion in 1865, of which military
expenses contributed 90 percent (U.S. Bureau of the Census 1961: 71),
and the Confederacy's to just under $500 million in 1864 (Todd 1954:
115, 153). This total far exceeded federal expenses in every succeeding
year (despite vastly growing national population and wealth) until
1917, during World War I. It then absorbed 28 percent of GNP. As
Table 11.3 reveals, this was about average for states caught in major
wars. Peace normally made the American state puny; wars suddenly
conjured up giants.

Table 11.3 also shows the impact of war on the other states. For
Prussia-Germany the highest expenditure, in 1760, involved the Seven
Years' War, and the rise of 1870 was for the Franco-Prussian War,
which gave the highest per capita real expenditure found in Table 11.2.
For Britain the eighteenth-century peaks of 1760 and 1780 involved
the Seven Years' War and the American Revolution, whereas the
enormous figures for 1800 and 1811 indicate the massive burden of the
Napoleonic Wars. For France the early peak figure is 1760, the Seven
Years' War, but the costs of the Revolution and the Napoleonic Wars
are not reflected in the figures of 1800 and 1811 because France was
subsidized by its occupied countries. Between 1740 and 1815, most
states were fighting major wars for two-thirds of the time, involving
progressively greater demands on manpower, taxation, and agricultural
and industrial production. Their states became militarized. To say this
of Prussia is to be entirely conventional, and Brewer (1989) has em-
phatically said it of constitutional Britain; but it needs saying of *all* late
eighteenth-century states. States began the modernization process
as little more than elaborated networks of drill sergeants, recruiting
officers, impressment gangs, and attendant tax officials.

The nineteenth century did not end such state activities. Immediately
after my present period ends, World War I had the normal effects. By
1918, total British government expenditures had rocketed to 52 percent
of GNP, and military and war-debt costs contributed more than 90
percent of expenditures (Peacock and Wiseman 1961: 153, 164, 186). It
is not easy to calculate French GNP during the war, but military and
war debt costs also contributed 90 percent of a vastly inflated state
budget (*Annuaire Statistique de la France* 1932, 490–1.) Similar increases occurred in Germany and probably Austria (whose figures
survive only for the first full year of war; see *Osterreiches Statistisches
Handbuch* 1918: 313). Only the United States escaped lightly during
World War I, its central government share of GNP trebling, but only
from 2 percent to 6 percent between 1914 and 1919.

This points directly to the principal cause of the relative decline of the nineteenth-century state: The frequency and duration of European wars was high in the eighteenth century and then diminished between 1815 and 1914. Nothing in Europe then paralleled the impact of the French Revolution and the Napoleonic Wars. Nothing even paralleled the mid-eighteenth-century struggles – the War of the Austrian Succession and the Seven Years' War. The Austro-Prussian and Franco-Prussian wars involved large armies but only for short periods. The Crimean War did not severely stretch France or Britain; nor did their perennial campaigns in their empires (though all impacted on state expenditures for the relevant years). Only the United States fought a (civil) war comparable to earlier ones. This largely explains why expenses declined in Austria, Britain, and Prussia-Germany and increased in the United States.

The second cause of the trends indicated in Table 11.3 was that developments in military tactics, organization, and technology lessened peacetime army costs in the nineteenth century. Bonaparte's success in throwing relatively untrained masses with guns at the enemy meant that soldiers' skills had declined. Fewer professional soldiers were required. The peacetime standing army consisted of a cadre of permanent professionals plus rotating cohorts of young conscripts and recalled reservists. This could be expanded rapidly at the onset of war. In the mid-eighteenth century, Prussian, Austrian, and French armies had doubled after a few months of war; in the Napoleonic Wars and the Austro-Prussian and Franco-Prussian wars, they rose four- to five-fold. In World War I, this trend continued, to an eightfold increase after two years of war. These army developments did not apply to navies, which remained professional. Thus Britain, predominantly a naval power, got fewer peacetime savings. I explore the changing nature of state militarism in Chapter 12.

The third cause of the trends revealed in Table 11.3 was traditional. The effect of war on state expenditures continued into peacetime, as it had done for most of the previous millennium. States borrow heavily in wartime, and when war ends, they have to repay the debt. After the Napoleonic Wars direct British military expenditures were tailing off, but debt repayment of war loans absorbed a high proportion of the budget for another fifty years. As Table 11.3 shows, British government expenditure in relation to national income and GNP declined slowly, not bottoming out until 1870. If wars are frequent, as they were in most of Europe between 1740 and 1815, or as in nineteenth-century Austria, the bottoming out occurred only in time for the next war. Only the nineteenth century allowed full bottoming out for most states.

Combined, these three military reasons explain the main discernible trends in Table 11.3. In fact their explanatory power raises the question

Table 11.4. Percentages of all government budgets allocated for civil and military expenditures, 1760–1910

	Austria		Prussia-Germany			France			Great Britain			United States		
	Central		Central		All	Central		All	Central		All	Central		All
Year	Civilian	Military	Civilian	Military	Civilian	Civilian	Military	Civilian	Civilian	Military	Civilian	Civilian	Military	Civilian
1760			9	86		14	50		6	75				
1770			9	90					15	39				
1780	28	51	8	84		24	33		7	66				
1790	21	62	25	75		21	27		13	31	36	26	19	
1800	14	61	22	74		24	64		5	31	36	12	56	
1810	15	57				9	75		11	59		16	49	
1820	33	35	45	38		48	25		17	29	31	16	56	60
1830	35	33	50	34		47	30		18	28	31	34	65	66
1840	35	33	53	35		49	34		19	26	31	34	65	72
1850	34	47	48	37		29	35		22	27	35	42	49	75
1860	39	51	49	36		17	39		34	25	41	49	46	79
1870	46	24	22	40	35	32	26	49	28	32	50	24	35	81
1880	45	19	15	82	63	39	30	54	35	53	61	24	41	80
1890	39	19	25	78	65	32	34	50	37	36	59	34	55	75
1900	47	17	35	59	64	36	38	54	36	48	65	28	64	74
1910	60	16	40	52	67	40	37	59	47	40	68	29	68	79

Note: Civil expenditures + military expenditures + debt charges (not listed here) = 100%.

Sources: See also Table 11.1.

Austria

1780–1860 Czoernig 1861: 123–7.

1870–1910 Wysocki 1975: 109–13; Wagner 1987: 300, 590–1; Mischler and Ulbrich 1905: II, 95 (Austrian *Reichshalf* only). This has sometimes involved recalculating source figures. All 1870 and 1910 figures and total expenditures from Wysocki; military expenditures from Wagner, recalculated to exclude the Hungarian military contribution to the joint army and to the Honved reserve force. Debt figures 1880–1900 from Mischler and Ulbrich. Civil expenditures = the residual. Hence Austrian figures must be treated with some caution.

(*Sources continue on next page.*)

Table 11.4. (cont.)

Prussia-Germany: 1820–70 = Prussia; 1880–1910 = Germany.

1760–1860   Riedel 1866: tables XV, XVI, XVIII, XX.

1820–1910   Andic and Veverka 1963–4: 262; Leineweber 1988: 312–6. I adjusted his 1820–70 figures to eliminate "civil debt costs" from civil expenditures (to make the German figures comparable with those of other countries).

France

1760   Riley 1986: 56–7, 138–48 (the year is 1761).

1780–90   Morineau 1980: 315, ordinary expenditures only (probably overstating civil expenditures by about 30%) for years 1775 and 1788.

1800–20   Marion 1927: IV, 234, 238, 241–2, 325, 1928: V, 14, 19; Block 1875: I, 495–512. 1800 average budgets for 1801, 1802, and 1803, which all allocate 23–25% for civil expenses. 1810 is actually 1811; 1820 is a composite of items from 1821 and 1822 budgets for which figures are available and is only approximate.

1830–60   *Annuaire statistique de la France* 1913; Block 1875: I, 491–3.

1870–1910   Delorme and André 1983: 722, 727.

Great Britain: Central government sources as for Table 11.1. Mitchell and Deane give only the "principal constituent items" of the budget. I have assumed that residual miscellaneous items are all civil. In 1860, these items amount to 12% of the total budget; in all other years, to much less. Local government, 1790 U.K. figure from Veverka 1963: 119; other local government from Mitchell and Deane 1980: public finance tables. Full data available from 1880 (actually 1884). Estimating procedures for earlier years: 1820–60, poor law receipts England and Wales plus county receipts England and Wales plus 12.5% additional Scottish expenditure. Note that Veverka 1963: 119 estimates U.K. expenses at 34% for 1840 and 47% for 1890.

United States: Sources as for Table 11.1. Payments to veterans counted as military expenditures. I assume no military expenses by local governments (state governments funded the national guard).

of why state expenditure did not decline more dramatically. The answer is that states were increasingly spending on other, civilian roles (cf. Grew 1984). Table 11.4 details the proportion of central-government expenses for civil and military functions and of all government (central plus local-regional) expenses for civil functions (local-regional government incurred few military costs). The residual, not given in the table, is debt repayment expenses. Indebtedness somewhat blurs the distinction between military and civil expenses because during the nineteenth century borrowing shifted from financing of wars to paying for large public capital projects such as railways and schools. In the case of Germany, the statistical sources give the exact purpose of each debt and we can correct for this understatement. Even without this correction, however, the table reveals a clear secular trend.

All the columns reveal that civil expenses increased relatively through the period. By 1911, between 60 percent and 80 percent of all government expenses was for civil functions. Adding civil debt increases the German figure from 67 percent to 75 percent (Leineweber 1988: 312–6), so the true range for total civilian expenditures among all the states is about 70 percent to 85 percent. For the beginning of the period, we cannot produce a clear-cut figure, because of the lack of local-regional government data. But the trends in the data that are available lead me to guess that the range in the mid-eighteenth century was only slightly higher than the central state figures given in the table – that is, they would be in the range of 15 percent to 35 percent. *This percentage increase in civilian expenses – from about 25 percent in the 1760s to about 75 percent in the 1900s – indicates a second sea change in the scope of the modern state, this one without parallel in history.* This growth was quite steady from the mid-nineteenth century on. It was not greatly affected by the economic cycle: the great agricultural depression from 1873 had no great impact (as Higgs's crisis theory might suggest). Nor, as we shall see, were most rising expenditures those normally associated with response to crisis, such as welfare spending.

Apart from Austria, most civil growth was at local-regional government levels. A division of labor devolved: Most of the new civil functions devolved to local or regional governments, with the central state retaining its historic militarism. Smaller central states remained most military. The extreme case is the post–Civil War United States, whose small federal state was predominantly military even in 1910. The moderate-sized central states, the British, French, and German, were fairly equally split between civil and military functions. In the Austrian lands, as we saw in Chapter 10, the failure to reach a constitutional settlement with the provinces meant that the central

Habsburg government retained most of its powers and most of the new civil funtions (after 1867, shared with the Hungarian central government in Budapest).

The division of functions between central and local varied among countries. American federal government spent less than local and state governments from the first point for which good figures are available. In the German Reich, local-regional quickly overtook central government, but this had a distinctive significance. The largest of the regional *Länder*, Prussia itself, spent more money than the central Reich government, yet was in a sense also the "German" state. In both countries the disparity was not reversed until involvement in World War II. Austrian, British, and French central exceeded regional-local expenditure for the whole period. Coordination also differed. In the centralized countries Britain and France, all levels of government began to coordinate their activities in the late nineteenth century and local-regional accounts were submitted to the national government. In part-federal Germany, coordination and accounting lagged a little. In confederal Austria, it was more particularistic, varying by province and *Reichshalf*. In the United States, the federal government had little contact with state or local government and knew nothing of their accounts for the whole of this period. Coordination would have been regarded as an infringement of liberties and disallowed by the Supreme Court. States varied substantially in what I term their "national" crystallization – how centralized or confederal they were.

These variations make similarities in overall trends all the more remarkable. As Grew (1984) has observed, the broadening of scope was occurring across European states of very different constitutions and levels of economic development. The nineteenth century introduced major nonmilitary government expenditures. In contrast to previous centuries, civil expenditures increased through periods of peace instead of being, as in the past, a by-product of war. In 1846, the civil expenditure of the British central state was more or less what it had been in 1820 and in every intervening year. But from 1847 on, a steady increase occurred in almost every year, war or peace. The pattern is confirmed in all available national statistics. War was no longer the only ratchet of state growth.

We can establish symbolic dates for the transition in the central state: the point at which civil outran military expenses for the first time, controlling for the effects of debt repayment. In the accounts this occurred as early as in 1820 in Prussia, although this is misleading, as the army was used in mainstream administration and was partly financed from there. But Britain reached this position in reality in 1881 – probably the first time in the entire history of organized states that the greatest Power of an era devoted more of its central state finances to peaceful than warlike activity. The central state remained a war-making machine, but it was now also at least half civil. We may begin the journey to a polymorphous model of the modern state (as promised in Chapter 3) by labeling this half-military, half-civil state a "dia-morphous state." As such it was novel in the world history of major successful states. We did not see such a state in Volume I. In the late nineteenth and early twentieth centuries such a state was not merely an isolate risking its survival by running down its military as a Saxony or a Poland had earlier. *All* the major Powers did this. So did such minor Powers as Belgium, Norway, and Sweden (*Annuaire Statistique de la Belgique* 1895; Woytinsky and Woytinsky 1955; *Norges Offisielle Statistikk* 1969: table 234; Therborn 1978: 114–6).

The similarity is striking. Minor Powers were slightly less militaristic than major ones, whereas U.S. total government was somewhat less militaristic and its central government much more militaristic than among the European Great Powers. But these are the only significant differences. There is little support here or in the personnel statistics given later for the frequently expressed notion that the Austrian, German, and French states were somehow uniquely oversized. I quoted Marx earlier on France, Kennedy (1988: 217) argues thus on nineteenth-century Austria, and Bruford (1965: 98–9) and Blanning (1974: 11–15) argue thus on German states of the eighteenth century. Neither fiscal nor personnel data deal kindly with such stereotypes.

I also qualify Davis and Huttenback's (1986) contention, repeated by O'Brien (1988), that in the late nineteenth century, British imperial military commitments were peculiarly draining. Per capita British expenses were the highest, but so were its civil state expenses. Britain was the richest European country and could afford both, as Kennedy (1989) also observes. As a proportion of GNP, neither British civil nor military expenses differed significantly from those of other European Great Powers. By 1910, military expenses as proportions of GNP ranged from 4.1 percent in France, about 2.9 percent in Germany, 2.8 percent in Britain, to 2.7 percent in Austria, with the United States trailing at 1.2 percent.[1] France (like Russia) was straining its economic resources to maintain its major-power status, whereas hemispheric isolation eased the pressure on America. These are the only deviations from a major-power norm.

---

[1] These figures are not dissimilar to Hobson's (1991) calculations of military expenditures as a percentage of national income: France 4.0 percent, Germany 3.3 percent, Britain 3.0 percent, the U.S. 1.1 percent, and with Russia in the range of 3.5 percent ot 3.8 percent.

We have seen two great sea changes in the life of the modern state. A massive militarist state had arrived in the eighteenth century, metamorphosing into a diamorphous civil-military state over the late nineteenth. Eighteenth-century states had been the first to thoroughly penetrate their territories – with networks of recruiting officers and tax assessors and collectors. Although these remained, they were no longer simply the "state" but, rather, shared state institutions with a host of civilian officials.

The scope of the state

The shift of expenditures (and also of personnel) from military to civil activities looks uncommonly like a widening state scope (as Grew 1984 emphasizes). Which civil functions were growing? The data are not easily comparable at this level of detail. I can be semi-systematic only for the period 1870–1911. Fortunately this is when almost all civil growth occurred.

The traditional war-dominated state had also fulfilled three main civil functions. (Chapter 4 shows that it also generated much particularistic local legislation.) Its heart had been the household and court of the monarch; its sinews, the fiscal apparatus necessary to support its military activities; and its head, the administration of law and order. In the mid-eighteenth century, these three disbursed more than 75 percent of the small civil expenditures of the Austrian, French, and British states. (We lack a Prussian breakdown, and the United States did not yet exist.) Yet Table 11.5 shows that these had declined by 1910 to between 5 percent and 20 percent of civil expenses, a remarkable change. After 1870, they increased in money terms (though not in France) but not in real or relative terms. There may actually have been fewer revenue collectors in 1911 than in 1760; royal households and courts were also smaller – and abolished in the United States and France; and though civil police forces were now increasing substantially, legal officials were not.

Table 11.5 shows that these traditional state functions had been overtaken everywhere by two principal growth areas, education and transport, followed by two lesser ones, postal and telegraph services and "other economic services" – principally environmental activities and agricultural and industrial subsidies. This was remarkably similar in all countries, although the division of functions between central and local-regional government differed considerably.

British increased central expenses were principally adjuncts to the growth of discursive literacy – education, post office, and telegraph. By 1901, these contributed 70 percent of total civil expenditure.

Table 11.5. *Percentage increase in civil expenditure items, 1870–1910, and their percentage contribution to total state budget in 1910*

	Austria Central		France Central		Germany All Government		Great Britain All Government		United States All Government	United States State Government
	Inc.	Cont.	Inc.	Cont.	Inc.	Cont.	Inc.	Cont.	Cont.	Inc.
Administration/Law and order	11	6	(33)	14	42	21	21	6	11	183
Education	67	3	429	9	248	19	531	19	18	400
Other welfare			70	3	151	10	152	8	5	432
Transport	398	29	34	9	89	11	338	12	17	238
Other economic services	14	2 }	83	2 }	188	2	385	14	13	
Postal and telegraph	74	6 }					259	8	8	
Other		14		1		4		0	8	

Note: Bracketed figure indicates decrease.

Sources: See also Table 11.1.

Austria: Wysocki 1975: 230–41. Figures for the Austrian *Reichshalf*. The large "other" category derives from the incomplete nature of Wysocki's presentation. I suspect that most "other expenses" were disbursed by the Ministry of Finance to various other departments.

Great Britain: Period covered is 1880–1910: Figures only available for period from 1880 (for some items 1884) to 1910 and for U.K. central government plus local government for England and Wales. Hence those figures will slightly overstate percentage contribution of items primarily provided by central government (i.e., postal services). They also understate administrative costs, as those are not given separately for local government.

United States: Contribution to 1913 federal, state, and local government expenses from U.S. 1976: table Y533–66. Only the increase during the period 1870–1900 at state government level is available – calculated from Holt 1977.

Local-regional expenditure was led by both symbolic and material communications, education and highways. In French budgets, education, postal and telegraph services, and roads, bridges, and docks also predominated; in American budgets, education, highways, and postal services led, only the postal service being a federal responsibility. Among the individual American states by far the biggest expansion was in education (Holt 1977).

In Germany, education was again the largest area of growth, followed by state subsidization and ownership of various enterprises, including railways. Here railways played a distinctive role in the largest government in the country, the Prussian regional government, absorbing just under half its total expenditure (and rather more of its revenue, as we see later). Railways absorbed the largest part of the Austrian civil budget, backed (as in Germany) by expenditure on other state and private enterprises. A similar pattern emerges among minor Powers: In Norway and Belgium, railways and other state-directed enterprises and education led. Remember these are *gross* expenditures; nationalized industries also brought in revenue, often profits. I consider this later.

These budgets reveal three forms of growth: the first universal, the other two more variable – more variable than Grew (1984) acknowledges:

1. The principal growth everywhere was in what I term *infrastructural* state functions (as does Wysocki 1975 commenting on Austrian growth). The infrastructures enabled states to extend material and symbolic communications throughout their territories. In fiscal terms this was easily the biggest, most universal extension of state function during the period.

2. Yet states varied significantly in the extent to which they *nationalized* material infrastructures and resources, especially railways. Britain, the United States, and France did not, though they regulated and often subsidized them; France owned the track, though not the rolling stock; other states ran railways and some ran many other enterprises too.

3. Table 11.5 also picks up the variable beginnings of *the welfare state*, especially in Germany. Local government had long provided poor relief (whose overall level is generally obscured by inadequate surviving records). Some central governments had long provided welfare for military veterans (whose level is obscured by my presentation of the data). Now central states were starting to provide the first rights of social citizenship.

Chapter 14 analyzes and explains these three increases in civilian scope. But let me here make a preliminary point: At least compared to the historic civil functions of the state, they might be quite popular, consensual extensions of scope, at least among most actors enjoying political power in this period. Of the old state functions, armies and law and order had contained considerable domestic militarism; armies and navies were also used abroad for the private glory of the ruler and old regimes; and court spending was for their private consumption. But new infrastructural spending could be plausibly claimed as useful for economic and military development alike; while welfare spending might supposedly contribute to the well-being of the people as a whole. The greater scope of the modern state might be more consensual than the lesser scope of the traditional state. I discuss this argument in Chapter 14. But of course, consensus would depend on how it was paid for.

Revenue and representation

Government revenues have already figured prominently in my narrative of political struggles, as they did in Volume I.[2] Attempts to increase or rationalize revenues caused revolution in France and America, national revolts in Austria, and reform in Britain; while Prussian ability to make do with traditional revenues enabled it to minimize both reform and revolution. At the end of the eighteenth century and the beginning of the nineteenth, politics *was* fiscal struggles, as it had been for centuries.

This intense fiscal-political relation weakened considerably during the nineteenth century. As we have just seen, a largely peaceful century plus the expansion of the capitalist economy reduced the fiscal strain. States needed proportionately less revenue than they had earlier (as Webber and Wildavsky 1986: 207 also note). Extracting it usually brought mutters, not howls, of principled protest (except in troubled Austria). Because the pain eased, something occurred that would have surprised earlier revolutionaries and reactionaries alike. Party democracies proved more amenable to this lower level of revenue extraction than monarchies. Parliaments could scrutinize accounts constitutionally presented to them, agree that certain moneys were required, debate alternatives, and vote the revenue. Representation made moderate revenue extraction more consensual. Monarchs

---

[2] The best general history of state revenues is given by Webber and Wildavsky (1986). Their chapters 6 and 7 discuss this period. See also Ardant (1975) and Woytinsky and Woytinsky (1955: 713–33). However, all their revenue figures are less comprehensive and reliable than those given here. Hobson (1991) gives the best comparative analysis of revenue for the period 1870–1914.

Table 11.6. *Percentage of state revenue coming from direct and indirect taxation and state property, 1760–1910*

Year	Austria			Great Britain			France			Prussia			United States		
	Dir.	Ind.	S.P.	Dir.	Ind.	S.P.	Dir.	Ind.	S.P.	Dir.	Ind.	S.P.	Dir.	Ind.	S.P.
1760	53	35	12	26	69	4	48	45	7						
1770	48	33	19	16	70	4									
1780	41	37	23	20	71	5	41	49	10						
1790	27	36		18	66	9	35	47	18						
1800	29	45		27	52	12									
1810	30	42		30	57	11									
1820	44	50	6+	14	68	16	40	22	38	36	33	30	10	62	26
1830	39	45	16	10	73	17							5	71	21
1840	25	49	29	8	73	19	c30			24	34	41	18	42	37
1850	29	44	22	18	65	16	c28			22	32	46	23	58	20
1860	27	42	35	18	64	16	c23						26	54	18
1870	35	30	26	26	59	12	26	31	44	20	24	55	26	58	16
1880	32	31	37	25	61	16	21	38	41	17	25	58	15	67	17
1890			26	50	18	18	36	42	8	30	62	16			
1900	28	20	42	27	47	22	21	36	43	7	28	65	64	20	
1910	28	29	43	(44)	(36)	(17)	22	33	45	9	22	69	16	58	26

Notes: Austrian, British, and French figures only for central government. Prussian and U.S. figures combine central and regional government figures as explained in the text and in Appendix Tables A.6 and A.12. For the U.S. states, business taxes have been included in direct taxes. British figures for 1910 actually 1911. The 1910 figure is also given in Appendix Table A.7.
Sources: See tables for individual countries in Appendix Tables A.6–A.12.

had to live under more particularistic restraints, accepting the yields of time-honored taxes and the tax exemptions of their political allies. In theory they could tax as they liked, but in practice – as I have emphasized throughout – monarchy involved continuous factional negotiation. Perhaps monarchies would remain more trapped in the politics of fiscal crisis than party democracies. But salvation came from an unexpected source.

Table 11.6 reveals the overall trend in the sources of ordinary gross revenues extracted by central states. Three preliminary points should be made:

1. "Gross" means that, wherever possible, the costs of collection have been added to the profit yielded by a revenue source (which is net revenue). This means that sometimes I have deviated from more commonly used statistics – for example, adding total expenditures of the U.S. Post Office to profit, which alone appears in the usual sources for U.S. revenue statistics.

2. "Ordinary" means I have excluded all loans (and the occasional surplus held over from previous years) from the calculation. The exclusion of loans is far from ideal, but source data on loans vary greatly among countries and are often incomplete. Nonetheless, the available loan data do reveal a trend: Loans were more frequent in the early part of the period because wars were more frequent. They revived during the financing of the midcentury railway boom, and then declined, appearing only at times of crisis (more frequent in Austria than elsewhere). The borrowing and issuing of money – now usually paper money – became less an ad hoc resort to moneylenders, wealthy foreign allies, and coinage debasement than a systematic, conscious attempt to finance expenditure through mild inflationary expansion. The policy indicated limited consciousness of the existence of an economic "system" and (along with tariff policy) a minimal sense of state economic responsibility. As long as the economy grew, which it usually did, the policy worked quite well at providing moderate sums of money painlessly. Hence Table 11.6 omits another minor, but nonetheless useful, fiscal painkiller.

3. Although my Austrian, British, and French data are straightforward, American and Prussian-German data present problems. The United States and Germany (after 1871) had federal regimes in which specific revenues were constitutionally transferred to the central government – almost entirely specified customs and excise taxes. Yet their regional governments drew from the varied resources found at all levels of government in other countries. Therefore, comparing the central-government revenue sources of Germany and the United States with those of the other countries would produce entirely artificial results.

We should also include data from their local-regional governments. In Germany my solution in Table 11.6 is to continue counting Prussian revenue data after 1871 (when Prussia became one of the *Länder* regional governments of the new Reich) and add to this the estimated Prussian contribution to the revenue of the federal Reich state. These two sums are separated in Appendix Table A.9. Prussia was, after all, the relevant state before 1871 and it still comprised almost two-thirds of Germany afterward. In the United States there was no individual state government as dominant as Prussia, so I have calculated per capita figures for states whose revenues are known and added them to the federal government's. Some estimated aggregation has been involved here, as in the early part of the period not all states preserved their revenue accounts. Details are given in Appendix Tables A.11 and A.12. These two levels of government in Prussia-Germany and the United States roughly correspond to central government in the other countries.

Each country has its own distinctive combination of revenues. There is no simple general explanation of differences. Level of economic development does not predict revenue sources. Representative state crystallizations help explain one revenue preference – monarchies preferred "state property" – but industrializing regimes apparently had choices and diverse influences entered into them. The most common overall pattern, with the United States deviating, is that taxation declined as a proportion of overall revenue as revenue from state property increased. In Austria, France, and Prussia, direct taxes fell dramatically; indirect taxes, far less so. In Britain and the United States, direct taxes fluctuated around a moderate norm, and indirect taxes declined slightly (only marginally in the United States). I consider the three revenue types in turn:

1. *Direct taxation* went through three modern phases, dominated by land taxes, wealth taxes, and finally (but only after our present period) by income tax. Land taxes had long been the staple direct tax, levied on the overall size and locally assessed value of land. Landowning notables had assessed themselves and their local peasants. In the more commercial Britain and the United States, flourishing land markets meant value could be assessed with some accuracy. All state elites were deeply embedded in their landowning classes and could not easily wriggle free of their control on an issue that affected so directly their economic interests. With industrialization, landowners' cooperation and peasant submissiveness declined. They protested it was unfair for agriculture to fund the state while industry escaped lightly. Notable parties warned ominously of peasant insurrection. They were heeded. British land taxes were abolished in 1816. Less advanced economies

continued longer with land taxes, but at lower rates of extraction – as with Austria's main land tax, the military contribution. States now had to turn elsewhere for major revenue.

They turned to taxes on external manifestations of wealth, such as houses and industrial buildings. Taxes on luxuries like carriages and servants were experimented with in the late eighteenth century, but the yield was hardly worth the high assessment costs. The French revolutionaries radically extended wealth taxes into what became later known as *les quatres vielles*, unchanged from 1799 to World War I. "The four old ones" were taxes on real property, on the rental value of lodgings, on commercial and professional license fees, and on the numbers of windows and doors in real property. Other states improvised on these models, but without a revolution they could exact less from those in whom they were so embedded. Around 1900, Britain, France, and Germany added inheritance taxes, levied with the aid of probate documents. The United States developed corporation taxes, especially on corporations that benefited from state regulation, like railroads and insurance. At maximum, in France, wealth taxes might generate about 20 percent of revenue. Other countries got far less. This was no major solution to their needs.

Unlike most historians of taxation (e.g., Webber and Wildavsky 1986: chapter 6), I skip quickly over the income tax because it contributed little to overall revenue. American Civil War politicians had high hopes for the income tax, but it yielded little and was then declared unconstitutional. Only after 1911 did it begin to have a permanent revival. British governments were rife with income tax schemes, from Pitt's 1799 scheme on (Levi 1988: chapter 6). At the height of the Napoleonic Wars, it provided almost 20 percent of total revenue. It was abandoned in 1816, modestly revived by Peel in 1842, intermittently expanded thereafter, and imitated across Scandinavia and Germany.

But income taxes yielded little, being really modest extensions of wealth taxes. They were levied at low rates only on some wealth sources and only on income above quite high levels. Income taxes were self-assessed; taxpayers filed their own worth to local commissioners under oath. This had worked during the Napoleonic Wars, when propertied classes felt they were fighting for their own "nation," but the practice could not be sustained in peacetime. An income tax was also difficult to assess. It could not be deducted "at source," except from government employees, until formally accounted waged and salaried employment predominated. Most people could not be assessed because they had no regular, formally recorded income. Income taxes were levied on only a minority of households in almost every country

(Denmark appears exceptional) until after World War I (Kraus 1981: 190–3).

Table 11.6 shows that only Britain and the United States maintained their level of direct taxation through most of the period. But their initial level was quite low. As the other countries' levels dropped, all except for Prussia ended, in 1910, with fairly similar levels, in the range of 16 percent to 28 percent of total revenue. But if we continue forward one more year, to 1911, we can see British direct taxes suddenly surge from 27 percent to 44 percent of total revenue. This surge was contributed by Lloyd George's radical extension of income tax and inheritance tax, a conscious attempt, the first since the French Revolution, to soak the rich. The Liberal party represented a mixed class-religious-regional constituency favoring redistributive politics, financing growing expenditures with progressive direct taxation rather than with regressive indirect taxes deriving from tariffs or sales taxes (Hobson 1991). American Progressives sought similar reforms, though as yet without success.

A reformist regime strategy was just emerging from some party democracies, embodying redistributive income taxes, later to dominate government theory, if not always government practice. Income tax became a potent form of social redistribution as well as of state revenue when its actual collection was both bureaucratized and legitimated. This was to happen during and after World War I, indicating considerable growth in state infrastructural powers.

But with this exception, direct taxes were not popular among nineteenth-century states. Society was no longer agrarian, but it was not yet industrial. Simple forms of direct taxation on agriculture were yielding less, and industry could not be milked, because it had not yet brought sufficient accounted waged and salaried employment. Moreover, during industrialization direct taxation was technically easier on the rich, but the rich controlled the state and were reluctant to tax themselves.

2. Could regimes turn to *indirect taxes*, the traditional regressive mainstay of agrarian states, passing the burden of taxation from those in whom they were embedded? Customs and excise-sales taxes were levied on goods in visible transit and at borders, ports, and marketplaces where even agrarian states had possessed a measure of infrastructural power. But even here levying techniques remained simple and particularistic. Throughout, at least half of indirect taxes came from a handful of goods, usually salt, sugar, tobacco, and alcohol. The last two taxes were (and still are) also legitimated by moral disapproval of vice, so were easier to impose. Such taxes were usually supplemented by more general customs revenues, especially on

imported foodstuffs. Indirect taxes thus fell disproportionately on subsistence items and on fairly universal drugs like alcohol and tobacco. They were regressive, especially hard on the urban poor. Eighteenth-century states were fiscal reactionaries, especially commercially buoyant states like the Netherlands and Britain, deriving 70 percent of revenue from indirect taxes (Mathias and O'Brien 1976). But the revolutionary decades taught propertied "peoples" to fear "populace" rioting against high prices on subsistence items. This spurred the successive hikes in income tax during the Napoleonic Wars. Reminded again in 1848, ruling classes eased the burden for good. Indirect taxation declined everywhere.

So were states caught in a more intense version of their traditional fiscal dilemma – to alienate their propertied supporters or their excluded populaces, to risk coup from within or revolution from below? Luckily, however, two solutions were at hand, the relative decline of total expenses and the growth of a third type of revenue.

3. *State property* consisted of revenue derived either from royal or from nationalized property or from selling government privileges and monopolies. Traditionally, such property had largely consisted of royal-domain land, supplemented by legal fees and the sale of privileges. These items declined greatly in relative (sometimes also in absolute) terms, although the U.S. federal government benefited during the mid-nineteenth century from its unique ability to sell off what it called "virgin" land – Indians simply were not counted as landowners.

But *regalian rights* could be modernized and extended. Fees could be charged and monopolies and privileges granted and then supposedly "regulated" over an expanding range of economic and professional services, from banking, insurance, and transportation to medical, architectural, and legal services. The state's cut was solemnized with an array of seals and stamps. Such revenue sometimes overlapped with direct taxes on corporations (making my allocation of a revenue item to one or the other category, direct taxes or state property, occasionally rather arbitrary). Other forms of state property are easier to distinguish. The state's postal monopoly could generate a profit. Then we must add the traditional peculiarity that private property had only ruled "above ground," as it were. The crown's regalian rights had included a share in the profits of mines and ports. Expanding mining and shipping brought increasing revenue, with or without outright state ownership. State roads, canals, and especially railways also generated tolls and fares. Canals dominated the revenue of some U.S. states in the early nineteenth century; railways were significant almost everywhere later. Most of these new or expanded state functions were useful services, noncontroversial, even popular. On the revenue side they had the advantage that they might pay for themselves and even turn a profit.

All states derived revenue from their property, but to different degrees. States benefiting most owned and ran railroads and other industries (usually mines and other communications industries). Railroads were the biggest money spinners, and Prussia was their main exploiter, taking over virtually all private railroads in the early 1880s. In 1911, Prussia drew no less than 58 percent of its own account revenue and 47 percent of total revenue (including its Reich contribution) from its ownership of the railways. Fremdling (1980: 38) observes that the Prussian state was probably the biggest entrepreneur in the world, yet had a statist conception of "profit." Freight and passenger rates were influenced by its fiscal-political goals, especially to evade direct or indirect taxation that involved negotiations with the Prussian or Reich legislative authorities.

The United States and Britain depended least on state property. It is difficult to know whether their laissez-faire economic philosophy or their party democracy accounted for this. The latter meant they had no political preferences among revenue sources, as all levies, including those from state property, required the assent of parliaments. It was otherwise in the two monarchies and (to a lesser extent) in more statist France. In Prussia choice of revenue was always as political as technical. As Richard Tilly (1966) emphasizes, direct and indirect taxation and borrowing implied consent from some organized body in civil society, which the regime preferred to avoid. State property offered "insulated" fiscal resources. But the Austrian regime failed to achieve this, in the late 1850s being forced to sell much of its railway network for cash. Autocratic Russia achieved greater revenue insulation: By 1910, a third of revenue came from railways and a third from its monopoly over liquor sales (Hobson 1991).

State property had broad appeal in monarchies. To the state elite it offered potentially autonomous fiscal resources; to political parties it appeared to offer less fiscal pain than taxes. Here representative crystallizations do predict: Party democracies had no political preferences for one type of revenue over another. Other regimes preferred, and sometimes attained, state property revenue because it provided insulated power from civil society. Monarchy had found tax relief.

In this period, states eased away from the fiscal crises that had fueled representative struggles for many centuries. Mainly at peace, with booming economies, and able to inflate the currency mildly, they were asked to perform new state functions that often could pay for themselves and sometimes could make large profits. The drive for representation was not at an end. With commercial and industrial capitalism generating extensive classes, how could it be? But it had lost its traditional fiscal bite. It would find new bites, but in the meantime the late nineteenth century provided tax relief on a world-historical scale.

Civil and military personnel and bureaucracy

The other measure of state size used in onward-and-upward stories is the number of personnel, but that presupposes we – or, indeed, the states of the period – could count them. Whether states could count is significant: If a state cannot count its officials, it cannot be remotely bureaucratic. Table 11.7 contains such personnel totals as I have unearthed. Though incomplete, especially on civil employment, they are more nearly complete than any previous compilation.

States at least knew the size of their armies. Available figures are of three types: the smallest comprise field armies and operational navies; the largest denote "paper strengths," or those notionally mobilizable; and middling numbers indicate those actually usable for all military purposes (i.e., not just fighting troops). I have tried to estimate this middling number: forces actually under military discipline at any one time – field armies, garrisons, headquarters and supply staff, and reserve troops and militias if actually mobilized ("embodied" in British source material), plus active naval personnel at sea and in port and supply establishments.

I have not used paper strengths and advance estimates for the purposes of extracting funds from parliaments. The paper strength of the *Grundbuchstand* has led to substantial overestimations of Austrian forces, and reliance on advance estimates to small inaccuracies for Britain (these are used, for example, by Flora 1983 and for the navy up to 1820 by Modelski and Thompson 1988). I exclude militias and reservists not actually called to the colors but include nationals serving abroad, including those in colonies, as well as European mercenaries financed by the state being counted. This is particularly important for eighteenth-century Britain, whose substantial Hessian and Hanoverian contingents are sometimes overlooked. But I have excluded troops recruited from colonies. Thus, for example, the total armed forces of the British Empire were greater than my figures indicate, but their proportion of the empire's population would be far less. In this case the small army necessary for keeping down India compared to its population of 200 million would give a severe underestimate of British militarism compared to that of other Western states. The reliability and validity of the military data for comparative purposes are good.

It is quite otherwise for civilian personnel. The most important finding of the research underlying Table 11.7 is that no state knew the number of public officials until the end of the nineteenth century. A thorough combing of the archives would unearth more figures comparable to these, but they would still not be figures of *total* public officials. My early figures, apart from France, total only officials countable by the central state. Where these counts were absurdly small, I have not included them. Thus Prussian government records for 1747–8 and 1753–4 enable Johnson (1975: appendix I) to construct a total of about 3,000 persons considered by the king and ministers as responsible to them. This does measure the Prussian "civil service," but it was a tiny proportion of all those who exercised public functions in Prussia. It is also far less than the 27,800 officials working on the Prussian royal estates in 1804 (Gray 1986: 21). The Prussian civil state thus consisted of a small administrative core, controllable from the center; a decentralized royal demesne administration; and an uncontrollable, unknowable but large administrative penumbra. The first two might be potentially insulated from civil society (in rather different ways); the third was thoroughly embedded. Thus it would be absurd to call the Prussian state "bureaucratic," as do most historians. (I pursue this issue further in Chapter 12.)

Austria (along with Sweden) was first to produce occupational censuses, including censuses of officials, in the mid-eighteenth century. Then, about 1800, the United States and Britain counted their central state officials. All counts were only of full-time officials above a certain level. The French figures in my table differ. They are the estimates of present-day historians as to the total numbers exercising public functions, far higher than contemporary counts for any country. If we could make such estimates for other countries we would arrive at much higher figures for them too. For example, in Table 11.7 British figures up to the 1840s do not include local land tax collectors for the very good reason that no one knew how many there were. They were guessed to be between 20,000 and 30,000, more than the total counted civil service personnel (Parris 1969: 22). In France, Finance Minister Necker estimated 250,000 people helped in the collection of revenue but guessed – admitting there was no precise record – that only perhaps 35,000 did it full time, depending on the office for their livelihood (1784: 194–7). Only with mid-nineteenth-century bureaucratization (discussed later) were most public functionaries counted.

The very concept of state employment, and consequently also of bureaucracy, is not applicable before the late nineteenth century. Who was "in" the state? The state elite comprised a few people working at the upper levels of ministries, departments, and boards in the capital, plus a few important regional officers. Courtiers were also at the heart of the state, as the court was the central political institution in most capitals. Yet courtiers were hardly state employees. They were privileged nobles and their clients, usually with hereditary embedded rights to their positions. What we might call the "local state elite" included some salaried officials, though not necessarily the highest ones. These might be part-time local notables acting as justices of the peace, *Landräte*, *maires*, and the like. Were these "in" the state? Were the members of semi-autonomous corporate organizations like the judges in the French parlements "in" the state? The universal uncertainty here is whether the embedded local notables who normally exercised the main civil functions of the state at regional and local levels were really "in" it at all. They were almost all part timers, yet their functions were central to the very existence of the state. The answer is clearly that when state administrations are so directly embedded in their civil societies, it makes only limited sense to talk of an "it" at all. The "state" was not as a totality a coherent elite, distinct from civil society. "It" did not exist.

The reach of "state employment" was also blurred at the lower levels and this lasted longer. Routine manual and clerical tasks were performed full time by casual workers, who were not at first counted in official records. The best-organized government office of the eighteenth century was probably the British Excise Department. In 1779, its central bureau employed almost 300 full-time officials. But in that year a document incidentally reveals a further 1,200 working as casual clerical labor (Brewer 1989: 69). Thuillier (1976: 11–15) notes that casual *auxiliaires* were still almost as numerous as *employés* in the Finance Ministry as late as 1899. Although by then they were counted in the French census (and so appear in Table 11.7), it is not clear when they had begun to enter the official statistics. Van Riper and Scheiber (1959: 56–9) estimate that American personnel were undercounted by perhaps 50 percent until 1816 and by about 25 percent for the rest of the period.

Undercounting also obscures the rise of female public employment. At the end of the century, most casual workers were women, but their rise remains obscure. By 1910, women composed half the public employees in Britain and the United States but represented only a quarter in France and Austria. Were these differences real? Confidence is undermined in the most detailed census of the period, that of France. This suggests a sudden discontinuity in female public employment. Having increased steadily to 333,000 in 1891, it then plummeted to 140,000 in the next census, that of 1901, before rising steadily again. This is probably an artifact, the result of suddenly excluding part-time employment and schoolteachers. Census estimates of female employment in this period are generally unreliable. Bose (1987) has reanalyzed U.S. census manuscripts for 1900 to guess that the official census figure of 20 percent for women working should be more than doubled. We cannot establish overall trends without further research on exact census procedures, work organization, and gender in each country.

My earlier figures derive from limited counting exercises – of what the two Germanic states called *Beamten* and the French called *fonctionnaires* – males of official, quasi-professional status formally employed by the state hierarchy (excluding the independent professionals counted among the *Beamten*). Then across midcentury counting ability extended across local-regional government and downward to manual and clerical workers. By about 1890, virtually all those exercising official public functions – *except* in the overlapping categories of the lowest level and female employment – were counted in censuses. They are so counted in Table 11.7. Subsequent civilian growth can be treated as largely real.

So we cannot interpret the upward civilian employment trend in the apparently obvious way (as do most writers, e.g., Anderson and Anderson 1967: 167; Flora 1984; Grew 1984). The absolute and proportionate trends seem dramatically upward. Yet the ability to count was also rising. Only after 1870 was growth almost certainly real. It was then rapid, especially in local-regional government. This reinforces the conclusion reached about expenditures. Late nineteenth-century states' civil activities grew substantially. Before then, the growth was less in real size than in the ability to count officials. Yet this ability was itself significant, reflecting a real growth in full-time state employment. States now had officials dispersed through 5 percent to 10 percent of the families of their territories, accountable to (and countable by) their superiors in local, regional, or central government. Outside of the United States, and sometimes of Austria, there was also considerable coordination between these levels. States were now potentially rooted amid a broad swathe of "state loyalists," whose distinctive politics I explore in Chapter 16.

The military trends are far clearer. Except for the United States, the highest armed forces, absolutely and in proportion to the population, appeared early, either in the Napoleonic Wars or the Seven Years' War. American military commitment was far lower except during the Civil War. Then it reached as high a proportion as that of any other country during this period: 4.3 percent of the North's population, 3.7 percent of the Confederacy, and 7.1 percent of the Confederacy excluding slaves. (Almost no slaves were in the Confederate armed

Table 11.7. *State employment for Austria-Hungary, France, Great Britain, Prussia-Germany, and the United States, 1760–1910 (as percentage of total population)*

	Civilian personnel										Military personnel				
	Central state					All levels									
Year	Austria-Hungary	France	Great Britain	Prussia-Germany	United States	Austria-Hungary	France	Great Britain	Prussia-Germany	United States	Austria-Hungary	France	Great Britain	Prussia-Germany	United States
1760	0.06		0.26			0.17					1.66	1.78	2.36	4.14	
1770	0.05										1.17	0.82	0.58		
1780							1.29				1.41	0.89	2.76	3.76	0.02
1790				0.37	0.02		1.01				1.52	0.85	0.97	3.42	0.12
1800			0.18		0.04	0.12	0.91				1.35	2.93	4.91	3.73	0.16
1810			0.24		0.05						2.38	3.66	5.30	3.88	0.16
1820			0.22		0.07								1.02	1.33	0.09
1830	0.35		0.17		0.09	0.37		0.29	0.33		1.38	1.23	1.01	1.15	0.13
1840	0.37	0.26		0.11+	0.11	0.41		0.41	0.47		1.56	1.02	1.10	1.05	0.09
1850	0.40	0.41	0.24	0.20+	0.11	0.45	0.84	0.41			1.56	1.09	1.20	1.04	0.09
1860					0.12	0.57		0.53			1.60	1.23	1.74	0.82	0.13
1870		0.60		0.55	0.13	0.50	1.11	0.46	1.15		0.86	1.66	1.14	0.98	0.07
1880		0.87	0.32		0.19	0.53	1.53	0.99	1.56		0.73	1.40	0.96	0.96	0.06
1890	1.06	0.91			0.25	2.92	1.83	1.66	1.70	1.36	0.79	1.47	0.96	1.07	
1900	1.14	1.10	0.40		0.31	3.30	1.80				0.88	1.59	1.51	1.12	0.17
1910	1.17	1.40	0.64		0.42	3.15	2.14	2.60	1.57	1.68	0.86	1.65	1.04	1.05	0.15

For sources and footnotes, see Appendix Tables A.1–A.5 containing data on the individual countries.

forces.)[3] This expansion was paralleled in civilian state employment. The federal state counted 37,000 officials in 1860. By 1861–2, the two warring states counted about 170,000 (Van Riper and Scheiber 1959: 450). In this respect, the American Civil War probably resembled World War I more than it resembled earlier European wars (which did not cause civilian personnel to rocket).

The high quality of military figures allows comparisons among states, and there were great differences among them. Prussia began the period with the largest military mobilization, then declined before partially reviving in the later German Reich. Contrary to popular liberal stereotypes, Great Britain managed the highest level of military mobilization seen in Europe during this period, in the Napoleonic Wars. Thereafter, France tended to have proportionately the largest armed forces, and Austria had the smallest among the European Powers. The decline of Austria as a Great Power was revealed in its falling behind its rivals' mobilizations, as contemporaries realized.

These figures permit two conclusions. First, they confirm, with admittedly imperfect figures, the fiscal trends. Although we cannot be certain about the nature of civilian employment, the overall growth in state employment was again less marked than the changes in its internal composition. Military employment declined greatly (except for the United States), and civilian employment grew formally over the earlier years of the period and in substance over later years. This is consistent with expenditure data. Second, taking the ability to count personnel as a minimal level of bureaucratization, this had already arrived in 1760 for the military but took at least another century for the civil state.

Provisional conclusions

I evidenced two great sea changes in the life of the modern state. Eighteenth-century states suddenly became massive in relation to their civil societies. Whether we regard nineteenth-century states as growing depends on the measure used. Expenditures grew enormously in money terms and moderately if we control for inflation and population growth. But in relation to the growth of civil society in this period, most states actually declined. The long nineteenth century was

---

[3] Civil War figures are from Coulter (1950: 68 – population); Kreidberg and Henry (1955: 95 – Union military actually serving in 1865); and Livermore (1900: 47 – Confederate military serving in 1864, assuming 80 percent of those enrolled were under arms, as in the Union forces). These are persons enrolled at any one time. Obviously the proportion enrolled at some point in the Civil War was very much higher.

dominated more by private economic growth than by state expansion – unless war dictated otherwise. Yet this conceals the second sea change – two great nineteenth-century shifts in the nature of states:

1. State functions shifted from their traditional narrow military crystallization toward three enlarged civilian roles. The greatest and most uniform provided new material and symbolic communications infrastructures. The second, found especially among monarchies and latecomer industrializers, increased state intervention in the economy. The third and latest, found at the very end of the period in some of the most advanced economies, provided modern forms of social welfare. Together these enlarged civil roles clearly mark the transition toward a new diamorphous half-military, half-civil state.

2. I have only provisionally suggested the second dramatic shift. States became largely bureaucratized during the period, but earlier in their military than their civilian administration. Bureaucratization lessened direct office embeddedness. Was this replaced by less direct, perhaps more democratic, forms of embedding? Or did bureaucratization lead to the insulation of a large number of state loyalists from civil society? Were the same patterns evident in civil and military state institutions?

The development of the modern state was a more complex, differentiated process than onward-and-upward theory suggests. There appeared a less fiscally exacting, more consensual state. But this overall trend emerged through three distinct processes: a military that was relatively declining but becoming more professionally and bureaucratically distinct and potentially insulated from civil society; increasing bureaucratization, first in the military, then in the civilian, state, and a civilian state perhaps consensually increasing its scope. These are the themes of the next three chapters, respectively.

Bibliography

This bibliography includes references cited in the appendix tables. It excludes official statistical sources adequately described in notes to the tables in this chapter or in Appendix A.

Abramovitz, M., and V. Eliasberg. 1957. *The Growth of Public Employment in Great Britain*. Princeton, N.J.: Princeton University Press.
Addington, L. 1984. *The Pattern of War Since the Eighteenth Century*. Bloomington: Indiana University Press.
Albrow, M. 1970. *Bureaucracy*. London: Pall Mall Press.
Anderson, E., and P. R. Anderson. 1967. *Political Institutions and Social Change in Continental Europe in the Nineteenth Century*. Berkeley: University of California Press.

Andic, S., and J. Veverka. 1963–4. The growth of government expenditure in Germany since the unification. *Finanzarchiv*, N.F. 23, 2.

Ardant, G. 1975. Financial policy and economic infrastructures of modern states and nations. In *The Formation of National States in Western Europe*, ed. C. Tilly. Princeton, N.J.: Princeton University Press.

Bean, R. 1973. War and the birth of the nation-state. *Journal of Economic History* 33.

Beer, A. de. 1871. *Die Finanzen Osterreiches*. Prague: n.p.

Beer, S. 1973. Modern political development. In his *Patterns of Government: The Major Political Systems of Europe*. New York: McGraw-Hill.

Blanning, T. C. W. 1974. *Reform and Revolution in Mainz, 1743–1803*. London: Cambridge University Press.

Block, M. 1875. *Statistique de la France Comparée avec les Divers Pays de l'Europe*, 2nd ed., 2 vols. Paris: Guillaumin.

Bolognese-Leuctenmuller, B. 1978. *Bevolkerungsentwicklung und Berufsstruktur, Gesundheits – und Fursorgewesen in Osterreich, 1750–1918*. Munich: Oldenbourg.

Bose, C. E. 1987. Devaluing women's work: the undercount in employment in 1900 and 1980. In *The Hidden Aspects of Women's Work*, ed. C. E. Bose et al. New York: Praeger.

Brandt, H.-H. 1978. *Die Osterreichische Neoabsolutismus und Politik, 1848–1860*. Göttingen: Vandenhoeck und Ruprecht.

Brewer, J. 1989. *The Sinews of Power*. London: Unwin Hyman.

Bruford, W. H. 1965. *Germany in the Eighteenth Century: The Social Background of the Literary Revival*. Cambridge: Cambridge University Press.

Bulow-Cummerow, E. 1842. *Preussen, seine Verfassung, seine Verwaltung, sein Verhaltnis zu Deutschland*. Berlin: n.p.

Chandler, D. G. 1966. *The Campaigns of Napoleon*. New York: Macmillan.

Church, C. H. 1981. *Revolution and Red Tape: The French Ministerial Bureaucracy, 1770–1850*. Oxford: Clarendon Press.

Corvisier, A. 1979. *Armies and Societies in Europe, 1494–1789*. Bloomington: University of Indiana Press.

Coulter, E. M. 1950. *The Confederate States of America, 1861–1865*. Baton Rouge: Louisiana State University Press.

Crafts, N. F. R. 1983. *British Economic Growth During the Industrial Revolution*. Oxford: Oxford University Press.

Czoernig, C., Freiherrn von. 1861. *Statistisches Handbuchlein fur die Oesterreichische Monarchie*. Vienna: K. K. Hof- und Staatsdruckerei.

Davis, L. E., and R. Huttenback. 1986. *Mammon and the Pursuit of Empire*. Cambridge: Cambridge University Press.

Davis, L. E., and J. Legler. 1966. The government in the American economy, 1815–1902: a quantitative study. *Journal of Economic History* 26.

Deane, P. 1968. New estimates of gross national product for the United Kingdom, 1830–1914. *Review of Income and Wealth* 3.

Deane, P., and W. A. Cole. 1962. *British Economic Growth, 1688–1959*. Cambridge: Cambridge University Press.

Delorme, R., and C. André. 1983. *L'Etat et L'économie: Un essai d'explication de l'évolution des dépenses publiques en France (1870–1980)*. Paris: Editions du Seuil.

Dickson, P. G. M. 1987. *Finance and Government Under Maria Theresa,*

1740–1780, 2 vols. Oxford: Clarendon Press.

Dull, J. R. 1975. *The French Navy and American Independence: A Study of Arms and Diplomacy, 1774–1787*. Princeton, N.J.: Princeton University Press.

Dupeux, G. 1976. *French Society, 1789–1970*. London: Methuen & Co.

Eckstein, H. 1982. The idea of political development: from dignity to efficiency. *World Politics* 35.

Fabricant, S. 1952. *The Trend in Government Activity Since 1900*. New York: National Bureau of Economic Research.

Finer, H. 1949. *The Theory and Practice of Modern Government*, 2nd ed. New York: Holt.

Fischer, F. W., et al. 1982. *Sozialgeschictliches Arbeitsbuch*. Vol. I: *Materialien zur Statistik des Deutschen Bundes, 1815–1870*. Munich: Beck.

Flora, P. 1983. *State, Economy and Society in Western Europe, 1815–1975*, 2 vols. Chicago: St. James Press.

Fortescue, J. W. 1915. *A History of the British Army*, 13 vols. London: Macmillan.

Foucault, M. 1975. *Discipline and Punish*. London: Lane.

Fremdling, R. 1980. Freight rates and state budget: the role of the national Prussian railways, 1880–1913. *Journal of European Economic History* 9.

Giddens, A. 1985. *The Nation-State and Violence*. Cambridge: Polity Press.

Goldsmith, R. W. 1987. *Premodern Financial Systems: A Historical Comparative Study*. Cambridge: Cambridge University Press.

Goldstone, J. 1991. *Revolutions and Rebellions in the Early Modern World*. Berkeley and Los Angeles: University of California Press.

Gratz, A. 1949. Die österreichische Finanzpolitik von 1848–1948. In *Hundert Jahre o Wirtschaftsentwicklung, 1848–1948*, ed. H. Mayer. Vienna: Springer Verlag.

Gray, M. 1986. Prussia in transition: society and politics under the Stein reform ministry of 1808. *Transactions of the American Philosophical Society* 76.

Grew, R. 1984. The nineteenth-century European state. In *Statemaking and Social Movements*, ed. C. Bright and S. Harding. Ann Arbor: University of Michigan Press.

Hampson, N. 1959. *La Marine de l'an II: Mobilisation de la flotte de l'Océan, 1793–1794*. Paris: M. Rivière.

Hansemann, D. J. L. 1834. *Preussen und Frankreich: Staatswirthschaftl. u. polit., unter vorzuegl. Beruecks. d. Rheinprovinz*. Leipzig: n.p.

Heitz, W. (ed.). 1980. *Quellen zur Deutschen Wirtschafts- und Sozialgeschichte im 18 Jahrhundert bis zur Reichsgrundung*. Darmstadt: Wiss. Buchgesellschaft.

Higgs, R. 1987. *Crisis and Leviathan. Critical Episodes in the Growth of American Government*. New York: Oxford University Press.

Hobson, J. 1991. The Tax-seeking State. Ph.D. diss., London School of Economics and Political Science.

Hohorst, G., et al. 1975. *Sozialgeschichtliches Arbeitsbuch. Materialien zur Statistik des Kaiserreichs, 1870–1914*. Munich: Beck.

Holt, C. F. 1977. *The Role of State Government in the Nineteenth-Century American Economy, 1840–1902*. New York: Arno Press.

Janetschek, K. 1959. Die Fiananzierung des Siebenjahrigen Krieges. Ein

Beitrag zur Finanzgeschichte des 18. Jahrhunderts. Ph.D. diss., University of Vienna.

Jany, C. 1967. *Geschichte den Preussischen Armee*, 4 vols. Osnabruck: Biblio Verlag.

Johnson, H. C. 1975. *Frederick the Great and His Officials*. New Haven, Conn.: Yale University Press.

Julien-Lafferrière, F. 1970. *Les députés fonctionnaires de France*. Paris: Presses Universitaires de France.

Kausel, A. 1979. Osterreichs Volkseinkommen 1830 bis 1913. In *Geschichte und Ergebnisse der Zentralen Amtlichen Statistik in Osterrich 1829–1979. Beitrage zur Osterreichischen Statistik*, Vol. 550.

Kennedy, P. 1988. *The Rise and Fall of the Great Powers*. London: Unwin Hyman.

1989. Debate: the costs and benefits of British imperialism, 1846–1914. *Past and Present*, no. 125.

Kennett, L. 1967. *The French Armies in the Seven Years' War*. Durham, N.C.: Duke University Press.

Kraus, A. 1980. *Quellen Zur Bevolkerungsstatistik Deutschlands, 1815–1875*. Boppard am Rhein: Harold Boldt.

Kraus, F. 1981. The historical development of income inequality in Western Europe and the United States. In *The Development of Welfare States in Europe and America*, ed. P. Flora and A. J. Heidenheimer. New Brunswick, N.J.: Transaction Books.

Kreidberg, M., and M. Henry. 1955. *History of Military Mobilization in the United States*. Washington, D.C.: U.S. Department of the Army.

Kunz, A. 1990. The state as employer in Germany, 1880–1918: from paternalism to public policy. In *The State and Social Change in Germany, 1880–1980*, ed. W. R. Lee and E. Rosenhaft. New York: Berg.

Legler, J. B., et al. 1988. U.S. city finances and the growth of government, 1850–1902. *Journal of Economic History* 48.

1990. Growth and trends in U.S. city revenues, 1820–1902. Unpublished paper, Department of Economics, University of Georgia.

Leineweber, N. 1988. *Das säkulare Wachstum der Staatsausgaben*. Göttingen: Vandenhoeck und Ruprecht.

Levi, M. 1988. *Of Rule and Revenue*. Berkeley: University of California Press.

Lévy-Leboyer, M. 1975. Histoire économique et histoire de l'administration. *Histoire de L'Administration Française Depuis 1800* 23.

Lindert, D. H., and J. G. Williamson. 1982. Revising England's social tables, 1688–1812. *Explorations in Economic History* 19.

1983. English workers' living standards during the Industrial Revolution: a new look. *Economic History Review* 36.

Livermore, T. L. 1900. *Numbers and Losses in the Civil War in America, 1861–65*. Boston: Houghton Mifflin.

Lynn, J. A. 1984. *The Bayonets of the Republic: Motivation and Tactics in the Army of Revolutionary France, 1791–94*. Urbana: University of Illinois Press.

Macartney, C. A. 1971. *The Habsburg Empire, 1790–1918*. London: Weidenfeld & Nicolson.

Maddison, A. 1983. Measuring long term growth and productivity change on a macro-economic level. In *Productivity in the Economies of Europe*, ed. R. Fremdling and P. K. O'Brien. Munich: Klett-Cotta.

Marczewski, J. 1965. Le produit physique de l'économie française de 1789 à 1913. *Cahiers de Institut de Science Economique Appliquées* I, no. 163.

Marion, M. 1927. *Histoire Financière de la France Depuis 1715*, 6 vols. Paris: Rousseau.

Markovitch, T. 1965. *L'industrie française de 1789 à 1964*. Paris: Institut de science économique appliqué.

Marx, K. 1968. The Eighteenth Brumaire of Louis Bonaparte. In *Selected Works*, K. Marx and F. Engels. London: Lawrence & Wishart.

Masson, P. 1968. *Napoléon et la Marine*. Paris: Peyronnet.

Mathias, P., and P. O'Brien. 1976. Taxation in England and France. *Journal of European Economic History* 5.

Miliband, R. 1969. *The Capitalist State*. London: Weidenfeld & Nicolson.

Mischler, E., and J. Ulbrich. 1905. *Osterreichisches Staatswörterbuch*, 2nd ed., 5 vols. Vienna: Hölder.

Mitchell, B. R. 1975. *European Historical Statistics, 1750–1970*. New York: Columbia University Press.

 1983. *International Historical Statistics. The Americas and Australasia*. Detroit: Gale Research.

Mitchell, B. R., and P. Deane. 1980. *Abstract of British Historical Statistics*, 2nd ed. Cambridge: Cambridge University Press.

Modelski, G., and W. R. Thompson. 1988. *Seapower in Global Politics, 1494–1993*. Seattle: University of Washington Press.

Morineau, M. 1980. Budgets de l'état et gestion des finances royales en France au dix-huitième siècle. *Revue Historique* 263.

Mühlpeck, V., et al. 1979. Index der Verbraucherpreise 1800 bis 1914. In *Geschichte und Ergebnisse der Zentralen Amlichen Statistik in Osterreich 1829–1979. Beitrage zur Osterreichischen Statistik 550*.

Necker, J. 1784. *De L'Administration des Finances de France*, 3 vols. Paris: n.p.

O'Brien, P. K. 1988. The costs and benefits of British imperialism, 1846–1914. *Past and Present*, no. 120.

Parris, H. 1969. *Constitutional Bureaucracy: The Development of British Central Administration Since the Eighteenth Century*. London: Allen & Unwin.

Peacock, A. T., and J. Wiseman. 1961. *The Growth of Public Expenditure in the United Kingdom*. Princeton, N.J.: Princeton University Press.

Poggi, G. 1990. *The State: Its Nature, Development and Prospects*. Stanford, Calif.: Stanford University Press.

Prochnow, P.-M. 1977. Staat im Wachstum Versuch einer finanzwirtschaftlichen Analyse der preussischen Haushaltsrechnungen, 1871–1913. Ph.D. diss., University of Munster.

Rasler, K., and W. Thompson. 1985. War making and state making: governmental expenditures, tax revenues, and global wars. *American Political Science Review* 79.

Riedel, A. F. 1866. *Der Brandenburgisch-Preussische Staatshaushalt in den likten beiden Jahrhunderten*. Berlin: n.p.

Riley, J. C. 1980. *International Government Finance and the Amsterdam*

Capital Market. Cambridge: Cambridge University Press.

1984. The Dutch economy after 1650: decline or growth? *Journal of European Economic History* 13.

1986. *The Seven Years' War and the Old Regime in France*. Princeton, N.J.: Princeton University Press.

Rothenberg, G. E. 1978. *The Art of Warfare in the Age of Napoleon*. Bloomington: Indiana University Press.

Scott, S. 1978. *The Response of the Royal Army to the French Revolution*. Oxford: Clarendon Press.

Skocpol, T. 1979. *States and Social Revolutions*. Cambridge: Cambridge University Press.

Tegeborski, M. L., de. 1843. *Des Finances et du Crédit Public de l'Autriche, de sa dette, de ses ressources financières et de son système d'imposition, avec quelques rapprochements entre ce pays, la Prusse et la France*, 2 vols. Paris: Jules Renouard.

Therborn, G. 1978. *What Does the Ruling Class Do When It Rules*? London: New Left Books.

Thuillier, G. 1976. *Bureaucratie et bureaucrates en France au XIXe siècle*. Geneva: Droz.

Tilly, R. 1966. The political economy of public finance and the industrialization of Prussia, 1815–1866. *Journal of Economic History* 26.

Todd, R. C. 1954. *Confederate Finance*. Athens: University of Georgia Press.

Turner, R. S. 1980. The *Bildungsbürgertum* and the learned professions in Prussia, 1770–1830: the origins of a class. *Histoire Sociale–Social History* 13.

U.S. Bureau of the Census. 1975. *Historical Statistics of the United States, Colonial Times to 1970*, Bicentennial Ed., Pt. 2. Washington, D.C.

U.S. Department of the Treasury. 1947. *Annual Report*. Washington, D.C.: U.S. Government Printing Office.

Van Riper, P. P., and H. N. Scheiber. 1959. The Confederate civil service. *Journal of Southern History* 25.

Veverka, J. 1963. The growth of government expenditure in the United Kingdom since 1790. *Scottish Journal of Political Economy* 10.

Vivien, A. F. A. 1859. *Etudes administratives*, 3rd ed. Paris: Guillaumin.

Vries. J. de. 1984. The decline and rise of the Dutch economy, 1675–1900. *Research in Economic History*, supplement 3.

Wagner, W. 1987. Armee-Gliederung und Aufgabenstellung, 1848–1866. In *Die Habsburgermonarchie, 1848–1918*. Vol. 5: *Die Bewaffnete Macht*, ed. A. Wandruszka and P. Urbanitsch. Vienna: Verlag de Osterreichischer Academie der Wissenschafter.

Webber, C., and A. Wildavsky. 1986. *A History of Taxation and Expenditure in the Western World*. New York: Simon & Schuster.

Weitzel, O. 1967. Die Entwicklung der Staatsaugaben in Deutschland. Ph.D. diss., University of Erlangen-Nurnberg.

Wolfe, A. 1977. *The Limits of Legitimacy: Political Contradictions of Contemporary Capitalism*. New York: Free Press.

Woytinsky, W. S., and E. S. Woytinsky. 1955. *World Commerce and Governments: Trends and Outlook*. New York: Twentieth Century Fund.

Wrigley, E. A., and R. Schofield. 1981. *The Population History of England,*

1541–1871: A Reconstruction. Cambridge, Mass.: Harvard University Press.

Wysocki, J. 1975. *Infrastructur und wachsende Staatsaufgaben. Das Fallbespiel Osterreich, 1868–1913.* Stuttgart: Fischer.

12 The rise of the modern state: II. The autonomy of military power

Chapter 11 shows that military activities dominated state functions in 1760 and still absorbed half of state resources in 1910. Militarism remained central to the modern state through 1914 – indeed, on into the twentieth century. Yet the unusual period of geopolitical and social peace dominating the West since World War II has led sociology to neglect the importance of military organization for modern society. This chapter shows the general relevance of three key issues of military power: who controlled the military, how it was internally organized, and what functions it served.[1]

1. The *control* issue can be posed in terms derived from the main theories of the state discussed in Chapter 3. Were the armed forces controlled by the dominant classes, by pluralist party democracy, or by an autonomous state elite? Alternatively, were they institutionally autonomous from all external control as a "military caste"? A single answer might not suffice for all the diverse times, places, and regimes covered here.

2. Military *organization* comprised the interaction of two hierarchies – relations between officers and men and their external relations with social classes – and two modernizing processes – bureaucratization and professionalization. It is often argued that the rise of "citizen armies" weakened both hierarchies (e.g., Best 1982). Yet military organization is essentially "concentrated-coercive." Soldiers need coercive discipline to risk their lives and take the lives of others in battle. Most armed forces are disciplined hierarchies. Because in this period most armies fought in orderly formations and campaigns, military hierarchy was unusually pronounced. Militaries were segmental power organizations, undercutting amd often repressing popular notions of class and citizenship. Yet military organization was transformed. It was bureaucratically absorbed into the state – yet this did not end its institutional autonomy. And it was professionalized while remaining entwined with classes and state bureaucracy.

3. Military *functions*, once they were monopolized by states, were

[1] General sources for this chapter were Vagts (1959), Janowitz (1960), Gooch (1980), Best (1982), McNeill (1983), Strachan (1983), Bond (1984), Anderson (1988), and Dandeker (1989).

402

what I term the state's "militarist crystallization." This was dual: geopolitical, prosecuting external war, and domestic, repressing discontent. Both remained, but they were also transformed.

Overall, I trace a surprising paradoxical trend: Despite the formal incorporation of military power into the state, despite the growth of broad national citizenship, military caste autonomy and segmental power *increased* through the period, bringing profound consequences and some danger for Western society. Why do you separate political and military power? critics have asked me (e.g., Runciman 1987 and Erik Wright in several friendly arguments). My answer is because they have been separated, autonomous, in our own era – with devastating consequences. This chapter ends as Western militaries geared themselves up for a "world-historical moment" of power demonstration.

Functions: I. Domestic militarism

Armies, rarely navies, remained essential for maintaining domestic order, yet their role changed greatly through the period.[2] I distinguish four levels of domestic repression. The least would be a state that solved public order by *conciliation, arbitration, and persuasion alone*, without any repression. Clearly, no state has ever been entirely pacific, and therefore all move occasionally or as a matter of routine to repression. The second level is *policing* in the modern sense – combating crime and disorder by a disciplined force possessing only simple weapons without recourse to a show of military force. This had rarely been a function of an army. Most eighteenth-century policing was by constables appointed and segmentally controlled by local notables. Even London, Europe's biggest city, was policed by a patchwork of parish constables. But if trouble escalated to a third level of riot, beyond the resources of constables, then regular army troops, militia, and other essentially *paramilitary* formations were called in for a show of force.

Riots were essentially demonstrations. If met by a demonstration of greater force, rioters normally dispersed. The authorities might then contemplate remedies. This was usually a ritual exchange of violences. When it did not work, there was escalation to the fourth level, of full-scale *military* repression: actual fighting and shooting, normally by regular troops. Neither regimes nor armies welcomed this state because it actually represented their failure to provide routinized order. Its instruments were also relatively uncontrollable. The behavior of rioters and soldiers once guns fired, horses charged, and sabers flailed, perhaps

---

[2] I have relied extensively in this section on Emsley's (1983) comparative study of policing.

in confined streets, could not easily be predicted. It could lead to even more disorderly outcomes – and regimes often jettisoned officials who ordered it.

Between 1600 and 1800, central states acquired more of the third and fourth levels of repression as the army took over from local notables and their retainers. Eighteenth-century absolutist regimes then added new paramilitary police organizations in their capitals and, occasionally, nationally. The most famous were the French Maréchaussée, more than three thousand men responsible to the minister of war. In the 1780s, a military police guard of more than three hundred men kept order in Vienna. These were paramilitaries whose routine presence was essentially a show of force, intended to increase general surveillance and to deter crime and disorder (Axtmann 1991). Constitutional regimes, wary of standing armies, developed militias but officered them with local gentry, loosely coordinating with the army.

The major nineteenth-century development was the emergence of municipal, regional, and national police forces with organizational abilities paralleling armies, though without their numbers, arsenals, or potential resort to the fourth level of violence. They were responsible not to army or parish but to broader civilian authorities. The British police force was at one extreme: unarmed, controlled locally-regionally by the borough and the county but coordinated from London in emergencies. Elsewhere civilian and paramilitary organizations developed alongside each other. In France the Sûreté Nationale, originally Parisian and responsible to the Ministry of the Interior, absorbed urban police forces, and the Gendarmerie developed from the Maréchaussée, armed and responsible to the minister of war. The Prussian police retained the most military flavor, though formally separate from the army and under increasing civilian control from about 1900. The U.S. Army cooperated with state militias, becoming the national guard, which in turn cooperated with local police authorities. These varied police forces and paramilitaries tended to remove armies from the third level of enforcement. Armies now specialized in the fourth level, confining themselves to serious outbreaks of organized violence, in close coordination with other authorities.

Contemporary sociologists have interpreted these developments under the influence of the two dominant and relatively pacific theories of modern times, liberalism and Marxism. They have read into them, especially into the growth of routinized policing, a more profound and essentially diffuse social transformation: the "pacification" of civil society itself through routinized policing and "internalized discipline." Foucault (1979) argued that punishment in society was transformed from authoritative, open, punitive, spectacular, and violent to diffuse, hidden, routinized, disciplinary, and internalized. His evidence concerned only prisons and mental asylums, of doubtful relevance to broader societies. Yet Giddens (1985: 181–92) and Dandeker (1989) extend his argument, arguing that broader "disciplinary power" came through the routinization and "surveillance" provided by the records and timetables of public and private administrations – the routines of factory production, offices and accountancy practices, the ubiquity of timetables, rationalized written law, the constraints of economic markets (especially the free labor contract), and the supervised routine of school instruction. Recalcitrance became disciplined into internalized compliance at the point of initial tension, before it might erupt into violence.

Giddens emphasizes the workplace, quoting Marx's comment that industrial capitalism introduced "dull economic compulsion" into class relations. This fits well with the arguments of Marxists like Anderson and Brenner that whereas historic modes of production extracted surplus labor with the help of violence, capitalism does it through the economic process itself. Violence recedes from class relations, a point also emphasized by Elias (1983) in his account of the development of the Western "civilizational process." Violence in modern society is hidden, institutionalized (though feminists insist family violence remains). We no longer count the bodies, we psychoanalyze the victims.

Neither Elias nor the Marxists have shown interest in the consequences of this for the military, but Giddens and Dandeker have. Giddens suggested that "it involves . . . not the decline of war but a concentration of military power 'pointing outwards' towards other states in the nation-state system" (1985: 192). Tilly (1990: 125) supports this, but adds the rider that no such transition has occurred in the twentieth-century Third World. Its armed forces point enormous military firepower inward against their own subjects, with few of the inhibitions shown by historic Western regimes. This differs from Western history, which, Tilly agrees, witnessed a major transformation of military power – from dual function (war/repression) to singular (war), detaching militaries from class struggle.

Is this true? Substantially, yes – but not during this period or primarily for the reasons cited by Foucault, Giddens, Dandeker, and Elias. They are right that social order in contemporary Western society – apart from American inner cities – is buttressed by far less repression than in most historic societies and that this leaves the military largely pointing outward. But this has been achieved predominantly in the *twentieth* century, due mostly to two other power achievements: political and social citizenship and the institutional conciliation of labor relations.

Though these began in this period, they were mostly attained in the twentieth century, in fact, mostly in the second half of the twentieth century. Because political and social citizenship has not been achieved in most of the Third World, this explains why militaries still point inward there.[3] The evidence will show that neither "discipline" nor the removal of the military from domestic repression had got far by 1914.

To establish a decline in overt violence, Dandeker and Giddens rely on two sources of evidence: contemporary descriptions of eighteenth-century society as characterized by petty theft, rowdyism, and unsafe highways, and the nineteenth-century reduction in common crimes of violence, evidenced, for example, by Gurr et al. (1977). Though criminal statistics are notoriously unreliable, the decline was probably real (though partly offset by a probable increase in nonviolent crimes against property; Emsley 1983: 115–31). Advanced capitalist society usually is more pacified in its interpersonal relations and everyday routines than were historic societies, and one stage of this transformation began in the eighteenth and continued through the nineteenth century, as Dandeker, Foucault, and Giddens argue (Elias argues that it began much earlier). Yet common crime (my second policing level) was not the concern of the eighteenth-century army, except in backward areas of Europe with organized banditry. Theft and rowdyism were suppressed by constables, magistrates, or the retainers of local notables, or they were tolerated as the normal condition of society. Armies and militias were called in only if violence escalated to the third level, to riots requiring a show of force – principally food riots, smuggling disturbances, labor disputes, and riots against military impressment (as we saw in Chapter 4).

Tilly (1986) has provided the best evidence for what then happened, in the case of France. He narrates not the decline of collective protest but its twofold transformation, from bread riot to labor strike, and from local to national organization – responses to the development of capitalism and national state. In the twentieth century, culminating in the 1950s, both became institutionalized so that labor union and political party agitation did not require suppression by the regular army. But before 1914 it was different. Strikers and political protesters were met by soldiers with the same frequency experienced earlier by bread rioters. More than 1,000 protesters were killed in fights with troops in 1830, 1848, and 1871. Though no later events matched these

---

[3] That the institutionalization of labor relations in the Third World has contributed less to demilitarization of society is probably due to the fact that industrialization is more narrowly based there than in the West. The industrial working class in countries like those of Latin America is far smaller proportionately than in their historical Western counterparts.

"revolutions," Tilly says that on dozens of occasions hundreds of people seized public spaces and held them against troops for more than a day. One of the biggest occurred near the end of the period, in the worker and farmer disturbances of 1905–7. There were also coups in 1851 and 1889 (failed).

Tilly labels the nineteenth "a rebellious century" (1986: 308–9, 358–66, 383–4). French armed forces were as active in repression in the nineteenth century as in the century before 1789. On the other hand, different departments of state also engaged in the opposite extreme, of conciliation. As we shall see in Chapter 18, French prefects and subprefects, aided at the end of the century by the Ministry of Labor, were attempting to defuse labor disputes before they escalated into violence. French domestic militarism was diversifying.

French history is distinctive, but its violence is not. In the United States, up to 1860, the army's main task was to kill Indians; then it fought a civil war that smoldered on in an occupation of the South while the large, reconstituted national guard switched from suppressing Indians and slaves to occupying the South and then to breaking up strikes and urban riots (Hill 1964: chapter 4; Dupuy 1971, esp. 76). Goldstein (1978: 1–102, 548) documents "massive and continuous" repression of American labor from 1870 to the 1930s, including repeated deployment of the national guard, backed where necessary by the army. It peaked in the 1880s and 1890s and then declined a little. But this was because regime and employers had devised a dual strategy for labor – repress broad and socialistic protest, conciliate the sectional protests of skilled workers (see Chapter 18). American domestic repression remained military and paramilitary, if becoming more selective. Only at the very beginning of the twentieth century were other government agencies beginning labor conciliation.

Austrian violence remained virtually unchanged. The army stationed garrisons in all major towns and repressed national disturbances in every decade. Though the Revolution of 1848–9 was not repeated, protest and repression did not decline, and the regime increasingly relied more on the regular joint army than on less reliable provincial paramilitaries (Deak 1990: esp. 65–7). There was little genuine labor arbitration by either the Austrian or Prussian-German states. Moreover, their militaries could also intervene in civil matters. German garrisons and citadel towns were the principal repressors of rioting right into the twentieth century. From 1820 on, local German army commanders had the right to intervene arbitrarily, without being asked by civilian authorities (though the two normally acted together). This culminated in the notorious Zabern incident of 1913, where a local colonel arbitrarily dispersed demonstrators and jailed their leaders. This stirred public outcry and the colonel was court-martialed – but he was acquitted and arbitrary military power upheld. There was no secular decline in German army intervention. In 1909, soldiers with machine guns, live ammunition, and fixed bayonets were still intimidating striking miners. Yet, by now, the German army rarely had to use much actual violence. Mostly a rather ritualized show of what was essentially paramilitary force sufficed (R. Tilly 1971; Ludtke 1989: esp. 180–98; see also Chapter 18).

In most countries military repression continued but *along with* the growth of new police and paramilitary authorities – and in the party-democratic states also eventually along with state conciliation of class conflict. Thus armies did not routinely face intermediate disturbance levels. Riots were as common as in the eighteenth century, but regimes found more forms of repression specifically geared to the actual level of threat. Very few regimes or military commanders had ever liked charging or firing at crowds. Only in Russia did they do this at all frequently; only in the United States, with its traditions of individual and local violence, did they routinely risk this (see Chapter 18). Repressive militarism remained in its three traditional forms – primarily a *presence*, secondarily a *show*, and only rather rarely actual *violence* – but it now had added a wider repertoire.

In fact, the British experience was the truly distinctive one, the one clear case of decline in military repression. During the eighteenth century the peacetime army, 10,000–15,000 strong, had been used repeatedly in riots, the last major occasion being the Gordon riots of 1780, when an astonishing 285 persons were killed. The army was kept ready for repression during the French wars, most of its barracks no longer in the smuggling areas but distributed for use against the French and domestic radicals. It was joined by two gentry militias, the Volunteers and the Yeomanry. Rioters were then suppressed by soldiers in 1816, 1821, and 1830–32 and Chartists between 1839 and 1848. Ireland was throughout a rebellious colony with an army of occupation. Thereafter (somewhat later in Ireland) there was relative peace until a series of strike waves between 1889 and 1912. But these were now handled differently.

From the 1840s on, the British authorities could also turn to borough and county police forces. If the large Manchester force (one constable per 633 of the population in 1849) could not cope with local strikers, the London Metropolitan Police and the Home Office could send ten times that number of policemen in a day. Though the army was used at least twenty-four times, probably more, between 1869 and 1910 (Emsley 1983: 178), most strikers were confronted by shows of strength from the boys in blue, not the redcoats (by now decked in khaki).

Military repression was still in evidence, but it had declined since 1848.

It was also substantially supplemented by the most substantial state agencies for the conciliation of labor disputes (see Chapter 17). Why had this unique change from the military to policing (plus a conciliation common to the party-democratic states) occurred in Britain, and what kind of pacification did it represent? There were three main causes:

1. Capitalist urbanization stimulated the fears of propertied classes, unable to control their localities by traditional segmental patronage power, bolstered by occasional resort to the army. They had to swallow their fear of centralized "despotic" police forces. They did this earlier than in other countries because the dislocations of urban, then industrial, capitalism uniquely coincided with the politicized rioting of the French wars and reform period through to Chartism (see Chapters 4 and 15). Moreover, a severe threat had already arisen in eighteenth-century Ireland. There the Protestant ascendancy had swallowed its fears of centralization to devise the police force that became the model for mainland Britain (Axtmann 1991).

2. The military itself wished to withdraw from repression, believing it damaged the troops' morale and interfered with Britain's imperial commitments. Britain had proportionately the smallest, most professional home army. It had no border regiments or other forces specializing in low-intensity pacification tasks that could easily switch to riot control.

3. The collapse of Chartism in 1848–9 demoralized radical protesters and enabled the new police forces a period to establish themselves efficiently at the lowest level of threat, dealing with crime, before they were asked to move up to riot control. The new system worked. By the time of the London dock strike of 1889, the police had developed the "keep moving, please" tactics that enabled shouting and marching to continue without culminating in head-on confrontation (McNeill 1983: 187–8). Now the regime could avoid the destabilizing, delegitimizing effects of all-out violence, freeing the army to defend the empire.

Did the new policing also work because of diffuse internalized "discipline" sweeping society? Giddens correctly stresses the nineteenth-century development of administrative and communications power capacities. But this was more authoritative than diffuse and *both* sides could use it. While fairly spontaneous local violence might reduce, organized class war might increase – as in the Chartist period. Thereafter, authoritative organization benefited the sectional trade unionism emerging out of the ruins of Chartism. The police also gained authoritative powers, responding swiftly and with flexible numbers in shows of force adequate to the intermediate level riot. The gun and cavalry charge were abandoned with relief.

There are few signs that potential rioters were being "disciplined" in the Foucault-Giddens sense, or exploited by purely economic means, in the Marxian sense. Chartists experienced physical and organizational defeat (Chapter 15 explains this); farm workers were cowed by declining numbers and transportation into local, covert protest (Tilly 1982); capitalism provided adequate food to the towns, reducing bread riots; and skilled workers turned to sectional, responsible protest. (See Chapter 15.) These causes stem from the balance of authoritative organized power, not from more diffuse "discipline." Because other regimes lacked such organizational superiority over their domestic opponents, they needed more military force to back up their emerging police.

Looking at repression historically and by level generates more complex conclusions than the single world-historical transformation suggested by Foucault, Giddens, and the Marxists. We must include the particularities of military and police organization and of regime strategies, neglected in their accounts. Actually, the earlier period, from about 1600 to 1800, had probably seen the greater transformation, when state-controlled armies became primarily responsible for the second as well as the third level of repression. Yet armies later became recognized as inappropriate instruments, especially in cities and when gun technology began to deliver too little show and bang, too much death, on crowds. We shall see later in the chapter that war was also becoming more professional, more concerned with concentrated firepower, less with sabers.

War was becoming more *different* from domestic repression. Regimes saw that the two military functions were diverging in tactics, weapons, barracking, and discipline. This threatened army efficiency in what had always been its primary external role. Thus it was absolutist regimes – closer to the military, not ruling with greater diffuse discipline – which moved first to police their biggest cities (Chapter 13 shows that they moved first toward more bureaucratic administration in general) and to institute paramilitary national police. Britain moved to police forces, partly from its Irish experience, partly because its army was the most stretched by its two roles.

Then a second transformation began about 1800, as the inappropriateness of the military instrument was exposed by the seditions of the revolutionary period and industrialization. A three-part division of labor (which still exists) appeared in the first half of the nineteenth century, as police, the paramilitary, and the regular army coped with ascending levels of threats to order. Two "pacifications" then furthered this transformation. The lowest level threat, ordinary crime, probably began to diminish, partly owing to the authoritative efficiency of the new police forces and perhaps, also, to broader social and disciplinary processes of the Giddens-Foucault-Marxist type. Second, and later, higher force levels were needed less as citizenship and the conciliation of labor relations developed, though this varied among regimes. Goldstein (1983) shows that, after 1900, the military was still involved everywhere, but its interventions were declining in the more constitutional, party-democratic regimes of northwest Europe.

Goldstein notes the particular effect of a "safety valve" without which things might have been worse: forty million young, vigorous, perhaps discontented Europeans departed for the New World between 1850 and 1914. But he attributes most of the decline in repression to politics. Regimes had promoted industrialization, literacy, and urbanization, yet this created a dissident petite bourgeoisie and working class. Eventually, after fifty years of turmoil and repression, regimes changed tack and began to conciliate selectively and incorporate middle- and working-class demands compatible with good order. Military repression would now be reserved for genuine extremists – a selective policy with profound implications for working-class movements (explored in Chapter 18). Some decline in military repression occurred in the three party-democratic regimes once they institutionalized political citizenship and labor relations. The British middle classes were incorporated in midcentury; the French republic and the American Union were entrenched rather later. Britain's industrial relations were the most institutionalized, then the French, but the major changes only occurred after the war (see Chapters 17 and 18). As Germany and Austria had not solved their representative, nor Austria its national, crystallization, their militaries were required as before.

Let me also draw attention to the biased nature of my own sample of states. They were all major Powers, wielding more military force than minor Powers. Most minor Powers of the West have shared many similarities – low regime capacity to repress, low levels of actual repression, early transition to full representative democracy (including early woman suffrage), early institutionalization of labor relations, and early transition to welfare states. It is difficult to believe that inhabitants of Australia, New Zealand, Scandinavia, and (after 1830) the Low Countries better internalized the "coercive disciplines" of modern society than did Germans or Americans. It is more likely they had less military coercion oppressing them and so were able to achieve greater citizen rights (as Stephens 1989 argues).

Most Great Power armies still pointed inward as well as outward, but they were now supplemented by police and paramilitary organizations and a few by conciliation. If society was becoming a little more disciplined, most of the discipline was still authoritatively imposed by hierarchical coercive organizations, not diffusely internalized by the citizens themselves. In the long run the development of the modern state was to "civilianize" more of the state, reducing its domestic militarism to lower levels. More of its staff were "conventionally attired, conventionally mannered people who operate in a most un-military fashion" and who pushed brute force into the background (Poggi 1990: 73–4). But in this period civilian officials pushed the brutes into a more specialized role, alongside a specialized "semibrutish" police role and (in some cases) a few "civil" conciliators – and with the compliance of the brutes themselves. This remained true in most countries until after 1945. Most domestic militarist crystallizations had declined toward lower force levels, but domestic militarism remained.

If some social groups in some countries now complied a little more actively and voluntarily, this resulted primarily from their attaining valued citizen rights, not from unconscious routinization of modern social life. Because both the balance of authoritative powers and the attainment of citizen rights varied, so did levels and types of military repression. For their part, regimes faced no less disorder from dissidents but possessed repressive resources with greater precision than musket volleys and flailing sabers. This left most militaries able to concentrate more on external war, modifying rather than ending their dual role. Domestic military repression remained directed against varied crystallizations of classes and ethnic, regional, and religious minorities fighting for greater citizenship rights. Thus the two hierarchies of army stratification – their class composition and their officer-men relations – remained relevant to their function of domestic repression. I show later that geopolitical militarism led to caste tendencies inside the military, but this was restrained by close relations with conservatives and propertied classes in domestic repression.

Functions: II. Geopolitical militarism

War and preparation for war had long been the predominant state function. Chapter 11 shows that this remained so until the mid-nineteenth century. In the eighteenth century the threat and use of military force was an unquestioned part of foreign policy. War is not the everyday stuff of foreign policy, and diplomats often avoided it. But eighteenth-century Great Powers were at war in 78 percent of years and nineteenth-century ones in 40 percent (Tilly 1990: 72). Because war is perhaps the most ruthless competition known to human societies, there was a continuous learning process – being at war or watching one closely, learning its lessons, modernizing the military, facing a threat, going to war or closely observing it, and on and on. A regime that did not pay close attention and was not modernizing its military would not survive long. Militarism also pervaded more pacific diplomacy – negotiating alliances, royal marriages, and trade treaties. Virtually no diplomatic arrangements were entered into without considering the military balance of power and the security of one's own state. War and the military were central to state leadership and foreign policy. All states crystallized as militaristic – as almost all do today.

Who controlled their geopolitical militarism, making decisions of war and peace? Traditional practices, enduring into the late eighteenth century in absolute regimes, were very clear. Foreign policy, including war, was the monarch's own private prerogative. Frederick II of Prussia described how in 1740 he came to win Silesia – crucial in the world-historical rise of Prussia:

At my father's death, I found all Europe at peace. . . . The minority of the youthful Tsar Ivan made me hope Russia would be more concerned with her internal affairs than with guaranteeing the Pragmatic Sanction [the treaty allowing a woman, Maria Theresa, to succeed to the Austrian throne]. Besides, I found myself with highly trained forces at my disposal, together with a well-filled exchequer, and I myself was possessed of a lively temperament. These were the reasons that prevailed upon me to wage war against Theresa of Austria, queen of Bohemia and Hungary. . . . Ambition, advantage, my desire to make a name for myself – these swayed me, and war was resolved upon. [Ritter 1969: I, 19]

Subtracting the affectation from Frederick's account still leaves formidable personal discretion to conduct wars. He also names his enemies personally, another attribute of dynastic diplomacy.

This constitutional prerogative was buttressed by a second. The monarch had become commander in chief of the armed forces. Maria Theresa (r. 1740–83) was the first Austrian ruler to obtain the final seal of authority: Austrian soldiers now swore an oath of allegiance to her rather than to their individual commander. She did not lead her soldiers into battle; no more did French or British kings; and Prussian kings soon ceased to. They needed hierarchical chains of command, (described later).

How did nineteenth-century democratization fare against these monarchical prerogatives? In a word – badly. Monarchs held out successfully on the conduct of foreign and military policy. As Chapter 10 shows, when in 1867 the Habsburgs conceded substantial autonomy to the Hungarian *Reichshalf*, foreign policy was still largely reserved as Franz Joseph's prerogative and the army was *his*. He was supposed to consult over commercial treaties, but he evaded this by dismissing foreign ministers who disagreed with him. Military affairs and budgets were under his personal control in his long reign and he put them first, above domestic considerations (Macartney 1971: 565–7, 586, passim). Of course, Austria was a distinctive, gigantic protection racket actually centered on the arbitrary dynastic, military powers of the Habsburgs to defend all their squabbling peoples from greater powers around. But Habsburg powers were not untypical. In the German Reich the Prussian king remained commander in chief. He did not need to consult the Reichstag over foreign policy or war. He required the consent of other German rulers in the Reichsrat, but his dominance ensured this was mere form. In these countries (and in Russia) a vigorous monarch could exercise close control of foreign policy or delegate it to chancellors and foreign ministers with his confidence.

We might assume things changed as regimes democratized, but not so. Consider first one of the most democratic constitutional monarchies in Europe, Norway after independence in 1905. The constitution typically reserved for the royal prerogative the executive and emergency powers to mobilize troops, declare war, make peace, enter and dissolve alliances, and send and receive envoys. In all respects he formally had to consult parliament but in practice parliament seemed indifferent. The Foreign Ministry had "hardly any strong feeling that foreign policy in a democratic society also concerns the people," concludes Riste (1965: 46). Norwegian classes and other interest groups were indifferent because they were *nationally* organized and preoccupied – as we shall see was (and still is) the nineteenth-century norm.

As nation-states emerged, classes and other major interest groups became nationally confined, leaving the conduct of foreign policy to supposedly "democratic" chief executives who in this respect actually resembled the old absolute monarchs. In mostly democratic Italy, the monarch had lost most domestic powers by 1900, but not his control over diplomacy. Bosworth (1983: 97) says, "Foreign policy was a matter for the King and his closest advisers. Nationalist 'public opinion' was tiresome, although, if organized and directed, it might have positive virtues. But it must never make decisions."

Because Britain was the greatest party democracy of the age, its decision making is of special significance. Its foreign policy plus "the government, command and disposition of the army" remained royal prerogatives, as was normal in constitutional monarchies. Yet, since 1688, military implementation had been severely constrained. Parliament determined army and navy size, funding, and internal regulations. Parliamentary assent was required to bring foreign troops into Britain and to maintain a peacetime standing army (Brewer 1989: 43–4). "Ultimate" decision making in foreign policy formally rested with Parliament.

Yet *routine* foreign policy did not require the consent of Parliament unless it broke the law of the land or incurred new financial obligations (Robbins 1977a). In 1914, Parliament had to approve the declaration of war (as in France, but unlike the other combatants), but everyday foreign policy during the crisis of July-August remained largely private. The foreign secretary ranked second only to the prime minister. Parliament did not exercise much control over him. Normally a hereditary peer, he sat in the Lords, not the Commons – a deliberate device for avoiding public discussion. Commons requests for information were regularly repulsed with the formula "not in the public interest." The foreign secretary consulted regularly the prime minister and intermittently at his discretion with relevant cabinet colleagues and experienced statesmen. He rarely consulted full cabinet. A commanding figure like Lord Rosebery ran his own foreign policy (Martel 1985), a moderately lazy one like Sir Edward Grey steered its general drift and did not bother to consult "outsiders." The few persons styling each other "statesmen" communicated through letters sent between country houses and conversations in gentlemen's clubs. In liberal diplomacy the court had been replaced by the club, not by the Commons (evidence from Steiner 1969; Steiner and Cromwell 1972; Robbins 1977a; Kennedy 1985: 59–65). In contrast to this tightly knit private group, public opinion was amorphous, disunited, and difficult to bring to bear on particular issues (Steiner 1969: 172–200; Robbins 1977b). An essentially old regime executive remained insulated in foreign policy even while worker MPs were crowding into the Commons. British classes were nationally pre-occupied. They left routine foreign policy to the experts.

In the most advanced party democracy, the United States, we might expect things to be different. After all, the Revolution had been squarely aimed against such practices – and specifically at executive taxes for foreign policy without consent. Indeed, the Constitution explicitly deprived the executive of taxation powers and vested war- and treaty-making powers with Congress. However, Article II of the Constitution vested in the president all executive powers not explicitly limited in other articles. These residual powers were assumed at the time, and were confirmed by nineteenth-century Supreme Courts, to center on the routine conduct of foreign policy. In practice this meant the president could conduct his own foreign policy as long as he did not declare war, make treaties, or need monies additional to those already slushing around the administration. This still seems the situation – and was roughly agreed on by all sides during the 1990–1 run-up to the Gulf War – though it can still occasion controversy. (See the exchange between Theodore Draper and President Bush's legal adviser in *The New York Review of Books*, March 1 and March 17, 1990.)

Early nineteenth-century presidents were in practice restrained by the fact that most foreign and military issues – relations with Britain, France, Spain, Mexico, and Indians – impacted directly on the territory of North America and on the lives of American settlers and interest groups. But as the continent was filled, foreign policy turned toward more distant imperialism, away from the predominantly national (or continental) preoccupations of Americans. Executive autonomy grew. After 1900, Presidents McKinley and Theodore Roosevelt manipulated Congress and public opinion into following foreign policies that were essentially made by executive actions. In 1908, Woodrow Wilson argued that imperialism had changed constitutional practice: "The initiative in foreign affairs, which the President possesses without any restriction whatever, is virtually the power to control absolutely" (LaFeber 1987: 708, on whom this paragraph relies). Even in this, the most constitutional state, once classes and other interest groups became nationally organized, foreign policy could be dominated by a fairly insulated state executive – with the formal backing of the Constitution. Public opinion and political parties played only a small part in formulating foreign policy before World War I (Hilderbrand 1981). Foreign policy remained the private domain of a small group of notables, plus special interest groups advising the few politicians who aspired to be "statesmen" (discussed further in Chapters 16 and 21). A state elite retained routine diplomatic autonomy in party democracies as well as in semiauthoritarian monarchies.

If a crisis reared, this changed. In the United States, major decisions of war and new taxes went (and still go) to Congress. In Britain, they went (and still go) to full cabinet and were (and are) discussed there in terms of what party, Parliament, or public opinion might wear. And if war loomed, there arose the one fundamental constraint on all regimes' freedom of action: money. If even an absolutist proposed a costly foreign policy, then whoever provided taxes or loans must normally consent. Public opinion among other power actors now became important.

But control only in crises or war is limited. Diplomacy is less regulated and predictable than domestic politics. Multistate diplomacy involves autonomous states with only limited normative ties, continuously recalculating geopolitical options. The actions of one – in rattling sabers, entering a new alliance, flaunting army or fleet exercises, increasing troop numbers beyond those required to enforce an existing policy of economic sanctions or mere defense of territory, privately offering support to aggressive pressure groups of merchants or white settlers – may seem provocative to other Powers. Their reverse might indicate weakness to them. Either may set up unpredictable ripple reactions among the Powers. Regimes find that routine diplomacy boxes them into a corner in an emerging crisis, facing them with unwelcome enemies or allies, or with a Hobson's choice between backing down or acting aggressively. Secret diplomacy further restricts options.

The crisis then suddenly confronts parliaments, dominant or taxpaying classes, and public opinion with potentially devastating but restricted policy choices. As we shall see in Chapter 21, in 1914, governments generally presented only two alternatives to parliaments and public opinion – to go to war or to back down and be humiliated, a boxed-in choice we have grown used to (and which recently occurred disastrously again in the Gulf War for both the United States and Iraq). It helps explain why regimes get support for war. State elite control over routine diplomacy and military deployments thus outflanks democratic checks. In fact, chief executives, not nations or classes, remained primarily responsible for American, British, and French diplomacy, just as monarchs decided Austrian and Prussian. Constitutions and representative crystallizations mattered less in foreign than in domestic policy. Citizenship proved national, narrow, blinkered. It still is.

But monarchs and executives did not alone decide routine foreign policy. They took advice from professional diplomats. These diplomats were drawn from a narrow social base, overwhelmingly from the old regime: monarchs' kin, aristocracy, gentry, and old money capitalists (for a general discussion, see Palmer 1983). In Austria and Germany, where the old regime survived best, the diplomatic service was dominated by aristocrats into the twentieth century. Preradovich (1955) attempted a standardized comparison of the two countries from 1804 to 1918. He found that the proportions of nobles among Prussian "high diplomats" fluctuated only between 68 percent and 79 percent (ending the period at 71 percent). In Austria it fluctuated between 63 percent and 84 percent (ending at 63 percent). The trends were similar for the old nobility alone (this controls for the possibility that diplomats might have been ennobled for their services). In 1914, the German corps of ambassadors consisted of eight princes, twenty-nine counts, twenty barons, fifty-four untitled nobles, and only eleven commoners. The lower-ranking consular service was wholly staffed by commoners, though usually wealthy and from the right universities and fraternities. But of the entire 548 Foreign Ministry officials 69 percent bore titles of nobility and they monopolized higher grades. The only discernible change between 1871 and 1914 was a decline in Junkers and in titles awarded before 1800, as opposed to more western and recent nobles. Both trends resulted from a shortage of Prussian and older nobles as the service expanded, not from an attempt to open up the service. Group solidarity was enhanced by kin connections, membership in reactionary fraternity organizations, and a preponderance of Protestants and total absence of Jews (Rohl 1967: 106–8; Cecil 1976: 66–8, 76, 79–86, 174–6).

In France the old regime suffered revolutions, yet its diplomats survived. Of all the ambassadors between 1815 and 1885, 73 percent had aristocratic surnames. During the Second Empire (1851–71) about 70 percent of senior officials in the Ministry of Foreign Affairs whose backgrounds are known came from landed, banking, or higher functionary backgrounds, a higher proportion than in any other government department (Wright 1972; Charle 1980a: 154, 172). Then, finally, a decline set in: Whereas 89 percent of accredited envoys were aristocrats in the period 1871–78, only 7 percent were during 1903–14, a rather remarkable change. Unfortunately, no details are given of this cohort. I would bet they represented the Republican equivalent of aristocracy, old money, but have no evidence to hand (the unpublished study cited by Cecil 1976: 67 may give this). Throughout the period, the British Foreign Office and diplomatic service remained dominated by the old regime. It was staffed at the top by the second sons of the aristocracy and wealthy gentry, educated at top public schools (especially Eton), and increasingly at Oxbridge (Cromwell and Steiner 1972).

The United States differed little, despite having lost its aristocracy in its revolution and despite having a foreign service of rather lower prestige than that of other countries. Its diplomats and State Department represented American old money, the Eastern Establishment – perhaps its more cultured, less dynamic scions (it was claimed at the time that the ablest children went into banking). Even into the twentieth century entrants to the diplomatic corps were required to have a private income, ostensibly because the pay was low. Ilchman (1961) says that the corps was staffed with sons of old, wealthy families throughout the period. Though personal patronage was replaced by qualifying examinations, "good breeding" was still considered essential: Between 1888 and 1906, at least 60 percent had attended Harvard, Yale, or Princeton and 64 percent were from the Northeast (by then providing only 28 percent of U.S. population).

In all countries such class imbalance was defended on supposedly technical grounds: The old regime spoke foreign languages, traveled extensively abroad, married foreign wives, and were cultural cosmopolitans. They would understand one another. There was little protest against this. This was – and still is – a bizarre feature of the modern state. At a time when the state's domestic activities were under attack from subordinate classes and others, when most domestic ministries and parliamentary assemblies were staffed by a broader cross section of bourgeois and professional classes (see Chapter 13), foreign policy was little scrutinized and narrowly staffed. It remained quite insulated and private, controlled by a particularistic alliance between a state executive elite and an old regime party whose economic power was in decline.

Thus the primary geopolitical function of the military pulled it in a slightly different direction to its secondary domestic function. The importance of militarism to foreign policy pushed it into close private relations with the state's old regime core, whereas repression pushed it toward the interests of the propertied classes as a whole, especially toward protecting the interests of modern industrial and landowning capitalists against discontented labor. The military might prove an important link between these formerly and presently dominant economic classes. I now turn to dissect the military itself.

The military: class, bureaucratization, and professionalization, 1760–1815

I first examine the social composition of the eighteenth-century officer corps. This was simple: Virtually all higher officers were noble; so were the vast majority of lower officers, except for navies, artillery, and in Britain (with the largest navy and the smallest nobility). The officer *was* noble, as he had long been. Only 5 percent to 10 percent of French army officers were nonnoble. Yet most nobles were not officers, except in Prussia (at some time in their lives). Elsewhere, officer corps had become a specialized noble network, and not its most socially powerful one. As Chapter 6 shows, in France this had been a controversial development, solved by privileging the older, often poorer *noblesse de l'épée*. In Austria, Maria Theresa attempted, with only limited success, to upgrade the aristocratic titles conferred on her officers, usually drawn from the poorer service nobility. War was no longer the central role of the nobility. The military, though still overwhelmingly old regime, was no longer quite at its core.

Britain had ostensibly the least militarized old regime. Yet the officer corps of the home army was almost entirely old regime: its highest ranks predominantly aristocratic; its lower, country gentry (Razzell 1963). Wealth was needed to purchase the commission and to afford regimental life. Life was cheaper and less desirable in the more marginal Indian army, whose officers were mostly from merchant and professional families. The navy was even more open, drawing officers from gentry, merchant, professional, and seafaring groups from coastal districts (as did the French navy). The navy required no prior wealth. Officers could live on their pay plus their distinctive bonus, prize money. Many were younger sons from respectable though not rich families. All officers served for two years as seamen, though with distinctive rank as midshipman or master's mate. About 10 percent of officers came from "nonrespectable" families, including that famous son of a farmhand, Captain James Cook (Rodger 1986: 252–72). His mobility would have been impossible in the army – and perhaps in the armed forces of any other country.

All armies and some navies also still contained elements of an international "service" mercenary nobility – from émigré families and from "marcher" or marginal areas like smaller German states, Scotland, or Ireland. These often moved around – Frederick von Schomberg served in five foreign armies (Brewer 1989: 55–6). Even in 1760, the officer corps was showing signs of being a distinct social group, not a caste still embedded in the old regime, but a professionalizing corps whose practices were no longer those of the upper classes as a whole.

Between officers and men lay a great gulf. Ordinary soldiers and sailors were portrayed by literate contemporaries as the dregs of society, the "scum" (Brodsky 1988). The label has stuck among scholars today (Jany 1967: 619ff.; Rothenberg 1978: 12; Dandeker 1989: 79; Holsti 1991: 102, 104; Berryman 1988 contests it for the United States), but its accuracy is questionable. Literate contemporaries were biased. As we have just seen, officers were drawn from unusually elevated strata. To them quite ordinary men might seem "dregs," especially conscripted and impressed men, trapped unwillingly, like caged animals, and held by cruel discipline. Civilians' contact with the military was mainly when impressment or quartering threatened them, so they were hostile, too. Up to one-third of soldiers were foreign mercenaries, sharing few values with local civilians. Civilians understandably hated soldiers and sailors, who stood somewhat apart from society.

We have reasonable data on two armies in the second half of the eighteenth century, French and British. French studies reveal its soldiers to be no dregs but disproportionately urban, artisan, and literate, peasants and farm workers being substantially underrepresented. By 1789, 63 percent of those with recorded occupations were artisans and shopkeepers (Corvisier 1964: I, 472–519; Scott 1978: 14–19; Lynn 1984: 46–7). The towns could release young men, probably surplus younger sons trained in their fathers' trades, and the army was happy to take skilled, literate men. British army recruits were mostly from manufacturing and laboring classes. They were slightly more urban and more Scottish, and perhaps slightly less literate, than the overall British population. This made them working class but hardly scum (see the data in Floud et al. 1990: 84–118; as the authors note, the apparently lower literacy of army recruits may be an artifact – individual officers made their own assessments of recruits' literacy, but were probably looking for more than mere signing ability). Central European armies were probably less skilled and literate than the French and British, for their conscription systems generally exempted skilled trades (and Austria's at first exempted peasant proprietors), and the ability to buy oneself out by paying for a substitute also depressed social levels. Yet some main recruiting areas, in the smaller German states, had high literacy rates. In the British and French peacetime navies, the sailors were largely a cross section of seafaring trades, though wartime impressment brought in poorer landlubbers (Hampson 1959; Rodger 1986). Perhaps the French and British armed forces had become more elevated than the rest, but I suspect officers, more than men, were from extreme social backgrounds.

The crucial mediating link between extreme ranks was the noncommissioned officer, who was almost always literate and usually was drawn from the middling classes. NCOs were recruited from the ranks and really formed the upper ranks of the soldiery, as promotion even to the junior levels of the officer corps was rare. Officers played little role in their regiments during peacetime: French officers took seven and a half months' leave every two years; British leave was generous and abused. NCOs were in close relations with soldiers while army officers were not. Navies differed, while at sea, where officers and men were in close living and working contact. Rodger (1986) portrays British ships as having relaxed discipline in which officers persuaded rather than commanded their men and in which professional skills mattered as much as the power of rank. Either this is a romantic view or conditions had changed by 1797, for the naval mutinies of that year revealed deep hostility toward discipline that was highly punitive.

Given such social distance and limited contact, all states and officer corps believed discipline must be punitive. Mid-eighteenth-century tactics required soldiers to stand exposed for long periods under fire that was not accurate but that was erratically and cumulatively lethal. Sailors in naval engagements had to take murderous short-range bursts of firepower. But at least they were kept busy while under fire. Soldiers were often standing passively waiting or walking slowly forward. Constant repetitive drilling to drive understandable terror to the fringes of consciousness might be required in any armed forces facing comparable danger. Such drilling was a notable feature of eighteenth-century armies. But even so, "discipline" was not fully internalized. Soldiers deserted en masse, not in battle, as this was difficult and conspicuous, but in peacetime. It was said that one-third of the Prussian army – a highly effective one – was employed rounding up another third deserting (leaving a third ready for war). Eighteenth-century officers coped by adding to drilling brutal, arbitrary corporal punishment and precious little humanity, as did many naval commanders whose authority at sea was quite arbitrary. Scott (1978: 35) says that many French soldiers had their first personal contact with their officer when facing disciplinary action from him.

Military society was thus distinctively, cruelly hierarchical, two-class, linked by arbitrary, punitive power. In this sense it was a segregated institution, no longer reflecting the more complex civil society outside. This distinctively hierarchical military society then confronted three processes of change: bureaucratization, professionalization, and democratization. The first two impacted fairly continuously right through the period, the last suddenly impacted through the French Revolution and Napoleonic Wars, and was later supposedly reinforced by the nineteenth-century development of industrial society (Huntington 1957 and Janowitz 1960 provide the classic accounts; Dandeker 1989, the best update).

I present my model of bureaucracy at the beginning of Chapter 13. Bureaucracy comprises five elements: two of personnel, two of office arrangements, and one of general structure. Bureaucratic *personnel* are salaried, without ownership or appropriation rights over administration; and they are appointed, promoted, and terminated according to impersonal measures of competence. *Offices* within bureaucratic departments are rationally arranged by function and hierarchy; and departments are similarly arranged into a single, centralized administration. Finally, the whole is *insulated* from the political struggles of civil society, except at the top where it receives political direction. Military bureaucratization from the beginning was directed by the state.

Professionalization is a general attribute of modernization, not confined to armed forces. But Teitler (1977: 6–8) observes that the military added a third professional element to two more general ones. Just like other professionals, soldiers and sailors acquired a monopoly of specialized skills, removing all others to the level of incompetent amateurs; and second, this specialized body acquired a distinct esprit de corps, anchored in tradition and a sense of honor. But third, military services were distinctively rendered to the state. Professionalization, like bureaucratization, developed within states.

Sociologists have often observed that bureaucracy and profession are intimately yet conflictually connected (e.g., Parsons 1964). In particular, bureaucracies develop a professional esprit de corps and distinct ethos as they become insulated from society. This may then conflict with the formal rationality of bureaucracy. In the case of the modern military, this entwined bureaucratic-professional ethos also involved distinctive class solidarity. The combination of the three encouraged the creation of a distinct officer caste.

Bureaucratization is ancient, though its main history occurred in my present period. It had mostly originated outside the state, first in the church, then in the private India companies – though the earliest of these, the Casa de Contratación de las Indias in Seville, was a monopoly controlled by the Spanish state.[4] Their orderly accounting systems, specified chains of command, and salaried civilian and military officials were responses to the difficulties of moderate-size administrations coping with a broad scope of functions spread over enormous geographic areas. Perhaps there was some pressure exerted by size, some threshold level beyond which administrative control became difficult without greater rationalized standardization. But in a study of ten modern organizations ranging in size from 65 to 3,096 employees, Hall (1963–4) found no significant relationship between their size and six measures of bureaucratization which are quite similar to my own measures. Similarly, in the premodern period, the main functional pressure for bureaucratization was less size than the problem of organizing diverse functions spread over large spaces.

The military revolution of 1500–1640 brought bureaucratization into the state. By 1760, armies and navies were divided into units of standardized size and specialized functions, related to each other and to headquarters through two linked chains of command. One, appearing in the eighteenth century, was that staple of modern business organization, the division between staff and line. The other was an integrated hierarchy, with standardized ranks running down from general officers, colonels, majors, captains, and lieutenants to noncommissioned officers and ordinary soldiers. The two command chains were integrated by the division (an army unit containing all the specialisms, coordinated by a staff, subordinated to a single commander), coordinated with other divisions by a "general" staff under a "general" officer. Navies also tightened coordination to overcome tactical difficulties presented by the dispersion of ships over vast oceans. Specialized standardized supply, artillery, and marine corps developed, as did signaling and manuals – all integrated into a formal "command, control, communication and intelligence" system (Dandeker 1989: 77). Offices were arranged bureaucratically, though at the very top monarchs and parliaments remained reluctant to entrust total operational command to one general

---

[4] Indeed, the seventeenth-century Spanish state may have some claim to have anticipated innovations I ascribe to my eighteenth-century states – though it seems to have had curiously little influence on them. Concentrating on a few country cases, as this volume does, carries the danger of exaggerating their collective significance.

officer. They preferred to divide and rule. Army (not usually navy) entrepreneurs survived; wealthy nobles funded and operated their own regiments. But mid-eighteenth-century monarchs and war ministers in Austria, Britain, France, and Prussia enacted centralizing regulations against them. When Maria Theresa secured control of army promotions in 1766, she eliminated the remaining proprietors, perhaps the last Western monarch to do so (Kann 1979: 118–9; cf. Scott 1978: 26–32; Brewer 1989: 57–8).

Military administration was relatively centralized, routinized, disciplined, homogeneous and bureaucratic – by far the most "modern" eighteenth-century power organization (Dandeker 1989: chapter 3). These characteristics had emerged directly from the logic of efficiency of military power, the requirements of war conducted between functionally varied and geographically dispersed armed forces. Again, size mattered less than functional and geographic scope, for the military revolution had centered on the emergence of clear-cut, formalized divisions between infantry, cavalry, and artillery and their engineering and supply departments. Specialization required new means of coordination over greater distances, especially for navies. Greater army and navy size was more product than cause: Bureaucratization enabled armies to grow. Bureaucratization won out as informal, looser military organization perished on the battlefield.

Personnel policy was less bureaucratized. True, salaries became normal. Sailors and soldiers were paid "employees," subordinated to an officer chain of command. Officers' status still varied. Most were state employees on fixed salaries, yet they also bought their initial commission and their subsequent promotions. Prussian officers were still entitled to appropriate fiscal resources flowing through their commands. Still, such practices were being phased out.

Bureaucratization lagged on the second personnel criterion, standards of competence. Literacy was required, but other formal qualifications and extensive training were rare, except among artillery and naval officers. The first general cadet academies were founded – the Maria Theresa Military Academy in 1748, the Ecole Militaire in 1751 (copied in twelve French provinces in 1776), many Prussian cadet schools throughout the century, with Sandhurst bringing up the British rear in 1802. But the main recruitment criterion was social background. It was assumed that an aristocratic or gentry upbringing produced officer potential – experience with physical exertion (especially riding), bravery, dignity, familiarity in giving orders to the lower classes, and a sense of honor. An Austrian field marshal once singled out his bourgeois officers for bravery in combat. He refused to praise his noble officers because, he said, a nobleman's bravery should be taken for granted (Kann 1979:

124). Most officers learned on the job, helped by drill books and simple manuals, and were plunged, young and inexperienced, into battle. Promotion would then be decided by a mixture of connections (justified in terms of ease with rank) and performance under fire.

The increased intensity of war then expanded a battle-hardened officer corps. Its experience was the core of a new professionalism. Amateur warriors were disappearing and despised: Only we professionals know what war is like. A distinct professional ethos, still noble, yet less particularistic and genealogical, was emerging.

The Revolution and the Napoleonic Wars impacted massively, reinforcing bureaucracy and profession and introducing limited democratization that seemed to threaten both noble domination and punitive discipline. Greater war intensity increased experienced professionalism. Amateurs perished before Bonaparte's troops while book learning and schooling made little progress. Connections remained important but fewer aristocratic dilettantes and incompetents or intellectuals of war were promoted. The rivalries and jealousies of officer corps, which, as any reader of military autobiographies knows, center on who gets promoted to command over whom, turned less on family connections, not yet on formal qualifications, more on job performance.

The impact was naturally greatest on the French revolutionary army. The Revolution brought noble emigration and purges. Opportunities for promotion suddenly expanded for NCOs, for the few promoted *officiers de fortune*, and even for ordinary soldiers. By 1793, 70 percent of officers had served some time as enlisted men, compared to 10 percent in 1789, though they were mostly in the lower officer grades. The highest grades still contained many former nobles: 40 percent to 50 percent of colonels and lieutenant colonels of the line army, compared to 10 percent to 20 percent of captains and lieutenants. But they shared rank with middle-class professionals, officials, businessmen, and bourgeois rentiers, comprising 40 percent of the higher grades and 30 percent of the lower. Artisans, shopkeepers, wage earners, and small peasants made up most of the remainder, providing 5 percent and 33 percent. Among the soldiers, bourgeois, middling groups, and artisans declined and peasants increased, though still underrepresented (Scott 1978: 186–206; Lynn 1984: 68–77).

Suddenly this army resembled the new society, rather than being a caricature of a very old one. Discipline was codified and applied to all ranks: French officers were now *more* likely than their men to go before a firing squad. It balanced punishment with enthusiasm, its high standard of combat performance individualized and partially internalized. The rank and file, concludes Lynn (1984: 118), were treated "as citizens and not as subjects." I find all such statements about armies somewhat exaggerated. Troops facing the distinct possibility of death almost never fully internalize discipline; it has to be supplemented by forms of concentrated coercion, *compelling* them to stand upright under fire or to charge, rather than to cower or flee.[5] But as a statement of trend, from eighteenth-century to revolutionary armies, Lynn's will suffice.

Over the next two decades, the officer corps became more bourgeois, as mobility through the ranks increased. In 1804, only three of Napoleon's eighteen marshals were former nobles, and half the officers were from the ranks (Chandler 1966: 335–8; Lefebvre 1969: 219). After Napoleon's fall, social background varied between subsequent regimes. The Bourbon monarchy, restored in 1815, increased nobles at the highest levels, but could not thoroughly purge a bourgeois army of its Republican sympathies. After two decades of trouble, expedients were found. Repression of army Republican clubs was coupled with three incentives – opportunities for promotion provided by the Algerian conquest, an increase in army pensions, and the end of the ministerial right to dismiss an officer. The French army remained divided, unable to move against revolution in 1848 or against Louis Bonaparte in 1851, but its radical "citizen" character was much diminished (Porch 1974: esp. 115–7, 138–9). Would the revolutionary wars transform other militaries?

Toward a military caste

The revolutionary wars transformed control over the rank and file and integrated and modernized officer corps. But this proved to contain fewer concessions to "national citizenship" than regimes and commanders had first feared.

Relations between officers and men were gradually transformed. The effectiveness of mass-mobilized morale and less cruel discipline was too striking to ignore. It actually reinforced the beliefs of "enlightened" factions in all officer corps. Naval and colonial campaigns had also repeatedly showed that when officers and men shared similar material hardships they fought better. Three years after its humiliation at Jena, the Prussian army abandoned arbitrary corporal punishment, extended its rule books, and began to write humanitarian injunctions into them. In 1818, they referred for the first time to the necessity to make discipline consonant with the sense of "honor" of the private soldier – a radical notion indeed (Craig 1955: 48; Demeter 1965: 178–80).

---

[5] I shall consider such coercive techniques in more detail in Volume III, when presenting the excellent research that has been done on the morale of World War I soldiers.

Under Maria Theresa, an enlightened code had been introduced in the artillery as early as 1759. It urged that the men be encouraged "through love of honor and good treatment than through brutality, untimely blows and beatings." But not until 1807 was the code extended to the infantry masses and not until late in the nineteenth century was it implemented frequently enough to deter brutal treatment (Rothenberg 1982: 117–8; Deak 1990: 106–8). Discipline remained essentially coercive – as it does today – but it gradually became rationalized and rule-governed. Officers and men were no longer so segregated; they were becoming subject to the rationality of a single emerging military caste.

During 1805–7 and 1813–14, it seemed that Austria and Prussia might go much farther than this, to become also "nations in arms," mobilizing patriotic enthusiasm and allowing freer relations between officers and men. The recruitment of foreign mercenaries dropped off so that armies became "national" in a minimal sense. Both regimes initiated reserve forces, the Landwehr. But after 1815, all regimes backed away from the citizen army, frightened by the notion of placing arms in the hands of a free people. The Archduke Charles, the great Austrian general, modestly suggested enlarging the pool of recruits while reducing the years of army service to eight (in many regiments it was lifelong). His scheme was rejected because discharged soldiers might contribute expert leadership for revolts. Count Colloredo clinched the argument at court by observing: "I can at any time stuff the mouth of a victorious enemy with a province, but to arm the people means literally to overturn the throne" (Langsam 1930: 52; Rothenberg 1982: 72). The Austrian Landwehr was abandoned in 1831. The Prussians retained their Landwehr, but they kept it disciplined. Throughout the nineteenth century, Prussians and other Germans debated the merits of "professional" versus "citizen" armies. The professionals always won if the debate was posed in these terms.

Yet the compromise notion of a "military citizenship" disciplined from above made some progress. In Germany it was influential in the granting of universal male suffrage (under controlled conditions) in return for their contribution of military service (Craig 1955; Ritter 1969: I, 93–119). The French definition of citizenship as the "blood tax" resonated across Europe and America. No country sustained popular citizen armies of the type that had worsted the Prussians at Valmy (see Chapter 6). Instead, mass armies embodied a more seg-mental form of participation, defined by their ruling regimes and dis-ciplined by a rationalized military hierarchy. As we shall see, under arms they were not really "citizens" but "nation-state loyalists."

Within military hierarchies nineteenth-century professional officers certainly treated their men better than their ancestors had done. Changes occurred in two phases, as army size declined after 1815, then after midcentury as it expanded again. In the first phase, budgetary constraints lessened. Welfare programs to buy the loyalty of officers and noncommissioned officers became general, including pensions and the offer of civilian state employment for veterans (discussed further in Chapter 14). Wages mostly kept pace with the civilian occupations that discharged officers and soldiers (except perhaps Austrian officers) might have undertaken. Armed forces also offered more secure employment, trapping most into long service (Porch 1974, 1981: 89; Berryman 1988: 26–7; Deak 1990: 105–6, 114–25).

Then, as the second expansionary phase hit, states coped by expanding their reserve forces. Long-service professionals at all levels became a cadre, leading and training the flood of conscript reservists who passed through for short terms (three years in Prussia) and then passed into reserve and territorial formations under regular-army supervision. Mobilized reservists now made up the bulk of armies when war actually threatened. Through the middle of the nineteenth century, armies recruited their soldiers more from the agrarian population, giving exemptions to skilled urban and industrial trades – and were more confident of their loyalty. As short-term conscription broadened in continental Europe, this bias declined. Nonetheless, major war would tend not to call up the organized core of the working class. In World War I, the working class "vanguard" – skilled workers in mining, transport, and metal manufacturing – were required to produce, not to fight. Only navies sought recruits from this background. Thus the soldiers, especially high-caliber frontline troops, tended to be recruited either from rural areas or from small towns or industries where working-class identities were weaker. Working class disloyalty affected armies less than either Engels or many conservative commentators had anticipated.

Giddens (1985: 230) argues that at the very time officers were becoming segregated specialists, soldiers became mass citizens. But they did not. Commanders were actually *tightening* military organization over their soldiers, reducing their ability to identify themselves as citizens or as members of classes. The lesson of the midcentury wars was that loose divisional coordination (developed by Bonaparte, as we saw in Chapter 8) was made obsolete by meticulous planning and coordination of maps and timetables. Prussian organization had devastated French élan in 1870. This enabled the generals to tighten discipline even over soldiers who were drilled less than their eighteenth-century forbears. Broader authoritative organization replaced narrower direct drilling. Railways, telegraph (eventually wireless telegraph), and staff systems enabled commanders to coordinate many units, each of which represented the individual soldier's far horizon. Most army units were recruited territorially, their unit morale based on local-regional solidarities and camaraderie.

The power of local morale was especially demonstrated in the American Civil War, when local recruitment ensured that most soldiers fought and died believing they were defending the integrity or values of their home community rather than larger units like the South or the Union (or the values with which these were associated). Six hundred thousand dead and low desertion rates testify to the astonishing power of this discipline, even over soldiers who had been rushed to the front with little training.

But other than the mass mobilization of the American Civil War and the overwhelmingly urban-industrial Britain, regional recruitment was also biased toward the most backward and conservative agrarian regions, able to provide surplus labor used to segmental discipline from above. After the Franco-Prussian War, a political battle was fought in France over the issues as Republicans sought to replace the regional recruitment system. But they lost before the combined weight of the conservatives and the army high command. Armies stayed regional and reactionary.

Just in case this was not enough, command structures reinforced conservatism. Local-regional unit organization was staffed by non-commissioned officers recruited from the same territorial pool. They welded local unit camaraderie into hierarchical discipline. Commissioned and noncommissioned officers thus developed fairly successful *segmental and local-regional* power relations at the heart of expanding and supposedly "class" and "national" citizen militaries. Outside of their immediate relations with their own officers, soldiers were organizationally outflanked. Their units and ships moved by higher line and staff commands for broader purposes that remained hidden from them. Soldiers now had little capacity for collective action outside their own unit or ship. As we shall see in Volume III, they had little organizational alternative to compliance even under the horrendous conditions of World War I, even if ineptly commanded – unless their officers also lacked loyalty. Both regular and reserve forces proved overwhelmingly loyal in war during this period.

McNeill (1983: 260) argues that a society that was becoming industrial was also enshrining the "primacy of the command principle." This is a little overgeneralized if referring to civil society, but is dead-on in describing its expanding armed forces. These were only deceptively "citizen," "national," or "class" armies. They were really *segmental* power organizations disciplined by social conservatives. By 1910, perhaps 20 percent of adult males in most countries had been so disciplined. The figure was to rise still further in World War I. Modern states were creating mass loyalists in their militaries (as in their civilian administrations; see Chapters 13 and 16). Between 1848 and 1917, virtually no armed force wavered in its segmental loyalties. That proved important, often decisive, in both principal military functions, war and repression, during the twentieth century.

There was also a lasting change within the officer corps, as notions of experienced competence continued to develop. Gradually the educational component of skill was upgraded. Cartography, logistics, and the comparative and historical study of tactics became a part of cadet and general staff training, emerging in the early nineteenth century. Then the massive increase in firepower under the industrialization of war required that some basic engineering knowledge be extended beyond the artillery branch. Prussian victories had clear technocratic lessons, learned especially quickly by the French. After about 1870, passing out from cadet college became necessary to entry, and attending further courses became a usual part of promotion, especially on the elite staff side. Files were routinely kept on officers' service record and qualifications, as patronage further declined in the face of universal technocratic criteria.

Britain and Austria lagged somewhat, for different reasons. As we shall see soon, the social composition of the British officer corps remained rural and reactionary and was out of sympathy with the only industrial society in the world. The British army remained conservative, spurning staff colleges and the efforts of a reform faction, until disasters in the Crimean and Boer wars forced laggard professionalization (Bond 1972; Harries-Jenkins 1977; Strachan 1984; Brodsky 1988: 72–82). Austria lagged because of political turmoil. Its main role being internal security, it was conservative, suspecting professionalization as "liberal" (Rothenberg 1976), but after 1870 it also moved. By 1900, its elite military schools and postgraduate training courses dominated long-range promotion chances (Deak 1990: 187–9).

In the end, reactionaries had little to fear. Education did not replace older, noble criteria or radicalize military politics. It was fused into them. In anticipation of more general twentieth-century mobility trends, as education became the principal avenue of upward mobility, direct promotion from the ranks actually was reduced. In the French army, 14 percent of division generals had come from the ranks in 1870, but less than 3 percent in 1901 (Serman 1978: 1325; Charle 1980b). Nobles had no choice but to give some ground, for a different reason – once armies began their late nineteenth-century expansion, there were simply not enough nobles to go around. They hung on remarkably well under the circumstances. Even in Republican France the highest ranks remained fairly aristocratic. In 1870, 39 percent of division generals were of noble origin; in 1901, they were still 20 percent. Lower down there was necessarily greater embourgeoisement, yet also greater recruitment from Roman Catholic rather than state schools. This officer corps remained socially and politically reactionary. Repeated clashes with Republican governments culminated in the Dreyfus affair, and not until just before 1914 were political compromises made that would shortly save the Republic (Girardet, 1953; Charle 1980a).

One military had no nobles, of course. The United States also had another unique feature: a major civil war that rapidly expanded both sides' officer corps to being representative of propertied and educated white males in general. But once settled back into small peacetime formations, American officers were less representative. Naval officers were overwhelmingly from the modern urban upper classes, that is, from capitalist and professional middle classes in the Northeast. They were disproportionately the sons of (in descending order) military officers, bankers, attorneys and judges, manufacturers, officials, "scientific" professionals (physicians, druggists, engineers), and merchants (Karsten 1972: table 1-2).

In contrast, army officers were strikingly – in view of the result of the American Civil War – southern and from the rural, perhaps decaying, old regime. Thirteen of the fourteen highest-ranking officers in 1910 were southerners, mostly from rural areas. Although broader data are scanty, most officers appear to have been either children of officers or of farmer-planters or of those professionals found in small towns as well as large – lawyers, doctors, teachers, officials, and ministers. Janowitz sums up the army officer corps as "old-family, anglo-saxon, Protestant, rural, upper-middle-class" – as close to being an old regime as the United States provides. But because such a class no longer ruled America (outside of the South), it was a somewhat segregated group. According to a northern account of 1890, the army was a "domain of its own, independent and isolated by its peculiar customs and discipline; an aristocracy by selection and the halo of traditions" (quotations from Janowitz 1960: 90, 100; cf. Huntington 1957: 227; Karsten 1980; Skelton 1980).

This small castelike corps also controlled its men distinctively. They were not conscripts, but professional volunteers, predominantly immigrants, especially from Ireland and Germany (descendants of earlier mercenaries?), but also blacks. They were content that the army gave them secure entry to (white) American society (Berryman 1988: chapter 2). Though not large or influential, the U.S. Army was loyal to its conservative masters, as we shall see in Chapter 18.

Elsewhere, noble and reactionary dominance remained impressive. Britain and Prussia were still the most extreme, with Austria at first similar. Razzell (1963) shows how little the social backgrounds of British army officers changed. Aristocrats and landed gentry (fewer than 1 percent of the population) supplied 40 percent of officers in the home army in 1780 and 41 percent in 1912. In the highest ranks (major generals and above), their dominance fell slightly, from 89 percent in 1830 to 64 percent in 1912; but this was countered by increasing stratification between regiments, as elite regiments became even more old regime in composition and socially reactionary in tone. At higher ranks the Prussian army also remained noble. In Preradovich's (1955) comparison of Prussian and Austrian general staffs from 1804 to 1918, nobles comprised about 95 percent of Austrian generals between 1804 and 1859, then the proportion plummeted to 41 percent by 1908. But in Prussia they held steady at about 90 percent until 1897 and then fell only to 71 percent in 1908. (Among enlarged general staffs during World War I both figures fell further.) Lower down the hierarchy, noble dominance dropped, and it dropped farther with expansion about 1900 – as we should expect, given the fixed numbers of nobles. Of generals and colonels, 86 percent were noble in 1860, and 52 percent in 1913. The integration of the more bourgeois Landwehr reserve force in 1860 made a big difference in the lower officer ranks. By 1873, only 38 percent of lieutenants were noble, down to 25 percent by 1913 – this was also the only drop in absolute numbers. Among all officers, nobles dropped from 65 percent to 52 percent (Demeter 1965: 28–9).

Thus the German and British pattern was late, *forced* decline of noble-gentry domination as officer numbers increased and nobles-gentry did not; a hierarchy still dominated at the top by the old nobility; and an almost total absence of sons of manufacturing or commercial capitalists. The dominant economic class left the army to the old regime. The army (along with diplomacy) gave the old regime a bridgehead into the core of the German state, ensuring more militarism in foreign policy and in class relations than would otherwise have occurred.

But the meaning of "nobility" also changed, becoming less particularistic as it merged into a distinct professional ethos, shared in common by officers. Rank within the German nobility had played a lesser role as early as the late eighteenth century, enabling poorer, lesser nobles, like Gneisenau, Scharnhorst, and Clausewitz, to move to the top. Early nineteenth-century reforms and the strengthening of military education institutionalized professional equality within the corps. Education in the university student corps, dueling fraternities, and staff colleges reinforced the ethos. The word *Bildung* did not just mean "education" but cultivation – in the military, the cultivation of honor. As a moral quality "nobility" now meant "honor," the distinctive attribute of officers.

The consequences can be seen in the rapidly expanding German navy, ostensibly the most bourgeois military branch. The navy required extensive technical training and recruited heavily from urban ports. Being recent, it lacked traditions and status. Thus it attracted few nobles. Of sea-cadet executive classes between 1890 and 1914, only 10 percent to 15 percent were from noble families, although this was more than the percentage from industrial or commercial capitalist backgrounds. In the well-documented class of 1907, professional backgrounds dominated: forty-five percent being sons of academics and 26 percent sons of nonnoble army or navy officers. The navy still wanted well-educated young men from "good families" and explicitly rejected applicants from lower social classes because these might deter good families from applying. Service experience was not bourgeois, however. Nobility was valued most, affluence came next. Successful executive officers were ennobled. Officers modeled their treatment of sailors on arrogant Prussian forms – costing them dearly in naval revolts at the end of World War I. Engineer-officer cadets came from somewhat lower backgrounds, primarily the lower or middle civil service. They were treated as "practical" personnel, unsuited to "command" positions. As in the army, Jews (unless baptized) and Socialists were anathema. Though army and navy ethos was not identical – navy militarism was more anti-British and imperialist – "the navy showed the way towards 'feudalizing' the upper bourgeoisie" (Herwig 1973: 39–45, 57–60, 76–8, 92, 103–4, 132). In armed forces dominated by reactionary nobles, even bourgeois branches imitated them. At a time when Germany was leading industrial capitalism, its industrial and commercial capitalists were shunning, and being shunned by, its armed forces.

World War I demonstrated that Germany had the best army in the world; 1866 and 1870 had already probably made this clear. Its navy was also technically excellent, though too small for the role asked of it. But the paradox is that its extraordinary professional modernity was essentially old regime. It was certainly technical, with a high standard of qualifications for officers, and, according to contemporary statistics, the only universal literacy of any army (*Annuaire Statistique de la France* 1913: 181). Its staff had an advanced understanding of the industrialization of war, including the best use of railway logistics. Because its officer and NCO corps was socially cohesive, officers were trusted to use their own initiative – more so, for example, than were officers in the strife-torn French army. This disparity was especially evident in the campaigns of 1870–1 (Gooch 1980: 107). Common speech has long understood the paradox in the expression "Prussian efficiency," for this officer corps was technically advanced and socially reactionary. The combination was a highly developed caste ethos, with the best NCO cadre in the world to segmentally instill its values below. But this was just the extreme version of a more general paradox: These socially reactionary officer corps were mobilizing the most advanced instruments of industrial capitalism, wielding the most advanced technocratic skills.

The Austrian officer corps was also socially conservative, but it also had unique qualities derived from the crystallizations of its state (discussed in Chapter 10). It remained dynastic and (unevenly) multinational. As late as 1859, a slight majority of its officers were recruited from abroad, especially from Germany but with a substantial British contingent. The dynasty also relied somewhat on Roman Catholics and heavily on Austro-Germans, who comprised 79 percent of regular officers in 1910 and only 23 percent of the population. All other nationalities were underrepresented. Nobles first dominated the corps but then declined, as in Prussia-Germany there were not enough German nobles to staff expansion. By 1870, only 20 percent of career lieutenants were noble, mostly from families recently ennobled for public service. The decline of noble generals occurred later, as we would expect and as evidenced above. There were concessions to Magyars after 1867: They dominated the Honved reserve army of their *Reichshalf*, and the few Magyar officers in the regular joint army benefited from positive discrimination in promotion.

After 1870, Austria also greatly expanded its reserve forces, and they became thoroughly embourgeoised, as the main qualifications were educational. This eliminated Roman Catholic overrepresentation, reduced German domination (to 60 percent), raised Czechs and Magyars to their rightful numbers, overrepresented Lutherans, and grossly overrepresented Jews (who comprised 17 percent to 18 percent of reserve officers, only 4 percent to 5 percent of the population). Other nationalities and religions remained underrepresented (Rothenberg 1976: 42, 128, 151; Deak 1990: 156–89).

This was a peculiar officer corps, bourgeois, highly educated and technocratic, but its essentially dynastic loyalty was mediated by particularistic national and religious identities. The army was tied more to the dual monarchy than to the dominant classes of its territories – and very little to the "nation." Its social isolation and its impractical rituals (like its pure-white uniforms) increased its castelike apartness and solidarity. Austrian officers, whatever their rank and status, even if strangers, showed their community by addressing each other with the familiar *Du* form of "you" (used elsewhere only for intimates and servants), rather than the more formal *Sie* usually used in other spheres of Germanic society. This later led to nasty scenes in World War I with German officers believing themselves insulted or propositioned by their Austrian allies!

The social isolation of Austrian officers was not unique. In the Russian army, the proportion of nonnoble officers also increased, from 26 percent in 1895 to 47 percent in 1911, while the remaining nobles were not tied to the great Russian aristocracy. By 1903, 91 percent of those with at least a major general's rank possessed no land or property, not even an urban dwelling (Wildman 1980: 23–4). This officer corps was also becoming segregated from class structure.

But Austrian officers were also more segregated from their men. Because the soldiers were recruited roughly proportionately and territorially from all nationalities, and because the monarchy was wary of homogeneous national regiments, officers and their men rarely shared a language. Thus the army's command structure got little reinforcement from social hierarchies provided either by class structure or local-regional linguistic community. Otto Bauer, the Socialist leader, describes what he believed were the effects of embourgeoisement (though not of nationality, for he appears to be describing an all-German regiment) in his own officer training. The army's professional ethos required the officer to treat the private first class with respect. But

the class hierarchy . . . distinguishes between a class of gentlemen and a class of workers and peasants. . . . The entire structure of the old army was to mark this separation between the class of gentlemen and the working class so clearly that it sometimes appeared not as a separation of classes but as one of castes. [But unlike the Prussian soldier confronting his Junker officer, the] Austrian peasant was required to see the son of the petty bourgeois with his sabre as an individual of exalted order. Particularly absurd was this . . . in relationship to the reserve officers. [Kann 1979: 122–3]

Absurd or not, the Austrian military hierarchy – viewed by contemporaries as the weakest among those of the Great Powers – still worked terrifyingly. Nothing testifies better to the castelike professionalism and segmental disciplinary powers of this embourgeoised-dynastic officer corps and its client noncommissioned officers than their ability to lead those peasants in the repeated suicidal infantry charges on Russian artillery postitions that destroyed half the Austrian army in the first year of the Great War.

Military old regimes were successfully absorbing all that the Age of Revolution and Industry could throw at them, yielding little to democratic citizenship. Bourgeois sons needed their manners smoothed to become officers; talented petit bourgeois, peasants, and workers needed noncommissioned officers' privileges; other ranks needed rule-governed rather than arbitrary discipline. Were these much of a concession? They were far less significant than the concessions made in civilian power networks in modernizing countries. This very difference added to the distinctive segregation and growing segmental power of nineteenth-century armed forces. An officer caste reached down through noncommissioned-officer and long-service cadres to segmentally discipline mass citizens, converting them into state loyalists. "Citizenship" was not merely the attainment of Marshall's universal rights; nor did it inaugurate pacific internationalism. It came entwined with military power relations. The "nation" was partially segmentally organized, statist, and violent.

Toward autonomous military power

Perhaps such forms of professional autonomy, approaching near to a distinct military caste, with excellent cadre and segmental control over its men, might not matter. Many historical societies and some contemporary ones (like Britain) possess a professional military caste without great social harm. True, if war breaks out, their power over society may be considerable, but in peacetime they may have autonomy from, but little power over, civil society. Yet, in peacetime nineteenth-century Europe "autonomy from" could lead to "power over." We saw earlier that diplomacy was little controlled by civil society. It was largely a private matter for state executives, dominated by similar old regime personnel as officer corps. This was not necessarily disastrous. Commanders are often cautious in their geopolitics, knowledgeable about the chaos and devastation of war, experienced in the fear of death. Officer corps often favored colonial ventures to play real war games and to open up promotion prospects. But they were cautious about war among the Great Powers. The industrialization of war brought another reason for caution as the increasing firepower available to the lightly trained soldier greatly increased the size of mobilizable armies. This meant going beyond peasants and marginal areas to arm the working class, a dangerous course of action – or so reactionary officer corps (largely unnecessarily) suspected.

Yet industrialization increased the *technocratic* powers and danger of the military. This happened in two ways. First, officer corps were at the forefront of nineteenth-century scientific and industrial development, using capitalism's most advanced products and forms of organization, sharing its positivistic optimism. The military came to believe that meticulous planning and coordination could give exact results and, in calculable conditions, victory. Although modernization benefited militaries, it could also induce overconfidence. Perhaps *the* lesson of war, *the* prediction that is possible about the next war, is that it is unpredictable. Because weaponry and tactics change between wars, because none is fought over precisely the same terrain as the last, and rarely against the same enemy, the fortunes of the next war are uncertain. A truly sensible military – concerned with whether devastating war can attain a precise policy objective – would only counsel war if possessing great apparent superiority over the enemy. Such superiority is usually provided by diplomacy, yielding powerful allies or depriving the enemy of allies. Yet the most "modern," technocratic, self-absorbed militaries were most apt to scorn foreign allies and rely on their own internal resources. Though diplomats and commanders were recruited from the same class, their training and professional experience diverged. Diplomats knew little of the new technocratic warfare, generals virtually nothing of alliance building. In the late nineteenth century the most modern, technocratic, self-absorbed, and politically ignorant army was the German army. It forgot that Bismarck's diplomacy had contributed as much as its own competence to the victories of 1865–7 and 1870–1 (see Chapter 9), and it neglected subsequent changes in other countries that were not purely technocratic, especially the consolidation of the French republic and of its new military discipline. Its self-absorbed militarism was to be its hubris.

Second, in the late nineteenth century, military technocracy privileged attack over defense. "Going to war" had traditionally involved three phases: mobilizing one's forces, concentrating them into campaign order, and marching them into actual battle. But industrialization, gunnery, and railways enabled an enormous weight of men and firepower to be delivered to the front. This advantaged swift, coordinated attack from railheads. The first to attack could achieve greater concentrated firepower, but defense must also be swift and coordinated, to concentrate fire on the attackers. General staff plans became complex and aggressive, detailing three preemptive moves in emergencies: mobilizing reservists, taking over the rail network, and using forward land and sea space, sometimes regardless of state frontiers or territorial waters. Seizing forward control of railway lines into neighboring states was the most provocative because it constituted actual invasion, though without a declaration of war. The Russian General Obruchev deemed mobilization tantamount to war. In his famous 1892 memorandum, he wrote that in modern war victory goes to the side that achieves the most rapid deployment, "beating the enemy to the punch." He concluded: "Mobilization can no longer be considered as a peaceful act; on the contrary it represents the most decisive act of war."

Blurring the line between defensive preparedness and aggression also preempted diplomacy. The Franco-Russian alliance in 1894 gave the high commands autonomous powers. If Austria, Germany, or Italy mobilized against either of them, they would both immediately mobilize. In 1900, the alliance was restricted to the case of German mobilization, and this agreement was actually implemented in 1914. Important aggressive steps, short of war but likely to precipitate war, were out of the hands of civilian politicians and diplomats (Kennan 1984: 248–53; he reproduces Obruchev's memorandum on p. 264). Similarly, the independent 1909 discussions between Generals Moltke (of Germany) and Conrad (of Austria) threatened to convert Bismarck's defensive alliance between the countries into an encouragement of each other's aggression (Albertini 1952: I, 73–7, 268–73). The Anglo-French entente led to military arrangements between the two Powers being long kept secret from their cabinets. (See Chapter 21.)

Whether the technocratic confidence and plans of the high commands could actually preempt the statesmen depended on channels of accountability. As we shall see in Chapter 21, the institutions of party democracies held their militaries more accountable than did those of the monarchies. In July 1914, the sequence of preemptive mobilizations by Austria, Russia, and Germany overwhelmed their own regimes and then Europe. Autonomous, cohesive military castes then proved to have decisive powers over society. Like ideology in the French Revolution, it was only a "world-historical moment" of power. But it devastated the Old World.

Conclusion

I have traced the development of military power relations through the long nineteenth century. Most internal developments supported military caste theory – the institutional autonomy of armed forces from both civilian and state control. Army and navy organization had tightened and become more segregated from civil society and state alike. In recruitment, training, and esprit de corps, the officer corps had turned in on itself. Its distinctive fusing of old regime and bourgeois sons, under the ideological domination of the former, resulted in an officer corps unlike any major class in advanced industrial society. The growth of internal bureaucracy, profession, and technocracy enhanced the privacy of their activities. Long-service and noncommissioned-officer cadres, plus tighter command structure coordinating individual local-regional military units, secured effective segmental control over a mass of soldiers and sailors without major concessions to citizens, nations, or classes. States had managed to lay down military infrastructures, tentacles, securely embracing parts of their territories and populations and disciplining their loyalties. Particular, segregated, and cohesive, armed forces had become castelike in modern industrializing society, producing a substantially autonomous *militarist* crystallization within the modern state and through civil society.

But I must qualify this. Their functions also entwined militaries with society and state, contradicting and reducing caste autonomy in several ways. Their most persistent embedding in civil society came from their secondary function, domestic repression. This embedded the officer corps in broader political power networks and in dominant economic classes. Because officers were imbued with reactionary old regime values, they generally shared old regime and capitalist hostility to urban riots and labor unrest. Yet, as rural reactionaries, officers were not mere stooges of modern industrial capitalists. Their professionalism also made them reluctant to employ their highest force levels beyond carefully managed shows of force into actual use of guns and sabers. Reluctance led them to collaborate with the expanding police and paramilitary institutions of the state. Professional caution often made them favor compromise between urban classes. For this pragmatic, moderated level of repression, their segmental disciplinary structures almost always provided loyal soldiers. In their repressive functions, the military thus represented an integration between old and new dominant classes. By 1900, military power networks had mediated and helped integrate two state crystallizations of class, as old regime and as capitalist. Their castelike cohesion and their segmental control over their men made dominant classes much more secure.

To some degree these close relations among military, old regime, and capital also permeated their primary function, war. They collaborated in foreign policy with the chief executive and its coterie of essentially old regime diplomats and statesmen, fairly independently of mass political parties or public opinion (I document this further in Chapters 16 and 21). They also collaborated technocratically with industrial capitalists whose products were their weapons, communications, and supplies (discussed in Chapter 14). This "military-industrial complex" sometimes also included broader relations with the state and with mass middle-class "statist" pressure groups (discussed in Chapter 21). But in other war-making respects the military were also private. Military technocracy encouraged caste privacy and insulated over-confidence. It also contributed its own secret time bomb – the internal development of tactics favoring attack over defense, especially escalated mobilization.

These entwinings fueled a dualism within the military crystallization – caste autonomy along with defense of old regime and capitalism. The autonomy came home to roost in 1914. The combination of bureaucratization, professionalization, military-industrial technocracy, old regime domination of high command and diplomacy, and insulation of military and diplomatic decision making had re-created an autonomy of military power that its formal incorporation into the state merely masked. This crystallization as militarism was significantly independent of, and powerful over, all other state crystallizations.

Some feared that this might recoil on old regime and capitalist crystallizations. Many commanders suspected class dangers if they pushed their troops toward mass-mobilization war. Revolution might threaten military caste, old regime, state, and capitalism alike. Most commanders worried needlessly; a few had their worst fears realized. But even amid the pointless slaughter of World War I, the segmental power of the military caste held together. Only the Russian armies broke apart to foment revolution. In all other cases segmental militarism survived: among the victorious troops reinforcing social conservatism, among the vanquished encouraging radical authoritarianism of the Right – and thence to fascism. Postwar class conflict over much of Europe now fused with conflict between military malcontents and loyalists. Most malcontents were inactive sailors and reserve troops, over whom discipline in the last war year had been lax, while most of the loyalists were frontline cadre troops. This difference in disciplined morale was to give a decisive edge to the *squadristi* and the *Freikorps* of the authoritarian and fascist Right. Military power – despite its neglect by twentieth-century sociology – proved to have massive and murderous effects on twentieth-century society. Its world-historical moment of 1914 was actually to last rather longer.

Bibliography

Albertini, L. 1952. *The Origins of the War of 1914*, Vol. I. Oxford: Oxford University Press.

Anderson, M. 1988. *War and Society in the Europe of the Old Regime*. London: Fontana.

Annuaire Statistique de la France. 1913.

Axtmann, R. 1991. Geopolitics and Internal Power Structures: The State, Police and Public Order in Austria and Ireland in the Late Eighteenth Century. Ph.D. diss., London School of Economics and Political Science.

Berryman, S. 1988. *Who Serves? The Persistent Myth of the Underclass Army*. Boulder, Colo.: Westview Press.

Best, G. 1982. *War and Society in Revolutionary Europe: 1770–1870*. Leicester: Leicester University Press.

Bond, B. 1972. *The Victorian Army and the Staff College, 1854–1914*. London: Eyre & Methuen.

1984. *War and Society in Europe, 1870–1970*. London: Fontana.

Bosworth, R. 1983. *Italy and the Approach of War*. London: Macmillan.

Brewer, J. 1989. *The Sinews of Power*. London: Unwin Hyman.

Brodsky, G. W. S. 1988. *Gentlemen of the Blade: A Social and Literary History of the British Army Since 1660*. New York: Greenwood Press.

Cecil, L. 1976. *The German Diplomatic Service, 1871–1914*. Princeton, N.J.: Princeton University Press.

Chandler, D. 1966. *The Campaigns of Napoleon*. New York: Macmillan.

Charle, C. 1980a. *Les hauts fonctionnaires en France au XIXième siècle*. Paris: Gallimard.

   1980b. Le recrutement des hauts fonctionnaires en 1901. *Annales, Economies, Sociétés, Civilisations*, no. 2.

Corvisier, A. 1964. *L'armée francaise de la fin du XVIIième siècle au ministère de Choiseul: Le soldat*. 2 vols. Paris: Presses Universitaires de France.

Craig, G. 1955. *The Politics of the Prussian Army, 1640–1945*. Oxford: Clarendon Press.

Dandeker, C. 1989. *Surveillance, Power and Modernity*. Oxford: Polity Press.

Deak, I. 1990. *Beyond Nationalism: A Social and Political History of the Habsburg Officer Corps, 1848–1918*. New York: Oxford University Press.

Demeter, K. 1965. *The German Officer Corps in Society and State, 1650–1945*. London: Weidenfeld & Nicolson.

Dupuy, R. E. 1971. *The National Guard: A Compact History*. New York: Hawthorn Books.

Elias, N. 1983. *The Court Society*. New York: Pantheon Books.

Emsley, C. 1983. *Policing and Its Context, 1750–1870*. London: Macmillan.

Floud, R., et al. 1990. *Height, Health and History*. Cambridge: Cambridge University Press.

Foucault, M. 1979. *Discipline and Punish*. Harmondsworth: Penguin Books.

Giddens, A. 1985. *The Nation-State and Violence*. Cambridge: Polity Press.

Girardet, R. 1953. *La société militaire dans la France contemporaine, 1815–1939*. Paris: Plon.

Goldstein, R. J. 1978. *Political Repression in Modern America*. Cambridge, Mass.: Schenkman.

   1983. *Political Repression in Nineteenth Century Europe*. London: Croom Helm.

Gooch, J. 1980. *Armies in Europe*. London: Routledge & Kegan Paul.

Gurr, T. R., et al. 1977. *The Politics of Crime and Conflict: A Comparative History of Four Cities*. Beverly Hills, Calif.: Sage Publications.

Hall, R. H. 1963–4. The concept of bureaucracy: an empirical assessment. *American Journal of Sociology* 69.

Hampson, N. 1959. *La Marine de l'an II: Mobilisation de la flotte de l'Océan, 1793–4*. Paris: M. Rivière.

Harries-Jenkins, G. 1977. *The Army in Victorian Society* London: Routledge & Kegan Paul.

Herwig, H. 1973. *The German Naval Officer Corps*. Oxford: Clarendon Press.

Hilderbrand, R. C. 1981. *Power and the People: Executive Management of Public Opinion in Foreign Affairs, 1897–1921*. Chapel Hill: University of North Carolina Press.

Hill, J. D. 1964. *The Minute Man in Peace and War. A History of the National Guard*. Harrisburg, Pa.: Stackpole.

Holsti, K. 1991. *Peace and War: Armed Conflicts and International Order,*

1648–1989. Cambridge: Cambridge University Press.

Huntington, S. 1957. *The Soldier and the State*. Cambridge, Mass.: Harvard University Press.

Ilchman, W. 1961. *Professional Diplomacy in the United States*. Chicago: University of Chicago Press.

Janowitz, M. 1960. *The Professional Soldier: A Social and Political Portrait*. New York: Free Press.

Jany, C. 1967. *Geschichte den Preussischen Armee*, 4 vols. Osnabruck: Biblio Verlag.

Kann, R. 1979. The social prestige of the officer corps in the Habsburg Empire from the eighteenth century to 1918. In *War and Society and East Central Europe*, Vol. I, ed. B. Kiraly and G. Rothenberg. New York: Brooklyn College Press.

Karsten, P. 1972. *Naval Aristocracy: The Golden Age of Annapolis and the Emergence of Modern American Navalism*. New York: Free Press.

  1980. Father's occupation of West Point cadets and Annapolis midshipmen. In *The Military in America: From the Colonial Era to the Present*, ed. P. Karsten. New York: Free Press.

Kennan, G. 1984. *The Fateful Alliance: France, Russia and the Coming of the First World War*. Manchester: Manchester University Press.

Kennedy, P. 1985. *The Realities Behind Diplomacy*. London: Fontana.

LaFeber, W. 1987. The Constitution and United States foreign policy: an interpretation. *Journal of American History* 74.

Langsam, W. C. 1930. *The Napoleonic Wars and German Nationalism in Austria*. New York: Columbia University Press.

Lefebvre, G. 1969. *Napoleon: From 18 Brumaire to Tilsit, 1799–1807*. New York: Columbia University Press.

Ludtke, A. 1989. *Police and State in Prussia, 1815–1850*. Cambridge: Cambridge University Press.

Lynn, J. 1984. *The Bayonets of the Republic*. Urbana: University of Illinois Press.

Macartney, C. A. 1971. *The Habsburg Empire, 1790–1918*. London: Weidenfeld & Nicolson.

McNeill, W. 1983. *The Pursuit of Power*. Oxford: Blackwell.

Martel, G. 1985. *Imperial Diplomacy. Rosebery and the Failure of Foreign Policy*. Montreal: McGill-Queen's University Press.

Palmer, A. 1983. *The Chancelleries of Europe*. London: Allen & Unwin.

Parsons, T. 1964. The professions and social structure. In his *Essays in Sociological Theory*, rev. ed. Glencoe, Ill.: Free Press.

Poggi, G. 1990. *The State. Its Nature, Development and Prospects*. Stanford, Calif.: Stanford University Press.

Porch, D. 1974. *Army and Revolution. France, 1815–1848*. London: Routledge & Kegan Paul.

  1981. *The March to the Marne: The French Army, 1871–1914*. Cambridge: Cambridge University Press.

Preradovich, N. von. 1955. *Die Führungsschichten in Österreich und Preussen, 1804–1918*. Wiesbaden: Steiner.

Razzell, P. E. 1963. Social origins of officers in the Indian and British home army: 1758–1962. *British Journal of Sociology* 14.

Riste, O. 1965. *The Neutral Ally: Norway's Relations with Belligerent Powers in the First World War*. London: Allen & Unwin.

Ritter, G. 1969. *The Sword and the Sceptre*. Vol. I: *The Prussian Tradition, 1740–1890*. Coral Gables, Fla.: University of Miami Press.

Robbins, K. G. 1977a. The foreign secretary, the cabinet, parliament and the parties, and

1977b. Public opinion, the press and pressure groups. Both in *British Foreign Policy Under Sir Edward Grey*, ed. F. H. Hinsley. Cambridge: Cambridge University Press.

Rodger, N. 1986. *The Wooden World*, London: Collins.

Rohl, J. 1967. Higher civil servants in Germany, 1890–1900. *Journal of Contemporary History* 2.

Rothenberg, G. 1976. *The Army of Francis Joseph*. West Lafayette, Ind.: Purdue University Press.

1978. *The Art of Warfare in the Age of Napoleon*. Bloomington: Indiana University Press.

1982. *Napoleon's Great Adversaries: The Archduke Charles and the Austrian Army, 1792–1814*. London: Batsford.

Runciman, W. G. 1987. The Old Question. *London Review of Books*, February 19.

Scott, S. 1978. *The Response of the Royal Army to the French Revolution*. Oxford: Clarendon Press.

Serman, S. 1978. Le corps des officiers francais sous la Deuxième République et la Second Empire. Thesis, University of Lille III.

Skelton, W. 1980. Officers and politicians: the origins of army politics in the United States before the Civil War. In *The Military in America: From the Colonial Era to the Present*, ed. P. Karsten. New York: Free Press.

Steiner, Z. 1969. *The Foreign Office and Foreign Policy, 1898–1914*. Cambridge: Cambridge University Press.

Steiner, Z., and V. Cromwell. 1972. The Foreign Office before 1914: a study in resistance. In *Studies in the Growth of Nineteenth Century Government*, ed. G. Sutherland. London: Routledge & Kegan Paul.

Stephens, J. 1989. Democratic transition and breakdown in Western Europe, 1870–1939. *American Journal of Sociology* 94.

Strachan, H. 1983. *European Armies and the Conduct of War*. London: Allen & Unwin.

1984. *Wellington's Legacy: The Reform of the British Army, 1830–54*. Manchester: Manchester University Press.

Teitler, G. 1977. *The Genesis of the Professional Officers Corps*. Beverly Hills, Calif.: Sage Publications.

Tilly, C. 1982. Proletarianization and rural collective action in East Anglia and elsewhere, 1500–1900. *Peasant Studies* 10.

1986. *The Contentious French*. Cambridge, Mass.: Harvard University Press.

1990. *Coercion, Capital and European States, AD 990–1990*. Oxford: Blackwell.

Tilly, R. 1971. Popular disorders in nineteenth-century Germany: a preliminary survey. *Journal of Social History* 4.

Vagts, A. 1959. *A History of Militarism*. Glencoe, Ill.: Free Press.

Wildman, A. 1980. *The End of the Imperial Russian Army*. Princeton, N.J.: Princeton University Press.

Wright, V. 1972. *Le conseil d'état sous le Second Empire*. Paris: Colin.

13   The rise of the modern state: III. Bureaucratization

The term "bureaucracy" is ubiquitous in historical work on the emergence of the modern state. Yet it is rarely defined and often misused. This is a pity, for since Weber, sociologists have generally used the term precisely. Weber (1978: I, 220–1) identified ten constituent elements of bureaucracy:

1. Officials are free, subject to authority only in their official tasks.
2. Officials are organized in a clearly defined hierarchy of offices.
3. Each office has a clearly defined sphere of competence.
4. Offices are filled by free contract.
5. Candidates for office are selected according to their qualifications, normally examinations and technical training.
6. Officials are salaried and granted pensions.
7. The office is the sole or primary occupation of the incumbent.
8. The office constitutes a career, involving promotion by seniority or for achievement.
9. The official is separated from ownership of the means of administration.
10. The official is subject to systematic discipline and control in official conduct.

This is surely more detail than we need – and research in modern-day offices demonstrates that most of the ten are closely interrelated (Hall 1963–4). For purposes of macrohistorical generalization, I have simplified Weber's ten into five key characteristics of bureaucracy, two of personnel, two of offices, and one indicating their relationship to the wider society:

Bureaucrats are officials (1) separated from ownership of office by an employed, salaried status and (2) appointed, promoted, and dismissed according to impersonal criteria of competence.

Bureaucratic offices are (3) organized within departments, each of which is centralized and embodies a functional division of labor; (4) departments are integrated into a single overall administration, also embodying functional division of labor and centralized hierarchy.

Finally, bureaucracy presupposes (5) *insulation* from the wider society's struggles over values. Weber saw bureaucracy as dominated by "formal" or "instrumental" rationality, insulating it from the "substantive" rationality embedded in the politics and values of society. Bureaucracies are efficient at implementing substantive goals set from outside their own administration. If an administration imports substantive or value rationality and party struggles, then it is embedded in society, reducing its formal rationality. Bureaucracy presupposes the insulation of administration from politics.

These five elements may be present in varying degrees, and each may be present without the others – although element 2 without 1 is unlikely and 5 tends to presuppose the rest. Administrations may be more or less bureaucratic, but full-fledged bureaucracy requires all five. It is also a universal, nationally uniform type of civil administration. Bureaucratization has accompanied and encouraged the growth of national states.

Given that most Western states are now largely bureaucratic, this chapter asks two simple empirical questions: When did they become so, and why? I claim not to give wholly original answers to these questions but, rather, to synthesize existing research literature. As is well known, states mostly bureaucratized in this period, but each of my five states proved at some point to be the pioneer as they all reacted to the entwinings of the sources of social power. Yet bureaucratization remained incomplete (as it still does today), especially at the top of administrations. As in militaries, bureaucratization and officials' social identities restrained one another to produce a dual crystallization within state administration: As an "elite," it was mildly technocratic-bureaucratic; as a "party," it largely reflected the policy of dominant classes. States were still not unitary.

Old regime administration

As Chapter 12 shows, bureaucracy entered states mainly through their armed forces, substantially bureaucratized well before civilian administrations. By 1760, military reforms were impacting on civil administration, especially in supply departments of navies and in fiscal departments. Yet this still had not gone very far. In eighteenth-century civil administration, the very notion of "employment" is dubious. There were five office-holding statuses and four forms of remuneration.

Office holding
1. At the highest levels office holding was dominated by hereditary ownership – the monarch's own position, of course. High offices could be passed directly to male heirs. Apart from royal families and ladies-in-waiting, there were no female holders of high office in this period.
2. The official could be elected, usually by his peers, holding office for life or a fixed term.
3. Offices could be purchased. In strict law these could rarely be transmitted to heirs, but in practice they often become hereditary, indistinguishable from status 1.

4. Offices could be acquired through the patronage of a higher official, often sweetened with a bribe. Ownership rights rested with the patron not the client official, who might be terminated at the patron's pleasure.
5. An office might be acquired and terminated in the modern way by impersonal criteria such as ability or experience, in which case no one owned it.

Remuneration

1. Many officials received no formal remuneration, but performed honorific duties flowing from their social rank.
2. Officials enjoyed the fruits of office, that is, to appropriate fees and perquisites flowing through it.
3. The salary was paid not to the person doing the office work (as in the modern manner) but to a sinecurist patron who then employed and paid a deputy to do the work.
4. A salary was paid in the modern way to the working official.

There are many possible combinations of office-holding statuses and remunerations, although a few combinations dominated. Only one combination – nonowning, salaried, working officials – can be regarded as potential bureaucrats, who were thus a small minority of mid-eighteenth-century state officials. The rest were embedded in particularistic, decentralized, and segmental forms of administrative control. As Weber noted, bureaucracy presupposes separating the official from his means of administration (he was playing upon Marx's definition of the proletariat). For administration to be bureaucratic, officials must find no profit in their decisions, they must be controllable by the administrative hierarchy, and they must be removable if they do not follow impersonal administrative rules. These conditions could not be met in the eighteenth century, because officials or their patrons *owned* offices and could derive profit from them. The property rights of owners and patrons blocked centralization, rationalization, and insulation of state administrations.

Their rights look to us like "corruption" – and they were eventually recognized as such and abolished. But in the eighteenth century such rights constituted a kind of "administrative representation," restraining royal despotism by allowing local-regional parties of the dominant classes to share control of state administration. Embryo party democracy in Britain and Holland meant not only parliaments; and in absolutist Austria, Prussia, and France, office ownership was the main restraint against centralized despotism, reducing state autonomy. In fact it makes it difficult to talk about the "state" as an actor. Old regime officials were highly embedded in civil society.

Then came two attempts at reform, the first from absolutism, the second a revolutionary and reformist redefinition of representation, from office owning toward democracy.

Phase 1: dynastic monarchy and war, 1700–1780

The first modern bureaucratic tracklayers were dynastic monarchs, formally above local-regional society in their military and civil powers. The administration of royal household and private domains actually belonged to the monarch, now also the undisputed commander in chief of the armed forces. The state elite did potentially exist as an "it," an actor, in the personages of the entourage, the friends, the relations, and the servants of the monarch. This "it" comprised only a fairly small part of the monarchical core, not the whole state. Outside were parties of nobles, high clerics, and local notables exercising effective autonomy in their own administrative spheres. Actual despotic power was limited by feeble infrastructural powers, typified by depending on local-regional – and sometimes also central – officials who owned their offices. Dynastic monarchies crystallized as dual: centralizing dynasts and decentralized old regime parties, played out as factionalism and intrigue at court and in administration.

For slightly different reasons, the two least representative regimes, the Hohenzollern and Habsburg dynasties of Prussia and Austria, launched an eighteenth-century bureaucratic offensive. Other German states, Sweden, and then Russia also joined in. The first major ideological movement for state reform, cameralism, appeared mainly in the universities of Lutheran North Germany and Roman Catholic Austria (Johnson 1969; Raeff 1975; Krygier 1979; Tribe 1984, 1988). Throughout the eighteenth century cameralists developed a "science of administration," arguing that state departments (*Kammer*) should be centralized, rationalized, informed by systematic statistics gathering, and subject to universal administrative and fiscal rules. This would better attain three policy goals: providing good order, encouraging subjects' (not citizens') economic activities, and routinely extracting their wealth as revenue. Their favorite metaphor was a machine.

A properly constituted state must be exactly analogous to a machine, in which all the wheels and gears are precisely adjusted to one another; and the ruler must be the foreman, the main-spring, or the soul . . . which sets everything in motion. [Justi, a cameralist, quoted by Krygier 1979: 17]

Early eighteenth-century cameralists were jurists, university professors, and prominent officials or their advisers, urging monarchs to abandon particularism. These "subservient bureaucrats" (Johnson's term) were then swept up into Central European enlightened absolutism, urging wholesale state reform. Anticlericalism also characterized Austrian cameralism. By 1790, there were more than thirty professors of cameralism in German and Austrian universities and about sixty published textbooks on the subject. Then cameralism faded before the influence of French Physiocrats and British political economists (Tribe 1988). The Central European statist phase of theorizing "modernization" gave ground before the British capitalist phase.

The Habsburg state was more dynastic and so more insulated from civil society than any state to the West. It was a gigantic confederation in which the royal central government and army constituted a separate tier apart from noble-dominated estate and lordship administrations of its many provinces and historic kingdoms. As Chapter 10 shows, the Habsburgs worked a protection racket: The provinces agreed to Habsburg despotic rule to avoid the potentially worse despotism of others and one another. The royal core was a neutral "it," relatively unconstrained by representative office holding – in this Catholic country many officials and officers were "neutral" foreigners and Protestants; later, many were Jews.

The main reform burst occurred in response to the War of the Austrian Succession (1740–8), a concerted attempt by surrounding Powers to dismember the Habsburg domains on the accession of a woman, Maria Theresa. Facing elimination, forced back on her core royal domains, the energetic queen economized and maximized the fiscal resources under the joint models provided by cameralism and Prussian military administration. Her high officials were particularly goaded by the sight of the Prussian army extracting double the revenue from Silesia that they themselves had managed before 1740, when it had been an Austrian province (Axtmann 1991). The Austrian army was finally subordinated to the monarchy and professionalized. Most high royal officials became salaried, and their pensions were converted into a single rationalized pension fund, earlier than elsewhere. From 1776 on, high officials had to show evidence of having studied cameralism, and universities and the press were liberalized and secularized. Most central state departments – especially the Vienna City Bank (effectively the treasury), the mines and coinage department, and the *Camerale* (core ministries) – now became bureaucratically organized. All this was reflected in the early emergence of Austrian census statistics revealed in Table 11.7.

Austrian bureaucratization, however, had two limits. First, individual departments were not integrated into a single functional and hierarchical structure. They coexisted in Vienna with earlier state institutions centered on the court. There was no single enduring cabinet, no effective first minister, but rather plural councils and ministers competing for access to the monarch and influence at court. Social ties among monarchy, court, church, high military officers, and administrators were so close that we can identify them as a state elite, if rarely a united one. But the Austrian state was not a single bureaucracy. It was a monarchy whose goals were implemented through interpenetrating administrations infiltrated by parties.

Second, this partial bureaucratization characterized only the central royal tier of government, mainly in Vienna, sitting above the local-regional administrations of Austria, Bohemia, Hungary, and so forth, whose offices were elected by the estates or owned by local notables and church dignitaries. As Table 4.2 indicates, the royal administration had less provincial infrastructural power than states whose officials were more embedded there. Maria Theresa and her son Joseph II were carrying out ambitious "enlightened" projects in the largest empire in Europe, but they could not institutionalize them there. Joseph II struggled hard and consciously against regional particularism, but he lost. Hungarian nobles and Low Country nobles, merchants, and clerics rebelled in the name of particularistic liberties and representative privileges. Both began negotiating with Prussia (offering a rival protection racket) when Joseph pushed them too far. His successor, Leopold, restored their liberties and offices. Enlightened absolutism retreated into its capital (Macartney 1969; Beales 1987; Dickson 1987; Axtmann 1991). An autonomous, protobureaucratic eighteenth-century state was infrastructurally a feeble one. The Austrian state failed to bureaucratize and modernize much further from this base.

Prussian administration is almost invariably (though not helpfully) called the "bureaucracy" by historians on whose empirical research I rely (Rosenberg 1958; Fischer and Lundgreen 1975: 509–27; Gray 1986; but Johnson 1975 differs). Its royal state core also moved early toward bureaucratic personnel – again under the pressure of war. Here the innovator was less directly cameralism, more the army. As Prussia triumphed through testing midcentury wars, an expanding military-fiscal administration enveloped the royal domains, regalian rights (the mint and mines), estates, and townships. Under Frederick William I, a general directory of four ministers supervised provincial boards of war and domains, overseeing tax commissars and county commissioners (*Landräte*). A minister famously commented: "Prussia was not a country with an army, but an army with a country which served as headquarters and food magazine" (Rosenberg 1958: 40).

Thus, after 1750, there was little office owning. Central and high-level local-regional officials drew salaries and pensions and were appointed and dismissed by the monarch. Under cameralist influence, the late 1730s saw training and examining of judges. By 1780, judges had to have earned a university law degree, undertaken two years of in-service training, and then passed an examination (Weill 1961; Johnson 1975: 106–33). The requirement of taking entrance examinations spread throughout the higher administration between 1770 and 1800. A university degree became the normal qualification, giving officials "national" cultural cohesion – the universities were the principal transmitters of "German" identity. The law code of 1794 reinforced all these and granted officials legal tenure conditional on competent performance of their duties. They were now titled not royal servants but "professional officials of the state" (*Beamten des Staats*). They were indeed bureaucrats, perhaps uniquely in the world at the time. Prussia had overtaken Austria as tracklayer of bureaucracy. As a "national" bureaucracy, Prussia was way ahead.

Yet Prussian bureaucratization also had limits. Like its progenitor, the army, it crystallized as *old regime* because it was a compromise with nobles, especially Junkers. As Table 4.2 indicates, the Prussian state was infrastructurally effective because it centrally coordinated the state elite with parties drawn from the dominant class. Then came the tensions of state modernization and bourgeois expansion. Until the 1820s, few nobles went to the universities, and the conflict between privately educated, "practical" notable officials and university-educated wealthy-commoner and "national" officials was openly acknowledged. Monarchs steered between them, wary of both too much noble control and the threat of a bureaucratic caste. In Prussia (and later in Russia) struggles between old regime and substantial bourgeoisie occurred within state administration.

The Prussian struggles were successfully compromised. Bourgeois professionals were admitted, and nobles became educated. Most high civil and military officers remained noble right up to the major expansion of army, navy, and civil administration just before 1900, when finally nobles could not supply enough sons (Bonin 1966; Koselleck 1967: 435; Gillis 1971: 30; military data presented in Chapter 12). Indeed, as the Junkers were now losing their economic power, they depended more on civil service careers (Muncie 1944). Examinations were also qualifying rather than competitive. Higher officials could select who they liked, provided the candidate passed. They selected their own, and administration remained embedded in the old regime. Thus officials served the crown, yet also enjoyed independence conferred by their class. Like officials of other German states, they often chose not to carry out directives they disliked (Blanning 1974: 191).

Prussian civil administration also crystallized as *militarist*. Administrators were put into uniforms and given formal rank. Militarism also spread through the middle and lower levels (Fischer and Lundgreen 1975: 520–1). Army mobilization depended on a large pool of trained reservists, especially noncommissioned officers. What to do with these veterans at war's end, and how to keep them motivated for the next one? Even in the eighteenth century, the Hohenzollerns urged ministers to find state employment for ex-soldiers. Veterans were preferred as city gate comptrollers, factory inspectors, policemen, elementary school teachers, even clergymen, and later as railway employees. From 1820 on, all noncommissioned officers with nine years' service could claim preferment in clerical and accounting jobs in the administration, provided they were literate and could count. Austria later guaranteed this for twelve-year noncommissioned officers, and France wrote similar practices into law in 1872. Even many twentieth-century German civil service rules concerned discipline and punishment, and regulations enshrined the primacy of public order over other goals and of the military in enforcing it. Martial law remained a hardy perennial of Prussian-German administration (Ludtke 1989).

These two crystallizations, as old regime and militarist, gave a distinctively "Prussian" cast to administration. Both enhanced control across and down the administration, less by Weber's rational accounting procedures than by that combination of esprit de corps and disciplined fear that is the hallmark of an effective military aristocracy. This modern administration was permeated by traditional class and military power relations.

The third limitation on Prussian bureaucracy operated in the opposite direction, to reduce state homogeneity. Prussia failed to integrate different administrative departments, just like Austria. Within departments arose hierarchy, order, and career structure. But relations between departments remained confused. The general directory had emerged from a wartime crisis, invasion. Some of its ministers had territorial, others functional, spheres of competence. At first they sat collectively in the royal privy council, but this body fell into disuse under Frederick the Great – he wanted power to centralize on him, not ministers. His segmental divide-and-rule policy reduced bureaucratization and aborted any prime minister who might constitute a power rival (Anderson and Anderson 1967: 37). The so-called cabinets were not councils of ministers but of court advisers liaising independently with ministries. As Prussia expanded, new agencies proliferated alongside old ministries:

Five primary bureaucracies operated at cross purposes, in opposition to one another and recognized only the king as a common master. . . . No single bureaucracy existed after 1740, and functions were not divided up logically and assigned to persons placed in a bureaucratic hierarchy. The Prussian government became more and more decentralized . . . divided into mutually antagonistic parts. [Johnson 1975: 274]

Administration mixed two principles of accountability, collegial decision making by corps of officials and the "one-man principle"

favored by most reformers. Prussian administration was not singular
and centralized. At its higher levels, it fed into an aristocratic court
centered on a monarch unwilling to abandon segmentalism. Ministers,
even chancellors after this post developed, relied on court intrigue
along with formal administrative position to exert influence. The goal
was to secure direct access to the monarch. Absolutism had only the
fictional unity of the monarch. It could not be bureaucratic, whatever
the employment status of its officials.

Yet the Austrian and Prussian states were the most bureaucratic of
the eighteenth century. Each reinforced dynastic monarchy with a
further autonomy, emerging from Austrian dynastic confederalism and
Prussian militarism. France, though formally absolutist, had no such
insulation. Centuries of accommodation to the privileges of provincial
nobles and corporate groups had embedded even its highest levels in
civil society in what can only be described as a peculiarly corrupt and
particularistic form of "representation" (Bosher 1970; Mousnier 1970:
17 ff.; Fischer and Lundgreen 1975: 490–509; Church 1981).

The French state had two main employment statuses. Most officials
were called *officiers*, owning their office, usually by purchase, their
property rights protected by corporate bodies. A minority were termed
commissaires, salaried working employees. The boundaries between
the two kept shifting, as *commissaires* sought ownership and the king
struggled to reduce venality. By the 1770s, there were at most 50,000
salaried, removable officials, predominantly in the ministries, customs
posts, and post offices. They were dwarfed by, and usually subordinate
to, *officiers*. Necker (1784) estimated 51,000 venal offices in law courts,
municipalities, and financial offices alone. To this we should add venal
offices in the royal household, in tax farming, and in other financial
companies used by the state and offices held by guild inspectors,
inspectors, and masters – even wigmakers. Taylor (1967: 477) and
Doyle (1984: 833) estimate the total at 2 percent to 3 percent of the
adult male population – about 200,000 persons. We should then add
perhaps 100,000 of the 215,000 part-time revenue collectors estimated
by Necker (the others may be already counted as venal offices above).
Some of these were venal, some salaried. I hazard a guess that at most
20 percent of the officials were salaried *commissaires*. But it is only a
guess, as nobody knew – which is actually the most significant finding
(as I noted more generally in Chapter 11).

There were no impersonal rules for appointment or promotion in
any department. Most high officials had prior legal training, but this
was normal for cultivated men, rather than technical administrative
training (which it partly was in Prussia). Perhaps 5 percent of French
officials can be called bureaucrats on our two Weberian indices of

personnel. The state was riddled with private and corporate property rights, thoroughly embedded in civil society.

Nor did its offices have much bureaucratic organization, within or between departments. Within the key ministries, hierarchy developed from the 1770s on, involving salary differentials and career lines. But even there, and rampant elsewhere, ownership rights cut across hierarchical and functional flows of information and control, as they did in relations between departments. French administration mixed collegial and one-man rule, and then aborted both. The old *conseil d'état* had specialized into various councils, some absorbed into the court. As in most countries the finance minister had emerged as the key official. But he had no particular status within councils or court, and he had little authority even over much of the sprawling financial administration. In the provinces much turned upon the energy of the individual intendant and his small staff, but they needed to collaborate amicably with local notables, replete with particularistic privileges.

Reformers knew what a rational, modern administration would look like, for the French Enlightenment drew upon cameralism (though with more explosive political demands). And in ministers like Necker they had patrons who counted numbers and costs, who eliminated what corruption they could, and who sought to reorganize broad administrative swathes (no one could comprehend, let alone reform, the whole). But their progress, as Necker admitted, was limited:

Subdelegates, officers of the *election*, managers, receivers and controllers of the *vingtièmes*, commissioners and collectors of the *taille*, officials of the *gabelles*, inspectors, process-servers, *corvée* bosses, agents of the *aides*, the *contrôle*, the reserved imposts; all these men of the fisc, each according to his character, subjugates to his small authority and entwines in his fiscal science the ignorant taxpayer, unable to know whether he is being cheated or not, but who constantly suspects and fears it. [quoted in Harris 1979: 97]

The principal twentieth-century scholar has agreed: "The old regime never had a budget, never had a legislative act foreseeing and authorising the total of receipts and expenses for a given period of time. . . . It only knew fragmented, incomplete states" (Marion 1927: I, 448).

Thus I find it bizarre that some historians are attracted to the word "bureaucracy" to describe this state. For example, Harris refers to the Royal General Farms – that monument to office holding as private property and profit – as "that enormous bureaucratic apparatus" (1979: 75). There were few traces of bureaucracy in old regime France.

Dynasticism saw some bureaucratic modernization, but administration was only insulated from classes at the highest royal level in Prussia and especially in Austria. Overall this seems less significant than party domination by an old regime that was simultaneously politicized classes and embedded officials. This was especially marked in France. In Britain and its American colonies we also find highly embedded old regimes – but in an embryo party democracy, containing parliamentary party factions as well as corrupt officeholders. This combination produced a British administration as cohesive as Prussia's, but one far less bureaucratized. (For the British-Prussian comparison, see Mueller 1984.)

Until nearly 1800 in Britain, salaried, working higher officials were greatly outnumbered by sinecurists drawing salary or fruits of office, employing deputies to do the actual work. Virtually all three hundred Exchequer offices were filled by deputies (Binney 1958: 232–3). In the Navy Department, the treasurer appointed and paid his own paymaster to do his work, and the two auditors of imprest kept most of their considerable salaries (more than £16,000 and £10,000 per year) even after paying all departmental expenses. In 1780, it was publicly revealed that neither had actually intervened in the work of his department for more than thirty years. In the office of the secretary of state, even the office cleaner employed another (Cohen 1941: 24–6). There were no preset qualifications or examinations for office and no formal criteria for promotion except in Customs and Excise and technical Navy departments. Even they had merely formalized patronage into written recommendations (Aylmer 1979: 94–5).

There could be no centralized chain of command between or even within departments. At every level it was frustrated by autonomous property rights to office. But in the eighteenth century changes occurred. The First Lord of the Treasury was gradually becoming "prime" minister, in the House of Lords representing the monarch to Parliament. Beneath him were two major secretaries of state and junior ministers and boards running specific departments. Yet monarch and members of both houses had independent channels of influence and patronage inside departments.

Public business was carried on in a number of more or less independent offices, which were subject to no supervision either as regards their methods of work or the details of their expenditure. . . . [T]he First Lord of the Treasury could not make a tolerable guess at the expenses of government for any one year. [Cohen 1941: 34]

There were no attempts to count officials until 1797.

As in France, "corruption" was sturdily defended, but in Britain it was centralized, national corruption, for its fountainheads were the sovereign and his ministries in Parliament. It brought rewards for owners and patrons, but it also ensured that royal administration could work only *through* the "protonational" parties of the propertied classes. Administration was not insulated from politics or class. Its corrupt, particularistic "representation" was appropriate to late agrarian societies like Britain and France. On the one hand, they lacked the communications and the party disciplines that later reinforced parliamentary representation in industrial capitalism; on the other hand, their populations and capitalisms were outgrowing rule by particularistic kin networks radiating downward from Royal Council or Parliament. In France administrative representation produced inefficient administration, but in Britain it was highly efficient. It remained virtually unchanged until the 1780s, despite the extraordinary transformation of civil society.

Yet British bureaucracy stirred when state militarism escalated fiscal pressures – first in the technical branches of the navy (not the more aristocratic army), then in the customs and excise tax offices. Brewer (1989) shows that the Excise Department became the first civilian administration directly controlled by higher state officials. Four thousand eight hundred persons, most of them salaried, were implicated in a "proto-organization chart" (although this figurative device had not yet been invented), embodying formal channels of functional and hierarchical communication and control, submitting regular written reports, actually delivering predictable revenues (unusual in the eighteenth century). It contrasted to the corrupt administration of the venerable land tax, bearing down on property owners who had elaborated office owning in self-defense. The excise tax had been introduced by an unusually effective despotic state, Cromwell's Commonwealth. Though constitutionally controversial, its extraction had not caused much pain among the old regime. It was a tax on the excess profits of commerce and on the consumption of the powerless poor – and it financed profitable global expansion. Yet the Excise Department was a potential Trojan horse. Its bureaucratic model was hailed in the 1780s by reformers urging parliamentary commissions of enquiry.

There were now also outside pressures toward a bureaucratic and, more ambivalently, toward a national administration. Chapter 4 charts the growth of a national "economic reform" movement inveighing against waste and corruption. It had two sources of inspiration. First, as elsewhere, came the fiscal pressure of modern war. The movement was created by the Seven Years' War, its first actual reforms pressured by the American Revolution. But second, it resonated ideologically amid the national alliance of old regime "outs" and emerging "excluded" petite bourgeoisie. This alliance also owed much to the diffusion of commercial, then industrial, capitalism. So did its theory of efficient administration. Utilitarianism differed from cameralism:

Its rationality was formal, systemic, and decentered, governed by principles underlying relations in civil society, needing less authoritative state guidance. I detect the influence of the "invisible hand" of the world's most capitalist economy.

I have charted a first phase of state modernization and bureaucratization. This was toward countable, working, salaried, qualified officials and toward functional and hierarchical rationalization of individual departments. As yet there was little change on the fourth and fifth criteria of bureaucracy, integrating different departments and separating party politics and administration. The main reforms had come from power relations that do not seem very "modern." The early moves came in the least representative monarchies, Austria and Prussia, absolute dynasties, poorly equipped with commerce, industry, and urbanization (as Aylmer 1979: 103 also notes). Dynasticism could be an "it," an insulated centralized actor capable of reorganizing "itself" with the aid of a conscious science of administration. Austrian and Prussian dynasticisms were reinforced by their confederal and militarist crystallizations. By contrast, in (embryo) party-democratic Britain, administration was royal *and* embedded – centralized and decentralized; so was Parliament, split between court and country parties, placemen and county gentry. Any reform must be agreed to by both parties. Yet corruption had been institutionalized by their historic compromise, buying the crown influence and notables freedom from despotism. In this respect the French regime, formally dynastic but embedded and "corruptly representative" almost up to its head, resembled the British. But Prussian and Austrian monarchs had higher administrations that were theirs to modernize. Cameralism could be thought there, not in Britain. True, dynasts could only penetrate their realms by compromising with nobility and church, embedded in local-regional administrations. But, unlike in Britain (or its American colonies), nobody questioned the monarch's right to administer his or her own.

Dynasts were also spurred toward reform by the pressure of land wars, which were most severe in Central Europe. The rhythms of state modernization were supplied by the fiscal and manpower strains of militarism; military-fiscal administrations were the first to be rationalized (the Prussian judiciary, an apparent exception, was closely linked to military administration); and, especially in Prussia, the military provided organizational models. The pressure was felt in France, too, but the regime was unable to carry military reforms into fiscal departments. When the Napoleonic Wars eventually brought comparable military-fiscal burdens to Britain, reform would come too, and through a similar departmental route.

Thus the first phase of bureaucratization was caused less by a "modern" capitalist civil society than by states' traditional military crystallizations, most intensely experienced in the least representative monarchies. There was one exception to this: pressures exerted by British bourgeois and petit bourgeois reformers, in this period unsuccessful. Bureaucratization was coming primarily from the old monarchical and military state, not the new civil society, its limits set primarily by that state's contradictions: rational administration versus segmental divide and rule and autonomy from, yet dependence on, the nobility.

Phase 2: revolution, reform, and representation, 1780-1850

In this period, state modernization shifted into tracks defined primarily by struggles over political representation and national citizenship that were led by revolutionaries. The American Revolution has historical precedence.[1] With independence achieved, there could be no American return to "old corruption." Despotism was to be avoided by making the state small and answerable to elected bodies. In principle, state rationalization was, for the first time, politically acceptable. Federalists were also steeped in cameralist, Enlightenment, and utilitarian ideas. Alexander Hamilton was an avid reader of Jacques Necker (McDonald 1982: 84-5, 135-6, 160-1, 234, 382-3). The European ideological community spanned the Atlantic.

The Constitution brought major development on four of my five indices of bureaucratization, though only at the federal level. *All* federal officials have been salaried, from the late 1780s to the present day. Each department was to be rationally organized by hierarchy and function. Authority was vested in the one-man principle urged by Hamilton. Hierarchy culminated in three secretaries (of the treasury, state, and war), later joined by the post office and navy heads and the attorney general. These departments were financially responsible to the treasury and met in cabinet under the chief executive, the president. They were to submit written reports to the president and Congress, and they imposed similar reports on subdepartments. A formal separation of powers divided administration from politics, except that the chief executive was also chief politician. By contrast, state and local governments devised far more embedded administrations. But at the federal level American government offices were

---

[1] My main sources on American administration have been Fish (1920), White (1951, 1954, 1958, 1965), Van Riper (1958), Keller (1977), Shefter (1978), and Skowroneck (1982).

intended as a full-fledged bureaucracy, the only one in the world for at least another fifty years. The international community of enlightened and utilitarian reformers hailed it as their ideal. The bureaucratic tracklayer had jumped the Atlantic.

Practice did not quite match theory. White's studies show that early administration depended as much on patron-client networks as on formal hierarchies. Reformers cut them down a little with rules governing accounting functions, contract bidding, and land grants. In 1822, Congress asked department heads to report on all employees' efficiency. The secretary of war listed his and added:

The only inefficient clerk in the Department is Colonel Henley, who is seventy-four years of age, and has been in the service . . . from the year 1775. . . . From his age he is incapable of performing the duties of a clerk, but, from his recollection of revolutionary events, he is useful in the examination of revolutionary claims. [American State Papers 1834: vol. 38, 983]

Maybe Colonel Henley was really the secretary's uncle, or maybe the department really liked hearing his stories about the Revolution. But the secretary had to account for him, as perhaps no department head in any other country yet would.

Yet personnel were not so bureaucratized and they became noticeably less so through most of the nineteenth century. They were salaried, but appointment, promotion, and dismissal criteria were fuzzy. Washington set up no rules other than against "family relationship, indolence and drink." This was progress. As Finer (1952: 332) ironically observes: In Britain the last two criteria were no barrier to office, and the first was a positive recommendation. But formal entry qualifications lagged. Qualifications and examinations were introduced in the military in 1818, but (apart from a few accountants) only in the civil service in 1853. They were not standardized until 1873 and not universal until 1883. Tenure during good behavior was the early norm but declined as the famous party spoils system developed.

All presidents had appointed political friends to office. As America democratized, notable rule gave way to party control of offices. In Jackson's watershed purge of 1828–9, 10 percent to 20 percent of all federal officials and 40 percent of higher officials were dismissed and replaced by loyalists from his Republican faction. Party purges continued through midcentury, and patronage dominated most state and local governments. Once the presidential party could subvert the bureaucracy, Congress and judiciary also intervened. Federal departments were constrained to submit budgets to congressional appropriations committees, undermining treasury centralized control. Regulating competition between parties and administrations fell onto the courts, becoming procedural surrogates for a more bureaucratized administration (Skowronek 1982: 24–30). As British reform steadily proceeded, U.S. government bureaucracy regressed, overtaken by business bureaucracy, especially in railroads (Finer 1952; Yeager 1988).

There were three reasons why federal government lagged. First, the United States was relatively uninvolved in foreign wars and had a tiny military budget. Elsewhere, military-fiscal pressures continued to increase the size and rationalize the structure of central state administration. In the United States, the War of 1812 did force reorganization of military and accounting departments, but this tiny state had no continental rivals into the twentieth century. The Civil War enormously increased both states' size, but only temporarily, for its result left the Union unchallenged. Second came an unanticipated peculiarity. This state, constitutionally entrusted with expanding customs revenues, proved surprisingly affluent, often blessed with surpluses, needing little of the "efficient or economical organization" that Congress in theory demanded. This state felt little of the geopolitical militarism that elsewhere pressured bureaucratization.

Third, the Constitution had not solved the two distinctively political crystallizations – representation and the national issue – and this blocked a bureaucracy seen as potentially despotic. The Constitution shows that contemporaries recognized the technical feasibility of bureaucracy – well before the emergence of an industrial society. But it turned out that they did not want it. Adult, white, male Americans disagreed about what government, especially central government, should do. Political power networks crystallized in complex political factions and parties representing class, religion, economic sector, regional economies, and individual states. Indeed, U.S. politics probably saw the greatest proliferation of such pluralist interest groups. To ensure that government actually represented their interests, parties and factions restrained centralized state power and embedded themselves in multiple assemblies and offices at the federal, state, and local levels.

The "confederal" solution was chosen in the absence of any single party strong enough to control the state. As American government grew, it became fractionalized by parties institutionalized at all levels of government. Then the result of the Civil War began to produce slow and partial recentralization (still within the limits of a federal constitution). The entwined politics of class and locality-region (as well as slavery-segregation, religion, etc.) kept this state puny, divided, only feebly bureaucratized throughout the period.

France was the home of the second, more ambitious revolution. On August 4, 1789, the French revolutionaries abolished office venality along with "feudalism." They intended to reduce the number of offices to a small salaried core and devolve most public functions onto unpaid, committed citizens. Its rationality would be as substantive as formal, embodying the morals and values of the new citizen. But neither idealism nor economy survived revolutionary war and terror. The need to supply armies and cities, to hunt out counterrevolutionaries, and to implement many new laws re-created the bulk of the old regime state. It was now salaried, not venal, committed to rational principles of hierarchy and function and ostensibly centralized. These were major modernizations. But it fell short of its goals and of modern claims on its behalf.

"As a flood spreads wider and wider, the water becomes shallower and dirtier. So the Revolution evaporates and leaves behind only the slime of a new bureaucracy. The chains of tormented mankind are made out of red tape." Kafka's bitter denunciation of the Bolshevik Revolution (Janouch 1953: 71) typifies twentieth-century cynicism about the legacy of revolution – the triumph not of liberty, equality, and fraternity but of state bureaucracy and despotism. The French Revolution led toward militant nationalism and statist communism not toward liberal freedom, says O'Brien (1990). For Skocpol, the French, Russian, and Chinese revolutions all increased state powers, especially their centralization and rationalization. In France the Revolution produced a "professional-bureaucratic state" existing "as a massive presence in society . . . as a uniform and centralized administrative framework," restrained only by a decentralized capitalist economy (1979: 161–2). Tilly (1990: 107–14) claims the French Revolution provided the "most sensational move" toward centralized "direct" government. Revolutionary armies then imposed this (with regional variations) on other countries.

Yet Skocpol's comparison with twentieth-century revolutions misleads. As we saw in Chapter 11, only at the end of the nineteenth century did state infrastructural powers develop much. They were also still restrained by competitive parties, rival state crystallizations, and market capitalism (Skocpol acknowledges this last restraint). If revolutionaries captured a twentieth-century state and abolished or bypassed the powers of capital and of party competition (as Bolsheviks and Fascists did), they might use these expanded infrastructures to increase enormously state despotic powers. But eighteenth- and early nineteenth-century revolutionaries had no such power potentiality at hand if they seized the state.

The French revolutionaries possessed, first, the distinct ideological power identified in Chapter 6. They *proclaimed* the most ambitious programs of state-led social regeneration and they could mobilize political support for them. Like the Americans, they knew in advance what a bureaucratic state looked like – borrowing cameralist mechanical models of administration (Bosher 1970: 296–7). In the fervent revolutionary climate they wiped some slates clean – abolishing office ownership and the particularisms of regional administrations at a stroke and formally replacing them with salaries and *départements*. This was important. As Tilly notes, it leveled French towns; no longer were bourgeois commercial towns subordinated to old regime administrative towns. Second, the revolutionaries centralized political representation so that dominant factions in the assembly and the two great committees could legislate for the whole of France. With these powers there is no question they modernized and bureaucratized state administration beyond old regime capacities. They aspired to direct, not indirect, rule – and in certain respects they achieved it.

Yet this did not increase the size or scope of total administration. Skocpol (1979: 199) uses Church's figures on the increase of salaried officials to assume such an increase. But as Table 11.7 and Appendix Table A.3 reveal, the *total* number of offices probably did not rise to old regime levels until after 1850. The core ministerial personnel did proliferate rapidly from 1791 on, and the convention and Committee of Public Safety introduced salary scales and office rationalization. The key fiscal department was integrated by function and hierarchy (Bosher 1970 calls it simply a "bureaucracy" by 1794). Yet its bureaucratic criteria were mixed with party ones. When the committee regulated office qualifications, they insisted on submission of a curriculum vitae containing evidence of loyalty to the Revolution.

Moreover, the *performance* of the revolutionary state, outside of the military sphere and outside of the erratic Terror, was minimal. Margadant (1988) shows that its inability to gather taxes was pathetic. Can a fiscal administration be called bureaucratic if it manages to collect 10 percent of the taxes it demands? As we saw in Chapter 6, the revolutionary state was forced – at the height of supposed centralization under the Committee of Public Safety – to send out politically reliable *députés en mission* to lead armed bands and allowed them much tactical discretion to extract its basic subsistence needs. We clearly see its penetrative powers through the memoirs of Madame de la Tour du Pin (1985: 202). After describing her counterrevolutionary network spread throughout France, she remarks how odd it is that their correspondence was not intercepted. They lived secretively in cellars and abandoned farms, they slipped out in disguise at night to the village postbox, and then the revolutionary postal service – inherited from the old regime – did the rest. The left hand of the Terror did not know what the right hand of the postal service was doing.

Once political compromise and consolidation became possible, under the Directory and Bonaparte, some state powers stressed by Skocpol became actuality. Ministries, prefects, and salaried officials governed France under the impersonal rules of Bonaparte's civil code (Richardson, 1966; Church 1981). Woolf (1984: 168) claims that under Napoleon, France acquired an "undoubted lead" in official statistics (though I doubt the data collected were in advance of earlier Austrian statistics). It still lacked bureaucratic characteristics: no impersonal preentry qualifications, no examinations, little integration of different ministries. Ministers reported either to the Council of State, a body of loyal notables without ministerial responsibilities, or to Bonaparte himself. He resorted to the segmental divide-and-rule strategies of monarchs seeking to prevent a unified bureaucracy. He also resorted to tax-farming arrangements with private financiers, reminiscent of the old regime (Bosher 1970: 315–7). Ministerial fragmentation then survived Bonaparte. Nineteenth-century France had not one administration but plural ministries, says Charle (1980: 14). Ministers imposed their own appointment, promotion, and dismissal criteria on their departments until after the 1848 revolution.

Most pervasive of all was the French practice of embedding administration in party politics: Officials remained divided between *employés* and *fonctionnaires* throughout the century (Charle 1980). *Employés* were the descendants of old regime *commissaires*, "bureaucrats" in its slightly pejorative modern usage, middle-to-lower level officials implementing impersonal rules laid down from above by *fonctionnaires*, descendants of old regime *officiers* married (metaphorically) to revolutionary citizen-officials. *Fonctionnaires*, organized into *corps*, staffed higher administration. Like military officers they were supposed to demonstrate party commitment to common ideals. Bonaparte sought to ensure this by recruiting only young men from families of imperial notables, given in-service training. His successors also imported loyalists but favored elite generalist education through the *grandes écoles*, and from 1872 from the academy still known as "Sciences Po" (Osborne 1983). The collegial *corps* imported substantive party rationality, reducing formal bureaucratization.

As no nineteenth-century French regime lasted longer than two decades, administrative parties kept changing as top personnel in ministries, prefectures, judiciary, and army were purged. As did American elections, this brought on a party spoils system. Monarchist notables changed places with députés-fonctionnaires (Julien-Laferrière 1970). Republicanism remained more solidly entrenched in local government, leading to midcentury conflict between central ministries and local communes, with prefects often acting as mediators (Ashford

1984: 49–68). Yet the secular drift toward Republicanism brought gradual bureaucratization. As Republican regimes institutionalized, they favored meritocracy and separated politics and administration. Competitive examinations spread after 1848, sharing the stage with informal on-the-job training and withstanding a final reaction under Louis Bonaparte (Thuillier 1976: 105–15; 1980: 334–62). Republicans finally captured the civil service in the 1880s. Now French administration became predominantly bureaucratic, though still ruled by a party collegial *corps*.

So the French Revolution, like the American, promised more bureaucracy than it delivered. The reason was the same: Party politics could not be separated from administration. Class and national politics were not yet settled. Party democracies were polymorphous, crystallizing in changing and entwined political-administrative shapes. Yet these complex administrative developments may be like a glass half drunk. We may emphasize the volume either of water or of air. Skocpol and Tilly emphasize bureaucratization and state power; I emphasize their limits. A better measure would be comparative. Had France been pushed – by revolution, directorate or Bonaparte – to greater bureaucracy than other countries? Yet the question cannot be posed this simply. As Tilly notes, revolution and its wars impacted on othei states, bureaucratizing them too. States were not just independent comparable cases but interdependent units in a European geopolitical, economic, and ideological community. I continue with the cases; then I turn to their interdependence.

Chapter 4 shows that the British struggle over political representation was linked to administrative economic reform. As geopolitical militarism brought fiscal pressures, economic reform rushed ahead, carrying franchise reform on its coattails. Wartime propertied taxpayers decided "old corruption" was too expensive. The old regime reformed itself, aided by class pressure from below. Parliamentary commissioners from the early 1780s on declared against corruption, Parliament legislated from the late 1780s on, and reforming ministers whittled away from the 1790s on. The proportion of the earnings of the top twenty Home Office officials coming from salaries rose from 56 percent in 1784 to 95 percent in 1796 (Nelson 1969: 174–5). By 1832, salaries were normal, office owning virtually gone. Abolition of sinecures enabled functional and hierarchical reorganization within most departments. Legislation prohibited placemen and barred members of Parliament from holding offices. The wars brought virtual cabinet government under a prime minister responsible to Parliament. Ministers spent more time in cabinet and Parliament, leaving their departments under the control of salaried permanent secretaries. An act of 1787 integrated the finances of departments hitherto paid out of separate earmarked funds. By 1828, all income and virtually all expenses went in and out of a single fund, its accounts presented to Parliament (although disbursements were not regulated by the treasury and remained political). By 1832, administration had been transformed (Cohen 1941; Finer 1952; Parris 1969).

On one criterion of bureaucracy Britain lagged: No standards of competence for employment or promotion were introduced until after midcentury – and even then reform was minimal. Although utilitarian and radical reformers demanded examinations and technical training, they got neither. By reforming itself, the old regime had held onto recruitment and some patronage. The impetus had been to cut administration and save money. Table 11.7 shows its success. Civil servants increased less than population between 1797 and 1830. Commissioners reported to Parliament that "old corruption" was gone and few further savings could be made. The reform movement subsided, no further bureaucratization occurring until after midcentury. The compromise endured.

In this second phase there had been two main causes of British bureaucratization. First, the traditional fiscal pressures of geopolitical militarism forced an old regime to raise taxes, cut costs, rationalize, centralize, and forget its ideological principles. Second, emerging bourgeois classes exerted a distinctively modern capitalist pressure for political citizenship and utilitarian administration. The two causes reinforced each other: The most advanced capitalist state was fighting for its geopolitical life. The resolution was a stabler settlement of old regime–emergent class struggles than in France and a more centralized settlement than in the United States. Added to the pressures of the third phase (discussed soon), this took Britain beyond the limits of bureaucracy found elsewhere. The bureaucratic tracklayer was now in offshore Europe.

After a promising beginning, Prussian dynasticism managed only limited modernization in the nineteenth century. By 1800, it was riven by party disputes. Reformers, mostly noble, though with some bourgeois professionals, sought administrative rationalization. In local administration they saw the obstacles as particularistic noble and gentry control and, at higher state levels, the court. Discreetly, cautiously, they suggested representative assemblies and a more open administration. War seemed to play into their hands. After Napoleon destroyed the Prussian army at Jena and Auerstadt in 1805–6, the monarchy sought reforms to enhance efficiency, avoid social upheaval, yet not antagonize its new French overlord. Reformers urged limited assemblies and a single administration to run right down from a chancellor to the villages. For a short time they gained the upper hand, but by 1808 they had antagonized much of the aristocracy and the French. The bourgeoisie and petite bourgeoisie were too small in backward Prussia to add much popular pressure. These absolutist modernizers could do little without their monarch. To appease the French, he abandoned them.

After Napoleon's defeat, a compromise was reached (Mueller 1984: 126–66; Gray 1986). At local-regional levels little changed. Junker and church institutions survived intact until the 1848 revolution. In the central administration academic qualifications and examinations were strengthened and the universities were reformed. Nobles began to go to university, gradually reducing the old party factionalism and solidifying the national cultural integration of officials. Collegiality weakened before one-man rule. A revived Council of State now sat ministers and courtiers together, with the more expert ministers having the upper hand. During the weak rule of Frederick William III (1797–1840) power accrued to the *Beamten*, less as a rationalized bureaucracy than as Hintze's "noble-bourgeois aristocracy of service," "feudalizing" its bourgeois members (Muncie 1944) while "enlightening" the Prussian nobility. But as absolutism revived, so did particularism. The "cabinets" revived, and *Immediatstellung*, the right of a military commander to see the king alone, was extended to civilian officials. Bureaucracy remained subordinate to whoever the monarch chose to confide in – professional ministers or noble cronies. Party conflicts reduced bureaucratic unity, splitting it apart in 1848 – civil servants and teachers were activists on both sides in that abortive revolution (Gillis 1971).

The state remained intriguing, its parties embedded in civil society. Not until class and national representation were faced squarely again, with the addition of bourgeoisie, petite bourgeoisie, and Roman Catholics at the end of the nineteenth century, could the state modernize into the semiauthoritarianism described in Chapters 9 and 21. Prussia helped pioneer bureaucracy, but for much of the century the state as "universal bureaucracy" was Hegelian ideology, not German reality.

Austria, the first bureaucratic tracklayer, faltered earlier and more completely. Being least embedded in provincial noble power, Austrian dynastic administration was panicked most by the French Revolution and representative movements. Joseph II's successors bolted into reaction in the 1790s – the main bureaucratization now occurred in police administration (Wangerman 1969; Axtmann 1991). Defeated, though not humiliated by Bonaparte, the Austrians confined reform to the army and leaned upon the Catholic church to mobilize support against the French. By 1815, the Austrian regime had become the hammer of reform across Europe. Chapters 7 and 10 showed this multiregional, dynastic state struggling against regional fragmenting movements. In 1867, even the royal government split into two.

This was a transitional period in the life of the state, from a predominantly military to a diamorphous military-civil state. The bureaucratic tracklaying crystallizations were changing from monarchism and geopolitical militarism to representative, national citizenship. Militarism continued to pressure toward bureaucratic efficiency, but about 1810, dynasticism had reached its bureaucratic limits, blocked by the contradiction between monarchical despotism and bureaucratic centralization and by the weakness of class pressure for citizenship. By contrast, French and "Anglo-Saxon" regimes, living in more commercialized civil societies containing extensive and political classes, institutionalized compromises among old regime, bourgeoisie, and petite bourgeoisie that allowed more party democracy and therefore more bureaucratic accountability in administration. But even there party democracy and bureaucracy were not in perfect harmony. Political parties often collided with elite technocratic bureaucracy. States remained polymorphous. Although most parties opposed old regime particularism, they were wary of state efficiency. Why give the state more efficient, cohesive, and bureaucratic infrastructures? That might aid the despotic strategy of the state elite, or it might aid rival parties. American parties changed strategies to ensure that their state became more embedded, less bureaucratic. British parties compromised. French parties compromised once the republic was saved.

What now of the Kafka-Skocpol-Tilly claim that revolution extended state power? I offer some support. Through revolution, French overtook Austrian and Prussian bureaucratization. Without revolution, France may have become an even more laggard state than Austria now became. The French state was transformed – perhaps because it had been so previously laggard and lackadasical. But French modernization went less far than American and less thoroughly than British. The American impetus was arguably revolutionary (though Skocpol has elsewhere denied this). Yet Britain did not have a revolution, and Austria and Prussia did not lag because they lacked one. My conclusion is not that revolution was necessary to state modernization, or that it provided a unique boost to state powers (this being the argument of Skocpol and Tilly). Rather, in this phase (though not in the earlier phase) movement toward party democracy through either reform or revolution increased state bureaucracy. Unlike the Bolshevik Revolution, it was the positive, democratic side of the French Revolution, not its negative, dictatorial side, that encouraged bureaucratization. Party democracies trusted bureaucracy more because they felt they could control it. Regimes that had settled both representative and national disputes trusted it most.

To these comparative points I add another about interdependence that does increase the causal, militarist significance of the French Revolution. This fits well enough into the more general theoretical models of Skocpol and Tilly, as they both emphasize militarism in social development. Wars continued to stretch and modernize states. But the leading actor of these wars, the French Army, differed from its military predecessors. Politicized and popular, it threatened all old regimes. The effects differed between Britain and continental Europe. Militarily, Britain experienced the semitotal war that Austria and Prussia had gone through in the mid-eighteenth century, converting old regimes to state modernization. The political effects on Britain are more difficult to assess, but Chapter 4 argues that the Revolutionary and French wars advanced the merger of old regime and bourgeoisie that enabled the institutionalization of limited representative government (avoiding more popular, democratic government). In turn this enabled gradual bureaucratic modernization. So the French Revolution probably speeded up British state modernization. But the same forces may have slowed down state modernization in Central Europe. There French pressure modernized armies more than states and set back political representation, and thus also bureaucracy, by tainting moderate reformers and weak bourgeoisies and petite bourgeoisies with Jacobinism. Regimes went reactionary. Despite Kafka, Skocpol, and Tilly, the French Revolution left a decidedly mixed legacy for state development.

Phase 3: state infrastructures and industrial capitalism, 1850–1914

Chapter 11 shows that all late nineteenth-century states greatly increased their civilian scope and personnel, especially at lower and middling and at local-regional levels. Bureaucratization developed from the 1880s, struggling to keep pace with this sprawl. By 1910, Britain and France were almost as bureaucratic as they were ever to become, the United States was beginning reforms culminating in the 1920s, and the two monarchies were as bureaucratic as they could allow. In this phase there were two connected causes of bureaucratization. States institutionalized citizenship (though to varying degrees), and capitalist industrialization boosted their infrastructural powers, national economic integration, and corporate business models of bureaucracy. Both tended to reduce (though not eliminate) conflict about the role of the state and the usefulness of administrative efficiency. Bureaucratization grew, with less direct opposition.

Yet the task facing would-be bureaucrats was daunting. Would the vast number of state employees be loyal to the hierarchy? Or would they represent their own private interests or those of their class or religious or linguistic community? Because much of the expansion was at the local-government level, would central coordination decline? And because no state was fully party democratic, would policy be determined by particularistic networks of academics, technocrats, and reform pressure groups scything right through formal state institutions?

Citizenship involved issues of both representation and nation, their entwinings varying by country. By 1850, the United States had institutionalized a two-party democracy for white males; yet it was entering the bitterest phase of its national struggle. While major disputes raged over the powers of the federal versus state governments, administration could not be divorced from politics. Effective government coordination at all three levels depended on party loyalty as well as bureaucracy. Under Lincoln, the spoils system reached its apogee: He removed 88 percent of all officials under presidential authority (Fish 1920: 170). The national issue was decided by force, in civil war, and then by the compromise of 1877. This reduced the political need for a partisan federal administration, though party politics returned to emasculate state and local levels in the short term. Britain and France experienced the opposite politics: more unanimity concerning the nation-state, less over (class) representation. But after the Reform Acts of 1867 and 1884 in Britain and the French Republican consolidation in the 1880s, those obstacles were being surmounted. All three party democracies could now locate sovereignty more precisely and then partially bureaucratize it.

The two semiauthoritarian monarchies moved less toward citizenship. In Prussia representation and nation were confronted together at mid-century. By 1880, as Chapter 9 shows, both were semiinstitutionalized. In Austria entwined representative and regional-national threats continued to politicize administration. Yet dissident nationalities were more at each other's than at Habsburg throats. (See Chapter 10.) A de facto compromise developed: Routine Habsburg central administration was allowed working autonomy, as turbulence persisted over political citizenship and over the language issue in administration.

The infrastructural growth of the state then somewhat reinforced this more consensual drift in all countries, even compensating for monarchical laggardness. Post offices and telegraph, canals, and railroads were not controversial. Schools were; for they normally involved a relatively secular central state against local-regional churches (plus the language issue in Austria). By just after 1900 these were generally resolved in favor of the central state. Semiauthoritarian monarchies especially used state infrastructures to sponsor late development, to the general satisfaction of major power actors. (See Chapter 14.) Classes and local-regional interest groups usually favored bureaucratic efficiency in expanding lower-level and technical branches of administration. (See Chapter 11.) Once salaries or examinations were accepted as the norm in some departments, their extension was relatively uncontroversial.

From the railway boom through the Second Industrial Revolution, state and large capitalist enterprise also converged on national economies and bureaucratic organization. The national economy (described for Britain in Chapter 17) reduced local-regional differences and further "naturalized" the population. The corporate organization chart, the multidivisional corporation, and the standardized sales catalog were analogous to state statistics, line-staff divisions and treasury control: bureaucratic responses to controlling organizations of increasing size and especially of increasing functional and geographic scope (Yeager 1980). With representative and national struggles becoming institutionalized, with consensus over many state functions, and with models also provided by industrial capitalism, national sovereignty and bureaucratization expanded.

In this phase bureaucratization impacted even more on local and regional government: British counties and boroughs, American state and local governments, Austrian and German *Länder* and *Gemeinde*, French *départements* and *communes*. Most remained controlled by local office-owning or honorific notables. But infrastructural and welfare state functions generated routine local administration uncongenial to unremunerated notables. A division of labor with central administrations developed, as revenue sharing grew – though not in the federal United States.

Bureaucratization remained weakest at the top levels of central policy making, especially in Austria and Prussia. Semiauthoritarian monarchy prolonged segmental divide-and-rule party tactics and blocked integrated cabinet government. Pressure group politics proliferated because ministries, court, and parliaments all remained autonomous sources of policy making. Along with and interpenetrating the Reich and Prussian civil services grew important academic and technocratic reform associations – some called "socialists of the chair" (Rosenhaft and Lee 1990). Avoiding fragmentation depended as much on the social solidarity of these *Bildungsbeamten* as on bureaucracy. About 1900, part of the bureaucratic civil service became "colonized" by aggressive nationalist pressure groups (see Chapter 16). The fragmentation of the state's foreign policy began in earnest – with disastrous consequences for the world (discussed in Chapter 21).

But bureaucracy also remained incomplete in party democracies. The British state now became ostensibly meritocratic. Civil service reforms were initiated from 1850 – usually to aid ministerial efficiency, without consulting Parliament where patronage still counted. Models were often drawn from British colonial practice. Internal auditing was improved. Entry and promotion on merit were instituted in 1853, boosted in 1879, and predominant by 1885 (Cohen 1941). Together with meritocratic reforms in the public schools, Oxford, Cambridge, and the church, this abolished patronage in recruitment. The top "intellectual grades" of the civil service were meritocratic, yet remained restrictive, almost all recruits coming from public or grammar schools and from the two ancient universities. Unlike Prussia, these academies were already dominated by gentry and higher professional families at the time reforms were made. Thus class composition and national solidarity of the higher civil service were confirmed (Mueller 1984: 108–25, 191–223). During 1904–14, 80 percent had been to Oxford or Cambridge.

Promotion from the lower "mechanical grades" became rare: During 1902–11, the annual promotion chance was 0.12 percent, concentrated in less prestigious departments such as customs. There were *no* promoted men in the War or Colonial Office (Kelsall 1955: 40–41, 139, 162–3). An ideology of rational, disinterested public service pervaded these men. The state was no longer an instrument of patriarchal household authority, staffed by "corrupt" patronage. Its "civil servants" were avowedly neutral, entrusted with the best interests of national civil society. Hegel's universal class of bureaucrats, always a curious concept applied to his own time and country, made a more plausible, if still ideological, appearance in the late nineteenth-century British civil service – confined within the British dominant class.

Chapter 11 shows that American government for most of the century (excluding the Civil War) was small, cheap, and easily financed. Its rapid growth in size in late century greatly expanded the spoils system and corruption, especially at the local-government level. Without bureaucratic controls, governments relied on bribery and kickbacks to get things done (Keller 1977: 245). But eventually demands for economy and efficiency arose, though much later than in Britain (Skowronek 1982). The American invention, the corporation, meant that bureaucratic models of efficiency were already available (Yeager 1980). The Pendleton Act of 1882 "classified" some federal civil service jobs – protecting them from political purges and allocating them by competitive examination. Classified positions rose from $10\frac{1}{2}$ percent in 1884 to 29 percent in 1895. Then they jumped to 45 percent the following year and to 64 percent in 1909. After World War I, they rose to more than 80 percent, where they remain today.

At first, motives behind protection were rather mixed, as parties leaving government sought to entrench their loyalists by giving them civil service status (Keller 1977: 313). But, borrowing from the corporation, the protected civil service gradually espoused the sciences of "personnel administration" (ordering of offices, careers, salaries, promotions, pensions, and efficiency reports) and "administrative management" (standardized accounting, archives and records, procurement and supply, and contracting procedures). Much of this was also implemented in northern state and local governments. The Taft Commission of 1913 drew from Chicago experience in recommending the creation of single budget and personnel bureaus to standardize federal accounts, examination and promotion criteria, position classification and salary systems, individual efficiency records, and disciplinary rules for all federal agencies. Yet neither this nor the consolidation of a single federal budget appeared until the 1920s, spurred by the administrative chaos of the American war effort (van Riper 1958: 191–223).

Much of this bureaucratization was achieved by the Progressive movement. In their administrative reforms, Progressives aimed at national "efficiency," the ideology of a coalition between rising careerist and professional middle classes (Wiebe 1967) and corporate liberalism (Weinstein 1968; Shefter 1978: 230–7). The ideology of a neutral, efficient national executive was more than a century old. It could now finally begin to overcome party patronage and confederalism because it entwined with powerful class actors in a national civil society. It also helped that Presidents Theodore Roosevelt and Taft had prior experience in civil service reform. Patronage remained – and still does today – at the top of all three levels of government. Political appointees usually have combined educational and technical qualifications with party loyalism.

Dualism also characterizes British and French top central government, and, unlike in the United States, local-regional has been subordinated to central government. The British recruited high-level civil servants almost entirely from elite public (i.e., private) schools and Oxbridge, from upper middle classes loyal to the national establishment. The French recruited theirs from *les grandes écoles* and "Sciences Po," well educated and technically qualified but also loyal to that combination of progressive capitalism and centralized Republicanism that has characterized twentieth-century French regimes.

Top administration has remained embedded in class and national party loyalists throughout the twentieth century. All regimes fought off both confederalism and a fully fledged Weberian bureaucracy. In this period the separation of administration from politics was completed at lower and middling – and in most countries, in local-regional – official levels, but not at the top of the nation-state. The commonsense notion of the "bureaucrat" as the lower-level pencil pusher has some truth. Top state administrators remained as much political as bureaucratic, although socialization into ideologies of disinterested public service partly conceals their party politics.

Conclusion

Over the long nineteenth century, my five bureaucratic components developed as follows:

1. By 1914, almost all central, and most local-regional, officials received salaries. Office owning by hereditary right or purchase had virtually disappeared. Only part-time honorific office holding survived in large numbers at the local level.
2. Appointment and promotion by impersonal measurement of competence also developed, but rather later and still incompletely in some countries by 1914.
3. The ordering of offices within departments at first varied considerably, but by the 1880s, virtually all resembled the bureaucratic model, divided by function under a centralized hierarchy.
4. The integration of all departments into a single, centralized national administration came early to the United States, which then regressed strongly away from it. It came later in Britain and France and had not come fully to Germany and Austria by the end of the period under discussion.
5. The insulation of party politics from administration came latest. At the top of central government it remained incomplete everywhere, but was feeblest in Germany and Austria.

Thus some bureaucratization on all five criteria occurred in all countries through the period. In 1760, states were not remotely bureaucratic; by 1914, national bureaucracy and administrative insulation were institutionalized, increasing state infrastructural powers and, to a much lesser extent, the internal cohesion of their civil administrations. Central state administrations had moved toward becoming unitary, either as semiauthoritarian – with bureaucrats implementing the decisions of monarchical regimes – or as party democratic – with bureaucrats implementing national parliamentary legislation.

Bureaucratization was everywhere preceded by its ideologies. Cameralism, the Enlightenment, utilitarianism, Progressivism, and other middle-class radicalisms came mainly from highly educated officials from the old regime and professional middle classes. All advocated what they called "rational administration" and what we would call bureaucracy. It is striking how conscious bureaucratization was, how it was clearly formulated throughout the West by ideologists before it was implemented. Ideologists could be persuasive partly because much bureaucratization was functional. It was an efficient cost-cutting response to administrations growing vastly in functional and geographic scope and diversity. Because ideologists communicated internationally, power actors in one country usually read of improved bureaucratic techniques in other countries before they adapted them at home (though I have not systematically researched this). The modern bureaucratic state appears as first imagined, then inexorably, functionally, in reality.

Yet an examination of states in detail modifies such appearances. Viewed from close up, the rise of modern state administration was not evolutionary or one-dimensional. Structural causes differed between periods. Ideologies proved ineffective without these causes, which also influenced ideological shifts (from cameralism to utilitarianism to radicalism, etc). Each one of my countries led bureaucratization at different periods, its surge then failing to surmount new barriers. I distinguished three phases in bureaucratization, dominated by (1) monarchical and militarist crystallizations, (2) representative and national citizenship crystallizations, and (3) the industrial capitalist crystallization. Underlying this was the transformation of the modern central state from being predominantly military to being diamorphous – half-civil, half-military.

Civil administration was the most important way state elites penetrated civil society. It was also, in 1760, the most important form of party penetration into absolutist states and perhaps even into party-democratic states (along with parliamentary assemblies). No eighteenth-century state possessed effective infrastructures to back up its formal despotic power over civil society because "its" civil administration was actually riddled with the ownership rights of dominant classes and churches. After the earlier military revolution, military administrations were not quite so riddled, somewhat more controlled by the state (Chapter 11 shows that the state then lost some control to a partially autonomous military caste).

From such military controls, pressured by war, dynasts launched the first bureaucratic offensive. However, their bureaucratic elements were entwined with, and restrained by, both segmental divide-and-rule strategy and dependence on old regime parties. In the second, transitional phase, pressured by popular (largely class-based) citizen movements as well as by war, revolutionary and party-democratic regimes took the lead and swept away "corrupt" office owning. But this second bureaucratic offensive also had limits, because such regimes did not satisfactorily solve enough of their major representative and national problems for them to be able to trust a cohesive, efficient, centralized bureaucratic state. In the third industrial capitalist phase some regimes made further progress in institutionalizing centralized party democracy and so could further bureaucratize. But bureaucratization, especially at lower and middling levels of administration, was now also aided considerably by the addition of new and largely consensual state infrastructures assisting national industrialization (and also national military rearmament). Only top administrative levels resisted full bureaucratization, as regimes continued to need party loyalists.

Civil administrations did not lose much cohesion, and they may even have gained some, as they grew during the period – but with two qualifications. First, cohesion was less a characteristic of an autonomous state than a relation between state and civil society – as I suggested it might be in Chapter 3. Whether states could act effectively and cohesively depended as much on officials being embedded in and expressing the national cohesion of dominant classes as on their own bureaucratic capacities. The form of this embedding and expression changed greatly through the period, from particularistic, predominantly decentralized office holding to supposedly universal and predominantly national meritocracy.

As Table 4.2 suggests, eighteenth-century Prussia and Britain were examples of states expressing relatively cohesive national civil societies and thus being infrastructurally effective. The old regime French state was less effective because it expressed (and contributed to) the incoherence of its society. And the Austrian state was about as effective as a highly autonomous state *not* embedded in its civil society could be, which is not very effective. Much later the three party-democratic states became more effective as they became genuinely representative of (males in) the dominant and nationally organized classes of early industrial society, especially of capitalists and the professional middle class. We have found little of *the* state as an autonomous actor, as suggested by elite theory. Where the state was relatively cohesive, this was mainly because central state actors remained embedded, if more universalistically, in civil society power networks, principally in national classes. Where state actors had more autonomy from civil society, they had difficulty in acting cohesively. Chapter 3 notes that autonomous earlier states (e.g., the feudal states) had usually been cohesive but feeble. Perhaps autonomous political power in modern society is actually the autonomy of the party factionalized state. Chapter 20 supports this suspicion.

Second, states were not fully unitary because their power networks extended beyond the departments of civil administration discussed in this chapter. Their armed forces were somewhat autonomous, somewhat more embedded in old regimes than were civilian administrators. Their diplomatic corps were even more old regime and closer to the supreme executive power of the state. Monarchical courts and political parties (of class, sector, locality-region, and religion) added their distinct factionalisms, social embeddings, and presumed capacities to coordinate some of this. Civil administrators' ability to coordinate all this was only moderate. As we saw, coordination of their own plural departments remained their weak points. Either they did coordinate, but through party loyalties as much as through bureaucracy – in which case they too might be a source of divisiveness – or they did not – in which case their own professional and technocratic capacities were applied to purposes defined more by a narrower technocratic-bureaucratic state crystallization than by the needs and purposes of the "whole" state. Chapter 14 discusses such possibilities.

Bibliography

Albrow, M. 1970. *Bureaucracy*. London: Pall Mall Press.

American State Papers. 1834. *Documents, Legislative and Executive, of the Congress of the U.S., 1809–1823*. Vol. 38, miscellaneous, Vol. 2, p. 983.

Anderson, E., and P. R. Anderson 1967. *Political Institutions and Social Change in Continental Europe in the Nineteenth Century*. Berkeley: University of California Press.

Ashford, D. 1982. *British Dogmatism and French Pragmatism. Central-Local Policymaking in the Welfare State*. London: Allen & Unwin.

Axtmann, R. 1991. Geopolitics and Internal Power Structures: The State, Police and Public Order in Austria and Ireland in the Late Eighteenth Century. Ph.D. diss., London School of Economics and Political Science.

Aylmer, G. E. 1979. From office-holding to civil service: the genesis of modern bureaucracy. *Transactions of the Royal Historical Society*, 30.

Beales, D. 1987. *Joseph II*. Vol. I: *In the Shadow of Maria Theresa, 1740–1780*. Cambridge: Cambridge University Press.

Binney, J. 1958. *British Public Finance and Administration, 1774–92*. Oxford: Clarendon Press.

Blanning, T. 1974. *Reform and Revolution in Mainz, 1743–1803*. Cambridge: Cambridge University Press.

Bonin, H. von. 1966. Adel und Burgertum in der hoheren Beamtenschaft der Preussischen Monarchie 1794–1806. *Jarhbuch für die Geschichte Mittle- und Ostdeutschlands* 15.

Bosher, J. F. 1970. *French Finances, 1770–1795*. Cambridge: Cambridge University Press.

Brewer, J. 1989. *The Sinews of Power: War, Money and the English State*. New York: Knopf.

Charle, C. 1980. *Les Hauts Fonctionnaires en France au XIXe siècle*. Gallimard/ Julliard.

Church, C. H. 1981. *Revolution and Red Tape: The French Ministerial Bureaucracy, 1770–1850*. Oxford: Clarendon Press.

Cohen, E. W. 1941. *The Growth of the British Civil Service, 1780–1939*. London: Allen & Unwin.

Dickson, P. G. M. 1987. *Finance and Government Under Maria Theresa, 1740–1780*, 2 vols. Oxford: Clarendon Press.

Doyle, W. 1984. *The Origins of the French Revolution*. Oxford: Oxford University Press.

Finer, S. E. 1952. Patronage and the public service: Jeffersonian bureaucracy and the British tradition. *Public Administration*, 30.

Fischer, W. and P. Lundgreen. 1975. The recruitment and training of administrative and technical personnel. In *The Formation of National States in Western Europe*, ed. C. Tilly. Princeton, N.J.: Princeton University Press.

Fish, C. R. 1920. *The Civil Service and the Patronage*. Cambridge, Mass.: Harvard University Press.

Gillis, J. R. 1971. *The Prussian Bureaucracy in Crisis, 1840–1860: Origins of an Administrative Ethos*. Menlo Park, Calif.: Stanford University Press.

Gray, M. 1986. Prussia in transition: society and politics under the Stein reform ministry of 1808. *Transactions of the American Philosophical Society* 76, pt. 1.

Hall, R. H. 1963–4. The concept of bureaucracy: an empirical assessment. *American Journal of Sociology* 69.

Harris, R. D. 1979. *Necker, Reform Statesman of the Ancien Régime*. Berkeley: University of California Press.

Janouch, G. 1953. *Conversations with Kafka*. London: Derek Verschoyle.

Johnson, H. C. 1969. The concept of bureaucracy in Cameralism. *Political Science Quarterly*, 79.

    1975. *Frederick the Great and His Officials*. New Haven Conn.: Yale University Press.

Julien-Laferrière, F. 1970. *Les députés fonctionnaires sous la monarchie de juillet*. Paris: PUF.

Keller, M. 1977. *Affairs of State: Public Life in Late Nineteenth Century America*. Cambridge, Mass.: Harvard University Press.

Kelsall, R. K. 1955. *Higher Civil Servants in Britain, from 1870 to the Present Day*. London: Routledge & Kegan Paul.

Koselleck, R. 1967. *Preussen zwischen Reform und Revolution*. Stuttgart: Klett.

Krygier, M. 1979. State and bureaucracy in Europe: the growth of a concept. In *Bureaucracy: The Career of a Concept*, ed. E. Kamenka and M. Krygier. London: Arnold.

Ludtke, A. 1989. *Police and State in Prussia, 1815–1850*. Cambridge: Cambridge University Press.

Macartney, C. A. 1969. *The Habsburg Empire, 1790–1918*. London: Weidenfeld & Nicolson.

McDonald, F. 1982. *Alexander Hamilton: A Biography*. New York: Norton.

Margadant, T. W. 1988. Towns, taxes, and state-formation in the French Revolution. Paper presented at the eleventh Annual Irvine Seminar on Social History and Theory, Department of History, University of California, Davis.

Marion, M. 1927. *Histoire Financière de la France Depuis 1715*. Paris: Rousseau.

Mousnier, R. 1979. *The Institutions of France Under the Absolute Monarchy, 1598–1789*. Chicago: University of Chicago Press.

Mueller, H.-E. 1984. *Bureaucracy, Education, and Monopoly: Civil Service Reforms in Prussia and England*. Berkeley: University of California Press.

Muncie, L. W. 1944. *The Junker in the Prussian Administration Under William II, 1888–1914*. Providence, R.I.: Brown University Press.

Necker, J. 1784. *De l'Administration des Finances de France*, 3 vols. Paris: n.p.

Nelson, R. R. 1969. *The Home Office, 1782–1801*. Durham, N.C.: Duke University Press.

O'Brien, C. C. 1990. The decline and fall of the French Revolution. *New York Review of Books*, February 13.

Osborne, T. R. 1983. *A Grande Ecole for the Grands Corps: The Recruitment and Training of the French Administrative Elite in the Nineteenth Century*. New York: Columbia University Press.

Parris, H. 1969. *Constitutional Bureaucracy: The Development of British Central Administration Since the Eighteenth Century*. London: Allen & Unwin.

Raeff, M. 1975. The well ordered police state and the development of modernity in seventeenth- and eighteenth-century Europe: an attempt at a comparative approach. *American Historical Review* 80.

Richardson, N. J. 1966. *The French Prefectoral Corps, 1814–1830*. Cambridge: Cambridge University Press.

Rosenberg, H. 1958. *Bureaucracy, Aristocracy, and Autocracy*. Cambridge, Mass.: Harvard University Press.

Rosenhaft, E., and W. R. Lee. 1990. State and society in modern Germany – *Beamtenstaat, Klassenstaat, Wohlfahrtstaat*. In *The State and Social Change in Germany, 1880–1980*, ed. E. Rosenhaft and W. R. Lee. New York: Berg.

Shefter, M. 1978. Party, bureaucracy, and political change in the United States. In *Political Parties: Development and Decay*. New York: Sage.

Skocpol, T. 1979. *States and Social Revolutions: A Comparative Analysis of France, Russia, and China*. Cambridge: Cambridge University Press.

Skowronek, S. 1982. *Building a New American State: The Expansion of National Administrative Capacities, 1877–1920*. Cambridge: Cambridge University Press.

Taylor, G. V. 1967. Non-capitalist wealth and the origins of the French Revolution. *American Historical Review* 72.

Thuillier, G. 1976. *La Vie Quotidienne dans les Ministères au XIXième Siècle*. Paris: Hachette.

   1980. *Bureaucratie et Bureaucrates en France au XIXième Siècle*. Geneva: Droz.

Tilly, C. 1990. *Coercion, Capital and European States, AD 990–1990*. Oxford: Blackwell.

Tour du Pin, Madame de la. 1985. *Memoirs*. London: Century.

Tribe, K. 1984. Cameralism and the science of government. *Journal of Modern History* 56.

1988. *Governing Economy: The Reformulation of German Economic Discourse, 1750–1840*. Cambridge: Cambridge University Press.

Van Riper, P. P. 1958. *History of the United States Civil Service*. New York: Row, Peterson.

Wangerman, E. 1969. *From Joseph II to the Jacobin Trials*, 2d ed. London: Oxford University Press.

Weber, M. 1978. *Economy and Society*, English ed., 3 vols. New York: Bedminster Press.

Weill, H. 1961. *Frederick the Great and Samuel von Cocceji*. Madison: University of Wisconsin Press.

Weinstein, J. 1968. *The Corporate Ideal in the Liberal State: 1900–1918*. Boston: Beacon Press.

White, L. D. 1951. *The Jeffersonians: A Study in Administrative History, 1801–1829*. New York: Macmillan.

1954. *The Jacksonians: A Study in Administrative History, 1829–1860*. New York: Macmillan.

1958. *The Republicans: A Study in Administrative History, 1869–1901*. New York: Macmillan.

1965. *The Federalists: A Study in Administrative History, 1789–1801*, 2d ed. New York: Free Press.

Wiebe, R. H. 1967. *The Search for Order, 1877–1920*. New York: Hill & Wang.

Woolf, S. J. 1984. Origins of statistics: France 1789–1815. In *States and Statistics in France*, ed. J. C. Perrot and S. J. Woolf. Chur, Switzerland: Harwood.

Yeager, M. A. 1988. Bureaucracy. In *Encyclopedia of American Economic History*. Vol. III, ed. G. Porter. New York: Scribner's.

14 The rise of the modern state: IV. The expansion of civilian scope

Chapter 11 identifies two sea changes in the development of the state. The first, lasting through the eighteenth century to 1815, saw great expansion in the state's size, due almost entirely to its geopolitical militarism. Earlier chapters show this greatly politicized social life intensifying the development of classes and nations. The second sea change is the concern of this chapter. Beginning about 1870, it greatly expanded not only size but civilian scope within the state as well. While retaining (a reduced) militarism plus traditional judicial and charitable functions, states acquired three new civilian functions, around which, as Chapter 13 shows, bureaucratization also centered:

1. All states massively extended infrastructures of material and symbolic communication: roads, canals, railways, postal service, telegraphy, and mass education.
2. Some states went into direct ownership of material infrastructures and productive industries.
3. Just before the end of the period, states began to extend their charity into more general welfare programs, embryonic forms of Marshall's "social citizenship."

Thus states increasingly penetrated social life. Despite a reduction in fiscal pain, civil society was further politicized. People could not return to their normal historical practice of ignoring the state. Class-national caging continued, if more quietly, with less world-historical drama. Social life was becoming more "naturalized," and states were becoming more "powerful" – but in what sense? Were autonomous states "intervening" more despotically in civil society, aided by greater infrastructural powers, as envisaged by elitist-managerialist state theory? Or was state growth merely a functional and infrastructural response to industrial capitalism? This might increase not state but civil society's collective powers (as in pluralist theory), or it might subordinate the state to the distributive power of the capitalist class (as in class theory). Or were these enlarged, more diverse states now more polymorphous, crystallizing in plural forms between which "ultimate" choices were not made? And if they became more polymorphous, did they also become less coherent?

Infrastructural growth, party democracy, and the nation

State infrastructures grew least in party-democratic regimes. These rarely nationalized economic resources, deferred more conspicuously to the needs of capital, and at first moved more slowly toward social citizenship. The three party democracies obviously differed – with the United States having easily the weakest, most federally divided government and France the most active state – but they did share many characteristics. I discuss these matters first for Britain. I argue that the British state became more polymorphous, crystallizing as militarist, as capitalist, as moral ideological, as federal national, and as more thoroughly party democratic. In this chapter, I discuss only some of the domestic repercussions of geopolitical militarism. Were there clear-cut relations, perhaps of "ultimate primacy," among these crystallizations? Chapter 3 argues that state crystallizations rarely confront one another in dialectical, head-on conflict, forcing direct political choice or compromise among them. Was this so in Victorian Britain and in other countries of the period?

The Victorian state certainly was capitalist. Almost all Victorians expected it to be. Even laissez-faire advocates had not doubted the need for state regulation. Adam Smith wanted the state to provide public goods that private actors had no personal interest in funding – external defense, internal security, national education, and a road network. Add railways, and this is what nineteenth-century states largely did. Smith rightly saw this less as state intervention than as civil society (by which he really meant market capitalism) coordinating itself. In the early nineteenth century in Britain, as in most other countries, activism by autonomous state elites was actually declining, as the court and royal licensing and patronage networks decayed. Then, after 1830, a kind of collective "party," rather than elitist, state activism began to grow, much of it concerned with assisting and regulating the development of industrial capitalism. Legislation became less ad hoc and more programmatic, continuing across parliamentary sessions, relying on public (not private) acts of Parliament initiated by cabinet ministers. Parliament also now routinely used select committees and royal commissions to investigate social conditions and recommend legislation. Other party democracies set up similar planning agencies. After midcentury, their administrative infrastructures also began to grow, though again mostly coordinating rather than intervening in civil society.

But civil society and state action involved more than capitalism. Moral-religious debates resonated strongly in Victorian politics (Marsh 1979; Weeks 1981: 81; Cronin 1988). Weeks and Foucault (for France) argue that this indicates "coercion" by dominant classes over a broader span of social life, a somewhat economic reductionist view of the moral-ideological crystallization. But as industrialization and state scope both increased, so moral rhetoric became more complex and more disputed. Many Victorians distinguished between commercial matters, on which the state should merely assist capitalist self-regulation, and social questions, which were legitimate matters of state intervention, even coercion. Thus declaimed Lord Macaulay, in defending the Ten Hours Bill in Parliament:

I am as firmly attached as any Gentlemen in this House to the principle of free trade properly stated . . . that it is not desirable that the state should interfere with the contracts of persons of ripe age and sound mind, touching matters purely commercial. I am not aware of any exception to that principle, but . . . the principle of the non-interference is one that cannot be applied without great restriction where the public health or the public morality are concerned. [Taylor 1972: 44]

In reality, though, as other contributors to the debate have observed, there was no simple division of labor between capitalism and "public health and morality." They interpenetrated one another. Victorian moralizing fused ideological currents with varying degrees of affinity to capitalism – moral Protestantism, Enlightenment, and utilitarian theories of progress, notions of individual and social "improvement," an imperial sense that Britain had global moral responsibilities, and regime fear of the "dangerous classes" below. Unless the lower classes were in actual revolt (as in Chartism or in 1848), regimes rarely focused on their political class interests. The lower classes were considered "dangerous" in a much broader sense than mere economic threat. Social-policy debates were pervaded by broad metaphors linking personal and class interest with health and morality, as in Lord Macaulay's speech. Social problems created "degradations" and "diseases" that spread "corruptions" and "infections." Industrialism and urbanization had greatly increased social density, so that lower-class immorality might infect all classes, as their germs certainly did. The 1851 census revealed few workers or their families attended church or chapel, which genuinely shocked the regime. It was both the duty and the interest of the governing class to guide the lower classes toward health, purity, morality, and religion.

Indeed, classical political economy and the public health movement, culminating in germ theory, actually shared the same metatheory: Invisible forces diffused through the unintended effects of countless social interactions, benign, chaotic, and malign alike. The state should assist benignity, preferably with relatively inconspicuous infrastructures – perhaps best typified by the introduction of underground glazed earthenware pipes channeling water and sewerage under the towns. The pipes represented a genuine increase in human collective powers, slashing mortality rates from the 1870s, and they were hailed as such. Policies gradually emerged for public health, street lighting, sewerage, minimum housing standards, rudimentary health care, a police force, the supervision of prisons and Poor Laws, the regulation of work hours and employment conditions, and primary and some secondary education for most children. Efficient communications, good public health, and mass literacy were believed to be functional for capitalism, national power, and human development in general. As Chapter 11 shows, even fiscal resistance to state broadening lessened as economic growth outstripped state expansion. Thus state civilian scope grew somewhat consensually among those who could organize effectively, that is, among dominant classes, regions, ethnic groups, and churches. As Grew (1984) notes, massive infrastructural growth was compatible with an emerging ideology of "state neutrality" and preservation of freedom, as most defined new "fields of play" in which civil-society actors could be expected to act without further state intervention.

Nonetheless, capitalism and morality might conflict and then set limits on each other, not fixed but fluctuating according to complex political processes. As the century neared its end, militarism started to influence social interactions. British imperial power was seen to depend more on "national efficiency," central to which were (barely) healthy mothers and children and a basic level of education for the nation. Indeed, in the notion of national efficiency capitalist and military rivalry tended to fuse, especially as Germany became perceived as the main rival Power. If reforms were demanded in the language of head-on class conflict, as in Chartism, they were forcibly repressed; then the capitalist state did assert itself. If reforms were presented merely as a rational mutual interest compromise to class conflict, they also normally failed to convert ruling old regime liberalism. The trick was to present reforms as ameliorating class conflict *and* having moral and national objectives. Then immoral or unpatriotic capitalists and taxpayers might be denounced, creating splits in the ruling regime. At the same time as Chartism, the Factory Acts movement denounced exploitation of the health and morals of working children and women – and so of family life – and was broadly successful. (See Chapter 15.) Most legislation mixed motives of social control, charity, and a recognition that increased social density made some state services functional for all. Social life was now inescapably collective. The national cage was tightening its bars yet, paradoxically, increasing genuine freedoms; for the pipes were dramatically lengthening the life span of fetuses, infants, and mothers.

Few thought yet in terms of Marshall's "social citizenship" – guaranteeing active citizen participation in the social and economic life of the nation beyond being barely healthy, then literate. No program redistributed much, as (until 1910) there was no progressive taxation to pay for it. But it was a conscious legislative reform program, fought over by enthusiasts, opponents, and compromisers, gradually making converts within state and party elites. By the 1860s, reform bills were being initiated by ministers rather than by private members. Liberal capitalism, influenced by Christian and secular morality and then by nationalism and by competitive parties responding to electoral pressure, could generate social reform – provided reform was not in the name of class, aimed squarely against capitalism.

Nor could capitalism or moral reform or militarism aim squarely against the further state crystallization, a moderately centralized yet still "federal" nation. In the terms of Table 3.3, Britain was in reality (if not in its constitution) still rather "federal," with considerable powers lodged in local government. True, Victorian acts, committees, and commissions also generated "technocrat-bureaucrats," conscious elite "incrementalists" seeking to extend the role of central government (Lubenow 1971). As long as they kept their heads down and attacked particular social ills with ad hoc remedies amid a smoke screen of moral and national rhetoric, reforms came. But if they advocated state intervention as a general principle of social amelioration, they fell afoul of the local party notables controlling the electoral process and Parliament.

When the national issue broke out in head-on confrontation, centralizers usually lost. The most they could do was pragmatically create state infrastructures staffed by local notables. On royal commissions technocrats were balanced by aristocrats, and centralizing recommendations were watered down in parliamentary legislation and then again when implemented. When the greatest Victorian technocrat, Edwin Chadwick, openly advocated central state intervention in municipal health, he was swiftly discredited, and his career of public service ended. From Poor Law reform, through factory acts to public health and education, social reform was proclaimed nationally by government and Parliament but implemented by local notables of boroughs, counties, parishes, and others of the 25,000 local instruments of mid-nineteenth century local government (Sutherland 1972; Mac-Donagh 1977; Digby 1982). Administration remained federal, though the British "constitution" was supposedly dominated by the doctrine of (centralized) parliamentary sovereignty. British administrations – state elites and parties, central and local – were still coordinating and disputing the moral and material anxieties of the ruling class-nation, not intervening as an autonomous central state in civil society.

At midcentury, three state crystallizations – as capitalist, as moral ideological, and as a federal nation-state – were setting broad limits for one another and for potential state autonomy as the scope of domestic civil policy broadened. Then, from the 1880s on, federalism weakened under the impact of growing national identities (discussed later), of imperial militarism, and of the fifth state crystallization, party democracy. Britain was not, of course, a full-fledged electoral democracy, even for men, but its franchise after 1832 was broad enough to gradually force party notables in some areas beyond mere segmental patron-client organization into programmatic competition with each other. This accelerated in 1867 and 1884 as the two parties extended the franchise to outbid each other. Now came more continuous and mass religious, regional, and class pressures. The Conservatives became Anglican and English, the Liberals partially Nonconformist and Celtic. Petite bourgeoisie and skilled workers became enfranchised, and the professional and careerist middle class politically influential. Some Liberal and Conservative party leaders switched sides over the national issue, and the ideological battle evened up. Moderate party and elite centralizers now commanded the rhetoric of "modernity," and local notables commanded those of "freedom." By 1900, partly centralized parties with national platforms and propaganda were appealing to a mass electorate sometimes over the heads of local notables, reducing their autonomy and moderating their preference for federalism.

The largest domestic responsibility of government was now education, geared (as Chapter 16 shows) to the middle class, the majority voters. An emerging "ideological citizenship" carried messages as diverse as its middle-class constituency: loyalty to capitalism, national efficiency, Anglicanism or Nonconformism, "social purity," temperance, and charity, even feminism. All this helped shift liberalism and the Liberal party toward more welfarism; it shifted Nonconformists from federalism toward state activism (provided education could be protected against Anglicanism); and it cemented the union of Scotland, Wales, and Ulster with England (largely through the medium of religion-party alliances). Education also locally politicized many workers, though their national politics centered on franchise reform and trade union rights. Most pressure for public welfare came from the Liberal middle class and moralists (Cronin 1988). Eventually, however, middle- and working-class political pressures joined to generate the policies of the last prewar Liberal government.

As Chapter 17 shows, active state intervention in industrial relations also began in the 1890s – in response to class pressures from below, but effective when able to find common pragmatic and moral ground to transcend the "selfish" interests of employers and unions. Moral pressures supplemented the few coercive powers contained by labor legislation. This was paralleled by more intervention, usually through fiscal incentives, in education, as inadequacies were revealed in the policy of plugging gaps between privately run schools. Public medical services crept surreptitiously through the Poor Laws to provide what was in effect a minimal state-funded health service of last resort. Local government reform provided more uniform services, especially in public health, guaranteed nationally, though decisions as to the exact level of services remained local, as did their administration. All this indicated a little more national centralization, limited party-democratic "interventions" in capitalism – often through moral persuasion, fiscal inducements, or covert technocracy, but sometimes through direct legislative coercion – and a limited state autonomy that had not derived from head-on challenges to capitalism or federalism, and not from direct class struggle, but rather from the unintended consequences of party politics in which moralism and nationalism entwined with mass regional, religious, and class crystallizations. As these had not challenged capitalism or federalism head-on, autonomous statism (of the kind envisaged by elite theory) had barely appeared. For the technocratic-bureaucratic interventionist state to emerge presupposed greater working-class pressure and mass-mobilization warfare, both lying beyond 1914. Prewar "statism" was predominantly moral and middle class. It was an implicit compromise between a federal and a centralized nation-state, mildly modifying the state's capitalist crystallization.

France and the United States moved along parallel tracks, France having stronger centralizers. Their most important state crystallizations were fairly similar to British ones, except that, from the 1870s on, American geopolitical militarism was far less pronounced. At the end of the nineteenth century the parties of centralizing Republicans eventually secured control of the French state against clerical, aristocratic, and finance capital resistance. As in earlier republics they designed a more centralized and somewhat more interventionist state than in Britain or the United States. But its major interventions were not directed against capitalism or class. Rather, the centralized nation-state fought principally on moral-ideological terrain – against the power of the Catholic church in education, family law, and social welfare, together with a Republican crusade against old regime control of the armed forces (focusing on the Dreyfus case). Capitalism continued to dominate political economy. Again we see a dual result, the triumph in political economy of the capitalist state, mediated by the party-democratic transformation of a second state crystallization, the moral ideological, from Catholicism into a secular, centralized welfarist morality, and by a late attempt to transform state militarism.

The United States was the homeland of capitalist liberalism, of party democracy, and of confederalism, with the weakest state in the Western world. The Civil War abruptly reversed this. The North, and especially the South, went much farther toward state intervention than any other nineteenth-century state did. The Confederacy interfered substantially and despotically with free labor and private property rights and rode roughshod over local and state governments and customs – an ironic performance from a regime fighting for states' rights. The Union, far larger and richer in its resource base, relied more on market incentives for the supply of manufactured goods. But this "Yankee Leviathan" was especially interventionist in creating the first national credit system and a finance capital class independent of Britain (Bensel 1990: chapter 3). After the war, the massive state administrations were quickly dismantled, but the victorious Union remained cohesive, sponsoring national economic development and directly ruling the entire South during Reconstruction. As Bensel observes, during the Civil War it had become a one-party state in which Republican party notables drawn from northern finance, industry, and free soil agriculture staffed the state themselves. Yet again we see that states effectively combining despotic and infra-structural powers depend not on autonomous elites but on elites institutionalized in a civil society party.

But this "strong state" alliance proved fragile. Most locally rooted conservative Republicans lost interest in Reconstruction and became prepared to deal with southern Democrats. Party factionalism resur-faced. To retain the presidency, conservative Republicans were forced to make an electoral deal restoring autonomy to the southern states in 1877. Government returned to its antebellum form: one of "courts and parties," small and predominantly confederal, controlled by locally rooted party factions, its law courts dominated by laissez-faire and localism, its most cohesive, purposive party faction (southern Demo-crats) resolutely opposing central state powers (Keller 1977; Skowronek 1982: 30; Bensel 1900: chapter 7).

American capitalism now developed as northern, its South a back-water, its institutionalized racism giving quite distinct hues to local capitalism, yet with entrenched blocking powers against the federal state. From the 1880s on, this northern capitalism also experienced tension with a middle class–centered religious moralism. But it also contained an internal tension: Its liberal individualism was stronger, yet its corporations grew bigger than in other countries. As corporations entwined with party factionalism and sought local and state government franchises, the stench of "corporate corruption" rose. Hence reformers, like their polar opposites, southern Democrats, sought to reduce, not expand, the infrastructures of government (Orloff 1988). Yet Washington differed from the other four (five, if we count Budapest) capitals in not being a major modernizing city. A small, preindustrial southern city, Washington was not easily controllable by the modern corporation. Therefore, some corporations favored "modernizing" reforms, starting at the federal level. The Progressive movement carried these somewhat contradictory currents, plus middle-class vested interest in education, sectarian religious welfarism, middle-class feminism, and the interests of skilled, unionized labor. All (except for feminists) were entrenched in the two parties. The complexity of these power relations, expressed differently at different levels of government, all the time forced to make deals at the federal level with alien southern Democrats, make it hard to sum up the Progressives (for specialist historians as well as this inexpert outsider). But the entwined entrenched powers of capitalist liberalism and southern states' rights allowed fewer central state moral restraints on capitalism (and on racist capitalism) once corporations were minimally regulated than in other countries.

In all three party democracies the capitalist crystallization continued to thrive. State intervention remained limited and often helpful to capitalism (with the exception of the American South). As yet little redistribution was occurring. In these arenas elite theory does not apply, pluralism is limited by the commanding power of capital over labor – and class theory does apply. But to focus on the limitations of state intervention would be to underestimate emerging crystallizations as nation-states. The British and French – even the puny confederal American – states were radical departures from history. The expansion of nineteenth-century state infrastructures did not greatly shift the balance of distributive power between state and civil society or among the classes of civil society. If that was the whole story, the capitalist crystallization would be ultimately primary. But these states *also* changed collective power relations, that is, the very identity of civil society and so of capitalism itself. Each infrastructure tended to increase the cohesion and boundedness of the territories and subjects of existing states as against the two historic alternative interaction networks, local-regional communities and the transnational arena.

Although capitalism also broke down local particularism into broader universalism, its classic ideologists (and opponents) expected this would be mostly transnational. Yet, without many intending it, "nationally" regulated railways, roads, public utilities, public health, police forces, courts and prisons, and above all, education and discursive literacy in the dominant language of the state provided centralized-territorial infrastructures for the further flowering of the nation-state. Because all of these infrastructures were deliberately held back by local notables in the South, the American nation remained distinctively *northern*. Across almost all the Western world capitalism and civil society were unintentionally steered away from transnational, toward national, power organization.

Such national infrastructural expansion occurred in all countries, not just party democracies. In only twenty-five years, between 1882 and 1907, the number of letters posted per person rose between two- and fourfold in the five countries. By 1907, the average French person was posting 34 letters or cards per year; the Austrian, 46; the German, 69; the Briton, 88; and the American, 89 (*Annuaire Statistique de la France* 1913: 205). Almost all these extensive networks of intimate and business communication were confined within single state territories. Mass schooling grew to astonishingly near-uniform levels throughout the West. The proportion of children aged five to fourteen in school ranged between 74 percent (in the Austrian *Reichshalf*) and 88 percent (France) among the five countries (Mitchell 1975: 29–54, 750–9; although the Hungarian *Reichshalf* lagged at 54 percent). There began the marked decline in regional disparities that has continued through the twentieth century. Variations in regional wage levels were either static or growing in the early phase of industrialization and then began to decline from about 1880 in all five countries. Regional variations in the assessed values of houses showed similar movement (Good 1984: 245–50; Soderberg 1985: tables 1 and 2). Not just the printed word but the reproduced photograph added to national integration. The monarch's or president's photograph on the wall symbolized the integration of local administrative offices into the national state; and newspapers and magazines reproduced national ceremonial scenes of coronations, military reviews, and openings of parliaments.

Demographic statistics – female fertility, illegitimacy rates, and age of marriage – might seem unconnected to the national state. After all, they indicate intimate behavior of which the major explicit regulators were transnational churches and local folk practices rather than states. Yet Watkins (1991) shows that in almost all European countries variations between the demographic statistics of regions were declining between the 1870s and the 1960s, as each nation-state acquired its own distinct, standardized national demographic profile. She presents no data on how far naturalization had proceeded by World War I (or by any other intermediate date); yet, in the long run, sex became national.

This should cause no surprise, in view of the discussion in Chapter 7. I there describe the mobilizing power of classes and nations as deriving from their ability to link extensive organization to the intensive organization provided by intimate family and local community. By the end of the nineteenth century this had become evident to national policymakers. British reformers began to nurture the intensive sphere as essential to the formation of national citizens. They influenced legislation regarding family arrangements, parental responsibilities, sexual morality, "health" as both physical and moral, "good mother-hood," and "healthy" (in physical and moral senses) homes, neighbor-hoods, and schools. Eugenics was the ideology that most closely linked family breeding to the nation. Politicians and popular writers of the 1900s often expressed it in strikingly imperialistic language:

I know Empire cannot be built on rickety and flat-chested citizens. And because I know that it is "not out of the knitted gun or the smoothed rifle, but out of the mouths of babes and sucklings that the strength is ordained which shall still the Enemy and the Avenger. . . ."

The history of nations is determined not on the battlefield but in the nursery, and the battalions which give lasting victory are the battalions of babies. [Davin 1978: 17, 29]

There were also softer, more permissive versions of eugenics. Edwardian Britain saw a move to reverse Victorian sexual prudery, encouraging girls' developing sexuality into marital, procreative love (Bland 1982). And British, French, German, and American feminists of the period employed a kind of "maternalist nationalist" rhetoric to seek welfare gains (Koven and Michel 1990; doubtless Austrian ones did too). Families and neighborhoods across all classes, not just male political citizens, were entering the nation as a bonded community of interaction and sentiment.

Though I know of little research on this, nineteenth-century senses of personal identity must have greatly changed. As personal practice, both private and public, became nationally confined, local and trans-national identities must have declined, largely unconsciously, with no great expressions of power conflict. Even most of those whose power derived from formally local or transnational organization – local notables, Catholic priests, Marxist militants – seem to have become more implicitly "national" in their sense of themselves. This clearly occurred among formerly notable political parties, and as I show in Chapter 21, it also undermined the transnational rhetoric of labor organization. The *national* organization of civil society, and of capitalism and its classes, greatly increased. The infrastructural state nourished the nation-state.

Of course, each country was unique. In Britain, state and a "ruling-class nation" had coincided for about a century before either industrialization or the extension of state functions. By 1800, this class-nation was homogeneous throughout England and, to a slightly lesser extent, Wales and Scotland. Its Protestant clients ruled Ireland. It spoke and wrote only in English; it produced, exchanged, and consumed in a capitalist market economy that was also for most practical purposes the territory of the British state and that for overseas trade relied heavily on its military arm; and it began to organize politically more at Westminster and Whitehall. In this context, industrialization and the rise of the bourgeoisie, followed by the growth of state infrastructural powers and the middle class, were two phases in the merging of state and nation. British social life became largely naturalized (in its distinctively dual British and English-Welsh-Scottish forms).

France and the United States differed somewhat. The French nation had been politicized earlier in the revolutionary and Napoleonic period among the urban bourgeoisie. The middle class thus had an earlier Republican nation to join (or to fight against) than in other countries. Eugen Weber (1976) shows that this bourgeois nation diffused into the provinces and peasantry only in the late nineteenth century, mainly carried by the material and symbolic infrastructures I identified – roads, rail, post, and education. Here, also, a mass citizen army (proportionately the largest in any country through much of the century) and the Republican political movement in a divided country also played a part. Indeed, Republican governments consciously extended national infrastructures to consolidate their own regime. Their opponents (especially the Catholic church) were decentralizers, more rooted in local communities. Thus a potent motive behind railway building was to bring scattered Republican strongholds into easier communication with each other and with the capital. The Republican nation-state triumphed from the 1880s.

The American dominant class also had a common language and culture, but state infrastructures outside the South assisted it in a distinctive task – the creation of a single English-speaking nation out of lower-class immigrants speaking many languages. Most educational institutions were run by the individual states, though based on a uniform model provided by national networks of professional educators. Relative American isolation from other advanced countries also facilitated a more self-contained national capitalism than in other countries, generating more national organization of markets and corporations. Federal government infrastructures may have been as much consequence as cause of a national civil society. (Skowronek

1982 suggests they were more consequence, but see later.) The American nation emerged more capitalist, less statist, than elsewhere.

But right across the Western world postal services, schools, and railways led to the nation and to nationally organized classes. A few state services – health regulations, police, courts, and prisons – also provided more substantive authoritative interventions. But most merely provided the "buried" facilities, like the glazed earthenware sewer pipes, by which diffuse intermingling of local-regional (or immigrant) diversities led toward nationally demarcated power networks. With few intending it, state infrastructures led toward nation-states.

A few states were not so favored. Linguistic and religious communities there crosscut states and ruling classes. Moreover, as the next section indicates, relative latecomers to industrialization experienced more uneven capitalist development. Parts of the economy might be more tightly integrated with a transnational than a national economy. Particularly diverse were the Russian, Austrian, and Ottoman empires. In the Austrian lands, state, industrialization, languages, and political citizenship struggles pulled in different territorial directions (as Chapter 10 shows). The monarchy desired industrialization, but this might increase either transnational or regional interdependencies more than those of its whole territories. It wished to promote literacy, but in what language if some carried dissident provincial-nationalism? If it conceded middle-class and worker demands for political participation, would this cement their loyalties to the existing state (as in nation-states) or to rival provincial states? Four mutually supportive forces were elsewhere creating nation-states – a state with stronger infrastructural coordination, the relatively even diffusion of capitalist industrialization, shared linguistic communities, and demands for political participation by mass, universal classes – but not in the Austrian, Ottoman, and Russian empires.

Late development and the military-industrial complex

The West was a single "multi-power-actor civilization," circulating cultural messages, goods, and services regulated by geopolitical rivalries, diplomacy, and war. Once industrialization was underway in some states, it was quickly diffused elsewhere. As it greatly boosted collective power, it was eagerly received and emulated elsewhere by most dominant power networks. This was conscious, aided by the communications networks of an emerging technocratic intelligentsia. In "latecomer" countries, intellectuals identified the strengths and weaknesses of early industrialization and urged state elites-parties to plan their own adaptations. It was an interactive process; for the challenges mounted by the latecomers forced early industrializers to adapt also. And, although the means were primarily economic (harnessing the enormous powers of industry), power actors and goals were varied. All four types of dominant power actor – ideological, economic, military, and political – collaborated in development strategies. Their collaborations usually, and unconsciously, tended to further the development of the centralized nation-state, although the United States and Austria lagged behind in this respect.

Development strategies have been treated, as usual, economistically by most economic historians. Gerschenkron (1962, 1965) offered the classic theory of late development. He attributed successful industrialization in latecomer countries to (1) a sharper "spurt" in growth than had occurred in Britain, (2) greater stress on producers' goods, (3) greater scale of industrial plant and enterprise, (4) greater pressure on mass consumption levels, (5) a lesser role for agriculture, (6) a more active role for large banks, and (7) a more active role for the state. Thus faster growth for latecomers was considerably aided by close coordination between an active state and authoritative industrial and financial corporations. State elites and parties reorganized state finances to pursue macroeconomic mildly inflationary credit policies. They sponsored credit banks to lend to industry and agriculture. They invited British skilled workmen and subsidized model workshops. They built or subsidized railways and other communications infrastructures. They especially expanded education. Finally, they encouraged mergers and cartels to found enterprises big enough to invest in science and machinery. It was primarily an alliance between state elites and capitalist parties in the common pursuit of profit (Senghaas 1985 has updated such late development theory).

With hindsight we can also perceive one precondition for success; relative economic evenness of state territories. If state-aided development was too lagged or uneven, then different economic sectors or regions might become more interdependent with the transnational economy than with a national economy. In this "enclave" path of development, increasingly prominent among twentieth-century developing countries, "comprador" classes may seek to keep their own state weak and ally with foreign capital, even with foreign states. Though transnational class alignments did not go this far in the nineteenth century, uneven development could destabilize a state, forcing elites-parties to concentrate on internal social tensions rather than on geo-economic development.

Among first-wave late developers, Prussia-Germany, Sweden, Japan, and Italy (but only in the north) possessed fairly evenly diffused, fairly commercialized civil societies. German success depended on particular agrarian-industrial relations mediated by the state (see Chapter 9). No doubt, the Swedish, Japanese, and north Italian cases would be equally contingent. But after these Powers came a divide. Russia and Austria, larger, more diverse empires using the late development repertoire, achieved rapid development at the cost of destabilization. In Russia, there were spurts of state aid to industry in the 1870s, the 1890s, and after 1908, the first two led by foreign capital and the last more indigenous. Russian industrialization was fairly successful in this last phase (McKay 1970). But agriculture was more critical, because grain exports paid for imported capital and capital goods. Agrarian reform preoccupied the regime, but bogged it down in social turbulence. Austria found that state aid to economic development did not much increase the territorial cohesion of its lands. (See Chapter 10.) Late development strategies might lead to economic growth but also to disintegration. The German late development act proved hard to transport eastward.

Why did state elites-parties adopt such late development strategies? Why should development be relatively statist? Centralized-territorial planning is not a necessary feature of development. Volume I analyzes two types of social development in agrarian societies, one the product of statist "empires of domination" and the other of decentralized "multi-power-actor civilizations." Europe had been a striking example of the latter, reaching its apogee with the "hidden hand" of the Industrial Revolution. Empires of domination had derived mainly from military conquest and rule: Obviously, nineteenth-century Europe witnessed a more pacific form of statist economic development. I shall identify six causes, the first four being congruent with the economism of the late-development literature (I draw especially from Pollard 1981; cf. Kemp 1978), the fifth and sixth deriving from noneconomic state crystallizations.

1. *The desired development is known and can be authoritatively planned for.* In late-developing Europe and in relatively developed non-European states affected by European power, the future seemed clear. Amid competitive geopolitics, industrializing countries could mobilize much greater collective power; others had to respond or be dominated. "Mr. Science and Mr. Industry" – as Chinese writers put it – were seen by virtually all power actors as necessary to their power.

2. *Development resources benefit from authoritative, centralized-territorial organization.* Some industry clearly was better served by large-scale authoritative organization. Railways required enormous capital investment and boosted capital-intensive industries: iron, coal mining, and engineering. After 1880, the Second Industrial Revolution

boosted scale, especially in metal manufacturing, chemicals, and mining. Authoritative organization might be supplied by corporations, but the state might be appropriate for more territorially centered resources like tariffs, currencies, and major credit ventures. Railways and other material and symbolic communications had a territorial, often a "national," base. Here the logistics of competition were important. If states built a national railway network, domestic marketing was stimulated. In nineteenth-century countries industry fanned out along lines of communication from the crucial natural resource: coal. Iron, steel, and engineering located near coalfields could produce less efficiently than the British and still compete in the domestic market because of lower transport costs. So could handicrafts and agricultural producers. Late twentieth-century transport networks are global, but communications in the nineteenth century resembled those national spiderwebs noted in Chapter 9. Markets were integrated within state territories.

3. *Civil society actors are unable to organize such centralized-territorial resources.* This capacity has varied considerably by time and place; but through the long nineteenth century, the scale of state organization and planning vastly exceeded that of private economic institutions. Compared to states, capitalist enterprises remained tiny. About 1910, Krupp was the largest capitalist enterprise in Europe, with 64,000 employees and a turnover of almost 600 million marks (Feldenkirchen 1988: 144). Yet the Prussian-Hessian state railway employed 560,000 and spent 3 billion marks, and a single government department, the Prussian Ministry of Public Works, was actually the largest employer in the world, a little bigger than the armed forces of 680,000 men (Kunz 1990: 37). Other civil services and armed forces were comparably sized, and capitalist corporations were smaller: The largest French company, Schneider, employed only 20,000 (Daviet 1988: 70).

In every country, large corporations were isolated whales amid shoals of small enterprises. About 1910, only 5 percent of the French labor force, 8 percent of the German, and 15 percent of the American were in establishments of more than 1,000 persons. By the early 1960s, these figures had risen to 28 percent, 20 percent, and 30 percent (Pryor 1973: 153; Mayer 1981: 35–78; Trebilcock 1981: 69). Concentration ratios rose during the Second Industrial Revolution, but only to between half and a third of 1960s levels: About 1910, the hundred biggest companies in France contributed 12 percent of national manufacturing output, in Britain 15 percent, and in the United States 22 percent (Hannah 1975; Prais, 1981: 4, appendix E; Daviet 1988: 70–3). All these figures show that only in the United States, with the smallest state(s) and the most corporations, was the state not the obvious agent for forward economic planning.

Banks, cartels, and trusts mobilized capital, but far less than state elites could. The British capitalist class basically had financed its own early industrial development, but in more backward or less centralized countries, private investors supplied such capital only if politically assisted. State elites protected producers with tariffs, arranged cartels of local investors and bankers, coordinated loans from bankers abroad, and used taxes to subsidize and guarantee interest rates. Planning for broad-scale economic development relied on the state.

4. *Development is favored by state elites and/or noneconomic power actors in civil society.*[1] An economic consensus appeared among most nineteenth-century dominant actors. Only the Catholic church for a time turned its back against state and "modernism." Midcentury industrial development was favored enthusiastically by most others. State infrastructures were accepted as technically useful for industry. We can add a Marxian to the neoclassical notion of interest: Old regimes and capitalist classes also looked to the state to defend their joint property rights against the propertyless. Richard Tilly (1966) argues that the regime-bourgeois solidarity forged in the 1848 revolution allowed them to expand jointly Prussian state infrastructures.

But even all four of these economic pressures combined did not positively *require* substantial state coordination of development. Oligarchies of financiers could have coordinated most tasks themselves with a little ad hoc regulatory help from the state. The late twentieth century has created a variety of planning agencies besides those of the singular nation-state – multinational corporations acting in concert, nongovernment organizations, the confederal EEC, and the like. Attempts at late development in the Third World today tend to swing in cycles between relatively statist and relatively market strategies. Economic relations and interests, though necessary, are an insufficient explanation of why nineteenth-century late development relied so much on the central state. I go on to identify two further influences.

5. *The militarist state crystallization favored statist economic development.* The expenditure figures in Chapter 11 showed that late nineteenth-century states began largely military and ended half military. Geopolitics and military pressures continued to boost scale and authoritative organization among late developers, and then they did so in all countries (Sen 1984). In all countries, even the United States,

---

[1] There may be cases where only state elites might favor this, yet be able to *compel* compliance from others – as the Bolsheviks did later. But no nineteenth-century state possessed such despotic powers.

the armed forces were by far the largest authoritative organization throughout the long nineteenth century. Peacetime armies were ten times – wartime armies, fifty times – the size of the largest private employer. In most major industries the largest customer was the state, buying armaments, uniforms, and fodder for soldiers and sailors, plus luxuries for officials, courts, and capital cities. The main products of most large enterprises were military goods. Previously military supplies had come from state-run dockyards and arsenals or from myriad artisanal workshops by way of autonomous subcontractors. Both practices had somewhat segregated state agencies from larger capitalistic enterprises, thus minimizing earlier statist economic development. But in the nineteenth century appeared the first integrated "military-industrial complex," in the familiar modern sense, propelled forward in two phases.

Railways provided the first phase by enhancing military motives to intervene in economic development. After an initial period of suspicion, high commands saw that railways could revolutionize military logistics. Even British line planning had been influenced by navy pressure to ensure communications for ports and dockyards. Elsewhere, high command, state elite, and the capitalist class cooperated more closely in building a national railway network. The later the development, the more the military helped plan the route, alerted by wars in which railway mobilization tipped the outcome – toward France in its Italian campaign of 1859, toward the North in the American Civil War, and toward Prussia in 1866 and 1870. Henceforth new lines in France, Russia, Austria, or Germany needed military permission and participation. State supervision increased (Pearton 1984: 24).

The second phase began with the arms race of the 1880s, developing what McNeill (1983: 279) calls "command technology." It was preceded across midcentury by capitalists pioneering mass production of guns and bullets – Prussian breech-loading guns, French Minié elongated bullets, and American Colt and Springfield guns using interchangeable machine parts. Then French naval dockyards pioneered iron warships, and an arms race ensued. The scale of production escalated through mergers and cartels (with state encouragement). Manufacturers (as in the United States today) had single dominant customers for whom the product was a use not an exchange value. Military states *had* to have these products, at almost whatever cost. They "intervened," though largely by inducement. States provided public credit for arms production on a scale at which the private capital market would have balked. Trebilcock (1973) believes that between 1890 and 1914 its scale rivaled that of earlier railway investment. Technological development was "commanded" forward by military

demand. From interchangeable machine parts through Bessemer's transformation of iron into steel, to a whole range of light metal alloys, to
turbines, diesels, and hydraulic machinery, most technological breakthroughs of the period were spun off this military-industrial complex.
The manufacturers had assured customers, faced dynamic international
competition, and were able to pump far more into research than other
industries (Trebilcock 1969: 481; Pearton 1984: 77–86).

Looking at photographs of HMS *Dreadnought*, the 1906 apogee of
the arms race, we find it difficult to appreciate that with its great,
bulbous hulk, its angular superstructure, and its innumerable protuber-
ances, this ship once seemed as hi-tech and futuristic as a sleek F-17
fighter or a *Trident*-class submarine does today. But dreadnoughts
were *the* symbol of the Second Industrial Revolution. They were built
by the largest industrial enterprises of the age, used the most advanced
technology, and produced the greatest concentration of firepower in
history. Unlike their counterparts today, they also generated mass
employment.

American military statist development first differed only in form,
then it lagged. Federal and state governments were concerned more
with expansion and integration of the continental Union than with
military rivalry with the major Powers. But the results were not dissimilar for much of the century. Governments chartered and subsidized
canals, then railroads, to penetrate the continent, lending the army as
Indian killers and engineers. The Civil War suddenly produced a
massive military-industrial complex and preserved the Union, integrating the continent and increasing industrial concentration. The
massive war debt, funded by government bonds, expanded the stock
market, which was also lending to the subsidized railroad companies.
As Bensel argues (1990), the state had effectively created an American
finance capitalism.

The rise of the great American corporation is often explained in
terms of a purely technological and capitalist logic (Chandler 1977;
Tedlow 1988), but as Roy (1990: 30) observes, "The decisive actor
creating corporations was the government." Actually, he means governments, as the individual states did most of the regulation. Yet near
century's end, with the continent penetrated, and under little geopolitical pressure, the American economy did become less statist than
those of other national countries. Its mass continental market generated
the famous corporate innovations – the Model T Ford assembly line,
the Sears Roebuck catalog, the light bulb – yet this was not a necessary
feature of capitalist development per se. Germany, the other corporate
pillar of the Second Industrial Revolution, had a substantially "commanded" economy.

6. *The monarchical state crystallization favored statist economic development.* Unlike most early industrializers, most late-developing states were monarchies centered on the old regime. Autonomous monarchical Powers were buttressed by old regime parties more particularistic than those of dominant classes. The monarchical–old regime alliance had its own private interests and goals, seeking fiscal resources bypassing representative assemblies. Chapters 8 and 11 show that such states used tariffs and revenue from state property to this end. State railways then gave a fiscal bonus, contributing half the revenue of the Prussian state. Other state infrastructures and nationalized industries were milked for revenue by all of them.

Thus there was a substantial military and a lesser monarchical boost to late development strategies; and then mixed military-capitalist motives spread to party democracies through geopolitical rivalry. Relations between the principal state crystallizations were thus largely consensual, reinforcing the fourth condition listed earlier. Increasingly the policies (though less the rhetoric) of state elites and parties, high commands, and capitalist classes presupposed that the desired goal of an industrial society (and in the United States also an integrated continental Union) would not be best encouraged if the transnational "invisible hand" of the market was let alone.

So, again, this was rarely a case of a state's intervening *against* civil society power actors. With their array of new powers, states might have become veritable Leviathans, as Giddens (1985) suggests. Logistic obstacles to territorial penetration were disappearing; state infrastructures sprawled evenly across civil society, reducing its historic privacy from the state; and some among dominant classes wished to give the political regime regulatory, even initiating, powers in the economy. But "intervention" in party democracies was largely coordination, persuasion, and inducement, not coercion. And though monarchies exploited fiscal opportunities to evade party democracy, they did not turn them against the capitalist class.

The idea rarely occurred to them. Monarchs, old regime parties, high commands, and bourgeois parties had different, sometimes competing, interests, but they were not in dialectical, head-on collision. Capitalists welcomed state credit, communications infrastructures, and protection. The arms race secured markets for their capital goods, and full employment created consumer goods markets. They recognized that high command and state elite interests were not theirs and niggled at both, but the overall trade-off was positive. Monarchical states claimed they built railways, established state industries, and licensed private industries in a neutral, technocratic spirit. A Prussian minister of commerce declared that "it did not matter who built railroads so long as someone built them" (Henderson 1958: 187). Latecomer states assisted private capitalists to achieve economic development and militaries to secure and perhaps extend it. They could also quietly use the ensuing revenues to evade party democracy.

As capitalist, military, and monarchical goals and crystallizations were broadly compatible, no one chose among them. State crystallizations were *additive*, which we shall see turned out to be disastrous. State elites and parties rarely opposed capitalism. Indeed, they needed profitable industries for goods and tax revenues. They had also for centuries supported private property rights. When states did confront class issues head-on, they usually sided with the dominant classes, though this might be mitigated by their pursuit of morality and public order. We shall see later that state autonomy was greater in foreign than in domestic policy. In domestic policy it was exercised more over subordinate than dominant classes.

But states did not only prop up capitalist property. Half their resources were still devoted to military rivalry with other states. As military and capitalist crystallizations entwined, both states and capitalist class were given greater national organization and more territorial conceptions of interest. This was not intended by either side. As geopolitical rivalry reacted back on the political economy of early industrializers, *their* organization became more national, *their* conceptions of profit more territorial. That was the principal power autonomy of nineteenth-century states, not the intended strategy of a state elite but principally the unintended consequence of four entwined state crystallizations: the capitalist, the military, the party-democratic or monarchical, and the emerging nation-state.

Social citizenship, militarism, and monarchism

Table 11.5 notes three great extensions of state civilian scope. Having discussed infrastructural expansion and nationalization of resources, I move to the least of the three, welfare, and to the first stirrings of Marshall's "social citizenship." As Table 11.5 shows, party democracies were not the biggest welfare spenders. True, Britain and France were just beginning modern welfare schemes and Britain moved decisively to progressive taxation at the very end of the period. But as yet welfare expenditure was mainly German. The most famous item was Bismarck's social insurance scheme, though not until 1913 did its cost exceed locally administered social assistance and Poor Law schemes (Steinmetz 1990a, 1990b). Table 11.5 also ignores the substantial welfare benefits being paid by France and the United States out of military expenditures. The earliest stirrings of the welfare state appear somewhat military and monarchical.

Regimes now had a broader "policing" problem. Capitalism and urbanization had weakened local-regional segmental controls over the lower classes. Propertyless laborers, subjected to capitalist markets, periodically were rendered destitute, migratory, and rebellious. Peasants were burdened by debts as commercialization swept the countryside. Because capitalism also conferred new powers of collective action on workers and peasants (see later chapters), more universal forms of social control were required, especially in the burgeoning towns.

Regime provision of "good order" had long been dual, combining "policing" with "welfare." We saw in Chapter 12 that policing now became more varied, as paramilitary, then civilian police forces appeared. Welfare also became more diverse. Traditionally, local Poor Laws had predominated. But these became strained as industrialization, geographic mobility, and sectoral unemployment spread their cost more unevenly. In Britain and across Germany (and probably also in countries with poorer records) the Poor Laws became the largest civil expenditure during the first half of the nineteenth century. Relief was minimal, involving little sense that the poor had rights – and certainly not to social citizenship. The destitute, infirm, or elderly might not starve if they showed themselves "deserving," often by placing themselves in workhouses. But two other forms of welfare developed: self-insurance and selective state welfare. These implied not universal social citizenship but sectional and especially segmental welfare, seeking to build up loyalist networks among workers and peasants.

Self-insurance emerged from below, from friendly societies, the principal "protectionist" function of early trade unions. (See Chapters 15 and 17.) They flourished among relatively skilled workers and in secure trades, and so were approved of, and sometimes encouraged, by dominant classes as indicating thrift and respectability, removing artisans from the "dangerous classes" below. They probably encouraged sectionalism among lower classes, but they did not much involve the state until the very end of the period.

Before then, some states had already introduced segmental welfare schemes. Modern France and the United States were born amid armed revolutionary struggle and mass mobilization wars. Many adult males lost life or limb in defense of "their" states. Old ad hoc payments to mutilated ex-soldiers and to widows and orphans of the dead were institutionalized and extended. A French pension scheme for veterans and wounded was introduced by the revolutionaries and strengthened by Bonaparte. By 1813, it cost 13 percent of the entire military budget, as more than 100,000 veterans received pensions. This percentage and number held until 1914 (Woloch 1979: 207–8).

The U.S. federal government paid disability and death benefits to veterans and dependents from the 1780s on, and by 1820, they exceeded all federal civil expenses. They rose to their peak during the second and third decades after each war, then declined. The Civil War extended them into a genuine old-age pension system. By 1900, half the elderly native-born white males received them. In the North and Midwest veterans constituted a vocal 12 percent to 15 percent of the electorate. Membership in their Grand Army of the Republic was 428,000 in 1890, more than half the membership of all labor unions. Military pensions again exceeded all federal civil expenses during 1892–1900, before declining. But from 1882 to 1916 they consumed between 22 percent and 43 percent of total federal expenses. Although the poorer Confederate state had given no pensions, most southern states (meagerly) granted them from the 1890s on. The United States had the first welfare state, a little-known fact, but it was confined to those who had demonstrated loyalty to their state. (This paragraph draws on the research of Orloff and Skocpol; see Orloff 1988.)

Indeed, the United States and France had a military tinge to citizenship. The French sometimes defined citizenship as *l'impôt du sang* – the blood tax of military service. The U.S. Constitution entrenches a citizen militia – in the clause often interpreted as guaranteeing the right to bear arms (including automatic weapons). These states were embedding themselves in citizen soldiers, rewarding past services and buying political support among the social groups from whom veterans were drawn. Nineteenth-century French bourgeois regimes tended to lack penetration among the peasant masses. A large, well-rewarded army established a loyal cell in every French village. By 1811, most departments had at least three pensioners per 1,000 population (Woloch 1979: 221–9). This may not seem many, but it was probably the most thorough penetration by the early nineteenth-century state into civil society. America differed. White adult male suffrage and the two-party system resulted in competition for farmer and worker votes. A Republican northern coalition between white workers and industrial capital emerged. The consent of northern workers to tariffs was bought partly by veterans' payments. These "social citizenships" were selective and segmental, not universal. Regimes obtained from peasants and workers not, as in agrarian societies, a particularistic loyalty to lineage and locality but an emerging loyalty to the universal nation-state.

Prussia-Germany and Austria did not follow France and the United States with these veterans' benefits. Yet their veterans, especially at the noncommissioned-officer level, were given preferential hiring rights in civil state employment (as also occurred in France), as Chapter 13 explains. Moreover, this policy was coupled with a second: selective welfare programs first introduced by Bismarck.

Latecomers could glance abroad and anticipate dangers as well as benefits. Foreign visitors to Britain reported not only on advanced technology, economic dynamism, and Parliament but also on urban squalor, criminality, and class conflict. German intelligentsia, increasingly state-centered, were well informed about Chartism and drew lessons about what might happen if industrialization was left to the "invisible hand." They identified the "British disease," class conflict, which Bismarck believed had also fatally undermined the French armies of 1870. They studied the English Poor Laws, co-ops, and friendly societies, French national workshops, Belgian and French sickness and old-age pension insurance funds, and Belgian mutual assurance societies. Model insurance schemes circulated in Germany, liberal self-help models competing with a "social" or "patriarchal monarchy" model (Reulecke 1981). Dynastic monarchies had practiced particularistic welfare. Prussia in 1776 restricted miners' working hours to eight, guaranteed a fixed income, prohibited child and female labor, and instituted a benefit scheme, all as a by-product of granting miners exemption from military conscription. Austrian ministers under Maria Theresa and Joseph II had introduced various welfare measures, which were then curtailed by lack of funds.

But Germany was the first to transform particular into fairly general benefits. Bismarck's social insurance legislation absorbed 10 percent of Reich expenditures from its inception in 1885, 20 percent after ten years of operation, and 30 percent by 1910. Inasmuch as almost all the remaining Reich budget was going for military expenditure, we can perceive its importance. Aiding workers to protect themselves against destitution, and persuading employers to help them, became a fundamental regime goal. Other countries did not yet follow suit. Austria did in 1885–7, but its coverage remained minimal (Macartney 1971: 633; Flora and Alber 1981). Even the German legislation was not all that generous. It provided low accident and sickness payments, covered just over half of those in employment, and granted a barely adequate pension at the age of seventy (later sixty-six) – if the worker had worked 300 days a year for 48 years. Only the pension contained a state contribution, so the scheme was mostly compulsory self-insurance. It did not touch the more contentious issue of factory safety or works inspection, which could have prevented accidents and illness in the first place (Tampke 1981). This would have infringed property rights.

Bismarck was attempting segmental control over labor, hoping to seduce skilled, organized workers away from socialism. The social insurance legislation was his carrot, the Anti-Socialist Laws his stick. He did not seek positive enthusiasm from workers, only that class struggle would not undermine the state and its armies. To relieve basic destitution among the more skilled industrial workers seemed adequate for this purpose.

But there was also a potentially more general cause: capitalist economic concentration. Bismarck's legislation extended policies already found in some large-scale heavy industry (Ullman 1981). Big industrialists were the main supporters of legislation introducing old-age and disability pensions and accident insurance (though they later opposed unemployment insurance), at first ranged against smaller employers. Indeed, shortage of funds forced Bismarck to adopt more of the self-insurance principle advocated by big employers than he had earlier intended. Thereafter the welfare schemes received considerable support from the newer, light manufacturing sector. Because their terms of eligibility embodied work incentives, they tended to "commodify" welfare along capitalist lines (Steinmetz 1990a, 1990b). Bismarck's legislation anticipated less the welfare state (as is often argued) than the late twentieth-century American or Japanese corporation: Workers benefiting from corporate internal labor markets became loyal to capitalism (and sometimes militarism), rejecting unions and socialism. It did seek to institutionalize class conflict, as Marshall argued, but by bypassing class with segmental organizations tying privileged workers to their employers and to the state.

Thus these early French, American, and German schemes for the relief of poverty embodied two principles, one a military citizen right deriving from the nation, the other a self-insurance encouraged by both monarchism and corporate capitalism. Neither was a right enjoyed by all citizens (still less by all adults). Rights were granted selectively, only to those providing key military or economic power resources to capital and regime. The intention, and sometimes the effect, was to redirect class consciousness into nationalism or sectionalism segmentally.

Yet both schemes radically extended state activities, reaching out far beyond local segmental power networks. They were also extendable – by the party democracies. Just before World War I, many British Liberals, American Democrats, and French Radicals began to link welfare to progressive taxes. Only the Liberal party, prodded by an inventive and persuasive politician, legislated before 1914. Lloyd George brought union and private insurance company schemes into a more comprehensive, government-regulated system. Its benefits still were not a universal citizen's right, because they were restricted to men in formal, stable employment, but they were too general for any segmental divide-and-rule strategy, although they were intended to undercut the

Labour party. More important, they were coupled with a progressive income tax. The poverty of some should be systematically relieved from the wealth of others: the first state recognition of social citizenship. The modern state was just beginning its third sea change.

Three main conditions underlay these varied schemes – the development of extensive and political lower classes, mass mobilization warfare, and corporate capitalism. If these persisted, then perhaps these segmental social-military and class-sectionalist rights might transform into universal social citizenship. All three conditions did persist. Indeed, in Europe in the two world wars, mass-mobilization war actually became total war, involving all citizens. Only in the United States did segmental rights significantly withstand the third sea change in the life of the state, the coming of social citizenship. But that occurred more recently, after the period discussed here.

Conclusion to Chapters 11–14

These four chapters have documented two modernizing sea changes in the life of Western states. Throughout the eighteenth century, these states had become much larger. Surprisingly, they were at their greatest size relative to their civil societies about 1800, after which they declined. But their scope remained traditional, narrow, and predominantly military. States were little more than revenue collectors and recruiting sergeants, although they were now biting deep and painfully into social life, thus politicizing it. In the second transformation, from the late nineteenth century on, they grew not in (relative) size but in scope. Their civilian functions were broad and still broadening. Much more of social life was now politicized, though with far less pain and intensity than in the late eighteenth century. By 1914, they were dual military-civil states. Both sea changes impacted considerably on the relations between states and civil societies. States became more representative and more bureaucratized, as state elites and parties sought to coordinate their expanded functions. And civil societies were becoming "naturalized" into nation-states, caged by state sovereignty and boundaries.

The second sea change, the expansion of state civilian functions, did not enlarge either the autonomous or the despotic power of state elites, as stressed by elite theory. Quite the reverse. States were dual, central place and territorial radii, elites and parties. As more of social life became politicized, parties strengthened more than did elites. Class reductionist theories of the "capitalist state" become plausible if we confine our gaze to its domestic civil activities vis-à-vis those of the dominant class. Within these blinkers Marx had a point when he described the British nineteenth-century state as a bourgeois "mutual insurance pact" or as an "executive committee for managing the common affairs of the bourgeoisie" – although he somewhat underestimated the constraints on capitalism that moral-ideological and party-democratic crystallizations might bring. These led states to many "interventions" against capitalist freedoms, though more usually through persuasion, inducement, and covert action than through openly hostile legislation. Overall, these states had crystallized more overtly as capitalist states than as anything else. Domestically, the state was in this respect less an actor, more a place in the arena of power. Its singular purpose conferred a degree of cohesion upon state institutions.

Much the same could be said of the American and French states, although the United States dispersed elites and parties amid various sites of government – and the South remained exceptional – whereas France centralized them even more in the capital. Of course, in the semiauthoritarian monarchies of Prussia and Austria, and even more in autocratic Russia, monarchical elites-parties possessed more power autonomy (though rarely elite cohesion). But overall, for particular historical reasons, *the* state – the one that mattered most in this period, the state of the Western Europeans and North Americans – was predominantly reducible in terms of open power struggles over domestic policy to the dominant capitalist class of civil society. It had not always been so. But a reductionist, economistic theory resonates strongly in domestic politics during the nineteenth century.

Such reductionism, however, would seriously neglect two further state crystallizations that, when combined, revolutionized capitalism and indeed social life around the globe. First, the growth in state infrastructural powers was not merely neutral. It reinforced the politicization and naturalization of social life prodded forward in earlier centuries. This was not through direct head-on struggles, like those ascribed by Marx to classes. Again, unconsciously, without anyone intending it, power networks were redirected toward the terrain of the state's territories, *caging*, naturalizing social life, even in its more intimate sphere, and subtly territorializing social conceptions of identity and interest. The modern state crystallized increasingly as the *nation-state*. This then entwined with long-lived political struggles over how centralized and national or decentralized and federal the state should become, producing interstitial forms of national centralization (although here the United States lagged and Austria deviated toward confederalism). Class reductionism would also neglect the third, *military*, crystallization of modern states. This was now not dominating states as formerly, but had become more autonomous within the state, more capable of insulated infrastructural control over "its" armed forces, and potentially extremely dangerous (as Chapter 12 suggests and Chapter 21 proves).

Throughout the nineteenth century, these two further crystallizations were, somewhat unevenly, retracking capitalism and social life into more national and more territorial forms – as capitalism was also retracking them. These three crystallizations – as capitalist, as nation-state, and as military – seem to have operated at a higher level of general causality over the period than others. Yet the three never met in head-on collision, from whose results we might "ultimately" rank them, or in systematic compromise, to which we might apply pluralist theory. Most states *appeared* to be relatively harmonious, their parties and elites sharing a broad consensus about the purposes of government – in Britain from midcentury, in France, Germany, and the United States from two or three decades later, in Austria not at all. Yet this was a casual, unconsidered, untested consensus. Crystallizations were "additive," added to each other without serious consideration of any ultimate contradictions among them – especially, as we glimpsed in Chapters 9 and 10, in semiauthoritarian monarchies. Party-democratic or monarchical crystallizations added more particular and variable influences through the period, as we shall see especially in later chapters, but because no state was yet fully representative, pluralist theory has only a limited explanatory role.

As states became more polymorphous, their seeming cohesion was potentially delusive. In earlier times, many states had been genuinely cohesive because they were controlled by small elites and their rather particular parties – princes, merchant oligarchies, priests, or warrior bands. They had enjoyed considerable autonomy in the political sphere they controlled, yet they had caged little of social life outside. We have seen autonomy decline but caging increase. States had become the elite center and the party radii through which much of civil society became organized. But as states did so, they lost their earlier, par-ticularistic coherence.

It is a basic tenet of my work that societies are not systems. There is no ultimately determining structure to human existence – at least none that social actors or sociological observers, situated in its midst, can discern. What we call societies are only loose aggregates of diverse, overlapping, intersecting power networks. States had now moved half-way to representing and bureaucratically organizing that diversity – but without systematically confronting, ranking, and compromising the ensuing polymorphous crystallizations. The danger of this for human existence was that these states were now mobilizing terrifying collective powers over which their – or, indeed, any collective – sovereign control was highly imperfect. Chapter 21 will show that in July 1914 the casual additive polymorphism of European states began to overwhelm the entire multi-power-actor civilization.

Bibliography

Bensel, R. 1990. *Yankee Leviathan: The Origins of Central State Authority in America, 1859–1877*. Cambridge: Cambridge University Press.

Bland, L. 1982. "Guardians of the race" or "vampires upon the nation's health"?: female sexuality and its regulations in early twentieth-century Britain. In *The Changing Experience of Women*, ed. E. Whitelegg et al. Oxford: Oxford University Press.

Chandler, A. D. 1977. *The Visible Hand: The Managerial Revolution in American Business*. Cambridge, Mass.: Belknap Press.

Cronin, J. E. 1988. The British state and the structure of political opportunity. *Journal of British Studies* 27.

Daviet, J.-P. 1988. Some features of concentration in France (end of the nineteenth century/twentieth century). In *The Concentration Process in the Entrepreneurial Economy Since the Late Nineteenth Century*, ed. H. Pohl. Wiesbaden: Steiner.

Davin, A. 1978. Imperialism and motherhood. *History Workshop* 5.

Digby, A. 1982. *The Poor Law in Nineteenth-Century England and Wales*. London: Historical Society.

Feldkirchen, W. 1988. Concentration in German industry, 1870–1939. In *The Concentration Process in the Entrepreneurial Economy Since the Late Nineteenth Century*, ed. H. Pohl. Wiesbaden: Steiner.

Flora, P., and J. Alber. 1981. Modernization, democratization, and the development of welfare states in Western Europe. In *The Development of Welfare States in Europe and America*, ed. P. Flora and A. J. Heidenheimer. New Brunswick, N.J.: Transaction Books.

Gerschenkron, A. 1962. *Economic Backwardness in Historical Perspective*. Cambridge, Mass.: Harvard University Press.

  1965. Typology of industrial development as a tool of analysis. *Second International Conference on Economic History*. Paris: Mouton.

Giddens, A. 1985. *The Nation-State and Violence*. Cambridge: Polity Press.

Good, D. F. 1984. *The Economic Rise of the Habsburg Empire, 1750–1914*. Berkeley and Los Angeles: University of California Press.

Grew, R. 1984. The nineteenth-century European state. In *Statemaking and Social Movements*, ed. C. Bright and S. Harding. Ann Arbor: University of Michigan Press.

Hannah, L. 1975. *The Rise of the Corporate Economy*. London: Methuen & Co.

Henderson, W. O. 1958. *The State and the Industrial Revolution in Prussia, 1740–1870*. Liverpool: Liverpool University Press.

Keller, M. 1977. *Affairs of State: Public Life in Late Nineteenth-Century America*. Cambridge, Mass.: Harvard University Press.

Kemp, T. 1978. *Historical Patterns of Industrialization*. London: Longman Group.

Koven, S., and S. Michel. 1990. Womanly duties: maternalist politics and the origins of the welfare states in France, Germany, Great Britain, and the United States, 1880–1920. *American Historical Review* 95.

Kunz, A. 1990. The state as employer in Germany, 1880–1918: from paternalism to public policy. In *The State and Social Change in Germany, 1880–1980*, ed. W. R. Lee and E. Rosenhaft. New York: Berg.

Lubenow, W. C. 1971. *The Politics of Government Growth: Early Victorian Attitudes Toward State Intervention, 1833–1848*. Hamden, Conn.: Archon Books.

Macartney, C. A. 1971. *The Hapsburg Empire, 1710–1918*. London: Weidenfeld & Nicolson.

MacDonagh, O. 1977. *Early Victorian Government, 1830–1870*. London: Weidenfeld & Nicolson.

McKay, J. P. 1970. *Pioneers for Profit: Foreign Entrepreneurship and Russian Industrialization, 1885–1913*. Chicago: University of Chicago Press.

McNeill, W. H. 1983. *The Pursuit of Power*. Oxford: Blackwell.

Marsh, P. (ed.). 1979. *The Conscience of the Victorian State*. Syracuse, N.Y.: Syracuse University Press.

Mayer, A. 1981. *The Persistence of the Old Regime*. New York: Pantheon.

Mitchell, B. R. 1975. *European Historical Statistics, 1750–1970*. New York: Columbia University Press.

Orloff, A. 1988. The political origins of America's belated welfare state. In *The Politics of Social Policy in the United States*, ed. M. Weir et al. Princeton, N.J.: Princeton University Press.

Pearton, M. 1984. *Diplomacy, War and Technology Since 1830*. Lawrence: University of Kansas Press.

Pollard, S. 1981. *Peaceful Conquest: The Industrialization of Europe, 1760–1970*. Oxford: Oxford University Press.

Prais, S. J. 1981. *The Evolution of Giant Firms in Britain*. Cambridge: Cambridge University Press.

Pryor, F. L. 1973. *Property and Industrial Organization in Communist and Capitalist Nations*. Bloomington: University of Indiana Press.

Reulecke, J. 1981. English social policy around the middle of the nineteenth century as seen by German social reformers. In *The Emergence of the Welfare State in Britain and Germany*, ed. W. J. Mommsen. London: Croom Helm.

Roy, W. G. 1990. Functional and historical logics in explaining the rise of the American industrial corporation. *Comparative Social Research* 12.

Sen, G. 1984. *The Military Origin of Industrialization and International Trade Rivalry*. New York: St. Martin's Press.

Senghaas, D. 1985. *The European Experience: A Historical Critique of Development Theory*. Leamington Spa: Berg.

Skowronek, S. 1982. *Building a New American State: The Expansion of National Administrative Capacities, 1877–1920*. Cambridge: Cambridge University Press.

Soderberg, J. 1985. Regional economic disparity and dynamics, 1840–1914: a comparison between France, Great Britain, Prussia and Sweden. *Journal of European Economic History* 14.

Steinmetz, G. 1990a. The local welfare state: two strategies for social domination in urban imperial Germany. *American Sociological Review* 55.

    1990b. The myth and the reality of an autonomous state: industrialists, Junkers and social policy in imperial Germany. *Comparative Social Research* 12.

Sutherland, G. (ed.). 1972. *Studies in the Growth of Nineteenth Century Government*. London: Routledge & Kegan Paul.

Tampke, J. 1981. Bismarck's social legislation: a genuine breakthrough? In *The Emergence of the Welfare State in Britain and Germany*, ed. J. Mommsen. London: Croom Helm.

Taylor, A. J. 1972. *Laissez-Faire and State Intervention in Nineteenth Century Britain*. London: Economic History Society.

Tedlow, R. S. 1988. The process of economic concentration in the American economy. In *The Concentration Process in the Entrepreneurial Economy Since the Late Nineteenth Century*, ed. H. Pohl. Wiesbaden: Steiner.

Tilly, R. 1966. The political economy of public finance and the industrialization of Prussia, 1815–1866. *Journal of Economic History* 26.

Trebilcock, C. 1969. "Spin-off" in British economic history: armaments and industry, 1760–1914. *Economic History Review*, 2d ser., 22.

1973. British armaments and European industrialization, 1890–1914. *Economic History Review*, 2d ser., 26.

1981. *The Industrialization of the Continental Powers, 1780–1914*. Essex: Longman Group.

Ullman, H.-P. 1981. German industry and Bismarck's social security legislation. In *The Emergence of the Welfare State in Britain and Germany*, ed. W. J. Mommsen. London: Croom Helm.

Watkins, S. C. 1991. *From Provinces into Nations. Demographic Integration in Western Europe, 1870–1960*. Princeton, N.J.: Princeton University Press.

Weber, E. 1976. *Peasants into Frenchmen*. Stanford, Calif.: Stanford University Press.

Weeks, J. 1981. *Sex, Politics and Society: The Regulation of Sexuality Since 1800*. London: Longman Group.

Woloch, I. 1979. *The French Veteran from the Revolution to the Restoration*. Chapel Hill: University of North Carolina Press.

15　The resistible rise of the British working class, 1815–1880

Theories of working-class movements

Most histories of working-class movements begin in Britain. During the nineteenth century, Britain was the only industrial nation, with the only large working class. Remarkably, as Table 15.1 indicates, there were more workers in manufacturing than in agriculture as early as the Battle of Waterloo, in 1815, virtually a hundred years earlier than in any other major Power (as Table 19.1 also reveals).

The early emergence of British labor made it unique. When, at the beginning of the twentieth century, other major Powers were industrialized, with comparably sized labor forces, the nature of industrialization, of the state, and of class had been transformed. What happened in Britain and in Chartism to the first proletariat was not repeatable. Nonetheless this first working class was then regarded – and often still is – as the prototype of the future. Britain housed Marx and Engels (who managed a factory in Stockport). Their theory of the working class drew principally on the British experience and has influenced virtually all subsequent writers. They argued four principal theses:

1. Capitalism diffused a qualitative divide between capital and labor throughout civil society as *similar* "universal classes."
2. Manufacturing capitalism massified the labor force, making workers collectively interdependent at the point of production and in the labor market. Workers became *interdependent* "collective laborers," forming trade unions and undertaking collective class action.
3. Similarity and interdependence are reinforced outside of work by dense worker *communities* capable of autonomous social and cultural organization.
4. These three capacities for collective action generate class politics and a *socialist party* capable of capturing political power, if necessary by revolution.

Though there is much here to accept, I depart from the Marx-Engels model in five ways:

1. Although workers did indeed develop into "collective laborers," this was rarely into a singular working class, especially in relatively pure economic conflict. As Weber argued, workers possessed more

510

Table 15.1. *Percentage of British labor force by sector, 1801–81*

	1801	1821	1841	1861	1881
Agriculture[a]	35	29	23	19	13
Industry, mining	29	39	44	49	49
Services	29	31	34	32	38

[a] Includes forestry and fisheries.
Sources: 1801–21: Evans (1983: 412), who also gives slightly lower industry figures for 1841 and 1861. 1841, 1861: Bairoch et al. (1968).

diverse economic power resources than Marx believed. Though none owned the means of production, many controlled the labor-market supply of their occupational skill, exercising what Parkin (1979) terms "closure," that is, closing the market to others seeking to use such skills. Because the nineteenth century had an abundant supply of labor, closure depended on preventing the use of "blacklegs" ("scabs" in America). Marx and Engels believed that capitalism homogenized workers' skills, rendering them interchangeable, easily replaceable. Thus, to exercise closure, workers would have to extend their combinations to the whole class, mutually agreeing not to be blacklegs. Yet capitalist development did not uniformly de-skill. Two alternative collectivities appeared:

A. Workers become *segmentally* interdependent with their co-workers *and* their employer, rather than with all workers. Employment relations are inherently dual: Although employers and workers conflict, they must also cooperate at an everyday level – the employer to realize profits, the worker wages. Conflict and interdependence are the Janus faces of labor relations. Interdependence is heightened if scarce labor skills are employer-specific and if skills are trained on the job. The worker is deprived of the power to leave, as in the outside labor market he or she is unskilled. But during strikes the employer may be reluctant to take on blackleg labor, because this involves training costs and short-term labor inefficiency. Employers and workers may mutually develop *internal labor markets* – jobs are stratified by the training required and promotion is from within, from lower to higher jobs. Employers and workers still are in conflict, but their interdependence also intensifies. Employees become segregated from the mass of workers outside, and conflict becomes employer-specific, not generalizable to a class.

B. The second form of interdependence does not involve employers, only workers, but within smaller *sectional* collectivities defined by trade, occupation, or industry. Skilled crafts or trades may especially act collectively to control the supply of their skill. If they do, they are less vulnerable to blacklegs and need not develop broader worker support to restrain them. Theirs can be the purely sectional strategy of an "aristocracy of labor." Skilled workers may oppose their employer quite strongly, but without sensing that they belong to a singular working class totality. Regimes and employers may also conciliate workers who have such market powers, reserving repression for less favored workers. Thus sectionalism among workers invites segmental strategies from their opponents.

Workers without either of these narrower interdependences are more vulnerable to blackleg labor. They must seek broader unity to restrain the supply of alternative labor, moving toward class definitions of identity and opposition. By contrast, both narrower collectivities sense two opponents – the employer *and* outside workers. Privileged insider workers struggle against the threat of replacement by outsiders. This fundamental sectional-segmental fault line divides skilled from unskilled occupations and craft or enterprise unions from industrial or general unions. These divisions will appear ubiquitously in these chapters, alongside elements of broader class organization.

2. Marx and Engels left unresolved a tension between diffused and authoritative aspects of capitalism. They sometimes emphasized the diffused nature of capitalism, sometimes a particular authoritative site of class struggle, variously described as the labor process, the point of production, and the direct relations of production. Until recently, most Marxists were "productivists," believing that production relations determine class and class politics – usually modeling production relations on the factory. Yet labor processes generate segmental or sectional as often as class conflict. In explaining broader, classlike labor movements, I focus less on factories and labor processes and more on the diffusion of capitalist commodity relations across civil society. Later chapters reveal this to be no mere academic debate. Productivist ideologies, especially Marxist ones, have weakened the potentially broader appeal of proletarian identities and socialist parties.

3. Marxism also tends to economic reductionism. Theses 3 and 4 – concerning working-class communities and politics – might seem to correct this, but Marx, Engels, and their followers viewed these as mostly determined by the economic power relations embedded in theses 1 and 2. I disagree, as many others have done.

Political power crystallizations have also shaped classes and class conflict. Marx, Engels, and most subsequent writers neglected the state, regarding worker politics as essentially determined by their economic conditions. Recent writers have amended this somewhat by observing how politics may be the outcome of struggles themselves, and not merely of original economic conditions. But this is still inadequate. Employer-worker conflicts came to involve the state, and so the other crystallizations of the state came to structure working-class movements, especially in bridging or reinforcing the working-class fault lines. Because, as Chapter 11 shows, states changed considerably through this period, so did their political structuring of labor. Political power relations profoundly shaped the emergence, or nonemergence, of the working class.

4. Similarly, worker communities have not been mere passive recipients of production-centered power relations. They also have shaped production relations, as has been recognized by research on American workers (discussed in Chapter 18). But this also raises the special influence of the more intimate social relations of family and gender. Marx had little interest in gender, Engels had more, but both regarded the working class as interchangeably male and universal. Yet class has always been entwined with family and gender. This chapter argues that nineteenth-century Britain saw a shift from a family- and community-oriented to a male- and employment-oriented working class, with consequences for segmental-sectional versus class organization.

5. The consequence of all of the preceding is that class conflict is rarely a dialectical head-on confrontation, for it involves numerous aspects with distinct, yet not contradictory, logics. On the occasions when there has been direct conflict, I shall argue, it is not resolved in the dialectical, revolutionary way envisaged by Marx. In head-on confrontation, the capitalist class clearly perceives the threat from below and restrains its internal factionalism. The working class is more likely to lose head-on class conflict than win it.

As usual, I center on class organization, but I also use the IOTA model of subjective class consciousness, introduced in Chapter 2. Remember that identity, opposition, totality, and alternative are ideal types, one-sided emphases on elements found only partially and imperfectly in social reality. Conceiving of oneself as working class or as opposed to a capitalist class will normally compete inside worker consciousness with other bases of collective identity and opposition, and a strong sense of class totality is rare, even among militants. I now explore more worker alternatives. Table 15.2 classifies the main alternatives conceived of by nineteenth- and twentieth-century workers (and peasants) to the capitalism confronting them.

Labor movements differ in how "radical" they are – the dimension running from competitive, through reformist, to revolutionary – and in

Table 15.2. *Worker and peasant alternatives to capitalism*

Tactical site of struggle	Strategy toward Capitalism		
	Competitive	*Reformist*	*Revolutionary*
Economy	Protectionism	Economism	Syndicalism
State	Mutualism	Social democracy	Marxism

whether they seek to transform the state as well as industrial relations. This yields three pairs of alternatives. The first pair is the most "moderate" – not changing capitalism but providing opportunities for workers to "compete" within capitalism. If they accept existing market rules and conditions, merely using collective solidarity to acquire market advantage, I term this *protectionism*. Cooperatives are usually protectionist, as are Robert Owen's model factories or the Chartist Land Plan or the massive Basque Mondragon enterprises today. They are internally collectivist, but they operate on external markets just like a capitalist enterprise. The most ubiquitous protectionism was provided by union insurance funds, which gave most nineteenth-century unions their actual names – "friendly societies" in Britain, "benevolent societies" in the United States, *Unterstüztungsverein* in Germany.

But workers were usually forced out of mere protectionism by biases in existing market rules and laws. They demanded legal recognition of unions and legislation to ease the credit and capital problems of cooperatives. This is *mutualism*, as advocated by Proudhon. Much of supposedly social democracy turns out to be mutualist, seeking state regulation only to preserve the rights and freedoms of labor organizations. Unions struggled principally for their own collective rights. Most nineteenth-century people did not experience states as "user-friendly" and tended to define freedom as freedom *from* the state. Mutualist rights plus reasonable and conciliatory employers were all that most labor unions probably wanted. I emphasize throughout this volume that, as in most prior history, people rarely wanted to be political. They would have preferred to avoid states, but were politicized when states interfered with them. Marshall has said that union organizing rights were anomalous to his concept of civil citizenship – though legal, they were essentially collective. But regimes resisted such rights throughout the nineteenth century, sometimes ferociously, thus vitiating Marshall's evolutionary stages of citizenship. In some cases, collective organizing rights were not granted until well into the twentieth century, long after most other civil and major political rights had been acquired. Regime resistance to union recognition was *the* major cause of worker politicization once state fiscal exactions began to decline in the early nineteenth century. If this state would not allow organizing freedoms, then perhaps it should be transformed. Workers moved toward the other alternatives specified in Table 15.2.

The second pair of alternatives sought to modify capitalism by reform from within. *Economism* describes unions seeking gains directly from bargaining with employers. Economism is not restricted to wage demands; control issues in the workplace can also be bargained over. *Social democracy* indicates political reformism (though the term confusingly originated as a label for Marxist revolutionary parties). The third pair of alternatives sought to overthrow capitalism by revolution. Those seeking revolution by economic means – industrial insurrection, the mass strike – were labeled *syndicalists* (sometimes anarchosyndicalists); those seeking to capture the state I label *Marxists*. Syndicalists deliberately eschew the state; Marxists advocate a centralized statist socialism (as a "temporary" stage of socialism). We shall see that, when faced with hostile capitalists and regimes, many militants skipped right from mutualism into the two revolutionary alternatives, bypassing reformism, which only came into its own after World War I.

These are ideal types. Rarely were workers driven single-mindedly; rather, they combined elements from all the alternatives. Their loose combinations were what was termed at the time as "socialism." As soon as labor moved into political alternatives, it also became, and stayed, prodemocratic. Rueschemeyer, Stephens, and Stephens (1992) show that workers throughout the modern world have consistently pressed for democracy. Because states controlled by dominant classes would not leave them alone, they demanded that states be controlled by the (initially male) people. I document one of the earliest democratic movements in this chapter.

Two final particulars should be noted. Because manufacturing capitalism spread steadily throughout nineteenth-century Britain, "productivist" Marxism should expect the working-class movement also to develop steadily. Yet aggressive working-class action in Britain peaked in the Chartist movement of the 1830s and 1840s and then transformed into a much milder and more sectional movement. The British working class has probably never been so united or militant as during its early Chartist phase. Why this nonlinear development? Second, the development of the working class involves an organizational novelty: Workers could counter the organizational outflanking that previously had buttressed social stratification. The people had only rarely constituted historical actors, because class structure had been asymmetric; dominant classes could organize more extensively than subordinate classes. Their outflanking was shaken in early nineteenth-century Britain and in the late nineteenth and early twentieth centuries elsewhere. How and why?

Entrepreneurial capitalism and popular politics, 1760–1832

Three late eighteenth-century revolutions, already discussed in Chapter 1, transformed British class relations: the rise of entrepreneurial capitalism, the modern state, and mass discursive literacy. I discuss the first two in turn and the third in the course of these two narratives.[1]

Uniquely, British agriculture was already capitalist by 1760, comprising almost entirely landlords, tenant farmers, and landless laboring families. Many landless men and women were now forced into urban employment provided by entrepreneurs, "takers-between," acquiring absolute private ownership of manufacturing and commercial resources. For these laborers, distinctions between manufacturing and service sectors and between the factory, the workshop, or the street as places of work had little meaning.

Entrepreneurs also threatened most artisans. Chapter 4 discusses how artisans possessed an ambiguous class position between propertied "people" and propertyless "populace." Perched uncertainly around the lower edges of the petite bourgeoisie historically they had possessed organizations quite their own. The *guild* fused urban neighborhood and skilled occupation into local communities formed of households of "masters," their families, and "men," loosely federated into a national political organization. The guild was licensed and regulated by the state, in return securing a monopoly over the supply of craft skills. Mobile maintenance workers, skilled workers in wood, stone, leather, and (increasingly) metal were organized as *journeymen* traveling the country, collectively controlling entry and wage rates (Leeson 1979). More recently most of these two organizations fused into looser craft organizations and spawned *tramping*. Artisans exploited differences in local trade conditions and used journeying networks to withdraw labor from one locality, receive traveling benefits, and find employment in another. All these organizations were essentially *protectionist*, setting their own rates and doing little bargaining with employers. Tramping enabled eighteenth-century trades to organize more extensively than entrepreneurs. In 1764, for example, six thousand striking London tailors "disappeared" into the country along the network. Tramping could also evade the Combination Acts (which outlawed unions be-

---

[1] The main sources for this section were Thompson (1968), Perkin (1969: 176–217), Musson (1972), Prothero (1979), Hunt (1981), and Calhoun (1982).

tween 1799 and 1824). Extensive organization and mobility enabled artisans to outflank employers and merchants.

But artisans comprised no more than 5 percent to 10 percent of the labor force, providing sectional, not class, organization, limited to each trade. Between them and the mass of agrarian laborers or casual urban workers had existed a great gulf. Then, in the early nineteenth century, artisans also felt entrepreneurial pressure. As the labor market became national, it weakened tramping's capacity to outflank the entrepreneurs. Artisans also lost control over the purchase of materials and the sale of their products. Some industrial crafts, especially millwrights and weavers, also lost their workplace and entry controls as entrepreneurs enveloped their markets and workshops and substituted machinery and unskilled workers. In the two great modern industries, cotton and iron, a factory proletariat was emerging – in cotton mostly young single women and children. The Napoleonic Wars heightened labor-market pressures on all, as they caused mass unemployment and lower wages, worsened by population growth and mass migration to the towns (O'Brien 1989). Much higher mortality (through contagious diseases) in the towns also leveled their working populations.

An entrepreneurial leveling offensive now aimed at artisans forced down wages, employed more low-wage women and children, introduced employer-controlled apprentice schemes, and eliminated artisans' direct access to raw materials and consumers. Trades became "crowded." Some artisans became sweated domestic outworkers; others survived by servicing the workshop factory.

But we must carefully appreciate the nature of what was to become a working class. Little of it was in factories, except in cotton, and even there most were small. In 1851, the average textile firm had just over 100 hands, though those combining spinning and weaving averaged just over 300. By 1890, these averages had less than doubled (Farnie, cited in Joyce 1980: 158; all other figures in this paragraph are from Clapham 1939: I, 184–93, II, 22–37, 116–33). There were a few large mines and ironworks. In 1838, Cornish tin mines averaged nearly 170 workers, in coal mining the national average was only 50, but a dozen northeastern pits each employed more than 300. In 1814, the Carron ironworks employed 2,000 ("the most extensive manufactory in Europe"), but the average Scottish ironworks employed only 20. There were a handful of factories making glass, cutlery, ceramics, or wool. The 1871 census estimated that half of manufacturing employment (a quarter of all employment) was in "factories," but these had an average of only 86 hands. The vast majority in manufacturing were in small workshops, most of which did not use steam power. Single pieces of machinery usually stood alone, manually operated, manually serviced at both ends. "The balance of advantage between steam power and hand technology was, in mid-Victorian times, very far from settled" (Samuels 1977: 58; Greenberg 1982).

Nor was most employment in "modern" industries. In the 1851 census, by far the largest sectors were agriculture and domestic service, followed by cotton, building trades, general laborers, milliners, shoemakers, miners, tailors, washerwomen, seamen, and silk workers. There were almost as many women as men. Most factory workers were young, unmarried women and children. Most men moved in and out, bringing goods they or their families worked at home or in small workshops, or they brought in their own tools to service machinery, or they negotiated prices for work done in the factory. In smaller towns and villages many households combined manufacturing and agricultural activities. Though craftsmen had lost some autonomy, they remained contractual free agents, controlling and paying their laborers, often their own family members. Yet now their control was rarely secure. Most factory work, like that in the home, workshop, fields, mines, or street, was casual. Diversity and irregularity were endemic.

Thus, concludes Joyce (1990: 145–53), there was little proletarianization and little sense of class identity. I draw the opposite conclusion: The entrepreneurial phase of capitalism produced the paradox of workers partly unified by their very heterogeneity. But to realize this, we must step outside productivism and the modern concept of employment or occupation and into the family and community. Artisanal sectionalism survived and employer segmentalism began to stir, but these rarely provided total identities for workers' families. "Factory" had emerged alongside "workshop," "household," and "street," and formal "employment" had emerged alongside the "trade" and the casual "hire." But these were not impenetrable boundaries. Rather, they interpenetrated, preventing any single employment status from enveloping many families or local communities. The clearest sectionalism would have pitted men against young women and children, yet they cohabited and often constituted a household production unit interpenetrating with workshop and factory.

In this period, the household contributed a measure of class solidarity across very different labor processes, generating close connections among work, home, and community. Secure versus casual employment was later to separate the factory from the household and street, the male from the female worker, and the skilled from the unskilled worker. But the heterogeneity of work in early industrialization reached through most workplaces, households, and families, homogenizing workers in a distinctive, underappreciated way – less the result of the factory labor process than of the diffusion of entrepreneurial capitalism across strikingly different labor processes and across workplace, household, and community.

Such class formation was only partial, and on its own it might have led to little class action. But this was boosted by three crystallizations of the British state – old regime capitalism, militarism, and a federalism (in the sense specified in Table 3.3) – now becoming strained by centralizing tendencies. During this period, the regime put classical political economy on the statute book of the central state, removing guild and journeymen's "restraints on trade." Between 1799 and 1813, minimum wages, apprentice rules defining entry to trades, and price fixing were swept away, and the Combination Acts of 1799 and 1800 prohibited unions. Artisans were bereft of legal protection against new market forces. Morally indignant, but at first apolitical, they attempted sectional resistance, trade by trade. But most trades faced the same threats, as did many less skilled workers. Thus craft unions abandoned protectionism for economistic bargaining. Regional strikes and lockouts resulted: London shoemakers were out in 1818 and again in 1824; Lancashire cotton spinners, in 1824 and 1828; shipwrights, in 1824; Bradford wool combers, in 1825; power-loom and handloom weavers, in 1826; Kidderminster carpet weavers, in 1828; London tailors, in 1834. All these strikes were defeated. There were more wage cuts, sweated labor, factory and "home work" employment of young women and children, diluting of skills, and greater crowding. Industrial action had somewhat enlarged some workers' class identity, but it had achieved nothing.

Thus workers were forced toward the national state, first to traditional demonstrating and petitioning of Parliament. Upper-level, better-organized trades took the lead: silk weavers, shoemakers, watchmakers, cordwainers, cabinetmakers, carpenters, tailors, saddlers, and printers. These commanded expanding infrastructures of discursive literacy among workers, dominating mechanics' institutes and Owenite "halls of science" (seven hundred of them with five hundred reading rooms by 1850), friendly societies, religious organizations, and journals and newspapers. Economic, political, and literary leadership extended over other groups affected by the offensive, especially domestic outworkers like weavers. Demands were now becoming *mutualist*, seeking central state recognition of union collective rights, regulation of apprenticeships, the setting of "fair" prices and wages, and the compensation of workers displaced by machinery.

In Parliament the two extremes of Radicals and High Tories gave sympathy but few results. The Combination Acts were indeed repealed in 1824, but an immediate strike wave prompted an 1825 act limiting workers' rights in what we shall see to be a typically bourgeois way, granting only collective organizing rights seen as closely connected to the expression of individual self-interest, which was considered morally legitimate. Only workers actually attending meetings that restricted themselves rigidly to their own wage, price, and hour levels had a legal right to combine. All other broader combinations were criminal conspiracies in unlawful restraint of trade. This meant proscription of all general and national unions, as well as most craft unions still enforcing controls over production. Though courts recognized that local meetings could not be effectively prosecuted, strikes could and were. Unions were repressed not much less than in the Combination Acts era, and with greater uniformity between laborers and artisans, earlier capable of bypassing the Combination Acts. The old regime felt that moral sympathy for workers' plight should not stop progress, whereas political economists believed that free trade laws actually *were* moral. Parliament refused to legislate, so stalling mutualism.

As we shall see, whenever centralized regimes repressed protectionist or mutualist workers fairly uniformly (though not with sufficient violence to cow resistance), worker agitation broadened toward class and the national level. For a time *reformism* predominated in their thinking: If the state would not protect them, then the state should be reformed. Chapter 4 shows that suffrage demands resonated amid some popular traditions. E. P. Thompson (1968: 213) observes that the working class was not created out of "some nondescript undifferentiated raw material of humanity." Other social identities conferred by historical traditions – religion, popular politics and national notions of the "free-born Englishman's rights," and Protestant moral equality (as later we see French and American republican traditions) – nourished workers' protests, though not always class consciousness. In the radical natural rights tradition from Locke to Paine, suffrage demands had been buttressed by social claims – the right to subsistence, that land belongs to the community for the common good, and the need to limit wealth. As we saw in Chapter 4, the emergence of civil society, the rise of the modern state, and geopolitical rivalries encouraged the downward diffusion of populism, a more popular, radical, and nationally centralized identity.

But this was also greatly assisted by the military crystallization of the state. As Chapter 11 shows, eighteenth-century wars required massive exactions of manpower and finances. Britain, with a capital-intensive navy and an army mostly recruited abroad and in Ireland, required more money than recruits. It raised money according to priorities largely set by its crystallization as old regime capitalist. It borrowed from the rich and repaid them; it raised taxes, mostly excise taxes on everyday consumables – beer, tobacco, salt, sugar, tea, coal, and housing. Between 1800 and 1834 (until the burden of debt repayment declined), the burden remained onerous and regressive, redistributing from those without to those with savings. This also had broader economic effects. During the wars inflation rose at 3 percent per annum while real wages fell. Mass unemployment continued in peacetime, so that poor relief remained the state's main civil activity. Almost a million people were claiming relief, subjected to humiliating control by the local ruling class, and many of their families were broken up by the poorhouse. Politics, like economics, exploited not just the male worker but the family. The central government had its priorities clear. During 1820–5, poor relief absorbed 6 percent of its expenditures, whereas cash transfers to bondholders absorbed 53 percent (O'Brien 1989). How could workers' families fail to be politicized by such fiscal exploitation impacting massively on their lives, embodying obvious class inequities? Agitation linked franchise reform with economic reform of state and social policy. Through artisan infrastructures of discursive literacy, the state was denounced as injurious to the people – in the sense of the populace.

Thus three agitations became entwined: protest spearheaded by artisans and outworkers against exploitation by capitalist entrepreneurs; the transmission of these discontents into mutualist and democratic politics aimed at the central state's political economy; and populist protest against fiscal-political exploitation of the people by the old regime capitalist state. Thus many workers were radicalized at the national level, their sense of class identity extended. After 1800, they routinely used the terms "working class" and, more commonly, "working classes" (Briggs 1960). They appropriated the petit bourgeois labor theory of value – we work, the idlers receive the fruits of our work. In 1834, the Owenite newspaper *Crisis* calculated the numbers of two "classes": To the "laboring population," the "producers of all wealth," and the "productive classes" belonged 8,892,731 persons, and 8,210,072 persons were "nonproducers." It complained that while producers received £100 million of annual wealth, nonproducers got £331 million (Hollis 1973: 6–8). Artisan writers proclaimed "we"-"they" dichotomies. "We" depend on collective action based on our ethic of mutual protection conferring a moral superiority over the selfishness of the opponent (E. P. Thompson 1968: 456–69).

Did we possess a clear sense of our class opponent? Not before 1832, for the political opponent was not the same as the economic. Indeed, political allies were often economic enemies. The petite bourgeoisie, including small entrepreneurs, were also consumers rather than savers, and they were also excluded from the franchise. The reform struggle was less class than populist, abused as democrat,

Jacobin, or Leveller, not with class labels. Radicals aimed less at the entrepreneur than at the rentier placeman of "old corruption" living off rents and state-licensed monopolies. Active capitalists puzzled radicals. *Crisis* distinguished a third intermediate "class" composed of "distributors, superintendents and manufacturers" who (it rather feebly complained) were "necessary, but too numerous." Some artisan newspapers identified entrepreneurs as a class enemy: "The interests of masters and men are as much opposed to each other as light is to darkness"; or "The capitalists produce nothing but themselves; they are fed, clothed and lodged by the working classes" (Hollis 1973: 45, 50). But workers also confronted Parliament, local magistrates, local parsons, political economists, spies and provocateurs, regular troops, and local yeoman militia. "Old corruption," "church and king," or "political economy" often seemed greater and more violent enemies than their own master. Attacks on them could also bring support from above, sometimes in segmental alliance with the "industrious classes" against "old corruption," sometimes with paternalist elements of the old order against political economy (more of this later), or sometimes with Protestant or Dissenter populism.

These diffused segmental, often local, links detracted from any purely class consciousness (Prothero 1979: 336; Stedman-Jones 1983; Joyce 1991). Indeed, before 1832 the opponent was not a singular class. Although most of "it" united against labor, on the franchise it was deeply divided over what classes should be represented and over how Protestant the state should be (as is discussed in Chapter 4). This weakened local segmental controls over workers, their political discontents encouraged by radical entrepreneurs and even, around 1830, by Whigs.

These political alignments undercut a class conception of an alternative. The most popular radical economic alternatives were Robert Owen's. His advocacy of protectionist producer cooperatives appealed to artisan and outworker desires to secure equal access to the market. Mutualist currents also flowed. During the 1820s, John Gray, Thomas Hodgkin, and William Thompson used *The Poor Man's Guardian* and *The Pioneer* to attack capitalists as parasitic middlemen, interfering in artisans' legitimate relationship to the market, which the state should guarantee. Noel Thompson (1988) calls them "Smithian socialists." Few advocated reorganizing production rather than market relations, as modern socialists do. This would not have been appropriate to artisan grievances of the period. But economic views were submerged in the political struggle over suffrage. Though many workers were skeptical about their political alliance with the radical bourgeoisie (especially when they saw the terms of the Reform Acts), they had

little alternative. They had no chance of achieving the desired mutualist legislation without it. An emerging class was uniting workers'
families across very different labor processes, but politics confused
their sense of the opponent and the alternative.

E. P. Thompson famously labeled this period as the "making of the
English working class," and he has been much criticized for it. Currie
and Hartwell (1965) proclaim his title "a myth, a construct of determined imagination and theoretical presuppositions." They note, as
others do for England (Prothero 1979: 337) and France (Sewell 1974:
106), that early nineteenth-century labor movements normally reached
only artisans; that Thompson wrongly assumes a unity between artisan
and laborer; and that the "apathetic and silent masses," under local
notable segmental control, were unaffected by turbulent protest
(Currie and Hartwell 1965: 639; Church and Chapman 1967: 165;
Morris 1979 discusses the conceptual issues). To speak of a singular
"working class" existing in 1830 would indeed be unhistorical. Yet to
arrive in some force, it needed only popular political struggle to array
the same opponent as economic struggle – and after 1832, this happened.

Chartist proletarian insurrections, 1832–1850

Worker militants saw their fears of the Great Reform Act confirmed.
As discussed in Chapter 4, much of the upper petite bourgeoisie and
old regime were merging toward a single capitalist class, while the state
crystallized as firmly capitalist and a little more centralized. Although
the enfranchised middling classes remained somewhat heterogeneous
and could be fractious, the Reform Act diminished their political
interest in those beneath them. A few radical members of Parliament
pressed for further suffrage reform, but the bourgeois electorate voted
most of them out by 1837. Parliament believed the suffrage issue
settled. "Radical" now meant two different things: To artisan groups
like the London Working Men's Association and to a few middle-class
activists, it still meant suffrage extension and state protection of living
standards. But to many others it meant merely laissez-faire.

The new Poor Law of 1834 epitomized the new regime, extending
harsher controls over workers' families while reducing notables' powers
to distribute particularistic charity. At workers' protest meetings it was
denounced as the "dissolution of the marriage tie – the annihilation of
every domestic affection, and the violent and most brutal oppression
ever yet practised among the poor of any country of the world"
(quoted in D. Thompson 1984: 35). General Napier, the commander
of the northern troops against Chartism, stressed the Poor Law in
explaining the insurrection: The working classes had "been shuffled

out of representative power," their resources, "dried up by indirect taxes for the debt," had been made "phantom" by the new Poor Law (Napier 1857: II, 1, 9). But reforms of municipal administration and the new police authorities also cemented the local power of the new regime, making it more representative of whatever were the local dominant classes. The Newspaper Act tightened press licensing. The Irish Coercion Act indicated willingness to repress. General unions were suppressed as "conspiracies," notably the Grand National Consolidated Trades Union of 1834, supposedly with 500,000 members.

Thus, during the 1830s, the new regime was galvanizing national working-class identity, opposition, and even totality. Its economic offensive reduced the effectiveness of narrow trade sectionalism and fueled the moral outrage of families. Its political offensive, especially the Poor Law, hurt the poorest most directly, but artisan militants were most threatened by harassment of unions' organizing rights. They all wanted suffrage, and because the franchise was now a class one, they had to organize as a class. Sectionalism and segmental controls declined; the working class developed. Its principal manifestation was Chartism – as "class-based," as "mass," and as "revolutionary" in its intent as was any movement discussed in this volume.

Chartism formed around a single issue, democracy for adult males, and a single document, the Charter.[2] Its Six Points demanded universal male suffrage, annual parliaments, a secret ballot, no property qualification for MPs, equal parliamentary constituencies, and payment for MPs. Many Chartists also supported woman suffrage, but the leaders claimed it would be counterproductive to demand this at the present time. But Chartists did not see the vote as an end. As I emphasize throughout this volume, political citizenship had not been sought as an intrinsically desirable goal. Most people preferred to avoid the state. But when states began to exploit and so politically cage them, they became politicized. Chartists wanted the vote to free themselves from novel social and economic exploitation. They urged lower, progressive taxation, reform of the Poor Law, fewer local government and police powers, a "ten hours'" act, and mutualist protections against "wage slavery," including union organizing rights. "The Charter and something more" was their most popular slogan. One arrested Chartist pleaded to his prison interrogator:

The great distress is the cause of our discontent – if the wages were what they ought to be we should not hear a word about the suffrage. If the masters will

---

[2] The main sources on Chartism were Briggs (1959b), Prothero (1971), Jones (1975), various essays in Epstein and Thompson (1982), Stedman-Jones (1983), and D. Thompson (1984).

only do something for the workmen to get them the common comforts of life, we should be the most contented creatures upon earth. [D. Thompson 1984: 211]

Enfranchised classes did not give the Chartists much support because they opposed most of these socioeconomic goals. Middle-class radical reformists did help with early leadership and later they reappeared ineffectually, seeking to moderate the movement. Between 10 and 46 MPs also supported pro-Chartist motions in the House of Commons, although only a handful gave any other support. Chartism became overwhelmingly a workers' movement.

The movement recruited a heterogeneous mass of workers. Several lists of militants, members, and arrested demonstrators survive, detailing their occupations (see D. Thompson 1984 for details). None is a representative sample, but they are all consistent with one another. There were a handful of those who were déclassé, a few professionals – schoolmasters, ministers, the odd doctor or lawyer – and rather more shopkeepers. But the vast bulk were workers. The only substantially underrepresented workers were agricultural laborers and domestic servants, kept under segmental control by their employers. There were few independent peasant proprietors in Britain; Chapter 19 shows that in other countries these were capable of organization and radicalism. Virtually all other manufacturing and service workers were present in large numbers. Depressed outworkers were overrepresented – weavers, framework knitters, wool combers, and nailers. So were the most crowded of the older artisanal trades, such as shoemaking, tailoring, and some of the building trades. Miners and textile factory operatives were well-represented "modern" occupations, although their fixed work routines meant that although they provided few organizers, they were often arrested. Miners achieved a special reputation for violence, and tailors, metalworkers, and woodworkers were overrepresented in peaceful protests.

Almost all artisanal tradesmen appeared, as did their trade unions. Only a few secure upper trades proved resistant. In London, almost all trade unions federated into Chartist organizations – both workers in threatened trades, such as shoemakers, carpenters, and tailors, and such relatively unthreatened "aristocrats" as stonemasons, hatters, leather finishers, carvers and gilders, and engineers (Goodmay 1982). In southeastern Lancashire only the securest unions – printers, bookbinders, and coachmakers – stayed away. Almost all other unions federated: cotton spinners, calico printers and dyers, tailors, shoemakers, construction workers, and engineers (Sykes 1982). Most Nottingham trades joined, though threatened framework knitters and shoemakers were overrepresented (Epstein 1982: 230–2). In every trade, concludes Dorothy Thompson, all branches "from the skilled society man to the slop man can be found among the Chartists, and indeed among the leadership" (1984: 233). Because of the communal nature of the movement (to be discussed soon), it was led by whatever were the locally dominant occupations. The occupational heterogeneity of workers was not preventing class action.

Occupational distributions alone do not convey the breadth of this class movement, for it was also community and family based – as was early manufacturing capitalism and as were most early radical workers' movements (as Calhoun 1982 emphasizes). Many manufacturing areas were composed of a city or town center surrounded by working-class villages. These offered organizing space relatively free from segmental control from above, as Napier noted with alarm. Mass demonstrations were boosted by contingents marching under these villages' banners. In workers' districts the movement centered on public meeting places of discursive and oral communication networks: chapels, reading rooms, schools, alehouses, and newsdealers' shops. Organization centered not on employment but the community.

Thus there were many Chartist women and women's associations. The authorities did not generally arrest (and so document) women; and as Victorian society turned against female agitation, later memoirs played down their role. But there may have been greater female participation in this, the first working-class movement, than in any following until the mid-twentieth century. The destruction of the working household, child and female factory labor, the Poor Law, and regressive taxation exploited families, not just, as later, predominantly male employees. Even male militants made this clear. One prominent banner motto (quoted in Bennett 1982: 96) read:

> For children and wife
> We war to the knife!
> So help us God.

Women also sponsored two lesser Chartist demands, for greater control of schooling and of alcohol. Dorothy Thompson (on whom this paragraph depends) believes that women's participation declined in the 1840s as the Poor Law became more humane and as factory conditions stabilized (1984: chapter 7). I argue later that the Factory Acts made Chartism more masculine. Chartism did not advocate equality of the sexes. Its leadership and program, especially the Charter itself, reflected the male domination normal to the times. But contemporary exploitation was of whole families, men and women were not clearly segregated in relation to exploitation, and men and women shared some common remedies for exploitation. The early working-class movement was not as male-dominated as later ones – and so was stronger.

The Chartists could certainly mobilize. The Charter was presented thrice to Parliament, backed by enormous petitions. Signing was the lowest level of participation in the movement. Just under 1.3 million signed in 1839, 3 million in 1842, and between 2 million and 5 million in 1847–8 (the two sides disputed this number). These are large numbers. Few signers can have worked in agriculture or domestic service. As the adult manufacturing population was fewer than 5 million, a majority of it probably signed at least one petition (there were not many middle-class signers). There was no comparable mass political activity in any country during the nineteenth century.

The number of militants was much smaller but still impressive. In 1842, the National Charter Association (NCA) had 50,000 members in 400 local clubs. In the late 1840s, the Chartist Land Company had about 70,000 members. The main Chartist newspaper, *Northern Star*, had 60,000 readers in its peak years. Public funerals of killed militants drew crowds of 50,000. Militants repeatedly brought out large demonstrations of between 4,000 and 70,000 persons (numbers are uncertain and were disputed at the time) in several towns at once. In 1842, the secretary of the NCA attended huge meetings around Birmingham, "and the universal cry is 'we must have the Charter' – and Wonderful! oh Wonderful, not one in a thousand has got a [membership] *Card*" (Epstein 1982: 229). There were three peaks of agitation: in 1839–40, 1842, and 1848. We do not know the numbers involved, but those on both sides anticipating events in 1839 were assuming a general strike until the leadership pulled back at the last moment; and the 1842 strike was the largest and most general in nineteenth-century Britain.

Chartism was not authoritatively organized, in the sense of being much directed from the center. Hence its ideology and sense of alternative (beyond the Charter) were little formalized and were fluctuating and diverse. But the movement was aggressive, fairly class-conscious, and hostile to capitalists. Feargus O'Connor, who considered himself no socialist, still thundered against capitalist employers as "traffickers in human blood and in infant gristle." A listener reported, "He divided society into just two classes – the rich oppressors and the poor oppressed. The whole question resolved itself into the battle between capital and labour" (D. Thompson 1984: 251). Bronterre O'Brien denounced "capitalist warfare." Militants now rarely railed against "old corruption" but against "class legislation" and the "Millocracy," "Shopocracy," "and every other Ocracy which feeds on human vitals," as the *Northern Star* put it (Stedman-Jones 1982: 14).

National leaders were wary of appearing inflammatory in public or in committee (for fear of police spies), but the actions and unguarded words of militants often went further. Strikes in 1842 were declared general in an attempt to force all workers out. As one intercepted letter said:

Now's the time for Liberty. We want the wages paid [at the] 1840 [level] if they won't give it us Revolution is the consequence we have stopt every trade – Tailors Cobblers Brushmakers Sweeps Tinkers Carters Masons Builders Colliers & c and every other trade.

One militant told a Manchester meeting:

The spread of the strike would and must be followed by a general outbreak. The authorities of the land would try to quell it; but we must resist them. There was nothing now but a physical force struggle to be looked for. We must get the people out to fight; and they must be irresistible, if they were united. [D. Thompson 1984: 287, 297]

Chartists have been often patronized by modern writers because few were socialists in any Marxian or productivist sense (e.g., Hobsbawm 1962: 252, 255; Musson 1976; Stedman-Jones 1983). But this is a partisan, teleological view, apparently deriving from disillusionment with "bourgeois democracy" and the Labour party. In view of the disastrous future of Marxism, it is not even convincing as teleology. Because the central state was the immediate cause of most of their exploitation, it was *rightly* the principal object of attack. Then (as now) the vote really did matter, and its attainment had a good chance of achieving what the militants wanted – a more humane Poor Law, mutualist organizing rights for unions, and more progressive taxation.

The Chartist combination of clear political objectives and mutualist economic goals seems appropriate to the exploitation of workers' families in the 1830s and 1840s. As Dorothy Thompson (1984: 337) concludes in her fine study, Chartism even had a plausible broader program – less rapid centralization (apart from state ownership of land and transport), much more local autonomy, a check on the size of economic units, and no new imperialism. To this we should add more humanity to children, including greater education, and restrictions on alcohol. She believes the Chartist program might have slowed economic growth. Yet, by focusing politics on manufacturing problems, it might have remedied the commercial bias of British capitalism (described in Chapter 4).

Some Chartists were prepared to go much farther, toward revolutionary methods, to achieve their goals. The "physical force" faction organized arms clubs with many thousands of pikes and hundreds of muskets; they drilled in military formations and paraded in torchlight processions to intimidate local authorities. There was some organization for a general rising in 1839, to begin in Newport, Newcastle, and the West Riding. Almost all the national leaders opposed this, although many favored slower, systematic drilling and arming. Something clearly went badly wrong in the planning, for the conspirators ran around like startled rabbits as soon as the Newport rising was botched and failed to spread. In Newport, about 5,000 pikemen had foolishly attempted to liberate Chartist prisoners from jail before 20,000 more marched in from the hills around. There was significant violence in 1840, with pitched battles in Bury, Birmingham, and the northeast coalfield, and much storming of food shops and workhouses, firing of vicarages and police stations, and stoning of troops. In 1842, Chartist crowds controlled Nottingham for four days before the military dispersed them, taking 400 prisoners. They also controlled the Potteries for two days, resulting in 49 transportations and 116 imprisonments; and in Halifax a mob seriously wounded 8 dragoons before being dispersed. In 1848, insurrectionary plans were laid in Lancashire, the West Riding, and London. In Glasgow an anti–Poor Law mob was fired on by troops, with 6 deaths. An armed mob in Bradford worsted the police and the special constables. Only the swords and guns of mounted dragoons dispersed them.

The Chartists did not fail because they were few or sectional or incoherent or timid. Their national organization was weak, and few intended a revolution, but this was true of all "revolutionary" movements until 1917. People became revolutionaries only when regimes refused their demands and, amid very confused escalation, they decided it was possible to overthrow them. True, the Chartists had one significant internal weakness. They found organizing the capital difficult, an important weakness for a movement aimed at the state (which became transparent in the debacle of 1848). When London's population rose from 1 million to 2.7 million between 1801 and 1851, collective mobilization chances in the capital diminished. The gap between amounts of organizable space at workshop and neighborhood level and at the political level of the entire city was too great (Goodmay 1982). Because Chartism was local community-based, it struggled in the great metropolis. But with this exception, if a revolution did not occur, this did not principally result from the Chartists' own shortcomings. Their agitation was as forceful as anything coming from below in France in 1789 or in the class (though not the national) movements of 1848. In particular, what the Chartists possessed (and shared with many nationalist dissidents) was the moral and emotional fervor their intense family and community organization provided.

What was lacking, rather, was weakness or division on the other side, although most historians have focused on the lower, not the upper, classes. Unlike in 1789 or 1848 or the early twentieth century in Russia, there was no significant split among regime or dominant classes.

In Chapter 5, we saw how essential regime splits – at court, in the Estates General and the National Assembly, in church, and in the army – were both to the unfolding of a true revolutionary crisis and to the Leftward, classward drift of insurgent leadership. But the British Parliament would not even discuss the Charter. There was now no evolution from individual civil citizenship to extended political citizenship, as Marshall suggested. Rather, the former firmly resisted the latter.

No one with national or regional authority sympathized enough to advocate conceding any of the Charter points. Moderate Chartist attempts to ally with middle-class reformers bore little fruit. When threatened, the middle classes rallied round property and order, enrolling as special constables in the thousands. There was, as John Saville sums up the matter in his fine study of the regime's response, "the closing of ranks among all those with a property stake in the country, however small that stake was" (1987: 227; cf. Weisser 1983). In the wake of the collapse of the last mass demonstration in 1848, after which Chartism rapidly declined, the wife of one cabinet minister wrote to the wife of another; "I am sure that it is very fortunate that the whole thing has occurred as it has shown the good spirit of our middle classes" (Briggs 1959a: 312).

So in the end Chartism evoked more persistent bourgeois than proletarian class consciousness. This was a case of head-on class struggle, and as usual there was no dialectical revolutionary synthesis but a victory for the dominant class.

Bourgeois unity enabled consistent, judicious repression – a state crystallization as mildly, orderly militarist. Chartism was not met with that oft-lauded English genius for compromise and pragmatism. Precious few such qualities had been revealed since 1832. Measured repression took their place. There were calm disagreements over tactics in the cabinet but no reversals of policy between factions and no sudden panics leading to overreaction and gross brutality. The military usually acted to minimize casualties. Severe sentences were meted out only in cases of violence and after due process – though the offender's violence usually paled in comparison with the punishments (execution, transportation, or a long jail sentence). Those who merely agitated and organized were charged with "sedition," "incitement," or "conspiracy," given due process, and merely removed by imprisonment for a year or so. Of the 20 Chartist commissioners elected in 1848, 14 were quickly arrested and imprisoned for up to a year (Saville 1987: 162).

It is important to understand the important and rather centralized role of law in Britain. As Saville argues, judicial-police institutions were centralized and firmly subordinated to a party-democratic Parliament that was the sovereign lawmaker. Unlike in most Continental regimes, the military, police, and judiciary had little autonomous crystallization in the state. As we shall also see later in discussing the United States, the law and constitution were sovereign. They did not share the state with more pragmatic or more monarchical preoccupations with riot control under which the law would be manipulated for the sake of order or for higher political goals. Britain in this period and the United States throughout the whole century had very different constitutions, but they shared a (restricted) party democracy and sovereign law embodying the rule of capitalist property. They both repressed labor agitation as "conspiracy" with a regime consistency and ruling class self-righteousness unparalleled elsewhere. As we shall see in the following chapters, the British state later lost some of this ideological self-righteousness (whereas the American state did not), but at mid-century it was strong. It was personified in the Tory General Napier, who sympathized with the Chartists, blamed the Whigs for the insurrection, yet argued that the constitution must be upheld at all costs.

Napier's army was also professional, with an almost unbroken record of success around the world, including extensive experience repressing popular disturbances in Ireland and the empire. Napier was confident of his soldiers' discipline. His tactics were also clear: Concentrate the troops so that small detachments were not left isolated to be over-whelmed in their billets – he believed such a mishap would be instantly propagandized by the Chartists into being a symbolic "Bastille," encouraging further uprisings. Break up pikemen with cavalry using the flats of their swords if possible, with infantry using musket and bayonet if the pikemen held ground. Use buckshot to reduce deaths. "The great point is to defeat without killing" (Napier 1857: II, 4). No police, militia, or troops refused to obey orders, and virtually no magistrates, officers, or soldiers panicked. The success of the risings – probably of all insurrections and revolutions – depended on this happening. Even in Newport, thirty-odd soldiers did not panic when encircled by 5,000 demonstrators brandishing pikes. The soldiers fired, and when the smoke from their second volley cleared (not buckshot here), the crowd fled, leaving at least twenty-two dead.

The major Chartist agitations were defeated by a professional, confident, disciplined army intelligently led, by class-conscious bourgeois militias, by newly organized local government authorities, and by newly institutionalized police authorities – all righteously implementing the law of the land. What could oratory, mobs, and pikes (which Napier says were designed too short) do against such efficient, centralized mobilization of force? No Bastille was stormed, and so no revolution commenced. Revolutions are more a product of irresolute regimes than of resolute, clear-sighted insurgency, as Lenin himself realized. Because the British regime was resolute, there was no British revolution.

When the events of 1839 first made this clear, the Chartists split over their response. Arguments about the merits of moral versus physical force had been heard already.[3] Most leaders knew Parliament would reject the moral force of the first petition. They had merely delayed their most difficult decision: Were they really to take the next logical step, to apply insurrectionary pressure? Probably even most of the physical-force faction saw this as pressure rather than a genuine seizure of state power, as also was the case in France between 1789 and mid-1791. But now the Chartist leaders also had tasted the bitter fruits of physical force. What could they possibly do if the regime was so united, so unresponsive to pressure?

Most rejected physical force on the grounds of "realism," as Wade did: "The cry of arms, without antecedent moral opinion and union of the middle classes with you, would only cause misery, blood and ruin" (Jones 1975: 151). O'Connor repeatedly argued that a crowd, however large, would always crumple before trained troops. So the major split was tactical, not ideological or political. From the beginning it had a sectional basis: between the more secure upper trades and the more crowded lower trades who favored physical force (Bennett 1982: 106–10). This was the beginning of further splits and weakenings that through the 1840s and 1850s finally ended British working-class aggression. But to understand this we must widen our focus.

It has become conventional to explain the decline of Chartism not only in terms of effective repression and consequent tactical split but also in terms of two general improvements occurring in the 1840s and 1850s in popular conditions. First, it is argued, the economy revived and did not turn down again until the 1870s, ending desperate times for workers. Second, the government moderated its harsh social policies, and this also cut the ground from under radical leaders urging political solutions.

These arguments have some truth, but they need amplification. There is no necessary relation between macroeconomic trends and social movements. Insurrections do not occur simply because economies improve or worsen. The best explanation along these lines is the famous J curve suggested by Davies (1970), whereby revolutions are said to occur after a long period of economic upswing followed by a short sharp downturn. Mass expectations have risen and are then abruptly frustrated. Such J curves often, though not always, do occur

---

[3] They may have originated from Irish emancipation struggles, as many Chartist leaders were Irish.

before revolutions. But with this theory mass insurrection should have happened again in Britain in the mid-1870s, after the upswing of the 1860s was sharply reversed. It did not. Insurrections are organizations (as resource mobilization theorists argue). Hence we need a more specific explanation of how economic improvement is linked to insurgent organization. I provide that in a moment.

Did the government moderate its social policies, so undermining Chartism (as Stedman-Jones 1982: 50–2 argues)? The decisive change was the decline in the tax burden on consumption in the 1840s (evidenced in Chapter 11). This resulted not from changing government sentiment but because (as Chapter 11 shows) the debt cycle incurred in the Napoleonic Wars ended and was not restarted by additional wars. Because regressive war finance had caused most class politicization since the 1760s, its decline now considerably depoliticized workers' families. Chapter 11 argues that tax relief was now occurring on a world-historical scale. Chartism was one of the last movements in which taxation played a significant role, at least in its early phase. In the late nineteenth century, new forms of class politicization would arise, but at midcentury there came a lull. Worker agitation became more economic, more confined to direct relations of production. Contrary to Marxian theory, this moderated and depoliticized it.

Two other signs of a more moderate regime are sometimes pointed to: more lenient administration of the Poor Law (D. Thompson 1984: 336) and collaboration among the "industrious classes" (especially among Dissenters) ranging workers with entrepreneurs against old regime to secure repeal of the Corn Laws in 1846 and to agitate for temperance and education reform. Yet anti–Poor Law riots still occurred in the 1840s, few Chartist militants were seduced by collaborative movements and these were not influential in Chartism's fall. Broader cross-class collaboration also occurred in the Factory Acts movement, but this – and the economic and tax upswings – was important less as "improvements" than as reinforcing the sectionalism into which defeated Chartism finally disintegrated. Let us consider this complex process.

The Factory Acts movements protested against exploitation of three different statuses of workers – men, women, and children. A few bourgeois radicals would support a "just wage" and "reasonable hours" for all three, but more wanted to regulate or terminate the factory employment of women, and far more – including even factory owners and their wives, mostly Evangelical Protestants and Temperance activists – attacked child labor. This support came from both extremes, Leftist Radicals and High Tories. The two identities sometimes merged, as in Michael Sadler, member of Parliament for Leeds, a "ten hours' bill" advocate, supported by Chartists against Liberal opponents in parliamentary elections. His alter ego was the Rochdale cotton factory owner, Radical yet laissez-faire John Bright, who opposed the Factory Acts as "restraining trade" and "infringing liberty." In Parliament, patrician Whigs and High Tories from the shires thundered against the immorality of factory owners. This *patriarchal* political crystallization provided the only significant regime disunity through which workers could make gains. Their gains came through interstitial cracks, not through dialectical, head-on confrontation or its systemic compromise.

Parliament had always legislated for children. The title of the elder Peel's 1802 bill, Health and Morals of Apprentices Act, indicates its moral paternalism. Peel, a Tory, may have been the only employer of apprentices in the House at this time. He appealed to moral paternalism over children without having to overcome the hostility of an entrenched parliamentary interest group. Next came a Tory act of 1819 forbidding the employment of children under nine in cotton mills. When the 1832 Parliament adequately represented factory owners, battle lines hardened. But the Factory Acts movement publicized the dreadful plight of children in mines and textiles and appealed to patriarchy by denouncing the sweated employment of women. Women, the carriers of domestic morality, were considered essential to the moral fabric of society by most Christians and conservatives. They believed unmarried women should do work training them for motherhood, like domestic service or retail trades. Married women should be in the home.

To secure these moral-patriarchal ends, acts were passed throughout the Chartist period. The Whig acts of 1833 and 1836 established factory commissioners to regulate factories and children's hours. The nonpartisan Mines Act of 1842 forbade underground employment of children under age ten and of women, and established an inspectorate to enforce the ban. The Tory Factory Act of 1844 applied to textiles. It fixed a 6.5-hour maximum for children under thirteen and a 12-hour maximum for women; it also fenced machinery and extended the inspectorate. The nonpartisan act of 1847 cut down women's hours to 10 in textiles. Acts in 1850 and 1853 laid down daytime hours for women. These acts also accepted responsibility for educating children when they were not working, although implementation was patchy. All passed the House of Lords with support from the bishops. Parliament extended the legislation to all industries between 1860 and 1867. Only in 1874 were men covered.

This legislative sequence reveals the sectional distinctions made on moral, predominantly patriarchal grounds among children, women, and men. Children were regulated and excluded first, with little disagreement. Working-class men and women whose voices were recorded were also unanimous: Children should not be used as wage slaves. It physically and morally degraded them, it destroyed the family and parental authority, and it lowered their own wages through competition. As Parliament agreed strongly with the first two sentiments, the third, "restraining trade," slipped through. One great cause of "crowding" was eliminated and wages might rise to the point where children could be supported at home. Moral arguments then also restricted female employment, though to a lesser extent. Workers were again fairly unanimous. Because all wanted reductions in hours and improvements in conditions, to secure them only for women was still a gain. Again restraint of trade and of crowding slipped through; again wages might rise.

But these gains also brought unintended consequences. Restrictions on one group's hours had implications for others. Because men and women worked together, different hours and conditions of employment interfered with productive efficiency (especially after the 1850 and 1853 acts). The movement realized this, hoping for shorter hours for men as well. Sometimes this happened. But coupled with the greater costs of child labor (especially if educational provision was made), the attractiveness to employers of children and female workers was reduced. Children were excluded from factory employment and women's formal employment declined. Men welcomed this, believing that their earnings would rise to provide a "family wage." Women had more mixed reactions, especially mature spinsters and widows, whose economic autonomy was now reduced. "Modern" enclosed places of employment – factories, mines, and railway workshops – became regulated and over-whelmingly male. Cotton textiles remained more mixed, but now with a stable hierarchical division of labor between men and women (and no children).

This is a narrative not only of legislative progress for workers but also of the unintended consequences of the entwining of capitalist and a combination of ideological-moral and patriarchal political crystal-lizations. These weakened the family-community class solidarity of Chartism and narrowed working-class action to the sectionalism of brotherhood. Britain is the only country in which we can clearly trace this, for patriarchal morality in other countries displaced women and children before a large working class appeared. Only in Britain was an insurrectionary workers' movement so family based. Now it sectionalized and further declined, reinforced as economy and taxes eased. Workers depoliticized, turning to workplace action, fuller order books streng-thening their economic weapons. It is amid such sectionalism and economism that the protectionist Chartist Land Company emerged in the mid-1840s, aiming to buy land for workers to till – a reaction to political defeat and a turning toward narrow (and backward-looking) economic action. And it is from the defeat of Chartist head-on class confrontation that "respectable trade unionism" rose after midcentury.

The rise of sectional trade unionism, 1850–1880

After midcentury,[4] trade union growth was slow but cumulative. The Webbs (1920: 472, 748) estimated membership as fewer than 100,000 in the early 1840s, and recent estimates put membership at 500,000 to 600,000 about 1860, 800,000 in 1867, and 1.6 million (which is probably too high) in 1876 (Fraser 1974: 16). But the unions swam amid larger cooperative societies and "friendly societies." In 1874, a royal commission estimated 4 million members and 8 million beneficiaries of friendly societies (Kirk 1985: 149–52). Most workers were implicated in forms of protectionism to which the regime had no objection.

Yet unions also changed their character. By 1860, most had become economistic, sectional, and to many writers conservative or aristocratic. Though no longer plainly illegal, unions remained harassed under the conspiracy laws. As we see later in the United States (Chapter 17), this privileged craft sectionalism could slip by the law easier than industrial or general unions, especially if they controlled labor supply. Most unions were thus confined to upper skill levels. To the city artisan core were added skilled engineers, ironworkers and miners encountering workshop and factory controls, and textile workers and others with more factory-created skills. The Unions' center of gravity shifted from artisan workshops to larger mechanized workshops and mines. Internal labor markets developed in railways, iron, and steel. Most unions sought to restrict entry to the trade, blocking "mates," "helpers," and "holders-up"; restricting female employment; and demanding the "family wage" – for men only (Savage 1987). They sought to institutionalize factory and workshop rules, to accommodate the employer, to conciliate strikes, to guarantee the efficiency of members' work, and to give respectability to members. There were few violent strikes, most in mining. Identity with the sectional trade and with the segmental enterprise strengthened more than with class (Joyce 1980: 50–89). A boilermaker (quoted in Fraser 1974: 59) rhapsodized:

> Capital and Labour seem
> By our Maker joined;
> Are they not like twin giants
> In the world of the mind?

---

[4] The main general sources on this period were Pelling (1963), Perkin (1969), Musson (1972), Fraser (1974), Tholfsen (1976), Hunt (1981), Evans (1983), and Kirk (1985).

What can Labour do alone?
Turn a gristless mill!
What can Capital indeed
By itself? But hoard its seed
Eat a golden pill.
Up the hill of progress bright
March we on in tether,
Making difficulties like,
Pulling all together.
So shall we in concord joined
Show to wondering mankind
Capital and Labour
Are the oars to pull the boat,
Are our wings to soar aloft,
In our high endeavour?
                    (Fraser, 1984: 59)

Yet respectable unions were moving toward one element of modern socialism, that of seeing society as an economic *totality*. They saw capitalism as a system, realizing that their terms of employment were linked to a trade cycle they could exploit (Hobsbawm 1964: 350). Another sign of their growing sense of totality – a "landmark in the history of trade unionism" Pelling (1963: 42) calls it – was the founding in 1851 of the first enduring national union, the Amalgamated Society of Engineers (ASE). Though confined to skilled male workers, it recognized their common national interests. The ASE provided a model for other unions moving up from local through regional to national organization.

The ASE rules stated the central paradox of craft unionism:

If constrained to make restrictions against the admission into our trade of those who have not earned a right by a probationary servitude (i.e., apprenticeship), we do so knowing that such encroachments are productive of evil, and when persevered in unchecked, result in reducing the condition of the artisan to that of the unskilled labourer, and confer no permanent advantage on those admitted. [Clegg et al. 1964: 4]

Although the union believed it was "constrained" to exclude unskilled workers, nonetheless this exclusion reinforced sectionalism. Yet the union was also extending and eventually politicizing the collective identities and organization of its members. At first the ASE was most concerned with standardizing friendly society benefits. But when employers locked the ASE out nationally in 1852, they and other craftsmen were forced into broader organization and politics. Class struggle had a cumulative, dialectical element. Union involvement in ten- and nine-hour movements pressured employers toward regional and national organization; this, in turn, further pressured union national organization. Membership rose from an initial 5,000 to 45,000 by 1880. The respectability of what were called the "new model unions" was not actually new (Musson 1972), but *national* unions were. The nation-state was becoming workers' *totality*.

Nonetheless, politicization was not primarily of class. Unions collaborated in the 1850s with middle-class reformers in the Reform League, whose motto was "working men are worthy of the vote." By the late 1860s, Liberalism had succeeded Chartism as the political creed of most labor militants. They also participated in cross-class cooperative, education, and temperance movements (Kirk 1985: 70, 132–73). In return, they received mutualist legislation securing the rights of cooperatives and friendly societies and improving education. Bourgeois reformers came to appreciate the mutualist argument that collective civil rights be granted to labor unions. Self-righteous bourgeois class unity was relaxing amid a more sectionalized, stable social order. Factionalism reappeared among the regime. More advocated the "liberal incorporation" of respectable workers.

Indeed, in relation to workers, the British state was now also crystallizing as party democratic. Some Tories, as well as Liberals, came to believe that the vote should be granted to such respectable men. The parties themselves were during this period becoming more mass, less notable, more involved in genuine electoral competition. Factions in both parties anticipated electoral benefits if they enacted reform. The 1867 Conservative Act granted householder suffrage in the boroughs, leaving Conservative power intact in the countryside – Lord Derby said his act would "dish the Whigs." The Liberals retaliated, extending the act to the counties in 1884. It turned out that the geographic concentration of coal miners gave them a majority in a few county constituencies. Miners, nominated by their union and loyal to the Liberal party, were elected to Parliament in 1885. Thus workers were in Parliament, as a result of segmental collaboration between unions and a party-democratic regime.

The Trades Union Congress (TUC) symbolized this national, mildly mutualist and collaborationist emergence. Founded in 1868–9 as a debating society, it was broadened (as had happened to labor organizations in the 1820s and 1830s) by legal repression of unions. The 1871 Criminal Law Amendment Act criminalized most picketing, threatening even craft unions. The TUC lobbied successfully for its repeal in 1875 among its bourgeois allies.

Unions also shared in Victorian attempts to understand the nature of "society." The notion that society was a systematic, bounded totality with its own laws was spreading through both political economy and the new discipline of sociology. English positivists popularized Comte, the coiner of the word; Spencer's books on social evolution achieved mass sales; and Marx debated the capitalist system with looser socialists who debated it with radicals and unionists. Most of their theories assumed a dual social totality – "society" was both a capitalist or an industrial system and it was a nation-state. And so it has remained for socialism and sociology alike.

Respectable trade unionism was not really a "labor aristocracy" and certainly not a "betrayal" (as Foster 1974 suggests). Chartism and the class movement were collapsing before unions turned respectable. Some insurrectionary constituencies then disappeared as a result of defeat, notably handloom weavers, largely extinct during the 1850s. Rather, respectability was a rational, sectional response to (1) the frontal defeat of Chartism's *class* tendencies; (2) the consequent diversion of class solidarity into economistic *sectional* strategies; (3) the recognition by party-democratic regime elements that sectionalism was no threat, and indeed embodied positive virtues; and (4) the boosting of sectionalism after midcentury by novel forms of economic *heterogeneity* amid economic growth. I turn to this fourth process, beginning with factories.

The growth of factories after midcentury did not strengthen class identities, as Marx expected. Joyce (1980) shows that cotton factories promoted segmental paternalism, even deference. This is consistent with Calhoun's (1982) evidence that earlier radicalism had survived better in towns with many small artisanal workshops rather than where factories predominated; with Rudé's (1964) demonstration that agitating crowds (except during Chartism's peak) were composed of workers more mobile, less subject to discipline, than factory operatives; and with F. M. L. Thompson's (1981) argument that from 1840 to 1880 the large factory was the main mechanism of segmental control exercised over the workers.

These findings also fit Newby's (1977) model of "deference." Deference, he notes, is relational rather than attitudinal, resulting in twentieth-century agriculture (his field of study) if the farmer controls the worker's whole life. The twentieth-century farmer and the late nineteenth-century manufacturer were not only active owner-managers but also magistrates and leaders of local social, educational, and political institutions. The worker lacks the extensive power to challenge this broad span but can achieve limited goals by manipulating a deferential style. He or she may even internalize deference: If the only possible reality *is* employer-dominated, then it becomes "natural" in the dual factual-normative meanings of this word. Thus Joyce shows enfranchised (male) cotton operatives voting with their employer, Whig or Tory. More conflict appeared in small enterprises because small masters had little more community control than artisans. Radicalism appeared more among big-city workers than in medium-sized towns; oligarchies of factory owners could control the Rochdales, Halifaxes, and Walsalls but not Manchester, Leeds, Nottingham, or London. The factory community discouraged class and encouraged segmental organization. The ability of upper classes to outflank lower classes organizationally had not ended. Marx was right to see it challenged. But the institutionalized factory helped stem the challenge, just as the emergent factory had helped begin it. The factory became less a "school for socialism" than the industrial equivalent of the medieval manor. Factory workers became the segmental retainers of their lord.

Moreover, where factories and prosperous stable firms intersected with craft controls over labor supply, unions "gendered" labor relations. Trade unions were overwhelmingly male, although women formed a substantial minority of employees. Labor notions of a family wage, the male breadwinner, and comradeship were masculine, as was the pub where most unions held their meetings (Hart 1989: 39–60). Outside the factory and the stable enterprise, and where they intersected with market uncertainties, casual unorganized labor, mostly males but with some females, predominated. In some areas Irish immigrants dominated among male casual workers, leading to serious ethnic-religious divisions and rioting (Kirk 1985: 310–48). In earlier days, when heterogeneity had not stabilized into sectionalism, Irish workers had been well represented in the Chartist movement. Lancashire militants from the two communities were now antagonists.

Victorians noted the new divisions, though usually only those among men. Marx had analyzed the divide between workers and casual lumpenproletariat in midcentury France; later he stressed English-Irish worker conflict. Other contemporaries pluraled the "working classes." As the radical *Bee-Hive* wrote in 1864:

The working classes . . . are divided into two large sections, one comprising the skilled artisan and mechanic and the other by the labourer, the costermonger, the men who find their daily living by means which they themselves would find difficult to describe . . . and the "roughs" of all description. [Fraser 1974: 209]

Mayhew noted that in the docks only skilled artisans had regular employment and wages:

The artisans are almost to a man red-hot politicians. . . . The unskilled labourers are a different class of people. As yet they are as unpolitical as footmen. . . . They appear to have no political opinions whatever, or if they do . . . they rather lead towards the maintenance of "things as they are" than towards the ascendancy of working people. [Evans 1983: 170]

Entwined skill and gender provided the major fault line in the Victorian working class. Contemporaries began to divide workers into "respectables" and "roughs." Gray (1976) and Crossick (1978) show that (male) artisans formed their own associations, intermarried, and transmitted their occupation to their sons; they saved moderate amounts through friendly societies and cultivated respectability. They were as divided from the middle class as from unskilled workers – not "embourgeoised" but, rather, constituting a distinct class fraction. They had one enormous advantage over the unskilled: security of employment because of labor market control. The unskilled were casual workers, not reaching family-wage levels. This precluded their contributing to friendly societies and other artisanal organizations. Perhaps the most telling comparison concerns the Victorian worker's worst fear, the workhouse (Crossick 1978: 112–3). In Greenwich, a laborer's chance of admission was five and a half times that of the population average; the traditional artisan's (tailor, mason, cooper) chance was only two-thirds of this average; and the engineering craftsman's, one-quarter. The engineer's life chances were more than twenty times better than the labourer's.

Gender differences, artisanal trades, domestic outwork, and casual factory labor – plus the more segmentally controlled agriculture and domestic service – could generate little class identity. Most collective action was restricted to skilled "brothers." The national state also blurred class by fostering segmental alliances. Thus before the working class could reemerge, both sectionalism and segmentalism would have to end. During the Second Industrial Revolution, after 1880, neither ended; but they did lessen, as Chapter 17 shows.

Conclusion

The early development of the British labor movement was unique. The main power relations charted in this chapter will not recur in later chapters. The early diffusion of manufacturing capitalism, reinforced by state militarism, made its historic "federal" crystallization rather more centralized. Entwined, these three forces generated a uniquely early and uniquely family- and community-oriented working-class movement. In the late 1830s and early 1840s, it launched Chartism, as insurrectionary a workers' movement as we find anywhere later in other countries. It encountered, however, an equally resolute, class-conscious, and self-righteous ruling regime and capitalist class, wielding greater, disciplined militarism. They clashed head-on, and there was no dialectical resolution. The working class lost, as it has lost all such head-on clashes. Its defeat was made final, with little apparent residue in subsequent decades, because workers' sectionalism could extract consolations for craft workers who possessed exclusionary powers in internal or external labor markets. Chapter 17 describes how these sectionalisms enountered the Second Industrial Revolution to develop again broader class organization, though far more moderate than Chartism.

The midcentury replacement of class with sectionalism also involved the family. Whereas the early class movement derived strong sustenance from family and community – stronger than Marx realized – later sectionalism became predominantly masculine, employment-centered, and productivist.

As Marx and Engels recommended, I have analyzed classes as relational. Neither regime, nor capitalist class, nor workers had a consistent strategy, whether reactionary, pragmatic, or progressive, through the period. Their strategies-drifts – indeed, their very identity – were forged as they interacted. The regime, for example, shifted from the pragmatic concessions amid factionalism of the Great Reform Act to the disciplined, self-righteous militarism of the Chartist period to the strengthening of pragmatic concessions from party democracy from the 1860s. It did so as its own identity, as external pressures, and as the identity of the labor movement all changed.

Unlike Marx and Engels, I have not treated class interactions as dialectical, composed of the head-on clash and resolution of whole organized classes. I have qualified this dialectic in two ways. First, segmentalism and sectionalism also inherently crosscut and weakened classes. In the present case, the decisive outcome of struggle was that whereas the regime retained identity and unity, militarism plus unanticipated consequences generated sectional worker identities. Later, when the regime relaxed, it too generated party factionalism. Second, class conflict is rarely pure and head-on, because it involves multiple power networks whose interrelations are not systemic or transparent to actors. Thus their resolution produces unanticipated consequences for one another. I have concentrated on nonsystemic entwinings between family and class and among capitalist, moral-ideological, patriarchal, and party-democratic state crystallizations. Their entwinings brought consequences no one intended. Through the Factory Acts, for example, workers made gains the regime did not wholly intend, while the labor movement became essentially masculine, which no one had intended. I might add that another set of nonsystemic interactions, between class and nation-state, was also proceeding during this period, but I have not yet traced their consequences.

Bibliography

Bairoch, P., et al. 1968. *The Working Population and Its Structure*. Brussels: Editions de l'Institut de Sociologie de l'Université Libre.

Bennett, J. 1982. The London Democratic Association, 1837–1841: a study in London radicalism. In *The Chartist Experience: Studies in Working-Class Radicalism and Culture, 1830–60*, ed. J. Epstein and D. Thompson. London: Macmillan.

Briggs, A. 1959a. *The Age of Improvement 1783–1867*. London: Longman Group.

1959b. *Chartist Studies*. London: Macmillan.

1960. The language of "class" in early nineteenth-century England. In *Essays in Labour History*, ed. A. Briggs and J. Saville. London: Macmillan.

Calhoun, C. 1982. *The Question of Class Struggle*. Oxford: Blackwell.

Church, R. A., and S. D. Chapman. 1967. Gravener Henson and the making of the English working class. In *Land, Labour and Population in the Industrial Revolution*, ed. E. C. James and G. E. Mingay. London: Arnold.

Clapman, J. H. 1939. *An Economic History of Modern Britain*. Cambridge: Cambridge University Press.

Clegg, H. A., et al. 1964. *A History of British Trade Unions Since 1889*, Vol. I. Oxford: Clarendon Press.

Crossick, G. 1978. *An Artisan Elite in Victorian Society*. London: Croom Helm.

Currie, R., and R. M. Hartwell. 1965. The making of the English working class. *Economic History Review*, 2nd ser. 18.

Davies, J. C. 1970. The J-curve of rising and declining satisfactions as a cause of some great revolutions and a contained rebellion. In *Violence in America*, ed. H. D. Graham and T. R. Gurr. New York: Bantam.

Epstein, J. 1982. Some organizational and cultural aspects of the Chartist movement in Nottingham. In *The Chartist Experience: Studies in Working-Class Radicalism and Culture, 1830–60*, ed. J. Epstein and D. Thompson. London: Macmillan.

Epstein, J., and D. Thompson (eds.). 1982. *The Chartist Experience*. London: Macmillan.

Evans, E. J. 1983. *The Forging of the Modern State: Early Industrial Britain, 1783–1870*. London: Longman Group.

Foster, J. 1974. *Class Struggle and the Industrial Revolution*. New York: St. Martin's Press.

Fraser, W. H. 1974. *Trade Unions and Society*. London: Allen & Unwin.

Goodmay, D. 1982. *London Chartism, 1838–1848*. Cambridge: Cambridge University Press.

Gray, R. Q. 1976. *The Labour Aristocracy in Victorian Edinburgh*. Oxford: Clarendon Press.

Greenberg, D. 1982. Reassessing the power patterns of the Industrial Revolution: an Anglo-American comparison. *American Historical Review* 87.

Hobsbawm, E. J. 1962. *The Age of Revolution, 1789–1848*. New York: Mentor. 1964. *Labouring Men*. London: Weidenfeld & Nicolson.

Hollis, P. 1973. *Class and Conflict in Eighteenth-Century England, 1815–1850*. London: Routledge & Kegan Paul.

Hunt, E. H. 1981. *British Labour History, 1815–1914*. London: Weidenfeld & Nicolson.

Jones, D. 1975. *Chartism and the Chartists*. London: Allen Lane.

Joyce, P. 1980. *Work, Society and Politics: The Culture of the Factory in Later Victorian England*. Brighton: Harvester.
    1990. Work. In *The Cambridge Social History of Britain, 1750–1950*. Vol. 2: *People and Their Environment*, ed. F. M. L. Thompson. Cambridge: Cambridge University Press.
    1991. *Visions of the People. Industrial England and the Question of Class, 1848–1914*. Cambridge: Cambridge University Press.
Kirk, N. 1985. *The Growth of Working Class Reformism in Mid-Victorian England*. London: Croom Helm.
Leeson, R. A. 1979. *Travelling Brothers*. London: Allen & Unwin.
Morris, R. J. 1979. *Class and Class Consciousness in the Industrial Revolution, 1780–1850*. London: Macmillan.
Musson, A. E. 1972. *British Trade Unions 1800–1875*. London: Macmillan.
    1976. Class struggle and the labour aristocracy, 1830–60. *Social History*, no. 3.
Napier, Sir W. F. P. 1857. *The Life and Opinions of General Sir Charles James Napier*, 4 vols. London: Murray.
Newby, H. 1977. *The Deferential Worker*. London: Allen Lane.
O'Brien, P. 1989. The impact of the revolutionary and Napoleonic wars, 1793–1815, on the long-run growth of the British economy. *Review* (Fernand Braudel Center) 12.
Parkin, F. 1979. *Marxism and Class Theory: A Bourgeois Critique*. London: Tavistock.
Pelling, H. 1963. *A History of British Trade Unions*. London: Macmillan.
Perkin, H. 1969. *The Origins of Modern English Society, 1780–1880*. London: Routledge & Kegan Paul.
Prothero, I. 1971. London Chartism and the trades. *Economic History Review* 24.
    1979. *Artisans and Politics in Early Nineteenth-Century London*. London: Methuen & Co.
Rudé, G. 1964. *The Crowd in History 1730–1848*. New York: Wiley.
Rueschemeyer, D., E. Stephens, and J. Stephens. 1992. *Capitalist Development and Democracy*. Chicago: University of Chicago Press.
Samuels, R. 1977. The workshop of the world: steam power and hand technology in mid-Victorian Britain. *History Workshop Journal*, no. 3.
Savage, M. 1987. *The Dynamics of Working-Class Politics*. Cambridge: Cambridge University Press.
Saville, J. 1987. *1848: The British State and the Chartist Movement*. Cambridge: Cambridge University Press.
Sewell, W. H. 1974. Social change and the rise of working-class politics in nineteenth-century Marseilles. *Past and Present* 65.
Stedman-Jones, G. 1975. Class struggle and the industrial revolution: a review article. *New Left Review*, no. 90.
    1982. The language of Chartism. In *The Chartist Experience: Studies in Working-Class Radicalism and Culture, 1830–60*, ed. J. Epstein and D. Thompson. London: Macmillan.
    1983. *Languages of Class*. Cambridge: Cambridge University Press.
Sykes, R. 1982. Early Chartism and trade unionism in south-east Lancashire. In *The Chartist Experience: Studies in Working-Class Radicalism and Culture, 1830–60*, ed. J. Epstein and D. Thompson. London: Macmillan.

Tholfsen, T. 1976. *Working Class Radicalism in Mid-Victorian England*. London: Croom Helm.

Thompson, D. 1984. *The Chartists*. New York: Pantheon.

Thompson, E. P. 1968. *The Making of the English Working Class*. Harmondsworth: Penguin Books.

Thompson, F. M. L. 1981. Social control in Victorian Britain. *Economic History Review*, 2d ser. 34.

Thompson, N. 1988. *The Market and Its Critics: Socialist Political Economy in Nineteenth Century Britain*. London: Routledge & Kegan Paul.

Webb, S., and B. Webb. 1920. *History of Trade Unionism*. London: Longman Group.

Weisser, H. 1983. *April 10: Challenge and Response in England 1848*. Lanham, Md.: University Press of America.

16 The middle-class nation

Theoretical issues

Chapters 4 and 9 discuss nineteenth-century regimes essentially composed of only a few thousand families. They could not rule unaided. True, workers provided little organized threat until the end of the century; peasants organized earlier but (as Chapter 19 shows) rarely subversively. It did not matter greatly whether most workers were enthusiasts for king, country, and capital or were disaffected. As they had few stable power organizations, their beliefs were largely irrelevant. Organizational outflanking, however, requires lower-level administrators and loyalists, formerly provided by particularistic segmental networks now somewhat reduced by the universalism of capitalism and modern state. Yet comfort emerged after midcentury from a group of predominantly loyal subalterns, the middle class.

Since then, this class has been mostly loyal to capitalism. Regimes seemingly have worried most about what many writers have believed to be its intermittent tendency to nationalist extremism. I shall look at bourgeois nationalism rather skeptically, finding a much more particularistic social location for what I term an overzealous, superloyal statism. Given such long-lived class loyalty, this chapter often breaks chronological boundaries, generalizing about continuities (where they exist) right up to today. The middle-class nation-state created in the late nineteenth century proved, in crucial respects, to be ours. The middle class has been as important as the working class in shaping Western society.

Defining of the middle class has always been contentious. The rise of "middling groups" immediately presented conceptual problems for nineteenth-century observers. Most used the plural "middle classes," impressed by their heterogeneity. The franchise acutely raised the problem of class definition: The middle classes should perhaps be allowed the vote, but who was middle class? But this was settled by pragmatic politics more than conceptual clarity. Contemporaries left definitions to us, but our historians have been no great help. Ryan (1981: 13) complains that American historians use "middle class" as a mere "residual category." Among British historians, Gray believes that "relations of production" distinguish capitalists and workers but establish only the "distinctness of the middle strata," so should not be applied "mechanistically" (1977: 134–5). This vague advice is echoed by Crossick for whom the "lower middle class" is "analytically" weak but useful as a "descriptive term for a contemporary observed reality" (1977: 14). Harrison (1971: 101) says that to define the middle classes is difficult in the twentieth century, but "in early Victorian England the tests of membership were more objective . . . though not by any means rigid or even definite." Can objectivity be indefinite? Can sociologists supply better concepts?

Sociologists certainly provide *more* concepts – the petite bourgeoisie, with its old, new, and traditional fractions; the middle class, old, new, and decomposed; the new working class; the service class; the professional and managerial class – all of these may be in "contradictory class locations." Alternatively, there are many middling strata, occupational strata, or status gradations; or mixed class-stratum terms like "white collar," "professions," or "semiprofessions." French terms parallel these. Germans combine class and "estate" terms – *Mittelstand*, *Burgertum*, divided into *Besitzburgertum* (propertied bourgeoisie) and *Bildungsburgertum* (highly educated bourgeoisie). This plethora embodies five alternative theories. Middling groups are

1. In the working class – the conclusion of orthodox Marxism
2. Part of the ruling bourgeois or capitalist class – an occasional, pessimistic Marxian response
3. In an ambiguous, contradictory class location (Wright 1985: 42–57)
4. "Decomposed," as various middling groups fall into different classes, or *Stande* – the most common view (e.g., Dahrendorf 1959)
5. A separate middle class (e.g., Giddens 1973)

There are endless debates among these five (reviewed by Abercrombie and Urry 1983: pt. I). I borrow from all of them but settle on a combination of theories 4 and 5. I argue for the emergence of a separate yet (like all classes) "impure" middle class containing three internal fractions, each with distinct power organizations. I also argue that most previous sociology has failed to appreciate sufficiently the complexity of the middle class, for three reasons:

1. Most writers have entered this debate concerned with another class problem: the relation between capitalist and working classes (Blumin 1989: 6–7 and Mayer 1975 also make this complaint). Middle classes (as the term implies) are seen in relation to the struggle between capital and labor, supposedly the defining characteristic of modern class relations. From this perspective, middling groups lack independence because most side with capital (see critics of the "professional-managerial class" theory of the Ehrenreichs 1979, such as Aronowitz 1979 or Goldthorpe 1982). If we focus only on capital-labor relations this view is correct. But as I have repeatedly argued, societies are not unitary, reducible to a single source of social power.

Modern Western society is not reducible to capitalism, nor are its class relations reducible to capital-labor relations.

2. Most Marxists and some non-Marxists share a narrow "productivism," focusing on direct employment relations, often those prevalent in large manufacturing industry. Some confine the working class to "productive labor," putting almost all middling groups on the side of capital, many exercising the "global functions of capital" (Poulantzas 1975; Carchedi 1977). Wright (1985) has sought to comprehend middling diversity with a rather original model of "relations of production." He identifies three power resources of employment – property, organizational power, and skills – each flowing from a distinct mode of production in modern society (though he views property power, and therefore the capitalist mode of production, as dominant). Middling groups tend to be high on one but not all three – thus they are in a "contradictory class location." I accept many of Wright's arguments, but his theory is productivist and functionalist: Only employment relations really count, and authority and education are introduced only insofar as they contribute functionally to economic production.

Some non-Marxists have shared the preoccupation with employment relations. Dahrendorf (1959) argues that authority relations in employment have replaced property ownership as the fundamental determinant of class in modern societies. Goldthorpe (1982) defines a "service class" in terms of trust conferred in employment upon professionals, managers, and higher technicians. He is sensitive to other qualities of his service class, like common educational experience, but these do not help define his class, which is essentially an aggregation of occupations. Again "relations to the means of production," interpreted as employment relations, supposedly are our guides through the middling morass.

3. Neo-Weberians only appear to trawl wider in dealing with middling groups. They count common life chances and life-styles, schooling, social interaction, and intermarriage, as well as formal employment relations, and they go beyond mere economic function. But they tend to integrate this diversity with the concept of common "market position," defined mostly by education. Parkin (1979) argues that educational "credentials" allow the middle class considerable "closure" of labor markets. Like Collins (1979), he is not functionalist but rather cynical about this: Education is not merely a response to economic needs; it is itself a form of power.

Giddens puts educational power into a broader theory of how market powers define classes. They form when "*mobility closure exists in relation to any specified form of market capacity*" (his emphasis). Partly paralleling Wright, he specifies three market powers: property, educational or technical qualifications, and manual-labor power. This gives three basic modern classes: capitalists, workers, and a middle class defined by education. This has the specific problem of leaving the classic petite bourgeoisie – small shopkeepers, independent artisans – outside the middle class, which is perhaps an odd conclusion. Giddens qualifies his model somewhat by adding secondary "proximate structurations of class relationships" like authority relations in the enterprise and consumption patterns. Yet, overall, his theory replaces employment-centered relations to the means of production with the market powers conferred by education (1973: 107–10).

Abercrombie and Urry (1983) have made the sensible observations that we should combine production and market relations and that collective action arising from both will also help define the middle class. These are necessary but still insufficient steps. I go three steps farther:

1. Three variably "impure" relations of production impinge on middling groups: (1) capitalist property ownership, (2) hierarchies specific to capitalist corporations and modern state bureaucracies, and (3) authoritative state-licensed professions. I sometimes distinguish within relation 2 between private and public hierarchies, but overall relations of production yield three distinct groups:

1. The *petite bourgeoisie*: proprietors of small, familial business
2. *Careerists*: wage or salaried employees moving up corporate and bureaucratic hierarchies
3. *Professionals*: "learned," collectively organized occupations licensed by the state

Of course, many persons lie in "contradictory class locations" between them, others mix them up (professionals employed by corporations), and still others may have idiosyncratic employment. But if we remained entirely at the level of direct relations of production, we might have to count these three as separate classes, as their employment relations are so different. Yet a common class position can be generated by steps 2 and 3.

2. I recall the distinction between *authoritative* and *diffused* power relations. Capitalism does not merely consist of authoritative employment organizations. These are embedded in diffused circuits of capital, including consumption (as many writers have noted). We will see that these help integrate our three class fractions.

3. Capitalism has never been self-constituting. As I have repeatedly argued, it is embedded in networks of ideological, military, and political power. We will see that ideological and political national citizenship also integrated the middle class.

Indeed, all three of these criteria – employment relations, diffused power relations, and all the sources of social power – confer an

additional common quality on middle-class persons: They have predominantly segmental relations with dominant classes above, reinforcing
their loyalty – if for some generating a worrying "superloyalty." Thus
they are fractions of a single middle class defined by the formula:
*segmental middling participation in the hierarchies of capitalism and
nation-state*. I start with economic relations.

Middle-class fractions

The petite bourgeoisie
The petite bourgeoisie owns and controls its means of production and
its own labor but employs no free wage labor (as in Marxian definitions).
The typical petit bourgeois business employs dependent family labor at
nonmarket rates (usually below them). The "owner" may be a person,
family, or a partnership of friends, usually on a substantially non-
contractual basis – profits, losses, and labor obligations are shared
according to diffused normative understandings of family and friendship,
unlike the more impersonal partnerships of larger business. The petite
bourgeoisie has capitalist property ownership but with "nonfree" wage
labor; it is familial and particularistic.

Obviously, the demarcation between petite bourgeoisie and capitalist
class is not absolute. Business comes in all sizes, and upper petite
bourgeoisie merges imperceptibly into the capitalist class. Because
capitalism is relatively diffuse, it does not often exclude, unlike some
other modes of production.

Chapter 4 discusses how the organization of early industrial capitalism
was essentially small and diffused. Artisans, jobbers, small traders,
and family business carried the Industrial Revolution. Petty "capital"
blurred into "skilled labor," as did nonmanual into manual work,
especially through artisans, preponderating among "middling ranks-
classes." Then both Chapters 4 and 15 discuss the artisanal world's
splitting apart. Most artisans in less secure trades dropped into the
working class, but in a prospering trade around midcentury perhaps 20
percent might rise in a decade to run small businesses. This new petite
bourgeoisie became "nonmanual," segregated from "workers" below,
and wealthier, securer, and of higher status (Blumin 1989: 66–137).
Small proprietors still dominated middling groups. "Dealers" formed
well over half those described by Victorians as middle class, and they
were increasing at midcentury (Booth 1886; Best 1979: 98–100, 104–6).

This nonmanual petite bourgeoisie enjoyed only moderate wealth
and status and was not received into the best circles. But it cooperated
with capitalists. Until the rise of the large corporation, after 1880 in
Germany and the United States (after 1900 in Britain, France, and

Austria), even the biggest enterprises generated small jobbers at both ends of the supply chain. Private unlimited companies and partnerships, subcontractors, and casual labor predominated, and both large and small capitalists were preoccupied with transmitting family property to their heirs. Small business jobbed for big business and dominated consumer industries, building, and services. Its savings were invested in government bonds or shares by solicitors, brokers, banks, and insurance companies. The petite bourgeoisie was participating happily in the expanded diffusion of capital.

Its loyalty helped defeat Chartism and the 1848 revolutions and continued thereafter. Mayer (1975) says that the petite bourgeoisie faced only one way after 1871 – backward. This is overstated, as Wiener (1976) argues. Its members remained mostly conservative, not reactionary. In Victorian Britain, they appear complacent. "The mellowing of middle-class liberalism" combined with the economic boom and British imperial dominance (Tholfsen 1976). The petite bourgeoisie comprised a near majority of the electorate between 1832 and 1867, about a third thereafter, but elections remained segmentally organized by "traditionally structured deference communities and deference networks" for a longer time (Moore 1976). Political quiescence went with a sentimental idealism. The paintings in petit bourgeois living rooms depicted scenes of domestic tranquillity, medieval and Scottish Highland romanticism, and the innocence of children. Blumin (1989: 138–91) and Ryan (1981) also paint a cosy domestic picture of the American petite bourgeoisie.

Yet, was this a fleeting golden era for the petite bourgeoisie? The Second Industrial Revolution developed corporations, cartels, trade associations, and protectionism amid intense international competition. It is usually argued that such "organized capitalism" was inimical to the petite bourgeoisie (e.g., Gellately 1974 and Lash and Urry 1987 synthesize this literature). British and French capitalism was less "organized" than American or German. But in the important petit bourgeois sector of retailing, department stores threatened small shopkeepers and dealers in all countries, and Britain and France suffered more from international competition. The petite bourgeoisie was supposedly menaced from the 1880s by corporate capitalism, numbers and power dwindling, reacting with vociferous and paranoid politics of status panic – volatile, usually rightist, eventually leading to extreme nationalism and fascism – an agitated class fraction.

Yet this turns out to be myth. The prewar petite bourgeoisie was bored, not excited. Indeed, there has been little organized petit bourgeois *economic* discontent right up to the present. In the countries we are discussing, by far the most organization came from Austro-

Hungarian nationalists and from the German *Mittelstand* – mainly political structurings of collective action whose narrowly economic manifestations tended to be pragmatic and moderate. For example, when German courts ruled that Bismarck's social insurance laws applied only to workers, the *Mittelstand* protested and got its own insurance law in 1911 (Kocka 1980: 258–9). The petite bourgeoisie in Britain and the United States only rarely agitated over domestic politics; it was not active in controversies over the Progressive movement. Chapman (1981: 236) notes little conflict between small and large British firms right from 1720 to the 1970s. Most trouble arose over retail price maintenance, but as the main rivals were co-ops, petit bourgeois protest voiced liberal capitalist ideology (Crossick 1977: 17). As we shall see, this class fraction was poorly represented in middle-class nationalist movements of the period. Even when discontented, the petite bourgeoisie rarely broke away to form its own parties.

Did the petite bourgeoisie nonetheless decline before the superior efficiency of the corporation? After half a century in which economists emphasized economies of scale, the efficiency issue was raised again in the 1980s. Prais (1981) failed to find economies of scale: The large swallowed up the small not because they were more efficient but because they exercised authoritative power over markets, and because of the characteristics of stock markets. Nikolaou's (1978) study of Greek enterprises found small or medium firms were the most efficient; Kiyonari (1981) found smaller Japanese firms were either very profitable or very unprofitable. There are few data on profits in earlier periods. The historical literature is full of petit bourgeois tales of woe, but no costings of profit and loss, no proof of economic decline (Gellately 1974 is a typical example). The death rate for small businesses was high, but it has probably always been so, certainly since the 1850s (Blumin 1989: 115).

Small business severely exploits family labor. Yet this is rarely *experienced* as exploitation. Bertaux and Bertaux-Wiame (1981) vividly describe the life of French bakers. The baker and his wife have a life of almost unremitting toil. During a six-day week the husband bakes from 3:00 or 4:00 A.M. to after midday, and the wife sells in the shop from 7:00 or 8:00 A.M. to 8:00 P.M. Yet the trade is their life and achievement, fulfilling both the idealist vision of "meaning" and the materialist vision of practical, creative self-expression. Few modern people experience autonomy and fulfillment at work, yet these goals remain highly valued. Even if profits and wages are low, many seek to enter the trade, and most experience it as satisfying, hardships and all. This does not generate discontent – nor do excessively long working hours facilitate class organization.

In the absence of data about profit, numbers are often used to indicate proletarianization. The conclusion has been almost unanimous: Numbers fell until the 1980s, indicating economic decline and proletarianization. The famous prediction of petit bourgeois proletarianization made by Marx and Engels (in the *Communist Manifesto*) has influenced disciples and critics alike. Marshaling rather slender evidence, Poulantzas proclaimed "a massive process of pauperization and proletarianisation of this petty bourgeoisie" (1975: 152). But even Marx's critics agree, adding only that a new salariat has arisen to compensate (Geiger 1969: 92–4). Giddens attempts more precision:

The figures . . . suggest a general pattern which applies, although with quite wide discrepancies, to most of the capitalist societies: a pattern of a steady relative diminution of small business . . . from the closing decades of the nineteenth century up to the early years of the 1930s; whence the decline continues, but at a considerably reduced gradient. [1973: 177–8]

The 1980s added a twist to this orthodox tale: the assertion that an era of corporate "organized" capitalism was succeeded by one of "disorganized" capitalism in which small business again flourished. Lash and Urry (1987) argue that corporate capitalism induced petit bourgeois decline from the 1880s to the 1950s and then decline reversed.

Yet these claims are all false. Petit bourgeois decline has been largely confined to manufacturing and to relative proportions, not absolute numbers. Giddens remarked the latter point, but he misread the timetable of relative decline. Most censuses do reveal a decline of small manufacturing until the 1970s. In Britain, in 1930, there were 93,000 establishments employing fewer than 10 persons; by 1968, only 35,000. A slightly lesser decline occurred in France, Germany, and the United States. Only Italy and Japan escaped decline. By the 1960s, establishments employing fewer than 10 persons made up only 2.1 percent of British manufacturing employment, 2.4 percent of American, 6.2 percent of West German, 10.8 percent of French, 12.2 percent of Japanese, and 18.2 percent of Italian (Pryor 1973: 153; Kiyonari 1981: 980; Prais 1981: 10–11, 160). But total employment trends are complex and differ between countries and periods.

The 1911 British census distinguished "employers," "own account workers," and "employees." The first two roughly indicate the petite bourgeoisie (although the first also includes the few large capitalists). Between 1911 and 1931, they increased absolutely by 14 percent, maintaining their exact relative contribution to the labor force. Between 1931 and 1951, numbers decreased by 21 percent; relative contribution, by slightly more. Exclusion of agriculture steepens the absolute decline to 28 percent, strongest in mining and manufacturing.

But "employers" declined earlier, and more than "own account workers." The latter at first increased, the 1951 figure being 141 percent of that of 1911, greatest in agriculture, then transport, catering, and distributive trades (Routh 1965: 20). Between 1951 and 1971, these trends reversed: Employers increased by nearly 50 percent, almost back to the 1931 level (the proportion went up by 25 percent), while the number of own-account workers went slightly down. This late increase in employers occurred in most sectors, including manufacturing (Routh 1980: 6–7, 18–20). Overall, absolute numbers increased after 1911, but relative contribution to the labor force slightly declined.

This suggests three British trends: (1) Although in midcentury the upper petite bourgeoisie (employers) declined slightly, this was balanced by an increasing familial petite bourgeoisie (own-account workers). (2) Overall trends may mask intersectoral shifts in opportunity. About 1900, opportunities were greatest in building, later in other service sectors. (3) Small business did relatively better in poor economic times. For example, in the textile industry during 1962–78, small firms weathered a difficult period better than large ones, some making large profits (Chapman 1981: 241). At present, in a stagnant economy, small manufacturers are increasing again (as in all countries).

If fuller occupational statistics existed for earlier periods, undoubtedly they would chart another form of petit bourgeois decline. The 1911 census found few own-account workers among managers and administrators, clerical workers, and skilled, semiskilled, and unskilled workers – only 3 percent of manual workers and 6 percent of skilled manual workers (Routh 1965: 4–5). Earlier, self-employment was much higher, especially among skilled artisans. This was almost certainly the most dramatic occupational shift affecting the petite bourgeoisie, severing its historic connections with manual artisans. The petite bourgeoisie also became workers' landlords (Bechhofer and Elliott 1976). But this is the opposite of proletarianization: The gulf between petite bourgeoisie and working class was widening around 1900, and little happened subsequently to narrow it.

Thus the British petite bourgeoisie became more distinct as a class *fraction*, insulated from below and, to a more variable extent, from above. The relative decline of small business reduced overlap with the capitalist class up to the mid-twentieth century, though this trend is now reversing. Below, the earlier collapse of self-employed artisans severely reduced overlap with the working class and reduced intragenerational mobility between the two. There was a time lag between the two barriers. Until the 1930s, reduced contact with the working class, plus continuing access to larger capitalism, might *increase* petit bourgeois loyalty to the established order. Though many suffered hard times, many in different sectors advanced their fortunes. Uneven experience might prevent collective politics from emerging. After the 1930s, the strengthening upper barrier might intensify fractional distinctiveness – centered on familial organization, informal normative understandings between family and friends, and shared labor exploitation.

Other countries developed differently, as Bairoch et al.'s (1968) compilation of historical censuses reveals. Their categories, "employers and independents" and "family workers," indicate the petite bourgeoisie – more reliably within single countries than in international comparisons, as census definitions vary. I add also the research of the Commission Internationale d'Histoire des Mouvements Sociaux et des Structures Sociales (1981), detailing petit bourgeois organization and politics.

First, agriculture was significant in every other country. Belgium, France, and Germany provide long-term agricultural figures. Although gross agricultural employment has declined through the twentieth century, peasant proprietorship ("employers and independents") has declined least. Peasant proprietors actually increased their dominance over agriculture until the late 1960s, when subsidies helped large farms make inroads throughout the European Economic Community. The number of farmers declined by more than half between 1960 and 1983 (a story outside the scope of this volume).

In other sectors, the earliest figures are Belgian, revealing long-run relative petit bourgeois decline: 40 percent of the 1846 nonagricultural labor force, 30 percent in 1880, 23 percent in 1910, stabilizing until 1945, then down to 19 percent by 1961. Decline occurred in most sectors but was greatest in manufacturing. But absolute numbers differ. Because the nonagricultural labor force increased by more than 250 percent between 1846 and 1910, petit bourgeois numbers increased by 50 percent. Then they held steady. Small business shifted out of heavy industry and textiles into consumer goods and retail trades, becoming complementary, not competitive, with big capital. Autonomous political organization appeared ostensibly as a "third force" between capital and labor, but actually an effective pragmatic pressure group in Belgian multiparty, multicleavage politics (Kurgan 1981: 189–223).

There was no overall relative or absolute French trend from 1866 to 1936. The petite bourgeoisie fluctuated between 33 percent and 43 percent of a fairly static nonagricultural work force. There was then a large relative decline to 19 percent by 1954, then 16 percent by 1962. Most sectors declined although construction rose. But absolute figures held steady as the nonagricultural work force rose. Distinctively French was the longer survival of independent artisans. While other countries moved into mass production, France supplied luxuries world-wide – there was not a fine plantation in Louisiana without a piano bought in Paris (Gaillard 1981: 131–88; Jaeger 1982). Even large enterprises produced in cooperation with small ones, which grew between 1901 and 1931, although tiny family units declined slightly (Bruchey 1981: 68). Small enterprises weathered recessions better. Artisan connections ensured that nineteenth-century petit bourgeois politics remained radical Republican, although it finally shifted right-ward after World War I. Petit bourgeois decline was late, only relative, and uneven.

German figures are difficult to interpret because of changes in territory and classification systems. From 1882 to 1936, there seems to have been a large absolute and a small relative increase in the petite bourgeoisie. Then both trends reversed until 1946, when slight absolute increase resumed as the work force expanded. This was unevenly distributed: Services increased by more than half, manufacturing declined, and construction and transport held steady. Kaufhold (1981: 273–98) dates the collapse of independent manufacturing craftsmen to just before 1900. The sudden collapse is sometimes used to explain why the remaining petite bourgeoisie moved to the extreme right (Haupt 1981: 247–72). But, of course, they were increasing during this period, and only decreased when the Nazis they supposedly supported were in power.

Kiyonari (1981: 961–89) shows that Japanese small business increased massively in absolute, and slightly in relative, employment during the twentieth century. But here booms, not slumps, have increased its share. Small business contains both more deficit-ridden and more highly profitable enterprises. Small business has fully participated in each phase of national development, the latest phase seeing symbiotic participation as subcontractors for assembly industries, high-technology innovation, and expansion in labor-intensive services. We do not find the politics of an autonomous, still less a discontented, petite bourgeoisie.

The U.S. census does not permit such breakdowns, but Bruchey summarizes the American case studies (1981: 995–1035). The collapse of artisans, the decline in small manufacturing, the resilience of small services – all occurred as elsewhere. The growth of manufacturing, both small and large, during the economic expansion of 1870–1900 mirrors the Japanese pattern; but this reverted to the French pattern in the post-1954 boom when numbers fell. The importance of fairly small business in banking is distinctively American, the product of federalism and capitalist liberalism.

Despite national peculiarities, we see three general trends:

1. The petite bourgeoisie has only declined in relative proportion, not absolute numbers, over the last hundred years.

2. The greatest relative decline occurred in the mid-twentieth century, not before, as in Giddens's timetable of decline and as suggested by the notion of an era of "organized capitalism." This was, of course, after the main extremist, Fascist phase of middle-class politics in the 1920s and 1930s. Thus a significant petit bourgeois economic decline (as measured by numbers) could not have been a major determinant of this turbulent politics.[1]

3. Declines, relative or absolute, have been unevenly distributed, leading to fluid movement across sectors.

These trends expose the supposed petit bourgeois decline, economic desperation, and consequent status-panic politics as myth. Moreover, there was a similarity across all countries: Because this was a substantially transnational economy, the period's tremendous economic growth boosted all classes. There were recessions and dislocations; but overall prosperity grew rapidly and included the petite bourgeoisie. Though no longer the leading edge, it was still increasing in absolute numbers. In most countries it was pushed to the manufacturing fringes but colonized services, new and old. Recall an argument of Chapter 4: British industrial enterprises remained small before World War I because they specialized in activities unsuited to corporate treatment. This argument was launched against social scientists' obsession with the corporation, with monopolies, and with authoritative organization in capitalist society. The same obsession has overstated petit bourgeois decline.

The petite bourgeoisie survived in two alternative ways: by following either (1) the pattern of Japan and the United States during 1870–1900 (and Italy after 1945; Weiss 1988) – small business participates fully in growth, finding new, profitable product and service lines; or (2) the French and more normal European pattern – small enterprise weathers recession better, increasing labor exploitation and forgoing profits. Berger (1981) sees this as a normal symbiosis of large and small capital. Where product parts are technologically simple and labor-intensive, or where demand is erratic, giant enterprises contract out to back-street enterprises using low-wage, nonunion labor. These are

[1] Other economic threats, such as inflation or taxation policies, might have disturbed the petite bourgeoisie in the 1920s or 1930s. They did not do so before 1914, that is, within this volume's time frame.

responses to market opportunities, reflecting the essentially diffused rather than authoritative organization of capitalist markets.

Symbiosis of large and small capital has been more prevalent than conflict. Subtracting *Mittelstand* politics and peasants (discussed in Chapter 19), the petite bourgeoisie has contributed little economic action that is distinctive, radical, or anti–big capital. It has remained wedded to capitalism and regimes because it is economically, segmentally dependent on them. Its loyalty has elicited concessions, either as a calculated move to build up support against labor, as in postwar Italy (see Weiss 1988), or as more spontaneous affirmation of capitalist liberalism, as in U.S. antitrust legislation or the politics of Thatcherism.

The gulf between petite bourgeoisie and working class yawned early, as artisans disappeared. Apart from artisans the petite bourgeoisie has not been proletarianized, but has participated segmentally in the circuits of capital. Its economic experience remains distinct as family entwines with work. But its economic power depends on capital, and it has done quite well out of dependence. Its conservatism has resulted not from status panic, ideology, or any of the other semiparanoid psychological reaction formations suggested by such writers as C. Wright Mills (1953) or Poulantzas (1975). Not failure but moderate success and energy-absorbing hard work has ensured petit bourgeois loyalty to capitalism. We shall see that, contrary to stereotype, the petite bourgeoisie was not overrepresented in extreme nationalist movements of this period.

Careerists

Careerists are people employed within, but mobile through, the hierarchical organizations of capitalist corporations and modern state bureaucracies. Before 1914, differences between the two hierarchies sometimes mattered, but they were rooted more in regime politics than in employment relations. Containment within graded, disciplined, segmental hierarchy distinguishes this from other classes or fractions. Containment is both cage and opportunity: *cage* because it cuts off the employee from collective action and allows capital or regime to outflank the careerist, *opportunity* because it permits career movement up (and in principle down) the hierarchy (cf. Abercrombie and Urry 1983: 121). Careerists include many white-collar workers, nonmanual workers, managers, civil servants, salesmen, higher technicians, and the like. They have the weekly or monthly salary, not payment by the hour, normal among manual workers; and some jobs confer a distinct collective identity (clerks are often similar in clothing, bearing, and life-style). But overall life chances are determined less by a single current job than by access to a *career*.

Dahrendorf argues that corporate and bureaucratic careers define a "new middle class" "born decomposed." He concludes (as I do not) that its two main halves belong in two different classes, the ruling and working classes:

A fairly clear as well as significant line can be drawn between salaried employees who occupy positions that are part of a bureaucratic hierarchy and salaried employees in positions that are not. The occupations of the post-office clerk, the accountant, and, of course, the senior executive are rungs on a ladder of bureaucratic positions: Those of the salesgirl [are not]. . . . [T]he ruling-class theory applies without exception to the social position of bureaucrats, and the working class theory equally generally to the social position of white-collar workers. [1959: 55]

This statement contains both sense and oddity. Although the job of the salesgirl may be similar to "working-class" jobs, why should those with careers be considered "ruling class"? It seems bizarre to so term postal clerks (and Dahrendorf later, 1969, modified his view). Highly formalized hierarchies, like that in the post office, "decompose" into distinct sections. Most clerks are mobile only through the lowest of these. They are better viewed as nonmanual versions of steel workers, moving up in an internal manual labor market, rarely attaining higher position. Steelworkers remain steelworkers, and postal clerks remain clerks, not managers, still less members of the ruling class. Actually, career opportunities are often greatest in less bureaucratized structures, as we shall see. Once again this is because capitalism is not very authoritatively organized.

Career employment is recent. The hierarchical organization centrally controlling its personnel was rare in agrarian societies except in some churches and in armies. Chapter 13 shows that early modern states were not bureaucratic. The two industrial revolutions brought only slow career development. The 1851 British census counted 1 percent to 2 percent of occupied persons in salaried employment (excluding armed forces and churches), mostly in railways and the post office, followed by commerce and finance. After 1870, commercial clerks and travelers, accountants, and banking and insurance workers were the fastest-growing salaried category throughout the West. Manufacturing and the civil service still offered few ordered careers. By 1911, clerical and managerial employees made up 7 percent of the British labor force, most in transport and commerce. Bairoch estimates 9 percent in Belgium, 12 percent in France, and 13 percent in Germany, but differences may result from different classification systems. Everywhere salaried employment was four-fifths male, but it was otherwise diverse. I distinguish clerical, sales, and managerial employment.

1. States, commerce, and corporations generated *clerks*. Work and

customer relations were routinized by collecting, storing, and recalling written measures of past and present activities. This required basic discursive literacy, at first in short supply (Perkin 1962). At the beginning, literate tasks were not separated from more senior tasks requiring experience; thus promotion from clerical (and sales) to managerial positions in commerce, industry, and civil service was frequent by midcentury and greater than upward mobility of manual workers (Blumin 1989: 120–1). But with further routinization, mere literacy became separated from other skills. Middle-class mass education, for both boys and girls, ended excess demand. Single women became a "reserve army," literate but not considered promotable by men. Thus clerical jobs deteriorated, though more in some sectors than others: In 1909, 46 percent of male insurance clerks earned more than 160 pounds a year (the income tax minimum), compared to only 10 of railway clerks (Klingender 1935: 20).

2. The diffusion of consumer goods and services expanded *sales* personnel, who needed literacy and "respectability," as most customers were middle class. Again a temporary excess of demand gave way to the same three pressures. Education and women exerted the same debasing pressures in the same periods. Technical requirements of jobs also became debased where sales were mass, low value, and routine, notably in large shops. Where selling affected enterprise fortunes, the connection to higher levels remained and sales careers were maintained.

3. Coordinating complex organizations generated *managers* with discursive literacy and experience in relating diverse pieces of information in an uncertain environment. Some information was learned on the job, but other skills were those cultivated by modern secondary and tertiary education, either technical or searching for relationships in a mass of empirical phenomena too large to memorize. Stratification in educational institutions (discussed later) impacted on the supply of managers: Multilevel recruitment stratified by differential educational qualifications heightened employment divisions within the salariat. About 1900, the gap widened between clerical or sales work and management, and in the civil service between "mechanical" and "intellectual" grades (as noted in Chapter 13).

Large organizations combining all three positions appeared in all sectors near 1900. Clerical, sales, and other specializations separated from managerial coordination. In state administration and in industry with stable product markets, short-distance career hierarchies were entered with distinct education and training. In organizations selling to middle-class customers, middle-class employees were preferred. Amid market uncertainty, especially in finance and commerce, there were more careers. The salaried middle class became decomposed as changes in education and gender relations reinforced the growth of large organizations, and career opportunities grew in financial and commercial sectors. Distinct careerists and a "lower middle class" – with proletarianized jobs and potential for collective action – separated just after 1900.

Thus white-collar jobs were proletarianized in the twentieth century. But the more significant sociological issue, from which class action might flow, is whether their incumbents were also proletarianized. Remember that all salaried employment was expanding. In Britain between 1911 and 1971, nonmanual employees increased almost fourfold in absolute numbers and threefold in relative contribution to the work force. The rate of expansion has been almost as great for managers as for clerical and sales workers (Routh 1980: 6–7). Because gross mobility opportunities rose, perhaps no one lost out in their own working lives or in comparison with fathers or mothers.

Stewart and co-workers conclude from their review of British, American, and Australian data since 1920: "No actual groups of individuals or types of employee has been proletarianized" (1980: 194). The expanding clerical and sales jobs had decomposed into three. First, most debased jobs, from which a career could rarely be expected, became filled by women recruited from manual jobs or from outside the work force (as female participation in education and the formal labor market grew). We can assess the true significance of this for social stratification only by analyzing gender relations (outside my scope here), but it has not been downward mobility or subjectively experienced proletarianization. Second, most other debased jobs, especially in manufacturing, were filled by older, ex–manually employed men moving laterally into less physically demanding work (perhaps with declining health) – again, not proletarianization. Third, true careers remained available to young men entering a low-level clerical or sales position. Their chances of upward mobility were the same in 1970 as in 1920. A current job title, like clerk or sales assistant, does not indicate an unequivocal class position. The destiny of the largest group of occupants, women, has been determined more by gender than by occupation, and younger men have remained middle-class careerists. As employment, educational, and gender relations have entwined, debasement of clerical and sales *jobs* has not proletarianized *people*.

These findings apply to the period since 1920. Some British writers have argued that proletarianization had occurred earlier. Yet their evidence is weak, largely the scattered complaints of young clerks, such as "How then is a man to live and keep a wife on this miserable pittance, and at the same time dress decently?" (quoted by Price 1977: 98; cf. Lockwood 1958: 62–3; Crossick 1977: 20–6). It never had been easy for a young man to maintain a household of a nonworking wife and children on his starting salary. The clerk had long depended on annual increments and promotion. There is no British evidence that these dried up before World War I for young men; there is American evidence that they did not (Blumin 1989: 267–75, 291–2). There is also evidence from several countries (Crew 1973, 1979) of virtually no downward mobility from nonmanual to manual employment. However, World War I did redistribute toward the poor, its burden falling mainly on the lesser salaried; and in Weimar Germany this was then worsened by galloping inflation. Such relative worsening may have influenced the middle class to swing to the extreme Right and to the Nazi party (Blackbourn 1977; Kocka 1980: 28–9). But before and after fascism, and in other countries, it is difficult to find much white-collar suffering.

We academics perch uneasily between profession and careerism. Most of us do not like careerists and clearly feel they *should* have suffered. Historians often depict unattractive personalities and neuroses among late nineteenth-century careerists, supposedly the inventors of a "classic" lower-middle value system. A desperate fear of falling and overweening individual ambition in a harsh environment allegedly isolated the suburban middle class. It became obsessively concerned with appearances, cleanliness, and propriety, suffering repression, tedium, loneliness, and frustration. This impressive catalog of neuroses is drawn by Crossick (1977: 27) from autobiographies by persons from this group. Perhaps academics, also mostly from this class (since the massive postwar university expansion), share a common distaste for origins. White-collar culture is regarded as pathological, only explicable in terms of social suffering turned inward into repression. Distaste clouds interpretation, as in Crossick's use of a contemporary account:

The lower middle class [was] frustrated and lonely. In autobiographies in particular there is an atmosphere of a self-imposed isolation and loneliness. "There is a real home life," wrote Masterman, "strong family affection, little gardens and ornamental villas, ambition for the children." [1977: 27]

Frustration and loneliness or strong family affection – which is it to be?

The careerist is easily mocked. The career integrates the manager and bureaucrat into a segmental hierarchy. Respect for that hierarchy is the condition of career promotion. Apart from the family, it is probably the organization on which the individual most depends. From the Grossmiths in *The Diary of a Nobody* (1892, 1965) to Whyte in *The Organization Man* (1956), writers have poked fun at careerists' conformity, neatness, and cleanliness, anxious yet calculated deference toward superiors, and mimicking of upper-class life-styles and values that gets them slightly, comically wrong. The absence of "masculinity" in such anxieties has been especially derided in what was long an all-male occupation. But none of this is pathological. The careerist's main source of power is movement up an organizational hierarchy determined by his superiors. His "dependents" depend on this. His vision of the world is affected by levels of the hierarchy he can see and those further up he must imagine (and may misperceive). He has been a loyal, disciplined subaltern of capitalism and bureaucracy. It looks as if she will be too.

Thus (along with many others) I reject the notion of a "managerial revolution" put forward by Berle and Means (1932), Burnham (1942), Chandler (1977), and Galbraith (1985). They all suggest that corporate managers have become a distinct class, often opposed to shareholding capitalists, changing enterprise goals – long-term corporate growth is maximized (because salaries depend on that) instead of short-term entrepreneurial profits. But studies have shown no significant differences in the goals or achievements of firms controlled by entrepreneurs and managers, and few managers identify interests opposed to those of shareholders (Nichols 1969; Scott 1979). This evidence was gathered before recent waves of corporate mergers, asset stripping, junk bonds, and so forth, further demonstrated that corporations are essentially capitalistic. Even the high point of "organized capitalism" is better described by C. Wright Mills's notion of the "managerial reorganization of capital." As Scott says:

By virtue of their structural location in the large enterprise the operational managers are committed to the forms of calculation and monetary accounting, criteria of profitability and growth... required by modern capitalist production.... The enterprise is hemmed in by the objective constraints of the market which serve to maintain the enterprise on the lines of capitalist rationality. [1982: 129]

Careerists depend directly on corporate authoritative hierarchies, but these rest on diffused commodity markets. As with all effective diffused power, it is not experienced as constraint but as rationality itself. The careerist's loyalty is rational and sincere. Capitalism works, especially for himself. The economic expansion and stability provided by corporate capitalism and bureaucratic states have been reflected in career development. As individuals, some careerists succeed and others fail, but collectively they have staffed the organizations responsible for most of the sustained economic development of the twentieth century.

Most of my evidence has been taken from the British experience. But there have been few economic differences among the careerists, or, indeed, among lower white-collar workers, of the countries discussed here. Kocka's (1980) comparison of American white-collar workers with German, Britain, and French reveals national differences in class organization. But he attributes them either to different political regimes or to different national working classes (which Chapter 18 also attributes largely to political power relations). None emerges from economic differences among national capitalisms. Across the West careerists experienced a successful, optimistic social milieu (as Blumin emphasizes for the nineteenth century). Their values have dominated our time. Individual mobility and achievement values dominate not in their original entrepreneurial form but as organizational career. The careerist's place in history is not as an individual (unlike the small entrepreneur who had made the Industrial Revolution) but as a loyal subaltern within broader segmental power organizations.

Professionals

The uniqueness of a profession does not easily fit into general theories of class. The word "profession" is routinely used by diverse occupations to claim privileges. No definition will apply equally to all of them – doctors, army officers, quantity surveyors, librarians, nurses – and to the different countries. But as an ideal type a profession is a "learned" (involving technically and culturally valued knowledge) occupation requiring special education, whose practice is formally licensed after negotiations between the state and an occupational organization. I distinguish degrees of professional power, according to the degree to which a license to restrict entry and control practice is in reality controlled by the profession. Thus professional power is essentially authoritative and particularistic, sharply distinguishing most professionals from most careerists – placed by Goldthorpe (1982) and Abercrombie and Urry (1983) in a single "service class."

I borrow most from sociologists of professions that emphasize power rather than function (Freidson 1970; Johnson 1972; Rueschemeyer 1973). Nonetheless, I also accept one functionalist argument: A profession rests partly on socially valued and relevant knowledge for which specialized training is functionally appropriate. This knowledge is never purely scientific and objective, for social power affects how we classify knowledge. In the West, knowledge about ultimate meaning requires only a clerical profession because of the organized power of churches; knowledge about sickness and health has been significantly influenced by doctors' power; nor is it obvious why professions need to acquire "elite" generalist education as well as narrow technical skills. Culturally constructed yet partly functional knowledge classifications form the background of my analysis and give professionals elevated credentials.

Modern society generated specialized knowledges whose practitioners could potentially develop professional power. Whether they did so depended on the ability of consumers to organize authoritatively the supply of these knowledges. There were three main consumers: the capitalist enterprise, the bourgeoisie/middle class; and the state. The first two were diffusely organized (see Chapter 4), and the nineteenth-century state was feeble (see Chapter 14). None could authoritatively control what their own demand generated. As occupations organized collectively in the interstices of authoritative power, they became professions. But professional opportunities declined in the early twentieth century as capitalist corporations and state bureaucracies increased authoritative powers. Thereafter, the strongest autonomous professions, notably medicine, serviced dispersed individuals and households (of whatever class), and weaker "semi-professions" serviced corporations and states. Yet this balance of authoritative power only explains the individual profession's power. To arrive at the common middle-class position of professions, I add more diffused power networks.

"Profession" originally referred to persons professing Christian faith as a life vocation. By 1700, it had expanded to four organizations: the church, law, medicine, and the military. These professions became (1) learned and (2) technical, (3) with an esprit de corps (weakest in medicine), and (4) professing an ethic of service to society mediated by (5) service to the state (weakest for most clerics). Chapter 12 discusses how officers became further professionalized as a distinct caste within the state. Then capitalist industrialization generated other occupations professing these same five qualities.

As capitalism became industrial, its technical base expanded. Fixed investment in machines and plant and the technical requirements of labor grew. Artisans and jobbing engineers led the early Industrial Revolution, along with entrepreneurs. Their guilds and journeymen organizations (discussed in Chapter 15) now split. Most of those whose skills, no matter how elevated, were central to the productive process of the capitalist enterprise and could be controlled and learned within it, became mere craftsmen. Most of those whose skills were interstitial to the enterprise and were too generalist to be profitably taught within it, might attain professional autonomy. Most industries now encountered science – making steel out of ores with low phosphorus content, or using electricity to power telegraphy. Other problems were more technical than scientific – buildings and vehicles containing heavy, juddering machines required architectural and surveying improvements. Business finance became complex, thus accountants, as did legal concerns, thus business lawyers. Enterprises remained small and these services were not the main point of their activity.

Both consumers and suppliers of knowledges turned to the state to issue licenses to bodies of competent specialists. As Chapter 11 shows, states were keen because they raised revenue from licensing. In Britain a wave of licensing lasted from 1818 (civil engineers) through 1848 (architects) and 1865 (chartered surveyors) to 1880 (chartered accountants) – taking in along the way gas engineers, electrical engineers, municipal engineers, and chemists. All professional bodies shared entry controls negotiated with state (and private) educational institutions. They still do.

The emerging corporation then extended authoritative controls over the work practices of employed "staff" professionals, who became subject to "line" management (a stronger distinction than in its original military manifestation). These staff moved halfway out of the profession toward the career. About 1900, accountancy became subject to the corporation, first through internal company control, then through accounting to the external risk bearer in joint-stock companies by public audit. In the twentieth century many professional firms themselves became large corporations. By the 1930s, a few large accountancy firms were auditing the books of most major corporations, parallel to the emergence of "corporate mega-lawyering" (Galanter 1983). Accountants' and lawyers' remaining professional autonomy probably derives from services provided to dispersed small businesses and middle-class families. But in business- and state-related professions, the practice (though not the initial entry) of professionals is not sharply distinguished from that of corporate and bureaucratic careerists.

Countries developed their own professional practices. The revolutionary American resistance to professional monopolies and weaker state regulation combined with earlier economic concentration to enhance corporate power over professionals. Elsewhere late industrialization brought large corporations and greater state regulation, both lessening professional educational autonomy. German and French professional qualifications came to matter more in combination with elite state education and the career civil service – in France the *grandes écoles*; and in Germany the state was even more dominant over the *Akademiker* and, through the notion of "professional bureaucrats," *Beamten*. Yet these are variations on a theme: Professional power was useful yet interstitial to the early organizations of capitalism and the modern state but then became more subjected to their growing authoritative power.

Medical professional power did not decline. Before the eighteenth century, physicians, surgeons, apothecaries, grocers, barbers, village priests, learned men, and village sages of both sexes all undertook diagnosis and cure. Then science and training increased and local medical associations appeared, then merged or standardized rules. Urban density spread diseases that threatened all classes. Class interest, charity, and enlightened and utilitarian faith in scientific progress all demanded state licensing. In 1855, the Worcester Medical and Surgical Society became the British Medical Association. Legislation in 1858 placed all licensing corporations under what became the association's general council, compiling a register of qualified practitioners. This state-licensed body still defines who is a doctor: "A doctor is a person endowed by the law of a sovereign state with certain rights, privileges and duties, not conferred on others within the jurisdiction of that state" (MacKenzie 1979: 55). Freidson comments sardonically: "The most strategic and treasured characteristic of the profession – its autonomy – is, therefore, owed to the sovereign state from which it is not ultimately autonomous" (1975: 23–4).

But as Freidson documents, authoritative powers over the medical profession failed. It controls its own licensing in all Western countries, as consumers and the state have been rendered ineffective. Although radicals argue that consumers could control their own health care (Illich 1977), a high-tech medical model of health predominates that consumers cannot evaluate – more the product of medical power than functional necessity, as medicine has contributed less to the massive health improvements of the last 150 years than improvements in diet, wages, housing, and environment (McKeown 1976; Hart 1985). Professional power was also achieved before the medical model was institutionalized. Medical power grew across the nineteenth century. Doctors previously treating prominent families now serviced many bourgeois and middle-class families in anonymous suburbs. Patients could no longer communicate collectively, and doctors could define their services in technical-professional terms (Waddington 1977). Goode (1969) also observes that doctors – and other autonomous professionals like psychotherapists, the clergy, lawyers, and university teachers – intrude into privacy. Client fears of ill health, madness, morality, and crime and retribution, and assessment of intellect, involve anxieties and vulnerabilities difficult to share with others. Clients are loath to organize, and therefore they defer. Need for personal privacy guarantees professional power. Professional power survives best when dealing with dispersed clients.

The state also lost control of licensing. As Chapter 14 emphasizes, nineteenth-century states rarely intervened in domestic civil society. The British state would do little without citizen pressure, and this pressure was for neutral infrastructures, not managerial intervention – except over the poor. The state lacked expert knowledge to check the profession, and its few specialists were themselves medical professionals.

The Privy Council was to supervise the 1858 license, but after an initial flurry of interest in public health, its medical office became controlled by the profession, which could now infiltrate higher education, municipal health, and the Poor Law. Poor Law hospitals pioneered twentieth-century "heroic surgery." Such professional power has endured through the creation of National Health Services.

Medical power over practice, and (to a slightly lesser extent) over qualifications, is now standard in the Western world, cutting across the formal employment relations stressed by many theorists of class. Whether employed by the state, capitalist insurance enterprises, or in partnerships or self-employment, doctors are preeminently professionals. Their skills, initially supplied to the bourgeois family, were supplied to all twentieth-century citizens. Neither citizens nor states have exercised authoritative control over them. Perhaps the greatest checks are now arising in countries like the United States, where large insurance companies are capable of greater authoritative power.

The state has been stronger dealing with more recent would-be professionals. The growth of state functions described in Chapter 14 – further expanding in the twentieth century – created new specialized knowledges. The first large group, appearing in the late nineteenth century, were schoolteachers, whose political significance will become clear later. They were followed, about 1900, by other learned occupations – social workers, librarians, town planners, and so forth – with lesser powers, often termed "semiprofessions." The state, often a monopoly employer, controls the supply of services more directly. In the twentieth century, the semiprofessions became feminized. Women now form a majority in most of them, and women have less power in society. Semiprofessionals blur the boundaries between career and lower white-collar employment.

But the direct "relations of production" of the higher professions differ from other classes and class fractions, and they distance them more from capitalism than the employment organizations of petite bourgeoisie or bureaucratic careerists. They do not fit well into Marxian classification schemes such as Wright's. But professionals also share common involvement in the more diffused organizations of capitalist nation-states. Considering these will lead us toward the integrating role of diffused power among all three fractions.

1. Professionals charge fees, determined partly by the profession (perhaps negotiating with the state, insurance companies, etc.) and partly by diffused market forces. They are less constrained by segmental, upward-oriented employment organizations than careerists. Fees also enable more of them to live and intermarry in upper-middle-class reaches and to purchase privileged consumer goods. The recent tendency

of corporations to subcontract out professional services has enhanced opportunity for fee-taking professionals.

2. Entry into the profession is affected by two diffuse characteristics of capitalist nation-states: elevated education and training and (less universally) wealth to finance unpaid apprenticeship and professional partnerships. These restrict entrants to relatively privileged families, and elevated education permits professional participation in elite culture. Yet dependence on education may separate them from the true capitalist class. As Parkin (1979: 54–73) observes, most capitalist property is inherited directly by sons and daughters from their parents, whereas most inheritance of educational credentials is indirect and imperfect. Education thrusts professionals' children into competitive mobility alongside other middle-class children, whereas as adults it puts them with higher social groups. Such differences reduce what might otherwise be a single capitalist-professional class.

3. As we have seen, clients affect professional power. Client demand has come from capitalist and middle-class families and businesses, the main exceptions being semiprofessions and medicine.(General access to health care is provided by the state and insurance plans.) Professionals perform class services for their clients. As Cain observes of English solicitors:

Clients are typically the institutions (legal persons) of capitalist society and middle class people [thus lawyers are] conceptive ideologists... who think, and therefore constitute the form of, the emergent relations of capitalist society . . . the organic intellectuals of the bourgeoisie. [1983: 111–2]

Lawyers participate diffusely in the circuits of capital.

4. Diffusion also affects professional organizations. They work for state or business, or they operate partnerships that are themselves capitalist enterprises (where fees are scaled by their profession, they are monopoly price-fixing corporations). Professional powers are partly expressed through quasi-capitalist enterprises or quasi-state departments.

Thus capitalist nation-states exert diffuse constraints on professions whose direct "labor process" otherwise confers autonomy. Thus, in matters of political economy, professionals are usually loyal allies of capital. Over redistribution, their interests lie with the wealthy, the secure, the work-controlling, the well educated. Over property ownership, they resist collective controls. True, on humanitarian and moral issues they are often liberal, partly because of elite education, through the twentieth century becoming more liberal. In such respects semiprofessionals are more autonomous. They have more diverse clients and are often torn in their professional role between citizen needs and social control. They depend on education but of a generalist, less privilege-protective kind; they rarely depend on wealth or corporate organization. Their incomes are usually lower, though comfortable. They are disproportionately women. Thus some semiprofessionals developed mildly radical politics through the twentieth century.

Three fractions of a single class

All three middle-class fractions have distinct relations of production. If used, as in some productivist theories, as the sole criterion of class position, this would yield three separate classes. But they also share segmental participation in capitalism and the nation-state. I begin with capitalism.

1. The three fractions participate in economic hierarchy. Dahrendorf believed this favored a decomposed theory. From investment consultants to jobbing building workers among the petite bourgeoisie, from surgeon to primary school teacher among professionals, from marketing director to salesman among careerists – differences between such positions are great. Yet this, paradoxically, integrates the middle class. This is obvious for careerists: "Anticipatory socialization" secures common consciousness across hierarchical levels. Among the petite bourgeoisie growth aspirations also integrate. Most small business gets bigger upgrading its clientele, developing symbiosis with bigger business or wealthier consumers. Professional hierarchy comprises securing partnerships and honors. All three structure mobility up through the middle class. Blockages may unionize erstwhile careerists and mildly radicalize semiprofessionals, but hierarchical mobility binds most of the middle class into upward disciplined loyalties.

2. The middle class consumes distinctively (as neo-Weberians note). The late nineteenth-century middle class participated in a consumer economy, purchasing variety in foodstuffs and clothing, purchasing or securely renting a separate dwelling, employing a servant girl. Its male household heads normally qualified to vote under property franchises. In broader franchises they might control local urban politics. The ability to employ the labor of another was a crucial class badge. In 1851, in York, 60 percent of "small shopkeepers, lower professionals, farmers, etc." employed at least one servant, compared to 10 percent of skilled and virtually no semiskilled or unskilled workers (Armstrong 1966: 234, 272–3). My grandmother's accounts for 1901 reveal the nonworking wife of a man with a small gardening business paying "2s 6d" weekly wages (about the price of a chicken) to a girl who slept in the kitchen.

Distinct middle-class consumption was then transformed and eventually declined. Progressive income tax and World War I reduced domestic service. The masses were slowly admitted to the economy of secure varied consumption. In all characteristics save one (employment of servants) working-class consumption tended to mirror middle-class consumption of the previous decade or two. Workers acquired variety of foodstuffs and clothing, secure dwellings, suburbs, cars, insurance, mortgages – eventually the cancerous substances – already associated with the middle class.

3. The three fractions can convert income into small investment capital. This was already happening in the railway boom of the 1840s. (See Chapter 4.) Investment in their own business is essential to the petite bourgeoisie, and many professionals buy a partnership or practice. Careerists receive stocks in their corporation and may use personal expertise in consultancy or investment. Most can pass a little capital to children. Middle-class marriage differed from working-class marriage from the 1930s to the early 1960s in Britain by parents' helping young couples with house purchase (Bell 1969). Through the mid-twentieth century, predominantly middle-class savings were channeled through occupational pension plans, insurance, and mortgages. Up to the 1950s in the United States, slightly later in Europe, such investments divided most middle-class from most working-class families. Their savings, debts, and life projects (housing, career, retirement) entered the central circuits of capital and benefited from capitalism's boom. Few workers had savings, and they often placed debts with subcultural talleymen (moneylenders) or pawnshops. Middle-class savings became identical in form to the property of the very wealthiest.

Thus whatever their peculiarities and internal diversity, the three fractions of the middle class have shared diffused capitalist participation in segmental hierarchies, class consumption badges, and the conversion of surplus income into supplementary investment capital. About 1900, the middle class was everywhere expanding, prospering, participating in a new form of economic society. Civil society *was* middle-class society, as the German term for both, *burgerlich Gesellschaft*, reveals. But this society was also entwined with, and partly defined by, ideological and political citizenship.

Middle-class ideological citizenship

Earlier chapters argue that "nations" emerging at the beginning of the nineteenth century centered on alliances between modernizing old regimes and the petite bourgeoisie. The core modernizers were liberal civil servants and professionals. Much national organization came through networks of discursive literacy, from ideological citizenship. Now new classes demanded political citizenship, and ideological citizenship – carried principally by state-financed or state-regulated education – helped merge nation and state into a nation-state.[2]

As we have seen, middle-class wealth depended increasingly on formal education. The petite bourgeoisie has been least dependent, but the others depended far more on education than either capitalist or working class, especially before World War I. The expansion of state education was partly a function of the job requirements of capitalism and modern states, as described earlier. But it also reflected dominant class desires for social control and subordinate class desires for "ideological citizenship" – revealing the class and national crystallizations of the state. The "credentialism" often identified as central to middle-class life was itself shaped by these.

Class biases in education were transparent. Tripartite segregation of schools existed throughout Europe (though not in America). Because fee paying was almost universal, wealth also stratified. The lowest level, the elementary school, was not usually preparatory to the secondary school. It comprised the entire educational experience of the lower classes. Secondary education then divided into lower "modern" schools and higher "classical" schools that controlled university entrance. Germany had most state control. Government ran the classical *Gymnasium* and the modern *Realgymnasium* and *Oberrealschule*, and set the qualifications necessary for entry (usually from the former) into universities and thence into the civil service and professions. The French government controlled the classical *lycées* and colleges and the "special" – from 1891 on the "modern" – schools and the different qualifications they conferred. The *lycées* were typical of classical schooling throughout Europe: The study of philosophy, letters, history and geography took up 77 percent of *lycée* hours in 1890. In Britain, most schools were private, but state regulation increased after 1902. Three separate royal commissions embodied British tripartism. The Clarendon Commission (1861) evaluated the nine great public (i.e., private) schools' training of national leaders. The Taunton Commission (1864) evaluated schools for "those large classes of English society which are comprised between the humblest and the very highest." The Newcastle

---

[2] My sources on nineteenth-century education were, for Britain, Musgrove (1959), Perkin (1961), Smith (1969), Sutherland (1971), Middleton and Weitzman (1976), Hurt (1979), Reeder (1987), Simon (1987), and Steedman (1987); for France, Harrigan (1975), Gildea (1980), and Ringer (1987); for Germany, Muller (1987) and Jarausch (1982, 1990); for the United States, Krug (1964), Collins (1979), Kocka (1980), and Rubinson (1986); plus the comparative analyses of Ringer (1979), Kaelble (1981), and Hobsbawm (1989: chapters 6 and 7).

Commission (1858) examined cheap schooling up to age eleven for the "laboring classes."

Because America lacked a cultured aristocracy and professions and a large civil service, its public education lagged. Until the end of the century, stratification was not much developed by schools or universities, except at the very top. Even when mass public schooling emerged, class segregation was restricted by party democracy's politicization of school issues. Most schools were run by local government, the most democratic of the three levels of the American federal polity. The exception of the South – effective schooling for whites only – remained.

In this period, the middle class became full or nearly full political citizens. Educational expansion was the principal result, enabling middle-class families to share in the cultural life of the nation and to distinguish themselves from workers and peasants below. This began to involve girls as well as boys. State-aided primary education and modern secondary education expanded between two- and fivefold, and university student numbers tripled in Western countries between the late 1870s and 1913. But European expansion remained segregated. British boys were taught mostly in private elementary schools to "read a short ordinary paragraph in a newspaper, write a similar passage of prose from dictation, and calculate 'sums in practice on bills of parcels.'" This was believed necessary to qualify the boy as a clerk and to enable him to participate in national cultural life. Only a few workers' children attended such schools and not all became literate. A series of education acts between 1870 and 1902 then expanded state elementary education, which was stratified between middle- and working-class children. Workers' children were taught discipline, reliability, and cleanliness as much as academic skills, and their education was usually not preparatory for secondary education. Middle-class children, including many girls, mostly continued on to secondary schools.

Expansion also segregated middling from upper-class occupations. The German higher civil service and professions were staffed overwhelmingly from the classical schools and universities; the middling civil service, lower professionals, and managerial positions, from the modern schools; and those who dropped out from schools or universities tended to staff lower positions than those who completed their studies – and dropouts from modern schools staffed lower white-collar occupations. In France and Britain, similar patterns were evident, except that most financial and commercial positions were also filled by the classically educated. In European and American universities, there was a net outflow from business: more children of businessmen entering universities than there were graduates going into business. Universities remained stratified, older upper-class universities (Oxbridge, the Ivy

League, etc.) remaining the elite ones, fraternities instilling traditional values in what might have otherwise been a "rising bourgeoisie."

Thus university-trained professionals, civil servants, and financial and commercial careerists became "learned" and "cultured," not just technically qualified like those below them and in manufacturing. Educational segregation also enabled "managers" to separate as an apparently functional category distinct from most clerks and salespersons; it then enabled literate middle-class girls to enter these positions in large numbers. Nonmanual separated ever more clearly from manual, though blurred by gender relations. Employment class relations were now thoroughly entwined with educational segregation.

Almost all contributors to the tangled debate on social mobility in this period agree that educational segregation was deliberately contrived by ruling regimes and that it prevented much long-range upward mobility. Because the highest positions increased far less than middling and technical positions, and because education was expanding, regimes became conscious of the potential overcrowding of "learned" occupations. Segregation was thus an attempt to protect their own children. Yet this did not result in mass discontent among the middle class. After all, middling-level occupational opportunities were expanding the most, segregation was also protecting them from competition below, and schooling itself socialized and disciplined children into loyalty to the tripartite hierarchy of "classical learning" over "modern technique" over "mere literacy."

During the twentieth century, most formal educational segregation ended. All children could enter (except at the highest level) without fees, and all formally progressed meritocratically. Education was not solely owned by the middle and upper classes after World War I. Selective secondary education expanded, bringing in many workers' children. Now the influence of class background became less direct. Twentieth-century attendance at British selective secondary shcools has hovered around 70 percent among children of professionals, managers, and large proprietors; 40 percent among those of lower non-manuals; and 20 percent to 25 percent among those of workers (Little and Westergaard 1964; Halsey et al. 1980: 18, 62–69). International comparisons reveal few differences in inequality of access to higher levels of education (although the United States seems somewhat more open than European countries). All admitted many workers' children in the early twentieth century while preserving middle-class dominance. First selective secondary, then tertiary education, integrated the twentieth-century middle class.

These are variations on a theme: the growth of a middle-class ideological citizenship. Economic power depended on state education and therefore on the struggle for citizenship. The middle class participated in an ideological citizenship whose content and opportunities was defined by its betters.

But this was not merely education reinforcing class. It also intensified the state's *national* crystallization. As I have argued throughout, political struggles concern what states actually *do* in any period. Chapter 14 shows that education was the principal state growth and the principal civil activity in the late nineteenth century. In most countries, government (central, regional, or local) took over private schools or expanded their own, leaving private schools as enclaves in an increasingly public system. Thus the period saw political conflict (often severe) between a secular, centralized state and a regional-religious alliance of decentralizers and churches. Where the state contained an established church, the dissidents' alliance was normally between regionalists and minority churches, as in Britain and Germany. Those depending most on education – teachers and state careerists above all, then other professionals, then private sector careerists – became most loyal to the secular centralizing state, identifying most strongly with the emerging nation-state. But as the states were themselves polymorphous and middle-class persons also had local-regional and religious community identities, emerging ideological citizenships and nationalisms varied.

Middle-class political nationalism

I have suggested that economic power relations would push middle-class men toward conservatism. Segmental hierarchical loyalties, prosperity, cultural privilege and complacency, rarity of proletarianization, integration into capitalist investment channels, desire to distinguish themselves in consumption, culture, and qualifications from workers – all these encouraged conservatism. We should not expect political excitement and extremism, nor proletarian alliances or socialist sympathies, but cosy middle-class conservatism. If states were merely capitalist, without other significant crystallizations, the middle class might bore the historian.

But it has not done so. Historians have detected an excited *political nationalism* among the middle class. Virtually every study of nationalism and every study of nationalist pressure groups burgeoning during this period conclude that nationalism was essentially middle class or petit bourgeois (with the qualification that, as in other nonlabor voluntary associations, most top positions in the pressure groups were held by notables). But the studies actually contain little evidence to test this assertion. They do only in Germany, where the evidence, cited here, actually shows a different pattern. Historians of other countries parrot one another's undocumented assertions and then proceed to explain *why* the middle class was nationalistic.

Hobsbawm (1990: 121–2), in defending his argument that *prewar* nationalism is essentially petit bourgeois, actually refers to *postwar* evidence on German Nazis. However, he is wrong even there: The Nazi evidence shows the same (non–petit bourgeois) patterns that I document for prewar Germany. Coetzee (1990) is an exception, admitting his data permit no generalizations about who the nationalists were. Supposed middle-class or petit bourgeois nationalism is said to reflect anxieties, insecurities, and desire for an authority figure in fatherland or motherland – "frustrated," "unhappy," "status panic" responses to economic concentration and the encroachments of labor (Howard 1970: 103–4; Wehler 1979: 131–2; Hobsbawm 1989: 152, 158–9, 181; Hobsbawm 1990: 117–22). Others see middle-class nationalism as the sublimation of economic and sexual frustrations by transferring evil to foreign agencies. I rejected pathological theories of the economic behavior of the petite bourgeoisie (since it was doing well). I do the same for middle-class politics now.

Pathological theories see a common Western pattern, caused by the impact on the middle class of the Second Industrial Revolution and the proletariat. Yet bourgeois nationalism was not uniform. It was also not very distinctive, for it reflected, sometimes exaggeratedly, the dilemmas of the various ruling regimes.

I first assess the threat from below. Mass worker and peasant movements impacted from the 1880s. Chapter 19 shows that peasant politics did not much threaten the middle class. Labor was more problematic. Yet in its direct relations of production, labor confronted only the petite bourgeoisie, whose interests lay in cheap labor and in resisting union organizing rights. Professionals were relatively uninvolved with capital-labor conflict; though careerists sometimes were involved, they had no direct interest in any single solution to labor relations. Although managers and bureaucrats might exercise the "global functions of capital" (Carchedi 1977), they could do this by repression or conciliation. Because in practice workers' parties sought mutualism and joint regulation, not the overthrow of capitalism, managers and bureaucrats might support them. From their direct relations of production, we might expect petit bourgeois hostility but varying professional and careerist stances to labor.

It was once again in "political economy," that is, in the economy of the state, that the interests of middle and working classes began to collide more. If workers were admitted in reality as well as formally to citizenship, states would no longer be essentially middle class. Workers would outnumber middle-class voters and might redirect political economy toward their own interests. Interests centered, as I have emphasized that politics usually had, on the costs and benefits of the state.

State *costs* meant revenue, now the choice between potentially progressive direct taxes and regressive indirect taxes and revenue from "state property." As Chapter 11 shows, although the tax burden was not now high, it remained regressive. When military expenditures rose after 1890, the protest of worker and peasant parties got louder. State *benefits* had shifted considerably over the century. The "fruits of office" no longer existed in the traditional corrupt sense. But bureaucratization meant offices went to the educated, and the best offices went to the "learned." So did careerist positions in commerce and manufacturing and so did professional monopolies. Technical credentials were embedded in a national cultural life that middle-class men (even women) shared in, while few workers did. The labor movement increasingly demanded ideological citizenship, that is, education, more than it demanded anything else from the state apart from union organizing rights. But because the state was now acquiring many other civil functions, other state services also became benefits. Labor was just beginning to seek to redirect services to itself and to convert state controls into services (for example, Poor Laws into social citizen rights). Class collision over political economy was not severe until late in World War I, but it had appeared by 1900. Fiscal redistribution and universal education now pitted middle against working class.

But this was not invariant, and rarely led to head-on class confrontation. In America the main political parties were not much divided by class; in Britain and France they were only a little more. Other political crystallizations crosscut class conflict, differing among regions and countries. Kocka (1980) shows that whereas American white-collar workers seem not to have feared the proletariat at all, German ones did greatly. The two American "classes" joined the same political parties – and if American clerks felt aggrieved, they joined similar unions. But Germans joined parties and unions antagonistic to workers and they were more conscious of being class opponents. Relations between these classes in Britain and France fell between these two extremes, though in different ways. National differences resulted because classes and political economy entwined with three main political crystallizations:

1. Although the middle class achieved *party democracy* during the nineteenth century, it did so to different degrees and in different ways. By the 1880s (earlier in the United States), it had full political citizenship in all three liberal countries. By 1900, their elections were less dominated by notables and segmental patron-client parties than by

mass membership parties and pressure groups. Mass meetings and impersonal electioneering were aimed primarily at the middle class. In Austria and Germany, property and curial franchises and limited parliamentary sovereignties had conferred somewhat lesser party democracy and regimes did more dividing and ruling. The middle class was admitted into the state only partly, and the working class was left quite outside and repressed. In Austria, divide and rule also involved nations and sometimes also excluded national middle classes. The United States was at the opposite extreme, with no exclusion by class. Britain and France were in the middle. British franchise extensions right through the century and French regime changes up to the 1880s allocated citizenship according to property, but this did not neatly separate classes. By 1900, for example, most British skilled workers possessed the vote (and collective organizing rights) alongside the middle class, while less skilled workers did not. Party democracy in the United States consisted of cross-class alliances; in Britain and France, this was partially so; and in Germany and Austria (such as it was), it was class-divided.

Thus German and Austrian political economy most pitted class against class, then French and British, with this happening least in America. Middle classes with similar economic power relations differed greatly in their stance toward lower classes because they were inserted differently into party democracy.

2. As indicated earlier, education also involved varied *national* crystallizations, centering on religious and regional networks. This created many possibilities for cross-class alliances – for example, a progressive alliance between secular centralizers (France), or between secularists and minority religions (Britain), or an antistatist alliance among excluded labor, regionalists, and minority religion (this alliance never quite materialized in Germany, but the possibility deeply affected nationalism there). These crystallizations actually dominated Austrian politics, bringing far broader and more state-subverting entwinings of class, regional-nation, and religion.

3. Prewar nationalisms differed considerably because states' *militarist* crystallizations so differed. America was expansionist, but not against other major Powers. Britain wished at first only to preserve global free trade and to defend the global empire it already had, but then turned to stiffen defenses against rising German power. France switched from colonial expansion to a defensive mode as its own and neighbors' territories seemed threatened by Germany. Though no Power of the period saw itself as an aggressor, the Austrian and German regimes came to believe attack was the best form of defense. Fear of cross-border nationalism (Austria) and encirclement (Germany) led them to

more aggressive geopolitics. It would indeed be proof of the irrational, paranoid character of the middle class if in countries in such different geopolitical cicumstances the middle class everywhere espoused militarist nationalism. But it did not. Indeed, all these three political crystallizations interacted with class conflict to generate very different nationalisms.

American imperial expansion in the nineteenth century ran little risk of war with other Great Powers. The United States sank only Spain's wooden navy. Because U.S. involvement in Cuba, the Philippines, and China was small in scale and carried few risks, there was little popular mobilization for or against imperialism. Nationalist pressure groups were weak and particularistic. Imperialism was driven more by presidential power and supported by interested senators, geopoliticians like Admiral Mahan, a few newspaper magnates, missionary groups, and (especially) sectional business groups with interests in those particular areas. It was opposed by a motley collection of other special business interests, liberals, racists seeking to avoid entanglements with nonwhite peoples, and Irish and German immigrants fleeing from militarism and conscription in Europe (Lasch 1958; Healy 1963, 1970; LaFeber 1963; Beisner 1975; Welch 1979; see also essays in Hollingsworth 1983). Rystad (1975: 167) dissents somewhat, emphasizing growing antiimperialism in the Democratic party in this period. But mass middle-class political nationalism is hard to find in America. Because (as we shall see later) state education contributed substantially to nationalism in other countries, the sparsity and local control of America's schools may have helped damp down nationalism.

There was not much more aggressive nationalism in nineteenth-century Britain. The British Empire was already in place and needed little citizen defense. Stiff resistance in India was countered by small professional armies reinforced with Indian levies, "natives" elsewhere in small contingents. British nationalism was more a firm sense of identity than of opposition – of who "we" were (though with our peculiar dual English-British, Scottish-British, etc., identities). Britain and America both developed rather idealized, liberal, and ostensibly pacific nationalisms. Britain had carried civilization, Parliament, and the Pax Britannica across the globe. America provided the "city on the hill," the shining beacon of the "freest people on earth." Both nations showed considerable savagery against "natives." But few in the party democracies saw much point in attacking other Great Powers. (I investigate the general argument that "liberal" states are pacific in Chapter 21.)

There was more aggressive nationalism in nineteenth-century France, but it was rarely middle class. True, *la grande (et bourgeoise) nation* had invented popular imperialism, but after 1815 it regretted its impetuosity. The middle class remained relatively indifferent to the imperialism espoused by monarchist regimes, by Louis Bonaparte, and by economic pressure groups seeking profits abroad. It was struggling to secure its republic against these very forces. When success eventually came after 1870, the middle-class nation remained Republican, anticlerical, and predominantly antimilitarist. Careerist and professional middle-class fractions were especially loyal, as educational institutions were firmly Republican. By contrast, petit bourgeois organizations moved to the right from the 1890s on, toward social Catholicism and a conservative, though not extremist, nationalism (Nord 1981). But in France nationalism was a contested ideology. Teachers and civil servants appear to have been the most "national" in the sense of being loyal to the Republic. Beginning in the 1870s, French education was gradually secularized and standardized, aimed at inculcating Republican virtues throughout the entire country (Moody 1978). In the villages and towns of France the schoolmaster personified and extolled the Republic, patriotism, and secular civic duty (Weber 1976: 332–8; Singer 1983) – but not aggressively: Textbooks contained little hostility toward other Western powers, although they taught that France had a special cultural duty to civilize backward races (Maingueneau 1979).

Paranoid theory ignores the success of liberal bourgeois civilization and the celebratory mood of its nationalisms. In Britain, it was more moralistic, romantic, and sentimental than aggressive; in America, a more positive affirmation of freedom and individual virility; and in France, essentially "modern" and secular. These middle classes had risen to full citizenship, transforming ruling class nations into nation-states. Their sense of nationhood represented bourgeois success, not failure.

The status quo held for America into World War I. But about 1900, British and French national feelings developed slightly more militarism as German Great Power aspirations seemed to rise. The French had been invaded and defeated in 1870–1 and many felt threatened again after 1900. Although the Left had been the main carrier of patriotism in the 1870s, the Right now took over – though its monarchism and clericalism weakened the appeal of its patriotism. The French middle class was also split by having two seeming class enemies, one above, the other below. Its antipathy to the old regime steered its large Radical party into an alliance with the Left to secure the triumph of the secular, educated state and Republican control of the military. Once this was secured, just after 1900, bourgeois parties moved somewhat to the Right, at the same time as the German threat revived. But this switched nationalism from global, colonial expansion to local national defense. The more aggressive nationalist parties dwindled (although they remained significant in the universities) before the war as Republican and Radical Centrist factions and French governments alike became more patriotic and accepted rearmament. But their patriotism was overwhelmingly defensive: rearmament to cope with an expected German attack. Many French patriots (somewhat overconfidently) exulted that this would lead to the recovery of Alsace-Lorraine, but no major politician advocated attacking Germany (all this is indebted to Eugen Weber 1968). They compromised conflicts over political economy and conscription, just in time to mount the defensive effort of 1914. French middle-class and working-class nationalism did not embarrass the regime but reinvigorated and saved it – with great heroism and sacrifice of life, thus strengthening the nation-state.

British imperialism, secure and more laissez-faire, had carried a liberal, ostensibly pacific ideology. Before 1880, imperialism had an architecture and statuary but little popular lobby. The few demonstrations were organized by humanitarian and religious groups attacking imperial policy (Eldridge 1973) or in the context of party politics or by pressure groups with economic interests abroad or in an expanded army. The death of General Gordon in the Sudan in 1885, marking a new phase of tougher "native" resistance, brought the first major imperialist demonstrations to the street. By the 1890s, imperialism was a "popular nostrum for curing depression and unemployment, for easing national insecurity and ensuring future greatness," says Robinson (1959: 180).

Imperialist ideology first centered more on anti-"native" than anti-European feeling, but France, then Germany also become objects of attack. Imperialism and a "quest for national efficiency" influenced both parties, resonating among the social Darwinism of the period. Liberal imperialists focused on building national strength through better physical and moral "health" and education for the working class; Conservatives, on empire and power abroad. I showed in Chapter 14 how all this was intended to rally the intense emotions of the family and "maternalism" to the extensive nation.

After about 1900, racism developed a peculiar ambivalence. It had earlier articulated Europeans' sense of superiority (sometimes mixed with vulnerability) in relation to "backward" peoples. Physical phenotypes defined race: The white race dominated the yellow, brown, and black races. Although imperial racism had largely perverted Enlightenment ideals, it was similarly transnational. But increasing social density, state infrastructures, and linguistic and sometimes also religious community now gave racism a national definition, especially among state-reinforcing nations (which by now also included Germany).

Ideologists for the Anglo-Saxon, the Frank, the Teuton, the Slav "race" developed a mythological history of common descent. In the 1900s, British politicians and popular writers used the word "race" in a perfectly routine way to refer to the British people, in discussing problems of the empire, *and* in regard to economic rivalry with Germany – even with the United States. Thus racism was not unitary but split, as Europe had always been split, between the transnational and the national.

But to go from a commonsense racial notion of the nation to the next step of advocating aggressive quasi-racist nationalism was far less common. It was far less sustainable than was imperial racism by contemporary biological science. In Britain, it was sometimes favored by newspaper magnates and Rightist pressure groups like the Navy League, the National Service League, the Imperial Maritime League, and the Primrose League. Some historians claim that these pressure groups had middle-class roots, though none provides any actual evidence of the class composition of members or activists (Fieldhouse 1973; Fest 1981; Summers 1981). Officer Training Corps and Reserves, Boy Scouts, and national cultural organizations provided a more respectable and, it is assumed, predominantly middle-class environment in which aggressive nationalists thrived (Kennedy 1980: 381–3). The most recent study, by Coetzee (1990), is obviously attracted by this "middle-class nationalist" model, yet rendered cautious by the paucity of evidence. In fact, Coetzee's limited data on the class background of activists in nationalist pressure groups suggests dominance by retired military officers, clerics, journalists, and businessmen with special material interests. Mangan (1986) has noted that imperial propaganda circulated most in the public (i.e., the private) schools for the regime's own children, not those of the middle class. When I turn to the better-documented German nationalists, I will give a different interpretation of pressure group composition.

Price (1977) assumes without giving evidence that jingoism was lower middle class. He then interprets this in terms of status panic by a middle class facing blocked mobility and a rising working class. I have already rejected the economic basis of his argument – the lower middle class was doing quite well during this period – while accepting that the working class might threaten over the state's political economy. The middle class might wish to keep the state theirs, keep taxation regressive, and keep the working class excluded.

But in British party democracy, class was crosscut by the national crystallization mobilizing regions, religions, and sectors. The Conservative leadership was unsympathetic to labor and opposed high social expenditures; but it had remained Anglican and agrarian-cum-commercial and favored military expenditures. Thus the British middle class split. Its manufacturing, Nonconformist, and Celtic bastions – and also many professionals, educated in the humane, liberal self-concept of Victorian Britain – stayed Liberal. Some followed the Liberal imperialism of Rosebery or Haldane. But others accepted the "new liberalism" (seemingly dominated by professionals) and urged electoral understandings with Labor. This encouraged further defections of industrialists and what some call the "upper middle class" to conservatism. Yet class tensions remained in the party. Although a genuinely Leftist redistributive party from 1906 on, the "Nonconformist businessman remained the backbone of the Liberal Party in the House of Commons" (Bernstein 1986: 14; cf. Clarke 1971; Emy 1973; Wald, 1983). Liberal sections of the middle class remained insulated from aggressive nationalism. The nationalist pressure groups mentioned earlier had close connections with Rightist Conservative circles – a few to the official Conservative party. They were matched by pacific internationalists connected to the Liberal Left. Imperialists and nationalists grew as German behavior seemed to vindicate their arguments, but in 1914 most were in opposition, while pacifists were in the Liberal cabinet.

Indeed, the British regime faced an ideological dilemma: to retain the old transnational moralistic liberalism or to strengthen militarism. But there was a compromise position, of *defensive* vigilance: We should fight if attacked, preparing our defenses now. This became the view of diplomats like Nicolson and Eyre Crowe, as well as the leadership of both parties. They could agree with moderate nationalists on a policy of firm national defense. Thus most British nationalism was neither particularly aggressive nor distinctively middle class – although it was also not working class. (See Chapter 21.)

In 1914, the Liberal government was constrained more by its own extremists' pacific liberalism than by extreme nationalists. If in power the Conservatives might have been constrained by their nationalist extremists (as in Germany). The British middle class remained loyal – but to its state's ambiguous crystallizations. I guess that the most highly educated and the state careerists were "superloyal schizoids," touched by *both* their state's traditional liberalism and its new imperialism. I have no actual evidence, but this would parallel the well-evidenced German outcome, detailed in a moment. It would also parallel state careerists' domestic politics. Most touched by this nation-state's self-image as uniquely capable of compromise and pragmatic evolution, they were mediating class conflict more than party leaders wished (as we see in Chapter 17). The highly educated middle class and state careerists overinternalized rival state doctrines, discomforting their political masters. Once both parties had gone to war, however, the middle class united and (apart from a few brave pacifists) loyally spilled its blood – furthering the downward spiral of the British nation-state.

In Germany and Austria, entwined class, national, and monarchist crystallizations generated middle-class nationalism that proved unsettling and, ultimately, disloyal. (Austria is discussed in Chapter 10.) Because class and nationality crosscut one another and loyalties to the regime, neither alone offered sufficient support to the Habsburgs. Uniquely, in the late nineteenth century, this regime deliberately played off against each other as many provincially dominant as subordinate classes and nations. Class and national loyalties remained calculative. Regional middle classes rarely had obvious hierarchies on which to fasten conservatism and loyalty. As we might have predicted from our discussion in this chapter, no Austro-Hungarian middle class went for a proletarian socialist alliance. But most other combinations occurred. Some middle-class notables (especially Czech and Slovak professionals and local state bureaucrats) controlled dissident nationalist movements; others (especially petites bourgeoisies) allied with peasants, nonsocialist workers, and the lower middle class in populist and social Christian dissidence (especially Austro-Germans and Czechs); still others (mostly in backward provinces and Hungary) allied with the local old regime against the Habsburgs; and manufacturers, financiers, corporate managers, and central state bureaucrats (especially if Austro-German or Jewish) supported the Habsburgs and their final aggression. It would take many pages to analyze all this, but middle-class loyal conservatism rarely found an appropriate object. Austro-Hungarian middle-class nationalisms were somewhat conservative, distinctly aggressive, always exciting, and usually state subverting – leading after defeat in war to numerous new nation-states.

German divide and rule differed, inasmuch as the regime brought the middle class into the edges of the state in order to keep labor and ethnic minorities well outside it. This moved the middle class rightward into hostility to the working class; and it moved the northern and Lutheran middle class (and peasantry) into centralizing statist loyalties, but Catholics and southerners into mild local-regional disloyalty. But middle-class parties were kept out of the state's core, which remained predominantly old regime and capitalist. As in Austria, but unlike liberal countries, mass parties did not control this state. So, although the middle class was strongly antisocialist and predominantly conservative and statist, it did not identify strongly with the present regime. Its autonomy was also fueled by its distinctive corporate organization. *Mittelstand* (middle estate) politics were sometimes radical, usually antiproletarian (Gellately 1974; Winkler 1976; Blackbourne 1977;

Kocka 1980) – their autonomy even encouraged by monarchical divide and rule as a counterweight to its enemies.

Nationalist pressure groups became influential after 1900, as German fears of encirclement grew. By 1911, the Colonial Society, the Pan-German League, the Society of the Eastern Marches, the Navy League, and the Defense League had much larger and more vocal memberships than did nationalists in other countries. Some smaller pressure groups (veterans associations, Young Germany Union) were regime propaganda arms. Some (the Society for the Eastern Marches) were single-issue groups linked to Junkers, army, and court. But the largest and most insistent (the Navy League and Pan-German League) became autonomous, popular, and aggressive, constraining regime and parties away from advocacy of diplomatic conciliation. Conservatives and National Liberals, having first despised such nationalism, wilted under its electoral pressure (Eley 1978, 1980, 1981).

Because there were few workers in any of these pressure groups and few peasants in most of them, it is usual to describe them as middle class (Wehler 1979; Eley 1981). Yet data (in Eley 1980: 61–7, 123–30, and Chickering 1975: tables 5.1–5.12; cf. Kehr 1977) permit greater precision.

The largest was the Navy League. Founded by wealthy businessmen, professors, and ex-officers, its national leaders remained notables. Of the 26 Presidium members between 1900 and 1908, 10 were big businessmen; 5, landed aristocrats; 9, former army and navy senior officers; 1, a professor; and 1, a retired civil servant. All were university graduates. Of its nine thousand branch officers in 1912, 20 percent were higher government officials (often mayors and *Landräte*); 19 percent, teachers; 18 percent, middling and lower officials (although, as often in German statistics, this category includes some clerical workers in the private sector); 11 percent, petit bourgeois; 9 percent, professionals; 8 percent, landowners or ex-military officers; 8 percent, industrialists and managers; and there were a few members of the clergy, artisans, and farmers, and virtually no workers. The over-representation of state employees is striking – 2 percent to 3 percent of the population, 50 percent to 60 percent of the Navy League's officers (including teachers and the few Protestant clergy). Equally striking is their elevated education: 1 percent of the population, 61 percent of local leaders, attended a university-level institution.

The Pan-German League was similarly skewed: Among nearly 2,500 local leaders, few were agrarians, workers, or artisans. Some 66 percent had received a university-level education, and 54 percent were state employees (half of these were teachers). Long-term activists were even more skewed: 77 percent had been to a university-level institution.

Chickering shows that in all the nationalist pressure groups most civil servants came from the middle to upper levels of the administration, few from its highest levels.

The Society of the Eastern Marches, centered in more rural eastern Prussia, had more peasants and artisans, each group providing about 20 percent of members. But, even here, civil servants and teachers dominated. In a sample of twenty-six branches during 1894–1900, they made up just under 50 percent of its members, the proportion rising later. Teachers alone provided between 10 percent and 14 percent of members, 22 percent of the society's functionaries, and 25 percent of its general committee, and other civil servants were a further 30 percent of the committee. In Chickering's sample of local society leaders, 74 percent had been to a university-level institution.

The composition of ordinary membership for the other organizations is largely guesswork. Eley guesses that the Navy League was disproportionately petit bourgeois but does not say why; Chickering guesses the Pan-Germans were broadly middle class, though disproportionately from the educated and from the public sector. All pressure groups were essentially from North Germany and Lutheran areas. The Catholic countryside and the Catholic petite bourgeoisie were relatively untouched by social imperialism (Blackbourne 1980: 238). Lutheranism was the official religion of Prussia, and so somewhat statist.

Chickering's study (1975: 73–6) of the pacifist peace movement permits an interesting contrast with extreme nationalists. Most pacifists were from the "nonrural middle to lower middle class," with small merchants and entrepreneurs the largest group (especially those doing business abroad), followed by elementary schoolteachers and professionals. Quite contrary to status-panic theories, the petite bourgeoisie was disproportionately pacifist. Women also constituted one-third of members, whereas the nationalist pressure groups were predominantly male. Chickering concludes that pacifists were those most removed from the principal institutions of the national state – the bureaucracy, universities, and army.

State education was officially nationalistic. Schools were supposed to encourage a rather military sense of nationhood. As the kaiser told a conference of educators: "I am looking for soldiers. We want a robust generation who can serve as the intellectual leaders and officials of the nation" (Albisetti 1989: 3). Whether primary school teachers obeyed is unclear. Many schools (most in Bavaria) were Catholic and resisted, and few working-class pupils seemed to get the message. State secondary school teachers did try, with greater success among their middle-class pupils. Yet children's enthusiasm focused less on regime and kaiser, more on an abstract *Volk* and *Reich* (Mosse 1964; Albisetti 1983; Schleunes 1989). The universities were most affected, losing their early nineteenth-century liberalism. The notion of humane, cultivated *Bildung* eroded. Academics became distinctly statist, and though only a minority were directly active in politics, these were almost all on the Right. Student social life saw the growth of "conservative-royalist" student corporations, the *Korps*, and other nationalist student organizations. Socialism made little impact and liberalism declined. A "'spiritual rebirth' of academic youth centered not on the present regime but around two slogans, *deutschnational* and *Weltpolitik*" (Jarausch 1982: 365): Because 20 million Germans were living abroad, the Reich should be expanded. State education did not socialize mere loyalty to the regime but a more abstract statist nationalism.

Thus not the middle class or the petite bourgeoisie but government employees – those most dependent on the state – and highly educated Lutherans – those most socialized into statist ideologies – were the most likely to be aggressive nationalists. Chickering (1984: 107, 111) suggests that these men were the cultural custodians of the *Kaiserreich*, yet they were perhaps moving somewhat beyond the kaiser. The petite bourgeoisie was not especially nationalist. Neither the old *Mittelstand* of artisans, peasants, or small businessmen nor the new *Mittelstand* of white-collar workers was well represented.

This puts a rather different complexion on nationalism. Perhaps we should really call it statism, not nationalism. Moreover, the mood of these movements rarely corresponded to the negative image presented by status-panic paranoid theory. It embodied an overzealous superloyal statism on the part of those within the state but not quite at the regime's core. Middling to upper state levels had been "colonized" by a particularistic pressure group. They were urging the regime on to implement what they argued were its true values, which the exigencies of practical politics – divide and rule at home, diplomacy abroad, the kaiser's own limitations – were subverting. Superloyalism did not see itself as anxious or reactionary, but as buoyant, affirmative, modern, with an image of the future – of a truly mobilized nation-state, united and solidary, as no historical regime (and certainly no dynastic monarchy) had been. Jews, Catholics, ethnic minorities, and socialists were attempting to subvert that national unity. But if the regime would give the true nation its head, they could be consigned to the dustbin of history. It is unfair to saddle these nationalists with the burden of subsequent history. Most intended no grievous bodily harm to the *Reichsfeinde*. Only when the old regime collapsed in 1918 and when those enemies grew stronger in Weimar did their successors – now with more rural and capitalist support, but still centered on state employment and Lutheranism – turn extremely nasty.

Through all the variations, there is probably a common pattern – at least in Britain, France, and Germany: Emerging nationalisms were less middle class, more specifically statist than has been generally believed. All three middle-class fractions showed loyalty on class issues to their regimes. Yet their politics varied, as religious and regional identities affected their stance on the national issue. Most nationalism was generated by state careerists and highly educated careerists and professionals. But it also varied according to the character of the regime. Nationalisms exaggerated, sometimes overzealously, regime preferences, producing a superloyal statist nationalism. But even in Germany this merely asked an ostensibly aggressive old regime to live up to its rhetoric and to become more populist. In Britain and France it produced party factionalized senses of nationhood congealing under external threat to firm defensive nationalisms. Austria and the United States developed unique variants of nationalism, the one aimed against the state, the other still not aroused by geopolitics into articulacy. These variations did not emerge from the direct relations of production, as these latter were fairly invariant among countries, but from different entwinings of political and ideological citizenship. Nationalism was more political than economic, whereas politics factionalized the state, reducing "its" cohesion. This will prove significant in Chapter 21, in my explanation of the causes of World War I.

Conclusion

Industrial capitalist society has had a middle class for about a hundred years. Only two middling groups were proletarianized, and neither resulted in much middle-class fuss. Most artisans were proletarianized so early and completely that they left little influence on the middle class. Then clerical, sales, and some technical jobs without career prospects became like manual work, yet few of their predominantly female incumbents experienced this as proletarianization. If lower white-collar workers have participated less in the labor movement than manual workers, this has not been because of supposed middle-class status consciousness but because of three factors that also reduced participation among manual workers: a high proportion of women, predominantly small employing organizations, and location in areas dominated by the middle class. The middle class has not been proletarianized; and appearances of middle-class "decomposition" mostly represent differences of gender.

The male-dominated middle class contains three fractions, each defined by distinct relations of production: petite bourgeoisie, corporate and bureaucratic careerists, and professionals. They are three fractions of one middle class because they have shared diffused features of capitalist nation-states. Some of these are primarily economic: middling participation in hierarchical segmental employment and market relations, privileged consumption badges, and the ability to convert income into small investment capital. But in this period they also shared an ideological citizenship linking state education to employment rights and a political citizenship denied to those beneath them. National civil societies and nation-states emerged ruled by capital and staffed at subaltern level by the middle class. Where this alliance was institutionalized by 1914, as in the three party democracies, no major class upheavals occurred. Working-class political and social citizenship was then mainly institutionalized on the model of middle-class national citizenship.

The middle class has been generally loyal to the capitalist class in its struggles with labor. No country neared the proletarian alliance envisaged by some Marxists. It came closest when they could ally on nonclass political crystallizations, like those of region and religion. The next chapters focus on how labor and peasants faced up to a middle-class conservatism that significantly limited their options. I do not, however, wish to fall into the trap I criticize others for falling into, that of viewing the middle class only in relation to capital and labor (plus peasants). The middle class cannot be reduced to mere loyal retainers of capitalism and regimes. At the beginning of the twentieth century, it was also the main reinforcer of the nation-state. Moreover, two subfractions – state careerists and highly educated careerists and professionals – were the main carriers of distinct and varied statist nationalisms.

In the United States, Britain, and France, there were few middle-class socialists (until the mid-twentieth-century expansion of state employment) but, rather, competing visions of the nation-state, from conservative (though somewhat defensive) nationalism to liberal pacifism. Across Austria-Hungary and Germany the middle class, especially the highly educated and state careerists, demonstrated more autonomous, aggressive, and abstract nationalisms capable of turning dramatically against the ruling regime. In Austria-Hungary, this now happened. In Germany, superloyal statism was already discomforting the regime and in less than twenty years would turn revolutionary. World War I intensified nation building in liberal countries and intensified conflicts over the meaning of the nation in other countries. Nation-states and nations have proved as decisive as capitalism and classes in structuring twentieth-century civilization. The middle class staffed its twentieth-century emergence, and its more statist fractions staffed their most intense and sometimes devastating forms.

A middle class emerged with a distinctive relation to power resources, with its own organizations and collective consciousness – a relation summed up by the "impure" dual formula: segmental middling participation in organizations generated by the diffused circuits of capital and more independent, varied participation in the authoritative nation-state. Once again the entwinings of diffuse capitalism and authoritative states were shaping the modern world.

Bibliography

Abercrombie, N., and J. Urry. 1983. *Capital, Labour and the Middle Classes.* London: Allen & Unwin.
Albisetti, J. 1983. *Secondary School Reform in Imperial Germany.* Princeton, N.J.: Princeton University Press.
Armstrong, W. A. 1966. Social structure from the early census returns. In *An Introduction to English Historical Demography*, ed. E. A. Wrigley. London: Weidenfeld & Nicolson.
Aronowitz, S. 1979. The professional-managerial class or middle strata? In *Between Labor and Capital*, ed. P. Walker. Boston: South End Press.
Bairoch, P. et al. 1968. *The Working Population and Its Structure.* Brussels: Editions de l'Institut de Sociologie de l'Université Libre (in English and French).
Bechhofer, F., and B. Elliott. 1976. Persistence and change: the *petite bourgeoisie* in the industrial society. *European Journal of Sociology* 17.
Beisner, R. 1975. *From the Old Diplomacy to the New, 1865–1900.* Arlington Heights, Il.: Harlan Davidson.
Bell, C. 1969. *Middle Class Families.* London: Routledge & Kegan Paul.
Berger, S. 1981. The uses of the traditional sector in Italy. In *The Petite Bourgeoisie: Comparative Studies of the Uneasy Stratum*, ed. F. Bechhofer and B. Elliott. London: Macmillan.
Berle, A., and G. Means. 1932. *The Modern Corporation and Private Property.* New York: Macmillan.
Bernstein, G. 1986. *Liberalism and Liberal Politics in Edwardian England.* Boston: Allen & Unwin.
Bertaux, D., and I. Bertaux-Wiame. 1981. Artisanal bakery in France: how it lives and why it survives. In *The Petite Bourgeoisie: Comparative Studies of the Uneasy Stratum*, ed. F. Bechhofer and B. Elliott. London: Macmillan.
Best, G. 1979. *Mid-Victorian Britain.* London: Fontana.
Blackbourn, D. 1977. The Mittelstand in German society and politics, 1871–1914. *Social History*, no. 4.
Blumin, S. 1989. *The Emergence of the Middle Class. Social Experience in the American City, 1760–1900.* Cambridge: Cambridge University Press.
Booth, C. 1886. On occupations of the people of the United Kingdom, 1801–81. *Journal of the Statistical Society* 49.
Bruchey, S. 1981. Remarques complétant les conclusions générales [and] Etats Unis. In Commission International d'Histoire des Mouvements

Sociaux et des Structures Sociales, *Petite Entreprise et Croissance Industrielle Dans le Monde Aux XIXe et XXe Siècles*, 2 vols. Paris.

Burnham, J. 1942. *The Managerial Revolution*. London: Putnam.

Cain, M. 1983. The general practice lawyer and client: towards a radical conception. In *The Sociology of the Professions*, ed. R. Dingwall and P. Lewis. London: Macmillan.

Carchedi, G. 1977. *On the Economic Identification of Social Classes*. London: Routledge & Kegan Paul.

Chandler, A. D., Jr. 1977. *The Visible Hand*. Cambridge, Mass.: Harvard University Press.

Chapman, S. 1981. Royaume-Uni. In Commission Internationale d'Histoire des Mouvements Sociaux et des Structures Sociales, *Petite Entreprise et Croissance Industrielle Dans le Monde Aux XIXe et XXe Siècles*. 2 vols. Paris.

Chickering, R. 1975. *Imperial Germany and a World Without War*. Princeton, N.J.: Princeton University Press.

1984. *We Men Who Feel Most German: A Cultural Study of the PanGerman League, 1886-1914*. Boston: Allen & Unwin.

Clarke, P. 1971. *Lancashire and the New Liberalism*. Cambridge: Cambridge University Press.

Coetzee, F. 1990. *For Party or Country: Nationalism and the Dilemmas of Popular Conservatism in Edwardian England*. New York: Oxford University Press.

Collins, R. 1979. *The Credential Society*. New York: Academic Press.

Commission Internationale d'Histoire des Mouvements Sociaux et des Structures Sociales. 1981. *Petite Entreprise et Croissance Industrielle Dans le Monde Aux XIXe et XXe Siècles*, 2 vols. Paris.

Crew, D. 1973. Definitions of modernity: social mobility in a German town, 1880-1901. *Journal of Social History* 7.

1979. *Town in the Ruhr: A Social History of Bochum, 1860-1914*. New York: Columbia University Press.

Crossick, G. 1977. The emergence of the lower middle class in Britain: a discussion. In *The Lower Middle Class in Britain, 1870-1914*, ed. G. Crossick. London: Croom Helm.

Cunningham, H. 1971. "Jingoism in 1877-88." *Victorian Studies* 14.

Dahrendorf, R. 1959. *Class and Class Conflict in Industrial Society*. London: Routledge & Kegan Paul.

1969. The service class. In *Industrial Man*, ed. T. Burns. Harmondsworth: Penguin Books.

Ehrenreich, B., and J. Ehrenreich. 1979. The profession-managerial class. In *Between Labor and Capital*, ed. P. Walker. Boston: South End Press.

Eldridge, G. C. 1973. *England's Mission*. London: Macmillan.

Eley, G. 1978. The Wilhelmine Right: how it changed. In *Society and Politics in Wilhelmine Germany*, ed. R. J. Evans. London: Croom Helm.

1980. *Reshaping the German Right*. New Haven, Conn.: Yale University Press.

1981. Some thoughts on the nationalist pressure groups in Imperial Germany. In *Nationalist and Racialist Movements in Britain and Germany Before 1914*, ed. P. Kennedy and A. Nicholls. London: Macmillan.

Emy, H. V. 1973. *Liberals, Radicals and Social Politics, 1892-1914*. Cambridge: Cambridge University Press.

Fest, W. 1981. Jingoism and xenophobia in the electioneering strategies of British ruling elites before 1914. In *Nationalist and Racialist Movements in Britain and Germany Before 1914*, ed. P. Kennedy and A. Nicholls. London: Macmillan.

Fieldhouse, D. K. 1973. *Economics and Empire, 1830–1914*. London: Weidenfeld & Nicolson.

Freidson, E. 1970. *Profession of Medicine*. New York: Dodd, Mead.

    1975. *Doctoring Together: A Study of Professional Social Control*. New York: Elsevier.

Gaillard, J. 1981. France. In Commission Internationale d'Histoire des Mouvements Sociaux et des Structures Sociales, *Petite Entreprise et Croissance Industrielle Dans le Monde Aux XIXe et XXe Siècles*, 2 vols. Paris.

Galanter, M. 1983. Mega-law and mega-lawyering in the contemporary United States. In *The Sociology of Professions*, ed. R. Dingwall and P. Lewis. London: Macmillan.

Galbraith, J. K. 1985. *The New Industrial State*, 4th ed. Boston: Houghton Mifflin.

Geiger, T. 1969. Class society in the melting pot. In *Structured Social Inequality*, ed. C. S. Heller. New York: Macmillan.

Gellately, R. 1974. *The Politics of Economic Despair: Shopkeepers and German Politics, 1890–1914*. London: Sage.

Giddens, A. 1973. *The Class Structure of the Advanced Societies*. London: Hutchinson.

Gildea, R. 1980. Education and the classes Moyennes in the nineteenth century. In *The Making of Frenchmen*, ed. D. Baker and P. Harrigan. Waterloo, Ont.: Historical Reflections Press.

Goldthorpe, J. H. 1982. On the service class, its formation and future. In *Social Class and the Division of Labour*, ed. A. Giddens and G. Mackenzie. Cambridge: Cambridge University Press.

Goode, W. J. 1969. The theoretical limits of professionalization. In *The Semi-Professions and Their Organization*, ed. A. Etzioni. New York: Free Press.

Gray, R. Q. 1977. Religion, culture and social class in late nineteenth and early twentieth century Edinburgh. In *The Lower Middle Class in Britain, 1870–1914*, ed. G. Crossick. London: Croom Helm.

Grossmith, G., and W. Grossmith. 1892 and 1965. *The Diary of a Nobody*. Harmondsworth: Penguin Books.

Halsey, A. H., et al. 1980. *Origins and Destinations*. Oxford: Clarendon Press.

Harrigan, P. 1975. Secondary education and the professions in France during the Second Empire. *Comparative Studies in Society and History* 17.

Harrison, J. F. C. 1971. *The Early Victorians, 1832–1851*. London: Weidenfeld & Nicolson.

Hart, N. 1985. *The Sociology of Health and Medicine*. Ormskirk, Lancs.: Causeway Press.

Haupt, H.-G. 1981. République Fédérale Allemande. In Commission Internationale d'Histoire des Mouvements Sociaux et des Structures Sociales, *Petite Entreprise et Croissance Industrielle Dans le Monde Aux XIXe et XXe Siècles*, 2 vols. Paris.

Healy, D. F. 1963. *The United States in Cuba, 1898–1902*. Madison: University of Wisconsin Press.

    1970. *U.S. Expansionism: The Imperialist Urge in the 1890s*. Madison:

University of Wisconsin Press.

Hobsbawm, E. 1989. *The Age of Empire, 1875–1914*. New York: Vintage.

1990. *Nations and Nationalism Since 1780*. Cambridge: Cambridge University Press.

Hollingsworth, J. R. (ed.). 1983. *American Expansion in the Late Nineteenth Century: Colonialist or Anticolonialist?* Malabar, Fla.: Krieger.

Howard, M. 1970. Reflections on the First World War. In his *Studies in War and Peace*. London: Temple Smith.

Hurt, J. S. 1979. *Elementary Schooling and the Working Classes, 1860–1918*. London: Routledge & Kegan Paul.

Illich, I. 1977. *Disabling Professions*. London: M. Boyars.

Jaeger, C. 1982. *Artisanat et Capitalisme*. Paris: Payot.

Jarausch, K. H. 1982. *Students, Society, and Politics in Imperial Germany: The Rise of Academic Illiberalism*. Princeton, N.J.: Princeton University Press.

1990. The German professions in history and theory. In *German Professions, 1800–1950*, ed. R. Cocks and K. H. Jarausch. Oxford: Oxford University Press.

Johnson, T. J. 1972. *Professions and Power*. London: Macmillan.

Joll, J. 1984. *The Origins of the First World War*. London: Longman.

Kaelble, H. 1981. Educational opportunities and government policies in Europe in the period of industrialization. In *The Development of Welfare States in Europe and America*, ed. P. Flora and A. J. Heidenheimer. New Brunswick, N.J.: Transaction Books.

Kaufhold, K. H. 1981. République Fédérale Allemande. In Commission Internationale d'Histoire des Mouvements Sociaux et des Structures Sociales, *Petite Entreprise et Croissance Industrielle Dans le Monde Aux XIXᵉ et XXᵉ Siècles*, 2 vols. Paris.

Kehr, E. 1977. *Economic Interest, Militarism and Foreign Policy*. Berkeley: University of California Press.

Kennedy, P. 1980. *The Rise of the Anglo-German Antagonism, 1860–1914*. London: Allen & Unwin.

Kiyonari, T. T. 1981. Japan. In the Commission Internationale d'Histoire des Mouvements Sociaux et des Structures Sociales, *Petite Entreprise et Croissance Industrielle Dans le Monde Aux XIXᵉ et XXᵉ Siècles*, 2 vols. Paris.

Klingender, F. D. 1935. *The Condition of Clerical Labour in Britain*. London: M. Lawrence.

Kocka, J. 1980. *White-Collar Workers in America, 1890–1940*. London: Sage.

Krug, E. 1964. *The Shaping of the American High School*. New York: Harper & Row.

Kurgan van Hentenryk, G. 1981. Belgique. In Commission Internationale d'Histoire des Mouvements Sociaux et des Structures Sociales, *Petite Entreprise et Croissance Industrielle Dans le Monde Aux XIXᵉ et XXᵉ Siècles*, 2 vols. Paris.

LaFeber, W. 1963. *The New Empire: An Interpretation of American Expansion, 1860–1898*. Ithaca, N.Y.: Cornell University Press.

Lasch, C. 1958. The anti-imperialists, the Philippines, and the inequality of man. *Journal of Southern History* 24.

Lash, S., and J. Urry. 1987. *The End of Organized Capitalism*. Oxford: Blackwell.

Little, A, and J. Westergaard. 1964. The trend of class differentials in educational opportunity in England and Wales. *British Journal of Sociology* 15.

Lockwood, D. 1958. *The Blackcoated Worker*. London: Allen & Unwin.

Mackenzie, W. 1979. *Power and Responsibility in Health Care*. Oxford: Oxford University Press.

McKeown, T. 1976. *The Modern Rise of Population*. London: Arnold.

Maingueneau, D. 1979. *Les Livres d'école de la République, 1870–1914*. Paris: Sycomore.

Mangan, J. 1986. "The grit of our forefathers": invented traditions, propaganda and imperialism. In *Imperialism and Popular Culture*. ed. J. MacKenzie. Manchester: Manchester University Press.

Mayer, A. J. 1975. The lower middle class as historical problem. *Journal of Modern History* 47.

Middleton, N., and S. Weitzman. 1976. *A Place for Everyone*. London: Gollancz.

Mills, C. W. 1953. *White Collar*. New York: Oxford University Press.

Moody, J. 1978. *French Education Since Napoleon*. Syracuse, N.Y.: Syracuse University Press.

Moore, D. C. 1976. *The Politics of Deference*. Hassocks, Sussex: Harvester.

Mosse, G. L. 1964. *The Crisis of German Ideology*. London: Weidenfeld & Nicolson.

Muller, D. 1987. The process of systematisation: the case of German secondary education. In *The Rise of the Modern Educational System*, ed. D. Muller, F. Ringer, and B. Simon. Cambridge: Cambridge University Press.

Musgrove, F. 1959. Middle-class education and employment in the nineteenth century. *Economic History Review* 12.

Nichols, T. 1969. *Ownership, Control and Ideology*. London: Allen & Unwin.

Nikolaou, K. 1978. *Inter-size Efficiency Differentials in Greek Manufacturing*. Athens: Center of Planning and Economic Research.

Nord, P. 1981. Le mouvement des petits commerçants et la politique en France de 1888 à 1914. *Mouvement Social* 114.

Parkin, F. 1979. *Marxism and Class Theory: A Bourgeois Critique*. London: Tavistock.

Perkin, H. 1961. Middle-class education and employment in the nineteenth century: a critical note. *Economic History Review* 14.

Poulantzas, N. 1975. *Classes in Contemporary Capitalism*. London: New Left Books.

Prais, S. J. 1981. *The Evolution of Giant Firms in Britain*. Cambridge: Cambridge University Press.

Price, R. N. 1977. Society, status and jingoism: the social roots of lower middle class patriotism, 1870–1900. In *The Lower Middle Class in Britain, 1870–1914*, ed. G. Crossick. London: Croom Helm.

Pryor, F. L. 1973. *Property and Industrial Organization in Communist and Capitalist Nations*. Bloomington: Indiana University Press.

Reeder, D. 1987. The reconstruction of secondary education in England, 1869–1920. In *The Rise of the Modern Educational System*, ed. D. Muller, F. Ringer, and B. Simon. Cambridge: Cambridge University Press.

Ringer, F. 1979. *Education and Society in Modern Europe*. Bloomington: Indiana University Press.

1987. On segmentation in modern European educational systems: the case of French secondary education, 1865–1920. In *The Rise of the Modern Educational System*, ed. D. Muller, F. Ringer, and B. Simon. Cambridge: Cambridge University Press.

Robinson, R. E. 1959. Imperial problems in British politics, 1880–95. In *The Cambridge History of the British Empire*. Vol. III, ed. E. A. Benians et al. Cambridge: Cambridge University Press.

Routh, B. 1965. *Occupation and Pay in Great Britain 1906–1960*. Cambridge: Cambridge University Press.

1980. *Occupation and Pay in Great Britain, 1906–1979*. London: Macmillan.

Rubinson, R. 1986. Class formation, politics, and institutions: schooling in the United States. *American Journal of Sociology* 92.

Rueschemeyer, D. 1973. *Lawyers and Their Society: A Comparative Study of the Legal Profession in Germany and in the United States*. Cambridge, Mass.: Harvard University Press.

Ryan, M. 1981. *Cradle of the Middle Class: The Family in Oneida County, New York, 1790–1865*. Cambridge: Cambridge University Press.

Rystad, G. 1975. *Ambiguous Imperialism: American Foreign Policy and Domestic Politics at the Turn of the Century*. Stockholm: Scandinavian University Books.

Schleunes, K. 1989. *Schooling and Society: The Politics of Education in Prussia and Bavaria, 1750–1900*. Oxford: Berg.

Scott, J. 1979. *Corporations, Classes and Capitalism*. London: Hutchinson.

1982. *The Upper Classes. Property and Privilege in Britain*. London: Macmillan.

Simon, B. 1987. Systematisation and segmentation in education: the case of England. In *The Rise of the Modern Educational System*, ed. D. Muller, F. Ringer, and B. Simon. Cambridge: Cambridge University Press.

Singer, B. 1983. *Village Notables in Nineteenth-Century France: Priests, Mayors, Schoolmasters*. Albany: State University of New York Press.

Smith, R. J. 1969. Education, society and literacy: Nottinghamshire in the mid-nineteenth century. *University of Birmingham Historical Journal* 12.

Steedman, H. 1987. Defining institutions: the endowed grammar schools and the systematisation of English secondary education. In *The Rise of the Modern Educational System*, ed. D. Muller, F. Ringer, and B. Simon. Cambridge: Cambridge University Press.

Stewart, A., et al. 1980. *Social Stratification and Occupations*. London: Macmillan.

Summers, A. 1981. The character of Edwardian nationalism: three popular leagues. In *Nationalism and Racialist Movements in Britain Before 1941*, ed. P. Kennedy and A. Nicholls. London: Macmillan.

Sutherland, G. 1971. *Elementary Education in the Nineteenth Century*. London: Macmillan.

Tholfsen, T. 1976. *Working Class Radicalism in Mid-Victorian England*. London: Croom Helm.

Waddington, I. 1977. General practitioners and consultants in early nineteenth century England: the sociology of an inter-professional conflict. In *Health Care and Popular Medicine in Nineteenth Century England*, ed. J. Woodward and D. Richards. London: Croom Helm.

Wald, K. 1983. *Crosses on the Ballot: Patterns of British Voter Alignment Since 1885*. Princeton, N.J.: Princeton University Press.

Weber, E. 1968. *The Nationalist Revival in France, 1905–1914*. Berkeley: University of California Press.

1976. *Peasants Into Frenchmen*. Stanford, Calif.: Stanford University Press.

Wehler, H.-U. 1979. Introduction to imperialism. In *Conflict and Stability in Europe*, ed. C. Emsley. London: Croom Helm.

Weiss, L. 1988. *Creating Capitalism: The State and Small Business Since 1945*. Oxford: Blackwell.

Welch, R., Jr. 1979. *Response to Imperialism: The United States and the Philippine-American War*. Chapel Hill: University of North Carolina Press.

Wertheimer, M. 1924. *The Pan-German League 1890–1914*. New York: Columbia University Press.

Whyte, W. M. 1956. *The Organization Man*. New York: Simon & Schuster.

Winkler, H. A. 1976. From social protectionism to National Socialism: the German small-business movement in comparative perspective. *Journal of Modern History* 48.

Wright, E. O. 1985. *Classes*. London: Verso.

17 Class struggle in the Second Industrial Revolution, 1880–1914: I. Great Britain

The Second Industrial Revolution

Between 1880 and 1914, most Western countries experienced their most rapid economic growth. (See Tables 8.2 and 8.4.) Agriculture was transformed, and migration from agriculture to the towns and overseas reached its highest levels. The "Second Industrial Revolution" brought big capital, high science, and complex technology especially into three industries – iron and steel, metal manufacturing, and chemicals. Agrarian and industrial commodities were distributed nationally by rail and internationally by steamships. Banks and stock markets channeled savings into global investment and then back as profits to enhance consumption. Thus the second revolution advanced the integration of economies, though their totality remained ambiguous because dual – national and transnational.

This second revolution in economic power changed societies. *Collective* powers were transformed qualitatively. Mass living standards throughout the West began to rise and remain securely above mere subsistence. Thus life expectancy began its dramatic, rapid rise, from about forty years in 1870 – which might have represented only the high point of yet another Malthusianlike historical cycle – to about seventy years by 1950. The life expectancy of women exceeded that of men. Societies became urbanized and industrialized. All this may have represented the most profound social change the world had ever seen. It resulted primarily from a revolution in economic power relations, from the industrializing phase of capitalism. Throughout this period, there has to be a residual economic determinism in our theories.

The economic revolution also transformed *distributive* power relations – the subject matter of the next three chapters. As Marx predicted, classes continued their rise, becoming more extensive and political. First, landed, commercial, and industrial wealth holders fused into a capitalist class, as we saw had already happened in Britain (see Chapter 4) and as was now happening in Germany (see Chapter 9). Second, the consolidation of petite bourgeoisie, professionals, and careerists into a middle class was under way. (See Chapter 16.) Third, agrarian classes were integrated into global commercial capitalism and into its overall

597

class conflicts. (See Chapter 19.) Most national economies were now split evenly between industry and agriculture. (Because Britain was the exception, the only overwhelmingly industrial country, I leave this dualism for the next chapters.) Fourth, a working-class movement emerged, centered in metalworking industries, mining, and transport and collectively organized in employment and politics. Class struggle between regimes–capitalist classes and workers became more extensive and political. Growing state infrastructural powers, the emergence of citizenship, and the partial caging of capital onto the terrain of the national state all channeled conflict into national organization. Classes became more symmetric, and class struggle could be evaded and outflanked no longer. Distributive power relations had been transformed – a process substantially begun in the late eighteenth century and completed at the beginning of the twentieth.

Yet the rise of such classes, and the "revolution" in distributive power relations, was actually more ambiguous than this – and more than Marx had realized. We saw in Chapter 16 that the middle class arose somewhat fragmented, with politics. Chapter 19 shows that agrarian classes (apart from large estate farmers) were extraordinarily diverse in their relations with each other and with urban-industrial classes. This chapter and the next will also evidence substantial ambiguities among workers – in their collective organizations, their ideologies, and their politics. In terms of organization the Second Industrial Revolution strengthened not just the working class but three forms of worker organization: class, section, and segment. Indeed, the core industries generating the most classlike tendencies were also the most sectionalized between skilled artisans and unskilled laborers and the most segmented by the internal labor market. All three were extensive and political forms of organization of a novel kind, all aspects of a genuine revolution in economic power relations. But combined they led not toward the dialectical totality culminating in revolution envisaged by Marx – nor simply in the evolutionary reformism envisaged by most other writers – but toward a tremendous ambiguity in distributive power relations. Western societies "solved" those ambiguities in various ways. Explaining those solutions is the main theoretical purpose of the next chapters.

Ambiguity was most evident in worker ideologies and politics in this period. In Table 15.1 I distinguished three pairs of strategic worker (and peasant) alternatives to complying with existing capitalism. All remained vibrant throughout this period. The two competitive strategies did not seek to change but to compete with capitalism. If economic, they were protectionist, ubiquitous within labor movements especially in their mildest form, whereby workers banded together to provide co-ops and friendly societies that offered benefits and insurance. Where this strategy turned political, seeking state assistance for worker ventures and organizing rights (collective civil citizenship), I have labeled it mutualism. Reformists also pursued two tactics. If political – social redistribution of wealth and power through taxation and social welfare provision – I have called this social democracy, still rare in this period. More common were economic tactics – industrial conciliation and collective bargaining over wages and conditions – which I have labeled economism. The pair of revolutionary strategies were the Marxist statist vision of the achievement of socialism through political revolution and syndicalist and anarchosyndicalist visions of revolution achieved through general economic strikes bypassing the state.

All six strategies had obvious attractions for workers brought into modern employment relations. Even revolutionaries must earn their daily subsistence and cooperate with their employer. Nor do they often reject friendly societies, ballot boxes, unemployment insurance, free schooling, or other lures of protectionism or reformism. Even conciliatory workers persistently discover that capitalism puts property rights first, that workers may be treated arbitrarily and made unemployed, if capitalist market forces so decree. Then they discover capitalist exploitation, the labor theory of value, and radical alternatives to capitalism. In this period, few would embrace statist solutions, as their experience was not of worker-friendly states. As Holton (1985) notes, syndicalism might be especially appropriate to these decades, especially as managerial controls extended among workers outside manufacturing, unused to disciplined factory life and routinized labor unions. By 1914, no single worker, or indeed employer, strategy had been thoroughly institutionalized in any country. All remained viable, attracting rival militant bands, and thus leaving distributive power relations highly ambiguous.

The attractions of the various alternatives depended crucially on the strategies-drifts of the ruling regime. Capitalists obviously would prefer to concede nothing, and states, ubiquitously crystallizing as capitalist, would prefer to support them with legal and, if necessary, military means. Yet if workers resisted tenaciously, collectively organized to exploit labor scarcities, and form alliances with other classes, then real dilemmas arose for regimes. If they offered mere repression, then reform and mutualism would achieve little and all workers would be in the same situation. Workers might accept sullenly their powerlessness, retreating perhaps to minimal covert protectionism, or they might follow those preaching mass strikes or political revolution, as in tsarist Russia. Most employers and regimes were also aware of alternative strategies. They repressed more carefully – selectively and segmentally.

Capitalists need worker cooperation; state elites need compliance with taxes, conscription, and public order; and parties need votes. Capitalists might conciliate and state elites and parties might be persuaded by their other crystallizations to pressure them to further conciliate. Because workers (and peasants) possessed varying organizing powers, capitalists, state elites, and parties might respond pragmatically and selectively, enhancing sectionalism, conciliating skilled, propertied, or enfranchised workers while repressing the rest.

Once segmental *incorporating* strategies were under way, protectionists, economists, and mutualists had an advantage over revolutionaries. The mass strike and the political revolution – even aggressive pressing for structural reforms – require weight of numbers and class unity. By contrast, "moderates" and sectionalism only need some concessions to some workers from some capitalists or elite or party factions to get started. Once some workers receive some benefits this way, they are less likely to rally behind revolutionaries. Class unity is broken, and the specter of revolution recedes. *Provided* some capitalists, state elites, and parties will compromise with some workers, protectionism, mild reform, sectionalism, segmentalism, and the weakening of revolutionary militants have been more likely in the long run than revolution.

But this likelihood now seemed to recede. Immediately after Marx died, in 1883, his theory seemed vindicated. The Second Industrial Revolution generated his "collective laborer." Actually, this was its second appearance. But unlike the first Chartist form, this working class formed around formal employment in large capitalist or state enterprises, especially in metal manufacturing, mines, and transport. Artisans largely disappeared. Skill differences remained, but they were mediated by increasing semiskilled occupations, all integrated by a single wage and managerial control system. This revolution also had macroeconomic consequences, intensifying international competition. Employers launched offensives against what they saw as obsolete craft protectionism, devising "scientific management" techniques to routinely control labor, sometimes aided by judicial and police repression. These aggressions increased the plausibility of class identities among workers, while often also reducing their capacities to do much about it.

The vital questions concerned the response of skilled workers. Would they use their organizations and surviving labor market powers for their own sectional, protectionist interest? Or would they unite with semiskilled and unskilled workers in a singular classlike movement, as Marx believed? Capitalists and state elites-parties were faced with a parallel choice: Repress all workers and risk polarizing class struggle, or segmentally conciliate the more respectable and repress the others.

In the next two chapters, I examine the varied ways these strategies-drifts interacted. I argue that *political* crystallizations played a large role in explaining outcomes. The economic revolution in distributive power relations remained intrinsically ambiguous. It needed help from other sources of social power to be completed. I begin with the "leading edge of power," the foremost Power in the first half of the period, the only industrial society throughout it, the country with the largest trade union movement in the world – Great Britain.

Explaining the rise of British labor

The general contours of labor during the period can be briefly summarized.[1] The first major change came in the late 1880s with the arrival of the "new unionism" – more aggressive, absorbing unskilled, semiskilled, and skilled workers alike, and becoming more extensive and political and less sectional. The movement was checked after 1890; then it stabilized and grew, especially from 1910 on. But union membership remained 90 percent male. Female membership grew but only from 2 percent to 10 percent between 1888 and 1914, and even in cotton and teaching most officials were men. Union growth among male manual workers was spectacular, from 12 percent to 32 percent. Among the 5 million men forming the working-class core – in factories supervised by the Factory Inspectorate, in mining, and in transport – unionists were probably a majority. In politics, unions first collaborated with the Liberal party; then some formed a Labour party to prosecute union interests. By 1914, more than half of all union members were affiliated with the Labour party. In the last prewar election, in 1910, Labour won 42 of the 56 working-class constituencies for which it fought – though with the help of an electoral pact with the Liberal party. British labor is usually portrayed in this period, as in subsequent ones, as reformist, combining economistic unions and a social democratic Labour party. But as yet it was even more moderate – its economic tactics usually lay between protectionism and economism, whereas mutualism predominated in politics. These competed with minority tendencies: Marxists and syndicalists agitated hopefully, and an unintentional reformism was generated as labor organizations became implicated in state administration.

Let us start with the unions. Many historians explain union growth

---

[1] General sources for this section were, on unions, the Webbs (1926), Pelling (1963: 85–148), Clegg et al. (1964), Cronin (1979, 1982), and Martin (1980: 58–131); and on the Labour party, McKibbin (1974) and Moore (1978).

with the aid of the four Marxian theses outlined in Chapter 15. They argue:

1. The qualitative divide between capital and labor became diffused across the whole economy, replacing more varied relations of production.

2. The transformation of the labor process in the Second Industrial Revolution led to the emergence of a "collective laborer," the singular working class.

3. This was reinforced by the growing density and segregation of workers' urban communities, although some argue that this produced a predominantly "defensive" solidarity.

4. Political demands emanating from the labor process, reinforced by the working-class community, drove toward a reformist Labour party.

In Chapter 15 I criticized this model in five ways:

1. Not one but three competing "collective laborers" rose up – the working *class*, the *sectional* craft, and the *segmental* employer-employee interdependence encouraged by the internal labor market.

2. There is a tension in the model between the *diffusion* of capitalism across a whole economy and the particular, *authoritative* organizational site represented by the factory labor process. In earlier periods diffusion determined more of working-class development than the labor process. Most historians of this period emphasize the transformation of the labor process. I dispute this.

3. As this economy was also predominantly the terrain of the national state, its *political crystallizations* helped determine the labor movement.

4. The emerging labor movement was sectional in a further sense: It was predominantly *male* and employment-centered. As production transformed, this influenced the relations between employment and community aspects of the labor movement.

5. The consequence of all this is that class conflict is not usually head-on confrontation and dialectical resolution, as in Marx's vision. The ruling regime will also normally be factionalized and sectionalized, producing more complex, competing outcomes. I have suggested that the working class would normally lose head-on class confrontation.

This chapter supports the idea that the Second Industrial Revolution furthered working-class identity; but this was only partial; and it segregated employment from family and community and so men from women. But outcomes were also structured by political crystallizations. The state's capitalist crystallization left mainly ambiguity, but other state crystallizations did not. The demilitarization of the state – its broadening scope of civilian functions and its pushing of militarism out to foreign (and Irish) parts – plus its party democracy entwined with a broadly centralized solution to the national issue (except for Ireland). All these pushed labor toward moderate mutualism. Largely because of the unintended consequences of varied actors, reformism did eventually become the dominant British worker strategy, but only during and after the Great War.

Working-class community and national civil society

Toward 1900, industrialization greatly affected residential communities. It reduced local, particularistic, segmental control and ecologically further segregated workers from others. Urban advanced further than economic concentration. By 1901, most workers had fewer than fifty co-workers yet lived in towns of more than 20,000 population. There were seventy-five towns of more than 50,000. Each town had many employers, sharing less cohesion and segmental community controls. Most organized conflict now occurred in stabilized factories or workshops in these towns. It touched about half of all workers, the other half still under segmental controls or in casual employment. Trams and railways also took the middle class into suburbs away from workers. Hierarchy was no longer reproduced locally but interlocally, even interregionally. Capitalists concentrated in London, salubrious spas, seasides, and the south; workers, in northern industrial grime. Remote control was necessary for social order as workers were left to their own culture and consciousness.

Stedman-Jones (1974) argues that a distinct "defensive" working-class culture was dominating large towns from the 1890s on. Traditional segmental controls like the charity school, the evening class, the library, the friendly society, the church, and the chapel gave ground to national state education, the pub, the sporting paper, the racecourse, the football match, and the music hall. Music-hall songs, he argues, show that working-class consciousness became defensive. Working-class identity was strengthened by a turning inward, away from aggressive socialism. (Turnings away from the supposed socialist destiny of workers tend to preoccupy Marxian historians.)

Some evidence supports this. In the community workers recognized their distinctiveness from even small masters. Although in Preston most workers voting before 1900 were Tories, they did not want to mix with middle-class Conservatives and established their own Conservative clubs (Savage 1987: 143). Yet their communities were not merely erecting barricades. Workers' families eagerly participated in mass consumer markets appearing from the 1870s and 1880s. Between 1870 and 1890, retail prices dropped by 20 percent, and weekly earnings rose by 20 percent (Feinstein 1976: table 65). Shops and distributive trades brought national marketing and uniform advertising billboards across towns, regions, even the whole country. Local protectionist networks of consumption and credit endured, but families also entered a national economy of consumer choice whose market controls were diffused, impersonal, and national (F. M. L. Thompson 1988). Sport moved from being rural to urban, generating a national leisure industry, with professional football its centerpiece. Here, market forces were diluted by direct segmental controls, as football, cricket, and other clubs were run by local notables (Hargreaves 1986). Sport provided metaphors for political activists of all classes – "It's not cricket," "Marquis of Queensberry Rules," "below the belt" – evidence of common adherence to the "rules of the game" (McKibbin 1990b). Such developments did not segregate workers but, rather, brought them into the national mainstream.

Ecological class segregation, the franchise for half of all male workers, and open electoral hustings brought workers into politics. But cross-class collaboration had so far dominated, centering on cooperation between skilled workers and middle-class Liberals and Nonconformists. Politics focused especially on education, now the state's main civil activity. Increasingly unionists and socialists sat on local school boards, cooperating with Liberals and Nonconformists. Literacy rocketed. In 1900, only 3 percent of those getting married could not sign their names in the register, compared to 30 percent in 1860 (Stone 1969). From 1892 on, compulsory schooling increased worker participation in national cultural life.

Segregation of men from women in working-class communities seems to have increased. This period saw dramatic changes in women's lives. The last great surge in discursive literacy was predominantly among workers' daughters, enabling female participation in national cultural life. Modern birth-control methods started to filter down, and mortality rates were reversed: Instead of dying younger than men, women began to outlive them. Rising wages, falling prices, and a consumer economy meant it mattered less that women still gave male breadwinners the lion's share of food. Their bodies could withstand childbirth (Hart 1989, 1991). Male breadwinners supported the household economy, though perhaps playing less of a role within it. There were two main practices. Either men handed over a portion of their wages to the women for household expenses, retaining personal discretion over the rest, or they handed over the entire wage, receiving back a fixed sum for their own use. Most women found casual part-time employment and normally spent their lesser wage for household and personal expenditures. Two spheres separated: male discretionary consumption and female-household consumption. Brewing, sports, and tobacco industries generated masculine leisure activities: "Respectable working men could gather, dressed in non-working clothes with watch, chain and bowler hat, removed from both work and the now female domain of home," remarks Davidoff (1990: 111).

Did the community life of men and women became more segregated and conflictual, weakening community *intensive* reinforcement for the *extensive* class polarization occurring in employment? We must be wary of romanticizing the earlier period. Temperance had been the principal form of nineteenth-century feminism, so some segregation and conflict had long been present. Yet the community lives of men and women remained partly segregated during this period of employment polarization. Previous chapters showed that in earlier petit bourgeois disturbances and in Chartism, community reinforced the *totality* of class movements. In the Second Industrial Revolution some of this reinforcement was lacking.

Thus community tendencies were rather complex. There was some segregation of class residence and culture. Some of this appears inward and defensive; some encouraged workers' political aggression; and some, their participation in the economic, cultural, and party-democratic life of the nation. Men and women experienced these developments differently. But overall, family and community life did not simply reinforce employment tendencies toward class polarization. Unlike nation, class was becoming more extensive but less intensive.

Economic strategies of capital and labor

The collective laborer thesis emphasizes the class-boosting effects of a deskilling process within Second Industrial Revolution factories. I now critically assess this thesis. It states that employers mechanized and rationalized production to attack craft privileges, thrusting artisans downward while thrusting up newly semiskilled workers. The two groups became more similar and many participated together in internal labor markets. The skilled workers were radicalized; semiskilled (and even some unskilled) workers developed their first unions. Gradually they fused, first in the "new unions," then more lastingly in radicalized older unions and in a social democratic Labour party. This is the main thrust of many historians' explanations – endorsed most fully by Price (1983, 1985) and to varying degrees by Pelling (1963: 85–6, 98–100), Gray (1976: 167–9), Crossick (1978: 248), Baines (1981: 162), Hunt (1981), and Thane (1981: 230).

Their arguments also resonate in the labor process and deskilling theories prevalent among industrial sociologists during the 1970s (e.g., Braverman 1974; Friedmann 1977; and Burawoy 1979; Hill 1981: 103–23 gives a critical account). These portrayed the labor process of the early twentieth century as typified by large corporations in manufacturing industry. More also resonate among current sociology's emphasis on the "Fordism" of the period, exemplified by the 1907 Model T assembly line of the Ford Motor Company. Drawing on Hilferding's classic theory, Lash and Urry (1987) characterize the period from the 1880s to the 1950s as the era of "organized capitalism," in contrast to the present era, which they see as dominated by "disorganized capitalism," "post-Fordism," and "flexible restructuring."

The enterprises of Edwardian Britain might seem to sit uneasily with this thesis. Joyce (1989) and McKibbin (1990) observe that only half of the labor force was in manufacturing-mining-transport "modern" sectors. The other half was in commerce, tiny establishment, or still working "on the streets," largely untouched by unions. Even the typical manufacturing enterprise was either a family firm or a federation of families (the private company). Joint-stock companies did not predominate until the 1920s. Of the 50 largest manufacturing enterprises (in assets) in 1905, 18 were in brewing and distilling (whose community significance I have already stressed); 10, in textiles; and only 23, in producer's goods (Payne 1967: 527; cf. Ashworth 1960: 90–102). About one hundred firms employed more than three thousand workers each, spread among an average of three factories per firm.

As in all countries even the largest factories were dwarfed by state organizations. After the armed forces, the largest department was the post office, its 114,000 work force (in 1908) four times larger than any private enterprise. The state provided 2 of the 10 largest manufacturing enterprises (the Royal Dockyards and the Royal Ordnance Factories). The other 8, each with more than 13,000 employees, were diverse: 2 textile conglomerates, each containing more than 25 establishments; 3 railway companies or workshops; 2 armaments firms closely linked to the state; and another engineering firm. Eleventh came the Co-operative Wholesale Society (Shaw 1983). If mines were included, 2 mining companies would be in the top 10 (Taylor 1968: 63–65). Could such diverse establishments have much in common?

Yes – the larger ones had in common steam power, *the* symbol of the first Industrial Revolution, not dominant until the second. Steam-engine capacity used for other than transport purposes increased by 25 percent during 1870–96. In 1870, more than half of steam power was confined to textiles, by 1907, under a fifth. Steam was especially used in mining, iron and steel, engineering, shipbuilding, railways; and public utilities. But other energy sources had also arrived. By 1907, electricity drove about one-quarter of engine capacity, and gas and internal-combustion engines (using coal gas and oil) rivaled steam in

Table 17.1. *Industrial distribution of the British labor force*
(percentages)

	1851	1881	1911
Agriculture, forestry, fishing	21.6	13.0	8.6
Mining, quarrying	4.1	4.6	6.5
Manufacturing	33.0	32.1	33.3
Building	5.2	6.9	6.5
Trade and transport	15.5	21.4	21.5
Public service, professional	5.2	6.1	8.1
Domestic, personal services	13.4	15.3	14.0
Total percentage	100.0%	100.0%	100.0%
Total working population (millions)	9.7	13.1	18.6

Source: Deane and Cole 1969: 143.

smaller establishments (Ashworth 1960: 86; Musson 1978: 166–70). Common technologies using these prime movers transformed workplaces throughout the economy, eliminating handicrafts from central production processes, reducing domestic outwork to 2 percent of employment according to the 1901 census (predominantly female outworkers in clothing, but presumably a considerable understatement), and mechanizing individual tasks (though rarely the linkages between machines).

In and around the core industries, this changed work tasks, de-skilled jobs, and increased management-machine pressure. But it also began to homogenize employment throughout the national economy, not just in manufacturing. The prime movers required feeding with mountains of coal, transported and deposited outside each workplace. Mining, transport, and distribution grew, although manufacturing remained static, as we see in Table 17.1.

The only declining group were agricultural workers, but manufacturing employment was only keeping pace with overall population and employment growth, outstripped by the rate of growth of mining, trade and transport, public employment, and professionals. In the 1907 census of production, mining's net output of £106 million dwarfed the next largest industries, engineering (£50 million), cotton (£45 million), construction (£43 million), and iron and steel (£30 million). Mining employment grew more than output over the period 1850–1913, indicating more labor rather than intensification of existing labor – probably also true in most tertiary areas.

Bain and Price (1980) provide statistics of union membership from the 1890s; I add 1888 figures from Clegg et al. (1964: 1). I identify two crude indicators of union power by their density level – the proportion of potential membership a union recruits. For an individual union this would be the labor force in its industry; for the labor movement as a whole, the national nonagricultural labor force.

1. At density levels of about 25 percent unions become significant *sectional* power actors. They can still be bypassed, employers can still control workers paternalistically, but this now involves risks. Unions mobilizing their members can now disrupt. If in crises they can mobilize outward among nonmembers, broad class conflict may result. This risk is reduced if union members are segregated from nonmembers by skill, industry, or religious, ethnic, or community identity. Then employers can segmentally divide and rule: incorporate and make concessions to organized and market-controlling workers, treat the rest harshly. British sectionalism was mainly by skill, and in some areas also by ethnicity (as, e.g., British versus Irish).

2. At about 50 percent density, unions may become *class* actors, with pretensions to lead a singular working class. Regimes may now prefer institutionalized national and local bargaining. Divide and rule is less practicable, and the main alternative to conciliation is costly full-scale repression.

In 1888, national density was only 5 percent. Three-quarters of union members were concentrated in four industries: engineering and shipbuilding (25 percent of union members), mining and quarrying (20 percent), textiles (16 percent), and construction (12 percent). Industry density rates were all under 20 percent, except for mining's more than 50 percent. Only mining unions approached all-grades class solidarity, though craftsmen in several industries had a sectional power presence. In national terms this amounted to a loose confederation of sectional, usually skilled power actors capable of disrupting key industries but not of class confrontation – as with all countries' labor movements at this time. Regimes and capitalists might attempt thoroughgoing repression with some prospect of success: Troops might be necessary in mining and some crafts, but such pockets of resistance could be isolated. Alternatively, segmental incorporation of these unions might avoid general concessions.

In only four years following 1888, the "new unionism" doubled in membership to 1.5 million and in density to 11 percent. Coal mining and engineering-shipbuilding each contributed 21 percent of national membership, twice that of cotton, construction, and transport workers. Density now curved upward. By 1901, it was 18 percent, and then it leveled off. By 1911, membership was 3.1 million, and density was 19 percent. Mining led, transport workers had leaped into second place – railway workers (whose density increased steadily) and road and sea transport workers (who surged in two bursts, 1888–92 and post-1910). Construction workers had been overtaken by local government and education workers. By 1914, membership had grown again to 4.1 million; density, to 25 percent. In all these industries, plus gas, printing, and postal services, density was now more than 50 percent.

Unions remained male. In 1901, women made up 30 percent of the labor force and only 8 percent of unionists. In 1914, male density was 32 percent and female 9 percent. All density rates given here would be much lower for women, about 30 percent higher for men, and even higher for men in the manufacturing-mining-transport core. Women were excluded from employment likely to generate unions. In 1911, 39 percent of employed women were still domestic servants. Nonetheless, many militants shared gas workers' leader Will Thorne's sexism: "Women do not make good trade unionists and for this reason we believe that our energies are better used towards the organisation of male workers" (Hinton 1983: 32).

In sum, unions first became significant sectional then class actors across several important industries, but only among men. Unions were strongest in coal mining, then engineering, shipbuilding and railways, then cotton, then construction and government employment. By now in mining, even sectional repression would be costly and might fail, and it was risky in other major industries. Employers were still relatively unconstrained in dealing with most female employees.

I begin discussion of individual union struggles with industries offering some support to the collective laborer thesis. Early construction unions grew amid small, dispersed workplaces and a mobile work force. As Chapter 15 showed, interstitial organization had been common in early unionism. Construction unions now lagged, but just before World War I, de-skilling, especially in bricklaying and masonry, broadened unionism and introduced radical syndicalism – which went down to heavy defeat (Holton 1976: 155–63).

Engineering was seriously affected by changes in the labor process, though in a double-edged way (Burgess 1985). From the 1880s on, mass production impacted on machine shops. Many new turret and capstan lathes, then mechanical milling, grinding, and boring machines were operated by semiskilled machinists who had replaced skilled fitters and turners. Apprenticeship declined as learning on the job increased. Yet these machines also upgraded the skills of maintenance workers and those who manufactured the machines.

This shifted rather than diluted skills and split the unions between old sectionalist leaders and new militants seeking all-grades unity. The employers attacked during this period of disunity, claiming their right to be "masters in their own shops," as American and German competitors already were. In the 1890s, they organized nationally and in 1897 provoked the Amalgamated Society of Engineers (ASE) to strike for an eight-hour day. The employers picked a time of slack demand. After six months, the ASE capitulated, withdrawing its eight-hour demand and conceding the employer's right to allocate men to machines. The ASE accepted apprenticeship decline, an increase in semiskilled workers (20 percent of the work force by 1914), and piecework. Unable to destroy the internal labor market, the union remained split. Many branches sought joint regulation of internal labor markets and accepted semiskilled and unskilled workers as members. The employers' victory slowly encouraged broader unity between grades. By 1911, though, the ASE had recovered and trouble was again brewing.

The employers' offensive spread to other manufacturing industries with entrenched craft unions – shipbuilding, printing, boots and shoes, and furniture. Pressured by international competition, employers organized nationally throughout the 1890s, using the trade cycle to choose the moment of confrontation. These became their two staple techniques: authoritative, national organization and exploitation of unplanned, diffused international markets, the two territorial sources of their class power, the national (soon to become their main area of weakness) and the transnational (eventually their main area of strength).

Employers could rarely smash unions, though some tried. British employers' strategies were at first more or less like those of employers everywhere. But craft unions in Britain had more weapons available than skilled workers in other countries had. They had been far longer entrenched, both in shop-floor bargaining and on the edges of state elites and parties. They influenced legislation improving their collective civil rights. After 1874 and again after 1906, British law was more favorable to unions, to strikes, and to picketing than the laws of any other major country. British employers thus were forced toward economic tactics, being deprived of much judicial or police repression. They did not have full public sympathy, and there was pressure from political parties and state elites to conciliate in labor disputes.

Nor were either side's economic weapons ideally suited for war to the death. Most rationalization and mechanization occurred in non-traditional firms where employers rarely confronted the best-entrenched craft unions. Newer industries like papermaking, milling, footwear, clothing, precious metals, bicycles, electrical and motor engineering, food processing, and chemicals generated new skilled grades into which production workers were upgraded rather than artisans downgraded. These skills were real, scarce, but learned more on the job than through apprenticeship. But in their heartland, in longer-established sectors of engineering, craftworkers were less challenged and held onto controls over apprenticeship and pay differentials, which remained fairly stable (Penn 1985).

Nonetheless, some changes were universal. Everywhere craftsmen lost their hiring-and-firing and subcontracting powers, and unskilled laborers were brought from casual work into the same organizations of production. All grades were now wage laborers with similar overall conditions of employment, not members of different classes, as artisans had been. Craft unions could maintain wholesale sectionalism only by abandoning newer industries and newer skilled and semiskilled workers, which they were reluctant to do. Employers had fewer black-leg (scab) options than in most countries. With agriculture already denuded of labor, only the Irish constituted "green" labor (and many employers shared English stereotypes of the feckless Irish). Employers also conferred powers on the newly skilled. They recruited to skilled grades through the internal labor market from responsible men in their own work forces. In this exchange the employer got control over labor but became dependent on the skilled. Workers got employment security and a decline in employer arbitrary power.

Doubtless, if British employers had been able to marshal law courts and paramilitary forces as could their American counterparts (see Chapter 18), most would have fought determinedly for the nonunion shop. Because Britain was the country that had most civilianized its regulation of domestic order (as Chapter 12 shows), they could not. Many negotiated. The legality of unions and bargaining rules were substantially secured by 1875, earlier than in other Western countries. Employers recognized in evidence to royal commissions and in conversations with contemporary inquirers that unions were there to stay. As one author noted in 1906:

I have not heard a single word in favour of trade unions from any employer in Germany or America. . . . Employers hate and dread the unions. In England I have met no such feeling at all. I have heard the unions unfavourably criticized and sometimes condemned, but without bitterness. I have far more often heard from employers and managers fair and even friendly expressions of opinion. [quoted in McKibbin 1990]

Unions also sought allies, aiming at middle-class liberalism and recruitment of the less skilled. They were driven toward politics and unskilled workers – both characteristics of the "new unionism."

That is all the confirming evidence for the labor process, factory-centered explanation of the rise of the collective laborer. No other union growth areas can be interpreted thus, and the character of emerging class consciousness cannot be explained in these terms alone, even in these industries. I now turn to other industries.

Coal mining was the most important. One union, the Miners Federation of Great Britain, grew at the expense of regional federations. This was partly a response to national organization by the mine owners, pressured by international competition but also because the federation championed two traditional demands uniting all grades, insistence on the eight-hour day and opposition to the sliding scale tying wages to the price of coal. Mining unions were also already traveling toward political incorporation, let in by the 1884 County Suffrage Act. Their unique geographic concentration enabled them to influence British party democracy by electing "Lib-Lab" members of Parliament.

All this was evident in the great strike of 1893. The Miners Federation resisted a 25 percent sliding scale wage reduction and were locked out nationally: 300,000 miners out for sixteen weeks. Alarmed and pressured by Lib-Lab MPs, the government intervened, apparently for the first time in an industrial dispute since the triumph of laissez-faire. The ensuing compromise was really a union victory. The strike encouraged solidarity among faceworkers (until now dominant in unions), other underground workers, and surface workers. The Miners Federation became "new," admitting the unskilled. Class unity had resulted from international pressure forcing employers into national organization, from traditional union demands, and from the party-democratic political crystallization. Mechanization and de-skilling barely came into it. Miners could withstand blackleg labor because they were united on wages and hours and because isolated solidary mining communities were not afraid of using violence. They sought mutualism – political regulation of industrial relations, a minimum wage, and limitation of hours – and remained Lib-Labs. Only in 1909 did they affiliate with the Labour party, retaining autonomy inside the party until after the war.

Although the labor process in mines was unique, the demands of mining unions were typical. The ten-, then nine-, then eight-hour day had been the main demands of nineteenth-century unions. After 1880, international competition pressured wages downward during recessions and led unions to demand minimum wages. The sliding scale was common in cotton, boots and shoes, and ironworking. Cotton workers did not restrict entry into their unions, but skilled spinners dominated them. This led lower grades to form a breakaway quasi-socialist "new union." Spinners' insertion in party democracy was halfway to the miners'. Concentrated as voters in Lancashire but still partly controlled by their employers (Joyce 1980), they exerted mild pressure on both parties through the United Textile Factory Workers Association – unlike the radical Yorkshire weavers, who launched the Independent Labour party (ILP), precursor of the Labour party. A national employers' offensive against wages was again led by employers' associations responding to international competition. The 1893 general cotton strike forced all grades closer together. Its settlement whittled down a 10 percent wage reduction to under 3 percent and instituted national procedures for settling disputes without strikes. This Brooklands Agreement set the pattern of conciliatory national bargaining.

So, in the principal "old unions," more extensive employers' organizations, pressured by international market forces, forced greater worker unity. It was either that or decline, even for many exclusive craft brotherhoods. The demands were mostly traditional, though in some sectors de-skilling was also an issue. Skill differentials and privileges in the workplace were being bypassed by wider economic forces leading to broader class organization by both sides. Unions were pushed toward more extensive and political organization. But various part-democratic insertions more than variations in the labor process were structuring political outcomes.

The "new unions" are conventionally dated back to the gas workers' and dockers' strikes of 1899 (Hobsbawm 1968: 158–78; Lovell 1985; Pollard 1985). Led by Will Thorne, a member of the Marxist Social Democratic Federation (SDF), with secretarial assistance from Eleanor Marx, Karl's daughter, the gas workers' union had 2,000 members in London within four months of formation. Gas production had been expanded by longer hours and harder work. Labor had been intensified, not de-skilled, as Hobsbawm (1985: 18) observes was the pattern among all new unions. The union demanded three shifts instead of two to reduce hours from twelve to eight. The union core was skilled stokers, with quite long training on the job and control over production, not easily replaceable with blacklegs. The London gas companies conceded without a fight. The internal labor market had worked against its creator. Gas workers' unions spread nationally, often with the aid of the SDF. Their example proved contagious. In August 1889, a pay dispute spread over the London docks. Massive orderly demonstrations brought public sympathy and intervention from the Lord Mayor and Cardinal Manning. The resulting compromise was a union triumph and membership shot up to 30,000. With the help of socialist organizations, new unions spread nationally among dockers, seamen, porters, carters, railway workers, and diverse groups in manufacturing, brick making, building, white-collar employment, and even agriculture. By 1890, these unions claimed more than 350,000 members.

Most could not hold on to their gains. The main success stories were in the gas, white-collar, and railway unions. White-collar unions grew faster than manual unions from 1901, mostly recruiting government employees, especially teachers (including many women) and postal workers. Clerks in commerce and industry were almost entirely unorganized; unionists in the sales sector were largely confined to the cooperative movement. Public employees have continued to dominate white-collar unions in the twentieth century, since the state has been more conciliatory than private employers (Bain 1970). Even a limited franchise party democracy constrained public employers toward conciliation.

The railways had long seen restrictive craft unions, but in 1889 they were suddenly rivaled by a General Railway Workers Union, open to all grades, aggressively deriding protectionism: "The Union shall remain a fighting one and shall not be encumbered with any sick or accident fund." It focused on hours, forcing craft unions to do likewise. Employers fought back, pressured, they argued, by the increasing ratio of working expenses to gross receipts. The General Union almost collapsed under their offensive, but in the 1890s, a craft union took over its cause. The Amalgamated Society of Railway Servants – the predecessor of the present National Union of Railwaymen – became "new" by opening up to all gardes. A new union had successfully fertilized an old one. Again the unity between grades was on a traditionally politicized issue, hours, rather than about any transformation of the labor process. And the fertilization was toward more extensive, classlike organization favoring joint regulation. By the end of the period governments had persuaded employers to achieve this (Bagwell 1985).

But most new unions failed, either dying quickly or declining slowly (until revived in the strike wave of 1911–14 from whence they spawned the General Unions of the twentieth century). From 1891 on, employers coordinated national offensives. New unions were rarely supported by old ones. Though their conditions stirred middle-class sympathy, their advocacy of socialism did not. When the recession of 1893 hit, employer lockouts and layoffs destroyed most of them. Yet they triumphed from the grave. Some of their class consciousness was now adopted by the old unions. I express this in terms of my IOTA model:

1. Unions new and old sought broader all-grades solidarity to form one great union. Class (more precisely general industrial) rather than sectional craft *identity* was strengthened.

2. They mobilized aggressive solidarity to impress employer and public opinion with strength and determination and to deter blackleg labor. Their lack of full entry controls made employers turn to blacklegging and they responded with violence. They resisted their class *opponent* forcefully and extensively, although in the end they aimed at conciliation.

3. These extensions encouraged class *totality*, though more exten-

sively than intensively. Unions grew – more full-time officials, executive bodies elected by whole membership rather than local affiliates, more interunion federations, and more national agreements on the cotton industry pattern. The TUC put representatives in Parliament and on government committees (Martin 1980: 58–96). Union involvement in local politics intensified. Union branches, trades councils, labor political committees, working men's clubs, co-ops, friendly societies, socialist clubs collaborated – most notably on school board elections – in a permanent "labor consciousness," combining mutualism and reformism (Thompson 1967; Crossick 1978: 245). This was predominantly male: Employment, family, and community were segregated by gender. Not all of a militant's life flowed from his employment identity. The intense commitment of the Chartist – deriving from entwined exploitation in employment, family, and community life – was lacking.

4. If the first three IOTA elements increased class formation, the fourth undercut it. Unions sought state elite and party aid against employers, renewing the cross-class segmental alliances common in recent British party democracy. State technocrats and some of the middle class showed sympathy. Probably half the unionists were enfranchised and the two parties competed for their votes to stave off an independent Labour party. Thus demands were compromised by the language of cross-class party democracy, lessening *alternative* socialisms.

Thus the development of unions contained an internal contradiction between socialist reformism and segmental alliances with incorporative liberalism. Nor was there yet a singular working class. Most union recruits had above-average earnings, security, and job skills. They were male insiders ranged against male and female outsiders. But unity and aggression grew. Unions and strikes were broader based than had been traditional among craftsmen, spanning many grades within an industry or locality, to create something a little more than Hobsbawm's "alliances of local job monopolies and closed shops" (1968: 179–203). Lest we get lost in the specifics of each industry, remember that the same pattern was occurring nationally: Virtually all unions were increasing membership density and affiliation with the TUC and the Labour party; most increases occurred in the same two bouts, 1889–92 and 1911–14 (as they did in all countries, as capitalism diffused its growth, its concentration, and its trade cycles throughout the West); and by 1914, density varied less among industries than at the beginning of the period. Almost everywhere density was above the "25 percent sectionalist" level. Unions were now a normal part of labor relations. All this is doubly impressive, given the variability of conditions and labor processes among industries. It pushes us toward explaining the rise of labor less as a response to the direct labor process than to diffused characteristics of overall economy and state.

Production relations mattered in the most general sense: A dichotomous, qualitative difference between capital and labor had spread across the economy. Other forms of employment – domestic outwork, subcontracting, casual employment – were in steep decline, especially among men. The first two now were relegated to minorities; the third was predominantly female, no longer typical of all nonskilled work. A large majority of those capable of collective action, whether formally skilled, semiskilled, or unskilled, entered a formal employment contract with an owner-manager. Two classes, in the sense specified by Marx and Engels, existed right across an extensive, diffused system recognized as such by them. Booms and slumps, relations between wages, hours, costs, prices, demand, supply, production, consumption, and competition, both national and international, forced uniform responses from both classes. National strikes and lockouts, government arbitration, and national agreements became routine. In 1899, there had been one industrywide agreement; by 1910, there were seven (Marks 1989: 86).

Employers' class identity was also expanded by the same forces. The coordinated employer offensive, mobilizing only civilian legal and police repression, relied mainly on economic organization – national lockouts, national organization of blackleg labor (protected by law and police) to sit out long confrontations without mutual competition. When employers organized nationally, no interstices remained. Artisan sectionalism was finally outflanked.

But employers' victories were achieved at a cost. Workers' organizational capacities grew, especially in the four industries (engineering, mining, transport, and government employment) now labor's core. Engineering artisans' insertion into industry made them leaders, used to organization and to exercising labor market controls. The large factory, railway shop, or mine located in a one-class residential community allowed space for workers to develop collective solidarity without meeting their master. The joint-stock company, especially in mining, provided even more space, leading to the "isolated mass" of workers removed from direct owner control (which Kerr and Siegel 1954 classically demonstrated increased class solidarity). Transport workers' distinctive mobility enabled them to organize contacts among dispersed occupations – workers had to comprehend a national economy and transport workers were best placed to pass discursive messages around a national work force. The importance of government employment provided further space: Workers in a giant naval dockyard or small post office or school did not interact with a "master" but with a more impersonal administration responsible to factionalized political masters and often committed to conciliation. The two sides were confronting each other over the same terrain, the territory of the national state, confronting each other's novel powers, uncertain about the future, and ambiguous about their own economic strategies.

Political strategies of labor and regime

To struggle for his interests, the masculine collective laborer was forced into politics, where he encountered the existing crystallizations of the state. Some political traditions emerged unscathed right through the period. Workers might remain in the embrace of Liberal political economy or Conservative paternalism (many still so remain), but most male heads of households were admitted to party democracy in the boroughs in 1867 and in the counties (along with agricultural workers with fixed abodes) in 1884. Sixty-six percent of adult males were now eligible to vote, including upward of 40 percent of male manual workers (although many were prevented from voting by biased registration procedures). Perhaps half the electorate were workers. With the decline in particularistic controls, party politics changed. The suffrage had been extended sectionally, by property franchises, as the parties competed for worker support. The 1867 act was Tory; the 1884 act, Liberal. In some areas Tories appeased workers' economism and mutualism (for Preston, see Savage 1987: 134–61); mostly the Liberals did this (for London, see P. Thompson 1967). Party divisions over tariffs strengthened cross-class sectoral alliances: Birmingham engineering favored protection; Lancashire, cotton free trade.

The widening civilian scope of the state ensured that party democracy acquired greater relevance for the regional-religious "national" crystallization, now focused on control of mass education: Anglican and English workers stayed more with the Conservative party; Nonconformists and Celts were Lib-Labs. Outside Ireland this secured the adherence of most regional (potentially national) dissidents to a national party democracy. The two mass parties finally institutionalized a predominantly centralized solution to its national issue. Britain was now a complete nation-state (in the terms of Table 3.3), at least on its mainland. Widening civilian scope also increased the number of government workers, which fostered relatively centralized conciliation and unionization, as it has done during the twentieth century. Town halls, under electoral pressure from local trades councils, accepted union rates for municipal employees. In 1891, the Conservative government's "fair wages resolution" agreed that central government contracts should be awarded at union rates. Civil servants were active conciliators, especially in the Board of Trade. By 1904, the board had used the Conciliation Act of 1896 to create 162 joint negotiating boards across industry. From 1909 on, Liberal legislation furthered this: Labour exchanges extended the board's consultation with unions and employers, and the inclusion of union benefit funds in the Health and Unemployment Insurance Act of 1911 brought the protectionist core of unions into state administration (Davidson 1972). National incorporation – centralized reforms in return for responsibility – furthered peace.

Nonetheless, incorporation by the existing parties faltered in the 1890s, and labor militants grew restive. The 1899 TUC congress voted narrowly to assist an independent Labour party. The Labour Representation Committee, founded the next year, had virtually no policy besides securing the "return of labour members to Parliament" and virtually no organization besides unions. But it found a potent issue after the Taff Vale judgment of 1901: Under a Conservative "law and order" government, the courts held unions legally liable for damages caused by individual striking members, another expression of a bourgeois-individualist concept of civil rights. Further legal judgments supported by the Conservative government made the legal blow serious. Conservative unionism evaporated and LRC membership more than doubled in two years. The Conservatives had become largely a class party. Workers would still vote for them – especially in the English south and midlands and among Anglicans – but not *as* workers. Their attempt to incorporate organized labor was over, even if their segmental controls remained effective in smaller towns and country regions.

But the Liberal party responded. Its left wing, the "New Liberals," offered mutualist guarantees of organizing rights plus social reforms: relief of poverty, more education, and other welfare. The moral-ideological crystallization of the British state now vigorously entwined with liberal Nonconformism. Booth's social surveys aroused liberal and religious outrage at poverty and unemployment, increasingly recognized as structural, not the fault of the poor and unemployed. Liberal moral sympathy was mobilized by journalists and professionals, rarely by business people (Emy 1973: 53). Booth himself called this program "limited socialism." It was largely mutualist. Under Lloyd George, it achieved substantial results: his 1911 scheme for health and unemployment insurance and his major switch from regressive indirect to more progressive direct taxation. The state would redistribute and encourage self-help through state-regulated insurance. Insurance covered only workers in larger firms, but brought together the state, most unions, large employers, and private insurance companies. This was the first genuine reformism, in a twentieth-century sense, to occur in any country. It had come less from labor, more from a cross-class party trying to rally workers, middle class, and some regions and religions.

Yet the Liberal party was not an ideal instrument to advance reformism. The two large parties had inherited the interests of the old regime, the Tories being (broadly) the party of the Anglican church, agriculture, and commercial capital; the Liberals, of Nonconformism and industry. The Tories became more English, especially southern English; the Liberals, more northern and Celtic (though not in Ireland). In these respects both were cross-class parties, including capitalists *and* workers. Despite the defection of many employers to the Conservative party in this period, the Liberals included industrialists and trade unions (because industry was more northern and Celtic). At a time of rising industrial confrontation, this caused internal party factionalism. Apart from Lloyd George, party leaders steered policy away from overall social strategy, for this might divide them. The new liberalism's overall reformist alternative was not adopted, though some reforms were. In local parties evasion was more difficult. All labor movements had as a key demand of political citizenship the election of workers – in practice, union officials – to political office. In Britain this was reinforced by militants' strong sense of class identity. In fact British labor became preoccupied with personnel and means rather than alternative ends: Its three overriding issues were universal suffrage (although such a male-dominated movement gave little real help to the woman suffragists), collective civil rights for unions, and the election of union officials to public office. The Liberals *had* to concede these to incorporate labor.

With the new infrastructural powers of the state, gone were the centuries when politics were irrelevant to the lives of the people. The state could not be evaded, better now to participate in the control of its multifarious benefits and costs impacting on many areas of social life. Suffrage was now desirable as the great symbol of citizenship, as feminists as well as workers made clear in all countries. But gone also was the half century when workers had experienced profound political exploitation. The tax burden and Poor Law had eased; worker representatives were participating in local government and half of all workers were voting. Labor wanted suffrage for all workers. The Liberals did not object, although they dragged their heels (their public reservations were mostly where labor also had private reservations, women). The Liberals would shortly have extended the franchise had the war not intervened. The Liberal leadership had also converted to collective civil rights for unions. Recognizing that union leaders were responsible and obsessed by the issue, they legislated the 1906 Trade Disputes Act, remedying the Taff Vale judgment, as soon as they regained office. Unions now enjoyed full collective organizing rights – the end in Britain (until the Thatcher period) of the major mutualist grievance, now finally institutionalized within the Lib-Lab tradition. Had this occurred in 1820, workers might even have been content not to have the vote. But the history of Chartism and later struggles over party democracy, reinforced by the widening civilian scope of the state, made this the centerpiece of class politics.

The real problem lay in choosing Liberal candidates. What good was the vote if it gave only a choice of voting for industrialists or lawyers? Precisely in industrial constituencies where Liberal candidates would be elected, their activists were most divided by class. In the West Riding of Yorkshire, for example, the industrial magnates, not the New Liberals, controlled the party and they excluded working-class candidates (Emy 1973: 289; Laybourn and Reynolds 1984). Even the most moderate labor activists were conscious of being kept at arm's length from real power – in what was supposed to be *their* political party. Though incorporative liberalism offered mutualist principles and policy reforms, it lacked comradeship. Its radicals were rationalist technocrats uneasy with mass electioning, puzzled by the lack of policy yet collective solidarity of the Labour party. The Liberal party was a party of notables, not a social movement. This was its main weakness.

Socialism offered comradeship – coherent, emotional, and totalizing – centered in the notion of workers controlling their own lives. Labor was, above all, a party of class identity. Its leaders were former workers. It had no individual party membership, only the collective membership of unions. Many militants also sensed class opposition when confronted by a coordinated employers' offensive backed by court rulings that union actions were illegal, and felt threatened by unemployment and cyclical economic trends, and patronized by the Liberals. British socialism emerged out of populism and radical non-conformity, yet added comprehension of the new economic system. It loosely Marxified the originally petit bourgeois labor theory of value and the comradeship of the male working class with a concept of the totality of society. British socialists – from Marx's disciple Hyndman, through the eclectic Tom Mann and William Morris, to the pragmatic Keir Hardie, the Labour party's first leader – shared one belief: The workers' material and moral ills were due to the laws of a capitalist economy that had to be confronted as a whole. The second revolution had increased class homogenization. Socialist ideology and comradeship could offer enlarged understanding in a literal sense. Tom Jones remembered South Wales during the 1880s and 1890s thus:

During this crusading period, Socialism swept through valleys like a new religion, and young men asked one another, Are you a Socialist? in the same tone as a Salvationist asks, Are you saved? In one generation the outlook of the miners was transformed.

Joyce shrewdly comments:

Socialism may most effectively have worked not as a received body of ideology but as a force breaching the understandings of decades on which paternalism and deference had subsisted. It broke in on the employer's mastery of the situation . . . penetrating the closed immediacy of the factory community. It was upon this capacity to define the boundaries of people's outlook that paternalism in large measure depended. [1980: 229, 335]

Workers were now organized over the same national terrain as employers and could use a systemic ideology to comprehend it. Labor was forced by the economy, by employers, and by hostile law courts and widening government administration toward the national state.

What would be its alternative? At that point socialism broke down and labor drifted back toward liberalism with mutualist hues. Most labor leaders before 1914 lacked even a reformist alternative. What labor should say when it got into Parliament was little debated. As a civil servant commented about his negotiations with labor leaders about the 1911 National Insurance Act: "They don't speak for their men, don't know what their men want, and can't bind their men to obey – rather difficult people to deal with" (Moore 1978: 113). There was no grand political design, rarely even great principled disputes. The Labour party and the TUC fought more for mutualism and means than for reformist ends. There was an interest in direct rather than indirect taxation (though the New Liberals made the running here) and in public works to alleviate unemployment, but no actual program. Unions preferred voluntary collective bargaining to state intervention, to the puzzlement of radical Liberals (Emy 1973: 264, 293–4). Labor, as in most other countries, showed little interest in welfare-state legislation. All labor movements distrusted state action, as states had generally harmed rather than benefited them.

Moreover, the national issue still impacted, though now *within* a centralized party democracy. It reinforced Labour party distrust of the state. The new industrial core, and therefore the labor core, was concentrated in Scotland, Wales, and northern England, regions suspicious of the power of the capital. This entwined with Nonconformist labor strength, suspicious of the established Anglican state church. Not until World War II did labor manage to identify itself fully with the English-British nation-state. Until then the state seemed ideologically conservative, best avoided (Pelling 1968: 1–18; Heclo 1974: 89–90; Cronin 1988; Brown 1971 dissents from this view).

Yet once welfare schemes were institutionalized, unions participated in their administration (Marks 1989: 105–6). Participation vastly enlarged during the war. Labor stumbled onto the reformist uses of the state, and liberal incorporation finally changed toward reformist socialism in two wartime bursts.

Divergences between Marxists, social democrats, and mutualists reflected the ambiguous identity of workers and of the labor movement in its civil society–national state. Was labor a citizen participant or was it not? After 1867 and 1884, many possessed the vote. Miners could determine their own MPs; others with a strong local presence could apply pressure. Many militants were in local government and on school boards. The collective civil citizenship of unions was eventually achieved but needed vigilance against judges. Practical state recognition was greater than employer recognition and sometimes greater than that of politicians. But this conciliatory state was not *their* state, not a state of genuine national citizenship, as the restricted franchise, the legal judgments and the London Anglican establishment revealed. Labor leaders, no matter how cautious, knew they were held away from the central councils of the realm.

It was difficult for all but hardened revolutionaries or Lib-Lab loyalists to decide what vision their ambiguous position might generate. Their divisions, partial incorporation and partial citizenship, made syndicalism, but above all Marxism, implausible. During 1913–14, in a time of mounting industrial confrontation, when Liberal and Labour politics were obtaining no concessions (politicians were obsessed with the Irish crisis), syndicalism rallied. Just under two thousand syndicalist militants influenced a wave of national strikes and the formation of broader industrial unions. But as these became implicated in the extension of state-aided collective bargaining, they became more like other unions. Thus practical activities doused the short-lived fire of British syndicalism (Holton 1976: 210; Hinton 1983: 90–93). Because so many had not been previously unionized, "they were striking for rather than against trade union controls" (Hyman 1985: 262).

Collective bargaining symbolized working-class progress, yet doused the fires of class hatred directed at the opponent. As Stedman-Jones puts it (and as Chapter 15 vindicates), aggressive as was the "new unionism," it did not conceive of the state as a "flesh and blood machine of coercion, exploitation and corruption as it had been in the period 1790–1850." The state, he says, was now viewed as a neutral agency for getting what one wanted (1974: 479). This chapter reveals that this was a largely correct view: The state had become less coercive, less corrupt; and its exploitations were not of workers' whole lives.

There were endless arguments whether to continue as Lib-Lab or press on with a Labour party. But this was just tactics. Labour's parliamentary breakthrough had come in the 1906 election (this paragraph depends on McKibbin 1974). Twenty-nine Labour Representative Committee MPs were elected, all of them workers and union officials, in striking contrast to the rest of the House of Commons. But 24 were elected as a result of an electoral pact with the Liberals. If Labour kept up its responsible pressure, its leaders believed the Liberals would concede universal suffrage. In the limited franchise, the pact gave both parties real but restricted gains. It was better than opposing each other, which might ensure a Conservative victory. In the two elections of 1910, Labour captured 40, then 42 seats, but only one had a Liberal candidate. During 1910–14, Labour increased its share of the vote but won no by-elections. Labour still depended overwhelmingly on the unions, yet the unions got only a bare majority of members to support the political levy. The Liberals only held seats in mining areas by grace of the pact, and their grass-roots activism had declined in industrial districts.

Hinton (1983: 80–1) believes that the likeliest sequence absent World War I would be the collapse of the pact (torn apart by the antipathy of the activists), electoral disaster for both parties, and the reconstitution of a Centrist Liberal party with Labour as a genuinely socialist party, which would have kept three-party democracy going much longer. McKibbin (1990) believes that the Liberal party was already failing to secure workers' votes. Suffrage extension, he believes, would have furthered their decline, and two-party (Conservative-Labour) democracy would have reemerged. Yet suffrage extension would be among the poor and women, both less unionized and probably less immediately attracted to Labour. Three-party democracy might have extended.

But the war did intervene. From 1920 on, Labour struck out for power on its own in a greatly enlarged electorate. The Liberal party now disintegrated, owing partly to internal class divisions, partly to the factionalism of Lloyd George and Asquith. It might have been otherwise had Liberal leaders been more astute. Labour militants and a class-conscious working class wanted their own MPs. The Liberals would not provide them.

British labor was pressured by others' actions toward reformism. It was pressured toward national organization by civilian state repression, widening of civilian state scope, and employer aggression. When possible, it cooperated with both parties to institutionalize mutualism and incorporation. Conservatives then decided to be a hostile class party and labor was pushed out of liberalism by the indifference of Liberal activists and the feuds of Liberal leaders. It was converted to the welfare state by administrative implication in Liberal and wartime government schemes. Subsequent to our period its electoral prospects and program adapted to the unforeseen consequences of total war and full male, then full female, suffrage. It then devised its program of statist social democracy. Class politics would out, but behind the backs of men.

Conclusion

The strategy chosen or drifted into by British labor had four principal determinants:

1. The collective class laborer partially emerged in the Second Industrial Revolution, as Marxian theory argues. In the economy this was due less to transformations in the labor process at the point of production than to the appearance of a total diffused economy. Capitalists experienced this totality as international but reacted to it with nationally organized class aggression against labor. In defense, a more national working class formed, though led by skilled workers with partly sectionalist interests and organized partly into segmental internal labor markets. Unions emerged as class actors in Britain while still pursuing sectional and segmental goals. The ambiguities of economic power relations did not resolve themselves.

2. This expanding movement remained masculine, and its gut sense of exploitation narrowed as employment polarization became segregated from more complex family and community trends. Class, though becoming more extensive, was probably becoming less intensive.

3. Because national and political, the still-ambiguous but masculine class struggle was largely "solved" by British political crystallizations, primarily by cross-class party democracy, the national issue, and the partial civilianization of the state. These restrained capitalist and regime repression, and its doppelgänger, revolutionary socialism, restrained sectoral and regional variations in class strategies and furthered centralized institutionalization of class conflict. National moderation would predominate, unless some major disaster, like defeat in war, struck.

4. The form of labor's national moderation was not decided by 1914, though the choices had narrowed. They would be predominantly mutualist, with some liberal and reformist hues, coming in one of two alternative politics – either from the Liberal party or from an autonomous Labour party.

Most of the parameters of British class struggle in the twentieth century seem to have been in place by 1914, as a result of interaction between the capitalist-driven Second Industrial Revolution, propelling forward an extensive, political, yet ambiguous labor movement and party-democratic, civilian, and national political crystallizations resolving most of those ambiguities. Yet I have neglected one important British peculiarity because it concerned an absence: Britain, uniquely, had no agrarian classes of great size or consequence.

Bibliography

Ashworth, W. 1960. *An Economic History of England, 1870–1939*. London: Methuen & Co.

Bagwell, P. 1985. The new unionism in Britain: the railway industry. In *The Development of Trade Unionism in Great Britain and Germany, 1880–1914*, ed. W. J. Mommsen and H.-G. Husung. London: German Historical Institute/Allen & Unwin.

Bain, G. 1970. *White Collar Trade Unionism*. Oxford: Clarendon Press.

Bain, G., and R. Price. 1980. *Profiles of Union Growth*. Oxford: Blackwell.

Baines, D. E. 1981. The labour supply and the labour market, 1860–1914. In *The Economic History of Britain Since 1700*, Vol. 2, ed. R. Floud and D. McCloskey. Cambridge: Cambridge University Press.

Braverman, H. 1974. *Labor and Monopoly Capital: The Degradation of Work in the Twentieth Century*. New York: Monthly Review Press.

Brown, K. D. 1971. *Labour and Unemployment, 1900–1914*. Newton Abbott: David & Charles.

Burawoy, M. 1979. *Manufacturing Consent: Changes in the Labor Process Under Monopoly Capitalism*. Chicago: University of Chicago Press.

Burgess, K. 1985. New unionism for old? The Amalgamated Society for Engineers in Britain. In *The Development of Trade Unionism in Great Britain and Germany, 1880–1914*, ed. W. J. Mommsen and H.-G. Husung. London: German Historical Institute/Allen & Unwin.

Clegg, H. A., et al. 1964. *A History of British Trade Unions Since 1889*, Vol. I. Oxford: Clarendon Press.

Cronin, J. 1979. *Industrial Conflict in Modern Britain*. London: Croom Helm.

1982. Strikes, 1870–1914. In *A History of British Industrial Relations, 1875–1914*, ed. C. Wrigley et al. Brighton: Harvester.

1988. The British state and the structure of political opportunity. *Journal of British Studies* 27.

Crossick, G. 1978. *An Artisan Elite in Victorian Society*. London: Croom Helm.

Davidoff, L. 1990. The family in Britain. In *The Cambridge Social History of Britain, 1750–1950*. Vol. 2: *People and Their Environment*, ed. F. M. L. Thompson. Cambridge: Cambridge University Press.

Davidson, R. 1972. Government administration. In *A History of British Industrial Relations, 1875–1914*, ed. C. Wrigley et al. Brighton: Harvester.

Deane, P., and W. A. Cole. 1969. *British Economic Growth, 1688–1959*. Cambridge: Cambridge University Press.

Emy, H. V. 1973. *Liberals, Radicals and Social Politics, 1892–1914*. Cambridge: Cambridge University Press.

Feinstein, C. 1976. *Statistical Tables of National Income, Expenditure and Output of the United Kingdom, 1855–1965*. Cambridge: Cambridge University Press.

Friedmann, A. 1977. *Industry and Labour: Class Struggle at Work and Monopoly Capitalism*. London: Macmillan.

Gray, R. Q. 1976. *The Labour Aristocracy in Victorian Edinburgh*. Oxford: Clarendon Press.

Hargreaves, J. 1986. *Sport, Power and Culture*. Cambridge: Polity Press.

Hart, N. 1989. Gender and the rise and fall of class politics. *New Left Review*, no. 175.

   1991. Female vitality and the history of human health. Paper presented to the Third Congress of the European Society for Medical Sociology, Marburg.

Heclo, H. 1974. *Modern Social Politics in Britain and Sweden*. New Haven, Conn.: Yale University Press.

Hill, S. 1981. *Competition and Control at Work: The New Industrial Sociology*. Cambridge, Mass.: MIT Press.

Hinton, J. 1983. *Labour and Socialism*. Sussex: Wheatsheaf.

Hobsbawm, E. J. 1968. *Labouring Men. Studies in the History of Labour*. London: Weidenfeld & Nicolson.

Holton, R. 1976. *British Syndicalism, 1900–1914*. London: Pluto Press.

   1985. Revolutionary syndicalism and the British labour movement. In *The Development of Trade Unionism in Great Britain and Germany, 1880–1914*, ed. W. J. Mommsen and H.-G. Husung. London: German Historical Institute/Allen & Unwin.

Hunt, E. H. 1981. *British Labour History, 1815–1914*. London: Heinemann.

Hyman, R. 1985. Mass organization and militancy in Britain: contrasts and continuities. In *The Development of Trade Unionism in Great Britain and Germany, 1880–1914*, ed. W. J. Mommsen and H.-G. Husung. London: German Historical Institute/Allen & Unwin.

Joyce, P. 1980. *Work, Society and Politics: The Culture of the Factory in Later Victorian England*. Brighton: Harvester.

   1989. Work. In *The Cambridge Social History of Britain, 1750–1950*. Vol. 2: *People and Their Environment*, ed. F. M. L. Thompson. Cambridge: Cambridge University Press.

Kerr, C., and A. Siegel. 1954. The inter-industry propensity to strike: an international comparison. In *Industrial Conflict*, ed. Kornhauser et al. New York: McGraw-Hill.

Lash, S., and J. Urry. 1987. *The End of Organized Capitalism*. Madison: University of Wisconsin Press.

Laybourn, K., and J. Reynolds. 1984. *Liberalism and the Rise of Labour, 1890–1918*. London: Croom Helm.

Lovell, J. 1985. The significance of the great dock strike of 1889 in British labour history. In *The Development of Trade Unionism in Great Britain and Germany, 1880–1914*, ed. W. J. Mommsen and H.-G. Husung. London: German Historical Institute/Allen & Unwin.

McKibbin, R. 1974. *The Evolution of the Labour Party, 1910–1924*. Oxford: Oxford University Press.

   1990. Why was there no Marxism in Great Britain? In his *Ideologies of*

Class. Social Relations in Britain, 1980–1950. Oxford: Clarendon Press.

Marks, G. 1989. *Unions in Politics: Britain, Germany and the United States in the Nineteenth and Early Twentieth Centuries*. Princeton, N.J.: Princeton University Press.

Martin, R. 1980. *T.U.C.: The Growth of a Pressure Group, 1868–1976*. Oxford: Clarendon Press.

Moore, R. 1978. *The Emergence of the Labour Party, 1880–1924*. London: Hodder & Stoughton.

More C. 1980. *Skill and the English Working Class, 1870–1914*. London: Croom Helm.

Musson, A. E. 1978. *The Growth of British Industry*. London: Batsford.

Payne, P. L. 1967. The emergence of the large scale company in Great Britain. *Economic History Review*, 2nd ser., 20.

Pelling, H. 1963. *A History of British Trade Unionism*. London: Macmillan.

1968. *Popular Politics and Society in Late Victorian Britain*. London: Macmillan.

Penn, R. 1985. *Skilled Workers in the Class Structure*. Cambridge: Cambridge University Press.

Pollard, S. 1985. The new unionism in Britain: its economic background. In *The Development of Trade Unionism in Great Britain and Germany, 1880–1914*, ed. W. J. Mommsen and H.-G. Husung. London: German Historical Institute/Allen & Unwin.

Price, R. 1983. The labour process and labour history. *Social History* 8.

1985. The new unionism and the labour process. In *The Development of Trade Unionism in Great Britain and Germany, 1880–1914*, ed. W. J. Mommsen and H.-G. Husung. London: German Historical Institute/Allen & Unwin.

Savage, M. 1987. *The Dynamics of Working-Class Politics*. Cambridge: Cambridge University Press.

Shaw, C. 1983. The large manufacturing employers of 1907. *Business History* 25.

Stedman-Jones, G. 1974. Working-class culture and working-class politics in London: 1870-1900. Notes on the remaking of a working class. *Journal of Social History* 7.

Stone, L. 1969. Literacy and education in England, 1640–1900. *Past and Present* 42.

Taylor, A. J. 1968. The coal industry. In *The Development of British Industry and Foreign Competition, 1875–1914*, ed. D. H. Aldcroft. London: Allen & Unwin.

Thane, P. 1981. Social history, 1860–1914. In *The Economic History of Britain Since 1700*, Vol. 2, ed. R. Floud and D. McCloskey. Cambridge: Cambridge University Press.

Thompson, F. M. L. 1988. *The Rise of Respectable Society: A Social History of Victorian Britain, 1830–1900*. London: Fontana.

Thompson, P. 1967. *Socialists, Liberals and Labour: The Struggle for London, 1885–1914*. London: Routledge & Kegan Paul.

Webb. S., and B. Webb. 1926. *History of Trade Unionism*. London: Longman Group.

18 Class struggle in the Second Industrial Revolution, 1880–1914: II. Comparative analysis of working-class movements

Theory

The Second Industrial Revolution brought nationally integrated economies, stiffer international competition, and commercialization of agriculture throughout the West. To each country it brought capital concentration, industrial science, expansion of the metallurgical and chemical industries, of mining, and of transport, and the corporation. In every country this greatly expanded and massified the urban-industrial labor force and led to employer pressure on wages, hours, and the de-skilling of artisans. This economic revolution was astonishingly similar in all countries, and workers responded with similar, though ambiguous, collective organizations.

This chapter charts the resulting conflict between capitalists and workers in several countries. It focuses on explaining the curious outcome that such marked economic similarities among countries generated varied worker ideologies – all six types distinguished in Chapter 15 – and varied outcomes of industrial class struggles. Russia was on the road toward revolution; Germany seemed on a different, quasi-revolutionary road; Britain was embarking on a mildly mutualist road; the United States, on a sectionalism largely devoid of socialism; and France still hotly debated all six options. Chapter 19 charts the similarly varied struggles in agriculture during the period. Both use a comparative method, taking national states as independent cases. I leave aside noncomparative aspects of labor movements – interactions among transnational, national, and nationalist organizations – until Chapter 21. I explain class conflicts in this period in terms of interaction between essentially similar industrial and agrarian economies with the variety provided primarily by political crystallizations and to a lesser extent by the structure of working-class communities. This reinforces one of the broadest generalizations of this volume: Modern society came to be increasingly structured by the entwining of economic and political power organizations.

628

As Chapter 17 shows for Britain, the Second Industrial Revolution hastened on three competing types of worker organizations: class, sectional, and segmental. Because all developed yet all undercut the others, worker-capitalist relations were profoundly ambiguous, offering no overall single logic of development. Yet struggles over citizenship had generated varied solutions for fifty to a hundred years before workers' class organizations joined in. As Rokkan (1970: 102–13) perceived, the struggle between capital and labor was the last to appear of the four major cleavages of the modernizing West – after struggles between centralized state building and peripheral regionalisms, between state and church, and between old landed regimes and an emerging manufacturing bourgeoisie. I should add that states had long been primarily militarist. Modern states thus crystallized on the "representative," "national," and "military-civil" issues before the working class appeared. Whereas capitalists and workers throughout the West responded similarly, and ambiguously, to similar changes in the sphere of production, worker politics differed considerably because influenced by these crystallizations.

A single great tendency underlay the complex economic-political entwinings that emerged. Where states favored the party-democratic incorporation of at least some workers, their political were separable from their economic demands. In this context class, sectional, and segmental organizations developed side by side, the last two undercutting potential class unity. Thus also socialist ideologies were milder and more economistic, at most amounting to mutualism or syndicalism, occasionally revolutionary in intent but deprived of the class unity to achieve it. Only where regimes did not make party-democratic concessions to some workers could sectionalism and segmentalism be overcome and class unity develop. This alone might lead toward aggressive reformism or even toward revolution.

This argument is not wholly original. I borrow, of course, from Lenin's famous declaration in 1902: "The history of all countries shows that the working class, solely by its own forces, is able to work out merely trade-union consciousness" (1970: 80).

By "trade-union consciousness," Lenin meant more than just economism, as narrow union interests also required mutualist legislation guaranteeing organizing freedoms. But Lenin argued that further elements of socialism had been added to workers' struggles from outside: "by the educated representatives of the propertied classes – the intelligentsia," "quite independently of the spontaneous growth of the labour movement."

Lenin was partly correct. The core theses of orthodox Marxism – its stress on relations of production, the labor process, and the extraction of surplus value – are insufficient to explain the emergence of working-class socialism. These economic experiences on their own produced far less than revolutionary socialism, even usually less than reformism, and they also produced less class than sectional agitation (cf. Marks 1989: 15). But the second half of Lenin's argument – socialism must be brought by outside intelligentsia – is not correct (as indeed Lenin elsewhere realized). Working classes, as well as intelligentsia, *have* generated socialism, though only when their diverse productive experiences are fused by experience of common political exploitations.

I borrow also from more recent writers. Wuthnow (1989: part III) has emphasized state influences on socialism in this period, though he generates no general theory of them. Lipset famously argued that party democracy defused workers' socialism (1977, 1984). Lipset believes that states can be placed on a single political continuum, from feudal to liberal, from which the extent and form of worker socialism can be predicted. Thus, he says, "feudal" regimes generated revolutionary socialism, mixed regimes generated reformist socialism, and liberal regimes generated no socialism. There is much truth in this, as we shall see. But I reject his overfree use of "feudal." I also reject his overbenign view of labor history and democracy (especially in America), which minimizes repression and neglects military-civil variations among states. Along with almost everyone else, he also neglects the national issue.

States are not one-dimensional. This volume has distinguished four principal types of state crystallization. All states crystallized as capitalist, so this does not help much in predicting variability in class outcomes over the period (except for an extreme case like that of the United States). Militarism and the growing civilian scope of states help a little more, if unevenly. But overall, the representative and national crystallizations of states explain most of the variability in capital-labor struggles.

Comparative data on national labor movements

I present brief comparative data on the labor movements in the five countries discussed, plus Sweden. Then I move to detailed analysis of countries, substituting Russia for Austria, as there are few Austrian and many Russian studies.[1]

Table 18.1 gives proportions of union members in civilian non-

---

[1] These two countries share a data deficiency that recent Eastern European revolutions may remedy: The *national* component of their proletarian class struggles has been neglected.

Table 18.1. *Union membership as percentage of nonagricultural civilian labor force, 1890–1914*

	Austria	Great Britain	France	Germany	United States	Sweden
1890	1.0	12.2	2.2	3.2	3.5	1.2
1895	2.0	11.6	4.0	2.7	3.5	1.6
1900	2.3	13.7	4.2	5.9	7.8	7.0
1905	3.4	14.0	6.6	10.2	14.3	10.2
1910	6.5	18.8	8.1	13.5	12.5	11.0
1914	6.5	23.6	8.3	12.5	13.4	12.2

Note: Nonagricultural labor force (NALF) figures also exclude members of armed forces. All estimated figures derive from straight-line extrapolations from available data for other years.
Austria: Union members – *Annuaire Statistique de la France* (1913: 183); 1914 is actually 1912. NALF – Bairoch et al. (1968: 85). All figures for Austrian *Reichshalf* only.
Great Britain: Union members – Bain and Price (1980: 37). NALF – Mitchell (1983: 171). Years are 1891, 1896, 1901, 1906, 1911, 1914. NALF for 1896, 1906, and 1914 estimated.
France: Union members – Shorter and Tilly (1974: appendix B). NALF – Mitchell (1983: 163). NALF for 1890 and 1914 estimated.
Germany: Union members – Bain and Price (1980: 133), excluding salaried employee associations. NALF – Mitchell (1983: 164). Figures are for 1882, 1895, and 1907. NALF figures are estimates from these.
United States: Lebergott (1984: 386–7). It is impossible to make the U.S. labor force figures exactly comparable to those of other countries. Lebergott's sources exclude domestic servants (Bain and Price include them but also double-count persons who had two jobs that year; their union membership figures include Canadian members). Thus my union density figures are probably slightly too high; by perhaps 1 percent to 2 percent.
Sweden: Union members – Bain and Price (1980: 142). NALF – Bairoch et al. (1968: 114).

agricultural labor forces, starting when data become available for all countries. The figures are only approximate. Union and government records contain many inaccuracies, and national statistics were collected using differing methods. I exclude agriculture and armed forces. They were little unionized in any country, yet the proportions in agriculture and the armed forces varied greatly among countries.

Union members remained a minority in all countries throughout the period. By 1914, the British rate was by far the highest, but it still amounted to only a quarter of the nonagricultural labor force. Because most union members everywhere were men, male densities were higher and female densities lower, by at least one-third. But the table shows a steady increase in membership throughout the period. Analysis by industry would reveal an avant-garde similar to Britain's

Table 18.2. *Percentage of civilian, nonagricultural labor force on strike, 1891–1913 (5-year averages)*

	Austria	Great Britain	France	Germany	United States
1891–95	—	2.5	1.0	0.1	2.7
1896–1900	1.4	1.1	1.1	0.7	2.3
1901–5	1.2	0.6	1.6	1.2	2.9
1906–10	2.2	1.3	2.5	1.4	—
1911–13	2.2	5.0	2.0	2.0	—

Sources: *Labor force*: See notes to Table 18.1. *Strikes*: Austria – *Annuaire Statistique de la France* (1913: 184). Great Britain – Cronin (1989: 82–3). France – Perrot (1974: I, 51). Germany – Cronin (1985: table 3.4); free trade union figures, 1890–98; official figures, 1899–1913. United States – Edwards (1981).

(discussed in Chapter 17): By 1914, density approached 50 percent among male skilled workers in mining, transport, construction, and metal manufacturing everywhere. The similarities among industries and occupations across countries are so striking that I rarely discuss relations in particular industries in this chapter. Unless I remark to the contrary, my discussion of Britain can stand as a rough proxy for what was occurring in the vanguard industries everywhere.

Differences among national union densities derive largely from levels of industrialization and urbanization. There were no serious laggards, rendered particularly congenial or uncongenial to unions by ideological or political antipathies, although French union density was somewhat lower than expected. This may be attributable partly to errors in the French data, partly to the early emergence of distinctively French unions, in which membership was confined to militants who could mobilize nonmembers in demonstrations and strikes. Overall, with industrialization, unions became the normal means by which male skilled workers, and then the unskilled and females, organized to remedy their grievances. Unions were the collective response of workers to industrial capitalism; they are rightly central to Marx's notion of the emerging collective laborer.

Strike rates are conventionally used to indicate the economic militancy of this collective laborer. Table 18.2 presents the proportion of the civilian nonagricultural labor force involved in strikes. I have preferred this measure to two others. The number of workdays lost in strikes is affected by single large strikes and so fluctuates erratically, whereas the number of strikes is inflated by very small strikes and measures general militancy less well.

Strikes were rare, annually involving about 4 percent of the labor force. A major strike wave could double this, as in Britain in 1912. The Revolution of 1905 in Russia increased it tenfold. Strikes were multiplying throughout the period, though not uniformly, and there was no consistent growth in the United States. In most decades countries had similar strike rates whatever their level of industrialization.

All countries were affected by the transnational diffusion of capitalism. Though some were more advanced or industrial, and although there were emerging national styles of industrial capitalism (German and American cartels-trusts, French rural industry, etc.), all capitalists reacted to transnational market conditions and technologies. Russia might have been backward, but it had large factories with the latest machinery, accountancy, scientific management, and so forth. Everywhere the three modern sectors of metalworking, mining, and transport were also somewhat dual. They contained most of the organized working-class core, yet they (plus chemicals) generated the largest enterprises with the most developed internal labor markets encouraging employer-employee segmental organization and with strong employer resistance to unions. But despite this dualism, most forms of worker action were "startlingly similar" in the same industry across diverse countries, as Grüttner (1985: 126) observes.

Because trade cycles and employer competition diffused across state boundaries, so did employer or union aggression. Strike waves spread right across the West. In four of the five countries for which data exist, there was a strike wave in 1889–90 and in 1899–1900; in five of the six with evidence in 1906 and in all six in 1910–12 – and there were no other strike waves in any of these countries between these dates (Boll 1985: 80, 1989; Cronin 1985; these authors also tentatively suggest an earlier transnational wave in 1870–3). Socialist leaders (as Chapter 21 shows) also constituted a dense network of transnational communication endorsing Marx's essentially transnational theory of working-class organization.

If economic power relations were similar, even transnational, politics were not. Table 18.3 shows the varied electoral fortunes of labor-socialist parties. Labor-socialist voting was increasing but at very different rates. Germany, Austria, and Sweden (plus other Scandinavian countries)[2] were at one extreme, their Socialists becoming the

[2] In 1912, the Norwegian Labor Party picked up 26 percent of votes, rising to 32 percent in 1915; and in 1913, the Danish Social Democrats picked up 30 percent. Most other European countries followed in the Anglo-French vote bracket: By 1909, the Italian Socialists received 19 percent, then in 1913, merging with Independents and Reformists, they garnered 23 percent (figures in Cook and Paxton 1978).

Table 18.3. *Percentage of (male) electorate voting socialist in national elections, 1906–14*

	1906–8	1909–11	1912–14
Austria	21	25	—
France	10	13	17
Germany	29	—	35
Great Britain	5	7[a]	—
Adjusted[b]	10–15	14–21	—
Sweden	15	29	33[d]
United States[c]	—	—	6

[a] In the two elections of 1910, Labour polled 6.4 percent and 7.6 percent.
[b] Adjusted to take account of exclusion of about 34 percent of British men (almost all manual workers) from the franchise. Assumes that with adult male suffrage, Labour would have doubled its candidates.
[c] Note that almost all black males were disenfranchised.
[d] In the two elections of 1914, the socialists polled 30.1 percent and 36.4 percent.
Source: Cook and Paxton (1978).

largest single parties by 1914, capturing most (male) workers' votes. At the other extreme the American Socialist party was struggling to get 5 percent – perhaps 10 percent of white male workers' votes. The British Labour party was also struggling against two established bourgeois parties amid a restricted franchise. Its actual vote understates worker support, as more than half of male workers were disenfranchised and the party only fielded candidates in overwhelmingly working-class constituencies. I have adjusted the Labour vote accordingly, in the second British row in Table 18.3. Any adjustment is guesswork, but I estimate British Labour voting as comparable to the French (and Italian) Socialist vote, somewhat less than northern European socialism.

It is harder to measure employer ideologies. A rough indicator of how extreme they were is how many workers they killed by acts of commission (they killed far more by acts of omission, in horrendous factory and mine accident rates). There was no systematic official recording of fatalities in labor disputes. I have constructed rough national estimates from combing the secondary literature for each country as listed in the bibliography of this chapter. (See Table 18.4.) Most violence against persons was initiated by employers and the authorities. Virtually all casualties were workers.

Britain had the least murderous record. Its 7 fatalities occurred in

Table 18.4. *Workers killed in labor disputes, 1872–1914*

Great Britain	Germany	France	United States	Russia
7	16	ca. 35	ca. 500–800	ca. 2,000–5,000

Sources: See text.

the 1870s and in 1910–13. Surprisingly, perhaps, semiauthoritarian Germany ranks next. Of its deaths, 8 occurred in 1889, 3 in 1899, 2 in 1905, and 3 during 1910–11. In France, there were 1 or 2 deaths in 1872, 9 in 1891, 1 in 1905, and 19 plus "several" more in 1907. The British, French, and German totals may be underestimates, but not by much. Their range is of a wholly different order to that of Russia and America. The U.S. estimate range is that suggested by American labor historians, although it may be an underestimate, because some of the many lynchings and shootings of southern blacks (excluded from my total) would have concerned labor disputes. Yet American violence was still not quite on the scale of Russian. The Russian toll can only be roughly approximate, because labor disputes merged into broader urban protests and peasant and national risings. But the differences are so marked as to be real. It seems that employers and regimes responded to industrial action in fundamentally different ways. But their level of domestic militarism did not correlate with their position on the representative state crystallization: Russia was the most authoritarian monarchy, but the United States the most advanced party democracy.

Union density, strikes, fatalities, and voting for parties with certain names are only crude measures of worker militancy and socialism. But they suggest a broad tendency: Economic relations tended to diffuse common patterns throughout the West, and political relations differed. I shall now examine individual countries more closely, concentrating on their political crystallizations. Unless stated otherwise, it should be assumed that the Second Industrial Revolution was diffusing roughly similarly through all countries.

The United States: political crystallizations and the decline of socialism

Thirteen answers to "why so little socialism?"
Discussion of U.S. labor history traditionally has centered on a supposed "American exceptionalism," especially the absence of socialism.

The question asked by Sombart's classic *Why Is There No Socialism in America?* (1906, 1976) has generated at least thirteen explanations for the absence of socialism (for reviews, see Lipset 1977; Foner 1984; and various essays in Laslett and Lipset 1974). These fall into three groups, according to whether America is thought to have substituted individualism, sectionalism, or democracy for socialism.

Individualism

1. *Dominance by small property ownership.* Most colonial settlement was by small farm proprietors who remained central to the Revolution and to the Jeffersonian and Jacksonian movements. The ideology of small property ownership dominated from the beginning. Early America was unsympathetic to "feudalism"; later America, to socialism (Hartz 1955; Grob 1961 emphasizes all five individualism arguments).

2. *The frontier thesis*, originally proposed by Turner in 1893, argues that the struggle to extend the American frontier in a harsh environment against warlike foes resulted in a rugged individualism hostile to collectivism. As the frontier acquired mythic cultural resonance, it influenced all of the United States, encouraging racial and spatial, not class, struggle (Slotkin 1985).

3. *Moral Protestantism* encouraged individualism. Without a state religion, yet with strong Protestant sects, America encouraged individuals to solve social problems from within their own moral resources.

4. *Mobility* opportunities encouraged individuals to seek personal, not collective, advancement.

5. *Capitalist prosperity* diffused among Americans. They have been reluctant to tamper with private property relations. American workers have been individually materialistic.

Sectionalism

6. *Racism.* Slavery divided the early working class. Segregation survived in the South until after World War II, and united class action of blacks and whites remained difficult everywhere, especially during the mass black migration to the North in the early twentieth century. (Laslett 1974 emphasizes all the sectionalism explanations.)

7. *Immigration.* Waves of immigrants added ethnic, linguistic, and religious divisions. Older immigrant groups became occupationally entrenched, reinforcing skilled sectionalism with ethnic stratification. Catholic immigration in the late nineteenth century impeded socialism because the church was then engaged in a crusade against socialism. Kraditor (1981) claims that immigrants were more attached to their ethnicity than their class. Their goal was to create self-sufficient ethnocultural enclaves, not a working-class community. Workers' com-

munities did not reinforce the collective laborer – they undermined it.

8. *Continental diversity*. The size and diversity of America ensured that industrialization differed among regions. Workers in different industries have been spatially segregated from each other and industry has kept moving into nonunionized regions. Workers migrated more, ensuring that hereditary working-class communities did not emerge. National class solidarity never really appeared.

9. *Sectarianism*. American labor was internally divided by factional fighting among groups like the Knights of Labor, the American Federation of Labor, rival socialist parties, syndicalists, the Congress of Industrial Organizations, and the Communist party. Had they fought capitalism more and one another less, the outcome would have differed (Weinstein 1967; Bell 1974).

American democracy

10. *Early male democracy*. The United States achieved adult white male democracy by the 1840s – before the working class emerged. It had, in Perlman's (1928: 167) famous words, the "free gift of the ballot." This is an upbeat, approving view of American democracy: Workers could remedy grievances through liberal democracy without recourse to alternative ideologies like socialism (Lipset 1984).

11. *Federalism*. The U.S. Constitution divides powers between a relatively weak federal government (with a small nonindustrial capital city) and stronger state governments, and among three branches of government – the presidency, two houses of Congress, and a separate judiciary. Workers had to divide their attention among government agencies, and this weakened national class politicization and unity (Lowi 1984).

12. *The two-party system*. By the time labor emerged, two cross-class parties were institutionalized. Congressional elections were based on large constituencies; presidential elections, on just one national constitutency. Emerging third parties, including labor parties, could not advance steadily by first obtaining minority representation in national politics. As labor was not at first strong enough to elect the president or senators, it worked within bourgeois parties that could win elections instead of forming a labor party that could not. The parties, however, were weaker in the federal system than in more centralized polities. This reduced party discipline and made them less responsive to broader class programs.

13. *Repression*. A more cynical view of American democracy emphasizes the extraordinary level of repression, judicial and military, mobilized against American working-class movements (Goldstein 1978; Forbath 1989).

All thirteen arguments have some merit in explaining the comparative weakness of American socialism. Did this massively overdetermine the outcome? That is, with all these odds stacked against them, how could socialists possibly win? But neither the odds nor the peculiarities in America were as great as this might suggest. America has not so much been exceptional as it has gradually come to represent one extreme on a continuum of class relations. America has never differed qualitatively from other national cases. Differences have been of degree, not kind – we have seen already that British socialism was fairly minimal before 1914. Nor was America born extreme; America became extreme. Thus explanations asserting an original and enduring American exceptionalism or extremism – most of the first group – have only a very limited truth. American extremism was born in this period, as we shall see.

The development of American labor up to World War I

I focus first on the precise nature and timing of American extremism. Several writers agree it lay in political rather than economic power relations (Montgomery 1979; Foner 1984: 59; Marks 1989: 198). America has differed from most continental European countries in that no socialist party ever gained more than the 6 percent vote obtained by Eugene Debs's party in the presidential election of 1912. And America differed from Britain and its white Commonwealth in not having a union-dominated labor party. America has had neither a significant socialist nor a union-dominated labor party. But extremism has not only been political: twentieth-century American unions have also become extreme, weakening into eventual insignificance. In 1990, American union membership was less than 15 percent of the labor force, by far the lowest in advanced capitalist countries, and still apparently declining. In 1958, May Day was redesignated by President Eisenhower as Law Day – with the approval of the American Federation of Labor (AFL) – an apt redesignation in the light of American labor history (as we shall see). As a resident foreigner I have been struck by the absence of unions from national or state politics. The *Communist Manifesto* seems about as alien to American college students as *The Epic of Gilgamesh*.

When did the two American extremisms, political and economic, arise? Tables 18.1 and 18.2 show that American unionization and strike participation before 1914 were more or less what we would expect from the level of industrialization. Indeed, according to the most precise comparative study, of the iron and steel industries, by Holt (1977: 14–16), American union density in 1892 was about 15 percent, whereas Britain's lagged at 11 percent to 12 percent. Earlier contemporary estimates of unions' national memberships indicate that, from the mid-1850s to the mid-1860s, British density was about 6 percent and American 5 percent. In the 1870s, British density was about 10 percent and American 9 percent. By 1880, American density was down to 4 percent, half the British figure, before rising again (Ulman 1955: 19; Rayback 1966: 104, 111; Montgomery 1967: 140–1; Fraser 1974: 76). As Britain was more industrialized, we would expect its union density to be higher and stabler. These figures suggest that America's unions were not at first weaker than British unions, as its lesser industrialization would suggest.

Such figures are rough. Even if entirely accurate, they provide only crude measures of class organization. A high union density or strike rate might indicate either highly class-conscious workers or the vigorous "business unionism" commonly identified as typically American. In an analysis of the character of nineteenth-century American labor relations, three points stand out.

1. Through most of the nineteenth century, American workers did not lag behind European workers experiencing comparable industrialization. American workers participated actively in the early struggle for the suffrage. No quasi-revolutionary movement like Chartism or 1848 insurrectionism was needed, but many American militants were radical, infused with populist republicanism. Because workers were mostly in the North, the main national issue of states' rights did not divide them. Radical but not revolutionary, American unions developed more or less as British ones did, lagging somewhat. Small craft brotherhoods cultivated respectability and benefit plans, attempted unilateral rate-setting practices, hired their own laborers, restricted entry to their craft, and gradually attained regional, then national organization. Beyond them were several attempts at large general industrial unions, vulnerable to trade cycles and employer onslaughts. Few unions were sympathetic to socialists; most were protectionist or mildly mutualist, expecting to enforce their own "legislation" – very similar to Britain's mid-nineteenth-century experience. There was little American extremism of either Left or Right before the 1870s (Ulman 1955; Rayback 1966: 47–128; Montgomery 1967, 1979: 9–31; Wilentz 1984).

One divisive feature of American working-class life, however, was already emerging. In other industrializing countries, family and local-community ties tended to support work solidarity. But in most American cities, support was undercut by ethnic-religious communities whose organizations reached more easily into the local patronage politics of two-party democracy than did labor unions (Hirsch 1978; Katznelson 1981).

2. American workers then responded assertively and in classlike forms to a Second Industrial Revolution that was more intensive than in Britain. Led by massive railroad integration, American industries, mines, and banks began to consolidate into larger units from 1870 on. Trusts and monopolies were erratically proscribed, but holding companies flourished. About 1900 began a wave of corporate mergers and the notion of scientific management. In 1905, the hundred largest companies made up 40 percent of the country's industrial capital, higher than in any other country. The corporation led perhaps the most severe employer offensive on craft autonomy, skills, wages, and working conditions in any country. Artisans and unions were especially assailed. De-skilling and antiunionism were spearheaded by massive hiring of scab labor, mostly immigrants and migrants from agriculture. Employers became better organized, more aggressive, more inventive. Their spies infiltrated every level of unions, up to the executive council of the AFL itself. The Goodyear Rubber Company hired a "flying squadron" of 800 men, training them over three years to cover any job in the plant in case of strikes (Montgomery 1979: 35, 59). Late nineteenth-century extremists were employers, not workers.

According to the argument of Chapters 15 and 17, employer extremism should have increased the unity and aggression of the labor movement. It did. Workers responded in several large strike waves and union expansions. The mass strike, the main weapon of syndicalism, was as common in the United States as in Britain or Germany during the three decades following 1870. In 1872, 100,000 New York building tradesmen struck, demanding an eight-hour day. The following year saw mass demonstrations against unemployment in at least eight major northern cities. An 1877 railway strike, aided by sympathy strikes and popular demonstrations in many towns, "involved the largest number of persons of any labor conflict in the nineteeth century" and gave "workingmen a class consciousness on a national scale" says Rayback (1966: 135–6). The 1880s saw a "one big union" movement, the Knights of Labor, urging class solidarity across craft and industrial lines and class opposition to capital. By 1886, the Knights had 703,000 members, 10 percent of the nonagricultural labor force. May Day 1886 saw a general strike for shorter hours; 190,000 workers walked out and another 150,000 were granted shorter hours without striking. At the end of the year, 100,000 Knights came out.

Like many early mass unions, the Knights could not stabilize their organization and declined. The AFL now began to coordinate predominantly craft unions. There were further strike waves. The secondary strikes of 1889–94 were twice as large as any subsequently (Montgomery 1979: 20–21). In 1892, a general strike paralyzed New

Orleans for three days; in 1894, a strike wave and marches of "unemployed armies" affected North and South alike, then the Pullman strike took out the national rail network. In 1897 and 1898, 100,000 mine workers struck. In 1902–4, the Western Federation of Miners struck, calling for a "complete revolution of present social and economic conditions." In all cases nonmembers struck and demonstrated alongside members. Many were led by socialists.

In numbers, and in militants' socialism, the American labor movement did not lag from the 1870s to near 1900 (Table 18.2 supports the first part of this statement). In Germany 109,000 workers struck in 1872, 394,000 in 1889–90, 132,000 in 1900, and about half a million in 1905 and 1912. France saw a similar rising trend of strike waves (Boll 1989). Britain had comparable waves in the early 1870s and in 1889–93, somewhat lesser waves in 1894–5, 1898, and 1908, and then the numbers rose to new heights in 1910–12, by which time more than a million were involved (Cronin 1989: 82–3). America seems distinct only at the end of the period, with no major escalation in labor unrest after about 1905. Foreign socialist observers like Engels, Edward Aveling, and Eleanor Marx remarked the early militancy. They appreciated that American socialism had distinctive republican hues. The Knights of Labor declared in their constitution: "We declare an inevitable and irresistible conflict between the wage-system of labor and republican system of government." But foreign socialists expected a creative compromise between native republicanism and the Marxism of small parties like DeLeon's Socialist Labor party and Debs's Socialist party. The Marxist Socialist party might seem unlikely in America, but why should not a British-style labor party and a merger between craft and industrial unionism develop a singular working-class movement?

3. Labor politics did not lag behind Britain's (the country with the most comparable political and ideological history) until about 1900. Earlier than Britain, in the 1870s, American socialists led large strikes. Their ideas influenced the Knights of Labor to fuse economics with politics in slogans such as the "abolition of the wages system" and the "emancipation of the working class." There were several attempts by AFL unions, the Knights of Labor, farmers, and political radicals to form united labor parties (discussed in Chapter 19). These succeeded in local and state elections in industrial cities and farming areas, in advance of British electoral gains by labor. British socialists pointed to the American model as one to be imitated.

In 1893–4, the AFL almost went much farther. It debated a reformist eleven-point program including an eight-hour day, public ownership of utilities, transport, and mines, the abolition of sweatshop and contract labor, and compulsory education. The preamble urged the "principle of independent labor politics" and culminated in a call for "collective ownership by the people of all means of production and distribution." It was to be discussed by individual unions and then voted on at the 1894 conference. Most unions approved it, but AFL leaders, especially Samuel Gompers, the union's president, opposed political unionism and organized to defeat it. The AFL constitution allowed national unions far more delegate votes than state and local unions, the main socialist bases (Grob 1961: 141). The 1894 convention was thus partly rigged, and it became deadlocked. The individual clauses were ratified, but the call for public ownership was weakened to refer only to land nationalization. The preamble was defeated by 1,345 votes to 861, and the program as a whole was defeated, 1,173 to 735. The socialists retaliated by voting Gompers out of office.

The 1895 convention began to clarify the outcome. Gompers recaptured office by conceding individual clauses but organized an overwhelming vote against party politics. He was aided by the constitutions of many unions that prohibited endorsement of candidates for political office – a legacy of a cross-class two-party system in which members could only be split by party politics. Thereafter Gompers remained in control, president until his death in 1924. Though socialists mobilized strong minorities (upwards of a third) on several occasions, the AFL consistently rejected a labor party. Socialists could pass all the legislative proposals they liked, but if the AFL relied on the two existing parties to implement them, they were dead letters.

In the mid-1890s, American unions had come close to a somewhat reformist labor party before Britain. The British TUC voted narrowly only in 1899 for a labor party that virtually had no policy. The American outcome was initially close, not overdetermined by that long list of explanations of American exceptionalism. Yet it was consistently ratified thereafter, and we cannot attribute that only to Gompers's machinations. The voting showed two related patterns:

1. The American "nation" was highly fragmented. Religion mattered, as in most countries, but here it was greatly reinforced by ethnicity, locally, communally concentrated. AFL membership and leadership was half Catholic. Socialist motions at AFL conventions received little support from Catholic delegates but mobilized two-thirds of Protestants and Jews. I explain the Catholic-Protestant differences of the period in the conclusion to this chapter.

2. The sectional fault line between craftworkers and other workers mattered. Five general industrial unions open to all grades (in mining, textiles, and brewing) provided less than 25 percent of AFL membership but 49 percent to 77 percent of Left votes at AFL conventions. Craft unions losing labor-market monopolies to internal labor

markets, such as boot and shoe workers, machinists, and carpenters, offered intermittent support. Securer closed craft unions, such as printers, molders, and locomotive engineers, voted overwhelmingly for Gompers's "pure and simple unionism" (Marks 1989: 204–10, 235–7; Laslett 1974). But the AFL constitution allowed these national craft unions to dominate the voting.

Thus the AFL's "collective laborer" was riven by religious-ethnic, local community, and craft sectionalisms. It was not much of a national class movement. I must try to explain why.

From this period on, American labor developed as distinct organizational "parties." Three tendencies competed, each predominating in distinct organizations – a different development to that of labor elsewhere. The majority of the AFL, and thus of the whole movement, championed *protectionist, sectional* craft unionism. Second, general industrial unions, a minority within the AFL, sought broader *mutualist class* action. The combined membership of the two, as Table 18.1 shows, did not lag behind comparable countries before World War I; and their divisions were intrinsically no worse than those among British or French unions. But radical industrial unionists also turned to the *syndicalist* International Workers of the World (the "Wobblies"). From 1905 on, the Wobblies organized short-lived strikes by unskilled and marginal workers, often unenfranchised women and immigrants. The Wobblies did not bother much about paid-up memberships (having only 18,000 members at their 1912 peak) or about negotiating contracts with employers, but their rhetoric and tumultuous mass strikes struck fear into the propertied classes (Dubofsky 1969). The war helped destroy them. Then the split took a new form. Industrial unions founded a rival to the AFL, the Congress of Industrial Organizations.

The third tendency was *reformist socialism*, developed by a minority mostly in industrial unions and in the West into the Socialist party. This grew to 118,000 members by 1912 before leveling off. In 1914, it elected 1,200 representatives to city and state offices and controlled the mayoralty or municipal county in more than thirty cities – mostly small industrial, mining, or railroad centers. But it declined sharply after 1920 and split, the more active group forming the Communist party (Weinstein 1984).

Thus factionalized, all three tendencies – craft unionism, industrial unionism, and reformist socialism – were diminished. Although there was a substantial boost in membership and militancy in the 1930s, it was still less than what occurred in Europe. Essentially fragmented, the American labor movement almost disappeared after the 1960s. The dominant form of labor relations in the United States is now nonunion, dominated by internal labor markets and employer-conferred privileges in the stabler, more corporate sector and by a high level of naked exploitation in the secondary sector.

Thus, in economic and political action alike the 1890s and early 1900s seem the first major turning point.[3] Broad national class identity and an emerging socialism were then retracked into a dominant and distinctively American fusion of localism, sectionalism, and factionalism. Elsewhere we find the craft-unskilled sectional fault line and in some countries (e.g., France, Germany) ideological factionalism, but America uniquely fused the two, adding a pronounced localism. Sectionalism was uniquely correlated with ideological factions and local communities, greatly enfeebling labor's class identity and power. Why the fusion? The chronology mostly invalidates those first group explanations – usually versions of nativist self-congratulation – that claim that an enduring "Americanism" or "individualism" was internalized by workers in this period. (Wilentz 1984 also makes this point.) Nineteenth-century American workers demonstrated as much class organization as did workers in other countries and as much early socialism as in some. What happened to that class organization and socialism at the very end of the century? My answer entwines four distinctive American political crystallizations.

Four American political crystallizations
1. *Domestic militarism.* We have glimpsed already the extremism of American employers. Thus one plausible answer is that the American working class was repressed by force. Most large strikes ended in violent defeat. After a relatively benign early nineteenth century (according to Katznelson 1981: 58–61), America swung to the opposite extreme after the Civil War. Taft and Ross (1970: 281) state the essential fact simply: "The United States has had the bloodiest and most violent labor history of any industrial nation in the world." Actually, tsarist Russia was worse, but apart from this case, what is strikingly exceptional or extreme about the United States in this period was its level of industrial violence and paramilitary repression. Most writers celebrating exceptionalism do not even mention this, or – even worse – they actually claim that America had little violence (Perlman 1928; Hartz 1955; Grob 1961; Lipset 1977, 1984). Quite the opposite is true.

---

[3] As American colleagues have tried to persuade me, perhaps there was a second (though I believe lesser) turning-point in the 1950s, when the growth of the 1930s and 1940s was (seemingly terminally) reversed – again more the result of political crystallizations rather than of the development of the American economy. I believe the die was substantially cast for American labor before 1914, but to sustain this argument properly requires full discussion of twentieth-century developments, not attempted in this volume.

From the 1870s on, American workers faced two forms of repression. First, they were harassed by (liberal-capitalist) judicial interpretations of the Constitution and freedom of contract. Civil rights were considered fundamentally individual, not collective – as we saw also in early nineteenth-century Britain. Although unions and strikes were in principle legal from 1842 on, most secondary actions, sympathy strikes and producers' and consumers' boycotts, were defined as "conspiracies" to deny employers lawful rights to control their own property. If employers then hired scabs, picketing against them was usually defined as unlawful. Employers persuaded the police to enforce the law or they went to court to obtain injunctions. There judges described worker tactics as "tyranny," "dictatorship," and "usurpation" over essential individual property rights. Labor law was largely set at the individual state level, but from 1894 on, the Supreme Court joined in, redirecting the Sherman Act from its original goal of preventing corporate monopolies to preventing union monopolies. If strikes or boycotts did not involve workers' own wages or working conditions, and so did not derive from legitimate individual interests, they were defined as "malicious." Injunctions were issued against more than 15 percent of sympathy strikes in the 1890s and more than 25 percent in the 1900s. Employers' secondary lockouts and open-shop drives were not proscribed; employers could do as they liked with their own property.

Courts also harassed pro-union legislation. By 1900, state and federal courts had invalidated about sixty labor laws, especially laws against victimization, the paying of wages in scrip (spent at company stores), laws setting hours and conditions for men (though courts usually upheld a moral responsibility for women and children), and laws reducing the scope of conspiracy – all these were struck down as "class legislation." Legal repression was severest against general unions or socialists because they initiated broader strikes and boycotts most removed from individual interests. Injunctions were issued against virtually all strikes bringing skilled and unskilled workers out together; these were described as "dictatorship," the negation of freedom (Fink 1987; Forbath 1989; Woodiwiss 1990).

Second, the law was buttressed by military or paramilitary force. From 1,000 to 2,000 workers were commonly arrested in big strikes; 100 to 200, in smaller ones. The police authorities, with hastily enlarged and armed deputy forces, sufficed for most strikes. But in the few big or supposedly dangerous strikes or when scabs needed protection, in came the regular army, state militias, and private employers' armies, often deputized with legal powers – a practice virtually unknown in Europe. State militias, aided occasionally by federal troops, were used in more than five hundred disputes between 1877 and 1903;

and the largest private army, the Pinkerton Detective Agency, had more men than the U.S. Army.

They did not only arrest. The death toll in American labor relations in this period was exceeded only by that in tsarist Russia, as Table 18.4 shows. Why was the United States so violent? Perhaps mainly because guns were more widespread. Anyone who has seen a strike knows that emotions usually run high, and along with jostling, blows are often exchanged, especially in active picketing of factories. Put guns in the hands of the two sides and deaths might easily result. Having witnessed British soccer hooligans and American ghetto rioters skirmishing with police, I cannot believe that more deaths result in the United States because young Americans are in their emotions more "violent" than their British counterparts. Rather, Americans carry guns. Yet we must add a second cause of the American slaughter: American employers and police refused to compromise so that violent tendencies might be ritualized into permitted yet contained "shows of force." This inflexibility America shared with tsarist Russia.

In both Russia and America, almost all violence against persons was initiated by employers and the authorities, and almost all casualties were workers. One single American strike, the railroad strike of 1877, caused at least 90 deaths inflicted by the 45,000 state militia and 2,000 federal troops brought into action. In the railroad strike of 1894, 34 workers were killed. In the strike wave of 1902–4, for which we have good figures, at least 198 people were killed, 1,966 injured, and more than 5,000 arrested. This was the end of the peak period of violence, although it continued sporadically, especially in the West – 74 died in the 1914 Colorado mining strike.

Violence, like legal repression, was concentrated against strikes led by socialists and against attempts to form big industrial unions uniting skilled and unskilled workers. Small wonder that the principal chronicler of violence, Robert Goldstein, concludes that repression played an important role in weakening American labor and was *the* reason for the disintegration of labor radicalism and socialism (1978: ix, 5–6, 550). Wilentz (1984: 15) specifically argues that the turning point was labor's defeat by repression in the period 1886–94. Shefter (1986: 252–3) agrees that AFL craft unionism triumphed over general unionism and socialism as these were physically defeated. Holt (1977) argues that repression accounted for the different trajectories of unions in the British and American iron and steel industries. Although American steel unions were at first more powerful than British, repression during the Homestead strike of 1892 virtually destroyed them. They were finished off by U.S. Steel in 1901, although the company was careful first to offer craftworkers divisive pension and stock-ownership benefits (Brody 1960: 78–95). Workers initially showed solidarity, but they had no ultimate answer to employers determined to drive out unions with massed scabs, Pinkerton men, and state troopers and to keep them out with blacklists and industrial espionage. Ultimately, employers could detach many craftworkers from class solidarity and repress the rest. This was the clearest American extremism of the period – one that has been appallingly repressed in American political and academic memories.

Militarism is necessary to our explanation, but it is not sufficient. Why did not American repression, like the European repression we observe later, merely increase workers' solidarity and socialism? We must bring in three further American political crystallizations. Then we can finally see why labor responded as it did.

2. *Capitalist liberalism.* The capitalist crystallization in America emerged extreme (as the first of the thirteen explanations listed earlier argues). Repression was wielded by a state that had crystallized especially in its judiciary as capitalist-liberal. It embodied a virtually sacred capitalist conception of legality. The Constitution had yoked two legal principles of freedom, of the person and of his property, and sacramented them in an *entrenched* document. If the most appropriate comparison in level of repression is with tsarist Russia, the difference between the two states is obvious. Russian repression came from an autocratic monarchy. Its law was the tsar's will moderated by what was politically expedient. Though Russian capitalists welcomed repression of their workers, they rarely initiated or controlled it. Even German and Austrian capitalists, with more power in their own states, had to share the regime with monarchs and nobilities whose commitment to order and force marched to principles besides the freedom of private property. American capitalists, as a "party" in Weber's sense, controlled their state, especially through the judiciary. Its sacred laws and therefore its policing enshrined their property rights and freedoms.

As I note in Chapter 5, America had enshrined a legal above a political conception of order and citizenship. No other country had done so. From 1900 on, this was slightly dented in mining and railroad strikes when presidents mediated because of disruption to the national economy (as regimes did in all countries, even Germany and Russia). But legal conceptions were especially revealed in the extent of scabbing in America. If European employers imported scabs, they could not count on unswerving police and military protection. State elites charged with preserving public order might decide that the scabs, not the strike, constituted the greater threat to order. They often pressured employers to conciliate (see Shorter and Tilly's 1974 quantitative French evidence referred to later). This rarely happened in America, where state elites were rigorously subjected to property law. Employers had the right to make private employment contracts with whomever they pleased. If employers entered into contracts with scabs, law and state would protect them, to the hilt. The capitalist crystallization predominated over the civilian-military.

American capitalists' own beliefs were buttressed by this sacred law. They believed self-righteously in the equation of their private economic interests, the rule of law, and ultimate values of freedom. God often figured in their arguments. The leader of the anthracite mine owners said in 1902: "the rights and interests of the laboring men will be protected and cared for – not by the labour agitators, but by the Christian men to whom God in his infinite wisdom has given control of the property interests of this country" (Rayback 1966: 211).

American capitalists were also on the crest of economic and political waves. Their invention, the corporate economy, was booming; they dominated national and non-southern state politics. Dubofsky (1974: 298) says: "the Wobblies and socialists failed not because American society was exceptional, but because they reached their respective peaks when the nation's rulers were most confident, united."

We saw ruling class solidarity destroy the Chartists in 1840s Britain. But now no other national capitalist class behaved with quite such righteous solidarity. By contrast, British employers, as the trade unionist (and later Labour cabinet minister) John Hodge observed, "are entitled to credit for always having played cricket" (quoted by Holt 1977: 30). The metaphor is apt. Industrialists had little choice because not they but the cricket-playing old regime constituted the core of state elites and parties. Having earlier destroyed an insurrectionary working class, the regime now confronted a responsible sectional labor movement whose votes they wanted and which they became prepared to conciliate. Neither Conservatives nor Liberals would let employers run their class policy; both regarded the law as the instrument of their political purpose – as indeed parliamentary sovereignty entailed. American state elites-parties upheld the law, and that was slower to change than political calculations of advantage. Thus individualism was internalized less by the workers (as in the first group of explanations of American exceptionalism), more by state elites centered on the judiciary and by the capitalist class.

Such pronounced American judicial repression did not characterize just this period. Modern versions flourish today. The remaining labor unions are still formidably intimidated by the courts, though less frequently than in the past by police and paramilitaries. The lower working class, predominantly black and Latino, is contained within its inner-city desperation by a substantial police and paramilitary presence. Neither repression appears much on the agenda of party democracy – these groups do not fund the parties, and few of them even vote.

This casts doubt on traditional one-dimensional conceptions of the state. The dominant tradition in comparative political sociology divides regimes into absolutist versus constitutional monarchies, authoritarian versus democratic regimes, on a single "right-left" continuum – what I term the representative crystallization. This infuses work from Moore (1973) and Lipset (1984) through to Rueschemeyer, Stephens, and Stephens (1992) and indeed through to my own later chapters of Volume I and even more recently (Mann 1988). Yet, as Rueschemeyer, Stephens, and Stephens recognize, U.S. history sits uncomfortably in this tradition. Following Moore, they ask why the United States became democratic, especially given the presence of substantial labor-repressive agriculture in the South. Like him, they seek to explain why a German-style authoritarian alliance between industrial and agrarian capitalists did not develop. Their reasons are good, and similar to mine.

First, federalism allowed southern landowners to repress anyway; second, industrialists seemed to be able to repress adequately even in a democracy. But I go farther. The diversity of American political institutions, given full rein by the federalism (discussed later), allows for polymorphous crystallizations that have significantly constrained expressions of popular sovereignty, as Chapter 5 shows they were deliberately designed to do. The first such crystallization has been a judicial-centered liberalism expressing the power of the capitalist class, constraining the social reality and strategic options of opposed power actors. Such constraints were not effected from "outside" political institutions, as many Marxian views of the "capitalist state" imply. Judicial power networks are a *part* of states, but then states are polymorphous. Let us turn to the third U.S. political crystallization:

3. *Party democracy.* America had the most institutionalized two-party democracy in the world in the nineteenth century. Repression was wielded by the two parties. Women could not vote, and blacks in the South had lost their short-lived votes. But unions were essentially male and northern, and almost all members had the vote. The male domination of work and republicanism may have been greater than in other countries. As Montgomery notes, a "manly" bearing toward the boss was *the* American working class virtue, "with all its connotations of dignity, respectability, defiant egalitarianism, and patriarchical male supremacy" (1979: 13). The swagger of American workingmen, the assertiveness of their speech, their tools carried around the belt in

(gun) holsters – all this strikes the foreign observer as a masculine claim to power. Male workers may have felt empowered by this state. Unlike Russian or even Austrian and German workers, American workers could not easily view violence and legal coercion as expected attributes of an alien state that should be overthrown. Until 1896, there was high voter turnout – up to 85 percent (75 percent in the cities) – and easy registration for immigrants. Most workers, including union members, were "freely" voting for the two parties whose administrations upheld their repression. Having fewer political grievances than European workers, Americans did not need to politicize their economic discontents into socialism, argues Lipset (1984). After 1896, white male democracy weakened. Residency and citizen requirements, aimed at immigrants, and Progressive legislation, aimed against city machines, considerably reduced turnout, especially worker turnout (Burnham 1965, 1970: 71–90).

But did this slightly weakening American party democracy bring workers gains? Was it as benign and as responsive a state as Lipset suggests? The repression suggests not. Remember two features of the organization of American party democracy. First, the parties were rooted more in local-regional, ethnic-religious segmental power networks than in national or class ones. Workers were voting neither for nor against labor repression but for *different* benefits concerned with "spoils" and the interests of their local, their ethnic, and their religious communities. Because unions were becoming sectional organizations of established workers, they themselves often supported antiimmigrant politics. Because under the U.S. Constitution repression was handled mainly by the courts rather than by politicians, it was somewhat removed from elections (as it is today).

Second, workers, as in all countries except Britain, were still a minority. They comprised somewhat more than a third of the population by 1914, about the same as farmers, perhaps double the burgeoning middle classes. Union workers were a small minority. They had to interest the mass of unorganized workers, many controlled segmentally by local notables, and they had to interest the other two class groups. Ultimately they failed. Labor advocated reducing property freedoms, yet farmers and the middle class were deeply attached to property and could sway many local laboring dependents. Labor failed in its ideological struggle to detach defense of small property from big, corporate property and so lost the electoral support of farmers, the lower middle class, and many unorganized workers. The loss of farmers was especially damaging. Though many opposed the authorities' violence against workers, and had their own radical grievances against corporate "monopolies," they did not favor solutions enhancing what were argued to be "union monopolies." The failure of farmer-labor parties (discussed in Chapter 19) was critical. Without such an alliance the majoritarian propertied classes could repress minority workers. Less the workers, more the majoritarian propertied classes (plus their segmental power dependents), internalized American individualism in this period.

American party democracy was not benign to workers. It did not give them more – it gave them less. Republican and Democratic parties were cross-class, local-regional, ethnic-religious, segmental coalitions. Workers did push for prolabor candidates (Bridges 1986), but the parties were ill suited to express class interests, especially in this period as the Democratic party became more rural and Catholic, with its distinctively reactionary southern, faction, and the dominant Republicans northern, industrial (labor and manufacturers), and Protestant. There were also many local exceptions, adding to segmentalism. Party national unity was weakened by the distinctively *federal* separation between parties and executive. The president, not the party, forms the cabinet and draws up a program. Therefore, the parties, unlike those under constitutions embodying parliamentary sovereignty, are less disciplined by the need to form a coherent program. They can remain more factionalized.

Labor had to pressure individual politicians in both parties: "Reward your friends and punish your enemies," said Gompers. Although in urban-industrial constituencies this could produce sympathetic politicians, it could not mobilize a national party with a legislative program. Nor could it elect senators, let alone a president, or appoint judges to the higher courts. Its successes were mostly in local and state politics, but their legislation could be set aside by the courts.

Labor's direct influence at the federal level was probably less than labor's influence in British or even in German national politics. This statement runs contrary to some interpretations of the period (e.g., Rayback 1966: 250–72). It also seems counterintuitive, as Germany was an authoritarian monarchy and half of British workers could not vote. But the German regime had to maneuver adroitly to mobilize an antilabor coalition, and it was not above inventing progressive programs, like social insurance, to keep socialism at bay. In Britain labor could elect members of Parliament and this influenced the two parties, especially the Liberals, needing its working-class constituencies. Parties in Parliament were also sovereign over the executive and the courts. Only five years after the judges in the Taff Vale case took away certain union organizing rights, the 1906 election of a Liberal government promptly secured a Trade Disputes Act granting unions the organizing freedoms they wanted. Unlike much Liberal legislation, this passed the Tory House of Lords with ease.

By contrast, American unions achieved little from the national political parties. The House of Representatives was sympathetic to bills restricting strike injunctions, but the Senate was not. Administrations enacted stringent child labor laws and restricted the conditions of female employment, but as in other countries a cross-class moral and male consensus existed to "protect" women and children. Factory safety regulation came less, and later, than in Britain or France. The founding of the U.S. Department of Labor introduced conciliation procedures and brought unions into the administrative corridors of power, but only in 1914, well after Britain and France. The eight-hour day on interstate railroads and improvements for federal government workers and seamen were genuine gains. The Clayton Act of 1914, regulating corporations, is sometimes regarded as labor's gain. It affirmed that the "labor of a human being is not a commodity or article of commerce" and that unions were not illegal or in violation of the antitrust laws. But this left "conspiracies" and secondary and sympathy actions exactly where they were (Sklar 1988: 331). The rate of antiunion injunctions actually increased after the Clayton Act, to 46 percent of all sympathy strikes in the 1920s (Forbath 1989: 1252–3). The Wobbly organizer also asked a simple skeptical question of new labor laws: "How are they *enforced*?" (Dubofsky 1969: 158).

Not until 1932 did the Norris–La Guardia Act give unions the organizing rights already granted in Britain in 1906. American democracy eventually secured collective civil rights for unions, after repression had taken its toll of them. Laslett (1974: 216–7) argues that concessions made by the Wilson administration fatally weakened the Socialist party: Most of its affiliated unions now turned away to the Democrats. If so, they were lured by promise rather than performance, and were already settling for less than their European counterparts. Workers made some mild gains, less as a working class than as mass voters, along with other mass constituencies such as the middle class and farmers. Reforms extending electoral control through the direct election of senators, regulating business monopolies, universal free education, and the progressive income tax were achieved by cross-class coalitions of Progressives in which organized labor played a subsidiary part (Lash 1984: 170–203; Mowry 1972; Wiebe 1967). Not all of Marshall's "social citizenship" had to come from class action. The progressive income tax, introduced in 1913 (though minor until the war), came from the competitive party system without much pressure from unions (as was also so in Britain). But overall, during the period of greatest repression, labor interests were not often helped, and they were more often hindered, by American party democracy.

4. *Federalism.* The American state crystallized on the "national"

issue first as confederal, then as federal. Repression was wielded by a fairly decentralized state rather than by a centralized nation-state. Worker resistance fragmented among federal, state, and local levels of government and between law courts and political administrations. During this period, the widening of civilian state scope, which tended in most countries to nationalize labor movements, served to fragment American labor further. Most new functions were wielded by state and local governments. Until the 1930s, the federal government was the least significant in matters relevant to labor (I draw freely here from Lowi 1984), and this fragmented potential national class unity. Most labor law was initiated by individual states. By 1900, industrial states like Massachusetts and Illinois had more conciliatory labor laws than existed at the federal level. Most were more repressive, some ferociously so. The unevenness of this enormous continental country is important. In any one year some northern states might be passing progressive legislation and seeking ways around reactionary court rulings, western states might be shooting Wobblies, southwestern states harassing Populists, and southern states intensifying racism. A notion of extensive class *totality* across the nation was hard to come by, even for those being shot at.

The South constituted a special federal problem. Racism buttressed domestic militarism to defeat attempts at class mobilization in the predominantly agrarian South. This meant that at the federal level a solid bloc of senators and congressmen, essentially unopposed in elections, used the seniority system of congressional committees to entrench their reactionary politics. As even Franklin D. Roosevelt was later to find, prolabor legislation was difficult to steer by them. Their "one-party state" in the South was increasingly the swing vote on Capitol Hill, since it was reactionary yet Democrat.

Local-regional party and community organization thrived under the entrenched federal Constitution, fed by waves of ethnic-religious immigration. City government could deliver benefits to its segmental clients, especially by issuing "variances" from state laws and by licensing and patronage over economic benefits. Many worker interests – community interests in housing, public health, control of transport and public utilities, and manual employment in the public sector – were determined at the city level, filtered through segmental power relations, not class ones. Goods were delivered through ethnic-religious communities and city patronage machines. Native-born skilled workers wielded substantial local influence inside machines, in cross-class alliances often directed against newer immigrant workers. Federalism and segmentalist political parties interacted with ethnicity to fragment total consciousness of class. Class and nation are not opposites. They reinforce one another – or their absence weakens each other, as in the United States. The narrowing of class to employment relations, a common tendency in this period, went much further there.

Domestic militarism, capitalist-liberalism, party democracy, and federalism – all had the same fragmenting effect on politics and classes in the United States. Skowronek (1982) justly observes that this "state of courts and parties" hindered the development of an American national state bureaucracy – but so did federalism. The American national state remained primarily military, as the data in Chapter 11 reveal. Thus, on the civilian-military issue, the United States crystallized domestically as predominantly militarist.

The worker response: sectionalism

But this capitalist-liberal, party-democratic, and federal militarism was ultimately uniquely successful against workers because it amplified their inherent tendencies to respond, not with class but with *sectionalism*. Repression was aimed more at general unionism and socialism than at craft unionism. Craftworkers could evade it better than could others. Employers chose selective or more general repression partly according to the trade cycle. When full-order books required production, they recognized craft union power and AFL pleas for national agreements. Most craft-union pressure was local and applied to particular employers, involving at most municipal political support and requiring little strike action. The solidarity of craftworkers was well established, informal, and relatively invulnerable to police infiltration or repression (Marks 1989: 53). Selective repression widened the normal division between craftworkers and other workers into a deep tactical and organizational sectionalism.[4] Craftworkers went their own way, leaving less favored comrades to their fate.

Here the United States differed sharply from tsarist Russia in two respects. First, regime violence in Russia was aimed equally at all skill levels. Second, the rapidity of Russian industrialization had not allowed artisan organization to mature gradually. Skilled workers did not have the organizational resources to go it alone. Whereas repression split the American working class, it united the Russian. Just as the Russian case was analyzed by socialism's greatest tactician, Lenin, so the American case was analyzed by the major tactician of sectionalism, Samuel Gompers.

---

[4] This is the missing element in Marks's otherwise excellent analysis of section-alism in the United States. He mistakenly classifies the United States with countries exhibiting little repression, such as Britain and Scandinavia (1989: 75).

Gompers and his American Federation of Labor generally avoided politics. Although the AFL set up a small lobbying organization in Washington in 1908, it was not active. Leaders such as Gompers and Mitchell placed more faith in their membership in the National Civic Foundation (NCF); a pressure group of progressive corporate leaders. Gompers and Mitchell wanted the NCF to persuade business leaders into national agreements between AFL unions and employer associations which would obviate the need for mass strikes. While many local unions were actively seeking pro-labor legislation at state and municipal levels, the AFL nationally advocated "voluntarism" (Fink 1973; Rogin 1961/62). This was partly under legal advice: Because the law proscribed union "coercion," informal voluntary agreements were unions' principal remaining power (Fink 1987: 915–7). But Gompers went farther. He opposed social insurance legislation as reducing the independence of workers. Even this was not unique. Because unions had such strongly protectionist and mutualist origins, many of their leaders were suspicious of such government intervention. But Gompers was extreme in opposing the regulation of factories and the arbitration of industrial disputes as ensnaring labor in "superlegalism." He even opposed laws banning victimizing union members:

I doubt the wisdom of trying to secure the passage of a bill interfering with the right of an employer to discharge an employee. . . . If we secure the enactment of a law making that act unlawful our enemies will certainly argue that the right to quit work singly or collectively (that is as a union) for any certain reasons ought to be made unlawful and they will endeavor to secure the enactment of a law to that effect. [Fink 1973, p. 816]

This may seem bizarre, but his own experience as a Cigarmakers Union organizer had taught him to eschew politics and legislation and concentrate on direct economic pressure on the individual employer. The union had lobbied hard to enact a New York State law to abolish tenement manufacturing (cigar-making families lived and worked in apartments in tenement blocks owned by the employer). The courts ruled the new law unconstitutional, the union successfully lobbied for a revised law, and the courts also ruled this unconstitutional. Gompers relates:

We talked over the possibilities of further legislative action and decided to concentrate on organization work. Through our trade unions we harassed the manufacturers by strikes and agitation until they were convinced . . . that it would be less costly for them to abandon the tenement manufacturing system and carry on the industry in factories under decent conditions. Thus we accomplished through economic power what we had failed to achieve through legislation. [1967: I, 197]

Because the law had done such damage to labor, it should be avoided in favor of "economic power." His mentor in the Cigarmakers Union, Adolph Strasser, declared in 1894:

You cannot pass a general eight hour day without changing the constitution of the United States and the constitution of every state in the Union. . . . I am opposed to wasting our time declaring for legislation being enacted for a time possibly, after we are dead. [Forbath 1989: 1145]

Alliances with political radicals and socialists only harmed labor. Gompers's autobiography evinces as much hostility toward socialists as capitalists. Although he always claimed to respect Marx and his ideas, he says his distrust of socialists began with the Tompkins Square Riot of 1874. He had narrowly avoided a police club by jumping into a cellar. His experiences there

became guide-posts for my understanding of the labor movement for years to come. I saw how professions of radicalism and sensationalism concentrated all the forces of organized society against a labor movement and nullified in advance normal, necessary activity. . . . I saw the danger of entangling alliances with intellectuals who did not understand that to experiment with the labor movement was to experiment with human life. [1967: I, 97–8]

Gompers advocated retreat to "pure and simple" trade unionism, conscious that it was a retreat. As he put it in 1914, the AFL "is guided by the history of the past, drawing its lessons from the past. . . . It works along the lines of least resistance" (Rogin 1961/62: 524).

Gompers believed that the mass movements of the 1880s and 1890s had been overextended. Labor had to rebuild slowly from its strongest redoubts with "permanent" organization, providing members with unemployment benefits, burial insurance, sick pay, and strike funds. Although these were intrinsically desirable, their main point was to establish a permanent relation between members and union (Gompers 1967: I, 166–8). Only well-financed organizations could withstand prolonged strikes and lockouts. It was futile to bring out masses who lacked such resources. They would be inevitably defeated. That was the lesson of this whole period, Gompers argued. It was why he so despised and hated the Wobblies, who led workers into strikes without permanent resources, without strike funds, without even formal members. *They* were the betrayers of the working class, he argued, not the AFL leadership.

But Gompers's tactics could not benefit the whole working class; in fact, they presupposed that class identity did not exist. The abandonment of politics narrowed the scope and weakened the totality of the "collective laborer" because it meant abandonment of social policies that might benefit working-class families and communities. The labor movement was confined, more than in any other country, to male employment economism. Even there Gompers's tactics were sectionalist, for they required workers to have strike funds and employers to be unable to find scab labor. In principle, scabs might be kept out by "one big union" of the entire working class, but this tactic had collapsed in mass violence and repression. Gompers believed that organizing masses of unskilled workers actually harmed his craft members. Some twentieth-century American unions, notably the Teamsters, have restrained scabs through violence. But scabs can rarely undertake skilled work successfully.

Although Gompers argued that patient permanent organization could slowly spread financial and skill resources to other workers, in practice not many workers besides craftsmen could either provide substantial union funds or restrict the training of skills in their occupation. In practice his tactics amounted to craft protectionism. The AFL had retreated to the position British unions had occupied between 1850 and 1890, after the collapse of Chartism, before the new unionism. After 1900, the American labor movement was becoming the weakest in any advanced country – partly because Gompers and the AFL possessed a sense of the art of the possible in the face of ruthless, righteous repression.

But AFL craft protectionism can be charged with further weakening of the labor movement, by focusing on restricting the supply of alternative labor. New labor market entrants increasingly came from different ethnic-religious groups of immigrants. Thus the second group of explanations of American extremism, concerning the "natural" sectionalism of America, have greater validity when applied to the period after 1900. Of course, from the first, racism and immigrant diversity had not helped American working-class unity, especially in politics. The black-white divide was largely confined to the South. The most enduring cleavage in economic struggle throughout the period was actually between Asian immigrants and the rest. Most American labor organizations showed deep hostility toward Chinese labor, partly because of gut racism against the "yellow races," partly because Chinese indentured labor was seriously undercutting Anglo workers in the West. Yet apart from this, American ethnic-religious divisions were not unique. They had only been on the scale of those in Lancashire between English and Irish workers or in Germany between Catholics and Protestants or Germans and Poles.

At first, America was not exceptional in this respect. Indeed, among the Knights of Labor and in major strikes like those of 1877 or at Homestead, or among miners, different ethnic groups, often including blacks, and men and women had shown considerable solidarity. Yet ethnic economic tensions now worsened. This was partly due to the increase in immigration from southern and eastern Europe. Neighborhoods and occupations became more ethnically segregated. But it was amplified by sectionalism in the labor movement itself: on the one hand, a predominantly craft AFL recruiting mostly native-born and northern Europeans, on the other, general unions and political groups recruiting southern and eastern Europeans and blacks (Shefter 1986: 205–7, 228–30). The AFL's antiimmigration lobbying was now a major legislative activity, reinforcing sectionalism.

American conclusions

I have not discussed all thirteen explanations of American exceptionalism, yet my own view should be clear: America was no more exceptional than all countries are. It was not even born extreme; it became extreme. The turning point was about 1900 and resulted primarily from a distinctive amplification of worker sectionalism by four "higher-level political crystallizations" – as domestically militarist, as (judicially centered) capitalist-liberal, as party democratic, and as federal. As Lipset argues, the regime form was the decisive determinant. Yet it was neither so benign nor so congenial to workers – so one-dimensionally "democratic" – as he suggests. States were polymorphous, not unitary. But faced with severe repression, American labor split more deeply than that of any other country to amplify the normal craft-noncraft sectional fault line. Uniquely the sectionalism of skill strata and internal labor markets coincided with ideological factionalism. The split institutionalized into factional worker organizations and deepened as the dominant AFL faction narrowed the scope of class and intensified sectionalism and ethnic-religious segmentalism.

Although there were still battles to be fought, and tactical decisions to be made, and though there was a labor revival in the 1930s and 1940s, working-class identity became un-American. Workers may label themselves as "workingmen" but not "working class," and they are significantly motivated by bourgeois individualism (Halle 1984). I have argued that this was consequence more than cause of the turning away from socialism.

Of course, as Lipset argues, and as these chapters confirm, the American state, unlike reactionary states elsewhere, has not reinforced working-class identity. No national class unity was conferred on workers by a common struggle for a national citizenship, unlike in most European countries. Thus normal divergencies between skilled and unskilled, between different industries and regions, and between ethnic and religious communities were not suppressed by common political exigencies. Indeed, they were reinforced by political federalism and factionalism.

In some continental European countries the working class was largely excluded from national citizenship and a common nationally organized repression was aimed against workers' demands for civil and political citizenship. Workers were forced to conceptualize a total struggle and forced toward national class unity and the national state by the strategies of its centralized class and regime enemies. This politically forced national class unity has been absent in the United States. The peculiarly fragmenting effects of the dominance of petit bourgeois ideology, the frontier, and ethnic divisions may have later "overdetermined" the outcome. But the early inclusion of white male workers in a militaristic, capitalist-liberal, party-democratic, and federal state intensified worker sectionalism and factionalism and made probable the decline of American class identity.

Socialist ideologies require a sense of totality and alternative. Yet capitalist production relations do not provide experience of a social totality. The closest approximation to a real, experienced totality is the individual enterprise or the single trade or industry – and these organizations crosscut one another. The only bounded network provided by capitalism itself is its entire global penetration, which is not experienced by anyone as a community. Thus the macroeconomic trends of capitalism are rarely experienced as totalities by everyone in the same way. Booms and slumps may impact differently on different firms, industries, and skill grades. Workers may respond aggressively, but sectionally by trade, industry, and region. Agitation aimed at national government gives totalizing unity to these disparate movements. Class and nation reinforce one another, as do sectionalism and local-regional identities. Without this, labor is divided between unionized, skilled insiders and unorganized, unskilled outsiders. Such a division has dominated U.S. labor history. American labor failed to articulate a sense of the totality of power relations or develop an alternative to them. This was already fairly clear by 1914.

The United States was not "exceptional," but it did become "extreme." This was not because workers lacked grievances but because American political crystallizations reinforced their segmentalism and sectionalism. Its extremism may reveal what might have happened in the nonexistent counterfactual case where capitalism was truly transnational – that is, if battles over the state were disconnected from the labor process. Far from this leading, as Marx believed, to the emergence of a singular working class aiming at socialism, it might have led to profoundly sectional and segmental struggles. Without battles over party democracy, the capitalist class might have been truly hegemonic. In the more transnational contemporary world, it again threatens to become truly hegemonic.

Imperial Russia: autocratic militarism and revolution

Russia industrialized and transformed its agriculture in great if uneven bursts throughout this period.[5] Serfdom had been abolished in 1861, fueling the agrarian struggles analyzed in Chapter 19. After about 1900, the Second Industrial Revolution arrived in Russia while the first one was still in its infancy. Bigger factories and denser proletarian suburbs came to the cities. Russian industrial capitalism generated a more logistically concentrated working class than in other countries, often assumed by historians to be an important cause of revolution. Concentration did indeed produce a more formidable, community-rooted working class than might have been expected by Russia's level of development or by the proportion of industrial workers in the labor force. But its veering toward revolution resulted far more from its political crystallizations than from the size of factories.

On representation, Russia was at the opposite extreme from the United States. By 1900, it remained the only autocratic monarchy in Europe, the only one without any pretense of party democracy, the one in which state elites and parties most interrelated as court factions. Its militarism was also distinctive in sustaining an empire surrounding the "Russian" core territories (though British militarism also sustained adjacent Ireland). Thus militarism was unusually pronounced domestically as well as geopolitically. The Russian state crystallized as capitalist but also as highly monarchical, militarist, and centralizing (though it rejected "national" or "nation-state" labels).

But even the eastern edge of the Western ideological community experienced the more liberal legacy of the Enlightenment. As we saw in Chapter 14 the later the economic development, the greater the emergence of a technocratic intelligentsia claiming knowledge of science and the future. Among Russian professionals, gentry and aristocrats, and state administrators, a self-conscious, partly autonomous intelligentsia emerged, advancing alternative versions of progress. State elites became factionalized. On the Right were court parties urging enlightened absolutism, urging the tsar toward essentially eighteenth-century strategies – property for exserfs, universal education, and civil citizenship. Conservatism could also be given a more populist tinge, urging the tsar to place himself at the head of the Russian or Slav people or

---

[5] For the working class I have depended principally on the studies of Bonnell (1983), Mandel (1983), Smith (1983: 5–53), and Swain (1983). For an interesting comparison of factory regimes in England, the United States, and Russia, see Burawoy (1984). For divisions among the regime and the intelligentsia, see Haimson (1964–5), Besançon (1986), and Hobson (1991). For tsarist labor policy, see McDaniel (1988), and for its repression, see Goldstein (1983: 278–87).

the Orthodox church community. There was also a Leftist populism. Liberals advocated civil and partial political citizenship. Out of the encounter between indigenous populism and European socialism came revolutionary anarchists and socialists. In other countries such varying strategies appeared in different social environments. Amid Russian ferment, the intelligentsia was debating all these patented prescriptions simultaneously – as Dostoevsky's novels vividly reveal. Alternative politics were confused, though somewhat restricted in penetrative powers.

The state was besieged by turbulence without and parties within. So as the civilian scope of the late nineteenth-century state expanded, so did its factionalism. Civilianization did, as elsewhere, lead to the proliferation of conciliatory state policies, but only by one faction and not usually the dominant one. Different state departments and officials with different backgrounds suggested strategies varying from military repression through paternalist, policed regulation to limited conciliation and autonomy for labor organizations. The finance and security ministries were notably at odds.

The regime had many options, and what it did was not inevitable. This state crystallized as autocratic. Ultimate power strategies were ratified by the autocrat, whose word was law, whose ministers reported personally to him, whose preferences, character, and determination mattered. But the talents of the last Romanovs were not distinguished. The last tsar with a clear strategy, toward enlightened if conservative absolutism, was Alexander II, murdered in 1881. Alexander III, reigning until 1894, combined industrialization with knee-jerk repression. Nicholas II then faced greater dislocation with irresolution, in marriage as well as affairs of state. Among autocrats such things matter. Lacking his own vision, besieged by the advice and visions of others – including the reactionary hysteria of Alexandra, his wife – he and his court veered around irresolute militarism.

To dignify the policy of these factionalized elites with the label "strategy" might mislead. Most traditions and instincts were reactionary and autocratic. But when faced with trouble, elites vacillated between minimal reform and brutal repression, an internal struggle usually resolved in favor of military repression by instinctive fear of autonomous powers arising in civil society. Autocratic repression in its Russian instance was more drift than strategy. It was a poor basis for providing order, for satisfying the claims of those outside the state, or for enhancing the morale of those inside. A better tsar might have done better.

In Russia, state elites, not capitalists, ran the show. They responded to unions, strikes, and socialist parties as they did to all such manifestations of collective organization. All were banned as a threat to public order. Armed police and troops were brought in routinely to disperse demonstrators or strikers. The army intervened almost two thousand times between 1895 and 1905 to suppress strikes and demonstrations. The government issued passports to workers migrating to the factories, revocable if they broke their employment contracts. Detailed rule books were drawn up by the government to regulate working practices. Physical beatings and personal servility to employers and managers were a part of this code, derived from the Russian army. How this particular unity of experience between workers and peasant-soldiers was to rebound on regime and capitalists in 1917! Even when state elites attempted conciliation, they did so with heavy-handed paternalism. Among the most curious trade unions spawned by capitalism were the Zubatov societies sponsored by the Moscow police chief from 1896, embodying the contradictions of, on the one hand, the genuine desire of reformers like Zubatov for "neutral" paternalism in labor relations, and on the other hand, an ultimate siding with the forces of order and property. The societies finally collapsed amid the 1905 revolution (McDaniel 1988: 64–88). There was no civil, let alone political, citizenship for workers, but there was not much more for peasants or middling classes either.

Thus *no* moderate worker strategy – protectionism, mutualism, economism, reformism – could freely organize to make gains. No stable legal or institutional framework emerged to handle labor relations. There was a fair amount of covert practical cooperation occurring within the factory gates, and many blind eyes were turned by individual ministers, provincial governors, and police chiefs. Some among these made promises of reforms that no reliable administration could enforce. Nor could syndicalism plausibly argue that this state could be bypassed by strikes, although its anarchist wing tried terrorism. Bourgeois democrats were driven toward statist socialists by common experience of militarism. By 1900, democrats – bourgeois and proletarian – were styling themselves "socialists," discussing Marx, and arguing that democracy required general economic and political transformation. Most socialists, driven underground to revolutionary dreams and plots, sought statist solutions.

Because the pace of industrialization had not allowed artisans to mature, craft organization and sectionalism were initially weak. They were destroyed by common experience of state repression. Thus state elites and employers rarely distinguished, as in other countries, between more and less "responsible" or "respectable" workers. Few concessions were made to skilled workers to separate them from the mass. There was little sectionalism in Russian labor. Even when mutualist schemes of state-aided social insurance were aired – in other countries an issue that divided workers according to level and security of their income – all worker organizations demanded a universal state-sponsored scheme. Elites and capitalists were, mostly unwittingly, forcing workers into class organizations led by revolutionaries. Lenin had realized this by 1899:

The Russian working class is burdened by a double yoke; it is robbed and plundered by the capitalists and the landlords, and to prevent it from fighting them, the police bind it hand and foot, gag it, and every attempt to defend the rights of the people is persecuted. Every strike against a capitalist results in the military and police being let loose on the workers. Every economic struggle necessarily becomes a political struggle, and Social-Democracy must indissolubly combine the one with the other into a *single class struggle of the proletariat.* [1969: 36, his emphasis; he repeated the argument in 1902, in *What Is to Be Done?*, 1970: 157]

In 1905, greater self-consciousness was forced on state elites. Their governing capacity was undermined by defeat in the war with Japan. In the Far Eastern provinces the army, poorly led and poorly supplied, fell apart; in the cities food distribution broke down; in many rural areas peasants exploited the power vacuum by seizing land. An estimated 2.8 million workers struck in 1905, more than twice the number in any other country in any year in the entire period. Their protest became entwined with community-based demonstrations and bread riots and with regional movements for "national" autonomies (under-researched by both Western and Soviet historians). The riots and demonstrations in 1905 and 1917 resembled in certain respects the street- and community-based revolutions of the earlier bourgeois and Chartist era rather than the employment-centered struggles of the modern working-class era. The Russian revolutions brought out masses of women as well as men, and the intensity of emotions owed much to a family and community reinforcement of narrower economic and political struggles. Russian working-class consciousness uniquely in this period became a *totality* – aimed at a state that brought a highly centralized and politicized exploitation into almost every aspect of life.

But as yet no large group had a revolutionary intent or, indeed, any coherent alternative beyond grievances expressed in traditional petitioning mode. In the urban centers the 1905 revolution was really a massive, broad-based demonstration of grievance. Nor was it yet a national movement. Locally-regionally organized rebellious soldiers, peasants, urban demonstrators, and regional-national dissidents acted separately and so could be repressed separately. Many regiments stayed disciplined and that was sufficient. In St. Petersburg, on "Bloody Sunday" alone, troops killed at least 130 demonstrators and wounded 300, at which Lenin (contradicting his earlier argument quoted at the beginning of this chapter) remarked, "The revolutionary education of the proletariat made more progress in one day than it could have made in months and years of drab, humdrum, wretched existence" (Kochan 1966: 80). The troops killed 2,500 the next year, in suppressing mainly national protests in Poland mixed with worker protests. The state responded to further scattered terrorism with mass hangings.

But the tsar was now frightened, and with reason, for the additive effects of mass peasant, regional-national, worker, and urban protests – all demanding citizenship – were straining the repressive resources of a regime just defeated in war. Moderates seized their chance and persuaded him that rivals like Germany or Japan could be defeated only if the state conjoined reforms with agrarian and industrial development. The state should grant partial civil and political citizenship. The Duma (parliament) was convoked, though with a strongly weighted suffrage system. Mutualist concessions were introduced in industry: For a short period from March 1906 trade unions were legalized, provided they stayed out of politics and refrained from secondary strikes. Even a paternalist conception of union rights was better than nothing. The labor movement split into optimistic mutualists and reformers (overlapping with regime liberals hoping for a more "Western" emergence of unions with socialist rhetoric and practical compromise) and skeptical revolutionaries.

The regime's brain was working, apparently toward German-style authoritarian incorporation. This required careful combination of segmental conciliation and repression. The obvious tactic was to conciliate bourgeois demands for citizenship, produce a divisive agrarian program, and repress worker and regional-national dissidents. But its heart despised bourgeois liberalism, just as its head feared the masses. For liberals to remain in control of a reform movement, worker, regional-national, and peasant restraint was required. But even the economistic unions, the "legalists," felt pressured toward demanding mutualist extensions of organizing rights and political citizenship. This was further than tsar or court would go. Nicholas vacillated and listened to his wife. The Duma was twice dissolved and its constitution modified in a futile attempt to make it compliant. The liberals lost office and influence over workers. An alternative brain emerged, belonging to the formidable Stolypin. He urged economic development, military modernization, and agrarian reform, all to divide the peasantry while resisting citizenship and repressing urban-industrial protest. The Duma's constitution was restricted a third time, giving 1 percent of landowners 50 percent of its seats. This finally ensured a compliant Duma able to last out its five-year term. Stolypin's strategy of segmentalism embodying repression of labor took over.

Bans on all unions followed in June 1907, leaving the legalists embittered yet with national organizational experience. Working-class leaders and radical bourgeois intelligentsia found more takers for revolutionary alternatives, though they could risk little open action. By about 1910, the dominant alternatives had narrowed to the interpretations of statist Marxism provided by three illegal parties: the Social Revolutionaries, the Mensheviks, and the Bolsheviks. But with massive state oppression within the factory and the community, neither economists, mutualists, reformists nor revolutionary syndicalists or anarchists could made much headway among workers and in working-class communities.

Stolypin was mysteriously assassinated in 1911 and the regime was beset by a second bout of vacillation. Censorship was eased. Unions were again allowed a half-life, partly legalized yet intermittently persecuted. Legalists experienced the same contradiction as in 1906–7 – permitted to organize, yet unable to deliver reforms. When strikes and demonstrations got too large, the troops stepped in. Yet military repression delivered worker leadership to revolutionaries, most dramatically after the Lena gold mine massacre of 1912: The deaths of two hundred miners triggered massive strikes in all major industrial centers, continuing until 1914.

The regime might have been persuaded to reform after army modernization and Stolypin's agrarian reforms were complete, which, ironically, would have happened about February 1917, but Germany struck first to forestall this. (See Chapter 21.) The war first strengthened the conservatives and repression tightened. But when the war went badly, army, bread distribution, and government disintegrated. When revolution erupted in 1917, it was even more broadly based: to workers, peasants, nationalists, and bread rioters were added discontented officers and insurrectionary soldiers and sailors. Core Bolshevik support among workers was provided by former legalists, now Marxist revolutionaries.

The sequence of repression, disturbances, mild reform schemes, vacillation, and then harsher repression alienated liberals and moderates within working class, bourgeoisie, and intelligentsie alike. By 1914, the regime's strategy was not definitively settled, but its enemies had proliferated. The principled claims of national citizenship had not been denied, and some of its detailed practices had been erratically accepted. State crystallizations had been varied and inconsistent. But in times of crisis the regime seemed to reveal its true nature. If reformers could make little headway, revolutionaries were prepared to lead.

Doubtless, most Russian workers in 1914, perhaps even in early 1917, were more "conservative" than the agitators, in the two senses of being skeptical of revolutionary alternatives and hopeful of reform from legalists, regime moderates, even the tsar. But no significant moderate or sectionalist movement had emerged for a decade among workers. Historians note the normal fault line of the working class – skilled metalworkers versus younger, ex-rural, unskilled, and often female factory and urban proletariat (this has been recently emphasized by McKean 1990). But this fault line did not generate different workers' organizations as it did in the United States and to a lesser extent in Britain. Rather, it produced the leadership of the former over the latter, in an increasingly common revolutionary struggle.

Unless a reform movement could deflect the monarchy onto a more Western incorporative path – whether Anglo-American or German – the labor movement would probably go through a revolutionary phase. Of course, it did so, and as in the case of the other superpower extreme, the United States, this proved to have immense global consequences. War and the peasantry both played obvious and necessary roles in this development. On their own, neither the small Russian proletariat nor its Marxist leaders could successfully undertake a revolution. I discuss the peasantry in Chapter 19 (and the war and Bolshevik Revolution in the next volume). But even without war and peasants, Russian workers had been made into a class and brought to the brink of insurrection, along with radical bourgeois and entwined with regional nationalists, by their common experience at the hands of a vacillating but ultimately highly militaristic, autocratic, centralized state – not only in employment but throughout the lives of their entire families. Exploitation was intensive as well as extensive. If that state was brought by other forces to its knees, its repressive arm broken, they would rise up in insurrection – though with unpredictable results.

France: contested political crystallizations, rival socialisms

I attribute most that is distinctive in the French labor movement, conventionally, to its political crystallizations.[6] This country's industrialization peculiarities, however, also contributed substantial influences. French industrialization began early but proceeded unusually slowly. For example, handloom weavers survived in the thousands even after the depression in their trade of 1882–90, long after their collapse in Britain and Germany. Similar early labor organizations as in other countries had greater survival powers. Craft artisans dominated unions for longer. Aided by the Revolution, peasant families held tenaciously

---

[6] For French labor history in this period, I have relied especially on Noland (1956), Lefranc (1967), Ridley (1970), Perrot (1974), and Moss (1976).

on to their farms and labor, slowing urban and manufacturing growth. In samples of workers in five towns in the Lyons area in the 1850s between 54 percent and 66 percent practiced the same trade as their fathers. Between 43 percent and 53 percent still did so in the ten years after 1902 (Lequin 1977: I, 222, 251). Labor shortages caused a shortage of potential blackleg labor and a high proportion of married women workers. Industry spread across rural France in order to be close to labor supply and consumers.

The proletariat thus emerged somewhat decentralized. Industry and agriculture and employment and local community were less segregated, with few households living only on industrial wages. Industrialization produced the usual union organizations. Journeymen's associations (*compagnonnages*) disintegrated, replaced by mutual benefit societies; artisans in handicraft were threatened by capitalist entrepreneurs using machines and female and child labor. Proletarianization was more gradual than in England, especially in the northern textile industry, which remained family-organized and employer-controlled, distinct from the centers of manufacturing artisans, of which the largest were in Paris and Lyons (Aminzade 1981, 1984). Not until the "new factories" in heavy engineering in the 1900s was there a clear-cut division of space between home, factory, and town, with unions centered in the male-dominated factory, though influencing the surrounding "red suburbs" (Perrot 1986; Cottereau 1986).

These distinctive features of French industrialization should have also slowed the development of the working-class movement. In numbers they probably did. But in their class consciousness and organization, French labor militants were precocious, mostly because contested political crystallizations kept the revolutionary tradition alive. Only the national crystallization was resolved, because all the contending parties favored a rather centralized state. But representation was contested among Republican democrats, Monarchists, and Bonapartists, causing capitalism to remain fairly reactionary and domestic militarism to thrive.

Faced with such threats, political socialists took early control of labor organizations in Paris and Lyons. Artisans demanded party democracy and organizing rights from the Monarchist regimes of the period 1815–48, and this spurred national class organization well beyond the level we should expect from rather halting industrialization. Sansculottism was transformed into artisanal socialism earlier than in other countries – as the exiled twenty-five year-old Marx discovered in 1843, in his first actual encounters with the working class, in Brussels and Paris. Republican socialists developed first a Parisian, then a national, ideological power network of journals, clubs with reading rooms, and cafés among artisans through the 1830s. By the 1840s, socialists were organizing benefit societies into a singular, centralized national organization, extending it in rudimentary fashion among less skilled workers.

In 1848, artisan associations formed "little republics" in the van of the Revolution, pushing it leftward (Gossez 1967; Lequin 1977; Aminzade 1981: Chapter 6; Sewell 1986; Traugott 1988). Though repressed and forced back to the local-regional level, socialists remained in clandestine control of labor organizations through the reign of Napoleon III (1851–70), rejecting his attempt to incorporate their mutual aid associations – by which he hoped to divide skilled from unskilled workers. Respectable, sectional trade unionism barely emerged, because the revolutionary tradition nourished class organization in the face of a broadly common repression. Labor transformed revolutionary rhetoric from petit bourgeois Jacobinism through the artisanal forms of Blanqism and Proudhon's mutualism to more proletarian Marxism and syndicalism.

From 1875 on, France superficially resembled the United States, enjoying male party democracy. Male workers possessed political citizenship. Yet a somewhat restricted party democracy was not safely institutionalized, surviving through precarious Centrist coalitions. In 1875, the Republic had triumphed by only one Senate vote over the divided Monarchists and received a clear-cut electoral mandate only in 1879. The regime resisted giving workers organizing rights. For the Left, the 1870s were dominated by the military repression meted out to the Paris Commune (30,000 deaths) and the regime's continuing hostility to labor. Red, the color of blood, became the workers' color. Left extremism remained vigorous, increasingly open, and widely rooted in local-regional working-class communities. About 1880, the regime began conciliating on collective civil citizenship, first amnestying surviving Communards and then legalizing unions and strikes in 1884. But Monarchist and Bonapartist threats remained, fueled by army factionalism, clericalism, and church-state contention. The limited party-democratic state had enemies on both the Left and Right, some of them (like the Rightist officer corps) entrenched within the state itself.

From the 1880s on, the civilian scope of the state expanded as elsewhere, coinciding with the entrenchment of Centrist Republicanism. Its domestic militarism became more even-handed and cautious. All state elites and dominant parties have an interest in order; its preservation is their principal domestic function; for, without order, they fall. They can respond to popular discontent with either paramilitary repression or concessions. If they believe that the riots rather than the granting of popular grievances constitute the main threat to order – and if they fear the army itself – they may urge concessions. The state may conciliate as long as basic property rights are not affected. Most nineteenth-century states were not totally dominated by industrial capital and, outside of Russia and America, their judicial-police power networks often intervened to conciliate. Because of their fear of Left and Right, including the officer corps, and because regimes were now party democratic, the French state was sensitive on the issue.

Shorter and Tilly's (1974: 30–32) quantitative analysis of nineteenth-century French strikes shows prefects repeatedly intervening, usually at the request of workers, to forestall or terminate riots. They also show an increasing trend for workers to achieve more of their demands when the state intervened than when it did not. Prefects and subprefects varied in their actions, some seeking conciliation, more siding with employers, but most seeking whatever means would speedily quieten their districts and preserve their personal administrative record for good order (Perrot 1974: II, 703–14). Bourgeois Republican parties also behaved erratically toward workers, alternately repressing and conciliating from above for support against the Right.

In response to such erratic state crystallizations, which (unlike in Russia) had no finally determining form, French labor acquired its principal distinctiveness: ideological factionalism. It oscillated between, on the one hand, mutualist and reformist cooperation with bourgeois radicalism and, on the other hand, more revolutionary alternatives born out of disillusionment with republican parties and state elites. Disillusion took three principal forms: a socialist version of the Jacobin tradition, predominantly political rather than economic; anarchist terrorism, which abated in the 1890s; and syndicalist trade unionism. Syndicalism was also encouraged by the relatively decentralized spread of industry. Economism, mutualism, social democracy, syndicalism, and Marxism – all emerged to compete and conflict, weakening overall working-class cohesion.

French capitalists, like their counterparts elsewhere, took the offensive about 1900 as their Second Industrial Revolution threatened craft controls. Artisans were forced to defend trade unionism. As in most countries, unions and strikes were more common in medium-size workshops than major factories (still effectively controlled by their owners) until the twentieth century (Lequin 1977: II, 129); and in towns where artisans existed alongside industrial workers, a stronger movement emerged than where artisans were absent (Hanager 1980). Nevertheless, most French unions lacked numbers and unity to defeat the employers. Ideological factionalism was encouraged.

Trade unions remained formally weak, with low dues-paying memberships, almost entirely male, though with little sectionalism by skill among men. Militants – unusually in the nineteenth century – looked predominantly to the state rather than to unions for social insurance and other collective benefits. When, at the end of the century, trade unions developed protectionist labor exchanges (*bourses de travail*), these quickly became broad-based organizations of "direct action syndicalism." Workers' political commitment increased during the struggle for male suffrage, during the radical-socialist coalition of the 1890s and during the post-1906 drive for reformist socialism. But these drives also split militants over their relations with the radical bourgeois parties, and concentration on politics to the neglect of industry alienated some militants toward revolutionary syndicalism. The main union federation, the CGT, was led from its 1895 inception by syndicalists. Yet they held power against a probable reformist majority among their members by the same constitutional bias (privileging national rather than local affiliated organizations) that sustained the conservative Gompers in the United States.

Syndicalists strengthened from 1899 as Alexandre Millerand became the first Western socialist to enter a bourgeois cabinet. Political socialists now split, the Right being incorporated with Millerand into the radical governments of the day, the Left joining syndicalists to eschew politics and proclaim the mass strike as the revolutionary weapon (Brecy 1969). CGT members were few (just under half of unionized workers, under 5 percent of all workers), but they led most mass strikes and demonstrations. But we should remember that during this period French politics crystallized less around class than around the radical *nation*, dominated by the centralizing drive of Republicans to seize secular control of education and family law from the anticentralist, locally-regionally rooted Catholic church. Because worker militants generally supported this drive, syndicalists could not mobilize a *totalizing* class consciousness – syndicalism was for economic issues; the parties for political ones. Such splits resulted less from the distinctiveness of French industry than from political crystallizations.

But, unlike in federal America, the broad thrust of the revolutionary Republican tradition, especially of Jacobinism, encouraged national centralizing and totalizing ideologies. Leaders were proud to style themselves "revolutionaries," recognizing the totality of French national capitalism, proclaiming rival alternative socialisms. Although the normal fault lines between trades, industries, and skill levels appeared, none converted into distinct sectional organizations, and they did not correspond to or reinforce the ideological factions. After defeat in the 1906 general strike, militants welcomed the unifying talents of Jean Jaurès. His Socialist party of 1905 blended revolutionary rhetoric and political reformism – universal suffrage, municipal socialism, and extension of social welfare. Even relations with the CGT improved as it learned to combine revolutionary rhetoric, centralized organization, and collective bargaining. By 1914, there was an ideological socialist-cum-syndicalist movement. Its proclaimed intentions were to make a revolution, though we may doubt its capacities (Gallie 1983: 182–95[7] and Lequin 1977 II: 297–370 are notably skeptical).

French socialism also focused on the economics and politics of male employment. The many married female workers did not join unions. Labor largely ignored them. The "red suburbs," despite their festivals and flags, rarely generated community politics that could activate entire working-class families. One important cause of this, as in the United States, was the existence of male suffrage. Active socialists and syndicalists had the vote already. They showed little interest in the predominantly bourgeois feminist movement, whose demands concentrated on nonemployment issues such as woman suffrage and matrimonial law. In most countries, the early attainment of male suffrage seems actually to have delayed the onset of woman suffrage. In a period in which employment struggles were male-dominated, political struggles within regimes embodying male suffrage also tended to separate men from women. Socialist ideologies were not strongly rooted in the total experience of working-class lives.

Overall, this factionalized but not usually sectional socialism is largely deducible from the insertion of French workers into a state institutionalized as highly centralized but factionalized with respect to everything else – especially party democracy and domestic militarism.

Germany: semiauthoritarian incorporation

By 1914, Germany was becoming the greatest industrial Power in Europe, with the largest socialist party in the world. It presents the clearest example of repressive domestic militarism being fairly calculatedly modernized. Tsarist labor relations were part knee-jerk reaction, part vacillation, but German regimes attempted a modernizing strategy to tame the working class yet leave it outside the regime – what Roth (1963) has termed the "negative incorporation" of the working class. But for the fortunes of war, this might have become the dominant way of institutionalizing class conflict in industrial capitalism.

---

[7] It is worth noting at this point my principal disagreement with Gallie. While he is correct to minimize the revolutionary strength of the prewar French labor movement (he attributes its later strength to World War I, which argument I assess in Volume III), he is not correct to minimize its revolutionary character, or rather characters, as it was factionalized. Marxism and syndicalism were well entrenched before 1914; they were not products of World War I as he suggests.

Germany's economic rise had come entwined with political and military power relations, as Chapter 9 shows. Industrialization was aided by the Prussian-led Zollverein, communications infrastructures, and national unification. It went farthest in Prussia and other conservative Lutheran states like Saxony rather than in liberal or Catholic states. Industrialization soon received the stamp of semiauthoritarian statism. But there were also economic peculiarities. Compared with the same occupations in Britain or America, small handicrafts industry, domestic outwork, and domestic service survived better, along with unusually concentrated heavy industry, to create a pronounced dualism of industrial structure. Most skilled industrial workers began in handicrafts before moving to large-scale industry, and they were early socialized in handicrafts into artisanal values. There was also a sharper gender divide, with few women in regular manufacturing employment, though their casual employment elsewhere was essential for family subsistence. In its industrial life, the organized German working class was as artisanal but even more male than its counterpart in France: Only 2 percent of socialist union members were female.

With these exceptions the economic contours of German labor roughly resembled those elsewhere (Kocka 1986). As usual, threatened journeymen and outworkers provided most early labor turbulence; artisans in securer handicrafts dominated the first stable trade unions; and factory workers (mostly in textiles) remained relatively docile, controlled by their masters, more likely to lose strikes. Artisans experienced the usual economic pressures, especially from a rapid and intense Second Industrial Revolution. Workers in metalworking industries and mining (though not in the railways, which were closely linked to state and army) joined with semi- and unskilled factory and workshop workers in a mass working-class movement about 1900. That this was a distinctive movement was due primarily to political power relations (as Tenfelde 1985 also argues).

Chapter 9 charts German representative and national political crystallizations. The 1848 revolution forced German states and classes to crucial decisions. German states accepted and were forced into a national, if partially federal, state under Prussian hegemony, and they offered limited party-democratic reforms to incorporate the bourgeoisie. Bourgeois notable parties hesitated, but disturbed by worker radicalism threw their weight behind social order, followed by much of the petite bourgeoisie. Radical artisans were isolated, increasing their Leftism. They began to describe themselves as "working class," coordinating artisans' clubs, educational societies, and local trade unions and in touch through political exiles with the most advanced European socialists. But they were a small minority, stranded and repressed, unable to fight the states or mobilize political sympathy to abort their militarism. State and local police authorities, assisted by the many internal frontier posts, controlled workers' associations more directly than in countries to the west (Ludtke 1979). Workers were driven into defensive class consciousness. But in Prussian and Lutheran areas, they also had internalized relatively national, statist politics.

Once Prussian authority was safely institutionalized, the regime relaxed somewhat. In the 1860s, unions (mainly benefit societies) and even strikes expressing direct worker interests were legalized by most German states, though closely supervised by the police (agricultural and domestic workers had no such rights even beyond 1914). The consequent expansion of unions and strikes was sectionalized by craft and factionalized by politics and religion expressed regionally. Of the seventy thousand union members in 1870, 40 percent were affiliated with liberal associations; 40 percent, with socialist ones; and 20 percent were independent or Catholic. Workers' political parties emerged in the 1860s out of the educational associations, restive at liberal failure to support demands for full civil and political citizenship. The sudden introduction of universal male suffrage in 1867 had the effect intended by the regime, undercutting liberal attempts to incorporate workers. Yet organized workers were unlikely to support regime parties, and proportional representation had the unanticipated consequence of allowing workers' parties to make gradual electoral headway. The workers' parties developed reformist socialism, later than in France but far earlier than in Britain or the United States, and before national unions formed. The parties coalesced into the forerunner of the Social Democratic party in 1875 and then helped federate local unions into a national union federation. The party was early acquiring its national, statist, and implicitly Lutheran influence over labor.

At this point much was still open. In the creation of the German Reich, between 1867 and 1871, Prussia made concessions to liberals and to states' rights. This complex process made the regime unusually conscious of alternative class and national strategies. Despite universal male suffrage, the Prussian monarchy retained formidable powers over the Reichstag as well as over the individual *Länder* (the old states). A mass party-democratic electoral process emerged, but the regime could choose which parties to admit into its counsels. The working-class male had only partial political citizenship, as he still had only partial civil citizenship. The Social Democrats were now winning elections in urban-industrial areas, but the Marxist character of their party was not set. Labor's party could still be incorporated as a "loyal opposition" alongside the bourgeois and Catholic parties, as in Britain and (more tenuously) in France.

Bismarck now took a hand, for a time consciously commanding a regime strategy of semiauthoritarian incorporation. Reich chancellor from 1871 to 1890, he offered a mixed bag of citizen rights designed to divide and rule – to exclude radical labor, ethnic minorities, and separatists from political power while neutralizing middle-class liberals, Catholics, and some workers. The policy had four main planks:

1. The extension of Prussian-German hegemony over Central Europe would distract attention from internal class struggle. Economic expansion was also to be identified with the military expansion of the state. This is discussed in Chapter 21.

2. Bismarck split the liberals, as described in Chapter 9. Most bourgeois notable parties were incorporated into the regime, leaving only a few liberal-radicals outside, tempted to ally with labor.

3. The Anti-Socialist Laws restricted workers' collective civil and political citizenship from 1878 until 1890. The Social Democratic party, its press, and virtually all its larger unions were banned; yet, in keeping with the political-military partial citizenship conferred on all men, they could organize during election campaigns. But this tactic did not really work. Sectionalism, which the regime otherwise fostered, was discouraged. Skilled and unskilled received the same treatment (unlike property franchises in more liberal countries). The electoral exceptions also handed hegemony over unions to the Social Democrats. Even after the Anti-Socialist Laws were rescinded, workers did not have full civil citizenship. Rights of association were incomplete, and police and military authorities intervened in labor disputes, almost always for the employers. Militarism was rather institutionalized. Though the soldiers were armed, their force was more ritual than violent. As we saw earlier, few German workers were actually killed in labor disputes – fewer than in France, far fewer than in the United States, both male democracies. This was authoritarian incorporation, not autocratic or party-democratic repression. For example, copying Austrian legislation, the police had to be notified about workers' meetings, and a policeman would sit on the platform. If he sensed subversion, he put on his helmet. This was the signal that the meeting was now illegal and must disperse. It almost always did. The policeman's helmet, sitting visibly on the speakers' table, was perhaps *the* symbol of the semiauthoritarian incorporation of labor.

Common exclusion plus leadership by socialists kept artisans and unskilled workers together, encouraging shared conceptions of class identity, in an increasingly Marxist Social Democratic party. The party embraced statist and ostensibly revolutionary Marxism in its 1891 Erfurt Program. Though the usual craft monopolies and insider versus outsider struggles occurred in employment, unions did not have sectional organization. The principal division was ideological: between the large socialist (implicitly Lutheran) "free unions," Catholic unions, and employer-sponsored "yellow unions," an expression of internal labor markets in heavy industries. There could be little syndicalism: There was no evading the alliance of monarchy, militarism, and capitalism right through the period (Saul 1985).

4. Bismarck sought to undercut the appeal of class identity and socialism by legislation embodying an ostensible social citizenship. National sickness benefits were introduced in 1883; accident insurance, in 1884; and old-age and disability insurance, in 1889. As noted in Chapter 14, this first welfare state had restricted coverage, aimed only at skilled workers and those privileged by internal labor markets in heavy industry. Large employers already provided housing and other welfare benefits to retain a stable labor force. Most supported the legislation. Collaboration between big industrialists and state elites (noted in Chapter 9) gave internal labor market sectionalism political significance. The Socialist party, socialist unions, and strikes remained concentrated among skilled workers in small and medium-sized enterprises right up to 1914, later than in other countries. In the very largest enterprises, workers were more insulated from class solidarity (though most Protestants voted for the Social Democrats) by internal labor market privileges. Bismarck was explicit about his welfare policies, arguing that pension levels should be graded according to income because this "will be more useful for the employer, since it will join the higher class of workers, that is, the most important support of every enterprise in the general security and thereby encourage striving for its achievement" (Crew 1979: 127). The "higher class of workers" could have a minimal, "sectional social citizenship."

Bismarck was a rare "statesman," sensitive to the widening scope of the modern state, his policies usually entwining domestic and foreign strategies. He drew his four policy lessons especially from his perception of French military weakness revealed in 1870. Unlike Napoleon III, he would carry most of the middle class and even some workers into support of German militarism. If petit bourgeois and worker radicals stayed without allies, they could develop revolutionary fantasies – but they would be unable to implement them or weaken Germany's power abroad. Gall (1986) is impressed by the coherence of Bismarck's strategy, which he labels "white revolutionary." But it was contradictory in the stance it took toward skilled workers, and Bismarck himself unraveled it. His fear of the Catholic church's rival authority and encouragement of southern separatism led him to attack it, in the Kulturkampf. This forced Catholic socialists Leftward. His contempt for parliament also led him into coup intrigues from 1888 and caused his fall. It was difficult to preserve authoritarian monarchy in a semiindustrial society without compromising with at least two among peasant farmers, the middle class, and important minority churches. As Fascist corporatism had not yet been invented, parliamentary institutions were the price.

After Bismarck's fall, the strategy was partially reinstated. Catholic and peasant support for the regime was restored, effecting the isolation of labor and ethnic and separatist radicals. I discuss this further in Chapter 19. The Anti-Socialist Laws were repealed as a failure; the socialists could weather suppression with a clandestine organization nourished by elections. But restrictions on workers' civil citizenship, especially their rights of association, remained. The welfare state continued along its Bismarckian path, expanding its coverage but insufficient on its own to sectionalize workers who continued to experience common exclusion from civil and political citizenship.

But the Social Democratic party remained isolated, lacking allies, tending in fact to alienate them. Its Marxist productivism deterred peasant support (see Chapter 19). Its implicitly Lutheran statism and Marxist godlessness alienated the Catholic church, preventing a formidable potential alliance among opponents of the regime. Thus the Catholic church moved to sponsor its own peasant and mutualist labor movements, the latter becoming important among the 20 percent to 25 percent of workers who were Catholic. Proletarian identity and socialism became isolated in urban-industrial Lutheran enclaves. Even in 1914, Germany was only semiindustrial. Its electorate was split nearly equally among agrarian, middle, and working classes, as well as 6.5:3.5 between Protestant and Catholic religions. The Socialist party dominated the Protestant working class and competed for Catholic worker votes – so electing many deputies – yet was unable to influence government to effect mutualist or reformist policies. And, without allies, it was incapable of effecting the revolution it formally espoused.

After Bismarck's fall, some Catholics and liberals, even a few industrialists, favored liberalization. Freedom of association – the last bastion right of individual civil citizenship – was finally granted in 1908. As union membership increased, unions developed more autonomy from the Socialist party and favored more mutualism (Mommsen 1985). But the regime did not favor further conciliation and had enough constitutional patronage to split liberals who did. Encouraged by ministries and police authorities, most employers continued to hinder union collective association, thus rendering the civil citizenship concessions more formal than real. Although Table 18.1 shows that unions were growing, apart from the yellow unions few were recognized by employers. Unions helped administer the broadening social welfare benefits and had de facto recognition when employers were forced to bargain during strikes. But there were few collective bargaining agreements (exact figures vary, see Schofer 1975: 137–64; Stearns 1975: 165, 180–1; Crew 1979: 146, 218, 250–1; and Mommsen 1985: 382; Spencer 1976 argues that by 1914 advocates of conciliatory bargaining were proliferating in the Ruhr). Thus the Social Democratic party and the socialist unions stayed outside state power, without significant allies, harassed but isolated.

The effects on labor have been often described (Roth 1963; Morgan 1975; Geary 1976; Kocka 1986; Nolan 1986; and various essays in Evans 1982). Excluded, yet greatly enlarged by the Second Industrial Revolution, the working-class Lutheran Marxist core turned inward to develop a socialist subculture, organizing workers' communities with choral societies, bands, gymnastic clubs, libraries, and festivals. These were primarily leisure activities, but they also totalized the identity of the *Arbeiter* (worker) across life activities (Lidtke 1985). Although most union members were skilled, sectionalism was discouraged by the socialists and by the Free Unions Central Commission. Unions kept their heads down and left most questions of strategies and alternatives to the party (Schönhoven 1985). As in other countries where most men were effectively excluded from political citizenship, the Socialist party supported universal and full parliamentary sovereignty, including votes for women. Because state elites staunchly advocated patriarchal values, the party also had a progressive family program, although its local associations remained overwhelmingly male (until 1908, the state banned women and minors from political organization). Although the party and the working-class culture embodied the normal gender inequalities of the period, there was less segregation between (male) employment and family and community organization than was the contemporary norm. A patriarchal regime kept up the sense of an intensive totality of German socialism.

The Social Democratic party developed into a powerful electoral force, taking one-third of the votes and constituting the largest Reichstag party by 1912, its politics dominating the major unions, expressing the productivist, state-centralized rhetoric and long-term goals of revolutionary Marxism. Yet it was without allies for extraparliamentary tactics, or even for the reform of parliament. It carried on doing what it was best at, fighting elections, but in a system rigged by the regime. "Negative integration," says Roth, "permits a hostile mass movement to exist legally, but prevents it from gaining access to the centers of power" (1963: 8). The party's Right favored mild reformism and compromise with the regime – but was only obliged during the brief chancellorship of Caprivi and occasionally under Bethmann-Hollweg. A small ultra-Left advocated revolution but lacked numbers and allies against a regime well equipped for repression. The majority followed the Center-Left, favoring revolution – but well in the future. Eventually Germany would become fully industrial, and the Social Democrats would become the majority party. As Kautsky expressed it, the party had to organize *for* the revolution, not organize *the* revolution.

The regime had partly drifted toward, partly consciously devised, a fairly successful semiauthoritarian strategy to incorporate labor. This strategy-drift deviated even more than the United States did from Marshall's evolutionary scheme of citizenship, because the regime conceded only partial civil and political citizenship throughout the period while experimenting with partial, sectional doses of social citizenship. Labor, wearing Marxist productivist, statist blinkers, contributed its own ineptitude to this success (documented more in Chapter 19).

Given the isolation and "negative integration" of labor, there seemed no obvious route toward liberal or social democracy, as envisaged by Marshall, or to revolution, as envisaged by Marx or Kautsky. This had resulted from an absolute military monarchy's confrontation with classes demanding party democracy and with regional states and a church demanding decentralization. Germany was distinctive less for its economy than for its representative and national crystallizations and, to a lesser extent, for its rather ritualized domestic militarism. True, "authoritarian national capitalism" and "negative integration" would have been inconceivable without the acceleration of the Second Industrial Revolution in Germany. But the closest comparable industrial revolution occurred in the United States, and that had developed very different class relations. The varying forms of institutionalization of class struggle in advanced capitalism were given less by industrialization than by the diverse crystallizations of states.

Other European countries

Most other industrializing countries fell somewhere between the semiauthoritarianism of Germany and the party democracy of Britain and France. Austria-Hungary was in many ways like Germany, repressing unions and workers' parties until 1891, turning workers Leftward to a Marxist socialist party. But the monarchy confronted far stronger confederalists. These also impacted on labor, converting it from a single transnational to many regional-national movements (Gulick 1948: 21–4; Shell 1962). The Swedish and Danish regimes, centralized but with weaker landholding nobilities and militaries, had already conceded some party-democratic rights to peasants and bourgeois liberals, and emerging labor allied with both and then steered well beyond British mutualism into reformist social democracy (see Chapter 19). The half-democratic Italian and Spanish regimes oscillated unevenly around the French model, though with more "national" contestation. In Japan, Meiji restorationists modified the German strategy.

In all these countries monarchies and old regimes tried to retain centralized authoritarian powers within semiparliamentary regimes (unsuccessfully in Scandinavia). The middle class had not been as fully incorporated into party democracy as in the United States, Britain, or France, yet was not wholly excluded from the state and repressed, as in Russia. Obviously these countries varied greatly. At one extreme radical regionalist bourgeoisies were still making fundamental demands on a monarchical state, as in Spain or (varying by regional nationality) Austria-Hungary. At the other the bourgeoisie was incorporated into an even more dependent position in the state than in Germany, as in Japan. The first extreme amplified confederalism, the second centralized nation-states.

As in Germany we can deduce most of the rights of labor from these dual representative and national crystallizations. In class terms, labor movements were neither partly inside the state (as in the United States, Britain, and France) nor totally excluded and militarily repressed (as in Russia). Because the Imperial German *Sonderweg* was not, in fact, "its own" but was adapted by much of Europe and by Japan, its viability was crucial to the development of modern society. The effects on workers were profound. These countries developed a more aggressive socialism than in Britain; a more consistent, united, and predominantly political strategy than in France (though Spain is exceptional); and a movement less committed to revolution than in Russia. Everywhere, class organization predominated over sectional. Everywhere except Spain the closest parallel was the negative incorporation of Imperial Germany: nominal and partial civil and political citizenship, but exclusion from the state and negative integration.

An exception was Spain, because of its distinctive entwining of class representation with the national issue.[8] In Spain, syndicalism reached its strongest European form; and its twentieth-century development has been deviant. Can such deviance be explained by my politically centered model? The answer is positive: Syndicalism was strong in Spain primarily because of its distinctive political constitution, which included a significant national-regional citizenship conflict. As in Austria, the question arose, From which state should classes demand citizenship?

From 1876 on, Spain had a constitutional monarchy, formal (if corrupted) adult male suffrage, and legal unions (though with the usual

---

[8] These paragraphs depend principally on Malefakis (1970), who overemphasizes class, and on Meaker (1974) and Giner (1984).

bourgeois restrictions on organizing rights). But it was economically backward (about Russia's level of development), without an extensive bourgeoisie. Political struggle was not predominantly between classes but between segmental patron-client networks. Liberal and Conservative parties alternated in office, backed by a mixture of banking and industrial class fractions and landed notables, the caciques. Party notables dispensed segmental patronage, controlled the local means of violence, and recruited clients among all classes. The pattern was common in countries on the semiperiphery of capitalism (Mouzelis 1986). Where would the emerging working class fit into this? Politics also contained class and Left-Right ideologies, appealing especially to the radical bourgeoisie and its enemies. The labor movement might attach itself to this radicalism, so developing French or British-style moderate socialism. But where caciques were firmly entrenched, such politics could not budge them. Workers and organized peasants became disillusioned with national politics altogether, and turned toward anarchist and syndicalist alternatives.

This possibility was fueled greatly by regional resentment at rule from Castile, sometimes amounting to nationalist separatism. Anarchist and syndicalist strategies, turning their back on the central state, became plausible in parts of Spain – anarchism in rural disaffected areas, syndicalism in industrial. I do not claim expertise on the complex differences among Spanish regions, but these two political causes – partial civil and political citizenship before extensive class organizations emerged, plus regional separatism – seem responsible for most of the factional splits in Spanish labor between Marxian socialism and syndicalism. The Second Industrial Revolution then entered in a distinctive regional form, accentuating industrialization in Catalonia, there reinforcing separatism and syndicalism, and strengthening Marxian statist socialism in Castile and the Asturias. The stage was now set for the tragic, divided socialist movements of 1917–18 and 1936–9. Spain deviates in its details, but not from my overall model. The distinctiveness of the Spanish class struggle was set less by the labor process than by the contested politics of national citizenship – in this case, as in Austria-Hungary, the politics of citizenship evoked severe "national" entwined with class conflict.

Conclusion

There is no need to cite myriad local details to support the overall argument of this chapter: Class struggle between capital and labor developed as a similar industrial transformation entwined with, principally, variations in representative, national, and civil-military political crystallizations and, secondarily, with various forms of worker communities. In Chapters 15, 17, and 18, I advance a three-part description of the nineteenth-century industrial transformation of labor:

1. Industrial capitalism generated not one collective laborer, as Marx envisaged, but three, competing and undercutting one another. As Marx noted, there emerged ubiquitously among workers a sense both of *class* identity and of a class opponent, the capitalist class. Some workers might even feel that class dominated the totality of their lives and generate socialist conceptions of an alternative society (though these alternatives were rather varied). Yet industrialization also encouraged two other smaller collective laborers, *sectional* collectivities, generated by skills and labor market powers, and *segmental* interdependences between workers and their employers. Extensive and political classes developed, but only imperfectly and in perennial competition with sectionalism and segmentalism.

2. I charted two phases in which class identity was strengthened. First (Chapter 15) came the (first) Industrial Revolution, but only to Britain. This was a peculiar collectivization, for the revolution cultivated heterogeneous employment situations: factories, artisan trades, street work, and domestic outwork, all interpenetrating one another. But because almost all skilled strata, neighborhoods, and family members were affected, this strengthened a familial sense of working-class identity, fusing employment, family, and local community against exploitation from outside. Second (Chapters 17 and 18), the Second Industrial Revolution came to all these countries (whether or not they had experienced a first one). Everywhere, this brought concentrated capital, the large factory, and employers' offensive de-skilling artisans while upgrading casual laborers to formal employment and semiskills. It developed broader unions and caged workers into their own residential communities. In response, workers developed extensive and political class organization evincing socialist tendencies.

Twice did a working *class* emerge. But its emergence was limited. In the first phase, it centered on artisans; in the second phase, on skilled and semiskilled metalworkers, miners, and transport workers in large towns. Outside these cores – in the first phase, in unthreatened trades, in most rural areas, and among domestic servants; in the second, in other industries and small towns – most workers were still under segmental controls, unconscious of or hostile to class identities. This made militants cautious, aware that they had limited influence over mass electorates and even less over armed forces. And even in the core, trade unionism and sectional labor market controls could narrow identity and compromise opposition away from class. Through the nineteenth century artisans did not so much disappear as transmute into skilled workers. The main sectional fault line now rested between skilled versus semiskilled and unskilled workers. The internal labor market developed in the core, bringing new segmental interdependencies between employers and workers and sectionalism between stably employed, organized workers against unorganized and casual workers outside. When these were defined as blacklegs or scabs, sectionalism became violent, yet also often was claimed to be socialist. Thus the rise of the industrial proletariat was not just as a class but also as *sections* and *segments*. The battle over workers' identities and souls continued.

3. Nor, after the first phase, did employment and family-community life simply reinforce one another as Marx expected. In the Second Revolution formal employment segregated the two spheres of life, the more so because formal waged employment – especially in industries and skilled strata generating most of the unions – became predominantly male. The collective laborer narrowed *his* sphere, his organization, his consciousness to become employment-centered and productivist. Socialism became less concerned with the totality of life, less capable of those intense revolutionary mobilizations we saw in the employment-street-community movements of the earlier bourgeois and Chartist era. Marxists had less moral fervor, less "immanent morale," than Chartists or Jacobins. As we shall see in Chapter 19, in most countries productivism and statism also led to a second crucial narrowing, which prevented an effective appeal to agrarian populations.

Thus labor's economic development was ambiguous, perhaps capable of turning into the kinds of tracks Marx expected or hoped for, perhaps turning down far more divided or conservative tracks. As we shall see, workers resembled peasants in being politically malleable. Like peasants, they turned down many different tracks. Variations in tracks were determined but little by variations in capitalist industrialization. Germany and the United States, the two leaders of the Second Industrial Revolution, developed the largest and the smallest socialist parties in the West. France, backward in its industrialization, was precocious in the socialism of its labor movement.

The decisive determinants of variations among labor movements were political power crystallizations, set in motion by earlier struggles between military monarchies and their representative and national enemies. These were not set in stone; for most states crystallized later as strongly capitalist, and most also began to civilianize significantly. but they had substantially institutionalized varied regime strategies to which workers might respond as class, sectional, or segmental actors and with varying forms of socialist ideology. When ruling regimes directly confronted workers as a class, there were four main strategies or drifts, mixing varying degrees of capitalism, militarism, and representation:

1. *Autocratic militarism* was exemplified by tsarist Russia. Workers were uniformly (though not entirely consistently) denied citizenship and repressed. In response, sectionalism, segmentalism, and milder socialist alternatives made only limited and erratic progress. Russian workers became a working class; their militants, revolutionary Marxists.

2. *Capitalist-liberal militarism* was exemplified by the United States. Workers' citizenship was highly uneven. Although individual civil and political citizenships were firmly institutionalized, collective civil rights were restricted and ferociously repressed. Because such repression was selective, worker responses divided. American labor became sectional and factional, rather than classlike, and predominantly without socialism.

3. *Liberal-reformist incorporation* was exemplified by Britain, and also included Britain's white dominions and the Netherlands and Belgium. France resembled this, though in the complex way described earlier. Capitalist liberalism was not so institutionalized in Europe – Switzerland would be the closest. Liberal democracy was extended more gradually, with greater attention paid to classes (and estates). Old regimes were incorporating the middle classes and farmers into the sovereign institutions of party democracy. Regime-bourgeois parties saw the necessity and often even the advantage in compromising sectionally and segmentally with workers, stratum by stratum, organization by organization, as they emerged through the first and second industrial revolutions. Reluctant to deploy domestic militarism, they compromised between liberalism and moderate mutualist and reformist forms of working-class socialism and between class and sectional forms of worker organization. Later, Scandinavian countries took this strategy/drift farther into full-scale *reformist incorporation*.

4. *Semiauthoritarian incorporation* was exemplified by Imperial Germany, then by Austria-Hungary and Japan (Italy and Spain were mixed cases between this and liberal incorporation). Here monarchies survived the first encounter with bourgeoisies, petite bourgeoisies, and farmers without conceding sovereign party democracy. This successfully split them, incorporating most into the regime, aided by semiparliamentary constitutions that institutionalized segmental divide-and-rule strategies and moderated militarism into ritual displays of force. The few excluded petit bourgeois radicals joined forces with artisans to form ostensibly revolutionary socialist parties and unions. Their isolation and their participation in limited party democracy, however, weakened their power actually to effect any revolutionary – or, indeed, any significant reformist or mutualist – alternative.

But these strategies or drifts cannot entirely explain outcomes because my cases also added varying *national* crystallizations. Let us consider the two extreme outcomes in terms of the presence or absence of class identities and socialism. Russian autocracy was highly centralized. Workers experienced such a "national" totality of repression and exploitation that they developed a strongly class and national sense of their own identity and of that of their opponents in employment, street and community alike. Their militants became committed to the revolutionary statist socialist alternative Marx had expected. Perhaps their revolutionary aspirations might be repressed indefinitely, but the regime also alienated urban liberals, regional-nationalists, and peasants and then lost a war of national mobilization. The proletariat and the nation rose together to overthrow it. The United States was the opposite extreme in outcome. But the United States was the next most severe case of domestic militarism. Here repression was wielded by a combination of intense capitalism and the two opposite political extremes to Russia, party democracy and federalism. It worked because it reinforced local-regional, ethnic-religious, and skill and internal labor market sectionalisms. American socialism factionalized and then disintegrated. These two extreme cases came to have critical significance in a mid-twentieth century dominated by these two powers.

Intermediate outcomes also resulted partly from distinctive entwinings of national with representative crystallizations. In Germany there was partial, rather more considered exclusion of workers from collective civil and political citizenship. As in Russia this extended class identity and weakened sectionalism, but the militants' Marxism was somewhat compromised by their electoralism. Moreover, class was substantially crosscut by contested national crystallizations. Although these reinforced class identity among Lutherans and northerners, they weakened it among Catholics and southerners, as they weakened the possibility of a worker-agrarian proletarian alliance. The German working class was as organized and perhaps as socialist as Marx might have wished for, but it was smaller and worse led. According to national crystallizations, mediated by the regional-religious insertion of industry and labor, workers' movements were sometimes highly statist (as in Germany), sometimes highly antistatist (as in parts of Spain), most often complex compromises.

As with peasants, national crystallizations help make sense of the *religious* differences. Why should Catholics be so much more resistant to socialism than Protestants? Most directly because their church hierarchy mobilized them to be. But why? Perhaps because socialism, especially Marxism, was godless – but this should alienate all churches. Perhaps this church was also in some general sense "conservative." It favored hierarchy, but then so did state Lutheranism, which was conducive to the state socialisms of social democracy and Marxism (and later fascism) in northern Europe, in the sense that a disproportionate number of persons with Lutheran backgrounds became social democrats and Marxists (or later, in Germany, fascists).

But additionally the Catholic church was antistatist in two senses. It was a *transnational* power organization, and it entered "national" politics as an advocate of *localism-regionalism*. It was particularly antistatist in this period because virtually all states were crystallizing as secular and encroaching on the two areas in which Catholic church local-regional power principally resided: education and the family. State education and civil, especially family, law were what it feared. Therefore, the church bitterly opposed all forms of centralized statism – most obviously in France, but also persistently in much of Austria, Germany, and the United States. Marxian socialism presented another statist alternative and so the church resolutely opposed it. Thus the church could sponsor its own protectionist, economist, and even mutualist unions. We find a tendency (though not a perfect association) for statist forms of socialism – Marxism and aggressive social democracy – to have developed either among Lutherans in northern Europe or as part of a secular nation-state offensive against Catholic domination in southern Europe. Conversely, nonstatist Protestantism (like English Nonconformism or most American Protestant churches) were associated with milder economism and mutualism among workers. Chapter 19 extends the argument to peasants. The political stances of churches were determined less by their formal dogmas, more by whether they were majority or minority churches and whether the identity of the state was religious or secular. In this period, church politics principally crystallized around the national issue. It did so even more strongly among agrarian classes.

Bibliography

Aminzade, R. 1981. *Class, Politics and Early Industrial Capitalism.* Albany: State University of New York Press.
    1984. Capitalist industrialization and patterns of industrial protest. *American Sociological Review* 49.
Bain, G. S., and R. Price. 1980. *Profiles of Union Growth.* Oxford: Blackwell.
Bairoch, P., et al. 1968. *The Working Population and Its Structure.* Brussels: Editions de l'Institut de Sociologie de l'Université Libre (in English and French).
Bell, D. 1974. The problem of ideological rigidity. In *Failure of a Dream?*, ed. J. H. M. Laslett and S. M. Lipset. Garden City, N.Y.: Anchor Books.
Besançon, A. 1986. The Russian case. In *Europe and the Rise of Capitalism*, ed. J. Baechler, J. A. Hall, and M. Mann. Oxford: Blackwell.
Boll, F. 1985. International strike waves: a critical assessment. In *The Devel-*

opment of Trade Unionism in Great Britain and Germany, 1880–1914, ed. W. J. Mommsen and H.-G. Husung. London: German Historical Institute/Allen & Unwin.

1989. Changing forms of labour conflict: secular development or strike waves? In *Strikes, War and Revolution*, ed. L. Haimson and C. Tilly. Cambridge: Cambridge University Press.

Bonnell, V. 1983. *Roots of Rebellion: Worker's Politics and Organizations in St. Petersburg and Moscow, 1900–1914*. Berkeley: University of California Press.

Brecy, R. 1969. *La grève générale en France*. Paris: Etudes et Documentation Internationales.

Bridges, A. 1986. Becoming American: the working classes in the United States before the Civil War. In *Working-Class Formation: Nineteenth Century Patterns in Western Europe and the United States*, ed. I. Katznelson and A. R. Zolberg. Princeton, N.J.: Princeton University Press.

Brody, D. 1960. *Steelworkers in America: The Non-union Era*. New York: Russell & Russell.

Burawoy, M. 1984. Karl Marx and the satanic mills: factory politics under early capitalism in England, the United States and Russia. *American Journal of Sociology* 90.

Burnham, W. D. 1965. The changing shape of the American political universe. *American Political Science Review* 59.

1970. *Critical Elections and the Mainspring of American Politics*. New York: Norton.

Cook, C., and J. Paxton. 1978. *European Political Facts, 1848–1918*. London: Macmillan.

Cottereau, A. 1986. The distinctiveness of working-class cultures in France, 1848–1900. In *Working-Class Formation: Nineteenth Century Patterns in Western Europe and the United States*, ed. I. Katznelson and A. R. Zolberg. Princeton, N.J.: Princeton University Press.

Crew, D. F. 1979. *Town in the Ruhr: A Social History of Bochum, 1860–1914*. New York: Columbia University Press.

Cronin, J. E. 1985. Strikes and the struggle for union organization: Britain and Europe. In *The Development of Trade Unionism in Great Britain and Germany, 1880–1914*, ed. W. J. Mommsen and H.-G. Husung. London: German Historical Institute/Allen & Unwin.

1989. Strikes and power in Britain, 1870–1920. In *Strikes, War and Revolution*, ed. L. Haimson and C. Tilly. Cambridge: Cambridge University Press.

Dubofsky, M. 1969. *We Shall Be All*. Chicago: Quadrangle Books.

1974. Socialism and syndicalism. In *Failure of a Dream?*, ed. J. H. M. Laslett and S. M. Lipset. Garden City, N.Y.: Anchor Books.

Edwards, P. K. 1981. *Strikes in the United States, 1881–1974*. Oxford: Blackwell Publisher.

Evans, R. J. (ed.). 1982. *The German Working Class, 1880–1933. The Politics of Everyday Life*. London: Croom Helm.

Fink, G. M. 1973. The rejection of voluntarism. *Industrial and Labor Relations Review* 26.

1987. Labor, liberty, and the law: trade unionism and the problem of the American constitutional order. *Journal of American History* 4.

Foner, E. 1984. Why is there no socialism in the United States? *History Workshop Journal* 17.

Forbath, W. E. 1989. The shaping of the American labor movement. *Harvard Law Review* 102.

Fraser, W. H. 1974. *Trade Unions in Society: The Struggle for Acceptance, 1850–1880*. London: Allen & Unwin.

Gall, L. 1986. *Bismarck, The White Revolutionary*. London: Allen & Unwin.

Gallie, D. 1983. *Social Inequality and Class Radicalism in France and Britain*. Cambridge: Cambridge University Press.

Geary, D. 1976. The German labour movement, 1848–1919. *European Studies Review* 16.

Giner, S. 1984. *The Social Structure of Catalonia*. Sheffield: Anglo-Catalan Society.

Goldstein, R. J. 1978. *Political Repression in Modern America*. Cambridge, Mass.: Schenkman.

1983. *Political Repression in Nineteenth Century Europe*. London: Croom Helm.

Gompers, S. 1967. *Seventy Years of Life and Labor: An Autobiography*, 2 vols., 2d ed. New York: Augustus M. Kelley Publishers.

Gossez, R. 1967. *Les ouvriers de Paris*. Vol. I: *L'organisation, 1848–1851*. Paris: Bibliothèque de la révolution de 1848.

Grob, G. N. 1961. *Workers and Utopia*. Evanston, Il.: Northwestern University Press.

Grüttner, M. 1985. The rank-and-file movements and the trade unions in the Hamburg docks from 1896–97. In *The Development of Trade Unionism in Great Britain and Germany, 1880–1914*, ed. W. J. Mommsen and H.-G. Husung. London: German Historical Institute/Allen & Unwin.

Gulick, C. A. 1948. *Austria from Habsburg to Hitler*. Vol. I: *Labor's Workshop of Democracy*. Berkeley: University of California Press.

Haimson, L. H. 1964–5. The problem of social stability in urban Russia, 1905–1917. *Slavic Review* 23 (1964), 24 (1965).

Halle, D. 1984. *America's Working Man: Work, Home, and Politics Among Blue-Collar Property Owners*. Chicago: University of Chicago Press.

Hanager, M. P. 1980. *The Logic of Solidarity: Artisans and Industrial Workers in Three French Towns*. Urbana: University of Illinois Press.

Hartz, L. 1955. *The Liberal Tradition in America*. New York: Harcourt, Brace & World.

Hirsch, S. 1978. *Roots of the American Working Class*. Philadelphia: University of Pennsylvania Press.

Hobson, J. 1991. The Tax Seeking State: Protectionism, Taxation and State Structures in Germany, Russia, Britain and America, 1870–1914. Ph.D. thesis, London School of Economics and Political Science.

Holt, J. 1977. Trade unionism in the British and U.S. steel industries, 1880–1914: a comparative study. *Labor History* 18.

Katznelson, I. 1981. *City Trenches: Urban Politics and the Patterning of Class in the United States*. New York: Pantheon.

Kochan, L. 1966. *Russia in Revolution, 1890–1918*. London: Weidenfeld & Nicolson.

Kocka, J. 1986. Problems of the working-class formation in Germany: the early years, 1800–1875. In *Working-Class Formation: Nineteenth Century Patterns in Western Europe and the United States*, ed. I.

Katznelson and A. R. Zolberg. Princeton, N.J.: Princeton University Press.

Kraditor, A. S. 1981. *The Radical Persuasion, 1890–1917.* Baton Rouge: Louisiana State University Press.

Lash, S. 1984. *The Militant Worker: Class and Radicalism in France and America.* London: Heinemann.

Laslett, J. H. M., and S. M. Lipset (eds.). 1974. *Labor and the Left.* New York: Basic Books.

Lebergott, S. 1984. *The Americans: An Economic Record.* New York: Norton.

Lefranc, G. 1967. *Le Mouvement Syndical Sous la Troisième République.* Paris: Payot.

Lenin, V. I. 1970. *What Is to Be Done?* Manchester: Panther Books.

Lequin, Y. 1977. *Les ouvriers de la région lyonnaise (1848–1914),* 2 vols. Lyons: Presses Universitaires de Lyons.

Lidtke, V. L. 1985. *The Alternative Culture: Socialist Labor in Imperial Germany.* New York: Oxford University Press.

Lipset, S. M. 1977. Why no socialism in the United States? In *Sources of Contemporary Radicalism,* ed. S. Bialer and S. Sluzar. Boulder, Colo.: Westview.

    1984. Radicalism or reformism: the sources of working-class politics. In his *Consensus and Conflict: Essays in Political Sociology.* New Brunswick, N.J.: Transaction Books.

Lowi, T. J. 1984. Why is there no socialism in the United States? A federal analysis. In *The Cost of Federalism,* ed. R. T. Golembiewski and A. Wildavsky. New Brunswick, N.J.: Transaction Books.

Ludtke, A. 1979. The role of state violence in the period of transition to industrial capitalism: the example of Prussia from 1815–1848. *Social History* 4.

McDaniel, T. 1988. *Autocracy, Capitalism and Revolution in Russia.* Berkeley: University of California Press.

McKean, R. 1990. *St. Petersburg Between the Revolutions.* New Haven, Conn.: Yale University Press.

Malefakis, E. M. 1970. *Agrarian Reform and Peasant Revolution in Spain.* New Haven, Conn.: Yale University Press.

Mandel, M. 1983. *The Petrograd Workers and the Fall of the Old Regime.* London: Macmillan.

Mann, M. 1988. Ruling class strategies and citizenship. In M. Mann, *States, War and Capitalism.* Oxford: Blackwell.

Marks, G. 1989. *Unions in Politics: Britain, Germany, and the United States in the Nineteenth and Early Twentieth Centuries.* Princeton, N.J.: Princeton University Press.

Meaker, G. H. 1974. *The Revolutionary Left in Spain, 1914–1923.*: Stanford, Calif.: Stanford University Press.

Mitchell, B. R. 1983. *International Historical Statistics. The Americas and Australasia.* Detroit: Gale Research.

Mommsen, H. 1985. The free trade unions and social democracy in imperial Germany. In *The Development of Trade Unionism in Great Britain and Germany, 1880–1914,* ed. W. J. Mommsen and H.-G. Husung. London: German Historical Institute/Allen & Unwin.

Montgomery, D. 1967. *Beyond Equality.* New York: Knopf.

1979. *Workers' Control in America*. Cambridge: Cambridge University Press.
    1980. Labor and the republic in industrial America: 1860–1920. *Le Mouvement Social*, no. 111.
Moore, B., Jr. 1973. *Social Origins of Dictatorship and Democracy*. Harmondsworth, Middlesex: Penguin.
Morgan, D. W. 1975. *The Socialist Left and the German Revolution*. Ithaca, N.Y.: Cornell University Press.
Moss, B. H. 1976. *The Origins of the French Labor Movement, 1830–1914: The Socialism of Skilled Workers*. Berkeley: University of California Press.
Mouzelis, N. 1986. *Politics in the Semi-Periphery: Early Parliamentarianism and Late Industrialization in the Balkans and Latin America*. New York: St. Martin's Press.
Mowry, G. E. 1972. *The Progressive Era, 1900–20*. Washington, D.C.: American Historical Association.
Nolan, M. 1986. Economic crisis, state policy, and working-class formation in Germany, 1870–1900. In *Working-Class Formation: Nineteenth Century Patterns in Western Europe and the United States*, ed. I. Katznelson and A. R. Zolberg. Princeton, N.J.: Princeton University Press.
Noland, A. 1956. *The Founding of the French Socialist Party, 1893–1905*. Cambridge, Mass.: Harvard University Press.
Perlman, S. 1928. *A Theory of the Labor Movement*. New York: Macmillan.
Perrot, M. 1974. *Les ouvriers en grève*. Paris: Menton.
    1986. On the formation of the French working class. In *Working-Class Formation: Nineteenth Century Patterns in Western Europe and the United States*, ed. I. Katznelson and A. R. Zolberg. Princeton, N.J.: Princeton University Press.
Rayback, J. G. 1966. *A History of American Labor*. New York: Free Press.
Ridley, F. F. 1970. *Revolutionary Syndicalism in France*. Cambridge: Cambridge University Press.
Rogin, M. 1961–62. Voluntarism: the political functions of an antipolitical doctrine. *Industrial and Labor Relations Review* 15.
Rokkan, S. 1970. *Citizens Elections Parties*. Oslo: Universitetsforlaget.
Roth, G. 1963. *The Social Democrats in Imperial Germany*. Totowa, N.J.: Bedminster Press.
Rueschemeyer, D., E. Stephens, and J. Stephens. 1992. *Capitalist Development and Democracy*. Chicago: University of Chicago Press.
Saul, K. 1985. Repression or integration? the state, trade unions and industrial disputes in imperial Germany. In *The Development of Trade Unionism in Great Britain and Germany, 1880–1914*, ed. W. J. Mommsen and H.-G. Husung. London: German Historical Institute/Allen & Unwin.
Schofer, L. 1975. *The Formation of a Modern Labor Force: Upper Silesia, 1865–1914*. Berkeley: University of California Press.
Schönhoven, K. 1985. Localism – craft union – industrial union: organizational patterns in German trade unions. In *The Development of Trade Unionism in Great Britain and Germany, 1880–1914*, ed. W. J. Mommsen and H.-G. Husung. London: German Historical Institute/Allen & Unwin.

Sewell, W. H., Jr. 1986. Artisans, factory workers, and the formation of the French working class, 1789–1848. In *Working-Class Formation: Nineteenth Century Patterns in Western Europe and the United States*, ed. I. Katznelson and A. R. Zolberg. Princeton, N.J.: Princeton University Press.

Shefter, M. 1986. Trade unions and political machines: the organization and disorganization of the American working class in the late nineteenth century. In *Working-Class Formation: Nineteenth Century Patterns in Western Europe and the United States*, ed. I. Katznelson and A. R. Zolberg. Princeton, N.J.: Princeton University Press.

Shell, K. L. 1962. *The Transformation of Austrian Socialism*. New York: University Publishers.

Shorter, E., and C. Tilly. 1974. *Strikes in France, 1830–1968*. Cambridge: Cambridge University Press.

Sklar, M. J. 1988. *The Corporate Reconstruction of American Capitalism, 1890–1916*. Cambridge: Cambridge University Press.

Skowronek, S. 1982. *Building a New American State: The Expansion of National Administrative Capacities, 1877–1920*. Cambridge: Cambridge University Press.

Slotkin, R. 1985. *The Fatal Environment: The Myth of the Frontier in the Age of Industrialization, 1800–1890*. New York: Atheneum.

Smith, S. A. 1983. *Red Petrograd: Revolution in the Factories, 1917–18*. Cambridge: Cambridge University Press.

Sombart, W. 1976. *Why Is There No Socialism in the United States?* London: Macmillan.

Spencer, E. G. 1976. Employer response to unionism: Ruhr coal industrialists before 1914. *Journal of Modern History* 48.

Stearns, P. 1975. *1848: The Revolutionary Tide in Europe*. New York: Norton.

Swain, G. 1983. *Russian Social Democracy and the Legal Labour Movement, 1906–14*. London: Macmillan.

Taft, P., and P. Ross. 1970. American labor violence: its causes, character and outcome. In *Violence in America*, ed. H. D. Graham and T. R. Gurr. New York: Praeger.

Tenfelde, K. 1985. Conflict and organization in the early history of the German trade union movement. In *The Development of Trade Unionism in Great Britain and Germany, 1880–1914*, ed. W. J. Mommsen and H.-G. Husung. London: German Historical Institute/Allen & Unwin.

Traugott, M. 1988. The crowd in the French Revolution of February, 1848. *American Historical Review* 93.

Ulman, L. 1955. *The Rise of the National Trade Union*. Cambridge, Mass.: Harvard University Press.

Weinstein, J. 1967. *The Decline of Socialism in America, 1912–1925*. New York: Monthly Review Press.

1984. *The Decline of Socialism in America, 1912–1925*, 2d ed. New Brunswick, N.J.: Rutgers University Press.

Wiebe, R. H. 1967. *The Search for Order, 1877–1920*. New York: Hill & Wang.

Wilentz, S. 1984. Against exceptionalism: class consciousness and the American labor movement, 1790–1920. *International Labor and Working Class History*, no. 26.

Woodiwiss, A. 1990. *Rights v. Conspiracy: A Sociological Essay on the History of American Labour Law*. Oxford: Berg.
Wuthnow, R. 1989. *Communities of Discourse. Ideology and Social Structure in the Reformation, the Enlightenment, and European Socialism*. Cambridge, Mass.: Harvard University Press.

19 Class struggle in the Second Industrial Revolution, 1880–1914: III. The peasantry

There has been little comparative work on agrarian classes. While workers have been done to death, peasants have been largely forgotten. Yet in almost all countries farmers constituted the largest population group, the largest voting bloc, and most of the soldiers. This chapter[1] compares agrarian class struggles in four of the five countries on which I have focused, plus Russia and the Scandinavian countries of Denmark, Norway, and Sweden – the additions enabling me to represent "Leftist" agrarian politics adequately. The missing country is Great Britain. Most stratification theories from Marx onward were based on the British experience. Table 19.1 shows how misleading this is.

We see that Britain (excluding its Irish colony) remained deviant throughout the nineteenth and early twentieth centuries. In 1911, only 9 percent of its labor force was in agriculture, less than one-third the percentage in any other major Power (minor Power Belgium had the next lowest, at 23 percent). In the other two most advanced economies, Germany and the United States, manufacturing and mining labor forces were only just then overtaking the agricultural and this had not occurred anywhere else besides Britain and Belgium. Whereas agriculture was insignificant in early twentieth-century British class relations, this was not true elsewhere. The outcome of the struggles charted in previous chapters among capital, labor, and the middle class would be decisively altered by agrarians. To theorize about modern class relations adequately, we must analyze the agrarian populations.

But three obstacles have blocked a general theory of agrarian politics. Marx's legacy has been disastrous. He expected agrarian populations to decline, as in Britain. They eventually did, but only in the mid-twentieth century, after capital-labor relations were largely institutionalized. He also wrongheadedly viewed peasants as incapable of class organization. His mistakes helped socialists make devastating political errors, as we shall see. Second, an antiagrarian bias has

---

[1] The research for this chapter was done jointly with Anne Kane, to whom I am greatly indebted. We have published a fuller joint article on our research (see Kane and Mann 1992).

Table 19.1. *Distribution of national labor force by sector (percent in each sector)*

Nation	Year	Agriculture[a]	Manufacturing	Services	Total
Great Britain	1871	15	47	38	100
	1911	9	52	40	100
France	1866	45	29	27	100
	1911	41	33	26	100
Denmark	1870	48	22	13	83[b]
	1911	42	24	30	96
Germany	1871	49	29	22	100
	1910	36	37	27	100
United States	1870	50	25	25	100
	1910	31	32	37	100
Sweden	1870	61	8	12	81[b]
	1910	46	26	14	96
Austria	1869	65	19	16	100
	1910	57	24	19	100
Hungary	1870	70	9	21	100
	1910	64	18	15	100
Russia	1897	59	14	25	100

[a] Agriculture includes forestry and fishing.
[b] Danish and Swedish census figures contain large numbers of "inadequately described" occupations, especially in early years.
Sources: Austria – Kausel (1979: 698). Germany – 1871 figures from Fischer et al. (1982: 52). All other figures from Bairoch et al. (1968).

dominated most Western thought, seeing agriculturalists as conservative and traditional, resisting modernization and doomed to the dustbin of history (Gerschenkron 1943; Moore 1973; E. Weber 1978; Jenkins 1986). Third, agrarian politics have in reality been diverse, presenting theory with a formidable task. What theoretical framework can integrate their clericalism, monarchism, fascism, populism, republicanism, social democracy, anarchism, and communism?

Theory has developed better on economics than on politics and better on the twentieth-century Third World than on the West. Linz (1976), Paige (1976), Sorokin et al. (1930), Stinchcombe (1961), and Wolf (1969) have mostly analyzed modern Third World economic interests, collective capacities, and responses to global commercialization. Yet, as I have emphasized throughout, class battles were also political. Some aimed at the main political exactions of the period, taxation and military conscription, but economic issues also became political, as parties sought to capture states – central, regional, and local – to achieve their goals. Thus political crystallizations also structured agrarian movements. Although these writers admit that economic variables are insufficient to explain outcomes, they treat politics as "outside" influences (Wolf 1969: 290–1; Paige 1976: 43, 47) or add them as empirical detail (Linz 1976). Others have theorized politics but deal only with class politics (Moore 1973; Rueschemyer, Stephens, and Stephens 1992). I shall argue that variations in agrarian politics principally resulted as party-democratic and national political crystallizations entwined, thus decisively structuring our modern world.

Agrarian classes

I identify three main agrarian classes. In this section I analyze their economic interests and powers. In the next I assess the impact on them of the agrarian dynamic of the Second Industrial Revolution period, the global commercialization of capitalism. Finally, I examine how political power relations entwined with these economic relations. The classes are:

1. *Estate farmers* – nobles, gentry, or commoners – own large tracts of land and employ labor on a moderate to large scale.
2. Smallholding farm proprietors – in continental European terminology, *peasants* – usually own their land and employ the labor of their own household.
3. *Landless laborers*, working for class 1 and occasionally for class 2, may be casual, seasonal, or permanent, waged or paid in kind, free or bonded.

Two caveats: First, tenant farming creates intermediate positions. Tenants possessing secure tenure and legal privileges converge on class 1 or class 2, according to size of holding and whether they employ labor. Conversely, tenants with lesser security or whose poverty endangers a loss of tenant rights are closer to landless laborers. Second, peasants are heterogeneous, varying from richer market-oriented farmers to subsistence "dwarfholders." Most richer peasants hire laborers, perhaps seasonally, from outside their household; whereas poorer peasants hire themselves out, freely or on bonded or share-cropping terms, to richer farmers as well as working their small plots. I take account of tenants and dwarfholders.

Two of the three classes will not detain me long. Class 1 interests and powers were straightforward. Estate farmers and landlords were at the heart of European ruling regimes (old and new); they dominated the American South and influenced the big business parties of other regions. Everywhere they organized conservative "parties of order," dedicated to preserve property relations and oppose democracy (Rueschemeyer, Stephens, and Stephens 1992).

The interests and powers of class 3, landless laborers, are also easy to grasp, though they were contradictory. They were proletarians, employed by large farmers, usually exploited transparently, suffering from low pay, arbitrary authority, and sparseness of legal rights. Most socialist parties working in the countryside concentrated their efforts among them. But laborers were poor at collective organization – territorially dispersed; barely literate; living and working under direct employer control, often accommodated in his or her farm, sometimes as bonded servants; and subject to farmer segmental control of local charity, church, magistracy, and government. Although a latent class, landless laborers rarely formed an extensive or political class.

Chapter 15 endorses Newby's (1977) explanation of how segmental control led more to "deference" than class consciousness: Farm workers obtained their wants through farmers, not against them, and so developed and internalized deferential strategies of appeal to them. Socialist agitators in the village might actually threaten the success of deference. Laborers (and tenant farmers) might identify themselves more as members of a cross-class village or estate community than as members of a class. Class identities and radical politics generally emerged amid absentee landlordism, where laborers and tenants had local autonomy, especially in the sharecropping common in southern Europe. (See, for example, Malefakis 1970 on Spain.) In the countries under discussion, this occurred only in southeast France and the western American states – and it did generate radicalism. The rural proletariat remained predominantly a latent class unless landlord segmental controls were removed.

Class 2, peasant proprietors, is the problem. Their economic position in relation to other classes is unclear. Although most peasants have a strong sense of collective identity, distinct from large landowners, landless laborers, and urban classes, they have no inherent class opponent in a Marxian production-centered sense, because their production is autonomous. Most production exploitation occurs within the household, normally by the senior male of the family. Most dwarf-holders experienced some labor exploitation, although this rarely provided a total class identity (as they were also property owners).

Yet a Weberian class analysis, based on credit struggles in markets rather than on production struggles, may be more applicable to peasants. Weber believed that class had been historically transformed: from struggles over "consumption credit toward, first, competitive struggles in the commodity market and then toward wage disputes on the labor market." Historically "peasants and . . . artisans [were] threatened by debt bondage and struggling against urban creditors" (1978: II, 931). As we shall see, this continued longer than Weber expected.

Late nineteenth-century peasants experienced major credit and price exploitation – over mortgages and foreclosures, crop lien systems, prices exacted by monopoly corporations – pitting them as a debtor class against the capitalist creditor class. Marx had also noted this occurring among nineteenth-century French peasants, threatening proletarianization. But he famously undercut this in *The 18th Brumaire* by doubting their ability to organize as a class. Peasants, though similar to each other, were not interdependent, he argued. Their mode of production separated them from each other – "mere local interconnectedness" made peasants like potatoes in a sack of potatoes, large but formless and inert, incapable of class organization. This is false. Peasants organized very effectively (as Wolf 1969 argues).

Yet whatever their class interests all three agrarian classes also share a *sectoral* identity. They are all vulnerable to climate and crop disease. They are "nearer to the soil," with all the subcultural, ideological resonance of that expression. They are territorially segregated into villages, giving them distinct *local-regional* organization and politics. Whereas most industrial workers organized by trade or enterprise, rural populations organized by community and locality. We shall see that this kept Rokkan's (1970) religious and center-periphery political cleavages relevant well beyond the time frame he imagined, into the twentieth century. Finally, European (though not American) agrarian populations were more traditional, with far older and more institutionalized relations with old regimes and churches than had urban-industrial populations. Rural politics was more concerned, positively or negatively, with old regime and clericalism.

Sectoralism pits farmers as producers against urban-industrial consumers. Farmers have an interest in high food prices, urban industrials in low prices – differences that were easily politicized, as prices were adjustable by price supports, taxes, and tariffs. Yet farmers usually buy some agrarian produce and all agrarian markets rarely vary together. When grain producers seek protection, root crop, wine, or dairy producers may seek open markets. Thus sectoral economic interests tend to be narrower in scope. Yet agrarians inhabit a different subculture from urban industrials. If their economic interests did conflict, ideological differences could quickly amplify them.

It is, therefore, difficult to deduce any *necessary* collective identities or politics from agrarian classes and sectors, apart from the conservatism of estate farmers. The most obvious Marxian class division, between large farmers and landless labor, was the most difficult to organize. Other conflict lines seem ambiguous. What Rokkan termed land versus industry conflict is especially ambiguous – actually a mixture of credit class struggle and producer-consumer sectoral struggle, each of which might range peasants against different opponents. They did so as the global transformation of capitalism impacted on late nineteenth-century agriculture.

The global commercialization of agriculture

As the West commercialized, urbanized, and industrialized, so agriculture fed it with produce and people. After railways (from the 1840s) and steamships (from the 1870s), even continental landmasses could be commercially integrated. Development favored farmers with investment capital and so rural stratification intensified. Estate farmers and richer peasants enlarged their landholdings at the expense of common lands, poor peasants, and the church. As Tilly (1979) notes, most proletarianization in the Industrial Revolution occurred in agriculture. Landless laborers supplied migrants to industry and overseas. Rural industry and handicrafts declined as manufacturing concentrated in towns (this happened less in France and Sweden, with important consequences). Rural society polarized faster than the urban-industrial polarization anticipated by the *Communist Manifesto*.

But then polarization stopped. Between 1860 and 1880, censuses and commissions were revealing that peasants were not disappearing as expected. This produced the best contemporary class analysis, Karl Kautsky's *The Agrarian Question* (1899, 1988). Kautsky saw that peasant household labor could be exploited more than free labor. Peasant families survived slumps by working harder and consuming less, so as to keep their land. Their self-exploitation – actually it was patriarchal exploitation, with the male household head exploiting underconsumption by females, junior males, and children – and their unwillingness to sell their land led the Russian Marxist Chayanov to proclaim a new "peasant mode of production." Yet Kautsky also noted that peasant households were not autonomous: Their production entwined with capitalism. The dwarfholder or cottager and the dual worker-peasant household performed day labor on a larger farm or in industry while producing part of its subsistence (and perhaps a little marketable produce) on its own cottage plot. The small farm also bred migrant and casual laborers and army recruits. A symbiotic relation had developed among peasant household, capitalism, and military state. Kautsky remained an orthodox Marxist, expecting agricultural employment to wither away in the face of industrial employment. But he saw that rural polarization was over.

Kautsky's arguments were correct, even understated. There were also positive reasons why peasants flourished. Concentration of landholding had cost and efficiency limits. In his 1894 thesis, Weber took note of Prussian Junker lords forced to sell land to peasants in order to raise capital to invest in the remainder of their estates. Also, as industry competed for labor, agricultural wages rose. Farm workers could save and invest in smallholdings; and the wage bill of estate farmers rose above that of peasants exploiting their households (Grantham 1975). Many foodstuffs were produced as cheaply on small as estate farms. This was less true of grain staples – and therefore of midwestern American farmers – but European peasants could specialize in root crops (as in West Germany; Perkins 1981), dairy produce (Denmark), or the vine (southern France; Smith 1975). Peasants could also form cooperatives to buy machinery and process and distribute produce, another organization refuting Marx's "sack of potatoes" metaphor. By 1900, most large estate areas were not advanced agrarian economies, as in early visions of development, but backward and reactionary – in Europe east of the Elbe, Russia, southern Italy and Spain, and the American South. In advanced regions, the economics of estates, peasants, and landless laborers was jointly linked to the most advanced industrial and financial sectors.

This led to two alternative rural politics: class populism and sectoral segmentalism. As farmers became enmeshed in global capitalism, credit conflicts intensified. Borrowing increased on the security of land (if a proprietor) or harvest (if a tenant). In the U.S. prairie states, farmers mortgaged land to buy shares in railroads, the lifeblood of their marketing capacities. But collusion between railroad companies and banks ensured losses on their investment, threatening foreclosure. Small farmers borrowed from large ones and from banks. Tenants were forced into crop lien or sharecropping systems. Poorer peasants were most threatened, especially where partible inheritance fragmented landholdings. Peasants saw that exploitation was by urban and rural big capital. They demanded cancellation or relief of debts, credit on favorable terms, and the regulation of banks, railroad companies, and corporate suppliers of fertilizer and machinery. This is *class populism*; a Weberian class conflict based on credit and market relations, pitting the "people" against corporate capitalism, potentially uniting peasants and workers, with similar opponents, in a Leftist alliance.

But market competition also intensified *sectoral* identity among farmers. Agricultural depressions were rapidly exported as producers were forced to reduce prices. Improvements a continent away could flood local markets with cheaper goods, as happened in Europe about 1880 with American grain and Argentine beef. Specialization increased vulnerability to changes in product markets. What if a natural disaster struck (like the phylloxera beetle that ravaged French vines in the 1880s) or foreign competitors increased their efficiency (as American farmers improved milling techniques in the 1880s to undersell Prussian rye)? There was a political remedy: state protection against market forces through subsidies, loans, and tariffs. But agrarian tariffs invited foreign retaliation, harming producers of other goods, so were usually opposed by the urban-manufacturing sector. Sectoral politics normally pitted peasants and workers against one another; if workers were Leftist, agrarians might swing to the Right. Much would depend on which farmers led the sectoral protest. Estate farmers might lead *segmental* and conservative movements; peasants, sectoral populism.

Thus agrarian political economy generated contradictory class and sectoral interests, politicized by debt, credit, and tariff demands, intensified from 1873 by the great agricultural depression. Many argue that the depression made peasants conservative, resisting a capitalist modernization threatening their existence (e.g., Jenkins 1986). But few peasants opposed modernization once proletarianization had ebbed. They did not need reaction or revolution but limited state intervention to relieve suffering in the short run and to enable equitable participation in long-run modernization. Grievances might be radical if aimed at capitalist actors like banks or railroad companies. But they implied pragmatic political remedies: tariff adjustment, credit, and cooperative assistance. Political activity went through states. What political crystallizations would agrarians face there?

States and agrarian classes: four general patterns

As earlier chapters show, later eighteenth- and nineteenth-century politics was dominated by representative and national struggles over citizenship. As Rokkan (1970) has argued, these were not just between classes and sectors but also between centralizers and decentralizers and between church and state. Representative movements resisted absolute monarchy in two ways: reducing central state powers or accepting centralization and democratizing it – raising national as well as party-democratic issues. In these struggles, churches were especially important in the countryside, where they provided the main infrastructures for local-regional mobilization. Catholic and Protestant churches had three possible situations: as a state church (more likely for Protestant than Catholic), majority church, or minority church. Their positions vis-à-vis party democracy and the national issue differed accordingly.

Although political crystallizations relevant to agrarians were complex and unique, they were in one respect simpler than industrial ones. By 1900, agrarians provided most of Europe's soldiers, and most regimes were compromising with agrarians (partly to avoid a combined agrarian-

Table 19.2. *Party democracy and the national question in nineteenth-century agrarian states*

Centralization versus confederalism	Monarchy versus party democracy		
	Evenly contested	Monarchy weakening	Party democracy institutionalized
Most parties centralizers Monarchy centralized, democrats confederal Most parties confederal	Germany Austro-Germany Most Austrian lands	Scandinavia Russia Minority nationalities in Russian empire	France United States

industrial workers' movement). Thus militarism declined in agrarian class relations, except where regional nationalism inflamed them (in the countries discussed here, principally in Austrian and Russian provinces and in the rather different case of the American South). Thus I simplify agrarian political crystallizations into two-dimensional space, distinguishing them in terms of three positions on each of two dimensions: party democracy and the national issue. In this period, monarchies in all advanced countries had been challenged by party democracy. Current outcomes varied from an even balance of forces, to monarchies in evident difficulty, to monarchies already abolished or rendered powerless by institutionalized party democracy. The national issue generated more diverse outcomes, but I have distinguished the three resulting in my countries. Table 19.2 specifies the nine resulting ideal types, though my countries only occupy six of the boxes.

International variations in agrarian politics can be predicted on the basis of these two combined political crystallizations. But because I do not cover many countries and because it makes narrative sense to discuss countries as single totalities, I simplify this into four broader patterns:

1. Party democracy (for most men) and a solution to the national issue were institutionalized. In France political institutions emerged centralized, in the United States, confederal. But in both cases existing political parties were firmly institutionalized and new parties, including peasant parties, were relatively ineffective. Because a confederal state allows for more regional variation, the main exceptions are found in America, in some local and state politics, temporarily captured by agrarian parties.

2. Party democracy was still contested by evenly balanced contending forces most of which accepted that the state should be centralized. This principally pitted authoritarian monarchy, with the support of a national bourgeoisie, against an equally centralizing statist working class. Here most peasant movements oscillated but eventually moved toward the Right, joining old regime parties or forming autonomous conservative or Center-Right parties acceptable to the monarchy. This was the main pattern in Germany and in the core Austro-German lands of Austria-Hungary.

3. Party democracy was still evenly contested, but between a centralizing authoritarian monarchy and confederal democratic parties. Here peasant politics moved toward class populism. Where peasants themselves dominated this, it was usually a Leftist populism; where they did not, it showed Rightist tendencies. This was the pattern across the rest of Austria-Hungary, and it was an ultimately unsuccessful pattern across southern and western Germany.

4. Party democracy was still contested, but ranged a weaker monarchy against an eventually triumphant alliance of urban liberals, peasants, and workers – both sides being centralizers. Here peasants moved toward the Left, to become potential allies of socialists. Where the old regime was toppled peacefully, social democracy resulted, as in Scandinavia; where toppling required revolution, peasants and workers alike were forced farther Left, as in Russia. The present inadequate state of research on minority nationalists within the Russian Empire prevents me from giving proper attention to the monarchy's struggle against confederal opponents.

Party democracy in France and the United States
The French state remained centralized in the nineteenth century, and its party democracy was institutionalized after 1880. Its economy was rather diverse. Agriculture differed among regions, and industrialization was slow and decentralized, dispersed through small towns and sharing its labor with farming households. In 1789, the revolutionaries had allied with peasants and institutionalized peasant property, but when they demanded high taxes, low food prices, and conscription, the rural population backed away. The tenants of the west went farthest, into armed revolt under landlord and clerical segmental control, which was maintained in the nineteenth century (Bois 1960). Some regions and cities dechristianized together; in others the church increased segmental controls through schools, charity, hospitals, and community recreation. Because centralization could not be directly challenged, clericalism was essentially covert confederalism: The scope of the central state was cut down by enlarging the scope of the sacred. There was an overall

difference between a conservative west and a radical southeast, plus many microschisms in which towns and their hinterlands remained factionalized by republican and conservative-clerical parties (Garrier 1973: I, 515–6; Merriman 1979). But French politics were too complex to be sectoral, rural versus urban, agrarian versus industrial.

Thus the agricultural depression channeled rural grievances into varied local-regional movements. In the southeast most peasants and dwarfholders specialized (in grapes, olives, fruits, or flowers) and were vulnerable to market fluctuations, to overproduction after 1900, to competition from large growers (also lowering dwarfholder wages), and to price and credit squeezes from merchant middlemen (Smith 1975; Judt 1979; Brustein 1988). They moved from republicanism toward socialism after 1880. The loose-knit French Left (described in Chapter 18) became adept at developing programs geared both to credit class peasant interests and the more production-oriented demands of sharecroppers and landless laborers. They muted land redistribution, spread tax concessions and subsidies around, advocated progressive taxes, encouraged cooperatives (not collective ownership of land), attacked monopolies, and mobilized anticlericalism in some areas (Loubère 1974: 206–33; Brustein 1988: 107, 169).

The depression also threatened the Right's rural bases, so the Right also learned political agility. Local notables mobilized peasants and tenants into credit, insurance, and cooperative schemes (Berger 1972; Garrier 1973: I, 518–22). The church also responded, fearing (as did the Catholic Center in Germany) that rural economic discontent might undermine its segmental control. One church faction abandoned its monarchism and its landlord allies and formed an effective rural social Christian movement.

Brustein (1988) has offered a class interpretation of the west-southeast schism. He shows that a positive correlation lasted more than a hundred years between areas of peasant proprietorship and areas of Left voting and between areas of medium and small tenancies (and landlord presence) and areas of Right voting. Reinterpreting earlier studies (Bois 1960; Tilly 1967; Le Goff and Sutherland, 1983), he suggests that these tenure differences had underlain rural support or opposition to the Revolution. Peasants are inherently Leftist and tenants inherently Rightist, he concludes. Judt (1979: 113–4, 134–6, 279–80) similarly concludes his study of Leftist peasants in the southeast: "The peasantry have *always* exhibited a greater propensity for revolutionary fervour than have the other constituent groups of modern societies." This chapter shows how overgeneralized this statement is. But why should it appear plausible for France?

Brustein argues that different relations of production ensured peasants' *interests* were Leftist and tenants' Rightist. He describes western landlords' relations with their impoverished dependents in somewhat rosy terms: Tenants shared "beneficial risk-taking arrangements" with their landlords; so did sharecroppers; while their bonded laborers actually had more security than wage laborers elsewhere. Yet this minimizes the exploitation experienced by all three, and some Rightist policies ran counter to all their interests – regressive taxation and opposition to rural democracy, for example. In fact, as is the general argument of this chapter, agrarian economic "interests" were ambivalent and more politically malleable than Brustein allows for. Relations of production involve control as well as interest. Local segmental control exercised by active farmer landlords over their dependents was more decisive in steering them in a conservative direction. As in other countries, economic and political power relations entwined to produce agrarian outcomes. It was distinctively French to transmit such varied definitions of rural interests into the twentieth century, primarily because of the unfinished local-regional effects of its revolution.

American party democracy and confederalism were institutionalized early, although a civil war and a failed period of southern reconstruction were needed to settle the latter fully. The war period also boosted agrarian commercialization (Bruchey 1965: 155–8; Danhof 1969: 11). International markets for cotton and foodstuffs stimulated cash crop production. As eastern farmers specialized in activities like dairying, plains and western farmers switched from self-sufficient cultivation to cash production of wheat and corn (maize). Farmers needed transport and credit but were vulnerable to lower agricultural prices and debts. The Civil War worsened this by producing a shortage of currency and credit, high taxes, high custom tariffs (to protect industries), and agricultural distress in the South.

This was not insurmountable, but unfortunately the American polity was becoming inhospitable to farmers. As discussed in Chapters 5 and 18, this state had crystallized as capitalist liberal (sacralizing property rights), party democratic, and federal. Its democracy was firmly in the hands of two parties. The Democratic party had inherited the agrarian interest but lost power in the Civil War. Republicans and industrial capital now dominated. A realigned electorate was polarized less by class than by local-regional and ethnic-religious communities (Burnham 1974: 688). Republicans now dominated the northern states and the federal level of government; Democrats held the southern states. To compete federally, Democrats also curried business and commercial support. Their representation of small farmers became sporadic, of labor negligible.

Political neglect produced growing farmer complaints. The high costs of transport motivated demands for railroad regulation. The high prices of manufactured goods purchased by farmers cultivated resentment toward urban industrial interests and local merchants. National banking operated against farmers. Returning the monetary system to the gold standard was good for business, but farmers got less money for their produce and had to pay more for purchases and to service debts. Lack of cash increased mortgage debt and dependence on moneylenders and creditor merchants. The crop lien credit system of the South spread elsewhere among small owners and tenant farmers. Credit class and sectoral tariff conflict intensified. Unlike most of Europe, American tariffs protected manufacturers and hurt farmers, particularly in the South and West (Buck 1913: 21).

Because the two existing parties remained unhelpful, farmers organized autonomously. The Grangers of the 1870s complained of low prices and high costs imposed by corporate railroads, machinery manufacturers, and middlemen. They turned to small third parties: the Reform, Greenback, and Anti-Monopoly parties. The more radical Farmers Alliance of the late 1880s attacked tenancy and one-crop dependency, especially in the South, demanding subsidies for cooperatives and farmer exchanges. Business domination of the two parties then moved them farther left, toward alliance with labor groups in the People's or Populist party, strongest in the South and West with additional midwestern strongholds. Its antimonopolist platform demanded more secure land for small farmers, protection from corporations, and a federal "subtreasury" to protect farmers from falling prices and high credit costs.

Leftward movement continued into the early twentieth century with the Socialist party, rurally centered on Oklahoma, Texas, Arkansas, and Louisiana. There farmers were forced into tenancy and crop liens, forced to farm cotton, and dominated by local regimes of large farmers, landlords, merchants, and creditors. Unlike the Populists exploited by outside metropolitan, commercial, and financial interests, southern and southwestern small farmers and tenants suffered at the hands of local notables. Thus cleavage was more by class than sector, politically fueled by capitalist control of the Democrats, dominant throughout the Southwest (Rosen 1978). Like their counterparts in France, Scandinavia, and Bavaria, southwestern Socialists advocated moderate agrarian socialism. They viewed small farmers not as capitalists but as active, laboring producers. They adopted a radical class populism – land to the direct producers – and competed electorally with the Democrats. Finally, they went beyond populism to demand the end of capitalist control.

These third parties enjoyed extensive local-regional support, winning many local and state elections (Fine 1928; Dyson 1986). Yet ultimately all went down to defeat, unable to break through two-party democracy in federal elections because of constituency size and capitalist-liberal domination of the two parties. The farm-labor alliance was necessary for both sides, but having the same opponent rarely generated genuine solidarity. Farm-labor parties were successfully established only in Wisconsin and Minnesota. Unlike Scandinavia, Russia, or parts of Austria-Hungary, there was no common exclusion from political citizenship to reinforce compatible, but different, economic programs.

With only a fragile alliance, faced with parties deeply infused with capitalist liberalism, both sides split. Chapter 18 shows how the AFL backed off from third-party politics in 1894–5, leaving the Socialist party a minority within labor. Farmers also split. The Populist party was co-opted by the Democrats, its policies diluted. South-western socialists began to moderate but then were suppressed by local Democrats (Burbank 1976: 188; Green 1976: 382). In the South, a multiracial populism protested the crop lien system, but black disenfranchisement weakened and split the movement along racial lines. The South remained politically controlled by local planter-merchant oligarchies until after World War II. Its congressional representatives remained cohesive and conservative in Washington, stymieing legislation favoring workers and small farmers. The continuing weakness of American labor also helped condemn radical farmers' movements to futility. Again we see the distinctively repressive effects of the capitalist-liberal, the party-democratic, and the federal crystallization of the American state.

In this period, American farmers' movements achieved little. Later in the twentieth century, after tenant and sharecropper movements collapsed, a combination of large and middling farmers achieved considerable influence through the existing two parties. Many of the sectoral demands of farmers were then achieved, in predominantly conservative segmental forms.

Strong monarchies challenged: Germany and Austria-Hungary

As Chapters 9 and 18 stress, German representation was always linked to national and religious issues, since the state was Prussian and Protestant. After the regime's Kulturkampf, in the 1870s, against the Catholic church failed, religion became less of a direct problem, but it still infused the national issue. This centralizing authoritarian monarchy depended on landlords and capitalists, plus increasingly the middle class, who therefore became national centralizers; its enemies were the labor movement and local-regional minorities favoring confederalism –

or even their own nation-states (Poles, Danes, Alsatians, and Hanoverian separatists).

Peasants were in the middle, neither inside the regime nor defined as its enemies. But having the expanding labor movement and the confederalists as enemies, the regime could hardly alienate a further third of the population. Moreover, having gambled on large farmers being able to control segmentally rural laborers and tenants, it had introduced an adult male suffrage weighted against the towns. Rural men had a disproportionate electoral voice and so peasants remained ambiguous about the extension of democracy (Rueschemeyer, Stephens, and Stephens 1992: chapter 4). Although German workers were united into a common class struggle for political citizenship, workers and peasants were not (unlike in) Scandinavia.

Thus peasants tended to move toward the Right. But the move varied regionally, as rural conditions differed between east and west. The abolition of serfdom had delivered eastern serfs as rural laborers to the Junkers, but western peasants had long been freer and they continued to flourish (Conze 1969: 54; Brenner 1976) across midcentury until the depression hit in 1873. This lowered prices and increased indebtedness, forstering both sectoral conflict between agrarians and urban-industrials and credit class populism against capitalists. After 1882, more than half of all German peasants were dwarfholders, forced to hire themselves out as laborers. Military conscription also hit hard, generating antimilitarism like that of the socialists. Peasants, like socialists, also opposed regressive indirect taxes favored by conservatives. But if peasant grievances were instead aired against the land tax and for tariff protection from foreign competition, a sectoral segmental alliance would result with Junkers and other estate farmers. Which way would they turn?

East of the Elbe, agrarians swung toward the Right, under Junker segmental control. But in western and in Catholic Germany, autonomous political mobilization occurred (Blackbourn 1977, 1984). Yet peasants were also ambivalent about the urban-industrial class struggle in ways that varied by region and religion. Lutherans in the Prussian North favored a centralized nation-state. Most Catholics – 37 percent of the Reich in 1905 – were in southern states favoring confederalism. Thus Catholics were mobilizable by their church against *both* the statist Lutheran old regime and the statist, godless proletariat. Northern Lutheran agrarians had no particular interest in repressing industrial workers, yet favored the centralized nation-state, whereas the rural Catholic South did not.

The Marxist Social Democratic party contributed to their decision (Hussain 1981). It had long ignored the rural population as doomed to

British-style decline, yet eventually began a rural electoral drive in 1890. It had some success in Protestant Hesse and in the rural hinterlands of its urban bases, among laborers in Mecklenburg and parts of East Prussia, where its statist socialism could be appreciated by Lutherans. But hindered by Marxian dogma, especially commitment to land socialization, and mobilized by its urban constituency into sectoral opposition to agrarian protection or subsidies, it had litle appeal for peasants. Because most laborers were dwarfholders, they wished to protect private property, not abolish it. Agrarians failed to comprehend Social Democratic ideology and looked in vain for sectoral concessions from them. The drive was largely a failure (Eley 1980: 23–24 emphasizes its few successes). The party could have done better, as its southern sister party proved: The Bavarian party dropped socialization and offered mortgage protection to peasants, who duly returned Social Democratic representatives to the Landtag.

Southern peasants as southerners and as Catholics favored confederalism. The Catholic Center party came to spearhead southern demands. Led by urban notables it did not at first respond to peasant discontents. When it supported the tariff reductions of the liberal Caprivi government in the early 1890s, peasant voters abandoned it and formed dissident peasant associations and leagues in Westphalia, the Rhineland, and Bavaria. The Bavarian leagues were radical, anticlerical, and antimilitarist, favoring progressive taxation and agrarian protection. Here was an opening for a Leftist alliance with the Social Democratic party. But an alarmed Center party formed its own Catholic peasant associations, moderated its tariff stance, and sponsored agrarian credit programs. The leagues now declined (Farr 1978). The Center had reasserted control by transforming itself into a partly peasant party, seeking redress of sectoral grievances. Allied with northern conservatives, it pressured the regime into agrarian protection. Southern peasants got much of what they wanted through a Center party with influence inside the regime.

In the North, the Caprivi government, disliked by agrarians, had depended on National Liberals and Progressives. Their agrarian wings now declined. Conservative parties dominated by large farmers jumped in, advocating protection and wooing peasants into their agrarian leagues. In Protestant areas where conservatives were weak, peasants moved instead to a Rightist populism whose antiurban, antimonopoly rhetoric became militantly Lutheran, nationalist, and anti-Semitic. Jews were an easy target for anticreditor populists in rural Hesse and Prussia, the same areas where the Social Democrats established a toehold and the same areas where the Nazis would later dominate (Eley 1980; Farr 1986).

Thus German peasants turned farther away from socialists than did peasants in most countries. They might adopt the mildly "Christian social" stance of the Catholic Center, or a sectoral segmentalism controlled by large farmer conservatives, or Rightist class populism. German agrarian discontent had drifted to the Right because of two features of the regime and one of the Social Democratic party. First, authoritarian monarchy advantaged top-down segmental divide-and-rule rural politics. If notable parties responded to rural grievances – conservatives and Catholic Center did, Progressives and National Liberals did not – their influence within the regime advantaged them over excluded popular parties and they could bend rural discontent toward the Right. Second, if notable parties were not responsive, then autonomous peasant movements emerged, influenced by the national issue and therefore by religion and region. Northern Lutherans favored nation-state centralization; some turned Right to national populism, a few turned Left to statist socialism. So began that intense competition between extreme Right and extreme Left in Lutheran Germany that eventually helped destroy the Weimar Republic. Ironically, the Catholic confederal South contained more potential for a radical agrarian move-ent, yet the godless, statist Socialist party was not the best agent for this, and the Center party recovered control. Third, the productivist Marxism of the Social Democrats further assisted the drift toward the Right by ignoring credit class grievance of farmers. These are all predominantly political crystallizations.

The Austrian lands were mainly agrarian, dominated by large estates worked by landless laborers or dwarfholders. Intense landlord ex-ploitation, high interest rates, and the backwardness of some provinces created severe poverty and debts barely relieved by mass emigration to the New World. Agrarian production and credit class and sectoral struggles might be ferocious – unless repressed by landlord segmental control – but they were structured by three distinctive Austro-Hungarian crystallizations over party democracy and the national issue (see Chapter 10).

First, the Habsburgs were not just monarchists but *dynasts*, with rather arbitrary if limited powers. Although they spent most of the century resisting all democracy, they then changed tack, seeking to use a limited party democracy to divide and rule segmentally between classes and "regional-nations." After experiments at local government level, in 1896 and 1907, the regime granted adult male suffrage to assemblies with limited sovereignty (implementation lagged in Hungary). Before then, urban liberal and rural conservative parties had taken little interest in disenfranchised peasants and landless laborers. The sudden franchise produced mass agrarian and industrial parties not already controlled segmentally by existing parties. They aimed for party democracy, that is, parliamentary sovereignty. Unlike Germany, but like Scandinavia, common political exclusion could potentially unite bourgeois radicals, workers, and peasants.

Second, with no parliamentary institutions, *churches* had informally represented most provinces and they now sponsored political parties. The Catholic church was a quasi-state church in some provinces, but it was ultimately transnational, not statist. In other provinces it expressed local-regional discontent. Minority Protestant churches did this more often. Rural movements were anticlerical or clerical according to the stance of the local church, but they were almost never indifferent to religion.

Third, most democrats favored *confederalism* (fitting the third of my patterns) except in the core Austro-German lands (which fit the second pattern). Most later became dissident nationalists. This forced the monarchy to depend more on Austro-Germans and after the 1867 compromise on other client nationalities. Thus landlord-laborer and creditor-debtor relations often also became "regional-national" because exploiters were often Germans or client Hungarians or Jews (entrenched in state administration and banking), whereas the exploited were usually of the local nationality. Economic grievances and nationalism reinforced each other. Austro-German democratic parties remained centralist, and non-Germans favored confederalism, then national autonomy. Hungarians were ambivalent, given their position as junior exploiters in the southeast.

Thus rural politics varied enormously among regions. In Austro-German Lower Austria all parties favored centralization. They were polarized by class and sectoral divisions surrounding rapid industrialization and urban secularization. The conservative, anti-Semitic Christian Social party, Catholic and predominantly peasant, won a two-thirds majority in the Landtag in 1903, vigorously pursuing peasant interests and securing debt moratoriums, mortgage limits, homestead laws, and cooperatives. Its main opponent was the Socialist party, garnering some landless laborer but virtually no peasant votes. Like their German counterparts, the Socialists had little in the way of a rural program and an unhelpful productivist, statist Marxian dogma (Lewis 1978).

Bohemia was the other main industrializing area. The Czech working class, like its Austro-German comrades, first espoused the statist Marxism of the Socialist party, but as Czech nationalism spread, Czech (like the Bavarian) Socialists became ambivalent. Many estate farmers were German and the majority Catholic church was implicated in Habsburg rule, which made nationalism anticlerical. All this weakened rural resistance to socialism. This was the area in Europe where a Marxist party most successfully attracted landless laborers. Indeed its main competitor among them was the National Socialist party, combining the ideologies its title suggests (not those of Hitler!). Most peasants went to the Center-Right Agrarian party, which favored Czech autonomy and greater democracy but was antisocialist and indifferent to landless labourers (Pech 1978).

In more backward Slovenia "national" dissidence was led by the Catholic church. Most peasants backed the clerical, radical Slovene People's party, committed to democratic reforms and peasant economic interests. Socialists made few converts, mostly in ethnically mixed areas where nationalism made little impact. Polish Galicia was also backward and rural, with a history of peasant insurrection and substantial provincial autonomy, allowing Polish nobles and rich peasants to exploit Ruthenian laborers and dwarfholders. Polish nationalism was thus muted, the Catholic church was neutral, and class dominated politics. Catholic and mutualist socialist parties competed for peasant votes and with the Socialist party for landless laborers.

Hungary's position in the monarchy was economically and politically unique, with the highest proportion of large estates and with firm Hungarian noble control institutionalized after 1867 over its *Reichshalf*. Magyar nationalism was thus muted and noble control damped down class organization among peasants and laborers in Hungary itself (Eddie 1967; Macartney 1969: 687–734; Hanak 1975). Yet the depression caused great suffering, and rural insurrections broke out in 1894 and 1897. The fledgling Hungarian Social Democratic party organized some of these but then faded as a radical populist smallholders party began to compete with landlord parties.

But elsewhere in this *Reichshalf*, rural discontent turned "regional-national," against Magyar domination. First Protestant, then Catholic churches led Slovak national resistance (Pech 1978). Liberals and socialists were not influential until after World War I. Peasant and landless discontents were ignored by national-religious politics. Croatia produced an almost opposite peasant reaction. Its local notables – a weak nobility, bourgeoisie, and Catholic hierarchy – were clients of Magyar overlords. With notables so compromised, a powerful dissident nationalism arose among the excluded peasant majority, glorifying the peasant – radical, anticlerical, and even socialist. In all Balkan provinces and states, nobles and gentry, decimated by Turkish rule, were weak. Peasants and dwarfholders dominated radical populist movements (Mouzelis 1986: 35–8).

Thus across Austria-Hungary class (production and credit) and sectoral interests rarely led directly to political organization. The national question – a debate over decentralized party democracy in a part-confessional state – interposed to generate diverse outcomes. Czech national discontent reinforced production class struggle to produce an alliance of industrial and agrarian proletarians. In the Balkans credit class and national struggles reinforced each other to produce radical class populism among peasants. Among Austro-Germans where industrialism was advanced and nationalism uniquely centralist, this consolidated statist Marxian socialism among industrial workers. But Austrian socialists were trapped, like their German comrades, into urban industrial enclaves. Elsewhere, outcomes were more conservative. Outside of Hungary and Slovakia, demands for national autonomy weakened aristocratic and clerical conservatism, but peasants were generally steered away from radical class populism by nationalism. Together with the urban bourgeoisie and petite bourgeoisie, they were moving toward Centrist and Rightist populism. Allied with anti-Semitism this later had some nasty outcomes.

Weak monarchies challenged: Scandinavia and Russia
I include Denmark, Norway, and Sweden in my coverage because they developed the most successful twentieth-century alliances between farmers and urban socialists. The three countries had varied economies but similar politics: A numerous peasantry was pushed toward the Left and into allying first with liberal bourgeois elements, then with workers. All had relatively weak landholding nobilities, important because this freed much of the countryside from strong segmental controls. Richer peasants generally had collective political rights, which proved extendable to poorer peasants through the nineteenth century. After Norway achieved independence in 1905, all three countries were fairly centralized and ethnically and religiously homogeneous. Their common destiny seems the product of similar state regimes and political alliances rather than of their economies. Rural like urban politics crystallized as party democratic and national centralizing.

Two issues, one economic, one political, brought peasants together, first with urban liberals, then with workers. First, most small farmers were free traders, "liberals" in the nineteenth-century sense. In Denmark this was because livestock and dairy farming remained successful in world markets. Danish urban liberals and socialists also favored legal freedoms for tenant crofters, an important semilaborer, semipeasant group. Norwegian peasants favored free trade because this meant free internal trade and freedom from taxation by foreign states ruling them until 1905. Swedish farmers, big and small, were more protectionist. But fewer sectoral conflicts divided agrarians from urban industrials in Scandinavia than in most of Europe. Swedish and Danish (along with

French) industrialization was also distinctive in scattering industry throughout the countryside, aiding contact between the two sectors, rather than concentrating it in urban ghettos.

Second, peasants allied with urban liberals in a struggle for political citizenship against relatively weak landed nobilities and monarchies. Swedish liberals came disproportionately from the Free (dissenting) churches and from the temperance movement. Their contacts with peasant farmers came especially from their sponsorship of national educational programs. As labor rose, much of the expanding urban middle class moved to the right as they began to oppose the spread of democracy. But the remaining liberals and the smaller farmers moved toward a democratic alliance with workers' socialist parties. Because the countries were centralized and Lutheran, the socialists at first were attracted to statist versions of socialism, many to Marxism. But they responded to urban liberalism and peasant radicalism by diluting their Marxian productivist orthodoxy (Danish socialists had never had any). The Swedish Social Democrats, for example, toned down the Erfurt Program they took from the German Social Democrats to remove any suggestion that a violent revolution might be desirable.

So developed a tripartite politics: urban and rural capitalists and much of the middle class forming conservative parties, peasants and a minority middle class forming liberal and radical parties, and workers (manual and then white-collar) becoming social democrats. Pragmatic alliances between the last two achieved the first electoral successes leading to that uniquely successful and Leftist form of modern civilization, Scandinavian social democracy (Munch 1954; Semmingsen 1954; Holmsen 1956; Kuuse 1971; Osterud 1971; Kuhnle 1975; Thomas 1977; Castles 1978; Stephens 1979: 129–39; Duncan 1982; Esping-Andersen 1985; and Rueschemeyer, Stephens, and Stephens 1992: chapter 4).[2] Agrarian classes were not themselves socialist, but their sectoral, their credit class, and above all their political citizenship interests led them Leftward.

So far, peasant politics centered on economic threats to peasant proprietorship and peasant activism in party democracy and on the national issue. Russia is a deviant case because neither condition initially existed. Russia also uniquely developed a revolutionary peasantry. Hence the Russian fusion of economic and political demands had a distinct character.

---

[2] These generalizations fit Norway less well than Denmark or Sweden. Norway's economy was more sectorally varied, its people more linguistically diverse, and this encouraged regional and religious fundamentalism and Marxian socialism. Only in 1935 did the DNA (Social Democrats) abandon Marxism and ally with farmers.

As Chapter 18 indicates, Russia remained an autocratic dynastic monarchy, making no motions toward party democracy until after 1905 and only puny motions thereafter. The regime was now opposed principally by urban-industrial and regional-national representative movements. The state seems to have been outside most peasants' reach. We lack evidence on dissident nationalism within the Russian Empire, and perhaps peasants from national minorities, like their decentralizing counterparts in other countries, were more politically engaged than is suggested here. But nobles seem to have dominated peasants through the regional zemstvos, local government units established in 1864, while at village level the historic egalitarian commune (*mir*) still functioned. As in France before its revolution, nobles were absent from most villages.

Emancipation from serfdom in 1862 did not give peasants autonomy. It bound them to the land in alternative ways and helped stifle agricultural productivity (for Russian peasants, see Pavlovsky 1930; Robinson 1932; Volin 1960; Wolf 1969; Shanin 1972, 1985; Haimson 1979; and Skocpol 1979). Unlike in Austria-Hungary, the abolition of serfdom produced few commercial large estates. The agricultural depression and declining prices forced nobles to sell or lease land to land-hungry peasants. But the peasants had to pay for emancipation through redemption payments, rents, and land purchases. Rapid regime-sponsored industrialization increased taxes, tariffs, and therefore prices. This forced peasants to sell produce on markets, and it forced markets to export to pay for the economy's manufactured imports and foreign loans. Economic pressure depleted oxen and cattle and forced the traditional three-field system to exhaust the soil (generally of poor quality), as fields were not left fallow. The *mir* began to polarize between rich peasants (kulaks) and the great majority of poor ones. Most had too little fertile land to feed themselves, generate a surplus for the market, and pay the various state exactions. Regime modernization plans seemed only to worsen their plight and to politicize them.

In 1905, the state fell apart in war defeat, and peasants seized their local chances. Insurgence was directed mostly at landlords and local government administration. Most rural strikes, attacks on property, and land confiscations in 1905 were directed against great landowners, especially in the central black-earth region and in the few areas where large capitalist estates had displaced peasants. Most consistent support came from middle peasants, and from young peasants exposed to revolutionary ideas through work in the cities (Perrie 1972: 127; Wolf 1979). Peasants demanded redistribution of land and abolition or reduction of rents, taxes, and service obligations. Violence was less directed against kulaks. Kulaks worked the land they owned; gentry did not. The peasant ideology "those that work the land have a right to it" papered over factionalism. This was a *peasant* uprising: Political agitation from outside was rarely successful, and attacks were often organized by the *mir* (Walkin 1962; Perrie 1972).

The 1905 revolution was repressed, but the frightened regime set up the limited Duma. Regime and noble landowners now appreciated agriculture's dangerous state. The regime abolished redemption payments, and landowners reduced rents and continued to sell off estates. When peasant demands continued, in the Duma and through rural violence, the regime changed direction. It rescinded most political reforms, depriving peasants of representation in the Duma, and Stolypin's agrarian reforms were an attempt to usher in capitalist farming among richer peasants.

Communes were factionalized by Stolypin's inducement for peasants to "separate" their title to land from the commune. Rich peasants could take advantage of this, and the poorest could "separate," sell their tiny plots, and use the money to migrate to the towns or abroad. The middle peasant majority opposed separation, wishing the commune to remain whole. This internal state-generated conflict meant separation rarely consolidated holdings into large private farms. Individual peasant strips remained integrated by the commune, which remained a powerful source for collective action. Middle peasants favored expropriation of noble and gentry land, perhaps its nationalization, but they did not want it reorganized on either a capitalist or a Bolshevik collectivist model. The local commune remained their ideal. The regime's attack on it was to worsen the fury unleashed in 1917.

Temporary Duma representation, then removed, deeply affected peasant politics (Haimson 1979; Vinogradoff 1979). Peasants were now brought into contact with Leftist political parties. Common exclusion from citizenship brought popular classes together and turned them Leftward, as we have also seen in other countries. Mensheviks and Bolsheviks were hindered by their orthodox Marxian concern with production relations, but the Social Revolutionary party stressed the more Weberian class issues of income distribution and credit, and their peasant unions played a major role in the 1917 revolution. The regime fell apart as it had in 1905 because of defeat in war and administrative breakdown; as in 1905, peasant insurrections were central to the revolutionary process; as in 1905, middle peasants took the lead; and as in 1905, the basis of peasant disorders was demand for land.

Thus Russian peasant movements must be understood in terms of virtually total exclusion, along with workers, from citizenship and of the regime's interference in their local economic position. Most Russian peasants were not independent proprietors, nor did they want to be.

Their demand for land and that it be farmed communally was not based on insecurity wrought by modernizing capitalism, as Wolf and Jenkins maintain, but on their negative experience of an autocratic capitalism that produced no benefits for them. Unlike in any other country, there was little successful capitalist agriculture in Russia, even on large estates. Only the Russian peasantry resisted modernization, simply demanding land, refusing to sever communal bonds, both before and after 1917. Russian peasants wished to remain apolitical, but they were forced by the regime into self-defense through revolution.

Conclusion

I have confirmed the complexity of agrarian politics. The problem lay neither with large estate farmers whose politics were uniformly conservative nor with landless laborers whose politics varied simply according to their ability to free themselves from local segmental controls. Peasant proprietors, many of them dwarfholders, posed the major problems for theory, as they did for contemporary politics. They had a strong sense of their own collective identity, and they organized effectively to secure their interests – quite the opposite of Marx's "sack of potatoes." They were intrinsically neither conservative (as Marx, Moore, Paige, and Stinchcombe argue) nor revolutionary (as Wolf, Brustein, and Judt argue). Most of their economic demands implied a moderate agrarian reformism mixing Weberian credit class with sectoral interests. Marxian production classes appeared among them only where tenancy and sharecropping predominated and they had space to organize. Creditor-debtor class conflict increased as agriculture became commercialized, reinforced by sectoral cleavage, since most creditors belonged to the urban capitalist class. Here their opponent was primarily the capitalist class.

Yet peasants were generally reformist; they sought specific government interventions against unregulated international markets dominated by big capital. Peasants outside of Russia made similar demands: usually for higher tariffs, always for reduced costs of credit, transport, and manufactured goods, equitable access to land, and legal protection of small proprietorship. Yet beyond this, peasants, like most agrarians, looked with suspicion at central states and wished to avoid them. Only in the sphere of education, and not even consistently there, did agrarian laborers and peasants much welcome the growing civilian scope of the late nineteenth-century state. Theirs was not reformist socialism, though it did seek limited state interventions for redistributive goals. Peasant collective identities and interests, even more than workers', were deeply ambiguous.

Thus reform movements spanned most of the political spectrum from Right to Left. Variation was not determined principally by economic factors, as most writers contend. True, economic variations did matter, as noted especially in France and Scandinavia, but political crystallizations mattered more. Peasant politics emanated primarily from their insertion in representative and national struggles for citizenship. These caught them up in the two great class struggles of urban-industrial politics – bourgeois liberalism versus landed old regime conservatism, then labor versus capital. But they were also caught up in struggles over how "national" and centralized the state should be. Because agrarians were territorially dispersed, they usually supported decentralizing local-regional movements.

The importance of churches in agrarian politics did not result primarily from greater peasant religiosity, although religiosity was at the forefront of many agrarian movements. Its roots lay, rather, in the common interests of some churches and rural populations in a relatively decentralized confederal state, as we saw in (Chapter 18) was also the case in worker politics. The agrarian politics of religion and region (eventually of "nation" in Austria) were entwined, politically structuring peasant identities and interests arising from the global commercialization of agriculture. This also made them usually ambivalent about the extension of state civilian scope, which centered in this period on state provision or regulation of mass education.

Peasants seldom formed a political majority. Where a numerical majority their power was lessened by restricted franchises and parliamentary sovereignties. They needed one or more of four main class-sectoral allies: bourgeois liberals, old regime conservatives, capitalists, or labor. In different regions and countries they allied with all four: across North Germany with old regime conservatives, then with capitalists; in Sweden with bourgeois liberals, then with labor; all four alliances occurred across France; and there were many varying alliances in other countries and regions. Peasants would seemingly ally with anyone – a third reason, besides their numbers and pragmatic moderation, why they constituted the crucial swing vote of the entire era.

Why did peasants choose or drift into one alliance rather than another? The definition of credit class and sectoral identities and opponents was malleable. Opponents and allies might choose themselves. Industrial labor was a problematic ally. Although both farmers and labor often viewed corporate capital as an opponent, their demands were rarely identical, except for lower, more progressive taxation and conscription. Sometimes peasant demands conflicted with labor's, as in calls for tariffs, reduced land taxes, and higher prices for agricultural products. More often they were just different. Urban-industrial movements of Right and Left often forgot that peasants had their own agenda. Conservatives mistakenly counted on supposedly traditional segmental controls over peasants, but peasant proprietors rarely accepted these controls without benefit. Leftist parties were generally worse offenders. There could have been more agrarian Leftism, more worker-peasant alliances than actually emerged. The Left was itself substantially to blame, blinkered by its experience in urban-industrial ghettos, concentrating on the mutualist needs of trade unions and debating productivist socialisms.

The worst offenders were Marxist parties, the German Social Democrats and Austrian socialists. Their productivism, also criticized in Chapters 15 and 17, was not merely academic. It had practical consequences. Marxist parties had a manufacturing-centered view of social development itself. They believed agriculture was collapsing and peasants were about to be proletarianized – hardly a message agrarians would warm to. Even pragmatic theorists like Kautsky and Lenin could not liberate themselves from this view. Because of the authoritative nature of manufacturing production and their own exclusion from citizenship in authoritarian states, Marxist parties developed a statist socialism. This also had little appeal to rural populations. Most peasants favored decentralized, confederal states. Long before the late twentieth century, workers were rejecting statist socialism in both East and West, and peasants were turning their backs on it.

Here the labor movement was making its most devastating mistake. The working class remained unarmed everywhere, and a minority in every country except Britain. It could not take on its class opponents without rural allies. Yet productivist statist ideologies blocked this very alliance. Labor was destroying its chances of achieving revolutionary change. Without farmers it would make little progress for another fifty years – until farmers finally did decline so far in numbers as to be largely ignored, in British fashion – and then it was probably too late. All that was left for the proletarian revolution in the twentieth century was the great and unpleasant opportunism of Lenin and Stalin. They manipulated peasant and national revolts against centralized autocracy and militarism and then subordinated them to productivist, statist, and eventually highly authoritarian Marxism.

This did not occur everywhere, however. In Scandinavia, Czech lands, and parts of France, worker-agrarian alliances were sought and achieved. Here were special circumstances. First, their states had early become relatively national; there were no significant decentralizing, confederal movements among the rural population (i.e., in Czech lands below the level of the provincial-national diet). Second, in Sweden, Denmark, and France, industrialization had also occurred in the countryside. There was less segregation between an urban-industrial and a rural-agrarian sector; they actually interpenetrated within households. In Sweden and Denmark, this encouraged a diffuse notion of social citizenship espoused by non-Marxist socialists; in France, it encouraged ideological factionalism. In neither country did there emerge two segregated political party movements, the one industrial, the other agrarian. This outcome was not rendered impossible elsewhere. Counterarguments to productivism and statism were heard and vigorously debated in most countries, but in the end they lost. It might have been otherwise. Just as some old regimes made disastrous mistakes and perished whereas others learned and adapted, so did workers' movements. When revolutionaries committed mistakes, they often paid with their lives.

Thus the mistakes of the Right and especially of the Left made a difference to outcomes. If peasants found no existing sympathetic party, they formed their own, as did American Populists (unsuccessfully) and various Austro-Hungarian peasantries (some highly successfully). Alternatively, adept mainstream parties, such as Germany's Catholic Center, Sweden's Social Democrats (eventually), and rival French parties, realized the importance of peasant support (especially as suffrages widened) and modified their platforms to win their votes.

Economic issues, though principally motivating political action, rarely determined peasant politics. Rather, the crystallizations of the states in which peasants pursued their interests explain the main colorations of rural struggles. I have not argued that politics simply determines class struggle, weighting economic versus political variables in some ultimate sense. Rather, outcomes were determined by (1) underlying *similarities* of class and sectoral interests, under the impact of an essentially similar global commercialization of capitalism, interacting with (2) very *different* political crystallizations on representation and the national question, connecting peasants to state regimes and party alliances in fundamentally different ways. This is strikingly similar to my conclusions about the outcomes of industrial class struggles.

Bibliography

Anderson, P. 1974. *Lineages of the Absolutist State*. London: New Left Books.
Bairoch, P., et al. 1968. *The Working Population and Its Structure*. Brussels: Editions de l'Institut de Sociologie de l'Université Libre.
Barral, P. 1968. *Les Agrariens Francais de Méline à Pisan*. Paris: Librairie Armand Colin.
Berger, S. 1972. *Peasants Against Politics*. Cambridge, Mass.: Harvard University Press.

Blackbourn, D. 1977. The Mittelstand in German society and politics, 1871–1914. *Social History*, no. 4.

    1984. Peasants and politics in Germany, 1871–1914. *European History Quarterly* 14.

Bois, P. 1960. *Paysans de l'Ouest*. Le Mans: Vilaire.

Boyer, J. W. 1981. *Political Radicalism in Late Imperial Vienna*. Chicago: University of Chicago Press.

Brenner, R. 1976. Agrarian class structure and economic development in pre-industrial Europe. *Past and Present*, no. 70.

Bruchey, S. 1965. *The Roots of American Economic Growth, 1607–1861*. New York: Harper & Row.

Brustein, W. 1988. *The Social Origins of Political Regionalism: France, 1849–1981*. Berkeley: University of California Press.

Buck, S. 1913. *The Granger Movement*. Cambridge, Mass.: Harvard University Press.

Burbank, G. 1976. *When Farmers Voted Red*. Westport, Conn.: Greenwood Press.

Burnham, W. 1974. The United States: the politics of heterogeneity. In *Electoral Behavior: A Comparative Handbook*, ed. R. Rose. New York: Free Press.

Castles, F. 1978. *The Social Democratic Image of Society*. London: Routledge & Kegan Paul.

Conze, W. 1969. The effects of nineteenth-century liberal agrarian reforms on social structure in central Europe. In *Essays in European Economic History, 1789–1914*, ed. Crouzet, Chaloner, and Stern. London: Arnold.

Danhof, C. 1969. *Change in Agriculture: The Northern United States, 1820–1870*. Cambridge, Mass.: Harvard University Press.

Dovring, F. 1965. *Land and Labor in Europe in the Twentieth Century*. The Hague: Nijhoff.

Duncan, S. 1982. Class relations and historical geography: the creation of the rural and urban questions in Sweden. *Research Papers in Geography* (University of Sussex), no. 12.

Dyson, L. 1986. *Farmers' Organizations*. New York: Greenwood Press.

Eddie, S. 1967. The changing pattern of leadership in Hungary, 1867–1914. *Economic History Review* 20.

Eley, G. 1980. *Reshaping the German Right: Radical Nationalism and Change After Bismarck*. New Haven, Conn.: Yale University Press.

Esping-Andersen, G. 1985. *Politics Against Markets: The Social Democratic Road to Power*. Princeton, N.J.: Princeton University Press.

Farr, I. 1978. Populism in the countryside: the peasant leagues in Bavaria in the 1890s. In *Society and Politics in Wilhelmine Germany*, ed. Richard J. Evans. London: Croom Helm.

    1986. Peasant protest in the empire – the Bavarian example. In *Peasants and Lords in Modern Germany: Recent Studies in Agricultural History*, ed. R. Moeller. Boston: Allen & Unwin.

Fine, N. 1928. *Labor and Farmer Parties in the United States, 1828–1928*. New York: Rand School of Social Science.

Fischer, F. W., et al. 1982. *Sozialgeschichtliches Arbeitsbuch*. Vol. I: *Materialien zur Statistik des Deutschen Bundes, 1815–1870*. Munich: Beck.

Garrier, G. 1973. *Paysans du Beaujolais et du Lyonnais, 1800–1970*. Grenoble: Presses Universitaires de Grenoble.

Gerschenkron, A. 1943. *Bread and Democracy in Germany*. Berkeley: University of California Press.

Goodwyn, L. 1976. *Democratic Promise: The Populist Moment in America*. New York: Oxford University Press.

Grantham, G. 1975. Scale and organization in French farming, 1840–1880. In *European Peasants and Their Markets*, ed. E. L. Jones and W. N. Parker. Princeton, N. J.: Princeton University Press.

Green, J. 1976. *Grass Roots Socialism*. Baton Rouge: Louisiana State University Press.

Haggard, H. R. 1971. *Rural Denmark and Its Lessons*. London: Longman Group.

Haimson, L. 1979. Introduction: the Russian landed nobility and the system of the third of June, and Conclusion: observations on the politics of the Russian countryside (1905–14). In *The Politics of Rural Russia*, ed. L. Haimson. Bloomington: Indiana University Press.

Hanak, P. 1975. Economics, society, and sociopolitical thought in Hungary during the age of capitalism. *Austrian History Yearbook 9*.

Hicks, J. 1931. *The Populist Revolt*. Minneapolis: University of Minnesota Press.

Hobsbawm, E. 1989. *The Age of Empire*. New York: Vintage Books.

Hohorst, V. G., et al. 1975. *Sozialgeschichtliches Arbeitsbuch*. Vol. I: *Materialien zur Statistik des Kaiserreichs, 1870–1914*. Munich: Beck.

Holmsen, A. 1956. Landowners and tenants in Norway. *Scandinavian Economic History Review 6*.

Hovde, B. 1943. *The Scandinavian Countries, 1720–1865*. Boston: Chapman & Grimes.

Hussain, A. 1981. *Marxism and the Agrarian Question*. Vol. 1: *German Social Democracy and the Peasantry, 1890–1907*. London: Macmillan.

Jenkins, J. C. 1986. Why do peasants rebel? structural and historical theories of modern peasant rebellions. *American Journal of Sociology 88*.

Jonasson, O. G. 1938. *Agricultural Atlas of Sweden*. Stockholm: Lantbruks-saellskapets.

Judt, T. 1979. *Socialism in Provence, 1871–1914*. Cambridge: Cambridge University Press.

Kane, A., and M. Mann. 1992. A theory of early twentieth-century agrarian politics. *Social Science History 16*.

Kausel, A. 1979. Osterreichs Volkseinkommen 1830 bis 1913. In *Geschichte und Ergebrisse der Zentralen Amtlichen Statistik in Osterreich 1829–1979. Beitrage zur Osterreichischen Statistik 550*.

Kautsky, K. 1988. *The Agrarian Question*. London: Zwan. (First published 1899.)

Kuhnle, S. 1975. *Patterns of Social and Political Mobilization: A Historical Analysis of the Nordic Countries*. London: Sage.

Kuuse, J. 1971. Mechanisation, commercialisation and the protectionist movement in Swedish agriculture, 1860–1910. *Scandinavian Economic History Review 19*.

Le Goff, T. J. A., and D. M. G. Sutherland. 1983. The social origins of counter-revolution in western France. *Past and Present*, no. 99.

Lewis, G. 1978. The peasantry, rural change and conservative agrarianism:

Lower Austria at the turn of the century. *Past and Present*, no. 81.

Linz, J. 1976. Patterns of land tenure, division of labor, and voting behavior in Europe. *Comparative Politics* 8.

Loubère, L. A. 1974. *Radicalism in Mediterranean France, 1848–1914*. Albany: State University of New York Press.

Lyashchenko, P. 1949. *History of the National Economy of Russia to the 1917 Revolution*. New York: Macmillan.

Macartney, C. A. 1969. *The Hapsburg Empire, 1790–1918*. London: Weidenfeld & Nicolson.

Malefakis, E. 1970. *Agrarian Reform and Peasant Revolution in Spain*. New Haven, Conn.: Yale University Press.

Margadant, T. W. 1979. *French Peasants in Revolt*. Princeton, N. J.: Princeton University Press.

Marx, K., and F. Engels. 1968. *Selected Works*. Moscow: Progress Publishers.

Medvedev, Z. 1987. *Soviet Agriculture*. New York: Norton.

Merriman, J. 1979. Incident at the statue of the Virgin Mary: the conflict of the old and the new in nineteenth century Limoges. In *Consciousness and Class Experience in Nineteenth Century Europe*, ed. J. Merriman. New York: Holmes & Meier.

Ministère de l'agriculture. 1897. *Statistique agricole de la France; résultats généraux de l'enquête decennale de 1892*. Paris.

Moore, B., Jr. 1973. *Social Origins of Dictatorship and Democracy*. Harmondsworth: Penguin Books.

Mouzelis, N. 1986. *Politics in the Semi-Periphery: Early Parliamentarianism and Late Industrialization in the Balkans and Latin America*. New York: St. Martin's Press.

Munch, P. 1954. The peasant movement in Norway: a study in class and culture. *British Journal of Sociology* 5.

Newby, H. 1977. *The Deferential Worker*. London: Lane.

Osterud, O. 1971. *Agrarian Structure and Peasant Politics in Scandinavia: A Comparative Study of Rural Response to Economic Change*. Oslo: Universitetsforlaget.

Paige, J. 1976. *Agrarian Revolution*. New York: Free Press.

Pavlovsky, G. 1930. *Agricultural Russia on the Eve of the Revolution*. London: Routledge & Kegan Paul.

Pech, S. 1978. Political parties in Eastern Europe, 1848–1939. *East Central Europe* 5.

Perkins, J. A. 1981. The agricultural revolution in Germany, 1850–1914. *Journal of European Economic History* 10.

Perrie, M. 1972. The Russian peasant movement of 1905–1907: its social composition and revolutionary significance. *Past and Present*, no. 57.

Raeff, M. 1966. *Origins of the Russian Intelligentsia: The Eighteenth Century Nobility*. New York: Harcourt, Brace & World.

Robinson, G. 1932. *Rural Russia Under the Old Regime*. Berkeley: University of California Press.

Rokkan, S. 1970. *Cities, Elections, Parties*. Oslo: Universitetsforlaget.

Rosen, E. 1978. Socialism in Oklahoma: a theoretical overview. *Politics and Society* 8.

Rothstein, M. 1988. Farmer movements and organizations: numbers, gains, and losses. *Agricultural History* 62.

Rueschemeyer, D., E. Stephens, and J. Stephens. 1992. *Capitalist Development and Democracy*. Chicago: University of Chicago Press.

Sandgruber, R. 1978. *Österreichische Agrärstatistik, 1750–1918*. Munich: Oldenbourg.

See, H. 1929. *Equisse d'une Histoire Economique et Sociale de la France*. Paris: Alcan.

Semmingsen, I. 1954. The dissolution of estate society in Norway. *Scandinavian Economic History Review* 2.

Shanin, T. 1972. *The Awkward Class*. Oxford: Clarendon Press.

1985. *Russia as a "Developing Society": The Roots of Otherness – Russia's Turn of the Century*, Vol. I. London: Macmillan.

Sked, A. 1989. *The Decline and Fall of the Hapsburg Empire, 1815–1918*. London: Arnold.

Skocpol, T. 1979. *States and Social Revolutions: A Comparative Analysis of France, Russia and China*. Cambridge: Cambridge University Press.

Smith, J. H. 1975. Work routine and social structure in a French village: Cruzy in the nineteenth century. *Journal of Interdisciplinary History* 3.

Sorokin, P. A., et al. 1930. *A Systematic Source Book in Rural Sociology*. Minneapolis: University of Minnesota Press.

Stephens, J. 1979. *The Transition from Capitalism to Socialism*. London: Macmillan.

Stinchcombe, A. L. 1961. Agricultural enterprise and rural class relations. *American Journal of Sociology* 67.

Thomas, A. 1977. Social democracy in Denmark. In *Social Democratic Parties in Western Europe*, ed. W. Paterson and A. Thomas. London: Croom Helm.

Tilly, C. 1967. *The Vendée*, 3d ed. New York: John Wiley.

1979. Did the cake of custom break? In *Consciousness and Class Experience in Nineteenth Century Europe*, ed. J. Merriman. New York: Holmes & Meier.

Tomasevich, J. 1955. *Peasants, Politics, and Economic Change in Yugoslavia*. Stanford, Calif.: Stanford University Press.

U.S. Census Bureau. 1910. *U.S. Census, 1910*. Washington, D.C.: U.S. Government Printing Office.

Vinogradoff, E. 1979. The Russian peasantry and the elections to the Fourth State Duma. In *The Politics of Rural Russia*, ed. L. Haimson. Bloomington: Indiana University Press.

Volin, L. 1960. The Russian peasant: from emancipation to kolkhoz. In *The Transformation of the Russian Peasantry*, ed. C. Black. Cambridge, Mass.: Harvard University Press.

Walkin, J. 1962. *The Rise of Democracy in Pre-revolutionary Russia*. New York: Praeger.

Weber, E. 1978. *Peasants Into Frenchmen*. Stanford, Calif.: Stanford University Press.

Weber, M. 1978. *Economy and Society*. Berkeley: Univeristy of California Press.

Wolf, E. 1969. *Peasant Wars of the Twentieth Century*. New York: Harper & Row.

20 Theoretical conclusions: Classes, states, nations, and the sources of social power

This volume has two concluding chapters. This, the first one, begins where Chapter 7 left off, generalizing about the rise of the two major actors of modern times – classes and nation-states – then about the four sources of social power during the period. Because the five countries covered (Austria, Britain, France, Prussia-Germany, and the United States) all differed, I must strike a balance between generalization and acknowledgment of uniqueness. But because history passed its own conclusion on the long nineteenth century, in the form of World War I, the final chapter will analyze the causes of that war, exemplifying and justifying the theory underlying this volume.

As we have seen, states were entwined with both classes and nations. I shall not once again summarize my research on states; rather, I refer the reader to the conclusion of Chapter 14. Here I repeat only the essential point: As the state became more socially significant through late eighteenth-century military and late nineteenth-century industrial capitalist expansion, it partially "naturalized" the West and its classes.

Classes and states

By the time of World War I, the entire West was becoming industrial. Britain and Belgium already were so, most countries were evenly balanced between industry and agriculture, and agriculture was also thoroughly commercialized. Capitalism had enormously accelerated human collective powers, predominantly diffusely, right across this multi-power-actor civilization. Its second industrial spurt, from the 1880s on, enhanced the material conditions of all classes and both sexes, enabling the conquest of bare subsistence and the near doubling of the human life span. Though unequally distributed, the benefits were spread so broadly that most power actors agreed that authoritative power institutions should support capitalist expansion. The scope of state civilian infrastructures now broadened. Capitalism and state bureaucratization developed similarly across the West.

Capitalism also transformed all countries' distributive power relations, generating extensive and political classes on a scale unparalleled in history. There emerged first a bourgeoisie and a petite bourgeoisie,

723

then a middle class, a working class, and a peasant class – all non-dominant classes with enlarged authoritative powers of collective organization. All these classes believed (despite the benefits) that they were exploited by dominant classes and political regimes, and all mounted collective protest seeking alternatives. This was evident to Marx and to most subsequent observers. More important, it was also evident to dominant classes and ruling regimes. Yet the outcomes of distributive conflict were not what Marx expected, for four reasons:

1. Because capitalism was predominantly a diffused power organization, its authoritative class organization emerged as essentially ambivalent. Bourgeoisies, petite bourgeoisies, and middle classes were economically heterogeneous. Without intervention from the other sources of social power, their conflicts with dominant classes and regimes turned out partial, mild, and particularistic. Over the first half of the period many compromised and even merged without much drama. Agrarian classes, especially the peasantry, developed as heterogeneous, generating three competing collective organizations: as "production classes," as "credit classes," and as an economic sector (in a segmental alliance with large estate farmers, their usual opponents on the other two dimensions). The proletariat also generated three collective organizational tendencies: class, sectionalism, and segmentalism. Thus the economic development of capitalism produced multiple collective organizations, among which classes, though inherently developing the dialectical conflict Marx expected, by no means dominated.

2. The outcomes of competition among these competing economic organizations were determined predominantly by the strategies or drifts of more authoritatively organized dominant classes and ruling regimes, which, after all, controlled existing authoritative states and armed forces. Providing they were concentrating hard on the emerging class confrontation (and that was not always so, as we shall see), most worked out an effective counterstrategy. This was not unusual. I have argued throughout that where class conflict is relatively transparent – that is, where it has the capacity to generate head-on class confrontation of the type Marx expected to result in revolution – then that is where ruling classes and regimes can most effectively use their greater institutionalized power to repress and to divide their opponent. Revolutions, I argued, occur where ruling classes and regimes become confused by the emergence of multiple, nondialectial but entwined conflicts. In this case the most effective regime strategy against transparent capital-labor conflict was to make concessions to some workers and peasants through sectionalism and segmentalism while repressing the rest. By this means they could undercut the class unity required for revolution or aggressive reform. The very emergence, simultaneously,

of three forms of worker organization undercut class because it required hegemony over workers, whereas the other two did not.

3. In turn, the strategies or drifts of dominant classes and regimes, and so therefore of workers themselves, were predominantly determined by the other three sources of social power. I refer the reader to Chapter 7 for my summary of the outcomes of economic struggles up to the 1830s or 1840s. There I stress diffuse ideological but especially authoritative military and then political power sources. Chapters 17–19 give a more political explanation of later worker and peasant movements. Thus, about 1900, outcomes of capital-labor conflict throughout the West were determined by (1) an essentially similar global diffusion of capitalism generating a common ambiguity of collective organizations and interests, interacting with (2) various crystallizations of authoritative states – ideological, patriarchal, military, but especially their two citizen crystallizations, on "representative" and "national" issues.

4. These interactions were not like billiard-ball collisions of separate objects. Classes, segments, and sections all "entwined nondialectically" with authoritative political crystallizations, thus helping to shape one another. Actors' very identities and interests were changed behind their backs by the unintended consequences of action. In such an uncertain environment, actors were prone to make "systemic mistakes." Chapter 6 shows how the French regime of 1789 made disastrous mistakes because it did not appreciate the emerging, developing nature of its opponent. Chapter 15 illustrates the inverse. Rather unusually, dominant classes controlling a state were faced "dialectically" by a single, fairly homogeneous class opponent, Chartism. Confronting the enemy squarely, they made no mistakes, firmly repressing its militants and forcing workers with greater market powers toward sectionalism. The last chapters have revealed more persistent world-historical mistakes made by excessively productivist and statist labor movements, under the influence of Marxism or Lutheranism, peculiarly unable to appreciate the distinctive complexities of agrarian struggles and thus converting potential peasant allies into enemies.

These four determinants were not merely external to one another. They were entwined, shaping one another's form. The relevance of regime strategies-drifts, of representative and national citizen struggles, of unintended consequences, and of mistakes derived from the way they strengthened class, sectional, or segmental identities according to context. Class, sectionalism, and segmentalism continued to battle over the souls of workers and peasants. In terms of their relations to the means of production, battle was joined in both industry and agriculture on deeply ambivalent terms, without decisive outcomes in this period. Of course, persistent sectionalism and segmentalism did undercut and undermine the broad unity required by class action. In a capitalist world without states this may have permanently weakened labor in relation to capital, and almost certainly it would have prevented revolutionary, even aggressively reformist, outcomes. Yet capitalism inhabited a world of states. In this period, ambivalent tendencies toward class, sectional, and segmental organization were mostly boosted or reversed, often unintentionally, by authoritative representative and national political crystallizations, especially as they impacted on labor-peasant alliances. Classes were not purely economic; nor were states purely political.

Capitalism and industrialism have both been overrated. Their diffused powers exceeded their authoritative powers, for which they relied more on, and were shaped by, military and political power organizations. Though both capitalism and industrialism vastly increased collective powers, distributive powers – social stratification – were less altered. Modern class relations were galvanized by the first and second industrial revolutions and by the global commercialization of agriculture, but they were propelled forward along inherently ambivalent tracks in which varying outcomes were determined by authoritative political crystallizations that had been mostly institutionalized rather earlier.

Why were states already so diverse? Charles Tilly reminds us that European states had originated in the medieval period in many forms – territorial monarchies, loose networks of prince-lord-vassal personal relations, conquest states, city-states, ecclesiastical city-states, leagues of cities, communes, and so forth. Although Tilly charts a decline in state types throughout the early modern period, as territorial states stabilized and came to dominate, much variety remained. The fragmenting of Christendom added religious variety. States varied especially in relations between the capital and the regions. In 1760, Anglican Britain was moderately homogeneous and centralized, absorbing Scottish, Welsh, and Nonconformist regionalism, but with an adjacent imperial colony, Catholic Ireland. Catholic France had a highly centralized monarchy, but with highly particularistic relations with its regions (which also fell into two distinct constitutional types). Lutheran Prussia was a fairly compact state closely integrating monarchy and the nobility of the dominant region. Catholic Austria was a confederal monarchy containing regional religious minorities and languages. America was a series of separate, expanding colonies. All states differed, grossly. States are territorial and territories are laid out in very particular fashion.

Territorial particularity was enhanced by agrarian economies, diminished by industrial ones. Today, in advanced (or post-) industrial society, the economic activities in Britain, France, and Germany are remarkably similar because modern economies transform most of the products of nature many times. But agrarian economies depend on ecology – on the soil, vegetation, climate, and water – and these vary by locality. The ecology of agrarian Europe was unusually varied, in economists' jargon offering a "dispersed portfolio of resources." But as capitalism developed, "national" economies became more similar (as Chapter 14 notes).

Capitalism is an unusually diffused form of power organization, whereas states are essentially authoritative. Especially in its industrial stage, increasingly liberated from the particularities of territory, capitalism spread right through the West in rather similar forms. Its diffused power also allows fairly "free" choice of alternative strategies, more unfinished competition, for collective as well as individual actors. Workers and employers, peasants and large estate farmers may make varied local arrangements that permit class, sectional, and segmental strategies to continue and compete. Yet states, by their very nature as a distinct source of social power, authoritatively allocate and institutionalize. Although parties and state elites may argue and reduce state coherence, laws regarding civil rights, suffrage, state centralization, conscription, tariffs, unions, and so forth, must be laid down authoritatively.

The modern state had first institutionalized the many territorial particularities of Europe. Then states greatly expanded as they faced two waves of common regulatory problems, emanating from the increased militarism of the eighteenth century and the capitalist development lasting through 1914. In this period, states became large, socially relevant, and distinctively "modern." The ways this happened now had an immense impact on social development. Yet, in their expanded roles, they first coped with the particular institutions developed amid the more "territorial" era. In the first phase of expansion, militarism interacted with these to result in distinctive "modernized" institutions in each state: America institutionalized its unique constitution; France institutionalized conflict over its constitution; Britain institutionalized old regime liberalism; Prussia, semiauthoritarianism; and Austria (less successfully) attempted to give its dynasticism more infrastructurally penetrative powers. Modern states – induced by eighteenth-century militarism and nineteenth-century industrial capitalism – now enormously increased their social significance. Thus the structuring power of their existing authoritative institutions, forged in interaction between an earlier age and the militarist phase, also grew. After about the 1830s, most countries' political institutions had a solidity absorbing almost all that industrial society could throw at them.

A second dialectic beside Marx's class dialectic was occurring, between what I label "interstitial emergence" and "institutionalization." Because societies are constituted by multiple, overlapping networks of interaction, they perennially produce emergent collective actors whose relations with older actors are not yet institutionalized but then become so. Classes and nations were emergent actors par excellence. They took dominant classes and regimes by surprise, and no existing institutions were directly designed to cope with them. Instead, dominant classes and regimes made do with the institutions designed for older, more territorially particular purposes. States did not grow primarily to cope with emerging classes and nations (but to fight costlier wars and then to assist industrialization), but their enlarged institutions bore much of the brunt of social control. Thus they increasingly determined class and national outcomes.

I give an example of this from Chapters 17 and 18: the diverging development of the American, British, and German labor movements. I focus here only on two forms of authoritative power, state representative and military crystallizations (for a fuller, more adequate explanation, consult those chapters). Eighteenth-century Britain had developed an embryonic form of party democracy primarily to institutionalize "court" and "country," dynastic and religious conflicts. Britain also lacked an effective home army (except in Ireland). Hence coping with emerging middling classes depended mostly on Parliament, and Parliament did cope. By 1820, Prussia had institutionalized noble-professional conflicts primarily within its royal administration and its army. These also helped the regime institutionalize middling classes, especially when the army gained legitimacy by turning Prussia into Germany. The German regime then also made innovative use of limited party democracy, which also bent the middle class Rightward. American party democracy originated primarily to institutionalize relations between large and small farmers. American military and paramilitary organizations developed largely to kill Indians.

When the proletariat emerged, dominant classes and regimes in the three countries handled it very differently. This was not because the British had a "genius for compromise" (until after midcentury they repressed more than they compromised) or because Germans were authoritarian or Americans schizophrenic. Most capitalists and politicians in all three countries wanted the same thing: to preserve order yet keep their privileges. But they had different authoritative state institutions already to hand for accomplishing these tasks. The British had competitive parties and a franchise whose relationship to class boundaries had varied and could vary again – but not much of a home army. The Germans had institutionalized a divide-and-rule party strategy excluding radical parties – and they had a large army whose shows of force had considerable domestic legitimacy. The Americans had competitive parties – but they also had military and paramilitary forces experienced in crude domestic repression. Thus similar emerging labor movements were deflected by different available state institutions along different tracks. Britain developed mild mutualism; Germany, a rather ritualized encounter between a reactionary state and capitalism and an ostensibly revolutionary Marxism, and America, greater violence and sectionalism and little socialism.

In all these encounters state institutions also changed, but more slowly than capitalism developed and classes emerged. The theoretical model appropriate for this phase of world history – with common diffusing capitalism entwined with more particular authoritative state institutions – is a kind of "political lag" theory, such as I teased out from the institutional theory of the state identified in Chapter 3. Variations between state institutions fostered various "collective laborers" in this period. This casts doubt on all theories asserting that capitalist development necessarily brings *any* determinant set of power relations between capital and labor – whether the theory is Marxist, reformist, or liberal. The collective laborer has been more malleable than these theories would suggest, compliant with (or unable to change) a number of regimes, and capable of crystallizing in many forms.

Indeed, this period seems to have institutionalized more diverse class relations than has more recent advanced capitalism, dominated by party democracies. Throughout most of the twentieth century, authoritarian regimes fared badly. Autocracy and semiauthoritarian monarchy disappeared as dominant strategies from the West, although comparable nonmonarchical regimes exist in many developing countries. Most Western theories have argued that this decline in variety and in authoritarianism was inevitable, the working out of the "logic of industrialism," of the "age of democracy" or of the "institutionalization of class conflict" – variant forms of modernization theory. Evolutionary theories have been boosted by the sudden collapse of twentieth-century authoritarian socialism in the Soviet bloc. But has there been such a "logic"? Why were tsarism, Imperial Germany – indeed, more than half the modernizing regimes – doomed? Were they stumbling and scheming to a viable alternative set of modern power relations to party democracy? These questions await Volume III. But one issue can be addressed here: Because authoritarian regimes bring militarism more directly into class regulation, this may make them vulnerable to war-induced demise. The causes of the Great War become critical to the first stage in assessing their viability.

Complexity in state crystallizations also turns us toward the war. Contemporary power actors found it as difficult to control outcomes as we find it to explain them. The consequences of their actions were often unintended. Class struggles – agrarian, industrial, or both – did not proceed according to their own pure logics. From beginning to end they were entwined with ideological, military, and political power relations that helped shape classes themselves. These now became even more complex as state militarism intensified. Chapter 21 traces the beginnings of this cataclysmic intervention.

Nations and states

Chapter 7 presents the first three phases of a four-phase theory of the nation. The religious and the commercial capitalist-statist phases occurred before the time period of this volume began, contributing only what I call "protonations." Then the militarist phase, detailed in Chapter 7, developed nations as real, partly cross-class, and occasionally aggressive actors. But nations came in three different types: state reinforcing (for example, England), state creating (Germany), and state subverting (across most Austrian lands). I now summarize the fourth, *industrial capitalist*, phase of these varied nations.

During the second half of the nineteenth century and the early twentieth, the industrial phase of capitalism, its class struggles, and its impact on the state reinforced emerging nations. States for the first time undertook major civilian functions, sponsoring communications systems; canals, roads, post offices, railways, telegraph systems, and, most significantly, schools. States were largely responding to the needs of industrialism, as articulated primarily by capitalists, but also by other classes, by militaries, and by state elites. Because almost all valued the increasing collective powers of an industrial society, they urged the state on toward greater social coordination. In turn, state infrastructures enhanced the density of social interaction, but bounded by the state's territorial reach. We saw that social behavior – even intimate social behavior such as sexual mores – became "naturalized," more nationally homogeneous. Quite unconsciously, most state activities furthered the nation as an experienced community, linking the intensive and emotional organizations of family and neighborhood with more extensive and instrumental power organizations.

The nation was not a total community. Localism survived, as did regional, religious, linguistic, and class barriers within the nation. The Western ideological community and global capitalism also maintained transnational organization. Because capitalism, the modern state, militarism, mass discursive literacy, and industrialism increased overall social density, there was room for more national and transnational organization.

Nor was the nation an uncontested community. The popular, cross-class nation necessarily involved conceptions of citizenship (though of varying types). But these raised the two dominant political crystallizations of the nineteenth century, turning on the "representative" issue – who should be full citizens – and the "national" issue – where citizenship should be located, that is, how centralized the state and nation should be. I have stressed throughout that the national issue was important and as contentious as was representation. Few states started the period as nationally homogeneous: Most contained regions with distinct religious and linguistic communities, and many regions had their own political institutions, or memories of them.

The military and industrial capitalist phases of state expansion intensified both representative and national issues. The late eighteenth-century fiscal and conscription consequences of increased militarism resulted in greater representative pressures but very different crystallizations on the national issue, ranging from the centralization attempted by Jacobin revolutionaries to the confederalism of most Austrian dissidents. Yet the later industrial capitalist phase intensified pressures toward both more representative and more national societies. "Naturalization" was especially effective because it was unconscious, unintended, interstitial, and so unopposed. It involved the emotions as well as instrumental reason, subtly changing conceptions of communities of attachment.

Yet one area of state expansion in industrial capitalism remained contentious. Though most state infrastructures were expanded fairly consensually, mass education generated conflict with minority churches and regional linguistic communities. If minority churches were regionally entrenched, this could intensify state-subverting nationalism (as in Ireland or some Austrian lands). Educational expansion could also convey a subtler antistatism. Under growing representative pressures from emerging classes, no central regime now could simply impose its language on provinces with their own native vernaculars. The expansion of education in the province of Bohemia, for example, diffused a Czech more than an Austrian sense of nation. Conversely, throughout "greater Germany" and throughout Italy education encouraged a sense of nationhood extending across existing state boundaries. Thus, according to context, the industrial capitalist phase of the nation encouraged three different types of nations: state reinforcing, state creating, and state subverting.

Capitalism's class conflicts also fueled all three types of nations, according to local circumstance. The middle class, peasants, and workers became literate in native vernaculars, which, according to context, either further naturalized the existing state or fragmented the state into more popular regional nations (state fragmenting) or cross-state nations (state creating). Middle class, peasants, and workers demanded political representation, again with the same alternative consequences. By the late nineteenth century, popular nations – in all three guises – were mobilizing the middle class and many peasants and workers in all European countries.

In this phase, nations also became more passionate and aggressive. Passion derived principally from the tighter links between the state and the intensive, emotional sphere of family and neighborhood interaction in which state education and physical and moral health infrastructures loomed large. Ideologies saw the nation as mother or father, hearth and home writ large. Aggression resulted because all states continued to crystallize as militarist; all were geopolitically militarist, and some remained domestically so.

State-subverting nationalism became increasingly violent where repressive imperial regimes would not grant regional-national autonomies and representation. Especially if reinforced by religion, regional dissidents developed intense, emotional protest. Their family and local community lives reinforced their sense of difference from the exploiting imperial nation. The latter returned the sentiments to justify using domestic militarism against them. Each fueled the passion and the violence of the other.

Thus state-subverting nationalism has been most passionate and "fanatical" when nonrepresentative imperial regimes begin to lose their repressive grip. Western states that institutionalized class, but especially regional-national, representation have not experienced fanatic violence even when beset by deeply rooted interethnic disputes. Belgium and Canada may break up, but this would probably occur without fatalities. In contrast, hundreds have been killed in Northern Ireland because the province never institutionalized representation of the minority community while segregating the intimate lives of both communities. Thousands are being killed in Yugoslavia, and may be in the future in more than one formerly Soviet country, precisely because they have not institutionalized representative government amid distinct linguistic, sometimes religious, regional communities, many with their own historical political institutions. State-subverting ethnic violence is a product of authoritarian regimes, not of party democracies. This was so in the long nineteenth century. It appears still true today.

The increasing violence of state-reinforcing nationalism has centered on interstate wars. In 1900, about 40 percent of state budgets still went toward preparation for war. The use and threat of war was still central to their diplomacy. Military virtues were still a valued part of masculine culture; women were valued as the bearers and nurturers of future warriors. But now these states were becoming more representative and more national. It is often asserted that the middle class, peasants, and even sometimes workers began to identify their interests and their sense of honor with those of their state against other nation-states, endorsing aggressive nationalism. A rival class theory looks to see exactly who was represented in these states. It concludes that full political citizens, primarily the middle class, were the bearers of aggressive nationalism in alliance with old regimes. Indeed, I have emphasized that conceptions of capitalistic profit were also becoming embedded in this period with a supposed "national interest."

Overall, however, I look rather skeptically at these rival theories. There is a considerable difference between conceiving of oneself as a member of a national community, even if socialized into a mythology of common ethnicity, even common "race," and supporting any particular national policy, abroad or at home. Most conceptions of what the nation stood for were strongly contested. In France this was obvious, as Republicans, Monarchists, and Bonapartists strongly, emotionally adhered to rival conceptions of the meaning of "France." But also in mainland Britain the old radical "Protestant" conception of the popular nation, now more secular, fought against more conservative imperialist conceptions, and some liberals advocated a softer imperialism. Everywhere classes and minorities who experienced the sharp end of domestic militarism opposed militarism in general and aggressive nationalism in particular. In all countries, as class theorists argue, full citizens were more likely to endorse the state and its militarism as *theirs*. But I also demonstrated that state diplomacy and militarism remained strongly private, largely hidden from the scrutiny of popular groups, enfranchised or not. Thus aggressive nationalism (or, indeed, any strong foreign policy commitment) did not in fact spread deeply among most middle-class groups – and especially not among the much-maligned petite bourgeoisie.

Yet aggressive nationalism had broadened its appeal. As industrialism expanded states, two sets of tentacles extended an embrace over national society: the civilian and military administrations. Hundreds of thousands of administrators now depended for their livelihood on the state; millions of young men were disciplined by a military cadre into the peculiar morale, coercive yet emotionally attached, that is the hallmark of the modern mass army. These two bodies of men, and their families – not broader classes or communities – provided most of the core of extreme nationalism. They were what I call "superloyalists," with an exaggerated loyalty to what they conceived to be the ideals of their state. Not all were militarists or aggressive nationalists, as state ideals varied. British civilian officials might be attached to liberal ideals; French, to Republican ones; and German and Austrian, to more authoritarian ideals. But because all states were militarist, their servants were generally mobilizable at least to an ostensibly "defensive" militarism.

So in the fourth, industrial capitalist, phase of its relatively short life, the nation had advanced in three essential ways. First, much of the population, largely unconsciously, had become naturalized, making the nation an extensive community of interaction and emotional attachment. Thus what I call "national" organization increased at the large expense of the local and the regional (unless that now turned into a nation itself) and at the lesser expense of transnational organization. This is where the nation rested for most of the population. Second, many citizens – at this point drawn from middling and upper classes and from dominant religious and linguistic communities – were drawn further toward nationalist organization, regarding national interests and honor as essentially conflicting with those of other nations. Third, the actually nationalist core was disproportionately drawn from state expansion itself, in civilian and military cadre employment. Its ideals then resonated rather shallowly among the families of the citizens. Combined, they could aspire to mobilize the merely national remainder. As we shall see in Chapter 21, the problem was that national populations were now more confined within cages whose relations with other national cages were defined not by the people as a whole but first by private state and military elites, second by the nationalists. Aggressive nationalism would out, but largely behind the backs of most men who composed the nation.

In the industrial capitalist phase the state-reinforcing nation can be simply represented as three concentric circular bands: the outer one circumscribed by and attached to the total national state, the middle more linked to the inner circle, the statist core. More graphically and more relevant to what was to follow, the nation can be represented as that cartoonist's delight, the late nineteenth-century anarchist's bomb, a black, pudding-shaped ball with a protruding fuse. The fuse is composed of the statist nationalists; the combustible material is composed of the full citizens, whose shallow aggressive pressure endures long enough to cause the explosion, which is the enormous power of the military state hurling outward the jagged fragments, coercively disciplined workers and peasants. The fuse needed igniting, however.

While Europe failed to curb the traditional militarism of its states, ignition could occur. Its violence could be peculiarly nasty when entwining nationalist with class, and sometimes with religious, ideologies. Extreme nationalists could entwine with citizen classes and religions to identify those outside national citizenship but wanting in – the working class and regional, linguistic, and religious minorities – as enemies of the nation-state, *Reichsfeinde* in Germany. The most violent of these statist nationalists directed emotional hatred simultaneously against foreigners and *Reichsfeinde* within. But my model views not even the most extreme as, as it were, "irrational demons." To anticipate Volume III: The Nazis were recognizably just more extreme versions of the European statist nationalists whose emergence I have here charted – more violent, more authoritarian, more racist. They represented the most extreme way in which three Western state crystallizations – militarist, authoritarian, and capitalist – entwined. They received disproportionate core support from "betrayed," "superloyal" ex-frontline troops and state employees, and their ideology resonated most in Lutheran bourgeois and agrarian Germany.

Have I not so far narrated a conventional evolutionary tale of the rise of the nation-state, ever strengthening its sovereignty, its infrastructural powers, and its powers of national mobilization? Obviously state sovereignty has both widened and deepened. Yet, I doubt if these later enlarged states were actually as coherent in many ways as had been the late eighteenth-century British and Prussian states. For as more of social life became politicized, so did its conflicts and its confusions. As the scope of state functions widened, parties and states became more polymorphous. By 1900, politics concerned diplomacy, militarism, nationalism, political economy, centralization, secularization, mass education, welfare programs, temperance, votes for women, plus many more particular issues. Thus politics mobilized state elites against mass parties, class against class, sector against sector, church against church and secular state, peripheral regions against center, feminists against patriarchs – and many others. By comparison, eighteenth-century politics had been relatively simple.

Were states merely in a transitional phase, acquiring modern crystallizations, without having shed all traditional ones? This was truer of the surviving semiauthoritarian monarchies – Germany and Austria, where parliaments competed with courts and factions swirled through ministries to culminate around the monarch. But everywhere foreign policy generated distinctive crystallizations. Diplomacy was conducted largely by a few old regime families, somewhat insulated from nationally caged classes and mass parties, though now buffeted erratically by nationalist parties. Officer corps retained autonomy by combining bureaucratic profession with old regime class composition and ethos.

Officers and noncommissioned officers became a military caste somewhat insulated from civil society and civilian state. More generally,
though democracy, bureaucracy, and rational budgeting all sought
to set coherent political priorities, all remained highly imperfect by
1914. Even today democratic control over diplomacy and the military
remains feeble. It is difficult to regard the whole state as a single
cohesive entity; rather, plural elites and parties entwine with one
another in confused, varying ways.

Throughout the twentieth century, as state functions continued
to broaden, political crystallizations further diversified. Today, the
American state might crystallize as conservative-patriarchal-Christian
one week when restricting abortion rights, as capitalist the next when
regulating the savings and loans banking scandal, as a superpower the
next when sending troops abroad for other than national economic
interests. These varied crystallizations are rarely in harmony or in
dialectical opposition to one another; usually they just differ. They
mobilize differing, if overlapping and intersecting, power networks,
and their solutions have consequences, some unintended for each
other. It is a basic tenet of my work that societies are not systems.
There is no ultimately determining structure to our entire social experience – at least, none that we, situated in its midst, can discern.
The elites of many historic states were controlled by particular social
groups – princes, priests, or warrior bands. They enjoyed considerable
autonomy, yet caged little of social life. Their states embodied systemic qualities arising from their own particularities. But when states
became the center and radii through which much of social life is
regulated, they lost that systemic coherence.

Polymorphism has proved an enduring feature of modern states.
When states became important regulators of material subsistence and
profit, of ideologies, of intimate family life, as well as of diplomacy,
war, and repression, many more parties became activated in politics.
In dealing with individual states, I listed their principal crystallizations
and showed how they entwined in nonsystemic, nondialectical ways.
These structured the very identity of classes and nations, often in ways
hidden from the actors themselves. I pursue this, as it was pursued in
reality, "over the top," in Chapter 21.

The sources of social power

This volume has sustained the general propositions stated at the beginning of Chapter 1. It is possible to steer between Marx and Weber,
to make significant yet non-materialist generalizations concerning the
"ultimate" structuring of human societies – at least within the confined

time and space discussed here. After all qualifications and disclaimers are made, we can discern two major phases in both of which the overall structuring of Western society from 1760 to 1914 appeared as predominantly dual.

During the first phase, lasting roughly through the eighteenth century to 1815, diffused economic and authoritative military power relations dominated Western societies. Commercial capitalism and the enduring consequences of the military revolution enabled Europeans and their colonists to dominate the globe; commercial capitalism and military states completed the expansion of mass discursive literacy begun earlier by churches, adding to social density, extensively, intensively, and across class boundaries. Capitalism increased collective human ability to exploit nature, it expanded population, and it propelled the emergence of extensive classes and industrialization. Militarism politicized civil societies, their classes and their religious and linguistic communities, around contentious representative and national issues. Militarism strengthened large states and wiped out small ones.

Thereafter, the national state (the main product of these dual determinations) shed its puny historical frame and emerged interstitially – without anyone intending it – as a major authoritative power organization in its own right. At the end of the eighteenth century, citizenship struggles were already being structured by the degree to which states had institutionalized conflicts over increased taxes and conscription. Nineteenth-century capitalism continued to revolutionize collective productive powers, as geopolitics became more pacific and militarism more variable among states (especially domestically), more "private" and castelike within the state. Thus a second phase of dual determination emerged after midcentury. A predominantly (though not entirely) diffused industrial capitalism and the authoritative nation-state became the principal restructurers of Western society, the former providing essentially similar thrusts because so diffuse (and because so desired by all), the latter – principally through diverse representative and national crystallizations – providing most of the authoritative, varied solutions.

Because in both phases the two principal transformers were not colliding billiard balls but entwined, and because they generated emergent, interpenetrating collective actors – classes, nations, and modern states, plus their rivals – it is not possible to weight *their* interrelations. Neither can be accorded a Marxian-style accolade as the wielder of a singular "ultimate primacy" in society, although of course, the economic power of capitalism uniquely remained a part of both phases of dualism.

This civilization during the period came as near to a single general developmental process as any ever has. In no other time or place has human collective power, over nature and over other civilizations, expanded so greatly or so rapidly. In no other time or place have all power actors except obscurantists and unconscious innovators at the leading edge had such a clear vision of how to increase powers. Desirable models of the future, wanted by almost everyone, were available in the latest, most "modern" form of capitalism, of the state, of military professionalism, and of scientific ideologies. Thus in no other time or place developed so many theories of progress and evolution.

Yet development was not unitary or systemic, "internal" to a single social organism. Even now this was not evolution. We can in principle abstract a single ideal-typical "logic" of capitalism. We may call it the "law of marginal utility" or the "law of value," according to preference. We can also abstract a "logic" of militarism: to concentrate superior coercion on the forces of the enemy. But as soon as we let *both* loose together in phase 1, and as soon as we add messier, polymorphous states in phase 2, then ideal-typical logics become decidedly impure and murky to their supposed carriers. I emphasize that the relative "efficiency" of market (i.e., pure capitalist) versus territorial (more military or political) conceptions of interest and profit remained unclear from beginning to end of the period. Competing political economies remained plausible means of enhancing collective and personal economic powers. Throughout the period, certain secular tendencies can be discerned: toward more capitalist industrialization, toward military professionalism, toward greater political representation, toward more state bureaucratization, toward the more centralized nation-state. Each of these "competed" with alternative structural arrangements and "won" – not in any final sense but as a definite tendency over the period. They won either because they were more desirable to a broad array of power actors or because they were genuinely more powerful. But none of these tendencies emerged from a single "logic." The nation-state was encouraged by all of them; so was capitalist industrialization.

Although I have simplified "ultimacy" into two phases of (roughly) dual determinism, I must also add caveats. The other sources of social power also added their weights, more particularistically and erratically. Ideological power relations, very significant at the beginning of the period, remained a force especially where religious and linguistic communities (the latter given more collective power over the period by the other power sources) did not coincide with existing state boundaries. Ideological power also made decisive contributions to classes and nations in the "world-historical moment" of the French Revolution. Militarism remained important in the West's dealings with the rest of the world and in the domestic politics of monarchies retaining despotic powers and of the United States. The military caste was also secretively flexing its muscles for its own world-historical moment, July–August 1914. For all these reasons, my overall generalizations remain limited and crude.

For these reasons, too, Western distributive power relations remained unclear to contemporary actors. Their identities and conceptions of interest and honor were subtly transformed by entwinings of more than one power source and by the unintended consequences of actions. For these reasons, too, distributive power relations also remained objectively ambiguous, difficult for anyone to fathom. Economic actors emerged simultaneously as classes, sections, and segments, rendering uncertain the future of the domestic stratification. Its states were now dual civilian-military ones, each *Reichshalf* facing in different directions, controlled by different balances of power between elites and parties.

More broadly, the West comprised simultaneously both a segmental series of nation-state "societies" and a broader transnational civilization. Its ideologies of peace and war; of conservatism, liberalism, and socialism; of religion; of racism – all oscillated uneasily between the national and the transnational. There was no systematic resolution of ambivalences. Yet there was a more particular one. Most ambiguities were resolved in reality, and all these ambivalent actors and ideologies contributed to the resolution. Reality interposed the Great War. So, finally, we go over the top.

21 Empirical culmination – over the top: Geopolitics, class struggle, and World War I

This volume culminates empirically, with an analysis of the cataclysm that ended the period and that ferociously illustrates my theory of modern society. World War I was a turning point in the history of society, its outcomes decisively determining the twentieth century. Establishing its causes is essential to understanding modern society. This war also draws our horrified fascination: It took more human lives than any other. The war's significance as a morality fable exceeds even its causal and its killing significance. For the multistate civilization of Europe, dominant in the world for centuries, almost committed suicide. Its leading philosophies of hope, liberalism and socialism, appeared to be extinguished in one crazed week in August 1914. Its leading Powers went with eyes apparently open into extinction or precipitate decline. Supposed practitioners of formal rationality, diplomats and capitalists, lent their techniques to a war that half destroyed them. Those four blood-drenched years raise the question, Are human beings, is human society, rational?

There have been countless attempts to answer. What can a non-specialist add to the enormous literature on the causes of the war? I cannot improve on Joll's (1984a) masterly synthesis of the historical literature. Yet a sociologist may have something distinctive to contribute: concern with underlying social patterns and a familiarity with general theories of society. Even empiricist historians recognize that theory helps establish the causes of the war.

Most debates have centered on whether domestic or foreign politics were the primary causes. Those favoring the primacy of domestic causes – *Primat der Innenpolitik* (the argument began in Germany) – have usually sought ultimate causes in two of the six international political economies distinguished in earlier chapters, economic and social imperialism. Under economic imperialism, the needs of capital supposedly generated nationalist economic rivalry and war. Under social imperialism, foreign aggression supposedly served as a regime strategy to allay domestic, especially class, struggle. Those who assert the primacy of foreign politics – realism or the *Primat der Aussenpolitik* – also divide. The "macrorealist" school emphasizes overall geopolitical logic articulated by the statesmen representing the Powers: the

740

war as a rational solution to the clash of states' interests. The "micro-realist" school of geopolitical crises resembles the "cock-up–foul-up" approach to state theory I identified in Chapter 3, emphasizing state incoherence and fallibility. Microrealism argues that particular geo-political configurations lead to unpredictability, crises, and miscalcu-lations. Those who stress cock-up–foul-up even more firmly reject all theory on the war, attributing it to sheer accident or to human irrationality.

A sociologist, accustomed to theories of imperialism, nationalism, and class struggle, can add generalizing talents to the *Innen* side of the argument. Indeed, most sociologists have a professional vested interest in reaching an *Innen* conclusion. It is our stock-in-trade to attribute social change to deep-rooted social-structural causes. Yet this particular sociologist recognizes the importance of *Aussenpolitik*. This particular sociologist will also entwine *Innenpolitik* and *Aussenpolitik* as part of his general theory of societies as multiple power networks impacting on essentially polymorphous states. The events of 1914 did not result primarily from the logic of either domestic structures or realist Power interests. Nor did they result quite from human irrationality or accident. World War I was principally caused by the unintended consequences of the interactions of four of the five overlapping power networks we saw impacting on foreign policy in Chapter 3: classes, "statesmen," militaries, and nationalist parties (the fifth, particularistic pressure groups, though important in colonial policy, barely figured in the slide toward World War I). Because these entwined in different ways in different regimes, the Powers also had difficulty understanding one another, adding miscalculations and unintended consequences. In 1914, their "nondialectical" entwinings provided a cataclysmic climax to the power processes described in this volume.

The slide toward war

World War I began as a fusion of two conflicts. First came a Balkan struggle between the Austro-Hungarian monarchy and its dissident South Slavs who were aided by neighboring Slav Serbia and protected by Slav Great Power Russia. Second was rivalry between two camps of Powers, the Triple Alliance of Austria, Germany, and Italy and the Entente of Russia, France, and Great Britain. Within each camp two of the Powers had pledged to come to the aid of their allies, if attacked. Italy and Britain had not formally committed themselves, although some support was expected from them. The Balkan conflict was not easily negotiable, and sooner or later Austria would seek to crush its troublesome Serbian neighbor. But why should this also be a world war between Great Power alliances? Fusion came in a sequence of events lasting only a month in all.

On June 28, 1914, Archduke Franz Ferdinand, heir to the Austrian throne, was murdered by Slav nationalists at Sarajevo in the Austrian province of Bosnia. An Austrian investigation showed the conspiracy led into Serb government circles (though it was not sanctioned by the Serb government). We have grown used to terrorism whose trail reaches murkily into sympathetic governments. Then it was rarer and evoked even more outrage. With the support of its ally Germany, the Austrian government delivered a stiff ultimatum to Serbia on July 23, demanding such controls over Serbian political movements as would infringe its territorial sovereignty. The Serbs appealed to Russia for help. If Russia or Austria moved, the alliances might be involved.

The Powers could see local crisis turning major. On July 25, the Serbs made a conciliatory reply to the ultimatum, but Austria, bent on a showdown, rejected it. On the same day Russia began to discuss mobilizing its army against Austria and invoking the Entente. For technical reasons (explained later), military mobilization was a step close to actual war. On July 28, Austria, now egged on by Germany, declared war on Serbia. Austrian offensive preparations proceeded slowly, leaving time for mediation. But Germany and Austria showed little interest. On July 30, the tsar ordered a general mobilization of Russian forces, on the German as well as the Austrian border. The terms of both Triple Alliance and Entente were speedily invoked. On July 31 and August 1, general mobilizations followed in Austria (against Russia as well as Serbia), Germany (against France as well as Russia), and France (against Germany). After August 1, declarations of war followed in quick succession. Fighting started in the west on August 4, when Germany invaded France and Belgium. Britain joined in on August 6. Italy declared neutrality on August 8 but joined the war on the side of the Entente in 1915.

Thus some Powers behaved more aggressively in the crisis than others. Serbia, Germany, and Austria initiated provocative action, and Germany and Austria actually invaded. Some see the war as the responsibility of Austria and Germany (Taylor 1954: 527; Lafore 1965: 268); others single out the dominant partner, Germany (Stone 1983: 326–39). Then came Russia, whose encouragement of Serbia was provocative and whose general mobilization was the intermediate escalation to war. Britain's direct responsibility was less, being the last combatant to move. But Germany claimed that British imperialism lay behind Great Power instabilities. In 1914, the German regime justified its "aggression" by casting blame beyond the immediate crisis: Germany was defending itself against encirclement by the longer-established Great Powers. Germany only wanted an equal "place in the sun" that Great Britain and France would not share. The war was rooted in broader Great Power rivalry, especially in British hegemony. I consider but largely reject this argument. Nonetheless, Britain can be "blamed," inasmuch as its diplomacy failed to give clear deterrent signals to Germany, which counted on British neutrality until July 30. France simply stood by its alliance with Russia and defended itself, as it had always said it would, although many French favored war to recover Alsace-Lorraine, and French secret diplomacy can be faulted, as we shall see.

This, then, is the order of priorities in establishing immediate causes: Ignoring the minor Power Serbia, I concentrate most on Germany and Austria, then Russia, and less on Britain and France. The first three were authoritarian monarchies, the last two liberal regimes. This raises an obvious *Innenpolitik* question related to the representative crystallization of states: Was there something peculiarly dangerous about monarchy when compared to party democracy (remembering that I classify Britain as the latter, not the former)? I will return to this question.

The depth of the problem lies revealed. Several causal processes rapidly became entwined. One particular structural conflict – the clash of nationalities in the Austro-Hungarian monarchy – fused with two general structural problems: Great Power rivalry and the apparent militarism of monarchies. These entwinings produced a two-week downward spiral of frenzied diplomatic and military scurrying, misunderstanding, and miscalculation, followed by the five-day eruption of a world war. *Innen* and *Aussen* became conjoined, as was deep structure, the tactical, the peculiar, and the cock-up–foul-up. As the war was fought for avowedly geopolitical reasons, I start with the broad sweep of *Aussenpolitik*.

Realist theories of the Great War

Diplomatic history, backed by realism (and, indeed, by any rational choice theory), looks for the general causes of war in terms of the geopolitical interests of states as interpreted by "statesmen," diplomats, and military commanders. It makes three assumptions: States have "interests," or at least statesmen articulate such interests; state interests persistently conflict; and war is a normal, if dangerous, means of securing interests. War is always a potential outcome because it can be a rational means to attain states' ends (unless it becomes too inherently destructive, as nuclear war has become). To explain when, where, and how actual wars break out, realism adds a second level of analysis.

War breaks out either (1) because a Power consciously provokes it to restructure the international order (the macroexplanation) or (2) because, amid complex conflicts, the misperceptions and suspicions of Powers lead to less mutual understanding and to wars at lower thresholds of acceptability (the microexplanation). In the macro case, war is straightforwardly rational for the aggressor; in the micro case, it is still rational but at a lower level of environmental certainty and human knowledge – it is an acceptable risk when all policy alternatives carry dangers.

Realism works to the extent that its presuppositions are shared by actors in the real world. This involves two preconditions:

1. If statesmen embody social identities carrying different presuppositions, realism will not work. Obviously, statesmen always do embody social identities; they are not merely neutral symbols of their states. But these identities might make little difference, or they might undermine realist presuppositions, persuading them to act in other ways. Finally, their social identities might actually persuade them to act as realists. Realist calculations might be less universal to human beings, more the product of statesmen embodying certain social identities. This is especially problematic because, as noted in Chapter 3, there are actually two motivations mixed up in realist diplomacy: material interests and ideological national honor.

2. Statesmen have to be responsible power actors, actually in charge of policy and events. If they are puppets of others, or buffeted around by the pressure of factionalized others, they may not act as realists. Rationality may or may not be the property of other power actors.

This chapter shows that social identities actually tended to reinforce realist behavior among statesmen but that this tendency was outweighed by confused, factionalized pressures to produce an outcome essentially incomprehensible from a realist perspective.

Chapter 12 shows that the principal social identity of nineteenth-century statesmen was as old regime. They were white male kinsmen and clients of monarchs, drawn from aristocracy, gentry, and "older" merchant groups and from dominant ethnic, religious, and regional communities. In republics, not dissimilar "notable" families had arisen, drawn from the surviving aristocracy, old rural notables, or the substantial "older" bourgeoisie. The "national" goals of statesmen might be partly defined by the distinctly reactionary goals of their class and other communities of attachment. This was clear, for example, during and immediately after the French Revolution and the Napoleonic Wars, when "international order" meant repressing social reform as well as France, and when diplomacy was highly colored by social ideologies. Was this still true just before 1914?

Most diplomats and historians have believed that social identities make little difference in statesmen's calculations. Many have depersonalized statesmen altogether, conferring on them an even grander title – they become the *Powers* – and thus are derived the perfectly routine statements in the documents and analyses of diplomacy that "Germany aggressed," "Britain dithered," and the like. Behind this lay a genuine transformation of social identities. Except for Russia and Austria-Hungary, statesmen now formally represented not dynasties but nation-states. "Reasons of state" became supposedly the "national interest" – unquestioned, even "sacred" in the Durkheimian sense of a goal set apart from, and superior to, material calculations of interest. As Kennan notes, gone was the cynicism of princes: "In the view [the nation-state] takes of itself it is admiring to the point of narcissism. *Its* symbols always require the highest reverence; *its* cause deserves the highest sacrifice; *its* interests are sacrosanct. . . . These are not limited aims" (1984: 256–7).

The state was not even usually referred to as an "it" at all but, rather, was personified and capitalized as a primordial authority figure, Mother or Father. The custom arose of assigning gender to states, according to the conventions of language – thus "Her" interests, morality, honor, dignity, and national security in Britain and Russia, "His" in the German Fatherland. Austrian statesmen deviated, often using the more archaic "the Monarchy" for the interests they pursued. Exchanges between statesmen also usually referred to two categories of actor, the statesman and the state, and to two places, the capital city and the address of the foreign office or chancellery (Quai d'Orsay or Wilhelmstrasse). The state (Mother or Father) acted, personified by its statesmen, domiciled in the diplomatic buildings of its capital city. The nation-state also had sacred symbols, especially flags and anthems. The public parade produced behavior like that in churches: reverential posture (in this case, standing to attention) and strong emotions (tears in the eyes, stirrings in the chest). The nation-state was – and still is – sacred.

Thus national interests often were not calculated as carefully as material interests really should be. They often were not explicitly traded off against other interests. If these were not carried unconsciously, they were rarely carried at all. Effective normative solidarities and prejudices, like the informal Anglo-American alliance or the contempt all these Powers shared for the nonwhite races, lay deep and were rarely articulated. Diplomats did acknowledge sectional interests, especially commercial interests, when dealing with colonies or negotiating trade treaties. Here economic pressure groups played their strongest role. But they are surprisingly absent from discussions of broader geopolitics. Thus Stone (1983: 331) remarks, with only a little exaggeration: Diplomatic documents and private papers of the period "indicate only a concern for questions of prestige, strategy, 'high politics.'" As we shall see, "honor" mattered greatly.

Few actors realized how socially created and peculiar was this state-centered view of the world. A relatively reflective participant, the Russian general Kireyev, confiding to his diary in 1910, concluded that it was part of the natural order: "We, like any powerful nation, strive to expand our territory, our 'legitimate' moral, economic, economic and political influence. This is in the order of things" (Lieven 1983: 22). Though Kireyev distances himself somewhat from the word "legit-imate" by putting it in quotation marks, he ultimately gives it the weight of the "order of things." Because most participants did so, geopolitics might approximate more to a rational realist system, con-taining common rules and signals. Residual old regime transnationalism even reinforced realist presuppositions. Ties of kinship and cosmo-politan aristocratic culture still bonded statesmen. Though most now wrote in their native vernaculars, most spoke at least three languages and their missives were peppered with French words and Latin tags. They normally understood one another very well, although we shall see that they understood one another's states much less well.

The late nineteenth-century science of geopolitics also systematized their pursuit of "national interests." The term *Geopolitik* was coined in the 1880s by Kjellen to signify "the science which conceives of the state as a geographical organism or as a phenomenon in space. . . . [V]ital vigorous states with limited space obey the categorical political importance of expanding their space by colonization, amalgamation and conquest" (Parker 1985: 55). The geopoliticians now defined four "vital" (the word means "necessary for life") national interests:

1. Above all else, to defend the territorial integrity of the realm
2. To extend control over territory by formal geopolitical imperialism, or by securing it as friendly ally or client state
3. To make use of the nineteenth-century revolution in extensive power to establish a global colonial and naval sphere of strategic control
4. To guarantee the first three by brandishing economic and military power within the system of Powers

These goals embody a markedly centralized and territorial conception of interest and community. "We" are defined territorially as the mem-bers of a state, not of localities, regions, or transnational collectivities. Acquiring control over further territory, not markets, might predo-minate in definitions or calculations of collective interest. Statesmen did not reject market acquisition and interest but assumed these would flow from territorial control. National interests were served by militarism and empire. The map room became the hub of diplomacy and high command; geographers became academic servants of state power. Diplomats mutually understood that regimes would act geopolitically: according to the geographic positioning of their territories and their political capacity to bring the mainly economic and military resources of their territories to bear on those of other powers. "Chaps and maps" is Palmer's succinct definition of such old regime geopolitics (1983: xi).

Not all Powers were equally committed to territorial expansion, and none pursued this to the exclusion of all other goals. The German Reich had only just been consolidated and there was discussion about whether its territorial appetite was "satiated" (Bismarck's contention). In fact, German foreign policy was rather conciliatory, given its military might, between 1871 and 1905. Because American statesmen did not count native Americans or the "yellow races" as fully human, they believed themselves pacific – and were so in relation to Western Powers. Britain had built its empire earlier and now wished only to keep it, which peace and the demonstration effect of navy maneuvers should ensure. French interest in new territory declined, apart from Alsace-Lorraine. So Anglo-Saxon and French statesmen preferred less territorial theories of power, especially Admiral Mahan's doctrine of sea power requiring only colonial ports and staging posts – "informal" not formal empire (Mahan 1918: 26–8). Geographers split between a predominantly German geopolitical school and a French-led emphasis on region, the permeability of frontiers, and international cooperation – an early expression of interdependence theory.

Nonetheless, throughout the long nineteenth century, the growth of state infrastructural powers and national citizenship diffused a "national" sense of identity and community. *Geopolitik* became more popular as an account of collective interest. Mackinder (1904) connected Mahan, territorial geopoliticians, and nationalism, arguing that world history was a recurring conflict between landsmen and seamen. Columbus had passed the edge to seamen; now the railway had swung it back again. Russia or Prussia was destined to found a world empire. The world was now the geopoliticians' oyster. In the "new imperialism" of the 1890s, the Powers scrambled for rather barren African territories, and they entered formal, committing alliances. By 1914, all statesmen thought geopolitically and globally, and their conceptions of "national interest" had some popular resonance.

The rise of the modern nation-state, with citizenship, nationalism, and sacred geopolitical interests, thus apparently reinforced realist presuppositions. Statesmen would be more likely to behave in a realist way than, say, if they were seeking to repress liberalism (as they had earlier). Thus realism might have a leg up from a more sociological explanation in interpreting 1914. Not that many realists have conceded this: Morgenthau (1978) attributes the war to statesmen operating a dangerous balance-of-power system, and thus it could have happened in any era, regardless of the other identities and motivations of statesmen. Rosecrance (1986: 86–8), however, notes the reinforcement. He argues that larger, more territorial states infused with popular nationalism had created more "military-political" definitions of national interest. Both writers agree, though, that aggressive geopolitics was systemic and seemingly realist – when viewed from the perspective of, respectively, the balance of power or the military-political world. I hope to show that rationality, consistency, and system were far weaker than either view implies.

What was the supposedly systemic, realist configuration of Powers that led to 1914? Geopolitics had changed somewhat since 1815. Then, as Chapter 8 describes, the two greatest Powers had been Russia and Great Britain, defensively invulnerable, straddling most European expansion routes – Russia into Asia, Britain across western sea-lanes. Britain's commercial power had also amounted to what I called a near or specialized hegemony. Then came France, Prussia, Austria, and the Ottoman Empire. During much of the century, diplomatic stability rested on Britain and Russia, on specialized British hegemony, and on the Concert, then the balance of power among all six. By 1910, Britannia still ruled the waves and led commerce, but it was slipping industrially behind Germany, which had defeated Austria and France and was dominant on the European continent. France was declining gradually, Austria more rapidly, and the Turks terminally. Russia remained defensively strong and was expanding in Asia and modernizing in Europe, but its regime was now unstable.

Transformation had occurred in two phases. In the first, from the late 1880s to about 1902, there were two separate spheres of conflict. The central Continental Powers, Austria, Germany, and Italy, formed a Triple Alliance against the flanking Entente of France and Russia. Germany and France were rivals on the Rhine, Austria and Russia in the Balkans, now a power vacuum with the Turkish collapse. In the global sphere each Power was on its own; the main conflicts, however, were between Britain and France and Russia (in Asia). But the continuing rise of Germany and its navy, and the 1905 collapse of Russia in war against Japan, produced realignment and a second phase. Britain now settled major differences with France and Russia and half joined their Entente, while actually promising nothing. This was the actual lineup in 1914, except that Italy declared neutrality (and later joined the Entente).

The first realist school asserts the primacy of a geopolitical logic flowing from these transformations. It asks some pointed rhetorical questions: How could such fundamental changes in world order *not* be accompanied by war? Had not the rise and decline of these very Powers *already* caused wars – the Crimean, Austro-Prussian, Franco-Prussian, and Russo-Japanese? What comparable changes in the balance of power in other periods of world history had not been sealed by war? Can we not even deduce the two fronts of 1914 from these changing parameters? In the east did not Austro-Russian rivalry make the Balkans unstable? Did not the western rivalry of Britain and Germany change a Balkan dispute into a world war? Did not German fear of Russian modernization – and fear that Germany had peaked and might be beginning a relative decline – lead to Germany striking first in 1914 on both fronts, integrating the two into a world war?

Macrorealism acknowledges difficulty in explaining the actual events of July 1914. In the slide toward war, there appeared precious little genius but, rather, massive human fallibility. Thus the second cock-up–foul-up microrealist school emphasizes the uncertainties and miscalculations of a rapidly shifting scenario. Mistakes certainly abounded: German leaders miscalculated on British neutrality and on the resilience of the French army; the British gave insufficient warning noises; the Russians botched their mobilization decisions; the Austrians were foolhardy. Albertini's monumental volumes (1952, 1953, 1957) on the diplomacy of June and July demonstrate that all this mattered; for without the stupidities and misunderstandings of Grey, Sazonov, Bethmann, Berchtold, and the rest, war may have been avoided.

But there were microrealist patterns even inside this diplomatic mess. As Morgenthau (1978: 212–8) emphasizes, a balance of power system, especially one based on alliances, introduces inherent uncertainties. No Power can calculate exactly what is "enough" power to preserve the status quo, nor can it entirely predict the behavior of allies or supposed enemies. Thus, though the system requires equality of power, each power must aim for a safety margin conferred by power superiority. But as the system is dynamic and not all Powers increase their powers at the same rate, preventive war (striking now before the relative power ratio worsens) is an inherent possibility in balances of power, recognized as potentially rational by the Powers. If Powers lose confidence in the balance, one may strike out.

Amid a worsening crisis, decision making may also become more narrowly based. Because the Powers cannot now predict the actions of others, they choose between narrower alternatives. Their choice then ripples back to other Powers, narrowing their choices. The slide toward war contained such a rippling, downward diplomatic spiral. Aggression started in the Balkans, its consequences then rippled to other Powers, and in turn their reactions rippled back through the diplomatic chain. War partly resulted because the original actors were farthest removed from the consequences of their actions. Were the murderers of the archduke or the Serbian or Austrian regimes responsible for the death of 55 million Europeans and Americans? To the end of his life Gavrilo Princip remained bewildered by the consequences of his shots. Near the beginning of the causal chain, desperate actors risked local war as the lesser of two, directly evident evils. A major war might not result – that depended on the uncertain responses of many others.

Thus Austrian statesmen decided that not to chastise Serbia would incite other dissident nationalities toward revolt. The regime could not survive the humiliation, whatever the risk of war. Conrad, the chief of staff, declared, "the Monarchy has been seized by the throat and forced to choose between letting itself be strangled and making a last effort to defend itself against attack" (Albertini 1953: II, 123). Surely the Russian regime could appreciate that and allow Serbia to be punished for encouraging terrorists. That was also the view of German statesmen: Austria, its only reliable ally, must be allowed to survive; the Balkan dispute should be localized between Austria and Serbia. This passed the buck to Russia. The Russian regime felt obliged to saber-rattle in defense of Serbia, yet also expected mediation and settlement of the dispute.

Only now, around July 25–28, when the Russians were evidently not backing down, were the Powers staring a major war in the face. Austria and Germany now found new reasons for risking it. Austrian statesmen felt themselves boxed into a corner: To avoid war, now they, not Serbia, would have to back down, inciting nationalists still further. Austrian and Serbian leaders both seemed unwilling to compromise, but the Austrians were also stiffened by German leaders. The buck passes to Germany. German statesmen panicked a little at the aggressive Russian response, but were now attracted by a preventive war. The Russians seemed surprisingly willing to fight Austria *and* Germany, despite realizing that under the Triple Alliance Germany would defend its ally. If Russia was bent on a showdown, from Germany's point of view better to have it now, before Russian military modernization was completed (in 1917) and before Austria further weakened. Had Germany peaked, to be permanently deprived of its place in the sun? Chancellor Bethmann-Hollweg gloomily said, "The future belongs to Russia which grows and grows, looming above us an increasingly terrifying nightmare." Bethmann and Moltke (the younger, not the victor of 1866–71), the German chief of staff, talked of the "calculated risk" of a preventive war against Russia (Stern 1968;

Jarausch 1969). They could put the blame on Russian "aggression." Blame mattered, for it could influence domestic public opinion as well as other Powers, especially apparently wavering Britain.

The British response now became crucial. It was a calculated risk for Germany to take on France and Russia; it would be near suicidal to take on Britain too. But most German leaders believed that until after July 29 Britain would either delay entry or declare neutrality. To keep Austria alive, Germany should encourage Austrian aggression against Serbia. Germany should strike swiftly against France, using the Austrians to hold up the Russians until resources could be switched from west to east. The French could be quickly forced to terms as in 1870, before the British committed themselves. Then the British could be bought off with French colonies. It was worth the risk now, because future odds against Germany would be greater. So the Germans declared war and closed down all choices for the French and Russians. They must now defend themselves under the military terms of the Entente. British statesmen hesitated but, believing German aggression threatened the Channel, resolved to fight. At the last moment all Powers tried to prove their opponents the aggressors.

No one backed down, for seemingly good, if narrowing, reasons. At each stage each Power's statesmen reasoned they had a choice only between escalation and something worse (Remak 1967: 147–50). Even in July 1914, statesmen were still rapidly calculating the odds of alternative courses of action within the broader geopolitical parameters analyzed earlier. Realist rationality was still evident. If it did not produce a rational end, that might be due to the difficulty of predicting the response of others in a rapidly changing situation and because the most "aggressive" actions (of Serbia, Austria, Russia, and Germany) were nearer the beginning of the chain of action and reaction. Such reasoning is added by the second cock-up–foul-up realist school.

A preliminary critique of the realist explanation

There are omissions and non sequiturs in this account. Yet the concepts of the two realist *Aussen* schools – sacred national geopolitical interests pursued by statesmen (and perhaps reinforced by popular nationalism), rationally pursued over the long run, confused in crises – might seem to explain much of the slide toward the Great War. Until the last two decades, explanations dealt almost entirely with diplomacy and were couched almost always in such terms (Mansergh 1949; Albertini 1952, 1953, 1957; Taylor 1954; Lafore 1965; Schmitt 1966). Yet there are three fundamental problems with this: War was not an inevitable consequence of geopolitical reordering of balances of power; this war was not perceived as the rational means of such reordering;

and *both* realist geopolitical logic and diplomatic mistakes were patterned partly by social-structural forces.

There are two reasons why the rise and decline of the Great Powers could have been handled peacefully in this period. The first is that this "balance of power" was actually quite unlike any other discussed in this volume, or indeed in European history, ever. For the first time it resembled a genuine zero-sum game in which for one Great Power to gain another must lose – and both probably would be devastated by modern warfare. Wars are not an inevitable consequence of certain lineups of Powers (as Morgenthau asserted). A more genuinely "realistic" approach would start from the fact that wars are oriented toward goals. As Weber would say, they are fought for "material or ideal interests," to secure profit or impose ideal values on the world. But now, suddenly, there were neither. As we have seen, war for centuries had secured for the major Powers both colonial and European trade and territory. But now there were no profitable colonies to be easily wrested away (and the "natives" were resisting harder, anyway). There were no minor Powers to be swallowed up, as Europe was divided only into Great Powers and small ones protected by all others. Only the Balkans were less institutionalized; a war there, but not a general conflagration, might be rational, goal-oriented activity. Also, unlike in past ages (and the later twentieth century), there was no great ideology to be imposed on conquered peoples: Catholicism, Democracy, Civilization, Socialism, or Fascism. Ideologically, all Powers initially claimed self-defense.

The most recent European wars had concerned the last profitable mopping-up operations in Europe, by Prussia (twice) of the small German states. This is highly significant: Massive territorial gains had been made in the 1860s and 1870s, at relatively low cost, and by Germany. As I have argued elsewhere (Mann 1988), Powers institutionalize those arrangements that make them great. Perhaps we should look a little harder at *states*, especially the German state, rather than at the general configuration of relations among the Powers, for the causes of this war.

The second reason reinforces the first. Britain was actually now matched by two Powers. War with Germany resulted, but not with the United States, nor was it remotely contemplated by either side. British diplomats looked realistically at the changes, shrugged their shoulders at the impossibility of matching American military resources in the Americas, withdrew most of the fleet, and secretly advised the politicians that if the United States wished to invade Canada, Britain could not stop them (Kennedy 1985: 107–9, 118–19). Over the next half century the replacement of Britain as near hegemon by the United

States was accomplished peacefully, even cooperatively. War does not inevitably accompany geopolitical reordering.

Of course, it might be replied, the United States was three thousand miles away, whereas Germany was only three hundred. Industrial, commercial, even naval rivalry might be troublesome, but the German threat to the North Sea, the Channel ports, and the English coast was of a different order. Britain had not the resources to stave off both Germany and the United States. Geopolitical logic suggested concentrating on the nearer German threat. Yet the Americans did not seize Canada, or even consider it. Nor did they use naval dominance to close the American continent to Britain. They were not uniquely virtuous, as they showed in their imperialism in the Pacific, but cooperation between these two Powers was grounded in a transnational economic and ideological solidarity. The two countries spoke the same language, were stocked (at leadership level) by the same ethnic and religious groups, shared similar party democracies, and were each other's largest trading and investment partners. The regimes did not *want* to war with each other; had they done so, they would have had difficulty persuading their citizens to fight in such a war. Anglo-Saxon society was, and still is, a diffused, normative community, an ideological power network that keeps war well away from its little squabbles.

These Anglo-Saxon norms were stronger than most operating transnationally. But, in a sense, they were merely exaggerated versions of those of the entire West. The West was a multi-power-actor civilization. Its religion, culture, secular philosophies, political institutions, economy, monarchical and noble genealogies, and increasingly its racism – all brought normative solidarity among and across the Powers. At the time many believed this could restrain growing geopolitical and territorial definitions of interest. And diplomacy was also designed to ensure peace and negotiate conflict. For example, colonial differences were generally settled in a regular sequence – from an "incident" arising from a rash act, to a "crisis" of mutual saber-rattling, to mediation, to a joint conference, and finally to a compromise settlement. Diplomacy was not all threat and strut in an anarchic black hole. It was also normative understandings and cultivated compromise.

Indeed, behind conciliatory diplomacy lay diffuse antiwar norms. The Enlightenment legacy, transmitted especially through liberalism, was that human societies could settle their differences through rational, peaceful discussion. As liberals emphasize, transnational aspects of capitalism greatly heightened economic interdependences among states. A peace lobby centered on liberals and finance capital. The power of *their* rationality might tip the scales away from war.

Peace lobbies could ask one very disconcerting "realistic" question of the realist account. Why *should* Germany risk devastating war with Britain when, like the United States, it was already overtaking Britain within the economic order supposedly dominated by Britain? Hugo Stinnes, a leading German industrialist, pleaded in fateful words in 1911: "Let us have another three to four years of peaceful development and Germany will be undisputed master of Europe" (Joll 1984a: 156). Stinnes was right; he would have been right again in the late 1930s; he might be right again in the 1990s. Let us hope his words, implying peaceful, predominantly market domination (combinations of the first three of my six types of international political economy), will be finally listened to – at the *third* chance for Germany and Europe – by a German regime (I write this on October 3, 1990, the date of German reunification). Had they listened, earlier regimes might have been saved a lot of trouble, for Germany and for the whole world.

Thus it simply was not true that Germany struck out either for gain or in mere self-defense against encirclement or British hegemony. Britain was no longer hegemonic, and, as we saw in Chapter 8, its specialized "hegemonic" commercial services were now provided with the active help of other Powers. We see later that "encirclement" was part consequence of German actions, part nationalist exaggeration. But above all, German aggression was not self-defense, for it did not actually defend. German realist and capitalist interests were better secured by the status quo – call it encirclement and British hegemony, if you like – than by encouraging war. Thus blame is as attributable to German power actors as most historians have assumed. Other Powers, too, were blameworthy. We still have to explain how collective interests and the West's more pacific norms were overcome. It clearly has sociological causes beyond mere realist or capitalist interests.

Perhaps we can return to the social composition of the statesmen, as they were recruited overwhelmingly from an old regime for whom war historically had been a normal sport. But aggression did not result directly from foaming-mouthed militarism among old regime soldiers and statesmen in monarchies. Many of them favored peace. Old regime transnationalism was not dead. Monarchs retained family solidarity; notables participated in transnational cultures of kinship, Enlightenment, and church. Though they honored war, this had been limited, private, professional war, not mass-mobilization war legitimated by the nation (which had badly scarred them during 1792–1815). The old regime was militaristic, but did not look forward to a mass mobilization war threatening to massively kill, dislocate economies, and topple regimes. Many generals understood what terrors might soon be unleashed; admirals did not want to send out their beautiful follies, the battleships, to be sunk.

Thus many statesmen and commanders in the more aggressive Powers actually warned against this war. Many Austrians argued that the monarchy could not survive a war with Russia. Austria's high command warned that its armies could not be effectively mobilized against Serbia and Russia simultaneously. Yet August 1914 required both. Germans warned against Austrian instability pulling them into war, against relying on Austria for effective military support, against fighting France and Russia simultaneously, against fighting anyone without first securing British neutrality. German admirals warned that they could not challenge the British navy. Yet all this was required in 1914. Russians argued stealth was the best route to Constantinople; war against Germany could only threaten regime survival. Russian generals argued against fighting a war halfway through a modernization program; admirals warned that the fleets would be trapped in the eastern Baltic and the Black Sea. Yet all this came to pass in 1914.

True, in all three monarchies other regime factions were not so pessimistic, and still others changed their minds or dithered. Even the Cassandras seemed to put fear behind them in late July and early August. Yet in calmer times many had calculated the odds and found them wanting. They were proved right. All these fears were justified. The war went badly for all three monarchies. None survived it.

Thus the war was not the rational outcome of rational geopolitics. Its principal initiators – the Austrian, German, and Russian monarchies – were destroyed by it, and many knew there was a strong possibility, even probability, this would occur. So as Europe slid toward war, statesmen found difficulty explaining what was going on and their own part in it. Many resorted to metaphors of fate. On August 3, at dusk, Sir Edward Grey looked out the Foreign Office windows at the street scene below and famously declared: "The lamps are going out all over Europe. We shall not see them lit again in our lifetime." Chancellor Bethmann-Hollweg pronounced that "things are out of control and the stone has started to roll. . . . I see a doom greater than human power hanging over Europe and our own people." Russian Foreign Minister Sazonov feared on July 25 that he was "being overwhelmed in this affair." The tsar, told by the German ambassador that war was inevitable unless he halted mobilization, pointed to the heavens and declared: "There is only One alone who can help." His interior minister added: "We cannot escape our fate." Even vigorous action could be seen as fate. Emperor Franz Josef finally resolved that Austria must punish Serbia and face the consequences. To his chief of staff he said, "If the Monarchy is doomed to perish, let it at least perish decorously." He had a bizarre sense of decor (Albertini 1953: II, 129, 543, 574; Joll 1984a: 21, 31).

These actors did not question their own rationality. They perceived forces greater than human reason at work. Later critics have not excused them so lightly. As the war was formally irrational (it could not achieve its stated goals), and as its initiators had a strong suspicion or even knew this was so, they must have been irrational. The argument is extended beyond them to entire old regimes and ruling classes, to nationalist movements, even to European civilization as a whole. The war is interpreted as the hubris of the old regime, "horsemen of the apocalypse . . . ready to crash into the past" in their "drive for retrogression" (Mayer 1981: 322); as the inevitable doom of the authoritarian, militaristic monarchy typified by Germany (Fischer 1967; Berghahn 1973; Geiss 1984); as the overthrowal of diplomacy by "intense nationalism" (Schmitt 1966: II, 482); as the triumph of social Darwinism (Joll 1984c; Koch 1984) or of the "organized," corporate, imperialist phase of capitalism over the liberalism of the Industrial Revolution (the interpretation of Hilferding and Lenin). For others, the emergence of Freud's theories in precisely these years and this context (Freud was an Austrian patriot in 1914) is too good an opportunity to miss: Europe was possessed by Thanatos, the death wish, induced by "statist delirium" (Todd 1979: 60–1).

But there is a problem with all such explanations, as there has been with my entire discussion so far. Quite contrary to realism, we cannot simply attribute the language of rationality or irrationality to the "Powers," as they were not in reality singular actors. In an important formal sense, they were singular. "They" negotiated, threatened, and declared war. Actually, statesmen did this. Yet statesmen were plural. "Austria-Hungary" started the war when the minister for foreign affairs, Berchtold, the Austrian and Hungarian prime ministers, Stuyck and Tisza, and the emperor, Franz Josef, approved the ultimatum to Serbia, when the emperor signed the general mobilization order submitted by the chief of staff, Conrad, and when the emperor signed telegrams declaring war submitted by Berchtold. Yet these five persons represented diverse characters and beliefs and they also represented points of crystallization for various networks of political power. The cautious old emperor was concerned to preserve his dynasty, preferably with Slav consent and without war. The chief of staff represented the war faction. He had long been convinced that the Serbs must be crushed to save the monarchy – and he seems to have wanted to become a war hero so that his true love would finally marry him (so suggests Williamson 1988: 816). The irresolute foreign minister was susceptible to German pressure, the Austrian prime minister was inexperienced, and the Hungarian premier was uninterested in foreign affairs.

The notion of "Austria" deciding or acting is mythical. Austria acted in the end boldly against Serbia because German pressure through Berchtold (who was also shocked by the archduke's murder) combined with Conrad's pressure to overcome the emperor's scruples and the two premiers' weakness. Even this oversimplifies the complexity of the power networks of Austrian politics. The "Power" Austria was less an actor than a field of forces, crystallizing in diverse nondialectical ways, with Franz Josef at its center. As we saw in Chapter 10, he had deliberately left the constitution and the powers and composition of his crown council vague so as to maximize his segmental divide-and-rule discretion. The result was factionalism.

The emperor sometimes experienced his centrality to all factions uncomfortably. In 1911, he gave a stormy audience to Chief of Staff Conrad, complaining of Conrad's treatment of Foreign Minister Aerenthal: "These incessant attacks on Aerenthal, these pin-pricks, I forbid them. . . . The ever-recurring reproaches on the question of Italy and the Balkans are directed at me. Policy – it is I who make it . . . and it is a policy of peace" (Albertini 1952: I, 351). But Franz Josef did not make policy. In this polymorphous state he was, rather, the central point at which crystallized a number of power networks, some domestic, others emanating from abroad (like German pressure), and others spanning across his borders (like South Slav nationalism). Realist "rationality" was a lot to ask for from him and his advisers: Consistency of goals and the selection of efficient means to reach them were subject to the entwined struggles of contending power crystallizations.

The problem was not a general irrationality of European society. Rather, two sets of rational calculations were interacting in two unpredictable ways. First, domestic and geopolitics entwined in all states, though in different, volatile fashion in each. Thus, second, it became difficult to predict the reactions of other Powers to one's own diplomacy. The problem was not irrational actors but plural actors with plural identities pursuing diverse strategies whose interactions were unpredictable and eventually devastating. So I must enumerate the principal power networks lying behind the statesmen and the "Powers." I will move outward from the statesmen and the military commanders, distinguishing between two principal ways states crystallized on the representative issue, as monarchies and as party democracies.

Statesmen in monarchies

Chapter 12 shows that foreign policy and war traditionally had been the private, and partly "insulated," prerogatives of the monarch. In the three monarchies they remained constitutionally private. Thus the monarch's opinions and temperament mattered. It made a difference in Anglo-German relations that Kaiser Wilhelm II respected the authority of his grandmother, Queen Victoria, but was infuriated by the cheek of her successor, his uncle Edward VII. This, plus Wilhelm's impulsive, bombastic temperament and his strutting in military uniform, "made a personal and substantial contribution to the worsening of Anglo-German relations," says Kennedy (1980: 400–9; cf. Steiner 1969: 200–8). But in the slide toward war no monarch actually had the character to dominate foreign policy, and no chief minister had since Bismarck. Tsar Nicholas II was feeble. His own sensibilities were for peace, but he was talked into war by his advisers. The elderly, limited Franz Josef had been rendered deeply cautious by long and bitter experience. Yet he, too, was persuaded into war. Kaiser Wilhelm II was unstable – aggressive, militarist, and racist in rhetoric, irresolute, sometimes even terrified, in an actual crisis. He was talked into backing words with actions. We must discover who was so honey-tongued in these regimes.

Access to and influence over the monarch *was* the political center under autocratic and semiauthoritarian regimes. These processes had become more complex as the countries modernized. We saw in Chapter 9 that in Germany no less than eleven distinct political power networks had crystallized around this center. In German foreign policy making, four distinct power networks channeled influence directly on the kaiser:

1. Civilian networks, headed by the chancellor, foreign minister, and Prussian war minister, channeled the advice of their ministries, including diplomats. They were responsive, though not constitutionally responsible, to the Reichstag and the Prussian Diet and, therefore, to public opinion, including that of the growing nationalist "parties" entrenched (as we saw in Chapter 16) within state administration itself. Civilian networks were incoherent, as the administration contained both realist statesmen and "superloyal" statist nationalists, now advocating more aggressive foreign policy than careful diplomatic calculations might favor.

2. Military networks, principally the army high command, plus the admiralty and ad hoc war councils, because these institutions were linked in no clear chain of command, were also institutionally incoherent, although they possessed social solidarity. They were drawn largely from Junkers and other aristocratic groups, partly represented them, and partly represented the narrow castelike militarism we have seen growing in this period.

As the vague constitution could not settle disputes within and between the first two networks, two other ad hoc power networks had emerged:

3. Three "cabinets" (army, navy, and civilian), originating in the monarch's household, supposedly channeled information between monarch and ministries but were actually court institutions, operating autonomously.

4. The system of *Immediatstellung*, originally the right of prominent military officers to have a personal audience with the kaiser without the presence of ministers, was expanded in the nineteenth century to include civilians and other officers. Thus persons of high family rank could bypass all other channels and seek to influence the kaiser directly.

Relations between, and sometimes within, these four networks were unclear and often unstable. They had arisen as ad hoc responses to particular crises, yet (as Chapter 9 shows) they were also part of the segmental divide-and-rule strategy of authoritarian monarchy that had done so well at preserving Hohenzollern powers in a modern industrial society. They were aimed at reducing the clarity of parliamentary, civilian-bureaucratic, and military-bureaucratic accountability (for evidence, unfortunately dominated by a controversy over how much personal power the kaiser wielded, see Hull 1982; essays by Rohl, Kennedy, and Deist in Rohl and Sombart 1982; and Eley 1985). Thus in foreign policy "intrigue, cabals and vendettas were able to proliferate," concludes Cecil (1976: 322). Previous chapters have traced this German tragedy. In contrast to its Prussian ancestor, the German state had institutionalized no single place in which ultimate decisions could be taken. Although there was a sovereign, there was no sovereignty.

Chapter 10 discusses how Austrian power networks were even looser, as Franz Josef's more dynastic version of divide and rule was more personal and dynastic, less institutionalized than the German version. This sovereign attempted to institutionalize real sovereignty on himself. But (as previous chapters show) the expanding scope of the modern state – exacerbated by the multinational complexities of this state – had made effective personal sovereignty a chimera (and this was no Nietzschean superman). Although I have not discussed Russian administration much, it too was dynastic, even autocratic, leading to bitter factionalism among ministries competing for the ear of the tsar and the gossip of the court. None of the three monarchies had institutionalized effective sovereignty.

But polymorphous intrigue and factionalism were not the same as chaos. Germany's intriguing political power networks cohered around the four higher-level crystallizations discussed in Chapter 9. There I noted that the result of divide-and-rule strategies was to fail to discard the competing goals of power actors (apart from those of socialists, Leftist liberals, and ethnic minority parties). Thus, as in domestic politics, the crystallizations were not prioritized but pursued "additively."

Few choices were made among them. We will see that this was an essential cause of war.

Two of the four crystallized less directly. The statesmen were drawn overwhelmingly from the old regime. Thus they crystallized only mildly as *nationalist*, a more popular ideology. But nationalism pressured them from without and within – since carried by middling to higher-level state employees and state educational institutions. Second, as an old regime they did not much directly crystallize as *capitalist*, or at least as modern industrial capitalist. Nonetheless as reactionaries they did have an abiding hatred of capitalism's enemies, the working class and socialism. To be firmly in the "party of order" by 1900 meant to be procapitalist. Statesmen crystallized as *monarchist* and *militarist* more directly. Almost all were courtiers. In the words of one of them, they constituted the "ruling herd." Herds stampede but are not courageous. Several chancellors and state secretaries doubted the kaiser's sanity and discussed putting him under restraint. But they never acted: "They dared not, because, whether brilliant or dull-witted, they all, with the exception of Bismarck, were courtiers before they were statesmen" (Albertini 1952: I, 160).

The monarch formally decided foreign policy; in reality, monarchism did, in the form of divide and rule and court intrigue. It played an unhelpful role in the slide toward war. So did soldiers. Most of the kaiser's entourage, of his cabinets, and of those enjoying *Immediatstellung* were officers from noble conservative families. The army was the old regime's training ground. Elite guards regiments surrounded the monarch. Martial law was used ubiquitously to preserve order.

High commands

Some of these characteristics of the German military were found in all regimes. Military service still dominated the old regime in all monarchies, constitutional as well as authoritarian. Monarchs, courts, and high commands played together, thought together, and fought together. The rituals of army life still emphasized aristocratic and royal connections (many still do). Passing out from staff college, promotion, decoration, maneuvers, and reviews all occurred under a dominating royal ethos. Outstanding officers were noble by birth or ennobled as reward for service. The officers' mess perpetuated the gentleman. As army size increased and conscription became general (except for Britain and the United States), middle-class sons experienced this world as cadets and reserve officers. All this might seem like a brilliant old regime strategy to clutch the middle class to its bosom, but it also contained two threats to old regime solidarity: one general, the other varying by country.

The variable consequence was that the officer corps now contained some of society's political tensions. Bourgeoisie versus "old corruption" was translated into technocratic modernism versus aristocratic conservatism. Where old regime–bourgeois conflict was largely solved, the army went through modernization relatively smoothly, as in Germany and Britain. In France, unity was achieved only after the struggles of the Dreyfus affair. The Austrian army remained factionalized between advocates of dynastic and parliamentary-ministerial control, reducing its fighting coherence (Stone 1975: 124; Rothenberg 1976: 79). By 1914, the Russian high command was split, unable to impose a single strategy on the different army corps. Russia entered the war with traditional generals defending fortresses while modernizers spread their forces across railway-defined fronts, and with northern and southern fronts poorly coordinated (Stone 1975: 17–27). The Russian officer corps now contained liberal technocrats becoming impatient with the monarchy. Their loyalty did not withstand three years of disastrous war.

But a more general problem faced all regimes, liberal as well as authoritarian. Even if the officer corps rallied middle class and old regime together, what it actually *did* became arcane, hidden from view, yet potentially devastating for regime and entire civil society. Military training and tactics were now removed from the everyday life of the aristocracy, indeed from the everyday life of anyone. Sports and playground fighting no longer related to war. The military was becoming a giant factory, effectively hierarchically integrated within, hidden from the outside, with little knowledge of the outside. But what was going on inside mattered very greatly because of the industrialization of war. Military tactics became aggressive, preemptive, and hampered narrow technocratic blinkers that hid the importance of diplomacy and alliance building to ultimate military victory.

The technocratic plans of high commands could preempt the statesmen. Whether they did so depended on channels of accountability. Party democracies provided more of these because they had been born in resistance to despotic monarchies using armies for internal repression. In Britain, France, the United States, and Italy, high command plans were usually vetted by the government (Steiner 1977: 189–214; Bosworth 1983: 44–60). In 1914, French mobilization was restricted by Poincaré to positions 10 kilometers behind the frontier to avoid precipitous border clashes, despite the grumblings of his generals. The French government also vetoed Marshal Joffre's plan for an offensive through Belgium, because this would alienate the British. Nonetheless, the consultations between the British and French militaries consequent upon the Entente were kept secret for five years from the cabinet and did constrain the diplomats. Exactly how much is currently controversial. In the three monarchies, controls were far less formal. Without cabinet government, with the monarch the titular commander in chief and a kinsman often in actual command, control depended on court intrigue. The Austrian army was, by 1914, the dynasty's main "transnational" prop. The Russian and German armies had seemingly *created* their empires. The German army owed its extraordinary degree of influence in the state to its string of dazzling, rapid, and low casualty victories. Powers tend to institutionalize what makes them great. After Bismarck's fall, the accountability of the German army actually reduced, as the authority of the minister of war, responsible to the Reichstag, faltered before that of the general staff and the military cabinets. The Reichstag could challenge this by rejecting the seven-year military budget, but it never dared do so (Craig 1955: chapter 6).

But militaries were not united on how military power should be employed. Various army and navy factions competed, with little political control or military consistency (Herwig 1973: 175–82; Kitchen 1968). Militaries lacked diplomatic competence or interest. The German army was casually anti-Russian, the navy anti-English; but the "ruling herd" paid little serious attention to geopolitics, to *Weltpolitik* or *Mitteleuropa* (discussed later), to the alliance system, or to economic mobilization. It concentrated on battlefield expertise and domestic conservatism. At the notorious German War Council of December 1912, the generals seemingly persuaded the kaiser of the need for a "preventive war" against Russia – supposedly a major escalation in German planning for war. Admiral Tirpitz, protesting that the fleet was not ready, got a delay of eighteen months (almost to the day war actually began). But this seemingly earth-shaking decision did not lead to any actual war preparations. No attention was paid to diplomatic preparations (to isolate Russia), to the problems of a war economy, or even to army-navy coordination (Rohl 1973: 28–32; Hull 1982: 261–5). Armies and navies were locked into a narrow technocratic militarism.

How monarchical statesmen and high commands went to war

Military power achieved its world-historical moment at the end of July and early August 1914. War actually started as a series of military mobilizations turned into declarations of war between July 28 and August 4. The Russian and German mobilizations were the key escalations.

In Russia, the tsar, most politicians, and the new chief of staff, Yanushkevich, favored partial mobilization against Austria alone rather than general mobilization against Germany too – to deter Austria but not provoke Germany. Yanushkevich suggested to the tsar (and to the Germans) on July 25 that a partial mobilization against Austria was possible. Yet his high command staff speedily informed him that the state of the railway network prevented anything short of a general mobilization. They exaggerated. Partial mobilization would have been possible, though it would have obstructed any later general mobilization. The generals were delivering a judgment on what concerned them – military efficiency. It was not their responsibility to cope with diplomatic repercussions, that is, to consider which Powers they might actually be fighting.

There was now a frenzy of court intrigue. On July 29, the tsar delayed his decision by signing two mobilization orders, one partial, the other general. Yanushkevich pocketed both, and over the next thirty-six hours was ordered to implement first the general, then the partial, then the general again. At 5 P.M. on July 30, he transmitted the general mobilization order, a decisive step toward war. Headquarters officers then supposedly tore out the telephones to prevent any further change of heart! The Germans heard of the mobilization immediately and assumed (as in their own planning) it meant actual war. Yet the high command had assured the tsar that Russian troops could be held in defensive mobilized positions for two to three weeks. Foreign Secretary Sazunov appeared baffled in an exchange with the German ambassador on July 26, asking, "Surely mobilization is not equivalent to war with you either. Is it?" "Perhaps not in theory," replied the ambassador, "but . . . once the button is pressed, and the machinery of mobilization set in motion there is no stopping it" (Albertini 1953: II, 481). So began that fateful metaphor, the button! But not even this warning conveyed to the Russians the precise, dangerous meaning that mobilization signified in Germany.

Neither Russian nor German leaders understood that the distinction between general and partial mobilization, over which they agonized, mattered little. The military clauses of the Triple Alliance compelled Germany to order general mobilization even if Russia mobilized only against Austria. This would immediately force Russia into general mobilization. Furthermore, *any* Russian mobilization was a mistake at this stage. It provoked Germany; and on the Austrian front it ignored the military consequences of diplomacy. The longer Russia sat quietly, the more Austrian mobilization carried the Austrian army south toward Serbia, away from the Russian border. Had Russia decided later to mobilize and invade, Austrian defenses would have been denuded

(Albertini 1953: II, 290–4, 479–85, 539–81; cf. Turner 1968; Schmitt 1966: 249–56, gives the Russian view).

Working out reasons of state and national interests is appropriate for realists in academic studies and seminars. But rapid decision making amid changing and dangerous circumstances is different. This court simply couldn't cope: The military courtiers wanted only what was narrowly technically efficient; the foreign secretary wanted to avoid war but knew nothing of military affairs and had little influence at court; the grand dukes were divided; the tsar's concentration span was limited; the tsarina was guided by Rasputin. Russian escalation resulted from the divided responsibilities, royal inadequacies, and inconclusive intrigue to which monarchy is peculiarly susceptible. Cock-up theory works for Russia.

The second escalation was the German response on July 31: the proclamation of war readiness (*Kriegsgefahr*) and a twelve-hour ultimatum to Russia to cancel its mobilization or be at war. German mobilization meant war, with no breathing space. The technical intricacies and precise timetables of the Schlieffen plan of 1905 had further developed the offensive military tactics discussed in Chapter 12. Troops were to be mobilized and concentrated *over* the border, in Holland, Belgium, and Luxembourg – all neutral countries. Holland was eliminated in Moltke's 1911 modification of the plan, but this made the other parts of the offensive essential. The Luxembourg railways must be occupied on day one of mobilization, Liège (in Belgium) on day three, the plan declared. German mobilization, once started, could not be held back from violations of neutrality and so from almost certain war with France and probable war with Britain.

Yet, astonishingly, this was not revealed by the German high command. The chancellor was not told until July 31 that mobilization involved immediate violation of Belgian neutrality. Nor was it known for sure by the Austrian allies, though all foreign high commands suspected it. The kaiser did not know about Liège until it happened, on August 4. As the chancellor realized, this would lead Britain into war, but it was too late to change the plan. The last German steps into war were taken by the high command independently of political channels. There was no overall cabinet. Chancellor Bethmann and Chief of Staff Moltke were equals, subject only to the kaiser, with their own channels of influence. Admiral Tirpitz ranked lower than the chief of staff but was a more influential courtier. As the kaiser was volatile, his moods were watched and exploited. Moltke had favored preventive war since 1912. Exploiting the kaiser's bellicosity, he persuaded him on August 30 to issue the *Kriegsgefahr* and the ultimatum next day. Through his own staff officers he personally guaranteed the Austrian high command German support if they mobilized against Russia. At this, Austrian Foreign Secretary Berchtold exclaimed, "Who rules in Berlin, Moltke or Bethmann?" (Turner 1970: 109). The answer, Tirpitz says, was neither:

Collective consultation between the political and military leaders never took place, either on the politico-strategical problems of the conduct of the war or even on the prospect of a world war at all. I was never even informed of the invasion of Belgium, which immediately raised naval questions when it took place. [Albertini 1957: III, 195, 250–1]

Since 1912, Moltke, Foreign Secretary Jagow, and Bethmann had been intermittently urging preventive war. Yet they had not consulted with industrialists or financiers to discuss the economic consequences of war (Turner 1970: 84–5). The military, diplomats, and capitalists went their own ways, influencing their different state power networks to undertake different specialized policies. Only a volatile kaiser was above them. In Berlin, too, there was cock-up.

In Vienna, the main cock-up–foul-up was between military and diplomatic power networks. Field Marshal Conrad's supremacy over military plans was unchallenged, but he had no competence or control over the diplomacy that decided who Austria's enemies were to be. Last-minute German pressure forced Austria to mobilize against Russia as well as Serbia. Hence the armies of the state that had started the war, that had longest to prepare its offensive, and that perhaps had the most united command structure were to be found on day one of the Great War frantically changing trains from the Serbian to the Russian border.

Cock-up–foul-up also went down through many diplomatic networks. Hartwig, Russian minister to Serbia, inflamed Belgrade against Austria for years. His government did not approve, but court patrons prevented his removal. The Serbian prime minister had actually got wind of the plot to assassinate the archduke in Bosnia (it was organized by his enemies within the government). But forgetting that the Austrian Finance Ministry ran Bosnia, he warned the wrong ministry, the bellicose Austrian Interior Ministry, which suppressed the message. German Ambassador Tschirschky encouraged Austrian bellicosity, transmitting in Vienna the views of hawkish Foreign Secretary Jagow rather than vacillating Chancellor Bethmann. Von Bulow commented sardonically that Bethmann and Jagow constituted "a committee for public catastrophe" (Turner 1970: 86). In London, German Ambassador Lichnovsky counseled caution to Berlin, but Jagow and sometimes Bethmann neutralized his dispatches.

The monarchies did aggress, but not because of any single-minded ruthless militarism. First, their aggression was rendered a distinct possibility from the regime's almost casual militarism, its readiness to defer to men in uniform more readily than liberal regimes in both domestic and geopolitics. This is the valid part of traditional liberal theories of war which assert that authoritarian, not liberal, regimes start wars (I consider them in a moment). Second, those militaries had developed a private castelike insulation whose very professionalism had led them toward more aggressive technical practices. Third, this major, catastrophic war was precipitated unintentionally by the segmental divide-and-rule strategies of monarchy. No one possessed supreme power and responsibility except the monarch. It was internal cock-up–foul-up, amid a general ethos of casual militarism, that made the monarchies dangerous. No one sufficiently controlled both military and diplomatic channels of influence to make rational realist decisions.

I have deconstructed the state or Power. True, the "Power" officially spoke as a single actor declaring war, and this determined the future of the world. Yet this "actor" was actually polymorphous, formed by factionalized power networks, embodying plural crystallizations, above which sat executives – mediocre monarchs and harassed chancellors, ministers, and foreign secretaries – all depending on intrigue for finding out what was going on. How different was it in the party democracies?

Party democracies

Since Kant, liberals (and, recently, conservatives such as Margaret Thatcher) have claimed that "republican," "constitutional," "liberal," or "democratic" states are inherently pacific whereas authoritarian states are warlike. This is partly because liberals have an optimistic view of human nature – the free individual will not want to go to war – and partly because they see liberal regimes as capitalistic and capitalism as transnational and cosmopolitan. There may be some truth in both propositions. But Doyle's research (1983) enables us to locate liberalism's pacific qualities rather more precisely.

Doyle defines regimes as liberal if they have market and private property economies, citizens possessing juridical rights (civil citizenship), and representative government in which the legislative branch has an effective role in public policy and is elected either by at least 30 percent of males or by a franchise achievable by inhabitants reaching a certain level of wealth (in the twentieth century, he adds criteria of woman suffrage). His political criteria amount to what I have termed party democracy. He lists three liberal regimes in the late eighteenth century – some Swiss cantons, the French republic between 1790 and 1795, and the United States. There were 8 liberal regimes (including

Britain) by 1850, 19 by 1914, and 72 by 1980. He then determines whether these regimes, or others, have started modern wars.

Doyle makes an apparently audacious claim: No two liberal regimes have ever gone to war with each other. But he has chosen his terrain carefully; yet even then his evidence strains at the seams. It is important to his claim that Britain not be considered liberal before the Great Reform Act of 1832, as shortly before then it had fought major wars against two of the only three regimes then classified as liberal (the French republic and America both before and after its independence). Yet Britain really meets Doyle's criteria because even its franchise was (unevenly) open to wealth achievement, and it clearly meets his other criteria. His restrictive historical time frame also enables him to exclude the later seventeenth-century Anglo-Dutch naval wars, ranging the two most liberal Powers of the age against each other. He cheats a little in including Italy but not Spain around 1900, when the two countries had rather similar "corrupt" constitutions. A cynic might observe that this avoids having to note the Spanish-American War as an exception. He also excludes civil wars, yet the American Civil War was between two predominantly liberal regimes (in his sense). If we limit his claim to the twentieth century, it becomes true (so far) – surely an impressive finding in itself.

But Doyle does not stop there, as liberal apologists tend to do. He also finds that liberal regimes have gone to war rather enthusiastically against nonliberal ones, especially in the modern Third World. Since World War II, they have positively foamed at the mouth and aggressed ferociously against regimes they define as "communist" (more recently as "dictatorships"). Why this extraordinary contrast between the behavior of liberal regimes toward each other and toward other types of regime? In the twentieth century, a Marxian answer contains some truth. Third World regimes, especially those designated communist, threaten capitalism, whereas other liberal regimes do not (although I do not consider this an ultimately adequate response, and the United States launched invasions of Central America during the twentieth century, well before communism could scare it). But this does not help much on the nineteenth century, when nonliberal regimes were also procapitalist. Doyle gives an alternative answer, arguing that liberal regimes believe they have a particularly strong claim to legitimacy because they rest on the consent of morally autonomous individuals. Liberal regimes respect one another's moral autonomy but see nonliberal regimes as lacking moral legitimacy and, therefore, attack them with ideological zeal.

I find virtues in Doyle's qualified defense of liberalism. It remains a little rosy, however, and somewhat neglects realist geopolitics. Before

World War I, the foreign policies of his liberal regimes were more geopolitically motivated than he suggests. The geopolitical interrelations of the three major liberal Powers – the United States, Britain, and France – were settled by major wars conveniently just before Doyle terms them liberal. Afterward, both Britain and the United States could expand freely by colonial genocide and wars in their agreed spheres of interest. They sought no wars against European Powers, liberal or not, unless their colonial expansion or naval power was threatened. Their liberalism (in dealing with each other) was also defined at the time as hard-nosed geopolitical interest. This was true of France as well. As Chapter 8 shows, France had been carefully neutralized from 1815 by the victorious Concert of Powers, which also guaranteed the neutrality of Belgium and the Netherlands (the next two liberal states). Thereafter it would have been dangerous for France to attack these and pointless for France to attack the much stronger Britain (though they did clash in the colonies).

After Piedmont-Italy became liberal, its motivations were similarly mixed. War with France was a geopolitical possibility and Italian diplomacy wavered through the period. But because France was threatened more by Germany, and because Piedmont-Italy could get pickings from war against Austria (and Turkey), Franco-Italian alliances resulted in the wars of 1859 and 1914. Italy decided its position in 1914–15 more by geopolitical reasoning than liberal solidarity (Doyle suggests the reverse). For Italy, it mattered more that (authoritarian) Russia was attacking Austria than that liberal Britain and France were attacking Germany. Allied with Russia (with France and Britain neutralizing Germany), Italy could grab territory from Austria.

Passing to the remaining European liberal states, Chapter 8 shows that the economies of the Low Country and Scandinavian states (the next liberal ones) depended on the British global economy. Their foreign policy was partly dominated by Britain, and Low Country geopolitics was also constrained by the Great Powers. During the nineteenth century, the only independent Scandinavian states were Sweden and Denmark. War between them would have to be naval, and after 1805, neither had major navies. In any case, Scandinavia had experienced a deterrent balance of power and small militaries for two centuries before it became liberal. Swiss cantons were neutral whether or not they were liberal, for traditional geopolitical reasons. Greece had no liberal rivals.

To proceed beyond Europe, the white dominions of the British Empire, dominated by London, were imbued with the same selective liberalism and had no geopolitical interest in attacking one another. Nor had Canada any desire to attack the United States. I do not know why Argentina and Chile did not make war on each other during the short period Doyle defines them as liberal (after 1891). It would have been geographically difficult for Colombia (liberal from 1910) to be at war with either of them.

That exhausts Doyle's pre-1914 liberal regimes. I have found geopolitical reasons why they did not war with each other. These seem insufficient to explain at most only two cases – Anglo-American and perhaps inter-Scandinavian peace (why had the northern balance of power never fully broken down?) – both resting on a much broader normative solidarity than the mere sharing of political liberalism. This is not to refute Doyle but to amend him in two ways:

1. In 1914, liberal party democracies, though because of entwined political and geopolitical causes, *were* less aggressive and militaristic than authoritarian regimes. Representative states *are* better at averting wars, though partly for a different reason than most liberals (including Doyle) suggest. Not many wars are simply "started" by a single belligerent. Most, like World War I, involve a downward spiral of diplomacy in which rapidly changing circumstances force rapid recalculations of interest. Liberals wrongly envy authoritarian regimes' supposed capacity to achieve "the privacy, the flexibility, and the promptness and incisiveness of decision and action . . . which are generally necessary to the conduct of an effective world policy by the rulers of a great state" (Kennan 1977: 4; he is also quoted approvingly by Doyle).

But this chapter shows the reverse. Although no regime was fully coherent (each being polymorphous), responsible liberal states are a little better at pursuing realist interests (including averting costly war) than monarchies were. I also believe that, being more internationalist and less oriented toward simple repression as a solution to problems, they are better at the diplomacy of acquiring allies than are authoritarian regimes. This is probably the decisive reason why democracies triumphed over authoritarian regimes in the major wars of the twentieth century. Though less good at militarism, they were better at mobilizing the bigger battalions mobilizable by alliances. But that is a matter for Volume III.

2. Doyle correctly emphasizes norms and ideology in geopolitics, but norms concern more than just regime form. Restraint in Anglo-American and in inter-Scandinavian relations partly resulted because the countries shared far more than just liberalism. Diffused norm sharing will help avert wars that do not fit rationally into realist schemes because they are in no one's interest to fight – as was World War I (although they will help prosecute wars that are partly defined by ideologies, as the Napoleonic Wars had been). Conversely, lack of shared norms worsens the misunderstandings of downward diplomatic

spirals. Thus the lack of shared norms between party democracies and monarchies worsened Great Power misunderstandings and steepened the spiral of 1914.

Chapter 12 shows that the party democracies had built more control over the regime in domestic and military than in diplomatic affairs. Indeed, the relative indifference of classes and political parties to foreign affairs may actually have conferred more insulated autonomy on the party democracy than on the monarchy in the routine conduct of foreign policy, as the cosmopolitan yet also militaristic old regime had more influence at court and more interest in foreign policy. But in a crisis it was different. Money could not be spent; formal commitments to other Powers could not be made; war could not be declared without the consent of suddenly interested majorities in cabinets and parliaments, mass media, and "public opinion." In Chapter 3, I distinguish classes, pressure groups, and nationalist parties as the principal power networks potentially pressuring statesmen and militaries. In crises their pressure was manifested. Yet by then policy options might have been already delimited. The liberal Power might be already boxed in by insulated routine diplomacy. This could lead into the tragic Hobson's choice between war or risking "national dishonor" by "backing down" – or, as Grey put it, "between war and diplomatic humiliation."

On the other hand, statesmen in party democracies were restrained by their perceptions of what the public would accept. What was perceived to be the expression of mass public opinion was rarely bellicose. In examining an age without polls, we must rely on what experienced politicians believed public opinion to be. Most politicians in Britain and France perceived the electorate as indifferent to routine Great Power diplomacy but opposed to war unless in self-defense. Gunboats in what would become the Third World were fine; "foreign entanglements," still less mobilization against a Great Power, were not. In 1914, Britain was ruled by a Liberal government, containing three virtual pacifist and a half-dozen Liberal internationalist cabinet members. In 1911, this cabinet had voted 15 to 5 against firming up the Entente. British politics were preoccupied with strikes and near civil war in Ulster (as they will probably be in the year 2014). French politics had been riven by debates about military conscription, but paid little attention to the Balkans or Alsace-Lorraine. The French media were preoccupied by a dramatic political murder trial. Amid popular indifference, Poincaré had achieved one-man control of foreign policy, manipulating the cabinet into "supine support of whatever he did" (Keiger 1983; cf. Bosworth 1983 on Italy). Statesmen were expected to solve the crisis in private, not by publicly threatening war. This created a difficulty for party-democratic regimes: Although they might believe geopolitical interests required firmness, even war readiness, they could not easily say so in public. Only right-wingers out of office did so freely.

There were – and still are – two solutions to the democratic dilemma, one exemplified at the time by French statesmen, the other by British. The French ambassador to Moscow, Paléologue, personified the French solution, of covert firmness. The French government had offered military and financial inducements to Russian generals and financiers to pressure the tsar into the Franco-Russian alliance. Believing now was the time to recover Alsace-Lorraine, Paléologue repeatedly urged Russian leaders to stand behind Serbia, assuring them of French support. He failed to report either Russian wavering or the provocative mobilization back to Paris. French public opinion must not glimpse either Russian hesitation or aggression. The appearance of firm self-defense must be maintained, if necessary into war. Much is uncertain about French diplomacy during the crisis (incriminating documents have probably been destroyed). It is difficult to assess how far French diplomatic trickery pushed Russian mobilization; it may have contributed but not decisively.

British Liberal statesmen took the opposite tack. (See especially Williamson 1969 and Wilson 1985 for sources of the next paragraphs.) Foreign Secretary Grey, with the tacit support of Prime Minister Asquith, felt unable to give even private assurances to France or Russia of British intentions. He was personally convinced that geopolitical logic meant honoring the Entente, as were his Foreign Office advisers, Eyre Crowe and Nicholson. They believed a showdown with Germany had become inevitable. This group of "statesmen" was thoroughly socialized into realist values, dedicated to the defense of British power and honor, not just material interests. By about 1912, it seemed clear to them that Germany was seeking to dominate Europe and displace Britain as its leading Power.

Being a near-hegemonic Power seems conducive to cultivating a high moral tone (as in American foreign policy today). It mattered less that, even if Germany did inflict another defeat on France, its navy was inadequate and would remain inadequate to threaten the British Isles. It mattered more in their expressed statements that such an outcome, amid British inactivity, would be a national "humiliation" and involve "reneging" on the implicit understanding they felt they had reached with the French. The French had, after all, withdrawn their fleet to the Mediterranean, assuming that the Royal Navy would police the Channel. Grey himself best expressed the sense of honor possessed by his generation of British statesmen: "When nations have gone down hill till they are at their last gasp their pride remains undiminished, if indeed it is not increased. It clings to them as Tacitus says the love of dissimulation clung to Tiberius at his last gasp" (quoted by Wilson at the opening of his 1985 study of the Entente).

Note how Grey personifies "nations." They have human attributes such as pride. There was also a more material realist dilemma in their position. British geopolitical interests lay in reaching an understanding with Russia – to prevent what was felt to be an unwinnable land war in Asia – and in keeping Germany from the Channel, which involved reaching an understanding with France. France and Russia should be friendly. Yet neither should be able to *count on* British support in case of war because they might then be tempted to act provocatively. Hence, there were geopolitical reasons for Grey's caution.

Innenpolitik, however, seems to have mattered most. Grey and his advisers believed that once Germany attacked France and Belgium and threatened Channel ports, British opinion would rally to back British "honor" with military intervention. But until that happened, Grey believed, public opinion and the cabinet majority would reject intervention. To convert the Entente into an alliance or to threaten Germany in advance would split the government because several ministers would resign (two did so when war was declared), and this would force its resignation. The Conservative party would support Grey and form the new government with Liberal imperialist support. This would destroy the Liberal party and might even lead to Irish civil war. So Grey did nothing. He kept the cabinet sketchily informed and did not ask for its collective advice. Foreign governments were told that Britain promised nothing and was keeping all options open. Grey's repeated public and private statements to this effect enabled the hawkish Jagow to discount Ambassador Lichowsky's warnings of British intervention at the Wilhelmstrasse (Williamson 1969: 340–2). German diplomats believed until July 30 that Britain would remain neutral. By then, they were losing control to the army. Had they not believed in British neutrality, they would not have stepped toward war.

After the war, Bethmann and Tirpitz complained bitterly of British deception: Britain had lured Germany toward destruction. But the opposite was true. Grey had acted pusillanimously, yet also as honorably as his perception of an essentially Liberal public opinion allowed. He did not want war; among British leaders, there were no advocates of a preventive war. But the situation cried out not for British pride but for Tiberian or Gallic dissimulation: Say nothing in public or full cabinet, but warn Germany privately that Britain would intervene if France was attacked and (unlike France) warn Russia privately that any provocation would lessen the chances of intervention. Unlike French duplicity, British honor may have been a necessary cause of a crisis becoming a world war. But Grey's mistakes were not idiosyncratic or socially inexplicable. They emerged from failure to resolve the militarist political crystallizations: British statesmen mixed insulated realism with a sense of national honor to espouse more militarism than did the Liberal ruling party and majority public opinion. There was no "ultimate" geopolitical identity of the British state, only confusion and world war.

Thus popular opinion played a destructive role in the party democracies during the crisis. As mediated by the party system, it granted routine insulation to the regime, yet restrained its freedom of action, specifically its ability to wield military threats, without giving the regime a realistic alternative policy. Regimes became boxed in during crises. Monarchical statesmen were less restrained and misunderstood the inaction of a party democracy as indifference or cowardice, both of which Britain had demonstrated forty to fifty years earlier, when Germany had attacked Denmark, Austria, and France (although then there had been no menacing German navy). Behavior that is rewarded will be repeated, unless the decision maker clearly perceives changed circumstances. This made it more likely that authoritarian regimes would attack, as occurred again just before World War II. As Doyle observed, lack of shared norms between democratic and authoritarian regimes mattered. In this case, however, it was less that they denied legitimacy to each other, more that they genuinely misunderstood each other's different polymorphous crystallizations. In crisis diplomacy, this accelerated the slide toward war.

Parliaments and parties rarely initiated foreign policy. The unstable semiinsulation of the regime tended to enfeeble geopolitics. It led either to vacillation, as in Britain, or to a covert regime strategy of manipulating opinion toward its desired goal. Both have appeared in twentieth-century party democracy, the first notably in Britain and the second notably in the United States as Presidents Wilson and Roosevelt manipulated American opinion toward world wars (for Wilson, see Hilderbrand 1981: 133–5).

To ram home this point, let me cite two present-day examples from regimes that are supposedly full democracies: U.S. entry into the Vietnam War and British involvement in the Falklands War of 1983. In both cases a small group of senior politicians and military men made minor decisions over several years concerning far-off countries, employing small discretionary resources, with virtually no public scrutiny or interest. The United States gradually and privately began to prop up the South Vietnam regime with aid, military hardware, and "advisers." Britain began to reduce its military presence in the South Atlantic without signaling any remaining defensive commitment. When the

South Vietnamese faded and the Argentines invaded, crises loomed. Neither the American nor the British government wished to be seen as "backing down," and for a time they manipulated uninformed public opinion by wrapping themselves in the flag and in shallow political nationalism. When fifty thousand Americans were killed in a futile war, nationalism weakened and the United States withdrew. The British, faced with a weaker enemy and good fortune, prevailed before they had exhausted shallow nationalism. Both became full-scale wars through the essentially private, autonomous decisions of statesmen. Although it is too early to understand all the moves that led up to the 1990–91 Gulf War, they have a similar appearance.

Is it mere naïveté to hope for the emergence of genuinely democratic foreign policy in which mass opinion and parties are not nationally obsessed and where they openly debate routine foreign policy, keeping regimes under restraints imposed by deep-rooted, general social interests – one of which is not to have large numbers of people killed in useless wars?

The party democracy also was polymorphous, leading to diplomacy that was incoherent, though less so than in monarchy. Democratic incoherence emerged, not among courtier factions, as in monarchies, and only partly in the institution that had supposedly replaced the court, the parliament, but more importantly in the contradiction between the everyday realist privacy and autonomy of the regime and the overall national climate of "pacific indifference" (which we shall see could be diverted in crises into shallow nationalist rhetoric). This raises puzzling questions: Were classes and nations so indifferent, allowing insulation to their regimes? And if so, why? Did the two regime types differ? I broaden my focus to more popular power actors, principally classes and nations.

Classes, nations, and geopolitics

I return to my three ideal-typical forms of class organization:

1. *Transnational*: When class identity and organization crosscut state boundaries, states and nations become largely irrelevant to class relations. Personal and collective interests are defined by global markets, not state territory. Modern transnational classes would be broadly pacific. They would possess foreign interests and would supervise regime geopolitics toward conciliatory diplomacy. If transnational classes had been dominant in 1914, war could not have resulted. The same reasoning applies to nonclass transnational actors. Had, for example, the Catholic church retained its transnational powers into the modern world, realist wars between nation-states would have been less likely

(though perhaps not religious wars). We may suspect that transnationalism had weakened through the modern period.

2. *Nationalist*: Where the interests of one nation conflict with another's, nationalist quasi-classes emerge, with distinct interests in relation to the international division of labor. Nationalist class relations encourage territorial definitions of identity and interest and aggressive geo-economics and geopolitics. If such class organization had dominated, the Great War might result from the conflicting material interests of (capitalist) nation-states.

3. *National*: Class identity and organization is here caged within each individual state, without significant reference to the world outside. Though classes get caught up in domestic struggles over the identity of the nation, they are inward-looking, incompetent in geopolitics. They have no serious geopolitical interests and no predisposition toward either war or peace. In their ignorance, national classes may leave geopolitics to the expertise of statesmen. Then war and peace are the responsibility of professionals (drawn from the old regime), not the masses, and predominantly insulated realism and the primacy of *Aussenpolitik* can continue right into modern society. Alternatively, the sentiments of national classes might be displaced onto nationalism that was essentially political rather than economic. Either ignorant, nationally obsessed classes may spontaneously displace their domestic frustrations onto foreigners (e.g., Howard 1970: 103–4) or ruling classes and regimes may create and manipulate national identity so as to displace domestic class antagonism onto international conflict (e.g., Mayer 1968, 1981). In both cases the flag is waved, the drums beaten, and foreigners rather than the rulers are attacked. In these approaches an essentially *political* nationalism resulted from nationally organized classes.

Transnational classes did not cause the Great War. They opposed it, but they were overruled in any of four ways:

1. Nationalist classes, with an aggressive geopolitical strategy based on their material interests, could have rationally started it. That is argued by theories of *economic imperialism*: The economic rivalry of capitalist nation-states led rationally and deliberately to geopolitics carrying a grave but acceptable risk of war. The interests directly conferred by economic power relations were responsible for war.

But national classes could also have caused the war in three alternative ways:

2. The frustrations and aggressions of domestic classes were manipulated by the rulers and displaced onto the foreign enemy: the theory of *social imperialism*. Class interests indirectly conferred by domestic economic power relations were responsible for war.

3. National classes developed spontaneous warlike xenophobia: the theory of *political nationalism*. Political power relations and identities were responsible for war.

4. Nationally obsessed classes left geopolitics to the old regime, pressured only by particularistic interest groups. These were responsible for the war. This I term *old regime* theory. Here economic power actors avoided foreign policy, leaving insulated or particularistically embedded diplomatic, military, and political power actors responsible for war.

All four explanations have some force, varying among types of regimes and classes. None offers a sufficient explanation of the war or of the aggression of any single Power. A sufficient explanation has to entwine them all. I consider the major classes in turn, starting with the capitalist class.

Capitalists and economic imperialism

To avoid war, nineteenth-century liberals pinned hopes on the predominantly transnational organization and "interdependence" of capital. Once capitalist property and market norms were institutionalized, entrepreneurs would pursue profit regardless of state boundaries. Classical economists did not ignore states but believed that international trade generated interdependence. As countries' resources differed, each would specialize in whatever it produced best – "comparative net advantages." Though disputes might arise about terms of trade, disruption by war would be mutually damaging. Trading also required transnational financial arrangements to guarantee currencies, credit, and convertibility. Thus capitalists would favor pacific geopolitics.

The real economy turned out not quite so harmoniously interdependent. The European Powers arose from a quite similar social base. As the Industrial Revolution took society away from nature, ecological differences became less important and collective power practices more important. It became easier to imitate other countries' manufacturing and agricultural techniques. Thus the major states became more economically similar than classical economists had expected. Rivalry for markets intensified. Theories of economic nationalism arose, asserting economic interest was being defined – for good or ill – by the nation-state.

The English liberal J. A. Hobson (1902) argued that, for considerable ill, imperialism was generated by the current needs of capital. Plutocratic British social structure denied workers an adequate share of the national product and so created surplus capital, which it then exported to the empire. Hobson's ideas were revised by the Marxists Hilferding, Lenin, and Luxemburg. They inserted the falling rate of profit, rather than underconsumption, as the original cause of capital export. For Hobson and the Marxists, capitalist rivalry pressured states toward territorial imperialism and war: The new imperialism and the scramble for Africa led to the Great War.

Yet this version of economic imperialism was largely wrong. There was no capital surplus. The most aggressive Powers, Germany, Austria, and Russia, had the least spare capital. Only a few colonies in this period were established because of specifically capitalist pressure; few were seen as good export markets; and colonial expansion in the late nineteenth century did not pay its way for any country. The eighteenth-century colonial bonanza had given way through the nineteenth century to the acquisition of poorer territories amid fiercer native resistance. This colonial rivalry then peaked during 1880–1900, and its principal protagonists were Britain versus France and Russia. Yet the war did not come then and was not fought between these Powers. These colonial rivals actually fought as allies in 1914. Though colonial clashes began to include Germany and often involved saber rattling, they were settled by diplomacy. Colonial rivalry in this period was not immediately profit seeking, and it did not cause the war (Robinson and Gallagher 1961; Fieldhouse 1973: 38–62; Kennedy 1980: 410–15; Mommsen 1980: 11–17).

But the theory of economic imperialism can still be partly saved. Though colonies were not that important, broader economic rivalries were. Fieldhouse is wrong to conclude that power and politics rather than profit lay behind imperialism. Some of the ventures he labels political, in Egypt, the Sudan, and central Asia, were designed to protect communications with India, which was economically vital to Britain. Moreover, almost no imperialism, no pursuit of power supposedly "for its own sake" is entirely divorced from considerations of economic gain. Even if the new imperialism in Britain was not caused by need to export capital, it included an important economic motive: to maintain British trade and finance in world markets amid German and American rivalry and the rise of protectionism (Platt 1979). No one knew how much African markets would be worth, but it was too risky to let others grab them and then find oneself excluded. After all, South Africa was transformed by the discovery of diamonds and gold from a worthless into a profitable colony over this period. From such considerations Wehler (1979) and Mommsen (1980) conclude that politics and economics should not be separated.

But I disagree. It is better to make definitions finer than to abandon them altogether. What is at stake is not economic versus political goals but, rather, varying mixtures of the two. Recall the six international political economies distinguished in Chapters 3 and 8.

At one extreme is *market profit*, a capitalist conception of profit resulting from exploiting superiority in markets through institutionalized free trade rules. The market is not viewed as a specific geographic area with territorial boundaries but as a set of functionally defined activities diffused transnationally, potentially over the globe. States are irrelevant to profit. This was the conception of the classical economists and still dominates the discipline of economics. This ideal type is transnational and pacific in its implications. It must have been overridden in the road to war.

The other conceptions all embody a more territorial sense of identity and interest carrying authoritative control of territory. The most territorial conception is *geopolitical imperialism*, defining interest as the invasion and control of as much territory as one's geopolitical power allows, seemingly for its own sake. Such aggression is never totally noneconomic; even Hitler (who gave no serious thought to economics) wanted to exploit the resources of conquered territories and sometimes directed assaults at economic targets (e.g., Romanian oil). But its predominant logic is not driven by the domestic economy. Targets for aggression are primarily selected not according to capitalist notions of profit but according to regime calculations of geopolitical alliance structures and military balances. If classes and other power actors support such geopolitical imperialism, they have subordinated themselves before political and military conceptions of interest, as the Germans did under Hitler, for example.

Between these two poles lie mixed market-territory conceptions of profit. *Protectionism* is the mildest, merely using legitimate state powers to protect the domestic economy on the international market through tariffs and import quotas. *Mercantilism* uses more aggressive techniques of disputed international legitimacy like subsidization and dumping of exports, state direction of domestic and foreign investment, and state support for monopolies or domestic corporations operating abroad. Where these two conceptions dominate, capitalist class organization becomes mildly nationalist. Protectionist and especially mercantilist policies may be defined by other Powers as hostile. But they will probably not threaten major war in response, as this will normally jeopardize profits even more. A more likely outcome is diplomatic compromise of protectionism or mercantilism.

We then proceed to two profit-led imperialisms. In *economic imperialism*, control of foreign territory, if necessary through war, is oriented to the needs of the domestic economy and of capital, as Hobson and the Marxists suggested. Capital organization itself becomes thoroughly nationalist. The capitalist class directs geopolitics and war, not vice versa. This was rarely so in the acquisition of late nineteenth-century colonies. Was it elsewhere? Finally, in *social imperialism* the profit motive is to damp down domestic class (or other) discontent, distracting it with foreign adventures. The adventures are not profitable, but heightened ability to exploit domestic classes and interest groups is.

War may have resulted from two broad economic paths: Either the geopolitical imperialism of political regimes and military castes may have overridden the market, possibly amplifying the mercantilist rationality of capitalists, or the economic or social imperialism of capital may have overridden its own market rationality and retracked the geopolitical imperialism of regimes and militaries. A third path, compromise, is also possible: War resulted from capitalists and state power networks coming together in a mutual, entwined conception of profit.

What did capitalists believe? Few thought about those issues in any systematic way, but their assumptions differed widely. As we saw in earlier chapters, capital split between relatively transnational and nationalist fractions. Some capitalists did band together nationally with state aid to control imports, exports, and foreign investment, but others were more interested in freedom of trade and open access to markets. Choices were affected by economic sector, the current terms and conditions of trade, their own size and profitability, and the like (Gourevitch 1986: 71–123). Many favored aggressive geopolitics toward Third World natives. But almost all were more cautious in their stances toward the European Powers, with which trade disruption and war would be very costly. In Europe, most went only as far as pragmatic protectionism, which did not denote fundamental national antagonism. Tariffs coexisted with economic and financial interdependence in global markets. The principal exception (explored later) was grain competition between Russia and Germany, whose high tariffs helped estrange the two countries and encourage German militarism.

Elsewhere the lineup of Powers was not caused by economic nationalism. The Austro-German alliance made little economic sense to Austria, in need of foreign capital and allied to the Power with least to spare (Joll 1984a: 134–5). France and Russia became financially interdependent, but more as consequence than cause of their Entente. French and German economic rivalry was not a major problem for either country. There was rivalry between Britain and Germany (varying between sectors), yet no more than with the United States, with which neither Power had hostile relations. In neither Germany nor Britain did aggressive nationalism directed against the other emerge from industrial or commercial capitalist rivalry; the two economies were actually becoming more interdependent. Between 1904 and 1914, Britain became Germany's best customer; and Germany, Britain's second best, after the United States (Steiner 1977: 41; Kennedy 1980: 41–58, 291–305). The lineup of Powers in the war was not caused fundamentally by protectionism, mercantilism, or economic imperialism.

By 1914, however, a sense of nationalist economic rivalry, hovering between mercantilism and economic imperialism, had spread, especially in Germany, as we saw in Chapter 9. Fewer German capitalists now advocated laissez-faire or mercantilism; more desired firmer territorial control abroad, as was expressed in slogans of *Mitteleuropa* and naval *Weltpolitik*, which made sense of the "encirclement" that alliances had brought about (discussed later). The Franco-Russian alliance had also cemented mutual economic interests: Whatever the geopolitical interests of France, there were now also good financial reasons for shoring up the tsar. Where aggressive territorial models of interest and rivalry existed, these worsened economic nationalism. But economic rivalry was more product than cause of geopolitical rivalry. Military and political power actors persuaded capitalists, more than vice versa, into imperialism.

Geopolitical power had always influenced economic theory. No conception of profit has a genuine and purely economic claim to "objectivity." Both their efficiency and adoption depend on other sources of social power. Market profit had recently been a British-cum-Enlightenment-cum-dynastic theory, depending on shared European ideology and diplomacy and on British naval and commercial power. It was vulnerable to List's accusation that it masked British interests. As British power and Continental involvement declined, market theories seemed less objectively based. Especially in Germany there developed a more protected, authoritatively organized, territorially centered capitalism. As Chapter 9 shows, this was neither more nor less correct as an economic theory than market alternatives. It worked and became influential partly because of the developing relationship between the Prussian state and bourgeois national citizenship. These power relations, more than the capitalist market, strengthened mercantilism and economic imperialism.

But even where nationalist economic rivalry was significant, it rarely fueled actual warmongering among capitalists. Capitalist pressure groups were often active in colonial policy, for particular industrial or commercial groups might have vital interests at stake in particular territories. For example, most countries saw the appearance of small but influential China lobbies, eager for further Western imperialism there (e.g., Campbell 1949). But economic interdependences among the Great Powers were strong, as were their fears of the cost of war for them. Therefore, few capitalists were as bellicose as popular press and nationalist "parties" in relation to other Great Powers. It was not in their economic interest to seek a war that would disrupt the global economy. Even arms manufacturers supplied transnationally – there were no government embargoes on military secrets – so they preferred cold to hot wars. The economic disruption of war seemed so self-evident that all Powers expected the war to be short: In months, the entire international economy would be at a standstill.

Yet although capitalists tended to give pacific advice, they were only marginal to the crucial decision-making arenas – cabinets, ministries, and courts. No government took more than cursory steps to develop economic planning machinery before the onset of hostilities. In Germany (as elsewhere in Europe) the Foreign Office was staffed almost exclusively by aristocrats with little knowledge or interest in economic affairs. Its nationalist critics in the Reichstag criticized this, but to no avail (Cecil 1976: 324–8). No government had plans for economic conquests before the outbreak of hostilities (German annexation plans, cataloged by Fischer 1975: 439–60, appeared during the war). Capitalists had developed some nationalist at the expense of transnational organization, but this was consequence more than cause of the rise of geopolitical rivalries. The war was not caused primarily by capitalist economic rationality, either of the mercantilist or the economic imperialist variety.

Social imperialism and the popular classes

Was geopolitical imperialism the result of *Innenpolitik* tensions displaced onto social imperialism? Did regimes see the war as the solution to these tensions? For one country the answers are clearly yes. The Austro-Hungarian monarchy came to see war with Serbia as the only solution to internal nationality problems. As Austrian aggression was a major cause of the war, this *Innenpolitik*, which, as Williamson (1988) observes, was indistinguishable from *Aussenpolitik* because it spread across Austrian borders, was decisive. Yet the monarchy was unique. Social imperialism is usually argued in relation to different domestic problems and strategies. The monarchy's problems were of regional nationality, not class, and Habsburg motives were dynastic, relatively unconcerned with popular manipulation or legitimation. Let us examine the other Powers. Was the spontaneous or manipulated political nationalism of classes responsible for the war?

As previous chapters have shown, over the course of the nineteenth century class struggles became more extensive and political. Organizations representing classes struggled over the whole terrain and constitution of the state, and some classes attained national citizenship. Mass public opinion became institutionalized through electoral campaigns fought between political parties and pressure groups, mediated by mass circulation newspapers. Conscription brought mass military experience. Thus the *Innenpolitik* of *national* classes became more relevant to the conduct of foreign policy (and vice versa).

The geopolitics of classes differed by how much citizenship they possessed. Political nationalism was greater where citizenship was fuller. I start with those who had least.

Workers and peasants were totally excluded in Russia, workers were largely excluded in Austria and Germany, and peasants were more variably excluded according to region. Though enfranchised and represented in sovereign parliaments in the three party democracies (least enfranchised in Britain), unions and workers' parties remained dissatisfied with the state's political economy – and so were many American farmers and French peasants.

Thus, for most workers and peasants, the state was not really *their* state. Of course, only a few worker militants were socialist converts, although socialist ideas were diffusing quite widely through the core industries (see Chapters 17 and 18), and peasants were attached to more conservative organizations than we might have expected (see Chapter 19). Many remained segmentally controlled by paternalistic employers, churches, and ethnic-linguistic communities. They might loyally follow their patrons into war, as retainers had done through the ages. Mass literacy and mass media might add more a modern, diffused rhetoric of attachment to the nation, flag, and monarch. But some segmental power organizations mobilizing workers and peasants, especially the Catholic church and regional-national minority communities, were ambivalent about the centralized nation-state.

Peasants were often also antiwar because they suffered most from conscription, wounds, and death. As I stress in Chapter 12, their military loyalty rested less on nationalism, more on military discipline that carefully molded local-regional unit loyalties into larger armies. The symbols of those armies were increasingly national. But the nationalism of soldiers and sailors was generated more by "organizational outflanking" and discipline than by "free" attachment to ideologies of genuine national citizenship.

Thus workers and peasants did not usually identify strongly and persistently with the nation-state. Because it was not their state, they had relatively little interest in its foreign policy. They were more concerned with national struggles for union-organizing rights, educational opportunities, and progressive taxation, or they were still caged by older local-regional community attachments. But they did tend to be antimilitarist – workers, because armies were still repressing them (Chapter 12) and because their liberal allies on domestic issues were often fervent antimilitarists; peasants, because they often identified militarism with centralism and conscription. Labor movements opposed military budgets, advocated socialist pacifism, and argued that capitalist or dynastic wars did not involve the interests of the people. In Russia, such sentiments were shared by peasant and middle-class organizations, also excluded from citizenship. In Austria, the exclusion of nationalities had similar radicalizing effects on some peasantries and middle classes. In the party democracies, with less exclusion, there was neither much militarism nor great suspicion of regime militarism among workers.

But in no country did working-class or peasant nationalism seriously exacerbate international tension. Some theorists of the "aristocracy of labor" assert that the working class was implicated in imperialism and nationalist rivalry. But they are wrong. The working class and peasantry were significantly underrepresented in all nationalist and imperialist movements of the period, including *all* the pressure groups discussed in Chapter 16, as well as in agitations concerning imperial ventures like the Boer War or U.S. intervention in the Philippines (Weber 1968; Price 1972; Eldridge 1973; Welch 1979: 88; Eley 1980). Whoever did cause the Great War, it was not the working class or the peasantry.

Working-class militants also identified with a larger, *transnational* community. Of its six principal ideologies (distinguished in Chapter 15), mutualism, syndicalism, Marxism, and social democracy were almost invariably transnational. So, even, were most versions of economism and protectionism. Gompers claimed to be as transnational as Marx. Although racism marred the transnationalism of American labor, it increased its antiimperialism (it opposed foreign ventures in order to keep America white). Almost all labor leaders endorsed the closing words of the *Communist Manifesto*: "Workers of all lands unite!" Their anthems were usually versions of the *Internationale*. Here is the Wobbly syndicalist version (Dubovsky 1969: 154):

> Arise, ye prisoners of starvation!
> Arise, ye wretched of the earth!
> For Justice thunders condemnation.
> A better world's in birth.
>
> The earth shall stand on new foundations;
> We have been *naught* – We shall be *All*!
> 'Tis the final conflict!
> Let each stand in his place.
> The Industrial Union
> Shall be the Human Race.

There was little overt nationalism in major labor movements; nor (remarkably for the period) was there much overt racism outside the

United States, because the "Human Race was One." Even the Jacobin identification of socialism with the French nation and republic – the revolutionary tradition of *tricoleur* and *Marseillaise* – was somewhat muted in this period. True, there were socialist "regionalist-nationalists" – Austro-Hungarian and Irish socialists sought their own national democracies – but few socialists supported military aggression or war abroad.

Socialism also possessed two small but influential transnational infrastructures, linking exiles and intelligentsia. Exiles had been forcibly rendered transnational; the intelligentsia enthusiastically embraced transnationalism. Artisan militants were punished with exile by monarchies throughout the nineteenth century. They congregated in small liberal German states, in London, Paris, Brussels, Switzerland, and the United States. Only in the United States did their socialism dissipate. Elsewhere, they interacted with native workers and with other displaced persons speaking their own language, principally exiled and cosmopolitan teachers and journalists – the socialist intelligentsia. These were the true inheritors of the transnational Enlightenment. Late nineteenth-century networks of exiles and intelligentsia in clubs, cafés, taverns, and journals became potent ideological infrastructures for communicating socialism across national boundaries. Few readers of Marx, Blanqui, Bakunin, Fourier, Lenin, Luxemburg, and their ilk could read a foreign language. A few bohemian cosmopolitans, often Jewish, sufficed as translators and publishers. Cells of artisan exiles and bohemian intelligentsia founded the First International in 1864, well before unions had established effective national organizations. Leftist intellectuals and militants were resolutely transnational.

But mass labor organizations became *national*. Whatever their ideologies, their activity went no farther than the nation-state. When protectionism, economism, or syndicalism sought to bypass the state, they usually organized locally or regionally, rarely abroad. Mutualists, social democrats, and Marxists took their demands to the national state and so strengthened it. Every success they achieved strengthened the national embrace. The national state was the only realistic context in which collective civil rights or redistribution of power, wealth, or security could occur. Labor was national because civil society became authoritatively regulated by the national state (which Marx never recognized). This set workers apart from capitalists, who now needed little national political regulation. They could allow the market, embodying capitalist property relations, to rule. In practice, capitalist organization varied considerably – some transnational, some national, some nationalist. By contrast, labor activity and organization was overwhelmingly nationally confined. As Jules Guesde said: "However internationalist we may be, it is on the national plane that the organized proletariat of each nation has to work for the emancipation of all humanity" (Weber 1968: 46).

The International might espouse transnational ideals, but by 1890 it had become a committee of national organizations, each representative pressing national interests. The national state was the real context for capital accumulation and for regulating labor (Olle and Schoeller 1977: 61). This left two weaknesses in labor's antiwar sentiments:

1. Because its praxis was overwhelmingly national, it was less active in than indifferent to geopolitics. British workers were not so much opposed as indifferent to the Boer War and to imperialism, concludes Price (1972: 238). The First International and other international labor congresses remained talk shops, without effective decision-making structures or mass followings. Faced with war, each national working class made its decisions independently of all others. Organizationally, this weakened labor's capacity to halt the slide toward war.

2. Militarism was feared primarily for national reasons, because of its role in domestic repression. Though the militarism of one's own regime was feared, that of foreign regimes was feared more if it seemed more repressive. French workers feared German aggression because of its reactionary threat to the republic; German and Austrian workers feared Russia because it threatened all workers' organizations. Only Russian workers, subject to the most reactionary regime, were immune. Elsewhere, fear could be manipulated to elicit worker support for the war.

In 1914, these weaknesses undermined the transnational rhetoric of the International and of labor leaders. In Germany, most leaders of the Social Democratic party feared that if they opposed the war their impressive party and union organization, built up over decades, would be promptly repressed with the full wartime support of other classes. The proletariat abroad could not protect them. German workers had only German organizations, and these must be protected at all costs. Nor were leaders confident that they could counter regime propaganda that the main enemy was reactionary Russia (Morgan 1975: 31). Similar motivations were found in the Austrian Socialist party. French socialists continued formal opposition to militarism right up to the war, but most also recognized that workers would and even should rally to defense of the Republic. British socialists had no foreign policy but followed their Liberal allies. Working class organizations followed sympathetic parties and regimes not because they were aggressive nationalists, either economically or politically, but because the working class was nationally caged. The working class could not stop others from perpetrating the Great War.

Classes with more secure citizenship were also nationally organized, but the state was *theirs*. Because it symbolized their imagined community, they might more easily identify with its "greatness," "honor," and geopolitical interests. As the state became the nation-state, sacred reasons of state might become sacred national interests. Earlier chapters showed the middle class joining national society, becoming voters, jurors, home owners, employers of servants, reserve officers, and participants in national education, culture, and markets. Mommsen (1990: 210–24) charts a major transformation of nineteenth-century liberalism. It had started the century liberal and fairly pacific, but from the 1880s on, national identities and emotions turned aggressive. Nationalist ideologies such as ethnic superiority, xenophobia, life-and-death struggle for national and racial survival, and popular militarism appeared. Yet in Chapter 16 I am somewhat skeptical of this widely held view of middle-class nationalism, finding little evidence to support it. The strength and character of nationalism varied considerably among countries. Nationalism caught up state careerists and the highly educated far more than the rest of the middle class. It also tended merely to amplify regime ideologies and dilemmas. Because party democracies were split between older cosmopolitan and newer imperial claims to national greatness, the middle class also became split.

Thus neither mass aggressive nationalism nor deliberate, manipulative social imperialism by party-democratic regimes was very significant. It was attempted by the far Right, but won few elections. It was trumpeted with bellicose sincerity by a few xenophobes, including press lords. They caused regimes intermittent discomfort, but they did not shift policy. Nationalism in Britain and France was ambiguous, containing liberal beliefs that the nation carried humanitarian, Christian, democratic civilization to the world as well as more imperial sentiments. Imperialism carried aggressive racist xenophobia to the colonies, but it was usually more defensive in Europe, where the war actually occurred. Political nationalism tended to amplify the ideologies of mainstream parties and the real defensive rearmament policies of French and British governments. Liberal regimes feared pacific public opinion more than they did aggressive nationalism. There were considerable social tensions – strike waves and Ulster in Britain, strike waves and conscription riots in France – but popular imperialism was not consistently wielded by governments as a solution to these tensions.

National identity was now deeply rooted in both intensive and extensive social practices, but aggressive nationalism was not. We saw earlier that economic imperialism had geopolitical roots. Hence political nationalism lacked the precise bite of economic interest that nationalist class organization would have provided. Although British informed opinion worried about German competition and protectionism, popular anti-German sentiment was more diffuse. Nationalists put the greatness of empire and navy ahead of direct economic appeal. French nationalists ignored economic competition, harping on Alsace-Lorraine and Germany's threat to the Republic and French military power. Such an unrooted nationalism, however, could be destabilizing. The identity of the opponent could be quickly switched. In less than a decade, British and French nationalism changed from being predominantly against each other to being anti-German. Aggressive chauvinism, seemingly prepared for war, appeared suddenly in crises, to decline equally rapidly afterward. A cynical Lloyd George commented, "The war had leaped into popularity between Saturday and Monday" as August 1914 began (Albertini 1957: 482; cf. Weber 1968: 31–2 on rapid French swings).

Such shallow volatility could disconcert or be exploited by regimes in crises. If the government declared war between Saturday and Monday, the (predominantly middle-class) nation would enthusiastically follow. That was the trick of managing shallow nationalism in a party democracy – it still is, except now the nation also includes the working class and women. But the trick, then as now, had limits: The essentially middle-class electorate did not look forward to the additional expense, let alone the sacrifice of life, of a war against another Great Power (Steiner 1977: 250–3). French and British regimes also doubted the loyalty of the working class even if Germany attacked first (from 1914 they were to be greatly cheered on this score). Party-democratic regimes warily watched political nationalism. But they were not seriously distracted by it, and they received most of its comforts after the war started.

At the opposite extreme, in autocratic Russia, social imperialism was even less evident (Lieven 1983: 38–46, 153–4; Kennan 1984). After 1900, Balkan crises increased pan-Slav populism. This urged Russian leadership of Slavs against Teutonic Germany and Austria. Pan-Slavism was, in a sense, middle class, having little worker, peasant, or noble support. But the citizenship rights of the Russian middle class were unclear. Unlike aggressive bourgeois nationalism in the West, pan-Slavism was not confined to the political Right. It spread all the way from tsar worship to violent anarchism. But the regime was not hospitable. The most reactionary monarchy in Europe did not intend even to tell the people about its conduct of foreign policy, still less legitimate it in terms of popular principles.

Thus, outside of Germany, manipulation of social imperialism and political nationalism were not major causes of the war. Public and regime were routinely too insulated from each other, the working class and peasantry too indifferent to foreign policy, the predominant strand of middle-class nationalism too defensive. There was relatively little nationalist or transnational organization among middle, peasant, or working classes. Their predominantly national or local-regional caging left considerable loopholes through which others could initiate war with their consent – excited but shallow among the middle class, resigned among peasants, grudging among the working class, disciplined among their soldiery.[1]

Social imperialism and regime drift in Germany

German aggression helped turn a Balkan conflict into a world war. Even if social imperialism were not significant elsewhere, if it flourished in Germany, so does the theory. The theory certainly flourishes among historians of Germany. Since Fritz Fischer's statement of *Der Primat der Innenpolitik* in German war aims (1961, English edition 1967; 1969, English edition 1975), many have affirmed his two basic points: German leadership was persistently aggressive, prepared and willing for a major war for a decade before 1914; and its motivation was as much to solve internal class tensions through social imperialism as to attain world domination (Berghahn 1973; Gordon 1974; Geiss 1976, 1984). Only Fischer's emphasis on consistency and coherence has given ground before an unearthing of regime contradictions (Wehler 1970, 1985). We cannot return to *Der Primat der Aussenpolitik* or dismiss the theory of social imperialism in Germany (Mommsen 1976; Joll 1984b).

German militarism is indisputable. Bismarck had also manipulated it toward a low-cost social imperialism, using colonies to divert domestic class and other social tensions (Pogge von Strandmann 1969; Wehler 1981). Subsequent governments copied. A Prussian minister said that he

entertained the hope that colonial policy would turn our attention outwards, but this had happened only to a limited extent. We would therefore have to introduce questions of foreign policy into the Reichstag, for in foreign affairs the sentiments of the nation would usually be united. Our undeniable successes in foreign policy would make a good impression in the Reichstag debates, and political divisions would thus be moderated. [Geiss 1976: 78]

Chancellor von Bülow went farther in conversation with one of the kaiser's confidants:

---

[1] The best confirming evidence comes from studies of the response of public opinion and of conscripted soldiers to the war. I analyze these in Volume III, but for a study of France that supports my argument, see Becker 1977.

The way to win popular support for the monarchy was to revive the "national idea." A victorious war would of course solve many problems, just as the wars of 1866 and 1870 had rescued the dynasty. [Geiss 1976: 78]

Max Weber had a liberal version of imperialism:

We have to grasp that the unification of Germany was a youthful prank which the nation committed in its olden days and which would have been better dispensed with because of its cost, if it were the end and not the beginning of a German *Weltmachtpolitik* [world-power politics]. [Geiss 1976: 80]

Weber advocated not imperialism *instead* of reforms but imperialism *plus* reforms, to stabilize and modernize Germany (Mommsen 1974: 22–46).

In other countries views embodying such aggressive imperialisms were rarer. Moreover, German social imperialism did not merely rally the nation against foreigners. *Reichsfeinde*, the enemies of the empire, were considered to be foreign Powers plus domestic enemies – socialists, Leftist liberals, and ethnic minorities, and, at first, Catholics. They were identified more or less sincerely with external enemies – socialists and Jews with international conspiracies, Catholics first with Austria, then with the Roman Curia, Poles with the Slav race and Russia, Alsatians with France, liberals with Britain and France (Wehler 1985: 102–13). Regime social imperialism embodied a segmental divide-and-rule strategy: rallying core loyalists, Protestant agrarians and industrialists, then middle class and Catholics, so as to isolate socialists, Leftist liberals, and ethnic minorities.

Yet German governments did not steadily manipulate social imperialism toward world war (as Fischer, Geiss, and Berghahn assert). Most regimes aspire to a foreign policy in which "greatness" may divert attention from domestic tension. But between this and starting a major war lies a great difference. Between this and starting a two-front war against the next three greatest Powers in Europe lies a yawning gulf. Could such a war have been designed as the solution to class struggle?

Bülow believed not. He continued his remark quoted above: "On the other hand, an unsuccessful war would mean the end of the dynasty." He expanded on this in 1911:

History shows us that every great war is followed by a period of liberalism, since a people demands compensation for the sacrifices and effort war has entailed. But any war which ends in a defeat obliges the dynasty that declared it to make concessions which before would have seemed unheard of.... Whoever would act, act prudently and consider the consequences. [Kaiser 1983: 455–6]

Bethmann, his successor as chancellor, went farther in July 1914:

World war with its unforeseeable consequences will greatly strengthen the power of social democracy since it preaches peace and will topple many a throne . . . a war, whatever its outcome, [will] result in an upheaval of all existing arrangements. [Jarausch 1973: 151–2]

These were not stray, unconsidered remarks. They were made by the last two prewar German chancellors in the context of a European debate on both Right and Left on the impact of mass mobilization warfare on class struggle. Though some ultra-Rightists thought war might rally support to the crown, most conservatives believed the opposite. So did most of the Left. As Lenin wrote from exile in Austria in 1912: "A war between Austria and Russia would be a very useful thing for the revolution in all of Eastern Europe, but it is not likely that Franz Joseph and [Tsar] Nikolasha will give us that pleasure."

If victory could be guaranteed, social imperialism would be a wonderful regime strategy. But war does not guarantee its victories in advance, and German statesmen did not enter the Great War in such a confident frame of mind. They knew war imperiled the social order. We cannot blame German aggression in 1914 on a considered, consistent strategy of social imperialism.

But *Innenpolitik* and bouts of social imperialism might have escalated German aggression in unintended ways (as Kaiser 1983 and Wehler 1985 have suggested). Domestic and geopolitics were entwined, as Chapter 9 shows. Domestically, the regime moved toward the *Sammlungspolitik*, the "politics of rallying together" of the "productive" (i.e., the possessing) classes against *Reichsfeinde* within and without. The regime would divide and rule among the productive classes – Bethmann described this as the "politics of the diagonal." Three competing combinations of international political economy and diplomacy emerged: liberalism, *Mitteleuropa*, and *Weltpolitik*, all entwined with domestic politics. The politics of the diagonal turned increasingly away from the first, so embracing more aggressive geopolitics. But they never chose between the other two alternatives, so drifting toward nonrealist disaster.

Liberalism centered on trade entrepôts like Hamburg, on light industry, and on finance capital. It found support within the regime, especially in the Wilhelmstrasse, whose diplomats often counseled international conciliation. They reasoned: France was alienated while Germany held Alsace-Lorraine; Britain and Russia must not also be antagonized. Caprivi, chancellor during 1890–4, moved toward a liberal package of domestic reform, laissez-faire political economy, and conciliation of the British. But the kaiser dismissed him rather than conciliate the working class. Thereafter liberalism weakened, out of regime favor, its political economy of little interest to conservatives or peasants, opposed by the military and political nationalists.

Agrarian conservatives, led by the Prussian Junkers, moved beyond protectionism to expansionism. Their main economic rival became Russia, their main domestic fear their Polish laborers. Tariffs closed the German market to Russian grain – a blow to Russian modernization, which needed grain export to pay for manufacturing imports and debts. Russia moved toward the French alliance – very bad diplomatic news for Germany. Many conservatives worsened the news by generalizing the conflict to Teuton versus Slav racism. Fiscally and socially conservative, the Junkers at first were reluctant to vote taxes and mobilize the mass army necessary for military aggression, but after 1909, political motivations lowered inhibitions as they sought to reverse declining power by allying with nationalist parties. Their chosen instrument was the army, their ideology was chauvinist and increasingly racist, and their geopolitics saw Russia as the enemy, Austria as the ally, and a German-dominated *Mitteleuropa* as the solution. They advocated mixed mercantilism, economic imperialism, and geopolitical imperialism, usually aimed eastward.

Some heavy industrialists also favored protection and expansion. Their motives were often pragmatic and market-oriented, but their incorporation into the regime had increased territorial conceptions of interest. Because the main competitor was Britain, along with the United States and France, many favored *Weltpolitik*, mercantilism on a world scale. In the 1890s, this escalated to economic imperialism (in alliance with the regime's own geopolitical imperialism) in the scramble for Africa. This subsided once it was realized that Germany had arrived too late on the colonial scene to find profits, unless willing to risk war with other European empires. Industrialists were not. Nor were they interested in expansion eastward. Yet market pressures, interpreted from within an authoritarian regime, favored aggressive mercantilism. In 1897, this brought them, and others, to the navy.

The German naval buildup had complex, even idiosyncratic causes. The kaiser's personal enthusiasm and Admiral Tirpitz's media skills and court influence were important. But the idea of a great German navy had domestic political attractions. Germany seemed created by militarism, yet army expansion was contentious. Expansion of the army was not favored by much of the middle class or by Catholic South Germany, because it could be used for domestic, centralized repression. Even the high command and the Junkers hesitated to arm the workers (conscription of supposedly loyal peasants was reaching its limits) or to allow bourgeois numerical domination of an enlarged officer corps. But a capital-intensive navy required little manpower, could not repress, and benefited heavy industry, employment, and economic modernization. As industrialists were persuaded of the economic advantages of battleships, they horse-traded with Junker conservatives and the Catholic Center representing peasants. In 1897, an increase in grain tariffs was agreed on in return for the second, decisive navy law. Minimal social reform won over the National Liberals (Kehr 1975, 1977: chapters 1–4).

Battleship building was supported by regime, industry, and much of the middle class, it was accepted by southerners and Catholics, and it was not energetically opposed by anyone – even Social Democrats (because it expanded employment). Traditional liberal marketeers like Hamburg shipping magnates became converts. It pandered to all four higher-level regime crystallizations – monarchism (because it was the kaiser's new toy), militarism, capitalism, and nationalism – without alienating the normal domestic enemies of these crystallizations. After 1900, the navy got almost all the resources it solicited. The battleships largely resulted from *Innenpolitik* – from sectional economic interest, from the regime's segmental divide-and-rule strategies, and from the state's almost casual institutionalized militarism.

But as a foreign policy, naval *Weltpolitik* was not very realist in a material sense. The fleet would supposedly protect German commercial and colonial interests. Yet battleships were designed less for commercial or colonial protection than for head-on confrontation with Britain in the North Sea. In fact, debate had focused less on the practical material utility of the fleet than on its symbolic status. A fleet was necessary for Germany, Bethmann argued, "for the general purpose of her greatness" (Jarausch 1973: 141–2). Such broad statist imperialism, entwining economics and geopolitics with national conceptions of honor, lacked the precise rationality that either realist or capitalist foreign interests might have provided. Though the fleet seemed aimed at Britain, its creation involved neither Anglophobia nor a cool assessment of either its impact abroad or its military utility.

The unintended diplomatic consequences were disastrous. Battleship building, accompanied by rhetoric about world power, alienated Great Britain and led to a naval arms race that Germany was bound to lose. Britain was well in the lead and able to transfer its large global navy to home waters. British diplomacy focused cohesively, as it had for 150 years, on "bluewater" policy. "We are fish," declared Lord Salisbury. The Royal Navy remained Britain's fundamental military arm, and home waters the absolute defense priority. Grey put it starkly in 1913: "The Navy is our one and only means of defense and our life depends upon it and on it alone." British statesmen believed that Britain must fight if Germany attacked France without guaranteeing Belgian neutrality: A large German navy in Low Country ports could deliver the death blow to British power.

Had Germany been able to lessen Continental commitments and conciliate Russia or France, German resources might have achieved Tirpitz's goal of a 2:3 ratio of German to British capital ships. This would have neutralized British naval power (though to what end is unclear). But the *Sammlungspolitik* meant a rallying together not only of German productive classes but also of their foreign enemies. German diplomacy did not conciliate Russia because Junkers had not been discarded from the regime. Nor did it attempt to break the Franco-Russian alliance. At home, the regime incorporated factions, added political crystallizations, and rejected none of their policies. A diplomatic consequence was that Germany was surrounded by its enemies. Without single-minded commitment of resources, the German navy could not command the North Sea. Germany had added Britain to the enemy Entente, yet would be quite unable to defeat Britain or cut off British aid to Continental allies (Kennedy 1980: 415–22).

And so it turned out. Deliberate, successful *Innenpolitik* had unintended, disastrous consequences for *Aussenpolitik*. Regime domestic success antagonized foreign Powers, increasing both objective foreign threat and German paranoia. As we intend no harm to Russia, Britain, and France, why are they so hostile to us? From 1906, the regime described Germany as "encircled," the victim of a geopolitical conspiracy. The Fischer school treats this as regime manipulation of public opinion, creating a climate to support a claim that aggression was only "defensive war" (Geiss 1976: 121–38). I prefer cock-up–foul-up to conspiracy: Drifting into decisions primarily for domestic reasons, with little thought of diplomatic consequences, the regime was surprised by foreign reaction. But the doctrine of encirclement made German retaliation more likely. It was a territorial and military metaphor, inviting what the kaiser described as a sally out across the "drawbridge" with the "sharp, good sword."

The final rallying together incorporated the middle class, South Germans, and Catholics within the gambit of segmental divide-and-rule strategies. Radical liberals, socialists, and ethnic-regional minorities were successfully isolated. But success deprived German politics of a center. As Chapters 18 and 19 show, a productivist, statist Marxism rampaged through the excluded Left, unhindered by pragmatic alliance with Centrist liberals, worsening its inability to recruit peasants or Catholics; while Center parties brought into the regime had to compromise with conservatism, not radical liberalism. As Chapter 16 shows, political nationalism centered on civil servants and state educational institutions and became somewhat more state-worshiping and racist than in other countries. In one sense, this merely amplified the preferences of the regime, but it also cut down its freedom of action.

Having alienated workers and ethnic minorities, the regime depended on middle-class votes. Having denied full parliamentary sovereignty, the regime depended on the loyalty of its own administrators. Their nationalist pressure was influential and destabilizing (Eley 1980).

With encirclement without and *Reichsfeinde* within, statist nationalists and regime began to develop paranoid tendencies. They became less capable of switching enemies than British or French nationalists were and less manipulable by either capitalist or realist definitions of interest. This is predominantly a *political* explanation of the "paranoid" element of German politics, not one based on the economic anxieties of classes or their supposed "status panic" (which theories I dismiss in Chapter 16).

In July 1914, Bethmann noted why Germany was in its predicament:

The earlier errors . . . challenge everybody, put yourself in everybody's path, and actually weaken no one in this fashion. Reason: aimlessness, the need for little prestige successes and solicitude for every current of public opinion. The "national" parties which with their racket about foreign policy want to preserve and strengthen their party position. [Stern 1968: 265]

That was shrewd but too late; he had already ceded diplomacy to the kaiser's "sharp, good sword."

Social imperialism *was* important to German diplomacy, but more as drift and unintended consequence than as deliberate regime strategy. Liberal historians argue that regime "failure" to solve domestic problems led to external aggression. On the contrary, its *success* in converting absolutism into modern semiauthoritarian monarchy led to geopolitical disaster. Order in court and Reichstag were bought by adding state crystallizations, by allowing most segmentally incorporated factions to maintain their sense of Germany's enemies. This is similar to Snyder's (1991: 66–7) theory of logrolling between "cartelized elites": Elites with highly concentrated powers and interests in imperial expansion, economic protectionism, and military preparedness agreed to trade positive votes with each other, producing an outcome more aggressive than any single one intended. Consequently, Germany was put in "everybody's path," as Bülow and Bethmann both realized. To avoid this would have required choice among Junkers, monarchy, army, navy, industrial capitalists, and statist nationalists. Bülow fell when he attacked Junker tax exemptions. Bethmann was pilloried and weakened by statist nationalists when he favored diplomatic conciliation.

The regime continued its casual, unconsidered drift toward militarism. The agrarians came back "in," and from 1912 on the army was expanded more than the navy. By 1914, only liberals and socialists had lost. No choice had been made between *Mitteleuropa* and *Weltpolitik* on their realist merits. Their regime factions remained intriguing; their foreign enemies had not been discarded. The regime remained capitalist *and* monarchist *and* militarist – *and* became nationalist – without choosing priorities among these crystallizations. No ultimacy test had been posed for what this regime finally stood for. Indeed, its popularity among diverse in and out factions depended on avoiding such a test. It was popular, but its popularity threatened peace and then its own survival. Never was the power of the unintended consequences of action so disastrously triumphant: The very domestic success of the strategy of semiauthoritarian incorporation proved its geopolitical hubris.

As if this were not enough, there was also a narrowly geopolitical contribution to German downfall. It was world-historical bad luck for Germany, resulting from its geographic position, that its militarism produced a *world* war. The enemy of its agrarian lords became its eastern neighbor and largest land rival, Russia; the enemy of its heavy (battleship-building) industry became westerly Britain, the greatest naval Power; and the obvious ally for both rivals was the still aggrieved and formidable southwesterly France. Once again a centrally located European Power fell into the trap of attacking both flanks at once – and went the way of the others mentioned in Chapter 8. Its territorial position in *Mitteleuropa* reinforced German hubris, in spades.

Conclusion

A singular event has particular causes. Take away the luck of Gavrilo Princip (the planned assassination had failed; Princip had retired to a café when the archduke's open carriage came unexpectedly right by him), or the rashness of a few Serbs and Austrians, or the mistakes of a few diplomats and generals, and the Great War might not have occurred when it did, or even at all. In dissecting more general, structural causes, I seek only to explain the general climate that made war somewhere between a possible and a probable outcome. Accidents may happen, but they may happen probabilistically. What may look random down on the ground, especially to the participants, may have an overall, long-term pattern *sub specie eternae*. This volume does not offer eternity. Nor do the 156 years it covers even offer enough of the very long term to test this possibility thoroughly, but it has begun. This chapter continues the beginning.

We can see clearly that explanation cannot concentrate exclusively or predominantly on either *Innen-* or *Aussenpolitik*. Decision making was determined by domestic and foreign politics always entwined both within and between the nation-states. The domestic consolidation of the nation-state led to the emergence of contending political nationalisms; the development of capitalism led to more struggle between extensive and political classes; and statesmen and militaries represented all these amid the intensifying geopolitics of the Powers. None developed in a vacuum isolated from the others; each affected all others in ways no one intended. No one controlled the whole or could predict the reactions of other nations, classes, statesmen, and militaries.

Both *Innen* and *Aussen* schools mistakenly see societies and states as systems, unitary and homogeneous. In the *Innen* vision, classes and other domestic power actors rationally scheme and compromise their interests through strategies such as economic or social imperialism. In the *Aussen* realist vision, statesmen rationally calculate geopolitical interests. Both schools admit that actors make mistakes, and realists attempt to incorporate mistakes into their micro explanation. Yet the scale of miscalculation was truly stupendous. Actors were indeed attempting rational action, calculating their national, class, and geopolitical interests and seeking the most economical means of attaining them. But none was successful. This was the most systematic feature of August 1914. It resulted from the unintended consequences of the interaction of overlapping, intersecting power networks. Actors pursued and drifted between strategies whose interactions were unpredictable and eventually devastating.

This "patterned mess" was worsened by an institutional contradiction at the heart of the modern state. On the one hand, the diplomacy of modern statesmen and the professionalism of modern militaries were systematic in their consequences because they commanded the massive power infrastructures described in Chapters 11–14. Regimes and Powers were toppled, economies devastated, millions killed or maimed – by their decisions to risk war. "Good reasons" adduced by *Innen* and *Aussen* theorists might *still* seem appropriate to this level of risk and danger. Yet neither statesmen nor militaries – nor classes nor nations – could act on the basis of such "good reasons." For, on the other hand, the structures whereby "sovereign" states made "their" decisions were disorderly, in four distinct ways. The modern state was unitary in its consequences but polymorphous and factionalized in its structure.

1. *Monarchies*: Here intrigue weaved intricate patterns through both routine and crisis policy making, while militaries could act autonomously in crises. Monarchs and their advisers had institutionalized segmental divide-and-rule strategies, deliberately avoiding locating ultimate responsibility for policy in any single body. They cultivated intrigue, hoping to center it on themselves. When industrial capitalists, bourgeois parliamentarians, and political nationalists arose, they were incorporated into divide-and-rule intrigue. In the three Great Powers disproportionately responsible for the war – Germany, Russia, and

Austria-Hungary – factions among nobles, generals, capitalists, party notables, and nationalist parties (absent in Russia) reached to the pinnacle of the state, the person of the monarch, pulling him this way and that, sometimes to caution and pusillanimity, eventually to rash action.

2. *Party democracies*: Here I distinguish routine from crisis decision making. Crisis decision making was concentrated in parliaments and cabinets, in which ultimate responsibilities were fairly clearly specified. Yet routine diplomatic decision making of old regime and republican notable statesmen was even more private, insulated, and autonomous than in monarchical regimes, as classes and parties were predominantly caged by national or local-regional organization. Their insulation had two major limitations: Statesmen could not arbitrarily allocate funds to foreign policy goals, nor could they threaten war. This meant they were short on deterrence, having to scheme dishonestly or wait until attacked before behaving aggressively. The party-democratic division was between half-insulated old regime and modern parliament and cabinet. Its factionalism was reflected in sharp changes of foreign policy during crises, mildly worsened by contending liberal and imperial forms of political nationalism.

3. *All states* moved toward somewhat more aggressive, territorial diplomacy. Statesmen believed Great Power shifts had made the world more dangerous. Militaries developed aggressive tactics and a disdain for diplomacy and imposed effective segmental discipline on masses of soldiers and sailors. But the growth of citizenship and of state infrastructures moved states toward being nation-states and reduced the insulation of regimes. Social life became naturalized, generating strong emotional attachments to the nation. Within such nations a more aggressive nationalism appeared, though limited largely to state administrators and state educational institutions, diffusing more shallowly among the middle class and dominant religious and linguistic communities. National definitions of community grew; local-regional and transnational ones weakened. Territorial definitions of economic interest, veering between peaceful protectionism, mercantilism, and economic imperialism, entwined with the regime's supposedly realist *geopolitik* and more popular conceptions of national identity and honor.

4. *All politics* thus demonstrated diplomatic incompetence and volatility. Militaries retreated into professional technocratic competence. Statesmen, now only semiinsulated, demonstrated marked inconsistency. A few *transnational* organizations favored pacific diplomacy; a few *nationalist* pressure groups favored aggressive geopolitics out of direct economic imperialism, especially in the colonies. But most classes and other power actors became caged into *national* organization and

politics, indifferent to routine foreign affairs but anxious in crises. Their foreign policies were mostly determined by domestic politics and were shallow and rhetorical. The working class, most of the peasantry and capitalist class, and some of the middle class in the party democracies opposed militarism for domestic reasons and remained rhetorically transnational and pacific. Other popular classes, especially among dominant religious and linguistic communities, could be aroused to shallow, volatile, but aggressive nationalism. But although their views erratically constrained statesmen, they could not initiate foreign policy.

Polymorphous factionalism went farthest in Germany and Austria-Hungary. These two Powers were inextricably caught between old regime monarchs, statesmen, and militaries, on the one hand, and the classes and nations of modern society, on the other. They carried to an extreme the polymorphous crystallization of modern states. The aggression of these two Powers (and of the Serbs) was directly responsible for the outbreak of war. I reject the German attempt to shift blame to encirclement and to British hegemony, as Germany derived more benefit from that very situation than it was likely to from war. German aggression was not considered or "realist." It was aggression born of monarchical regime – plus military caste – plus class – plus nation – cock-up–foul-up. Austria-Hungary added its distinctive cock-up–foul-up: a desperate dynast and generals ranged against regional-nationalists. The Russian court added its militarist cock-up–foul-up of escalatory mobilization. Party democracies added their cock-up–foul-up: statesmen's erratic half insulation restricted by their inability to alarm their citizens by threatening war. Regimes shared to varying degrees the underlying contradiction of the modern state: The powers of states had become gigantic in their effects, polymorphous and factionalized in their processes. But states were only reflecting modern society, equipped with massive collective powers, their distributive power networks entwining nondialectically. The Great War exemplifies, horrifically, the structure of modern states and modern societies, as I have analyzed them and theorized about them.

Less has changed today than should make us entirely comfortable. Have we learned from the Great War how to avoid an even greater one? Or will we stumble to repeat the tragic vision and fate of this young poet in the trenches?

To Germany
You are blind like us. Your hurt no man designed.
And no man claimed the conquest of your land.
But gropers both through fields of thought confined
We stumble and we do not understand.

You only saw your future bigly planned,
And we, the tapering paths of our own mind,
And in each other's dearest ways we stand,
And hiss and hate. And the blind fight the blind.
[Charles Hamilton Sorley –
b. 1895, Aberdeenshire, Scotland;
d. 1915, Battle of Loos, Flanders]

Bibliography

Albertini, L. 1952, 1953, 1957. *The Origins of the War of 1914*, 3 vols. Oxford: Oxford University Press.

Becker, J.-J. 1977. *1914: Comment les Français sont entrés dans la guerre*. Paris: PUF.

Berghahn, V. R. 1973. *Germany and the Approach of War in 1914*. London: St. Martin's Press.

Bosworth, R. 1983. *Italy and the Approach of War*. London: Macmillan.

Campbell, C. 1949. American interests and the open door. In *American Expansion in the Late Nineteenth Century*, ed. J. R. Hollingsworth. Malabar, Fla.: Krieger.

Cecil, L. 1976. *The German Diplomatic Service, 1871–1914*. Princeton, N.J.: Princeton University Press.

Craig, G. 1955. *The Politics of the Prussian Army, 1640–1945*. Oxford: Clarendon Press.

Deist, W. 1982. Kaiser Wilhelm II in the context of his military and naval entourage. In *Kaiser Wilhelm II: New Interpretations*, ed. J. Rohl and N. Sombart. Cambridge: Cambridge University Press.

Doyle, M. 1983. Kant, liberal legacies and foreign affairs, parts 1 and 2. *Philosophy and Public Affairs* 12.

Dubovsky, M. 1969. *We Shall Be All*. Chicago: Quadrangle Books.

Eldridge, G. C. 1973. *England's Mission*. London: Macmillan.

Eley, G. 1980. *Reshaping the German Right*. New Haven, Conn.: Yale University Press.

1985. The view from the throne: the personal rule of Kaiser Wilhelm II. *Historical Journal* 28.

Fieldhouse, D. K. 1973. *Economics and Empire, 1830–1914*. London: Weidenfeld & Nicolson.

Fischer, F. 1967. *Germany's Aims in the First World War*. London: Chatto & Windus.

1975. *War of Illusions: German Policies from 1911 to 1914*. London: Chatto & Windus.

Geiss, I. 1976. *German Foreign Policy, 1871–1914*. London: Routledge & Kegan Paul.

1984. Origins of the First World War. In *Origins of the First World War*, ed. H. W. Koch. London: Macmillan.

Gordon, M. R. 1974. Domestic conflict and the origins of the First World War: the British and German cases. *Journal of Modern History* 46.

Gourevitch, P. 1986. *Politics and Hard Times*. Ithaca, N.Y.: Cornell University Press.

Herwig, H. 1973. *The German Naval Officer Corps*. Oxford: Clarendon Press.

Hilderbrand, R. C. 1981. *Power and the People: Executive Management of Public Opinion in Foreign Affairs, 1897–1921.* Chapel Hill: University of North Carolina Press.

Hobson, J. A. 1902. *Imperialism: A Study.* London: Nislet.

Howard, M. 1970. Reflections on the First World War. In his *Studies in War and Peace.* London: Temple Smith.

Hull, I. V. 1982. *The Entourage of Kaiser Wilhelm II, 1888–1918.* Cambridge: Cambridge University Press.

Jarausch, K. H. 1969. The illusion of limited war: Chancellor Bethmann Hollweg's calculated risk, July 1914. *Central European History* 2.

   1973. *The Enigmatic Chancellor: Bethmann Hollweg and the Hubris of Imperial Germany.* New Haven, Conn.: Yale University Press.

Joll, J. 1984a. *The Origins of the First World War.* London: Longman Group.

   1984b. The 1914 debate continues: Fritz Fischer and his critics. In *Origins of the First World War*, ed. H. W. Koch. London: Macmillan.

   1984c. 1914: the unspoken assumptions. In *Origins of the First World War*, ed. H. W. Koch. London: Macmillan.

Kaiser, D. E. 1983. Germany and the origins of the First World War. *Journal of Modern History* 55.

Kehr, E. 1975. *Battleship Building and Party Politics in Germany.* Chicago: University of Chicago Press.

   1977. *Economic Interest, Militarism and Foreign Policy.* Berkeley: University of California Press.

Keiger, J. 1983. *France and the Origins of the First World War.* London: Macmillan.

Kennan, G. F. 1977. *A Cloud of Danger.* Boston: Little, Brown.

   1984. *The Fateful Alliance: France, Russia and the Coming of the First World War.* Manchester: Manchester University Press.

Kennedy, P. 1980. *The Rise of the Anglo-German Antagonism, 1860–1914.* London: Allen & Unwin.

   1982. The kaiser and German Weltpolitik. In *Kaiser Wilhelm II: New Interpretations*, ed. J. Rohl and N. Sombart. Cambridge: Cambridge University Press.

   1985. *The Realities Behind Diplomacy.* London: Fontana.

Kitchen, M. 1968. *The German Officer Corps, 1890–1914.* Oxford: Clarendon Press.

Koch, H. W. 1984. Social Darwinism as a factor in the new imperialism. In his *Origins of the First World War.* London: Macmillan.

Lafore, L. 1965. *The Long Fuse: An Interpretation of the Origins of World War I.* London: Weidenfeld & Nicolson.

Lieven, D. C. B. 1983. *Russia and the Origins of the First World War.* London: Macmillan.

Mackinder, H. 1904. The geographical pivot of history. *Geographical Journal* 23 (reprinted by the Royal Geographical Society, London, 1951).

Mahan, A. T. 1918. *The Influence of Sea Power upon History 1660–1783.* Boston: Little, Brown.

Mann, M. 1988. The decline of Great Britain. In M. Mann, *States, War and Capitalism.* Oxford: Blackwell.

Mansergh, N. 1949. *The Coming of the First World War.* London: Longman Group.

Mayer, A. J. 1968. Domestic causes of the First World War. In *The Respon-

sibility of Power: Historical Essays in Honor of Hajo Holborn, ed. L. Krieger and F. Stern. London: Macmillan.

1981. *The Persistence of the Old Regime.* London: Croom Helm.

Mommsen, W. J. 1974. *The Age of Bureaucracy: Perspectives on the Political Sociology of Max Weber.* Oxford: Blackwell.

1980. *Theories of Imperialism.* London: Weidenfeld & Nicolson.

1990. The varieties of the nation state in modern history: liberal, imperialist, fascist and contemporary notions of nation and nationality. In *The Rise and Decline of the Nation State*, ed. M. Mann. Oxford: Blackwell.

Morgan, D. W. 1975. *The Socialist Left and the German Revolution.* Ithaca, N.Y.: Cornell University Press.

Morgenthau, H. 1978. *Politics Among Nations.* New York: Knopf.

Olle, W., and W. Schoeller. 1977. World market competition and restrictions upon international trade union policies. *Capital and Class* 1.

Palmer, A. 1983. *The Chancelleries of Europe.* London: Allen & Unwin.

Parker, G. 1985. *Western Geopolitical Thought in the Twentieth Century.* London: Croom Helm.

Platt, D. C. 1979. Economic factors in British policy during the new imperialism. In *Conflict and Stability in Europe*, ed. C. Emsley. London: Croom Helm.

Pogge von Strandmann, H. 1969. Domestic origins of Germany's colonial expansion under Bismarck. *Past and Present*, no. 45.

Price, R. 1972. *An Imperial War and the British Working Class.* London: Routledge & Kegan Paul.

Remak, J. 1967. *The Origins of World War I: 1871–1914.* New York: Holt, Rinehart & Winston.

Robinson, R., and J. Gallagher. 1961. *Africa and the Victorians: The Official Mind of Imperialism.* London: Macmillan.

Rohl, J. 1973. Introduction. In *1914: Delusion or Design? The Testimony of Two German Diplomats*, ed. J. Rohl. London: Elek.

1982. Introduction. In *Kaiser Wilhelm II: New Interpretations*, ed. J. Rohl and N. Sombart. Cambridge: Cambridge University Press.

Rohl, J., and N. Sombart (eds.). 1982. *Kaiser Wilhelm II: New Interpretations.* Cambridge: Cambridge University Press.

Rosecrance, R. 1986. *The Rise of the Trading State: Commerce and Conquest in the Modern World.* New York: Basic Books.

Rothenberg, G. 1976. *The Army of Francis Joseph.* West Lafayette, Ind.: Purdue University Press.

Schmitt, B. E. 1966. *The Coming of the War 1914*, 2 vols. New York: Fertig.

Snyder, J. 1991. *Myths of Empire: Domestic Politics and International Ambition.* Ithaca, N.Y.: Cornell University Press.

Steiner, Z. S. 1969. *The Foreign Office and Foreign Policy, 1898–1914.* Cambridge: Cambridge University Press.

1977. *Britain and the Origins of the First World War.* London: Macmillan.

Stern, F. 1968. Bethmann Hollweg and the war: the limits of responsibility. In *The Responsibility of Power: Historical Essays in Honor of Hajo Halborn*, ed. L. Krieger and F. Stern. London: Macmillan.

Stone, N. 1975. *The Eastern Front, 1914–1917.* New York: Scribner's.

1983. *Europe Transformed, 1878–1919.* London: Fontana.

Taylor, A. J. P. 1954. *The Struggle for Mastery in Europe, 1848–1918.* Oxford: Clarendon Press.

Todd, E. 1979. *Le fou et le proletaire*. Paris: Laffont.
Turner, L. C. F. 1967. The significance of the Schlieffen plan. *American Journal of Politics and History* 4.
    1968. The Russian mobilization in 1914. *Journal of Contemporary History* 3.
    1970. *Origins of the First World War*. London: Arnold.
Weber, E. 1968. *The Nationalist Revival in France, 1905–1914*. Berkeley: University of California Press.
Wehler, H.-U. 1979. Introduction to Imperialism. In *Conflict and Stability in Europe*, ed. C. Emsley. London: Croom Helm.
    1981. Bismarck's imperialism, 1862–1890. In *Imperial Germany*, ed. J. J. Sheehan. New York: Franklin Watts.
    1985. *The German Empire 1871–1918*. Leamington Spa: Berg.
Welch, R. 1979. *Response to Imperialism: The United States and the Philippine-American War*. Chapel Hill: University of North Carolina Press.
Williamson, S. R., Jr. 1969. *The Politics of Grand Strategy: Britain and France Prepare for War, 1904–1914*. Cambridge, Mass.: Harvard University Press.
    1988. The origins of World War I. *Journal of Interdisciplinary History* 18.
Wilson, K. 1985. *The Policy of the Entente*. Cambridge: Cambridge University Press.

Appendix:
Additional tables on state finances and state employment

Table A.1. *State employment: Austria (Austria-Hungary 1760–1860 and Austria 1830–1910)*

Year	Population (millions)		Civilian personnel				Military personnel			
			Central state total (thousands)	%	All levels total (thousands)	%	Austria (thousands)	%	Austria-Hungary (thousands)	%
	Austria	Austria-Hungary								
1760		15.00	10A-H	0.06	26	0.17			250	1.66
1770		17.00							200	1.17
1780		22.00	11A-H	0.05					310	1.41
1790		23.00							350	1.52
1800		24.00							325	1.35
1810		25.00			31	0.12			594	2.38
1820		27.00								
1830	15.83	29.63	55A	0.35	111A-H	0.37	242	1.53	410	1.38
1840	16.86	30.50	62A	0.37	126A-H	0.41	280	1.66	475	1.56
1850	17.82	31.10	72A	0.40	140A-H	0.45	318	1.79	485	1.56
1860	19.13	33.50	190A-H	0.57			308	1.61	535	1.60
1870	20.60	35.90	102A	0.50			177	0.86		
1880	22.14	39.04	118A	0.53			162	0.73		
1890	23.90	42.69	254A	1.06	697A	2.92	188	0.79		
1900	26.15	46.81	297A	1.14	864A	3.30	230	0.88		
1910	28.57	51.39	334A	1.17	899A	3.15	247	0.86		

Notes:

1. All figures before 1830 refer to the entire Austrian (Austro-Hungarian) Empire, whereas all after 1860 refer only to the Austrian *Reichshalf* (sometimes called Cisleithenia), thus excluding Hungary (for which comparable figures are generally unavailable).

2. Until 1880, personnel figures generally come from internal administrative sources, after they come from national censuses. Thus the large jump in civil servants in 1890 should be treated with caution.

3. See the bibliography in Chapter 11 for references cited.

Sources: Population: Austria-Hungary – 1760–90, Dickson 1987: I, 36; 1790–1910, *Beitrage zur Osterreichischen Statistik* 550, 1979, I: 13–14 – figures available for 1786, 1828, 1857, 1869, and 1880–1910 (these also include Bosnia-Herzegovina); I have projected estimates for missing decades. *Austria* – 1830–1910, Bolognese-Leuchtenmuller 1979: II, 1. *Military:* 1760–90, Dickson 1987: II, 343–55; 1800, Rothenberg 1978– field army plus garrisons and other sedentary but mobilized reserves; 1810, Rothenberg 1982: 126 – the "realistic 1809 mobilization plan"; 1830– 1910, Bolognese-Leuchtenmuller 1979: I, 57–60 and II, 5 – active army and navy personnel; 1850 and 1860 (actually 1857) are for Austria- Hungary but exclude Lombardy-Venetia; later years are Austrian *Reichshalf* only. *Civilian:* 1760–1810 (actually 1806), Dickson 1987, I: 306–10; 1830–50 central (actually 1828, 1838, and 1848), *K. K. Statistiche Monatschrift* 1890: 532–4; 1830, all levels (actually 1828), Macartney 1969: 263; 1840 all levels, projection between similar totals given by Tegeborski 1843: 360 for 1839, and by Macartney 1969: 263 for 1842; 1850 all levels, *K. K. Statistiche Jahrbuch* 1863: 104–5 – total of 52,000 *Beamten* (established civil servants) assumed to comprise 26% of all officials (as *Beamten* did in 1845 and 1848); 1870–80 all levels, *K. K. Statistiche Jahrbuch* 1873: 22, 1881: 54 – includes public officials plus 67% of legal and health workers (classified in later censuses as in the public sector); 1890–1910, *Osterreichisches Statistisches Handbuch*, 1890, 1900, 1910, 1914, *K. K. Statistiche Monatschrift* 1904: 696 – note, however, that Bolognese-Leuchtenmuller 1978: II, table 60, reproduces the 1910 census figures, but lowers those for 1890 and 1900 to 495,000 and 617,000 without explanation.

Table A.2. *State employment: Great Britain 1760–1910*

Year	Total population (millions)	Civilian personnel					Military personnel	
		Central state		All levels				
		Total (thousands)	%	Total (thousands)	%		Total	%
1760	6.10	16	0.26				144	2.36
1770	6.41						37	0.58
1780	6.99						193	2.76
1790	7.65						74	0.97
1800	8.61	16	0.18				422	4.91
1810	9.76	23	0.24				517	5.30
1820	11.30	24	0.22				115	1.02
1830	13.11	23	0.17				132	1.01
1840	14.79			43	0.29		163	1.10
1850	16.52	40	0.24	67	0.41		197	1.20
1860	18.68			76	0.41		325	1.74
1870	21.24			113	0.53		242	1.14
1880	25.71			118	0.46		246	0.96
1890	28.76	90	0.32	285	0.99		276	0.96
1900	32.25	130	0.40	535	1.66		486	1.51
1910	35.79	229	0.64	931	2.60		372	1.04

Notes:
1. Military figure for 1840 includes embodied militia and police but not volunteer corps. 1850 includes embodied militia, police, and enrolled pensioners (the last amounting to 16,720).
2. See the bibliography in Chapter 11 for references cited.

Sources: *Population*: Wrigley and Schofield 1981. *Civilian*: Central – 1800–30 calculated from figures in House of Commons, *British Sessional Papers*, Establishments of Public Offices, 1797, 1810, 1819, and 1827; 1840–80, Mitchell and Deane 1962; 1890–1910, Flora 1983: I, 242. All levels – 1840–80, Mitchell and Deane 1980; 1890–1910, Abramovitz and Eliasberg 1957: 25. Years are actually 1891, 1901, 1911. *Military*: 1760–90 and 1810–60 calculated from House of Commons, *British Sessional Papers*: 1760–70 in 1816, 12: 399 and 1860, 42: 547–9; 1780 (actually 1781) in 1813–14, 11: 306–7 and 1860, 42: 547–49; 1790 (actually 1792) and 1810–30 in 1844, 42: 169 and 1860, 42: 547–9; 1840–50 in 1852, 30: 1–3; 1860–1910 in Flora 1983, I: 247–50. 1800 combines army figures in Fortescue 1915, vol. 4, part 2: 939 and navy figures calculated from *British Sessional Papers* 1860, 42: 547–49.

Table A.3. *State employment: France, 1760–1910*

Year	Total population (millions)	Civilian personnel — Central state Total (thousands)	%	Civilian personnel — All levels Total (thousands)	%	Military personnel Total (thousands)	%
1760	25.70					460	1.78
1770	26.60					220	0.82
1780	27.00			350	1.29	240	0.89
1790	27.19			275	1.01	230	0.85
1800	27.35			250	0.91	800	2.93
1810	27.35					1,000	3.66
1820	30.46						
1830	32.57					400	1.23
1840	34.23	90	0.26			350	1.02
1850	35.78	146	0.41	300	0.84	390	1.09
1860	37.39					460	1.23
1870	36.10	220	0.60	374	1.03	600	1.66
1880	37.67	331	0.87	483	1.28	540	1.44
1890	38.34	348	0.91	472	1.23	600	1.55
1900	38.96	430	1.10	583	1.50	620	1.59
1910	39.61	556	1.40	562	1.42	650	1.65

Notes:
1. Military recruits from France itself totaled about 350,000 in 1800 and 450,000 in 1812.
2. See the bibliography in Chapter 11 for references cited.

Sources: Population: 1760–80, Riley 1986: 5; 1790–1910, Dupeux 1976: 37. *Civilian*: All levels – 1780 estimate derived from Necker 1784 (see text); 1790 and 1800 estimates (actually 1794 and 1798) from Church 1981; 1850 (actually 1846) list of government officers in Block 1875: 117–9; 1870–1910, Flora 1983: I, 211. Central – 1850 (actually 1846) figure of Vivien 1859: 172–8 as amended by Julien-Lafferrière 1970 and excluding military officers; 1870–1900, *Recensement général* and *Résultats Statistiques du Dénombrement*, for years 1866, 1876, 1891, and 1901; 1910, *Annuaire statistique de la France* 1913: 264. Year is actually 1913. *Military*: Army – 1760, Kennett 1967: 77–8; 1770–90, Lynn 1984: 44, Scott 1978: 5; 1800, 1810 (actually 1812), Addington 1984: 26, Rothenberg 1978: 43, 51–5, Chandler 1966; 1830–70, Block 1875: I, 566 (excluding troops stationed in Algeria). Navy – 1780, Dull 1975: 144; 1790, Hampson 1959: 209; 1810, Masson 1968: 257; 1870, Block 1875: I, 583. All other years before 1860 include extrapolated estimates for naval personnel. Army and navy: 1880–1910, *Annuaire statistique de la France* 1913: "Résumé rétrospectif," 132.

Table A.4. *State employment: Prussia-Germany, 1760–1910*

| | Total population (millions) | | Civilian personnel | | | | | | Military personnel | |
| | | | Central state | | All levels | | | | | |
Year	Prussia	Germany	Prussia total (thousands)	%	Prussia total (thousands)	%	Germany total (thousands)	%	Total (thousands)	%
1760	3.62								150	4.14
1770	4.10									
1780	5.00								188	3.76
1790	5.70								195	3.42
1800	6.16		23	0.37					230	3.73
1810	7.00								272	3.88
1820	11.27								150	1.33
1830	13.00								150	1.15
1840	14.93		16+	0.11+	55+	0.33+			157	1.05
1850	16.61		32+	0.20+	86	0.47			173	1.04
1860	18.27								149	0.82
1870	24.57	41.01	135	0.55	283	1.15			400	0.98
1880	27.19	45.23			413	1.51	704	1.56	434	1.07
1890	29.84	49.43			535	1.80	900	1.70	529	1.12
1900	34.27	56.37							629	1.05
1910	39.92	64.93			c. 1,000	3.92	1,700	2.35	680	1.05

Notes:

1. Pre-1870 military personnel figures are Prussian; thereafter they are German.

2. See the bibliography in Chapter 11 for references cited.

Sources: Population: Prussia – 1760–1810, Turner 1980; 1820–70, Kraus 1980: 226; 1870–1910, *Statistische Jahrbuch für den Preussischen Staat* 1912. Germany: 1870–1900, Hohorst et al. 1975: 22; 1870–1860, Jany 1967; actual years are 1763, 1777, 1789, 1813, 1820, 1830, 1840, 1850, 1859. Jany's 1820–40 figures do not include noncommissioned officers or officers and have been upwardly adjusted by 23% (this being the normal proportion of NCOs and officers in the nineteenth-century Prussian army); 1870 Prussian total is 315,000 (Jany plus 2,400 naval personnel). Germany – 1870, Weitzel 1967: table 8; 1872 figure. 1880–1910, Hohorst et al. 1975: 171; 1890 figure actually 1891. *Civil:* Prussia – 1800 estimate provided "with reserve" by a senior Prussian official to Finer 1949: 710 (as his 1850 estimate was far too low, his reserve may be justified); 1840, Bülow-Cummerow 1842: 225, number of *Beamten* for 1839; 1850, *Tabellen und amtlichen Nachrichten den Preussischen Staat für das Jahr 1849*, number *Beamten* for 1849, thus the 1840 and 1850 figures underestimate total state employment by perhaps 20%–30%; 1860 (actually 1861), *Jahrbuch für die Amliche Statistik* 1863; 1870, 1880, 1890 (actually 1869, 1882, and 1895), *Statistisches Handbuch für den Preussischen Staat*, 1869, 1898; 1910 (actually 1907) Kunz 1990. Germany – 1880–1910, *Statistisches Jahrbuch für das Deutche Reich* 1884: 19, 1889: 14, 1909: 33 (actually 1882 and 1895); 1910 (actually 1907) Kunz 1990.

Table A.5. *State employment: United States, 1760–1910*

Year	Total population (millions)	Civilian personnel Central state Total (thousands)	%	All levels Total (thousands)	%	Military personnel Total (thousands)	%
1760	1.59						
1770	2.15						
1780	2.78						
1790	3.93	0.7	0.02			0.7	0.02
1800	5.93	2.6	0.04			7	0.12
1810	7.24	3.8 (est.)	0.05 (est.)			12	0.16
1820	9.62	7	0.07			15	0.16
1830	12.90	11	0.09			12	0.09
1840	17.12	18	0.11			22	0.13
1850	23.26	26	0.11			21	0.09
1860	31.51	37	0.12			28	0.09
1870	39.91	51	0.13			50	0.13
1880	50.26	100	0.19			38	0.07
1890	63.06	157	0.25			39	0.06
1900	76.09	239	0.31	1,034	1.36	126	0.17
1910	92.41	389	0.42	1,552	1.68	139	0.15

Note: See the bibliography in Chapter 11 for references cited.
Sources: *Population*: 1760–80 in U.S., Bureau of the Census 1975: tables A.6–8. *Civilian*: Central – 1790–1810, calculated from figures in U.S., *American State Papers*, vol. 38, *Miscellaneous*: 1790 (actually 1792) in 1: 57–68; 1800 (actually 1802) in 1: 260–308; 1810 extrapolated from 1810 and 1816 figures in 2: 307–96; 1820–1910 in U.S. 1975: table Y308–17. All levels – 1900–10 in Fabricant 1952: 29. *Military*: U.S. 1975: table Y 904–16. Actual years are 1789, 1801, 1821, 1831, 1841, 1851, 1861, 1871, 1891, 1901, and 1911.

Table A.6. *State revenue: Austria, 1760–1910 (total and principal sources as percentage of total)*

Year	Total (millions of florins)	Direct taxes	Indirect taxes General	Salt, tobacco monopolies	State property Stamps, fees	Profits of monopolies
1760	35.0	53	19	16	2	10
1770	39.5	48	17	16	9	10
1780	50.1	41	18	19	13	10
1790	85.6	27	36		NA	
1800	65.5	29	45		NA	
1810	25.0	30	42		NA	
1820	112.2	44	20	30	4	2+
1830	123.0	39	23	22	4	12
1840	193.3	25	23	26	4	25
1850	202.5	29	24	24	4	18
1860	355.1	27	17	25	9	26
1870	259.6	35	30		15	21
1880		32	31		20	17
1890		NA	NA		NA	NA
1900		28	30		17	25
1910	1,159.2	28	29		17	26

Notes:
1. Actual years used: 1763, 1770, 1778, 1821, 1830, 1841, 1850, 1859, 1868, 1883, 1898, 1913.
2. See the bibliography in Chapter 11 for references cited.
Sources: 1760–80: Dickson 1987: II, 382–3; peacetime ordinary net revenue, "Stamps and fees" equals Dickson's "other" category. 1790–1810: Czoernig 1861: 122; total revenue for 1800 and 1810 as recalculated by Beer 1871: 390–1, to allow for currency changes (this massively reduces the 1810 total revenue, probably by a little too much). The bulk of the remaining revenue for those years is classified by Czoernig as "extra-ordinary," probably a mixed category. 1820–60: Brandt 1978: II, 1072–3, 1100. 1820–30 ordinary revenue; "profits of monopoly" industries missing during these years, assumed to be the residue after subtracting direct taxes, indirect taxes, and stamps and fees from total revenue (this is unbelievably low in 1821; perhaps it has been confused in the unusually high "salt monopoly" category). 1870–1910: Gratz 1949: 229–30.

Table A.7. *State revenue: Britain, 1760–1911 (total and principal sources as percentage of total)*

Year	Total (millions of pounds)	Taxes		State property
		Direct	Indirect	(stamps and post office)
1760	9.2	26	69	4
1770	11.4	16	70	4
1780	12.5	20	71	5
1790	17.0	18	66	9
1800	31.6	27	52	12
1810	69.2	30	57	11
1820	58.1	14	68	16
1830	55.3	10	73	17
1840	51.8	8	73	19
1850	57.1	18	65	16
1860	70.1	18	64	16
1870	73.7	26	59	12
1880	73.3	25	61	16
1890	94.6	26	50	18
1900	129.9	31	47	22
1910	131.7	27	47	22
1911	(203.9)	(44)	(36)	(17)

Notes:
1. Figures for 1800 are actually for 1802.
2. See the bibliography in Chapter 11 for references cited.
Source: Mitchell and Deane 1980: public finance tables.

Table A.8. *State revenue: France, 1760–1910 (total and principal sources as percentage of total)*

Year	Total (millions of francs)	Taxes		State property
		Direct	Indirect	
1760	259 *l.t.*	48	45	7
1770				
1780	377 *l.t.*	41	49	10
1790	472 *l.t.*	35	47	18
1800				
1810				
1820	933			
1830	978	40	22	38
1840	1,160	c. 30		
1850	1,297	c. 28		
1860	1,722	c. 23		
1870	1,626	26	31	44
1880	2,862	21	38	41
1890	3,221	18	36	42
1900	3,676	21	36	43
1910	4,271	22	33	45

Notes:
1. Ordinary revenue, excluding all loans.
2. Adjacent years used: 1751, 1775, 1788, 1828.
3. See the bibliography in Chapter 11 for references cited.
Sources: 1760–90: Morineau 1980: 314, classifying the contribution of the clergy as direct tax and *dons gratuit* as state property. Total in *livres tournois* (*l.t.*). 1830 (actually 1828): Hansemann 1834. 1844–1910: *Annuaire Statistique de la France* 1913: 134–9; 1840 direct tax figure equals sum of central government's *quatres contributions direct* plus estimated 5% for missing capital gains tax.

Table A.9. *State revenue: Prussia, 1820–1910 (total and principal sources as percentage of total)*

Year	Total (millions of marks)	Taxes Direct	Indirect	State property Railways	Other industries	All
1820	96	36	33			30
1840	169	24	34			41
1850	183	22	32			46
1870	550 (651)	24 (20)	10 (24)	24 (20)	30 (25)	65 (55)
1880	805 (982)	21 (17)	8 (25)	30 (25)	22 (18)	71 (58)
1890	1,744 (2,140)	10 (8)	14 (30)	51 (42)	15 (12)	76 (62)
1900	2,607 (3,139)	8 (7)	13 (28)	54 (44)	16 (13)	79 (65)
1910	3,732 (4,630)	11 (9)	3 (22)	58 (47)	16 (13)	86 (69)

Notes:
1. All figures for ordinary revenue, excluding all loans and surpluses.
2. Adjacent years used: 1821, 1844, 1871.
3. In 1870 and after: Figures relate only to Prussia (not the entire German Reich). Unbracketed figures derived from Prussian state revenue accounts. Bracketed figures add 60% of Reich revenue (almost all derived from indirect taxes). Prussia contributed 60% of Reich population, and revenue contribution to the Reich from individual states was usually assessed on their populations. Therefore bracketed figures are probably roughly accurate estimates.
4. See the bibliography in Chapter 11 for references cited.
Sources: 1820–50: Leineweber 1988: 315. Note that in 1850 Prussian revenue sources were about average among the larger German states, though smaller ones tended to rely more on traditional state property sources for their revenue (figures in Heitz 1980: 406–8). 1870–1910: Prochnow 1977: 5–7.

Table A.10. *Federal plus state revenue: United States, 1820–1900 (total and principal sources as percentage of total)*

Year	Total (millions of dollars)	Taxes Direct	Indirect	State property
1820	25	10	62	26
1830	31	5	71	21
1840	33	18	42	37
1850	69	23	58	20
1860	100	26	54	18
1870	501	26	58	16
1880	446	15	67	17
1890	584	16	64	20
1900	837	16	58	26

Notes:
1. Method of calculation: state revenues are available for about half the contemporary states in 1820, for about three-quarters by 1870, and for all by 1900. Per capita revenues were calculated for these states, and the sums were multiplied by the total U.S. population for that year. The total state estimates were then added to the federal government totals.
2. State property includes postal revenue. The figures in U.S. 1975 do not include postal revenue, except when the post office generated a surplus, in which case only the surplus is included.
3. State property revenue derived from the post office in all periods, canal tolls in earlier years, and land grants in the mid-nineteenth century.
4. See the bibliography in Chapter 11 for references cited.
Source: Calculated from U.S. 1975: table Y352–7; U.S. 1947: 419–22; Holt 1977: 99–324.

Table A.11. *Federal revenue: United States, 1792–1910 (total and principal sources as percentage of total)*

| | | Taxes | | |
Year	Total (millions of dollars)	Direct	Indirect	State property
1792	4		98	2
1800	11		89	11
1810	10		87	13
1820	19		80	20
1830	27		82	18
1840	24		56	44
1850	49		81	19
1860	65		82	18
1870	430	17	68	15
1880	367	1	82	17
1890	464	0.2	80	20
1900	670	2	71	27
1910	900		69	31

Notes:
1. State property is mostly postal revenue. The figures in U.S. 1975 are net postal revenue, except when the post office generated a surplus, in which case only the surplus is included. I have included all postal revenues.
2. See the bibliography in Chapter 11 for references cited.
Sources: Population: U.S. 1975: Tables A.6–A.8. Revenue: calculated from U.S. 1975: table Y352–7; U.S. 1947: 419–22.

Table A.12. *State revenue: United States, 1820–1900 (estimated aggregated total and by principal source in percentage of total)*

| | | Principal source of revenue | | | | |
| | | Taxation | | | State | |
Year	Total revenue	Direct	Indirect	Business	property	Other
1820	5,930	25	7	17	43	8
1830	4,263	25	1	14	42	18
1840	9,085	24	4	40	19	13
1850	19,462	53	1.5	23	22	1
1860	35,643	62	1.6	13	18	6
1870	70,911	64	1	17	16	3
1880	79,125	63	0.1	19	18	1
1890	119,988	60	1	20	18	2
1900	167,407	52	4	23	20	2

Notes:
1. Figures for 1820–1900 are aggregated for total U.S. population based on available state data (see Table A.10, note 1).
2. See the bibliography in Chapter 11 for references cited.
Source: 1820–1900: calculated from Holt 1977: 99–324.

Index

Africa, 72, 262, 348, 747, 777
Agriculture, 94, 102, 138–9, 141–2, 171,
    263–4, 268, 272, 298, 314, 379,
    492–3, 510–11, 516, 527, 539, 554,
    595, 597–8, 607, 625, 660, 664–6,
    692, 722, 723, 726–7
Alliances, 70, 246, 259–60, 267, 269–71,
    276–82, 290, 343, 348–9, 353, 437–8,
    741–3, 745, 748–54, 769, 771–2,
    779–80, 793–5
American colonies, 37, 97, 108, 115, 117,
    118, 137–66, 220–3, 269, 454, 456
    see also United States
Armed forces, 144, 148, 149, 152–4, 179,
    181, 195–6, 203–5, 207, 215, 217,
    241–4, 271–3, 308, 319, 331, 337–8,
    340–1, 347–50, 372, 376, 389,
    402–43, 445, 448–9, 494–7, 502,
    505–6, 520, 531–2, 631, 713, 733–4,
    760–6, 797
    NCOS in, 179, 204, 271, 421, 425,
    428–9, 433–5, 438, 451, 502, 736
    officers in, 179, 189, 192, 196, 202–4,
    246, 271, 275, 322, 338, 419, 436,
    450–1, 475, 564–9, 582, 735–6, 761
    ranks in, 179, 196, 204, 271, 420–2,
    424–30, 435–6, 699, 788
Artisans, 3, 29, 96, 97, 98, 100–1, 105,
    110, 124, 140, 146, 153, 154, 159, 188,
    202, 204, 206, 220, 231, 233, 307–8,
    420–1, 425, 516–26, 536, 540–7, 549,
    550, 554, 558, 565, 588, 598, 600, 616,
    666–8, 672–4, 681–2
Austria, Austria-Hungary, 5, 16, 38–9,
    79, 80, 82, 84–5, 109, 115, 131, 152,
    177, 181, 203–4, 215, 218, 219,
    222–4, 226, 229, 232, 236, 239,
    241–8, 250, 255, 259, 262–4, 271,
    273, 276–7, 279–81, 284, 287–8,
    290–8, 301–3, 307, 309–11, 317,
    330–57, 362–84, 388–94, 404, 407,
    411, 413–14, 417, 419–20, 424,
    427–8, 430, 432, 434–5, 438, 447–9,
    453, 456, 465–6, 468–9, 491, 493,
    501–2, 505–6, 578, 584, 588, 630–4,
    678–9, 683, 693, 700–1, 708–11,
    716–18, 726, 727, 730, 731, 734, 735,
    741–3, 745, 748–51, 755–66, 768,
    781–5, 798, 804–5, 811
Authoritative power, 1, 2, 6, 310, 321,
    503, 512, 549, 558, 559, 567, 590, 602,
    610, 724, 726–30, 736, 784

Belgium, Austrian Netherlands, 281, 284,
    286, 288, 290, 301, 330, 338, 370, 377,
    380, 502, 555, 559, 683, 692, 723, 732,
    742, 764, 768, 792
Bismarck, Otto von, 64, 180, 249, 261,
    288, 309–18, 322, 324, 326, 343, 437,
    438, 502–3, 552, 674–5, 747, 788
Bourgeoisie, 71, 92, 96, 102, 130, 168,
    173, 187–8, 194–5, 202, 206–8,
    218–21, 233, 239, 244–5, 247, 279,
    306–8, 310, 313, 318, 337, 353,
    424–5, 432–3, 438, 467, 490, 504–5,
    522, 547, 565, 629, 679–80, 683,
    723–4, 744
    see also Middle class; Petite bourgeoisie
Bureaucracy, 51, 57–8, 60, 67–8, 79, 119,
    317–19, 322, 352, 358–61, 390, 395,
    402, 422–5, 438–40, 444–79, 506,
    559, 563, 577, 723, 736, 738, 759

Cage, caging (social), 8, 20, 72, 224, 250,
    252, 482, 505, 558, 598, 734, 775, 797
Cameralism, 300, 447–50, 453, 455, 456,
    461, 472–3
Capital, see Finance capital
Capitalism, 1, 23–34, 37–9, 93–4, 132,
    141–2, 155, 173–4, 215, 217–20, 228,
    232, 234, 244, 247–51, 254–7, 306,
    314, 317, 333–6, 353, 360, 388, 405,
    455–6, 490–9, 503–4, 510–18,
    548–9, 558, 563, 606, 723–7, 730–4,
    737–8, 753–4, 766
Capitalist crystallizations, 76–82, 86, 88,
    129, 214, 268, 303–4, 313, 322–5,
    331, 345, 439, 464, 473, 480–7, 499,
    504–6, 519, 535, 542, 575, 599, 630,
    647–9, 658–9, 683, 684, 703–5, 726,
    760, 792–5
Capitalists, 28, 72, 96–7, 219–21, 322,
    346, 522, 597, 599–600, 603, 605–17,

Capitalists (*cont.*)
  633, 647–8, 697–8, 765, 776–81,
    791–2, 798
Careerists, 29, 99, 308, 314, 471, 549,
    558–64, 570–1, 574, 576–7, 580, 588
  defined, 558
Catholic church, 17, 37, 80, 81, 82, 84,
    113, 124, 174, 175, 177–8, 181,
    185–6, 195, 197, 202, 207, 216, 226,
    231, 236, 237, 243, 297, 300, 312–13,
    315–17, 320, 321, 332, 447, 485–6,
    490, 495, 584–7, 642, 670, 672–3,
    675–6, 684–5, 699, 701–3, 705–10,
    774, 782, 789, 791–3
Chartism, 80, 122, 130, 339, 409–10, 482,
    502, 510, 519, 523–36, 538, 539,
    541–2, 551, 600, 605, 615, 620, 639,
    648, 725
China, 14, 36, 261–3, 275, 493
Cities, *see* Towns and cities
Citizenship, 19–20, 66, 68, 110, 117, 118,
    157–8, 208, 217, 226, 238, 239, 248,
    337, 339, 352, 359, 402, 405–6, 412,
    417, 425–9, 436, 464, 466–8, 479,
    480, 483, 499–504, 514, 524, 530, 549,
    571–5, 577, 619, 647, 658, 660–6,
    668, 673–80, 712, 713, 717–18, 732,
    735, 747, 782
Civil society, 23, 39–40, 42, 95, 96, 107,
    109, 111, 137, 141, 177–8, 207, 208,
    254, 297, 306, 318, 335, 338, 361, 394,
    404–5, 456, 457, 479, 480, 498, 510,
    520, 571, 603–5, 784
Civil War, American, 364–5, 369–71,
    375, 385, 392–3, 429, 431, 459, 484,
    496, 501, 703
Class, class conflict, 2, 24–34, 44–6,
    70–1, 77, 80, 96–103, 110, 114–15,
    121–4, 149–53, 158, 160–1, 167–8,
    173–5, 187, 193, 197–203, 208, 214–
    53, 306–7, 402, 405, 501–4, 510–91,
    730, 740, 774–6, 781–95
  defined, 7–8, 26–8
  see also Class consciousness; Marx, Karl,
    and Marxian theories, class theories
Class consciousness, 25–8, 105–7, 110–
    11, 195, 233, 308, 513, 518–23, 527,
    530–1, 536–42, 602–5, 614–17, 619,
    640, 658, 667, 670, 673, 681–5, 695,
    715–16, 735
Clientelism, patronage, 17, 111–12, 140,
    143, 152–4, 160–1, 446, 454–5,
    458–9, 468, 480, 639, 653, 680
Cock-up, foul-up theories, 44, 53–4, 76,
    88, 740, 743, 749, 751, 764–6, 793,
    798
Collective power, 2–3, 12–15, 24, 59–61,

74, 218–19, 254, 491, 597, 723, 730
Colonial empires, colonies, 35, 70, 131,
    255, 264, 280, 281, 284, 285, 289, 293,
    377, 489, 578–83, 751, 752, 753, 777,
    779–81, 786, 788, 791
Communications infrastructures, 94–5,
    127–8, 137–8, 160, 287, 288, 303–5,
    312, 337, 375, 378–80, 387–8, 395,
    428–9, 437, 459, 461, 479, 490,
    492–9, 616, 698, 704, 730–1
Community, 107, 139, 145, 153, 174,
    200–2, 227, 246, 321, 344, 449, 510,
    513, 518, 526, 528–9, 539–42, 602–5,
    615, 616, 624, 628, 639, 663, 667, 677,
    681, 696, 713, 730, 732
Conservative parties, 121, 122, 124–5,
    128–9, 146, 311–16, 318, 320, 344,
    484, 486, 519, 533–4, 538, 539, 603,
    617–18, 623–4, 648, 650, 694, 701–
    10, 716–18, 772, 791–2
Corporations, 551–2, 557–66, 616, 640,
    652
Courts, royal, 64, 97, 108, 114, 176,
    194–6, 198–9, 207, 319, 322, 331,
    378, 391, 448–9, 475, 480, 660,
    758–60, 764, 798

Democracy, party democracy,
    parliaments, 44, 47, 57, 76, 78–9,
    83–4, 92, 108–12, 114, 116, 125, 131,
    151, 153–5, 162–4, 178, 248–52,
    305–7, 311, 319–20, 323, 337, 338,
    340–1, 344, 346, 351–4, 381–8, 408,
    411–18, 438, 446, 456, 466–8, 472–4,
    480–91, 498, 506, 515, 524–36, 538,
    542, 577–8, 582, 589, 613–15, 617–
    25, 629–30, 635, 637, 649–52, 654,
    658, 668, 671, 673, 678, 683–4, 694,
    700–5, 708, 711–13, 728–9, 732, 743,
    766–74, 786–7, 797–8
Despotic power, 19, 59–64, 108–10, 146,
    155, 159, 207, 251–2, 331, 448, 457,
    473
Dialectical conflict, 16–17, 31, 130, 158,
    164, 176–8, 324, 352, 480, 498, 505,
    513, 541–2, 577, 598, 602, 724–5,
    728, 741
Diffused power, 1, 6, 117, 512, 549, 550,
    558, 568–71, 590, 602, 610, 624,
    724–30, 736
Diplomats, statesmen, 49, 62, 72–3,
    417–19, 437–9, 735, 744–8, 771, 775,
    781, 796
Distributive power, 2–3, 12, 15–18,
    59–61, 218–19, 597–8, 601, 723, 739
Dutch Republic, *see* Holland, Dutch
    Republic

Economic power, 1, 7–8, 23–34, 79,
    256–8, 261–6, 271–2, 492, 597, 638,
    718, 730
Economism among workers, 514–15,
    519–20, 536, 599, 601, 629, 657,
    662–5, 669, 685, 783–4
Education, 37–9, 67, 129, 175, 228, 238,
    242, 304–5, 310, 375, 378–80, 430,
    432–3, 447–50, 462–3, 470–1,
    480–5, 488, 490, 492, 526, 538, 548,
    560, 564–70, 572–5, 577, 578, 580,
    585–7, 652, 685, 715, 730–1, 735, 786
Elite theories, 44, 48, 54, 58, 62–6, 85,
    87–8, 107, 168, 318, 358–9, 391, 479
Enlightenment, 36, 39–41, 96, 103,
    145–6, 176–8, 181–3, 189–95, 205,
    235, 237, 255, 426, 449, 453, 457, 472,
    481, 660–1, 753, 780, 784
Entwinings of power relations, 2, 21, 30,
    41, 71, 87, 93, 250–5, 307, 315, 345,
    439, 535, 541, 584, 590, 671, 680, 684,
    694, 725, 730, 735, 737, 741, 748, 757,
    779, 790, 795–8
Ethnicity, race, 35, 72, 74, 84, 137, 139–
    40, 155–6, 215–16, 244, 320, 321,
    337, 348, 387, 392–3, 407, 482,
    579–83, 635–7, 639, 642–3, 649, 650,
    653, 657–8, 684, 703, 705–6, 732,
    733, 747, 753, 782–4, 786, 789, 791
Evolution, 92, 111, 130, 332, 353, 358–60,
    395, 629, 729–30, 735–8

Factories, workshops, 96, 123, 405,
    482–3, 512, 516–19, 533–6, 539–40,
    599, 601, 603, 606–7, 655, 660
Family, kinship, 96, 98–9, 127, 219, 220,
    225, 227, 249, 482, 488–9, 513, 518,
    521, 523–4, 526, 528–9, 533–6,
    540–2, 550–2, 562–3, 571, 603–5,
    615, 624, 685, 695, 697, 730, 732, 746,
    754
Farmers, see Peasants, farmers
Federal and confederal societies, states, 4,
    44, 81, 84–5, 137, 142, 156–62,
    205–6, 208, 241–2, 247, 250, 255,
    297–8, 300–1, 303, 307–12, 331–3,
    337–47, 352–4, 448, 452, 459, 483–8,
    505–6, 519, 541, 637, 652–4, 679–80,
    684, 700–1, 708–15, 731
Feudalism, 60, 162, 167, 173–4, 180, 199–
    200, 247, 322, 331, 433, 460, 465, 630,
    636
Finance capital, 97, 128–30, 172, 257, 266
    268, 274, 292, 335, 495, 497, 597, 696,
    698, 704
Foreign policy, see Geopolitics, foreign
    policy

France, 29, 37, 84, 96, 97, 101, 109, 115,
    130, 131, 132, 149, 160, 164, 167–213,
    215, 218, 219, 220, 222–3, 232, 237,
    241, 246, 247, 255, 262–4, 267–77,
    279–83, 286, 288, 290–1, 301, 303,
    309–10, 334, 337, 352, 353, 362–7,
    369–86, 388, 390–4, 404, 406–7, 411,
    417–22, 424–7, 429–31, 433, 437,
    452–6, 464, 466–7, 471, 480, 490,
    499–501, 505–6, 552, 553, 555–6,
    559, 564, 566, 572–3, 577–81, 628,
    631–5, 644, 652, 666–71, 674, 675,
    678–9, 682, 683, 685, 698, 700–3,
    712, 716–18, 726, 727, 733, 734,
    741–3, 745, 748, 751, 761–2, 766–8,
    770–3, 785, 807, 813

Geopolitics, foreign policy, 49–50, 56, 62,
    69–75, 85–7, 92, 112, 115–16, 132,
    143, 149, 161, 162, 167–8, 171, 203,
    249, 254–98, 300–5, 309–11, 325–6,
    338, 341–2, 346–50, 354, 412–19,
    437–9, 464, 578–90, 675, 735, 740–98
    defined, 746
Germany, 30, 33, 37, 58, 63, 70, 76, 84–5,
    131, 219, 236–7, 243, 244, 250, 259,
    262–4, 283, 288, 290–2, 297–329,
    333, 334, 335, 341, 347, 348, 350,
    352–4, 362–9, 371–7, 379–80,
    383–5, 392–4, 407–8, 411, 432–4,
    438, 492–3, 501–3, 506, 552–3, 555,
    556, 559, 562, 564, 566, 572–3,
    577–8, 584–9, 628, 631–5, 640–1,
    644, 651, 671–9, 682, 684–5, 692–3,
    698, 700–1, 705–8, 728–31, 734, 735,
    741–3, 745, 747–66, 768, 771–3, 785,
    788–95, 798, 808–9
    see also Prussia
Great Britain, 1, 15, 79, 82, 83, 92–136,
    140, 142–3, 160, 207, 208, 214, 215,
    218, 222, 232, 238, 239, 247, 255–9,
    262–71, 280–93, 309, 333, 352, 353,
    362–9, 371–91, 393–4, 414–17, 419–
    21, 424, 429–30, 432, 446, 456,
    463–4, 466–7, 480–5, 492, 505–6,
    510–45, 552–5, 559, 564, 566–8,
    592–5, 597–628, 631–5, 638–42, 646,
    651–2, 657, 678–9, 683, 692–3, 717,
    723, 726–30, 733, 734, 741–3, 745,
    748–55, 761–2, 767–74, 785, 792–3,
    806, 812

Hegemony, international, 2, 33, 256–8,
    260, 270–2, 274–8, 280–8, 291–3,
    301, 743, 748, 752–4, 771, 798

819 Index

Holland, Dutch Republic, 257, 265, 268,
273, 279, 281, 284, 288, 369, 387, 446,
683, 764, 768
Hungary, 281, 330, 331, 335, 337, 339–41,
343–9, 370, 376, 413, 449, 584, 693,
708, 710–11, 756

Ideological power, 2, 7, 30–1, 35–42,
103–7, 130, 144–5, 163, 167–70,
175–8, 184, 195–7, 215, 227–37, 249,
258–9, 272, 278, 438, 473, 491, 549,
564, 571–5, 725, 730
Ideological power elite, intelligentsia, 41,
170, 191, 193–4, 196–7, 200, 202,
206–8, 228–37, 239, 460, 492, 502,
629, 660–1, 665
Imperialism, 34, 241, 264, 298–9, 416,
578–83, 660, 733, 742–3, 747, 752–3,
783–5
  economic, 34, 72, 266–7, 289, 298, 740,
  775–81, 791, 797
  geopolitical, 34, 267, 271, 288, 298, 778,
  781, 791
  social, 34, 298, 740, 775–6, 779, 781–95
India, 262, 267, 269, 280, 579
Industrial Revolution, industrialization,
11–18, 92–6, 115, 126, 129–30, 164,
244, 284, 333, 353, 368, 436–7,
491–9, 550, 565, 606, 639, 666–7,
672, 681, 697, 701, 703, 711–12, 717–
18, 723, 726–7, 730–1, 776
  Second, 12, 73, 297, 469, 493–9, 542,
  551, 576, 597–602, 605, 624–5,
  628–9, 635, 640, 660, 672, 677, 678,
  680, 681, 682, 697
Infrastructural power, 59–61, 107–9, 331,
338
Institutional statism, 44, 52–4, 59, 88,
130–1, 163, 251, 319–22, 512–13,
727–9, 737
Interstitial emergence, 35, 39, 41, 105,
565, 727–8
Ireland, Irish, 1, 91, 102, 112, 121, 124,
129, 149, 239, 408–9, 420, 431, 490,
520, 531, 540, 579, 602–3, 608, 611,
726, 731, 732, 770, 772, 784
Italy, 77–8, 84, 238–42, 244, 245, 259,
262, 281, 284, 291, 301, 307, 309, 330,
335, 338–40, 342, 414, 438, 492–3,
553, 557, 633, 683, 698, 731, 741–2,
761, 768

Japan, 14, 30, 36, 40–1, 262–3, 306, 317,
353–4, 492–3, 553, 556, 557, 679,
683, 748

Labor parties, see Socialist and labor
parties
Laissez-faire, see Market, market
organization, laissez-faire
Language, linguistic communities, 236,
239–47, 305, 335–7, 339–40, 344,
346, 351, 490, 491, 731, 734, 738, 753,
782, 798
Late development theories, 159–60, 170,
299, 333, 335, 491–9
Law, law courts, lawyers, 38, 65–6, 78,
111, 113, 114, 117–18, 138, 145–6,
156–8, 172, 175, 177, 181–3, 186–9,
192, 195, 212, 230, 231, 232, 237, 239,
240, 248, 311, 331, 337, 340, 378, 405,
449, 519–20, 530–1, 536, 538, 565,
569, 610–11, 618–20, 645–8, 651,
655–6
Liberal parties, 119–21, 124–5, 129, 308,
311–16, 320, 344–5, 471, 484, 486–7,
503, 519, 522, 533–4, 538, 539, 552,
556, 579–83, 601, 604, 612, 617–24,
648, 650, 652, 653, 703–5, 708,
770–3, 785, 789, 792
Liberalism, 39, 71, 86, 126–30, 137, 143,
162–4, 218, 251, 256, 305–6, 308–11,
313, 318, 324, 337, 344–5, 353, 369,
404, 471, 482–7, 538, 551, 552, 569,
579–83, 611, 615, 647–9, 654, 658,
664, 673, 676, 683, 701, 703–5, 711–
12, 716, 727, 734, 747, 753–4,
766–74, 776, 786, 790
Literacy, 36–8, 97, 102–5, 117, 139, 145,
175–7, 184, 196, 201, 215–18, 225,
228–33, 235–7, 242, 245–6, 248, 254,
297, 300–1, 305, 307, 336, 378,
420–1, 451, 516, 519, 521, 560–1,
571, 604, 731, 732
Local government, 63, 83–5, 313, 361–9,
373–6, 378–9, 383–4, 387–8, 390–5,
449, 459, 461, 465, 468–71, 483–4,
497, 524, 528, 693, 700, 708
Local-regional power, 3, 5, 17, 84–5,
105–7, 113, 132, 156, 159–60, 207,
215, 228, 231, 238–9, 246, 267, 320,
342, 343, 346, 429, 491, 629, 684, 685,
696, 702–11, 726, 730–2, 734, 782
Logistics, 13–14, 61, 137, 143, 273, 288,
428–9, 494, 498
Lutheranism, see Protestantism,
Lutheranism

Manufacturing, 93–7, 100, 102, 128–9,
171, 173, 191, 202, 220, 245, 262–5,
270, 281, 301–5, 335, 339, 469,
493–9, 503, 510–11, 515–23, 548,

551–8, 600, 606–7, 609–11, 697, 717, 723

Market, market organization, laissez-faire, 33–4, 92, 101–2, 220–1, 228, 254–5, 267, 279, 284–93, 298–300, 302–5, 318, 335, 480–7, 519–20, 523, 534, 711–12, 738, 754, 778, 780

Marshall, T. H., 19–20, 66, 68, 157–8, 311, 359, 436, 479, 483, 499, 503, 514, 652, 678

Marx, Karl, and Marxian theories, class theories, 1, 7–8, 11, 16, 23–34, 41, 44–6, 51, 55, 58, 59, 62, 65, 68–9, 71, 75–8, 82, 88, 92, 218–21, 227, 229, 255–7, 299, 300, 306–7, 310, 317, 323, 324, 345, 360, 377, 404–5, 410, 446, 479, 495, 504–6, 510–15, 528, 533, 542, 547–8, 550, 553, 568, 589, 597–8, 600, 602–3, 616, 629–30, 659, 665, 667, 680–2, 684, 692, 695–7, 709–10, 712, 714, 717–18, 724, 725, 784

Marxism among workers, 315–16, 514–15, 599–601, 613, 622, 624, 665–6, 669, 673, 677–8, 683–5, 706–8, 783–4

Mercantilism, 34, 154, 255, 267, 270, 287, 289, 298–9, 302–3, 305, 778–81, 791, 797

Middle class, 5, 28–9, 97, 102, 314, 316, 411, 431, 433–6, 485, 523, 525, 530, 532, 538, 546–98, 614, 615, 675–6, 679, 705, 711–12, 724, 732–3, 783, 786–7, 791, 794, 798
  defined, 546–50
  see also Bourgeoisie; Petite bourgeoisie

Militarism, militarist crystallization, 76, 81–2, 85–6, 88, 131, 137, 164, 167, 174, 207, 214–16, 221–6, 237–47, 255, 268, 288, 304, 306, 310, 313, 322–5, 331–3, 338, 345, 351–2, 354, 370–8, 381, 395, 402–19, 439, 450–1, 455, 457, 459, 463–4, 466–7, 473, 479, 482, 485, 495–7, 499, 519–21, 526–7, 542, 549, 578–88, 602, 629–30, 644–7, 654, 658, 660, 666, 667, 671, 674, 675, 678, 680–1, 683, 684, 699–700, 727, 729–30, 732–5, 737–9, 743, 754–6, 760, 766, 773, 785, 788–95, 798

Military caste, 73–4, 402, 412, 420, 423, 426–36, 438–40, 473, 739, 758, 766, 779, 798

Military conscription, 100, 107, 121, 222, 240, 406, 411, 428–9, 579, 581, 693, 706, 731, 760–1, 770, 782–3

Military mobilization, 437–8, 742, 755, 761–6

Military power, 1, 8–9, 30–1, 37, 44, 55, 69, 73–4, 79–80, 92–4, 115–20, 152–5, 162–3, 196, 203, 249, 259, 371–8, 351, 402, 443, 492, 725, 726, 730, 762

Monarchical crystallizations (autocratic, authoritarian, absolutist, dynastic), 15, 44, 60, 62–8, 76, 79, 83–4, 172, 174, 177–8, 180–1, 187, 208, 232, 251, 254, 297–301, 304, 306–7, 311, 321–5, 331–3, 338–9, 341–54, 381–8, 404, 413–14, 438, 446–56, 464–9, 472–3, 498–506, 635, 647, 660–1, 666, 674–8, 683, 700–1, 705–15, 727–9, 732, 735–6, 743, 757–66, 769, 773, 780–1, 787, 792–8

Moral-ideological crystallization, 44, 81, 480–7, 533–5, 542

Multi-power-actor civilizations, 10, 69, 254, 266, 491, 493, 507, 753

Mutualism, 514, 519, 521, 523, 524, 528, 538, 576, 599–601, 603, 615, 620–4, 629, 639, 655, 662–5, 668–9, 683, 685, 729, 783–4

Napoléon Bonaparte, 119, 180, 237–44, 259, 261, 271–8, 280, 293, 426, 428, 462–5, 500

Nation, 1–2, 5, 36, 73, 93, 102, 106, 187, 193, 196, 204–5, 208, 214–53, 282, 299, 301, 331, 336–54, 436, 450, 488–9, 546, 571–96, 605, 642, 653, 658, 728, 730–6, 771–2, 774–6

Nation-state, national state, 3, 29–30, 33, 44, 57, 205–7, 234, 237, 255–6, 268–70, 297–9, 331, 332, 350, 354, 359, 488–9, 499, 504–6, 550, 569–90, 602, 617, 629, 735, 737–8, 745–8, 784–6, 795, 797

National crystallization, 20, 44, 81, 86, 88, 129, 155–6, 159, 205–6, 214, 245, 307, 313, 316, 323–5, 338, 376, 411, 473, 499, 505–6, 572, 575, 578, 582, 584, 617–21, 624, 629–30, 652–3, 667, 672, 678, 679, 683–4, 694, 699–701, 725, 731, 775–6, 784–6

National organization, 32–3, 71–2, 102, 254–5, 298–305, 339, 479, 488–91, 505–6, 571, 597, 610, 616–17, 731, 734, 784–5, 797–8

Nationalism, nationalist organization, 32–3, 71, 74–5, 102, 106, 119, 204–7, 216, 225, 227, 237, 240–1, 244–7, 249–50, 255–6, 282, 292, 298–9, 301,

Nationalism (*cont.*)
310, 311, 312, 314, 323–5, 332, 335,
336, 352, 470, 489, 546, 551–2, 559,
575–88, 709–11, 713, 716–18, 732–5,
740–2, 747–8, 751, 754, 756, 758,
760, 770, 774–6, 778–81, 783–7,
792–8
Navies, naval power, 34, 70, 257, 264–5,
268, 273–4, 285, 288, 354, 403,
419–33, 440, 445, 496–7, 582, 747,
752–3, 755, 762, 771–3, 791–3
Norms, 31, 49–50, 69, 72, 227, 257–8,
270, 278–9, 284–5, 287, 293, 745–6,
753–4, 769–70, 773

Old regime, nobles, landowners, 17, 28,
62–5, 71–4, 92, 96–9, 101–2, 104–5,
124–5, 128–30, 140, 142, 147, 167–8,
185, 191, 196, 202, 219, 220, 222, 230,
245, 247, 268, 279, 306–8, 310, 313–
14, 318, 337, 384, 417–20, 424, 426,
430–6, 438–40, 450–1, 464, 467, 475,
519, 520, 522, 571, 584, 598, 629, 649,
679, 696–9, 701–3, 708–11, 713–16,
727, 735, 744, 754, 756, 760–1, 775,
776, 791
Organizational outflanking, 429, 515, 540,
546, 558, 616
Ottoman Empire, Turkey, 281, 287, 291,
301, 331, 348, 491, 748

Parliaments, *see* Democracy, party
democracy, parliaments
Particularism, 15, 62–4, 71–2, 112, 114,
116, 119, 125, 172, 187, 193, 208, 222,
225, 230, 248, 334, 345, 351–2, 455,
474, 523, 546, 603, 710, 724
Parties, 58, 62, 68, 74, 108–11, 113–15,
131, 148, 159–61, 168, 194, 223–4,
247–9, 311, 313–22, 386, 439, 445,
459, 463, 464, 475, 492, 526, 577–8,
584, 599–600, 610, 648, 718, 760, 773
Patriarchy, 44, 81, 155, 526, 534–5, 677,
725, 735
Patronage, *see* clientelism, patronage
Peasants, farmers, 5, 25–6, 97, 123, 138–
42, 145, 154, 164, 168, 172, 174–5,
180, 185, 188, 199–200, 202, 222, 224,
241, 242, 306, 313, 339, 345, 346, 384,
420–1, 425, 490, 501, 513, 525, 546,
576–7, 650–1, 663, 664, 666–7, 676,
680, 683, 684, 692–722, 724, 727, 732,
782–3, 798
People, populace, 99–101, 106, 116–17,
121, 123, 125, 140, 146, 151–2, 187,
193, 194, 198, 200, 203, 204, 207, 219,
225, 240, 247, 249, 516

Petite bourgeoisie, 28, 38, 92, 96–7, 100,
102–7, 110–19, 121, 125, 126, 129,
140, 148, 168, 188, 202, 205–8, 219–
22, 224, 238, 239, 247–9, 279, 307–8,
314, 339–41, 345, 425, 467, 516,
521–3, 547, 549–58, 570–2, 575–6,
584–8, 605, 625, 683, 723–4, 733
defined, 550
Pluralism, 44, 46–7, 50, 54, 58, 59, 63, 75,
76, 82, 85, 88, 359, 479
Police, 65, 403–12, 500, 524
Political power, 1, 9, 30–4, 44–91, 249,
259, 278, 492, 512–13, 549, 638, 718,
225, 226, 730
Polymorphous crystallizations, 5, 44,
75–88, 108, 132, 260, 300, 321–6,
345, 349, 351–2, 463, 479, 480,
506–7, 575, 649, 658, 678, 735–6,
741, 757, 759, 766, 769, 774, 796–8
Population, 13, 93, 125, 154, 171, 272, 517
Primacy, ultimate, 1, 76–88, 251, 323–5,
480, 736–9
Private property, 23, 107, 157–8, 267,
324, 445–6, 449, 452–6, 531, 540,
636, 694
Professionals, 29, 97–9, 101, 102, 186–9,
233, 308, 314, 402, 420, 422, 425–36,
438–40, 450–1, 471, 529, 549, 562,
564–71, 573–6, 580, 586–8, 735
defined, 564
Proletariat, *see* Working class, workers,
proletariat
Property, *see* Private property
Protectionism
trade, 33–4, 267, 279, 286, 288–9, 298–
302, 305, 312–13, 551, 696, 698–9,
703, 706–8, 713, 715, 778–80, 791–2,
794, 797
among workers, 514, 516–19, 522, 598–
601, 639, 655, 657, 662, 683, 783
Protestantism, Lutheranism, 36–7, 81, 82,
84, 106–7, 113, 114, 118, 124, 139,
145, 216, 226, 231, 235–6, 239, 243,
292, 300, 305, 308, 312, 315–16, 319–
20, 323–5, 417, 447, 484, 520, 522,
533–5, 581–2, 584–7, 604, 636, 642,
673, 675–7, 684–5, 699, 705–12,
725
Prussia, 16, 27, 31, 38, 79, 84, 108–10,
115, 131, 152, 181, 184, 203–4, 215,
218, 222–4, 232, 242–3, 247, 248,
259, 269, 271, 273, 276–7, 279–82,
284, 287–8, 297–311, 330, 331, 333,
337, 362–9, 371–4, 376, 378, 381–4,
386, 388, 390, 392–4, 404, 407,
413–14, 417, 419–20, 424, 426–8,
430, 432–4, 447–53, 456, 464–70,

492–6, 505, 699, 726, 747, 748,
    808–9, 814
see also Germany

Race, *see* Ethnicity, race
Realism, 44, 49–50, 54, 55, 58, 75, 76,
    256–8, 740–1, 743–57, 764, 767–9,
    771, 798
Reformism, 218, 221, 308–9, 386, 514–15,
    520, 599–600, 603, 615, 617–25, 630,
    643–4, 662, 669–71, 673, 683, 715–
    18, 725
Regime strategies, 18–21, 39, 105, 215,
    279, 298–9, 314–16, 322–5, 338–54,
    386, 466, 473, 491–504, 542, 584–5,
    588, 599–601, 617–24, 661–6, 668,
    671, 673–8, 682–4, 708, 714–15, 724,
    728–9, 757–9, 766, 781–95
Religion, 2, 15, 37–9, 77, 81, 116, 121,
    124, 139–40, 215–17, 228, 236,
    280–1, 307, 482–3, 575, 589, 629,
    642, 648, 657, 684, 696, 697, 699, 703,
    726, 731–2, 734–5, 738, 786, 798
Representative crystallization, 5, 20, 81,
    86, 88, 110, 172, 214, 331, 384, 411,
    452, 454, 466, 473, 629–30, 649, 660,
    667, 672, 678, 679, 699–711, 716–18
Repression, 123–4, 139, 148, 306, 308,
    321–2, 324, 340–2, 348, 403–12, 426,
    439, 530–3, 599–600, 608–11, 630,
    634–5, 637, 644–50, 653, 654, 656–7,
    661–6, 668–9, 672, 674, 678, 679,
    684, 714, 724–5, 760, 783, 791–2
Revolutionaries, 146–7, 149–53, 155–6,
    182–3, 186–94, 199–200, 229, 248,
    307–8, 338, 528–9, 599–600, 663,
    713, 718, 731
Revolutions, 11–18, 92, 120–5, 214, 221,
    224, 316, 359, 440, 457–67, 500,
    514–15, 528–32, 541, 599–600, 628,
    668–71, 676–8, 725, 794
    American, 18, 46, 122, 132, 137–66,
    180, 214, 222, 232, 371, 455, 457–9
    of 1848, 224, 281, 307–8, 339–41, 465,
    495, 551, 639
    French, 2, 18, 30, 41, 65, 74, 80, 87,
    119, 123, 149, 150, 167–214, 221, 222,
    232, 234, 237, 241, 270–1, 307, 385,
    459–61, 466–7, 701–2, 738
    Russian, 628, 633, 663–6, 713–15
Riots, mobs, revolts, 119, 121–5, 142–3,
    145–7, 156, 200–1, 220, 234, 237,
    243, 347, 384, 403–12, 439, 500,
    528–33, 539, 635, 662–6, 713–14
Russia, 57, 84, 177, 238, 247, 259, 262–3,
    274–7, 279–80, 286–8, 290–1, 331,
    338, 342, 347–50, 377, 408, 438, 440,

447, 450, 491–2, 599, 628, 630, 633,
    635, 644, 646, 647, 654, 660–6, 671,
    679, 683, 684, 693, 698, 700–1,
    713–15, 729, 732, 741–3, 745–51,
    755, 759, 761, 763–6, 768, 771,
    782–3, 785, 787, 798

Science, technology, 13–14, 95–6, 310,
    492, 495–7, 597, 738
Sections, sectionalism, 3, 8, 28–9, 248,
    503–4, 739
    among workers, 511–12, 517–19, 524,
    532–42, 598–602, 608–17, 628, 629,
    636–7, 642–4, 654–9, 662–3, 666,
    668, 670–1, 673–5, 681–3, 724, 725,
    727, 729
Segments, segmentalism, 3, 8, 28–9, 64,
    82, 111, 113–15, 123, 127, 130–2,
    140–1, 163, 173, 187, 207, 221, 225,
    239, 241, 248, 249, 288, 314, 320–1,
    325, 342–6, 402–3, 429–36, 438–40,
    457, 469, 484, 501–4, 522, 546, 550,
    558, 564, 571, 575, 577, 590, 650, 664,
    680, 695, 698–9, 701–3, 708, 724,
    739, 759, 782, 796
    among workers, 511–12, 518, 536,
    539–40, 542, 598–600, 602–3, 608,
    615, 624, 629, 633, 653, 659, 681–3,
    724–7
Socialist and labor parties, 86, 314–16,
    320, 345, 503–4, 510, 514–15, 528,
    589, 599–602, 605, 612, 615, 617–24,
    628, 630, 633–8, 641–4, 647, 650,
    652, 656, 659, 661, 664–71, 673–80,
    682–5, 695, 702–12, 714–15, 717–18,
    729, 782–5, 792
Spain, 149, 238, 241, 262, 265, 267,
    273–4, 279–81, 284, 330, 423, 579,
    679–80, 683, 684, 695, 698
State
    autonomy of, 44–54, 59–77, 88, 108,
    110, 300, 305–9, 317–26, 446–9,
    474–5, 479, 483–4, 499, 504–7,
    735–6
    defined, 55–6
    elites of, 48–52, 54, 58–9, 61, 64–8,
    72–3, 75, 87–8, 131, 248, 250–1, 269,
    310, 318, 338, 390–1, 445, 447, 450,
    473, 480, 483–4, 491–9, 504–6, 599–
    600, 610, 647–8, 660–1, 677, 727,
    730, 734
    expenditures of, 66, 78, 85–6, 112–16,
    179–80, 214–15, 221–3, 286, 288,
    334, 360–81, 577
    institutions of, 37, 62–75, 112–15,
    156–60, 180–1, 198, 221–6, 268, 311,
    340–2, 606

State (*cont.*)
  modern, rise of, 1, 4–5, 44–91, 107–15,
    300, 349, 358–61, 456–509, 516,
    726–8, 735–6, 796–8
  officials of, 67–8, 97, 113–14, 118,
    172–3, 186–9, 308, 338, 344, 360–1,
    389–95, 444–78, 571–6, 580, 584–9,
    613–14, 616–18, 733–4, 758, 786,
    804–10
  revenues of, 60–1, 63, 66, 69, 107,
    112–13, 115–16, 118, 144–7, 155,
    171, 179–80, 183–4, 221–6, 235,
    245–6, 286, 302–3, 311, 313, 316,
    334, 337–8, 342, 361, 381–9, 452–3,
    461–2, 499, 503, 515, 520–1, 524–8,
    533, 570, 572, 599, 618, 652, 693,
    702–3, 706, 731, 794
Statesmen, *see* Diplomats, statesmen
Statists, state loyalists, 344, 392, 395, 436,
    546, 575–88, 733–4, 793–4
Strikes, 406–12, 511, 519–21, 527–8, 536,
    600, 610–12, 632–5, 640–1, 644–7,
    656, 663, 665, 667–70, 673–4, 677
Sweden, 37, 333, 335, 377, 390, 447,
    492–3, 630–1, 678, 693, 711–12,
    716–18, 768
Syndicalism, 514–15, 599–601, 622, 640,
    662, 668–71, 679–80, 783–4

Technocratic-bureaucratic crystallization,
    67–8, 72, 436–8, 445, 466, 475,
    483–5, 615, 761
Technology, *see* Science, technology
Territorial organization, 33–4, 255, 282,
    288–93, 298–9, 726–7, 738, 746, 775,
    778–81, 797
Towns and cities, 92–3, 117, 123, 141,
    145, 152–3, 172, 200–1, 404, 405,
    420, 526, 539–40, 603, 660, 702
Transcendence, ideological, 35, 106, 197,
    204–5, 207, 235
Transition from feudalism to capitalism,
    11–13, 167, 218–21, 331
Transnational organization, 3, 31–2, 71,
    217–18, 231, 239, 254–6, 267, 269–
    70, 276–7, 278, 286–93, 297–301,
    303, 310, 335, 345, 488, 597, 610, 659,
    678, 685, 731, 734, 746, 753, 754, 766,
    774–81, 783–5, 797
Turkey, *see* Ottoman Empire, Turkey

Unions, 122, 500, 503, 514, 520, 524–5,
    536–42, 601–2, 605–17, 629–33,
    637–59, 662, 667–70, 672–7, 704–5,
    782–5
United States, 36, 54, 57, 68, 72, 78,
    80–1, 83–5, 101, 180, 206, 234, 247,
    248, 250, 256–8, 262–6, 280, 283,
    287, 289–92, 309, 312, 321, 324, 333,
    335, 339, 348, 352, 353, 354, 362–7,
    369–88, 390–4, 404, 407, 411, 414–
    18, 420, 429–31, 457–9, 464, 466,
    468, 470–1, 480, 490, 494–7, 499–
    501, 505–6, 531, 536, 551, 553,
    556–7, 562–4, 566, 568, 572–4, 577–
    80, 588, 611, 631–59, 674, 678, 679,
    682, 683, 685, 692–3, 698–700,
    703–5, 726–9, 739, 747, 752–4, 761,
    766–8, 773–4, 783, 810, 815–17
see also American colonies

War, 69–70, 171, 224–6, 256–7, 266–70,
    293, 325, 337, 352, 354, 358–9, 405,
    454, 456, 459, 732–4, 743–4, 751–4,
    766–70
  Austro-Prussian War, 303, 309–11, 343,
    372, 496
  Franco-Prussian War, 308–9, 371, 372,
    496, 675, 749
  Revolutionary and Napoleonic wars,
    118–20, 149–55, 203–7, 221, 237–48,
    271–9, 282, 369, 371–2, 385, 387,
    392–3, 408, 412–19, 425–8, 456,
    463–6, 517, 520–1, 533, 744, 769
  Seven Years' War, 115–20, 144, 179,
    269, 371, 372, 392
  World War I, 87, 224, 260, 292, 332,
    349–50, 368, 371, 386, 428, 433, 438,
    448, 506–7, 570, 588, 603, 623–4,
    665–6, 671, 729, 740, 802
Weber, Max, and Weberian theories, 1,
    11, 18, 44, 54–9, 61, 72–3, 79, 85, 88,
    108, 154, 300, 306, 312–19, 322, 359,
    370, 440, 446, 452, 472, 510, 547–9,
    570, 695, 697–8, 752, 789
Welfare policies, 321, 324, 358, 380–1,
    395, 428, 479, 481–7, 499, 504, 533,
    599, 618–22, 670, 675–6, 735
Women, 16, 77, 78, 104, 110, 121, 152,
    220–1, 223, 391–2, 489, 513, 516–18,
    524, 526, 533–6, 540–1, 560–1, 563,
    573–4, 588, 597, 601, 604–5, 607,
    609, 613, 615, 616, 631, 649, 652, 667,
    671, 682, 733, 735, 787
Working class, workers, proletariat, 24–9,
    98, 100–1, 164, 202, 206, 224, 227,
    306, 307, 311, 314–16, 324, 339–41,
    346, 347, 415, 420–1, 428, 481–5,
    502–3, 510–46, 558, 559, 561–2, 571,
    573–8, 581, 585, 588, 597–691,
    703–5, 707, 709–12, 717, 724–5,
    727–9, 732, 782–5, 787, 798
Workshops, *see* Factories, workshops